Department of International Economic and Social Affairs, Statistical Office of the United Nations

Industrial Statistics Yearbook 1985

Volume I

General Industrial Statistics

United Nations
New York, 1987

NOTE

Symbols of United Nations documents are composed of capital letters combined with figures. Mention of such a symbol indicates a reference to a United Nations document.

GENERAL DISCLAIMER

The designations employed and the presentation of material in this publication do not imply the expression of any opinion whatsoever on the part of the Secretariat of the United Nations concerning the legal status of any country, territory, city or area or of its authorities, or concerning the delimitation of its frontiers or boundaries.

Where the designation "country or area" appears in the headings of tables, it covers countries, territories, cities or areas. In prior issues of this publication, where the designation "country" appears in the headings of tables, it should be interpreted to cover countries, territories, cities or areas.

In some tables, the designation "developed" and "developing" economies is intended for statistical convenience and does not necessarily express a judgement about the stage reached by a particular country or area in the development process.

ST/ESA/STAT/SER.P/24 (Vol.I)

UNITED NATIONS PUBLICATION

Sales No. E.87.XVII.8

05000H
(only hardbound edition for sale)

ISBN 92-1-161288-8
ISBN 92-1-161289-6 (Vols. I and II the set)

Inquiries should be directed to:

PUBLISHING DIVISION
UNITED NATIONS
NEW YORK, N.Y. 10017

CONTENTS

INTRODUCTION

This is the nineteenth in a series of annual compilations of statistics on world industry designed to meet both the general demand for information of this kind and the special requirements of the United Nations, particularly the United Nations Industrial Development Organization (UNIDO), and related international bodies. The first seven editions in this series were published under the title The Growth of World Industry and, from the 1974 edition to the 1981 edition, under the title of Yearbook of Industrial Statistics.

The Industrial Statistics Yearbook consists of two volumes, Volume I: General Industrial Statistics and Volume II: Commodity Production Statistics. Volume I is divided into two parts; the first part contains the basic data for each country or area in the form of separate chapters and the second part gives a selection of indicators showing global and regional trends in industrial activity. The first part is primarily based on replies to the United Nations General Industrial Statistics Questionnaire, distributed in 1986. The second part is drawn from the work undertaken by the Statistical Office of the United Nations on the compilation of the United Nations indexes of industrial production and employment published in the United Nations Statistical Yearbook and Monthly Bulletin of Statistics.

The present edition covers the five-year period from 1981 through 1985. Efforts are continually being made to expand the representation of countries in part one and to increase the number of items of information for which data are shown, particularly in the case of the developing countries.

Volume II contains detailed information on world production of industrial commodities for the period 1976-1985. This information supplements at the commodity level the information presented on an industry basis in the present volume and provides a more specific indication of the nature and importance of the industrial activities undertaken in each country. In this comparison volume, a standard list of about 530 commodities has been adopted for the publication of production data and estimates for most of these commodities are published for about 200 countries or areas, including all major industrialized countries. Beginning with the 1982 edition, Volume II has been prepared in a bilingual form, English and French. For Volume I, the bilingual form will be introduced in the near future.

The co-operation of national statistical offices in the provision of the information included in this volume is gratefully acknowledged.

Explanation of symbols

The following symbols have been employed in making entries in the tables:

-	Magnitude nil or less than half of the unit of measurement employed
...	Data not available
*	Provisional figure
.	Category not applicable

Decimal figures are always preceded by a period (.).

Rounding of figures

The original figures have, in many cases, been rounded to the nearest final digit for the purposes of presentation. The totals shown generally represent the sum of the constituent items.

PART ONE: NATIONAL TABLES

INTRODUCTION TO THE NATIONAL TABLES

The information presented in the tables is primarily derived from replies to the United Nations Questionnaire on General Industrial Statistics. This edition presents the results of the 1985 inquiry, which was conducted by means of a questionnaire distributed in 1986. The questionnaires distributed by the United Nations are designed to collect internationally comparable annual statistics on industrial activity in accordance with the priorities suggested in the international recommendations. As the recommendations contain separate priorities for countries with developed industrial statistics and for countries beginning to develop, or in the process of developing, their industrial statistics, the questionnaire is distributed in two versions. Countries falling into the first of the above categories are requested to complete a comprehensive questionnaire covering 20 items of industrial activity. The remaining countries receive a modified version of the questionnaire covering 11 items of information.

The data shown have been compiled bearing in mind the requirements of international comparability and the standards for this work promulgated by the United Nations. The concepts and definitions of the items of data are drawn from the International Recommendations for Industrial Statistics (ST/STAT/SER.M/48, Rev.1) 1/ and the classification by industry from the International Standard Industrial Classification of All Economic Activities (ISIC) (ST/STAT/SER.M/4 Rev.2). 2/ Deviations from these standards, where known, are mentioned in the introductory note to each country chapter or in the footnotes to each table.

System of tables

The selection of the indicators of industrial activity for which data were requested is based on the priorities suggested in the international recommendations. The 20 tables included in the comprehensive edition of the questionnaire covered the following items classified by industry:

I Number of establishments

II Number of persons engaged

III Number of employees

IV Wages and salaries of employees

V Supplements to wages and salaries

VI Number of operatives

VII Wages and salaries of operatives

VIII Hours or days worked by operatives

IX Quantity of electricity consumed

X Output

XI Cost of goods and industrial services consumed

XII Cost of materials and supplies consumed

XIII Cost of purchased fuels and electricity consumed

XIV Value added

XV Gross fixed capital formation - Total

XVI Gross fixed capital formation - Machinery and equipment

XVII Value of stocks - Total

XVIII Value of stocks - Materials, fuels and supplies

XIX Value of stocks - Work in progress

XX Value of stocks - Finished goods

Of these, for the purposes of publication, items XI-XIII and XVIII-XX have been omitted, principally owing to the limitations of the present publications programme. In the case of countries with developing economies, these items were not requested, nor were items V, XVI and XVII.

The countries receiving the comprehensive edition of the questionnaire are as follows: Australia, Austria, Belgium, Bulgaria, Canada, Czechoslovakia, Denmark, Finland, France, German Democratic Republic, Federal Republic of Germany, Greece, Hungary, Ireland, Israel, Italy, Japan, Luxembourg, Netherlands, New Zealand, Norway, Poland, Portugal, Romania, South Africa, Spain, Sweden, Switzerland, Turkey, Union of Soviet Socialist Republics, United Kingdom of Great Britain and Northern Ireland, United States of America and Yugoslavia.

Industrial classification

The classification of industrial activity set out in the tables follows the three-digit or major group level of the present version of ISIC, supplemented by a number of selected four-digit groups. Aggregates at the major division level and for industry as a whole are included. Where information was not provided in this form, the estimates are shown in the most applicable category.

1/ United Nations publication, Sales No. E.83.XVII.8.

2/ United Nations publication, Sales No. E.68.XVII.8.

Reference unit

For most countries represented, the data shown relate to the activity of "establishments" in the specified industries rather than the activity of any other type of industrial unit. In a few cases, however, the concepts of "kind-of-activity unit", "local unit" or "enterprise" are found. An "establishment" is ideally a unit which engages, under a single ownership or control, in one, or predominantly one, kind of activity at a single location; for example, an individual mine, workshop, factory or generating station. A "kind-of-activity unit" differs from the establishment in that there is no restriction in respect of the geographical area in which a given kind of activity is carried on by a single legal entity. A "local unit", on the other hand, comprises all activities carried on under a single ownership or control at a single location and differs from the establishment-type of unit in that there is no restriction on the range of these activities. An "enterprise" is a legal entity possessing the right to conduct business in its own name; for example, to enter into contracts, own property, incur liability for debts, and establish bank accounts. In countries with centrally planned economies, the reference unit is normally the enterprise and this is usually defined as the unit having a single administration with the right to conclude contracts, an independent production plan, an independent current bank account and a self-contained system of book-keeping with independent balance-sheets and profit-and-loss statements. Specific information on the character of the units covered in the tables for each country is set out in the introductory note to each chapter.

Reference period

The statistics in the tables relate, in general, to the calendar year. It should be noted, however, that in many cases where the basic reference period of the industrial inquiry is the calendar year, returns covering proximate financial years may be accepted for reporting purposes and the data for these years incorporated in the calendar-year aggregates without adjustment. In a few countries, financial years normally used for public accounting purposes have been adopted as the basic reference periods. In the case of financial-year coverage, the year indicated in the tables refers to the calendar year in which the major part of the financial year falls. In the case of financial years from 1 July to 30 June, the year referred to is normally the one in which the financial year ends. In the text, an oblique stroke is used to connect the two years which the financial period overlaps.

Concepts and definitions of the items

The United Nations standards which have been applied in preparing the tables are set out below. All values are in national currencies and are at current prices unless otherwise indicated.

Number of persons engaged, number of employees and number of operatives

The number of persons engaged is defined as the total number of persons who worked in or for the establishment during the reference year. However, homeworkers are excluded. The concept covers working proprietors, active business partners and unpaid family workers as well as regular employees. The figures reported refer normally to the average number of persons engaged during the reference year, obtained as the sum of the "average number of employees" during the year and the total number of other persons engaged measured for a single period of the year.

The category "employees" is intended to include all persons engaged other than working proprietors, active business partners, unpaid family workers and homeworkers.

The category "operatives" refers to all employees directly engaged in the production or related activities of the establishment, including any clerical or working supervisory personnel whose function is to record or expedite any step in the production process. Employees of a similar type engaged in activities ancillary to the main activity of the establishment are considered to be operatives.

Wages and salaries

The estimates of wages and salaries include all payments in cash or in kind made to "employees" and "operatives" during the reference year in relation to work done for the establishment. The payments include: (a) direct wages and salaries; (b) remuneration for time not worked; (c) bonuses and gratuities; (d) housing allowances and family allowances paid directly by the employer; and (e) payments in kind. Social insurance contributions and contributions to pension and welfare funds payable by the employer, together with pension payments, family allowances not paid directly by the employer and similar social benefits, are excluded.

Supplements to wages and salaries

This item covers all payments made by the employer on behalf of his or her employees which are normally considered in national accounting practice to form part of compensation of employees, but not of wages and salaries. Examples are: (a) statutory social security contributions; (b) collectively agreed, contractual and non-obligatory contributions to private pension and insurance schemes; (c) direct payments to employees in respect of absence from work owing to sickness, maternity or employment injury, to compensate for loss of earnings; other direct payments to employees comparable to social security benefits; (d) cost of medical care and health services provided by outside organizations; and (e) severance and termination pay. The sum of this item and "wages and salaries" equals total compensation of employees as defined for national accounting purposes.

Hours or days worked by operatives

Hours worked by operatives refer to the total number of hours actually spent by operatives at work, including waiting time. Overtime is included and calculated in terms of actual hours spent at work and not in terms of time paid for. Since the concept refers to hours worked rather than hours paid for, time spent on vacation and casual or sick leave are excluded.

Days worked by operatives refer to the total number of days actually spent at work. In other respects, the concept corresponds to that defined for hours worked.

Quantity of electricity consumed

The quantity of electricity consumed is defined as the sum of the quantity of electricity purchased and generated less the quantity of electricity sold to others.

Output

The value of output in the case of estimates compiled on a production basis comprises: (a) the value of all products of the establishment; (b) the net change between the beginning and the end of the reference period in the value of work in progress; (c) the value of industrial services rendered to others; (d) the value of goods shipped in the same condition as received less the amount paid for these goods; and (e) the value of fixed assets produced during the period by the unit for its own use. In the case of estimates compiled on a shipment basis, the net change between the beginning and the end of the reference period in the value of stocks of finished goods is also included. Valuation may be in factor values, excluding all indirect taxes falling on production and including all current subsidies received in support of production activity, or in producers' prices, including all indirect taxes and excluding all subsidies.

Value added

Value added is, ideally, represented by the contribution of the establishments in each branch of activity to the gross domestic product in terms of the national accounting concept. In the case of estimates derived from industrial inquiries, however, as generally reported in the tables, the measure normally used is the "census value added" concept. This can be defined as the value of output less the cost of (a) materials, fuels and other supplies consumed; (b) contract and commission work done by others; (c) repair and maintenance work done by others; and (d) electricity purchased. If input estimates are compiled on a "received" rather than on a "consumed" basis, the result is adjusted for the net change between the beginning and the end of the period in the value of stocks of materials, fuels and supplies. For estimates compiled according to the "national accounting" value-added concept, the cost of non-industrial services is deducted and the receipts for non-industrial services are included. The estimates, whether in terms of census value added or in terms of the national accounting concept, are gross of depreciation and other provisions for capital consumption, unless otherwise stated. The valuation may be in factor values or in producers' prices, depending on the treatment of indirect taxes and subsidies.

Gross fixed capital formation

The estimates refer to the value of purchases and own-account construction of fixed assets during the reference year less the value of corresponding sales. The fixed assets covered are those, whether new or used, with a productive life of one year or more which are intended for the use of the establishment, including fixed assets made by the establishment's own labour force for its own use. Major additions, alterations and improvements to existing assets which extend their normal economic life or raise their productivity are also included.

Assets acquired from others are valued at the full cost incurred, that is, at the delivered price plus the cost of installation and any necessary fees and taxes. Assets produced by the establishment for its own use are valued at the cost of work put in place during the reference year, including the cost of labour, materials and other supplies and also an allocation for overheads. Used assets sold are valued at the actual amount realized.

The category "machinery and equipment" covers transport equipment; industrial machinery and equipment; office machinery, equipment and furniture; professional instruments and equipment; and any other machinery and equipment. Major alterations and improvements of existing machinery and equipment are included.

Value of stocks

The estimates relate to the value of all stocks owned by the parent enterprise and under the control of the reporting establishment, at the establishment itself or in ancillary warehouses, at the end of each reference year. The estimates correspond to the sum of "value of stocks of materials, fuels and supplies", "value of work in progress" and "value of stocks of finished goods". In principle, stocks of materials are valued at current replacement cost; an imputed valuation of the work done, including an imputed margin for overhead costs and profits, is used for work in progress; and stocks of finished goods are valued in terms of prices at which similar goods have been shipped immediately prior to the reference date. In practice, the book values are frequently used.

Index numbers of industrial production

The index numbers of industrial production are compiled by national authorities and provided in response to the United Nations Questionnaire on Indexes of Industrial Production. A brief description of the source and coverage is given in the introductory note to each chapter. A more complete description of the methodology and definitions appears in the 1977 Supplement to the Statistical Yearbook and the Monthly Bulletin of Statistics. 3/ As recommended internationally, for most countries the indexes relate to the value at constant prices of census value added or to the contributions to the gross or net domestic product. These measures are usually in factor values.

3/ United Nations publication, Sales No: E.78.XVII.10

AFGHANISTAN

The information in the tables is based on the reply to the United Nations Questionnaire on General Industrial Statistics from the Central Statistics Office, Kabul. The concepts, definitions and classification by branches of industry are generally in accordance with United Nations standards.

The estimates are derived from the monthly survey conducted by the statistical office mentioned above. All registered establishments are covered. The estimates in the tables are based on the national data which are available only by broad groupings of industries. They have been arranged by the national statistical authorities to represent appropriate ISIC categories as far as details permit. It should be noted that up until 1983 the manufacture of wearing apparel except footwear (ISIC 322) was out of the scope of the survey. It should also be noted that the manufacture of coal products (ISIC 354) is included in ISIC 36.

The number of establishments is as of 21 March of the year indicated. Other estimates refer to the fiscal year beginning 21 March of the year indicated.

Wages and salaries represent all payments made for work done by all persons included in the count of employees, including fringe benefits. The value of output is the value of sales of all commodities.

Related national publications:
Statistical Information (annual); *Statistical Research* (quarterly), both published by the Central Statistics Office, Kabul.

ISIC	INDUSTRY	1. NUMBER OF ESTABLISHMENTS a/ (NUMBER) 1981	1982	1983	1984	1985	2. AVERAGE NUMBER OF EMPLOYEES b/ (NUMBER) 1981	1982	1983	1984	1985	ISIC
210	Coal mining	2	2	2	1	2	2086	1672	2417	...	...	210
220	Petroleum and gas	2	2	2	2	2	1225	1344	...	...	...	220
230	Metal ore mining	-	-	16	...	...	-	-	...	...	...	230
290	Other mining	11	11	12	...	...	821	...	...	...	...	290
2	Mining, quarrying .	15	15	32	...	...	4132	...	...	...	...	2
311/2	Food products	60	67	65	70	73	8233	6579	4877	...	...	311/2
313	Beverages	2	2	2	2	2	248	287	358	...	...	313
314	Tobacco	-	-	-	-	-	-	-	-	...	...	314
321	Textiles	56	63	66	75	84	15068	13387	10176	...	...	321
3211	Spinning,weaving etc..	15	14	25	27	29	294	236	289	...	...	3211
322	Wearing apparel	.	.	3	3	3	.	.	...	...	...	322
323	Leather and products ...	4	4	9	9	10	236	162	161	...	...	323
324	Footwear	3	3	...	...	...	461	422	716	...	...	324
331	Wood products	[5	4	3	11	13	1090	852	1002]	...	...	331
332	Furniture, fixtures									...	...	332
341	Paper and products	-	-	-	-	-	-	-	-	...	...	341
3411	Pulp,paper etc.	-	-	-	-	-	-	-	-	...	...	3411
342	Printing,publishing	18	18	20	24	24	2230	1810	2317	...	...	342
351	Industrial chemicals ...	1	1	1	1	1	2308	2198	1983	...	...	351
3511	Basic excl fertilizers	...	...	...	...	...	...	...	...	...	...	3511
3513	Synthetic resins etc .	...	...	...	...	...	...	...	...	...	...	3513
352	Other chemical products.	4	4	4	4	4	547	480	770	...	...	352
3522	Drugs and medicines ..	4	4	4	4	4	547	480	770	...	...	3522
353	Petroleum refineries ...	-	-	-	-	-	-	-	-	...	...	353
354	Petroleum,coal products. c/	...	...	...	...	...	...	...	...	...	...	354
355	Rubber products	-	-	-	-	-	-	-	-	...	...	355
356	Plastic products n.e.c..	32	27	27	30	31	828	716	446	...	...	356
361	Pottery,china etc								...	...	...	361
362	Glass and products ..... c/	[9	10	1	1	1	1343	1526]	...	...	...	362
369	Non-metal products n.e.c								...	...	...	369
371	Iron and steel	-	-	-	-	-	-	-	-	...	...	371
372	Non-ferrous metals	-	-	-	-	-	-	-	-	...	...	372
381	Metal products .... d/	[17	16	16	22	20	2378	2359	2359]	...	...	381
382	Machinery n.e.c.									...	...	382
3825	Office,computing etc..	...	...	...	...	...	...	...	...	...	...	3825
383	Electrical machinery ... d/	...	...	...	...	...	...	...	...	...	...	383
3832	Radio,television etc..	...	...	...	...	...	...	...	...	...	...	3832
384	Transport equipment .... d/	...	...	...	...	...	...	...	...	...	...	384
3841	Shipbuilding, repair..	...	...	...	...	...	...	...	...	...	...	3841
3843	Motor vehicles	...	...	...	...	...	...	...	...	...	...	3843
385	Professional goods	-	-	-	-	-	-	-	-	...	...	385
390	Other industries	-	-	-	-	-	-	-	-	...	...	390
3	Manufacturing	211	219	e/ 217	e/ 252	e/ 266	34970	30778	...	...	...	3
410	Electricity,gas,steam ..	...	...	...	...	...	...	...	...	...	...	410
4101	Electricity	...	...	...	...	...	...	...	...	...	...	4101
420	Water works and supply .	...	...	...	...	...	...	...	...	...	...	420
4	Electricity,gas etc	42	42	40	42	48	3621	3615	3507	...	...	4
2-4	All industry	268	276	e/ 289	...	...	42723	...	...	...	...	2-4

a/ As at 21 March of the year indicated.
b/ Twelve months beginning 21 March of the year indicated.
c/ Major group 354 is included in 361 to 369 combined.
d/ Major groups 383 and 384 are included in 381 and 382 combined.
e/ Excluding major group 324.

ISIC	INDUSTRY	3. WAGES AND SALARIES OF EMPLOYEES a/ (MILLION AFGHANIS)					4. AVERAGE NUMBER OF OPERATIVES a/ (NUMBER)					ISIC
		1981	1982	1983	1984	1985	1981	1982	1983	1984	1985	
210	Coal mining	82.1	65.8	101.2	119.7	...	1323	1120	1568	...	...	210
220	Petroleum and gas	39.5	42.3	...	240.5	...	765	651	...	...	...	220
230	Metal ore mining	-	-	...	...	...	-	-	...	...	...	230
290	Other mining	24.0	...	...	...	...	428	119	...	...	...	290
2	Mining, quarrying .	145.6	...	...	...	...	2516	1890	...	...	...	2
311/2	Food products	258.6	241.8	170.5	...	...	4932	4951	3109	...	...	311/2
313	Beverages	16.4	14.5	14.5	...	...	90	96	114	...	...	313
314	Tobacco	-	-	-	-	...	-	-	-	...	...	314
321	Textiles	499.5	495.6	413.2	...	...	10609	8645	7321	...	...	321
3211	Spinning,weaving etc..	15.4	9.0	11.1	...	...	207	134	171	...	...	3211
322	Wearing apparel	.	.	...	...	...	.	.	...	...	...	322
323	Leather and products ...	12.2	7.2	8.2	...	...	193	109	109	...	...	323
324	Footwear	19.9	23.8	34.9	...	...	374	344	499	...	...	324
331	Wood products	[41.4	26.0	47.4]	...	...	[811	577	665]	...	...	331
332	Furniture, fixtures				...	...				...	...	332
341	Paper and products	-	-	-	-	...	-	-	-	...	...	341
3411	Pulp,paper etc.	-	-	-	-	...	-	-	-	...	...	3411
342	Printing,publishing	74.0	73.0	109.2	68.0	...	1429	1108	1589	...	...	342
351	Industrial chemicals ...	38.3	79.1	83.0	120.8	...	2006	1542	...	...	...	351
3511	Basic excl fertilizers	...	...	...	...	...	...	...	...	...	...	3511
3513	Synthetic resins etc .	...	...	...	...	...	...	...	...	...	...	3513
352	Other chemical products.	30.4	29.4	37.2	33.2	...	232	216	203	...	...	352
3522	Drugs and medicines ..	30.4	29.4	37.2	33.2	...	232	216	203	...	...	3522
353	Petroleum refineries ...	-	-	-	-	...	-	-	-	...	...	353
354	Petroleum,coal products. b/	...	...	...	...	...	...	...	...	...	...	354
355	Rubber products	-	-	-	-	...	-	-	-	...	...	355
356	Plastic products n.e.c..	17.6	23.2	16.8	...	...	605	211	259	...	...	356
361	Pottery,china etc			...	...	...			...	...	...	361
362	Glass and products ..... b/	[29.7	46.1]	...	...	...	[1152	1093]	...	...	...	362
369	Non-metal products n.e.c			...	...	...			...	...	...	369
371	Iron and steel	-	-	-	-	...	-	-	-	...	...	371
372	Non-ferrous metals	-	-	-	-	...	-	-	-	...	...	372
381	Metal products .... c/	[75.9	79.1]	...	...	...	[1344	2337]	...	...	...	381
382	Machinery n.e.c.			...	...	...			...	...	...	382
3825	Office,computing etc..	...	...	...	...	...	...	...	...	...	...	3825
383	Electrical machinery ... c/	...	...	...	...	...	...	...	...	...	...	383
3832	Radio,television etc..	...	...	...	...	...	...	...	...	...	...	3832
384	Transport equipment .... c/	...	...	...	...	...	...	...	...	...	...	384
3841	Shipbuilding, repair..	...	...	...	...	...	...	...	...	...	...	3841
3843	Motor vehicles	...	...	...	...	...	...	...	...	...	...	3843
385	Professional goods	-	-	-	-	...	-	-	-	...	...	385
390	Other industries	-	-	-	-	...	-	-	-	...	...	390
3	Manufacturing	1113.9	1138.8	...	...	...	23777	21229	...	...	...	3
410	Electricity,gas,steam ..	...	...	...	...	...	...	...	...	...	...	410
4101	Electricity	...	...	...	...	...	...	...	...	...	...	4101
420	Water works and supply .	...	...	...	...	...	...	...	...	...	...	420
4	Electricity,gas etc	111.9	114.3	157.6	...	...	946	946	669	...	...	4
2-4	All industry	1371.4	...	...	...	...	27239	24065	...	...	...	2-4

a/ Twelve months beginning 21 March of the year indicated. b/ Major group 354 is included in 361 to 369 combined.
c/ Major groups 383 and 384 are included in 381 and 382 combined.

ISIC	INDUSTRY	5. WAGES AND SALARIES OF OPERATIVES a/ (MILLION AFGHANIS) 1981	1982	1983	1984	1985	6. OUTPUT a/b/ (MILLION AFGHANIS) 1981	1982	1983	1984	1985	ISIC
210	Coal mining	60.4	25.7	49.4	78.5	47.2	105	113	191	226	205	210
220	Petroleum and gas	34.7	28.2	23.9	161.2	33.3	13675	14226	...	...	...	220
230	Metal ore mining	-	-	...	...	...	-	-	...	...	...	230
290	Other mining	14.5	3.5	...	...	...	24	19	...	...	...	290
2	Mining, quarrying .	109.6	57.4	...	...	...	13804	14358	...	...	...	2
311/2	Food products	...	...	...	...	...	3762	3867	4991	...	...	311/2
313	Beverages	...	...	...	...	...	160	194	312	327	412	313
314	Tobacco	-	-	-	-	-	-	-	-	-	-	314
321	Textiles	338.7	299.0	296.0	...	...	2770	1651	1671	...	...	321
3211	Spinning,weaving etc..	10.4	5.1	6.7	...	...	80	67	75	111	91	3211
322	Wearing apparel	.	.	...	...	...	.	.	...	...	...	322
323	Leather and products ...	8.8	5.1	4.6	...	...	325	236	246	...	...	323
324	Footwear	15.1	18.7	26.3	...	...	196	172	150	...	...	324
331	Wood products	[31.2	16.7	30.6]	...	...	[207	195	125]	...	...	331
332	Furniture, fixtures				...	...				...	...	332
341	Paper and products	-	-	-	-	-	-	-	-	-	-	341
3411	Pulp,paper etc.	-	-	-	-	-	-	-	-	-	-	3411
342	Printing,publishing	43.9	43.4	69.9	47.3	83.2	539	...	941	...	...	342
351	Industrial chemicals ...	28.8	...	33.5	57.5	56.9	748	711	707	861	859	351
3511	Basic excl fertilizers	...	...	...	...	...	...	...	...	...	...	3511
3513	Synthetic resins etc .	...	...	...	...	...	...	...	...	...	...	3513
352	Other chemical products.	...	...	8.8	...	...	459	496	541	...	...	352
3522	Drugs and medicines ..	...	...	8.8	...	...	459	496	541	...	...	3522
353	Petroleum refineries ...	-	-	-	-	-	-	-	-	-	-	353
354	Petroleum,coal products. c/	...	...	...	...	...	...	...	...	...	...	354
355	Rubber products	-	-	-	-	-	-	-	-	-	-	355
356	Plastic products n.e.c..	...	7.9	9.4	...	...	235	241	285	...	...	356
361	Pottery,china etc		...	...	...	...			...	...	...	361
362	Glass and products ..... c/	[14.5]	...	...	...	...	[274	238]	...	...	...	362
369	Non-metal products n.e.c		...	...	...	...			...	...	...	369
371	Iron and steel	-	-	-	-	-	-	-	-	-	-	371
372	Non-ferrous metals	-	-	-	-	-	-	-	-	-	-	372
381	Metal products .... d/	[42.9]	...	...	...	...	[387	312	237]	...	...	381
382	Machinery n.e.c.		...	...	...	...				...	...	382
3825	Office,computing etc..	...	...	...	...	...	...	...	...	...	...	3825
383	Electrical machinery ... d/	...	...	...	...	...	...	...	...	...	...	383
3832	Radio,television etc..	...	...	...	...	...	...	...	...	...	...	3832
384	Transport equipment .... d/	...	...	...	...	...	...	...	...	...	...	384
3841	Shipbuilding, repair..	...	...	...	...	...	...	...	...	...	...	3841
3843	Motor vehicles	...	...	...	...	...	...	...	...	...	...	3843
385	Professional goods	-	-	-	-	-	-	-	-	-	-	385
390	Other industries	-	-	-	-	-	-	-	-	-	-	390
3	Manufacturing	...	...	...	...	...	10062	e/ 8313	...	...	...	3
410	Electricity,gas,steam ..	...	...	...	...	...	...	...	...	...	...	410
4101	Electricity	...	...	...	...	...	...	...	...	...	...	4101
420	Water works and supply .	...	...	...	...	...	...	...	...	...	...	420
4	Electricity,gas etc	54.8	37.0	28.8	3.5	71.4	722	688	709	695	775	4
2-4	All industry	...	...	...	...	...	24588	e/ 23359	...	...	...	2-4

a/ Twelve months beginning 21 March of the year indicated.
b/ Value of sales only.
c/ Major group 354 is included in 361 to 369 combined.
d/ Major groups 383 and 384 are included in 381 and 382 combined.
e/ Excluding major group 342.

ARGENTINA

The information in the tables, except for the indexes, is based on the reply to the United Nations Questionnaire on General Industrial Statistics from the Instituto Nacional de Estadistica y Censos, Buenos Aires. The concepts, definitions and classification by branches of industry are generally in accordance with United Nations standards.

The estimates are derived from information collected monthly by the Instituto Nacional de Estadistica y Censos from establishments engaged in selected industries. The number of employees relates to annual averages, excluding homeworkers. Wages and salaries include family allowances, bonuses, bounties, payments for vacations and leave etc. The industries for which estimates are shown in the tables are as follows:

ISIC 311/312: vegetable oils, wheat mill products and by-products, rice, sugar; ISIC 313: beer; ISIC 314: cigarettes and cigars; ISIC 321: wool cleaning; ISIC 341: paper, paperboard, cardboard and pulp for paper; ISIC 351: industries enumerated under ISIC 3511 and ISIC 3513; ISIC 3511: tanning extracts, compressed and liquid gas, sulphuric acid; ISIC 3513 : cellulosic and non-cellulosic synthetic filament and fibres, plastic materials; ISIC 352: antibiotics; paints, lacquers and varnishes; matches; soap; ISIC 3522: antibiotics; ISIC 355: tyres and tubes; ISIC 356: plastic footwear; ISIC 369: cement, fibro cement products; ISIC 371: iron smelting, iron and steel pipes and tubes; ISIC 381: gas heating apparatus and cooking ranges; ISIC 382: sewing machines; refrigerators and washing machines; ISIC 383: electric light bulbs and tubes, television receiving sets, phonograph records; ISIC 3832: television receiving sets, phonograph records; ISIC 384: motor-vehicle bodies; motor vehicles, motorcycles, scooters, including agricultural tractors (ISIC 382).

The indexes of industrial production are compiled by the Banco Central de la Republica Argentina and provided in response to the United Nations Questionnaire on Indexes of Industrial Production. In principle, the indexes cover all establishments.

Related national publications:
<u>Indicadores Industriales Serie I</u> (annual); <u>Boletin Estadistico Trimestral</u>, both published by the Instituto Nacional de Estadistica y Censos, Buenos Aires.

ARGENTINA

ISIC	INDUSTRY	1. NUMBER OF ESTABLISHMENTS a/ (NUMBER)					2. AVERAGE NUMBER OF EMPLOYEES a/ (THOUSANDS)					ISIC
		1981	1982	1983	1984	1985	1981	1982	1983	1984	1985	
210	Coal mining	...	...	...	...	...	...	...	...	...	...	210
220	Petroleum and gas	...	...	...	...	...	...	...	...	...	...	220
230	Metal ore mining	...	...	...	...	...	...	...	...	...	...	230
290	Other mining	...	...	...	...	...	...	...	...	...	...	290
2	Mining, quarrying .	...	...	...	...	...	...	...	...	...	...	2
311/2	Food products	253	211	207	230	237	30.38	30.56	31.78	33.55	32.26	311/2
313	Beverages	8	9	8	8	8	2.78	2.96	3.42	3.78	3.60	313
314	Tobacco	26	25	31	31	31	5.71	5.18	4.95	4.72	4.48	314
321	Textiles	24	24	25	21	21	0.88	0.88	0.83	0.81	0.79	321
3211	Spinning,weaving etc..	...	...	...	...	...	...	...	...	...	...	3211
322	Wearing apparel	...	...	...	...	...	...	...	...	...	...	322
323	Leather and products ...	...	...	...	...	...	...	...	...	...	...	323
324	Footwear	...	...	...	...	...	...	...	...	...	...	324
331	Wood products	...	...	...	...	...	...	...	...	...	...	331
332	Furniture, fixtures	...	...	...	...	...	...	...	...	...	...	332
341	Paper and products	122	127	115	114	115	12.64	12.76	14.13	15.45	15.08	341
3411	Pulp,paper etc.	...	...	...	...	...	...	...	...	...	...	3411
342	Printing,publishing	...	...	...	...	...	...	...	...	...	...	342
351	Industrial chemicals ...	166	165	155	167	164	13.60	12.18	13.04	13.92	13.78	351
3511	Basic excl fertilizers	71	65	67	66	65	3.12	2.93	2.85	2.73	2.66	3511
3513	Synthetic resins etc .	95	100	102	101	99	10.48	9.25	10.19	11.19	11.12	3513
352	Other chemical products.	165	159	157	158	146	10.20	10.42	10.55	10.14	10.01	352
3522	Drugs and medicines ..	4	3	4	3	3	0.19	0.17	0.14	0.15	0.16	3522
353	Petroleum refineries ...	...	...	...	...	...	...	...	...	...	...	353
354	Petroleum,coal products.	...	...	...	...	...	...	...	...	...	...	354
355	Rubber products	11	10	12	12	13	6.17	5.60	6.84	6.54	6.39	355
356	Plastic products n.e.c..	4	4	4	4	4	0.12	0.15	0.21	0.26	0.34	356
361	Pottery,china etc	...	...	...	...	...	...	...	...	...	...	361
362	Glass and products	...	...	...	...	...	...	...	...	...	...	362
369	Non-metal products n.e.c	32	32	32	30	30	10.07	8.88	8.50	8.27	7.45	369
371	Iron and steel	70	63	62	58	59	14.90	18.98	13.82	15.06	15.20	371
372	Non-ferrous metals	...	...	...	...	...	...	...	...	...	...	372
381	Metal products	65	61	70	57	55	4.58	4.12	4.49	4.79	4.10	381
382	Machinery n.e.c.	53	49	49	45	42	3.58	3.13	3.32	3.65	3.04	382
3825	Office,computing etc..	...	...	...	...	...	...	...	...	...	...	3825
383	Electrical machinery ...	29	27	25	24	21	4.37	4.08	4.21	5.05	5.24	383
3832	Radio,television etc..	22	21	19	18	16	2.78	2.69	2.78	3.54	3.79	3832
384	Transport equipment	107	102	108	104	100	40.12	28.39	29.21	30.89	29.43	384
3841	Shipbuilding, repair..	...	...	...	...	...	...	...	...	...	...	3841
3843	Motor vehicles	...	...	...	...	...	...	...	...	...	...	3843
385	Professional goods	...	...	...	...	...	...	...	...	...	...	385
390	Other industries	...	...	...	...	...	...	...	...	...	...	390
3	Manufacturing	...	...	...	...	...	...	...	...	...	...	3
410	Electricity,gas,steam ..	...	...	...	...	...	...	...	...	...	...	410
4101	Electricity	...	...	...	...	...	...	...	...	...	...	4101
420	Water works and supply .	...	...	...	...	...	...	...	...	...	...	420
4	Electricity,gas etc	...	...	...	...	...	...	...	...	...	...	4
2-4	All industry	...	...	...	...	...	...	...	...	...	...	2-4

a/ Selected industries; for coverage, see country note.

ISIC	INDUSTRY	3. WAGES AND SALARIES OF EMPLOYEES a/ (MILLION PESOS)					4. AVERAGE NUMBER OF OPERATIVES a/ (THOUSANDS)					ISIC
		1981	1982	1983 b/	1984 b/	1985 b/	1981	1982	1983	1984	1985	
210	Coal mining	...	...	...	...	...	...	...	...	...	...	210
220	Petroleum and gas	...	...	...	...	...	...	...	...	...	...	220
230	Metal ore mining	...	...	...	...	...	...	...	...	...	...	230
290	Other mining	...	...	...	...	...	...	...	...	...	...	290
2	Mining, quarrying .	...	...	...	...	...	...	...	...	...	...	2
311/2	Food products	954473	c/ 2354	1440	12422	76696	23.18	23.38	24.33	25.90	24.80	311/2
313	Beverages	93909	258069	184	2008	12811	1.97	2.10	2.47	2.83	2.65	313
314	Tobacco	307432	709927	333	2615	18175	3.23	2.77	2.71	2.57	2.48	314
321	Textiles	40418	90623	42	355	2304	0.70	0.73	0.69	0.68	0.66	321
3211	Spinning,weaving etc..	...	...	...	...	...	...	...	...	...	...	3211
322	Wearing apparel	...	...	...	...	...	...	...	...	...	...	322
323	Leather and products ...	...	...	...	...	...	...	...	...	...	...	323
324	Footwear	...	...	...	...	...	...	...	...	...	...	324
331	Wood products	...	...	...	...	...	...	...	...	...	...	331
332	Furniture, fixtures	...	...	...	...	...	...	...	...	...	...	332
341	Paper and products	424252	c/ 1096	517	7000	44111	9.64	9.73	10.56	11.39	11.10	341
3411	Pulp,paper etc.	...	...	...	...	...	...	...	...	...	...	3411
342	Printing,publishing	...	...	...	...	...	...	...	...	...	...	342
351	Industrial chemicals ...	500239	c/ 1253	732	6668	40003	9.13	8.24	8.92	9.75	9.59	351
3511	Basic excl fertilizers	110212	260610	136	1083	6980	2.10	1.96	1.87	1.81	1.77	3511
3513	Synthetic resins etc .	390027	992172	596	5585	33023	7.03	6.28	7.05	7.94	7.82	3513
352	Other chemical products.	499339	c/ 1079	551	4759	21447	5.58	5.96	5.95	5.66	5.38	352
3522	Drugs and medicines ..	12016	25017	9	83	622	0.10	0.10	0.07	0.08	0.09	3522
353	Petroleum refineries ...	...	...	...	...	...	...	...	...	...	...	353
354	Petroleum,coal products.	...	...	...	...	...	...	...	...	...	...	354
355	Rubber products	313667	760994	437	4459	26181	4.30	3.76	4.94	4.58	4.43	355
356	Plastic products n.e.c..	5575	9668	11	102	521	0.10	0.13	0.18	0.21	0.24	356
361	Pottery,china etc	...	...	...	...	...	...	...	...	...	...	361
362	Glass and products	...	...	...	...	...	...	...	...	...	...	362
369	Non-metal products n.e.c	480379	c/ 1002	499	3679	20453	7.38	6.27	5.92	5.72	5.23	369
371	Iron and steel	648861	c/ 1445	849	8199	54297	10.61	14.79	9.96	10.77	10.85	371
372	Non-ferrous metals	...	...	...	...	...	...	...	...	...	...	372
381	Metal products	163146	344376	208	1871	9921	3.22	2.85	3.17	3.50	2.99	381
382	Machinery n.e.c.	128014	215102	132	1366	7404	2.28	2.08	2.29	2.53	2.03	382
3825	Office,computing etc..	...	...	...	...	...	...	...	...	...	...	3825
383	Electrical machinery ...	153637	337417	210	6134	23131	3.09	2.93	3.09	3.83	4.03	383
3832	Radio,television etc..	93615	199228	135	5389	18494	2.00	2.00	2.07	2.72	2.98	3832
384	Transport equipment	c/ 2570	c/ 3887	2029	21037	129119	27.67	19.20	20.04	21.78	20.85	384
3841	Shipbuilding, repair..	...	...	...	...	...	...	...	...	...	...	3841
3843	Motor vehicles	...	...	...	...	...	...	...	...	...	...	3843
385	Professional goods	...	...	...	...	...	...	...	...	...	...	385
390	Other industries	...	...	...	...	...	...	...	...	...	...	390
3	Manufacturing	...	...	...	...	...	...	...	...	...	...	3
410	Electricity,gas,steam ..	...	...	...	...	...	...	...	...	...	...	410
4101	Electricity	...	...	...	...	...	...	...	...	...	...	4101
420	Water works and supply .	...	...	...	...	...	...	...	...	...	...	420
4	Electricity,gas etc	...	...	...	...	...	...	...	...	...	...	4
2-4	All industry	...	...	...	...	...	...	...	...	...	...	2-4

a/ Selected industries; for coverage, see country note.
b/ In million Argentine pesos (10,000 pesos per Argentine peso).
c/ In billion pesos.

ISIC	INDUSTRY	5. WAGES AND SALARIES OF OPERATIVES a/ (MILLION PESOS) 1981	1982	b/ 1983	b/ 1984	b/ 1985	6. HOURS WORKED BY OPERATIVES a/ (MILLIONS) 1981	1982	1983	1984	1985	ISIC
210	Coal mining	...	...	...	...	...	...	...	...	...	...	210
220	Petroleum and gas	...	...	...	...	...	...	...	...	...	...	220
230	Metal ore mining	...	...	...	...	...	...	...	...	...	...	230
290	Other mining	...	...	...	...	...	...	...	...	...	...	290
2	Mining, quarrying .	...	...	...	...	...	...	...	...	...	...	2
311/2	Food products	601020	c/ 1533	1007	8828	53283	55.52	56.82	58.95	61.72	57.86	311/2
313	Beverages	52743	156783	125	1373	8055	3.97	4.42	5.46	6.11	5.56	313
314	Tobacco	106673	239134	121	978	7020	5.98	5.21	5.26	5.07	4.86	314
321	Textiles	32008	70308	33	285	1827	1.68	1.55	1.47	1.52	1.38	321
3211	Spinning,weaving etc..	...	...	...	...	...	...	...	...	...	...	3211
322	Wearing apparel	...	...	...	...	...	...	...	...	...	...	322
323	Leather and products ...	...	...	...	...	...	...	...	...	...	...	323
324	Footwear	...	...	...	...	...	...	...	...	...	...	324
331	Wood products	...	...	...	...	...	...	...	...	...	...	331
332	Furniture, fixtures	...	...	...	...	...	...	...	...	...	...	332
341	Paper and products	271878	733470	492	2104	28153	21.15	22.47	25.32	26.38	24.16	341
3411	Pulp,paper etc.	...	...	...	...	...	...	...	...	...	...	3411
342	Printing,publishing	...	...	...	...	...	...	...	...	...	...	342
351	Industrial chemicals ...	248717	668372	418	3941	22592	17.85	18.24	19.74	21.20	19.28	351
3511	Basic excl fertilizers	56631	136323	78	609	3853	4.53	4.38	4.18	3.94	3.77	3511
3513	Synthetic resins etc .	192086	532049	341	3332	18239	13.32	13.86	15.56	17.26	15.51	3513
352	Other chemical products.	206362	453439	243	2104	14021	12.67	12.57	12.68	11.96	11.63	352
3522	Drugs and medicines ..	4337	8722	4	39	315	0.26	0.26	0.19	0.20	0.24	3522
353	Petroleum refineries ...	...	...	...	...	...	...	...	...	...	...	353
354	Petroleum,coal products.	...	...	...	...	...	...	...	...	...	...	354
355	Rubber products	180443	413556	261	2750	15020	8.35	8.28	9.59	10.45	9.00	355
356	Plastic products n.e.c..	4248	8263	9	81	350	0.24	0.27	0.43	0.45	0.38	356
361	Pottery,china etc	...	...	...	...	...	...	...	...	...	...	361
362	Glass and products	...	...	...	...	...	...	...	...	...	...	362
369	Non-metal products n.e.c	278084	569175	292	2219	12420	15.81	13.74	12.86	12.22	11.21	369
371	Iron and steel	387832	899046	542	5243	34526	21.80	20.64	21.39	21.90	21.24	371
372	Non-ferrous metals	...	...	...	...	...	...	...	...	...	...	372
381	Metal products	89050	191050	126	1204	6129	6.26	5.71	6.77	7.06	5.71	381
382	Machinery n.e.c.	64905	125157	85	856	4423	4.85	4.30	5.01	5.53	4.15	382
3825	Office,computing etc..	...	...	...	...	...	...	...	...	...	...	3825
383	Electrical machinery ...	80688	184355	130	2283	15975	6.20	6.11	6.27	7.75	8.09	383
3832	Radio,television etc..	51295	113828	90	1857	13670	4.03	3.95	4.01	5.40	5.96	3832
384	Transport equipment	c/ 1295	c/ 1883	1036	11914	70512	45.40	37.00	42.76	45.81	39.42	384
3841	Shipbuilding, repair..	...	...	...	...	...	...	...	...	...	...	3841
3843	Motor vehicles	...	...	...	...	...	...	...	...	...	...	3843
385	Professional goods	...	...	...	...	...	...	...	...	...	...	385
390	Other industries	...	...	...	...	...	...	...	...	...	...	390
3	Manufacturing	...	...	...	...	...	...	...	...	...	...	3
410	Electricity,gas,steam ..	...	...	...	...	...	...	...	...	...	...	410
4101	Electricity	...	...	...	...	...	...	...	...	...	...	4101
420	Water works and supply .	...	...	...	...	...	...	...	...	...	...	420
4	Electricity,gas etc	...	...	...	...	...	...	...	...	...	...	4
2-4	All industry	...	...	...	...	...	...	...	...	...	...	2-4

a/ Selected industries; for coverage, see country note.
c/ In billion pesos.
b/ In million Argentine pesos (10,000 pesos per Argentine peso).

7. OUTPUT a/ (BILLION PESOS)

ISIC	INDUSTRY	1981	1982	1983 b/	1984 b/	1985 c/	ISIC
210	Coal mining	...	...	...	...	...	210
220	Petroleum and gas	...	...	...	...	...	220
230	Metal ore mining	...	...	...	...	...	230
290	Other mining	...	...	...	...	...	290
2	Mining, quarrying .	...	...	...	...	...	2
311/2	Food products	18519	41896	20259	149074	1114	311/2
313	Beverages	1178	1787	1105	8794	53	313
314	Tobacco	7228	20429	8410	48443	461	314
321	Textiles	304	1002	494	3614	28	321
3211	Spinning,weaving etc..	...	...	...	...	...	3211
322	Wearing apparel	...	...	...	...	...	322
323	Leather and products ...	...	...	...	...	...	323
324	Footwear	...	...	...	...	...	324
331	Wood products	...	...	...	...	...	331
332	Furniture, fixtures	...	...	...	...	...	332
341	Paper and products	3494	11277	8156	61981	441	341
3411	Pulp,paper etc.	...	...	...	...	...	3411
342	Printing,publishing	...	...	...	...	...	342
351	Industrial chemicals ...	3049	12826	8817	59102	297	351
3511	Basic excl fertilizers	794	2630	1325	9514	81	3511
3513	Synthetic resins etc .	2256	10195	7491	49588	215	3513
352	Other chemical products.	2763	9900	4139	25024	205	352
3522	Drugs and medicines ..	81	178	152	1059	8	3522
353	Petroleum refineries ...	...	...	...	...	...	353
354	Petroleum,coal products.	...	...	...	...	...	354
355	Rubber products	2014	9509	5537	27103	209	355
356	Plastic products n.e.c..	27	47	51	204	2	356
361	Pottery,china etc	...	...	...	...	...	361
362	Glass and products	...	...	...	...	...	362
369	Non-metal products n.e.c	3286	8651	3904	20055	179	369
371	Iron and steel	7447	28299	11780	79086	767	371
372	Non-ferrous metals	...	...	...	...	...	372
381	Metal products	775	2552	1335	8777	60	381
382	Machinery n.e.c.	631	2114	1143	8655	47	382
3825	Office,computing etc..	...	...	...	...	...	3825
383	Electrical machinery ...	2289	5783	2418	14788	173	383
3832	Radio,television etc..	2004	4563	1835	14205	142	3832
384	Transport equipment	9779	10321	19351	150856	1035	384
3841	Shipbuilding, repair..	...	...	...	...	...	3841
3843	Motor vehicles	...	...	...	...	...	3843
385	Professional goods	...	...	...	...	...	385
390	Other industries	...	...	...	...	...	390
3	Manufacturing	...	...	...	...	...	3
410	Electricity,gas,steam ..	...	...	...	...	...	410
4101	Electricity	...	...	...	...	...	4101
420	Water works and supply .	...	...	...	...	...	420
4	Electricity,gas etc	...	...	...	...	...	4
2-4	All industry	...	...	...	...	...	2-4

a/ Selected industries; for coverage, see country note. b/ In million Argentine pesos (10,000 pesos per Argentine peso).
c/ In billion Argentine pesos (10,000 pesos per Argentine peso).

8. INDEX NUMBERS OF INDUSTRIAL PRODUCTION (1980 = 100)

ISIC	INDUSTRY	1976	1977	1978	1979	1981	1982	1983	1984	1985	RATE a/	ISIC
210	Coal mining	121	134	95	144	117	114	116	106	82	-4.2	210
220	Petroleum and gas	80	85	88	94	102	104	107	109	105	3.1	220
230	Metal ore mining	101	120	108	98	104	107	101	103	109	0.9	230
290	Other mining	77	87	87	92	89	77	64	56	51	-4.5	290
2	Mining, quarrying .	80	87	89	95	101	101	101	102	98	2.3	2
311/2	Food products	98	99	98	100	98	92	94	97	99	0.1	311/2
313	Beverages	96	85	77	91	91	76	85	101	95	-0.1	313
314	Tobacco	97	97	97	100	33	86	91	103	103	0.7	314
321	Textiles	116	123	106	120	82	82	97	101	76	-4.6	321
3211	Spinning,weaving etc..	...	...	...	...	...	...	...	...	...	...	3211
322	Wearing apparel	130	123	96	112	63	55	60	62	43	-11.6	322
323	Leather and products ...	121	132	135	119	96	108	94	79	88	-3.5	323
324	Footwear	129	120	103	103	88	80	75	85	70	-6.6	324
331	Wood products	109	107	101	105	83	68	70	69	56	-7.1	331
332	Furniture, fixtures	58	72	80	100	93	83	72	60	58	0.0	332
341	Paper and products	100	106	109	122	75	94	105	105	97	-0.3	341
3411	Pulp,paper etc.	...	...	...	...	...	...	...	...	...	...	3411
342	Printing,publishing	104	99	102	94	88	80	81	83	84	-2.3	342
351	Industrial chemicals ...	98	106	96	116	90	109	121	126	107	1.0	351
3511	Basic excl fertilizers	...	...	...	...	...	...	...	...	...	...	3511
3513	Synthetic resins etc .	...	...	...	...	...	...	...	...	...	...	3513
352	Other chemical products.	105	98	86	94	102	90	97	113	113	0.8	352
3522	Drugs and medicines ..	...	...	...	...	...	...	...	...	...	...	3522
353	Petroleum refineries ...	85	89	90	94	97	96	100	97	100	1.8	353
354	Petroleum,coal products.	83	103	85	100	107	92	100	96	104	2.5	354
355	Rubber products	101	101	85	106	67	68	94	98	71	-3.8	355
356	Plastic products n.e.c..	82	89	80	100	75	80	91	105	81	-0.1	356
361	Pottery,china etc	116	96	86	101	50	61	83	77	48	-9.3	361
362	Glass and products	97	89	99	110	77	71	83	82	54	-6.3	362
369	Non-metal products n.e.c	96	98	98	102	88	78	84	76	63	-4.6	369
371	Iron and steel	90	104	99	113	90	102	107	101	97	0.8	371
372	Non-ferrous metals	69	79	69	93	75	83	93	100	78	1.4	372
381	Metal products	96	109	94	104	82	76	93	100	84	-1.5	381
382	Machinery n.e.c.	114	141	104	114	71	66	72	68	49	-9.0	382
3825	Office,computing etc..	...	...	...	...	...	...	...	...	...	...	3825
383	Electrical machinery ...	96	111	97	104	78	73	78	86	74	-2.9	383
3832	Radio,television etc..	...	...	...	...	...	...	...	...	...	...	3832
384	Transport equipment	78	105	78	96	62	55	71	78	64	-2.2	384
3841	Shipbuilding, repair..	...	...	...	...	...	...	...	...	...	...	3841
3843	Motor vehicles	...	...	...	...	...	...	...	...	...	...	3843
385	Professional goods	130	131	135	149	72	60	76	90	81	-5.1	385
390	Other industries	98	106	94	104	84	80	89	92	83	-1.8	390
3	Manufacturing	104	105	94	104	84	80	89	92	83	-2.5	3
410	Electricity,gas,steam ..	73	77	81	92	99	102	110	116	117	5.4	410
4101	Electricity	71	76	80	93	99	101	109	114	116	5.6	4101
420	Water works and supply .	...	...	...	...	...	...	...	...	...	...	420
4	Electricity,gas etc	74	77	81	93	98	101	110	116	118	5.3	4
2-4	All industry	102	104	93	103	85	81	90	94	85	-2.0	2-4

a/ Annual growth rate 1976-1985.

The information on industrial activity is based on the reply to the United Nations Questionnaire on General Industrial Statistics from the Australian Bureau of Statistics, Canberra. The concepts, definitions and classification by branches of industry are generally in accordance with United Nations standards.

The estimates are derived from annual censuses of mining, manufacturing and electricity and gas. These censuses are conducted within the framework of an integrated census programme which also covers, on a periodic basis, retail and wholesale trade. A standard industrial classification has been adopted for the integrated censuses and the census units are consistently defined to cover all activities carried out under one ownership at a single physical location. For the industrial censuses, all establishments in the industries surveyed are covered, but water works and supply are not surveyed and the manufacturing data shown in the tables exclude single-establishment enterprises with fewer than 4 employees. Only a limited range of data (employment and earnings) is collected from these small manufacturing units and their contribution to statistical aggregates is stated to be marginal. The reference period is the fiscal year from 1 July to 30 June; the period referred to in the tables is the fiscal year ending in the year indicated.

In application of the standardized concept of the census unit, mining excludes establishments at which the mining activity is subsidiary to a non-mining activity at the same location. Itinerant and part-time miners are omitted because of their limited operations and consequent difficulties in collecting returns. For manufacturing, data supplied for the establishment cover, in addition to manufacturing activities primary to the industry class to which the establishment is classified, the following activities, subject to certain exceptions mentioned below: any other manufacturing activity (that is, production of goods primary to another class of industry); any selling and distribution activities connected with the products manufactured; any non-manufacturing activity (for example, merchanting of goods not manufactured by the establishment, extraction of raw materials for use by the establishment); activities of separately located administrative offices and ancillary units serving the establishment. Exceptions are made in the case of locations where subsidiary activities exceed a specified amount in gross value (currently $4.3 million), the units in such cases being treated as two or more establishments corresponding to the kinds of activity carried on. The census unit for electricity and gas, an exception to the general concept, consists of all locations, including administrative offices and ancillary units, operated by the particular undertaking in the one State, including own account construction.

The estimates, which are based on the 1978 edition of the Australian Standard Industrial Classification, generally have been adjusted to the present version of ISIC. However, it should be noted that the national concept of manufacturing excludes making up of curtains, custom dressmaking and tailoring, and repair and servicing of agricultural machinery (these activities are included in the retail and wholesale trade censuses). Also, manufacture of refrigerators (ISIC 382) is included in ISIC 383, manufacture of hard surface floor covering n.e.c. (ISIC 321) is included in ISIC 356, and steam and hot water supply (ISIC 410) are included in ISIC 390.

The information relates to the numbers of establishments which operated at any time during the year. For mining, manufacturing and electricity and gas, the count of establishments in table 1 relates to those operating at 30 June. Separately located administrative offices and ancillary units are not included in the establishment count but activities of these units are included in the establishment statistics.

The employment data for mining and electricity and gas are as of 30 June. For manufacturing, the estimates of persons engaged and employees are annual averages, but numbers of operatives are as of 30 June.

The concept of output comprises (a) sales (exclusive of excise and sales tax) of goods, whether produced by the establishment or not, (b) transfers out of goods to other establishments of the same enterprise, (c) bounties and subsidies on production, (d) all other operating revenue from outside the enterprise (such as commission, repair and service revenue), (e) capital work done for own use, or for rental or lease and (f) rent, leasing and hiring revenue. Adjustments are made for changes in the value of stocks of finished goods and work in progress.

Value added is calculated as the value of output less the following inputs: (a) purchases of materials, fuel, power, containers etc. and of goods for resale, adjusted for stock changes, (b) transfers in of goods from other establishments of the enterprise, (c) charges for commission and subcontract work, (d) repair and maintenance expenses, (e) outward freight and cartage, motor vehicle running expenses, sales commission payments made outside the enterprise and (f) rent, leasing and hiring expenses.

Gross fixed capital formation represents the outlay on new and used fixed tangible assets less disposals. Expenditure on establishments not yet in operation is included.

The indexes of industrial production are compiled by the Australia and New Zealand Banking Group Limited and provided in response to the United Nations Questionnaire on Indexes of Industrial Production. In principle, the indexes cover establishments with 4 or more persons engaged or with installed power equipment. All figures relate to the 12-month period ending 30 June of the year indicated.

Related national publications:
<u>Mining Establishments</u> (annual); <u>Manufacturing Establishments</u> (annual); <u>Electricity and Gas Establishments</u> (annual); <u>Year Book Australia</u>, all published by the Australian Bureau of Statistics, Canberra.

ISIC	INDUSTRY	1. NUMBER OF ESTABLISHMENTS a/b/ (NUMBER) 1981	1982	1983	1984	1985	2. AVERAGE NUMBER OF PERSONS ENGAGED b/c/d/ (THOUSANDS) 1981	1982	1983	1984	1985	ISIC
210	Coal mining	[140	147]	137	136	132	[33	37]	35	34	34	210
220	Petroleum and gas			18	22	27			3	4	4	220
230	Metal ore mining	250	237	257	310	330	35	35	32	31	31	230
290	Other mining	1124	1107	1130	1162	1160	10	9	9	9	9	290
2	Mining, quarrying .	1514	1491	1542	1630	1649	78	81	79	78	78	2
311/2	Food products	3002	3071	3032	3049	3030	158	152	150	145	144	311/2
313	Beverages	407	408	386	380	351	21	21	20	19	18	313
314	Tobacco	6	6	6	6	6	5	5	5	5	5	314
321	Textiles	904	924	899	897	921	50	49	45	45	47	321
3211	Spinning,weaving etc..	253	250	243	240	253	25	23	21	21	22	3211
322	Wearing apparel	1523	1548	1486	1474	1544	52	52	46	47	49	322
323	Leather and products ...	207	211	201	190	187	5	5	4	4	4	323
324	Footwear	206	215	212	201	202	13	13	11	12	13	324
331	Wood products	2610	2681	2536	2420	2452	50	51	44	43	45	331
332	Furniture, fixtures	1465	1503	1492	1554	1571	29	30	27	27	28	332
341	Paper and products	267	273	258	243	241	25	25	23	22	23	341
3411	Pulp,paper etc.	19	21	21	26	33	10	9	9	8	8	3411
342	Printing,publishing	2549	2673	2651	2668	2731	77	78	77	77	79	342
351	Industrial chemicals ...	267	285	277	272	270	20	20	19	18	18	351
3511	Basic excl fertilizers	142	157	146	147	148	9	9	8	8	8	3511
3513	Synthetic resins etc .	69	67	66	60	62	6	6	6	5	5	3513
352	Other chemical products.	601	621	617	603	579	34	35	34	33	32	352
3522	Drugs and medicines ..	121	127	131	127	124	10	11	10	10	10	3522
353	Petroleum refineries ...	12	12	13	13	15	5	5	5	5	5	353
354	Petroleum,coal products.	24	24	24	22	23	1	1	1	1	1	354
355	Rubber products	227	245	219	212	198	14	14	11	10	10	355
356	Plastic products n.e.c..	923	968	914	961	971	33	34	32	31	32	356
361	Pottery,china etc	52	60	59	62	57	3	2	2	2	2	361
362	Glass and products	38	43	41	41	40	7	7	6	6	6	362
369	Non-metal products n.e.c	1608	1674	1612	1610	1614	39	37	32	30	31	369
371	Iron and steel	305	319	331	317	306	69	67	56	49	48	371
372	Non-ferrous metals	224	229	217	216	223	28	29	27	28	29	372
381	Metal products	4272	4509	4272	4165	4137	113	116	102	94	93	381
382	Machinery n.e.c.	2537	2614	2449	2402	2364	94	94	78	69	68	382
3825	Office,computing etc..	1121	1149	1093	1054	1053	31	32	27	24	24	3825
383	Electrical machinery ...	981	1009	975	963	969	63	65	58	54	54	383
3832	Radio,television etc..	272	272	286	293	313	21	21	19	18	19	3832
384	Transport equipment	1370	1356	1270	1264	1280	124	126	116	112	115	384
3841	Shipbuilding, repair..	335	319	308	277	268	15	15	14	14	13	3841
3843	Motor vehicles	917	911	840	830	845	72	75	67	62	65	3843
385	Professional goods	321	391	411	478	428	10	11	10	10	11	385
390	Other industries	773	834	809	789	811	12	12	11	11	11	390
3	Manufacturing	27681	28706	27696	27472	27611	1154	1156	1053	1010	1021	3
410	Electricity,gas,steam ..	124	119	122	116	117	82	92	93	93	93	410
4101	Electricity	86	85	85	82	83	72	82	82	83	83	4101
420	Water works and supply .	...	...	...	...	...	...	...	...	...	...	420
4	Electricity,gas etc	...	...	...	...	...	...	...	...	...	...	4
2-4	All industry	...	...	...	...	...	...	...	...	...	...	2-4

Note. For certain differences in classification, see country note.

a/ At 30 June of the year indicated.
b/ Manufacturing: excluding single-establishment enterprises with fewer than 4 employees.
c/ Twelve months ending 30 June of the year indicated.
d/ Mining and electricity and gas: at 30 June of the year indicated.

ISIC	INDUSTRY	3. AVERAGE NUMBER OF EMPLOYEES a/b/d/ (THOUSANDS)					4. WAGES AND SALARIES OF EMPLOYEES a/b/c/ (MILLION DOLLARS)					ISIC
		1981	1982	1983	1984	1985	1981	1982	1983	1984	1985	
210	Coal mining	[33	37]	35	34	34	[775	970]	1052	1065	1138	210
220	Petroleum and gas			3	4	4			81	113	131	220
230	Metal ore mining	35	35	32	31	31	670	755	765	776	850	230
290	Other mining	9	9	8	9	8	149	157	165	175	188	290
2	Mining, quarrying .	77	81	78	78	77	1594	1882	2063	2129	2307	2
311/2	Food products	156	150	148	144	142	1980	2171	2392	2418	2520	311/2
313	Beverages	21	21	20	19	18	306	345	355	372	382	313
314	Tobacco	5	5	5	5	5	76	91	107	116	109	314
321	Textiles	50	49	45	45	47	590	657	672	715	782	321
3211	Spinning,weaving etc..	25	23	21	21	22	305	340	349	368	399	3211
322	Wearing apparel	51	51	46	46	48	487	547	546	580	634	322
323	Leather and products ...	5	5	4	4	4	53	62	58	59	58	323
324	Footwear	13	13	11	12	12	136	145	142	158	176	324
331	Wood products	48	49	43	41	44	552	625	609	634	703	331
332	Furniture, fixtures	28	29	26	26	27	301	342	341	371	399	332
341	Paper and products	25	25	23	22	23	384	419	447	451	501	341
3411	Pulp,paper etc.	10	9	9	8	8	176	176	193	190	205	3411
342	Printing,publishing	76	77	76	76	78	1019	1172	1264	1321	1468	342
351	Industrial chemicals ...	20	20	19	18	18	338	388	405	405	448	351
3511	Basic excl fertilizers	9	9	8	8	8	153	180	181	178	190	3511
3513	Synthetic resins etc .	6	6	5	5	5	98	113	131	133	141	3513
352	Other chemical products.	34	35	34	33	32	476	545	591	635	669	352
3522	Drugs and medicines ..	10	11	10	10	10	148	171	184	205	212	3522
353	Petroleum refineries ...	5	5	5	5	5	109	126	137	148	138	353
354	Petroleum,coal products.	1	1	1	1	1	10	11	11	11	14	354
355	Rubber products	14	14	11	10	10	179	212	185	183	197	355
356	Plastic products n.e.c..	33	34	31	31	32	411	488	502	516	579	356
361	Pottery,china etc	3	2	2	2	2	30	33	32	31	33	361
362	Glass and products	7	7	6	6	6	111	135	138	141	138	362
369	Non-metal products n.e.c	39	36	32	30	31	533	601	591	569	631	369
371	Iron and steel	69	67	56	49	48	1111	1247	1109	1020	1080	371
372	Non-ferrous metals	28	29	27	28	29	450	537	573	627	702	372
381	Metal products	111	114	100	93	93	1395	1625	1584	1543	1604	381
382	Machinery n.e.c.	93	93	77	68	68	1205	1376	1278	1167	1237	382
3825	Office,computing etc..	28	32	27	24	24	405	482	464	433	444	3825
383	Electrical machinery ...	63	65	58	54	54	785	916	955	921	985	383
3832	Radio,television etc..	21	21	19	18	19	272	307	333	328	373	3832
384	Transport equipment	123	123	116	112	115	1624	1893	2075	2043	2244	384
3841	Shipbuilding, repair..	15	15	14	14	13	179	210	225	237	246	3841
3843	Motor vehicles	72	75	67	62	65	947	1115	1197	1103	1247	3843
385	Professional goods	10	10	10	10	11	132	148	154	164	188	385
390	Other industries	12	12	11	11	11	131	148	149	151	162	390
3	Manufacturing	1143	1141	1043	1000	1014	14914	17005	17403	17467	18781	3
410	Electricity,gas,steam ..	82	92	93	93	93	1290	1645	1896	2050	2230	410
4101	Electricity	72	82	82	83	83	1139	1474	1690	1833	2001	4101
420	Water works and supply .	...	...	...	...	...	...	...	...	...	...	420
4	Electricity,gas etc	...	...	...	...	...	...	...	...	...	...	4
2-4	All industry	...	...	...	...	...	...	...	...	...	...	2-4

Note. For certain differences in classification, see country note.

a/ Twelve months ending 30 June of the year indicated.
b/ Manufacturing: excluding single-establishment enterprises with fewer than 4 employees.
c/ Excluding payments in kind.
d/ Mining and electricity and gas: at 30 June of the year indicated.

ISIC	INDUSTRY	5. AVERAGE NUMBER OF OPERATIVES a/b/ (THOUSANDS)					6. WAGES AND SALARIES OF OPERATIVES b/c/d/ (MILLION DOLLARS)					ISIC
		1981	1982	1983	1984	1985	1981	1982	1983	1984	1985	
210	Coal mining	[28	30]	27	27	27	[619	763]	860	845	892	210
220	Petroleum and gas			1	2	2			36	54	61	220
230	Metal ore mining	24	23	22	21	20	448	509	518	513	547	230
290	Other mining	7	6	6	6	6	107	114	122	128	139	290
2	Mining, quarrying .	59	59	56	56	55	1174	1386	1536	1540	1638	2
311/2	Food products	115	113	108	108	107	1431	1564	1741	1749	1817	311/2
313	Beverages	13	13	11	11	11	182	205	211	223	226	313
314	Tobacco	4	4	4	4	4	54	62	71	80	73	314
321	Textiles	40	38	34	36	37	428	478	480	520	576	321
3211	Spinning,weaving etc..	19	18	16	17	17	214	238	238	255	283	3211
322	Wearing apparel	44	44	39	41	42	400	447	451	480	531	322
323	Leather and products ...	4	4	3	3	3	41	49	45	45	45	323
324	Footwear	12	11	10	11	11	113	121	117	134	151	324
331	Wood products	38	37	33	33	34	423	476	460	479	529	331
332	Furniture, fixtures	23	23	20	21	22	231	263	262	287	306	332
341	Paper and products	19	18	17	17	17	274	302	329	331	366	341
3411	Pulp,paper etc.	7	7	6	6	6	131	133	145	143	156	3411
342	Printing,publishing	48	48	47	47	49	629	721	792	817	905	342
351	Industrial chemicals ...	13	13	12	11	11	204	232	244	250	271	351
3511	Basic excl fertilizers	5	6	5	5	5	90	105	105	107	110	3511
3513	Synthetic resins etc .	4	4	3	3	3	63	72	83	82	90	3513
352	Other chemical products.	19	19	18	18	18	237	271	293	313	334	352
3522	Drugs and medicines ..	6	6	6	6	6	74	84	92	99	107	3522
353	Petroleum refineries ...	3	3	3	3	3	71	83	87	95	98	353
354	Petroleum,coal products.	-	-	-	-	-	6	7	6	7	8	354
355	Rubber products	11	11	8	8	8	138	157	131	134	144	355
356	Plastic products n.e.c..	24	24	22	23	24	282	335	340	352	401	356
361	Pottery,china etc	2	2	2	2	1	22	25	25	24	25	361
362	Glass and products	5	5	5	5	4	82	97	104	105	106	362
369	Non-metal products n.e.c	26	25	22	22	23	370	423	404	395	449	369
371	Iron and steel	51	48	37	36	35	780	874	765	705	740	371
372	Non-ferrous metals	21	21	19	21	21	320	369	380	429	496	372
381	Metal products	86	85	71	68	68	1016	1187	1142	1098	1138	381
382	Machinery n.e.c.	70	67	52	50	48	863	987	915	821	861	382
3825	Office,computing etc..	23	23	19	17	17	287	350	333	301	310	3825
383	Electrical machinery ...	48	47	41	40	41	552	632	660	632	668	383
3832	Radio,television etc..	15	15	14	13	14	182	193	218	219	238	3832
384	Transport equipment	99	101	86	90	92	1189	1412	1543	1494	1679	384
3841	Shipbuilding, repair..	11	11	10	10	10	126	149	160	165	169	3841
3843	Motor vehicles	58	60	48	51	53	688	834	888	803	932	3843
385	Professional goods	8	8	7	8	8	96	108	110	118	138	385
390	Other industries	8	8	7	7	7	86	98	116	98	106	390
3	Manufacturing	854	838	738	746	750	10520	11985	12203	12217	13187	3
410	Electricity,gas,steam ..	50	53	54	55	54	778	913	1053	1164	1288	410
4101	Electricity	45	48	49	50	49	699	833	959	1064	1188	4101
420	Water works and supply .	...	...	...	...	...	...	...	...	...	...	420
4	Electricity,gas etc	...	...	...	...	...	...	...	...	...	...	4
2-4	All industry	...	...	...	...	...	...	...	...	...	...	2-4

Note. For certain differences in classification, see country note.

a/ At 30 June of the year indicated.
b/ Manufacturing: excluding single-establishment enterprises with fewer than 4 employees.
c/ Twelve months ending 30 June of the year indicated. d/ Excluding payments in kind.

ISIC	INDUSTRY	7. OUTPUT IN FACTOR VALUES a/b/ (MILLION DOLLARS)					8. VALUE ADDED IN FACTOR VALUES a/b/ (MILLION DOLLARS)					ISIC
		1981	1982	1983	1984	1985	1981	1982	1983	1984	1985	
210	Coal mining	[4711	5665]	4610	4869	5904	[3352	4088]	2876	2776	3341	210
220	Petroleum and gas			2170	2889	3894			1984	2712	3601	220
230	Metal ore mining	4005	3855	4526	4655	5166	2459	2147	2799	2763	2999	230
290	Other mining	792	893	955	1086	1247	413	463	486	574	669	290
2	Mining, quarrying .	9508	10413	12261	13499	16211	6224	6698	8145	8825	10610	2
311/2	Food products	13822	14465	15617	16503	17554	4053	4291	4663	5115	5302	311/2
313	Beverages	2065	2296	2496	2814	2927	822	877	1025	1161	1208	313
314	Tobacco	382	410	494	527	547	175	157	239	238	255	314
321	Textiles	2632	2877	2782	3085	3512	1027	1170	1077	1223	1363	321
3211	Spinning,weaving etc..	1282	1332	1311	1441	1670	481	513	507	552	616	3211
322	Wearing apparel	1700	1843	1820	2027	2197	793	883	862	969	1030	322
323	Leather and products ...	266	311	306	373	408	92	105	101	110	109	323
324	Footwear	442	470	452	527	594	217	235	221	261	292	324
331	Wood products	2522	2805	2670	2981	3391	1089	1191	1114	1318	1467	331
332	Furniture, fixtures	1196	1332	1307	1462	1610	520	579	560	639	723	332
341	Paper and products	1965	2245	2348	2474	2756	726	859	845	903	1003	341
3411	Pulp,paper etc.	823	919	933	1014	1112	329	373	334	356	393	3411
342	Printing,publishing	3331	3878	4154	4632	5434	1842	2107	2227	2478	3041	342
351	Industrial chemicals ...	3151	3430	3442	3738	4078	1007	1097	1036	1179	1155	351
3511	Basic excl fertilizers	1200	1392	1416	1461	1561	424	501	496	492	583	3511
3513	Synthetic resins etc .	982	1064	1054	1229	1283	293	329	309	416	442	3513
352	Other chemical products.	2576	2933	3127	3440	3734	1153	1327	1440	1584	1699	352
3522	Drugs and medicines ..	738	841	938	1061	1142	371	424	482	528	587	3522
353	Petroleum refineries ...	1348	1430	1537	1626	1914	320	310	329	311	406	353
354	Petroleum,coal products.	112	105	101	118	142	33	32	29	32	36	354
355	Rubber products	779	857	740	756	829	343	356	307	341	377	355
356	Plastic products n.e.c..	2034	2270	2380	2577	2948	784	864	954	984	1153	356
361	Pottery,china etc	76	84	83	80	90	46	55	50	53	59	361
362	Glass and products	407	501	512	580	624	237	291	281	343	363	362
369	Non-metal products n.e.c	2836	3287	3156	3392	3954	1139	1339	1228	1335	1549	369
371	Iron and steel	5241	5613	4721	5568	5868	2776	1832	1185	1931	1985	371
372	Non-ferrous metals	4675	4591	4669	5321	6721	1342	1248	1315	1427	2011	372
381	Metal products	5927	6838	6371	6549	6962	2502	2860	2650	2763	2912	381
382	Machinery n.e.c.	4666	5350	4536	4464	4907	2088	2317	1960	1990	2247	382
3825	Office,computing etc..	1464	1733	1569	1474	1610	686	802	727	697	770	3825
383	Electrical machinery ...	3106	3627	3582	3598	4032	1344	1005	1626	1631	2897	383
3832	Radio,television etc..	984	1171	1174	1180	1498	450	536	579	568	754	3832
384	Transport equipment	6248	7457	7930	8143	9583	2455	3634	3189	3220	3680	384
3841	Shipbuilding, repair..	482	544	563	620	610	260	302	312	345	347	3841
3843	Motor vehicles	4644	5634	5865	5862	7245	1591	2521	1980	1843	2283	3843
385	Professional goods	559	648	653	748	815	282	312	345	370	398	385
390	Other industries	500	557	571	651	726	243	268	275	312	351	390
3	Manufacturing	74564	82510	82481	88754	98927	29450	31601	31059	34221	39071	3
410	Electricity,gas,steam ..	...	...	9508	10742	11806	...	...	4952	5472	5681	410
4101	Electricity	...	...	8344	9356	10153	...	...	4326	4720	4856	4101
420	Water works and supply .	...	...	...	...	...	...	...	...	...	...	420
4	Electricity,gas etc	...	...	...	...	...	...	...	...	...	...	4
2-4	All industry	...	...	...	...	...	...	...	...	...	...	2-4

Note. For certain differences in classification, see country note.

a/ Twelve months ending 30 June of the year indicated.
b/ Manufacturing: excluding single-establishment enterprises with fewer than 4 employees.

ISIC	INDUSTRY	9. GROSS FIXED CAPITAL FORMATION TOTAL a/b/ (MILLION DOLLARS)					10. GROSS FIXED CAPITAL FORMATION MACHINERY AND EQUIPMENT a/b/ (MILLION DOLLARS)					ISIC
		1981	1982	1983	1984	1985	1981	1982	1983	1984	1985	
210	Coal mining	[1295	2018]	1598	808	532	[619	971]	894	456	234	210
220	Petroleum and gas			1406	1141	631			630	791	256	220
230	Metal ore mining	605	559	422	413	542	369	302	203	227	255	230
290	Other mining	129	75	71	95	226	79	56	48	62	144	290
2	Mining, quarrying .	2029	2652	3497	2457	1931	1067	1329	1775	1536	889	2
311/2	Food products	382	375	356	378	440	299	308	295	338	378	311/2
313	Beverages	103	165	212	138	45	85	138	182	93	99	313
314	Tobacco	13	10	26	10	59	12	7	11	9	30	314
321	Textiles	45	82	66	64	125	42	71	60	59	91	321
3211	Spinning,weaving etc..	26	56	39	41	89	26	51	36	38	59	3211
322	Wearing apparel	17	16	16	23	30	15	15	15	19	23	322
323	Leather and products ...	4	5	3	6	5	2	3	2	3	5	323
324	Footwear	5	9	5	7	10	5	7	4	7	9	324
331	Wood products	71	77	81	63	95	57	57	67	54	79	331
332	Furniture, fixtures	20	18	10	14	21	13	13	10	11	15	332
341	Paper and products	109	185	79	55	86	92	163	70	50	65	341
3411	Pulp,paper etc.	76	133	37	9	44	66	129	36	14	26	3411
342	Printing,publishing	95	109	127	127	224	76	98	106	112	211	342
351	Industrial chemicals ...	125	155	168	108	105	114	142	155	94	89	351
3511	Basic excl fertilizers	67	73	91	68	45	62	71	89	58	41	3511
3513	Synthetic resins etc	26	54	36	23	35	23	49	33	22	29	3513
352	Other chemical products.	63	84	76	95	121	46	62	52	76	88	352
3522	Drugs and medicines ..	28	33	31	27	36	18	22	17	20	26	3522
353	Petroleum refineries ...	108	69	83	63	65	98	62	77	58	61	353
354	Petroleum,coal products.	6	1	1	-	3	5	2	2	1	3	354
355	Rubber products	18	21	23	21	23	17	19	17	20	22	355
356	Plastic products n.e.c..	66	80	93	93	104	56	64	76	76	93	356
361	Pottery,china etc	1	2	2	3	2	2	1	2	2	1	361
362	Glass and products	32	25	26	44	23	28	24	31	42	22	362
369	Non-metal products n.e.c	165	152	116	107	143	147	130	104	78	110	369
371	Iron and steel	294	384	213	109	177	233	323	202	101	158	371
372	Non-ferrous metals	652	1302	1219	666	494	419	971	1054	573	450	372
381	Metal products	138	167	147	123	152	98	124	112	104	125	381
382	Machinery n.e.c.	106	130	99	79	89	89	101	81	69	87	382
3825	Office,computing etc..	39	48	39	35	33	26	35	28	27	28	3825
383	Electrical machinery ...	58	103	98	78	113	53	81	83	68	99	383
3832	Radio,television etc..	16	30	29	26	41	15	25	25	24	39	3832
384	Transport equipment	152	321	295	265	335	95	267	257	193	298	384
3841	Shipbuilding, repair..	27	28	22	38	31	8	9	5	6	7	3841
3843	Motor vehicles	95	256	214	155	244	71	227	215	140	240	3843
385	Professional goods	19	22	20	21	31	15	18	20	21	29	385
390	Other industries	16	18	15	17	13	12	11	9	12	11	390
3	Manufacturing	2883	4087	3678	2778	3133	2225	3282	3157	2343	2751	3
410	Electricity,gas,steam ..	1943	2528	3433	4116	3146	1051	1189	2231	2163	1418	410
4101	Electricity	1839	2367	2953	3547	2762	1024	1137	1840	2138	1329	4101
420	Water works and supply .	...	...	...	...	...	...	...	...	...	...	420
4	Electricity,gas etc	...	...	...	...	...	...	...	...	...	...	4
2-4	All industry	...	...	...	...	...	...	...	...	...	...	2-4

Note. For certain differences in classification, see country note.

a/ Twelve months ending 30 June of the year indicated.
b/ Manufacturing: excluding single-establishment enterprises with fewer than 4 employees.

11. VALUE OF STOCKS AT END OF PERIOD
TOTAL a/b/
(MILLION DOLLARS)

ISIC	INDUSTRY	1981	1982	1983	1984	1985	ISIC
210	Coal mining	[398	553]	658	673	661	210
220	Petroleum and gas			74	108	196	220
230	Metal ore mining	577	694	854	777	738	230
290	Other mining	89	103	124	143	121	290
2	Mining, quarrying .	1064	1350	1710	1701	1716	2
311/2	Food products	1316	1294	1389	1467	1564	311/2
313	Beverages	438	465	481	519	554	313
314	Tobacco	182	188	195	205	209	314
321	Textiles	489	537	494	526	632	321
3211	Spinning,weaving etc..	238	249	225	246	292	3211
322	Wearing apparel	292	308	279	311	323	322
323	Leather and products ...	40	41	40	47	54	323
324	Footwear	64	71	67	82	92	324
331	Wood products	356	407	398	413	461	331
332	Furniture, fixtures	160	178	169	187	199	332
341	Paper and products	327	329	302	308	345	341
3411	Pulp,paper etc.	133	127	110	115	131	3411
342	Printing,publishing	377	444	440	424	537	342
351	Industrial chemicals ...	585	626	626	617	675	351
3511	Basic excl fertilizers	177	188	186	188	188	3511
3513	Synthetic resins etc .	195	237	210	217	207	3513
352	Other chemical products.	511	535	586	618	690	352
3522	Drugs and medicines ..	201	212	230	253	279	3522
353	Petroleum refineries ...	189	152	211	202	186	353
354	Petroleum,coal products.	16	19	21	16	19	354
355	Rubber products	117	114	81	83	81	355
356	Plastic products n.e.c..	319	364	363	379	417	356
361	Pottery,china etc	13	16	18	17	16	361
362	Glass and products	68	93	107	102	103	362
369	Non-metal products n.e.c	352	405	448	419	441	369
371	Iron and steel	1131	1142	1009	1024	1076	371
372	Non-ferrous metals	846	930	932	995	1160	372
381	Metal products	969	1074	957	1011	1037	381
382	Machinery n.e.c.	1079	1220	1066	973	1065	382
3825	Office,computing etc..	295	339	275	272	286	3825
383	Electrical machinery ...	710	798	787	797	890	383
3832	Radio,television etc..	261	281	292	280	375	3832
384	Transport equipment	1257	1338	1365	1206	1377	384
3841	Shipbuilding, repair..	57	73	77	81	74	3841
3843	Motor vehicles	877	920	989	823	992	3843
385	Professional goods	106	100	95	108	117	385
390	Other industries	100	107	109	124	154	390
3	Manufacturing	12409	13295	13035	13182	14474	3
410	Electricity,gas,steam ..	431	580	742	786	701	410
4101	Electricity	382	530	670	713	631	4101
420	Water works and supply .	...	...	...	...	...	420
4	Electricity,gas etc	...	...	...	...	...	4
2-4	All industry	...	...	...	...	...	2-4

Note. For certain differences in classification, see country note.

a/ At 30 June of the year indicated.
b/ Manufacturing: excluding single-establishment enterprises with fewer than 4 employees.

12. INDEX NUMBERS OF INDUSTRIAL PRODUCTION (1980 = 100) a/

ISIC	INDUSTRY	1976	1977	1978	1979	1981	1982	1983	1984	1985	b/ RATE	ISIC
210	Coal mining	...	...	...	...	...	...	...	...	...	...	210
220	Petroleum and gas	...	...	...	...	...	...	...	...	...	...	220
230	Metal ore mining	...	...	...	...	...	...	...	...	...	...	230
290	Other mining	...	...	...	...	...	...	...	...	...	...	290
2	Mining, quarrying .	...	...	...	...	...	...	...	...	...	...	2
311/2	Food products	106	108	112	102	103	102	...	...	...	d/ -0.6	311/2
313	Beverages	95	98	97	96	99	96	...	...	...	d/ 0.2	313
314	Tobacco	99	101	99	98	102	99	...	...	...	d/ 0.0	314
321	Textiles	98	97	99	100	100	92	...	...	...	d/ -1.0	321
3211	Spinning,weaving etc..	...	...	...	...	...	...	...	...	...	...	3211
322	Wearing apparel	79	80	87	93	101	87	...	...	...	d/ 1.6	322
323	Leather and products ...	...	...	...	...	...	...	...	...	...	...	323
324	Footwear	78	82	89	94	94	91	...	...	...	d/ 2.6	324
331	Wood products	[94	94	86	95	95	92	...	...	...	d/ -0.4]	331
332	Furniture, fixtures											332
341	Paper and products	83	86	90	98	93	90	...	...	...	d/ 1.4	341
3411	Pulp,paper etc.	...	...	...	...	...	...	...	...	...	...	3411
342	Printing,publishing	...	...	...	...	...	...	...	...	...	...	342
351	Industrial chemicals ...	74	79	89	104	98	96	...	...	...	d/ 4.4	351
3511	Basic excl fertilizers	...	...	...	...	...	...	...	...	...	...	3511
3513	Synthetic resins etc .	...	...	...	...	...	...	...	...	...	...	3513
352	Other chemical products.	94	92	95	101	103	102	...	...	...	d/ 1.4	352
3522	Drugs and medicines ..	...	...	...	...	...	...	...	...	...	...	3522
353	Petroleum refineries ...	99	103	102	103	102	100	...	...	...	d/ 0.2	353
354	Petroleum,coal products.	...	...	...	...	...	...	...	...	...	...	354
355	Rubber products	...	...	...	...	...	...	...	...	...	...	355
356	Plastic products n.e.c..	...	...	...	...	...	...	...	...	...	...	356
361	Pottery,china etc											361
362	Glass and products	[93	89	88	95	101	88	...	...	...	d/ -0.9]	362
369	Non-metal products n.e.c											369
371	Iron and steel	[88	93	96	98	95	79	...	...	...	d/ -1.8]	371
372	Non-ferrous metals											372
381	Metal products	94	95	97	101	96	76	...	...	...	d/ -3.5	381
382	Machinery n.e.c.	88	82	90	103	104	73	...	...	...	d/ -3.1	382
3825	Office,computing etc..	...	...	...	...	...	...	...	...	...	...	3825
383	Electrical machinery ...	94	81	84	92	97	78	...	...	...	d/ -3.1	383
3832	Radio,television etc..	...	...	...	...	...	...	...	...	...	...	3832
384	Transport equipment	117	103	115	108	111	108	...	...	...	d/ -1.3	384
3841	Shipbuilding, repair..	...	...	...	...	...	...	...	...	...	...	3841
3843	Motor vehicles	125	106	120	111	112	108	...	...	...	d/ -2.4	3843
385	Professional goods	...	...	...	...	...	...	...	...	...	...	385
390	Other industries	80	81	91	103	103	87	...	...	...	d/ 1.4	390
3	Manufacturing	93	92	94	99	100	88	93	95	98	0.6	3
410	Electricity,gas,steam ..	79	83	87	93	105	106	111	118	125	5.2	410
4101	Electricity	82	85	90	95	106	108	112	119	...	e/ 4.8	4101
420	Water works and supply .	.	.	.	.	.	.	.	.	...	.	420
4	Electricity,gas etc	...	...	...	...	...	...	...	...	...	...	4
2-4	All industry c/	92	91	94	99	101	90	94	98	102	1.2	2-4

a/ Twelve months beginning 1 July of the year stated.
b/ Annual growth rate 1976-1985.
c/ Excluding mining.
d/ Annual growth rate 1976-1982.
e/ Annual growth rate 1976-1984.

The information on industrial activity is based on the reply to the United Nations Questionnaire on General Industrial Statistics from the Austrian Central Statistical Office, Vienna. The concepts, definitions and classification by branches of industry are generally in accordance with United Nations standards.

In general, the estimates are derived from the results of annual surveys conducted by the Austrian Central Statistical Office under the terms of a statistical law introduced in 1969. The figures presented in the tables generally cover all establishments affiliated with the Industry Section of the Federal Economic Chamber (membership is compulsory for specific commodity-producing units), and establishments with 20 or more employees of the "Gewerbesektion". The latter are generally handicraft-type units, but for certain branches of industry they account for a considerable share of total output. Establishments below this size are also surveyed annually but the results are not included. Also, up to 1982, data shown for ISIC 331 exclude sawmills as activities of this industry were not surveyed annually before 1983.

The estimates, which are based on the national classification scheme, have generally been adjusted to the present version of ISIC. Certain differences are annotated in the tables.

In principle, the reporting unit is the local self-contained unit capable of reporting production costs. However, a deviation from this practice is used for units engaged in multiple economic activities at one location; these units are whenever possible subdivided by their activities.

The employment figures represent the numbers on 31 December of each year. Homeworkers are included in the estimates of persons engaged and employees, and payments to homeworkers are included in remuneration of employees. Homeworkers are also included in the tables relating to operatives.

The estimates of wages and salaries represent gross pay-roll earnings of salary and wage earners, including apprentices paid at apprenticeship rates. They include both regular pay and irregular allowances, such as employee profit sharing and dismissal pay. Commission earnings, daily allowances etc. paid to independent agents are excluded. Supplements to wages and salaries comprise (a) social security contributions paid by the employer (health, old-age, accident and unemployment insurance); contributions to the equalization fund for child allowance; contributions to the residential construction fund and lodging allowance; and (b) all (net) expenditures of the employer for non-obligatory social services (payments in case of accident, decease and distress; canteen services, mileage allowance etc.).

The estimates of output comprise turnover of own production, receipts for goods sold in the same condition as received and receipts for repair, installation, maintenance and other work done. Adjustments are made for changes in the value of stocks of finished goods and work in progress. The estimates of value added are derived as the difference between output and the cost of the following inputs: raw materials, supplies, semi-manufactures, fuels and electricity; work contracted out, including repair work; other operating expenses, including the cost of goods to be sold as received and non-industrial services. Adjustments are made for changes in stocks. The valuation is in producers' prices but the value-added tax is not included.

Gross fixed capital formation relates to acquisitions of fixed capital assets; sales are not deducted. Improvements and repair of a capital nature are included. Also included are rights treated as assets under the national concept, such as licences and rights to the use of trade marks. For machinery and equipment, second-hand plant and minor assets are excluded.

The estimates of stocks cover all commodities owned by the establishments at the end of the year. Valuation is in purchasers' prices or producers' prices depending on the category of the stock.

The indexes of industrial production are compiled by the Austrian Central Statistical Office and provided in response to the United Nations Questionnaire on Indexes of Industrial Production. The indexes cover all establishments affiliated with the Industry Section of the Federal Economic Chamber.

Related national publications:
Statistisches Handbuch fur die Republik Osterreich (annual); Industriestatistik, 2.Teil (annual); Gewerbestatistik, 2. Teil (annual); Statistische Nachrichten (monthly - selected issues), all published by the Austrian Central Statistical Office, Vienna. Betriebsstatistik-Erzeugung und Verbrauch Elektrischer Energie in Osterreich, 1. Teil, Gesamtergebnisse (annual), published by the Ministry of Trade and Industry, Vienna.

ISIC	INDUSTRY	1. NUMBER OF ESTABLISHMENTS a/ (NUMBER) 1981	1982	1983	1984	1985	2. AVERAGE NUMBER OF PERSONS ENGAGED a/b/c/ (THOUSANDS) 1981	1982	1983	1984	1985	ISIC
210	Coal mining	10	10	10	9	...	3.8	3.4	3.2	3.0	...	210
220	Petroleum and gas	15	15	14	15	...	6.2	6.1	4.5	4.2	...	220
230	Metal ore mining	10	10	11	11	...	3.1	2.9	2.8	2.8	...	230
290	Other mining	175	169	167	153	...	4.5	4.4	3.9	3.6	...	290
2	Mining, quarrying .	210	204	202	188	...	17.6	16.8	14.4	13.6	...	2
311/2	Food products	772	778	830	830	...	53.1	52.3	52.3	52.7	...	311/2
313	Beverages	215	211	219	253	...	14.4	13.9	13.3	13.5	...	313
314	Tobacco	14	15	15	15	...	1.7	1.6	1.6	1.5	...	314
321	Textiles	583	566	543	530	...	50.1	46.2	41.1	43.3	...	321
3211	Spinning,weaving etc..	301	295	280	263	...	26.7	24.7	22.8	22.2	...	3211
322	Wearing apparel	550	534	513	479	...	34.7	33.1	35.0	31.8	...	322
323	Leather and products ...	60	61	56	49	...	3.7	3.5	3.4	3.1	...	323
324	Footwear .... d/	92	88	84	85	...	13.8	13.8	13.9	13.3	...	324
331	Wood products	223	e/ 214	2325	2248	...	8.0	e/ 7.6	20.6	19.6	...	331
332	Furniture, fixtures	552	548	572	565	...	28.7	28.1	29.3	28.2	...	332
341	Paper and products	181	175	162	158	...	22.0	20.7	19.5	19.4	...	341
3411	Pulp,paper etc.	54	51	48	48	...	13.9	13.4	12.4	12.6	...	3411
342	Printing,publishing	314	299	311	296	...	26.1	24.3	24.3	25.4	...	342
351	Industrial chemicals ...	109	107	126	132	...	21.5	20.8	21.5	21.6	...	351
3511	Basic excl fertilizers	...	...	...	...	...	...	...	...	...	...	3511
3513	Synthetic resins etc .	59	59	54	77	...	9.1	8.5	9.6	10.1	...	3513
352	Other chemical products.	298	296	289	295	...	18.9	18.0	18.3	18.4	...	352
3522	Drugs and medicines ..	61	65	66	67	...	5.4	5.3	6.0	6.1	...	3522
353	Petroleum refineries ...	15	16	23	23	...	2.7	2.6	4.1	4.1	...	353
354	Petroleum,coal products.	16	17	15	15	...	1.2	1.1	1.1	1.1	...	354
355	Rubber products	37	35	38	34	...	8.9	7.7	7.9	7.9	...	355
356	Plastic products n.e.c..	272	274	256	244	...	13.9	13.6	12.0	12.0	...	356
361	Pottery,china etc	29	33	30	28	...	2.9	2.8	2.7	2.7	...	361
362	Glass and products	80	80	82	78	...	8.8	8.5	8.4	8.5	...	362
369	Non-metal products n.e.c	509	480	473	452	...	26.9	25.6	25.6	25.3	...	369
371	Iron and steel .... f/	124	121	122	119	...	56.4	59.8	51.5	48.2	...	371
372	Non-ferrous metals ..... f/	50	48	49	49	...	9.8	9.4	9.5	9.4	...	372
381	Metal products	917	935	902	860	...	62.6	59.3	65.0	54.9	...	381
382	Machinery n.e.c.	695	687	706	713	...	70.7	68.0	58.2	67.1	...	382
3825	Office,computing etc..	...	...	...	...	...	...	...	...	...	...	3825
383	Electrical machinery ...	469	466	459	450	...	76.3	73.9	72.1	73.9	...	383
3832	Radio,television etc..	45	46	47	44	...	16.6	15.9	14.7	15.2	...	3832
384	Transport equipment	115	118	105	111	...	32.1	31.6	30.8	32.5	...	384
3841	Shipbuilding, repair..	3	4	4	5	...	1.8	1.8	1.7	1.7	...	3841
3843	Motor vehicles	72	69	58	66	...	16.8	16.9	22.0	23.1	...	3843
385	Professional goods	88	82	81	82	...	6.4	6.8	6.6	7.0	...	385
390	Other industries	56	48	58	63	...	6.4	6.2	6.6	7.3	...	390
3	Manufacturing ..... d/	7435	e/ 7332	9444	9256	...	682.7	e/ 660.8	656.2	653.7	...	3
410	Electricity,gas,steam ..	g/ 335	g/ 361	g/ 358	g/ 361	...	35.6	36.2	35.5	35.5	...	410
4101	Electricity	g/ 264	g/ 289	g/ 286	g/ 288	...	31.6	32.1	31.5	31.4	...	4101
420	Water works and supply .	172	184	188	188	...	2.3	2.3	2.3	2.3	...	420
4	Electricity,gas etc	507	545	546	549	...	37.9	38.5	37.8	37.8	...	4
2-4	All industry d/	...	...	...	...	...	738.2	e/ 716.1	708.4	705.1	...	2-4

a/ All establishments affiliated with the Industry Section of the Federal Economic Chamber and establishments with 20 or more employees of the "Gewerbesektion".
b/ At 31 December of the year indicated.
c/ Including homeworkers.
d/ Including repair of footwear.
e/ Up to 1982, excluding sawmills.
f/ Non-ferrous metal foundries are included in major group 371.
g/ Number of enterprises.

ISIC	INDUSTRY	3. AVERAGE NUMBER OF EMPLOYEES a/b/c/ (THOUSANDS)					4. WAGES AND SALARIES OF EMPLOYEES a/d/ (BILLION SCHILLINGS)					ISIC
		1981	1982	1983	1984	1985	1981	1982	1983	1984	1985	
210	Coal mining	3.8	3.4	3.2	3.0	...	0.80	0.80	0.73	0.74	...	210
220	Petroleum and gas	6.2	6.1	4.4	4.2	...	2.05	2.18	1.61	1.59	...	220
230	Metal ore mining	3.1	2.9	2.8	2.8	...	0.64	0.66	0.64	0.64	...	230
290	Other mining	4.5	4.3	3.9	3.5	...	0.99	1.01	0.95	0.88	...	290
2	Mining, quarrying .	17.6	16.7	14.3	13.5	...	4.48	4.65	3.93	3.85	...	2
311/2	Food products	52.6	51.7	51.7	52.1	...	9.23	9.77	10.25	10.79	...	311/2
313	Beverages	14.3	13.7	13.2	13.4	...	3.16	3.26	3.31	3.44	...	313
314	Tobacco	1.7	1.6	1.6	1.5	...	0.44	0.46	0.46	0.47	...	314
321	Textiles	49.6	45.7	40.7	42.9	...	7.13	7.22	6.69	7.25	...	321
3211	Spinning,weaving etc..	26.4	24.4	22.6	22.0	...	4.07	4.10	4.01	4.07	...	3211
322	Wearing apparel	34.3	32.7	34.7	31.5	...	3.72	3.81	4.23	3.86	...	322
323	Leather and products ...	3.7	3.5	3.4	3.1	...	0.45	0.46	0.46	0.47	...	323
324	Footwear .... e/	13.7	13.8	13.9	13.3	...	1.69	1.74	1.80	1.93	...	324
331	Wood products	7.8	f/ 7.5	18.2	17.3	...	1.28	f/ 1.32	3.11	3.12	...	331
332	Furniture, fixtures	28.2	27.6	28.8	27.8	...	4.31	4.46	4.76	4.91	...	332
341	Paper and products	21.9	20.6	19.5	19.3	...	4.73	4.89	5.01	5.10	...	341
3411	Pulp,paper etc.	13.9	13.4	12.4	12.6	...	3.31	3.46	3.53	3.67	...	3411
342	Printing,publishing	25.9	24.1	24.1	25.2	...	5.56	5.58	5.86	6.25	...	342
351	Industrial chemicals ...	21.5	20.8	21.4	21.5	...	5.12	5.32	5.61	6.02	...	351
3511	Basic excl fertilizers	...	...	...	...	...	...	...	...	...	...	3511
3513	Synthetic resins etc .	9.1	8.5	9.6	10.1	...	1.97	2.02	3.32	2.58	...	3513
352	Other chemical products.	18.8	17.9	18.2	18.3	...	3.92	3.04	2.30	4.54	...	352
3522	Drugs and medicines ..	5.4	5.3	6.0	6.0	...	1.12	1.19	1.41	1.53	...	3522
353	Petroleum refineries ...	2.7	2.6	4.1	4.1	...	0.80	0.83	1.51	1.63	...	353
354	Petroleum,coal products.	1.2	1.1	1.1	1.1	...	0.28	0.28	0.29	0.31	...	354
355	Rubber products	8.9	7.7	7.8	7.9	...	1.83	1.78	1.85	1.90	...	355
356	Plastic products n.e.c..	13.8	13.5	12.0	12.0	...	2.36	2.47	2.18	2.25	...	356
361	Pottery,china etc	2.9	2.8	2.7	2.7	...	0.50	0.52	0.52	0.56	...	361
362	Glass and products	8.8	8.5	8.3	8.4	...	1.68	1.81	1.90	1.99	...	362
369	Non-metal products n.e.c	26.7	25.4	25.5	25.2	...	6.04	6.14	6.21	6.45	...	369
371	Iron and steel .... g/	56.4	52.7	51.4	48.2	...	12.41	12.55	12.30	12.21	...	371
372	Non-ferrous metals ..... g/	9.8	9.4	9.5	9.4	...	2.01	2.06	2.17	2.28	...	372
381	Metal products	62.1	58.8	64.5	54.4	...	11.25	11.69	13.86	11.54	...	381
382	Machinery n.e.c.	70.4	67.8	58.1	66.8	...	14.72	15.18	13.03	16.15	...	382
3825	Office,computing etc..	...	...	...	...	...	...	...	...	...	...	3825
383	Electrical machinery ...	76.1	73.7	72.0	73.8	...	14.31	15.41	15.74	16.67	...	383
3832	Radio,television etc..	16.6	15.9	14.7	15.2	...	2.63	2.92	2.69	2.87	...	3832
384	Transport equipment	32.1	31.6	30.7	32.5	...	6.55	6.90	6.78	7.57	...	384
3841	Shipbuilding, repair..	1.8	1.8	1.7	1.7	...	0.35	0.40	0.40	0.42	...	3841
3843	Motor vehicles	16.8	16.9	22.0	13.0	...	3.39	3.72	4.83	5.35	...	3843
385	Professional goods	6.3	6.8	6.5	6.9	...	1.15	1.16	1.13	1.26	...	385
390	Other industries	6.4	6.2	6.6	7.3	...	1.04	1.07	1.20	1.40	...	390
3	Manufacturing ..... e/	678.6	f/ 649.8	650.2	647.9	...	127.67	f/ 131.18	134.52	142.32	...	3
410	Electricity,gas,steam ..	35.5	36.0	35.4	35.4	...	9.47	10.27	10.62	11.03	...	410
4101	Electricity	31.5	32.0	31.3	31.3	...	8.52	9.24	9.46	9.87	...	4101
420	Water works and supply .	2.3	2.3	2.3	2.3	...	0.48	0.53	0.59	0.58	...	420
4	Electricity,gas etc	37.8	38.3	37.7	37.7	...	9.95	10.80	11.21	11.61	...	4
2-4	All industry e/	734.0	f/ 704.9	702.2	699.1	...	142.10	f/ 146.63	149.66	157.78	...	2-4

a/ All establishments affiliated with the Industry Section of the Federal Economic Chamber and establishments with 20 or more employees of the "Gewerbesektion".
b/ At 31 December of the year indicated.
c/ Including homeworkers.
d/ Including payments to homeworkers.
e/ Including repair of footwear.
f/ Up to 1982, excluding sawmills.
g/ Non-ferrous metal foundries are included in major group 371.

ISIC	INDUSTRY	5. SUPPLEMENTS TO WAGES AND SALARIES a/b/ (BILLION SCHILLINGS)					6. AVERAGE NUMBER OF OPERATIVES a/c/ (THOUSANDS)					ISIC
		1981	1982	1983	1984	1985	1981	1982	1983	1984	1985	
210	Coal mining	0.21	0.22	0.20	0.21	...	3.3	2.9	2.8	2.7	...	210
220	Petroleum and gas	0.64	0.70	0.37	0.36	...	3.8	3.7	3.2	3.1	...	220
230	Metal ore mining	0.21	0.26	0.25	0.26	...	2.4	2.3	2.2	2.2	...	230
290	Other mining	0.27	0.28	0.26	0.24	...	3.4	3.3	3.0	2.7	...	290
2	Mining, quarrying .	1.33	1.46	1.08	1.07	...	12.9	12.2	11.2	10.7	...	2
311/2	Food products	2.36	2.54	2.80	2.91	...	35.4	34.8	34.8	35.3	...	311/2
313	Beverages	0.84	0.85	0.91	0.95	...	9.6	9.2	8.8	8.8	...	313
314	Tobacco	0.24	0.28	0.27	0.29	...	1.1	1.0	1.0	0.9	...	314
321	Textiles	1.79	1.83	1.71	1.90	...	36.8	33.8	29.9	31.7	...	321
3211	Spinning,weaving etc..	1.02	1.05	1.01	1.06	...	19.2	17.6	16.3	15.9	...	3211
322	Wearing apparel	0.93	0.97	1.08	1.02	...	28.0	26.8	28.4	25.9	...	322
323	Leather and products ...	0.11	0.11	0.12	0.12	...	3.0	2.8	2.7	2.5	...	323
324	Footwear .... d/	0.43	0.46	0.48	0.52	...	11.6	11.6	11.7	11.3	...	324
331	Wood products	0.32	e/ 0.33	0.75	0.77	...	6.2	e/ 5.9	14.8	14.1	...	331
332	Furniture, fixtures	1.05	1.08	1.17	1.24	...	21.9	21.4	22.4	21.6	...	332
341	Paper and products	1.31	1.37	1.38	1.43	...	16.7	15.5	14.5	14.4	...	341
3411	Pulp,paper etc.	0.97	1.01	1.01	1.05	...	11.0	10.5	9.7	9.7	...	3411
342	Printing,publishing	1.22	1.29	1.31	1.41	...	16.7	15.2	15.1	16.0	...	342
351	Industrial chemicals ...	1.35	1.41	1.50	1.71	...	14.3	13.8	14.4	14.5	...	351
3511	Basic excl fertilizers	...	...	...	...	...	...	...	...	...	...	3511
3513	Synthetic resins etc .	0.53	0.53	0.60	0.73	...	6.3	5.9	6.8	7.1	...	3513
352	Other chemical products.	1.03	1.10	1.16	1.30	...	9.0	8.4	8.9	8.8	...	352
3522	Drugs and medicines ..	0.30	0.32	0.39	0.46	...	2.1	2.0	2.3	2.3	...	3522
353	Petroleum refineries ...	0.18	0.19	0.56	0.63	...	1.8	1.7	2.1	2.0	...	353
354	Petroleum,coal products.	0.07	0.06	0.08	0.08	...	0.9	0.8	0.8	0.8	...	354
355	Rubber products	0.49	0.48	0.50	0.53	...	6.9	5.9	6.0	6.1	...	355
356	Plastic products n.e.c..	0.59	0.63	0.56	0.59	...	9.7	9.6	8.5	8.5	...	356
361	Pottery,china etc	0.13	0.14	0.14	0.15	...	2.4	2.3	2.2	2.2	...	361
362	Glass and products	0.47	0.51	0.51	0.57	...	6.7	6.5	6.4	6.6	...	362
369	Non-metal products n.e.c	1.72	1.71	1.73	1.90	...	19.1	17.9	18.1	18.0	...	369
371	Iron and steel .... f/	3.59	3.73	3.80	3.84	...	42.7	39.4	38.8	36.5	...	371
372	Non-ferrous metals ..... f/	0.59	0.64	0.64	0.67	...	6.8	6.5	6.6	6.6	...	372
381	Metal products	2.81	3.01	3.70	3.13	...	44.7	42.3	44.6	39.6	...	381
382	Machinery n.e.c.	3.58	4.08	3.33	4.37	...	45.8	43.4	38.0	42.6	...	382
3825	Office,computing etc..	...	...	...	...	...	...	...	...	...	...	3825
383	Electrical machinery ...	3.92	4.12	4.33	4.76	...	48.0	45.7	44.2	45.4	...	383
3832	Radio,television etc..	0.71	0.77	0.74	0.84	...	12.7	12.1	10.9	11.4	...	3832
384	Transport equipment	1.80	1.89	1.92	2.12	...	23.0	22.9	22.7	23.9	...	384
3841	Shipbuilding, repair..	0.09	0.10	0.11	0.11	...	1.3	1.3	1.3	1.3	...	3841
3843	Motor vehicles	0.97	1.04	1.42	1.55	...	11.8	12.2	16.5	17.3	...	3843
385	Professional goods	0.30	0.32	0.33	0.36	...	4.3	4.6	4.6	5.1	...	385
390	Other industries	0.26	0.29	0.32	0.38	...	4.9	4.8	5.2	5.9	...	390
3	Manufacturing ..... d/	33.48	e/ 35.42	37.09	39.65	...	478.0	e/ 454.5	456.2	455.6	...	3
410	Electricity,gas,steam ..	3.57	4.59	4.04	4.39	...	14.6	14.6	14.4	14.2	...	410
4101	Electricity	3.11	4.09	3.53	3.85	...	12.2	12.1	12.0	10.5	...	4101
420	Water works and supply .	0.20	0.22	0.31	0.25	...	1.2	1.2	1.2	1.2	...	420
4	Electricity,gas etc	3.77	4.81	4.35	4.64	...	15.8	15.8	15.6	15.4	...	4
2-4	All industry d/	38.58	e/ 41.69	42.52	45.36	...	506.7	e/ 482.5	483.0	481.7	...	2-4

a/ All establishments affiliated with the Industry Section of the Federal Economic Chamber and establishments with 20 or more employees of the "Gewerbesektion".
b/ Including payments to homeworkers.
c/ At 31 December of the year indicated.
d/ Including repair of footwear.
e/ Up to 1982, excluding sawmills.
f/ Non-ferrous metal foundries are included in major group 371.

ISIC	INDUSTRY	7. WAGES AND SALARIES OF OPERATIVES a/ (BILLION SCHILLINGS) 1981	1982	1983	1984	1985	8. OUTPUT IN PRODUCERS' PRICES a/b/ (BILLION SCHILLINGS) 1981	1982	1983	1984	1985	ISIC
210	Coal mining	0.61	0.62	0.59	0.60	...	1.75	2.04	2.07	2.00	...	210
220	Petroleum and gas	1.08	1.14	1.05	1.08	...	25.28	22.19	17.76	22.75	...	220
230	Metal ore mining	0.47	0.47	0.46	0.46	...	1.58	1.65	1.66	1.94	...	230
290	Other mining	0.67	0.69	0.64	0.60	...	4.88	5.01	4.29	4.29	...	290
2	Mining, quarrying .	2.83	2.92	2.74	2.74	...	33.49	30.89	25.78	30.98	...	2
311/2	Food products	5.20	5.49	5.75	6.08	...	81.89	87.14	94.15	99.09	...	311/2
313	Beverages	1.85	1.90	1.92	1.99	...	17.10	18.86	19.00	19.87	...	313
314	Tobacco	0.23	0.24	0.23	0.23	...	12.72	14.24	15.86	16.78	...	314
321	Textiles	4.16	4.17	3.81	4.20	...	33.81	34.37	31.82	35.84	...	321
3211	Spinning,weaving etc..	2.31	2.31	2.25	2.30	...	19.70	20.21	19.16	20.10	...	3211
322	Wearing apparel	2.57	2.65	2.92	2.68	...	14.25	14.43	16.18	15.42	...	322
323	Leather and products ...	0.31	0.31	0.31	0.32	...	2.08	2.24	2.49	2.93	...	323
324	Footwear .... c/	1.24	1.27	1.31	1.41	...	8.06	8.13	8.79	9.15	...	324
331	Wood products	0.91	d/ 0.94	2.33	2.35	...	7.69	d/ 7.68	23.31	24.00	...	331
332	Furniture, fixtures	2.96	3.04	3.24	3.37	...	18.25	18.21	19.53	19.60	...	332
341	Paper and products	3.07	3.10	3.15	3.21	...	29.03	29.48	28.79	34.21	...	341
3411	Pulp,paper etc.	2.29	2.36	2.38	2.46	...	21.10	21.50	21.13	26.28	...	3411
342	Printing,publishing	2.95	2.91	3.01	3.18	...	17.06	17.66	18.83	20.55	...	342
351	Industrial chemicals ...	2.87	2.96	3.14	3.39	...	34.44	33.70	38.95	46.61	...	351
3511	Basic excl fertilizers	...	...	...	...	...	...	...	...	...	...	3511
3513	Synthetic resins etc .	1.19	1.21	1.38	1.57	...	13.66	12.61	16.34	19.92	...	3513
352	Other chemical products.	1.35	1.36	1.43	1.52	...	23.86	24.92	26.50	28.44	...	352
3522	Drugs and medicines ...	0.28	0.29	0.32	0.34	...	6.80	7.44	8.74	9.68	...	3522
353	Petroleum refineries ...	0.47	0.48	0.62	0.62	...	49.12	43.54	38.88	49.64	...	353
354	Petroleum,coal products.	0.18	0.17	0.18	0.18	...	1.90	1.98	2.00	2.21	...	354
355	Rubber products	1.20	1.12	1.19	1.25	...	8.32	8.51	9.49	10.48	...	355
356	Plastic products n.e.c..	1.35	1.42	1.25	1.29	...	11.24	12.09	10.82	11.16	...	356
361	Pottery,china etc	0.37	0.38	0.38	0.41	...	1.47	1.47	1.54	1.51	...	361
362	Glass and products	1.10	1.20	1.27	1.30	...	6.94	7.39	7.66	8.12	...	362
369	Non-metal products n.e.c	3.86	3.83	3.83	4.00	...	30.11	31.33	32.20	34.01	...	369
371	Iron and steel .... e/	8.48	8.43	8.27	8.37	...	51.71	54.27	52.82	56.86	...	371
372	Non-ferrous metals ..... e/	1.18	1.21	1.28	1.37	...	14.33	13.78	16.26	19.21	...	372
381	Metal products	6.97	7.21	7.89	7.12	...	42.96	47.09	65.40	44.44	...	381
382	Machinery n.e.c.	8.00	8.11	7.10	8.45	...	65.67	74.95	56.26	75.64	...	382
3825	Office,computing etc..	...	...	...	...	...	...	...	...	...	...	3825
383	Electrical machinery ...	7.04	7.43	7.34	7.78	...	61.04	66.76	69.90	75.46	...	383
3832	Radio,television etc..	1.63	1.84	1.60	1.72	...	15.27	18.82	15.17	16.78	...	3832
384	Transport equipment	4.04	4.17	4.15	4.61	...	28.98	28.74	33.25	36.59	...	384
3841	Shipbuilding, repair..	0.23	0.25	0.26	0.27	...	1.11	1.12	1.10	1.49	...	3841
3843	Motor vehicles	2.03	2.20	3.00	3.35	...	16.39	17.56	26.71	28.64	...	3843
385	Professional goods	0.56	0.62	0.64	0.74	...	3.62	3.88	3.67	4.46	...	385
390	Other industries	0.70	0.70	0.80	0.94	...	4.20	4.63	5.24	5.99	...	390
3	Manufacturing ..... c/	75.17	d/ 76.82	78.74	82.36	...	681.85	d/ 711.47	749.59	808.27	...	3
410	Electricity,gas,steam ..	2.75	2.97	3.09	3.14	...	74.57	85.68	84.49	88.77	...	410
4101	Electricity	2.28	2.47	2.54	2.52	...	57.19	66.49	66.66	69.02	...	4101
420	Water works and supply .	0.22	0.24	0.25	0.26	...	2.48	2.68	2.86	2.93	...	420
4	Electricity,gas etc	2.97	3.21	3.34	3.40	...	77.05	88.36	87.35	91.70	...	4
2-4	All industry c/	80.97	d/ 82.95	84.82	88.50	...	792.39	d/ 830.72	862.72	930.95	...	2-4

a/ All establishments affiliated with the Industry Section of the Federal Economic Chamber and establishments with 20 or more employees of the "Gewerbesektion".
b/ Excluding value-added tax.
c/ Including repair of footwear.
d/ Up to 1982, excluding sawmills.
e/ Non-ferrous metal foundries are included in major group 371.

ISIC	INDUSTRY	9. VALUE ADDED IN PRODUCERS' PRICES a/b/c/ (BILLION SCHILLINGS) 1981	1982	1983	1984	1985	10. GROSS FIXED CAPITAL FORMATION TOTAL a/d/ (BILLION SCHILLINGS) 1981	1982	1983	1984	1985	ISIC
210	Coal mining	1.18	1.29	1.34	1.31	...	0.11	0.15	0.18	0.15	...	210
220	Petroleum and gas	9.83	9.49	8.01	8.68	...	1.34	1.72	1.02	0.92	...	220
230	Metal ore mining	0.85	0.93	0.99	1.03	...	0.15	0.13	0.10	0.25	...	230
290	Other mining	2.12	2.05	1.94	1.90	..	0.53	0.43	0.45	0.39	...	290
2	Mining, quarrying .	13.98	13.76	12.28	12.92	...	2.13	2.43	1.75	1.71	...	2
311/2	Food products	17.03	17.86	19.59	20.97	...	2.89	2.73	2.98	3.27	...	311/2
313	Beverages	6.68	7.16	7.45	7.44	...	1.21	1.31	1.60	1.74	...	313
314	Tobacco	11.15	12.44	13.41	14.28	...	0.20	0.26	0.30	0.27	...	314
321	Textiles	12.02	12.37	11.44	13.04	...	1.63	1.50	1.44	1.57	...	321
3211	Spinning,weaving etc..	6.92	7.18	6.90	7.10	...	0.98	0.89	0.98	0.96	...	3211
322	Wearing apparel	5.95	6.07	6.85	6.18	...	0.40	0.39	0.54	0.46	...	322
323	Leather and products ...	0.72	0.72	0.69	0.74	...	0.08	0.12	0.09	0.11	...	323
324	Footwear .... e/	2.69	2.65	2.86	2.87	...	0.29	0.28	0.30	0.29	...	324
331	Wood products	2.40	f/ 2.45	6.33	5.99	...	0.50	f/ 0.46	1.36	1.50	...	331
332	Furniture, fixtures	7.55	7.57	8.18	8.08	...	0.89	0.82	0.87	0.97	...	332
341	Paper and products	8.67	8.52	8.62	10.32	...	2.05	2.33	3.22	6.49	...	341
3411	Pulp,paper etc.	5.96	5.73	5.89	7.70	...	1.53	1.98	2.86	6.11	...	3411
342	Printing,publishing	8.29	8.38	9.08	9.77	...	0.92	0.91	0.90	1.35	...	342
351	Industrial chemicals ...	8.21	7.76	9.21	11.52	...	1.51	1.30	1.23	1.98	...	351
3511	Basic excl fertilizers	...	...	...	...	...	...	...	...	...	...	3511
3513	Synthetic resins etc .	3.24	3.04	4.19	5.52	...	0.46	0.49	0.63	1.15	...	3513
352	Other chemical products.	7.22	7.27	7.47	7.81	...	1.19	0.97	1.19	1.22	...	352
3522	Drugs and medicines ..	2.08	2.15	2.23	2.35	...	0.49	0.39	0.60	0.54	...	3522
353	Petroleum refineries ...	2.68	1.07	0.77	4.51	...	1.63	1.51	0.96	0.95	...	353
354	Petroleum,coal products.	0.37	0.42	0.47	0.49	...	0.07	0.11	0.07	0.09	...	354
355	Rubber products	3.06	3.13	3.47	3.67	...	0.27	0.27	0.33	0.37	...	355
356	Plastic products n.e.c..	3.91	4.36	4.10	4.08	...	0.66	0.67	0.66	0.75	...	356
361	Pottery,china etc	0.88	0.87	0.92	0.87	...	0.09	0.06	0.08	0.06	...	361
362	Glass and products	3.16	3.40	3.57	4.12	...	0.94	1.02	0.53	0.62	...	362
369	Non-metal products n.e.c	10.89	11.77	12.14	12.77	...	2.24	1.86	1.98	2.21	...	369
371	Iron and steel .... g/	15.36	17.36	16.95	17.79	...	3.90	4.42	2.55	1.75	...	371
372	Non-ferrous metals ..... g/	3.46	3.13	4.05	4.91	...	0.51	0.54	0.53	0.72	...	372
381	Metal products	17.53	19.07	23.14	17.87	...	2.62	2.13	2.80	2.18	...	381
382	Machinery n.e.c.	23.90	26.08	20.28	24.72	...	2.88	2.87	2.37	2.60	...	382
3825	Office,computing etc..	...	...	...	...	...	...	...	...	...	...	3825
383	Electrical machinery ...	22.63	23.91	25.15	28.08	...	3.72	2.83	3.21	3.80	...	383
3832	Radio,television etc..	3.88	3.88	4.02	4.80	...	1.42	0.63	1.24	1.60	...	3832
384	Transport equipment	10.03	9.45	12.73	14.30	...	7.73	5.84	1.71	1.48	...	384
3841	Shipbuilding, repair..	0.55	0.51	...	0.81	...	0.06	0.03	0.02	0.03	...	3841
3843	Motor vehicles	5.50	5.24	9.87	10.67	...	7.11	5.47	1.59	1.21	...	3843
385	Professional goods	1.64	1.72	1.68	2.04	...	0.19	0.20	0.16	0.20	...	385
390	Other industries	1.75	1.88	2.18	2.37	...	0.17	0.14	0.22	0.24	...	390
3	Manufacturing ..... e/	219.83	f/ 228.84	242.78	261.60	...	41.38	f/ 37.85	34.18	39.24	...	3
410	Electricity,gas,steam ..	31.80	36.15	37.06	36.55	...	16.41	18.08	18.06	20.36	...	410
4101	Electricity	28.21	32.26	32.68	31.98	...	15.07	16.45	16.65	18.52	...	4101
420	Water works and supply .	1.68	1.85	2.01	2.05	...	0.87	0.99	0.98	0.93	...	420
4	Electricity,gas etc	33.48	38.00	39.07	38.60	...	17.28	19.07	19.04	21.29	...	4
2-4	All industry e/	267.29	f/ 280.60	294.13	313.12	...	60.79	f/ 59.35	54.97	62.24	...	2-4

a/ All establishments affiliated with the Industry Section of the Federal Economic Chamber and establishments with 20 or more employees of the "Gewerbesektion".
b/ Net of non-industrial costs.
c/ Excluding value-added tax.
d/ The value of sales is not deducted.
e/ Including repair of footwear.
f/ Up to 1982, excluding sawmills.
g/ Non-ferrous metal foundries are included in major group 371.

ISIC	INDUSTRY	11. GROSS FIXED CAPITAL FORMATION MACHINERY AND EQUIPMENT a/b/ (BILLION SCHILLINGS)					12. VALUE OF STOCKS AT END OF PERIOD TOTAL a/ (BILLION SCHILLINGS)					ISIC
		1981	1982	1983	1984	1985	1981	1982	1983	1984	1985	
210	Coal mining	0.09	0.12	0.15	0.12	...	0.19	0.18	0.23	0.30	...	210
220	Petroleum and gas	1.19	1.35	0.98	0.88	...	0.81	0.85	0.77	0.72	...	220
230	Metal ore mining	0.08	0.10	0.07	0.18	...	0.23	0.24	0.24	0.21	...	230
290	Other mining	0.31	0.26	0.30	0.28	...	0.38	0.43	0.39	0.33	...	290
2	Mining, quarrying .	1.67	1.83	1.50	1.46	...	1.61	1.70	1.63	1.56	...	2
311/2	Food products	1.78	1.80	1.96	2.30	...	7.39	7.67	8.04	8.47	...	311/2
313	Beverages	0.63	0.71	0.93	1.03	...	2.59	2.67	2.77	3.39	...	313
314	Tobacco	0.15	0.13	0.12	0.16	...	1.39	1.50	1.54	1.49	...	314
321	Textiles	1.12	1.07	1.11	1.18	...	7.68	7.47	6.67	7.49	...	321
3211	Spinning,weaving etc..	0.73	0.65	0.79	0.76	...	4.17	4.20	3.94	4.20	...	3211
322	Wearing apparel	0.25	0.21	0.26	0.28	...	2.79	2.82	3.21	2.92	...	322
323	Leather and products ...	0.05	0.07	0.04	0.07	...	0.51	0.52	0.56	0.53	...	323
324	Footwear .... c/	0.15	0.17	0.18	0.18	...	1.44	1.54	1.63	1.63	...	324
331	Wood products	0.33	d/ 0.29	0.97	1.08	...	1.33	d/ 1.28	4.24	4.66	...	331
332	Furniture, fixtures	0.53	0.45	0.54	0.63	...	3.54	3.48	3.61	3.65	...	332
341	Paper and products	1.46	1.82	2.45	5.24	...	4.25	4.28	3.79	4.22	...	341
3411	Pulp,paper etc.	1.06	1.52	2.18	4.93	...	3.25	3.30	2.84	3.26	...	3411
342	Printing,publishing	0.72	0.62	0.74	1.12	...	1.44	1.43	1.41	1.59	...	342
351	Industrial chemicals ...	0.97	0.92	0.99	1.20	...	5.29	5.28	4.97	5.64	...	351
3511	Basic excl fertilizers	...	...	...	...	...	...	...	...	...	...	3511
3513	Synthetic resins etc .	0.33	0.41	0.52	0.59	...	1.89	1.70	1.97	2.48	...	3513
352	Other chemical products.	0.70	0.63	0.81	0.82	...	4.75	4.74	4.77	5.31	...	352
3522	Drugs and medicines ..	0.27	0.24	0.43	0.30	...	1.79	1.90	1.99	2.30	...	3522
353	Petroleum refineries ...	1.44	1.40	0.85	0.76	...	7.40	6.12	6.85	8.30	...	353
354	Petroleum,coal products.	0.04	0.05	0.04	0.06	...	0.16	0.15	0.15	0.17	...	354
355	Rubber products	0.23	0.17	0.26	0.30	...	1.52	1.30	1.32	1.53	...	355
356	Plastic products n.e.c..	0.44	0.46	0.52	0.59	...	1.69	1.66	1.65	1.72	...	356
361	Pottery,china etc	0.07	0.05	0.06	0.05	...	0.28	0.30	0.29	0.32	...	361
362	Glass and products	0.73	0.64	0.42	0.45	...	1.12	1.28	1.31	1.43	...	362
369	Non-metal products n.e.c .	1.48	1.33	1.54	1.62	...	5.05	4.86	4.63	4.88	...	369
371	Iron and steel .... e/	3.08	3.59	2.27	1.41	...	14.09	14.49	13.58	14.07	...	371
372	Non-ferrous metals ..... e/	0.33	0.35	0.34	0.50	...	3.11	2.97	3.20	3.90	...	372
381	Metal products	1.67	1.46	1.97	1.54	...	11.44	12.52	16.23	12.82	...	381
382	Machinery n.e.c.	1.76	1.75	1.48	1.79	...	19.98	20.48	17.08	20.92	...	382
3825	Office,computing etc..	...	...	...	...	...	...	...	...	...	...	3825
383	Electrical machinery ...	2.12	2.06	2.45	2.92	...	16.37	16.60	15.66	15.77	...	383
3832	Radio,television etc..	0.76	0.55	1.04	1.31	...	4.73	4.88	2.18	2.39	...	3832
384	Transport equipment	1.62	4.78	1.41	1.15	...	10.42	10.33	9.46	10.38	...	384
3841	Shipbuilding, repair..	0.02	0.02	0.01	0.02	...	0.52	0.59	0.70	0.61	...	3841
3843	Motor vehicles	1.29	4.48	1.32	0.94	...	6.51	6.76	7.46	8.03	...	3843
385	Professional goods	0.13	0.17	0.13	0.15	...	0.95	0.96	0.90	1.04	...	385
390	Other industries	0.11	0.11	0.16	0.19	...	1.07	1.04	1.13	1.21	...	390
3	Manufacturing ..... c/	24.09	d/ 27.26	25.00	28.77	...	139.04	d/ 139.74	140.65	149.45	...	3
410	Electricity,gas,steam ..	10.52	11.03	10.29	12.32	...	9.99	9.47	7.44	9.03	...	410
4101	Electricity	9.92	10.20	9.55	10.87	...	4.22	4.45	4.14	4.43	...	4101
420	Water works and supply .	0.15	0.10	0.10	0.20	...	0.12	0.12	0.11	0.12	...	420
4	Electricity,gas etc	10.67	11.13	10.39	12.52	...	10.11	9.59	7.55	9.15	...	4
2-4	All industry c/	36.43	d/ 40.22	36.89	42.75	...	150.76	d/ 151.03	149.83	160.16	...	2-4

a/ All establishments affiliated with the Industry Section of the Federal Economic Chamber and establishments with 20 or more employees of the "Gewerbesektion".
b/ The value of sales is not deducted.
c/ Including repair of footwear.
d/ Up to 1982, excluding sawmills.
e/ Non-ferrous metal foundries are included in major group 371.

13. INDEX NUMBERS OF INDUSTRIAL PRODUCTION (1980 = 100)

ISIC	INDUSTRY		1976	1977	1978	1979	1981	1982	1983	1984	1985	a/ RATE	ISIC
210	Coal mining		...	...	...	...	...	...	...	...	...	...	210
220	Petroleum and gas		...	...	...	...	...	...	...	...	...	...	220
230	Metal ore mining		...	...	...	...	...	...	...	...	...	...	230
290	Other mining	b/	94	84	84	99	105	108	105	117	112	2.0	290
2	Mining, quarrying .		97	90	87	100	104	109	107	113	110	1.4	2
311/2 313	Food products .... Beverages		86	90	91	97	105	107	108	109	112	3.0	311/2 313
314	Tobacco		92	94	99	102	97	102	102	98	105	1.5	314
321	Textiles		94	94	91	96	99	91	86	89	91	-0.4	321
3211	Spinning,weaving etc..		...	...	...	...	...	...	...	...	...	...	3211
322	Wearing apparel		95	93	88	96	98	96	96	95	93	-0.2	322
323 324	Leather and products ... Footwear		83	88	86	95	98	97	95	98	95	1.5	323 324
331 332	Wood products .... Furniture, fixtures		89	98	96	101	94	94	95	96	100	1.3	331 332
341	Paper and products		86	87	89	97	104	105	107	114	123	4.1	341
3411	Pulp,paper etc.		87	89	90	99	102	103	107	114	124	4.0	3411
342	Printing,publishing		...	...	...	...	...	...	...	...	...	...	342
351	Industrial chemicals ...	c/	80	85	89	95	101	97	106	123	118	4.4	351
3511	Basic excl fertilizers		...	...	...	...	...	...	...	...	...	...	3511
3513	Synthetic resins etc .		...	...	...	...	...	...	...	...	...	...	3513
352	Other chemical products.	c/	...	...	...	...	...	...	...	...	...	...	352
3522	Drugs and medicines ..		...	...	...	...	...	...	...	...	...	...	3522
353	Petroleum refineries ...		111	108	112	113	107	101	96	96	94	-1.8	353
354	Petroleum,coal products.		...	...	...	...	...	...	...	...	...	...	354
355	Rubber products		...	...	...	...	...	...	...	...	...	...	355
356	Plastic products n.e.c..		...	...	...	...	...	...	...	...	...	...	356
361	Pottery,china etc		96	98	96	97	101	90	96	100	97	0.1	361
362	Glass and products		58	64	70	87	100	100	104	111	127	9.1	362
369	Non-metal products n.e.c		...	...	...	...	...	...	...	...	...	...	369
371	Iron and steel	d/	97	92	97	106	95	90	93	103	104	0.8	371
372	Non-ferrous metals	d/	87	91	92	99	100	96	110	116	116	3.2	372
381	Metal products		83	87	93	97	97	96	103	113	120	4.2	381
382	Machinery n.e.c.		78	80	87	98	89	95	87	86	96	2.3	382
3825	Office,computing etc..		...	...	...	...	...	...	...	...	...	...	3825
383	Electrical machinery ...		77	86	90	96	106	109	112	121	132	6.2	383
3832	Radio,television etc..		...	...	...	...	...	...	...	...	...	...	3832
384	Transport equipment		80	88	78	81	98	92	103	110	134	5.9	384
3841	Shipbuilding, repair..		...	...	...	...	...	...	...	...	...	...	3841
3843	Motor vehicles		...	...	...	...	...	...	...	...	...	...	3843
385	Professional goods		...	...	...	...	...	...	...	...	...	...	385
390	Other industries		...	...	...	...	...	...	...	...	...	...	390
3	Manufacturing		85	88	91	97	98	97	99	104	109	2.8	3
410	Electricity,gas,steam ..		...	...	...	...	...	...	...	...	...	...	410
4101	Electricity		83	89	90	96	102	104	102	102	108	3.0	4101
420	Water works and supply .		.	.	.	.	.	.	.	.	.	.	420
4	Electricity,gas etc		...	...	...	...	...	...	...	...	...	...	4
2-4	All industry	e/	85	88	91	97	99	98	99	104	109	2.8	2-4

a/ Annual growth rate 1976-1985.
b/ Excluding stone quarrying.
c/ Major group 352 is included in 351.
d/ Non-ferrous metal foundries are included in major group 371.
e/ Excluding gas and steam.

BANGLADESH

The information in the tables, except for the indexes, is based on the reply to the United Nations Questionnaire on General Industrial Statistics from the Statistics Division, Ministry of Planning, Dhaka. The concepts, definitions and classification by branches of industry are generally in accordance with United Nations standards.

The estimates are derived from the census of manufacturing industries taken annually by the Statistics Divison. The census covers registered establishments which employ 10 or more workers. Hand-loom weaving is out of the scope of inquiries. The estimates in the tables have been adjusted for non-response.

The estimates are based on the national classification, which generally follows the present version of ISIC. It should be noted, however, that the repair of mechanically propelled vehicles and watches and clocks (ISIC major division 9) is included in ISIC 384 and 390 respectively. The reference period is the fiscal year 1 July to 30 June; in the tables, the period referred to is the fiscal year ending in the year indicated.

Data on employees and operatives include persons employed through labour contractors. Wages and salaries include payments made to labour contractors. The estimates of output and value added are compiled in accordance with the definitions set out in the international recommendations. The valuation of these estimates is in producers' prices.

The indexes of industrial production are compiled by the Statistics Division, Ministry of Planning. The indexes cover about 83.7 per cent of the total value added by manufacturing for 1969/70.

Related national publications:
Census of Manufacturing Industries in Bangladesh (annual); Statistical Yearbook of Bangladesh, both published by the Statistics Division, Ministry of Planning, Dhaka.

BANGLADESH

ISIC	INDUSTRY	1. NUMBER OF ESTABLISHMENTS a/b/ (NUMBER)					2. AVERAGE NUMBER OF PERSONS ENGAGED a/b/ (THOUSANDS)					ISIC
		c/ 1981	c/ 1982	c/ 1983	1984	1985	1981	1982	1983	1984	1985	
210	Coal mining	...	...	...	...	...	...	...	...	...	...	210
220	Petroleum and gas	...	...	...	...	...	...	...	...	...	...	220
230	Metal ore mining	...	...	...	...	...	...	...	...	...	...	230
290	Other mining	...	...	...	...	...	...	...	...	...	...	290
2	Mining, quarrying .	...	...	...	...	...	...	...	...	...	...	2
311/2	Food products	479	490	517	...	...	42.45	43.31	45.05	...	...	311/2
313	Beverages	5	6	6	...	...	0.62	0.76	0.84	...	...	313
314	Tobacco	29	29	28	...	...	6.30	6.39	6.96	...	...	314
321	Textiles	1195	1298	1459	...	...	291.08	299.97	292.38	...	...	321
3211	Spinning,weaving etc..	164	175	185	...	...	259.46	262.70	254.89	...	...	3211
322	Wearing apparel	14	22	26	...	...	0.37	2.75	4.30	...	...	322
323	Leather and products ...	118	117	119	...	...	2.70	2.85	3.24	...	...	323
324	Footwear	6	6	6	...	...	0.23	1.13	1.16	...	...	324
331	Wood products	22	24	22	...	...	1.82	2.23	1.93	...	...	331
332	Furniture, fixtures	17	16	15	...	...	1.17	1.12	1.12	...	...	332
341	Paper and products	30	29	29	...	...	11.26	11.23	10.84	...	...	341
3411	Pulp,paper etc.	4	4	4	...	...	9.67	9.72	9.42	...	...	3411
342	Printing,publishing	127	152	156	...	...	5.27	6.27	7.54	...	...	342
351	Industrial chemicals ...	21	20	23	...	...	5.80	5.40	5.90	...	...	351
3511	Basic excl fertilizers	5	5	7	...	...	0.22	0.23	0.37	...	...	3511
3513	Synthetic resins etc .	7	8	8	...	...	0.42	0.39	0.39	...	...	3513
352	Other chemical products.	398	399	406	...	...	27.76	29.48	30.52	...	...	352
3522	Drugs and medicines ..	177	194	199	...	...	12.62	13.94	14.89	...	...	3522
353	Petroleum refineries ...	1	1	1	...	...	0.51	0.54	0.58	...	...	353
354	Petroleum,coal products.	1	1	1	...	...	0.01	0.01	0.01	...	...	354
355	Rubber products	33	30	33	...	...	2.32	2.24	1.46	...	...	355
356	Plastic products n.e.c..	30	40	42	...	...	0.72	0.90	1.04	...	...	356
361	Pottery,china etc	5	5	5	...	...	1.18	1.35	1.14	...	...	361
362	Glass and products	36	37	37	...	...	1.37	1.45	1.61	...	...	362
369	Non-metal products n.e.c	15	16	17	...	...	3.31	3.22	3.06	...	...	369
371	Iron and steel	44	47	52	...	...	11.03	10.71	9.78	...	...	371
372	Non-ferrous metals	-	-	-	...	...	-	-	-	...	...	372
381	Metal products	237	260	268	...	...	9.45	10.35	10.37	...	...	381
382	Machinery n.e.c.	106	121	122	...	...	6.02	8.02	6.83	...	...	382
3825	Office,computing etc..	-	-	-	...	...	-	-	-	...	...	3825
383	Electrical machinery ...	53	60	60	...	...	7.11	7.21	4.44	...	...	383
3832	Radio,television etc..	12	13	13	...	...	1.76	1.71	0.64	...	...	3832
384	Transport equipment	27	32	38	...	...	4.78	4.51	4.64	...	...	384
3841	Shipbuilding, repair..	5	7	9	...	...	2.59	2.48	2.54	...	...	3841
3843	Motor vehicles	6	8	10	...	...	1.17	1.07	1.15	...	...	3843
385	Professional goods	[103	98	95]	...	...	[3.23	3.08	3.30]	...	...	385
390	Other industries				...	...				...	...	390
3	Manufacturing ..... d/e/	3152	3356	3583	...	...	447.87	466.48	460.04	...	...	3
410	Electricity,gas,steam ..	...	...	...	...	...	...	...	...	...	...	410
4101	Electricity	...	...	...	...	...	...	...	...	...	...	4101
420	Water works and supply .	...	...	...	...	...	...	...	...	...	...	420
4	Electricity,gas etc	...	...	...	...	...	...	...	...	...	...	4
2-4	All industry	...	...	...	...	...	...	...	...	...	...	2-4

a/ Establishments with 10 or more workers.
b/ Twelve months ending 30 June of the year indicated.
c/ Reporting establishments.
d/ Including some repair services; see country note.
e/ For certain differences in classification, see country note.

ISIC	INDUSTRY	3. AVERAGE NUMBER OF EMPLOYEES a/b/ (THOUSANDS) 1981	1982	1983	1984	1985	4. WAGES AND SALARIES OF EMPLOYEES a/b/ (MILLION TAKA) 1981	1982	1983	1984	1985	ISIC
210	Coal mining	...	...	...	...	...	...	...	...	...	...	210
220	Petroleum and gas	...	...	...	...	...	...	...	...	...	...	220
230	Metal ore mining	...	...	...	...	...	...	...	...	...	...	230
290	Other mining	...	...	...	...	...	...	...	...	...	...	290
2	Mining, quarrying .	...	...	...	...	...	...	...	...	...	...	2
311/2	Food products	41.22	41.68	43.20	...	...	322.8	388.8	476.7	...	...	311/2
313	Beverages	0.62	0.76	0.83	...	...	9.4	12.1	14.3	...	...	313
314	Tobacco	6.19	6.29	6.70	...	...	94.8	121.7	109.8	...	...	314
321	Textiles	289.36	297.80	289.71	...	...	3035.4	3115.2	3152.5	...	...	321
3211	Spinning,weaving etc..	259.39	262.61	254.77	...	...	2868.9	2903.2	2897.4	...	...	3211
322	Wearing apparel	0.35	2.71	4.24	...	...	1.8	18.5	34.6	...	...	322
323	Leather and products ...	2.50	2.62	3.02	...	...	20.5	23.5	30.0	...	...	323
324	Footwear	0.22	1.12	1.15	...	...	2.0	18.2	20.1	...	...	324
331	Wood products	1.81	2.18	1.89	...	...	18.9	22.7	23.9	...	...	331
332	Furniture, fixtures	1.15	1.11	1.06	...	...	13.2	11.4	11.3	...	...	332
341	Paper and products	9.29	9.23	9.00	...	...	132.8	140.4	142.6	...	...	341
3411	Pulp,paper etc.	7.72	7.74	7.60	...	...	116.6	122.1	125.9	...	...	3411
342	Printing,publishing	5.08	6.04	7.32	...	...	66.8	78.1	81.8	...	...	342
351	Industrial chemicals ...	5.49	5.31	5.80	...	...	90.1	99.3	102.1	...	...	351
3511	Basic excl fertilizers	0.22	0.23	0.36	...	...	...	2.7	4.4	...	...	3511
3513	Synthetic resins etc .	0.42	0.39	0.38	...	...	5.0	5.3	4.7	...	...	3513
352	Other chemical products.	26.82	28.26	29.21	...	...	334.6	394.4	464.3	...	...	352
3522	Drugs and medicines ..	12.36	13.64	14.57	...	...	189.8	218.7	277.0	...	...	3522
353	Petroleum refineries ...	0.51	0.54	0.58	...	...	22.4	32.3	32.4	...	...	353
354	Petroleum,coal products.	0.01	0.01	0.01	...	...	0.2	0.4	0.4	...	...	354
355	Rubber products	2.28	2.20	1.43	...	...	24.9	25.0	16.4	...	...	355
356	Plastic products n.e.c..	0.69	0.85	0.98	...	...	4.2	5.8	7.8	...	...	356
361	Pottery,china etc	1.15	1.34	1.13	...	...	9.2	11.2	10.7	...	...	361
362	Glass and products	1.33	1.41	1.58	...	...	13.1	14.4	17.7	...	...	362
369	Non-metal products n.e.c	3.24	3.15	2.98	...	...	32.4	33.2	33.9	...	...	369
371	Iron and steel	9.64	9.57	9.03	...	...	161.6	164.1	213.5	...	...	371
372	Non-ferrous metals	-	-	-	...	...	-	-	-	...	...	372
381	Metal products	8.60	9.98	9.97	...	...	69.6	86.3	95.1	...	...	381
382	Machinery n.e.c.	5.95	7.86	6.65	...	...	62.6	73.4	78.0	...	...	382
3825	Office,computing etc..	-	-	-	...	...	-	-	-	...	...	3825
383	Electrical machinery ...	7.06	7.13	4.37	...	...	96.0	111.1	57.7	...	...	383
3832	Radio,television etc..	1.75	1.70	0.63	...	...	23.6	30.4	19.2	...	...	3832
384	Transport equipment	4.75	4.46	4.55	...	...	75.8	71.5	73.2	...	...	384
3841	Shipbuilding, repair..	2.59	2.46	2.47	...	...	39.9	38.5	40.5	...	...	3841
3843	Motor vehicles	1.16	1.07	1.14	...	...	24.9	21.3	19.1	...	...	3843
385	Professional goods	[2.74	2.68	2.56]	...	...	[21.8	21.9	22.7]	...	...	385
390	Other industries				...	...				...	...	390
3	Manufacturing ..... c/d/	438.05	456.29	448.95	...	...	4736.9	5094.9	5323.5	...	...	3
410	Electricity,gas,steam ..	...	...	...	...	...	...	...	...	...	...	410
4101	Electricity	...	...	...	...	...	...	...	...	...	...	4101
420	Water works and supply .	...	...	...	...	...	...	...	...	...	...	420
4	Electricity,gas etc	...	...	...	...	...	...	...	...	...	...	4
2-4	All industry	...	...	...	...	...	...	...	...	...	...	2-4

a/ Establishments with 10 or more workers.
c/ Including some repair services; see country note.
b/ Twelve months ending 30 June of the year indicated.
d/ For certain differences in classification, see country note.

ISIC	INDUSTRY	5. AVERAGE NUMBER OF OPERATIVES a/b/ (THOUSANDS) 1981	1982	1983	1984	1985	6. WAGES AND SALARIES OF OPERATIVES a/b/ (MILLION TAKA) 1981	1982	1983	1984	1985	ISIC
210	Coal mining	...	...	...	...	...	...	...	...	...	...	210
220	Petroleum and gas	...	...	...	...	...	...	...	...	...	...	220
230	Metal ore mining	...	...	...	...	...	...	...	...	...	...	230
290	Other mining	...	...	...	...	...	...	...	...	...	...	290
2	Mining, quarrying	...	...	...	...	...	...	...	...	...	...	2
311/2	Food products	28.06	27.15	27.02	...	...	170.3	191.9	222.8	...	...	311/2
313	Beverages	0.26	0.31	0.36	...	...	3.4	4.3	5.3	...	...	313
314	Tobacco	4.67	4.68	5.04	...	...	58.8	80.1	72.2	...	...	314
321	Textiles	243.68	251.78	244.15	...	...	2334.0	2392.4	2419.0	...	...	321
3211	Spinning,weaving etc.	220.32	223.39	215.95	...	...	2212.4	2235.6	2224.1	...	...	3211
322	Wearing apparel	0.29	2.40	3.71	...	...	1.2	13.8	25.0	...	...	322
323	Leather and products	1.81	1.85	2.17	...	...	12.8	14.1	18.2	...	...	323
324	Footwear	0.14	0.66	0.69	...	...	1.1	7.9	8.6	...	...	324
331	Wood products	1.18	1.51	1.30	...	...	10.5	12.7	12.8	...	...	331
332	Furniture, fixtures	0.90	0.85	0.86	...	...	10.5	8.0	8.3	...	...	332
341	Paper and products	5.78	5.73	5.57	...	...	67.9	86.5	84.0	...	...	341
3411	Pulp,paper etc.	4.70	4.69	4.61	...	...	58.2	76.2	74.2	...	...	3411
342	Printing,publishing	3.68	4.37	5.72	...	...	46.4	49.7	55.8	...	...	342
351	Industrial chemicals	2.88	2.73	3.36	...	...	43.7	46.0	49.7	...	...	351
3511	Basic excl fertilizers	0.15	0.14	0.21	...	...	1.5	1.5	2.1	...	...	3511
3513	Synthetic resins etc	0.21	0.20	0.20	...	...	2.0	2.0	1.7	...	...	3513
352	Other chemical products	11.13	11.38	17.86	...	...	151.8	178.5	211.4	...	...	352
3522	Drugs and medicines	5.28	5.93	6.49	...	...	53.9	64.9	89.0	...	...	3522
353	Petroleum refineries	0.20	0.22	0.26	...	...	7.9	12.4	13.3	...	...	353
354	Petroleum,coal products	0.01	0.01	0.01	...	...	0.2	0.3	0.3	...	...	354
355	Rubber products	1.70	1.63	1.06	...	...	16.5	15.9	10.1	...	...	355
356	Plastic products n.e.c.	0.57	0.69	0.79	...	...	3.3	4.4	5.7	...	...	356
361	Pottery,china etc	0.92	1.09	0.90	...	...	6.3	7.8	7.6	...	...	361
362	Glass and products	0.99	1.01	1.19	...	...	6.6	8.4	11.2	...	...	362
369	Non-metal products n.e.c	2.10	2.11	2.04	...	...	17.4	17.7	20.2	...	...	369
371	Iron and steel	5.31	5.40	5.03	...	...	78.1	77.7	103.2	...	...	371
372	Non-ferrous metals	-	-	-	...	...	-	-	-	...	...	372
381	Metal products	6.83	7.89	7.76	...	...	50.4	61.8	65.0	...	...	381
382	Machinery n.e.c.	4.08	5.82	4.70	...	...	35.3	42.4	45.2	...	...	382
3825	Office,computing etc.	-	-	-	...	...	-	-	-	...	...	3825
383	Electrical machinery	4.37	4.35	2.88	...	...	50.0	53.3	32.8	...	...	383
3832	Radio,television etc.	0.90	0.83	0.42	...	...	10.3	11.9	5.0	...	...	3832
384	Transport equipment	3.00	2.77	2.83	...	...	43.3	39.7	43.3	...	...	384
3841	Shipbuilding, repair	1.77	1.63	1.64	...	...	25.8	24.2	25.8	...	...	3841
3843	Motor vehicles	0.53	0.51	0.59	...	...	11.5	9.5	10.6	...	...	3843
385	Professional goods	[1.61	1.82	1.67]	...	...	[10.7	12.3	12.2]	...	...	385
390	Other industries				...	...				...	...	390
3	Manufacturing c/d/	336.15	350.21	348.93	...	...	3238.4	3440.0	3563.2	...	...	3
410	Electricity,gas,steam	...	...	...	...	...	...	...	...	...	...	410
4101	Electricity	...	...	...	...	...	...	...	...	...	...	4101
420	Water works and supply	...	...	...	...	...	...	...	...	...	...	420
4	Electricity,gas etc	...	...	...	...	...	...	...	...	...	...	4
2-4	All industry	...	...	...	...	...	...	...	...	...	...	2-4

a/ Establishments with 10 or more workers.
b/ Twelve months ending 30 June of the year indicated.
c/ Including some repair services; see country note.
d/ For certain differences in classification, see country note.

ISIC	INDUSTRY	7. DAYS WORKED BY OPERATIVES a/b/ (THOUSANDS)					8. QUANTITY OF ELECTRICITY CONSUMED a/b/ (MILLION KWH)					ISIC
		1981	1982	1983	1984	1985	1981	1982	1983	1984	1985	
210	Coal mining	...	...	...	...	...	...	...	...	...	...	210
220	Petroleum and gas	...	...	...	...	...	...	...	...	...	...	220
230	Metal ore mining	...	...	...	...	...	...	...	...	...	...	230
290	Other mining	...	...	...	...	...	...	...	...	...	...	290
2	Mining, quarrying .	...	...	...	...	...	...	...	...	...	...	2
311/2	Food products	7511	7209	6839	...	...	34.6	40.3	42.9	...	...	311/2
313	Beverages	78	88	107	...	...	0.6	0.8	0.9	...	...	313
314	Tobacco	1331	1355	1439	...	...	6.7	7.3	6.5	...	...	314
321	Textiles	73444	73232	72822	...	...	427.4	468.2	531.3	...	...	321
3211	Spinning,weaving etc..	66773	65181	64663	...	...	375.3	392.0	474.3	...	...	3211
322	Wearing apparel	55	594	1032	...	...	...	0.5	0.9	...	...	322
323	Leather and products ...	525	517	602	...	...	2.1	2.8	3.7	...	...	323
324	Footwear	40	185	194	...	...	0.6	0.6	1.0	...	...	324
331	Wood products	307	386	423	...	...	5.3	3.7	4.7	...	...	331
332	Furniture, fixtures	192	227	241	...	...	0.5	0.6	0.6	...	...	332
341	Paper and products	1812	1667	1612	...	...	53.0	48.7	23.3	...	...	341
3411	Pulp,paper etc.	1463	1375	1352	...	...	51.0	47.9	21.5	...	...	3411
342	Printing,publishing	1118	1267	1383	...	...	2.2	6.0	3.5	...	...	342
351	Industrial chemicals ...	960	889	1059	...	...	48.5	51.4	59.1	...	...	351
3511	Basic excl fertilizers	38	36	55	...	...	...	...	...	...	...	3511
3513	Synthetic resins etc .	64	58	54	...	...	0.9	0.9	3.3	...	...	3513
352	Other chemical products.	5554	4948	5067	...	...	12.9	15.0	15.5	...	...	352
3522	Drugs and medicines ..	1718	1679	1843	...	...	6.8	8.9	9.2	...	...	3522
353	Petroleum refineries ...	63	71	71	...	...	1.6	1.9	2.5	...	...	353
354	Petroleum,coal products.	3	3	4	...	...	...	-	-	...	...	354
355	Rubber products	493	466	296	...	...	4.2	2.2	1.9	...	...	355
356	Plastic products n.e.c..	158	194	221	...	...	0.4	0.6	0.7	...	...	356
361	Pottery,china etc	278	325	259	...	...	1.6	1.6	2.0	...	...	361
362	Glass and products	314	283	319	...	...	2.6	2.9	2.7	...	...	362
369	Non-metal products n.e.c	621	626	597	...	...	9.4	10.4	10.9	...	...	369
371	Iron and steel	5506	1596	1384	...	...	49.0	47.2	40.4	...	...	371
372	Non-ferrous metals	-	-	-	...	...	-	-	-	...	...	372
381	Metal products	2110	2213	2101	...	...	6.2	7.9	8.0	...	...	381
382	Machinery n.e.c.	1126	1250	1313	...	...	3.3	3.2	5.4	...	...	382
3825	Office,computing etc..	-	-	-	...	...	-	-	-	...	...	3825
383	Electrical machinery ...	1171	1187	755	...	...	3.0	3.5	3.5	...	...	383
3832	Radio,television etc..	235	218	119	...	...	...	0.6	0.6	...	...	3832
384	Transport equipment	856	849	811	...	...	3.4	3.6	4.0	...	...	384
3841	Shipbuilding, repair..	528	542	489	...	...	...	2.6	2.6	...	...	3841
3843	Motor vehicles	130	131	148	...	...	0.2	0.1	0.3	...	...	3843
385	Professional goods	[420	479	425]	...	...	...	[2.4	1.4]	...	...	385
390	Other industries				...	...	...			...	...	390
3	Manufacturing ..... c/d/	106046	102106	101376	...	...	e/ 679.1	733.3	777.3	...	...	3
410	Electricity,gas,steam ..	...	...	...	...	...	...	...	...	...	...	410
4101	Electricity	...	...	...	...	...	...	...	...	...	...	4101
420	Water works and supply .	...	...	...	...	...	...	...	...	...	...	420
4	Electricity,gas etc	...	...	...	...	...	...	...	...	...	...	4
2-4	All industry	...	...	...	...	...	...	...	...	...	...	2-4

a/ Establishments with 10 or more workers.
b/ Twelve months ending 30 June of the year indicated.
c/ Including some repair services; see country note.
d/ For certain differences in classification, see country note.
e/ Excluding major groups 385 and 390.

ISIC	INDUSTRY	9. OUTPUT IN PRODUCERS' PRICES a/b/ (MILLION TAKA) 1981	1982	1983	1984	1985	10. VALUE ADDED IN PRODUCERS' PRICES a/b/ (MILLION TAKA) 1981	1982	1983	1984	1985	ISIC
210	Coal mining	...	...	...	...	...	...	...	...	...	...	210
220	Petroleum and gas	...	...	...	...	...	...	...	...	...	...	220
230	Metal ore mining	...	...	...	...	...	...	...	...	...	...	230
290	Other mining	...	...	...	...	...	...	...	...	...	...	290
2	Mining, quarrying .	...	...	...	...	...	...	...	...	...	...	2
311/2	Food products	4695	6104	7236	...	...	1484	1879	2415	...	...	311/2
313	Beverages	194	234	214	...	...	138	163	156	...	...	313
314	Tobacco	2566	3162	3553	...	...	1750	2093	2497	...	...	314
321	Textiles	11319	11990	14561	...	...	4948	4805	6157	...	...	321
3211	Spinning,weaving etc..	10233	10692	12880	...	...	4554	4351	5600	...	...	3211
322	Wearing apparel	14	149	296	...	...	5	47	84	...	...	322
323	Leather and products ...	1196	1321	1621	...	...	275	212	253	...	...	323
324	Footwear	163	267	309	...	...	62	95	118	...	...	324
331	Wood products	136	164	139	...	...	47	75	58	...	...	331
332	Furniture, fixtures	53	60	95	...	...	23	28	35	...	...	332
341	Paper and products	1373	1582	1689	...	...	351	396	433	...	...	341
3411	Pulp,paper etc.	1226	1364	1502	...	...	295	313	352	...	...	3411
342	Printing,publishing	342	425	450	...	...	133	167	172	...	...	342
351	Industrial chemicals ...	1512	1781	1850	...	...	728	826	830	...	...	351
3511	Basic excl fertilizers	20	22	24	...	...	5	5	10	...	...	3511
3513	Synthetic resins etc .	45	44	61	...	...	18	20	30	...	...	3513
352	Other chemical products.	3682	4105	3983	...	...	1705	1955	1756	...	...	352
3522	Drugs and medicines ..	1903	2310	2106	...	...	789	1206	970	...	...	3522
353	Petroleum refineries ...	5477	6988	7045	...	...	c/ 16	c/ 29	1572	...	...	353
354	Petroleum,coal products.	129	90	151	...	...	25	27	50	...	...	354
355	Rubber products	174	227	109	...	...	63	105	40	...	...	355
356	Plastic products n.e.c..	37	52	73	...	...	10	15	20	...	...	356
361	Pottery,china etc	69	79	86	...	...	44	47	47	...	...	361
362	Glass and products	109	150	184	...	...	56	68	89	...	...	362
369	Non-metal products n.e.c	684	699	724	...	...	248	245	211	...	...	369
371	Iron and steel	3250	4202	2519	...	...	839	1250	541	...	...	371
372	Non-ferrous metals	-	-	-	...	...	-	-	-	...	...	372
381	Metal products	627	799	880	...	...	173	233	239	...	...	381
382	Machinery n.e.c.	480	563	789	...	...	176	215	409	...	...	382
3825	Office,computing etc..	-	-	-	...	...	-	-	-	...	...	3825
383	Electrical machinery ...	1035	1114	822	...	...	428	459	283	...	...	383
3832	Radio,television etc..	259	257	145	...	...	80	82	57	...	...	3832
384	Transport equipment	919	750	594	...	...	276	146	243	...	...	384
3841	Shipbuilding, repair..	197	201	221	...	...	63	61	86	...	...	3841
3843	Motor vehicles	578	369	249	...	...	165	...	122	...	...	3843
385	Professional goods	[482	573	671]	...	...	[127	131	124]	...	...	385
390	Other industries				...	...				...	...	390
3	Manufacturing ..... d/e/	40717	47630	50643	...	...	14130	15711	18832	...	...	3
410	Electricity,gas,steam ..	...	...	...	...	...	...	...	...	...	...	410
4101	Electricity	...	...	...	...	...	...	...	...	...	...	4101
420	Water works and supply .	...	...	...	...	...	...	...	...	...	...	420
4	Electricity,gas etc	...	...	...	...	...	...	...	...	...	...	4
2-4	All industry	...	...	...	...	...	...	...	...	...	...	2-4

a/ Establishments with 10 or more workers.
b/ Twelve months ending 30 June of the year indicated.
c/ Value added is less than corresponding wages and salaries due to operating losses.
d/ Including some repair services; see country note.
e/ For certain differences in classification, see country note.

11. INDEX NUMBERS OF INDUSTRIAL PRODUCTION (1980 = 100) a/

ISIC	INDUSTRY	1976	1977	1978	1979	1981	1982	1983	1984	1985	b/ RATE	ISIC
210	Coal mining	...	...	...	...	...	...	...	...	...	...	210
220	Petroleum and gas	65	69	79	90	130	144	170	184	204	13.5	220
230	Metal ore mining	...	...	...	...	...	...	...	...	...	...	230
290	Other mining	...	...	...	...	..	...	...	...	...	...	290
2	Mining, quarrying	73	77	86	94	123	129	153	170	177	10.3	2
311/2	Food products	98	114	97	87	124	119	100	66	69	-3.8	311/2
313	Beverages	67	87	112	102	112	85	143	105	102	4.8	313
314	Tobacco	78	80	91	94	106	94	99	99	100	2.8	314
321	Textiles	81	92	91	92	95	100	97	94	88	0.9	321
3211	Spinning,weaving etc.	...	...	...	...	...	...	...	...	...	...	3211
322	Wearing apparel	...	...	...	...	...	...	...	...	...	...	322
323	Leather and products	...	...	...	...	...	...	...	...	...	...	323
324	Footwear	...	...	...	...	...	...	...	...	...	...	324
331	Wood products	...	...	...	...	...	...	...	...	...	...	331
332	Furniture, fixtures	...	...	...	...	...	...	...	...	...	...	332
341	Paper and products	77	101	102	109	109	80	92	105	125	5.5	341
3411	Pulp,paper etc.	...	...	...	...	...	...	...	...	...	...	3411
342	Printing,publishing	...	...	...	...	...	...	...	...	...	...	342
351	Industrial chemicals	77	61	85	95	95	100	152	183	211	11.9	351
3511	Basic excl fertilizers	81	102	183	99	77	87	102	120	123	4.8	3511
3513	Synthetic resins etc.	...	...	...	...	...	...	...	...	...	...	3513
352	Other chemical products. c/	66	71	85	95	122	112	136	140	137	8.5	352
3522	Drugs and medicines	59	64	78	93	128	106	142	149	137	9.8	3522
353	Petroleum refineries	90	87	99	100	94	74	77	79	76	-1.9	353
354	Petroleum,coal products.	...	...	...	...	...	...	...	...	...	...	354
355	Rubber products	183	197	94	91	88	78	268	175	172	-0.7	355
356	Plastic products n.e.c.	...	...	...	...	...	...	...	...	...	...	356
361	Pottery,china etc	...	...	...	...	...	...	...	...	...	...	361
362	Glass and products	89	116	132	139	145	158	194	198	122	3.6	362
369	Non-metal products n.e.c	91	99	94	98	95	89	79	70	83	-1.0	369
371	Iron and steel	74	80	101	92	86	33	66	79	72	-0.3	371
372	Non-ferrous metals	...	...	...	...	...	...	...	...	...	...	372
381	Metal products	...	...	...	...	...	...	...	...	...	...	381
382	Machinery n.e.c.	26	19	21	61	84	551	199	416	95	15.5	382
3825	Office,computing etc.	...	...	...	...	...	...	...	...	...	...	3825
383	Electrical machinery	61	91	105	114	74	99	117	158	202	14.2	383
3832	Radio,television etc.	...	...	...	...	...	...	...	...	...	...	3832
384	Transport equipment	130	89	89	113	92	39	69	59	97	-3.2	384
3841	Shipbuilding, repair.	...	...	...	...	...	...	...	...	...	...	3841
3843	Motor vehicles	...	...	...	...	...	...	...	...	...	...	3843
385	Professional goods	...	...	...	...	...	...	...	...	...	...	385
390	Other industries	213	112	122	129	86	119	118	51	140	-4.6	390
3	Manufacturing	79	87	92	93	100	95	99	103	97	2.3	3
410	Electricity,gas,steam	...	...	...	...	...	...	...	...	...	...	410
4101	Electricity	61	72	80	88	114	129	143	164	179	12.7	4101
420	Water works and supply	...	...	...	...	...	...	...	...	...	...	420
4	Electricity,gas etc	...	...	...	...	...	...	...	...	...	...	4
2-4	All industry d/	79	86	92	92	101	96	101	105	99	2.5	2-4

a/ Twelve months beginning 1 July of the year stated.
c/ Matches only.
b/ Annual growth rate 1976-1985.
d/ Excluding gas, steam, water works and supply.

BARBADOS

The information in the tables, except for the indexes, is based on the reply to the United Nations Questionnaire on General Industrial Statistics from the Barbados Statistical Service, Bridgetown. The concepts, definitions and classification by branches of industry are generally in accordance with United Nations standards.

The estimates are derived from the annual survey of industrial establishments conducted since 1972 by the Barbados Statistical Service. The survey covers on a complete enumeration basis all establishments engaged in mining and manufacturing. The inquiry is conducted by mail and field contact, if necessary. The response rate is reported to be approximately 75 per cent. In the tables, no adjustments are made for non-response.

The estimates are based on the present version of ISIC. However, in order to avoid disclosing confidential information, certain ISIC groups have been combined. It should be noted that manufacturing estimates do not include sugar manufacturing (ISIC 311/2).

The period of reference is, in general, the calendar year. Where only data for a financial year are available for certain establishments, such data are incorporated for the calendar year in which the major part of the financial year falls.

Employment numbers relate to averages of four quarters. Output is the value of gross receipts adjusted for inventory changes. Value added represents output less the cost of goods and services purchased during the year. In several instances, the estimates of wages and salaries of employees exceed the corresponding data for value added. This is because one or more relatively important establishments within the industry have been highly subsidized.

Gross fixed capital formation refers to the value of fixed assets acquired from others and produced on own account during the year less the value of sales of fixed assets during the year. Expenditures for current repair and maintenance are not included.

The indexes of industrial production are compiled by the Barbados Statistical Service.

Related national publication:
    Statistical Bulletin: Survey of Industrial Establishments (occasional), published by the Barbados Statistical Service, Bridgetown.

ISIC	INDUSTRY		1. NUMBER OF ESTABLISHMENTS (NUMBER) 1981	1982	1983	*1984	1985	2. AVERAGE NUMBER OF PERSONS ENGAGED (NUMBER) 1981	1982	1983	*1984	1985	ISIC
210	Coal mining		-	-	-	-	...	-	-	-	-	...	210
220	Petroleum and gas	a/	...	...	...	...	...	...	...	...	...	...	220
230	Metal ore mining		-	-	-	-	...	-	-	-	-	...	230
290	Other mining	a/	5	6	6	7	...	213	250	247	272	...	290
2	Mining, quarrying .		5	6	6	7	...	213	250	247	272	...	2
311/2	Food products	b/	30	37	28	38	...	1472	2030	1659	1613	...	311/2
313	Beverages		[10	12	11	11]	...	[789	823	737	755]	...	313
314	Tobacco						...					...	314
321	Textiles	c/	2	4	6	12	...	43	55	72	111	...	321
3211	Spinning,weaving etc..		...	...	...	...	...	...	...	...	...	...	3211
322	Wearing apparel		18	19	28	30	...	2200	2303	3316	2408	...	322
323	Leather and products ...	c/	...	...	...	...	...	...	...	...	...	...	323
324	Footwear	c/	...	...	...	...	...	...	...	...	...	...	324
331	Wood products		[9	21	17	24]	...	[175	474	379	391]	...	331
332	Furniture, fixtures						...					...	332
341	Paper and products	d/	15	15	20	22	...	531	588	720	710	...	341
3411	Pulp,paper etc.		...	...	...	...	...	...	...	...	...	...	3411
342	Printing,publishing	d/	...	...	...	...	...	...	...	...	...	...	342
351	Industrial chemicals ...	e/	14	16	18	22	...	369	437	552	442	...	351
3511	Basic excl fertilizers		...	...	...	...	...	...	...	...	...	...	3511
3513	Synthetic resins etc .		...	...	...	...	...	...	...	...	...	...	3513
352	Other chemical products.		5	7	6	9	...	148	180	167	198	...	352
3522	Drugs and medicines ..		...	...	...	...	...	...	...	...	...	...	3522
353	Petroleum refineries ...	e/	...	...	...	...	...	...	...	...	...	...	353
354	Petroleum,coal products.		-	-	-	-	...	-	-	-	-	...	354
355	Rubber products	e/	...	...	...	...	...	...	...	...	...	...	355
356	Plastic products n.e.c..	e/	...	...	...	...	...	...	...	...	...	...	356
361	Pottery,china etc		-	-	-	-	...	-	-	-	-	...	361
362	Glass and products		[9	10	9	13]	...	[322	409	298	529]	...	362
369	Non-metal products n.e.c						...					...	369
371	Iron and steel		-	-	-	-	...	-	-	-	-	...	371
372	Non-ferrous metals		-	-	-	-	...	-	-	-	-	...	372
381	Metal products		11	21	21	21	...	393	778	680	...	...	381
382	Machinery n.e.c.	f/	8	12	13	15	...	1594	2424	2618	2756	...	382
3825	Office,computing etc..		...	...	...	...	...	...	...	...	...	...	3825
383	Electrical machinery ...	f/	...	...	...	...	...	...	...	...	...	...	383
3832	Radio,television etc..		...	...	...	...	...	...	...	...	...	...	3832
384	Transport equipment	g/	5	8	9	9	...	151	194	320	307	...	384
3841	Shipbuilding, repair..		...	...	...	...	...	...	...	...	...	...	3841
3843	Motor vehicles		...	...	...	...	...	...	...	...	...	...	3843
385	Professional goods	g/	...	...	...	...	...	...	...	...	...	...	385
390	Other industries		4	6	6	11	...	104	136	56	158	...	390
3	Manufacturing	b/	140	188	192	237	...	8291	10831	11574	h/ 10378	...	3
410	Electricity,gas,steam ..		...	...	...	...	...	...	...	...	...	...	410
4101	Electricity		...	...	...	...	...	...	...	...	...	...	4101
420	Water works and supply .		...	...	...	...	...	...	...	...	...	...	420
4	Electricity,gas etc		...	...	...	...	...	...	...	...	...	...	4
2-4	All industry		...	...	...	...	...	...	...	...	...	...	2-4

a/ Major group 220 is included in 290.
c/ Major groups 323 and 324 are included in 321.
e/ Major groups 353, 355 and 356 are included in 351.
g/ Major group 385 is included in 384.
b/ Excluding sugar factories and refineries.
d/ Major group 342 is included in 341.
f/ Major group 383 is included in 382.
h/ Excluding major group 381.

ISIC	INDUSTRY	3. AVERAGE NUMBER OF EMPLOYEES (NUMBER)					4. WAGES AND SALARIES OF EMPLOYEES (THOUSAND DOLLARS)					ISIC
		1981	1982	1983	*1984	1985	1981	1982	1983	*1984	1985	
210	Coal mining	-	-	-	-	...	-	-	-	-	...	210
220	Petroleum and gas ...... a/	...	...	...	...	...	...	...	...	...	...	220
230	Metal ore mining	-	-	-	-	...	-	-	-	-	...	230
290	Other mining .... a/	213	249	247	272	...	2647	3223	4324	4496	...	290
2	Mining, quarrying .	213	249	247	272	...	2647	3223	4324	4496	...	2
311/2	Food products .... b/	1461	2018	1650	1568	...	16597	24436	24035	27235	...	311/2
313	Beverages	[789	823	737	754]	...	[11186	12818	13779	15595]	...	313
314	Tobacco					...					...	314
321	Textiles .... c/	41	51	68	107	...	160	387	599	1003	...	321
3211	Spinning,weaving etc..	...	...	...	...	...	...	...	...	...	...	3211
322	Wearing apparel	2145	2298	3314	2403	...	13127	18786	29191	21129	...	322
323	Leather and products ... c/	...	...	...	...	...	...	...	...	...	...	323
324	Footwear .... c/	...	...	...	...	...	...	...	...	...	...	324
331	Wood products	[173	462	368	378]	...	[1240	4126	4079	4782]	...	331
332	Furniture, fixtures					...					...	332
341	Paper and products ..... d/	526	575	706	703	...	7251	7767	11719	15408	...	341
3411	Pulp,paper etc.	...	...	...	...	...	...	...	...	...	...	3411
342	Printing,publishing .... d/	...	...	...	...	...	...	...	...	...	...	342
351	Industrial chemicals ... e/	368	433	552	441	...	4892	6730	8878	9791	...	351
3511	Basic excl fertilizers	...	...	...	...	...	...	...	...	...	...	3511
3513	Synthetic resins etc .	...	...	...	...	...	...	...	...	...	...	3513
352	Other chemical products.	148	178	167	196	...	1696	2454	2567	3287	...	352
3522	Drugs and medicines ..	...	...	...	...	...	...	...	...	...	...	3522
353	Petroleum refineries ... e/	...	...	...	...	...	...	...	...	...	...	353
354	Petroleum,coal products.	-	-	-	-	...	-	-	-	-	...	354
355	Rubber products .... e/	...	...	...	...	...	...	...	...	...	...	355
356	Plastic products n.e.c.. e/	...	...	...	...	...	...	...	...	...	...	356
361	Pottery,china etc	-	-	-	-	...	-	-	-	-	...	361
362	Glass and products	[318	408	297	528]	...	[3967	5516	4661	10556]	...	362
369	Non-metal products n.e.c					...					...	369
371	Iron and steel	-	-	-	-	...	-	-	-	-	...	371
372	Non-ferrous metals	-	-	-	-	...	-	-	-	-	...	372
381	Metal products	388	768	673	637	...	4008	9750	9397	9319	...	381
382	Machinery n.e.c. .... f/	1594	2424	2618	2756	...	11988	20746	25901	31896	...	382
3825	Office,computing etc..	...	...	...	...	...	...	...	...	...	...	3825
383	Electrical machinery ... f/	...	...	...	...	...	...	...	...	...	...	383
3832	Radio,television etc..	...	...	...	...	...	...	...	...	...	...	3832
384	Transport equipment .... g/	148	192	318	307	...	1672	2472	3225	3184	...	384
3841	Shipbuilding, repair..	...	...	...	...	...	...	...	...	...	...	3841
3843	Motor vehicles	...	...	...	...	...	...	...	...	...	...	3843
385	Professional goods ..... g/	...	...	...	...	...	...	...	...	...	...	385
390	Other industries	102	131	52	153	...	698	1311	339	1190	...	390
3	Manufacturing ..... b/	8201	10761	11520	10931	...	78482	117299	138370	154375	...	3
410	Electricity,gas,steam ..	...	...	...	...	...	...	...	...	...	...	410
4101	Electricity	...	...	...	...	...	...	...	...	...	...	4101
420	Water works and supply .	...	...	...	...	...	...	...	...	...	...	420
4	Electricity,gas etc	...	...	...	...	...	...	...	...	...	...	4
2-4	All industry	...	...	...	...	...	...	...	...	...	...	2-4

a/ Major group 220 is included in 290.
b/ Excluding sugar factories and refineries.
c/ Major groups 323 and 324 are included in 321.
d/ Major group 342 is included in 341.
e/ Major groups 353, 355 and 356 are included in 351.
f/ Major group 383 is included in 382.
g/ Major group 385 is included in 384.

ISIC	INDUSTRY		5. AVERAGE NUMBER OF OPERATIVES (NUMBER) 1981	1982	1983	*1984	1985	6. OUTPUT IN PRODUCERS' PRICES (THOUSAND DOLLARS) 1981	1982	1983	*1984	1985	ISIC
210	Coal mining		-	-	-	-	...	-	-	-	-	...	210
220	Petroleum and gas	a/	...	...	...	...	...	...	...	...	...	...	220
230	Metal ore mining		-	-	-	-	...	-	-	-	-	...	230
290	Other mining	a/	176	203	201	209	...	13299	29934	36936	46328	...	290
2	Mining, quarrying .		176	203	201	209	...	13299	29934	36936	46328	...	2
311/2	Food products	b/	1124	1541	1239	1144	...	137758	178024	165255	185688	...	311/2
313	Beverages		[425	460	377	448]	...	[77040	87465	91546	98716]	...	313
314	Tobacco						...					...	314
321	Textiles	c/	36	46	61	88	...	703	1300	1516	2636	...	321
3211	Spinning,weaving etc..		...	...	...	...	...	...	...	...	...	...	3211
322	Wearing apparel		1832	1936	2578	1998	...	53169	60951	77133	73835	...	322
323	Leather and products ...	c/	...	...	...	...	...	...	...	...	...	...	323
324	Footwear	c/	...	...	...	...	...	...	...	...	...	...	324
331	Wood products		[150	403	310	312]	...	[6185	13879	14897	14998]	...	331
332	Furniture, fixtures						...					...	332
341	Paper and products	d/	401	373	498	476	...	26237	23882	43201	48531	...	341
3411	Pulp,paper etc.		...	...	...	...	...	...	...	...	...	...	3411
342	Printing,publishing	d/	...	...	...	...	...	...	...	...	...	...	342
351	Industrial chemicals ...	e/	257	317	400	282	...	150533	162563	167784	173256	...	351
3511	Basic excl fertilizers		...	...	...	...	...	...	...	...	...	...	3511
3513	Synthetic resins etc .		...	...	...	...	...	...	...	...	...	...	3513
352	Other chemical products.		102	110	102	116	...	13698	18711	22195	21864	...	352
3522	Drugs and medicines ..		...	...	...	...	...	...	...	...	...	...	3522
353	Petroleum refineries ...	e/	...	...	...	...	...	...	...	...	...	...	353
354	Petroleum,coal products.		-	-	-	-	...	-	-	-	-	...	354
355	Rubber products	e/	...	...	...	...	...	...	...	...	...	...	355
356	Plastic products n.e.c..	e/	...	...	...	...	...	...	...	...	...	...	356
361	Pottery,china etc		-	-	-	-	...	-	-	-	-	...	361
362	Glass and products		[286	363	234	411]	...	[22946	23556	19981	32566]	...	362
369	Non-metal products n.e.c						...					...	369
371	Iron and steel		-	-	-	-	...	-	-	-	-	...	371
372	Non-ferrous metals		-	-	-	-	...	-	-	-	-	...	372
381	Metal products		294	588	505	458	...	25073	62054	53206	40519	...	381
382	Machinery n.e.c.	f/	1250	1850	1882	2275	...	32831	51861	117834	174785	...	382
3825	Office,computing etc..		...	...	...	...	...	...	...	...	...	...	3825
383	Electrical machinery ...	f/	...	...	...	...	...	...	...	...	...	...	383
3832	Radio,television etc..		...	...	...	...	...	...	...	...	...	...	3832
384	Transport equipment	g/	102	139	265	256	...	7931	10333	14703	12719	...	384
3841	Shipbuilding, repair..		...	...	...	...	...	...	...	...	...	...	3841
3843	Motor vehicles		...	...	...	...	...	...	...	...	...	...	3843
385	Professional goods	g/	...	...	...	...	...	...	...	...	...	...	385
390	Other industries		90	125	42	112	...	1979	3654	2296	4300	...	390
3	Manufacturing	b/	6349	8251	8493	8376	...	556083	698233	791547	884413	...	3
410	Electricity,gas,steam ..		...	...	...	...	...	...	...	...	...	...	410
4101	Electricity		...	...	...	...	...	...	...	...	...	...	4101
420	Water works and supply .		...	...	...	...	...	...	...	...	...	...	420
4	Electricity,gas etc		...	...	...	...	...	...	...	...	...	...	4
2-4	All industry		...	...	...	...	...	...	...	...	...	...	2-4

a/ Major group 220 is included in 290.
b/ Excluding sugar factories and refineries.
c/ Major groups 323 and 324 are included in 321.
d/ Major group 342 is included in 341.
e/ Major groups 353, 355 and 356 are included in 351.
f/ Major group 383 is included in 382.
g/ Major group 385 is included in 384.

ISIC	INDUSTRY		7. VALUE ADDED IN PRODUCERS' PRICES a/ (THOUSAND DOLLARS) 1981	1982	1983	*1984	1985	8. GROSS FIXED CAPITAL FORMATION TOTAL (THOUSAND DOLLARS) 1981	1982	1983	*1984	1985	ISIC
210	Coal mining		-	-	-	..	...	-	-	-	-	...	210
220	Petroleum and gas	b/	...	...	...	...	...	...	...	...	...	...	220
230	Metal ore mining		-	-	-	-	...	-	-	-	-	...	230
290	Other mining	b/	3510	18656	22774	25016	...	2941	28181	21093	4632	...	290
2	Mining, quarrying .		3510	18656	22774	25016	...	2941	28181	21093	4632	...	2
311/2	Food products	c/	25007	34732	37442	41413	..	6330	4119	4689	6087	...	311/2
313	Beverages		[26572	20738	25205	28755]	...	[2790	3312	2058	3766]	...	313
314	Tobacco						...					...	314
321	Textiles	d/	276	401	602	693	...	8	-	93	479	...	321
3211	Spinning,weaving etc..		...	...	...	...	...	...	...	...	...	...	3211
322	Wearing apparel		21182	23413	30874	25844	...	2977	1445	1481	718	...	322
323	Leather and products ...	d/	...	...	...	...	...	...	...	...	...	...	323
324	Footwear	d/	...	...	...	...	...	...	...	...	...	...	324
331	Wood products		[1959	4966	4885	4563]	...	[1841	1253	1904	759]	...	331
332	Furniture, fixtures						...					...	332
341	Paper and products	e/	10458	8215	19008	19565	...	862	2114	1167	3476	...	341
3411	Pulp,paper etc.		...	...	...	...	...	...	...	...	...	...	3411
342	Printing,publishing	e/	...	...	...	...	...	...	...	...	...	...	342
351	Industrial chemicals ...	f/	4022	11951	22577	18734	...	3497	2891	5573	4830	...	351
3511	Basic excl fertilizers		...	...	...	...	...	...	...	...	...	...	3511
3513	Synthetic resins etc .		...	...	...	...	...	...	...	...	...	...	3513
352	Other chemical products.		2480	3339	4313	4313	...	439	823	817	1032	...	352
3522	Drugs and medicines ..		...	...	...	...	...	...	...	...	...	...	3522
353	Petroleum refineries ...	f/	...	...	...	...	...	...	...	...	...	...	353
354	Petroleum,coal products.		-	-	-	-	...	-	-	-	-	...	354
355	Rubber products	f/	...	...	...	...	...	...	...	...	...	...	355
356	Plastic products n.e.c..	f/	...	...	...	...	...	...	...	...	...	...	356
361	Pottery,china etc		-	-	-	-	...	-	-	-	-	...	361
362	Glass and products		[8153	6578	6052	-8744]	...	[2425	350	680	188990]	...	362
369	Non-metal products n.e.c						...					...	369
371	Iron and steel		-	-	-	-	...	-	-	-	-	...	371
372	Non-ferrous metals		-	-	-	-	...	-	-	-	-	...	372
381	Metal products		6530	20736	12530	10826	...	1812	8923	4124	759	...	381
382	Machinery n.e.c.	g/	12622	27434	86438	79063	...	5830	2308	1793	11932	...	382
3825	Office,computing etc..		...	...	...	...	...	...	...	...	...	...	3825
383	Electrical machinery ...	g/	...	...	...	...	...	...	...	...	...	...	383
3832	Radio,television etc..		...	...	...	...	...	...	...	...	...	...	3832
384	Transport equipment	h/	2451	3837	5752	3872	...	1302	1525	568	2012	...	384
3841	Shipbuilding, repair..		...	...	...	...	...	...	...	...	...	...	3841
3843	Motor vehicles		...	...	...	...	...	...	...	...	...	...	3843
385	Professional goods	h/	...	...	...	...	...	...	...	...	...	...	385
390	Other industries		754	1075	539	1124	...	114	229	465	358	...	390
3	Manufacturing	c/	122466	167415	256217	230021	...	30227	29292	25412	225198	...	3
410	Electricity,gas,steam ..		...	...	...	...	...	...	...	...	...	...	410
4101	Electricity		...	...	...	...	...	...	...	...	...	...	4101
420	Water works and supply .		...	...	...	...	...	...	...	...	...	...	420
4	Electricity,gas etc		...	...	...	...	...	...	...	...	...	...	4
2-4	All industry		...	...	...	...	...	...	...	...	...	...	2-4

a/ Net of non-industrial costs.
c/ Excluding sugar factories and refineries.
e/ Major group 342 is included in 341.
g/ Major group 383 is included in 382.

b/ Major group 220 is included in 290.
d/ Major groups 323 and 324 are included in 321.
f/ Major groups 353, 355 and 356 are included in 351.
h/ Major group 385 is included in 384.

9. INDEX NUMBERS OF INDUSTRIAL PRODUCTION (1980 = 100)

ISIC	INDUSTRY	1976	1977	1978	1979	1981	1982	1983	1984	1985	a/ RATE	ISIC
210	Coal mining	...	...	...	...	...	...	...	...	...	...	210
220	Petroleum and gas	...	...	...	...	...	...	...	...	...	...	220
230	Metal ore mining	...	...	...	...	...	...	...	...	...	...	230
290	Other mining	88	75	77	78	116	96	113	154	166	7.3	290
2	Mining, quarrying .	88	75	77	78	111	95	113	154	165	7.2	2
311/2	Food products	86	88	92	97	96	88	87	88	89	0.4	311/2
313	Beverages	[87	99	111	90	95	89	88	81	81	-0.8]	313
314	Tobacco											314
321	Textiles	...	...	...	...	...	...	...	...	...	...	321
3211	Spinning,weaving etc..	...	...	...	...	...	...	...	...	...	...	3211
322	Wearing apparel	94	100	95	99	101	103	109	114	96	0.2	322
323	Leather and products ...	...	...	...	...	...	...	...	...	...	...	323
324	Footwear	...	...	...	...	...	...	...	...	...	...	324
331	Wood products	...	...	...	...	...	...	...	...	...	...	331
332	Furniture, fixtures	...	...	...	...	...	...	...	...	...	...	332
341	Paper and products	...	...	...	...	...	...	...	...	...	...	341
3411	Pulp,paper etc.	...	...	...	...	...	...	...	...	...	...	3411
342	Printing,publishing	...	...	...	...	...	...	...	...	...	...	342
351	Industrial chemicals ... b/	90	74	80	79	101	88	86	74	66	-3.4	351
3511	Basic excl fertilizers	...	...	...	...	...	...	...	...	...	...	3511
3513	Synthetic resins etc .	...	...	...	...	...	...	...	...	...	...	3513
352	Other chemical products. b/	...	...	...	...	...	...	...	...	...	...	352
3522	Drugs and medicines ..	...	...	...	...	...	...	...	...	...	...	3522
353	Petroleum refineries ...	86	87	89	96	103	102	100	102	106	2.4	353
354	Petroleum,coal products.	...	...	...	...	...	...	...	...	...	...	354
355	Rubber products	...	...	...	...	...	...	...	...	...	...	355
356	Plastic products n.e.c..	...	...	...	...	...	...	...	...	...	...	356
361	Pottery,china etc											361
362	Glass and products	[73	73	77	93	110	96	80	74	83	1.4]	362
369	Non-metal products n.e.c											369
371	Iron and steel	...	...	...	...	...	...	...	...	...	...	371
372	Non-ferrous metals	...	...	...	...	...	...	...	...	...	...	372
381	Metal products	...	...	...	...	...	...	...	...	...	...	381
382	Machinery n.e.c.	...	...	...	...	...	...	...	...	...	...	382
3825	Office,computing etc..	...	...	...	...	...	...	...	...	...	...	3825
383	Electrical machinery ...	...	...	...	...	...	...	...	...	...	...	383
3832	Radio,television etc..	...	...	...	...	...	...	...	...	...	...	3832
384	Transport equipment	...	...	...	...	...	...	...	...	...	...	384
3841	Shipbuilding, repair..	...	...	...	...	...	...	...	...	...	...	3841
3843	Motor vehicles	...	...	...	...	...	...	...	...	...	...	3843
385	Professional goods	...	...	...	...	...	...	...	...	...	...	385
390	Other industries	119	113	109	106	89	82	84	78	71	-5.6	390
3	Manufacturing	97	98	100	98	95	89	91	92	84	-1.6	3
410	Electricity,gas,steam ..	64	74	85	94	100	102	118	124	132	8.4	410
4101	Electricity	...	...	...	...	...	...	...	...	...	...	4101
420	Water works and supply .	.	.	.	.	.	.	.	.	.	.	420
4	Electricity,gas etc	...	...	...	...	...	...	...	...	...	...	4
2-4	All industry	90	93	97	97	97	93	97	100	95	0.6	2-4

a/ Annual growth rate 1976-1985.

b/ Major group 352 is included in 351.

BELGIUM

The information on industrial activity is based on the reply to the United Nations Questionnaire on General Industrial Statistics from the Institut national de statistique, Brussels. The concepts, definitions and classification by branches of industry are generally in accordance with United Nations standards.

The estimates of establishments, employment and earnings are derived from social security records maintained by the Office national de securite sociale. The records cover all workers subject to social security for whom contributions are received during the second quarter of each year. Data are compiled on an establishment basis, whereby employers possessing more than one producing unit, or exercising more than one activity, are treated as more than one unit.

The employment numbers are as of 30 June of each year. Heads of establishments covered by social security regulations are included in the figures for employees. The figures shown for operatives refer to employees subject to social security regulations in the "worker" category. Apprentices are included in both the "employee" and "worker" categories. The estimates of wages and salaries are the gross wage and salary payments reported by employers to social security, including commissions and payments in kind.

The estimates of electricity consumed are derived from information compiled by the Federation professionnelle des producteurs et distributeurs d'electricite de Belgique (FPE). The data cover the consumption of all producers, including those producing for their own use. The classification is that followed by FPE.

The estimates of value added are derived from national accounts statistics. They are based on the results of the annual statistics of industrial production inquiry, generally covering establishments with 5 or more employees.

The estimates based on social security records are compiled according to the General Industrial Classification of Economic Activities within the European Communities (NACE). Other estimates are compiled according to the classifications used by the authorities concerned adjusted, as far as possible, to the present version of ISIC. For the national accounts estimates, retailing of meat and bakery products (ISIC major division 6) is included in ISIC 311/2; activities of railway company workshops are not covered; electric power stations producing for coal mining establishments are included in ISIC 210; manufacture of plaster and plaster and stone products (ISIC 369) is included in ISIC 290; manufacture of artificial and synthetic fibres (ISIC 3513) is included in ISIC 321 and manufacture of made-up textile goods, except wearing apparel (ISIC 321) is included in ISIC 322; processing of waste and recovery of fibres and flock (ISIC 321) is included in ISIC 390; manufacture of leather gloves and some other leather wearing apparel (ISIC 322) and leather products (ISIC 323) is included in ISIC 324; for ISIC 331, only sawmills are covered and other activities of this industry are included in ISIC 332; manufacture of miscellaneous wooden transport equipment (ISIC 384) is also included in ISIC 332; manufacture of paints, varnishes and lacquers (ISIC 352) is included in ISIC 351; gas manufacture (ISIC 410) and coke ovens in steel mills (ISIC 371) are included in ISIC 353-354 combined; ship breaking yards (ISIC 3841) are included in ISIC 390.

The indexes of industrial production are compiled by the Institut national de statistique and provided in response to the United Nations Questionnaire on Indexes of Industrial Production. In principle, the indexes cover all establishments.

Related national publications:
<u>Annuaire statistique de la Belgique</u>; <u>Bulletin de statistique</u> (monthly), both published by the Institut national de statistique, Brussels.
<u>Annuaire statistique</u>, published by the Federation professionnelle des producteurs et distributeurs d'electricite de Belgique (FPE).

ISIC	INDUSTRY	1. NUMBER OF ESTABLISHMENTS a/ (NUMBER) 1981	1982	1983	1984	1985	2. AVERAGE NUMBER OF PERSONS ENGAGED b/c/ (THOUSANDS) 1981	1982	1983	1984	1985	ISIC
210	Coal mining	26	24	22	...	...	21	21	21	...	...	210
220	Petroleum and gas	-	-	-	...	...	-	-	-	...	...	220
230	Metal ore mining	-	-	-	...	...	-	-	-	...	...	230
290	Other mining	243	249	226	...	...	10	10	9	...	...	290
2	Mining, quarrying .	269	273	248	...	...	31	31	30	...	...	2
311/2	Food products	6576	6596	6603	...	...				...	...	311/2
313	Beverages	332	313	298	...	...	[113	112	110]	...	...	313
314	Tobacco	65	64	63	...	...				...	...	314
321	Textiles	1390	1328	1303	...	...	65	62	62	...	...	321
3211	Spinning,weaving etc..	...	...	...	...	...	...	...	...	...	...	3211
322	Wearing apparel	2262	2169	2111	...	...	49	47	46	...	...	322
323	Leather and products ...	208	193	180	...	...	3	3	3	...	...	323
324	Footwear	138	134	134	...	...	3	3	3	...	...	324
331	Wood products	[2399	2320	2231]	...	...	[47	45	44]	...	...	331
332	Furniture, fixtures				...	...				...	...	332
341	Paper and products	357	338	321	...	...	19	18	18	...	...	341
3411	Pulp,paper etc.	...	...	...	...	...	...	...	...	...	...	3411
342	Printing,publishing	2137	2080	2063	...	...	38	38	38	...	...	342
351	Industrial chemicals ... d/	733	731	719	...	...	72	72	71	...	...	351
3511	Basic excl fertilizers	...	...	...	...	...	...	...	...	...	...	3511
3513	Synthetic resins etc .	...	...	...	...	...	...	...	...	...	...	3513
352	Other chemical products. d/	...	...	...	...	...	...	...	...	...	...	352
3522	Drugs and medicines ..	...	...	...	...	...	...	...	...	...	...	3522
353	Petroleum refineries ...	25	24	23	...	...	[6	6	5]	...	...	353
354	Petroleum,coal products.	6	6	6	...	...				...	...	354
355	Rubber products	108	102	99	...	...	[22	21	21]	...	...	355
356	Plastic products n.e.c..	420	419	421	...	...				...	...	356
361	Pottery,china etc	e/	e/	e/	...	...				...	...	361
362	Glass and products	126	133	134	...	...	[49	45	43]	...	...	362
369	Non-metal products n.e.c	e/ 1421	e/ 1335	e/ 1304	...	...				...	...	369
371	Iron and steel	[166	158	147]	...	...	[77	74	70]	...	...	371
372	Non-ferrous metals				...	...				...	...	372
381	Metal products	3144	3098	3086	...	...	[f/ 300	f/ 280	f/ 274]	...	...	381
382	Machinery n.e.c.	885	875	851	...	...				...	...	382
3825	Office,computing etc..	...	...	...	...	...	...	...	...	...	...	3825
383	Electrical machinery ...	609	617	628	...	...	f/	f/	f/	...	...	383
3832	Radio,television etc..	...	...	...	...	...	...	...	...	...	...	3832
384	Transport equipment	476	481	492	...	...	f/	f/	f/	...	...	384
3841	Shipbuilding, repair..	...	...	...	...	...	...	...	...	...	...	3841
3843	Motor vehicles	...	...	...	...	...	...	...	...	...	...	3843
385	Professional goods	483	479	456	...	...	f/	f/	f/	...	...	385
390	Other industries	988	977	984	...	...	15	15	15	...	...	390
3	Manufacturing	25464	24970	24657	...	...	878	841	823	...	...	3
410	Electricity,gas,steam ..	...	...	...	...	...	...	...	...	...	...	410
4101	Electricity	...	...	...	...	...	...	...	...	...	...	4101
420	Water works and supply .	...	...	...	...	...	...	...	...	...	...	420
4	Electricity,gas etc	605	604	568	...	...	33	33	33	...	...	4
2-4	All industry	26338	25847	25473	...	...	942	905	886	...	...	2-4

Note. For description of classification, see country note.

a/ Estimates derived from social security records.
b/ Estimates relate to total employment.
c/ At 30 June of the year indicated.
d/ Major group 352 is included in 351.
e/ Major group 361 is included in 369.
f/ Major groups 383 to 385 are included in 381 and 382 combined.

BELGIUM

ISIC	INDUSTRY	3. AVERAGE NUMBER OF EMPLOYEES a/b/ (THOUSANDS) 1981	1982	1983	1984	1985	4. WAGES AND SALARIES OF EMPLOYEES a/ (BILLION FRANCS) 1981	1982	1983	1984	1985	ISIC
210	Coal mining	21	21	21	...	...	12.85	13.48	...	...	...	210
220	Petroleum and gas	-	-	-	...	...	-	-	...	...	...	220
230	Metal ore mining	-	-	-	...	...	-	-	...	...	...	230
290	Other mining	6	6	6	...	...	2.94	3.05	...	...	...	290
2	Mining, quarrying .	27	27	27	...	...	15.79	16.53	...	...	...	2
311/2	Food products	74	74	73	...	...	33.87	35.85	...	...	...	311/2
313	Beverages	17	16	15	...	...	9.28	9.28	...	...	...	313
314	Tobacco	7	6	6	...	...	3.20	3.29	...	...	...	314
321	Textiles	63	60	59	...	...	22.87	23.74	...	...	...	321
3211	Spinning,weaving etc..	...	...	...	...	...	...	...	...	...	...	3211
322	Wearing apparel	45	43	42	...	...	12.19	13.04	...	...	...	322
323	Leather and products ...	3	3	3	...	...	1.01	1.05	...	...	...	323
324	Footwear	3	2	2	...	...	0.79	0.87	...	...	...	324
331	Wood products	[36	35	34]	...	...	[15.27	15.48]	...	...	...	331
332	Furniture, fixtures				...	...			...	...	...	332
341	Paper and products	18	18	18	...	...	9.93	10.32	...	...	...	341
3411	Pulp,paper etc.	...	...	...	...	...	...	...	...	...	...	3411
342	Printing,publishing	33	32	32	...	...	18.40	19.32	...	...	...	342
351	Industrial chemicals ... c/	72	71	70	...	...	50.34	54.46	...	...	...	351
3511	Basic excl fertilizers	...	...	...	...	...	...	...	...	...	...	3511
3513	Synthetic resins etc .	...	...	...	...	...	...	...	...	...	...	3513
352	Other chemical products. c/	...	...	...	...	...	...	...	...	...	...	352
3522	Drugs and medicines ..	...	...	...	...	...	...	...	...	...	...	3522
353	Petroleum refineries ...	6	6	5	...	...	4.96	5.43	...	...	...	353
354	Petroleum,coal products.	2	2	1	...	...	0.67	0.67	...	...	...	354
355	Rubber products	7	7	6	...	...	3.78	3.81	...	...	...	355
356	Plastic products n.e.c..	14	14	14	...	...	6.62	7.27	...	...	...	356
361	Pottery,china etc ...... d/	...	...	...	...	...	...	...	...	...	...	361
362	Glass and products	16	15	15	...	...	8.24	8.63	...	...	...	362
369	Non-metal products n.e.c d/	31	28	26	...	...	14.14	14.01	...	...	...	369
371	Iron and steel	[77	74	70]	...	...	[49.20	48.97]	...	...	...	371
372	Non-ferrous metals				...	...			...	...	...	372
381	Metal products	77	74	72	...	...	36.60	37.60	...	...	...	381
382	Machinery n.e.c.	52	50	47	...	...	28.45	28.83	...	...	...	382
3825	Office,computing etc..	...	...	...	...	...	...	...	...	...	...	3825
383	Electrical machinery ...	78	75	72	...	...	45.09	46.91	...	...	...	383
3832	Radio,television etc..	...	...	...	...	...	...	...	...	...	...	3832
384	Transport equipment	76	71	72	...	...	40.33	42.49	...	...	...	384
3841	Shipbuilding, repair..	...	...	...	...	...	...	...	...	...	...	3841
3843	Motor vehicles	...	...	...	...	...	...	...	...	...	...	3843
385	Professional goods	5	5	5	...	...	2.50	2.51	...	...	...	385
390	Other industries	13	13	13	...	...	4.06	4.19	...	...	...	390
3	Manufacturing	825	794	772	...	...	421.79	438.02	...	...	...	3
410	Electricity,gas,steam ..	...	...	...	...	...	...	...	...	...	...	410
4101	Electricity	...	...	...	...	...	...	...	...	...	...	4101
420	Water works and supply .	...	...	...	...	...	...	...	...	...	...	420
4	Electricity,gas etc	33	33	32	...	...	28.16	29.80	...	...	...	4
2-4	All industry	885	854	831	...	...	465.74	484.35	...	...	...	2-4

Note. For description of classification, see country note.

a/ Estimates derived from social security records.
b/ At 30 June of the year indicated.
c/ Major group 352 is included in 351.
d/ Major group 361 is included in 369.

ISIC	INDUSTRY	5. AVERAGE NUMBER OF OPERATIVES a/b/ (THOUSANDS) 1981	1982	1983	1984	1985	6. WAGES AND SALARIES OF OPERATIVES a/ (BILLION FRANCS) 1981	1982	1983	1984	1985	ISIC
210	Coal mining	20	20	20	...	...	11.70	12.28	...	...	...	210
220	Petroleum and gas	-	-	-	...	...	-	-	...	...	...	220
230	Metal ore mining	-	-	-	...	...	-	-	...	...	...	230
290	Other mining	5	5	5	...	...	1.97	2.04	...	...	...	290
2	Mining, quarrying .	25	25	25	...	...	13.67	14.32	...	...	...	2
311/2	Food products	55	55	54	...	...	21.36	22.64	...	...	...	311/2
313	Beverages	12	11	11	...	...	5.51	5.49	...	...	...	313
314	Tobacco	5	5	5	...	...	1.93	1.92	...	...	...	314
321	Textiles	54	51	51	...	...	16.68	17.37	...	...	...	321
3211	Spinning,weaving etc..	...	...	...	...	...	...	...	...	...	...	3211
322	Wearing apparel	40	38	37	...	...	9.02	9.69	...	...	...	322
323	Leather and products ...	2	2	2	...	...	0.72	0.76	...	...	...	323
324	Footwear	2	2	2	...	...	0.64	0.72	...	...	...	324
331	Wood products	[31	30	29]	...	...	[12.00	12.20]	...	...	...	331
332	Furniture, fixtures				...	...			...	...	...	332
341	Paper and products	14	13	13	...	...	6.23	6.53	...	...	...	341
3411	Pulp,paper etc.	...	...	...	...	...	...	...	...	...	...	3411
342	Printing,publishing	21	20	20	...	...	10.00	10.47	...	...	...	342
351	Industrial chemicals ... c/	39	38	37	...	...	20.63	21.98	...	...	...	351
3511	Basic excl fertilizers	...	...	...	...	...	...	...	...	...	...	3511
3513	Synthetic resins etc .	...	...	...	...	...	...	...	...	...	...	3513
352	Other chemical products. c/	...	...	...	...	...	...	...	...	...	...	352
3522	Drugs and medicines ..	...	...	...	...	...	...	...	...	...	...	3522
353	Petroleum refineries ...	3	2	2	...	...	1.67	1.74	...	...	...	353
354	Petroleum,coal products.	1	1	1	...	...	0.55	0.57	...	...	...	354
355	Rubber products	5	5	5	...	...	2.27	2.33	...	...	...	355
356	Plastic products n.e.c..	11	10	11	...	...	4.02	4.42	...	...	...	356
361	Pottery,china etc ...... d/	...	...	...	...	...	...	...	...	...	...	361
362	Glass and products	12	12	11	...	...	5.22	5.42	...	...	...	362
369	Non-metal products n.e.c d/	25	23	21	...	...	9.76	9.50	...	...	...	369
371	Iron and steel	[61	58	55]	...	...	[33.73	33.09]	...	...	...	371
372	Non-ferrous metals				...	...			...	...	...	372
381	Metal products	61	58	57	...	...	24.53	25.19	...	...	...	381
382	Machinery n.e.c.	36	34	32	...	...	16.03	15.86	...	...	...	382
3825	Office,computing etc..	...	...	...	...	...	...	...	...	...	...	3825
383	Electrical machinery ...	50	47	45	...	...	21.22	21.68	...	...	...	383
3832	Radio,television etc..	...	...	...	...	...	...	...	...	...	...	3832
384	Transport equipment	62	58	59	...	...	28.63	30.92	...	...	...	384
3841	Shipbuilding, repair..	...	...	...	...	...	...	...	...	...	...	3841
3843	Motor vehicles	...	...	...	...	...	...	...	...	...	...	3843
385	Professional goods	3	3	3	...	...	1.10	1.14	...	...	...	385
390	Other industries	11	11	11	...	...	2.53	2.63	...	...	...	390
3	Manufacturing	616	587	574	...	...	255.98	264.26	...	...	...	3
410	Electricity,gas,steam ..	...	...	...	...	...	...	...	...	...	...	410
4101	Electricity	...	...	...	...	...	...	...	...	...	...	4101
420	Water works and supply .	...	...	...	...	...	...	...	...	...	...	420
4	Electricity,gas etc	...	...	...	...	...	...	...	...	...	...	4
2-4	All industry	...	...	...	...	...	...	...	...	...	...	2-4

Note. For description of classification, see country note.

a/ Estimates derived from social security records.
b/ At 30 June of the year indicated.
c/ Major group 352 is included in 351.
d/ Major group 361 is included in 369.

ISIC	INDUSTRY	7. QUANTITY OF ELECTRICITY CONSUMED a/ (MILLION KWH)					8. VALUE ADDED IN FACTOR VALUES b/c/ (BILLION FRANCS)					ISIC
		1981	1982	1983	1984	1985	1981	1982	1983	1984	1985	
210	Coal mining	630	663	644	...	...	13.8	10.2	10.3	...	...	210
220	Petroleum and gas	-	-	-	...	...	-	-	-	...	...	220
230	Metal ore mining	-	-	-	...	..	-	-	-	...	...	230
290	Other mining	261	272	282	...	...	10.9	10.3	10.2	...	...	290
2	Mining, quarrying	891	935	926	...	...	24.7	20.5	20.5	...	...	2
311/2	Food products	1550	1622	1613	...	...	121.4	137.8	148.8	...	...	311/2
313	Beverages	281	288	304	...	...	17.5	19.7	21.3	...	...	313
314	Tobacco	36	36	35	...	...	5.7	6.5	7.2	...	...	314
321	Textiles	1020	1019	1070	...	...	46.2	48.2	54.7	...	...	321
3211	Spinning, weaving etc.	942	942	989	...	...	36.0	37.9	43.7	...	...	3211
322	Wearing apparel	38	37	40	...	...	19.2	20.8	21.5	...	...	322
323	Leather and products	11	12	11	...	...	d/	d/	d/	...	...	323
324	Footwear	8	8	8	...	...	1.9	2.2	2.3	...	...	324
331	Wood products	[318	400	412]	...	...	3.7	3.9	4.1	...	...	331
332	Furniture, fixtures				...	...	34.3	36.3	38.1	...	...	332
341	Paper and products	1120	1066	1084	...	...	19.4	21.5	22.2	...	...	341
3411	Pulp, paper etc.	...	...	...	...	...	8.6	9.3	9.3	...	...	3411
342	Printing, publishing	153	160	175	...	...	27.7	28.7	29.0	...	...	342
351	Industrial chemicals	e/ 7630	e/ 7794	e/ 7950	...	...	77.3	88.8	98.5	...	...	351
3511	Basic excl fertilizers	...	...	...	...	...	...	...	...	...	...	3511
3513	Synthetic resins etc	...	...	...	...	...	...	...	...	...	...	3513
352	Other chemical products	e/	e/	e/	...	...	21.1	24.0	25.2	...	...	352
3522	Drugs and medicines	...	...	...	...	...	14.5	15.8	16.2	...	...	3522
353	Petroleum refineries	709	630	631	...	...	[17.6	17.2	15.0]	...	...	353
354	Petroleum, coal products	24	18	16	...	...				...	...	354
355	Rubber products	101	102	113	...	...	5.4	5.5	6.4	...	...	355
356	Plastic products n.e.c.	...	...	...	...	...	d/	d/	d/	...	...	356
361	Pottery, china etc	36	42	46	...	...				...	...	361
362	Glass and products	463	448	453	...	...	[32.6	34.4	33.8]	...	...	362
369	Non-metal products n.e.c	1178	1014	951	...	...				...	...	369
371	Iron and steel	5020	4421	4461	...	...	40.1	36.4	32.9	...	...	371
372	Non-ferrous metals	1545	1468	1655	...	...	14.4	16.2	18.2	...	...	372
381	Metal products	[1139	1129	1151]	...	...	[f/ 259.6	f/ 279.2	f/ 301.0]	...	...	381
382	Machinery n.e.c.				...	...				...	...	382
3825	Office, computing etc.	...	...	...	...	...	...	...	...	...	...	3825
383	Electrical machinery	519	510	507	...	...	f/	f/	f/	...	...	383
3832	Radio, television etc.	...	...	...	...	...	...	...	...	...	...	3832
384	Transport equipment	668	706	734	...	...	f/	f/	f/	...	...	384
3841	Shipbuilding, repair	...	...	...	...	...	...	...	...	...	...	3841
3843	Motor vehicles	...	...	...	...	...	...	...	...	...	...	3843
385	Professional goods	...	...	...	...	...	f/	f/	f/	...	...	385
390	Other industries	436	422	435	...	...	d/ 43.0	d/ 47.3	d/ 54.1	...	...	390
3	Manufacturing	24003	23352	23855	...	...	808.1	874.6	934.3	...	...	3
410	Electricity, gas, steam	...	...	...	...	...	89.5	94.0	113.0	...	...	410
4101	Electricity	3500	3699	3882	...	...	64.2	65.0	80.5	...	...	4101
420	Water works and supply	...	...	...	...	...	16.5	17.8	18.8	...	...	420
4	Electricity, gas etc	...	...	...	...	...	106.0	111.8	131.8	...	...	4
2-4	All industry	...	...	...	...	...	938.8	1006.9	1086.6	...	...	2-4

Note. For description of classification, see country note.

a/ Total industrial consumption. Derived from data compiled by FPE; see country note.
b/ Contributions to the gross domestic product.
c/ Estimates derived from national accounts calculations.
d/ Major groups 323 and 356 are included in 390.
e/ Major group 352 is included in 351.
f/ Major groups 383 to 385 are included in 381 and 382 combined.

9. INDEX NUMBERS OF INDUSTRIAL PRODUCTION (1980 = 100)

ISIC	INDUSTRY	1976	1977	1978	1979	1981	1982	1983	1984	1985	a/ RATE	ISIC
210	Coal mining	135	124	111	98	95	99	92	91	84	-5.1	210
220	Petroleum and gas	...	...	...	...	...	...	...	...	...	...	220
230	Metal ore mining	...	...	...	...	...	...	...	...	...	...	230
290	Other mining	98	97	90	91	88	83	80	85	82	-2.0	290
2	Mining, quarrying .	123	115	105	97	94	95	89	90	84	-4.1	2
311/2	Food products	88	92	95	98	105	111	113	117	121	3.6	311/2
313	Beverages	103	100	96	98	100	104	104	104	101	-0.2	313
314	Tobacco	101	102	97	101	102	108	108	103	104	0.3	314
321	Textiles	107	94	89	97	97	96	103	104	104	-0.3	321
3211	Spinning,weaving etc..	...	...	...	...	...	...	...	...	...	...	3211
322	Wearing apparel	113	105	109	103	98	100	98	94	93	-2.1	322
323	Leather and products ...	222	192	153	125	109	119	119	124	118	-6.8	323
324	Footwear .... b/	143	115	100	102	89	100	101	94	86	-5.5	324
331	Wood products .... b/	[99	98	94	93	98	99	96	95	96	-0.3]	331
332	Furniture, fixtures											332
341	Paper and products	94	91	94	101	101	102	105	111	113	2.1	341
3411	Pulp,paper etc.	...	...	...	...	...	...	...	...	...	...	3411
342	Printing,publishing	...	...	...	...	...	...	...	...	...	...	342
351	Industrial chemicals ... c/	90	95	98	106	102	104	109	115	118	3.1	351
3511	Basic excl fertilizers	...	...	...	...	...	...	...	...	...	...	3511
3513	Synthetic resins etc .	...	...	...	...	...	...	...	...	...	...	3513
352	Other chemical products. c/	...	...	...	...	...	...	...	...	...	...	352
3522	Drugs and medicines ..	...	...	...	...	...	...	...	...	...	...	3522
353	Petroleum refineries ...	[92	110	102	103	87	75	63	71	66	-3.6]	353
354	Petroleum,coal products.											354
355	Rubber products	90	89	88	92	90	84	82	90	94	0.5	355
356	Plastic products n.e.c..	85	88	94	102	103	112	120	124	135	5.3	356
361	Pottery,china etc	122	117	116	106	89	88	83	85	79	-4.7	361
362	Glass and products	79	90	90	95	91	86	84	91	72	-1.0	362
369	Non-metal products n.e.c	100	104	101	103	89	84	76	76	74	-3.3	369
371	Iron and steel	94	88	99	107	98	79	82	92	89	-0.6	371
372	Non-ferrous metals	89	102	96	102	89	94	93	96	100	1.3	372
381	Metal products	95	96	93	100	94	95	96	97	99	0.5	381
382	Machinery n.e.c.	98	97	97	105	97	92	91	101	109	1.2	382
3825	Office,computing etc..	...	...	...	...	...	...	...	...	...	...	3825
383	Electrical machinery ...	101	98	103	102	93	93	96	93	94	-0.8	383
3832	Radio,television etc..	...	...	...	...	...	...	...	...	...	...	3832
384	Transport equipment	83	90	98	106	103	114	122	112	120	4.2	384
3841	Shipbuilding, repair..	...	...	...	...	...	...	...	...	...	...	3841
3843	Motor vehicles	...	...	...	...	...	...	...	...	...	...	3843
385	Professional goods	63	67	72	77	104	107	119	121	122	7.6	385
390	Other industries	...	...	...	...	...	...	...	...	...	...	390
3	Manufacturing	94	94	97	102	98	98	100	102	104	1.1	3
410	Electricity,gas,steam ..	...	...	...	...	...	...	...	...	...	...	410
4101	Electricity	88	88	95	97	94	94	98	102	106	2.1	4101
420	Water works and supply .	95	95	97	98	100	103	103	104	110	1.6	420
4	Electricity,gas etc	...	...	...	...	...	...	...	...	...	...	4
2-4	All industry d/	95	95	97	101	97	98	99	102	104	1.0	2-4

a/ Annual growth rate 1976-1985.
b/ Wooden shoes are included in major group 324.
c/ Major group 352 is included in 351.
d/ Excluding gas and steam.

BOLIVIA

The information in the tables, except for the indexes, is based on the reply to the United Nations Questionnaire on General Industrial Statistics from the Instituto Nacional de Estadistica, Ministerio de Planeamiento y Coordinacion, La Paz. The concepts, definitions and classification by branches of industry are generally in accordance with United Nations standards.

The estimates for 1981 and 1982 are derived from annual returns submitted by industrial enterprises with a capital of 50 thousand pesos or more to the Instituto Nacional de Estadistica as required by law. Beginning 1983, the estimates refer to establishments with 20 or more persons engaged and all multi-establishment enterprises regardless of size. It is estimated that these large establishments account for 85 per cent of the output in manufacturing. The data include estimates for non-response, except for 1982. The estimates in the tables are tabulated according to the present version of ISIC. Employment numbers and wages and salaries of both employees and operatives relate to persons employed on the permanent and temporary employment basis. Permanent workers are defined as those who work at least one-third of daily working hours for the establishment.

Estimates of output represent the sum of the value of goods produced by the establishment during the year, receipts from industrial services rendered to others and value of goods sold in the same condition as purchased. Value added is calculated as the value of output less the value of intermediate consumption, consisting of the value of raw materials, supplies and packing materials consumed, value of electricity purchased, oils and fuels consumed, other costs (freightage, insurance, advertisement etc.) and the cost of goods sold in the same condition as purchased. The valuation of output and value added is in producers' prices.

Gross fixed capital formation is the difference between the gross value of purchases of fixed assets acquired during the year and the value of sales of fixed assets owned by the establishment.

The indexes of industrial production are compiled by the Instituto Nacional de Estadistica. The indexes provided by the national authorities are compiled according to the preceding version of ISIC. Wherever possible, adjustments have been incorporated to convert the data to the present version; owing to lack of detail, the conversion is not complete for all industries.

Related national publication:
Bolivia en Cifras 1985 (annual), published by the Instituto Nacional de Estadistica, La Paz.

ISIC	INDUSTRY	1. NUMBER OF ESTABLISHMENTS (NUMBER)					2. AVERAGE NUMBER OF PERSONS ENGAGED a/ (NUMBER)					ISIC
		b/ 1981	b/c/ 1982	d/ 1983	d/ 1984	1985	b/ 1981	b/c/ 1982	d/ 1983	d/ 1984	1985	
210	Coal mining	...	...	...	...	...	...	...	...	...	...	210
220	Petroleum and gas	...	...	...	...	...	...	...	...	...	...	220
230	Metal ore mining	42	43	43	43	...	83404	84150	84150	84100	...	230
290	Other mining	...	...	...	...	...	...	...	...	...	...	290
2	Mining, quarrying .	...	...	...	...	...	...	...	...	...	...	2
311/2	Food products	266	221	123	163	...	7268	6666	8627	5946	...	311/2
313	Beverages	55	51	37	36	...	3618	3554	3946	3688	...	313
314	Tobacco	1	2	1	2	...	180	170	160	148	...	314
321	Textiles	130	130	53	67	...	4845	4923	4430	4705	...	321
3211	Spinning,weaving etc..	55	55	30	35	...	3824	4074	3597	3645	...	3211
322	Wearing apparel	75	71	22	35	...	1097	1009	616	662	...	322
323	Leather and products ...	29	31	19	18	...	664	697	821	882	...	323
324	Footwear	19	18	13	25	...	517	1442	1418	1863	...	324
331	Wood products	147	133	55	78	...	2751	2997	1943	1335	...	331
332	Furniture, fixtures	58	46	35	68	...	526	404	436	375	...	332
341	Paper and products	12	10	7	6	...	131	132	187	202	...	341
3411	Pulp,paper etc.	1	1	1	1	...	52	26	7	93	...	3411
342	Printing,publishing	117	115	28	36	...	1731	1469	1082	1236	...	342
351	Industrial chemicals ...	17	16	10	9	...	312	279	184	229	...	351
3511	Basic excl fertilizers	12	14	8	7	...	233	275	175	204	...	3511
3513	Synthetic resins etc .	4	...	...	...	...	75	...	...	...	...	3513
352	Other chemical products.	68	61	29	30	...	1878	1741	1593	1542	...	352
3522	Drugs and medicines ..	28	27	14	13	...	1096	1002	937	906	...	3522
353	Petroleum refineries ...	2	3	3	3	...	...	798	811	938	...	353
354	Petroleum,coal products.	5	5	-	-	...	14	32	-	-	...	354
355	Rubber products	11	7	3	3	...	226	138	44	57	...	355
356	Plastic products n.e.c..	37	43	20	23	...	966	946	849	873	...	356
361	Pottery,china etc	...	-	1	-	...	112	-	114	-	...	361
362	Glass and products	7	4	4	5	...	826	287	557	691	...	362
369	Non-metal products n.e.c	70	71	33	48	...	1977	1791	1731	1759	...	369
371	Iron and steel	4	7	2	5	...	175	121	87	98	...	371
372	Non-ferrous metals	6	5	8	6	...	2196	2185	2226	1569	...	372
381	Metal products	94	68	41	57	...	1879	1457	856	936	...	381
382	Machinery n.e.c.	14	12	4	7	...	448	366	241	141	...	382
3825	Office,computing etc..	...	...	...	...	...	...	...	...	...	...	3825
383	Electrical machinery ...	14	14	9	13	...	277	255	211	333	...	383
3832	Radio,television etc..	...	...	...	...	...	...	...	...	...	...	3832
384	Transport equipment	22	14	9	14	...	598	377	326	437	...	384
3841	Shipbuilding, repair..	...	...	...	...	...	...	...	...	...	...	3841
3843	Motor vehicles	16	11	8	11	...	474	303	281	379	...	3843
385	Professional goods	9	9	4	6	...	119	123	85	113	...	385
390	Other industries	25	19	13	16	...	312	329	277	193	...	390
3	Manufacturing	e/ 1314	1186	586	779	...	f/ 35643	34688	33858	30951	...	3
410	Electricity,gas,steam ..	...	...	...	...	...	...	...	...	...	...	410
4101	Electricity	...	...	...	...	...	...	...	...	...	...	4101
420	Water works and supply .	...	...	...	...	...	...	...	...	...	...	420
4	Electricity,gas etc	...	...	...	...	...	...	...	...	...	...	4
2-4	All industry	...	...	...	...	...	...	...	...	...	...	2-4

a/ For one period of the year indicated. b/ Enterprises with a capital of 50 thousand pesos or more.
c/ Reporting establishments without estimate for non-response.
d/ Establishments with 20 or more persons engaged and all multi-establishment enterprises regardless of size.
e/ Excluding major group 361. f/ Excluding major group 353.

ISIC	INDUSTRY	3. AVERAGE NUMBER OF EMPLOYEES a/ (NUMBER)					4. WAGES AND SALARIES OF EMPLOYEES (BILLION PESOS)					ISIC
		b/ 1981	b/c/ 1982	1983	1984	1985	b/ 1981	b/c/ 1982	d/ 1983	1984	1985	
210	Coal mining	...	...	...	...	...	...	...	...	...	...	210
220	Petroleum and gas	...	...	...	...	...	...	...	...	...	...	220
230	Metal ore mining	...	...	...	...	...	...	...	...	...	...	230
290	Other mining	...	...	...	...	...	...	...	...	...	...	290
2	Mining, quarrying .	...	...	...	...	...	...	...	...	...	...	2
311/2	Food products	7035	6510	...	...	...	0.6	1.0	6.2	...	...	311/2
313	Beverages	3587	3515	...	...	...	0.3	0.4	3.8	...	...	313
314	Tobacco	176	166	...	...	...	-	-	0.2	...	...	314
321	Textiles	4694	4788	...	...	...	0.3	0.5	3.2	...	...	321
3211	Spinning,weaving etc..	3782	4031	...	...	...	0.2	0.4	2.7	...	...	3211
322	Wearing apparel	990	883	...	...	...	0.1	0.1	0.4	...	...	322
323	Leather and products ...	633	676	...	...	...	-	0.1	0.4	...	...	323
324	Footwear	494	1431	...	...	...	-	0.2	2.7	...	...	324
331	Wood products	2729	2867	...	...	...	0.1	0.2	0.9	...	...	331
332	Furniture, fixtures	475	353	...	...	...	-	-	0.2	...	...	332
341	Paper and products	121	124	...	...	...	-	-	0.1	...	...	341
3411	Pulp,paper etc.	52	26	...	...	...	-	-	-	...	...	3411
342	Printing,publishing	1641	1356	...	...	...	0.1	0.2	1.0	...	...	342
351	Industrial chemicals ...	309	274	...	...	...	-	-	0.1	...	...	351
3511	Basic excl fertilizers	231	270	...	...	...	-	-	0.1	...	...	3511
3513	Synthetic resins etc .	74	...	...	...	...	-	-	-	...	...	3513
352	Other chemical products.	1822	1690	...	...	...	0.2	0.2	1.8	...	...	352
3522	Drugs and medicines ..	1071	981	...	...	...	0.1	0.2	1.2	...	...	3522
353	Petroleum refineries ...	...	...	...	...	...	...	...	1.3	...	...	353
354	Petroleum,coal products.	13	29	...	...	...	-	-	-	...	...	354
355	Rubber products	212	119	...	...	...	-	-	-	...	...	355
356	Plastic products n.e.c..	939	916	...	...	...	0.1	0.1	0.9	...	...	356
361	Pottery,china etc	112	-	...	...	...	-	-	0.1	...	...	361
362	Glass and products	823	285	...	...	...	0.1	-	0.6	...	...	362
369	Non-metal products n.e.c	1911	1724	...	...	...	0.1	0.2	1.6	...	...	369
371	Iron and steel	174	120	...	...	...	-	-	-	...	...	371
372	Non-ferrous metals	2194	2184	...	...	...	0.1	0.4	2.7	...	...	372
381	Metal products	1560	1139	...	...	...	0.1	0.1	0.5	...	...	381
382	Machinery n.e.c.	441	359	...	...	...	-	-	0.2	...	...	382
3825	Office,computing etc..	...	...	...	...	...	-	-	-	...	...	3825
383	Electrical machinery ...	256	243	...	...	...	-	-	0.1	...	...	383
3832	Radio,television etc..	...	...	...	...	...	-	-	-	...	...	3832
384	Transport equipment	577	363	...	...	...	-	-	0.2	...	...	384
3841	Shipbuilding, repair..	...	...	...	...	...	-	-	-	...	...	3841
3843	Motor vehicles	453	290	...	...	...	-	-	0.2	...	...	3843
385	Professional goods	111	116	...	...	...	-	-	0.1	...	...	385
390	Other industries	281	311	...	...	...	-	-	0.1	...	...	390
3	Manufacturing	e/ 34310	e/ 32541	...	...	...	e/ 2.2	e/ 3.7	29.4	...	...	3
410	Electricity,gas,steam ..	...	...	...	...	...	...	...	...	...	...	410
4101	Electricity	...	...	...	...	...	...	...	...	...	...	4101
420	Water works and supply .	...	...	...	...	...	...	...	...	...	...	420
4	Electricity,gas etc	...	...	...	...	...	...	...	...	...	...	4
2-4	All industry	...	...	...	...	...	...	...	...	...	...	2-4

a/ For one period of the year indicated.
b/ Enterprises with a capital of 50 thousand pesos or more.
c/ Reporting establishments without estimate for non-response.
d/ Establishments with 20 or more persons engaged and all multi-establishment enterprises regardless of size.
e/ Excluding major group 353.

ISIC	INDUSTRY	5. AVERAGE NUMBER OF OPERATIVES (NUMBER)					6. WAGES AND SALARIES OF OPERATIVES (BILLION PESOS)					ISIC
		a/ 1981	a/b/ 1982	1983	1984	1985	a/ 1981	a/b/ 1982	c/ 1983	1984	1985	
210	Coal mining	...	...	...	...	...	...	...	...	...	...	210
220	Petroleum and gas	...	...	...	...	...	...	...	...	...	...	220
230	Metal ore mining	...	...	...	...	...	...	...	...	...	...	230
290	Other mining	...	...	...	...	...	...	...	...	...	...	290
2	Mining, quarrying .	...	...	...	...	...	...	...	...	...	...	2
311/2	Food products	4740	4189	...	...	...	0.3	0.6	1.7	...	...	311/2
313	Beverages	2422	2337	...	...	...	0.2	0.3	...	...	...	313
314	Tobacco	145	138	...	...	...	-	-	0.1	...	...	314
321	Textiles	3959	3999	...	...	...	0.2	0.4	1.9	...	...	321
3211	Spinning,weaving etc..	3178	3409	...	...	...	0.2	0.3	1.8	...	...	3211
322	Wearing apparel	826	741	...	...	...	-	0.1	0.2	...	...	322
323	Leather and products ...	548	567	...	...	...	-	-	0.2	...	...	323
324	Footwear	443	1180	...	...	...	-	0.1	...	...	...	324
331	Wood products	2357	2551	...	...	...	0.1	0.2	0.4	...	...	331
332	Furniture, fixtures	419	307	...	...	...	-	-	0.1	...	...	332
341	Paper and products	105	103	...	...	...	-	-	-	...	...	341
3411	Pulp,paper etc.	44	20	...	...	...	-	-	-	...	...	3411
342	Printing,publishing	1135	948	...	...	...	0.1	0.1	0.3	...	...	342
351	Industrial chemicals ...	192	160	...	...	...	-	-	0.1	...	...	351
3511	Basic excl fertilizers	125	158	...	...	...	-	-	0.1	...	...	3511
3513	Synthetic resins etc .	65	...	...	...	...	-	-	-	...	...	3513
352	Other chemical products.	1036	953	...	...	...	0.1	0.1	0.3	...	...	352
3522	Drugs and medicines ..	499	440	...	...	...	-	-	0.2	...	...	3522
353	Petroleum refineries ...	...	...	...	...	...	...	...	...	...	...	353
354	Petroleum,coal products.	9	27	...	...	...	-	-	-	...	...	354
355	Rubber products	161	93	...	...	...	-	-	...	...	...	355
356	Plastic products n.e.c..	700	690	...	...	...	-	0.1	0.3	...	...	356
361	Pottery,china etc	83	-	...	...	...	-	-	-	...	...	361
362	Glass and products	707	245	...	...	...	0.1	-	0.3	...	...	362
369	Non-metal products n.e.c	1580	1366	...	...	...	0.1	0.2	0.7	...	...	369
371	Iron and steel	147	83	...	...	...	-	-	-	...	...	371
372	Non-ferrous metals	1158	1111	...	...	...	0.1	0.2	0.6	...	...	372
381	Metal products	1274	900	...	...	...	0.1	0.1	0.2	...	...	381
382	Machinery n.e.c.	331	258	...	...	...	-	-	0.1	...	...	382
3825	Office,computing etc..	...	...	...	...	...	-	-	...	...	...	3825
383	Electrical machinery ...	189	182	...	...	...	-	-	-	...	...	383
3832	Radio,television etc..	...	...	...	...	...	-	-	-	...	...	3832
384	Transport equipment	384	161	...	...	...	-	-	0.1	...	...	384
3841	Shipbuilding, repair..	...	...	...	...	...	-	-	-	...	...	3841
3843	Motor vehicles	292	109	...	...	...	-	-	0.1	...	...	3843
385	Professional goods	82	88	...	...	...	-	-	0.1	...	...	385
390	Other industries	183	190	...	...	...	-	-	...	...	...	390
3	Manufacturing ..... d/	25315	23567	...	...	...	1.4	2.4	...	...	...	3
410	Electricity,gas,steam ..	...	...	...	...	...	...	...	...	...	...	410
4101	Electricity	...	...	...	...	...	...	...	...	...	...	4101
420	Water works and supply .	...	...	...	...	...	...	...	...	...	...	420
4	Electricity,gas etc	...	...	...	...	...	...	...	...	...	...	4
2-4	All industry	...	...	...	...	...	...	...	...	...	...	2-4

a/ Enterprises with a capital of 50 thousand pesos or more. b/ Reporting establishments without estimate for non-response.
c/ Establishments with 20 or more persons engaged and all multi-establishment enterprises regardless of size.
d/ Excluding major group 353.

ISIC	INDUSTRY	7. OUTPUT IN PRODUCERS' PRICES (BILLION PESOS) b/ 1981	b/c/ 1982	d/ 1983	d/ 1984	1985	8. VALUE ADDED IN PRODUCERS' PRICES a/ (BILLION PESOS) b/ 1981	b/c/ 1982	d/ 1983	d/ 1984	1985	ISIC
210	Coal mining	...	...	...	...	...	...	...	...	...	...	210
220	Petroleum and gas	...	...	...	...	...	...	...	...	...	...	220
230	Metal ore mining	15.2	22.3	20.2	22.1	...	1.1	1.0	1.0	1.0	...	230
290	Other mining	...	...	...	...	...	...	...	...	...	...	290
2	Mining, quarrying	...	...	...	...	...	...	...	...	...	...	2
311/2	Food products	12.3	25.4	102.4	1696.4	...	3.7	17.1	47.5	997.1	...	311/2
313	Beverages	3.8	7.7	36.4	382.9	...	2.1	3.4	23.4	268.3	...	313
314	Tobacco	0.7	1.7	3.6	27.7	...	0.5	1.3	2.7	23.6	...	314
321	Textiles	1.6	5.3	14.2	214.3	...	0.7	2.3	6.6	131.9	...	321
3211	Spinning,weaving etc.	1.2	4.3	11.4	156.0	...	0.5	1.9	5.7	90.4	...	3211
322	Wearing apparel	0.4	0.6	2.8	33.3	...	0.1	0.3	1.8	21.8	...	322
323	Leather and products	0.3	0.8	2.5	34.3	...	0.1	0.3	1.0	14.6	...	323
324	Footwear	0.1	2.3	8.3	112.7	...	0.1	0.9	5.0	67.5	...	324
331	Wood products	1.0	1.6	3.9	47.2	...	0.3	0.6	2.0	29.6	...	331
332	Furniture, fixtures	0.1	0.1	0.6	4.9	...	-	-	0.3	2.5	...	332
341	Paper and products	0.1	0.2	0.6	6.3	...	-	-	0.2	3.4	...	341
3411	Pulp,paper etc.	-	-	-	3.0	...	-	-	-	2.0	...	3411
342	Printing,publishing	1.0	2.0	6.3	83.0	...	0.4	0.8	2.9	45.9	...	342
351	Industrial chemicals	0.1	0.4	1.0	54.4	...	0.1	0.2	0.4	29.9	...	351
3511	Basic excl fertilizers	0.1	0.4	0.9	53.8	...	0.1	0.2	0.4	29.5	...	3511
3513	Synthetic resins etc	-	-	...	...	...	-	-	-	...	...	3513
352	Other chemical products.	1.4	3.9	11.7	145.0	...	0.6	1.6	5.1	90.1	...	352
3522	Drugs and medicines	0.8	2.1	5.6	68.5	...	0.4	1.1	3.2	43'.4	...	3522
353	Petroleum refineries	9.3	17.4	35.1	305.7	...	5.3	...	...	105.7	...	353
354	Petroleum,coal products.	-	-	-	-	...	-	-	-	-	...	354
355	Rubber products	0.2	0.8	0.5	2.0	...	-	0.2	0.1	0.4	...	355
356	Plastic products n.e.c..	0.5	1.3	3.7	37.8	...	0.3	0.5	2.2	21.7	...	356
361	Pottery,china etc	-	-	0.5	-	...	-	-	0.3	-	...	361
362	Glass and products	0.3	0.1	2.4	37.7	...	0.1	-	1.6	28.4	...	362
369	Non-metal products n.e.c	1.3	3.9	8.4	98.2	...	0.7	2.3	4.5	65.9	...	369
371	Iron and steel	0.1	0.2	0.5	3.5	...	-	0.1	0.2	1.9	...	371
372	Non-ferrous metals	7.6	31.5	60.6	752.7	...	1.0	19.0	21.4	472.1	...	372
381	Metal products	1.2	2.8	4.4	43.5	...	0.3	0.7	2.3	27.5	...	381
382	Machinery n.e.c.	0.3	0.2	0.8	2.4	...	0.2	0.1	0.5	1.3	..	382
3825	Office,computing etc..	...	...	...	...	...	...	...	...	...	...	3825
383	Electrical machinery	0.2	0.4	1.3	16.7	...	0.1	0.2	0.7	9.9	...	383
3832	Radio,television etc..	...	...	...	...	...	...	...	...	...	...	3832
384	Transport equipment	0.4	0.3	0.5	10.1	...	0.2	0.1	0.3	6.0	...	384
3841	Shipbuilding, repair..	...	...	...	...	...	...	-	...	...	...	3841
3843	Motor vehicles	0.2	0.1	0.3	6.6	...	0.1	0.1	0.1	4.3	...	3843
385	Professional goods	-	0.1	0.2	4.1	...	-	-	0.1	3.2	...	385
390	Other industries	0.1	0.4	0.5	3.1	...	0.1	0.3	0.3	2.0	...	390
3	Manufacturing	111.4	111.3	313.7	4159.9	...	17.0	e/ 52.5	e/ 136.9	2472.2	...	3
410	Electricity,gas,steam	...	...	...	...	...	...	...	...	...	...	410
4101	Electricity	...	...	...	...	...	...	...	...	...	...	4101
420	Water works and supply	...	...	...	...	...	...	...	...	...	...	420
4	Electricity,gas etc	...	...	...	...	...	...	...	...	...	...	4
2-4	All industry	...	...	...	...	...	...	...	...	...	...	2-4

a/ Net of non-industrial costs.
b/ Enterprises with a capital of 50 thousand pesos or more.
c/ Reporting establishments without estimate for non-response.
d/ Establishments with 20 or more persons engaged and all multi-establishment enterprises regardless of size.
e/ Excluding major group 353.

9. GROSS FIXED CAPITAL FORMATION
TOTAL
(BILLION PESOS)

ISIC	INDUSTRY	a/ 1981	a/b/ 1982	c/ 1983	c/ 1984	1985	ISIC
210	Coal mining	...	...	...	...	...	210
220	Petroleum and gas	...	...	...	...	...	220
230	Metal ore mining	...	...	...	...	...	230
290	Other mining	...	...	...	...	...	290
2	Mining, quarrying .	...	...	...	...	...	2
311/2	Food products	0.9	3.5	6.6	708.5	...	311/2
313	Beverages	0.7	2.3	2.6	24.4	...	313
314	Tobacco	-	-	-	0.5	...	314
321	Textiles	0.1	1.2	0.7	26.0	...	321
3211	Spinning,weaving etc..	0.1	1.0	0.4	22.1	...	3211
322	Wearing apparel	0.1	-	-	0.4	...	322
323	Leather and products ...	-	0.1	0.1	14.4	...	323
324	Footwear	-	0.1	0.2	2.7	...	324
331	Wood products	0.1	0.4	0.3	1.7	...	331
332	Furniture, fixtures	-	-	-	-	...	332
341	Paper and products	-	-	0.3	9.5	...	341
3411	Pulp,paper etc.	-	-	-	9.1	...	3411
342	Printing,publishing	-	0.2	0.2	11.0	...	342
351	Industrial chemicals ...	-	0.1	-	2.0	...	351
3511	Basic excl fertilizers	-	0.1	-	2.0	...	3511
3513	Synthetic resins etc .	-	-	-	-	...	3513
352	Other chemical products.	0.1	0.4	0.9	25.4	...	352
3522	Drugs and medicines ..	-	0.2	0.3	22.6	...	3522
353	Petroleum refineries ...	0.1	1.4	0.2	1.0	...	353
354	Petroleum,coal products.	-	-	-	-	...	354
355	Rubber products	-	-	0.1	-	...	355
356	Plastic products n.e.c..	-	0.2	0.2	4.1	...	356
361	Pottery,china etc	-	-	-	-	...	361
362	Glass and products	-	0.1	-	0.3	...	362
369	Non-metal products n.e.c	0.5	5.4	4.5	1.3	...	369
371	Iron and steel	-	-	-	-	...	371
372	Non-ferrous metals	0.2	0.1	0.2	2.7	...	372
381	Metal products	0.1	0.2	0.1	1.9	...	381
382	Machinery n.e.c.	-	-	-	-	...	382
3825	Office,computing etc..	-	-	-	-	...	3825
383	Electrical machinery ...	-	-	-	0.3	...	383
3832	Radio,television etc..	-	-	-	-	...	3832
384	Transport equipment	-	-	0.1	0.3	...	384
3841	Shipbuilding, repair..	-	-	-	-	...	3841
3843	Motor vehicles	-	-	0.1	0.3	...	3843
385	Professional goods	-	-	-	0.2	...	385
390	Other industries	-	-	-	-	...	390
3	Manufacturing	2.9	15.7	17.3	838.6	...	3
410	Electricity,gas,steam ..	...	...	...	...	...	410
4101	Electricity	...	...	...	...	...	4101
420	Water works and supply .	...	...	...	...	...	420
4	Electricity,gas etc	...	...	...	...	...	4
2-4	All industry	...	...	...	...	...	2-4

a/ Enterprises with a capital of 50 thousand pesos or more. b/ Reporting establishments without estimate for non-response.
c/ Establishments with 20 or more persons engaged and all multi-establishment enterprises regardless of size.

10. INDEX NUMBERS OF INDUSTRIAL PRODUCTION (1980 = 100)

ISIC	INDUSTRY		1976	1977	1978	1979	1981	1982	1983	1984	1985	RATE a/	ISIC
210	Coal mining		...	...	...	...	...	...	...	...	...	...	210
220	Petroleum and gas		...	...	108	102	101	108	102	99	97	-1.5	220
230	Metal ore mining		...	...	[109	98	102	89	91	72	59	-8.4]	230
290	Other mining		...	...									290
2	Mining, quarrying .		...	...	107	98	102	92	...	...	...	d/ -3.7	2
311/2	Food products		...	...	...	...	[					]	311/2
313	Beverages		...	...	...	...	98	96	57	78	76	e/ -5.3	313
314	Tobacco		...	...	...	...							314
321	Textiles	b/	...	...	...	...	98	97	82	78	60	e/ -9.7	321
3211	Spinning,weaving etc..		...	...	...	...	...	...	...	...	...	...	3211
322	Wearing apparel	b/	...	...	...	...	...	...	...	...	...	...	322
323	Leather and products ...	b/	...	...	...	...	...	...	...	...	...	...	323
324	Footwear	b/	...	...	...	...	...	...	...	...	...	...	324
331	Wood products		...	...	...	...	96	96	78	100	48	e/ -13.7	331
332	Furniture, fixtures		...	...	...	...	...	...	...	...	...	...	332
341	Paper and products		...	...	...	...	...	...	...	...	...	...	341
3411	Pulp,paper etc.		...	...	...	...	...	...	...	...	...	...	3411
342	Printing,publishing		...	...	...	...	96	96	86	68	54	e/ -11.6	342
351	Industrial chemicals ...	c/	...	...	...	...	98	96	93	87	83	e/ -3.7	351
3511	Basic excl fertilizers		...	...	...	...	...	...	...	...	...	...	3511
3513	Synthetic resins etc .		...	...	...	...	...	...	...	...	...	...	3513
352	Other chemical products.	c/	...	...	...	...	...	...	...	...	...	...	352
3522	Drugs and medicines ..		...	...	...	...	...	...	...	...	...	...	3522
353	Petroleum refineries ...	c/	...	...	...	...	...	...	...	...	...	...	353
354	Petroleum,coal products.	c/	...	...	...	...	...	...	...	...	...	...	354
355	Rubber products	c/	...	...	...	...	...	...	...	...	...	...	355
356	Plastic products n.e.c..	c/	...	...	...	...	...	...	...	...	...	...	356
361	Pottery,china etc		...	...	...	...	...	...	...	...	...	...	361
362	Glass and products		...	...	...	...	[98	98	113	85	87	e/ -2.7]	362
369	Non-metal products n.e.c		...	...	...	...							369
371	Iron and steel		...	...	...	...	...	...	...	...	...	...	371
372	Non-ferrous metals		...	...	...	...	100	98	68	74	60	e/ -9.7	372
381	Metal products		...	...	...	...	95	90	50	35	25	e/ -24.2	381
382	Machinery n.e.c.		...	...	...	...	...	...	...	...	...	...	382
3825	Office,computing etc..		...	...	...	...	...	...	...	...	...	...	3825
383	Electrical machinery ...		...	...	...	...	...	...	...	...	...	...	383
3832	Radio,television etc..		...	...	...	...	...	...	...	...	...	...	3832
384	Transport equipment		...	...	...	...	...	...	...	...	...	...	384
3841	Shipbuilding, repair..		...	...	...	...	...	...	...	...	...	...	3841
3843	Motor vehicles		...	...	...	...	...	...	...	...	...	...	3843
385	Professional goods		...	...	...	...	...	...	...	...	...	...	385
390	Other industries		...	...	...	...	...	...	...	...	...	...	390
3	Manufacturing		...	...	96	99	96	81	...	...	...	d/ -4.2	3
410	Electricity,gas,steam ..		...	...	...	...	...	...	...	...	...	...	410
4101	Electricity		...	...	82	90	110	110	110	111	112	4.6	4101
420	Water works and supply .		...	...	...	...	...	...	...	...	...	...	420
4	Electricity,gas etc		...	...	...	...	...	...	...	...	...	...	4
2-4	All industry		...	...	99	98	99	87	...	...	...	d/ -3.2	2-4

a/ Annual growth rate 1978-1985.
b/ Major groups 322 to 324 are included in 321.
c/ Major groups 352 to 356 are included in 351.
d/ Annual growth rate 1978-1982.
e/ Annual growth rate 1980-1985.

BOTSWANA

The information in the tables is based on the reply to the United Nations Questionnaire on General Industrial Statistics from the Central Statistics Office, Ministry of Finance and Development Planning, Gaborone. The concepts and definitions are generally in accordance with United Nations standards.

The estimates for ISIC 4 cover large parastatal water utilities and electric power corporations. The estimates for output and value added are derived from national accounts calculations and cover all establishments. Value added relates to the contribution of industry to the gross domestic product.

The reference period is the fiscal year 1 July to 30 June; the period referred to in the tables is the fiscal year ending in the year indicated, except where footnoted otherwise.

Related national publications:
Statistical Bulletin (monthly); Employment Survey Report (annual); National Accounts of Botswana (annual), all published by the Central Statistics Office, Ministry of Finance and Development Planning, Gaborone.

ISIC	INDUSTRY	1. NUMBER OF ESTABLISHMENTS a/ (NUMBER) b/ 1981	b/ 1982	b/ 1983	b/ 1984	c/ 1985	2. AVERAGE NUMBER OF PERSONS ENGAGED a/ (THOUSANDS) 1981	1982	1983	1984	c/ 1985	ISIC
210	Coal mining	1	1	1	1	1	...	...	...	...	0.2	210
220	Petroleum and gas	-	-	-	-	-	...	...	...	...	-	220
230	Metal ore mining	5	5	5	4	5	...	...	...	...	4.5	230
290	Other mining	10	9	14	14	27	...	...	...	...	2.6	290
2	Mining, quarrying	16	15	20	19	33	...	...	...	...	7.3	2
311/2	Food products	26	20	23	31	85	...	...	...	...	3.3	311/2
313	Beverages	2	4	5	12	19	...	...	...	...	0.4	313
314	Tobacco	-	-	-	-	-	...	...	...	...	-	314
321	Textiles d/	40	47	48	56	89	...	...	...	...	1.6	321
3211	Spinning, weaving etc.	...	...	...	...	...	...	...	...	...	...	3211
322	Wearing apparel d/	...	...	...	...	...	...	...	...	...	...	322
323	Leather and products	[16	10	10	2	35]	...	...	...	...	[0.3]	323
324	Footwear						...	...	...	...		324
331	Wood products	[16	11	16	31	40]	...	...	...	...	[0.4]	331
332	Furniture, fixtures						...	...	...	...		332
341	Paper and products e/	10	19	18	17	36	...	...	...	...	0.5	341
3411	Pulp, paper etc.	...	...	...	...	...	...	...	...	...	...	3411
342	Printing, publishing e/	...	...	...	...	...	...	...	...	...	...	342
351	Industrial chemicals f/	11	5	17	19	28	...	...	...	...	0.3	351
3511	Basic excl fertilizers	...	...	...	...	...	...	...	...	...	...	3511
3513	Synthetic resins etc	...	...	...	...	...	...	...	...	...	...	3513
352	Other chemical products f/	...	...	...	...	...	...	...	...	...	...	352
3522	Drugs and medicines	...	...	...	...	...	...	...	...	...	...	3522
353	Petroleum refineries	-	-	-	-	-	...	...	...	...	-	353
354	Petroleum, coal products	-	-	-	-	-	...	...	...	...	-	354
355	Rubber products f/	...	...	...	...	...	...	...	...	...	...	355
356	Plastic products n.e.c. f/	...	...	...	...	...	...	...	...	...	...	356
361	Pottery, china etc	-	-	-	-	-	...	...	...	...	-	361
362	Glass and products	-	-	-	-	-	...	...	...	...	-	362
369	Non-metal products n.e.c	-	-	-	-	-	...	...	...	...	-	369
371	Iron and steel	-	-	-	-	-	...	...	...	...	-	371
372	Non-ferrous metals	-	-	-	-	-	...	...	...	...	-	372
381	Metal products g/	[21	37	48	68	108]	...	...	...	...	[2.0]	381
382	Machinery n.e.c.						...	...	...	...		382
3825	Office, computing etc.	...	...	...	...	...	...	...	...	...	...	3825
383	Electrical machinery g/	...	...	...	...	...	...	...	...	...	...	383
3832	Radio, television etc.	...	...	...	...	...	...	...	...	...	...	3832
384	Transport equipment g/	...	...	...	...	...	...	...	...	...	...	384
3841	Shipbuilding, repair	-	-	-	-	-	...	...	...	...	-	3841
3843	Motor vehicles	...	...	...	...	...	...	...	...	...	...	3843
385	Professional goods	-	-	-	-	-	...	...	...	...	-	385
390	Other industries	42	52	94	84	200	...	...	...	...	1.4	390
3	Manufacturing	184	205	279	320	640	...	...	...	...	10.2	3
410	Electricity, gas, steam h/	15	10	11	5	12	...	...	...	...	1.2	410
4101	Electricity	15	10	11	5	12	...	...	...	...	1.2	4101
420	Water works and supply	6	11	7	9	15	...	...	...	...	0.7	420
4	Electricity, gas etc h/	21	21	18	14	27	...	...	...	...	1.9	4
2-4	All industry h/	221	241	317	353	700	...	...	...	...	19.4	2-4

a/ Mining and manufacturing: licensed establishments with one or more paid employees.
b/ At 31 August of the year indicated.
c/ At 30 September of the year indicated.
d/ Major group 322 is included in 321.
e/ Major group 342 is included in 341.
f/ Major groups 352, 355 and 356 are included in 351.
g/ Major groups 383 and 384 are included in 381 and 382 combined.
h/ Excluding gas and steam.

ISIC	INDUSTRY		3. AVERAGE NUMBER OF EMPLOYEES a/ (THOUSANDS)					4. WAGES AND SALARIES OF EMPLOYEES a/d/ (MILLION PULA)					ISIC
			b/ 1981	b/ 1982	b/ 1983	b/ 1984	c/ 1985	e/ 1981	e/ 1982	e/ 1983	e/ 1984	f/ 1985	
210	Coal mining		0.2	0.2	0.2	0.2	0.2	...	...	...	...	1.5	210
220	Petroleum and gas		-	-	-	-	-	...	...	...	...	-	220
230	Metal ore mining		4.6	4.3	4.4	4.5	4.5	...	...	...	...	23.2	230
290	Other mining		2.6	2.6	2.6	2.8	2.6	...	...	...	...	18.8	290
2	Mining, quarrying .		7.4	7.1	7.2	7.5	7.3	30.7	41.8	50.2	39.1	43.5	2
311/2	Food products		2.4	2.2	2.5	2.9	3.2	...	...	...	...	13.2	311/2
313	Beverages		0.3	0.4	0.4	0.5	0.4	...	...	...	...	2.2	313
314	Tobacco		-	-	-	-	-	...	...	...	...	-	314
321	Textiles	g/	1.1	1.6	1.7	1.9	1.5	...	...	...	...	3.6	321
3211	Spinning,weaving etc..		...	...	...	...	...	...	...	...	...	...	3211
322	Wearing apparel	g/	...	...	...	...	...	...	...	...	...	...	322
323	Leather and products ...		[0.3	0.2	0.2	0.1	0.3]	...	...	...	...	[0.5]	323
324	Footwear							...	...	...	...		324
331	Wood products		[0.4	0.1	0.3	0.3	0.4]	...	...	...	...	[0.9]	331
332	Furniture, fixtures							...	...	...	...		332
341	Paper and products	h/	0.1	0.2	0.5	0.3	0.5	...	...	...	...	2.0	341
3411	Pulp,paper etc.		...	...	...	...	...	...	...	...	...	...	3411
342	Printing,publishing	h/	...	...	...	...	...	...	...	...	...	...	342
351	Industrial chemicals ...	i/	0.1	0.1	0.4	0.4	0.3	...	...	...	...	1.7	351
3511	Basic excl fertilizers		...	...	...	...	...	...	...	...	...	...	3511
3513	Synthetic resins etc .		...	...	...	...	...	...	...	...	...	...	3513
352	Other chemical products.	i/	...	...	...	...	...	...	...	...	...	...	352
3522	Drugs and medicines ..		...	...	...	...	...	...	...	...	...	...	3522
353	Petroleum refineries ...		-	-	-	-	-	...	...	...	...	-	353
354	Petroleum,coal products.		-	-	-	-	-	...	...	...	...	-	354
355	Rubber products	i/	...	...	...	...	...	...	...	...	...	...	355
356	Plastic products n.e.c..	i/	...	...	...	...	...	...	...	...	...	...	356
361	Pottery,china etc		-	-	-	-	-	...	...	...	...	-	361
362	Glass and products		-	-	-	-	-	...	...	...	...	-	362
369	Non-metal products n.e.c		-	-	-	-	-	...	...	...	...	-	369
371	Iron and steel		-	-	-	-	-	...	...	...	...	-	371
372	Non-ferrous metals		-	-	-	-	-	...	...	...	...	-	372
381	Metal products	j/	[0.5	1.1	1.8	1.9	2.0]	...	...	...	...	[13.2]	381
382	Machinery n.e.c.							...	...	...	...		382
3825	Office,computing etc..		...	...	...	...	...	...	...	...	...	...	3825
383	Electrical machinery ...	j/	...	...	...	...	...	...	...	...	...	...	383
3832	Radio,television etc..		...	...	...	...	...	...	...	...	...	...	3832
384	Transport equipment	j/	...	...	...	...	...	...	...	...	...	...	384
3841	Shipbuilding, repair..		-	-	-	-	-	...	...	...	...	-	3841
3843	Motor vehicles		...	...	...	...	...	...	...	...	...	...	3843
385	Professional goods		-	-	-	-	-	...	...	...	...	-	385
390	Other industries		1.3	1.3	1.9	1.2	1.4	...	...	...	...	3.2	390
3	Manufacturing		6.5	7.2	9.7	9.5	10.0	21.0	26.6	31.7	34.8	40.5	3
410	Electricity,gas,steam ..	k/	1.0	1.5	1.4	1.4	1.2	...	...	...	...	8.7	410
4101	Electricity		1.0	1.5	1.4	1.4	1.2	...	...	...	...	8.7	4101
420	Water works and supply .		0.6	0.7	0.5	0.6	0.7	...	...	...	...	3.0	420
4	Electricity,gas etc	k/	1.6	2.2	1.9	2.0	1.9	9.5	9.1	13.1	15.1	11.7	4
2-4	All industry	k/	15.5	16.5	18.8	19.6	19.2	61.2	77.5	95.0	89.0	95.7	2-4

a/ Mining and manufacturing: licensed establishments with one or more paid employees.
b/ At 31 August of the year indicated.
c/ At 30 September of the year indicated.
d/ Excluding payments in kind.
e/ Month of August multiplied by 12.
f/ Month of September multiplied by 12.
g/ Major group 322 is included in 321.
h/ Major group 342 is included in 341.
i/ Major groups 352, 355 and 356 are included in 351.
j/ Major groups 383 and 384 are included in 381 and 382 combined.
k/ Excluding gas and steam.

ISIC	INDUSTRY		5. OUTPUT IN FACTOR VALUES a/b/ (MILLION PULA) 1981	1982	1983	1984	1985	6. VALUE ADDED IN FACTOR VALUES a/c/ (MILLION PULA) 1981	1982	1983	1984	1985	ISIC
210	Coal mining		...	...	...	...	...	...	...	...	...	...	210
220	Petroleum and gas		...	...	...	...	...	...	...	...	...	...	220
230	Metal ore mining		...	...	...	...	...	...	...	...	...	...	230
290	Other mining		...	...	...	...	...	...	...	...	...	...	290
2	Mining, quarrying .		306.9	259.3	443.0	586.6	...	208.8	139.3	285.3	405.3	...	2
311/2	Food products		80.8	96.4	124.3	109.5	...	14.6	24.7	26.5	28.7	...	311/2
313	Beverages		22.7	29.5	33.7	40.0	...	9.2	14.5	13.8	15.8	...	313
314	Tobacco		-	-	-	-	...	-	-	-	-	...	314
321	Textiles	d/	17.5	24.5	32.3	32.9	...	5.6	7.3	9.5	5.7	...	321
3211	Spinning,weaving etc..		...	...	...	...	...	...	...	...	...	...	3211
322	Wearing apparel	d/	...	...	...	...	...	...	...	...	...	...	322
323	Leather and products ...		[5.0	3.6	4.2	1.9]	...	[1.5	0.3	0.9	0.4]	...	323
324	Footwear						...					...	324
331	Wood products		[2.4	1.7	3.4	5.6]	...	[0.7	0.6	0.9	1.1]	...	331
332	Furniture, fixtures						...					...	332
341	Paper and products	e/	2.1	2.9	5.9	7.4	...	0.9	0.7	2.3	2.5	...	341
3411	Pulp,paper etc.		...	...	...	...	...	...	...	...	...	...	3411
342	Printing,publishing	e/	...	...	...	...	...	...	...	...	...	...	342
351	Industrial chemicals ...	f/	2.7	5.7	8.7	11.0	...	0.8	1.6	0.6	3.4	...	351
3511	Basic excl fertilizers		...	...	...	...	...	...	...	...	...	...	3511
3513	Synthetic resins etc .		...	...	...	...	...	...	...	...	...	...	3513
352	Other chemical products.	f/	...	...	...	...	...	...	...	...	...	...	352
3522	Drugs and medicines ..		...	...	...	...	...	...	...	...	...	...	3522
353	Petroleum refineries ...		-	-	-	-	...	-	-	-	-	...	353
354	Petroleum,coal products.		-	-	-	-	...	-	-	-	-	...	354
355	Rubber products	f/	...	...	...	...	...	...	...	...	...	...	355
356	Plastic products n.e.c..	f/	...	...	...	...	...	...	...	...	...	...	356
361	Pottery,china etc		-	-	-	-	...	-	-	-	-	...	361
362	Glass and products		-	-	-	-	...	-	-	-	-	...	362
369	Non-metal products n.e.c		-	-	-	-	...	-	-	-	-	...	369
371	Iron and steel		-	-	-	-	...	-	-	-	-	...	371
372	Non-ferrous metals		-	-	-	-	...	-	-	-	-	...	372
381	Metal products	g/	[4.2	6.0	10.5	13.9]	...	[0.9	1.9	3.3	8.3]	...	381
382	Machinery n.e.c.						...					...	382
3825	Office,computing etc..		...	...	...	...	...	...	...	...	...	...	3825
383	Electrical machinery ...	g/	...	...	...	...	...	...	...	...	...	...	383
3832	Radio,television etc..		...	...	...	...	...	...	...	...	...	...	3832
384	Transport equipment	g/	...	...	...	...	...	...	...	...	...	...	384
3841	Shipbuilding, repair..		-	-	-	-	...	-	-	-	-	...	3841
3843	Motor vehicles		...	...	...	...	...	...	...	...	...	...	3843
385	Professional goods		-	-	-	-	...	-	-	-	-	...	385
390	Other industries		27.8	40.6	42.5	38.4	...	15.1	19.6	20.9	16.1	...	390
3	Manufacturing		165.2	210.9	265.5	260.6	...	49.3	71.2	78.7	82.0	...	3
410	Electricity,gas,steam ..		...	...	...	...	...	...	...	...	...	...	410
4101	Electricity		...	...	...	...	...	...	...	...	...	...	4101
420	Water works and supply .		...	...	...	...	...	...	...	...	...	...	420
4	Electricity,gas etc		45.4	53.9	88.3	67.4	...	19.3	21.8	29.7	32.3	...	4
2-4	All industry		517.5	524.1	796.8	914.6	...	277.4	232.3	393.7	519.6	...	2-4

a/ Twelve months ending 30 June of the year indicated.
b/ Estimates derived from national accounts calculations.
c/ Contributions to the gross domestic product.
d/ Major group 322 is included in 321.
e/ Major group 342 is included in 341.
f/ Major groups 352, 355 and 356 are included in 351.
g/ Major groups 383 and 384 are included in 381 and 382 combined.

BULGARIA

The information on industrial activity is based on the reply to the United Nations Questionnaire on General Industrial Statistics from the Central Statistical Office of the Council of Ministers, Sofia. The concepts, definitions and classification by branches of industry have been adjusted as far as possible to comply with United Nations standards.

The estimates are derived from statistical reports collected regularly by the office mentioned above. The figures given in the tables relate to the socialist sector, covering all State and co-operative industrial enterprises with independent balance-sheets; subsidiary industrial activity of non-industrial enterprises and organizations and private industrial activities are excluded. The socialist sector accounted for 99.8 per cent of all industrial production in 1978.

The statistical unit is the enterprise (or co-operative) and the classification by branches of industry of all its primary and subsidiary units is determined by the basic activity. Where the enterprise engages in more than one kind of activity, the nature of the main product (in terms of constant prices) determines the classification; if no product accounts for more than 80 per cent of total output, the enterprise is classified under miscellaneous manufacturing. It should also be noted that in the tables all activities of co-operatives are included in the miscellaneous manufacturing branch.

The estimates, which are based on the national classification scheme, have been adjusted as far as possible to ISIC. The figures do not include information on publishing, gas manufacture and distribution, and water works and supply. Owing to lack of detail, adjustments have not been made for the following differences: logging and fishing (ISIC major division 1) are included in other mining, ISIC 290; manufacture of made-up textile goods except wearing apparel (ISIC 321) is included in ISIC 322; manufacture of wearing apparel of leather and fur (ISIC 322) is included in ISIC 323; cellulose manufacturing (ISIC 351) is included in ISIC 341; manufacture of electrical household appliances (ISIC 383) is included in ISIC 381; data shown for ISIC 3511 include fertilizers; and data shown for ISIC 3843 include motorcycles and bicycles. It has not been possible to adopt the principles of the revised version of ISIC in respect of repair services for the general public. Such services are included in the following industries: manufacture of textiles (ISIC 321), wearing apparel (ISIC 322), leather and leather products (ISIC 323), footwear (ISIC 324), machinery except electrical (ISIC 382), electrical machinery (ISIC 383), transport equipment (ISIC 384) and other manufacturing industries (ISIC 390). Since 1981 television and radio repair establishments are included in major group 383 and in group 3832 and excluded from major group 382; transport repair establishments are included in major group 384 and repair of motor vehicles in group 3843 and excluded from major group 382.

The number of enterprises shown in table 1 refers to State and co-operative industrial enterprises as of 31 December of the reference year. The estimates of total employment relate to the average annual number of workers and other employees, including apprentices and non-industrial staff. Working proprietors and unpaid family workers are not found in the socialist sector. Data on wages and salaries relate to the average annual payment per person. Estimates for numbers of operatives relate to persons directly engaged in the main production process of the enterprise; apprentices are not included nor are persons engaged in non-industrial activities. The estimates of fixed capital formation refer to net increases in fixed assets other than land during the reference year. Valuation is at full original cost.

The indexes of industrial production are compiled by the Central Statistical Office of the Council of Ministers in response to the United Nations Questionnaire on Indexes of Industrial Production. In principle, the indexes cover all industrial establishments.

Related national publication:
Statisticheski Godishnik Na Narodna Republika Bulgaria (Statistical Yearbook of the People's Republic of Bulgaria), published by the Central Statistical Office of the Council of Ministers, Sofia.

ISIC	INDUSTRY	1. NUMBER OF ENTERPRISES (NUMBER) 1981	1982	1983	1984	1985	2. AVERAGE NUMBER OF PERSONS ENGAGED a/ (THOUSANDS) 1981	1982	1983	1984	1985	ISIC
210	Coal mining	6	6	5	6	5	45.7	46.5	37.1	45.7	42.8	210
220	Petroleum and gas						0.5	0.5				220
230	Metal ore mining	221	225	226	227	228			76.1	67.4	66.8	230
290	Other mining						65.5	66.1				290
2	Mining, quarrying .	227	231	231	233	233	111.7	113.1	113.2	113.1	109.6	2
311/2	Food products	192	191	186	177	175	117.3	116.5	112.5	107.5	106.6	311/2
313	Beverages	60	61	63	63	64	19.4	19.8	20.3	20.5	20.5	313
314	Tobacco	23	23	23	23	23	20.3	20.3	20.4	19.0	19.4	314
321	Textiles	128	126	139	136	133	129.0	129.7	129.7	124.9	120.7	321
3211	Spinning,weaving etc..	89	86	89	84	82	92.5	90.0	86.8	83.1	80.5	3211
322	Wearing apparel	48	49	60	69	73	48.3	47.7	51.5	57.2	59.1	322
323	Leather and products ...	16	16	17	17	19	10.3	10.5	11.6	11.6	11.8	323
324	Footwear	14	14	15	17	19	18.3	18.5	18.7	19.3	20.5	324
331	Wood products	58	58	59	58	58	28.2	28.2	28.2	26.1	25.5	331
332	Furniture, fixtures	48	50	51	50	50	22.9	23.3	24.1	25.4	25.0	332
341	Paper and products	18	18	18	18	18	15.1	15.7	15.9	16.0	16.0	341
3411	Pulp,paper etc.	11	11	11	10	9	11.3	11.7	11.9	11.2	10.9	3411
342	Printing,publishing	36	36	36	36	36	11.5	11.2	11.0	10.9	10.7	342
351	Industrial chemicals ...	14	14	13	12	12	35.2	35.5	35.6	35.5	34.9	351
3511	Basic excl fertilizers	...	...	...	...	...	...	...	...	...	...	3511
3513	Synthetic resins etc .	...	...	...	...	...	...	...	...	...	...	3513
352	Other chemical products.	32	44	42	45	46	21.4	24.7	24.4	26.5	27.3	352
3522	Drugs and medicines ..	9	9	9	9	9	11.2	11.8	12.2	13.2	13.7	3522
353	Petroleum refineries ...	-	-	-	-	-	-	-	-	-	-	353
354	Petroleum,coal products.	3	3	5	4	5	11.7	12.9	22.4	12.7	15.6	354
355	Rubber products	12	12	14	14	13	17.4	18.8	19.3	20.2	19.4	355
356	Plastic products n.e.c..	19	21	22	21	22	10.9	12.2	12.6	12.5	12.6	356
361	Pottery,china etc	11	11	11	10	10	7.9	7.9	7.8	6.9	7.0	361
362	Glass and products	10	10	10	10	10	18.5	18.8	19.0	18.8	18.9	362
369	Non-metal products n.e.c	98	100	95	94	98	54.6	53.1	43.6	50.0	49.7	369
371	Iron and steel	3	3	5	5	5	33.2	33.8	35.3	35.0	35.0	371
372	Non-ferrous metals ..... b/	...	...	...	...	...	...	...	...	...	...	372
381	Metal products	118	116	118	118	120	50.6	48.1	48.1	49.5	50.0	381
382	Machinery n.e.c. .... c/	237	246	239	237	242	144.7	149.9	151.7	153.8	158.8	382
3825	Office,computing etc..	...	...	...	...	...	...	...	...	...	...	3825
383	Electrical machinery ...	116	114	124	128	132	94.3	96.4	101.3	106.4	107.8	383
3832	Radio,television etc..	54	52	57	56	58	35.7	34.9	38.5	40.2	41.3	3832
384	Transport equipment	120	119	119	122	121	73.3	74.1	75.7	76.7	77.2	384
3841	Shipbuilding, repair..	10	10	10	10	10	15.5	15.6	15.6	15.5	15.3	3841
3843	Motor vehicles	83	82	82	83	82	29.6	30.1	29.9	30.7	30.8	3843
385	Professional goods ..... c/	...	...	...	...	...	...	...	...	...	...	385
390	Other industries .... b/d/	455	452	431	429	441	219.9	216.5	213.1	207.7	206.2	390
3	Manufacturing ..... e/	1889	1907	1915	1913	1945	1234.2	1244.1	1253.8	1250.6	1256.2	3
410	Electricity,gas,steam ..	19	19	18	18	18	27.1	28.4	28.8	29.4	30.1	410
4101	Electricity	19	19	18	18	18	27.1	28.4	28.8	29.4	30.1	4101
420	Water works and supply .	.	.	.	.	.	.	.	.	.	.	420
4	Electricity,gas etc	19	19	18	18	18	27.1	28.4	28.8	29.4	30.1	4
2-4	All industry e/	2135	2157	2164	2164	2196	1373.0	1385.6	1395.8	1393.1	1395;9	2-4

Note. For certain deviations in classification, see country note.

a/ Number of employees; working proprietors and unpaid family workers are not found in socialist industry.
b/ Major group 372 is included in 390.
c/ Major group 385 is included in 382.
d/ Including all industrial activities of co-operatives.
e/ Including repair services for the general public.

ISIC	INDUSTRY		3. AVERAGE NUMBER OF EMPLOYEES (THOUSANDS)					4. WAGES AND SALARIES OF EMPLOYEES a/ (LEVA)					ISIC
			1981	1982	1983	1984	1985	1981	1982	1983	1984	1985	
210	Coal mining		45.7	46.5	37.1	45.7	42.8	3495	3554	3610	3634	3869	210
220	Petroleum and gas		0.5	0.5				3124	...	...	...	...	220
230	Metal ore mining		65.5	66.1	76.1	67.4	66.8	...	...	...	...	...	230
290	Other mining							...	...	...	...	...	290
2	Mining, quarrying .		111.7	113.1	113.2	113.1	109.6	3207	3255	3305	3374	3526	2
311/2	Food products		117.3	116.5	112.5	107.5	106.6	2145	2187	2227	2309	2345	311/2
313	Beverages		19.4	19.8	20.3	20.5	20.5	2069	2162	2231	2302	2370	313
314	Tobacco		20.3	20.3	20.4	19.0	19.4	2124	2195	2246	2367	2398	314
321	Textiles		129.0	129.7	129.7	124.9	120.7	2078	2137	2170	2242	2456	321
3211	Spinning,weaving etc..		92.5	90.0	86.8	83.1	80.5	2152	2204	2256	2315	2568	3211
322	Wearing apparel		48.3	47.7	51.5	57.2	59.1	1870	1872	1898	1952	2047	322
323	Leather and products ...		10.3	10.5	11.6	11.6	11.8	2134	2193	2286	2357	2459	323
324	Footwear		18.3	18.5	18.7	19.3	20.5	2001	2037	2000	2096	2216	324
331	Wood products		28.2	28.2	28.2	26.1	25.5	2342	2449	2453	2521	2606	331
332	Furniture, fixtures		22.9	23.3	24.1	25.4	25.0	2355	2405	2430	2504	2548	332
341	Paper and products		15.1	15.7	15.9	16.0	16.0	2369	2420	2444	2470	2585	341
3411	Pulp,paper etc.		11.3	11.7	11.9	11.2	10.9	2420	2464	2505	2521	2651	3411
342	Printing,publishing		11.5	11.2	11.0	10.9	10.7	2409	2456	2499	2536	2608	342
351	Industrial chemicals ...		35.2	35.5	35.6	35.5	34.9	2674	2743	2773	2849	2968	351
3511	Basic excl fertilizers		...	...	...	...	...	...	...	...	...	...	3511
3513	Synthetic resins etc .		...	...	...	...	...	...	...	...	...	...	3513
352	Other chemical products.		21.4	24.7	24.4	26.5	27.3	...	...	...	...	...	352
3522	Drugs and medicines ..		11.2	11.8	12.2	13.2	13.7	2419	2464	2600	2675	2794	3522
353	Petroleum refineries ...		-	-	-	-	-	-	-	-	-	-	353
354	Petroleum,coal products.		11.7	12.9	22.4	12.7	15.6	...	...	...	...	...	354
355	Rubber products		17.4	18.8	19.3	20.2	19.4	...	...	...	...	...	355
356	Plastic products n.e.c..		10.9	12.2	12.6	12.5	12.6	2353	2403	2528	2604	2673	356
361	Pottery,china etc		7.9	7.9	7.8	6.9	7.0	2166	2230	2274	2323	2436	361
362	Glass and products		18.5	18.8	19.0	18.8	18.9	2457	2517	2549	2621	2867	362
369	Non-metal products n.e.c		54.6	53.1	43.6	50.0	49.7	2612	2668	2526	2730	2796	369
371	Iron and steel		33.2	33.8	35.3	35.0	35.0	3044	3085	3189	3299	3431	371
372	Non-ferrous metals	b/	...	...	...	...	...	...	...	...	...	...	372
381	Metal products		50.6	48.1	48.1	49.5	50.0	2496	2581	2644	2726	2832	381
382	Machinery n.e.c.	c/	144.7	149.9	151.7	153.8	158.8	2595	2687	2788	2864	3011	382
3825	Office,computing etc..		...	...	...	...	...	...	...	...	...	...	3825
383	Electrical machinery ...		94.3	96.4	101.3	106.4	107.8	2325	2421	2502	2614	2758	383
3832	Radio,television etc..		35.7	34.9	38.5	40.2	41.3	2179	2270	2375	2534	2703	3832
384	Transport equipment		73.3	74.1	75.7	76.7	77.2	2661	2731	2828	2928	3051	384
3841	Shipbuilding, repair..		15.5	15.6	15.6	15.5	15.3	2775	2833	2930	3124	3252	3841
3843	Motor vehicles		29.6	30.1	29.9	30.7	30.8	2510	2597	2688	2753	2885	3843
385	Professional goods	c/	...	...	...	...	...	...	...	...	...	...	385
390	Other industries	b/d/	219.9	216.5	213.1	207.7	206.2	...	...	...	...	...	390
3	Manufacturing	e/	1234.2	1244.1	1253.8	1250.6	1256.2	2314	2380	2439	2519	2637	3
410	Electricity,gas,steam ..		27.1	28.4	28.8	29.4	30.1	2848	2872	2925	2989	3135	410
4101	Electricity		27.1	28.4	28.8	29.4	30.1	2848	2872	2925	2989	3135	4101
420	Water works and supply .		.	.	.	.	.	.	.	.	.	.	420
4	Electricity,gas etc		27.1	28.4	28.8	29.4	30.1	2848	2872	2925	2989	3135	4
2-4	All industry	e/	1373.0	1385.6	1395.8	1393.1	1395.9	2397	2462	2520	2598	2717	2-4

Note. For certain deviations in classification, see country note.

a/ Annual average per employee.
b/ Major group 372 is included in 390.
c/ Major group 385 is included in 382.
d/ Including all industrial activities of co-operatives.
e/ Including repair services for the general public.

ISIC	INDUSTRY	5. AVERAGE NUMBER OF OPERATIVES (THOUSANDS)					6. WAGES AND SALARIES OF OPERATIVES a/ (LEVA)					ISIC
		1981	1982	1983	1984	1985	1981	1982	1983	1984	1985	
210	Coal mining	37.4	37.0	29.7	37.7	35.2	3525	3536	3645	3631	3871	210
220	Petroleum and gas	0.4	0.4				3122	...	...	...	...	220
230	Metal ore mining	[48.5	48.9]	[57.0	49.7	49.6]	...	...	...	...	...	230
290	Other mining						...	...	...	...	...	290
2	Mining, quarrying .	86.3	86.3	86.7	87.4	84.8	3272	3282	3359	3416	3570	2
311/2	Food products	81.7	81.6	79.1	76.2	75.8	2123	2171	2222	2307	2348	311/2
313	Beverages	16.0	16.3	16.7	16.9	16.8	2003	2079	2138	2209	2280	313
314	Tobacco	17.9	17.8	17.8	16.5	16.9	2046	2101	2160	2268	2308	314
321	Textiles	114.2	114.7	114.4	110.2	106.7	2030	2081	2118	2193	2411	321
3211	Spinning,weaving etc..	82.0	79.6	76.5	73.3	71.2	2111	2154	2211	2277	2535	3211
322	Wearing apparel	42.9	42.3	45.3	50.3	51.9	1814	1809	1833	1879	1960	322
323	Leather and products ...	9.1	9.2	10.3	10.2	10.5	2103	2147	2229	2301	2401	323
324	Footwear	16.5	16.7	16.8	17.3	18.5	1959	1995	1939	2042	2160	324
331	Wood products	23.9	23.7	23.7	21.9	21.5	2344	2445	2467	2524	2615	331
332	Furniture, fixtures	19.7	19.9	20.6	21.7	21.3	2305	2354	2380	2462	2519	332
341	Paper and products	13.0	13.6	13.6	13.7	13.6	2305	2343	2390	2400	2518	341
3411	Pulp,paper etc.	9.7	10.1	10.2	9.6	9.3	2359	2394	2453	2456	2590	3411
342	Printing,publishing	10.0	9.7	9.5	9.4	9.2	2374	2404	2440	2482	2542	342
351	Industrial chemicals ...	28.0	28.1	27.5	27.6	27.1	...	...	...	...	...	351
3511	Basic excl fertilizers	...	...	...	...	...	...	...	...	...	...	3511
3513	Synthetic resins etc .	...	...	...	...	...	...	...	...	...	...	3513
352	Other chemical products.	17.3	18.8	18.5	20.1	20.6	...	...	...	...	...	352
3522	Drugs and medicines ..	9.5	9.9	10.3	10.9	11.2	2339	2389	2500	2578	2686	3522
353	Petroleum refineries ...	-	-	-	-	-	-	-	-	-	-	353
354	Petroleum,coal products.	9.4	10.4	18.0	9.8	12.3	...	...	...	...	...	354
355	Rubber products	15.0	15.9	16.4	17.1	16.3	...	...	...	...	...	355
356	Plastic products n.e.c..	9.1	10.1	10.3	10.3	10.5	2267	2331	2460	2538	2599	356
361	Pottery,china etc	6.8	6.8	6.7	5.9	6.1	2134	2190	2235	2273	2380	361
362	Glass and products	16.2	16.5	16.7	16.5	16.6	2412	2481	2539	2607	2860	362
369	Non-metal products n.e.c	45.5	44.2	36.2	41.6	41.6	2610	2676	2529	2745	2806	369
371	Iron and steel	27.0	27.5	28.7	28.6	28.6	3117	3149	3273	3373	3504	371
372	Non-ferrous metals ..... b/	...	...	...	...	...	...	...	...	...	...	372
381	Metal products	41.4	39.0	38.7	40.0	40.4	2496	2582	2640	2716	2824	381
382	Machinery n.e.c. .... c/	116.5	120.3	121.5	123.4	127.4	2614	2703	2791	2881	3027	382
3825	Office,computing etc..	...	...	...	...	...	...	...	...	...	...	3825
383	Electrical machinery ...	78.8	80.1	84.6	89.1	90.2	2290	2387	2454	2563	2692	383
3832	Radio,television etc..	29.8	29.0	32.3	33.8	34.6	2102	2196	2279	2436	2578	3832
384	Transport equipment	58.5	59.0	60.3	61.3	61.9	2713	2788	2880	2974	3090	384
3841	Shipbuilding, repair..	12.0	12.1	12.1	12.1	11.8	2863	2959	3056	3220	3342	3841
3843	Motor vehicles	24.4	24.7	24.6	25.3	25.6	2532	2615	2707	2782	2899	3843
385	Professional goods ..... c/	...	...	...	...	...	...	...	...	...	...	385
390	Other industries .... b/d/	181.2	178.5	173.4	168.1	167.1	...	...	...	...	...	390
3	Manufacturing ..... e/	1015.6	1020.7	1025.3	1023.7	1029.4	2286	2349	2407	2485	2602	3
410	Electricity,gas,steam ..	18.7	19.7	20.1	20.7	21.4	2811	2834	2896	2955	3136	410
4101	Electricity	18.7	19.7	20.1	20.7	21.4	2811	2834	2896	2955	3136	4101
420	Water works and supply .	.	.	.	.	.	.	.	.	.	.	420
4	Electricity,gas etc	18.7	19.7	20.1	20.7	21.4	2811	2834	2896	2955	3136	4
2-4	All industry e/	1120.6	1126.7	1132.1	1131.8	1135.6	2370	2429	2488	2565	2684	2-4

Note. For certain deviations in classification, see country note.

a/ Annual average per operative.
c/ Major group 385 is included in 382.
e/ Including repair services for the general public.
b/ Major group 372 is included in 390.
d/ Including all industrial activities of co-operatives.

ISIC	INDUSTRY	7. HOURS WORKED BY OPERATIVES (MILLIONS) 1981	1982	1983	1984	1985	8. QUANTITY OF ELECTRICITY CONSUMED (MILLION KWH) 1981	1982	1983	1984	1985	ISIC
210	Coal mining	68.2	67.0	54.4	68.9	65.0	682	710	701	748	738	210
220	Petroleum and gas	0.8	0.7				12	16	16	17	13	220
230	Metal ore mining	97.2	95.3	96.2	95.9	95.7	...	...	...	...	...	230
290	Other mining						...	...	...	...	...	290
2	Mining, quarrying .	166.2	163.0	150.6	164.8	160.7	a/ 694	a/ 726	a/ 717	a/ 765	a/ 751	2
311/2	Food products	160.7	160.2	154.9	151.1	149.4	1138	920	856	809	796	311/2
313	Beverages	31.2	31.8	32.4	32.6	32.1	110	121	128	129	123	313
314	Tobacco	33.6	33.7	33.9	30.3	32.2	68	70	72	73	72	314
321	Textiles	197.1	198.2	198.2	192.1	187.2	787	803	812	786	767	321
3211	Spinning,weaving etc..	142.8	138.3	133.2	128.6	125.7	683	684	680	673	660	3211
322	Wearing apparel	72.9	71.5	77.5	85.8	89.1	54	41	50	53	54	322
323	Leather and products ...	16.3	16.5	18.5	18.5	19.1	25	29	31	32	32	323
324	Footwear	29.0	29.3	29.1	30.2	32.2	18	19	21	22	20	324
331	Wood products	45.2	45.3	45.4	41.7	41.0	280	262	263	246	241	331
332	Furniture, fixtures	36.9	37.0	38.7	40.5	40.4	83	89	92	106	105	332
341	Paper and products	24.0	25.2	24.9	24.8	24.8	616	586	654	667	714	341
3411	Pulp,paper etc.	17.9	18.7	18.6	17.3	17.0	594	567	634	598	574	3411
342	Printing,publishing	18.0	17.5	17.0	17.2	16.5	31	31	30	39	37	342
351	Industrial chemicals ...	50.2	50.0	48.7	48.4	47.5	4570	4165	4276	4298	4229	351
3511	Basic excl fertilizers	...	...	...	...	...	...	...	...	...	...	3511
3513	Synthetic resins etc .	...	...	...	...	...	...	...	...	...	...	3513
352	Other chemical products.	30.4	33.9	33.3	35.8	37.0	365	374	364	403	421	352
3522	Drugs and medicines ..	16.5	17.5	18.5	19.2	20.0	234	250	252	282	305	3522
353	Petroleum refineries ...	-	-	-	-	-	-	-	-	-	-	353
354	Petroleum,coal products.	16.5	18.4	32.1	17.3	21.1	1354	1419	1462	1714	1560	354
355	Rubber products	27.4	29.1	29.7	31.0	29.6	79	417	421	440	422	355
356	Plastic products n.e.c..	16.2	17.8	18.5	18.6	19.0	157	192	228	243	237	356
361	Pottery,china etc	12.4	12.4	12.1	10.6	11.0	132	130	127	114	114	361
362	Glass and products	29.5	30.0	30.2	29.8	30.3	330	342	360	351	354	362
369	Non-metal products n.e.c	83.9	82.4	81.1	79.6	79.0	1883	1102	1128	1143	1082	369
371	Iron and steel	50.3	49.4	52.2	51.9	52.3	2470	2559	2722	2848	2759	371
372	Non-ferrous metals ..... b/	...	...	...	...	...	...	...	...	...	...	372
381	Metal products	77.5	72.9	72.2	73.9	75.2	500	473	415	420	403	381
382	Machinery n.e.c. .... c/	219.2	224.9	228.3	230.8	238.5	1503	948	1015	1021	1016	382
3825	Office,computing etc..	...	...	...	...	...	...	...	...	...	...	3825
383	Electrical machinery ...	141.9	144.4	153.0	161.0	162.7	485	542	556	563	546	383
3832	Radio,television etc..	52.6	51.0	57.0	59.8	61.0	98	64	59	62	60	3832
384	Transport equipment	110.2	111.1	114.4	116.1	117.1	416	472	478	493	478	384
3841	Shipbuilding, repair..	22.5	22.5	22.9	22.7	22.0	85	88	88	87	82	3841
3843	Motor vehicles	46.3	47.1	47.6	48.5	49.3	178	195	188	202	200	3843
385	Professional goods ..... c/	...	...	...	...	...	...	...	...	...	...	385
390	Other industries .... b/d/	332.8	329.6	319.3	307.8	306.2	1347	2569	2657	2733	2778	390
3	Manufacturing ..... e/	1863.3	1872.5	1895.6	1877.4	1890.5	18801	18675	19218	19746	19360	3
410	Electricity,gas,steam ..	35.9	37.4	38.6	39.7	41.3	6075	6601	6889	7703	7002	410
4101	Electricity	35.9	37.4	38.6	39.7	41.3	6075	6601	6889	7703	7002	4101
420	Water works and supply .	.	.	.	.	.	.	.	.	.	.	420
4	Electricity,gas etc	35.9	37.4	38.6	39.7	41.3	6075	6601	6889	7703	7002	4
2-4	All industry e/	2065.4	2072.9	2084.8	2081.9	2092.5	a/ 25570	a/ 26002	a/ 26824	a/ 28214	a/ 27113	2-4

Hours worked: in the printed table, 97.2 and 95.3 (1981, 1982) are bracketed for rows 230 and 290. 96.2, 95.9 and 95.7 (1983–1985) are bracketed for rows 220 to 290.

Note. For certain deviations in classification, see country note.

a/ Excluding major groups 230 and 290.
b/ Major group 372 is included in 390.
c/ Major group 385 is included in 382.
d/ Including all industrial activities of co-operatives.
e/ Including repair services for the general public.

ISIC	INDUSTRY	9. GROSS FIXED CAPITAL FORMATION TOTAL a/ (MILLION LEVA) 1981	1982	1983	1984	1985	10. GROSS FIXED CAPITAL FORMATION MACHINERY AND EQUIPMENT (MILLION LEVA) 1981	1982	1983	1984	1985	ISIC
210	Coal mining	99.8	156.5	119.1	81.4	106.0	77.0	102.8	76.2	31.3	55.8	210
220	Petroleum and gas	30.7	26.1	17.0	14.8	[	29.5	11.5	3.0	2.6	3.2	220
230	Metal ore mining	[137.8	170.3	124.3	92.6]	161.2	...	...	...	...	...	230
290	Other mining					]	...	...	...	...	...	290
2	Mining, quarrying .	268.3	352.9	260.4	188.8	267.2	b/ 106.5	b/ 114.3	b/ 79.2	b/ 33.9	b/ 59.0	2
311/2	Food products	128.0	99.3	102.4	70.5	114.2	86.5	47.3	45.7	20.1	62.0	311/2
313	Beverages	15.4	61.0	29.4	23.9	16.2	7.0	36.2	16.5	10.6	4.3	313
314	Tobacco	-1.3	15.9	10.9	15.1	14.6	-3.3	5.1	6.9	9.6	12.8	314
321	Textiles	64.2	54.5	51.4	36.4	42.3	49.7	33.2	32.9	18.2	25.9	321
3211	Spinning,weaving etc..	48.9	36.4	39.6	26.0	28.9	26.0	22.4	27.3	12.5	15.7	3211
322	Wearing apparel	0.4	6.5	11.3	11.3	16.2	4.1	3.0	3.1	5.8	10.6	322
323	Leather and products ...	7.2	5.1	7.2	2.3	2.3	1.8	2.6	3.0	0.7	1.2	323
324	Footwear	2.6	7.1	6.2	2.3	6.3	2.2	5.2	4.4	1.9	3.1	324
331	Wood products	39.9	54.1	31.9	15.6	17.3	14.3	23.5	8.5	3.9	5.2	331
332	Furniture, fixtures	6.4	8.8	13.4	12.6	9.2	3.1	3.1	5.7	7.8	3.5	332
341	Paper and products	64.2	19.7	73.2	39.1	31.7	43.2	10.7	41.4	29.7	21.1	341
3411	Pulp,paper etc.	63.1	17.1	67.2	27.9	10.3	42.2	8.3	36.8	22.2	6.3	3411
342	Printing,publishing	1.1	2.2	4.0	17.5	2.4	0.9	2.7	2.4	8.4	0.5	342
351	Industrial chemicals ...	60.0	118.4	109.5	30.5	37.2	60.9	94.2	57.9	10.7	9.0	351
3511	Basic excl fertilizers	...	...	...	...	...	...	...	...	...	...	3511
3513	Synthetic resins etc .	...	...	...	...	...	...	...	...	...	...	3513
352	Other chemical products.	21.7	112.9	39.8	72.2	60.7	10.6	52.8	22.9	32.1	40.3	352
3522	Drugs and medicines ..	15.7	34.7	23.9	36.9	33.3	9.2	23.7	14.6	21.4	25.7	3522
353	Petroleum refineries ...	-	-	-	-	-	-	-	-	-	-	353
354	Petroleum,coal products.	293.7	280.9	61.5	93.1	49.5	204.2	202.3	27.9	45.6	21.7	354
355	Rubber products	59.4	58.7	23.2	36.2	35.8	26.1	48.0	8.9	25.4	20.0	355
356	Plastic products n.e.c..	28.6	73.5	51.8	16.5	12.9	17.9	51.3	32.1	8.1	7.1	356
361	Pottery,china etc	4.1	2.5	2.4	5.0	21.4	5.2	10.0	0.3	7.2	10.6	361
362	Glass and products	13.2	17.2	6.2	5.9	34.1	9.8	11.3	3.9	1.7	18.6	362
369	Non-metal products n.e.c	90.3	98.1	86.1	102.1	29.5	32.6	32.1	34.5	36.8	13.3	369
371	Iron and steel	61.1	292.6	167.6	76.2	151.8	97.5	141.9	122.4	64.7	-1.0	371
372	Non-ferrous metals ..... c/	...	...	...	...	...	...	...	...	...	...	372
381	Metal products	157.6	50.7	114.5	65.9	76.1	90.8	31.8	49.9	42.3	65.6	381
382	Machinery n.e.c. .... d/	121.0	275.3	458.5	465.7	551.9	52.4	139.4	221.6	222.8	301.8	382
3825	Office,computing etc..	...	...	...	...	...	...	...	...	...	...	3825
383	Electrical machinery ...	47.2	86.0	131.5	81.9	107.5	27.7	61.4	85.7	57.0	84.7	383
3832	Radio,television etc..	2.3	11.6	35.8	12.4	23.3	1.1	8.7	17.7	5.4	16.9	3832
384	Transport equipment	57.6	91.8	116.8	94.9	105.1	42.2	40.4	52.2	65.0	69.3	384
3841	Shipbuilding, repair..	13.5	27.3	39.2	16.1	9.5	12.1	8.9	7.7	6.8	4.3	3841
3843	Motor vehicles	41.1	41.4	41.7	33.8	55.3	28.9	23.4	25.6	23.4	33.9	3843
385	Professional goods ..... d/	...	...	...	...	...	...	...	...	...	...	385
390	Other industries .... c/e/	66.1	81.4	84.6	49.5	65.2	129.7	86.5	49.5	7.9	55.8	390
3	Manufacturing ..... f/	1409.7	1974.2	1795.3	1442.2	1611.4	1017.1	1176.0	940.2	744.0	867.0	3
410	Electricity,gas,steam ..	437.1	373.3	312.8	316.9	467.9	292.7	287.7	209.3	266.7	318.8	410
4101	Electricity	437.1	373.3	312.8	316.9	467.9	292.7	287.7	209.3	266.7	318.8	4101
420	Water works and supply .	.	.	.	.	.	.	.	.	.	.	420
4	Electricity,gas etc	437.1	373.3	312.8	316.9	467.9	292.7	287.7	209.3	266.7	318.8	4
2-4	All industry f/	2115.1	2700.4	2368.5	1947.9	2346.5	b/ 1416.3	b/ 1578.0	b/ 1228.7	b/ 1044.6	b/ 1244.8	2-4

Note. For certain deviations in classification, see country note.

a/ Excluding land.
b/ Excluding major groups 230 and 290.
c/ Major group 372 is included in 390.
d/ Major group 385 is included in 382.
e/ Including all industrial activities of co-operatives.
f/ Including repair services for the general public.

11. INDEX NUMBERS OF INDUSTRIAL PRODUCTION (1980 = 100)

ISIC	INDUSTRY	1976	1977	1978	1979	1981	1982	1983	1984	1985	a/ RATE	ISIC
210	Coal mining	82	82	83	92	98	104	88	104	100	2.2	210
220	Petroleum and gas	...	...	...	...	...	...	...	...	...	...	220
230	Metal ore mining .... b/	102	102	98	101	106	131	150	152	155	4.8	230
290	Other mining	84	87	96	96	110	112	113	116	115	3.6	290
2	Mining, quarrying . c/	92	91	95	100	97	102	103	106	105	1.5	2
311/2	Food products	[94	97	101	104	102	106	103	102	104	1.1]	311/2
313	Beverages											313
314	Tobacco	100	94	84	97	100	111	109	103	111	1.2	314
321	Textiles	83	86	92	97	105	110	113	115	112	3.4	321
3211	Spinning,weaving etc..	...	...	...	...	...	...	...	...	...	...	3211
322	Wearing apparel	92	95	98	98	106	110	113	117	121	3.1	322
323	Leather and products ...	89	95	92	92	105	108	121	125	131	4.4	323
324	Footwear	85	93	95	95	110	113	115	123	140	5.7	324
331	Wood products	82	88	90	91	103	108	108	103	104	2.7	331
332	Furniture, fixtures	90	92	93	100	116	121	130	145	149	5.8	332
341	Paper and products	84	87	92	94	107	111	110	112	118	3.8	341
3411	Pulp,paper etc.	...	...	...	...	...	...	...	...	...	...	3411
342	Printing,publishing .... d/	65	85	91	95	104	104	106	106	109	5.9	342
351	Industrial chemicals ...	73	82	88	96	132	133	142	146	142	7.7	351
3511	Basic excl fertilizers	...	...	...	...	...	...	...	...	...	...	3511
3513	Synthetic resins etc .	...	...	...	...	...	...	...	...	...	...	3513
352	Other chemical products.	57	66	80	88	114	129	135	154	167	12.7	352
3522	Drugs and medicines ..	...	...	...	...	...	...	...	...	...	...	3522
353	Petroleum refineries ...	...	...	...	...	...	...	...	...	...	...	353
354	Petroleum,coal products.	...	...	...	...	...	...	...	...	...	...	354
355	Rubber products	75	84	86	92	107	116	131	137	142	7.3	355
356	Plastic products n.e.c..	...	...	...	...	...	...	...	...	...	...	356
361	Pottery,china etc	59	69	77	88	102	106	110	90	91	4.9	361
362	Glass and products	84	88	91	98	102	109	111	113	116	3.7	362
369	Non-metal products n.e.c	78	84	94	98	107	112	112	110	108	3.7	369
371	Iron and steel	86	92	96	98	107	105	112	117	115	3.3	371
372	Non-ferrous metals ..... b/	...	...	...	...	...	...	...	...	...	...	372
381	Metal products	95	102	101	107	102	108	108	117	124	3.0	381
382	Machinery n.e.c.	63	77	87	90	108	122	136	143	163	11.1	382
3825	Office,computing etc..	...	...	...	...	...	...	...	...	...	...	3825
383	Electrical machinery ...	72	76	84	89	109	116	130	150	167	9.8	383
3832	Radio,television etc..	...	...	...	...	...	...	...	...	...	...	3832
384	Transport equipment	70	77	90	100	96	102	112	121	128	6.9	384
3841	Shipbuilding, repair..	...	...	...	...	...	...	...	...	...	...	3841
3843	Motor vehicles	...	...	...	...	...	...	...	...	...	...	3843
385	Professional goods	...	...	...	...	...	...	...	...	...	...	385
390	Other industries	40	48	54	57	63	65	78	88	91	9.6	390
3	Manufacturing ..... d/	80	85	91	96	106	110	115	120	124	5.0	3
410	Electricity,gas,steam .. e/	74	80	86	90	107	119	126	132	124	5.9	410
4101	Electricity	...	...	...	...	...	...	...	...	...	...	4101
420	Water works and supply .	.	.	.	.	.	.	.	.	.	.	420
4	Electricity,gas etc	...	...	...	...	...	...	...	...	...	...	4
2-4	All industry c/d/e/	80	85	91	96	105	110	115	120	124	5.0	2-4

a/ Annual growth rate 1976-1985.
b/ Major group 372 is included in 230.
c/ Including logging and fishing.
d/ Excluding publishing.
e/ Excluding gas manufacture and distribution.

CANADA

The information on industrial activity is based on the reply to the United Nations Questionnaire on General Industrial Statistics from Statistics Canada, Ottawa. The concepts, definitions and classification by branches of industry are generally in accordance with United Nations standards.

In general, the estimates are derived from annual censuses of mining and manufacturing, and annual surveys of electric power and gas utilities. The censuses are conducted by mail and cover all establishments principally engaged in mining and all manufacturing establishments with paid employees. For electricity and gas, the surveys cover all establishments engaged in the generation and distribution of electric power and companies engaged in the sale of manufactured or natural gas to consumers through distribution pipelines. Data on steam and hot water supply are not collected. For water works and supply, the employment and pay-roll data cover waterworks in municipalities with populations of ten thousand or more; for other estimates the coverage is unrestricted.

Data for small manufacturing establishments are generally obtained from administrative records or imputed from the available information. The criteria used for differentiating between large and small establishments vary by industry and province and from year to year, but are governed, in general, by the objective of minimizing the burden on respondents without the loss of a significant amount of detail on shipments of products.

The statistical unit is the establishment, defined as the smallest operating unit capable of reporting specified input and output data. All activities, including non-industrial activities of industrial establishments, are covered. The number of establishments represents the number of operating units that are principally engaged in the activities of the industry to which they have been classified. The operational activities of head offices and auxiliary units are reflected in the industry data.

The estimates, which are based on the national classification scheme (1980 edition), generally have been adjusted to the present version of ISIC. However, it should be noted that the national concept of manufacturing excludes custom tailoring, dressmaking, blacksmithing and welding. Also, manufacture of metal furniture and fixtures (ISIC 381), which in the national scheme is treated as an integral part of the furniture industry, is included in ISIC 332; manufacture of motorcycles and bicycles (ISIC 384) is included in ISIC 390; manufacture of musical instruments (ISIC 390) is included in ISIC 383 and manufacture of synthetic oil (part of ISIC 3540) is included in ISIC 220. For the estimates of gross fixed capital formation, data are compiled only at the 3-digit level of the national scheme and it has not been possible to incorporate all of the adjustments made in other tables.

The estimates of persons engaged include employees and working owners or partners; unpaid family workers are not normally found in industry. The number of employees refers to the average number employed during the reporting period comprising operatives (defined as production and related workers directly engaged in production activities of the classified industry), workers engaged in secondary activities, such as own-account construction work, and other employees (administrative, sales etc.). Homeworkers are excluded from all employment figures and their remuneration treated as contract work done by others.

Wages and salaries refer to gross earnings before deductions for income tax and employees' contributions to social services. They include all salaries, wages, payments for overtime, bonuses, profits shared with employees, the value of room and board where provided, commissions (paid to regular employees only), as well as any other allowance forming part of the worker's earnings.

The value of output for mining and manufacturing is the total value f.o.b. plant of production (for mining) or shipments adjusted for changes in inventories (for manufacturing), including repair and custom revenue, plus non-manufacturing revenues (goods purchased for resale, fixed assets produced by own work force for own use, revenue from product rentals etc.). The valuation is net of sales and excise taxes and duties; subsidies, when they occur, are included. Data for electricity and gas refer to total operating revenues. For water works and supply, the figures are derived from summaries of municipal revenues prepared by the provincial government authorities.

The estimates of value added for mining and manufacturing relate to output, as defined above, less the cost of the relevant commodity inputs (materials and supplies, fuels and electricity consumed etc.) and amounts paid to others for work done. The cost of repair and maintenance work done by other establishments is not deducted. Value added for electricity and gas represents total operating revenues reduced by operating expenditures other than wages and salaries.

The estimates of gross fixed capital formation are based on results of annual questionnaire surveys of capital expenditures, which cover larger business establishments. Extension to full coverage is made by the inclusion of imputed expenditures for non-response and for the smaller firms not surveyed. The estimates relate to the current value of purchases and own-account construction of new fixed assets, including delivery, installation and any necessary fees and taxes. Also included are expenditures for major additions, alterations and improvements to existing assets, and for imported used fixed assets. No deduction is made for scrap or trade-in value of used assets. The estimates shown for manufacturing and for electricity, gas and water exclude investments charged to operating accounts which are not available at the major group level. The amounts excluded are set out in footnotes to the tables.

Stocks are valued at book values and relate to owned inventories held in the country, including goods in transit and on consignment.

The indexes of industrial production are compiled by Statistics Canada and provided in response to the United Nations Questionnaire on Indexes of Industrial Production. In principle, the indexes cover all establishments.

Related national publications:

<u>General Review of the Mineral Industries</u> (annual); <u>Manufacturing Industries of Canada</u> (annual); <u>Electric Power Statistics, Volume II - Annual Statistics</u>; <u>Gas Utilities (Transport and Distribution Systems)</u> (annual); <u>Survey of Production</u> (annual); <u>Canada Year Book</u>; <u>Private and Public Investment in Canada, Outlook</u> (annual), all published by Statistics Canada, Ottawa.

ISIC	INDUSTRY	1. NUMBER OF ESTABLISHMENTS (NUMBER)					2. AVERAGE NUMBER OF PERSONS ENGAGED (THOUSANDS)					ISIC
		1981	a/ 1982	1983	1984	1985	1981	a/ 1982	1983	1984	1985	
210	Coal mining	27	30	28	29	...	11	13	12	12	...	210
220	Petroleum and gas	862	758	928	911	...	b/ 35	b/ 38	b/ 39	b/ 45	...	220
230	Metal ore mining	125	126	114	116	...	69	62	52	53	...	230
290	Other mining	343	334	338	326	...	21	17	17	17	...	290
2	Mining, quarrying .	1357	1248	1408	1382	...	136	130	120	127	...	2
311/2	Food products	4153	3209	3192	3249	...	202	191	187	187	...	311/2
313	Beverages	339	309	292	296	...	33	32	31	32	...	313
314	Tobacco	25	24	25	25	...	9	9	8	8	...	314
321	Textiles	1229	1176	1216	1245	...	91	71	76	76	...	321
3211	Spinning,weaving etc..	296	292	297	301	...	37	29	31	30	...	3211
322	Wearing apparel	2152	2192	2230	2320	...	97	97	100	101	...	322
323	Leather and products ...	214	229	224	226	...	8	8	7	7	...	323
324	Footwear	196	165	176	174	...	18	16	17	17	...	324
331	Wood products	3394	2770	2796	2856	...	114	91	95	96	...	331
332	Furniture, fixtures	2464	2099	2272	2310	...	54	46	47	48	...	332
341	Paper and products	742	658	655	661	...	130	116	113	114	...	341
3411	Pulp,paper etc.	144	143	137	142	...	88	83	79	79	...	3411
342	Printing,publishing	4508	4622	5155	5275	...	108	108	111	114	...	342
351	Industrial chemicals ...	316	344	337	349	...	34	36	34	35	...	351
3511	Basic excl fertilizers	150	157	147	153	...	27	28	22	22	...	3511
3513	Synthetic resins etc .	61	73	74	79	...	7	6	6	6	...	3513
352	Other chemical products.	916	987	1020	1050	...	56	60	60	59	...	352
3522	Drugs and medicines ..	134	135	129	131	...	16	15	15	15	...	3522
353	Petroleum refineries ...	60	65	66	60	...	22	21	18	17	...	353
354	Petroleum,coal products.	67	76	82	76	...	2	2	2	2	...	354
355	Rubber products	142	145	146	145	...	29	25	25	26	...	355
356	Plastic products n.e.c..	888	1042	1086	1143	...	33	36	37	43	...	356
361	Pottery,china etc	47	62	66	67	...	2	1	1	1	...	361
362	Glass and products	125	137	148	160	...	12	11	12	13	...	362
369	Non-metal products n.e.c	1402	1355	1369	1392	...	42	36	34	35	...	369
371	Iron and steel	196	206	198	202	...	72	67	60	62	...	371
372	Non-ferrous metals	243	252	239	249	...	53	47	47	47	...	372
381	Metal products	3957	3475	3509	3518	...	145	122	113	111	...	381
382	Machinery n.e.c.	2735	3461	3613	3797	...	123	129	119	125	...	382
3825	Office,computing etc..	71	92	106	135	...	16	17	16	17	...	3825
383	Electrical machinery ...	1175	1141	1127	1197	...	131	111	105	113	...	383
3832	Radio,television etc..	496	519	504	555	...	52	51	50	56	...	3832
384	Transport equipment	1270	1154	1224	1329	...	179	160	159	177	...	384
3841	Shipbuilding, repair..	395	361	391	424	...	21	19	15	14	...	3841
3843	Motor vehicles	684	609	629	676	...	107	98	106	124	...	3843
385	Professional goods	1122	434	458	511	...	27	19	19	19	...	385
390	Other industries	1703	2332	2366	2564	...	35	38	38	40	...	390
3	Manufacturing	35780	34121	35287	36446	...	1861	1706	1675	1727	...	3
410	Electricity,gas,steam ..	126	124	124	...	...	84	82	85	...	...	410
4101	Electricity	63	61	58	...	...	71	69	66	...	...	4101
420	Water works and supply . c/	198	198	192	192	...	9	8	8	8	...	420
4	Electricity,gas etc	324	322	316	...	...	93	90	93	...	...	4
2-4	All industry	37461	35691	37011	...	...	2090	1926	1888	...	...	2-4

Note. For certain differences in classification, see country note.

a/ Data are based on the 1980 edition of national classification. Prior to 1982, data were compiled according to the 1970 classification.

b/ Including estimates for synthetic oil plants.

c/ Municipalities with populations of 10 000 or more.

ISIC	INDUSTRY	3. AVERAGE NUMBER OF EMPLOYEES (THOUSANDS) 1981	1982 a/	1983	1984	1985	4. WAGES AND SALARIES OF EMPLOYEES (MILLION DOLLARS) 1981	1982 a/	1983	1984	1985	ISIC
210	Coal mining	11	13	12	12	...	300	394	361	458	...	210
220	Petroleum and gas ...... b/	35	38	39	45	...	975	1260	1489	1704	...	220
230	Metal ore mining	69	62	52	53	...	1851	1766	1644	1815	...	230
290	Other mining	21	17	16	17	...	481	439	443	493	...	290
2	Mining, quarrying .	136	130	119	127	...	3607	3859	3937	4470	...	2
311/2	Food products	201	191	187	187	...	3610	3815	4012	4170	...	311/2
313	Beverages	33	32	31	32	...	753	827	885	941	...	313
314	Tobacco	9	9	8	8	...	202	222	236	240	...	314
321	Textiles	91	71	76	75	...	1425	1199	1384	1468	...	321
3211	Spinning,weaving etc..	37	29	31	30	...	610	528	609	626	...	3211
322	Wearing apparel	97	97	100	101	...	1237	1294	1369	1445	...	322
323	Leather and products ...	8	8	7	7	...	113	109	104	110	...	323
324	Footwear	18	16	17	17	...	234	231	253	277	...	324
331	Wood products	113	91	95	96	...	2286	1995	2298	2408	...	331
332	Furniture, fixtures	53	46	47	48	...	823	743	823	882	...	332
341	Paper and products	130	116	113	114	...	3119	3153	3305	3478	...	341
3411	Pulp,paper etc.	88	83	79	79	...	2310	2442	2528	2638	...	3411
342	Printing,publishing	107	107	110	113	...	2105	2287	2545	2761	...	342
351	Industrial chemicals ...	34	36	34	35	...	943	1109	1133	1225	...	351
3511	Basic excl fertilizers	27	28	22	22	...	757	886	773	828	...	3511
3513	Synthetic resins etc .	7	6	6	6	...	167	176	176	205	...	3513
352	Other chemical products.	56	60	60	59	...	1139	1378	1468	1552	...	352
3522	Drugs and medicines ..	16	15	15	15	...	338	365	390	419	...	3522
353	Petroleum refineries ...	22	21	18	17	...	674	754	742	714	...	353
354	Petroleum,coal products.	2	2	2	2	...	40	40	48	51	...	354
355	Rubber products	29	25	25	26	...	585	582	616	683	...	355
356	Plastic products n.e.c..	33	36	37	43	...	526	644	718	858	...	356
361	Pottery,china etc	2	1	1	1	...	32	26	22	23	...	361
362	Glass and products	12	11	12	13	...	246	254	296	333	...	362
369	Non-metal products n.e.c	41	36	34	35	...	910	862	875	922	...	369
371	Iron and steel	72	67	60	62	...	1749	1855	1770	2056	...	371
372	Non-ferrous metals	53	47	47	47	...	1310	1329	1427	1562	...	372
381	Metal products	145	122	113	111	...	2874	2656	2604	2646	...	381
382	Machinery n.e.c.	123	129	119	124	...	2545	2904	2812	3082	...	382
3825	Office,computing etc..	16	17	16	17	...	334	391	415	452	...	3825
383	Electrical machinery ...	130	111	105	113	...	2510	2408	2457	2774	...	383
3832	Radio,television etc..	52	51	50	56	...	1036	1141	1225	1449	...	3832
384	Transport equipment	179	159	159	177	...	4084	3966	4334	5261	...	384
3841	Shipbuilding, repair..	21	19	14	14	...	475	490	390	364	...	3841
3843	Motor vehicles	107	98	106	124	...	2473	2414	2949	3792	...	3843
385	Professional goods	27	19	19	19	...	484	361	437	432	...	385
390	Other industries	35	38	37	39	...	548	622	639	721	...	390
3	Manufacturing	1855	1704	1673	1721	...	37106	37625	39612	43075	...	3
410	Electricity,gas,steam ..	84	82	85	...	...	2301	2639	2808	...	...	410
4101	Electricity	71	69	66	...	...	1984	2283	2419	...	...	4101
420	Water works and supply . c/	9	8	8	8	...	181	201	212	219	...	420
4	Electricity,gas etc	93	90	93	...	...	2482	2840	3020	...	...	4
2-4	All industry	2084	1924	1885	...	...	43195	44324	46569	...	...	2-4

Note. For certain differences in classification, see country note.

a/ Data are based on the 1980 edition of national classification. Prior to 1982, data were compiled according to the 1970 classification.

b/ Including estimates for synthetic oil plants.

c/ Municipalities with populations of 10 000 or more.

ISIC	INDUSTRY	5. SUPPLEMENTS TO WAGES AND SALARIES (MILLION DOLLARS)					6. AVERAGE NUMBER OF OPERATIVES (THOUSANDS)					ISIC
		1981	1982	1983	1984	1985	1981	1982 a/	1983	1984	1985	
210	Coal mining	...	...	...	...	...	9	10	8	9	...	210
220	Petroleum and gas ...... b/	...	...	...	...	...	11	11	12	14	...	220
230	Metal ore mining	...	...	...	...	...	50	44	37	39	...	230
290	Other mining	...	...	...	...	...	16	13	13	13	...	290
2	Mining, quarrying .	704	757	790	858	...	86	78	70	75	...	2
311/2	Food products	...	...	...	...	...	142	132	129	130	...	311/2
313	Beverages	...	...	...	...	...	18	17	17	18	...	313
314	Tobacco	...	...	...	...	...	6	6	5	5	...	314
321	Textiles	...	...	...	...	...	73	56	62	61	...	321
3211	Spinning,weaving etc..	...	...	...	...	...	29	22	24	24	...	3211
322	Wearing apparel	...	...	...	...	...	84	84	88	89	...	322
323	Leather and products ...	...	...	...	...	...	7	7	6	6	...	323
324	Footwear	...	...	...	...	...	16	14	14	15	...	324
331	Wood products	...	...	...	...	...	94	75	79	80	...	331
332	Furniture, fixtures	...	...	...	...	...	44	38	39	40	...	332
341	Paper and products	...	...	...	...	...	99	87	85	87	...	341
3411	Pulp,paper etc.	...	...	...	...	...	67	63	60	61	...	3411
342	Printing,publishing	...	...	...	...	...	64	62	64	65	...	342
351	Industrial chemicals ...	...	...	...	...	...	18	19	19	19	...	351
3511	Basic excl fertilizers	...	...	...	...	...	14	15	12	12	...	3511
3513	Synthetic resins etc .	...	...	...	...	...	4	3	3	4	...	3513
352	Other chemical products.	...	...	...	...	...	28	30	31	30	...	352
3522	Drugs and medicines ..	...	...	...	...	...	7	7	7	7	...	3522
353	Petroleum refineries ...	...	...	...	...	...	8	8	7	6	...	353
354	Petroleum,coal products.	...	...	...	...	...	1	1	1	1	...	354
355	Rubber products	...	...	...	...	...	20	17	18	18	...	355
356	Plastic products n.e.c..	...	...	...	...	...	26	29	30	35	...	356
361	Pottery,china etc	...	...	...	...	...	2	1	1	1	...	361
362	Glass and products	...	...	...	...	...	9	9	9	10	...	362
369	Non-metal products n.e.c	...	...	...	...	...	29	24	24	25	...	369
371	Iron and steel	...	...	...	...	...	56	50	45	48	...	371
372	Non-ferrous metals	...	...	...	...	...	36	32	33	34	...	372
381	Metal products	...	...	...	...	...	108	91	84	84	...	381
382	Machinery n.e.c.	...	...	...	...	...	83	85	78	85	...	382
3825	Office,computing etc..	...	...	...	...	...	7	6	7	8	...	3825
383	Electrical machinery ...	...	...	...	...	...	86	72	67	74	...	383
3832	Radio,television etc..	...	...	...	...	...	35	33	32	36	...	3832
384	Transport equipment	...	...	...	...	...	136	118	118	133	...	384
3841	Shipbuilding, repair..	...	...	...	...	...	17	15	11	10	...	3841
3843	Motor vehicles	...	...	...	...	...	83	75	84	99	...	3843
385	Professional goods	...	...	...	...	...	18	11	11	11	...	385
390	Other industries	...	...	...	...	...	26	30	29	31	...	390
3	Manufacturing	4035	4190	4559	4886	...	1337	1205	1193	1241	...	3
410	Electricity,gas,steam .. c/	...	...	...	...	...	10	10	10	...	...	410
4101	Electricity	...	...	...	...	...	...	...	...	...	...	4101
420	Water works and supply .	...	...	...	...	...	...	...	...	...	...	420
4	Electricity,gas etc	370	420	447	493	...	...	...	...	...	...	4
2-4	All industry	5109	5367	5796	6237	...	...	...	...	...	...	2-4

Note. For certain differences in classification, see country note.

a/ Data are based on the 1980 edition of national classification. Prior to 1982, data were compiled according to the 1970 classification.
b/ Including estimates for synthetic oil plants. c/ Gas only.

ISIC	INDUSTRY	7. WAGES AND SALARIES OF OPERATIVES (MILLION DOLLARS)					8. HOURS WORKED BY OPERATIVES (MILLIONS)					ISIC
		1981	a/ 1982	1983	1984	1985	1981	a/ 1982	1983	1984	1985	
210	Coal mining	237	293	245	324	...	17	18	15	16	...	210
220	Petroleum and gas ...... b/	313	383	419	487	...	23	23	23	26	...	220
230	Metal ore mining	1266	1180	1110	1296	...	92	71	66	71	...	230
290	Other mining	352	310	329	357	...	30	24	24	24	...	290
2	Mining, quarrying .	2168	2166	2103	2464	...	162	136	128	137	...	2
311/2	Food products	2354	2418	2537	2619	...	266	247	240	241	...	311/2
313	Beverages	391	422	460	489	...	33	32	32	33	...	313
314	Tobacco	119	128	132	132	...	9	9	8	7	...	314
321	Textiles	1016	842	1002	1065	...	138	105	117	117	...	321
3211	Spinning,weaving etc..	430	360	428	439	...	55	41	45	44	...	3211
322	Wearing apparel	964	999	1072	1136	...	150	150	157	161	...	322
323	Leather and products ...	92	85	81	88	...	13	12	11	11	...	323
324	Footwear	183	169	188	205	...	29	25	27	28	...	324
331	Wood products	1824	1571	1846	1924	...	172	131	145	146	...	331
332	Furniture, fixtures	631	562	627	672	...	86	72	74	77	...	332
341	Paper and products	2229	2201	2367	2502	...	181	158	156	158	...	341
3411	Pulp,paper etc.	1670	1729	1838	1922	...	123	113	110	110	...	3411
342	Printing,publishing	1184	1256	1404	1494	...	114	112	114	115	...	342
351	Industrial chemicals ...	470	559	575	626	...	35	36	36	37	...	351
3511	Basic excl fertilizers	372	461	395	425	...	27	28	24	24	...	3511
3513	Synthetic resins etc .	88	84	91	110	...	7	6	6	7	...	3513
352	Other chemical products.	487	584	631	655	...	53	57	57	56	...	352
3522	Drugs and medicines ..	119	127	140	142	...	13	12	13	12	...	3522
353	Petroleum refineries ...	241	258	258	254	...	16	15	14	12	...	353
354	Petroleum,coal products.	24	23	31	34	...	2	2	2	3	...	354
355	Rubber products	373	371	398	458	...	37	32	32	34	...	355
356	Plastic products n.e.c..	373	455	507	613	...	49	54	56	65	...	356
361	Pottery,china etc	25	18	16	17	...	3	2	2	2	...	361
362	Glass and products	182	182	214	247	...	18	16	17	19	...	362
369	Non-metal products n.e.c	612	556	571	619	...	55	46	45	48	...	369
371	Iron and steel	1274	1326	1296	1552	...	105	92	83	94	...	371
372	Non-ferrous metals	846	842	929	1024	...	68	60	60	63	...	372
381	Metal products	1988	1833	1814	1862	...	207	170	157	158	...	381
382	Machinery n.e.c.	1613	1784	1691	1921	...	157	159	145	160	...	382
3825	Office,computing etc..	115	130	141	169	...	12	12	13	15	...	3825
383	Electrical machinery ...	1471	1352	1390	1587	...	159	133	125	137	...	383
3832	Radio,television etc..	611	645	701	800	...	65	62	60	66	...	3832
384	Transport equipment	2944	2778	3076	3785	...	252	214	228	267	...	384
3841	Shipbuilding, repair..	383	394	293	267	...	32	29	21	19	...	3841
3843	Motor vehicles	1814	1746	2208	2902	...	153	133	163	203	...	3843
385	Professional goods	265	173	200	214	...	33	20	20	21	...	385
390	Other industries	365	433	450	499	...	49	55	54	57	...	390
3	Manufacturing	24540	24179	25763	28293	...	2489	2216	2214	2327	...	3
410	Electricity,gas,steam .. c/	223	239	261	...	...	...	...	...	...	...	410
4101	Electricity	...	...	...	...	...	...	...	...	...	...	4101
420	Water works and supply .	...	...	...	...	...	...	...	...	...	...	420
4	Electricity,gas etc	...	...	...	...	...	...	...	...	...	...	4
2-4	All industry	...	...	...	...	...	...	...	...	...	...	2-4

Note. For certain differences in classification, see country note.

a/ Data are based on the 1980 edition of national classification. Prior to 1982, data were compiled according to the 1970 classification.

b/ Including estimates for synthetic oil plants.

c/ Gas only.

ISIC	INDUSTRY	9. QUANTITY OF ELECTRICITY CONSUMED a/b/ (MILLION KWH) 1981	1982 c/	1983	1984	1985	10. OUTPUT IN PRODUCERS' PRICES (BILLION DOLLARS) 1981	1982 c/	1983	1984	1985	ISIC
210	Coal mining	699	729	692	906	...	1.05	1.23	1.25	1.72	...	210
220	Petroleum and gas ...... d/	3240	3688	4466	5134	...	17.96	21.59	25.56	28.31	...	220
230	Metal ore mining	10494	9891	9660	11672	...	8.59	6.83	6.96	8.33	...	230
290	Other mining	2100	1782	1928	2120	...	2.39	1.70	1.77	2.19	...	290
2	Mining, quarrying .	16533	16090	16746	19832	...	29.99	31.35	35.54	40.55	...	2
311/2	Food products	4041	4052	4166	4348	...	33.04	33.76	34.81	37.40	...	311/2
313	Beverages	663	663	662	709	...	4.25	4.55	4.87	5.30	...	313
314	Tobacco	124	142	149	153	...	1.49	1.63	1.59	1.72	...	314
321	Textiles	2185	1752	2000	2117	...	6.84	5.27	6.48	6.65	...	321
3211	Spinning,weaving etc..	1542	1181	1378	1373	...	3.08	2.29	2.79	2.71	...	3211
322	Wearing apparel	306	317	282	303	...	4.41	4.47	4.82	5.23	...	322
323	Leather and products ...	65	64	63	62	...	0.48	0.44	0.45	0.48	...	323
324	Footwear	79	71	77	105	...	0.90	0.84	0.89	1.01	...	324
331	Wood products	3476	3198	3558	3818	...	8.75	6.93	9.41	9.86	...	331
332	Furniture, fixtures	387	371	391	421	...	2.93	2.50	2.90	3.21	...	332
341	Paper and products	29530	27849	31175	37710	...	16.25	14.84	15.35	17.91	...	341
3411	Pulp,paper etc.	28720	27263	30578	37026	...	12.23	11.38	11.54	13.69	...	3411
342	Printing,publishing	696	734	765	814	...	6.75	7.06	7.98	9.11	...	342
351	Industrial chemicals ...	11829	11745	12566	12865	...	9.00	9.85	10.92	12.27	...	351
3511	Basic excl fertilizers	10493	10506	9871	10030	...	6.88	7.53	7.10	7.89	...	3511
3513	Synthetic resins etc .	1319	1219	1269	1320	...	1.79	1.52	1.81	2.26	...	3513
352	Other chemical products.	750	844	907	967	...	6.93	7.59	8.27	9.13	...	352
3522	Drugs and medicines ..	167	170	181	181	...	1.67	1.81	1.99	2.25	...	3522
353	Petroleum refineries ...	3640	3448	3466	3492	...	22.29	22.59	23.87	24.88	...	353
354	Petroleum,coal products.	84	73	86	107	...	0.47	0.44	0.56	0.53	...	354
355	Rubber products	739	733	771	1037	...	2.80	2.61	2.80	3.43	...	355
356	Plastic products n.e.c..	900	1094	1195	1417	...	2.77	3.14	3.69	4.43	...	356
361	Pottery,china etc	30	25	22	23	...	0.09	0.07	0.06	0.06	...	361
362	Glass and products	567	559	588	617	...	0.95	0.96	1.17	1.34	...	362
369	Non-metal products n.e.c	3976	3393	3373	3799	...	4.31	3.80	3.96	4.49	...	369
371	Iron and steel	9448	8123	8256	8894	...	9.13	7.43	7.71	9.60	...	371
372	Non-ferrous metals	10981	8739	9284	10025	...	6.96	6.37	6.63	7.75	...	372
381	Metal products	1886	1690	1647	1859	...	12.94	11.43	11.05	12.04	...	381
382	Machinery n.e.c.	1209	1401	1331	1981	...	11.22	11.24	10.70	12.98	...	382
3825	Office,computing etc..	149	159	187	146	...	1.60	1.73	1.78	2.30	...	3825
383	Electrical machinery ...	1681	1385	1370	1595	...	11.07	9.68	9.68	11.53	...	383
3832	Radio,television etc..	394	395	400	543	...	4.01	4.22	4.44	5.44	...	3832
384	Transport equipment	3087	3129	3386	3906	...	29.96	30.03	37.20	49.88	...	384
3841	Shipbuilding, repair..	178	189	159	169	...	1.37	1.27	0.97	1.34	...	3841
3843	Motor vehicles	2320	2381	2685	3094	...	24.26	25.15	33.10	44.49	...	3843
385	Professional goods	160	141	135	174	...	1.82	1.38	1.44	1.58	...	385
390	Other industries	288	263	254	339	...	2.81	2.49	2.66	3.03	...	390
3	Manufacturing	92807	85998	91925	103657	...	221.61	213.39	231.92	266.83	...	3
410	Electricity,gas,steam ..	...	...	...	...	...	17.41	20.01	22.47	...	...	410
4101	Electricity	e/ 1591	e/ 1850	e/ 1996	...	...	12.68	14.30	16.08	...	...	4101
420	Water works and supply .	...	...	...	...	...	0.87	0.97	1.02	1.08	...	420
4	Electricity,gas etc	...	...	...	...	...	18.28	20.98	23.49	...	...	4
2-4	All industry	...	...	...	...	...	269.88	265.72	290.95	...	...	2-4

Note. For certain differences in classification, see country note.

a/ Purchased electricity only.
b/ Manufacturing: Prior to 1982, excluding small establishments.
c/ Data are based on the 1980 edition of national classification. Prior to 1982, data were compiled according to the 1970 classification.
d/ Including estimates for synthetic oil plants.
e/ Consumption in own plant by utilities.

ISIC	INDUSTRY	11. VALUE ADDED IN PRODUCERS' PRICES (BILLION DOLLARS) 1981	1982 c/	1983	1984	1985	12. GROSS FIXED CAPITAL FORMATION TOTAL a/b/ (MILLION DOLLARS) 1981	1982 c/	1983	*1984	1985	ISIC
210	Coal mining	0.67	0.84	0.89	1.31	...	576	1030	1225	783	...	210
220	Petroleum and gas	d/ 16.76	d/ 19.90	d/ 23.35	d/ 26.34	...	7031	7440	6915	7177	...	220
230	Metal ore mining	4.70	3.50	3.73	4.66	...	1908	1470	1151	1299	...	230
290	Other mining	1.79	1.19	1.20	1.56	...	490	422	333	394	...	290
2	Mining, quarrying .	23.92	25.43	29.17	33.87	...	10005	10362	9624	9653	...	2
311/2	Food products	8.11	8.64	9.35	10.13	...	598	729	675	678	...	311/2
313	Beverages	2.25	2.47	2.65	2.84	...	146	156	218	314	...	313
314	Tobacco	0.64	0.73	0.75	0.79	...	32	47	43	38	...	314
321	Textiles	2.86	2.09	2.67	2.78	...	181	160	180	214	...	321
3211	Spinning,weaving etc..	1.22	0.91	1.17	1.19	...	143	126	135	164	...	3211
322	Wearing apparel	2.17	2.21	2.36	2.55	...	37	19	23	28	...	322
323	Leather and products ...	0.21	0.19	0.19	0.20	...	10	6	8	8	...	323
324	Footwear	0.41	0.40	0.43	0.49	...	7	6	16	13	...	324
331	Wood products	3.44	2.53	3.76	3.82	...	449	320	289	344	...	331
332	Furniture, fixtures	1.46	1.25	1.48	1.62	...	53	35	26	32	...	332
341	Paper and products	6.87	5.77	5.84	7.36	...	2178	1852	993	1174	...	341
3411	Pulp,paper etc.	5.40	4.52	4.38	5.80	...	2052	1743	903	1014	...	3411
342	Printing,publishing	4.08	4.28	4.96	5.61	...	205	176	176	252	...	342
351	Industrial chemicals ...	2.73	2.55	2.99	3.38	...	1879	2036	1451	700	...	351
3511	Basic excl fertilizers	2.29	2.08	2.02	2.25	...	1678	1695	1316	636	...	3511
3513	Synthetic resins etc .	0.37	0.27	0.42	0.52	...	100	71	40	50	...	3513
352	Other chemical products.	3.37	3.76	4.14	4.55	...	271	241	176	242	...	352
3522	Drugs and medicines ..	0.97	1.06	1.23	1.38	...	65	86	66	68	...	3522
353	Petroleum refineries ...	2.86	2.19	2.59	2.54	...	842	1223	840	534	...	353
354	Petroleum,coal products.	0.14	0.15	0.15	0.17	...	8	5	7	4	...	354
355	Rubber products	1.13	1.05	1.14	1.40	...	209	214	95	110	...	355
356	Plastic products n.e.c..	1.15	1.31	1.52	1.88	...	76	70	84	121	...	356
361	Pottery,china etc	0.05	0.04	0.04	0.04	...	13	9	6	6	...	361
362	Glass and products	0.51	0.50	0.61	0.72	...	50	29	37	55	...	362
369	Non-metal products n.e.c	1.95	1.75	1.86	2.03	...	284	128	97	117	...	369
371	Iron and steel	3.40	2.75	3.00	3.78	...	906	621	243	306	...	371
372	Non-ferrous metals	2.44	2.10	2.63	3.14	...	714	585	420	804	...	372
381	Metal products	5.69	4.93	4.82	5.23	...	351	229	198	358	...	381
382	Machinery n.e.c.	5.14	5.34	5.09	6.16	...	328	320	246	331	...	382
3825	Office,computing etc..	0.67	0.77	0.79	1.00	...	...	...	...	...	...	3825
383	Electrical machinery ...	5.28	4.94	4.82	5.79	...	345	340	413	436	...	383
3832	Radio,television etc..	2.23	2.48	2.44	3.02	...	196	186	224	281	...	3832
384	Transport equipment	8.04	7.50	9.80	12.67	...	1210	688	767	659	...	384
3841	Shipbuilding, repair..	0.73	0.71	0.53	0.57	...	48	58	29	22	...	3841
3843	Motor vehicles	4.99	5.00	7.63	9.89	...	972	425	616	465	...	3843
385	Professional goods	0.90	0.69	0.76	0.85	...	58	51	66	64	...	385
390	Other industries	1.17	1.25	1.30	1.54	...	51	46	50	62	...	390
3	Manufacturing	78.45	73.36	81.70	94.06	...	e/ 11491	e/ 10343	e/ 7843	e/ 8004	...	3
410	Electricity,gas,steam ..	8.47	10.32	10.99	...	...	7828	8926	8287	7218	...	410
4101	Electricity	7.29	8.17	9.43	...	...	7319	8408	7770	6643	...	4101
420	Water works and supply .	0.35	0.36	0.39	0.39	...	4	5	6	7	...	420
4	Electricity,gas etc	8.82	18.85	20.81	...	...	f/ 7832	f/ 8931	f/ 8293	f/ 7225	...	4
2-4	All industry	111.19	117.64	131.68	...	...	29328	29634	25760	24882	...	2-4

Note. For certain differences in classification, see country note.

a/ Excluding used fixed assets.
b/ Manufacturing and electricity, gas and water: excluding capital items charged to operating expenses.
c/ Data are based on the 1980 edition of national classification. Prior to 1982, data were compiled according to the 1970 classification.
d/ Including estimates for synthetic oil plants.
e/ Capital items charged to operating expenses amounted to (in millions of dollars):1981 1252; 1982 1149; 1983 1017; 1984 1087
f/ Capital items charged to operating expenses amounted to (in millions of dollars): 1981 44; 1982 58; 1983 44; 1984 52.

ISIC	INDUSTRY	13. GROSS FIXED CAPITAL FORMATION MACHINERY AND EQUIPMENT a/b/ (MILLION DOLLARS)					14. VALUE OF STOCKS AT END OF PERIOD TOTAL (MILLION DOLLARS)					ISIC
		1981	c/ 1982	1983	*1984	1985	1981	c/ 1982	1983	1984	1985	
210	Coal mining	157	367	283	350	...	...	-	81	-	...	210
220	Petroleum and gas	1206	1420	881	711	...	...	...	...	...	...	220
230	Metal ore mining	576	371	312	362	...	1801	1450	1345	1281	...	230
290	Other mining	261	196	151	228	...	377	334	312	325	...	290
2	Mining, quarrying .	2200	2354	1627	1651	...	...	...	...	...	...	2
311/2	Food products	412	524	521	545	...	2908	2944	2975	3202	...	311/2
313	Beverages	108	123	179	266	...	977	1003	1015	1054	...	313
314	Tobacco	25	37	37	32	...	616	685	682	829	...	314
321	Textiles	157	135	147	180	...	1255	949	1051	1101	...	321
3211	Spinning,weaving etc..	123	106	113	137	...	562	398	437	461	...	3211
322	Wearing apparel	24	15	19	24	...	878	852	915	1003	...	322
323	Leather and products ...	6	6	7	8	...	90	86	84	91	...	323
324	Footwear	5	4	12	11	...	160	148	163	196	...	324
331	Wood products	340	238	236	284	...	1554	1295	1500	1579	...	331
332	Furniture, fixtures	29	20	19	26	...	522	450	489	528	...	332
341	Paper and products	1786	1518	842	998	...	2063	2086	1971	1221	...	341
3411	Pulp,paper etc.	1676	1420	762	877	...	1492	1613	1468	659	...	3411
342	Printing,publishing	168	150	150	217	...	560	542	586	709	...	342
351	Industrial chemicals ...	1399	1638	1175	561	...	1564	1873	1906	2160	...	351
3511	Basic excl fertilizers	1312	1350	1057	507	...	1250	1461	1288	1463	...	3511
3513	Synthetic resins etc .	86	54	35	43	...	256	227	229	311	...	3513
352	Other chemical products.	141	163	134	186	...	1265	1380	1397	1524	...	352
3522	Drugs and medicines ..	...	41	46	42	...	358	360	378	397	...	3522
353	Petroleum refineries ...	212	332	210	...	...	3359	3256	2797	3097	...	353
354	Petroleum,coal products.	7	4	6	...	...	30	34	40	47	...	354
355	Rubber products	129	184	86	99	...	551	515	516	592	...	355
356	Plastic products n.e.c..	63	62	74	102	...	417	429	507	574	...	356
361	Pottery,china etc	9	8	6	6	...	19	18	16	11	...	361
362	Glass and products	44	26	35	52	...	169	169	184	192	...	362
369	Non-metal products n.e.c	201	100	85	98	...	585	534	521	542	...	369
371	Iron and steel	757	520	225	273	...	2306	2031	1999	2216	...	371
372	Non-ferrous metals	533	407	326	547	...	1173	1045	1075	1188	...	372
381	Metal products	266	186	166	284	...	2478	2062	1915	1961	...	381
382	Machinery n.e.c.	199	199	186	273	...	2714	2791	2686	2984	...	382
3825	Office,computing etc..	...	...	...	...	...	437	438	440	524	...	3825
383	Electrical machinery ...	248	254	328	359	...	2523	2090	2157	2824	...	383
3832	Radio,television etc..	141	147	...	...	...	947	912	978	1481	...	3832
384	Transport equipment	963	520	652	499	...	4099	3595	3442	3965	...	384
3841	Shipbuilding, repair..	19	16	12	9	...	267	180	108	143	...	3841
3843	Motor vehicles	804	365	541	343	...	2188	1934	2154	2475	...	3843
385	Professional goods	31	29	46	49	...	407	316	291	321	...	385
390	Other industries	36	32	37	45	...	562	540	542	619	...	390
3	Manufacturing	d/ 8298	d/ 7434	d/ 5946	d/e/ 6164	...	35804	33718	33422	36330	...	3
410	Electricity,gas,steam ..	2994	3904	3814	3342	...	1811	2300	2094	...	...	410
4101	Electricity	2905	3788	3701	3220	...	1392	1684	1578	...	...	4101
420	Water works and supply .	-	-	-	-	...	...	...	...	...	...	420
4	Electricity,gas etc f/	2994	3904	3814	3342	...	...	...	...	...	...	4
2-4	All industry	13492	13692	11387	11157	...	...	...	...	...	...	2-4

Note. For certain differences in classification, see country note.

a/ Excluding used fixed assets.
b/ Manufacturing and electricity, gas and water: excluding capital items charged to operating expenses.
c/ Data are based on the 1980 edition of national classification. Prior to 1982, data were compiled according to the 1970 classification.
d/ Capital items charged to operating expenses amounted to (in millions of dollars): 1981 1252; 1982 1149; 1983 1017; 1984 1087
e/ Including major groups 353 and 354.
f/ Capital items charged to operating expenses amounted to (in millions of dollars): 1981 44; 1982 58; 1983 44; 1984 52.

15. INDEX NUMBERS OF INDUSTRIAL PRODUCTION (1980 = 100)

ISIC	INDUSTRY	1976	1977	1978	1979	1981	1982	1983	1984	1985	a/ RATE	ISIC
210	Coal mining	68	74	81	91	105	98	101	148	158	9.8	210
220	Petroleum and gas	90	91	91	103	92	93	95	100	105	1.7	220
230	Metal ore mining	113	118	87	92	98	86	89	102	105	-0.8	230
290	Other mining	95	99	95	103	95	69	72	85	77	-2.3	290
2	Mining, quarrying .	97	100	89	98	94	89	92	100	104	0.8	2
311/2	Food products	93	94	96	98	102	100	100	100	104	1.2	311/2
313	Beverages	94	97	97	101	102	96	98	98	100	0.7	313
314	Tobacco	100	100	97	100	102	102	96	92	95	-0.6	314
321	Textiles	88	91	96	104	104	86	104	106	106	2.1	321
3211	Spinning,weaving etc..	...	...	...	...	...	...	...	...	...	...	3211
322	Wearing apparel	102	96	102	108	100	88	93	98	98	-0.4	322
323	Leather and products ... b/	102	95	107	104	103	83	79	75	75	-3.4	323
324	Footwear	98	90	100	108	107	92	97	106	104	0.7	324
331	Wood products	89	95	98	103	98	82	100	103	112	2.6	331
332	Furniture, fixtures .... c/	97	88	96	102	109	87	96	98	107	1.1	332
341	Paper and products	88	88	98	98	99	88	97	100	104	1.9	341
3411	Pulp,paper etc.	82	84	100	99	97	87	94	98	...	g/ 2.3	3411
342	Printing,publishing	81	82	87	92	102	97	104	110	113	3.8	342
351	Industrial chemicals ... d/	74	80	83	102	100	86	98	109	112	4.7	351
3511	Basic excl fertilizers	...	...	...	...	...	...	...	...	...	...	3511
3513	Synthetic resins etc .	...	...	...	...	...	...	...	...	...	...	3513
352	Other chemical products. d/	84	88	94	98	104	98	102	106	111	3.1	352
3522	Drugs and medicines ..	84	90	98	103	105	104	111	117	...	g/ 4.2	3522
353	Petroleum refineries ...	123	114	115	100	105	90	85	85	84	-4.1	353
354	Petroleum,coal products.	90	87	96	103	92	89	112	109	112	2.5	354
355	Rubber products	103	110	107	118	105	98	102	130	123	2.0	355
356	Plastic products n.e.c..	78	83	96	105	106	102	118	130	142	6.9	356
361	Pottery,china etc ...... e/	101	101	105	111	98	78	79	85	93	-0.9	361
362	Glass and products	90	86	99	106	98	93	109	120	123	3.5	362
369	Non-metal products n.e.c e/	...	...	...	...	...	...	...	...	...	...	369
371	Iron and steel	89	90	99	108	100	76	80	94	93	0.5	371
372	Non-ferrous metals	82	95	95	88	101	82	97	106	85	0.4	372
381	Metal products .... c/	94	92	95	102	100	92	87	92	99	0.6	381
382	Machinery n.e.c. .... f/	70	72	82	95	102	83	78	89	95	3.5	382
3825	Office,computing etc..	...	...	...	...	...	...	...	...	...	...	3825
383	Electrical machinery ... f/	91	89	90	100	107	99	95	102	87	-0.5	383
3832	Radio,television etc..	64	50	53	80	119	104	117	122	...	g/ 8.4	3832
384	Transport equipment	109	116	118	122	101	91	104	124	133	2.2	384
3841	Shipbuilding, repair..	94	88	74	90	97	88	61	51	...	g/ -7.4	3841
3843	Motor vehicles	128	138	138	138	101	97	126	158	...	g/ 2.7	3843
385	Professional goods	75	76	83	91	96	92	86	95	102	3.5	385
390	Other industries	107	99	106	107	102	87	92	99	99	-0.9	390
3	Manufacturing	91	93	97	103	101	90	95	102	107	1.8	3
410	Electricity,gas,steam ..	82	86	91	96	102	102	106	115	122	4.5	410
4101	Electricity	80	86	90	96	103	103	107	116	...	g/ 4.8	4101
420	Water works and supply .	...	...	...	...	...	...	...	...	...	...	420
4	Electricity,gas etc	82	86	91	96	103	103	108	116	123	4.6	4
2-4	All industry	91	93	96	102	101	92	97	104	109	2.0	2-4

a/ Annual growth rate 1976-1985.
b/ Excluding fur dressing and dyeing industries.
c/ Manufacture of metal furniture and fixtures is included in major group 332.
d/ Synthetic resins and plastic materials are included in major group 352.
e/ Major group 369 is included in 361.
f/ Electronic computers and their accessories are included in major group 383.
g/ Annual growth rate 1976-1984.

CENTRAL AFRICAN REPUBLIC

The information in the tables is based on the reply to the United Nations Questionnaire on General Industrial Statistics from the Direction de la statistique generale et des etudes economiques, Ministere du plan, des statistiques et de la cooperation internationale, Bangui. The concepts and definitions are generally in accordance with United Nations standards.

The estimates are derived from the industrial survey conducted since 1969, by the Service des enquetes economiques et sociales of the above-mentioned office. The survey covers all enterprises in the modern sector which keep records sufficient for providing information on management characteristics and other statistical data. The inquiry is made by mail supplemented by visits of field enumerators, if necessary.

The estimates are compiled according to the national classification system which is not strictly comparable with ISIC. Adjustments to ISIC have been made by the national authorities. Data are available only by broad groupings of industries because of statistical secrecy regulations.

Estimates of output and value added are compiled in accordance with the definitions set out in the international recommendations. The valuation is in factor values.

Related national publication:

Enquete sur les entreprises du secteur moderne (formerly, Recensement des entreprises du secteur moderne) (annual), published by the Direction de la statistique generale et des etudes economiques, Ministere du plan, des statistiques et de la cooperation internationale, Bangui.

ISIC	INDUSTRY		1. NUMBER OF ENTERPRISES a/ (NUMBER) 1981	1982	1983	1984	1985	2. AVERAGE NUMBER OF EMPLOYEES a/ (NUMBER) 1981	1982	1983	1984	1985	ISIC
210	Coal mining		...	...	...	...	...	...	...	...	...	...	210
220	Petroleum and gas		...	...	...	...	...	...	...	...	...	...	220
230	Metal ore mining		...	...	...	...	...	...	...	...	...	...	230
290	Other mining		...	...	...	...	...	...	...	...	...	...	290
2	Mining, quarrying .		...	...	...	...	...	...	...	...	...	...	2
311/2	Food products					...	...				...	...	311/2
313	Beverages		[13	17	15]	...	...	[1346	1509	1450]	...	...	313
314	Tobacco					...	...				...	...	314
321	Textiles	b/	4	4	4	...	...	670	694	723	...	...	321
3211	Spinning,weaving etc..		...	...	...	...	...	...	...	...	...	...	3211
322	Wearing apparel	b/	...	...	...	...	...	...	...	...	...	...	322
323	Leather and products ...	b/	...	...	...	...	...	...	...	...	...	...	323
324	Footwear		-	-	-	...	...	-	-	-	...	...	324
331	Wood products		-	-	-	...	...	-	-	-	...	...	331
332	Furniture, fixtures	c/	[4	4	11]	...	...	[278	241	2679]	...	...	332
341	Paper and products					...	...				...	...	341
3411	Pulp,paper etc.		...	...	...	...	...	...	...	...	...	...	3411
342	Printing,publishing	c/	...	...	...	...	...	...	...	...	...	...	342
351	Industrial chemicals ...	d/	5	5	5	...	...	225	216	209	...	...	351
3511	Basic excl fertilizers		...	...	...	...	...	...	...	...	...	...	3511
3513	Synthetic resins etc .		...	...	...	...	...	...	...	...	...	...	3513
352	Other chemical products.	d/	...	...	...	...	...	...	...	...	...	...	352
3522	Drugs and medicines ..		...	...	...	...	...	...	...	...	...	...	3522
353	Petroleum refineries ...		-	-	-	...	...	-	-	-	...	...	353
354	Petroleum,coal products.		-	-	-	...	...	-	-	-	...	...	354
355	Rubber products		-	-	-	...	...	-	-	-	...	...	355
356	Plastic products n.e.c..		-	-	-	...	...	-	-	-	...	...	356
361	Pottery,china etc		-	-	-	...	...	-	-	-	...	...	361
362	Glass and products		-	-	-	...	...	-	-	-	...	...	362
369	Non-metal products n.e.c		-	-	-	...	...	-	-	-	...	...	369
371	Iron and steel		-	-	-	...	...	-	-	-	...	...	371
372	Non-ferrous metals		-	-	-	...	...	-	-	-	...	...	372
381	Metal products	e/	[8	8	4]	...	...	[438	387	214]	...	...	381
382	Machinery n.e.c.					...	...				...	...	382
3825	Office,computing etc..		...	...	...	...	...	...	...	...	...	...	3825
383	Electrical machinery ...	e/	...	...	...	...	...	...	...	...	...	...	383
3832	Radio,television etc..		...	...	...	...	...	...	...	...	...	...	3832
384	Transport equipment	e/	...	...	...	...	...	...	...	...	...	...	384
3841	Shipbuilding, repair..		...	...	...	...	...	...	...	...	...	...	3841
3843	Motor vehicles		...	...	...	...	...	...	...	...	...	...	3843
385	Professional goods		-	-	-	...	...	-	-	-	...	...	385
390	Other industries		4	8	8	...	...	167	308	320	...	...	390
3	Manufacturing		38	46	47	...	...	3124	3355	5595	...	...	3
410	Electricity,gas,steam ..		...	...	...	...	...	...	...	...	...	...	410
4101	Electricity		...	...	...	...	...	...	...	...	...	...	4101
420	Water works and supply .		...	...	...	...	...	...	...	...	...	...	420
4	Electricity,gas etc		2	2	2	...	...	853	777	779	...	...	4
2-4	All industry		...	...	...	...	...	...	...	...	...	...	2-4

a/ Enterprises keeping modern accounting records.
b/ Major groups 322 and 323 are included in 321.
c/ Major group 342 is included in 332 and 341 combined.
d/ Major group 352 is included in 351.
e/ Major groups 383 and 384 are included in 381 and 382 combined.

ISIC	INDUSTRY		3. WAGES AND SALARIES OF EMPLOYEES a/ (MILLION FRANCS) 1981	1982	1983	1984	1985	4. AVERAGE NUMBER OF OPERATIVES a/ (NUMBER) 1981	1982	1983	1984	1985	ISIC
210	Coal mining		...	...	...	...	...	...	...	...	...	...	210
220	Petroleum and gas		...	...	...	...	...	...	...	...	...	...	220
230	Metal ore mining		...	...	...	...	...	...	...	...	...	...	230
290	Other mining		...	...	...	...	...	...	...	...	...	...	290
2	Mining, quarrying .		...	...	...	...	...	...	...	...	...	...	2
311/2	Food products					...	...				...	...	311/2
313	Beverages		[1073	1347	1706]	...	...	[1053	911	954]	...	...	313
314	Tobacco					...	...				...	...	314
321	Textiles	b/	791	705	1138	...	...	608	610	610	...	...	321
3211	Spinning,weaving etc..		...	...	...	...	...	...	...	...	...	...	3211
322	Wearing apparel	b/	...	...	...	...	...	...	...	...	...	...	322
323	Leather and products ...	b/	...	...	...	...	...	...	...	...	...	...	323
324	Footwear		-	-	-	...	...	-	-	-	...	...	324
331	Wood products		-	-	-	...	...	-	-	-	...	...	331
332	Furniture, fixtures	c/	[208	179	1846]	...	...	[242	187	2342]	...	...	332
341	Paper and products					...	...				...	...	341
3411	Pulp,paper etc.		...	...	...	...	...	...	...	...	...	...	3411
342	Printing,publishing	c/	...	...	...	...	...	...	...	...	...	...	342
351	Industrial chemicals ...	d/	220	232	329	...	...	132	123	121	...	...	351
3511	Basic excl fertilizers		...	...	...	...	...	...	...	...	...	...	3511
3513	Synthetic resins etc .		...	...	...	...	...	...	...	...	...	...	3513
352	Other chemical products.	d/	...	...	...	...	...	...	...	...	...	...	352
3522	Drugs and medicines ..		...	...	...	...	...	...	...	...	...	...	3522
353	Petroleum refineries ...		-	-	-	...	...	-	-	-	...	...	353
354	Petroleum,coal products.		-	-	-	...	...	-	-	-	...	...	354
355	Rubber products		-	-	-	...	...	-	-	-	...	...	355
356	Plastic products n.e.c..		-	-	-	...	...	-	-	-	...	...	356
361	Pottery,china etc		-	-	-	...	...	-	-	-	...	...	361
362	Glass and products		-	-	-	...	...	-	-	-	...	...	362
369	Non-metal products n.e.c		-	-	-	...	...	-	-	-	...	...	369
371	Iron and steel		-	-	-	...	...	-	-	-	...	...	371
372	Non-ferrous metals		-	-	-	...	...	-	-	-	...	...	372
381	Metal products	e/	[295	298	229]	...	...	[380	341	175]	...	...	381
382	Machinery n.e.c.					...	...				...	...	382
3825	Office,computing etc..		...	...	...	...	...	...	...	...	...	...	3825
383	Electrical machinery ...	e/	...	...	...	...	...	...	...	...	...	...	383
3832	Radio,television etc..		...	...	...	...	...	...	...	...	...	...	3832
384	Transport equipment	e/	...	...	...	...	...	...	...	...	...	...	384
3841	Shipbuilding, repair..		...	...	...	...	...	...	...	...	...	...	3841
3843	Motor vehicles		...	...	...	...	...	...	...	...	...	...	3843
385	Professional goods		-	-	-	...	...	-	-	-	...	...	385
390	Other industries		126	278	579	...	...	125	241	209	...	...	390
3	Manufacturing		2713	3039	5827	...	...	2540	2413	4411	...	...	3
410	Electricity,gas,steam ..		...	...	...	...	...	...	...	...	...	...	410
4101	Electricity		...	...	...	...	...	...	...	...	...	...	4101
420	Water works and supply .		...	...	...	...	...	...	...	...	...	...	420
4	Electricity,gas etc		719	736	946	...	...	405	123	133	...	...	4
2-4	All industry		...	...	...	...	...	...	...	...	...	...	2-4

a/ Enterprises keeping modern accounting records.
b/ Major groups 322 and 323 are included in 321.
c/ Major group 342 is included in 332 and 341 combined.
d/ Major group 352 is included in 351.
e/ Major groups 383 and 384 are included in 381 and 382 combined.

ISIC	INDUSTRY		5. WAGES AND SALARIES OF OPERATIVES a/ (MILLION FRANCS) 1981	1982	1983	1984	1985	6. OUTPUT IN FACTOR VALUES a/ (MILLION FRANCS) 1981	1982	1983	1984	1985	ISIC
210	Coal mining		...	...	...	...	...	...	...	...	...	...	210
220	Petroleum and gas		...	...	...	...	...	...	...	...	...	...	220
230	Metal ore mining		...	...	...	...	...	...	...	...	...	...	230
290	Other mining		...	...	...	...	...	...	...	...	...	...	290
2	Mining, quarrying		...	...	...	...	...	...	...	...	...	...	2
311/2	Food products					...	...				...	...	311/2
313	Beverages		[363	322	412]	...	...	[7371	9408	9161]	...	...	313
314	Tobacco					...	...				...	...	314
321	Textiles	b/	521	446	551	...	...	4896	3727	7065	...	...	321
3211	Spinning, weaving etc.		...	...	...	...	...	...	...	...	...	...	3211
322	Wearing apparel	b/	...	...	...	...	...	...	...	...	...	...	322
323	Leather and products	b/	...	...	...	...	...	...	...	...	...	...	323
324	Footwear		-	-	-	...	...	-	-	-	...	...	324
331	Wood products		-	-	-	...	...	-	-	-	...	...	331
332	Furniture, fixtures	c/	[118	66	668]	...	...	[631	508	9982]	...	...	332
341	Paper and products					...	...				...	...	341
3411	Pulp, paper etc.		...	...	...	...	...	...	...	...	...	...	3411
342	Printing, publishing	c/	...	...	...	...	...	...	...	...	...	...	342
351	Industrial chemicals	d/	45	44	52	...	...	1274	1317	1252	...	...	351
3511	Basic excl fertilizers		...	...	...	...	...	...	...	...	...	...	3511
3513	Synthetic resins etc		...	...	...	...	...	...	...	...	...	...	3513
352	Other chemical products	d/	...	...	...	...	...	...	...	...	...	...	352
3522	Drugs and medicines		...	...	...	...	...	...	...	...	...	...	3522
353	Petroleum refineries		-	-	-	...	...	-	-	-	...	...	353
354	Petroleum, coal products		-	-	-	...	...	-	-	-	...	...	354
355	Rubber products		-	-	-	...	...	-	-	-	...	...	355
356	Plastic products n.e.c.		-	-	-	...	...	-	-	-	...	...	356
361	Pottery, china etc		-	-	-	...	...	-	-	-	...	...	361
362	Glass and products		-	-	-	...	...	-	-	-	...	...	362
369	Non-metal products n.e.c		-	-	-	...	...	-	-	-	...	...	369
371	Iron and steel		-	-	-	...	...	-	-	-	...	...	371
372	Non-ferrous metals		-	-	-	...	...	-	-	-	...	...	372
381	Metal products	e/	[156	148	53]	...	...	[2136	2362	2030]	...	...	381
382	Machinery n.e.c.					...	...				...	...	382
3825	Office, computing etc.		...	...	...	...	...	...	...	...	...	...	3825
383	Electrical machinery	e/	...	...	...	...	...	...	...	...	...	...	383
3832	Radio, television etc.		...	...	...	...	...	...	...	...	...	...	3832
384	Transport equipment	e/	...	...	...	...	...	...	...	...	...	...	384
3841	Shipbuilding, repair		...	...	...	...	...	...	...	...	...	...	3841
3843	Motor vehicles		...	...	...	...	...	...	...	...	...	...	3843
385	Professional goods		-	-	-	...	...	-	-	-	...	...	385
390	Other industries		36	63	119	...	...	982	1823	3706	...	...	390
3	Manufacturing		1239	1089	1855	...	...	17290	19145	33196	...	...	3
410	Electricity, gas, steam		...	...	...	...	...	...	...	...	...	...	410
4101	Electricity		...	...	...	...	...	...	...	...	...	...	4101
420	Water works and supply		...	...	...	...	...	...	...	...	...	...	420
4	Electricity, gas etc		65	84	90	...	...	1864	2307	2961	...	...	4
2-4	All industry		...	...	...	...	...	...	...	...	...	...	2-4

a/ Enterprises keeping modern accounting records.
b/ Major groups 322 and 323 are included in 321.
c/ Major group 342 is included in 332 and 341 combined.
d/ Major group 352 is included in 351.
e/ Major groups 383 and 384 are included in 381 and 382 combined.

ISIC	INDUSTRY		7. VALUE ADDED IN FACTOR VALUES a/ (MILLION FRANCS) 1981	1982	1983	1984	1985	8. GROSS FIXED CAPITAL FORMATION TOTAL a/ (MILLION FRANCS) 1981	1982	1983	1984	1985	ISIC
210	Coal mining		...	...	...	...	...	...	...	...	...	...	210
220	Petroleum and gas		...	...	...	...	...	...	...	...	...	...	220
230	Metal ore mining		...	...	...	...	...	...	...	...	...	...	230
290	Other mining		...	...	...	...	...	...	...	...	...	...	290
2	Mining, quarrying .		...	...	...	...	...	...	...	...	...	...	2
311/2	Food products		[		]	...	...	[		]	...	...	311/2
313	Beverages		2975	3051	3203	...	...	552	719	283	...	...	313
314	Tobacco		[		]	...	...	[		]	...	...	314
321	Textiles	b/	1345	-174	1482	...	...	65	77	445	...	...	321
3211	Spinning,weaving etc..		...	...	...	...	...	...	...	...	...	...	3211
322	Wearing apparel	b/	...	...	...	...	...	...	...	...	...	...	322
323	Leather and products ...	b/	...	...	...	...	...	...	...	...	...	...	323
324	Footwear		-	-	-	...	...	-	-	-	...	...	324
331	Wood products		-	-	-	...	...	-	-	-	...	...	331
332	Furniture, fixtures	c/	[363	280	3829]	...	...	[21	23	721]	...	...	332
341	Paper and products					...	...				...	...	341
3411	Pulp,paper etc.		...	...	...	...	...	...	...	...	...	...	3411
342	Printing,publishing	c/	...	...	...	...	...	...	...	...	...	...	342
351	Industrial chemicals ...	d/	543	504	467	...	...	26	30	24	...	...	351
3511	Basic excl fertilizers		...	...	...	...	...	...	...	...	...	...	3511
3513	Synthetic resins etc .		...	...	...	...	...	...	...	...	...	...	3513
352	Other chemical products.	d/	...	...	...	...	...	...	...	...	...	...	352
3522	Drugs and medicines ..		...	...	...	...	...	...	...	...	...	...	3522
353	Petroleum refineries ...		-	-	-	...	...	-	-	-	...	...	353
354	Petroleum,coal products.		-	-	-	...	...	-	-	-	...	...	354
355	Rubber products		-	-	-	...	...	-	-	-	...	...	355
356	Plastic products n.e.c..		-	-	-	...	...	-	-	-	...	...	356
361	Pottery,china etc		-	-	-	...	...	-	-	-	...	...	361
362	Glass and products		-	-	-	...	...	-	-	-	...	...	362
369	Non-metal products n.e.c		-	-	-	...	...	-	-	-	...	...	369
371	Iron and steel		-	-	-	...	...	-	-	-	...	...	371
372	Non-ferrous metals		-	-	-	...	...	-	-	-	...	...	372
381	Metal products	e/	[509	506	457]	...	...	[40	-7	20]	...	...	381
382	Machinery n.e.c.					...	...				...	...	382
3825	Office,computing etc..		...	...	...	...	...	...	...	...	...	...	3825
383	Electrical machinery ...	e/	...	...	...	...	...	...	...	...	...	...	383
3832	Radio,television etc..		...	...	...	...	...	...	...	...	...	...	3832
384	Transport equipment	e/	...	...	...	...	...	...	...	...	...	...	384
3841	Shipbuilding, repair..		...	...	...	...	...	...	...	...	...	...	3841
3843	Motor vehicles		...	...	...	...	...	...	...	...	...	...	3843
385	Professional goods		-	-	-	...	...	-	-	-	...	...	385
390	Other industries		245	478	1018	...	...	366	1325	860	...	...	390
3	Manufacturing		5980	4645	10456	...	...	1070	2167	2353	...	...	3
410	Electricity,gas,steam ..		...	...	...	...	...	...	...	...	...	...	410
4101	Electricity		...	...	...	...	...	...	...	...	...	...	4101
420	Water works and supply .		...	...	...	...	...	...	...	...	...	...	420
4	Electricity,gas etc		1188	1495	1338	...	...	212	337	492	...	...	4
2-4	All industry		...	...	...	...	...	...	...	...	...	...	2-4

a/ Enterprises keeping modern accounting records.
b/ Major groups 322 and 323 are included in 321.
c/ Major group 342 is included in 332 and 341 combined.
d/ Major group 352 is included in 351.
e/ Major groups 383 and 384 are included in 381 and 382 combined.

CHILE

The information in the tables, except for the indexes, is based on the reply to the United Nations Questionnaire on General Industrial Statistics from the Instituto Nacional de Estadisticas, Santiago. The concepts, definitions and classification by branches of industry are generally in accordance with United Nations standards.

The estimates are derived from the annual industrial survey conducted by the Instituto Nacional de Estadisticas. The survey covers establishments with 50 or more persons engaged on a complete enumeration basis. The inquiry is carried out by enumerators of the Instituto Nacional de Estadisticas. The estimates are compiled according to the present version of ISIC.

The number of establishments represents the number estimated by taking account of the number of new establishments and those closed down during the year. Estimates of employment relate to averages of four periods (February, May, August and November) during the reference year. Wages and salaries include commissions, overtime payments, bonuses, rewards, profit shares paid to employees and other payments directly related with the work of employees. Employers' contributions to the social security fund are excluded.

Output is the sum of the value of sales of products, net change between the beginning and the end of the year in the value of work in progress and finished goods, value of goods sold in the same condition as purchased, value of work done for others, value of electricity sold and value of fixed assets produced by the establishment for its own use. Value added is the difference between the value of output and the value of inputs (i.e., the cost of materials, supplies, fuels, and electricity purchased, cost of goods sold in the same condition as purchased, value of work done by others and net change between the beginning and the end of the year in the value of stocks of materials, fuels etc.). Valuation of output and value added is in producers' prices.

Gross fixed capital formation represents the sum of purchase values of fixed capital assets, new and used, less the value of assets sold plus the value of improvements of land and the value of new assets produced and developments made by workers of the establishments for their own use.

The indexes of industrial production are compiled by the Instituto Nacional de Estadisticas and provided in response to the United Nations Questionnaire on Indexes of Industrial Production. The indexes cover, in principle, all establishments employing 10 or more persons.

Related national publication:
Industrias Manufactureras (annual), published by the Instituto Nacional de Estadisticas, Santiago.

ISIC	INDUSTRY	1. NUMBER OF ESTABLISHMENTS a/ (NUMBER)					2. AVERAGE NUMBER OF PERSONS ENGAGED a/ (THOUSANDS)					ISIC
		1981	1982	1983	1984	1985	1981	1982	1983	1984	1985	
210	Coal mining	...	...	...	...	...	...	...	...	...	...	210
220	Petroleum and gas	...	...	...	...	...	...	...	...	...	...	220
230	Metal ore mining	...	...	...	...	...	...	...	...	...	...	230
290	Other mining	...	...	...	...	...	...	...	...	...	...	290
2	Mining, quarrying .	...	...	...	...	...	...	...	...	...	...	2
311/2	Food products	233	214	227	257	...	38.38	32.69	36.57	40.30	...	311/2
313	Beverages	66	61	58	56	...	7.97	7.29	7.09	6.66	...	313
314	Tobacco	3	3	2	2	...	1.10	0.78	0.57	0.62	...	314
321	Textiles	100	68	67	68	...	19.78	13.13	14.47	15.91	...	321
3211	Spinning,weaving etc..	57	44	42	42	...	15.04	10.56	11.66	13.12	...	3211
322	Wearing apparel	81	66	56	69	...	10.47	7.79	6.23	8.07	...	322
323	Leather and products ...	16	16	12	12	...	1.80	1.61	1.26	1.28	...	323
324	Footwear	33	29	30	38	...	5.47	4.64	4.75	6.05	...	324
331	Wood products	86	64	80	81	...	12.08	7.60	9.72	11.83	...	331
332	Furniture, fixtures	22	21	18	21	...	2.63	2.15	1.53	1.96	...	332
341	Paper and products	22	21	20	22	...	6.20	5.02	5.21	5.58	...	341
3411	Pulp,paper etc.	10	10	9	8	...	4.63	3.99	3.82	3.71	...	3411
342	Printing,publishing	41	38	38	36	...	7.58	6.98	6.41	5.91	...	342
351	Industrial chemicals ...	17	15	15	15	...	1.75	1.51	1.55	1.96	...	351
3511	Basic excl fertilizers	8	8	9	10	...	0.76	0.80	0.94	1.40	...	3511
3513	Synthetic resins etc .	8	6	4	3	...	0.73	0.47	0.33	0.24	...	3513
352	Other chemical products.	70	67	68	65	...	10.74	10.08	9.50	9.70	...	352
3522	Drugs and medicines ..	32	33	33	31	...	4.87	4.93	4.65	4.51	...	3522
353	Petroleum refineries ...	3	4	3	5	...	1.66	1.37	1.27	1.37	...	353
354	Petroleum,coal products.	3	3	3	5	...	0.40	0.39	0.36	0.50	...	354
355	Rubber products	13	12	13	17	...	3.05	2.24	2.21	2.72	...	355
356	Plastic products n.e.c..	36	30	26	36	...	4.32	3.21	3.05	4.07	...	356
361	Pottery,china etc	2	3	5	5	...	0.34	0.73	1.25	1.57	...	361
362	Glass and products	11	7	7	9	...	1.68	0.96	0.89	1.13	...	362
369	Non-metal products n.e.c	35	25	23	27	...	5.04	3.51	3.17	3.51	...	369
371	Iron and steel	16	17	17	17	...	6.59	6.40	5.97	6.21	...	371
372	Non-ferrous metals	18	15	14	16	...	8.51	7.85	7.78	7.63	...	372
381	Metal products	110	88	72	97	...	12.89	10.93	8.27	10.61	...	381
382	Machinery n.e.c.	47	31	28	31	...	10.47	6.49	7.01	7.26	...	382
3825	Office,computing etc..	2	2	1	-	...	0.32	0.31	0.22	-	...	3825
383	Electrical machinery ...	29	24	21	23	...	4.72	2.98	2.66	2.88	...	383
3832	Radio,television etc..	4	3	2	2	...	1.27	0.57	0.43	0.43	...	3832
384	Transport equipment	35	25	19	21	...	5.74	3.62	2.47	3.14	...	384
3841	Shipbuilding, repair..	3	3	3	5	...	0.44	0.35	0.38	0.79	...	3841
3843	Motor vehicles	24	15	12	10	...	3.97	2.18	1.35	1.47	...	3843
385	Professional goods	4	4	4	5	...	0.34	0.27	0.26	0.30	...	385
390	Other industries	10	4	4	6	...	0.93	0.27	0.30	0.51	...	390
3	Manufacturing	1162	975	950	1062	...	192.63	152.49	151.78	169.24	...	3
410	Electricity,gas,steam ..	...	...	...	...	...	...	...	...	...	...	410
4101	Electricity	...	...	...	...	...	...	...	...	...	...	4101
420	Water works and supply .	...	...	...	...	...	...	...	...	...	...	420
4	Electricity,gas etc	...	...	...	...	...	...	...	...	...	...	4
2-4	All industry	...	...	...	...	...	...	...	...	...	...	2-4

a/ Establishments with 50 or more persons engaged.

ISIC	INDUSTRY	3. AVERAGE NUMBER OF EMPLOYEES a/ (THOUSANDS)					4. WAGES AND SALARIES OF EMPLOYEES a/ (MILLION PESOS)					ISIC
		1981	1982	1983	1984	1985	1981	1982	1983	1984	1985	
210	Coal mining	...	...	...	...	...	...	...	...	...	...	210
220	Petroleum and gas	...	...	...	...	...	...	...	...	...	...	220
230	Metal ore mining	...	...	...	...	...	...	...	...	...	...	230
290	Other mining	...	...	...	...	...	...	...	...	...	...	290
2	Mining, quarrying .	...	...	...	...	...	...	...	...	...	...	2
311/2	Food products	38.26	32.57	36.43	40.12	...	11377	10727	12737	16140	...	311/2
313	Beverages	7.95	7.27	7.07	6.65	...	2647	2643	3035	3332	...	313
314	Tobacco	1.10	0.78	0.57	0.62	...	675	501	492	610	...	314
321	Textiles	19.70	13.07	14.41	15.86	...	4357	3248	3806	4557	...	321
3211	Spinning,weaving etc..	15.02	10.54	11.64	13.09	...	3474	2699	3155	3907	...	3211
322	Wearing apparel	10.37	7.69	6.13	7.95	...	1995	1501	1357	2041	...	322
323	Leather and products ...	1.79	1.60	1.25	1.27	...	451	423	450	456	...	323
324	Footwear	5.43	4.61	4.71	6.01	...	1091	1048	1195	1568	...	324
331	Wood products	12.00	7.53	9.64	11.75	...	2033	1515	1945	2693	...	331
332	Furniture, fixtures	2.60	2.12	1.52	1.93	...	520	460	320	434	...	332
341	Paper and products	6.20	5.02	5.20	5.57	...	2769	2319	2851	3487	...	341
3411	Pulp,paper etc.	4.63	3.99	3.82	3.71	...	2251	1900	2295	2545	...	3411
342	Printing,publishing	7.56	6.97	6.40	5.90	...	3136	3135	3055	3650	...	342
351	Industrial chemicals ...	1.75	1.51	1.55	1.95	...	799	839	906	1368	...	351
3511	Basic excl fertilizers	0.75	0.80	0.94	1.40	...	359	407	498	872	...	3511
3513	Synthetic resins etc .	0.72	0.47	0.33	0.24	...	293	287	220	240	...	3513
352	Other chemical products.	10.73	10.07	9.49	9.69	...	5209	5508	6647	7730	...	352
3522	Drugs and medicines ..	4.87	4.93	4.64	4.50	...	2542	2654	3367	3879	...	3522
353	Petroleum refineries ...	1.66	1.37	1.27	1.37	...	1036	996	1272	1618	...	353
354	Petroleum,coal products.	0.40	0.39	0.36	0.50	...	159	168	153	242	...	354
355	Rubber products	3.03	2.22	2.20	2.70	...	1085	819	935	1249	...	355
356	Plastic products n.e.c..	4.30	3.20	3.04	4.05	...	1169	872	955	1340	...	356
361	Pottery,china etc	0.34	0.73	1.25	1.57	...	87	109	298	404	...	361
362	Glass and products	1.67	0.96	0.88	1.12	...	552	352	368	513	...	362
369	Non-metal products n.e.c	5.01	3.49	3.15	3.50	...	1666	1478	1569	1967	...	369
371	Iron and steel	6.59	6.40	5.97	6.20	...	2888	3285	3689	4550	...	371
372	Non-ferrous metals	8.51	7.85	7.78	7.63	...	4243	4124	5298	6242	...	372
381	Metal products	12.79	10.86	8.22	10.53	...	3519	3162	2922	4027	...	381
382	Machinery n.e.c.	10.45	6.47	6.99	7.25	...	4155	3376	4425	5227	...	382
3825	Office,computing etc..	0.32	0.31	0.22	-	...	171	179	147	-	...	3825
383	Electrical machinery ...	4.70	2.96	2.66	2.87	...	1970	1416	1533	2027	...	383
3832	Radio,television etc..	1.26	0.57	0.43	0.43	...	505	205	186	295	...	3832
384	Transport equipment	5.71	3.60	2.45	3.12	...	1651	1078	877	1459	...	384
3841	Shipbuilding, repair..	0.44	0.35	0.37	0.78	...	118	124	163	455	...	3841
3843	Motor vehicles	3.95	2.16	1.33	1.45	...	1264	705	494	659	...	3843
385	Professional goods	0.34	0.26	0.26	0.30	...	108	99	120	109	...	385
390	Other industries	0.92	0.27	0.30	0.50	...	301	81	95	150	...	390
3	Manufacturing	191.86	151.84	151.15	168.48	...	61648	55282	63305	79190	...	3
410	Electricity,gas,steam ..	...	...	...	...	...	...	...	...	...	...	410
4101	Electricity	...	...	...	...	...	...	...	...	...	...	4101
420	Water works and supply .	...	...	...	...	...	...	...	...	...	...	420
4	Electricity,gas etc	...	...	...	...	...	...	...	...	...	...	4
2-4	All industry	...	...	...	...	...	...	...	...	...	...	2-4

a/ Establishments with 50 or more persons engaged.

CHILE

ISIC	INDUSTRY	5. AVERAGE NUMBER OF OPERATIVES a/ (THOUSANDS)					6. WAGES AND SALARIES OF OPERATIVES a/ (MILLION PESOS)					ISIC
		1981	1982	1983	1984	1985	1981	1982	1983	1984	1985	
210	Coal mining	...	...	...	...	...	...	...	...	...	...	210
220	Petroleum and gas	...	...	...	...	...	...	...	...	...	...	220
230	Metal ore mining	...	...	...	...	...	...	...	...	...	...	230
290	Other mining	...	...	...	...	...	...	...	...	...	...	290
2	Mining, quarrying .	...	...	...	...	...	...	...	...	...	...	2
311/2	Food products	28.69	24.09	27.26	30.38	...	5354	4807	5859	7111	...	311/2
313	Beverages	5.25	4.73	4.59	4.41	...	951	935	1059	1092	...	313
314	Tobacco	0.64	0.45	0.31	0.38	...	239	138	158	184	...	314
321	Textiles	14.79	9.63	10.67	12.14	...	2117	1462	1826	2290	...	321
3211	Spinning,weaving etc..	11.11	7.65	8.51	9.93	...	1594	1162	1468	1909	...	3211
322	Wearing apparel	8.45	6.11	4.99	6.52	...	1249	854	808	1232	...	322
323	Leather and products ...	1.36	1.23	0.95	1.02	...	237	214	250	281	...	323
324	Footwear	4.59	3.83	3.98	5.01	...	667	626	742	1022	...	324
331	Wood products	10.49	6.30	8.23	10.37	...	1329	931	1187	1711	...	331
332	Furniture, fixtures	2.16	1.74	1.27	1.58	...	320	261	192	255	...	332
341	Paper and products	3.34	2.81	3.46	3.88	...	861	805	1078	1252	...	341
3411	Pulp,paper etc.	2.20	2.08	2.43	2.46	...	589	611	810	795	...	3411
342	Printing,publishing	4.80	4.35	4.12	3.58	...	1196	1317	1307	1176	...	342
351	Industrial chemicals ...	1.18	0.96	0.96	1.30	...	352	361	366	621	...	351
3511	Basic excl fertilizers	0.54	0.56	0.61	0.97	...	167	199	202	409	...	3511
3513	Synthetic resins etc .	0.49	0.28	0.19	0.15	...	114	99	85	103	...	3513
352	Other chemical products.	5.68	5.49	4.88	5.03	...	1398	1451	1578	1657	...	352
3522	Drugs and medicines ..	2.34	2.66	2.22	2.13	...	601	681	717	794	...	3522
353	Petroleum refineries ...	1.14	0.89	0.82	0.84	...	538	390	614	634	...	353
354	Petroleum,coal products.	0.28	0.25	0.25	0.38	...	63	53	54	91	...	354
355	Rubber products	2.19	1.66	1.63	2.12	...	493	387	437	593	...	355
356	Plastic products n.e.c..	3.08	2.21	2.16	3.03	...	535	369	401	636	...	356
361	Pottery,china etc	0.25	0.60	0.95	1.23	...	43	54	151	219	...	361
362	Glass and products	1.17	0.64	0.63	0.83	...	227	155	133	248	...	362
369	Non-metal products n.e.c	4.00	2.65	2.23	2.58	...	889	782	571	759	...	369
371	Iron and steel	4.95	4.70	4.42	4.80	...	1639	1791	2045	2736	...	371
372	Non-ferrous metals	5.41	5.26	5.08	5.32	...	1880	2063	2682	3022	...	372
381	Metal products	9.55	7.80	5.92	7.72	...	1780	1456	1394	1930	...	381
382	Machinery n.e.c.	7.01	4.12	4.36	4.66	...	1877	1631	2160	2355	...	382
3825	Office,computing etc..	0.19	0.18	0.12	-	...	69	77	60	-	...	3825
383	Electrical machinery ...	2.93	1.93	1.67	1.85	...	846	551	633	796	...	383
3832	Radio,television etc..	0.74	0.33	0.23	0.25	...	218	74	65	135	...	3832
384	Transport equipment	4.30	2.62	1.78	2.28	...	878	500	432	749	...	384
3841	Shipbuilding, repair..	0.36	0.27	0.29	0.59	...	78	54	77	241	...	3841
3843	Motor vehicles	2.85	1.45	0.88	1.02	...	619	278	184	275	...	3843
385	Professional goods	0.25	0.19	0.18	0.21	...	57	43	53	59	...	385
390	Other industries	0.69	0.18	0.22	0.39	...	137	39	45	68	...	390
3	Manufacturing	138.62	107.42	107.97	123.84	...	28152	24426	28215	34779	...	3
410	Electricity,gas,steam ..	...	...	...	...	...	...	...	...	...	...	410
4101	Electricity	...	...	...	...	...	...	...	...	...	...	4101
420	Water works and supply .	...	...	...	...	...	...	...	...	...	...	420
4	Electricity,gas etc	...	...	...	...	...	...	...	...	...	...	4
2-4	All industry	...	...	...	...	...	...	...	...	...	...	2-4

a/ Establishments with 50 or more persons engaged.

ISIC	INDUSTRY	7. QUANTITY OF ELECTRICITY CONSUMED a/ (MILLION KWH)					8. OUTPUT IN PRODUCERS' PRICES a/ (BILLION PESOS)					ISIC
		1981	1982	1983	1984	1985	1981	1982	1983	1984	1985	
210	Coal mining	...	...	...	...	...	...	...	...	...	...	210
220	Petroleum and gas	...	...	...	...	...	...	...	...	...	...	220
230	Metal ore mining	...	...	...	...	...	...	...	...	...	...	230
290	Other mining	...	...	...	...	...	...	...	...	...	...	290
2	Mining, quarrying .	...	...	...	...	...	...	...	...	...	...	2
311/2	Food products	277	269	323	376	...	107.3	114.0	154.5	231.9	...	311/2
313	Beverages	49	43	43	31	...	26.2	28.6	29.7	36.9	...	313
314	Tobacco	6	6	5	6	...	15.2	17.8	24.4	29.9	...	314
321	Textiles	120	96	116	135	...	19.7	14.6	23.6	35.5	...	321
3211	Spinning,weaving etc..	111	89	108	129	...	14.4	11.7	19.2	30.7	...	3211
322	Wearing apparel	12	8	7	14	...	12.2	9.6	10.6	16.3	...	322
323	Leather and products ...	9	8	9	9	...	3.4	2.7	3.9	6.2	...	323
324	Footwear	8	6	7	9	...	7.6	6.4	8.1	11.5	...	324
331	Wood products	56	45	65	74	...	14.5	12.4	18.7	27.3	...	331
332	Furniture, fixtures	6	5	4	4	...	3.3	2.7	2.0	2.9	...	332
341	Paper and products	727	742	833	879	...	24.7	23.5	40.9	65.2	...	341
3411	Pulp,paper etc.	711	732	817	852	...	20.7	20.2	34.0	51.0	...	3411
342	Printing,publishing	16	26	27	22	...	18.9	15.4	17.3	21.9	...	342
351	Industrial chemicals ...	131	31	133	222	...	7.5	7.8	12.1	16.7	...	351
3511	Basic excl fertilizers	97	15	105	193	...	3.3	4.1	6.0	8.2	...	3511
3513	Synthetic resins etc .	27	12	22	23	...	3.0	2.7	4.1	4.9	...	3513
352	Other chemical products.	28	24	26	31	...	32.1	32.6	41.5	56.7	...	352
3522	Drugs and medicines ..	8	8	8	9	...	12.0	13.1	15.7	19.6	...	3522
353	Petroleum refineries ...	85	49	86	84	...	78.0	71.1	124.1	157.7	...	353
354	Petroleum,coal products.	2	2	2	3	...	1.2	1.1	1.6	2.8	...	354
355	Rubber products	22	13	20	27	...	6.3	4.4	8.7	12.6	...	355
356	Plastic products n.e.c..	30	23	28	37	...	7.0	5.2	7.4	12.3	...	356
361	Pottery,china etc	2	3	10	11	...	0.3	0.5	1.4	2.1	...	361
362	Glass and products	17	11	13	13	...	2.9	1.8	2.6	4.2	...	362
369	Non-metal products n.e.c	221	136	181	170	...	17.1	10.5	15.0	21.2	...	369
371	Iron and steel	442	275	420	409	...	24.1	26.9	39.6	52.1	...	371
372	Non-ferrous metals	815	836	1044	1106	...	84.2	109.9	177.6	228.6	...	372
381	Metal products	43	42	36	48	...	19.2	15.0	19.2	31.9	...	381
382	Machinery n.e.c.	47	28	41	40	...	12.4	9.1	12.2	15.4	...	382
3825	Office,computing etc..	-	-	-	-	...	0.5	0.3	0.2	-	...	3825
383	Electrical machinery ...	13	9	11	12	...	9.2	4.9	6.5	10.7	...	383
3832	Radio,television etc..	2	1	1	1	...	2.5	1.0	1.2	2.8	...	3832
384	Transport equipment	19	19	18	16	...	18.4	8.1	6.3	13.0	...	384
3841	Shipbuilding, repair..	1	1	1	4	...	0.5	0.5	0.9	2.0	...	3841
3843	Motor vehicles	12	9	8	8	...	17.1	7.1	5.0	10.0	...	3843
385	Professional goods	1	1	1	1	...	0.5	0.4	0.6	0.7	...	385
390	Other industries	2	-	-	1	...	1.1	0.3	0.5	0.8	...	390
3	Manufacturing	3206	2756	3509	3790	...	574.5	557.3	810.6	1124.9	...	3
410	Electricity,gas,steam ..	...	...	...	...	...	...	...	...	...	...	410
4101	Electricity	...	...	...	...	...	...	...	...	...	...	4101
420	Water works and supply .	...	...	...	...	...	...	...	...	...	...	420
4	Electricity,gas etc	...	...	...	...	...	...	...	...	...	...	4
2-4	All industry	...	...	...	...	...	...	...	...	...	...	2-4

a/ Establishments with 50 or more persons engaged.

ISIC	INDUSTRY	9. VALUE ADDED IN PRODUCERS' PRICES a/ (MILLION PESOS)					10. GROSS FIXED CAPITAL FORMATION TOTAL a/ (MILLION PESOS)					ISIC
		1981	1982	1983	1984	1985	1981	1982	1983	1984	1985	
210	Coal mining	...	...	...	...	...	...	...	...	...	...	210
220	Petroleum and gas	...	...	...	...	...	...	...	...	...	...	220
230	Metal ore mining	...	...	...	...	...	...	...	...	...	...	230
290	Other mining	...	...	...	...	...	...	...	...	...	...	290
2	Mining, quarrying .	...	...	...	...	...	...	...	...	...	...	2
311/2	Food products	42426	48118	64491	89055	...	4192	3292	3723	5807	...	311/2
313	Beverages	14886	16259	16901	22246	...	1021	556	-52	580	...	313
314	Tobacco	12052	14822	21191	26442	...	326	323	223	160	...	314
321	Textiles	11089	8702	12339	18817	...	251	285	295	907	...	321
3211	Spinning,weaving etc..	8234	6895	10033	16213	...	183	255	233	818	...	3211
322	Wearing apparel	5344	4828	4735	8446	...	214	74	115	378	...	322
323	Leather and products ...	1562	1216	1433	2200	...	77	33	7	118	...	323
324	Footwear	4559	4221	3618	5634	...	147	61	68	504	...	324
331	Wood products	6960	7018	10542	14545	...	438	744	597	673	...	331
332	Furniture, fixtures	1736	1484	1239	1481	...	241	-48	33	35	...	332
341	Paper and products	12780	13383	24746	38138	...	1919	1315	4183	849	...	341
3411	Pulp,paper etc.	11427	11902	21676	32444	...	1803	1256	3952	544	...	3411
342	Printing,publishing	13187	9929	9843	12905	...	1417	1495	398	520	...	342
351	Industrial chemicals ...	3444	4403	5812	7438	...	139	287	201	467	...	351
3511	Basic excl fertilizers	2355	2755	3253	4759	...	126	279	-88	351	...	3511
3513	Synthetic resins etc .	971	1431	2050	1868	...	16	1	22	49	...	3513
352	Other chemical products.	20440	21835	25311	33726	...	793	570	640	912	...	352
3522	Drugs and medicines ..	8768	10027	10866	13626	...	316	95	270	226	...	3522
353	Petroleum refineries ...	18614	16997	25605	34577	...	209	336	377	444	...	353
354	Petroleum,coal products.	639	515	585	777	...	65	66	49	123	...	354
355	Rubber products	2623	2492	4509	5521	...	43	56	78	176	...	355
356	Plastic products n.e.c..	3546	2868	3586	5800	...	514	201	136	363	...	356
361	Pottery,china etc	258	312	763	1345	...	-2	-	44	53	...	361
362	Glass and products	1782	1363	1696	2755	...	402	285	12	421	...	362
369	Non-metal products n.e.c	11114	6698	9196	12445	...	1658	3656	5513	1050	...	369
371	Iron and steel	8121	11949	18738	21797	...	564	326	326	1072	...	371
372	Non-ferrous metals	40674	52276	79888	110371	...	2077	2362	1761	4423	...	372
381	Metal products	10653	8833	10123	15720	...	696	634	480	868	...	381
382	Machinery n.e.c.	5596	4189	5549	6936	...	453	376	677	333	...	382
3825	Office,computing etc..	430	283	183	-	...	5	7	5	-	...	3825
383	Electrical machinery ...	5913	3098	4124	6979	...	298	236	325	426	...	383
3832	Radio,television etc..	1397	516	634	1859	...	8	9	13	16	...	3832
384	Transport equipment	7542	3383	2911	5703	...	189	103	101	201	...	384
3841	Shipbuilding, repair..	336	258	661	1295	...	120	6	11	101	...	3841
3843	Motor vehicles	6867	2835	2097	3761	...	68	96	90	61	...	3843
385	Professional goods	282	279	358	408	...	5	8	4	6	...	385
390	Other industries	535	254	298	413	...	166	1	3	15	...	390
3	Manufacturing	268357	271724	370130	512620	...	18512	17633	20317	21884	...	3
410	Electricity,gas,steam ..	...	...	...	...	...	...	...	...	...	...	410
4101	Electricity	...	...	...	...	...	...	...	...	...	...	4101
420	Water works and supply .	...	...	...	...	...	...	...	...	...	...	420
4	Electricity,gas etc	...	...	...	...	...	...	...	...	...	...	4
2-4	All industry	...	...	...	...	...	...	...	...	...	...	2-4

a/ Establishments with 50 or more persons engaged.

11. INDEX NUMBERS OF INDUSTRIAL PRODUCTION (1980 = 100)

ISIC	INDUSTRY	1976	1977	1978	1979	1981	1982	1983	1984	1985	a/ RATE	ISIC
210	Coal mining	123	128	108	92	84	98	108	131	138	1.3	210
220	Petroleum and gas ...... b/	69	58	52	61	124	128	118	116	107	5.0	220
230	Metal ore mining .... c/	94	97	95	99	103	120	120	126	132	3.8	230
290	Other mining	94	88	84	98	102	90	99	113	79	-1.9	290
2	Mining, quarrying . b/c/	92	94	91	96	108	119	119	125	129	3.8	2
311/2	Food products .... d/	97	93	95	96	106	108	109	126	123	2.7	311/2
313	Beverages	70	84	93	103	108	92	96	97	100	4.0	313
314	Tobacco	84	90	94	95	88	73	73	77	77	-1.0	314
321	Textiles	88	97	104	103	94	69	78	98	105	2.0	321
3211	Spinning,weaving etc..	...	...	...	...	...	...	...	...	...	...	3211
322	Wearing apparel	67	84	81	81	118	64	66	78	84	2.5	322
323	Leather and products ...	124	108	120	92	111	83	83	82	70	-6.2	323
324	Footwear	139	144	140	144	104	86	103	101	96	-4.0	324
331	Wood products .... e/	111	121	104	125	94	75	88	99	94	-1.8	331
332	Furniture, fixtures	76	63	61	87	95	59	49	68	77	0.1	332
341	Paper and products	93	106	102	110	109	91	104	109	115	2.4	341
3411	Pulp,paper etc.	...	...	...	...	...	...	...	...	...	...	3411
342	Printing,publishing	49	46	48	54	100	91	88	90	80	5.6	342
351	Industrial chemicals ...	80	101	94	100	89	70	84	89	91	1.4	351
3511	Basic excl fertilizers	...	...	...	...	...	...	...	...	...	...	3511
3513	Synthetic resins etc .	...	...	...	...	...	...	...	...	...	...	3513
352	Other chemical products.	72	91	95	115	105	95	94	103	98	3.5	352
3522	Drugs and medicines ..	...	...	...	...	...	...	...	...	...	...	3522
353	Petroleum refineries ...	85	88	100	105	95	74	84	84	85	0.0	353
354	Petroleum,coal products.	...	...	...	...	...	...	...	...	...	...	354
355	Rubber products	70	90	71	81	91	62	89	103	99	3.9	355
356	Plastic products n.e.c..	...	...	...	...	...	...	...	...	...	...	356
361	Pottery,china etc	28	30	38	39	65	12	60	115	131	18.7	361
362	Glass and products	91	86	89	106	93	50	83	79	92	0.1	362
369	Non-metal products n.e.c	59	65	72	86	115	64	83	89	92	5.1	369
371	Iron and steel	60	70	75	87	90	60	76	91	90	4.6	371
372	Non-ferrous metals ..... c/	77	75	93	103	99	108	109	114	110	4.0	372
381	Metal products	65	69	99	99	106	83	82	83	90	3.7	381
382	Machinery n.e.c.	61	85	57	75	98	44	37	48	42	-4.1	382
3825	Office,computing etc..	...	...	...	...	...	...	...	...	...	...	3825
383	Electrical machinery ...	50	56	75	88	96	52	62	74	76	4.8	383
3832	Radio,television etc..	...	...	...	...	...	...	...	...	...	...	3832
384	Transport equipment	29	47	79	85	92	54	37	38	48	5.8	384
3841	Shipbuilding, repair..	...	...	...	...	...	...	...	...	...	...	3841
3843	Motor vehicles	...	...	...	...	...	...	...	...	...	...	3843
385	Professional goods	...	...	...	...	...	...	...	...	...	...	385
390	Other industries	120	108	116	90	151	70	72	74	57	-7.9	390
3	Manufacturing ..... c/d/e/	74	81	87	94	101	85	89	98	98	3.2	3
410	Electricity,gas,steam ..	...	...	...	...	...	...	...	...	...	...	410
4101	Electricity	...	...	...	...	...	...	...	...	...	...	4101
420	Water works and supply .	...	...	...	...	...	...	...	...	...	...	420
4	Electricity,gas etc	...	...	...	...	...	...	...	...	...	...	4
2-4	All industry	...	...	...	...	...	...	...	...	...	...	2-4

a/ Annual growth rate 1976-1985.
b/ Excluding natural gas.
c/ Smelting and refining of copper is included in major group 230.
d/ Excluding slaughtering.
e/ Excluding sawmills.

CHINA

The information in the tables is based on the reply to the United Nations Questionnaire on General Industrial Statistics from the State Statistical Bureau, Beijing. The concepts, definitions and classification by branches of industry have been adjusted as far as possible to comply with United Nations standards.

The estimates are based on regular reports of industrial undertakings. The coverage of estimates in the tables is different from table to table. The number of enterprises and the estimates of output and value added relate to whole-people-owned and collectively-owned industrial enterprises whether they keep independent account or non-independent account. The average number of employees and wages and salaries of employees relate to industrial enterprises owned by the whole people with independent account. "Employees" are defined as workers and staff members enrolled in these enterprises. Data on quantity of electricity consumed refer to the consumption of electricity by whole-people-owned and collectively-owned enterprises with independent account. Estimates of gross fixed capital formation relate to the value of investment covered by the State budget and investment put up by various departments, localities and enterprises.

The classification system on which the data are based is not comparable with ISIC. In the tables, the grouping by branches of industry has been adjusted as far as possible to comply with ISIC. Principal differences from ISIC are footnoted in each table. It should be noted that ISIC 390 includes the data for mining and manufacturing activities for which separate data are not shown in the tables. In the table for quantity of electricity consumed, estimates for ISIC 390 further include logging (ISIC 122) and processing of wood and wood products (part of ISIC 331). The totals shown for manufacturing include data for mining and quarrying.

Estimates of output and value added are at constant prices of 1980. The estimates of gross fixed capital formation represent investment in capital construction at budget prices, not including investment of renewal and replacement of fixed assets and investment put up by collectively-owned organizations in urban and rural areas.

ISIC	INDUSTRY	1. NUMBER OF ENTERPRISES a/ (NUMBER) 1981	1982	1983	1984	1985	2. AVERAGE NUMBER OF EMPLOYEES (THOUSANDS) b/ 1981	b/ 1982	1983	1984	1985	ISIC
210	Coal mining	8217	8346	8548	10034	10255	c/ 3867	c/ 3945	...	...	...	210
220	Petroleum and gas	19	22	23	24	27	d/	d/	...	...	...	220
230	Metal ore mining	2315	2419	2357	2887	3246	e/	e/	...	...	...	230
290	Other mining	...	...	...	...	...	f/	f/	...	...	...	290
2	Mining, quarrying .	...	...	...	...	...	...	...	...	...	...	2
311/2	Food products					61130			...	...	...	311/2
313	Beverages	55627	60107	62547	74010	17757	2349	2587	...	...	...	313
314	Tobacco					399			...	...	...	314
321	Textiles	17068	18116	18404	19681	21631	3590	3960	...	...	...	321
3211	Spinning,weaving etc..	...	...	...	...	...	...	...	...	...	...	3211
322	Wearing apparel	...	...	...	...	...	...	...	...	...	...	322
323	Leather and products ...	6306	6491	6390	6895	7735	...	...	...	...	...	323
324	Footwear	...	...	...	...	...	...	...	...	...	...	324
331	Wood products	13732	14436	14408	16819	6773	...	...	...	...	...	331
332	Furniture, fixtures	...	...	...	...	12993	...	...	...	...	...	332
341	Paper and products	4690	4680	4504	4439	9243	477	497	...	...	...	341
3411	Pulp,paper etc.	...	...	...	...	4551	...	...	...	...	...	3411
342	Printing,publishing	...	...	...	...	12175	...	...	...	...	...	342
351	Industrial chemicals ...	9346	9227	9497	10439	15297	f/g/ 2991	f/g/ 3080	...	...	...	351
3511	Basic excl fertilizers	2587	2564	2662	3068	3683	...	...	...	...	...	3511
3513	Synthetic resins etc .	...	...	...	...	...	...	...	...	...	...	3513
352	Other chemical products.	2778	2840	2818	3224	2731	g/	g/	...	...	...	352
3522	Drugs and medicines ..	992	1016	1010	1103	...	...	...	...	...	...	3522
353	Petroleum refineries ...	345	310	312	421	470	c/d/ 552	c/d/ 590	...	...	...	353
354	Petroleum,coal products.								...	...	...	354
355	Rubber products	2929	2843	2857	3060	3619	g/	g/	...	...	...	355
356	Plastic products n.e.c..	7996	8606	9173	10901	13519	g/	g/	...	...	...	356
361	Pottery,china etc	h/ 501	h/ 565	h/ 624	h/ 657	3367			...	...	...	361
362	Glass and products	i/ 687	i/ 723	i/ 765	i/ 1064	2967	j/k/ 1939	j/k/ 1984	...	...	...	362
369	Non-metal products n.e.c	j/ 39532	l/	...	...	...			...	...	...	369
371	Iron and steel	4602	4631	4793	5747	2471	e/ 3123	e/ 3204	...	...	...	371
372	Non-ferrous metals					1488			...	...	...	372
381	Metal products	43702	43648	43070	45405	32032	...	...	...	...	...	381
382	Machinery n.e.c.	104112	102286	101649	107570	45934	9951	10197	...	...	...	382
3825	Office,computing etc..	...	...	...	...	...	...	...	...	...	...	3825
383	Electrical machinery ...	...	...	...	...	4010	...	...	...	...	...	383
3832	Radio,television etc..	...	...	...	...	1026	...	...	...	...	...	3832
384	Transport equipment	...	...	...	...	11219	...	...	...	...	...	384
3841	Shipbuilding, repair..	...	...	...	...	6123	...	...	...	...	...	3841
3843	Motor vehicles	...	...	...	...	3659	...	...	...	...	...	3843
385	Professional goods	...	...	...	...	...	...	...	...	...	...	385
390	Other industries .... m/	46744	l/ 87402	...	...	...	3221	3366	...	...	...	390
3	Manufacturing ..... n/	371248	377698	o/ 292739	o/ 323277	o/ 302488	32060	33410	...	...	...	3
410	Electricity,gas,steam ..	...	...	...	...	11790	...	...	...	...	...	410
4101	Electricity	10295	10923	11118	12241	11674	887	955	...	...	...	4101
420	Water works and supply .	...	...	...	...	2460	...	...	...	...	...	420
4	Electricity,gas etc .	...	...	...	...	14250	...	...	...	...	...	4
2-4	All industry	...	...	...	...	316738	...	...	...	...	...	2-4

a/ Whole-people-owned and collectively-owned enterprises with either independent account or non-independent account.
b/ Whole-people-owned enterprises with independent account.
c/ Part of major group 354 is included in 210.
d/ Major group 220 is included in 353 and 354 combined.
e/ Major group 230 is included in 371 and 372 combined.
f/ Extraction of minerals for chemical industry is included in major group 351.
g/ Major groups 352, 355 and 356 are included in 351.
h/ Manufacture of pottery and china products for construction use only.
i/ Manufacture of glass and glass products for construction use only.
j/ Manufacture of non-metallic mineral products for construction use only.
k/ Including extraction of corresponding non-metallic minerals.
l/ Major group 369 is included in 390.
m/ Including mining and manufacturing activities for which separate data are not shown.
n/ Including mining and quarrying.
o/ Excluding major groups 369 and 390.

ISIC	INDUSTRY		3. WAGES AND SALARIES OF EMPLOYEES (MILLION YUAN) 1981 a/	1982 a/	1983	1984	1985	4. QUANTITY OF ELECTRICITY CONSUMED b/ (MILLION KWH) 1981	1982	1983	1984	1985	ISIC
210	Coal mining	c/	3962	4190	...	...	...	17772	18746	20075	...	...	210
220	Petroleum and gas	d/	...	...	...	...	...	...	...	...	...	...	220
230	Metal ore mining	e/	...	...	...	...	...	...	...	...	...	...	230
290	Other mining	f/	...	...	...	...	...	...	...	...	...	...	290
2	Mining, quarrying .		...	...	...	...	...	...	...	...	...	...	2
311/2	Food products				...	...	...				...	...	311/2
313	Beverages		1820	2016	...	...	...	6054	7038	8007	...	...	313
314	Tobacco				...	...	...				...	...	314
321	Textiles		2828	3072	...	...	...	14002	15229	15914	...	...	321
3211	Spinning,weaving etc..		...	...	...	...	...	...	...	...	...	...	3211
322	Wearing apparel		...	...	...	...	...	...	...	...	...	...	322
323	Leather and products ...		...	...	...	...	...	...	...	...	...	...	323
324	Footwear		...	...	...	...	...	...	...	...	...	...	324
331	Wood products		...	...	...	...	...	...	...	...	...	...	331
332	Furniture, fixtures		...	...	...	...	...	...	...	...	...	...	332
341	Paper and products		373	391	...	...	...	5707	6081	6578	...	...	341
3411	Pulp,paper etc.		...	...	...	...	...	...	...	...	...	...	3411
342	Printing,publishing		...	...	...	...	...	...	...	...	...	...	342
351	Industrial chemicals ...	f/g/	2411	2546	...	...	...	52474	55596	59069	...	...	351
3511	Basic excl fertilizers		...	...	...	...	...	...	...	...	...	...	3511
3513	Synthetic resins etc .		...	...	...	...	...	...	...	...	...	...	3513
352	Other chemical products.	g/	...	...	...	...	...	...	...	...	...	...	352
3522	Drugs and medicines ..		...	...	...	...	...	...	...	...	...	...	3522
353	Petroleum refineries ...	c/d/	536	600	...	...	...	10327	10744	11558	...	...	353
354	Petroleum,coal products.				...	...	...				...	...	354
355	Rubber products	g/	...	...	...	...	...	...	...	...	...	...	355
356	Plastic products n.e.c..	g/	...	...	...	...	...	...	...	...	...	...	356
361	Pottery,china etc				...	...	...				...	...	361
362	Glass and products	h/i/	1573	1676	...	...	...	11245	12395	13988	...	...	362
369	Non-metal products n.e.c				...	...	...				...	...	369
371	Iron and steel	e/	2875	2984	...	...	...	45319	47079	50921	...	...	371
372	Non-ferrous metals				...	...	...				...	...	372
381	Metal products		...	...	...	...	...	...	...	...	...	...	381
382	Machinery n.e.c.		8141	8458	...	...	...	20398	21841	23837	...	...	382
3825	Office,computing etc..		...	...	...	...	...	...	...	...	...	...	3825
383	Electrical machinery ...		...	...	...	...	...	...	...	...	...	...	383
3832	Radio,television etc..		...	...	...	...	...	...	...	...	...	...	3832
384	Transport equipment		...	...	...	...	...	...	...	...	...	...	384
3841	Shipbuilding, repair..		...	...	...	...	...	...	...	...	...	...	3841
3843	Motor vehicles		...	...	...	...	...	...	...	...	...	...	3843
385	Professional goods		...	...	...	...	...	...	...	...	...	...	385
390	Other industries	j/	2780	2933	...	...	...	k/ 14232	k/ 14584	k/ 14940	...	...	390
3	Manufacturing	l/	27299	28866	...	...	...	k/ 197530	k/ 209333	k/ 224887	...	...	3
410	Electricity,gas,steam ..		...	...	...	...	...	...	...	...	...	...	410
4101	Electricity		760	829	...	...	...	45604	47065	49473	...	...	4101
420	Water works and supply .		...	...	...	...	...	...	...	...	...	...	420
4	Electricity,gas etc		...	...	...	...	...	...	...	...	...	...	4
2-4	All industry		...	...	...	...	...	...	...	...	...	...	2-4

a/ Whole-people-owned enterprises with independent account.
b/ Whole-people-owned and collectively-owned enterprises with independent account.
c/ Part of major group 354 is included in 210.
d/ Major group 220 is included in 353 and 354 combined.
e/ Major group 230 is included in 371 and 372 combined.
f/ Extraction of minerals for chemical industry is included in major group 351.
g/ Major groups 352, 355 and 356 are included in 351.
h/ Manufacture of non-metallic mineral products for construction use only.
i/ Including extraction of corresponding non-metallic minerals.
j/ Including mining and manufacturing activities for which separate data are not shown.
k/ Including logging.
l/ Including mining and quarrying.

ISIC	INDUSTRY	5. OUTPUT a/b/ (MILLION YUAN)					6. VALUE ADDED a/ (MILLION YUAN)					ISIC
		1981	1982	1983	1984	1985	1981	1982	1983	1984	b/ 1985	
210	Coal mining	14560	15446	16587	18062	19375	...	...	...	...	12444	210
220	Petroleum and gas	13049	13231	13234	14250	16132	...	...	...	...	14439	220
230	Metal ore mining	5058	4141	3655	4439	4907	...	...	...	...	2885	230
290	Other mining	...	...	...	...	...	...	...	...	...	...	290
2	Mining, quarrying .	...	...	...	...	...	...	...	...	...	...	2
311/2	Food products					63323	...	...	...	...	10803	311/2
313	Beverages	[69012	75552	79425	86584]	13539	...	...	...	...	5343	313
314	Tobacco					17197	...	...	...	...	11834	314
321	Textiles	85602	86685	95604	108294	115540	...	...	...	...	27128	321
3211	Spinning,weaving etc..	...	...	...	...	...	...	...	...	...	...	3211
322	Wearing apparel	...	...	...	...	...	...	...	...	...	...	322
323	Leather and products ...	5858	5567	5701	6221	7654	...	...	...	...	2369	323
324	Footwear	...	...	...	...	...	...	...	...	...	...	324
331	Wood products	4003	4393	4695	5259	1825	...	...	...	...	613	331
332	Furniture, fixtures	...	...	...	...	4994	...	...	...	...	1631	332
341	Paper and products	6940	7396	8141	9222	14722	...	...	...	...	4961	341
3411	Pulp,paper etc.	...	...	...	...	10768	...	...	...	...	3989	3411
342	Printing,publishing	...	...	...	...	8964	...	...	...	...	3088	342
351	Industrial chemicals ...	31090	34244	38047	41604	54569	...	...	...	...	19132	351
3511	Basic excl fertilizers	7176	7924	9063	9797	8257	...	...	...	...	3179	3511
3513	Synthetic resins etc .	...	...	...	...	...	...	...	...	...	...	3513
352	Other chemical products.	11106	12363	13754	15616	14271	...	...	...	...	3928	352
3522	Drugs and medicines ..	4209	5232	6123	6828	...	...	...	...	...	...	3522
353	Petroleum refineries ...	[15230	15635	17852	19321	21132]	...	...	...	...	11400	353
354	Petroleum,coal products.						...	...	...	...	...	354
355	Rubber products	8290	9369	10866	12264	14445	...	...	...	...	4906	355
356	Plastic products n.e.c..	8105	9320	10769	12838	15822	...	...	...	...	4235	356
361	Pottery,china etc	c/ 572	c/ 697	c/ 833	c/ 964	c/ 2968	...	...	...	...	1424	361
362	Glass and products	d/ 1166	d/ 1375	d/ 1583	d/ 1880	d/ 5481	...	...	...	...	2700	362
369	Non-metal products n.e.c	e/ 14245	e/f/	...	...	e/ 1576	...	...	...	...	586	369
371	Iron and steel	[45669	48523	52368	57936]	42964	...	...	...	...	19039	371
372	Non-ferrous metals					18533	...	...	...	...	5714	372
381	Metal products	27068	30430	34648	40800	23328	...	...	...	...	8207	381
382	Machinery n.e.c.	107995	122506	144048	175710	91230	...	...	...	...	35735	382
3825	Office,computing etc..	...	...	...	...	...	...	...	...	...	...	3825
383	Electrical machinery ...	...	...	...	...	29156	...	...	...	...	8411	383
3832	Radio,television etc..	...	...	...	...	12061	...	...	...	...	2553	3832
384	Transport equipment	...	...	...	...	35363	...	...	...	...	13395	384
3841	Shipbuilding, repair..	...	...	...	...	8451	...	...	...	...	2916	3841
3843	Motor vehicles	...	...	...	...	19024	...	...	...	...	7507	3843
385	Professional goods	...	...	...	...	...	...	...	...	...	...	385
390	Other industries .... g/	23897	f/ 40165	...	...	...	...	...	...	...	...	390
3	Manufacturing ..... h/	498515	537038	i/ 551810	i/ 631264	j/ 659010	...	...	...	...	j/ 236350	3
410	Electricity,gas,steam ..	...	...	...	...	26296	...	...	...	...	16612	410
4101	Electricity	19486	20707	22023	23558	25847	...	...	...	...	16495	4101
420	Water works and supply .	...	...	...	...	1752	...	...	...	...	1060	420
4	Electricity,gas etc	...	...	...	...	28048	...	...	...	...	17672	4
2-4	All industry	...	...	...	...	687058	...	...	...	...	254022	2-4

a/ Whole-people-owned and collectively-owned enterprises with either independent account or non-independent account.
b/ At constant prices of 1980.
c/ Manufacture of pottery and china products for construction use only.
d/ Manufacture of glass and glass products for construction use only.
e/ Manufacture of non-metallic mineral products for construction use only.
f/ Major group 369 is included in 390.
g/ Including mining and manufacturing activities for which separate data are not shown.
h/ Including mining and quarrying.
i/ Excluding major groups 369 and 390.
j/ Excluding major group 390.

7. GROSS FIXED CAPITAL FORMATION
TOTAL a/b/
(MILLION YUAN)

ISIC	INDUSTRY		1981	1982	1983	1984	1985	ISIC
210	Coal mining		2285	2848	...	...	...	210
220	Petroleum and gas		2314	2152	...	...	...	220
230	Metal ore mining	c/	...	...	...	...	...	230
290	Other mining		...	...	...	...	...	290
2	Mining, quarrying .		...	...	...	...	...	2
311/2	Food products		[926	1407]	...	...	...	311/2
313	Beverages				...	...	...	313
314	Tobacco				...	...	...	314
321	Textiles		1986	2116	...	...	...	321
3211	Spinning,weaving etc..		...	...	...	...	...	3211
322	Wearing apparel		...	...	...	...	...	322
323	Leather and products ...		...	...	...	...	...	323
324	Footwear		...	...	...	...	...	324
331	Wood products		15	21	...	...	...	331
332	Furniture, fixtures		...	...	...	...	...	332
341	Paper and products		191	169	...	...	...	341
3411	Pulp,paper etc.		...	...	...	...	...	3411
342	Printing,publishing		70	72	...	...	...	342
351	Industrial chemicals ...		1389	2238	...	...	...	351
3511	Basic excl fertilizers		947	1657	...	...	...	3511
3513	Synthetic resins etc .		...	...	...	...	...	3513
352	Other chemical products.		158	158	...	...	...	352
3522	Drugs and medicines ..		...	110	...	...	...	3522
353	Petroleum refineries ...		[511	514]	...	...	...	353
354	Petroleum,coal products.				...	...	...	354
355	Rubber products		43	35	...	...	...	355
356	Plastic products n.e.c..		225	23	...	...	...	356
361	Pottery,china etc	d/	...	...	...	...	...	361
362	Glass and products		100	132	...	...	...	362
369	Non-metal products n.e.c	d/e/	820	1068	...	...	...	369
371	Iron and steel	c/	[2735	4300]	...	...	...	371
372	Non-ferrous metals				...	...	...	372
381	Metal products		...	...	...	...	...	381
382	Machinery n.e.c.		2439	2712	...	...	...	382
3825	Office,computing etc..		...	...	...	...	...	3825
383	Electrical machinery ...		...	...	...	...	...	383
3832	Radio,television etc..		...	...	...	...	...	3832
384	Transport equipment		...	...	...	...	...	384
3841	Shipbuilding, repair..		...	...	...	...	...	3841
3843	Motor vehicles		...	...	...	...	...	3843
385	Professional goods		...	...	...	...	...	385
390	Other industries	f/	657	706	...	...	...	390
3	Manufacturing	g/	16864	20671	...	...	...	3
410	Electricity,gas,steam ..		...	...	...	...	...	410
4101	Electricity		4014	4623	...	...	...	4101
420	Water works and supply .		...	...	...	...	...	420
4	Electricity,gas etc		...	...	...	...	...	4
2-4	All industry		...	...	...	...	...	2-4

a/ Investment in capital construction at budget prices by the State, various departments, localities and enterprises.
b/ Excluding investment of renewal and replacement of fixed assets and investment put up by collectively-owned organizations in urban and rural areas.
c/ Major group 230 is included in 371 and 372 combined. d/ Major group 361 is included in 369.
e/ Manufacture of non-metallic mineral products for construction use only.
f/ Including mining and manufacturing activities for which separate data are not shown.
g/ Including mining and quarrying.

COLOMBIA

The information in the tables, except for the indexes, is based on the reply to the United Nations Questionnaire on General Industrial Statistics from the Departamento Administrativo Nacional de Estadistica, Bogota. The concepts, definitions and classification by branches of industry are generally in accordance with United Nations standards.

The estimates are derived from the annual manufacturing survey undertaken by the Departamento Administrativo Nacional de Estadistica. The inquiry covers establishments with 10 or more persons engaged. It should be noted, however, that those establishments which were covered in the preceding year but have less than 10 persons engaged during the year of reference are also included in the survey. The estimates are based on the national classification system which follows the present version of ISIC.

Employment numbers are as of the pay period which includes 15 November or the nearest date to it. Persons on strike are excluded. Apprentices are included in numbers of persons engaged and employees, but excluded in the tables relating to operatives. Estimates of wages and salaries represent all payments, in cash and in kind, made to employees during the year. Employers' contributions to social insurance, welfare funds and other similar schemes are excluded, unless otherwise footnoted.

Output is the sum of the value of goods produced by the establishment, adjusted for the net change in the value of work in progress, receipts for industrial services rendered to others, value of goods shipped in the same condition as received and value of electricity sold. Value added is the difference between output and the cost of the following inputs: raw materials, supplies, fuels, electricity purchased and industrial services rendered by others. The valuation of output and value added is in producers' prices.

The estimates of gross fixed capital formation refer to the current value of purchases and own-account construction of fixed assets, less the value of sales and depreciation. The revaluation of fixed assets in the year is taken into account.

The indexes of industrial production are compiled by the Banco de la Republica. The indexes provided by the national authorities are compiled according to the present version of ISIC. The indexes cover, in principle, all establishments with 10 or more persons engaged, adjusted with estimates for small and handicraft industries.

Related national publications:
Industria Manufacturera (annual); Boletin Mensual de Estadistica (La Industria Manufacturera); Anuario General de Estadistica, Tomo IV; Informe al Congreso Nacional (annual), all published by the Departamento Administrativo Nacional de Estadistica, Bogota.

COLOMBIA

ISIC	INDUSTRY	1. NUMBER OF ESTABLISHMENTS b/ (NUMBER)					2. AVERAGE NUMBER OF PERSONS ENGAGED a/b/ (THOUSANDS)					ISIC
		1981	1982	1983	1984	1985	1981	1982	1983	1984	1985	
210	Coal mining	...	...	...	...	...	...	...	...	...	...	210
220	Petroleum and gas	...	...	...	...	...	...	...	...	...	...	220
230	Metal ore mining	...	...	...	...	...	...	...	...	...	...	230
290	Other mining	...	...	...	...	...	...	...	...	...	...	290
2	Mining, quarrying	...	...	...	...	...	...	...	...	...	...	2
311/2	Food products	1212	1246	1077	1086	...	74.9	76.3	77.2	72.5	...	311/2
313	Beverages	130	131	127	125	...	27.1	27.2	27.5	26.9	...	313
314	Tobacco	23	22	16	15	...	3.9	3.3	3.7	3.0	...	314
321	Textiles	491	478	435	426	...	64.9	57.3	53.3	52.7	...	321
3211	Spinning,weaving etc.. c/	124	105	107	112	...	15.5	12.5	12.3	12.0	...	3211
322	Wearing apparel	878	963	906	928	...	51.3	49.9	47.2	45.3	...	322
323	Leather and products	104	105	87	92	...	7.5	7.1	6.3	6.4	...	323
324	Footwear	220	259	211	226	...	10.5	10.9	10.4	10.1	...	324
331	Wood products	183	202	174	167	...	5.9	6.3	6.3	5.6	...	331
332	Furniture, fixtures	195	224	179	167	...	6.8	7.3	6.8	6.6	...	332
341	Paper and products	144	148	133	143	...	11.6	11.2	10.6	11.0	...	341
3411	Pulp,paper etc.	28	30	29	31	...	5.6	5.7	5.3	5.7	...	3411
342	Printing,publishing	365	385	340	338	...	20.6	20.1	20.1	20.0	...	342
351	Industrial chemicals	105	110	107	115	...	14.7	16.6	14.4	15.1	...	351
3511	Basic excl fertilizers	68	69	66	73	...	6.4	6.2	6.0	6.3	...	3511
3513	Synthetic resins etc	23	22	21	21	...	4.3	6.4	4.4	5.1	...	3513
352	Other chemical products.	288	291	270	264	...	23.9	24.8	23.4	22.8	...	352
3522	Drugs and medicines	124	127	113	103	...	11.4	12.5	11.6	11.3	...	3522
353	Petroleum refineries	7	7	6	5	...	6.1	5.1	6.3	5.6	...	353
354	Petroleum,coal products.	19	18	17	22	...	0.7	0.7	0.8	0.8	...	354
355	Rubber products	89	90	82	78	...	9.1	8.7	7.3	7.1	...	355
356	Plastic products n.e.c..	241	268	255	267	...	15.1	16.5	16.4	17.9	...	356
361	Pottery,china etc	42	38	27	28	...	5.4	5.0	4.8	4.6	...	361
362	Glass and products	52	54	42	46	...	6.9	6.0	6.3	5.8	...	362
369	Non-metal products n.e.c	329	343	294	286	...	21.1	21.4	21.5	21.0	...	369
371	Iron and steel	54	54	50	53	...	14.3	14.1	12.9	11.7	...	371
372	Non-ferrous metals	35	36	26	28	...	2.4	2.2	2.0	1.9	...	372
381	Metal products	614	627	552	505	...	31.6	29.6	28.9	28.4	...	381
382	Machinery n.e.c.	330	314	268	278	...	14.6	14.3	14.0	13.1	...	382
3825	Office,computing etc..	13	11	7	9	...	0.5	0.4	0.3	0.3	...	3825
383	Electrical machinery	197	200	181	173	...	17.2	16.9	16.0	16.4	...	383
3832	Radio,television etc..	44	42	43	39	...	4.8	4.5	4.3	4.3	...	3832
384	Transport equipment	222	240	201	199	...	21.9	20.8	18.8	19.2	...	384
3841	Shipbuilding, repair..	15	19	17	14	...	1.6	2.1	2.0	1.8	...	3841
3843	Motor vehicles	164	176	143	143	...	14.6	13.3	11.6	12.1	...	3843
385	Professional goods	62	58	58	59	...	3.2	2.5	2.8	2.8	...	385
390	Other industries	161	156	12	139	...	7.5	7.0	6.1	7.1	...	390
3	Manufacturing	6792	7067	6133	6258	...	500.7	489.1	472.1	461.4	...	3
410	Electricity,gas,steam	...	...	...	...	...	...	...	...	...	...	410
4101	Electricity	...	...	...	...	...	...	...	...	...	...	4101
420	Water works and supply	...	...	...	...	...	...	...	...	...	...	420
4	Electricity,gas etc	...	...	...	...	...	...	...	...	...	...	4
2-4	All industry	...	...	...	...	...	...	...	...	...	...	2-4

a/ In the pay period including 15 November of the year indicated or the nearest date to it.
b/ Establishments with 10 or more persons engaged.
c/ Excluding manufacture of wool, cotton and synthetic fabrics.

ISIC	INDUSTRY	3. AVERAGE NUMBER OF EMPLOYEES a/b/ (THOUSANDS)					4. WAGES AND SALARIES OF EMPLOYEES b/ (MILLION PESOS)					ISIC
		1981	1982	1983	1984	1985	1981	1982	1983	1984	1985	
210	Coal mining	...	...	...	...	...	...	...	...	...	...	210
220	Petroleum and gas	...	...	...	...	...	...	...	...	...	...	220
230	Metal ore mining	...	...	...	...	...	...	...	...	...	...	230
290	Other mining	...	...	...	...	...	...	...	...	...	...	290
2	Mining, quarrying .	...	...	...	...	...	...	...	...	...	...	2
311/2	Food products	73.4	74.6	75.9	71.2	...	11067	14230	18184	21733	...	311/2
313	Beverages	27.1	27.1	27.5	26.9	...	5591	7058	9111	11067	...	313
314	Tobacco	3.9	3.3	3.7	3.0	...	670	652	855	1120	...	314
321	Textiles	64.4	56.8	52.8	52.2	...	9628	10397	11637	14826	...	321
3211	Spinning,weaving etc.. c/	15.5	12.4	12.2	12.0	...	2153	2114	2481	3042	...	3211
322	Wearing apparel	50.0	48.6	46.0	44.1	...	4840	5976	6797	8052	...	322
323	Leather and products ...	7.4	7.0	6.2	6.4	...	932	1180	1275	1605	...	323
324	Footwear	10.2	10.5	10.1	9.8	...	1148	1529	1687	2098	...	324
331	Wood products	5.7	6.1	6.0	5.4	...	662	953	1229	1284	...	331
332	Furniture, fixtures	6.6	7.0	6.6	6.4	...	669	877	1048	1243	...	332
341	Paper and products	11.5	11.1	10.5	10.9	...	2448	3071	3820	4831	...	341
3411	Pulp,paper etc.	5.6	5.6	5.3	5.7	...	1471	1914	2414	3087	...	3411
342	Printing,publishing	20.2	19.6	19.6	19.4	...	3074	3795	4734	5982	...	342
351	Industrial chemicals ...	14.6	16.6	14.3	15.1	...	3883	5495	6327	7735	...	351
3511	Basic excl fertilizers	6.4	6.2	6.0	6.3	...	1346	1643	2118	2560	...	3511
3513	Synthetic resins etc	4.3	6.4	4.4	5.1	...	1073	1940	1782	2558	...	3513
352	Other chemical products.	23.7	24.5	23.2	22.6	...	4752	6251	7381	9191	...	352
3522	Drugs and medicines ..	11.4	12.4	11.5	11.3	...	2626	3626	4267	5325	...	3522
353	Petroleum refineries ...	6.1	5.1	6.3	5.6	...	1860	2021	3066	3706	...	353
354	Petroleum,coal products.	0.7	0.6	0.7	0.8	...	92	135	181	259	...	354
355	Rubber products	9.1	8.6	7.2	7.1	...	1743	2152	2379	2950	...	355
356	Plastic products n.e.c..	14.9	16.3	16.1	17.6	...	1917	2670	3418	4635	...	356
361	Pottery,china etc	5.4	5.0	4.7	4.6	...	784	962	1048	1369	...	361
362	Glass and products	6.9	6.0	6.3	5.8	...	1229	1368	1830	2002	...	362
369	Non-metal products n.e.c	20.8	21.1	21.2	20.8	...	3218	4383	5438	6747	...	369
371	Iron and steel	14.3	14.0	12.9	11.7	...	2838	3574	4307	4909	...	371
372	Non-ferrous metals	2.4	2.1	1.9	1.9	...	374	468	557	731	...	372
381	Metal products	30.9	28.8	28.2	27.8	...	4164	4856	5868	7485	...	381
382	Machinery n.e.c.	14.3	14.0	13.8	12.9	...	1979	2486	3123	3332	...	382
3825	Office,computing etc..	0.5	0.4	0.3	0.3	...	102	104	95	90	...	3825
383	Electrical machinery ...	17.0	16.8	15.9	16.2	...	2800	3629	4446	5428	...	383
3832	Radio,television etc..	4.8	4.4	4.3	4.3	...	608	753	955	1125	...	3832
384	Transport equipment	21.6	20.6	18.6	19.1	...	3941	4776	5563	7001	...	384
3841	Shipbuilding, repair..	1.6	2.1	2.0	1.8	...	228	492	588	623	...	3841
3843	Motor vehicles	14.6	13.1	11.4	12.0	...	2732	3125	3442	4583	...	3843
385	Professional goods	3.2	2.4	2.8	2.8	...	491	395	695	883	...	385
390	Other industries	7.3	6.8	6.0	7.0	...	1058	1221	1166	1712	...	390
3	Manufacturing	493.6	481.0	465.0	455.1	...	77852	96560	117170	143916	...	3
410	Electricity,gas,steam ..	...	...	...	...	...	...	...	...	...	...	410
4101	Electricity	...	...	...	...	...	...	...	...	...	...	4101
420	Water works and supply .	...	...	...	...	...	...	...	...	...	...	420
4	Electricity,gas etc	...	...	...	...	...	...	...	...	...	...	4
2-4	All industry	...	...	...	...	...	...	...	...	...	...	2-4

a/ In the pay period including 15 November of the year indicated or the nearest date to it.
b/ Establishments with 10 or more persons engaged.
c/ Excluding manufacture of wool, cotton and synthetic fabrics.

ISIC	INDUSTRY	5. AVERAGE NUMBER OF OPERATIVES a/b/ (THOUSANDS)					6. WAGES AND SALARIES OF OPERATIVES b/ (MILLION PESOS)					ISIC
		1981	1982	1983	1984	1985	1981	1982	1983	1984	1985	
210	Coal mining	...	...	...	...	...	...	...	...	...	...	210
220	Petroleum and gas	...	...	...	...	...	...	...	...	...	...	220
230	Metal ore mining	...	...	...	...	...	...	...	...	...	...	230
290	Other mining	...	...	...	...	...	...	...	...	...	...	290
2	Mining, quarrying	...	...	...	...	...	...	...	...	...	...	2
311/2	Food products	51.8	52.0	52.7	48.2	...	6234	7875	9954	11841	...	311/2
313	Beverages	14.4	14.5	14.3	13.5	...	2545	3247	4279	5014	...	313
314	Tobacco	2.8	2.2	2.4	1.9	...	379	349	428	586	...	314
321	Textiles	52.7	46.0	42.8	42.5	...	6887	7539	8399	10792	...	321
3211	Spinning,weaving etc.. c/	12.5	10.1	10.1	9.9	...	1514	1485	1747	2168	...	3211
322	Wearing apparel	41.2	40.1	38.2	37.8	...	3493	4296	4967	6132	...	322
323	Leather and products	6.0	5.6	4.9	4.9	...	640	798	872	1080	...	323
324	Footwear	8.4	8.6	8.3	8.1	...	827	1107	1239	1542	...	324
331	Wood products	4.6	4.7	4.6	4.1	...	457	624	798	812	...	331
332	Furniture, fixtures	5.3	5.7	5.2	4.9	...	483	651	752	870	...	332
341	Paper and products	7.8	7.5	7.0	7.5	...	1458	1771	2115	2797	...	341
3411	Pulp,paper etc.	3.7	3.7	3.4	3.8	...	866	1078	1337	1780	...	3411
342	Printing,publishing	12.6	12.3	12.0	11.1	...	1547	2125	2550	3120	...	342
351	Industrial chemicals	8.7	9.4	8.5	9.3	...	1727	2370	2828	3744	...	351
3511	Basic excl fertilizers	4.3	4.1	3.9	4.1	...	725	900	1136	1407	...	3511
3513	Synthetic resins etc	...	3.7	2.8	3.4	...	544	932	955	1407	...	3513
352	Other chemical products	12.6	13.4	12.4	11.9	...	1552	2188	2531	3049	...	352
3522	Drugs and medicines	5.6	6.1	5.4	5.2	...	731	1060	1222	1438	...	3522
353	Petroleum refineries	3.8	3.6	4.8	4.3	...	764	916	1877	2345	...	353
354	Petroleum,coal products	0.4	0.4	0.5	0.6	...	47	69	91	127	...	354
355	Rubber products	6.9	6.4	5.4	5.4	...	1084	1313	1409	1835	...	355
356	Plastic products n.e.c..	11.2	12.3	12.1	13.0	...	1153	1654	2075	2729	...	356
361	Pottery,china etc	4.4	4.0	3.8	3.7	...	576	696	736	974	...	361
362	Glass and products	5.3	4.6	4.9	4.5	...	757	856	1190	1346	...	362
369	Non-metal products n.e.c	16.3	16.6	16.3	15.9	...	2163	2930	3451	4291	...	369
371	Iron and steel	10.6	10.0	9.1	8.3	...	1691	2032	2350	2755	...	371
372	Non-ferrous metals	1.7	1.5	1.3	1.3	...	209	248	296	399	...	372
381	Metal products	23.5	21.8	21.3	20.9	...	2636	3064	3708	4606	...	381
382	Machinery n.e.c.	10.6	10.4	9.9	9.6	...	1299	1606	1871	2157	...	382
3825	Office,computing etc..	0.3	0.3	0.2	0.2	...	52	50	39	39	...	3825
383	Electrical machinery	11.6	11.4	10.4	11.1	...	1477	1956	2230	2846	...	383
3832	Radio,television etc..	3.2	2.9	2.7	2.7	...	310	404	473	579	...	3832
384	Transport equipment	15.4	14.6	13.2	13.7	...	2235	2800	3134	4067	...	384
3841	Shipbuilding, repair..	1.2	1.6	1.5	1.4	...	139	348	407	424	...	3841
3843	Motor vehicles	10.4	9.4	8.1	8.7	...	1534	1803	1831	2660	...	3843
385	Professional goods	2.2	1.7	1.9	1.9	...	262	225	343	449	...	385
390	Other industries	5.3	4.9	4.5	5.2	...	563	662	714	952	...	390
3	Manufacturing	358.1	346.2	332.7	325.1	...	45145	55967	67187	83257	...	3
410	Electricity,gas,steam	...	...	...	...	...	...	...	...	...	...	410
4101	Electricity	...	...	...	...	...	...	...	...	...	...	4101
420	Water works and supply	...	...	...	...	...	...	...	...	...	...	420
4	Electricity,gas etc	...	...	...	...	...	...	...	...	...	...	4
2-4	All industry	...	...	...	...	...	...	...	...	...	...	2-4

a/ In the pay period including 15 November of the year indicated or the nearest date to it.
b/ Establishments with 10 or more persons engaged.
c/ Excluding manufacture of wool, cotton and synthetic fabrics.

ISIC	INDUSTRY	7. QUANTITY OF ELECTRICITY CONSUMED a/ (MILLION KWH)					8. OUTPUT IN PRODUCERS' PRICES a/ (BILLION PESOS)					ISIC
		1981	1982	1983	1984	1985	1981	1982	1983	1984	1985	
210	Coal mining	...	...	...	...	...	...	...	...	...	...	210
220	Petroleum and gas	...	...	...	...	...	...	...	...	...	...	220
230	Metal ore mining	...	...	...	...	...	...	...	...	...	...	230
290	Other mining	...	...	...	...	...	...	...	...	...	...	290
2	Mining, quarrying .	...	...	...	...	...	...	...	...	...	...	2
311/2	Food products	723	759	797	809	...	211	271	339	418	...	311/2
313	Beverages	203	219	238	244	...	91	107	136	157	...	313
314	Tobacco	14	13	14	15	...	14	15	24	32	...	314
321	Textiles	653	552	550	611	...	81	88	100	143	...	321
3211	Spinning,weaving etc.. b/	192	132	129	136	...	17	15	17	25	...	3211
322	Wearing apparel	51	51	51	58	...	30	36	40	51	...	322
323	Leather and products ...	32	33	33	33	...	8	10	10	15	...	323
324	Footwear	21	24	20	20	...	8	10	11	14	...	324
331	Wood products	33	38	37	39	...	6	8	10	11	...	331
332	Furniture, fixtures	10	11	17	12	...	3	5	6	7	...	332
341	Paper and products	404	417	393	503	...	36	45	53	76	...	341
3411	Pulp,paper etc.	375	393	370	475	...	22	28	34	48	...	3411
342	Printing,publishing	53	46	52	54	...	22	29	36	49	...	342
351	Industrial chemicals ...	757	765	747	820	...	55	66	78	113	...	351
3511	Basic excl fertilizers	466	437	445	449	...	15	16	18	24	...	3511
3513	Synthetic resins etc .	190	229	199	269	...	17	23	26	44	...	3513
352	Other chemical products.	74	83	84	82	...	56	72	87	108	...	352
3522	Drugs and medicines ..	30	32	31	30	...	23	29	36	44	...	3522
353	Petroleum refineries ...	567	625	613	625	...	68	59	91	115	...	353
354	Petroleum,coal products.	2	3	4	6	...	4	5	6	9	...	354
355	Rubber products	89	87	81	86	...	18	21	20	27	...	355
356	Plastic products n.e.c..	132	150	159	175	...	22	28	35	53	...	356
361	Pottery,china etc	38	39	41	49	...	5	6	6	9	...	361
362	Glass and products	143	100	120	132	...	8	11	15	16	...	362
369	Non-metal products n.e.c	603	593	638	702	...	31	40	48	61	...	369
371	Iron and steel	403	541	773	1163	...	25	30	39	54	...	371
372	Non-ferrous metals	33	33	37	34	...	5	5	6	9	...	372
381	Metal products	139	134	143	154	...	34	38	47	63	...	381
382	Machinery n.e.c.	57	62	60	58	...	15	19	25	28	...	382
3825	Office,computing etc..	1	1	1	1	...	1	1	1	1	...	3825
383	Electrical machinery ...	67	74	69	72	...	30	35	38	53	...	383
3832	Radio,television etc..	11	11	11	11	...	6	7	8	12	...	3832
384	Transport equipment	75	68	67	74	...	46	54	53	89	...	384
3841	Shipbuilding, repair..	5	6	7	7	...	1	2	3	4	...	3841
3843	Motor vehicles	56	47	44	51	...	38	44	39	72	...	3843
385	Professional goods	7	6	8	10	...	4	3	5	7	...	385
390	Other industries	24	26	21	36	...	8	10	9	13	...	390
3	Manufacturing	5407	5552	5867	6676	...	944	1126	1373	1800	...	3
410	Electricity,gas,steam ..	...	...	...	...	...	...	...	...	...	...	410
4101	Electricity	...	...	...	...	...	...	...	...	...	...	4101
420	Water works and supply .	...	...	...	...	...	...	...	...	...	...	420
4	Electricity,gas etc	...	...	...	...	...	...	...	...	...	...	4
2-4	All industry	...	...	...	...	...	...	...	...	...	...	2-4

a/ Establishments with 10 or more persons engaged.

b/ Excluding manufacture of wool, cotton and synthetic fabrics.

ISIC	INDUSTRY	9. VALUE ADDED IN PRODUCERS' PRICES a/ (MILLION PESOS)					10. GROSS FIXED CAPITAL FORMATION TOTAL a/b/c/ (MILLION PESOS)					ISIC
		1981	1982	1983	1984	1985	1981	1982	1983	1984	1985	
210	Coal mining	...	...	...	...	...	...	...	...	...	...	210
220	Petroleum and gas	...	...	...	...	...	...	...	...	...	...	220
230	Metal ore mining	...	...	...	...	...	...	...	...	...	...	230
290	Other mining	...	...	...	...	...	...	...	...	...	...	290
2	Mining, quarrying	...	...	...	...	...	...	...	...	...	...	2
311/2	Food products	55837	70903	90336	113300	...	5280	8271	12427	6972	...	311/2
313	Beverages	59066	67685	84851	101171	...	1625	820	2401	4053	...	313
314	Tobacco	9777	9638	16938	22686	...	30	602	343	1019	...	314
321	Textiles	38745	41854	47153	67066	...	4329	7458	7302	3849	...	321
3211	Spinning,weaving etc.. d/	8457	7783	9040	12371	...	1196	338	1051	184	...	3211
322	Wearing apparel	13692	16551	18491	22885	...	768	1152	309	704	...	322
323	Leather and products	3279	4102	3972	5252	...	177	204	197	223	...	323
324	Footwear	3608	4635	5041	6352	...	167	214	331	424	...	324
331	Wood products	3027	4529	5043	6401	...	620	1104	1428	1059	...	331
332	Furniture, fixtures	1798	2335	2840	3245	...	104	370	298	288	...	332
341	Paper and products	13143	16655	21302	28870	...	1875	1666	2756	1214	...	341
3411	Pulp,paper etc.	8584	11234	14809	20350	...	1412	1215	2324	1120	...	3411
342	Printing,publishing	11697	14588	17360	24443	...	1051	2094	3710	2379	...	342
351	Industrial chemicals	21198	27652	29460	42344	...	7930	1060	3527	3409	...	351
3511	Basic excl fertilizers	6345	7720	8250	10869	...	1287	338	781	-58	...	3511
3513	Synthetic resins etc	6713	10297	9575	17362	...	6318	446	2524	2122	...	3513
352	Other chemical products.	26378	34460	41482	50780	...	1824	4329	1002	1426	...	352
3522	Drugs and medicines	12715	15682	19152	23003	...	879	1695	784	502	...	3522
353	Petroleum refineries	37273	...	9198	18584	...	-299	-253	6414	831	...	353
354	Petroleum,coal products.	1101	1855	1902	2937	...	80	118	182	150	...	354
355	Rubber products	7508	9595	9359	11769	...	249	278	558	140	...	355
356	Plastic products n.e.c..	7866	10353	13077	19121	...	1138	1798	1576	1684	...	356
361	Pottery,china etc	2550	3216	3480	5157	...	311	238	633	527	...	361
362	Glass and products	4481	6721	7446	8895	...	-2	-183	2198	46	...	362
369	Non-metal products n.e.c	14394	19924	24708	31684	...	1618	3251	9522	7724	...	369
371	Iron and steel	12411	13810	17463	25673	...	1798	20152	14285	4536	...	371
372	Non-ferrous metals	1952	2317	3080	4030	...	197	277	118	146	...	372
381	Metal products	15413	16727	21517	28022	...	1606	1726	1098	2694	...	381
382	Machinery n.e.c.	6758	8636	11672	12352	...	570	614	446	564	...	382
3825	Office,computing etc..	431	829	817	598	...	...	15	4	-7	...	3825
383	Electrical machinery	13901	15959	17212	22892	...	837	1231	532	810	...	383
3832	Radio,television etc..	2848	3349	3817	4882	...	202	265	171	249	...	3832
384	Transport equipment	15285	19255	16799	25560	...	2770	2932	1322	1000	...	384
3841	Shipbuilding, repair..	674	1520	1910	2995	...	...	333	531	-24	...	3841
3843	Motor vehicles	11538	14497	10193	17049	...	1319	2530	829	982	...	3843
385	Professional goods	2096	1445	2788	3879	...	88	126	122	10	...	385
390	Other industries	4914	5500	5664	7489	...	140	1233	151	502	...	390
3	Manufacturing	409148	e/ 450900	549634	722839	...	36881	62882	75188	48383	...	3
410	Electricity,gas,steam	...	...	...	...	...	...	...	...	...	...	410
4101	Electricity	...	...	...	...	...	...	...	...	...	...	4101
420	Water works and supply	...	...	...	...	...	...	...	...	...	...	420
4	Electricity,gas etc	...	...	...	...	...	...	...	...	...	...	4
2-4	All industry	...	...	...	...	...	...	...	...	...	...	2-4

a/ Establishments with 10 or more persons engaged.
b/ Net of depreciation.
c/ Including value of revaluation of fixed assets effected in the year.
d/ Excluding manufacture of wool, cotton and synthetic fabrics.
e/ Excluding major group 353.

11. INDEX NUMBERS OF INDUSTRIAL PRODUCTION (1980 = 100)

ISIC	INDUSTRY	1976	1977	1978	1979	1981	1982	1983	1984	1985	a/ RATE	ISIC
210	Coal mining	...	...	...	...	...	...	...	...	...	...	210
220	Petroleum and gas	116	109	104	99	107	113	121	135	143	2.4	220
230	Metal ore mining	46	41	40	39	96	87	85	135	211	18.4	230
290	Other mining	92	95	106	104	80	72	122	138	160	6.3	290
2	Mining, quarrying	93	90	94	93	107	115	130	161	...	b/ 7.1	2
311/2	Food products	78	77	89	96	94	92	95	107	115	4.4	311/2
313	Beverages	68	76	86	93	97	92	97	101	107	5.2	313
314	Tobacco	98	98	95	94	108	113	116	132	137	3.8	314
321	Textiles	97	99	108	104	102	96	88	100	104	0.8	321
3211	Spinning,weaving etc.	...	...	...	...	...	...	...	...	...	...	3211
322	Wearing apparel	82	84	89	94	101	93	85	82	81	-0.1	322
323	Leather and products	78	101	95	104	103	96	77	79	79	0.1	323
324	Footwear	...	...	...	...	103	92	94	80	80	c/ -4.4	324
331	Wood products	79	90	95	93	106	113	109	110	113	4.1	331
332	Furniture, fixtures	...	...	...	...	92	71	61	64	66	c/ -8.0	332
341	Paper and products	85	85	91	99	98	94	92	103	111	3.0	341
3411	Pulp,paper etc.	...	...	...	...	...	...	...	...	...	...	3411
342	Printing,publishing	96	96	97	96	95	98	96	86	81	-1.9	342
351	Industrial chemicals	81	88	91	96	88	88	101	124	136	5.9	351
3511	Basic excl fertilizers	...	...	...	...	...	...	...	...	...	...	3511
3513	Synthetic resins etc	...	...	...	...	...	...	...	...	...	...	3513
352	Other chemical products	...	...	...	...	95	101	97	105	119	c/ 3.5	352
3522	Drugs and medicines	...	...	...	...	...	...	...	...	...	...	3522
353	Petroleum refineries	101	105	94	92	113	113	124	126	133	3.1	353
354	Petroleum,coal products	...	...	...	...	113	107	114	113	137	c/ 6.5	354
355	Rubber products	90	96	90	102	106	95	89	97	103	1.5	355
356	Plastic products n.e.c.	...	...	...	...	94	94	100	93	90	c/ -2.1	356
361	Pottery,china etc	...	...	...	...	96	93	84	88	101	c/ 0.2	361
362	Glass and products	81	85	95	101	97	96	93	89	108	3.2	362
369	Non-metal products n.e.c	...	...	...	...	98	102	99	114	111	c/ 2.1	369
371	Iron and steel	95	94	106	104	104	110	119	110	110	1.6	371
372	Non-ferrous metals	...	...	...	...	100	91	91	110	82	c/ -3.9	372
381	Metal products	71	77	91	99	96	88	88	95	92	2.9	381
382	Machinery n.e.c.	...	...	...	...	99	96	87	85	63	c/ -8.8	382
3825	Office,computing etc.	...	...	...	...	...	...	...	...	...	...	3825
383	Electrical machinery	...	...	...	...	107	104	88	89	87	c/ -2.7	383
3832	Radio,television etc.	...	...	...	...	...	...	...	...	...	...	3832
384	Transport equipment	...	...	...	...	89	75	65	101	80	c/ -4.4	384
3841	Shipbuilding, repair	...	...	...	...	...	...	...	...	...	...	3841
3843	Motor vehicles	...	...	...	...	...	...	...	...	...	...	3843
385	Professional goods	...	...	...	...	119	121	120	154	169	c/ 11.1	385
390	Other industries	...	...	...	...	93	69	78	96	101	c/ 0.2	390
3	Manufacturing	83	86	94	98	97	94	94	103	106	2.8	3
410	Electricity,gas,steam	...	...	...	...	...	...	...	...	...	...	410
4101	Electricity	74	77	76	84	105	112	114	116	117	5.2	4101
420	Water works and supply	...	...	...	...	...	...	...	...	...	...	420
4	Electricity,gas etc	77	78	86	93	102	108	113	119	...	b/ 5.6	4
2-4	All industry	83	86	93	97	100	100	101	108	...	b/ 3.3	2-4

a/ Annual growth rate 1976-1985.
b/ Annual growth rate 1976-1984.
c/ Annual growth rate 1980-1985.

COSTA RICA

The information in the tables is based on the reply to the United Nations Questionnaire on General Industrial Statistics from the Direccion General de Estadistica y Censos, Ministerio de Economia y Comercio, San Jose. The concepts, definitions and classification by branches of industry are generally in accordance with United Nations standards.

The data in the tables are based on the national classification which follows the present version of ISIC. The data for output are derived from national accounts statistics compiled by the Seccion de Cuentas Nacionales of the Banco Central de Costa Rica; the estimates cover all establishments in the country and the period of reference is the calendar year. The estimates of value added refer to the contribution of industry to the gross domestic product. The valuation of output and value added is in producers' prices.

ISIC	INDUSTRY	1. OUTPUT IN PRODUCERS' PRICES a/b/ (MILLION COLONES)					2. VALUE ADDED IN PRODUCERS' PRICES b/c/ (MILLION COLONES)					ISIC
		1981	1982	1983	1984	1985	1981	1982	1983	1984	1985	
210	Coal mining	...	...	...	...	...	...	...	...	...	...	210
220	Petroleum and gas	...	...	...	...	...	...	...	...	...	...	220
230	Metal ore mining	...	...	...	...	...	...	...	...	...	...	230
290	Other mining	...	...	...	...	...	...	...	...	...	...	290
2	Mining, quarrying .	...	...	...	...	...	...	...	...	...	...	2
311/2	Food products	16645	29000	36591	46030	...	3218	5092	7266	9836	...	311/2
313	Beverages	1675	3401	5793	6867	...	889	1536	2971	3734	...	313
314	Tobacco	535	1065	1285	1668	...	343	523	730	1002	...	314
321	Textiles	1066	2164	2705	2867	...	424	685	1008	1129	...	321
3211	Spinning,weaving etc..	517	1143	1355	1461	...	213	419	521	592	...	3211
322	Wearing apparel	1207	2603	3522	4000	...	404	820	1174	1418	...	322
323	Leather and products ...	213	376	446	447	...	72	122	157	165	...	323
324	Footwear	422	947	1127	1166	...	141	122	318	350	...	324
331	Wood products	885	1306	1796	2398	...	319	471	763	1075	...	331
332	Furniture, fixtures	831	1164	1374	1646	...	278	296	458	581	...	332
341	Paper and products	1337	2453	3525	3434	...	271	698	891	936	...	341
3411	Pulp,paper etc.	...	...	...	...	...	...	...	...	...	...	3411
342	Printing,publishing	545	959	1351	1744	...	159	314	458	626	...	342
351	Industrial chemicals ...	1678	3452	3792	4458	...	366	820	700	972	...	351
3511	Basic excl fertilizers	17	37	71	76	...	8	17	39	42	...	3511
3513	Synthetic resins etc .	172	241	188	251	...	30	70	46	62	...	3513
352	Other chemical products.	1841	3742	5173	5613	...	575	1430	2015	2125	...	352
3522	Drugs and medicines ..	824	1880	2670	2235	...	322	924	1377	1225	...	3522
353	Petroleum refineries ...	3473	5328	6234	8436	...	438	262	1114	1622	...	353
354	Petroleum,coal products.	12	14	21	22	...	4	1	4	4	...	354
355	Rubber products	607	1363	1794	1842	...	185	471	629	691	...	355
356	Plastic products n.e.c..	871	1747	2121	2921	...	230	628	598	881	...	356
361	Pottery,china etc	81	162	160	218	...	20	52	48	69	...	361
362	Glass and products	262	407	648	796	...	88	174	205	268	...	362
369	Non-metal products n.e.c	585	1065	1314	2104	...	224	296	451	776	...	369
371	Iron and steel	340	642	545	785	...	81	227	117	180	...	371
372	Non-ferrous metals	...	72	213	294	...	...	17	60	87	...	372
381	Metal products	974	1100	1562	2093	...	260	349	397	570	...	381
382	Machinery n.e.c.	376	788	1167	1548	...	120	228	382	540	...	382
3825	Office,computing etc..	...	...	...	...	...	...	...	...	...	...	3825
383	Electrical machinery ...	1410	2688	2875	3412	...	409	1064	723	913	...	383
3832	Radio,television etc..	791	1574	1561	1984	...	235	732	401	543	...	3832
384	Transport equipment	892	1247	871	1417	...	337	542	362	557	...	384
3841	Shipbuilding, repair..	8	10	41	120	...	2	2	10	27	...	3841
3843	Motor vehicles	779	1060	560	1025	...	276	453	187	360	...	3843
385	Professional goods	...	...	...	...	...	...	...	...	...	...	385
390	Other industries	84	165	231	294	...	29	59	90	122	...	390
3	Manufacturing	d/ 38847	e/ 69348	e/ 88236	e/ 108520	...	d/ 9884	e/ 17299	e/ 24089	e/ 31229	...	3
410	Electricity,gas,steam ..	...	...	...	...	...	...	...	...	...	...	410
4101	Electricity	...	...	...	...	...	...	...	...	...	...	4101
420	Water works and supply .	...	...	...	...	...	...	...	...	...	...	420
4	Electricity,gas etc	...	...	...	...	...	...	...	...	...	...	4
2-4	All industry	...	...	...	...	...	...	...	...	...	...	2-4

a/ Estimates derived from national accounts calculations.
b/ Excluding indirect taxes.
c/ Contributions to the gross domestic product.
d/ Excluding major groups 372 and 385.
e/ Excluding major group 385.

COTE D'IVOIRE

The information in the tables is based on the reply to the United Nations Questionnaire on General Industrial Statistics from the Direction de la statistique, Ministere du plan et de l'industrie, Abidjan. The concepts, definitions and classification by branches of industry are generally in accordance with United Nations standards.

The data in the tables for number of enterprises, number of employees and wages and salaries of employees are derived from the annual survey of industrial activity carried out by the Chambre d'industrie de Cote d'Ivoire and cover enterprises with annual turnover of 12 million francs or more. The data for output and value added are from national accounts calculations which cover all enterprises.

The estimates are based on the present version of ISIC. It should be noted, however, that repair services of transport equipment (ISIC major division 9) are included in ISIC 384.

The number of enterprises is as of 1 October of the year indicated and the number of employees relates to the mid-year number of persons who work in or for the enterprise and receive pay.

Related national publication:
    L'industrie ivoirienne (annual), published by the Chambre d'industrie de Cote d'Ivoire, Abidjan.

ISIC	INDUSTRY		1. NUMBER OF ENTERPRISES a/ (NUMBER) 1981	1982	1983	1984	1985	2. AVERAGE NUMBER OF EMPLOYEES a/b/ (NUMBER) 1981	1982	1983	1984	1985	ISIC
210	Coal mining		...	...	...	...	...	...	...	...	...	...	210
220	Petroleum and gas		...	...	...	...	...	...	...	...	...	...	220
230	Metal ore mining		...	...	...	...	...	...	...	...	...	...	230
290	Other mining		...	...	...	...	...	...	...	...	...	...	290
2	Mining, quarrying .		1	2	2	...	...	...	242	554	...	...	2
311/2	Food products	c/	257	272	290	...	...	21926	22279	20287	...	...	311/2
313	Beverages		9	9	8	...	...	3335	3278	2509	...	...	313
314	Tobacco	c/	...	...	...	...	...	...	...	...	...	...	314
321	Textiles	d/	39	40	37	...	...	11710	11604	9136	...	...	321
3211	Spinning,weaving etc..		...	...	...	...	...	...	...	...	...	...	3211
322	Wearing apparel	d/	...	...	...	...	...	...	...	...	...	...	322
323	Leather and products ...		[41	35	36]	...	...	[1218	1121	762]	...	...	323
324	Footwear					...	...				...	...	324
331	Wood products		[107	107	104]	...	...	[10492	9653	3894]	...	...	331
332	Furniture, fixtures					...	...				...	...	332
341	Paper and products	e/	96	100	100	...	...	1459	1491	1672	...	...	341
3411	Pulp,paper etc.		...	...	...	...	...	...	...	...	...	...	3411
342	Printing,publishing	e/	...	...	...	...	...	...	...	...	...	...	342
351	Industrial chemicals ...	f/	55	55	55	...	...	4400	4427	2425	...	...	351
3511	Basic excl fertilizers		...	...	...	...	...	...	...	...	...	...	3511
3513	Synthetic resins etc .		...	...	...	...	...	...	...	...	...	...	3513
352	Other chemical products.	f/	...	...	...	...	...	...	...	...	...	...	352
3522	Drugs and medicines ..		...	...	...	...	...	...	...	...	...	...	3522
353	Petroleum refineries ...		[4	4	4]	...	...	[961	969	876]	...	...	353
354	Petroleum,coal products.					...	...				...	...	354
355	Rubber products		7	6	5	...	...	648	726	2206	...	...	355
356	Plastic products n.e.c..	f/	...	...	...	...	...	...	...	...	...	...	356
361	Pottery,china etc					...	...				...	...	361
362	Glass and products		[20	20	20]	...	...	[1437	1144	222]	...	...	362
369	Non-metal products n.e.c					...	...				...	...	369
371	Iron and steel		[1	1	1]	...	...	[204	117	302]	...	...	371
372	Non-ferrous metals					...	...				...	...	372
381	Metal products	g/	[39	38	40]	...	...	[4494	3655	1756]	...	...	381
382	Machinery n.e.c.					...	...				...	...	382
3825	Office,computing etc..		...	...	...	...	...	...	...	...	...	...	3825
383	Electrical machinery ...	g/	...	...	...	...	...	...	...	...	...	...	383
3832	Radio,television etc..		...	...	...	...	...	...	...	...	...	...	3832
384	Transport equipment	h/	22	21	18	...	...	1803	1916	1762	...	...	384
3841	Shipbuilding, repair..		...	...	...	...	...	...	...	...	...	...	3841
3843	Motor vehicles		...	...	...	...	...	...	...	...	...	...	3843
385	Professional goods		-	-	-	...	...	-	-	-	...	...	385
390	Other industries		11	15	11	...	...	765	713	1131	...	...	390
3	Manufacturing	h/	708	723	729	...	...	64852	63093	48940	...	...	3
410	Electricity,gas,steam ..		...	...	...	...	...	...	...	...	...	...	410
4101	Electricity		...	...	...	...	...	...	...	...	...	...	4101
420	Water works and supply .		...	...	...	...	...	...	...	...	...	...	420
4	Electricity,gas etc		2	2	2	...	...	4743	5024	4890	...	...	4
2-4	All industry	h/	711	727	733	...	...	...	68359	54384	...	...	2-4

a/ Enterprises with annual turnover of 12 million francs or more.
b/ Mid-year numbers.
c/ Major group 314 is included in 311/2.
d/ Major group 322 is included in 321.
e/ Major group 342 is included in 341.
f/ Major groups 352 and 356 are included in 351.
g/ Major group 383 is included in 381 and 382 combined.
h/ Including repair services of transport equipment.

ISIC	INDUSTRY		3. WAGES AND SALARIES OF EMPLOYEES a/ (MILLION FRANCS) 1981	1982	1983	1984	1985	4. OUTPUT IN PRODUCERS' PRICES b/ (BILLION FRANCS) 1981	1982	1983	1984	1985	ISIC
210	Coal mining		...	...	...	...	...	...	...	...	...	...	210
220	Petroleum and gas		...	...	...	...	...	...	...	...	...	...	220
230	Metal ore mining		...	...	...	...	...	...	...	...	...	...	230
290	Other mining		...	...	...	...	...	...	...	...	...	...	290
2	Mining, quarrying .		...	1271	5319	...	...	33.8	62.8	...	...	...	2
311/2	Food products	c/	24844	27367	41533	...	...	286.4	327.8	...	...	...	311/2
313	Beverages		6197	6309	6359	...	...	33.3	34.2	...	...	...	313
314	Tobacco	c/	...	...	...	...	...	...	...	...	...	...	314
321	Textiles	d/	15387	17345	17045	...	...	114.8	130.3	...	...	...	321
3211	Spinning,weaving etc..		...	...	...	...	...	...	...	...	...	...	3211
322	Wearing apparel	d/	...	...	...	...	...	...	...	...	...	...	322
323	Leather and products ...		[1474	1750	1882]	...	...	[8.0	10.1]	...	...	...	323
324	Footwear					...	...			...	...	...	324
331	Wood products		[6995	7065	9456]	...	...	[58.2	57.2]	...	...	...	331
332	Furniture, fixtures					...	...			...	...	...	332
341	Paper and products	e/	2622	2798	4975	...	...	22.7	25.9	...	...	...	341
3411	Pulp,paper etc.		...	...	...	...	...	...	...	...	...	...	3411
342	Printing,publishing	e/	...	...	...	...	...	...	...	...	...	...	342
351	Industrial chemicals ...	f/	8806	9648	7748	...	...	60.3	64.9	...	...	...	351
3511	Basic excl fertilizers		...	...	...	...	...	...	...	...	...	...	3511
3513	Synthetic resins etc .		...	...	...	...	...	...	...	...	...	...	3513
352	Other chemical products.	f/	...	...	...	...	...	...	...	...	...	...	352
3522	Drugs and medicines ..		...	...	...	...	...	...	...	...	...	...	3522
353	Petroleum refineries ...		[4050	4679	4671]	...	...	[156.2	220.5]	...	...	...	353
354	Petroleum,coal products.					...	...			...	...	...	354
355	Rubber products		759	698	4698	...	...	7.4	7.8	...	...	...	355
356	Plastic products n.e.c..	f/	...	...	...	...	...	...	...	...	...	...	356
361	Pottery,china etc					...	...			...	...	...	361
362	Glass and products		[2471	2522	629]	...	...	[26.1	28.2]	...	...	...	362
369	Non-metal products n.e.c					...	...			...	...	...	369
371	Iron and steel		[388	261	1449]	...	...	[2.6	1.5]	...	...	...	371
372	Non-ferrous metals					...	...			...	...	...	372
381	Metal products	g/	[8287	7784	6131]	...	...	[52.9	60.2]	...	...	...	381
382	Machinery n.e.c.					...	...			...	...	...	382
3825	Office,computing etc..		...	...	...	...	...	...	...	...	...	...	3825
383	Electrical machinery ...	g/	...	...	...	...	...	...	...	...	...	...	383
3832	Radio,television etc..		...	...	...	...	...	...	...	...	...	...	3832
384	Transport equipment	h/	3588	4163	5213	...	...	70.0	77.1	...	...	...	384
3841	Shipbuilding, repair..		...	...	...	...	...	...	...	...	...	...	3841
3843	Motor vehicles		...	...	...	...	...	...	...	...	...	...	3843
385	Professional goods		-	-	-	...	...	-	-	...	...	...	385
390	Other industries		1064	1121	3497	...	...	9.7	9.2	...	...	...	390
3	Manufacturing	h/	86932	93510	115286	...	...	908.6	1054.9	...	...	...	3
410	Electricity,gas,steam ..		...	...	...	...	...	...	...	...	...	...	410
4101	Electricity		...	...	...	...	...	...	...	...	...	...	4101
420	Water works and supply .		...	...	...	...	...	...	...	...	...	...	420
4	Electricity,gas etc		14265	16258	17207	...	...	63.0	74.2	...	...	...	4
2-4	All industry	h/	...	111039	137812	...	...	1005.4	1191.9	...	...	...	2-4

a/ Enterprises with annual turnover of 12 million francs or more.
b/ Estimates derived from national accounts calculations.
c/ Major group 314 is included in 311/2.
d/ Major group 322 is included in 321.
e/ Major group 342 is included in 341.
f/ Major groups 352 and 356 are included in 351.
g/ Major group 383 is included in 381 and 382 combined.
h/ Including repair services of transport equipment.

5. VALUE ADDED IN PRODUCERS' PRICES a/ (MILLION FRANCS)

ISIC	INDUSTRY		1981	1982	1983	1984	1985	ISIC
210	Coal mining		...	...	...	...	...	210
220	Petroleum and gas		...	...	...	...	...	220
230	Metal ore mining		...	...	...	...	...	230
290	Other mining		...	...	...	...	...	290
2	Mining, quarrying .		27425	52245	...	...	...	2
311/2	Food products	b/	67385	78488	...	...	...	311/2
313	Beverages		15746	15357	...	...	...	313
314	Tobacco	b/	...	...	...	...	...	314
321	Textiles	c/	40853	47555	...	...	...	321
3211	Spinning,weaving etc..		...	...	...	...	...	3211
322	Wearing apparel	c/	...	...	...	...	...	322
323	Leather and products ...		[2960	4557]	...	...	...	323
324	Footwear				...	...	...	324
331	Wood products		[19176	15463]	...	...	...	331
332	Furniture, fixtures				...	...	...	332
341	Paper and products	d/	7475	7337	...	...	...	341
3411	Pulp,paper etc.		...	...	...	...	...	3411
342	Printing,publishing	d/	...	...	...	...	...	342
351	Industrial chemicals ...	e/	17213	16406	...	...	...	351
3511	Basic excl fertilizers		...	...	...	...	...	3511
3513	Synthetic resins etc .		...	...	...	...	...	3513
352	Other chemical products.	e/	...	...	...	...	...	352
3522	Drugs and medicines ..		...	...	...	...	...	3522
353	Petroleum refineries ...		...	[44820]	...	...	...	353
354	Petroleum,coal products.		...		...	...	...	354
355	Rubber products		645	176	...	...	...	355
356	Plastic products n.e.c..	e/	...	...	...	...	...	356
361	Pottery,china etc				...	...	...	361
362	Glass and products		[5053	6284]	...	...	...	362
369	Non-metal products n.e.c				...	...	...	369
371	Iron and steel		[460	288]	...	...	...	371
372	Non-ferrous metals				...	...	...	372
381	Metal products	f/	[17795	19232]	...	...	...	381
382	Machinery n.e.c.				...	...	...	382
3825	Office,computing etc..		...	...	...	...	...	3825
383	Electrical machinery ...	f/	...	...	...	...	...	383
3832	Radio,television etc..		...	...	...	...	...	3832
384	Transport equipment	g/	21951	38041	...	...	...	384
3841	Shipbuilding, repair..		...	...	...	...	...	3841
3843	Motor vehicles		...	...	...	...	...	3843
385	Professional goods		-	-	...	...	...	385
390	Other industries		7424	6864	...	...	...	390
3	Manufacturing	g/	h/ 224136	300868	...	...	...	3
410	Electricity,gas,steam ..		...	...	...	...	...	410
4101	Electricity		...	...	...	...	...	4101
420	Water works and supply .		...	...	...	...	...	420
4	Electricity,gas etc		40980	52903	...	...	...	4
2-4	All industry	g/	h/ 292541	406016	...	...	...	2-4

a/ Contributions to the gross domestic product.
b/ Major group 314 is included in 311/2.
c/ Major group 322 is included in 321.
d/ Major group 342 is included in 341.
e/ Major groups 352 and 356 are included in 351.
f/ Major group 383 is included in 381 and 382 combined.
g/ Including repair services of transport equipment.
h/ Excluding major groups 353 and 354.

CUBA

The information on industrial activity is based on the reply to the United Nations Questionnaire on General Industrial Statistics from the Comite Estatal de Estadisticas, Habana and the Council for Mutual Economic Assistance (CMEA), Moscow. The concepts, definitions and classification by branches of industry are generally in accordance with United Nations standards.

The estimates are based on regular monthly and annual reports of enterprises. The statistical unit is the industrial enterprise or the industrial unit of the non-industrial enterprise; industrial units of collective farms and small subsidiary industrial enterprises, however, are not covered.

The estimates, which are based on the national classification, are shown in the most appropriate category of ISIC. The national classification includes logging; commercial fishing; repair of motor vehicles, household appliances, furniture and footwear; repair and restoration of knitted goods and apparel; film copying and cleaning and dyeing. The following industries are excluded: (a) prospecting and drilling for minerals, crude petroleum and natural gas, and preparing sites for extracting; (b) gas distribution; and (c) water supply.

Employment numbers are annual averages of monthly figures and relate to persons engaged in the industrial activities of enterprises classified under mining, manufacturing, electricity and gas. They comprise production workers, apprentices, engineers and technicians, office staff, minor service personnel and guards.

The average monthly earnings per employee was recorded as 178 pesos for 1981, 184 pesos for 1982, 189 pesos for 1983, 192 pesos for 1984 and 194 pesos for 1985.

Value of resale of commodities without further processing is not included in output.

The estimates of gross fixed capital formation represent acquisitions of new fixed assets and relate to the "productive" investments of industrial enterprises, valued at current prices; they do not include capital repair and compensation of losses of fixed assets; the investments of industrial enterprises in dwellings, public utilities, social facilities and other "non-productive" assets are not included.

Related national publications:
<u>Republica de Cuba, Anuario Estadistico de Cuba</u> (annual), <u>Cuba en Cifras</u> (annual) both published by the Comite Estatal de Estadisticas, Habana; <u>Statistical Yearbook</u> published by the Council for Mutual Economic Assistance (CMEA), Moscow.

ISIC	INDUSTRY		1. NUMBER OF ENTERPRISES (NUMBER) 1981	1982	1983	1984	1985	2. AVERAGE NUMBER OF EMPLOYEES (THOUSANDS) 1981	1982	1983	1984	1985	ISIC
210	Coal mining	a/b/	[4	4	4	4	4	3.8	3.8	3.9	4.0	4.5]	210
220	Petroleum and gas												220
230	Metal ore mining	c/	...	...	...	...	...	...	...	...	...	...	230
290	Other mining	d/	...	...	...	...	...	...	...	...	...	...	290
2	Mining, quarrying .		...	...	...	...	...	...	...	...	...	...	2
311/2	Food products	e/f/	296	297	299	294	291	178.3	190.1	205.5	231.6	237.1	311/2
313	Beverages		[44	44	44	43	43	37.2	44.1	43.4	46.3	49.2]	313
314	Tobacco												314
321	Textiles		15	15	15	14	14	21.6	21.0	22.3	26.2	27.3	321
3211	Spinning,weaving etc..		...	...	...	...	...	...	...	...	...	...	3211
322	Wearing apparel		14	14	14	14	15	27.7	28.3	28.6	29.3	31.2	322
323	Leather and products ...		[15	15	15	15	15	17.5	18.6	19.5	19.4	19.4]	323
324	Footwear												324
331	Wood products		[18	18	18	18	18	16.4	15.7	16.2	17.1	16.5]	331
332	Furniture, fixtures												332
341	Paper and products		9	9	9	11	11	4.6	6.2	6.4	7.1	8.3	341
3411	Pulp,paper etc.		...	...	...	...	...	...	...	...	...	...	3411
342	Printing,publishing		16	17	18	18	17	12.4	9.1	10.2	10.3	10.3	342
351	Industrial chemicals ...	g/	42	43	42	40	38	26.8	26.5	25.7	28.7	29.3	351
3511	Basic excl fertilizers		...	...	...	...	...	...	...	...	...	...	3511
3513	Synthetic resins etc .		...	...	...	...	...	...	...	...	...	...	3513
352	Other chemical products.	g/	...	...	...	...	...	...	...	...	...	...	352
3522	Drugs and medicines ..		...	...	...	...	...	...	...	...	...	...	3522
353	Petroleum refineries ...	a/	...	...	...	...	...	...	...	...	...	...	353
354	Petroleum,coal products.	a/	...	...	...	...	...	...	...	...	...	...	354
355	Rubber products	g/	...	...	...	...	...	...	...	...	...	...	355
356	Plastic products n.e.c..	g/	...	...	...	...	...	...	...	...	...	...	356
361	Pottery,china etc		[5	6	6	6	6	3.9	5.8	6.0	6.2	6.4]	361
362	Glass and products												362
369	Non-metal products n.e.c	d/	43	43	40	41	43	46.0	43.3	43.7	46.9	49.2	369
371	Iron and steel		4	5	6	5	6	8.1	8.1	8.8	8.7	8.3	371
372	Non-ferrous metals	c/	5	5	6	7	7	10.4	10.6	11.7	12.3	12.5	372
381	Metal products		21	21	22	23	25	11.2	12.9	14.0	14.6	14.8	381
382	Machinery n.e.c.	h/	125	136	134	134	142	70.5	74.4	78.5	82.8	87.8	382
3825	Office,computing etc..		...	...	...	...	...	...	...	...	...	...	3825
383	Electrical machinery ...		17	18	18	18	17	12.3	11.8	12.6	14.2	14.2	383
3832	Radio,television etc..		...	...	...	...	...	...	...	...	...	...	3832
384	Transport equipment	h/	...	...	...	...	...	...	...	...	...	...	384
3841	Shipbuilding, repair..		...	...	...	...	...	...	...	...	...	...	3841
3843	Motor vehicles		...	...	...	...	...	...	...	...	...	...	3843
385	Professional goods	h/	...	...	...	...	...	...	...	...	...	...	385
390	Other industries		39	40	40	41	42	i/ 26.4	i/ 26.0	i/ 28.0	i/ 29.6	i/ 33.4	390
3	Manufacturing	e/f/i/	732	750	750	746	...	k/ 535.1	k/ 556.3	k/ 585.0	k/ 635.3	k/ 659.7	3
410	Electricity,gas,steam ..		10	10	16	16	15	l/ 15.5	l/ 16.4	l/ 17.0	l/ 17.8	l/ 18.7	410
4101	Electricity		10	10	16	16	15	15.5	16.4	17.0	17.8	18.7	4101
420	Water works and supply .		.	.	.	.	.	.	.	.	.	.	420
4	Electricity,gas etc		10	10	16	16	15	i/ 15.5	i/ 16.4	i/ 17.0	i/ 17.8	i/ 18.7	4
2-4	All industry		742	760	766	762	769	k/ 550.6	k/ 572.7	k/ 602.0	k/ 653.1	k/ 678.4	2-4

Note. For certain deviations in classification see country note.

a/ Major groups 353 and 354 are included in 210 and 220 combined.
b/ Combustible industries only.
c/ Non-ferrous ore mining is included in major group 372.
d/ Major group 290 is included in 369.
e/ Including sugar-cane cropping.
f/ Excluding Processing of fish, crustacea and other sea foods.
g/ Major groups 352, 355 and 356 are included in 351.
h/ Major groups 384 and 385 are included in 382.
i/ Including industries not shown separately.
j/ Including mining and quarrying.
k/ Including some repair establishments.
l/ Excluding gas and steam.

ISIC	INDUSTRY		3. WAGES AND SALARIES OF EMPLOYEES (MILLION PESOS) 1981	1982	1983	1984	1985	4. AVERAGE NUMBER OF OPERATIVES (THOUSANDS) 1981	1982	1983	1984	1985	ISIC
210	Coal mining	a/b/	10.3	10.6	11.0	12.0	13.0	2.3	2.4	2.3	2.4	2.6	210
220	Petroleum and gas												220
230	Metal ore mining	c/	...	...	...	...	...	...	...	...	...	...	230
290	Other mining	d/	...	...	...	...	...	...	...	...	...	...	290
2	Mining, quarrying .		...	...	...	...	...	...	...	...	...	...	2
311/2	Food products	e/f/	408.2	448.1	488.5	517.0	548.8	131.7	150.2	159.8	169.1	172.1	311/2
313	Beverages		67.5	81.0	80.0	88.1	95.3	34.5	38.2	37.4	38.9	40.3	313
314	Tobacco												314
321	Textiles		44.1	43.2	47.7	56.6	61.7	18.0	18.0	18.1	20.7	23.5	321
3211	Spinning,weaving etc..		...	...	...	...	...	...	...	...	...	...	3211
322	Wearing apparel		43.1	44.3	46.9	49.2	54.8	23.4	22.8	23.2	24.4	26.7	322
323	Leather and products ...		35.5	36.7	39.0	39.5	39.8	14.1	15.0	15.3	15.6	16.2	323
324	Footwear												324
331	Wood products		30.0	29.6	31.9	35.8	36.3	12.0	10.8	11.0	11.8	11.0	331
332	Furniture, fixtures												332
341	Paper and products		10.2	13.6	14.2	16.4	19.7	4.0	4.2	4.4	5.4	5.8	341
3411	Pulp,paper etc.		...	...	...	...	...	...	...	...	...	...	3411
342	Printing,publishing		24.1	19.1	21.6	22.5	22.6	5.5	4.2	5.5	6.5	6.7	342
351	Industrial chemicals ...	g/	55.2	56.0	55.4	64.6	68.0	17.8	16.8	17.5	18.5	19.4	351
3511	Basic excl fertilizers		...	...	...	...	...	...	...	...	...	...	3511
3513	Synthetic resins etc .		...	...	...	...	...	...	...	...	...	...	3513
352	Other chemical products.	g/	...	...	...	...	...	...	...	...	...	...	352
3522	Drugs and medicines ..		...	...	...	...	...	...	...	...	...	...	3522
353	Petroleum refineries ...	a/	...	...	...	...	...	...	...	...	...	...	353
354	Petroleum,coal products.	a/	...	...	...	...	...	...	...	...	...	...	354
355	Rubber products	g/	...	...	...	...	...	...	...	...	...	...	355
356	Plastic products n.e.c..	g/	...	...	...	...	...	...	...	...	...	...	356
361	Pottery,china etc		8.3	12.4	13.7	14.9	15.9	3.4	4.8	4.5	4.8	4.9	361
362	Glass and products												362
369	Non-metal products n.e.c	d/	98.6	96.8	102.7	112.8	118.0	34.4	30.0	31.0	34.0	35.5	369
371	Iron and steel		20.5	21.8	24.5	23.8	24.2	6.1	5.4	6.2	6.5	6.5	371
372	Non-ferrous metals	c/	24.7	25.4	29.9	33.3	35.9	7.4	8.4	8.5	9.2	9.2	372
381	Metal products		24.5	29.1	32.5	35.3	36.5	8.6	9.0	9.6	9.5	10.7	381
382	Machinery n.e.c.	h/	156.2	171.0	184.7	203.9	219.6	48.5	51.0	53.0	60.1	60.5	382
3825	Office,computing etc..		...	...	...	...	...	...	...	...	...	...	3825
383	Electrical machinery ...		25.2	24.7	27.4	32.1	32.3	8.1	7.2	8.1	9.5	9.7	383
3832	Radio,television etc..		...	...	...	...	...	...	...	...	...	...	3832
384	Transport equipment	h/	...	...	...	...	...	...	...	...	...	...	384
3841	Shipbuilding, repair..		...	...	...	...	...	...	...	...	...	...	3841
3843	Motor vehicles		...	...	...	...	...	...	...	...	...	...	3843
385	Professional goods	h/	...	...	...	...	...	...	...	...	...	...	385
390	Other industries	i/	46.8	48.3	55.2	59.9	69.5	19.6	15.5	19.2	19.1	19.7	390
3	Manufacturing	e/f/i/k/	1133.0	1211.7	1306.8	1417.7	1511.9	399.4	413.9	434.6	466.0	481.0	3
410	Electricity,gas,steam ..	l/	37.6	41.5	43.6	46.4	49.2	7.5	8.4	8.4	9.0	9.6	410
4101	Electricity		37.6	41.5	43.6	46.4	49.2	7.5	8.4	8.4	9.0	9.6	4101
420	Water works and supply .		.	.	.	.	.	.	.	.	.	.	420
4	Electricity,gas etc	l/	37.6	41.5	43.6	46.4	49.2	7.5	8.4	8.4	9.0	9.6	4
2-4	All industry	k/	1170.6	1253.2	1350.4	1464.1	1561.1	406.9	422.3	443.0	475.0	490.6	2-4

Note. For certain deviations in classification see country note.

a/ Major groups 353 and 354 are included in 210 and 220 combined.
b/ Combustible industries only.
c/ Non-ferrous ore mining is included in major group 372.
d/ Major group 290 is included in 369.
e/ Including sugar-cane cropping.
f/ Excluding Processing of fish, crustacea and other sea foods.
g/ Major groups 352, 355 and 356 are included in 351.
h/ Major groups 384 and 385 are included in 382.
i/ Including industries not shown separately.
j/ Including mining and quarrying.
k/ Including some repair establishments.
l/ Excluding gas and steam.

ISIC	INDUSTRY		5. OUTPUT IN PRODUCERS' PRICES (MILLION PESOS) 1981	1982	1983	1984	1985	6. VALUE ADDED (MILLION PESOS) 1981	1982	1983	1984	1985	ISIC
210	Coal mining	a/b/	513	531	536	540	552	50	56	52	56	54	210
220	Petroleum and gas												220
230	Metal ore mining		...	...	...	...	...	...	...	...	...	...	230
290	Other mining	c/	...	...	...	...	...	...	...	...	...	...	290
2	Mining, quarrying .		...	...	...	...	...	...	...	...	...	...	2
311/2	Food products	d/e/	3316	3458	3530	3951	4018	587	679	590	771	871	311/2
313	Beverages		1726	1995	1995	2262	2448	1440	1665	1701	1914	2072	313
314	Tobacco												314
321	Textiles		163	164	180	185	228	35	32	36	23	37	321
3211	Spinning,weaving etc..		...	...	...	...	...	...	...	...	...	...	3211
322	Wearing apparel		196	193	223	224	243	58	51	73	78	89	322
323	Leather and products ...		153	158	178	166	167	78	76	90	79	73	323
324	Footwear												324
331	Wood products		129	130	138	159	162	68	67	78	90	87	331
332	Furniture, fixtures												332
341	Paper and products		137	145	149	173	198	49	31	37	48	40	341
3411	Pulp,paper etc.		...	...	...	...	...	...	...	...	...	...	3411
342	Printing,publishing		81	90	93	105	115	21	23	27	52	54	342
351	Industrial chemicals ...	f/	634	555	613	679	764	273	248	287	326	364	351
3511	Basic excl fertilizers		...	...	...	...	...	...	...	...	...	...	3511
3513	Synthetic resins etc .		...	...	...	...	...	...	...	...	...	...	3513
352	Other chemical products.	f/	...	...	...	...	...	...	...	...	...	...	352
3522	Drugs and medicines ..		...	...	...	...	...	...	...	...	...	...	3522
353	Petroleum refineries ...	a/	...	...	...	...	...	...	...	...	...	...	353
354	Petroleum,coal products.	a/	...	...	...	...	...	...	...	...	...	...	354
355	Rubber products	f/	...	...	...	...	...	...	...	...	...	...	355
356	Plastic products n.e.c..	f/	...	...	...	...	...	...	...	...	...	...	356
361	Pottery,china etc		32	43	41	46	53	6	6	5	3	8	361
362	Glass and products	g/											362
369	Non-metal products n.e.c	c/g/	369	354	352	383	406	106	87	82	87	97	369
371	Iron and steel		109	119	130	125	145	26	34	42	35	40	371
372	Non-ferrous metals	h/	136	131	147	144	148	41	38	47	40	30	372
381	Metal products		141	158	186	204	202	56	70	84	92	84	381
382	Machinery n.e.c.	i/	554	644	748	876	959	263	307	382	449	470	382
3825	Office,computing etc..		...	...	...	...	...	...	...	...	...	...	3825
383	Electrical machinery ...		101	89	120	145	152	41	41	53	46	53	383
3832	Radio,television etc..		...	...	...	...	...	...	...	...	...	...	3832
384	Transport equipment	i/	...	...	...	...	...	...	...	...	...	...	384
3841	Shipbuilding, repair..		...	...	...	...	...	...	...	...	...	...	3841
3843	Motor vehicles		...	...	...	...	...	...	...	...	...	...	3843
385	Professional goods	i/	...	...	...	...	...	...	...	...	...	...	385
390	Other industries	j/	409	409	454	521	550	102	106	143	169	171	390
3	Manufacturing	d/e/k/l/	8899	9366	9813	10888	11510	3300	3617	3809	4379	4694	3
410	Electricity,gas,steam ..	m/	452	488	502	535	475	216	239	247	262	190	410
4101	Electricity		452	488	502	535	475	216	239	247	262	190	4101
420	Water works and supply .		.	.	.	.	.	.	.	.	.	.	420
4	Electricity,gas etc	m/	452	488	502	535	475	216	239	247	262	190	4
2-4	All industry	l/	9351	9854	10315	11423	11985	3516	3856	4056	4620	4884	2-4

Note. For certain deviations in classification see country note.

a/ Major groups 353 and 354 are included in 210 and 220 combined.
b/ Combustible industries only.
c/ Major group 290 is included in 369.
d/ Including sugar-cane cropping.
e/ Excluding Processing of fish, crustacea and other sea foods.
f/ Major groups 352, 355 and 356 are included in 351.
g/ Part of major group 369 is included in 362.
h/ Non-ferrous ore mining is included in major group 372.
i/ Major groups 384 and 385 are included in 382.
j/ Including industries not shown separately.
k/ Including mining and quarrying.
l/ Including some repair establishments.
m/ Excluding gas and steam.

ISIC	INDUSTRY		7. GROSS FIXED CAPITAL FORMATION TOTAL (MILLION PESOS) 1981	1982	1983	1984	1985	8. GROSS FIXED CAPITAL FORMATION MACHINERY AND EQUIPMENT (MILLION PESOS) 1981	1982	1983	1984	1985	ISIC
210	Coal mining	a/b/	[60.8	67.1	77.1	100.4	104.5	33.2	35.0	34.3	25.4	32.1]	210
220	Petroleum and gas												220
230	Metal ore mining	c/	...	...	...	...	...	...	...	...	...	...	230
290	Other mining	d/	...	...	...	...	...	...	...	...	...	...	290
2	Mining, quarrying .		...	...	...	...	...	...	...	...	...	...	2
311/2	Food products	e/f/	268.6	267.1	345.7	411.4	525.7	121.8	138.1	179.8	180.5	258.2	311/2
313	Beverages		[12.3	16.3	24.6	44.0	53.5	6.8	8.4	15.1	27.2	29.4]	313
314	Tobacco												314
321	Textiles		83.5	77.4	58.5	43.1	39.0	44.1	22.9	14.8	14.4	10.1	321
3211	Spinning,weaving etc..		...	...	...	...	...	...	...	...	...	...	3211
322	Wearing apparel		3.5	3.3	3.2	3.4	7.3	2.4	2.3	2.0	1.7	3.6	322
323	Leather and products ...		[2.4	6.1	8.9	8.3	7.1	2.0	4.8	6.9	5.0	4.5]	323
324	Footwear												324
331	Wood products		[3.4	2.8	3.0	6.7	3.8	1.5	1.3	1.2	2.2	1.7]	331
332	Furniture, fixtures												332
341	Paper and products		122.3	39.2	34.7	29.2	23.0	81.2	13.5	11.0	5.9	16.8	341
3411	Pulp,paper etc.		...	...	...	...	...	...	...	...	...	...	3411
342	Printing,publishing		2.4	0.8	2.3	1.9	3.0	1.1	0.4	1.8	0.9	2.2	342
351	Industrial chemicals ...	g/	29.8	31.7	27.8	44.0	75.2	14.3	21.2	11.5	16.6	40.7	351
3511	Basic excl fertilizers		...	...	...	...	...	...	...	...	...	...	3511
3513	Synthetic resins etc .		...	...	...	...	...	...	...	...	...	...	3513
352	Other chemical products.	g/	...	...	...	...	...	...	...	...	...	...	352
3522	Drugs and medicines ..		...	...	...	...	...	...	...	...	...	...	3522
353	Petroleum refineries ...	a/	...	...	...	...	...	...	...	...	...	...	353
354	Petroleum,coal products.	a/	...	...	...	...	...	...	...	...	...	...	354
355	Rubber products	g/	...	...	...	...	...	...	...	...	...	...	355
356	Plastic products n.e.c..	g/	...	...	...	...	...	...	...	...	...	...	356
361	Pottery,china etc		[13.0	10.2	4.9	10.1	16.5	3.4	3.7	1.6	4.1	8.6]	361
362	Glass and products												362
369	Non-metal products n.e.c	d/	62.6	60.2	63.8	124.2	123.2	18.8	30.9	23.4	50.0	57.5	369
371	Iron and steel		10.5	19.3	34.2	46.7	76.8	2.5	10.3	22.2	21.7	42.5	371
372	Non-ferrous metals	c/	172.4	122.3	160.3	185.0	231.1	109.7	51.3	77.5	74.3	90.4	372
381	Metal products		10.0	12.4	12.4	19.8	32.6	4.0	8.3	5.1	10.8	20.1	381
382	Machinery n.e.c.	h/	112.9	118.0	102.2	108.2	115.5	55.1	76.0	53.0	49.1	62.8	382
3825	Office,computing etc..		...	...	...	...	...	...	...	...	...	...	3825
383	Electrical machinery ...		19.7	13.1	10.9	13.1	15.0	10.0	6.6	4.2	6.4	8.0	383
3832	Radio,television etc..		...	...	...	...	...	...	...	...	...	...	3832
384	Transport equipment	h/	...	...	...	...	...	...	...	...	...	...	384
3841	Shipbuilding, repair..		...	...	...	...	...	...	...	...	...	...	3841
3843	Motor vehicles		...	...	...	...	...	...	...	...	...	...	3843
385	Professional goods	h/	...	...	...	...	...	...	...	...	...	...	385
390	Other industries	i/	51.3	32.5	43.3	44.7	54.6	2.2	5.0	5.2	7.8	5.9	390
3	Manufacturing	e/f/i/k/	1041.4	899.8	1017.8	1244.2	1507.4	514.1	440.0	470.6	504.0	695.1	3
410	Electricity,gas,steam ..	l/	116.4	143.2	204.0	284.9	277.3	49.1	64.3	96.6	121.9	82.5	410
4101	Electricity		116.4	143.2	204.0	284.9	277.3	49.1	64.3	96.6	121.9	82.5	4101
420	Water works and supply .		.	.	.	.	.	.	.	.	.	.	420
4	Electricity,gas etc	l/	116.4	143.2	204.0	284.9	277.3	49.1	64.3	96.6	121.9	82.5	4
2-4	All industry	k/	m/ 1157.8	m/ 1043.0	m/ 1221.8	1529.1	1784.7	563.2	504.3	567.2	625.9	777.6	2-4

Note. For certain deviations in classification see country note.

a/ Major groups 353 and 354 are included in 210 and 220 combined.
b/ Combustible industries only.
c/ Non-ferrous ore mining is included in major group 372.
d/ Major group 290 is included in 369.
e/ Including sugar-cane cropping.
f/ Excluding Processing of fish, crustacea and other sea foods.
g/ Major groups 352, 355 and 356 are included in 351.
h/ Major groups 384 and 385 are included in 382.
i/ Including industries not shown separately.
j/ Including mining and quarrying.
k/ Including some repair establishments.
l/ Excluding gas and steam.
m/ Excluding capital repair and compensation of losses.

CYPRUS

The information in the tables, except for the indexes, is based on the reply to the United Nations Questionnaire on General Industrial Statistics from the Department of Statistics and Research, Ministry of Finance, Nicosia. The concepts, definitions and classification by branches of industry are generally in accordance with United Nations standards.

The estimates are derived from the survey on industrial production conducted annually by the Department of Statistics and Research. The inquiry is carried out on a sample basis and the relevant information is obtained through personal interviews of the respondents by enumerators of the Department. The estimates in the tables relate to all establishments in mining, quarrying, manufacturing, electricity, gas and water. Every five years, the Department also conducts a census of industrial production covering large establishments with 5 or more persons engaged on a complete enumeration basis and small establishments with 4 or less persons engaged on a sample basis. The census provides the basis for reviewing intercensal estimates of output, value added and employment which are compiled from the annual industrial production survey. The frame for the census as well as for the annual survey is provided by a registration of establishments held prior to each census. Since independence in 1960, five censuses have been taken, for 1962, 1967, 1972 , 1976 and 1981. The estimates in the tables refer only to the industrial activity in the Government controlled areas and have been adjusted on the basis of the results of the 1981 census. Manufacturing data exclude the cottage industry; the most important branches of that industry are embroidery, weaving and the manufacture of cane products. It should be noted that many of the figures published in official reports are revised in subsequent reports in the light of more complete information from later surveys. The estimates in the tables are based on the national classification scheme, which is comparable with the present version of ISIC.

Data shown in Table 1 for electricity, gas and water refer to number of enterprises. Employment numbers relate to annual averages. The quantity of electricity consumed relates to the supply of electric energy to industrial consumers by the Electricity Authority of Cyprus and other electricity producers. Except for electricity, output is the value of all goods produced, value of services rendered to others by the establishment and other receipts. The valuation of output is at prices secured by the establishment or the enterprise including excise tax, but excluding discounts, commissions and subsidies. If transportation costs are paid by the producer for its products, the value of output includes these costs. Otherwise, the valuation is at ex-factory prices. For electricity, output refers to the value of sales, excluding losses in the distribution and unbilled consumption. Value added refers to the value of output minus the costs of all materials, fuels and electricity used and the amount paid for work given out. Estimates of gross fixed capital formation relate to the current value of purchases minus disposals of all fixed assets, covering buildings, transport equipment, machinery and other equipment. Major additions, alterations and improvements to existing fixed assets are included. The value of fixed assets produced by the establishment for its own use is also included.

The indexes of industrial production are compiled by the Department of Statistics and Research and provided in response to the United Nations Questionnaire on Indexes of Industrial Production. The indexes cover a representative sample of establishments.

Related national publications:
Industrial Production Survey (annual until 1983); Industrial Statistics (annual beginning 1984); Census of Industrial Production, 1981; Statistical Abstract (annual); Index Numbers of Industrial Production (irregular), all published by the Department of Statistics and Research, Ministry of Finance, Nicosia.

ISIC	INDUSTRY	1. NUMBER OF ESTABLISHMENTS (NUMBER)					2. AVERAGE NUMBER OF PERSONS ENGAGED (NUMBER)					ISIC
		1981	1982	1983	1984	1985	1981	1982	1983	1984	1985	
210	Coal mining	-	-	-	-	-	-	-	-	-	-	210
220	Petroleum and gas	-	-	-	-	-	-	-	-	-	-	220
230	Metal ore mining	10	10	6	6	6	527	334	207	180	148	230
290	Other mining	204	160	130	105	111	984	939	908	888	831	290
2	Mining, quarrying .	214	170	136	111	117	1511	1273	1115	1068	979	2
311/2	Food products	643	668	653	687	910	4330	4705	4779	5100	5316	311/2
313	Beverages	42	47	48	48	52	1893	1720	1751	1841	1784	313
314	Tobacco	4	4	4	4	4	528	480	500	468	454	314
321	Textiles	189	188	190	194	203	2286	2228	2218	2269	2180	321
3211	Spinning,weaving etc..	27	28	27	27	23	311	288	289	302	269	3211
322	Wearing apparel	1322	1329	1327	1344	1306	9049	9105	9355	10278	9910	322
323	Leather and products ...	79	80	80	81	84	920	848	840	931	991	323
324	Footwear	146	148	156	158	169	3122	2962	3024	2903	2848	324
331	Wood products	777	799	801	816	922	2636	2717	2753	2755	2963	331
332	Furniture, fixtures	726	735	733	736	774	2508	2619	2735	2828	3001	332
341	Paper and products	44	46	47	47	52	819	828	676	584	636	341
3411	Pulp,paper etc.	1	1	1	-	-	125	122	60	-	-	3411
342	Printing,publishing	167	169	170	173	218	1615	1572	1469	1473	1640	342
351	Industrial chemicals ...	7	7	7	7	8	201	540	466	282	182	351
3511	Basic excl fertilizers	1	1	1	1	1	25	25	26	26	26	3511
3513	Synthetic resins etc .	-	-	-	-	-	-	-	-	-	-	3513
352	Other chemical products.	91	101	108	108	101	974	1146	1173	1154	1177	352
3522	Drugs and medicines ..	-	-	4	4	4	-	-	79	84	103	3522
353	Petroleum refineries ...	1	1	1	1	1	147	159	167	179	183	353
354	Petroleum,coal products.	-	-	-	-	-	-	-	-	-	-	354
355	Rubber products	16	17	14	15	18	276	288	132	145	144	355
356	Plastic products n.e.c..	26	28	37	38	45	817	830	1057	1074	1112	356
361	Pottery,china etc	26	28	28	28	41	64	77	73	70	107	361
362	Glass and products	11	11	11	11	17	18	18	21	21	28	362
369	Non-metal products n.e.c	151	154	152	152	170	2474	2425	2335	2298	2234	369
371	Iron and steel	-	-	-	-	-	-	-	-	-	-	371
372	Non-ferrous metals	-	-	-	-	-	-	-	-	-	-	372
381	Metal products	629	651	661	675	850	2655	2867	2869	2956	3192	381
382	Machinery n.e.c.	184	188	186	189	224	1309	1380	1297	1348	1428	382
3825	Office,computing etc..	2	2	2	2	2	16	17	17	17	18	3825
383	Electrical machinery ...	36	40	40	41	64	499	496	519	544	649	383
3832	Radio,television etc..	4	4	4	4	5	86	89	88	76	45	3832
384	Transport equipment	61	69	66	66	78	593	417	385	383	415	384
3841	Shipbuilding, repair..	15	17	16	16	26	113	125	113	108	140	3841
3843	Motor vehicles	45	52	50	50	52	345	292	272	275	275	3843
385	Professional goods	-	-	-	-	-	-	-	-	-	-	385
390	Other industries	235	242	237	246	305	640	658	661	728	895	390
3	Manufacturing	5613	5750	5757	5865	6616	40373	41085	41255	42612	43469	3
410	Electricity,gas,steam ..	a/ 9	a/ 9	a/ 9	a/ 9	a/ 9	1259	1253	1212	1185	1256	410
4101	Electricity	a/ 1	a/ 1	a/ 1	a/ 1	a/ 1	1182	1169	1128	1099	1170	4101
420	Water works and supply .	a/ 5	a/ 5	a/ 5	a/ 5	a/ 5	219	230	242	257	275	420
4	Electricity,gas etc	a/ 14	a/ 14	a/ 14	a/ 14	a/ 14	1478	1483	1454	1442	1531	4
2-4	All industry	5841	5934	5907	5990	6747	43362	43841	43824	45122	45979	2-4

a/ Electricity, gas and water: number of enterprises.

ISIC	INDUSTRY	3. AVERAGE NUMBER OF EMPLOYEES (NUMBER)					4. WAGES AND SALARIES OF EMPLOYEES (THOUSAND POUNDS)					ISIC
		1981	1982	1983	1984	1985	1981	1982	1983	1984	1985	
210	Coal mining	-	-	-	-	-	-	-	-	-	-	210
220	Petroleum and gas	-	-	-	-	-	-	-	-	-	-	220
230	Metal ore mining	527	334	207	180	148	1535	1112	731	693	674	230
290	Other mining	962	916	883	868	814	2718	3127	3079	3248	3504	290
2	Mining, quarrying .	1489	1250	1090	1048	962	4253	4239	3810	3941	4178	2
311/2	Food products	3847	4180	4283	4578	4686	7215	8968	9995	11330	12847	311/2
313	Beverages	1881	1702	1729	1819	1774	5057	5740	6468	7204	7499	313
314	Tobacco	527	479	498	466	452	1216	1645	1560	1627	1706	314
321	Textiles	2158	2108	2098	2151	2089	3336	3652	4041	4552	4715	321
3211	Spinning,weaving etc..	300	277	275	290	263	555	582	591	669	653	3211
322	Wearing apparel	7970	8009	8269	9192	8975	10427	12039	13972	16765	17644	322
323	Leather and products ...	867	794	785	876	940	1299	1355	1513	1849	2042	323
324	Footwear	3032	2870	2929	2810	2763	5356	5759	6344	6974	7197	324
331	Wood products	1847	1909	1947	1936	2112	3542	4232	4837	5303	6153	331
332	Furniture, fixtures	1797	1877	2003	2096	2334	3137	3766	4448	5080	6218	332
341	Paper and products	803	804	653	558	622	1706	1931	1845	1667	1990	341
3411	Pulp,paper etc.	125	122	60	-	-	325	306	176	-	-	3411
342	Printing,publishing	1473	1432	1331	1332	1525	3778	4243	4386	4957	5809	342
351	Industrial chemicals ...	201	540	466	282	182	513	1435	1721	1069	771	351
3511	Basic excl fertilizers	25	25	26	26	26	81	97	109	120	143	3511
3513	Synthetic resins etc .	-	-	-	-	-	-	-	-	-	-	3513
352	Other chemical products.	914	1083	1108	1091	1144	1864	2443	2761	2993	3290	352
3522	Drugs and medicines ..	-	-	79	84	103	-	-	164	198	255	3522
353	Petroleum refineries ...	147	159	167	179	183	813	1011	1051	1314	1572	353
354	Petroleum,coal products.	-	-	-	-	-	-	-	-	-	-	354
355	Rubber products	273	285	127	137	137	534	663	356	420	439	355
356	Plastic products n.e.c..	808	821	1049	1066	1105	1671	1998	2800	3163	3433	356
361	Pottery,china etc	45	60	56	53	81	65	92	99	94	178	361
362	Glass and products	7	7	10	10	13	14	14	20	28	35	362
369	Non-metal products n.e.c	2384	2340	2247	2213	2158	5867	6572	7202	7935	8481	369
371	Iron and steel	-	-	-	-	-	-	-	-	-	-	371
372	Non-ferrous metals	-	-	-	-	-	-	-	-	-	-	372
381	Metal products	2097	2269	2261	2339	2551	4272	5272	5597	6420	7465	381
382	Machinery n.e.c.	1134	1202	1121	1171	1266	2503	3104	3063	3494	4219	382
3825	Office,computing etc..	15	16	16	16	17	30	37	40	44	48	3825
383	Electrical machinery ...	476	472	491	518	613	878	1134	1205	1277	1664	383
3832	Radio,television etc..	86	89	87	75	44	135	181	182	177	141	3832
384	Transport equipment	542	354	326	331	365	1459	970	1021	1099	1223	384
3841	Shipbuilding, repair..	100	110	100	95	127	289	390	399	419	531	3841
3843	Motor vehicles	307	244	226	236	238	768	580	622	680	692	3843
385	Professional goods	-	-	-	-	-	-	-	-	-	-	385
390	Other industries	403	414	429	496	658	664	775	797	1102	1591	390
3	Manufacturing	35633	36170	36383	37700	38728	67186	78813	87102	97716	108181	3
410	Electricity,gas,steam ..	1259	1253	1212	1185	1256	5834	6363	6776	7202	8084	410
4101	Electricity	1182	1169	1128	1099	1170	5586	6073	6459	6859	7711	4101
420	Water works and supply .	219	230	242	257	275	666	822	981	1059	1201	420
4	Electricity,gas etc	1478	1483	1454	1442	1531	6500	7185	7757	8261	9285	4
2-4	All industry	38600	38903	38927	40190	41221	77939	90237	98669	109918	121644	2-4

CYPRUS

ISIC	INDUSTRY	5. AVERAGE NUMBER OF OPERATIVES (NUMBER)					6. WAGES AND SALARIES OF OPERATIVES (THOUSAND POUNDS)					ISIC
		1981	1982	1983	1984	1985	1981	1982	1983	1984	1985	
210	Coal mining	-	-	-	-	-	-	-	-	-	-	210
220	Petroleum and gas	-	-	-	-	-	-	-	-	-	-	220
230	Metal ore mining	469	287	155	136	106	1314	886	486	463	415	230
290	Other mining	863	827	802	788	738	2375	2749	2693	2848	3039	290
2	Mining, quarrying .	1332	1114	957	924	844	3689	3635	3179	3311	3454	2
311/2	Food products	2815	3109	3132	3290	3520	4644	5997	6601	7368	8870	311/2
313	Beverages	1037	1004	1025	1076	1114	2489	3254	3698	3964	4171	313
314	Tobacco	424	387	397	362	368	831	1172	1038	990	1134	314
321	Textiles	1959	1897	1880	1933	1875	2929	3118	3410	3896	3982	321
3211	Spinning,weaving etc..	271	251	246	256	235	491	501	465	549	523	3211
322	Wearing apparel	7409	7335	7557	8447	8398	9204	10380	12077	14561	15626	322
323	Leather and products ...	784	717	693	784	854	1101	1147	1276	1570	1766	323
324	Footwear	2620	2473	2492	2407	2473	4351	4690	5019	5652	6095	324
331	Wood products	1716	1794	1835	1814	1986	3199	3897	4464	4863	5667	331
332	Furniture, fixtures	1611	1705	1816	1867	2153	2783	3389	4016	4490	5659	332
341	Paper and products	653	665	541	447	477	1279	1462	1470	1241	1412	341
3411	Pulp,paper etc.	91	100	50	-	-	177	261	141	-	-	3411
342	Printing,publishing	1181	1115	1035	1038	1196	3034	3276	3185	3702	4302	342
351	Industrial chemicals ...	81	417	358	211	109	204	1068	1365	818	446	351
3511	Basic excl fertilizers	17	17	18	18	18	57	68	78	86	106	3511
3513	Synthetic resins etc .	-	-	-	-	-	-	-	-	-	-	3513
352	Other chemical products.	606	701	741	726	757	1133	1393	1719	1811	2035	352
3522	Drugs and medicines ..	-	-	61	59	77	-	-	111	127	181	3522
353	Petroleum refineries ...	99	111	119	130	136	485	633	646	873	1064	353
354	Petroleum,coal products.	-	-	-	-	-	-	-	-	-	-	354
355	Rubber products	230	232	106	112	108	426	516	280	310	335	355
356	Plastic products n.e.c..	629	618	785	817	840	1257	1488	2122	2434	2601	356
361	Pottery,china etc	44	57	54	49	78	64	84	93	85	165	361
362	Glass and products	7	7	10	10	13	14	14	20	28	35	362
369	Non-metal products n.e.c	2151	2109	2010	1987	1922	5153	5827	6316	7020	7441	369
371	Iron and steel	-	-	-	-	-	-	-	-	-	-	371
372	Non-ferrous metals	-	-	-	-	-	-	-	-	-	-	372
381	Metal products	1811	1973	1975	2037	2257	3562	4441	4772	5451	6436	381
382	Machinery n.e.c.	959	1010	944	987	1069	2044	2540	2561	2935	3541	382
3825	Office,computing etc..	11	11	11	12	13	21	24	26	33	35	3825
383	Electrical machinery ...	368	393	391	409	512	631	826	859	939	1283	383
3832	Radio,television etc..	73	75	73	63	35	99	135	130	132	104	3832
384	Transport equipment	468	293	275	284	327	1198	776	826	932	1061	384
3841	Shipbuilding, repair..	77	91	86	79	111	208	314	332	368	463	3841
3843	Motor vehicles	256	202	189	205	216	589	462	494	565	598	3843
385	Professional goods	-	-	-	-	-	-	-	-	-	-	385
390	Other industries	327	347	346	407	581	496	592	619	895	1350	390
3	Manufacturing	29989	30469	30517	31631	33123	52511	61980	68452	76828	86477	3
410	Electricity,gas,steam ..	682	516	508	480	488	2993	2649	2853	2966	3211	410
4101	Electricity	632	455	448	418	422	2876	2485	2672	2765	2968	4101
420	Water works and supply .	108	118	128	135	149	294	367	430	455	530	420
4	Electricity,gas etc	790	634	636	615	637	3287	3016	3283	3421	3741	4
2-4	All industry	32111	32217	32110	33170	34604	59487	68631	74914	83560	93672	2-4

ISIC	INDUSTRY	7. DAYS WORKED BY OPERATIVES (THOUSANDS) 1981	1982	1983	1984	1985	8. QUANTITY OF ELECTRICITY CONSUMED a/ (MILLION KWH) 1981	1982	1983	1984	1985	ISIC
210	Coal mining	-	-	-	-	-	-	-	-	-	-	210
220	Petroleum and gas	-	-	-	-	-	-	-	-	-	-	220
230	Metal ore mining	104	61	33	33	25	...	...	...	...	...	230
290	Other mining	192	191	160	173	167	...	...	...	...	...	290
2	Mining, quarrying .	296	252	193	206	192	27.4	26.5	21.9	17.3	23.5	2
311/2	Food products	721	783	796	816	880	24.4	26.9	29.2	30.0	31.7	311/2
313	Beverages	240	230	235	245	252	9.0	9.3	9.7	10.5	11.2	313
314	Tobacco	101	90	93	83	86	2.4	2.4	2.3	2.3	2.4	314
321	Textiles	453	446	447	452	435	4.1	3.9	3.9	4.1	4.0	321
3211	Spinning,weaving etc..	62	59	58	...	54	...	...	...	...	...	3211
322	Wearing apparel	1726	1709	1783	1968	1932	b/ 8.0	b/ 8.3	b/ 8.7	b/ 9.6	b/ 9.9	322
323	Leather and products ...	185	169	163	184	194	0.8	1.0	1.0	1.1	1.0	323
324	Footwear	610	571	581	551	566	b/	b/	b/	b/	b/	324
331	Wood products	407	420	422	421	463	[7.3	8.3	8.6	8.7	9.0]	331
332	Furniture, fixtures	379	401	427	437	502						332
341	Paper and products	150	150	120	105	112	c/ 11.9	c/ 9.8	c/ 7.8	c/ 6.3	c/ 6.5	341
3411	Pulp,paper etc.	21	20	7	-	-	...	...	...	...	...	3411
342	Printing,publishing	279	266	249	249	281	c/	c/	c/	c/	c/	342
351	Industrial chemicals ...	17	98	83	50	25	d/ 15.1	d/ 16.4	d/ 24.9	d/ 20.0	d/ 21.0	351
3511	Basic excl fertilizers	4	4	5	...	5	...	...	...	...	...	3511
3513	Synthetic resins etc .	-	-	-	-	-	...	...	...	...	...	3513
352	Other chemical products.	142	162	173	171	174	d/	d/	d/	d/	d/	352
3522	Drugs and medicines ..	-	-	14	...	18	-	-	-	-	-	3522
353	Petroleum refineries ...	30	31	38	37	33	10.2	10.2	11.4	10.3	8.8	353
354	Petroleum,coal products.	-	-	-	-	-	-	-	-	-	-	354
355	Rubber products	54	54	25	26	25	1.0	1.1	1.3	1.8	2.1	355
356	Plastic products n.e.c..	155	151	189	199	201	d/	d/	d/	d/	d/	356
361	Pottery,china etc	11	14	13	13	18	[0.3	0.4	0.5	0.6	0.7]	361
362	Glass and products	2	2	3	3	3						362
369	Non-metal products n.e.c	521	510	484	485	475	108.1	105.0	99.0	96.4	79.8	369
371	Iron and steel	-	-	-	-	-	-	-	-	-	-	371
372	Non-ferrous metals	-	-	-	-	-	-	-	-	-	-	372
381	Metal products	420	464	460	477	526	[e/ 8.4	e/ 9.2	e/ 10.0	e/ 11.2	e/ 11.6]	381
382	Machinery n.e.c.	226	238	221	230	248						382
3825	Office,computing etc..	3	3	2	...	3	...	...	...	...	...	3825
383	Electrical machinery ...	91	92	92	96	121	e/	e/	e/	e/	e/	383
3832	Radio,television etc..	17	17	16	...	8	...	...	...	...	...	3832
384	Transport equipment	125	71	65	66	76	0.6	0.5	0.5	0.5	0.5	384
3841	Shipbuilding, repair..	18	23	20	...	26	...	...	...	...	...	3841
3843	Motor vehicles	62	48	45	...	50	...	...	...	...	...	3843
385	Professional goods	-	-	-	-	-	-	-	-	-	-	385
390	Other industries	81	84	79	96	143	0.3	0.3	0.3	0.4	0.5	390
3	Manufacturing	7126	7206	7241	7460	7771	211.9	213.0	219.1	213.8	200.7	3
410	Electricity,gas,steam ..	219	163	160	168	170	1.2	1.2	1.2	1.2	1.3	410
4101	Electricity	207	149	147	153	154	1.0	1.0	1.0	1.0	1.1	4101
420	Water works and supply .	24	27	29	33	37	21.4	23.5	26.0	27.6	29.8	420
4	Electricity,gas etc	243	190	189	201	207	22.6	24.7	27.2	28.8	31.1	4
2-4	All industry	7665	7648	7623	7867	8170	261.9	264.2	268.2	259.9	255.3	2-4

a/ Quantity of electricity supplied by the Electric Authority of Cyprus and other electricity producers to industrial consumers.
b/ Major group 324 is included in 322.
c/ Major group 342 is included in 341.
d/ Major groups 352 and 356 are included in 351.
e/ Major group 383 is included in 381 and 382 combined.

ISIC	INDUSTRY	9. OUTPUT IN PRODUCERS' PRICES (THOUSAND POUNDS)					10. VALUE ADDED IN PRODUCERS' PRICES (THOUSAND POUNDS)					ISIC
		1981	1982	1983	1984	1985	1981	1982	1983	1984	1985	
210	Coal mining	-	-	-	-	-	-	-	-	-	-	210
220	Petroleum and gas	-	-	-	-	-	-	-	-	-	-	220
230	Metal ore mining	2874	2326	1443	1198	1650	1939	1542	962	664	939	230
290	Other mining	15778	14988	14275	13986	12532	9193	8652	8169	8329	6596	290
2	Mining, quarrying .	18652	17314	15718	15184	14182	11132	10194	9131	8993	7535	2
311/2	Food products	64367	76218	84755	103859	116167	17544	24815	24350	28400	29866	311/2
313	Beverages	32464	32519	36063	39257	39431	14520	15668	16738	19788	17596	313
314	Tobacco	23327	23653	23552	25050	26068	14104	14151	15789	17190	16015	314
321	Textiles	16780	18456	19435	22029	20623	6928	7826	8482	9794	8791	321
3211	Spinning,weaving etc..	2585	2727	2601	2998	2858	1146	1304	1286	1461	1290	3211
322	Wearing apparel	55879	58241	68059	89251	85275	21507	25372	28362	35600	32837	322
323	Leather and products ...	6815	6679	7357	8984	10262	2383	2475	2795	3334	3519	323
324	Footwear	24369	23680	26015	29984	29706	9618	9938	11087	12907	11610	324
331	Wood products	18369	21165	23920	26627	32076	8355	10246	11146	12412	13876	331
332	Furniture, fixtures	15340	18840	22119	23470	29707	7560	9260	10806	11828	13379	332
341	Paper and products	14244	13980	12342	14092	16306	4052	3819	3590	4261	4709	341
3411	Pulp,paper etc.	952	706	283	-	-	a/ 290	a/ 58	a/ 44	-	-	3411
342	Printing,publishing	15283	16851	16922	20939	24460	6998	7328	8151	10321	10819	342
351	Industrial chemicals ...	3016	5074	7828	3142	3301	1021	a/ 1310	1895	889	1022	351
3511	Basic excl fertilizers	287	316	349	417	499	133	152	180	242	274	3511
3513	Synthetic resins etc .	-	-	-	-	-	-	-	-	-	-	3513
352	Other chemical products.	15311	18092	20356	23544	25575	5071	5994	6713	7396	7285	352
3522	Drugs and medicines ..	-	-	2004	2465	3399	-	-	595	635	913	3522
353	Petroleum refineries ...	65988	68111	73523	77687	64923	2304	2508	2565	2853	2931	353
354	Petroleum,coal products.	-	-	-	-	-	-	-	-	-	-	354
355	Rubber products	3338	3710	2178	2643	2868	1109	1324	770	912	954	355
356	Plastic products n.e.c..	10773	12793	17297	20149	19195	3959	4603	6199	7063	6600	356
361	Pottery,china etc	220	245	291	295	771	162	174	197	199	444	361
362	Glass and products	123	80	142	183	129	68	71	90	111	102	362
369	Non-metal products n.e.c	42071	42197	39446	41183	41528	16048	15508	13451	14750	14750	369
371	Iron and steel	-	-	-	-	-	-	-	-	-	-	371
372	Non-ferrous metals	-	-	-	-	-	-	-	-	-	-	372
381	Metal products	25846	33221	33755	37023	45582	9773	12361	12723	14227	15803	381
382	Machinery n.e.c.	11986	13143	13364	15967	17173	5604	6508	6442	7738	7427	382
3825	Office,computing etc..	72	86	95	95	105	51	61	68	70	69	3825
383	Electrical machinery ...	7232	9226	9689	9714	13724	2581	3319	3246	3612	3797	383
3832	Radio,television etc..	2490	3549	3185	2228	2043	780	1118	858	754	360	3832
384	Transport equipment	5522	4390	4182	4181	4884	2891	2001	2109	2059	2217	384
3841	Shipbuilding, repair..	1091	1293	1214	1206	1667	595	683	756	660	840	3841
3843	Motor vehicles	3681	3097	2968	2975	3217	1607	1318	1353	1399	1377	3843
385	Professional goods	-	-	-	-	-	-	-	-	-	-	385
390	Other industries	6256	7320	9273	11432	14490	2041	2422	3131	3557	4269	390
3	Manufacturing	484919	527884	571863	650685	684224	166201	189001	200827	231201	230618	3
410	Electricity,gas,steam ..	41664	47107	53880	64911	70379	14167	16249	21117	26626	30872	410
4101	Electricity	37535	42417	48910	59723	65048	13255	15348	20157	25588	29802	4101
420	Water works and supply .	1616	2959	3416	4191	5191	973	1643	1630	1883	2464	420
4	Electricity,gas etc	43280	50066	57296	69102	75570	15140	17892	22747	28509	33336	4
2-4	All industry	546851	595264	644877	734971	773976	192473	217087	232705	268703	271489	2-4

a/ Value added is less than corresponding Wages and salaries due to operating losses.

11. GROSS FIXED CAPITAL FORMATION
TOTAL
(THOUSAND POUNDS)

ISIC	INDUSTRY	1981	1982	1983	1984	1985	ISIC
210	Coal mining	-	-	-	-	-	210
220	Petroleum and gas	-	-	-	-	-	220
230	Metal ore mining	322	364	-	26	46	230
290	Other mining	1169	511	382	758	439	290
2	Mining, quarrying .	1491	875	382	784	485	2
311/2	Food products	2478	4059	3545	4510	5854	311/2
313	Beverages	1364	1950	2523	3786	3604	313
314	Tobacco	138	157	182	119	341	314
321	Textiles	1208	1265	997	1821	1378	321
3211	Spinning,weaving etc..	244	211	182	523	259	3211
322	Wearing apparel	1612	1716	2650	3452	3156	322
323	Leather and products ...	152	121	174	208	266	323
324	Footwear	1143	866	1187	1961	1263	324
331	Wood products	749	1119	879	1068	1148	331
332	Furniture, fixtures	946	838	1520	1361	1450	332
341	Paper and products	795	275	439	1170	485	341
3411	Pulp,paper etc.	22	9	-	-	-	3411
342	Printing,publishing	537	1117	659	1035	793	342
351	Industrial chemicals ...	2433	2418	496	70	160	351
3511	Basic excl fertilizers	22	46	12	12	75	3511
3513	Synthetic resins etc .	-	-	-	-	-	3513
352	Other chemical products.	971	1519	1186	889	1081	352
3522	Drugs and medicines ..	-	-	287	82	67	3522
353	Petroleum refineries ...	86	238	180	591	1149	353
354	Petroleum,coal products.	-	-	-	-	-	354
355	Rubber products	225	376	77	81	298	355
356	Plastic products n.e.c..	677	738	883	1315	2153	356
361	Pottery,china etc	8	26	18	254	133	361
362	Glass and products	-	17	49	9	2	362
369	Non-metal products n.e.c	5159	5460	3698	2701	2583	369
371	Iron and steel	-	-	-	-	-	371
372	Non-ferrous metals	-	-	-	-	-	372
381	Metal products	2208	1680	1401	2525	4117	381
382	Machinery n.e.c.	870	890	697	902	1274	382
3825	Office,computing etc..	-	10	20	10	17	3825
383	Electrical machinery ...	244	299	236	348	535	383
3832	Radio,television etc..	44	50	9	3	22	3832
384	Transport equipment	511	106	183	169	434	384
3841	Shipbuilding, repair..	214	60	82	107	22	3841
3843	Motor vehicles	13	46	101	62	412	3843
385	Professional goods	-	-	-	-	-	385
390	Other industries	143	161	371	581	500	390
3	Manufacturing	24657	27411	24230	30926	34157	3
410	Electricity,gas,steam ..	16523	17049	9517	5950	6601	410
4101	Electricity	16180	16796	9291	5567	6138	4101
420	Water works and supply .	268	408	456	292	693	420
4	Electricity,gas etc	16791	17457	9973	6242	7294	4
2-4	All industry	42939	45743	34585	37952	41936	2-4

12. INDEX NUMBERS OF INDUSTRIAL PRODUCTION (1980 = 100)

ISIC	INDUSTRY	1976	1977	1978	1979	1981	1982	1983	1984	1985	a/ RATE	ISIC
210	Coal mining	...	...	...	...	...	...	...	...	...	...	210
220	Petroleum and gas	...	...	...	...	...	...	...	...	...	...	220
230	Metal ore mining	825	675	525	325	73	62	50	41	62	-25.0	230
290	Other mining	52	66	79	92	88	83	77	67	71	3.5	290
2	Mining, quarrying	97	103	103	99	85	79	75	65	71	-3.4	2
311/2	Food products	79	80	87	92	108	118	127	135	140	6.6	311/2
313	Beverages	69	79	88	97	109	116	122	125	119	6.2	313
314	Tobacco	68	80	95	98	116	114	98	93	84	2.4	314
321	Textiles	74	85	93	95	99	101	97	101	95	2.8	321
3211	Spinning, weaving etc.	...	...	...	...	...	...	...	...	...	...	3211
322	Wearing apparel	60	77	89	97	106	87	102	126	102	6.1	322
323	Leather and products	54	63	73	93	122	119	122	132	152	12.2	323
324	Footwear	53	72	82	90	117	116	121	128	127	10.2	324
331	Wood products	74	77	78	89	97	112	119	126	131	6.6	331
332	Furniture, fixtures	72	82	86	94	112	122	144	143	145	8.1	332
341	Paper and products	41	50	73	76	105	101	103	94	90	9.1	341
3411	Pulp, paper etc.	...	...	...	...	...	...	...	...	...	...	3411
342	Printing, publishing	68	82	86	96	124	129	108	138	131	7.6	342
351	Industrial chemicals	62	100	90	95	96	147	205	91	101	5.6	351
3511	Basic excl fertilizers	...	...	...	...	...	...	...	...	...	...	3511
3513	Synthetic resins etc	...	...	...	...	...	...	...	...	...	...	3513
352	Other chemical products	54	72	77	81	116	122	127	134	150	12.0	352
3522	Drugs and medicines	...	...	...	...	...	...	...	...	...	...	3522
353	Petroleum refineries	...	...	...	...	...	...	...	...	...	...	353
354	Petroleum, coal products	...	...	...	...	...	...	...	...	...	...	354
355	Rubber products	57	68	75	86	101	98	121	105	101	6.6	355
356	Plastic products n.e.c.	...	...	...	...	...	...	...	...	...	...	356
361	Pottery, china etc	52	70	79	84	130	122	135	100	139	11.5	361
362	Glass and products	...	...	...	...	...	...	...	...	...	...	362
369	Non-metal products n.e.c	71	80	86	93	90	91	86	84	77	0.9	369
371	Iron and steel	...	...	...	...	...	...	...	...	...	...	371
372	Non-ferrous metals	...	...	...	...	...	...	...	...	...	...	372
381	Metal products	57	71	90	95	103	125	100	103	104	6.9	381
382	Machinery n.e.c.	66	86	97	98	103	121	126	140	173	11.3	382
3825	Office, computing etc.	...	...	...	...	...	...	...	...	...	...	3825
383	Electrical machinery	56	70	75	81	159	190	198	170	181	13.9	383
3832	Radio, television etc.	...	...	...	...	...	...	...	...	...	...	3832
384	Transport equipment	56	78	79	90	160	148	149	159	142	10.9	384
3841	Shipbuilding, repair	...	...	...	...	...	...	...	...	...	...	3841
3843	Motor vehicles	...	...	...	...	...	...	...	...	...	...	3843
385	Professional goods	...	...	...	...	...	...	...	...	...	...	385
390	Other industries	77	74	85	94	111	125	125	146	165	8.8	390
3	Manufacturing	65	76	85	93	107	109	112	118	115	6.5	3
410	Electricity, gas, steam	...	...	...	...	...	...	...	...	...	...	410
4101	Electricity	77	83	89	95	102	108	114	118	123	5.3	4101
420	Water works and supply	.	.	.	.	.	.	.	.	.	.	420
4	Electricity, gas etc	...	...	...	...	...	...	...	...	...	...	4
2-4	All industry b/	70	80	87	94	104	106	108	113	112	5.4	2-4

a/ Annual growth rate 1976-1985.

b/ Excluding gas and steam.

CZECHOSLOVAKIA

The information on industrial activity is based on the reply to the United Nations Questionnaire on General Industrial Statistics from the Federal Statistical Office of Czechoslovakia, Prague. The concepts, definitions and classification by branches of industry have been adjusted as far as possible to comply with United Nations standards.

The estimates are derived from annual industrial inquiries covering activities of industrial enterprises in socialist industry. Socialist industry comprises State national and local industries and co-operatives. State national enterprises are relatively independent economic units under socialist ownership. The difference between State national and local enterprises is organizational only. The latter are those under the control of national committees at regional, district or local level, usually producing goods or services of local importance. Industrial activity of a secondary or ancillary character in non-industrial enterprises is not included and private handicrafts are not covered. The figures given in the tables generally relate to all socialist industry, but the number of enterprises and the estimates of output relate to State national industry only; the estimates of gross fixed capital formation exclude co-operatives.

The estimates, which are based on the national classification scheme, have been adjusted as far as possible to ISIC. It should be noted that publishing is not covered and for water works and supply, only selected items of information are available. It should also be noted that repair of footwear is included in ISIC 324 and repair of motor vehicles in ISIC 384. All data for electric light and power include steam and hot water supply. It has not been possible to adjust the classification for the following differences: peat extraction (ISIC 290) is included in ISIC 210; stone processing (ISIC 369) in ISIC 290; salt mining (ISIC 290) in ISIC 351; matches (ISIC 352) in ISIC 331; boiler products (ISIC 381) in ISIC 382; and office machines (ISIC 3825) in ISIC 385. In the case of most figures, the estimates are compiled according to the principles of organization and methodology in effect during each year. For this reason, the estimates so annotated are not fully comparable from year to year.

The employment estimates relate to the average number of persons employed in industrial enterprises of socialist industry, including those engaged in non-industrial activities. Averages are calculated for operatives as the average daily number and for other employees as the average of numbers at the beginning and end of the year. Included are temporary workers, homeworkers, persons under military training and persons working outside the enterprise or outside the industry if at least partly paid by the enterprise. Apprentices are not included and working proprietors and unpaid family workers are not found in socialist industry. All estimates of operatives relate to workers employed in industrial activities only and exclude those engaged in activities of a non-industrial character. Homeworkers are included in the estimates of number of operatives and wages and salaries, but not in hours worked.

Wages and salaries relate to the gross earnings of employees (including payments in kind and employees' shares in the economic results of the enterprise) before deduction of income tax. No other deductions are made; health and pension contributions are paid by the employer. Payments to homeworkers are included in the estimates. Value added relates to net output and is the difference between the value of sales of output, adjusted for changes in the value of stocks, and the cost of materials and services (including non-industrial) consumed. The estimates are net of depreciation allowances. The estimates of gross fixed capital formation refer to investment outlays of State industry on new fixed assets and on the expansion, reconstruction and renewal of existing fixed assets.

The indexes of industrial production are compiled by the Federal Statistical Office of Czechoslovakia and provided in response to the United Nations Questionnaire on Indexes of Industrial Production. In principle, the indexes cover all publicly-owned enterprises and co-operatives.

Related national publications:
Statisticka Rocenka CSSR (Statistical Yearbook); Statistical Abstract (irregular), both published by the Federal Statistical Office of Czechoslovakia, Prague.

ISIC	INDUSTRY	1. NUMBER OF ENTERPRISES a/ (NUMBER)					2. AVERAGE NUMBER OF PERSONS ENGAGED b/c/d/ (THOUSANDS)					ISIC
		1981	1982	1983	1984	1985	1981	1982	1983	1984	1985	
210	Coal mining	37	37	37	38	38	139	143	146	146	148	210
220	Petroleum and gas	2	2	2	2	2	3	3	3	3	3	220
230	Metal ore mining	4	4	4	4	4	21	21	21	21	22	230
290	Other mining	12	12	12	12	12	19	19	19	19	18	290
2	Mining, quarrying .	55	55	55	56	56	182	186	189	189	191	2
311/2	Food products	92	93	93	93	93	173	173	174	175	176	311/2
313	Beverages	24	24	24	25	25	33	33	34	34	34	313
314	Tobacco	2	2	2	2	2	4	4	4	4	4	314
321	Textiles	55	55	55	56	56	222	221	220	219	217	321
3211	Spinning,weaving etc..	40	40	40	41	41	157	158	156	155	154	3211
322	Wearing apparel	18	17	17	17	17	107	107	106	105	105	322
323	Leather and products ...	7	7	7	7	7	27	26	26	26	27	323
324	Footwear	6	6	6	6	6	71	72	71	71	70	324
331	Wood products	18	18	18	18	18	67	66	66	65	65	331
332	Furniture, fixtures	9	9	9	9	9	62	63	63	62	62	332
341	Paper and products	18	18	18	18	18	49	49	49	49	49	341
3411	Pulp,paper etc.	...	...	...	...	...	...	...	...	...	...	3411
342	Printing,publishing	18	18	18	18	18	31	31	30	29	29	342
351	Industrial chemicals ...	29	29	29	30	30	96	96	96	97	98	351
3511	Basic excl fertilizers	...	...	...	...	...	...	...	...	...	...	3511
3513	Synthetic resins etc .	...	...	...	...	...	...	...	...	...	...	3513
352	Other chemical products.	19	19	19	18	18	24	24	24	24	24	352
3522	Drugs and medicines ..	14	14	14	14	14	14	14	14	14	15	3522
353	Petroleum refineries ...	6	6	6	6	6	23	23	23	23	23	353
354	Petroleum,coal products.	6	6	6	6	6	10	10	10	10	10	354
355	Rubber products	13	13	13	13	13	26	27	26	26	27	355
356	Plastic products n.e.c..	2	2	2	2	2	8	8	8	8	8	356
361	Pottery,china etc	2	2	2	2	2	9	9	9	9	9	361
362	Glass and products	20	20	20	20	20	74	76	75	76	76	362
369	Non-metal products n.e.c	46	46	46	46	46	89	88	87	87	86	369
371	Iron and steel	13	13	13	13	13	162	162	161	171	170	371
372	Non-ferrous metals	16	16	16	16	16	28	28	28	28	28	372
381	Metal products	54	54	54	54	54	171	172	173	164	164	381
382	Machinery n.e.c.	153	153	153	155	155	522	526	536	540	545	382
3825	Office,computing etc..	...	...	...	...	...	...	...	...	...	...	3825
383	Electrical machinery ...	47	47	47	47	47	153	154	153	159	164	383
3832	Radio,television etc..	...	...	...	...	...	...	...	...	...	...	3832
384	Transport equipment	56	56	56	57	57	247	250	252	254	255	384
3841	Shipbuilding, repair..	...	...	...	...	...	...	...	...	...	...	3841
3843	Motor vehicles	...	...	...	...	...	...	...	...	...	...	3843
385	Professional goods	7	7	7	7	7	16	16	16	16	15	385
390	Other industries	15	15	15	15	15	44	46	47	47	48	390
3	Manufacturing ..... e/f/	771	771	771	776	776	2548	2560	2567	2578	2588	3
410	Electricity,gas,steam ..	32	33	33	33	33	65	66	68	69	70	410
4101	Electricity .... g/	28	29	29	29	29	59	60	62	63	64	4101
420	Water works and supply .	.	.	.	.	.	.	.	.	.	.	420
4	Electricity,gas etc	32	33	33	33	33	65	66	68	69	70	4
2-4	All industry e/f/	858	859	859	865	865	2795	2812	2824	2836	2849	2-4

Note. For certain deviations in classification, see country note.

a/ State national industry only.
b/ Number of employees, including homeworkers; working proprietors and unpaid family workers are not found in socialist industry.
c/ Data are not fully comparable from year to year owing to organizational changes.
d/ Including persons engaged in non-industrial activities of enterprises in socialist industry.
e/ Including repair of footwear.
f/ Including repair of motor vehicles.
g/ Including steam and hot water supply.

ISIC	INDUSTRY	3. AVERAGE NUMBER OF EMPLOYEES a/b/ (THOUSANDS)					4. WAGES AND SALARIES OF EMPLOYEES a/c/ (BILLION KORUNAS)					ISIC
		1981	1982	1983	1984	1985	1981	1982	1983	1984	1985	
210	Coal mining	139	143	146	146	148	6.72	7.52	7.82	7.97	8.10	210
220	Petroleum and gas	3	3	3	3	3	0.09	0.10	0.11	0.11	0.12	220
230	Metal ore mining	21	21	21	21	22	0.82	0.85	0.89	0.91	0.92	230
290	Other mining	19	19	19	19	18	0.67	0.68	0.68	0.68	0.69	290
2	Mining, quarrying .	182	186	189	189	191	8.30	9.15	9.50	9.67	9.83	2
311/2	Food products	173	173	174	175	176	5.26	5.41	5.59	5.75	5.92	311/2
313	Beverages	33	33	34	34	34	1.03	1.08	1.12	1.15	1.17	313
314	Tobacco	4	4	4	4	4	0.12	0.12	0.12	0.13	0.13	314
321	Textiles	222	221	220	219	217	6.10	6.22	6.30	6.36	6.44	321
3211	Spinning,weaving etc..	157	158	156	155	154	4.45	4.54	4.58	4.61	4.66	3211
322	Wearing apparel	107	107	106	105	105	2.77	2.82	2.85	2.89	3.10	322
323	Leather and products ...	27	26	26	26	27	0.75	0.77	0.79	0.81	0.64	323
324	Footwear	71	72	71	71	70	2.18	2.25	2.27	2.33	2.34	324
331	Wood products	67	66	66	65	65	2.02	2.05	2.04	2.08	2.11	331
332	Furniture, fixtures	62	63	63	62	62	1.80	1.82	1.87	1.89	1.93	332
341	Paper and products	49	49	49	49	49	1.47	1.52	1.55	1.59	1.62	341
3411	Pulp,paper etc.	...	...	...	...	...	...	...	...	...	...	3411
342	Printing,publishing	31	31	30	29	29	0.96	0.98	0.97	0.95	0.95	342
351	Industrial chemicals ...	96	96	96	97	98	3.31	3.43	3.54	3.68	3.78	351
3511	Basic excl fertilizers	...	...	...	...	...	...	...	...	...	...	3511
3513	Synthetic resins etc .	...	...	...	...	...	...	...	...	...	...	3513
352	Other chemical products.	24	24	24	24	24	0.72	0.76	0.76	0.79	0.81	352
3522	Drugs and medicines ..	14	14	14	14	15	0.43	0.46	0.47	0.50	0.51	3522
353	Petroleum refineries ...	23	23	23	23	23	0.87	0.91	0.93	0.97	0.98	353
354	Petroleum,coal products.	10	10	10	10	10	0.36	0.38	0.38	0.39	0.40	354
355	Rubber products	26	27	26	26	27	0.88	0.90	0.92	0.95	0.98	355
356	Plastic products n.e.c..	8	8	8	8	8	0.24	0.24	0.24	0.25	0.25	356
361	Pottery,china etc	9	9	9	9	9	0.25	0.25	0.26	0.27	0.27	361
362	Glass and products	74	76	75	76	76	2.19	2.28	2.33	2.40	2.44	362
369	Non-metal products n.e.c	89	88	87	87	86	3.00	3.07	3.11	3.14	3.19	369
371	Iron and steel	162	162	161	171	170	6.42	6.58	6.67	7.18	7.27	371
372	Non-ferrous metals	28	28	28	28	28	1.00	1.03	1.06	1.08	1.10	372
381	Metal products	171	172	173	164	164	5.37	5.52	5.70	5.50	5.65	381
382	Machinery n.e.c.	522	526	536	540	545	18.26	18.80	19.60	20.19	20.69	382
3825	Office,computing etc..	...	...	...	...	...	...	...	...	...	...	3825
383	Electrical machinery ...	153	154	153	159	164	4.56	4.70	4.80	5.14	5.48	383
3832	Radio,television etc..	...	...	...	...	...	...	...	...	...	...	3832
384	Transport equipment	247	250	252	254	255	8.56	8.83	9.12	9.33	9.51	384
3841	Shipbuilding, repair..	...	...	...	...	...	...	...	...	...	...	3841
3843	Motor vehicles	...	...	...	...	...	...	...	...	...	...	3843
385	Professional goods	16	16	16	16	15	0.52	0.53	0.54	0.56	0.53	385
390	Other industries	44	46	47	47	48	1.23	1.29	1.35	1.39	1.43	390
3	Manufacturing ..... d/e/	2548	2560	2567	2578	2588	82.20	84.54	86.78	89.14	91.11	3
410	Electricity,gas,steam ..	65	66	68	69	70	2.41	2.55	2.64	2.75	2.89	410
4101	Electricity .... f/	59	60	62	63	64	2.22	2.35	2.44	2.53	2.67	4101
420	Water works and supply .	.	.	.	.	.	.	.	.	.	.	420
4	Electricity,gas etc	65	66	68	69	70	2.41	2.55	2.64	2.75	2.89	4
2-4	All industry d/e/	2795	2812	2824	2836	2849	92.91	96.24	98.92	101.56	103.83	2-4

Note. For certain deviations in classification, see country note.

a/ Data are not fully comparable from year to year owing to organizational changes.
b/ Including homeworkers.
c/ Including payments to homeworkers.
d/ Including repair of footwear.
e/ Including repair of motor vehicles.
f/ Including steam and hot water supply.

ISIC	INDUSTRY	5. SUPPLEMENTS TO WAGES AND SALARIES a/ (MILLION KORUNAS) 1981	1982	1983	1984	1985	6. AVERAGE NUMBER OF OPERATIVES a/b/ (THOUSANDS) 1981	1982	1983	1984	1985	ISIC
210	Coal mining	672	752	782	797	810	112	116	118	118	119	210
220	Petroleum and gas	9	10	11	11	12	2	2	2	2	2	220
230	Metal ore mining	82	85	89	91	92	16	16	15	16	16	230
290	Other mining	67	68	68	68	69	14	14	14	14	14	290
2	Mining, quarrying	830	915	950	967	983	144	148	149	150	151	2
311/2	Food products	526	541	559	575	592	130	130	130	130	131	311/2
313	Beverages	103	108	112	115	117	24	25	25	25	25	313
314	Tobacco	12	12	12	13	13	3	3	3	3	3	314
321	Textiles	610	622	630	636	644	176	175	174	172	171	321
3211	Spinning,weaving etc.	445	454	458	461	466	124	123	122	121	120	3211
322	Wearing apparel	276	282	285	289	310	88	87	86	86	85	322
323	Leather and products	75	77	79	81	64	21	21	21	21	21	323
324	Footwear	218	225	227	233	234	58	58	58	57	56	324
331	Wood products	203	205	204	208	211	53	52	52	52	51	331
332	Furniture, fixtures	180	182	187	189	193	51	51	51	50	50	332
341	Paper and products	147	152	155	159	162	36	36	36	36	36	341
3411	Pulp,paper etc.	...	...	...	...	...	...	...	...	...	...	3411
342	Printing,publishing	96	98	97	95	95	23	23	22	21	21	342
351	Industrial chemicals	331	343	354	368	378	65	65	65	66	66	351
3511	Basic excl fertilizers	...	...	...	...	...	...	...	...	...	...	3511
3513	Synthetic resins etc	...	...	...	...	...	...	...	...	...	...	3513
352	Other chemical products.	72	76	76	79	81	16	16	16	16	16	352
3522	Drugs and medicines	43	46	47	50	51	9	9	9	9	9	3522
353	Petroleum refineries	87	91	93	97	98	15	15	15	15	15	353
354	Petroleum,coal products.	36	38	38	39	40	7	7	7	7	7	354
355	Rubber products	88	90	92	95	98	20	21	20	20	20	355
356	Plastic products n.e.c.	24	24	24	25	25	6	6	6	6	6	356
361	Pottery,china etc	25	25	26	27	27	7	7	7	7	7	361
362	Glass and products	219	228	233	240	244	57	59	59	59	59	362
369	Non-metal products n.e.c	300	307	311	314	319	66	65	65	64	64	369
371	Iron and steel	642	658	667	718	727	119	119	119	126	125	371
372	Non-ferrous metals	100	103	106	108	110	20	20	20	20	20	372
381	Metal products	537	552	570	550	565	134	134	134	127	127	381
382	Machinery n.e.c.	1826	1880	1960	2019	2069	342	346	352	353	355	382
3825	Office,computing etc.	...	...	...	...	...	...	...	...	...	...	3825
383	Electrical machinery	456	470	480	514	548	104	105	104	107	111	383
3832	Radio,television etc.	...	...	...	...	...	...	...	...	...	...	3832
384	Transport equipment	856	883	912	933	951	168	171	172	173	173	384
3841	Shipbuilding, repair.	...	...	...	...	...	...	...	...	...	...	3841
3843	Motor vehicles	...	...	...	...	...	...	...	...	...	...	3843
385	Professional goods	52	53	54	56	53	12	12	12	12	11	385
390	Other industries	123	129	135	139	143	34	35	36	38	37	390
3	Manufacturing c/d/	8220	8454	8678	8914	9111	1855	1864	1867	1869	1869	3
410	Electricity,gas,steam	241	255	264	275	289	42	42	43	43	45	410
4101	Electricity e/	212	235	244	253	267	39	39	39	39	41	4101
420	Water works and supply	.	.	.	.	.	.	.	.	.	.	420
4	Electricity,gas etc	241	255	264	275	289	42	42	43	43	45	4
2-4	All industry c/d/	9291	9624	9892	10156	10383	2041	2054	2059	2062	2065	2-4

Note. For certain deviations in classification, see country note.

a/ Data are not fully comparable from year to year owing to organizational changes.
b/ Including homeworkers.
c/ Including repair of footwear.
d/ Including repair of motor vehicles.
e/ Including steam and hot water supply.

ISIC	INDUSTRY	7. WAGES AND SALARIES OF OPERATIVES a/b/ (BILLION KORUNAS)					8. HOURS WORKED BY OPERATIVES a/ (MILLIONS)					ISIC
		1981	1982	1983	1984	1985	1981	1982	1983	1984	1985	
210	Coal mining	5.41	6.12	6.38	6.46	6.55	212	218	218	218	218	210
220	Petroleum and gas	0.06	0.07	0.07	0.08	0.08	3	4	4	4	4	220
230	Metal ore mining	0.58	0.61	0.64	0.65	0.66	29	29	29	29	29	230
290	Other mining	0.49	0.49	0.49	0.50	0.50	28	27	27	26	27	290
2	Mining, quarrying .	6.54	7.29	7.58	7.69	7.79	272	278	278	277	278	2
311/2	Food products	3.82	3.93	4.05	4.16	4.28	261	270	268	268	269	311/2
313	Beverages	0.72	0.76	0.79	0.81	0.82	49	51	50	50	49	313
314	Tobacco	0.09	0.09	0.09	0.09	0.09	6	6	6	6	6	314
321	Textiles	4.63	4.70	4.75	4.81	4.87	325	322	318	315	312	321
3211	Spinning,weaving etc..	3.34	3.40	3.43	3.46	3.50	230	229	225	223	220	3211
322	Wearing apparel	2.18	2.21	2.23	2.27	2.30	160	158	156	155	154	322
323	Leather and products ...	0.58	0.59	0.60	0.62	0.63	40	39	39	39	39	323
324	Footwear	1.70	1.74	1.75	1.80	1.81	107	107	105	103	103	324
331	Wood products	1.56	1.58	1.58	1.61	1.63	103	103	100	100	98	331
332	Furniture, fixtures	1.43	1.45	1.48	1.49	1.52	97	97	97	96	95	332
341	Paper and products	1.06	1.10	1.12	1.14	1.16	70	71	71	70	70	341
3411	Pulp,paper etc.	...	...	...	...	...	...	...	...	...	...	3411
342	Printing,publishing	0.69	0.69	0.68	0.67	0.67	45	44	43	40	40	342
351	Industrial chemicals ...	2.16	2.25	2.32	2.41	2.48	122	123	123	123	124	351
3511	Basic excl fertilizers	...	...	...	...	...	...	...	...	...	...	3511
3513	Synthetic resins etc .	...	...	...	...	...	...	...	...	...	...	3513
352	Other chemical products.	0.45	0.47	0.47	0.49	0.51	31	31	30	30	30	352
3522	Drugs and medicines ..	0.24	0.25	0.26	0.27	0.28	16	16	4	16	16	3522
353	Petroleum refineries ...	0.56	0.58	0.60	0.62	0.63	29	28	28	28	28	353
354	Petroleum,coal products.	0.24	0.25	0.25	0.25	0.25	13	13	13	13	13	354
355	Rubber products	0.67	0.69	0.70	0.71	0.74	39	39	38	38	38	355
356	Plastic products n.e.c..	0.16	0.16	0.16	0.17	0.17	10	10	10	10	10	356
361	Pottery,china etc	0.18	0.19	0.19	0.20	0.20	13	13	13	13	13	361
362	Glass and products	1.65	1.73	1.76	1.81	1.84	109	113	112	112	112	362
369	Non-metal products n.e.c	2.20	2.25	2.27	2.29	2.32	132	131	129	127	126	369
371	Iron and steel	4.68	4.81	4.86	5.23	5.29	228	228	226	240	239	371
372	Non-ferrous metals	0.70	0.72	0.74	0.76	0.77	38	37	37	38	38	372
381	Metal products	4.03	4.13	4.25	4.09	4.20	259	259	258	244	245	381
382	Machinery n.e.c.	11.93	12.30	12.84	13.19	13.51	679	685	697	698	701	382
3825	Office,computing etc..	...	...	...	...	...	...	...	...	...	...	3825
383	Electrical machinery ...	2.93	3.00	3.05	3.26	3.49	199	199	196	204	210	383
3832	Radio,television etc..	...	...	...	...	...	...	...	...	...	...	3832
384	Transport equipment	5.74	5.92	6.12	6.26	6.38	332	335	337	339	340	384
3841	Shipbuilding, repair..	...	...	...	...	...	...	...	...	...	...	3841
3843	Motor vehicles	...	...	...	...	...	...	...	...	...	...	3843
385	Professional goods	0.38	0.38	0.39	0.41	0.39	23	23	23	23	21	385
390	Other industries	0.91	0.96	1.01	1.05	1.07	64	67	69	71	71	390
3	Manufacturing ..... c/d/	58.03	59.63	61.10	62.67	64.02	3583	3602	3592	3593	3594	3
410	Electricity,gas,steam ..	1.53	1.60	1.64	1.68	1.80	82	83	83	83	87	410
4101	Electricity .... e/	1.41	1.48	1.51	1.55	1.67	75	76	76	76	80	4101
420	Water works and supply .	.	.	.	.	.	.	.	.	.	.	420
4	Electricity,gas etc	1.53	1.60	1.64	1.68	1.80	82	83	83	83	87	4
2-4	All industry c/d/	66.10	68.52	70.32	72.04	73.61	3937	3963	3953	3953	3959	2-4

Note. For certain deviations in classification, see country note.

a/ Data are not fully comparable from year to year owing to organizational changes.
b/ Including payments to homeworkers.
c/ Including repair of footwear.
d/ Including repair of motor vehicles.
e/ Including steam and hot water supply.

ISIC	INDUSTRY	9. QUANTITY OF ELECTRICITY CONSUMED (MILLION KWH)					10. OUTPUT a/b/c/ (BILLION KORUNAS)					ISIC
		1981	1982	1983	1984	1985	1981	1982	1983	1984	1985	
210	Coal mining	3726	3791	3903	4022	4114	25.41	25.88	26.81	33.24	33.16	210
220	Petroleum and gas	8	7	6	6	6	0.54	0.55	0.44	0.60	0.85	220
230	Metal ore mining	374	368	381	385	393	3.33	3.40	3.37	3.53	3.75	230
290	Other mining	213	212	211	216	221	3.10	3.33	3.27	3.65	3.71	290
2	Mining, quarrying .	4321	4378	4501	4629	4734	32.38	33.16	33.89	41.02	41.47	2
311/2	Food products	1320	1357	1392	1439	1505	88.94	103.12	106.37	116.54	121.96	311/2
313	Beverages	293	299	297	295	296	10.42	11.88	12.24	12.70	13.22	313
314	Tobacco	12	13	13	13	13	1.75	1.87	1.89	1.93	1.90	314
321	Textiles	1592	1607	1644	1662	1695	35.12	35.70	36.29	37.93	38.92	321
3211	Spinning,weaving etc..	157	160	165	165	170	28.08	28.56	28.90	30.23	30.92	3211
322	Wearing apparel	84	84	87	92	93	9.59	9.96	10.11	10.39	10.48	322
323	Leather and products ...	60	60	59	61	63	4.28	4.74	4.68	4.78	4.68	323
324	Footwear	250	251	253	262	263	10.16	11.30	11.30	11.41	11.44	324
331	Wood products	557	571	596	619	624	12.55	13.00	13.19	13.76	14.50	331
332	Furniture, fixtures	168	169	175	178	182	6.81	7.20	7.57	7.78	7.98	332
341	Paper and products	1740	1844	1905	1999	2126	12.69	13.61	13.89	16.11	17.43	341
3411	Pulp,paper etc.	...	...	...	...	...	...	...	...	...	...	3411
342	Printing,publishing	78	79	80	81	84	3.81	3.93	4.02	4.90	4.37	342
351	Industrial chemicals ...	4424	4330	4396	4385	4512	45.75	46.86	49.73	55.94	58.54	351
3511	Basic excl fertilizers	...	...	...	...	...	...	...	...	...	...	3511
3513	Synthetic resins etc .	...	...	...	...	...	...	...	...	...	...	3513
352	Other chemical products.	885	886	905	908	931	7.98	8.11	7.23	7.47	7.96	352
3522	Drugs and medicines ..	104	107	112	113	128	5.10	5.04	5.09	5.02	5.49	3522
353	Petroleum refineries ...	483	426	447	450	438	33.51	32.29	32.89	44.31	45.27	353
354	Petroleum,coal products.	2737	2743	2838	2842	2914	4.57	5.25	5.18	6.51	5.57	354
355	Rubber products	349	346	357	362	365	8.09	8.72	9.21	9.42	9.70	355
356	Plastic products n.e.c..	84	80	83	85	88	1.63	1.65	1.69	1.69	1.78	356
361	Pottery,china etc	505	506	513	525	529	0.95	1.05	1.10	1.14	1.17	361
362	Glass and products	928	911	931	938	965	8.88	9.27	9.28	9.76	10.02	362
369	Non-metal products n.e.c	1951	1872	1826	1689	1825	17.58	19.56	19.69	22.08	25.76	369
371	Iron and steel	6587	6564	6600	6775	7116	59.80	67.41	69.39	83.95	85.56	371
372	Non-ferrous metals	1870	1798	1843	1827	1841	18.66	19.44	17.65	18.35	18.77	372
381	Metal products	1138	1132	1318	1160	992	27.09	29.23	30.16	27.92	28.95	381
382	Machinery n.e.c.	2456	2480	2513	2602	2666	91.51	97.67	103.06	107.30	112.35	382
3825	Office,computing etc..	...	...	...	...	...	...	...	...	...	...	3825
383	Electrical machinery ...	665	666	680	720	794	29.85	31.67	31.68	34.65	36.28	383
3832	Radio,television etc..	...	...	...	...	...	...	...	...	...	...	3832
384	Transport equipment	1457	1445	1426	1516	1562	53.99	57.68	60.49	63.66	65.40	384
3841	Shipbuilding, repair..	...	...	...	...	...	...	...	...	...	...	3841
3843	Motor vehicles	...	...	...	...	...	...	...	...	...	...	3843
385	Professional goods	231	226	239	243	245	2.32	2.49	2.75	2.79	2.57	385
390	Other industries	4667	5120	5220	5474	5616	8.59	9.67	9.88	10.28	10.62	390
3	Manufacturing ..... d/e/	37571	37865	38636	39202	40343	616.87	664.33	682.61	745.45	773.15	3
410	Electricity,gas,steam ..	2494	2543	2764	2750	2723	24.06	24.58	25.75	28.21	38.84	410
4101	Electricity .... f/	1207	1310	1310	1394	1606	22.59	23.09	24.25	25.76	36.85	4101
420	Water works and supply .	.	.	.	.	.	.	.	.	.	...	420
4	Electricity,gas etc	2494	2543	2764	2750	2723	24.06	24.58	25.75	28.21	38.84	4
2-4	All industry d/e/	44386	44786	45901	46581	47800	673.31	722.07	742.25	814.68	853.46	2-4

Note. For certain deviations in classification, see country note.

a/ State national industry only.
b/ Data are not fully comparable from year to year owing to organizational changes.
c/ Excluding turnover taxes.
d/ Including repair of footwear.
e/ Including repair of motor vehicles.
f/ Including steam and hot water supply.

ISIC	INDUSTRY	11. VALUE ADDED a/ (BILLION KORUNAS)					12. GROSS FIXED CAPITAL FORMATION TOTAL b/c/ (BILLION KORUNAS)					ISIC
		d/ 1981	1982	1983	1984	1985	e/ 1981	e/ 1982	f/ 1983	f/ 1984	g/ 1985	
210	Coal mining	15.74	15.44	16.04	20.87	20.73	5.70	6.32	6.98	7.28	6.87	210
220	Petroleum and gas	0.44	0.44	0.32	0.47	0.70	0.28	0.50	0.34	0.36	0.35	220
230	Metal ore mining	2.09	2.12	1.95	1.90	2.00	0.24	0.26	0.37	0.42	0.36	230
290	Other mining	1.55	1.70	1.69	1.94	1.96	0.41	0.39	0.36	0.42	0.45	290
2	Mining, quarrying .	19.82	19.70	20.00	25.18	25.39	6.63	7.47	8.05	8.48	8.03	2
311/2	Food products	13.03	13.13	13.64	14.11	15.61	2.99	2.98	3.28	3.66	4.22	311/2
313	Beverages	2.60	3.33	3.58	3.31	3.58	0.53	0.63	0.75	0.91	0.91	313
314	Tobacco	0.45	0.40	0.42	0.40	0.40	0.03	0.04	0.04	0.04	0.04	314
321	Textiles	13.54	13.85	14.06	14.17	14.54	2.00	1.80	1.68	1.91	2.29	321
3211	Spinning,weaving etc..	10.47	10.71	10.78	10.76	11.06	1.61	1.39	1.38	1.50	1.75	3211
322	Wearing apparel	3.70	3.88	4.02	4.07	4.04	0.22	0.24	0.23	0.29	0.41	322
323	Leather and products ...	1.20	1.16	1.20	1.18	1.18	0.18	0.12	0.12	0.15	0.18	323
324	Footwear	3.72	3.86	3.99	4.02	4.19	0.35	0.33	0.38	0.43	0.41	324
331	Wood products	4.33	4.55	4.68	4.54	4.44	1.34	0.93	0.84	0.61	0.65	331
332	Furniture, fixtures	2.39	2.57	2.72	2.75	2.78	0.23	0.19	0.22	0.23	0.25	332
341	Paper and products	3.84	4.18	4.22	4.73	4.92	2.79	3.58	1.93	1.42	1.16	341
3411	Pulp,paper etc.	...	...	...	...	...	...	...	...	...	...	3411
342	Printing,publishing	1.62	1.65	1.68	1.71	1.77	0.79	0.25	0.23	0.28	0.36	342
351	Industrial chemicals ...	12.06	12.66	14.22	13.50	14.78	2.94	3.06	3.29	3.24	2.95	351
3511	Basic excl fertilizers	...	...	...	...	...	...	...	...	...	...	3511
3513	Synthetic resins etc .	...	...	...	...	...	...	...	...	...	...	3513
352	Other chemical products.	2.27	2.38	2.37	2.00	2.23	0.36	0.44	0.49	0.56	0.58	352
3522	Drugs and medicines ..	1.80	1.80	1.87	1.55	1.72	0.24	0.33	0.40	0.52	0.52	3522
353	Petroleum refineries ...	5.25	5.72	6.47	6.04	6.68	0.98	0.79	0.79	0.76	0.55	353
354	Petroleum,coal products.	1.50	1.26	1.25	1.43	1.27	0.52	0.51	0.35	0.34	0.33	354
355	Rubber products	2.56	2.50	2.83	2.66	2.71	0.46	0.43	0.53	0.58	0.55	355
356	Plastic products n.e.c..	0.61	0.59	0.61	0.53	0.58	0.06	0.09	0.09	0.07	0.09	356
361	Pottery,china etc	0.55	0.63	0.67	0.66	0.66	0.11	0.10	0.09	0.09	0.11	361
362	Glass and products	4.14	4.26	4.41	4.24	4.50	0.77	0.76	0.94	1.23	1.10	362
369	Non-metal products n.e.c	7.38	7.85	8.04	8.26	8.37	1.50	1.38	0.99	0.98	1.75	369
371	Iron and steel	16.68	15.61	16.27	20.57	22.49	3.46	3.24	3.43	2.90	3.03	371
372	Non-ferrous metals	3.50	3.30	3.45	3.45	3.67	0.36	0.37	0.44	0.50	0.65	372
381	Metal products	9.14	9.26	10.12	10.46	10.11	1.27	1.37	1.53	1.64	1.54	381
382	Machinery n.e.c.	41.77	42.48	45.64	45.06	48.46	5.80	6.09	6.39	6.67	7.75	382
3825	Office,computing etc..	...	...	...	...	...	...	...	...	...	...	3825
383	Electrical machinery ...	11.21	11.79	12.57	13.69	14.19	1.49	1.42	2.01	2.40	2.64	383
3832	Radio,television etc..	...	...	...	...	...	...	...	...	...	...	3832
384	Transport equipment	19.74	20.64	22.58	22.41	22.54	3.03	3.19	3.27	3.17	3.85	384
3841	Shipbuilding, repair..	...	...	...	...	...	...	...	...	...	...	3841
3843	Motor vehicles	...	...	...	...	...	...	...	...	...	...	3843
385	Professional goods	1.13	1.25	1.25	1.22	1.15	0.13	0.16	0.12	0.19	0.31	385
390	Other industries	2.57	2.75	2.79	2.32	2.40	0.33	0.29	0.27	0.40	0.49	390
3	Manufacturing ..... h/i/	192.48	197.49	209.75	213.49	224.24	35.02	34.78	34.72	35.65	39.15	3
410	Electricity,gas,steam ..	8.65	9.44	10.21	11.07	11.49	6.00	6.60	8.15	7.02	7.53	410
4101	Electricity .... j/	7.84	8.63	9.35	9.72	10.53	5.65	6.17	7.80	6.73	7.27	4101
420	Water works and supply .	.	.	.	.	.	.	.	.	.	.	420
4	Electricity,gas etc	8.65	9.44	10.21	11.07	11.49	6.00	6.60	8.15	7.02	7.53	4
2-4	All industry h/i/	220.95	226.63	239.96	249.74	261.12	47.65	48.85	50.92	51.15	54.71	2-4

Note. For certain deviations in classification, see country note.

a/ Net of depreciation and non-industrial costs.
b/ State industry only.
c/ Excluding used fixed assets.
d/ Owing to the changes in methodology, data are not comparable with those for previous years.
e/ At prices of 1 January 1967.
f/ At 1983 prices.
g/ At current prices.
h/ Including repair of footwear.
i/ Including repair of motor vehicles.
j/ Including steam and hot water supply.

13. GROSS FIXED CAPITAL FORMATION
MACHINERY AND EQUIPMENT a/b/c/
(BILLION KORUNAS)

ISIC	INDUSTRY	1981	1982	1983	1984	d/ 1985	ISIC
210	Coal mining	3.56	3.64	3.88	3.83	3.46	210
220	Petroleum and gas	0.10	0.10	0.08	0.10	0.12	220
230	Metal ore mining	0.13	0.13	0.22	0.23	0.18	230
290	Other mining	0.27	0.26	0.25	0.27	0.32	290
2	Mining, quarrying .	4.06	4.13	4.43	4.43	4.08	2
311/2	Food products	1.84	1.81	2.03	2.22	2.75	311/2
313	Beverages	0.35	0.40	0.46	0.50	0.54	313
314	Tobacco	0.02	0.02	0.02	0.03	0.01	314
321	Textiles	1.57	1.37	1.25	1.46	1.80	321
3211	Spinning,weaving etc..	1.28	1.04	1.02	1.11	1.35	3211
322	Wearing apparel	0.14	0.15	0.13	0.14	0.24	322
323	Leather and products ...	0.12	0.08	0.07	0.07	0.10	323
324	Footwear	0.24	0.23	0.24	0.28	0.33	324
331	Wood products	0.99	0.57	0.54	0.40	0.42	331
332	Furniture, fixtures	0.14	0.13	0.13	0.15	0.18	332
341	Paper and products	1.67	2.48	1.27	1.00	0.83	341
3411	Pulp,paper etc.	...	...	...	...	...	3411
342	Printing,publishing	0.12	0.18	0.18	0.22	0.28	342
351	Industrial chemicals ...	2.01	2.11	2.35	2.22	1.99	351
3511	Basic excl fertilizers	...	...	...	...	...	3511
3513	Synthetic resins etc .	...	...	...	...	...	3513
352	Other chemical products.	0.20	0.24	0.31	0.30	0.33	352
3522	Drugs and medicines ..	0.13	0.18	0.25	0.27	0.28	3522
353	Petroleum refineries ...	0.77	0.55	0.57	0.60	0.34	353
354	Petroleum,coal products.	0.09	0.11	0.09	0.13	0.12	354
355	Rubber products	0.32	0.28	0.37	0.42	0.40	355
356	Plastic products n.e.c..	0.05	0.06	0.04	0.05	0.07	356
361	Pottery,china etc	0.07	0.07	0.06	0.04	0.05	361
362	Glass and products	0.56	0.42	0.44	0.73	0.52	362
369	Non-metal products n.e.c	0.92	0.83	0.82	0.56	1.08	369
371	Iron and steel	2.30	2.18	2.39	1.96	2.24	371
372	Non-ferrous metals	0.27	0.28	0.34	0.37	0.52	372
381	Metal products	0.87	0.90	1.04	1.12	1.06	381
382	Machinery n.e.c.	3.67	3.95	4.29	4.27	5.30	382
3825	Office,computing etc..	...	...	...	...	...	3825
383	Electrical machinery ...	1.09	0.93	1.39	1.62	1.88	383
3832	Radio,television etc..	...	...	...	...	...	3832
384	Transport equipment	1.87	1.88	1.94	1.73	2.24	384
3841	Shipbuilding, repair..	...	...	...	...	...	3841
3843	Motor vehicles	...	...	...	...	...	3843
385	Professional goods	0.09	0.09	0.08	0.12	0.23	385
390	Other industries	0.21	0.19	0.13	0.23	0.30	390
3	Manufacturing ..... e/f/	22.56	22.49	22.97	22.94	26.15	3
410	Electricity,gas,steam ..	4.02	4.74	4.48	3.29	4.13	410
4101	Electricity .... g/	3.98	4.69	4.40	3.23	4.09	4101
420	Water works and supply .	.	.	.	.	.	420
4	Electricity,gas etc	4.02	4.74	4.48	3.29	4.13	4
2-4	All industry e/f/	30.64	31.36	31.88	30.66	34.36	2-4

a/ At 1983 prices.
b/ State industry only.
c/ Excluding used fixed assets.
d/ At current prices.
e/ Including repair of footwear.
f/ Including repair of motor vehicles.
g/ Including steam and hot water supply.

14. INDEX NUMBERS OF INDUSTRIAL PRODUCTION (1980 = 100)

ISIC	INDUSTRY	1976	1977	1978	1979	1981	1982	1983	1984	1985	a/ RATE	ISIC
210	Coal mining	98	97	100	102	99	100	101	102	100	0.2	210
220	Petroleum and gas	116	124	138	113	115	117	120	144	156	3.3	220
230	Metal ore mining	84	89	94	97	97	96	98	100	104	2.4	230
290	Other mining	81	85	90	96	102	98	97	99	100	2.4	290
2	Mining, quarrying .	94	95	98	101	99	99	101	102	101	0.8	2
311/2	Food products	87	93	96	98	101	100	103	106	108	2.4	311/2
313	Beverages	92	96	96	99	102	102	106	108	106	1.6	313
314	Tobacco	99	104	104	102	105	102	104	106	104	0.5	314
321	Textiles	86	89	92	96	103	104	106	108	111	2.9	321
3211	Spinning,weaving etc..	...	...	...	...	...	...	...	...	...	...	3211
322	Wearing apparel	86	90	93	97	103	106	108	111	116	3.4	322
323	Leather and products ...	89	91	94	98	102	102	101	103	107	2.1	323
324	Footwear	88	92	94	97	101	103	102	104	107	2.2	324
331	Wood products	81	86	92	96	102	106	109	114	115	4.0	331
332	Furniture, fixtures	77	82	88	94	100	100	104	107	110	4.0	332
341	Paper and products	88	91	94	97	102	106	108	115	121	3.6	341
3411	Pulp,paper etc.	...	...	...	...	...	...	...	...	...	...	3411
342	Printing,publishing .... b/	86	89	94	97	103	105	107	111	114	3.2	342
351	Industrial chemicals ...	83	88	93	95	101	103	106	110	116	3.8	351
3511	Basic excl fertilizers	...	...	...	...	...	...	...	...	...	...	3511
3513	Synthetic resins etc .	...	...	...	...	...	...	...	...	...	...	3513
352	Other chemical products.	78	84	89	94	105	105	110	118	131	5.9	352
3522	Drugs and medicines ..	...	...	...	...	...	...	...	...	...	...	3522
353	Petroleum refineries ...	84	93	98	101	100	97	98	100	104	2.4	353
354	Petroleum,coal products.	96	96	97	97	98	95	88	80	80	-2.0	354
355	Rubber products	80	86	91	96	103	104	107	111	115	4.1	355
356	Plastic products n.e.c..	...	...	...	...	...	...	...	...	...	...	356
361	Pottery,china etc	86	90	92	94	102	106	111	115	116	3.4	361
362	Glass and products	87	91	94	99	102	105	105	110	112	2.8	362
369	Non-metal products n.e.c	89	92	96	97	102	101	102	102	103	1.6	369
371	Iron and steel	89	91	95	96	101	100	101	103	104	1.7	371
372	Non-ferrous metals	90	93	97	100	100	98	100	100	103	1.5	372
381	Metal products	83	87	91	97	103	104	107	110	116	3.8	381
382	Machinery n.e.c.	78	84	90	96	104	109	115	122	129	5.7	382
3825	Office,computing etc..	...	...	...	...	...	...	...	...	...	...	3825
383	Electrical machinery ...	78	84	90	95	107	112	121	136	149	7.5	383
3832	Radio,television etc..	...	...	...	...	...	...	...	...	...	...	3832
384	Transport equipment	79	83	89	95	140	144	150	159	168	8.7	384
3841	Shipbuilding, repair..	...	...	...	...	...	...	...	...	...	...	3841
3843	Motor vehicles	...	...	...	...	...	...	...	...	...	...	3843
385	Professional goods	77	84	90	95	104	108	112	114	114	4.5	385
390	Other industries	89	90	94	97	103	103	105	107	110	2.4	390
3	Manufacturing ..... b/	84	89	93	97	102	104	107	111	116	3.7	3
410	Electricity,gas,steam ..	84	89	93	94	101	103	105	108	112	3.2	410
4101	Electricity	...	...	...	...	...	...	...	...	...	...	4101
420	Water works and supply .	87	90	94	96	107	113	115	119	...	c/ 4.0	420
4	Electricity,gas etc	85	89	93	94	105	106	108	112	116	3.5	4
2-4	All industry b/	84	89	93	97	102	104	107	111	115	3.6	2-4

a/ Annual growth rate 1976-1985.
b/ Excluding publishing.
c/ Annual growth rate 1976-1984.

DENMARK

The information on industrial activity is based on the reply to the United Nations Questionnaire on General Industrial Statistics from Danmarks Statistik, Copenhagen. The concepts, definitions and classification by branches of industry are generally in accordance with United Nations standards. The estimates relate to Denmark exclusive of the Faeroe Islands and Greenland.

The data presented in the tables are principally obtained from the results of three separate industrial inquiries conducted annually by Danmarks Statistik. These relate to employment, accounts and investments. The employment inquiry, which includes information on earnings and hours worked, covers establishments with 6 or more employees. The accounts inquiry covers enterprises with 20 or more employees and collects detailed profit and loss statistics. The investments inquiry covers enterprises with 20 or more employees; based on the results obtained from this inquiry, estimates are made to cover industrial establishments with 6 or more employees. For the electricity industry, the accounts and investments inquiries cover 10 major enterprises which account for 98 per cent of the total electricity consumption in the country. Excluded from the annual inquiries are production of crude petroleum and natural gas, metal ore mining, water works and supply and for manufacturing, casing factories, periodical publishing, manual industries such as bakeries, tailoring and basket work.

The estimates are compiled according to the national classification which follows the present version of ISIC.

The total number of persons engaged comprises employees, proprietors (whether working or not) and unpaid family members. Homeworkers and persons working less than 15 hours a week are not included in the employment numbers or hours worked, but payments to these workers are included in data on wages and salaries. Apprentices are included in the category of operatives. The employment numbers are measured as annual averages for employees, based on enumerations in four months of the year (March, June, September and November) and the numbers at 30 November for proprietors and unpaid family workers.

Wages and salaries include regular payments, overtime pay, holiday allowances and sick pay. The estimates of supplements to wages and salaries are based on enterprise statistics. Included are the employers' expenditures on social security and other pension schemes, staff insurances, vocational training and all other compulsory or voluntary social expenses for the benefit of the staff.

The estimates of electricity consumed are derived from the results of special investigations into energy consumption in industry. The inquiry covers establishments with 20 or more employees, which account for about 87 per cent of the total number of industrial employees.

The estimates of output comprise the value of sales of own products, payments received for contract, repair and installation work done for others, the value of goods shipped in the same condition as received, receipts from other sources and the value of production of plant and equipment for own use. Adjustments are made for stock changes in the value of finished goods and work in progress. Output is valued exclusive of the value-added tax and any other taxes or duties on turnover.

Value added is the value of output as defined above less the cost of purchases of raw materials, semi-manufactures, auxiliary materials and packing; fuel and power purchased; contract work performed by others; and goods shipped in the same condition as received. Adjustments are made for changes in the value of stocks of materials, fuels and supplies and goods to be sold in the same condition as received. No deduction is made for the cost of repair and maintenance work done by others. Input is valued exclusive of the value-added tax but including other taxes and duties.

The estimates of gross fixed capital formation relate to the current value of purchases and own-account construction of fixed assets less the value of corresponding sales. Valuation is exclusive of the value-added tax.

The indexes of industrial production are compiled by Danmarks Statistik and provided in response to the United Nations Questionnaire on Indexes of Industrial Production. The indexes cover, in principle, manufacturing enterprises with 6 or more operatives and all electricity and gas undertakings.

Related national publications:
Industristatistik (annual); Regnskabsstatistik for industrien (annual); Statistisk Arbog (Statistical Yearbook); Statistisk Tiars-oversigt (Statistical Ten-Year Survey) (annual); Statistiske Efterretninger (Statistical News) (irregular - selected issues), all published by Danmarks Statistik, Copenhagen.

ISIC	INDUSTRY	1. NUMBER OF ESTABLISHMENTS a/ (NUMBER)					2. AVERAGE NUMBER OF PERSONS ENGAGED a/ (THOUSANDS)					ISIC
		1981	1982	1983	1984	1985	1981	1982	1983	1984	1985	
210	Coal mining	-	-	-	-	-	-	-	-	-	-	210
220	Petroleum and gas	.	.	.	.	.	.	.	.	.	.	220
230	Metal ore mining	.	.	.	.	.	.	.	.	.	.	230
290	Other mining	84	78	80	82	80	1.1	1.0	1.1	1.1	1.1	290
2	Mining, quarrying .	84	78	80	82	80	1.1	1.0	1.1	1.1	1.1	2
311/2	Food products	850	846	826	779	814	61.5	61.5	62.1	63.2	66.5	311/2
313	Beverages	55	52	49	48	48	10.8	10.7	10.3	10.0	9.8	313
314	Tobacco	16	15	15	14	15	2.8	2.4	2.2	2.1	2.2	314
321	Textiles	339	351	343	359	380	13.5	14.2	14.0	14.6	15.5	321
3211	Spinning,weaving etc..	61	61	61	65	71	4.3	4.4	4.6	4.8	5.2	3211
322	Wearing apparel	303	294	293	291	312	10.3	10.8	11.1	11.6	12.3	322
323	Leather and products ...	37	34	30	33	29	1.3	1.2	1.1	1.1	1.0	323
324	Footwear	50	46	41	34	32	2.5	2.7	2.3	2.2	2.0	324
331	Wood products	303	279	281	297	310	8.9	8.6	8.9	9.7	10.2	331
332	Furniture, fixtures	386	379	402	438	461	11.7	11.6	12.1	14.3	15.6	332
341	Paper and products	115	112	119	118	116	8.6	8.4	8.7	8.9	9.2	341
3411	Pulp,paper etc.	9	10	12	12	11	2.2	2.1	2.2	2.1	2.0	3411
342	Printing,publishing	644	643	665	713	726	24.0	24.4	24.1	24.6	25.6	342
351	Industrial chemicals ...	133	120	117	123	129	10.7	10.6	10.5	11.2	11.9	351
3511	Basic excl fertilizers	40	36	34	33	34	4.7	4.8	4.8	5.0	5.4	3511
3513	Synthetic resins etc .	86	76	75	81	86	4.6	4.3	4.4	4.9	5.1	3513
352	Other chemical products.	153	151	155	170	170	12.1	11.9	12.2	13.1	13.4	352
3522	Drugs and medicines ..	34	33	37	43	43	6.0	5.9	6.3	6.8	7.1	3522
353	Petroleum refineries ...	3	3	3	3	3	0.6	0.6	0.5	0.6	0.6	353
354	Petroleum,coal products.	77	74	73	68	70	1.2	1.1	1.3	1.1	1.3	354
355	Rubber products	43	41	46	46	48	2.4	2.2	2.2	2.5	2.5	355
356	Plastic products n.e.c..	201	204	217	237	244	7.7	7.8	8.0	8.8	9.7	356
361	Pottery,china etc	25	24	25	28	28	3.3	3.0	2.6	2.6	2.3	361
362	Glass and products	41	39	41	36	42	2.9	2.5	2.3	2.3	2.5	362
369	Non-metal products n.e.c	365	334	312	336	345	12.6	12.0	12.0	12.8	13.4	369
371	Iron and steel	39	39	38	39	38	4.6	4.2	3.9	4.2	4.3	371
372	Non-ferrous metals	36	38	40	40	40	2.0	1.9	1.8	1.9	1.8	372
381	Metal products	679	687	714	760	803	28.5	29.2	30.7	33.6	37.2	381
382	Machinery n.e.c.	855	815	853	910	965	54.1	52.1	52.2	56.7	62.7	382
3825	Office,computing etc..	24	24	22	23	26	2.1	2.0	1.7	1.9	2.4	3825
383	Electrical machinery ...	247	250	274	276	288	23.6	23.5	23.1	24.4	27.3	383
3832	Radio,television etc..	91	98	103	109	105	10.9	10.9	10.8	11.1	12.6	3832
384	Transport equipment	248	242	267	277	294	27.4	29.0	26.4	25.2	27.4	384
3841	Shipbuilding, repair..	133	133	151	157	166	20.8	22.3	19.8	19.5	20.3	3841
3843	Motor vehicles	95	88	95	101	105	4.5	4.5	4.4	4.7	5.1	3843
385	Professional goods	101	108	114	127	130	8.9	9.1	9.7	10.6	11.6	385
390	Other industries	141	136	138	135	137	5.9	5.7	5.3	5.6	6.3	390
3	Manufacturing	6485	6356	6491	6735	7017	364.4	362.9	361.6	379.5	406.1	3
410	Electricity,gas,steam ..	...	...	...	...	...	...	...	...	...	...	410
4101	Electricity	...	...	...	...	...	...	...	...	...	...	4101
420	Water works and supply .	.	.	.	.	.	.	.	.	.	.	420
4	Electricity,gas etc	...	...	...	...	...	...	...	...	...	...	4
2-4	All industry	...	...	...	...	...	...	...	...	...	...	2-4

a/ Establishments with 6 or more employees.

ISIC	INDUSTRY	3. AVERAGE NUMBER OF EMPLOYEES a/ (THOUSANDS)					4. WAGES AND SALARIES OF EMPLOYEES a/b/ (MILLION KRONER)					ISIC
		1981	1982	1983	1984	1985	1981	1982	1983	1984	1985	
210	Coal mining	-	-	-	-	-	-	-	-	-	-	210
220	Petroleum and gas	.	.	.	.	.	.	.	.	.	.	220
230	Metal ore mining	.	.	.	.	.	.	.	.	.	.	230
290	Other mining	1.1	1.0	1.0	1.1	1.1	130	133	147	164	173	290
2	Mining, quarrying	1.1	1.0	1.0	1.1	1.1	130	133	147	164	173	2
311/2	Food products	61.3	61.4	62.0	63.1	66.4	7070	7841	8518	9115	9724	311/2
313	Beverages	10.8	10.7	10.3	10.0	9.8	1512	1642	1697	1726	1647	313
314	Tobacco	2.8	2.4	2.2	2.1	2.2	289	278	281	294	300	314
321	Textiles	13.3	14.0	13.9	14.5	15.4	1314	1546	1653	1859	2028	321
3211	Spinning,weaving etc.	4.3	4.4	4.6	4.8	5.2	457	526	596	654	708	3211
322	Wearing apparel	10.2	10.7	10.9	11.5	12.2	855	980	1079	1221	1314	322
323	Leather and products	1.2	1.2	1.1	1.1	1.0	117	129	124	130	124	323
324	Footwear	2.5	2.7	2.3	2.2	2.0	226	277	255	255	250	324
331	Wood products	8.8	8.5	8.8	9.6	10.1	912	975	1099	1284	1405	331
332	Furniture, fixtures	11.5	11.4	11.9	14.1	15.5	1130	1264	1412	1753	1984	332
341	Paper and products	8.6	8.4	8.7	8.9	9.2	1056	1165	1308	1408	1487	341
3411	Pulp,paper etc.	2.2	2.1	2.2	2.1	2.0	264	281	323	341	340	3411
342	Printing,publishing	23.8	24.1	23.8	24.4	25.4	3456	3995	4217	4501	4837	342
351	Industrial chemicals	10.7	10.6	10.5	11.1	11.9	1397	1536	1642	1835	2036	351
3511	Basic excl fertilizers	4.7	4.8	4.8	5.0	5.4	634	727	769	847	969	3511
3513	Synthetic resins etc	4.5	4.3	4.4	4.9	5.1	558	588	644	757	822	3513
352	Other chemical products	12.1	11.9	12.2	13.1	13.4	1541	1686	1865	2144	2313	352
3522	Drugs and medicines	6.0	5.9	6.3	6.8	7.1	798	881	1005	1164	1280	3522
353	Petroleum refineries	0.6	0.6	0.5	0.6	0.6	100	107	105	116	125	353
354	Petroleum,coal products	1.1	1.1	1.3	1.1	1.3	147	158	190	181	208	354
355	Rubber products	2.4	2.2	2.2	2.5	2.5	258	276	299	348	367	355
356	Plastic products n.e.c.	7.6	7.7	8.0	8.8	9.6	863	968	1090	1252	1425	356
361	Pottery,china etc	3.3	2.9	2.6	2.5	2.3	338	340	339	342	313	361
362	Glass and products	2.9	2.5	2.3	2.3	2.5	338	319	311	326	360	362
369	Non-metal products n.e.c	12.5	12.0	12.0	12.8	13.3	1496	1588	1725	1932	2091	369
371	Iron and steel	4.6	4.1	3.9	4.1	4.3	530	523	538	592	620	371
372	Non-ferrous metals	2.0	1.9	1.8	1.9	1.8	244	248	246	268	259	372
381	Metal products	28.3	29.0	30.5	33.5	37.1	3236	3713	4215	4842	5464	381
382	Machinery n.e.c.	53.9	51.9	52.0	56.5	62.5	6385	6825	7360	8290	9598	382
3825	Office,computing etc.	2.1	2.0	1.7	1.9	2.4	268	296	298	321	475	3825
383	Electrical machinery	23.6	23.5	23.1	24.4	27.3	2744	3036	3238	3591	4149	383
3832	Radio,television etc.	10.9	10.9	10.8	11.1	12.6	1255	1389	1523	1629	1889	3832
384	Transport equipment	27.3	28.9	26.3	25.1	27.3	3246	3857	3841	3769	4207	384
3841	Shipbuilding, repair.	20.7	22.3	19.8	19.5	20.3	2532	3068	2996	3003	3212	3841
3843	Motor vehicles	4.5	4.4	4.4	4.7	5.1	491	533	570	648	722	3843
385	Professional goods	8.9	9.1	9.7	10.6	11.6	1088	1242	1431	1625	1866	385
390	Other industries	5.9	5.7	5.3	5.6	6.3	620	677	684	762	877	390
3	Manufacturing	362.5	361.1	360.1	378.0	404.8	42508	47191	50762	55761	61378	3
410	Electricity,gas,steam	...	...	...	...	...	...	...	...	...	...	410
4101	Electricity	...	...	...	...	...	...	...	...	...	...	4101
420	Water works and supply	.	.	.	.	.	.	.	.	.	.	420
4	Electricity,gas etc	...	...	...	...	...	...	...	...	...	...	4
2-4	All industry	...	...	...	...	...	...	...	...	...	...	2-4

a/ Establishments with 6 or more employees.

b/ Including payments to homeworkers.

ISIC	INDUSTRY	5. SUPPLEMENTS TO WAGES AND SALARIES b/ (MILLION KRONER)					6. AVERAGE NUMBER OF OPERATIVES a/ (THOUSANDS)					ISIC
		1981	1982	c/ 1983	c/ 1984	c/ 1985	1981	1982	1983	1984	1985	
210	Coal mining	-	-	-	-	-	-	-	-	-	-	210
220	Petroleum and gas	.	.	.	.	.	.	.	.	.	.	220
230	Metal ore mining	.	.	.	.	.	.	.	.	.	.	230
290	Other mining	3.0	3.4	4.3	5.5	5.3	0.8	0.7	0.8	0.8	0.8	290
2	Mining, quarrying .	3.0	3.4	4.3	5.5	5.3	0.8	0.7	0.8	0.8	0.8	2
311/2	Food products	214.5	253.4	376.4	446.7	486.8	47.7	47.9	48.4	49.6	52.4	311/2
313	Beverages	134.0	164.5	193.4	192.9	165.4	8.1	8.0	7.6	7.3	7.2	313
314	Tobacco	18.7	20.8	20.7	24.6	26.0	2.2	1.8	1.7	1.6	1.7	314
321	Textiles	34.6	45.7	67.1	84.9	92.9	10.2	10.8	10.7	11.2	11.8	321
3211	Spinning,weaving etc..	13.9	17.9	26.5	30.7	28.7	3.3	3.4	3.5	3.7	3.8	3211
322	Wearing apparel	17.2	21.7	36.9	55.4	64.8	8.3	8.7	9.0	9.5	10.1	322
323	Leather and products ...	1.5	2.3	4.3	5.2	4.6	1.0	0.9	0.8	0.8	0.7	323
324	Footwear	4.6	6.8	9.4	11.3	10.6	2.1	2.3	1.9	1.8	1.6	324
331	Wood products	22.0	24.9	34.4	52.0	63.0	6.8	6.6	6.9	7.7	8.0	331
332	Furniture, fixtures	19.5	25.7	41.5	64.5	86.0	9.1	9.1	9.7	11.5	12.6	332
341	Paper and products	49.6	66.7	80.2	95.2	99.2	6.3	6.2	6.4	6.6	6.9	341
3411	Pulp,paper etc.	16.2	17.3	19.9	25.4	24.1	1.7	1.6	1.7	1.6	1.6	3411
342	Printing,publishing	170.5	215.0	229.4	243.7	243.4	13.7	14.1	13.8	14.1	14.6	342
351	Industrial chemicals ...	80.8	101.1	118.8	139.6	147.6	6.6	6.3	6.3	6.7	7.1	351
3511	Basic excl fertilizers	...	...	...	...	...	2.5	2.6	2.5	2.5	2.7	3511
3513	Synthetic resins etc .	16.6	19.7	30.6	36.7	44.2	3.2	2.9	3.1	3.4	3.6	3513
352	Other chemical products.	120.1	130.0	124.5	158.3	175.0	5.1	5.0	5.0	5.3	5.4	352
3522	Drugs and medicines ..	66.3	74.3	...	90.2	99.7	2.5	2.5	2.6	2.8	2.8	3522
353	Petroleum refineries ...					3.5	0.1	0.1	0.1	0.1	0.1	353
354	Petroleum,coal products.	16.0	22.0	24.6	26.3	8.2	0.7	0.7	0.8	0.7	0.8	354
355	Rubber products					17.0	1.7	1.6	1.6	1.8	1.8	355
356	Plastic products n.e.c..	21.2	26.8	37.3	48.4	56.9	5.4	5.4	5.6	6.2	6.8	356
361	Pottery,china etc	14.6	17.3	39.6	45.8	48.8	2.8	2.4	2.1	2.0	1.8	361
362	Glass and products	16.0	21.8	19.6	20.7	6.9	2.2	.1.9	1.7	1.8	1.9	362
369	Non-metal products n.e.c	73.2	77.4	78.9	116.2	110.3	8.7	8.4	8.5	9.1	9.5	369
371	Iron and steel	18.9	18.5	14.7	22.4	24.4	3.5	3.2	3.0	3.2	3.4	371
372	Non-ferrous metals	8.2	8.5	11.1	15.4	13.7	1.4	1.4	1.3	1.5	1.4	372
381	Metal products	80.4	88.0	130.7	173.4	208.8	21.0	21.4	22.5	25.0	27.7	381
382	Machinery n.e.c.	166.5	159.1	241.8	301.5	378.3	36.6	35.0	34.6	38.0	42.1	382
3825	Office,computing etc..	...	...	...	...	...	1.0	1.0	0.5	0.6	0.6	3825
383	Electrical machinery ...	114.8	129.0	150.7	186.3	208.5	14.8	14.7	14.4	15.3	17.1	383
3832	Radio,television etc..	29.5	35.6	55.2	71.3	83.4	6.7	6.7	6.7	6.9	7.8	3832
384	Transport equipment	98.1	111.5	168.5	192.2	196.9	21.4	22.5	20.0	19.0	20.9	384
3841	Shipbuilding, repair..	80.2	90.5	134.7	150.2	154.4	16.4	17.4	15.1	14.7	15.5	3841
3843	Motor vehicles	...	...	...	...	...	3.4	3.4	3.3	3.6	3.9	3843
385	Professional goods	25.8	31.3	50.0	61.6	68.5	5.0	5.0	5.3	5.8	6.4	385
390	Other industries	20.0	25.6	23.4	29.1	33.2	4.1	4.0	3.6	3.8	4.4	390
3	Manufacturing	1561.3	1815.4	2327.9	2813.6	3049.2	256.6	255.4	253.3	267.0	286.2	3
410	Electricity,gas,steam ..	...	...	...	...	...	...	...	...	...	...	410
4101	Electricity	...	...	...	...	...	...	...	...	...	...	4101
420	Water works and supply .	.	.	.	.	.	.	.	.	.	.	420
4	Electricity,gas etc	...	...	...	...	...	...	...	...	...	...	4
2-4	All industry	...	...	...	...	...	...	...	...	...	...	2-4

a/ Establishments with 6 or more employees. b/ Enterprises with 20 or more employees.
c/ Estimates derives from new inquiry form with specifications for enterprises.

ISIC	INDUSTRY	7. WAGES AND SALARIES OF OPERATIVES a/b/ (MILLION KRONER)					8. HOURS WORKED BY OPERATIVES a/ (MILLIONS)					ISIC
		1981	1982	1983	1984	1985	1981	1982	1983	1984	1985	
210	Coal mining	-	-	-	-	-	-	-	-	-	-	210
220	Petroleum and gas	.	.	.	.	.	.	.	.	.	.	220
230	Metal ore mining	.	.	.	.	.	.	.	.	.	.	230
290	Other mining	88	90	101	115	120	1.4	1.3	1.4	1.5	1.5	290
2	Mining, quarrying .	88	90	101	115	120	1.4	1.3	1.4	1.5	1.5	2
311/2	Food products	5208	5771	6272	6735	7163	78.7	79.7	81.0	82.8	83.3	311/2
313	Beverages	1053	1142	1169	1161	1060	13.0	13.0	12.4	11.8	10.4	313
314	Tobacco	194	186	187	199	206	3.2	2.7	2.6	2.6	2.6	314
321	Textiles	886	1050	1136	1275	1372	15.9	16.9	17.0	18.1	18.5	321
3211	Spinning,weaving etc..	314	364	412	455	484	5.4	5.5	5.8	6.1	6.1	3211
322	Wearing apparel	625	718	800	909	963	11.8	12.5	13.0	14.1	14.3	322
323	Leather and products ...	83	92	86	91	84	1.4	1.5	1.3	1.3	1.2	323
324	Footwear	176	220	195	195	189	3.2	3.5	3.0	2.8	2.6	324
331	Wood products	654	705	812	950	1024	11.1	10.8	11.8	13.0	13.3	331
332	Furniture, fixtures	818	923	1062	1331	1491	14.9	15.2	16.4	19.5	20.6	332
341	Paper and products	720	803	901	986	1032	10.2	10.3	10.7	11.1	11.0	341
3411	Pulp,paper etc.	190	204	236	244	241	2.8	2.8	2.8	2.8	2.6	3411
342	Printing,publishing	1936	2327	2426	2565	2707	21.4	23.6	23.4	23.9	24.4	342
351	Industrial chemicals ...	760	819	871	980	1057	11.1	10.8	10.7	11.4	11.7	351
3511	Basic excl fertilizers	298	337	347	370	404	4.2	4.3	4.2	4.2	4.4	3511
3513	Synthetic resins etc .	352	368	409	487	523	5.3	4.9	5.1	5.7	5.9	3513
352	Other chemical products.	529	573	624	706	739	8.2	7.9	8.0	8.6	8.5	352
3522	Drugs and medicines ..	271	296	338	378	402	3.9	3.8	4.1	4.4	4.4	3522
353	Petroleum refineries ...	8	7	6	7	6	0.1	0.1	0.1	0.1	0.1	353
354	Petroleum,coal products.	80	86	107	97	116	1.3	1.2	1.4	1.3	1.4	354
355	Rubber products	169	180	199	237	242	2.7	2.6	2.7	3.0	2.9	355
356	Plastic products n.e.c..	539	604	687	790	886	8.8	8.9	9.4	10.3	11.1	356
361	Pottery,china etc	262	262	261	258	229	4.0	3.5	3.3	3.2	2.7	361
362	Glass and products	239	226	218	231	251	3.6	3.2	2.9	3.0	3.1	362
369	Non-metal products n.e.c	954	1018	1123	1264	1359	14.6	14.2	14.7	15.7	16.1	369
371	Iron and steel	383	377	384	429	445	6.0	5.3	5.1	5.4	5.4	371
372	Non-ferrous metals	153	153	158	181	175	2.3	2.2	2.2	2.4	2.2	372
381	Metal products	2194	2507	2860	3320	3705	35.0	36.4	38.8	43.0	46.0	381
382	Machinery n.e.c.	3876	4110	4361	4916	5609	61.6	59.8	59.6	64.4	70.1	382
3825	Office,computing etc..	108	109	66	78	77	1.7	1.6	1.0	1.0	1.0	3825
383	Electrical machinery ...	1471	1614	1715	1891	2122	24.1	24.2	23.9	25.4	27.5	383
3832	Radio,television etc..	644	703	782	830	937	10.8	10.8	11.1	11.5	12.4	3832
384	Transport equipment	2371	2786	2711	2602	2938	35.3	37.5	34.6	32.1	34.2	384
3841	Shipbuilding, repair..	1870	2222	2121	2065	2245	27.0	29.1	26.2	24.7	25.3	3841
3843	Motor vehicles	344	380	399	454	515	5.7	5.7	5.7	6.1	6.6	3843
385	Professional goods	499	553	613	708	785	8.1	8.2	8.5	9.5	10.0	385
390	Other industries	391	423	418	468	542	6.5	6.2	5.8	6.2	6.8	390
3	Manufacturing	27231	30235	32362	35482	38497	418.1	421.9	424.3	446.0	462.0	3
410	Electricity,gas,steam ..	...	...	...	...	...	...	...	...	...	...	410
4101	Electricity	...	...	...	...	...	...	...	...	...	...	4101
420	Water works and supply .	.	.	.	.	.	.	.	.	.	.	420
4	Electricity,gas etc	...	...	...	...	...	...	...	...	...	...	4
2-4	All industry	...	...	...	...	...	...	...	...	...	...	2-4

a/ Establishments with 6 or more employees.

b/ Including payments to homeworkers.

ISIC	INDUSTRY	9. QUANTITY OF ELECTRICITY CONSUMED (MILLION KWH) 1981	1982	1983 a/	1984	1985 a/	10. OUTPUT IN FACTOR VALUES b/ (BILLION KRONER) 1981	1982	1983	1984	1985	ISIC
210	Coal mining	...	...	-	...	-	-	-	-	-	-	210
220	Petroleum and gas	...	...	.	...	.	.	.	.	.	.	220
230	Metal ore mining	...	...	.	...	.	.	.	.	.	.	230
290	Other mining	...	...	38	...	42	0.38	0.41	0.45	0.53	0.66	290
2	Mining, quarrying .	...	...	38	...	42	0.38	0.41	0.45	0.53	0.66	2
311/2	Food products	...	...	1279	...	1372	59.65	68.37	75.52	83.46	85.44	311/2
313	Beverages	...	...	166	...	164	5.10	5.91	6.45	6.66	6.93	313
314	Tobacco	...	...	16	...	19	1.20	1.37	1.57	1.79	2.03	314
321	Textiles	...	...	153	...	173	5.10	5.77	6.28	6.97	7.93	321
3211	Spinning,weaving etc..	...	...	105	...	116	1.83	2.10	2.56	2.71	2.90	3211
322	Wearing apparel	...	...	18	...	22	2.29	2.72	2.84	3.42	3.83	322
323	Leather and products ...	...	...	6	...	4	0.33	0.39	0.41	0.45	0.45	323
324	Footwear	...	...	9	...	9	0.74	0.97	0.90	1.02	1.02	324
331	Wood products	...	...	167	...	199	3.18	3.12	3.47	4.43	4.80	331
332	Furniture, fixtures	...	...	73	...	110	2.96	3.59	4.15	5.29	6.39	332
341	Paper and products	...	...	331	...	358	4.32	5.03	5.42	6.23	6.76	341
3411	Pulp,paper etc.	...	...	247	...	255	1.22	1.50	1.51	1.89	2.00	3411
342	Printing,publishing	...	...	96	...	104	6.71	8.15	8.85	9.81	11.18	342
351	Industrial chemicals ...	...	...	444	...	545	7.76	8.41	10.64	12.50	11.83	351
3511	Basic excl fertilizers	...	...	197	...	277	...	...	...	...	...	3511
3513	Synthetic resins etc .	...	...	105	...	136	2.63	2.69	3.13	3.89	4.20	3513
352	Other chemical products.	...	...	212	...	252	7.18	8.21	9.20	10.85	11.93	352
3522	Drugs and medicines ..	...	...	173	...	206	3.51	4.22	4.92	5.87	6.49	3522
353	Petroleum refineries ...	...	...	213	...	209					9.28	353
354	Petroleum,coal products.	...	...	38	...	41	14.89	10.95	10.35	11.59	1.92	354
355	Rubber products	...	...	37	...	44					1.11	355
356	Plastic products n.e.c..	...	...	158	...	200	2.65	2.99	3.37	4.06	4.64	356
361	Pottery,china etc	...	...	17	...	16	0.56	0.56	0.58	0.57	0.51	361
362	Glass and products	...	...	50	...	50	1.02	0.95	0.97	0.98	1.02	362
369	Non-metal products n.e.c	...	...	418	...	433	5.17	5.33	6.00	7.32	8.07	369
371	Iron and steel	...	...	485	...	546	2.18	2.26	2.12	2.54	2.98	371
372	Non-ferrous metals	...	...	52	...	56	1.21	1.10	1.28	1.80	1.51	372
381	Metal products	...	...	235	...	317	8.91	11.09	12.07	15.07	17.98	381
382	Machinery n.e.c.	...	...	299	...	347	17.27	18.43	20.92	23.55	27.70	382
3825	Office,computing etc..	...	...	9	...	-	...	...	...	...	...	3825
383	Electrical machinery ...	...	...	168	...	191	7.39	8.77	9.58	11.17	12.68	383
3832	Radio,television etc..	...	...	45	...	54	3.38	3.85	4.42	5.10	6.14	3832
384	Transport equipment	...	...	232	...	213	9.97	12.32	13.62	12.61	13.93	384
3841	Shipbuilding, repair..	...	...	164	...	173	7.54	9.55	10.90	9.62	10.55	3841
3843	Motor vehicles	...	...	55	...	29	...	...	...	...	...	3843
385	Professional goods	...	...	33	...	42	2.85	3.16	3.72	4.38	5.05	385
390	Other industries	...	...	37	...	49	2.14	2.39	2.43	2.93	3.56	390
3	Manufacturing	...	...	5442	...	6181	182.73	202.31	222.71	251.45	272.46	3
410	Electricity,gas,steam ..	...	...	...	...	...	...	...	...	...	...	410
4101	Electricity	...	...	...	...	...	...	...	...	...	...	4101
420	Water works and supply .	...	...	...	...	...	.	.	.	.	.	420
4	Electricity,gas etc	...	...	...	...	...	...	...	...	...	...	4
2-4	All industry	...	...	...	...	...	...	...	...	...	...	2-4

a/ Establishments with 20 or more employees.
b/ Kind-of-activity units of enterprises with 20 or more employees.

ISIC	INDUSTRY	11. VALUE ADDED IN FACTOR VALUES a/ (BILLION KRONER) 1981	1982	1983	1984	1985	12. GROSS FIXED CAPITAL FORMATION TOTAL b/ (MILLION KRONER) 1981	1982	1983	1984	1985	ISIC
210	Coal mining	-	-	-	-	-	-	-	-	-	-	210
220	Petroleum and gas	.	.	.	.	.	.	.	.	.	.	220
230	Metal ore mining	.	.	.	.	.	.	.	.	.	.	230
290	Other mining	0.26	0.28	0.31	0.38	0.49	21	65	38	70	76	290
2	Mining, quarrying .	0.26	0.28	0.31	0.38	0.49	21	65	38	70	76	2
311/2	Food products	14.42	15.84	17.54	19.48	20.40	1435	1419	1535	2068	2339	311/2
313	Beverages	3.00	3.51	3.79	3.88	4.04	335	239	246	502	352	313
314	Tobacco	0.65	0.69	0.79	0.90	1.01	47	25	36	59	58	314
321	Textiles	2.32	2.63	2.92	3.12	3.43	138	202	199	353	398	321
3211	Spinning,weaving etc..	0.80	0.94	1.21	1.25	1.26	55	72	72	140	172	3211
322	Wearing apparel	1.17	1.34	1.46	1.64	1.86	57	66	95	124	125	322
323	Leather and products ...	0.16	0.19	0.19	0.20	0.19	7	15	8	8	20	323
324	Footwear	0.33	0.39	0.37	0.40	0.40	25	27	31	21	44	324
331	Wood products	1.38	1.38	1.55	1.92	2.05	137	128	141	202	338	331
332	Furniture, fixtures	1.56	1.87	2.14	2.69	3.23	98	146	154	401	576	332
341	Paper and products	1.87	2.11	2.37	2.68	2.78	248	245	307	352	353	341
3411	Pulp,paper etc.	0.44	0.54	0.56	0.72	0.74	116	58	134	44	44	3411
342	Printing,publishing	4.42	5.39	5.81	6.47	7.15	286	333	459	501	923	342
351	Industrial chemicals ...	3.49	3.83	4.65	5.04	5.11	505	537	620	677	857	351
3511	Basic excl fertilizers	...	...	...	...	...	...	...	...	...	...	3511
3513	Synthetic resins etc .	1.09	1.13	1.36	1.62	1.80	152	153	193	191	244	3513
352	Other chemical products.	3.81	4.51	5.05	5.65	6.35	359	490	644	736	786	352
3522	Drugs and medicines ..	2.15	2.69	3.13	3.46	3.98	276	381	478	548	515	3522
353	Petroleum refineries ...					0.54					159	353
354	Petroleum,coal products.	1.53	1.33	1.53	1.77	0.62	145	218	178	338	158	354
355	Rubber products					0.59					105	355
356	Plastic products n.e.c..	1.37	1.51	1.74	2.00	2.80	135	172	183	348	464	356
361	Pottery,china etc	0.47	0.47	0.48	0.48	0.42	17	8	9	10	10	361
362	Glass and products	0.55	0.51	0.55	0.57	0.61	41	75	25	37	51	362
369	Non-metal products n.e.c	2.93	3.00	3.47	4.17	4.58	843	474	354	523	989	369
371	Iron and steel	0.95	1.05	0.97	1.09	1.25	42	70	93	103	145	371
372	Non-ferrous metals	0.34	0.31	0.42	0.49	0.45	91	42	32	36	31	372
381	Metal products	4.48	5.52	5.99	7.31	8.46	376	473	449	714	1013	381
382	Machinery n.e.c.	9.50	10.06	11.47	12.50	14.70	808	809	890	1093	1757	382
3825	Office,computing etc..	...	...	...	...	...	...	...	...	...	...	3825
383	Electrical machinery ...	4.13	4.88	5.16	5.96	6.59	291	381	414	571	776	383
3832	Radio,television etc..	1.95	2.25	2.40	2.72	3.12	137	189	206	252	373	3832
384	Transport equipment	4.29	5.39	6.21	6.03	6.06	272	321	369	354	417	384
3841	Shipbuilding, repair..	3.20	4.15	4.97	4.66	4.61	153	245	270	232	238	3841
3843	Motor vehicles	...	...	...	...	...	...	...	...	...	...	3843
385	Professional goods	1.80	2.06	2.41	2.80	3.11	120	144	161	220	349	385
390	Other industries	1.30	1.46	1.49	1.73	1.96	77	95	80	109	153	390
3	Manufacturing	72.22	81.23	90.52	100.97	110.74	6935	7154	7712	10460	13746	3
410	Electricity,gas,steam ..	...	...	...	...	...	...	...	...	...	...	410
4101	Electricity	...	...	...	...	...	...	...	...	...	...	4101
420	Water works and supply .	.	.	.	.	.	.	.	.	.	.	420
4	Electricity,gas etc	...	...	...	...	...	...	...	...	...	...	4
2-4	All industry	...	...	...	...	...	...	...	...	...	...	2-4

a/ Kind-of-activity units of enterprises with 20 or more employees.
b/ Establishments with 6 or more employees.

ISIC	INDUSTRY	13. GROSS FIXED CAPITAL FORMATION MACHINERY AND EQUIPMENT a/ (MILLION KRONER)					14. VALUE OF STOCKS AT END OF PERIOD TOTAL b/ (MILLION KRONER)					ISIC
		1981	1982	1983	1984	1985	1981	1982	1983	1984	1985	
210	Coal mining	-	-	-	-	-	-	-	-	-	-	210
220	Petroleum and gas	.	.	.	.	.	.	.	.	.	.	220
230	Metal ore mining	.	.	.	.	.	.	.	.	.	.	230
290	Other mining	53	49	29	49	67	41	51	40	48	53	290
2	Mining, quarrying .	53	49	29	49	67	41	51	40	48	53	2
311/2	Food products	900	959	1050	1425	1664	4975	5539	6144	6878	7226	311/2
313	Beverages	275	169	170	302	271	547	557	578	650	674	313
314	Tobacco	41	30	29	51	48	1009	1198	1386	1473	1846	314
321	Textiles	111	150	138	240	307	994	1091	1193	1390	1516	321
3211	Spinning,weaving etc..	46	59	57	106	136	351	350	435	508	519	3211
322	Wearing apparel	50	48	65	89	99	508	568	550	685	767	322
323	Leather and products ...	4	5	7	7	12	69	80	86	97	101	323
324	Footwear	14	18	19	17	34	120	167	140	204	193	324
331	Wood products	95	95	98	149	236	603	590	625	727	787	331
332	Furniture, fixtures	65	91	101	226	342	611	698	735	986	1207	332
341	Paper and products	189	175	267	292	285	664	685	653	831	800	341
3411	Pulp,paper etc.	91	33	116	42	24	219	221	161	221	222	3411
342	Printing,publishing	232	246	406	396	723	567	579	633	621	716	342
351	Industrial chemicals ...	327	352	406	501	694	1605	1412	1548	1829	2013	351
3511	Basic excl fertilizers	...	...	...	...	...	...	...	...	...	...	3511
3513	Synthetic resins etc .	91	120	155	153	217	443	429	488	591	589	3513
352	Other chemical products.	246	312	352	466	409	1515	1693	1990	2371	2409	352
3522	Drugs and medicines ..	29	226	223	324	283	873	1068	1302	1568	1554	3522
353	Petroleum refineries ...					141					845	353
354	Petroleum,coal products.	[123	192	153	322]	140	[1775	1908	1397	1326]	284	354
355	Rubber products					94					231	355
356	Plastic products n.e.c..	108	141	147	281	373	431	433	482	557	670	356
361	Pottery,china etc	9	7	8	9	10	202	236	261	249	225	361
362	Glass and products	29	69	21	39	57	151	127	126	110	126	362
369	Non-metal products n.e.c	612	374	272	408	758	832	815	779	1070	1067	369
371	Iron and steel	40	57	86	93	110	328	328	358	418	391	371
372	Non-ferrous metals	46	22	32	34	27	243	204	263	254	205	372
381	Metal products	262	358	342	551	763	2082	2537	2534	2980	3337	381
382	Machinery n.e.c.	506	602	695	871	1224	4108	4057	4684	5515	6609	382
3825	Office,computing etc..	...	...	...	...	...	...	...	...	...	...	3825
383	Electrical machinery ...	244	318	304	471	595	1931	2086	2233	2632	2980	383
3832	Radio,television etc..	103	168	162	209	284	937	976	1060	1259	1491	3832
384	Transport equipment	166	214	211	230	304	3539	4839	4329	4205	4535	384
3841	Shipbuilding, repair..	110	153	157	155	171	2957	4212	3710	3515	3700	3841
3843	Motor vehicles	...	...	...	...	...	...	...	...	...	...	3843
385	Professional goods	90	107	115	151	238	737	807	892	1049	1278	385
390	Other industries	64	46	55	75	112	388	416	418	465	649	390
3	Manufacturing	4848	5157	5549	7696	10070	30534	33650	35017	39572	43687	3
410	Electricity,gas,steam ..	...	...	...	...	...	...	...	...	...	...	410
4101	Electricity	...	...	...	...	...	...	...	...	...	...	4101
420	Water works and supply .	.	.	.	.	.	.	.	.	.	.	420
4	Electricity,gas etc	...	...	...	...	...	...	...	...	...	...	4
2-4	All industry	...	...	...	...	...	...	...	...	...	...	2-4

a/ Establishments with 6 or more employees.
b/ Kind-of-activity units of enterprises with 20 or more employees.

15. INDEX NUMBERS OF INDUSTRIAL PRODUCTION (1980 = 100)

ISIC	INDUSTRY	1976	1977	1978	1979	1981	1982	1983	1984	1985	a/ RATE	ISIC
210	Coal mining	...	...	...	...	...	...	...	...	...	...	210
220	Petroleum and gas	...	...	...	...	...	...	...	...	...	...	220
230	Metal ore mining	...	...	...	...	...	...	...	...	...	...	230
290	Other mining	99	102	101	106	81	75	80	90	98	-0.1	290
2	Mining, quarrying .	98	102	101	106	80	84	89	100	110	1.3	2
311/2	Food products	84	88	90	95	106	108	112	116	120	4.0	311/2
313	Beverages	101	99	97	95	99	106	96	102	102	0.1	313
314	Tobacco	98	99	98	99	102	106	103	108	109	1.2	314
321	Textiles	108	97	98	102	102	103	107	117	116	0.8	321
3211	Spinning,weaving etc..	...	...	...	...	...	...	...	...	...	...	3211
322	Wearing apparel	113	104	97	99	99	97	99	112	119	0.6	322
323	Leather and products ...	145	126	119	113	110	116	106	95	88	-5.4	323
324	Footwear	96	87	85	97	113	127	110	115	110	1.5	324
331	Wood products	108	103	105	112	95	96	108	122	121	1.3	331
332	Furniture, fixtures	103	97	97	102	111	114	127	159	158	4.9	332
341	Paper and products	86	88	91	98	104	104	112	122	120	3.8	341
3411	Pulp,paper etc.	...	...	...	...	...	...	...	...	...	...	3411
342	Printing,publishing	97	98	104	105	92	103	108	118	123	2.7	342
351	Industrial chemicals ...	93	95	96	103	106	113	120	124	126	3.4	351
3511	Basic excl fertilizers	...	...	...	...	...	...	...	...	...	...	3511
3513	Synthetic resins etc .	...	...	...	...	...	...	...	...	...	...	3513
352	Other chemical products.	86	90	91	95	109	113	116	122	134	5.1	352
3522	Drugs and medicines ..	...	...	...	...	...	...	...	...	...	...	3522
353	Petroleum refineries ...	115	109	107	122	91	79	85	104	99	-1.7	353
354	Petroleum,coal products.	96	104	101	99	87	89	108	114	106	1.1	354
355	Rubber products	97	95	100	100	104	96	82	97	94	-0.3	355
356	Plastic products n.e.c..	98	97	106	104	102	110	114	123	131	3.3	356
361	Pottery,china etc	[107	102	97	100	92	79	77	76	71	-4.5]	361
362	Glass and products											362
369	Non-metal products n.e.c	116	120	124	119	81	75	85	96	101	-1.5	369
371	Iron and steel .... b/	[93	99	111	100	94	84	80	101	97	0.5]	371
372	Non-ferrous metals											372
381	Metal products	85	89	91	104	94	95	102	128	146	6.2	381
382	Machinery n.e.c. .... b/	92	93	95	100	98	98	101	111	115	2.5	382
3825	Office,computing etc..	...	...	...	...	...	...	...	...	...	...	3825
383	Electrical machinery ...	86	89	92	97	94	98	104	119	132	4.9	383
3832	Radio,television etc..	...	...	...	...	...	...	...	...	...	...	3832
384	Transport equipment	105	102	98	93	104	110	102	95	104	-0.1	384
3841	Shipbuilding, repair..	108	103	99	92	102	106	100	90	99	-1.0	3841
3843	Motor vehicles	...	...	...	...	...	...	...	...	...	...	3843
385	Professional goods	64	74	85	91	109	120	120	142	151	10.0	385
390	Other industries	104	101	105	102	129	136	141	154	136	3.0	390
3	Manufacturing	92	93	96	100	100	102	106	117	122	3.2	3
410	Electricity,gas,steam ..	...	...	...	...	...	...	...	...	...	...	410
4101	Electricity	76	82	76	82	72	88	81	83	107	3.9	4101
420	Water works and supply .	...	...	...	...	...	...	...	...	...	...	420
4	Electricity,gas etc	...	...	...	...	...	...	...	...	...	...	4
2-4	All industry c/d/	93	94	97	100	100	102	106	116	121	3.0	2-4

a/ Annual growth rate 1976-1985.
b/ Iron foundries are included in major group 382.
c/ Excluding ship building and repairing.
d/ Excluding gas, steam, water works and supply.

DOMINICAN REPUBLIC

The information in the tables, except for the indexes, is based on the reply to the United Nations Questionnaire on General Industrial Statistics from the Oficina Nacional de Estadistica, Santo Domingo. The concepts, definitions and classification by branches of industry are generally in accordance with United Nations standards.

With the exception of data on value added, the estimates are derived from the results of quarterly inquiries undertaken on a sample basis which generally relate to establishments with 5 or more employees or with a sales value of 31 630 pesos or more. For the following activities, these limits are disregarded in order to permit the inclusion of establishments with one or more employees: manufacture of grainmill products, manufacture of bakery products, manufacture of cocoa, chocolate and sugar confectionery, manufacture of miscellaneous food preparations, manufacture of footwear, manufacture of wearing apparel, manufacture of cork and wood products not elsewhere classified, manufacture of furniture and fixtures and manufacture of leather products. The inquiry is carried out by mail by the Oficina Nacional de Estadistica. Estimates of value added are derived from national accounts statistics compiled by the Banco Central de la Republica Dominicana, Santo Domingo. These estimates cover all establishments except handicrafts. The estimates in the tables are based on the national classification system which follows the present version of ISIC.

The number of establishments refers to the sample population or universe. Employment numbers for manufacturing include persons engaged on sugar plantations and persons engaged in cropping sugar-cane. Wages and salaries relate to payments in cash only and, for manufacturing, include payments made to persons engaged on sugar plantations and persons engaged in cropping sugar-cane. Value added is the contribution to the gross domestic product. Valuation of output and value added is in producers' prices.

The indexes of industrial production are compiled by the Oficina Nacional de Estadistica and provided by the national authorities in response to the United Nations Questionnaire on Indexes of Industrial Production. In principle, the indexes cover all establishments.

Related national publications:

<u>Boletin Estadistica Industrial de la Republica Dominicana 1979-81</u>, published by the Oficina Nacional de Estadistica, Santo Domingo.
<u>Cuentas Nacionales (Producto Nacional Bruto)</u> (annual), published by the Banco Central de la Republica Dominicana.

ISIC	INDUSTRY	1. NUMBER OF ESTABLISHMENTS a/ (NUMBER) 1981	1982	1983	1984	1985	2. AVERAGE NUMBER OF EMPLOYEES a/ (THOUSANDS) 1981	1982	1983	1984	1985	ISIC
210	Coal mining	-	-	-	-	...	-	-	-	...	...	210
220	Petroleum and gas	-	-	-	-	...	-	-	-	...	...	220
230	Metal ore mining	3	3	3	3	...	3.17	2.27	2.14	...	...	230
290	Other mining	12	12	13	14	...	0.60	0.63	0.83	...	...	290
2	Mining, quarrying .	15	15	16	17	...	3.77	2.90	2.97	...	...	2
311/2	Food products	932	1009	1029	1038	...	b/ 106.50	b/ 107.89	b/ 107.50	...	...	311/2
313	Beverages	35	35	36	36	...	3.59	3.86	4.51	...	...	313
314	Tobacco	18	21	21	21	...	1.69	1.84	1.84	...	...	314
321	Textiles	34	34	34	34	...	4.12	3.60	3.71	...	...	321
3211	Spinning,weaving etc..	15	17	17	17	...	2.15	1.57	1.71	...	...	3211
322	Wearing apparel	120	123	125	126	...	2.30	2.50	2.95	...	...	322
323	Leather and products ...	16	16	16	16	...	0.73	0.73	0.69	...	...	323
324	Footwear	45	46	47	47	...	1.99	1.96	2.10	...	...	324
331	Wood products	28	28	28	28	...	0.14	0.14	0.14	...	...	331
332	Furniture, fixtures	82	84	87	87	...	1.75	1.86	2.00	...	...	332
341	Paper and products	19	19	19	19	...	2.13	2.29	2.30	...	...	341
3411	Pulp,paper etc.	2	2	2	2	...	0.71	0.67	0.74	...	...	3411
342	Printing,publishing	46	47	50	54	...	1.75	1.83	1.97	...	...	342
351	Industrial chemicals ...	19	21	21	21	...	1.57	1.69	1.74	...	...	351
3511	Basic excl fertilizers	7	8	8	8	...	0.81	0.91	0.93	...	...	3511
3513	Synthetic resins etc .	4	5	5	5	...	0.28	0.29	0.31	...	...	3513
352	Other chemical products.	85	85	87	88	...	3.06	3.13	3.27	...	...	352
3522	Drugs and medicines ..	23	24	24	24	...	0.51	0.61	0.62	...	...	3522
353	Petroleum refineries ...	[3	3	3	3]	...	[0.11	0.17	0.18]	...	...	353
354	Petroleum,coal products.					...				...	...	354
355	Rubber products	20	22	22	22	...	1.14	1.24	1.23	...	...	355
356	Plastic products n.e.c..	30	31	30	30	...	2.11	2.16	2.28	...	...	356
361	Pottery,china etc	3	3	5	5	...	0.18	0.25	0.27	...	...	361
362	Glass and products	8	8	8	8	...	0.81	1.03	1.00	...	...	362
369	Non-metal products n.e.c	68	65	60	63	...	4.73	4.65	4.39	...	...	369
371	Iron and steel	6	6	6	6	...	0.89	0.89	0.96	...	...	371
372	Non-ferrous metals	3	3	3	3	...	0.13	0.13	0.13	...	...	372
381	Metal products	49	50	51	51	...	2.94	2.70	2.69	...	...	381
382	Machinery n.e.c.	4	5	6	7	...	0.44	0.47	0.48	...	...	382
3825	Office,computing etc..	...	...	...	...	...	...	...	...	...	...	3825
383	Electrical machinery ...	17	18	17	17	...	0.91	0.80	0.71	...	...	383
3832	Radio,television etc..	3	3	2	2	...	0.04	0.02	0.02	...	...	3832
384	Transport equipment	3	4	4	4	...	0.05	0.07	0.07	...	...	384
3841	Shipbuilding, repair..	-	-	-	-	...	-	-	-	...	...	3841
3843	Motor vehicles	3	4	4	4	...	...	0.07	0.07	...	...	3843
385	Professional goods	2	2	2	2	...	0.07	0.07	0.08	...	...	385
390	Other industries	13	13	14	14	...	0.24	0.23	0.26	...	...	390
3	Manufacturing	1708	1801	1831	1850	...	b/ 146.07	b/ 148.18	b/ 149.45	...	...	3
410	Electricity,gas,steam ..	...	...	...	...	...	...	...	...	...	...	410
4101	Electricity	7	7	7	7	...	5.49	5.59	5.59	...	...	4101
420	Water works and supply .	...	...	...	...	...	...	...	...	...	...	420
4	Electricity,gas etc	...	...	...	...	...	...	...	...	...	...	4
2-4	All industry	...	...	...	...	...	...	...	...	...	...	2-4

a/ In general, establishments with 5 or more employees.
b/ Including persons engaged on sugar plantations or in cropping sugar-cane.

ISIC	INDUSTRY	3. WAGES AND SALARIES OF EMPLOYEES a/b/ (THOUSAND PESOS)					4. AVERAGE NUMBER OF OPERATIVES b/ (NUMBER)					ISIC
		1981	1982	1983	1984	1985	1981	1982	1983	1984	1985	
210	Coal mining	-	-	-	...	...	-	-	-	...	...	210
220	Petroleum and gas	-	-	-	...	...	-	-	-	...	...	220
230	Metal ore mining	32677	29103	26141	...	...	2306	1605	1513	...	...	230
290	Other mining	1389	1680	1846	...	...	433	455	322	...	...	290
2	Mining, quarrying .	34066	30783	27987	...	...	2739	2060	1835	...	...	2
311/2	Food products	c/ 162525	c/ 190820	c/ 189006	...	...	d/ 92132	d/ 92401	d/ 91206	...	...	311/2
313	Beverages	14323	15988	19294	...	...	2274	2412	2939	...	...	313
314	Tobacco	5237	6458	6456	...	...	1088	1183	1174	...	...	314
321	Textiles	10961	9622	10810	...	...	3350	2890	3052	...	...	321
3211	Spinning,weaving etc..	5852	4367	5290	...	...	1746	1262	1423	...	...	3211
322	Wearing apparel	4519	5141	6392	...	...	1912	2022	2513	...	...	322
323	Leather and products ...	1958	2058	1963	...	...	587	576	509	...	...	323
324	Footwear	4240	4682	4789	...	...	1754	1690	1767	...	...	324
331	Wood products	304	325	308	...	...	112	91	130	...	...	331
332	Furniture, fixtures	4348	4851	5696	...	...	1475	1614	1791	...	...	332
341	Paper and products	7950	8865	9401	...	...	1701	1793	1785	...	...	341
3411	Pulp,paper etc.	3071	2886	3231	...	...	617	579	640	...	...	3411
342	Printing,publishing	6151	6435	6982	...	...	866	898	1058	...	...	342
351	Industrial chemicals ...	6203	6867	6812	...	...	1074	1116	1146	...	...	351
3511	Basic excl fertilizers	2750	3716	4049	...	...	670	736	732	...	...	3511
3513	Synthetic resins etc .	1060	1131	1295	...	...	193	200	219	...	...	3513
352	Other chemical products.	12064	13625	15811	...	...	1745	1716	1682	...	...	352
3522	Drugs and medicines ..	1783	2332	2801	...	...	260	280	275	...	...	3522
353	Petroleum refineries ...	[3277	3341	3673]	...	...	[25	47	52]	...	...	353
354	Petroleum,coal products.				...	...				...	...	354
355	Rubber products	3372	3748	3877	...	...	841	918	856	...	...	355
356	Plastic products n.e.c..	5995	7045	7580	...	...	1592	1556	1670	...	...	356
361	Pottery,china etc	725	1141	1259	...	...	157	219	245	...	...	361
362	Glass and products	2222	2835	3571	...	...	673	864	820	...	...	362
369	Non-metal products n.e.c	16612	16708	15268	...	...	3548	3457	3340	...	...	369
371	Iron and steel	4059	4114	5501	...	...	579	578	634	...	...	371
372	Non-ferrous metals	488	480	505	...	...	111	107	95	...	...	372
381	Metal products	9890	10163	10504	...	...	2248	2044	1965	...	...	381
382	Machinery n.e.c.	1100	1190	1769	...	...	322	338	310	...	...	382
3825	Office,computing etc..	...	...	...	...	...	...	...	...	...	...	3825
383	Electrical machinery ...	3083	3070	2930	...	...	640	506	433	...	...	383
3832	Radio,television etc..	109	40	41	...	...	32	13	12	...	...	3832
384	Transport equipment	165	198	224	...	...	32	46	40	...	...	384
3841	Shipbuilding, repair..	-	-	-	...	...	-	-	-	...	...	3841
3843	Motor vehicles	...	...	...	...	...	32	46	40	...	...	3843
385	Professional goods	215	226	244	...	...	46	46	48	...	...	385
390	Other industries	591	695	777	...	...	177	169	178	...	...	390
3	Manufacturing	c/ 292577	c/ 330691	c/ 341402	...	...	d/ 121061	d/ 121297	d/ 121438	...	...	3
410	Electricity,gas,steam ..	...	...	...	...	...	...	...	...	...	...	410
4101	Electricity	26904	34292	40971	...	...	3159	3145	3150	...	...	4101
420	Water works and supply .	...	...	...	...	...	...	...	...	...	...	420
4	Electricity,gas etc	...	...	...	...	...	...	...	...	...	...	4
2-4	All industry	...	...	...	...	...	...	...	...	...	...	2-4

a/ Payments in cash only.
b/ In general, establishments with 5 or more employees.
c/ Including payments to persons engaged on sugar plantations or in cropping sugar-cane.
d/ Including persons engaged on sugar plantations or in cropping sugar-cane.

ISIC	INDUSTRY	5. WAGES AND SALARIES OF OPERATIVES a/ (THOUSAND PESOS)					6. QUANTITY OF ELECTRICITY CONSUMED a/ (MILLION KWH)					ISIC
		1981	1982	1983	1984	1985	1981	1982	1983	1984	1985	
210	Coal mining	-	-	-	...	...	-	-	-	...	...	210
220	Petroleum and gas	-	-	-	...	...	-	-	-	...	...	220
230	Metal ore mining	19020	16246	15626	...	...	620.3	223.1	468.0	...	...	230
290	Other mining	760	957	529	...	...	2.5	4.0	3.0	...	...	290
2	Mining, quarrying .	19780	17203	16155	...	...	622.8	227.1	471.0	...	...	2
311/2	Food products	b/ 105317	b/ 129571	b/ 122542	...	...	267.9	259.5	239.2	...	...	311/2
313	Beverages	7675	6461	10611	...	...	22.1	25.7	30.0	...	...	313
314	Tobacco	2446	2678	2639	...	...	4.9	4.8	5.6	...	...	314
321	Textiles	7482	6307	7269	...	...	20.5	22.6	20.3	...	...	321
3211	Spinning,weaving etc..	4099	2960	3617	...	...	10.5	11.5	10.5	...	...	3211
322	Wearing apparel	2972	3313	4361	...	...	3.4	3.8	5.2	...	...	322
323	Leather and products ...	1247	1307	1109	...	...	2.3	1.0	2.1	...	...	323
324	Footwear	3283	3635	3668	...	...	3.6	3.3	4.0	...	...	324
331	Wood products	233	246	273	...	...	0.2	0.2	0.2	...	...	331
332	Furniture, fixtures	3006	3485	3122	...	...	2.3	2.9	3.0	...	...	332
341	Paper and products	5241	5374	5528	...	...	33.7	32.7	32.8	...	...	341
3411	Pulp,paper etc.	2355	2220	2575	...	...	27.2	25.5	25.9	...	...	3411
342	Printing,publishing	2357	2495	3044	...	...	7.4	7.5	9.6	...	...	342
351	Industrial chemicals ...	3292	3508	3633	...	...	24.3	31.7	23.2	...	...	351
3511	Basic excl fertilizers	2077	2526	2618	...	...	20.8	28.3	18.9	...	...	3511
3513	Synthetic resins etc .	473	465	539	...	...	2.1	1.0	3.4	...	...	3513
352	Other chemical products.	4495	3801	5708	...	...	9.7	10.1	11.9	...	...	352
3522	Drugs and medicines ..	474	574	628	...	...	1.7	1.7	1.7	...	...	3522
353	Petroleum refineries ...	[46	75	114]	...	...	[16.6	16.1	17.3]	...	...	353
354	Petroleum,coal products.				...	...				...	...	354
355	Rubber products	1686	1881	1817	...	...	8.5	7.1	6.7	...	...	355
356	Plastic products n.e.c..	3192	3169	3522	...	...	25.2	24.1	22.8	...	...	356
361	Pottery,china etc	596	854	1122	...	...	2.8	3.5	3.7	...	...	361
362	Glass and products	1713	2175	2716	...	...	6.7	7.8	7.9	...	...	362
369	Non-metal products n.e.c	10449	9967	9284	...	...	161.7	119.8	132.0	...	...	369
371	Iron and steel	1743	1800	2405	...	...	42.2	42.3	44.7	...	...	371
372	Non-ferrous metals	266	266	275	...	...	1.4	1.4	1.4	...	...	372
381	Metal products	5370	5132	5357	...	...	10.6	11.6	11.8	...	...	381
382	Machinery n.e.c.	497	550	781	...	...	1.5	1.1	1.8	...	...	382
3825	Office,computing etc..	...	...	...	...	...	...	...	...	...	...	3825
383	Electrical machinery ...	1556	1423	1002	...	...	5.4	4.2	4.1	...	...	383
3832	Radio,television etc..	50	16	18	...	...	-	-	-	...	...	3832
384	Transport equipment	74	95	91	...	...	-	-	-	...	...	384
3841	Shipbuilding, repair..	-	-	-	...	...	-	-	-	...	...	3841
3843	Motor vehicles	74	95	91	...	...	-	-	-	...	...	3843
385	Professional goods	94	93	99	...	...	0.5	0.4	0.4	...	...	385
390	Other industries	341	353	367	...	...	0.3	0.2	0.5	...	...	390
3	Manufacturing	b/ 176669	b/ 200014	b/ 202459	...	...	685.7	645.4	642.2	...	...	3
410	Electricity,gas,steam ..	...	...	...	...	...	...	...	...	...	...	410
4101	Electricity	14570	13506	19080	...	...	...	...	...	...	...	4101
420	Water works and supply .	...	...	...	...	...	...	...	...	...	...	420
4	Electricity,gas etc	...	...	...	...	...	...	...	...	...	...	4
2-4	All industry	...	...	...	...	...	...	...	...	...	...	2-4

a/ In general, establishments with 5 or more employees.
b/ Including payments to persons engaged on sugar plantations or in cropping sugar-cane.

ISIC	INDUSTRY	7. OUTPUT IN PRODUCERS' PRICES b/ (MILLION PESOS)					8. VALUE ADDED IN PRODUCERS' PRICES a/ (MILLION PESOS)					ISIC
		1981	1982	1983	1984	1985	1981	1982	*1983	1984	1985	
210	Coal mining	-	-	-	...	...	...	...	...	...	...	210
220	Petroleum and gas	-	-	-	...	...	...	...	...	...	...	220
230	Metal ore mining	342.6	186.7	253.3	...	...	...	...	...	...	...	230
290	Other mining	14.7	17.2	16.0	...	...	...	...	...	...	...	290
2	Mining, quarrying .	357.3	203.9	269.3	...	...	...	...	...	...	...	2
311/2	Food products	1469.5	1560.3	1559.0	...	...	595.1	631.9	626.0	...	...	311/2
313	Beverages	211.9	319.7	362.2	...	...	118.0	182.1	207.4	...	...	313
314	Tobacco	84.0	118.8	130.8	...	...	49.9	70.2	77.3	...	...	314
321	Textiles	48.1	79.9	83.6	...	...	27.6	46.0	48.1	...	...	321
3211	Spinning,weaving etc..	21.2	23.0	20.0	...	...	...	...	...	...	...	3211
322	Wearing apparel	27.1	36.6	38.3	...	...	13.2	17.6	18.4	...	...	322
323	Leather and products ...	22.6	26.6	27.9	...	...	11.3	13.8	14.5	...	...	323
324	Footwear	22.8	33.3	34.8	...	...	14.8	21.7	22.7	...	...	324
331	Wood products	2.9	6.6	7.0	...	...	2.5	4.3	4.6	...	...	331
332	Furniture, fixtures	17.4	30.0	31.3	...	...	11.2	19.3	20.2	...	...	332
341	Paper and products	48.1	83.2	87.1	...	...	21.8	37.6	39.3	...	...	341
3411	Pulp,paper etc.	16.7	19.6	22.9	...	...	...	...	...	...	...	3411
342	Printing,publishing	25.2	36.6	38.3	...	...	15.5	22.5	23.6	...	...	342
351	Industrial chemicals ...	53.6	88.4	72.7	...	...	21.8	34.2	27.9	...	...	351
3511	Basic excl fertilizers	36.8	38.2	36.9	...	...	...	...	...	...	...	3511
3513	Synthetic resins etc .	12.3	13.1	16.9	...	...	...	...	...	...	...	3513
352	Other chemical products.	67.3	120.6	118.9	...	...	34.1	52.3	51.6	...	...	352
3522	Drugs and medicines ..	12.7	15.3	19.3	...	...	...	...	...	...	...	3522
353	Petroleum refineries ...	285.3	391.5	424.8	...	...	[79.0	108.4	117.7]	...	...	353
354	Petroleum,coal products.	0.2	6.7	7.0	...	...				...	...	354
355	Rubber products	15.6	26.6	26.8	...	...	6.0	10.2	10.3	...	...	355
356	Plastic products n.e.c..	50.9	53.2	55.0	...	...	23.2	24.3	25.1	...	...	356
361	Pottery,china etc	...	3.3	3.9	...	...	...	1.3	1.6	...	...	361
362	Glass and products	6.4	16.0	19.6	...	...	...	7.3	9.0	...	...	362
369	Non-metal products n.e.c	76.9	117.6	139.0	...	...	30.0	47.4	56.1	...	...	369
371	Iron and steel	29.1	54.4	72.9	...	...	10.4	19.5	26.1	...	...	371
372	Non-ferrous metals	2.8	3.3	4.4	...	...	1.0	1.2	1.6	...	...	372
381	Metal products	59.8	96.6	111.1	...	...	24.4	44.3	51.0	...	...	381
382	Machinery n.e.c.	10.5	15.9	18.3	...	...	4.1	6.1	7.0	...	...	382
3825	Office,computing etc..	...	...	...	...	...	...	...	...	...	...	3825
383	Electrical machinery ...	14.8	26.6	30.6	...	...	1.4	8.3	11.6	...	...	383
3832	Radio,television etc..	0.6	0.2	0.2	...	...	...	...	...	...	...	3832
384	Transport equipment	0.2	-	-	...	...	-	-	-	...	...	384
3841	Shipbuilding, repair..	-	-	-	...	...	-	-	-	...	...	3841
3843	Motor vehicles	-	-	-	...	...	-	-	-	...	...	3843
385	Professional goods	1.7	2.3	3.8	...	...	0.8	1.5	1.7	...	...	385
390	Other industries	1.6	11.4	13.2	...	...	0.3	2.2	2.7	...	...	390
3	Manufacturing	c/ 2656.3	3366.0	3522.3	...	...	d/ 1126.4	1435.5	1503.1	...	...	3
410	Electricity,gas,steam ..	...	...	...	...	...	...	...	...	...	...	410
4101	Electricity	352.4	308.1	379.1	...	...	...	...	...	...	...	4101
420	Water works and supply .	...	...	...	...	...	...	...	...	...	...	420
4	Electricity,gas etc	...	...	...	...	...	...	...	...	...	...	4
2-4	All industry	...	...	...	...	...	...	...	...	...	...	2-4

a/ Contributions to the gross domestic product. Excluding handicrafts.
b/ In general, establishments with 5 or more employees. c/ Excluding major group 361.
d/ Excluding major groups 361 and 362.

9. INDEX NUMBERS OF INDUSTRIAL PRODUCTION (1980 = 100)

ISIC	INDUSTRY	1976	1977	1978	1979	1981	1982	1983	1984	1985	a/ RATE	ISIC
210	Coal mining	...	...	...	...	...	...	...	...	...	...	210
220	Petroleum and gas	...	...	...	...	...	...	...	...	...	...	220
230	Metal ore mining	...	...	...	...	...	...	...	...	...	...	230
290	Other mining	...	...	...	...	...	...	...	...	...	...	290
2	Mining, quarrying .	...	...	...	...	...	...	...	...	...	...	2
311/2	Food products	113	113	109	109	110	127	120	112	94	-2.0	311/2
313	Beverages	70	81	84	88	97	105	115	147	141	8.1	313
314	Tobacco	95	92	96	100	102	108	107	110	114	2.0	314
321	Textiles	76	80	90	104	82	92	102	108	116	4.8	321
3211	Spinning,weaving etc..	...	...	...	...	...	...	...	...	...	...	3211
322	Wearing apparel	59	56	70	106	78	83	107	141	156	11.4	322
323	Leather and products ...	124	124	129	109	104	108	114	121	139	1.3	323
324	Footwear	60	79	75	87	92	92	86	92	99	5.7	324
331	Wood products	94	93	93	99	101	116	98	103	115	2.3	331
332	Furniture, fixtures	61	62	72	89	91	98	101	110	121	7.9	332
341	Paper and products	43	64	65	96	83	90	109	118	129	13.0	341
3411	Pulp,paper etc.	...	...	...	...	...	...	...	...	...	...	3411
342	Printing,publishing	63	69	83	87	117	111	112	121	134	8.7	342
351	Industrial chemicals ...	74	78	84	95	97	85	97	99	108	4.3	351
3511	Basic excl fertilizers	...	...	...	...	...	...	...	...	...	...	3511
3513	Synthetic resins etc .	...	...	...	...	...	...	...	...	...	...	3513
352	Other chemical products.	65	68	73	89	88	101	104	109	120	7.0	352
3522	Drugs and medicines ..	...	...	...	...	...	...	...	...	...	...	3522
353	Petroleum refineries ...	...	...	...	...	...	...	...	...	...	...	353
354	Petroleum,coal products.	...	...	...	...	...	...	...	...	...	...	354
355	Rubber products	110	110	118	82	86	88	85	95	103	-0.7	355
356	Plastic products n.e.c..	42	51	52	69	83	91	94	97	102	10.4	356
361	Pottery,china etc	...	...	...	...	...	...	...	...	...	...	361
362	Glass and products	67	76	72	96	103	80	100	106	109	5.6	362
369	Non-metal products n.e.c	66	76	79	88	86	89	102	109	115	6.4	369
371	Iron and steel	341	357	152	145	106	87	104	127	153	-8.5	371
372	Non-ferrous metals	...	...	...	...	...	...	...	...	...	...	372
381	Metal products	56	69	80	83	81	85	99	101	102	6.9	381
382	Machinery n.e.c.	...	...	...	...	...	...	...	...	...	...	382
3825	Office,computing etc..	...	...	...	...	...	...	...	...	...	...	3825
383	Electrical machinery ...	74	74	84	85	97	108	95	98	101	3.5	383
3832	Radio,television etc..	...	...	...	...	...	...	...	...	...	...	3832
384	Transport equipment	...	...	...	...	...	...	...	...	...	...	384
3841	Shipbuilding, repair..	...	...	...	...	...	...	...	...	...	...	3841
3843	Motor vehicles	...	...	...	...	...	...	...	...	...	...	3843
385	Professional goods	...	...	...	...	...	...	...	...	...	...	385
390	Other industries	89	65	61	64	102	324	268	298	328	15.6	390
3	Manufacturing ..... b/	76	84	86	93	96	104	104	112	116	4.8	3
410	Electricity,gas,steam ..	...	...	...	...	...	...	...	...	...	...	410
4101	Electricity	...	...	...	...	...	...	...	...	...	...	4101
420	Water works and supply .	...	...	...	...	...	...	...	...	...	...	420
4	Electricity,gas etc	...	...	...	...	...	...	...	...	...	...	4
2-4	All industry	...	...	...	...	...	...	...	...	...	...	2-4

a/ Annual growth rate 1976-1985.

b/ Relates to industries for which indexes are shown.

ECUADOR

The information in the tables, except for the indexes, is based on the reply to the United Nations Questionnaire on General Industrial Statistics from the Instituto Nacional de Estadistica y Censos, Quito. The concepts, definitions and classification by branches of industry are generally in accordance with United Nations standards.

The data in the tables are derived from the survey of manufacture and mining undertaken annually by the Instituto Nacional de Estadistica y Censos. The inquiry covers establishments with 10 or more persons engaged. The enumeration is based on a mail inquiry followed by field visit. Handicraft and home industries are excluded. Approximately 90 per cent response is normally obtained; non-response is mainly attributed to establishments which have been liquidated or which do not satisfy the requisites mentioned above at the time of inquiry. All data in the tables refer to reporting establishments as no adjustments are made for non-response. The estimates in the tables are based on the present version of ISIC.

Employment data refer to the last pay period of November of the year under review. Homeworkers are excluded from the estimates of persons engaged and employees. Wages and salaries relate to payments to all employees, including paid apprentices.

The value of output is the sum of (a) total value of all goods sold during the year, adjusted for annual changes in stocks of finished goods, (b) receipts for work done for others with materials supplied, (c) receipts from repair services and (d) value of goods sold without transformation. The following values are not taken into account in the calculation of output: value of electricity sold, net change between the beginning and the end of the year in the value of work in progress and value of fixed assets produced by the establishment for its own use. Estimates of value added are obtained by subtracting the cost of input from the value of output, plus the value of electricity sold and the net change between the beginning and the end of the year in the value of work in progress. The following input items are deducted: (a) cost of materials and supplies consumed, (b) cost of fuels used, (c) cost of electricity purchased, (d) cost of water consumed, (e) other operating costs. For alcoholic beverages, tobacco and petroleum products, indirect taxes are deducted.

Estimates of gross fixed capital formation relate to expenditure on new and used fixed assets during the year. New establishments not in operation during the year are not covered.

The indexes of industrial production are compiled by the Banco Central del Ecuador and provided in response to the United Nations Questionnaire on Indexes of Industrial Production.

Related national publication:
<u>Encuesta de Manufactura y Mineria</u> (annual), published by the Instituto Nacional de Estadistica y Censos, Quito.

ISIC	INDUSTRY	1. NUMBER OF ESTABLISHMENTS b/ (NUMBER) 1981	1982	1983	1984	1985	2. AVERAGE NUMBER OF PERSONS ENGAGED a/b/ (NUMBER) 1981	1982	1983	1984	1985	ISIC
210	Coal mining	...	...	...	...	...	...	...	...	...	...	210
220	Petroleum and gas	3	4	4	...	...	1064	1393	1442	...	...	220
230	Metal ore mining	3	c/	c/	...	...	134	d/	d/	...	...	230
290	Other mining	15	13	12	...	...	357	302	254	...	...	290
2	Mining, quarrying .	e/ 21	f/ 17	f/ 16	...	...	e/ 1555	f/ 1695	f/ 1696	...	...	2
311/2	Food products	309	297	279	...	...	24585	26272	22720	...	...	311/2
313	Beverages	56	56	57	...	...	4890	4569	4692	...	...	313
314	Tobacco	4	4	4	...	...	1165	1060	1239	...	...	314
321	Textiles	164	153	141	...	...	15703	15109	14810	...	...	321
3211	Spinning,weaving etc..	67	59	57	...	...	11244	10610	10681	...	...	3211
322	Wearing apparel	68	60	61	...	...	3392	3256	3159	...	...	322
323	Leather and products ...	19	18	19	...	...	912	930	965	...	...	323
324	Footwear	15	9	9	...	...	939	825	874	...	...	324
331	Wood products	53	49	41	...	...	3574	3107	2619	...	...	331
332	Furniture, fixtures	60	58	51	...	...	3385	3362	2884	...	...	332
341	Paper and products	28	26	24	...	...	3502	3179	3043	...	...	341
3411	Pulp,paper etc.	9	8	7	...	...	1816	1642	1338	...	...	3411
342	Printing,publishing	89	82	75	...	...	3741	3260	2947	...	...	342
351	Industrial chemicals ...	26	24	27	...	...	1243	1005	1113	...	...	351
3511	Basic excl fertilizers	17	16	18	...	...	387	382	479	...	...	3511
3513	Synthetic resins etc .	5	4	5	...	...	322	257	283	...	...	3513
352	Other chemical products.	84	86	83	...	...	5450	5453	5381	...	...	352
3522	Drugs and medicines ..	31	31	31	...	...	2486	2443	2480	...	...	3522
353	Petroleum refineries ...	3	4	4	...	...	1237	1291	1305	...	...	353
354	Petroleum,coal products.	6	4	4	...	...	136	118	113	...	...	354
355	Rubber products	12	11	12	...	...	1253	1286	1309	...	...	355
356	Plastic products n.e.c..	57	55	54	...	...	4371	4241	4306	...	...	356
361	Pottery,china etc	4	5	5	...	...	550	607	613	...	...	361
362	Glass and products	16	13	15	...	...	832	714	673	...	...	362
369	Non-metal products n.e.c	63	56	57	...	...	4790	4435	4404	...	...	369
371	Iron and steel	11	12	12	...	...	886	903	1014	...	...	371
372	Non-ferrous metals	6	6	6	...	...	300	337	319	...	...	372
381	Metal products	163	151	129	...	...	7318	6712	6096	...	...	381
382	Machinery n.e.c.	25	23	21	...	...	860	790	776	...	...	382
3825	Office,computing etc..	c/	c/	c/	...	...	d/	d/	d/	...	...	3825
383	Electrical machinery ...	46	46	43	...	...	4993	4391	4091	...	...	383
3832	Radio,television etc..	16	15	14	...	...	1104	963	874	...	...	3832
384	Transport equipment	40	36	33	...	...	2247	2108	1816	...	...	384
3841	Shipbuilding, repair..	...	...	...	...	...	...	...	...	...	...	3841
3843	Motor vehicles	36	32	29	...	...	2020	1896	1585	...	...	3843
385	Professional goods	12	10	10	...	...	488	487	497	...	...	385
390	Other industries	23	22	21	...	...	774	809	797	...	...	390
3	Manufacturing	1462	1376	1297	...	...	103516	100616	94575	...	...	3
410	Electricity,gas,steam ..	...	...	...	...	...	...	...	...	...	...	410
4101	Electricity	...	...	...	...	...	...	...	...	...	...	4101
420	Water works and supply .	...	...	...	...	...	...	...	...	...	...	420
4	Electricity,gas etc	...	...	...	...	...	...	...	...	...	...	4
2-4	All industry	...	...	...	...	...	...	...	...	...	...	2-4

a/ In the last pay period in November of the year indicated.
b/ Establishments with 10 or more persons engaged.
c/ Less than 3 establishments.
d/ Disclosure prohibited.
e/ Excluding major group 210.
f/ Excluding major groups 210 and 230.

ISIC	INDUSTRY	3. AVERAGE NUMBER OF EMPLOYEES a/b/ (NUMBER)					4. WAGES AND SALARIES OF EMPLOYEES b/ (MILLION SUCRES)					ISIC
		1981	1982	1983	1984	1985	1981	1982	1983	1984	1985	
210	Coal mining	...	...	...	...	...	...	...	...	...	...	210
220	Petroleum and gas	1064	1393	1442	...	...	408	515	843	...	...	220
230	Metal ore mining	50	c/	c/	...	...	6	c/	c/	...	...	230
290	Other mining	355	300	252	...	...	45	41	36	...	...	290
2	Mining, quarrying .	d/ 1469	e/ 1693	e/ 1694	...	...	d/ 459	e/ 556	e/ 879	...	...	2
311/2	Food products	24505	26218	22675	...	...	3723	4192	4806	...	...	311/2
313	Beverages	4872	4563	4685	...	...	725	775	939	...	...	313
314	Tobacco	1165	1060	1239	...	...	239	333	467	...	...	314
321	Textiles	15612	15048	14761	...	...	1743	1942	2376	...	...	321
3211	Spinning,weaving etc..	11228	10606	10616	...	...	1311	1470	1797	...	...	3211
322	Wearing apparel	3360	3235	3143	...	...	249	289	362	...	...	322
323	Leather and products ...	907	928	962	...	...	87	102	171	...	...	323
324	Footwear	930	824	871	...	...	87	95	131	...	...	324
331	Wood products	3549	3080	2604	...	...	418	485	456	...	...	331
332	Furniture, fixtures	3359	3348	2871	...	...	356	386	465	...	...	332
341	Paper and products	3501	3177	3042	...	...	554	602	703	...	...	341
3411	Pulp,paper etc.	1816	1642	1338	...	...	257	265	288	...	...	3411
342	Printing,publishing	3711	3239	2921	...	...	523	603	636	...	...	342
351	Industrial chemicals ...	1241	1004	1112	...	...	187	214	273	...	...	351
3511	Basic excl fertilizers	385	381	478	...	...	61	70	108	...	...	3511
3513	Synthetic resins etc .	322	257	283	...	...	49	51	62	...	...	3513
352	Other chemical products.	5437	5437	5374	...	...	983	1217	1591	...	...	352
3522	Drugs and medicines ..	2482	2437	2476	...	...	531	618	770	...	...	3522
353	Petroleum refineries ...	1237	1291	1305	...	...	399	465	602	...	...	353
354	Petroleum,coal products.	136	118	113	...	...	44	52	88	...	...	354
355	Rubber products	1251	1285	1308	...	...	249	280	360	...	...	355
356	Plastic products n.e.c..	4363	4235	4305	...	...	525	600	762	...	...	356
361	Pottery,china etc	550	607	613	...	...	68	95	148	...	...	361
362	Glass and products	823	713	670	...	...	157	156	154	...	...	362
369	Non-metal products n.e.c	4728	4413	4369	...	...	821	896	1104	...	...	369
371	Iron and steel	884	900	1012	...	...	190	274	309	...	...	371
372	Non-ferrous metals	300	337	319	...	...	42	61	97	...	...	372
381	Metal products	7279	6686	6067	...	...	949	1069	1250	...	...	381
382	Machinery n.e.c.	845	778	768	...	...	94	123	126	...	...	382
3825	Office,computing etc.. c/	...	...	...	...	...	...	...	...	...	...	3825
383	Electrical machinery ...	4990	4389	4088	...	...	737	888	1006	...	...	383
3832	Radio,television etc..	1104	962	871	...	...	134	143	166	...	...	3832
384	Transport equipment	2230	2095	1805	...	...	284	338	381	...	...	384
3841	Shipbuilding, repair..	...	...	...	...	...	...	...	...	...	...	3841
3843	Motor vehicles	2003	1883	1576	...	...	259	313	348	...	...	3843
385	Professional goods	484	484	496	...	...	94	107	175	...	...	385
390	Other industries	768	805	791	...	...	91	124	136	...	...	390
3	Manufacturing	103017	100297	94289	...	...	14618	16763	20074	...	...	3
410	Electricity,gas,steam ..	...	...	...	...	...	...	...	...	...	...	410
4101	Electricity	...	...	...	...	...	...	...	...	...	...	4101
420	Water works and supply .	...	...	...	...	...	...	...	...	...	...	420
4	Electricity,gas etc	...	...	...	...	...	...	...	...	...	...	4
2-4	All industry	...	...	...	...	...	...	...	...	...	...	2-4

a/ In the last pay period in November of the year indicated.
b/ Establishments with 10 or more persons engaged.
c/ Disclosure prohibited.
d/ Excluding major group 210.
e/ Excluding major groups 210 and 230.

ISIC	INDUSTRY	5. AVERAGE NUMBER OF OPERATIVES a/c/ (NUMBER)					6. OUTPUT IN PRODUCERS' PRICES b/c/ (MILLION SUCRES)					ISIC
		1981	1982	1983	1934	1985	1981	1982	1983	1984	1985	
210	Coal mining	...	...	...	...	...	...	...	...	...	...	210
220	Petroleum and gas	279	297	303	...	...	36335	51060	72213	...	...	220
230	Metal ore mining	45	d/	d/	...	...	4	d/	d/	...	...	230
290	Other mining	276	236	187	...	...	200	186	169	...	...	290
2	Mining, quarrying .	e/ 600	f/ 533	f/ 490	...	...	e/ 36539	f/ 51246	f/ 72382	...	...	2
311/2	Food products	18264	20065	17086	...	...	31334	34958	51516	...	...	311/2
313	Beverages	3610	3391	3694	...	...	4664	5269	7232	...	...	313
314	Tobacco	820	722	879	...	...	1937	2821	4501	...	...	314
321	Textiles	12964	12643	12468	...	...	8320	9923	13427	...	...	321
3211	Spinning,weaving etc..	9266	8922	9028	...	...	6356	7594	10535	...	...	3211
322	Wearing apparel	2660	2556	2465	...	...	1149	1351	1634	...	...	322
323	Leather and products ...	733	735	754	...	...	482	561	906	...	...	323
324	Footwear	753	639	688	...	...	393	456	737	...	...	324
331	Wood products	3060	2643	2191	...	...	1581	1997	1971	...	...	331
332	Furniture, fixtures	2585	2315	1947	...	...	1319	1523	1472	...	...	332
341	Paper and products	2372	2132	2147	...	...	4689	5370	5987	...	...	341
3411	Pulp,paper etc.	1213	989	861	...	...	1928	1913	2024	...	...	3411
342	Printing,publishing	1934	1961	1638	...	...	2351	2719	3054	...	...	342
351	Industrial chemicals ...	634	599	574	...	...	1900	2284	2807	...	...	351
3511	Basic excl fertilizers	187	191	266	...	...	407	519	868	...	...	3511
3513	Synthetic resins etc .	203	171	181	...	...	417	577	723	...	...	3513
352	Other chemical products.	2855	3011	2769	...	...	5985	8548	12493	...	...	352
3522	Drugs and medicines ..	1175	1272	1189	...	...	2286	3109	4694	...	...	3522
353	Petroleum refineries ...	914	915	925	...	...	1931	3442	5170	...	...	353
354	Petroleum,coal products.	75	55	54	...	...	591	794	1205	...	...	354
355	Rubber products	863	906	855	...	...	1368	1979	2805	...	...	355
356	Plastic products n.e.c..	3558	3357	3379	...	...	3267	3944	5374	...	...	356
361	Pottery,china etc	423	473	466	...	...	381	502	746	...	...	361
362	Glass and products	618	497	472	...	...	725	839	1065	...	...	362
369	Non-metal products n.e.c	3694	3502	3360	...	...	4565	5928	7462	...	...	369
371	Iron and steel	591	616	720	...	...	2114	2841	4331	...	...	371
372	Non-ferrous metals	235	265	244	...	...	639	912	1432	...	...	372
381	Metal products	5553	5081	4518	...	...	5917	7036	8307	...	...	381
382	Machinery n.e.c.	582	524	517	...	...	380	504	769	...	...	382
3825	Office,computing etc.. d/	...	...	...	...	...	...	...	...	...	...	3825
383	Electrical machinery ...	3283	2802	2528	...	...	4588	5967	6715	...	...	383
3832	Radio,television etc..	673	636	574	...	...	1001	1183	1194	...	...	3832
384	Transport equipment	1724	1575	1345	...	...	2433	2925	3718	...	...	384
3841	Shipbuilding, repair..	...	...	...	...	...	...	...	...	...	...	3841
3843	Motor vehicles	1552	1420	1168	...	...	2082	2627	3514	...	...	3843
385	Professional goods	252	276	293	...	...	543	655	870	...	...	385
390	Other industries	580	608	599	...	...	504	1004	789	...	...	390
3	Manufacturing	76189	74864	69575	...	...	96050	117052	158495	...	...	3
410	Electricity,gas,steam ..	...	...	...	...	...	...	...	...	...	...	410
4101	Electricity	...	...	...	...	...	...	...	...	...	...	4101
420	Water works and supply .	...	...	...	...	...	...	...	...	...	...	420
4	Electricity,gas etc	...	...	...	...	...	...	...	...	...	...	4
2-4	All industry	...	...	...	...	...	...	...	...	...	...	2-4

a/ In the last pay period in November of the year indicated.
c/ Establishments with 10 or more persons engaged.
e/ Excluding major group 210.
b/ For concept, see country note.
d/ Disclosure prohibited.
f/ Excluding major groups 210 and 230.

ISIC	INDUSTRY	7. VALUE ADDED IN PRODUCERS' PRICES a/c/ (MILLION SUCRES)					8. GROSS FIXED CAPITAL FORMATION TOTAL b/c/ (MILLION SUCRES)					ISIC
		1981	1982	1983	1984	1985	1981	1982	1983	1984	1985	
210	Coal mining	...	...	...	...	...	...	...	...	...	...	210
220	Petroleum and gas	33472	44641	65539	...	...	998	394	3940	...	...	220
230	Metal ore mining	-	d/	d/	...	...	-	d/	d/	...	...	230
290	Other mining	101	56	68	...	...	54	11	14	...	...	290
2	Mining, quarrying .	e/ 33573	f/ 44697	f/ 65607	...	...	e/ 1052	f/ 405	f/ 3954	...	...	2
311/2	Food products	8510	6445	15443	...	...	1517	2863	2704	...	...	311/2
313	Beverages	2155	2416	3613	...	...	322	423	295	...	...	313
314	Tobacco	1139	1400	3092	...	...	36	97	92	...	...	314
321	Textiles	3597	3508	5833	...	...	655	1263	708	...	...	321
3211	Spinning,weaving etc..	2597	2606	4397	...	...	535	1137	550	...	...	3211
322	Wearing apparel	512	511	607	...	...	26	48	40	...	...	322
323	Leather and products ...	163	147	264	...	...	2	49	62	...	...	323
324	Footwear	209	169	298	...	...	28	25	28	...	...	324
331	Wood products	685	736	916	...	...	130	197	177	...	...	331
332	Furniture, fixtures	745	590	621	...	...	203	87	28	...	...	332
341	Paper and products	1285	835	1692	...	...	209	361	196	...	...	341
3411	Pulp,paper etc.	674	344	654	...	...	147	249	135	...	...	3411
342	Printing,publishing	945	989	1198	...	...	128	289	84	...	...	342
351	Industrial chemicals ...	442	330	835	...	...	53	105	214	...	...	351
3511	Basic excl fertilizers	126	131	322	...	...	38	32	178	...	...	3511
3513	Synthetic resins etc .	105	91	191	...	...	7	63	21	...	...	3513
352	Other chemical products.	2142	2642	4113	...	...	201	417	446	...	...	352
3522	Drugs and medicines ..	1001	1057	1740	...	...	74	165	138	...	...	3522
353	Petroleum refineries ...	851	735	1205	...	...	51	33	663	...	...	353
354	Petroleum,coal products.	160	240	434	...	...	14	37	71	...	...	354
355	Rubber products	531	788	1409	...	...	263	159	151	...	...	355
356	Plastic products n.e.c..	1207	1172	1849	...	...	317	452	601	...	...	356
361	Pottery,china etc	277	299	459	...	...	14	13	41	...	...	361
362	Glass and products	390	202	522	...	...	807	49	471	...	...	362
369	Non-metal products n.e.c	2106	2233	3520	...	...	356	713	1033	...	...	369
371	Iron and steel	646	597	1319	...	...	152	349	168	...	...	371
372	Non-ferrous metals	178	190	509	...	...	54	76	47	...	...	372
381	Metal products	2322	1907	3165	...	...	545	557	399	...	...	381
382	Machinery n.e.c.	152	191	362	...	...	26	33	12	...	...	382
3825	Office,computing etc.. d/	...	...	...	...	...	...	...	...	...	...	3825
383	Electrical machinery ...	1324	1376	2801	...	...	391	493	49	...	...	383
3832	Radio,television etc..	375	238	412	...	...	31	21	-	...	...	3832
384	Transport equipment	705	519	919	...	...	103	102	148	...	...	384
3841	Shipbuilding, repair..	...	...	...	...	...	...	...	...	...	...	3841
3843	Motor vehicles	654	488	858	...	...	103	96	106	...	...	3843
385	Professional goods	251	304	401	...	...	22	57	32	...	...	385
390	Other industries	150	288	314	...	...	54	15	12	...	...	390
3	Manufacturing	33779	31759	57713	...	...	6679	9362	8972	...	...	3
410	Electricity,gas,steam ..	...	...	...	...	...	...	...	...	...	...	410
4101	Electricity	...	...	...	...	...	...	...	...	...	...	4101
420	Water works and supply .	...	...	...	...	...	...	...	...	...	...	420
4	Electricity,gas etc	...	...	...	...	...	...	...	...	...	...	4
2-4	All industry	...	...	...	...	...	...	...	...	...	...	2-4

a/ For concept, see country note.
c/ Establishments with 10 or more persons engaged.
e/ Excluding major group 210.

b/ The value of sales is not deducted.
d/ Disclosure prohibited.
f/ Excluding major groups 210 and 230.

9. INDEX NUMBERS OF INDUSTRIAL PRODUCTION (1980 = 100)

ISIC	INDUSTRY	1976	1977	1978	1979	1981	1982	1983	1984	1985	a/ RATE	ISIC
210	Coal mining	...	...	...	...	...	...	...	...	...	...	210
220	Petroleum and gas	...	...	...	...	...	...	...	...	...	...	220
230	Metal ore mining	...	...	...	...	...	...	...	...	...	...	230
290	Other mining	...	...	...	...	...	...	...	...	...	...	290
2	Mining, quarrying	...	...	...	...	...	...	...	...	...	...	2
311/2	Food products	90	88	93	99	96	89	85	92	97	0.8	311/2
313	Beverages	69	76	79	87	101	96	98	94	91	3.1	313
314	Tobacco	86	103	110	110	104	126	86	93	104	2.1	314
321	Textiles	77	87	90	94	102	107	105	94	98	2.7	321
3211	Spinning,weaving etc.	...	...	...	...	...	...	...	...	...	...	3211
322	Wearing apparel	...	...	...	...	...	...	...	...	...	...	322
323	Leather and products	77	87	90	94	102	107	105	94	98	2.7	323
324	Footwear	58	71	86	97	99	105	107	112	114	7.8	324
331	Wood products	55	78	89	102	103	112	116	122	126	9.6	331
332	Furniture, fixtures	...	...	...	...	...	...	...	...	...	...	332
341	Paper and products	78	83	88	95	92	89	60	65	72	-0.9	341
3411	Pulp,paper etc.	...	...	...	...	...	...	...	...	...	...	3411
342	Printing,publishing	60	69	81	92	110	115	123	138	143	10.1	342
351	Industrial chemicals	68	74	84	86	105	115	105	125	132	7.6	351
3511	Basic excl fertilizers	...	...	...	...	...	...	...	...	...	...	3511
3513	Synthetic resins etc	...	...	...	...	...	...	...	...	...	...	3513
352	Other chemical products	68	74	84	86	105	114	105	125	132	7.6	352
3522	Drugs and medicines	...	...	...	...	...	...	...	...	...	...	3522
353	Petroleum refineries	61	77	86	93	88	98	99	108	117	7.5	353
354	Petroleum,coal products	58	51	71	77	88	98	99	108	117	8.1	354
355	Rubber products	60	72	81	92	111	124	125	137	148	10.6	355
356	Plastic products n.e.c.	60	72	81	92	111	124	125	136	148	10.6	356
361	Pottery,china etc	73	86	94	96	106	112	107	113	118	5.5	361
362	Glass and products	73	86	94	96	106	112	107	113	118	5.5	362
369	Non-metal products n.e.c	59	58	95	97	111	142	130	153	175	12.8	369
371	Iron and steel	64	87	96	114	105	149	159	187	150	9.9	371
372	Non-ferrous metals	...	...	...	...	...	...	...	...	...	...	372
381	Metal products	58	78	82	92	108	111	105	113	122	8.6	381
382	Machinery n.e.c.	...	...	...	...	...	...	...	...	...	...	382
3825	Office,computing etc.	...	...	...	...	...	...	...	...	...	...	3825
383	Electrical machinery	54	72	79	88	92	92	82	81	101	7.2	383
3832	Radio,television etc.	...	...	...	...	...	...	...	...	...	...	3832
384	Transport equipment	56	62	70	89	131	146	155	164	197	15.0	384
3841	Shipbuilding, repair	...	...	...	...	...	...	...	...	...	...	3841
3843	Motor vehicles	...	...	...	...	...	...	...	...	...	...	3843
385	Professional goods	...	...	...	...	...	...	...	...	...	...	385
390	Other industries	59	66	78	89	104	109	76	81	79	3.3	390
3	Manufacturing	70	79	86	94	102	105	101	107	113	5.5	3
410	Electricity,gas,steam	...	...	...	...	...	...	...	...	...	...	410
4101	Electricity	...	...	...	...	...	...	...	...	...	...	4101
420	Water works and supply	...	...	...	...	...	...	...	...	...	...	420
4	Electricity,gas etc	...	...	...	...	...	...	...	...	...	...	4
2-4	All industry	...	...	...	...	...	...	...	...	...	...	2-4

a/ Annual growth rate 1976-1985.

EL SALVADOR

The information in the tables is based on the reply to the United Nations Questionnaire on General Industrial Statistics from the Direccion General de Estadistica y Censos, Ministerio de Economia, San Salvador. The concepts, definitions and classification by branches of industry are generally in accordance with United Nations standards.

The estimates are derived from the quarterly survey of manufacturing undertaken by the Direccion General de Estadistica y Censos. The inquiry covers selected industries which are considered more important for the economic activity of the country. The industries are selected from those included in the directory prepared annually by the Direccion General de Contribuciones Directas for establishments registered under law (coverage: approximately 60 per cent).

Estimates are based on the national classification system which follows the present version of ISIC. It should be noted that (a) manufacture of hygienic paper and similar products, including sanitary towels (ISIC 385) is included in ISIC 341, (b) manufacture of matches (ISIC 352) is included in ISIC 351 and (c) sugar factories and refineries are excluded.

Employment numbers relate to 31 August of the reference year. Output is the sum of (a) total value of goods produced, (b) value of industrial services rendered to others, (c) value of fixed assets produced by the establishment for its own use and (d) receipts from the sale of waste and scrap and rents for buildings, machinery and transport equipment. Value of goods sold without transformation is not taken into account. Value added is calculated as the difference between the value of output defined above and the value of input, comprising the costs of materials and supplies, oils and fuels, electricity purchased and payments for industrial services rendered by others.

Related national publication:
Boletin Estadistica Industrial (quarterly), published by the Direccion General de Estadistica y Censos, San Salvador.

ISIC	INDUSTRY	1. NUMBER OF ESTABLISHMENTS a/ (NUMBER) 1981	1982	1983	1984	1985	2. AVERAGE NUMBER OF PERSONS ENGAGED a/b/ (NUMBER) 1981	1982	1983	1984	1985	ISIC
210	Coal mining	...	...	...	...	...	...	...	...	...	...	210
220	Petroleum and gas	...	...	...	...	...	...	...	...	...	...	220
230	Metal ore mining	...	...	...	...	...	...	...	...	...	...	230
290	Other mining	...	...	...	...	...	...	...	...	...	...	290
2	Mining, quarrying	...	...	...	...	...	...	...	...	...	...	2
311/2	Food products	78	84	79	...	...	7746	6344	6580	...	...	311/2
313	Beverages	17	17	19	...	...	2815	2433	2511	...	...	313
314	Tobacco	2	2	2	...	...	455	444	448	...	...	314
321	Textiles	40	47	44	...	...	6663	6323	6138	...	...	321
3211	Spinning,weaving etc.	23	23	25	...	...	4544	4410	4522	...	...	3211
322	Wearing apparel	54	54	47	...	...	3186	2730	2341	...	...	322
323	Leather and products	8	10	11	...	...	628	657	723	...	...	323
324	Footwear	4	5	5	...	...	1685	1735	1724	...	...	324
331	Wood products	7	4	3	...	...	188	133	117	...	...	331
332	Furniture, fixtures	8	11	12	...	...	402	339	530	...	...	332
341	Paper and products	8	9	11	...	...	1858	1842	1912	...	...	341
3411	Pulp,paper etc.	3	3	4	...	...	600	451	598	...	...	3411
342	Printing,publishing	18	24	23	...	...	1040	1174	1405	...	...	342
351	Industrial chemicals	7	8	9	...	...	208	229	242	...	...	351
3511	Basic excl fertilizers	5	5	7	...	...	82	65	98	...	...	3511
3513	Synthetic resins etc	1	2	-	...	...	20	61	-	...	...	3513
352	Other chemical products.	36	41	42	...	...	2760	2908	3280	...	...	352
3522	Drugs and medicines	16	19	22	...	...	1124	1344	1675	...	...	3522
353	Petroleum refineries	1	1	1	...	...	60	60	58	...	...	353
354	Petroleum,coal products.	2	1	-	...	...	37	29	-	...	...	354
355	Rubber products	8	10	8	...	...	429	464	376	...	...	355
356	Plastic products n.e.c.	17	21	25	...	...	1261	1385	1693	...	...	356
361	Pottery,china etc	-	-	-	...	...	-	-	-	...	...	361
362	Glass and products	-	2	-	...	...	-	54	-	...	...	362
369	Non-metal products n.e.c	17	22	16	...	...	1272	1344	1255	...	...	369
371	Iron and steel	5	5	6	...	...	705	701	683	...	...	371
372	Non-ferrous metals	1	1	1	...	...	154	5	6	...	...	372
381	Metal products	24	21	20	...	...	1258	1064	1025	...	...	381
382	Machinery n.e.c.	10	15	14	...	...	606	622	569	...	...	382
3825	Office,computing etc.	-	-	-	...	...	-	-	-	...	...	3825
383	Electrical machinery	10	9	10	...	...	776	614	572	...	...	383
3832	Radio,television etc.	4	4	4	...	...	169	143	124	...	...	3832
384	Transport equipment	4	-	-	...	...	101	-	-	...	...	384
3841	Shipbuilding, repair.	1	-	-	...	...	14	-	-	...	...	3841
3843	Motor vehicles	2	-	-	...	...	13	-	-	...	...	3843
385	Professional goods	4	4	7	...	...	44	39	124	...	...	385
390	Other industries	11	20	20	...	...	428	686	729	...	...	390
3	Manufacturing	401	448	435	...	...	36765	34358	35041	...	...	3
410	Electricity,gas,steam	...	...	...	...	...	...	...	...	...	...	410
4101	Electricity	...	...	...	...	...	...	...	...	...	...	4101
420	Water works and supply	...	...	...	...	...	...	...	...	...	...	420
4	Electricity,gas etc	...	...	...	...	...	...	...	...	...	...	4
2-4	All industry	...	...	...	...	...	...	...	...	...	...	2-4

Note. For certain differences in classification, see country note.

a/ Data derived from the quarterly survey covering important industries for the national industrial statistics.
b/ At 31 August of the year indicated.

ISIC	INDUSTRY	3. AVERAGE NUMBER OF EMPLOYEES a/b/ (NUMBER) 1981	1982	1983	1984	1985	4. WAGES AND SALARIES OF EMPLOYEES b/ (MILLION COLONES) 1981	1982	1983	1984	1985	ISIC
210	Coal mining	...	...	...	...	...	...	...	...	...	...	210
220	Petroleum and gas	...	...	...	...	...	...	...	...	...	...	220
230	Metal ore mining	...	...	...	...	...	...	...	...	...	...	230
290	Other mining	...	...	...	...	...	...	...	...	...	...	290
2	Mining, quarrying	...	...	...	...	...	...	...	...	...	...	2
311/2	Food products	7676	6290	6525	...	...	70.72	67.83	80.49	...	...	311/2
313	Beverages	2807	2430	2507	...	...	31.88	32.47	35.41	...	...	313
314	Tobacco	455	444	448	...	...	7.55	8.94	9.86	...	...	314
321	Textiles	6631	6288	6107	...	...	64.49	61.51	62.07	...	...	321
3211	Spinning,weaving etc.	4524	4389	4506	...	...	44.42	44.87	47.36	...	...	3211
322	Wearing apparel	3126	2686	2302	...	...	19.77	17.84	17.04	...	...	322
323	Leather and products	619	649	714	...	...	5.11	7.13	6.43	...	...	323
324	Footwear	1680	1733	1719	...	...	14.81	16.50	17.88	...	...	324
331	Wood products	184	130	116	...	...	1.51	1.07	1.08	...	...	331
332	Furniture, fixtures	396	330	521	...	...	2.02	2.27	4.27	...	...	332
341	Paper and products	1857	1837	1912	...	...	23.87	23.09	28.70	...	...	341
3411	Pulp,paper etc.	599	449	598	...	...	7.90	4.93	9.34	...	...	3411
342	Printing,publishing	1014	1144	1388	...	...	9.01	12.97	17.18	...	...	342
351	Industrial chemicals	205	224	242	...	...	2.27	2.88	3.15	...	...	351
3511	Basic excl fertilizers	81	64	98	...	...	0.85	0.90	1.02	...	...	3511
3513	Synthetic resins etc	18	57	-	...	...	0.15	0.50	-	...	...	3513
352	Other chemical products	2735	2885	3253	...	...	30.60	34.36	41.94	...	...	352
3522	Drugs and medicines	1108	1328	1652	...	...	11.99	15.26	22.23	...	...	3522
353	Petroleum refineries	60	60	58	...	...	2.26	2.48	2.62	...	...	353
354	Petroleum,coal products	36	29	-	...	...	0.39	0.48	-	...	...	354
355	Rubber products	424	460	373	...	...	3.64	5.04	3.73	...	...	355
356	Plastic products n.e.c.	1252	1366	1676	...	...	11.15	13.21	16.87	...	...	356
361	Pottery,china etc	-	-	-	...	...	-	-	-	...	...	361
362	Glass and products	-	52	-	...	...	-	0.45	-	...	...	362
369	Non-metal products n.e.c	1264	1338	1248	...	...	15.11	16.07	15.87	...	...	369
371	Iron and steel	703	698	683	...	...	5.36	5.88	6.60	...	...	371
372	Non-ferrous metals	153	5	6	...	...	1.86	0.06	0.06	...	...	372
381	Metal products	1245	1048	1014	...	...	11.95	12.48	12.82	...	...	381
382	Machinery n.e.c.	599	615	558	...	...	6.12	6.97	6.81	...	...	382
3825	Office,computing etc.	-	-	-	...	...	-	-	-	...	...	3825
383	Electrical machinery	770	612	569	...	...	10.28	9.27	10.47	...	...	383
3832	Radio,television etc.	167	142	122	...	...	1.47	1.43	1.36	...	...	3832
384	Transport equipment	100	-	-	...	...	0.81	-	-	...	...	384
3841	Shipbuilding, repair.	14	-	-	...	...	0.09	-	-	...	...	3841
3843	Motor vehicles	12	-	-	...	...	0.06	-	-	...	...	3843
385	Professional goods	42	39	121	...	...	0.34	0.53	1.48	...	...	385
390	Other industries	423	675	716	...	...	3.45	5.37	6.11	...	...	390
3	Manufacturing	36456	34067	34776	...	...	356.33	367.15	408.94	...	...	3
410	Electricity,gas,steam	...	...	...	...	...	...	...	...	...	...	410
4101	Electricity	...	...	...	...	...	...	...	...	...	...	4101
420	Water works and supply	...	...	...	...	...	...	...	...	...	...	420
4	Electricity,gas etc	...	...	...	...	...	...	...	...	...	...	4
2-4	All industry	...	...	...	...	...	...	...	...	...	...	2-4

Note. For certain differences in classification, see country note.

a/ At 31 August of the year indicated.
b/ Data derived from the quarterly survey covering important industries for the national industrial statistics.

ISIC	INDUSTRY	5. AVERAGE NUMBER OF OPERATIVES a/b/ (NUMBER)					6. WAGES AND SALARIES OF OPERATIVES b/ (MILLION COLONES)					ISIC
		1981	1982	1983	1984	1985	1981	1982	1983	1984	1985	
210	Coal mining	...	...	...	...	...	...	...	...	...	...	210
220	Petroleum and gas	...	...	...	...	...	...	...	...	...	...	220
230	Metal ore mining	...	...	...	...	...	...	...	...	...	...	230
290	Other mining	...	...	...	...	...	...	...	...	...	...	290
2	Mining, quarrying .	...	...	...	...	...	...	...	...	...	...	2
311/2	Food products	6090	4844	5213	...	...	35.81	33.25	40.96	...	...	311/2
313	Beverages	1544	1357	1301	...	...	10.11	10.12	11.33	...	...	313
314	Tobacco	163	148	140	...	...	1.14	1.11	1.22	...	...	314
321	Textiles	5722	5513	5291	...	...	35.21	34.42	34.99	...	...	321
3211	Spinning,weaving etc..	4115	3967	4088	...	...	...	...	...	...	...	3211
322	Wearing apparel	2669	2361	1994	...	...	11.75	11.29	9.91	...	...	322
323	Leather and products ...	531	546	592	...	...	3.10	4.62	3.92	...	...	323
324	Footwear	1044	1145	1304	...	...	7.51	8.90	8.93	...	...	324
331	Wood products	147	99	86	...	...	0.73	0.46	0.45	...	...	331
332	Furniture, fixtures	318	255	402	...	...	1.02	1.30	2.41	...	...	332
341	Paper and products	1200	1210	1330	...	...	9.06	8.21	11.92	...	...	341
3411	Pulp,paper etc.	396	296	411	...	...	...	...	...	...	...	3411
342	Printing,publishing	780	848	998	...	...	4.59	6.36	6.89	...	...	342
351	Industrial chemicals ...	163	178	176	...	...	1.11	1.30	1.32	...	...	351
3511	Basic excl fertilizers	55	44	74	...	...	...	...	...	...	...	3511
3513	Synthetic resins etc .	10	39	-	...	...	...	...	-	...	...	3513
352	Other chemical products.	1807	1799	2069	...	...	10.33	10.27	13.39	...	...	352
3522	Drugs and medicines ..	623	746	902	...	...	...	...	...	...	...	3522
353	Petroleum refineries ...	36	32	32	...	...	0.66	0.78	0.81	...	...	353
354	Petroleum,coal products.	25	20	-	...	...	0.14	0.16	-	...	...	354
355	Rubber products	311	327	248	...	...	1.76	2.06	1.44	...	...	355
356	Plastic products n.e.c..	913	1019	1233	...	...	4.96	5.83	7.95	...	...	356
361	Pottery,china etc	-	-	-	...	...	-	-	-	...	...	361
362	Glass and products	-	39	-	...	...	-	0.23	-	...	...	362
369	Non-metal products n.e.c	1053	1023	957	...	...	7.73	8.53	7.80	...	...	369
371	Iron and steel	575	580	554	...	...	2.97	3.42	3.71	...	...	371
372	Non-ferrous metals	99	5	4	...	...	0.78	0.04	0.03	...	...	372
381	Metal products	942	752	747	...	...	5.12	5.70	5.76	...	...	381
382	Machinery n.e.c.	497	506	465	...	...	3.15	3.37	3.27	...	..:	382
3825	Office,computing etc..	-	-	-	...	...	-	-	-	...	...	3825
383	Electrical machinery ...	527	429	365	...	...	3.64	3.25	3.43	...	...	383
3832	Radio,television etc..	148	125	107	...	...	...	...	...	...	...	3832
384	Transport equipment	77	-	-	...	...	0.40	-	-	...	...	384
3841	Shipbuilding, repair..	13	-	-	...	...	...	-	-	...	...	3841
3843	Motor vehicles	11	-	-	...	...	...	-	-	...	...	3843
385	Professional goods	23	13	64	...	...	0.15	0.11	0.57	...	...	385
390	Other industries	332	546	568	...	...	1.53	2.46	2.77	...	...	390
3	Manufacturing	27588	25594	26133	...	...	164.46	167.55	185.18	...	...	3
410	Electricity,gas,steam ..	...	...	...	...	...	...	...	...	...	...	410
4101	Electricity	...	...	...	...	...	...	...	...	...	...	4101
420	Water works and supply .	...	...	...	...	...	...	...	...	...	...	420
4	Electricity,gas etc	...	...	...	...	...	...	...	...	...	...	4
2-4	All industry	...	...	...	...	...	...	...	...	...	...	2-4

Note. For certain differences in classification, see country note.

a/ At 31 August of the year indicated.
b/ Data derived from the quarterly survey covering important industries for the national industrial statistics.

ISIC	INDUSTRY	7. OUTPUT a/ (MILLION COLONES)					8. VALUE ADDED IN PRODUCERS' PRICES a/ (MILLION COLONES)					ISIC
		1981	1982	1983	1984	1985	1981	1982	1983	1984	1985	
210	Coal mining	...	...	...	...	...	...	...	...	...	...	210
220	Petroleum and gas	...	...	...	...	...	...	...	...	...	...	220
230	Metal ore mining	...	...	...	...	...	...	...	...	...	...	230
290	Other mining	...	...	...	...	...	...	...	...	...	...	290
2	Mining, quarrying .	...	...	...	...	...	...	...	...	...	...	2
311/2	Food products	620	578	712	...	...	198	195	262	...	...	311/2
313	Beverages	255	236	254	...	...	174	159	176	...	...	313
314	Tobacco	86	98	108	...	...	61	72	83	...	...	314
321	Textiles	308	281	333	...	...	154	133	178	...	...	321
3211	Spinning,weaving etc..	219	216	277	...	...	108	101	136	...	...	3211
322	Wearing apparel	83	69	64	...	...	45	35	35	...	...	322
323	Leather and products ...	27	27	30	...	...	14	13	14	...	...	323
324	Footwear	69	80	75	...	...	38	35	35	...	....	324
331	Wood products	4	3	6	...	...	2	1	3	...	...	331
332	Furniture, fixtures	14	10	21	...	...	8	6	11	...	...	332
341	Paper and products	175	156	220	...	...	90	67	104	...	...	341
3411	Pulp,paper etc.	49	34	87	...	...	19	6	34	...	...	3411
342	Printing,publishing	54	68	86	...	...	27	32	44	...	...	342
351	Industrial chemicals ...	27	29	47	...	...	9	11	19	...	...	351
3511	Basic excl fertilizers	4	5	13	...	...	3	3	6	...	...	3511
3513	Synthetic resins etc .	1	5	-	...	...	-	1	-	...	...	3513
352	Other chemical products.	238	260	330	...	...	129	137	180	...	...	352
3522	Drugs and medicines ..	79	101	131	...	...	52	63	83	...	...	3522
353	Petroleum refineries ...	479	477	504	...	...	63	40	68	...	...	353
354	Petroleum,coal products.	22	14	-	...	...	4	2	-	...	...	354
355	Rubber products	21	27	21	...	...	10	14	11	...	...	355
356	Plastic products n.e.c..	57	68	102	...	...	28	32	48	...	...	356
361	Pottery,china etc	-	-	-	...	...	-	-	-	...	...	361
362	Glass and products	-	2	-	...	...	-	1	-	...	...	362
369	Non-metal products n.e.c	105	96	107	...	...	42	47	59	...	...	369
371	Iron and steel	43	32	44	...	...	14	14	17	...	...	371
372	Non-ferrous metals	11	1	-	...	...	4	1	-	...	...	372
381	Metal products	63	52	55	...	...	30	24	29	...	...	381
382	Machinery n.e.c.	30	29	33	...	...	17	17	21	...	...	382
3825	Office,computing etc..	-	-	-	...	...	-	-	-	...	...	3825
383	Electrical machinery ...	77	67	81	...	...	36	28	34	...	...	383
3832	Radio,television etc..	22	24	25	...	...	8	10	9	...	...	3832
384	Transport equipment	3	-	-	...	...	1	-	-	...	...	384
3841	Shipbuilding, repair..	1	-	-	...	...	-	-	-	...	...	3841
3843	Motor vehicles	-	-	-	...	...	-	-	-	...	...	3843
385	Professional goods	2	2	8	...	...	1	1	5	...	...	385
390	Other industries	17	24	25	...	...	10	15	15	...	...	390
3	Manufacturing	2890	2786	3266	...	...	1209	1132	1451	...	...	3
410	Electricity,gas,steam ..	...	...	...	...	...	...	...	...	...	...	410
4101	Electricity	...	...	...	...	...	...	...	...	...	...	4101
420	Water works and supply .	...	...	...	...	...	...	...	...	...	...	420
4	Electricity,gas etc	...	...	...	...	...	...	...	...	...	...	4
2-4	All industry	...	...	...	...	...	...	...	...	...	...	2-4

Note. For certain differences in classification, see country note.

a/ Data derived from the quarterly survey covering important industries for the national industrial statistics.

9. GROSS FIXED CAPITAL FORMATION
TOTAL a/
(MILLION COLONES)

ISIC	INDUSTRY	1981	1982	1983	1984	1985	ISIC
210	Coal mining	...	...	...	...	...	210
220	Petroleum and gas	...	...	...	...	...	220
230	Metal ore mining	...	...	...	...	...	230
290	Other mining	...	...	...	...	...	290
2	Mining, quarrying .	...	...	...	...	...	2
311/2	Food products	12.87	10.83	16.19	...	...	311/2
313	Beverages	3.34	7.04	8.13	...	...	313
314	Tobacco	0.12	4.15	0.47	...	...	314
321	Textiles	4.11	4.28	9.99	...	...	321
3211	Spinning,weaving etc..	2.76	3.77	6.18	...	...	3211
322	Wearing apparel	0.91	0.55	0.46	...	...	322
323	Leather and products ...	0.50	0.31	0.25	...	...	323
324	Footwear	0.68	4.58	1.26	...	...	324
331	Wood products	0.08	0.02	0.11	...	...	331
332	Furniture, fixtures	0.08	0.07	0.93	...	...	332
341	Paper and products	3.67	1.40	8.56	...	...	341
3411	Pulp,paper etc.	0.57	0.26	4.18	...	...	3411
342	Printing,publishing	0.47	1.93	2.53	...	...	342
351	Industrial chemicals ...	0.25	0.56	0.65	...	...	351
3511	Basic excl fertilizers	0.17	0.27	0.16	...	...	3511
3513	Synthetic resins etc .	-	0.21	-	...	...	3513
352	Other chemical products.	1.73	3.42	7.02	...	...	352
3522	Drugs and medicines ..	0.60	1.35	5.13	...	...	3522
353	Petroleum refineries ...	2.03	2.66	1.75	...	...	353
354	Petroleum,coal products.	0.23	0.11	-	...	...	354
355	Rubber products	0.34	0.39	-1.17	...	...	355
356	Plastic products n.e.c..	4.04	0.79	4.18	...	...	356
361	Pottery,china etc	-	-	-	...	...	361
362	Glass and products	-	0.02	-	...	...	362
369	Non-metal products n.e.c	0.95	1.22	1.38	...	...	369
371	Iron and steel	3.22	0.87	0.17	...	...	371
372	Non-ferrous metals	0.13	-	0.02	...	...	372
381	Metal products	1.27	1.27	0.96	...	...	381
382	Machinery n.e.c.	0.47	0.45	0.39	...	...	382
3825	Office,computing etc..	-	-	-	...	...	3825
383	Electrical machinery ...	0.96	0.99	0.70	...	...	383
3832	Radio,television etc..	0.07	0.04	0.10	...	...	3832
384	Transport equipment	0.19	-	-	...	...	384
3841	Shipbuilding, repair..	-	-	-	...	...	3841
3843	Motor vehicles	-	-	-	...	...	3843
385	Professional goods	0.01	0.02	0.07	...	...	385
390	Other industries	0.15	0.75	1.00	...	...	390
3	Manufacturing	42.80	48.68	66.00	...	...	3
410	Electricity,gas,steam ..	...	...	...	...	...	410
4101	Electricity	...	...	...	...	...	4101
420	Water works and supply .	...	...	...	...	...	420
4	Electricity,gas etc	...	...	...	...	...	4
2-4	All industry	...	...	...	...	...	2-4

Note. For certain differences in classification, see country note.

a/ Data derived from the quarterly survey covering important industries for the national industrial statistics.

ETHIOPIA

The information in the tables is based on the reply to the United Nations Questionnaire on General Industrial Statistics from the Central Statistical Office, Addis Ababa. The concepts, definitions and classification by branches of industry are generally in accordance with United Nations standards.

The estimates for manufacturing are derived from the annual survey of manufacturing industry conducted by the Central Statistical Office. The inquiry is carried out primarily by mail and covers establishments with 10 or more employees and using power driven machines. Data on electricity relate to the Ethiopian Electric Light and Power Authority. In the tables, the estimates have been adjusted for non-responding establishments.

The estimates in the tables are based on the national classification, which follows the present version of ISIC. The reference period is the fiscal year ending 30 June of the year indicated.

The establishment is defined as an entity comprising the whole of the premises under the same ownership or management at a particular address. The number of employees refers to all persons on the pay-roll, whether employed on a full-time or part-time basis. The number of part-time workers has been adjusted to give the equivalent of full-time workers, taking into account the number of months worked.

The value of output represents the sum of (a) value of goods produced, (b) value of industrial services rendered to others, (c) value of goods sold in the same condition as purchased, (d) net change between the beginning and the end of the reference year in the value of work in progress, (e) value of electricity sold and (f) value of fixed assets produced during the reference year by the establishment for its own use. Value added is defined as the difference between output and industrial costs (the cost of materials, supplies, fuels and electricity consumed, cost of repair and maintenance, cost of contract and commission work done by others and cost of goods sold in the same condition as purchased). The valuation of output and value added is in producers' prices.

Estimates for gross fixed capital formation relate to additions of new and second-hand assets valued at purchase price. Custom duties, other taxes, transfer fees, delivery and installation costs are included. Also included is the value of work done by the establishment's own labour for construction of buildings and structures (including materials used), for installation of machinery and equipment, and for capitalized alterations, improvements or rebuilding.

Related national publications:
<u>Statistical Abstract</u> (annual) and <u>Results of Annual Survey of Manufacturing Industries</u>, both published by the Central Statistical Office, Addis Ababa.

ISIC	INDUSTRY	1. NUMBER OF ESTABLISHMENTS a/b/ (NUMBER)					2. AVERAGE NUMBER OF PERSONS ENGAGED a/b/ (NUMBER)					ISIC
		1981	1982	1983	1984	1985	1981	1982	1983	1984	1985	
210	Coal mining	...	...	...	...	...	...	...	...	...	...	210
220	Petroleum and gas	...	...	...	...	...	...	...	...	...	...	220
230	Metal ore mining	...	...	...	...	...	...	...	...	...	...	230
290	Other mining	...	...	...	...	...	...	...	...	...	...	290
2	Mining, quarrying .	...	...	...	...	...	...	...	...	...	...	2
311/2	Food products	123	134	128	128	...	15600	16671	16789	16687	...	311/2
313	Beverages	28	28	28	28	...	6210	7159	6953	6921	...	313
314	Tobacco	2	2	2	2	...	849	1289	1719	1854	...	314
321	Textiles	51	58	58	52	...	30057	31676	32281	36447	...	321
3211	Spinning,weaving etc..	22	21	21	21	...	24752	26213	26726	30782	...	3211
322	Wearing apparel	6	8	9	11	...	2297	2462	2594	3154	...	322
323	Leather and products ...	10	10	10	10	...	2067	2124	2186	2596	...	323
324	Footwear	10	14	15	15	...	2474	2542	2516	2493	...	324
331	Wood products	51	25	25	19	...	4321	2159	1978	1705	...	331
332	Furniture, fixtures	17	19	17	14	...	965	956	1007	949	...	332
341	Paper and products	6	5	6	5	...	1400	903	985	1158	...	341
3411	Pulp,paper etc.	...	...	...	...	...	...	...	...	...	...	3411
342	Printing,publishing	22	24	23	23	...	2394	2512	2605	2752	...	342
351	Industrial chemicals ...	4	4	4	3	...	256	257	246	294	...	351
3511	Basic excl fertilizers	...	...	...	...	...	...	...	...	...	...	3511
3513	Synthetic resins etc .	...	...	...	...	...	...	...	...	...	...	3513
352	Other chemical products.	14	15	15	15	...	1802	1768	1901	2494	...	352
3522	Drugs and medicines ..	...	...	...	...	...	...	...	...	...	...	3522
353	Petroleum refineries ...	1	1	1	1	...	1039	1038	976	1070	...	353
354	Petroleum,coal products.	-	-	-	-	...	-	-	-	-	...	354
355	Rubber products	3	4	4	4	...	1352	1500	1548	1636	...	355
356	Plastic products n.e.c..	9	9	10	9	...	1158	1232	1304	1418	...	356
361	Pottery,china etc	-	-	-	-	...	-	-	-	-	...	361
362	Glass and products	2	2	2	2	...	407	749	812	762	...	362
369	Non-metal products n.e.c	25	27	28	28	...	2604	2777	2843	3190	...	369
371	Iron and steel	3	3	3	3	...	681	709	758	752	...	371
372	Non-ferrous metals	-	-	-	-	...	-	-	-	-	...	372
381	Metal products	18	24	24	24	...	1363	1601	1642	1643	...	381
382	Machinery n.e.c.	-	-	-	-	...	-	-	-	-	...	382
3825	Office,computing etc..	-	-	-	-	...	-	-	-	-	...	3825
383	Electrical machinery ...	3	3	3	3	...	74	81	89	95	...	383
3832	Radio,television etc..	...	...	...	...	...	...	...	...	...	...	3832
384	Transport equipment	-	-	-	-	...	-	-	-	-	...	384
3841	Shipbuilding, repair..	-	-	-	-	...	-	-	-	-	...	3841
3843	Motor vehicles	-	-	-	-	...	-	-	-	-	...	3843
385	Professional goods	-	-	-	-	...	-	-	-	-	...	385
390	Other industries	-	-	-	-	...	-	-	-	-	...	390
3	Manufacturing	408	419	415	399	...	79370	82165	83732	90070	...	3
410	Electricity,gas,steam ..	...	...	...	...	...	...	...	...	...	...	410
4101	Electricity	44	...	...	...	...	5275	...	...	...	...	4101
420	Water works and supply .	...	...	...	...	...	...	...	...	...	...	420
4	Electricity,gas etc	...	...	...	...	...	...	...	...	...	...	4
2-4	All industry	...	...	...	...	...	...	...	...	...	...	2-4

a/ Manufacturing: establishments with 10 or more employees and using power-driven machines.
b/ Twelve months ending 30 June of the year indicated.

ISIC	INDUSTRY	3. AVERAGE NUMBER OF EMPLOYEES a/b/ (NUMBER)					4. WAGES AND SALARIES OF EMPLOYEES a/b/ (THOUSAND BIRR)					ISIC
		1981	1982	1983	1984	1985	1981	1982	1983	1984	1985	
210	Coal mining	...	...	...	...	...	...	...	...	...	...	210
220	Petroleum and gas	...	...	...	...	...	...	...	...	...	...	220
230	Metal ore mining	...	...	...	...	...	...	...	...	...	...	230
290	Other mining	...	...	...	...	...	...	...	...	...	...	290
2	Mining, quarrying .	...	...	...	...	...	...	...	...	...	...	2
311/2	Food products	15502	16547	16664	16551	...	33379	37623	41696	43238	...	311/2
313	Beverages	6194	7143	6936	6896	...	16202	17551	18879	21422	...	313
314	Tobacco	849	1289	1719	1854	...	2267	2332	3511	4861	...	314
321	Textiles	30012	31604	32206	36389	...	59186	64083	68596	72441	...	321
3211	Spinning,weaving etc..	24751	26212	26725	30780	...	50956	55610	59768	62779	...	3211
322	Wearing apparel	2293	2459	2587	3139	...	3423	3892	4899	5463	...	322
323	Leather and products ...	2066	2122	2184	2594	...	4216	4777	5020	5924	...	323
324	Footwear	2471	2531	2504	2479	...	5222	6011	6263	6471	...	324
331	Wood products	4286	2127	1948	1682	...	9066	5005	5960	4821	...	331
332	Furniture, fixtures	951	939	990	940	...	2801	2990	3107	2976	...	332
341	Paper and products	1396	900	982	1156	...	2323	2411	2510	2984	...	341
3411	Pulp,paper etc.	...	...	...	...	...	...	...	...	...	...	3411
342	Printing,publishing	2380	2496	2587	2739	...	6992	7406	8411	8646	...	342
351	Industrial chemicals ...	255	256	245	294	...	463	611	679	810	...	351
3511	Basic excl fertilizers	...	...	...	...	...	...	...	...	...	...	3511
3513	Synthetic resins etc .	...	...	...	...	...	...	...	...	...	...	3513
352	Other chemical products.	1796	1758	1896	2488	...	4489	5023	5507	6002	...	352
3522	Drugs and medicines ..	...	...	...	...	...	...	...	...	...	...	3522
353	Petroleum refineries ...	1039	1038	976	1070	...	8928	9004	10392	14749	...	353
354	Petroleum,coal products.	-	-	-	-	...	-	-	-	-	...	354
355	Rubber products	1347	1494	1543	1629	...	4759	4981	5171	5512	...	355
356	Plastic products n.e.c..	1153	1226	1299	1413	...	2238	2545	3085	3830	...	356
361	Pottery,china etc	-	-	-	-	...	-	-	-	-	...	361
362	Glass and products	407	749	812	762	...	1307	1801	2137	2110	...	362
369	Non-metal products n.e.c	2587	2761	2821	3170	...	7328	7172	7151	7496	...	369
371	Iron and steel	681	709	758	752	...	2516	2625	2919	2984	...	371
372	Non-ferrous metals	-	-	-	-	...	-	-	-	-	...	372
381	Metal products	1353	1590	1632	1631	...	4383	5113	5598	5720	...	381
382	Machinery n.e.c.	-	-	-	-	...	-	-	-	-	...	382
3825	Office,computing etc..	-	-	-	-	...	-	-	-	-	...	3825
383	Electrical machinery ...	73	80	88	94	...	240	284	320	349	...	383
3832	Radio,television etc..	...	...	...	...	...	...	...	...	...	...	3832
384	Transport equipment	-	-	-	-	...	-	-	-	-	...	384
3841	Shipbuilding, repair..	-	-	-	-	...	-	-	-	-	...	3841
3843	Motor vehicles	-	-	-	-	...	-	-	-	-	...	3843
385	Professional goods	-	-	-	-	...	-	-	-	-	...	385
390	Other industries	-	-	-	-	...	-	-	-	-	...	390
3	Manufacturing	79091	81818	83377	89722	...	181728	193240	211811	228809	...	3
410	Electricity,gas,steam ..	...	...	...	...	...	...	...	...	...	...	410
4101	Electricity	5275	...	...	...	...	14131	...	...	...	...	4101
420	Water works and supply .	...	...	...	...	...	...	...	...	...	...	420
4	Electricity,gas etc	...	...	...	...	...	...	...	...	...	...	4
2-4	All industry	...	...	...	...	...	...	...	...	...	...	2-4

a/ Manufacturing: establishments with 10 or more employees and using power-driven machines.
b/ Twelve months ending 30 June of the year indicated.

ISIC	INDUSTRY	5. AVERAGE NUMBER OF OPERATIVES a/b/ (NUMBER)					6. WAGES AND SALARIES OF OPERATIVES a/b/ (THOUSAND BIRR)					ISIC
		1981	1982	1983	1984	1985	1981	1982	1983	1984	1985	
210	Coal mining	...	...	...	...	...	...	...	...	...	...	210
220	Petroleum and gas	...	...	...	...	...	...	...	...	...	...	220
230	Metal ore mining	...	...	...	...	...	...	...	...	...	...	230
290	Other mining	...	...	...	...	...	...	...	...	...	...	290
2	Mining, quarrying .	...	...	...	...	...	...	...	...	...	...	2
311/2	Food products	11237	11761	12203	11497	...	18309	19152	23848	24586	...	311/2
313	Beverages	3009	3806	3543	3282	...	4988	6250	7016	7249	...	313
314	Tobacco	563	889	1103	1291	...	1028	1043	1590	2801	...	314
321	Textiles	25854	27343	28142	31525	...	40548	44233	48169	51094	...	321
3211	Spinning,weaving etc..	21208	22461	23128	26402	...	34646	38295	42171	44119	...	3211
322	Wearing apparel	1934	2018	2142	2620	...	2240	2363	3112	3313	...	322
323	Leather and products ...	1585	1617	1591	1914	...	2354	2812	2688	3044	...	323
324	Footwear	2025	2019	1847	1796	...	3198	3642	3879	3610	...	324
331	Wood products	3509	1753	1523	1320	...	4537	3238	3988	2848	...	331
332	Furniture, fixtures	803	784	791	746	...	1919	2188	2217	2102	...	332
341	Paper and products	1135	624	685	817	...	1247	1216	1230	1393	...	341
3411	Pulp,paper etc.	...	...	...	...	...	...	...	...	...	...	3411
342	Printing,publishing	1883	1975	2032	2141	...	5027	5418	5899	6025	...	342
351	Industrial chemicals ...	189	185	176	197	...	271	425	464	511	...	351
3511	Basic excl fertilizers	...	...	...	...	...	...	...	...	...	...	3511
3513	Synthetic resins etc .	...	...	...	...	...	...	...	...	...	...	3513
352	Other chemical products.	1163	1066	1161	1810	...	1906	1805	2085	2344	...	352
3522	Drugs and medicines ..	...	...	...	...	...	...	...	...	...	...	3522
353	Petroleum refineries ...	341	295	264	332	...	1218	1481	1377	2484	...	353
354	Petroleum,coal products.	-	-	-	-	...	-	-	-	-	...	354
355	Rubber products	920	1051	1171	1273	...	2284	2255	3502	3270	...	355
356	Plastic products n.e.c..	927	965	989	1043	...	1290	1229	1481	2030	...	356
361	Pottery,china etc	-	-	-	-	...	-	-	-	-	...	361
362	Glass and products	189	545	611	608	...	464	1013	1028	1141	...	362
369	Non-metal products n.e.c	1919	2099	2101	2524	...	3521	4509	4718	5025	...	369
371	Iron and steel	442	457	486	521	...	1419	1413	1391	1722	...	371
372	Non-ferrous metals	-	-	-	-	...	-	-	-	-	...	372
381	Metal products	1081	1226	1285	1188	...	2804	3145	3121	3083	...	381
382	Machinery n.e.c.	-	-	-	-	...	-	-	-	-	...	382
3825	Office,computing etc..	-	-	-	-	...	-	-	-	-	...	3825
383	Electrical machinery ...	61	64	65	74	...	165	175	193	237	...	383
3832	Radio,television etc..	...	...	...	...	...	...	...	...	...	...	3832
384	Transport equipment	-	-	-	-	...	-	-	-	-	...	384
3841	Shipbuilding, repair..	-	-	-	-	...	-	-	-	-	...	3841
3843	Motor vehicles	-	-	-	-	...	-	-	-	-	...	3843
385	Professional goods	-	-	-	-	...	-	-	-	-	...	385
390	Other industries	-	-	-	-	...	-	-	-	-	...	390
3	Manufacturing	60769	62542	63911	68519	...	100737	109005	122996	129912	...	3
410	Electricity,gas,steam ..	...	...	...	...	...	...	...	...	...	...	410
4101	Electricity	...	...	...	...	...	...	...	...	...	...	4101
420	Water works and supply .	...	...	...	...	...	...	...	...	...	...	420
4	Electricity,gas etc	...	...	...	...	...	...	...	...	...	...	4
2-4	All industry	...	...	...	...	...	...	...	...	...	...	2-4

a/ Manufacturing: establishments with 10 or more employees and using power-driven machines.
b/ Twelve months ending 30 June of the year indicated.

ISIC	INDUSTRY	7. OUTPUT IN PRODUCERS' PRICES a/b/ (MILLION BIRR)					8. VALUE ADDED IN PRODUCERS' PRICES a/b/ (MILLION BIRR)					ISIC
		1981	1982	1983	1984	1985	1981	1982	1983	1984	1985	
210	Coal mining	...	...	...	...	...	...	...	...	...	...	210
220	Petroleum and gas	...	...	...	...	...	...	...	...	...	...	220
230	Metal ore mining	...	...	...	...	...	...	...	...	...	...	230
290	Other mining	...	...	...	...	...	...	...	...	...	...	290
2	Mining, quarrying	...	...	...	...	...	...	...	...	...	...	2
311/2	Food products	565.5	566.7	618.3	623.8	...	244.3	246.1	302.0	278.1	...	311/2
313	Beverages	274.1	291.6	296.1	326.2	...	189.9	199.1	218.2	238.5	...	313
314	Tobacco	111.9	128.6	128.6	160.4	...	54.0	65.2	58.9	76.5	...	314
321	Textiles	403.9	414.5	404.9	401.6	...	197.1	200.0	182.9	180.3	...	321
3211	Spinning, weaving etc.	357.6	365.6	352.6	346.4	...	177.6	176.8	154.5	150.9	...	3211
322	Wearing apparel	32.7	37.5	40.0	51.3	...	11.7	13.1	17.5	18.7	...	322
323	Leather and products	72.7	71.6	79.9	80.9	...	25.6	21.2	27.6	27.3	...	323
324	Footwear	44.3	46.7	49.9	53.1	...	17.3	17.2	21.0	20.9	...	324
331	Wood products	36.7	26.3	25.8	24.4	...	18.8	15.3	13.9	15.3	...	331
332	Furniture, fixtures	10.6	11.5	17.3	17.0	...	5.0	6.3	6.7	7.0	...	332
341	Paper and products	34.6	40.1	38.5	40.9	...	6.1	15.1	16.1	18.5	...	341
3411	Pulp, paper etc.	...	...	...	...	...	...	...	...	...	...	3411
342	Printing, publishing	37.2	42.1	46.4	54.1	...	23.0	25.8	28.4	33.0	...	342
351	Industrial chemicals	6.9	7.0	6.6	6.5	...	3.2	3.1	4.7	3.0	...	351
3511	Basic excl fertilizers	...	...	...	...	...	...	...	...	...	...	3511
3513	Synthetic resins etc	...	...	...	...	...	...	...	...	...	...	3513
352	Other chemical products	63.8	78.0	94.8	97.3	...	20.6	26.6	36.2	41.2	...	352
3522	Drugs and medicines	...	...	...	...	...	...	...	...	...	...	3522
353	Petroleum refineries	353.6	491.1	502.7	533.2	...	15.8	57.0	29.7	120.5	...	353
354	Petroleum, coal products	-	-	-	-	...	-	-	-	-	...	354
355	Rubber products	44.9	51.5	54.4	58.6	...	13.0	19.0	22.2	25.7	...	355
356	Plastic products n.e.c.	30.4	38.0	42.6	44.3	...	12.8	20.2	21.7	19.9	...	356
361	Pottery, china etc	-	-	-	-	...	-	-	-	-	...	361
362	Glass and products	4.5	15.7	15.5	11.4	...	1.6	7.4	7.3	6.4	...	362
369	Non-metal products n.e.c	40.9	43.3	42.4	46.8	...	22.8	22.0	20.0	24.2	...	369
371	Iron and steel	73.9	73.7	75.8	82.0	...	20.4	17.2	16.6	19.3	...	371
372	Non-ferrous metals	-	-	-	-	...	-	-	-	-	...	372
381	Metal products	44.2	45.1	49.1	54.9	...	18.1	19.2	18.7	20.9	...	381
382	Machinery n.e.c.	-	-	-	-	...	-	-	-	-	...	382
3825	Office, computing etc.	-	-	-	-	...	-	-	-	-	...	3825
383	Electrical machinery	1.6	2.6	2.0	2.1	...	0.8	1.4	1.0	1.2	...	383
3832	Radio, television etc.	...	...	...	...	...	...	...	...	...	...	3832
384	Transport equipment	-	-	-	-	...	-	-	-	-	...	384
3841	Shipbuilding, repair	-	-	-	-	...	-	-	-	-	...	3841
3843	Motor vehicles	-	-	-	-	...	-	-	-	-	...	3843
385	Professional goods	-	-	-	-	...	-	-	-	-	...	385
390	Other industries	-	-	-	-	...	-	-	-	-	...	390
3	Manufacturing	2288.9	2523.2	2631.6	2770.8	...	921.9	1017.5	1071.3	1196.4	...	3
410	Electricity, gas, steam	...	...	...	...	...	...	...	...	...	...	410
4101	Electricity	72.9	...	...	...	...	...	...	...	...	...	4101
420	Water works and supply	...	...	...	...	...	...	...	...	...	...	420
4	Electricity, gas etc	...	...	...	...	...	...	...	...	...	...	4
2-4	All industry	...	...	...	...	...	...	...	...	...	...	2-4

a/ Manufacturing: establishments with 10 or more employees and using power-driven machines.
b/ Twelve months ending 30 June of the year indicated.

9. GROSS FIXED CAPITAL FORMATION
TOTAL a/b/c/
(MILLION BIRR)

ISIC	INDUSTRY	1981	1982	1983	1984	1985	ISIC
210	Coal mining	...	...	...	...	...	210
220	Petroleum and gas	...	...	...	...	...	220
230	Metal ore mining	...	...	...	...	...	230
290	Other mining	...	...	...	...	...	290
2	Mining, quarrying .	...	...	...	...	...	2
311/2	Food products	8.10	25.08	30.83	16.14	...	311/2
313	Beverages	6.13	9.05	4.90	6.16	...	313
314	Tobacco	0.87	1.47	2.60	1.96	...	314
321	Textiles	17.70	26.81	7.71	10.32	...	321
3211	Spinning,weaving etc..	15.85	25.21	7.30	9.68	...	3211
322	Wearing apparel	0.61	0.22	0.28	0.05	...	322
323	Leather and products ...	1.19	0.43	1.94	1.63	...	323
324	Footwear	0.49	0.59	1.03	0.95	...	324
331	Wood products	0.51	1.03	0.73	0.99	...	331
332	Furniture, fixtures	0.14	0.28	0.38	0.31	...	332
341	Paper and products	0.47	0.77	1.75	0.79	...	341
3411	Pulp,paper etc.	...	...	...	...	...	3411
342	Printing,publishing	1.12	0.64	2.55	1.96	...	342
351	Industrial chemicals ...	0.10	0.08	0.04	0.13	...	351
3511	Basic excl fertilizers	...	...	...	...	...	3511
3513	Synthetic resins etc .	...	...	...	...	...	3513
352	Other chemical products.	0.85	1.30	1.00	2.53	...	352
3522	Drugs and medicines ..	...	...	...	...	...	3522
353	Petroleum refineries ...	3.18	3.19	9.73	26.47	...	353
354	Petroleum,coal products.	-	-	-	-	...	354
355	Rubber products	0.88	1.62	0.97	0.85	...	355
356	Plastic products n.e.c..	1.35	1.05	1.34	1.28	...	356
361	Pottery,china etc	-	-	-	-	...	361
362	Glass and products	8.63	0.20	0.48	1.49	...	362
369	Non-metal products n.e.c	1.42	0.79	0.96	0.37	...	369
371	Iron and steel	0.17	0.74	0.27	1.86	...	371
372	Non-ferrous metals	-	-	-	-	...	372
381	Metal products	1.14	0.28	0.58	1.31	...	381
382	Machinery n.e.c.	-	-	-	-	...	382
3825	Office,computing etc..	-	-	-	-	...	3825
383	Electrical machinery ...	0.01	0.02	0.24	0.12	...	383
3832	Radio,television etc..	-	-	-	-	...	3832
384	Transport equipment	-	-	-	-	...	384
3841	Shipbuilding, repair..	-	-	-	-	...	3841
3843	Motor vehicles	-	-	-	-	...	3843
385	Professional goods	-	-	-	-	...	385
390	Other industries	-	-	-	-	...	390
3	Manufacturing	55.06	75.64	70.31	77.67	...	3
410	Electricity,gas,steam ..	...	...	...	...	...	410
4101	Electricity	...	...	...	...	...	4101
420	Water works and supply .	...	...	...	...	...	420
4	Electricity,gas etc	...	...	...	...	...	4
2-4	All industry	...	...	...	...	...	2-4

a/ The value of sales is not deducted.
b/ Manufacturing: establishments with 10 or more employees and using power-driven machines.
c/ Twelve months ending 30 June of the year indicated.

FIJI

The information in the tables is based on the reply to the United Nations Questionnaire on General Industrial Statistics from the Bureau of Statistics, Suva. The concepts, definitions and classification by branches of industry are generally in accordance with United Nations standards.

The estimates are derived from the annual census of industries conducted by the Bureau of Statistics. The census covers all establishments irrespective of size, including handicrafts. However, due to the difficulties involved in identifying the small producing units in the villages, activities such as handicrafts are considerably underestimated. The inquiry is conducted by mail, but includes some field enumeration. The data in the tables relate only to establishments submitting returns in the private sector, except for ISIC 4 in which the activities of government and statutory authorities categorized in ISIC 4 are included. Non-response rate is reported approximately 15 per cent and data in the tables do not include estimates for non-responding establishments. The data for 1981 and 1982 are based on the previous national classification system and that for 1983 on the present version of the national classification system. Both systems are based on ISIC but are modified to accommodate national needs. Major deviations from ISIC are footnoted.

Wages and salaries of employees refer to the compensation of employees made during the year, i.e. the sum of wages and salaries in cash, remuneration in kind and contributions made by employers in respect of their employees to social security schemes, private pension arrangements, health insurance and similar schemes (Fiji National Provident Fund). Wages and salaries of operatives relate to cash payments only.

Output is defined as the gross value of all goods and services produced during the year. Output comprises the value of all goods manufactured, value of own capital construction, value of industrial services rendered to others, value of work in progress, difference between purchases and sales of goods sold without further processing and miscellaneous receipts including rent. Value added is the difference between output and the cost of raw materials, supplies, fuels, water and electricity consumed and payments for industrial and non-industrial services. The valuation of output and value added is in producers' prices.

Gross fixed capital formation is the value of purchases of new and used fixed assets less the sales of used assets plus the value of own account capital construction work done by the establishment.

Related national publication:
Census of Industrial Production (annual), published by the Bureau of Statistics, Suva.

ISIC	INDUSTRY	1. NUMBER OF ESTABLISHMENTS a/ (NUMBER)					2. AVERAGE NUMBER OF PERSONS ENGAGED a/ (NUMBER)					ISIC
		1981	1982	1983	1984	1985	1981	1982	1983	1984	1985	
210	Coal mining	-	-	-	...	...	-	-	-	...	...	210
220	Petroleum and gas	-	-	-	...	...	-	-	-	...	...	220
230	Metal ore mining	15	15	16	...	...	1222	1210	1149	...	...	230
290	Other mining	12	8	8	...	...	129	107	78	...	...	290
2	Mining, quarrying .	27	23	24	...	...	1351	1317	1227	...	...	2
311/2	Food products	70	76	103	...	...	5107	5614	5683	...	...	311/2
313	Beverages	[15	18	17]	...	...	[610	579	576]	...	...	313
314	Tobacco				...	...				...	...	314
321	Textiles	b/ 106	b/ 117	c/ 134	...	...	b/ 954	b/ 1029	c/ 1213	...	...	321
3211	Spinning, weaving etc..	...	...	...	...	...	...	...	...	...	...	3211
322	Wearing apparel	b/	b/	c/	...	...	b/	b/	c/	...	...	322
323	Leather and products ...	b/	b/	[8]	...	...	b/	b/	[106]	...	...	323
324	Footwear	8	6		...	...	36	54		...	...	324
331	Wood products	52	49	47	...	...	1000	948	945	...	...	331
332	Furniture, fixtures	73	83	89	...	...	448	798	855	...	...	332
341	Paper and products	8	7	8	...	...	184	190	189	...	...	341
3411	Pulp, paper etc.	-	-	-	...	...	-	-	-	...	...	3411
342	Printing, publishing	31	33	39	...	...	806	811	784	...	...	342
351	Industrial chemicals ...	-	-	-	...	...	-	-	-	...	...	351
3511	Basic excl fertilizers	-	-	-	...	...	-	-	-	...	...	3511
3513	Synthetic resins etc .	-	-	-	...	...	-	-	-	...	...	3513
352	Other chemical products.	16	16	d/ 19	...	...	302	287	d/ 357	...	...	352
3522	Drugs and medicines ..	-	-	-	...	...	-	-	-	...	...	3522
353	Petroleum refineries ...	-	-	-	...	...	-	-	-	...	...	353
354	Petroleum, coal products.	-	-	-	...	...	-	-	-	...	...	354
355	Rubber products	8	6	6	...	...	135	100	106	...	...	355
356	Plastic products n.e.c..	16	15	17	...	...	190	252	251	...	...	356
361	Pottery, china etc	-	-	-	...	...	-	-	-	...	...	361
362	Glass and products	-	-	-	...	...	-	-	-	...	...	362
369	Non-metal products n.e.c	10	8	[14]	...	...	419	398	[419]	...	...	369
371	Iron and steel	-	-		...	...	-	-		...	...	371
372	Non-ferrous metals	-	-	-	...	...	-	-	-	...	...	372
381	Metal products	47	49	53	...	...	887	819	816	...	...	381
382	Machinery n.e.c.	21	24	25	...	...	229	164	153	...	...	382
3825	Office, computing etc..	-	-	-	...	...	-	-	-	...	...	3825
383	Electrical machinery ...	4	4	9	...	...	58	63	126	...	...	383
3832	Radio, television etc..	-	-	-	...	...	-	-	-	...	...	3832
384	Transport equipment	12	8	9	...	...	603	362	368	...	...	384
3841	Shipbuilding, repair..	5	[8]	4	...	...	332	[362]	236	...	...	3841
3843	Motor vehicles	7		5	...	...	271		132	...	...	3843
385	Professional goods	-	-	-	...	...	-	-	-	...	...	385
390	Other industries	14	16	19	...	...	114	196	130	...	...	390
3	Manufacturing	511	535	d/ 616	...	...	12082	12664	d/ 13077	...	...	3
410	Electricity, gas, steam ..	...	...	...	...	...	...	...	...	...	...	410
4101	Electricity	...	...	...	...	...	...	...	...	...	...	4101
420	Water works and supply .	...	...	...	...	...	...	...	...	...	...	420
4	Electricity, gas etc	4	4	d/ 2	...	...	1122	1213	d/ 1256	...	...	4
2-4	All industry	542	562	642	...	...	14555	15194	15560	...	...	2-4

a/ Except for major division 4, private establishments submitting returns only.
b/ Major groups 322 and 323 are included in 321. c/ Major group 322 is included in 321.
d/ Manufacture of gas (ISIC 410) is included in major group 352.

ISIC	INDUSTRY	3. AVERAGE NUMBER OF EMPLOYEES a/ (NUMBER) 1981	1982	1983	1984	1985	4. WAGES AND SALARIES OF EMPLOYEES a/b/ (THOUSAND DOLLARS) 1981	1982	1983	1984	1985	ISIC
210	Coal mining	-	-	-	...	...	-	-	-	...	...	210
220	Petroleum and gas	-	-	-	...	...	-	-	-	...	...	220
230	Metal ore mining	1222	1210	1149	...	...	5778	5388	5708	...	...	230
290	Other mining	129	107	74	...	...	445	299	240	...	...	290
2	Mining, quarrying .	1351	1317	1223	...	...	6223	5687	5948	...	...	2
311/2	Food products	5049	5565	5641	...	...	19687	21434	18467	...	...	311/2
313	Beverages	[601	570	568]	...	...	[2808	3130	3154]	...	...	313
314	Tobacco				...	...				...	...	314
321	Textiles	c/ 822	c/ 888	d/ 1056	...	...	c/ 1121	c/ 1200	d/ 1692	...	...	321
3211	Spinning,weaving etc..	...	...	...	...	...	...	...	...	...	...	3211
322	Wearing apparel	c/	c/	d/	...	...	c/	c/	d/	...	...	322
323	Leather and products ...	c/	c/	[103]	...	...	c/	c/	[103]	...	...	323
324	Footwear	32	42		...	...	43	56		...	...	324
331	Wood products	967	904	911	...	...	4657	3809	3721	...	...	331
332	Furniture, fixtures	369	711	743	...	...	876	1682	1882	...	...	332
341	Paper and products	179	183	184	...	...	849	1145	1022	...	...	341
3411	Pulp,paper etc.	-	-	-	...	...	-	-	-	...	...	3411
342	Printing,publishing	781	785	773	...	...	3100	3450	3802	...	...	342
351	Industrial chemicals ...	-	-	-	...	...	-	-	-	...	...	351
3511	Basic excl fertilizers	-	-	-	...	...	-	-	-	...	...	3511
3513	Synthetic resins etc .	-	-	-	...	...	-	-	-	...	...	3513
352	Other chemical products.	297	284	e/ 357	...	...	1520	1668	e/ 2067	...	...	352
3522	Drugs and medicines ..	-	-	-	...	...	-	-	-	...	...	3522
353	Petroleum refineries ...	-	-	-	...	...	-	-	-	...	...	353
354	Petroleum,coal products.	-	-	-	...	...	-	-	-	...	...	354
355	Rubber products	132	97	106	...	...	389	310	474	...	...	355
356	Plastic products n.e.c..	182	241	243	...	...	863	1063	1184	...	...	356
361	Pottery,china etc	-	-	-	...	...	-	-	-	...	...	361
362	Glass and products	-	-	-	...	...	-	-	-	...	...	362
369	Non-metal products n.e.c	414	393	[412]	...	...	2250	2412	[3300]	...	...	369
371	Iron and steel	-	-		...	...	-	-		...	...	371
372	Non-ferrous metals	-	-	-	...	...	-	-	-	...	...	372
381	Metal products	838	765	794	...	...	3200	3082	2729	...	...	381
382	Machinery n.e.c.	198	133	130	...	...	351	369	359	...	...	382
3825	Office,computing etc..	-	-	-	...	...	-	-	-	...	...	3825
383	Electrical machinery ...	58	63	121	...	...	292	342	728	...	...	383
3832	Radio,television etc..	-	-	-	...	...	-	-	-	...	...	3832
384	Transport equipment	595	355	364	...	...	2448	2066	2060	...	...	384
3841	Shipbuilding, repair..	330	[355]	234	...	...	1900	[2066]	1360	...	...	3841
3843	Motor vehicles	265		130	...	...	548		700	...	...	3843
385	Professional goods	-	-	-	...	...	-	-	-	...	...	385
390	Other industries	99	178	116	...	...	170	288	363	...	...	390
3	Manufacturing	11613	12157	e/ 12622	...	...	44624	47506	e/ 47107	...	...	3
410	Electricity,gas,steam ..	...	...	...	...	...	...	...	...	...	...	410
4101	Electricity	...	...	...	...	...	...	...	...	...	...	4101
420	Water works and supply .	...	...	...	...	...	...	...	...	...	...	420
4	Electricity,gas etc	1122	1213	e/ 1256	...	...	7210	7897	e/ 6572	...	...	4
2-4	All industry	14086	14687	15101	...	...	58057	61090	59627	...	...	2-4

a/ Except for major division 4, private establishments submitting returns only.
b/ Including employers' contributions to national provident fund.
c/ Major groups 322 and 323 are included in 321.
d/ Major group 322 is included in 321.
e/ Manufacture of gas (ISIC 410) is included in major group 352.

ISIC	INDUSTRY	5. AVERAGE NUMBER OF OPERATIVES a/b/ (NUMBER) 1981	1982	1983	1984	1985	6. WAGES AND SALARIES OF OPERATIVES a/b/c/ (THOUSAND DOLLARS) 1981	1982	1983	1984	1985	ISIC
210	Coal mining	-	-	-	...	...	-	-	-	...	...	210
220	Petroleum and gas	-	-	-	...	...	-	-	-	...	...	220
230	Metal ore mining	809	808	837	...	...	3030	3108	3499	...	...	230
290	Other mining	115	97	71	...	...	385	279	214	...	...	290
2	Mining, quarrying .	924	905	908	...	...	3415	3387	3713	...	...	2
311/2	Food products	4323	4788	4803	...	...	17641	14238	14151	...	...	311/2
313	Beverages	[477	431	427]	...	...	[1566	1690	1606]	...	...	313
314	Tobacco				...	...				...	...	314
321	Textiles	d/ 753	d/ 867	e/ 1012	...	...	d/ 819	d/ 1044	e/ 1497	...	...	321
3211	Spinning,weaving etc..	...	...	...	...	...	...	...	...	...	...	3211
322	Wearing apparel	d/	d/	e/	...	...	d/	d/	e/	...	...	322
323	Leather and products ...	d/	d/	[99]	...	...	d/	d/	[82]	...	...	323
324	Footwear	29	38		...	...	34	43		...	...	324
331	Wood products	835	876	874	...	...	3527	2976	2857	...	...	331
332	Furniture, fixtures	350	664	573	...	...	781	1561	1406	...	...	332
341	Paper and products	134	151	139	...	...	443	675	544	...	...	341
3411	Pulp,paper etc.	-	-	-	...	...	-	-	-	...	...	3411
342	Printing,publishing	565	527	544	...	...	1745	1681	2204	...	...	342
351	Industrial chemicals ...	-	-	-	...	...	-	-	-	...	...	351
3511	Basic excl fertilizers	-	-	-	...	...	-	-	-	...	...	3511
3513	Synthetic resins etc .	-	-	-	...	...	-	-	-	...	...	3513
352	Other chemical products.	236	223	f/ 280	...	...	817	906	f/ 1083	...	...	352
3522	Drugs and medicines ..	-	-	-	...	...	-	-	-	...	...	3522
353	Petroleum refineries ...	-	-	-	...	...	-	-	-	...	...	353
354	Petroleum,coal products.	-	-	-	...	...	-	-	-	...	...	354
355	Rubber products	107	81	90	...	...	237	198	277	...	...	355
356	Plastic products n.e.c..	150	216	212	...	...	544	620	785	...	...	356
361	Pottery,china etc	-	-	-	...	...	-	-	-	...	...	361
362	Glass and products	-	-	-	...	...	-	-	-	...	...	362
369	Non-metal products n.e.c	349	322	[313]	...	...	1461	1526	2280	...	...	369
371	Iron and steel	-	-		...	...	-	-	...	...	...	371
372	Non-ferrous metals	-	-	-	...	...	-	-	-	...	...	372
381	Metal products	702	630	694	...	...	2261	2016	1876	...	...	381
382	Machinery n.e.c.	157	121	119	...	...	272	287	256	...	...	382
3825	Office,computing etc..	-	-	-	...	...	-	-	-	...	...	3825
383	Electrical machinery ...	49	51	106	...	...	148	198	469	...	...	383
3832	Radio,television etc..	-	-	-	...	...	-	-	-	...	...	3832
384	Transport equipment	536	319	331	...	...	1733	1476	1500	...	...	384
3841	Shipbuilding, repair..	275	[319]	214	...	...	1244	[1476]	949	...	...	3841
3843	Motor vehicles	261		117	...	...	489		551	...	...	3843
385	Professional goods	-	-	-	...	...	-	-	-	...	...	385
390	Other industries	85	160	83	...	...	103	181	185	...	...	390
3	Manufacturing	9837	10465	f/ 11711	...	...	34132	31316	f/ 33058	...	...	3
410	Electricity,gas,steam ..	...	...	...	...	...	...	...	...	...	...	410
4101	Electricity	...	...	...	...	...	...	...	...	...	...	4101
420	Water works and supply .	...	...	...	...	...	...	...	...	...	...	420
4	Electricity,gas etc	g/ 884	g/ 982	f/g/ 1023	...	...	h/ 1836	h/ 2005	f/h/ 1339	...	...	4
2-4	All industry	g/ 11645	g/ 12352	g/ 12630	...	...	h/ 39383	h/ 36708	h/ 38110	...	...	2-4

a/ Except for major division 4, private establishments submitting returns only.
b/ Operatives: Fiji citizens only.
c/ Payments in cash only.
d/ Major groups 322 and 323 are included in 321.
e/ Major group 322 is included in 321.
f/ Manufacture of gas (ISIC 410) is included in major group 352.
g/ Excluding operatives of the Public Works Department Water Supplies.
h/ Excluding payments to operatives of the Public Works Department Water Supplies.

ISIC	INDUSTRY	7. OUTPUT IN PRODUCERS' PRICES b/ (THOUSAND DOLLARS) 1981	1982	1983	1984	1985	8. VALUE ADDED IN PRODUCERS' PRICES a/b/ (THOUSAND DOLLARS) 1981	1982	1983	1984	1985	ISIC
210	Coal mining	-	-	-	...	...	-	-	-	...	...	210
220	Petroleum and gas	-	-	-	...	...	-	-	-	...	...	220
230	Metal ore mining	14320	16828	22265	...	...	-89	5141	5639	...	...	230
290	Other mining	2536	2395	2007	...	...	707	977	833	...	...	290
2	Mining, quarrying	16856	19223	24272	...	...	618	6118	6472	...	...	2
311/2	Food products	253109	268101	190777	...	...	49320	57826	30753	...	...	311/2
313	Beverages	[40301	46002	48507]	...	...	[7339	7404	8510]	...	...	313
314	Tobacco				...	...				...	...	314
321	Textiles	c/ 6861	c/ 7602	d/ 9230	...	...	c/ 2404	c/ 2650	d/ 3083	...	...	321
3211	Spinning,weaving etc.	...	...	...	...	...	...	...	...	...	...	3211
322	Wearing apparel	c/	c/	d/	...	...	c/	c/	d/	...	...	322
323	Leather and products	c/	c/	[599]	...	...	c/	c/	[155]	...	...	323
324	Footwear	226	431		...	...	50	82		...	...	324
331	Wood products	16931	13262	16298	...	...	5697	5023	5644	...	...	331
332	Furniture, fixtures	4743	6842	8135	...	...	1198	2129	2906	...	...	332
341	Paper and products	5405	6424	5828	...	...	1975	1965	2010	...	...	341
3411	Pulp,paper etc.	-	-	-	...	...	-	-	-	...	...	3411
342	Printing,publishing	9719	11419	12083	...	...	4152	4662	4991	...	...	342
351	Industrial chemicals	-	-	-	...	...	-	-	-	...	...	351
3511	Basic excl fertilizers	-	-	-	...	...	-	-	-	...	...	3511
3513	Synthetic resins etc	-	-	-	...	...	-	-	-	...	...	3513
352	Other chemical products.	13483	14566	e/ 18838	...	...	3212	3355	e/ 5545	...	...	352
3522	Drugs and medicines	-	-	-	...	...	-	-	-	...	...	3522
353	Petroleum refineries	-	-	-	...	...	-	-	-	...	...	353
354	Petroleum,coal products.	-	-	-	...	...	-	-	-	...	...	354
355	Rubber products	2335	2286	2926	...	...	455	372	713	...	...	355
356	Plastic products n.e.c.	5967	5994	7837	...	...	2083	1765	2356	...	...	356
361	Pottery,china etc	-	-	-	...	...	-	-	-	...	...	361
362	Glass and products	-	-	-	...	...	-	-	-	...	...	362
369	Non-metal products n.e.c	13870	15787	[22008]	...	...	4843	4710	[7799]	...	...	369
371	Iron and steel	-	-		...	...	-	-		...	...	371
372	Non-ferrous metals	-	-	-	...	...	-	-	-	...	...	372
381	Metal products	23979	23688	23421	...	...	5233	5132	5708	...	...	381
382	Machinery n.e.c.	1546	1509	1102	...	...	600	492	347	...	...	382
3825	Office,computing etc.	-	-	-	...	...	-	-	-	...	...	3825
383	Electrical machinery	1178	1799	2842	...	...	339	401	633	...	...	383
3832	Radio,television etc.	-	-	-	...	...	-	-	-	...	...	3832
384	Transport equipment	6651	9153	6776	...	...	f/ 1979	2591	3097	...	...	384
3841	Shipbuilding, repair.	4222	[9153]	3792	...	...	f/ 1298	[2591]	1806	...	...	3841
3843	Motor vehicles	2429		2984	...	...	681		1291	...	...	3843
385	Professional goods	-	-	-	...	...	-	-	-	...	...	385
390	Other industries	2091	2516	2945	...	...	503	522	829	...	...	390
3	Manufacturing	408395	437381	e/ 380152	...	...	91382	101081	e/ 85079	...	...	3
410	Electricity,gas,steam	...	...	...	...	...	...	...	...	...	...	410
4101	Electricity	...	...	...	...	...	...	...	...	...	...	4101
420	Water works and supply	...	...	...	...	...	...	...	...	...	...	420
4	Electricity,gas etc	49367	...	e/ 54170	...	...	19978	21966	e/ 27240	...	...	4
2-4	All industry	474618	...	458594	...	...	111978	129165	118791	...	...	2-4

a/ Net of non-industrial costs.
b/ Except for major division 4, private establishments submitting returns only.
c/ Major groups 322 and 323 are included in 321.
d/ Major group 322 is included in 321.
e/ Manufacture of gas (ISIC 410) is included in major group 352.
f/ Value added is less than corresponding wages and salaries due to operating losses.

9. GROSS FIXED CAPITAL FORMATION
TOTAL a/
(THOUSAND DOLLARS)

ISIC	INDUSTRY	1981	1982	1983	1984	1985	ISIC
210	Coal mining	-	-	-	...	...	210
220	Petroleum and gas	-	-	-	...	...	220
230	Metal ore mining	929	504	3490	...	...	230
290	Other mining	-10	343	33	...	...	290
2	Mining, quarrying .	919	847	3523	...	...	2
311/2	Food products	11931	20118	7201	...	...	311/2
313	Beverages	[860	1295	1711]	...	...	313
314	Tobacco				...	...	314
321	Textiles	b/ 231	b/ 526	c/ 408	...	...	321
3211	Spinning,weaving etc..	...	...	...	...	...	3211
322	Wearing apparel	b/	b/	c/	...	...	322
323	Leather and products ...	b/	b/	[11]	...	...	323
324	Footwear	7	17		...	...	324
331	Wood products	1588	2842	3803	...	...	331
332	Furniture, fixtures	242	410	536	...	...	332
341	Paper and products	889	503	377	...	...	341
3411	Pulp,paper etc.	-	-	-	...	...	3411
342	Printing,publishing	594	452	825	...	...	342
351	Industrial chemicals ...	-	-	-	...	...	351
3511	Basic excl fertilizers	-	-	-	...	...	3511
3513	Synthetic resins etc .	-	-	-	...	...	3513
352	Other chemical products.	182	716	d/ 537	...	...	352
3522	Drugs and medicines ..	-	-	-	...	...	3522
353	Petroleum refineries ...	-	-	-	...	...	353
354	Petroleum,coal products.	-	-	-	...	...	354
355	Rubber products	169	67	222	...	...	355
356	Plastic products n.e.c..	241	229	746	...	...	356
361	Pottery,china etc	-	-	-	...	...	361
362	Glass and products	-	-	-	...	...	362
369	Non-metal products n.e.c	1299	2573	[4035]	...	...	369
371	Iron and steel	-	-		...	...	371
372	Non-ferrous metals	-	-	-	...	...	372
381	Metal products	539	314	951	...	...	381
382	Machinery n.e.c.	111	17	39	...	...	382
3825	Office,computing etc..	-	-	-	...	...	3825
383	Electrical machinery ...	13	19	40	...	...	383
3832	Radio,television etc..	-	-	-	...	...	3832
384	Transport equipment	185	314	56	...	...	384
3841	Shipbuilding, repair..	139	[314]	57	...	...	3841
3843	Motor vehicles	46		-1	...	...	3843
385	Professional goods	-	-	-	...	...	385
390	Other industries	121	143	253	...	...	390
3	Manufacturing	19202	30555	d/ 21751	...	...	3
410	Electricity,gas,steam ..	...	...	...	...	...	410
4101	Electricity	...	...	...	...	...	4101
420	Water works and supply .	...	...	...	...	...	420
4	Electricity,gas etc	94267	63335	d/ 51753	...	...	4
2-4	All industry	114388	94737	77027	...	...	2-4

a/ Except for major division 4, private establishments submitting returns only.
b/ Major groups 322 and 323 are included in 321.
c/ Major group 322 is included in 321.
d/ Manufacture of gas (ISIC 410) is included in major group 352.

FINLAND

The information on industrial activity is based on the reply to the United Nations Questionnaire on General Industrial Statistics from the Central Statistical Office of Finland, Helsinki. The concepts, definitions and classification by branches of industry are generally in accordance with United Nations standards.

The estimates are derived from the annual industrial statistics inquiry conducted by the Central Statistical Office. The inquiry is carried out on the basis of a complete enumeration of all establishments with an annual average of 5 or more persons engaged, or the equivalent in terms of a combination of installed power equipment and employment (five kilowatts of installed power equipment is equated to one person engaged). However, in a few branches exceptions are made. For publishing and electric light and power, all establishments are covered irrespective of size; in the case of sawmills, the cut-off limit is the production of less than 100 standards a year on average.

For manufacturing, the coverage of the annual inquiry, in relation to total manufacturing activity, can best be measured by comparing the annual results with those obtained from a special inquiry which is conducted every second year into the activities of units liable to taxation on their turnover, as obtained from the general economic register. For 1980, the results of this inquiry show that the annual inquiry covered 41 per cent of the manufacturing establishments, 97 per cent of all manufacturing employment and 99 per cent of gross output.

The estimates are based on the national classification which follows the present version of ISIC.

The estimates of persons engaged relate to owners working in the establishment and employees. The number of employees is calculated as the number of wage earners averaged over twelve periods of the year and the average number of salaried employees during the year. Operatives are defined as wage earners and cover production workers, workers of industrial auxiliary sections, transport workers and other auxiliary workers.

The estimates of output relate to the gross value of production (excluding indirect taxes and including subsidies) comprising the sales value of goods produced, income from repair work and income from contract work. The value of electricity sold is included and adjustments are made for changes in the value of work in progress during the year. The value of goods shipped in the same condition as received is not included, nor is the value of fixed assets produced by the establishment for its own use. The estimates of value added are derived as the difference between the value of output and the cost of the following inputs: raw materials and semi-finished products, packages and packaging materials, purchased fuel, steam and electricity, lubricants, other auxiliary materials and accessories, and repair and contract work performed by other establishments.

The estimates of gross fixed capital formation relate to the acquisition of new and used fixed assets less sales, and improvements of a capital nature. Progress payments are included and also fixed capital formation in establishments not yet in operation, which is classified according to the probable future activity of the establishment.

The indexes of industrial production are compiled by the Central Statistical Office and provided in response to the United Nations Questionnaire on Indexes of Industrial Production. In principle, the indexes cover all establishments with 5 or more persons engaged.

Related national publications:
<u>Teollisuustilasto, Osa I</u> (Industrial Statistics, Volume I) (annual); <u>Tilastotiedotus TE. Teollisuustilasto, ennakkotietoja</u> (Statistical Report TE. Industrial Statistics, preliminary data); <u>Suomen Tilastollinen Vuosikirja</u> (Statistical Yearbook of Finland); <u>Tilastokatsauksia</u> (Bulletin of Statistics)(monthly), all published by the Central Statistical Office of Finland, Helsinki.

ISIC	INDUSTRY	1. NUMBER OF ESTABLISHMENTS a/ (NUMBER) 1981	1982	1983	1984	1985	2. AVERAGE NUMBER OF PERSONS ENGAGED a/ (THOUSANDS) 1981	1982	1983	1984	*1985	ISIC
210	Coal mining	-	-	-	-	...	-	-	-	-	-	210
220	Petroleum and gas	-	-	-	-	...	-	-	-	-	-	220
230	Metal ore mining	13	13	12	12	...	4.6	4.3	4.2	3.8	3.7	230
290	Other mining	97	101	102	102	...	3.0	3.4	3.2	3.1	3.1	290
2	Mining, quarrying .	110	114	114	114	...	7.6	7.7	7.4	6.9	6.8	2
311/2	Food products	1065	1069	1055	1025	...	54.2	53.5	53.1	52.3	51.8	311/2
313	Beverages	27	27	27	27	...	5.6	5.4	5.2	5.1	5.0	313
314	Tobacco	4	4	4	4	...	1.7	1.4	1.3	1.3	1.3	314
321	Textiles	286	304	303	295	...	22.2	20.8	18.9	17.5	16.0	321
3211	Spinning,weaving etc..	75	72	73	69	...	8.7	8.0	7.3	6.7	5.8	3211
322	Wearing apparel	461	459	441	440	...	33.1	31.9	31.0	30.9	29.6	322
323	Leather and products ...	76	79	80	80	...	2.8	2.7	2.7	2.7	2.6	323
324	Footwear	107	113	104	93	...	8.2	8.1	7.5	7.2	7.4	324
331	Wood products	763	787	760	739	...	45.0	40.4	39.4	38.3	36.6	331
332	Furniture, fixtures	357	388	381	375	...	13.4	13.4	13.2	12.7	12.1	332
341	Paper and products	196	191	194	196	...	50.2	47.0	45.1	44.6	43.7	341
3411	Pulp,paper etc.	117	113	110	112	...	40.6	38.5	36.0	35.1	33.7	3411
342	Printing,publishing	729	776	767	768	...	36.9	37.4	37.6	38.8	39.1	342
351	Industrial chemicals ...	150	158	165	163	...	14.4	14.1	14.6	14.3	14.1	351
3511	Basic excl fertilizers	62	62	67	68	...	5.1	5.0	5.3	5.6	5.3	3511
3513	Synthetic resins etc .	75	83	86	83	...	7.2	7.1	7.2	6.7	6.5	3513
352	Other chemical products.	115	115	111	104	...	10.6	10.4	10.4	10.5	10.6	352
3522	Drugs and medicines ..	18	16	16	16	...	2.9	2.9	3.2	3.6	3.5	3522
353	Petroleum refineries ...	2	2	2	2	...	2.6	2.7	2.7	2.9	2.7	353
354	Petroleum,coal products.	24	26	28	26	...	0.9	1.0	1.0	0.9	0.9	354
355	Rubber products	18	18	18	18	...	4.8	4.6	4.6	4.3	4.0	355
356	Plastic products n.e.c..	148	153	156	155	...	6.8	7.1	6.9	6.9	7.7	356
361	Pottery,china etc	10	11	13	13	...	1.4	1.5	1.5	1.5	1.4	361
362	Glass and products	46	50	50	49	...	3.9	3.8	3.7	3.4	3.2	362
369	Non-metal products n.e.c	366	373	384	385	...	15.9	16.0	16.4	16.5	16.5	369
371	Iron and steel	58	59	57	59	...	14.8	14.0	13.6	13.6	13.6	371
372	Non-ferrous metals	30	30	30	31	...	5.2	5.1	5.1	5.0	4.9	372
381	Metal products	648	831	808	840	...	31.7	33.9	35.4	34.5	34.2	381
382	Machinery n.e.c.	718	792	810	806	...	66.3	65.7	61.2	60.2	59.4	382
3825	Office,computing etc..	50	56	58	57	...	2.7	2.9	3.5	3.8	4.1	3825
383	Electrical machinery ...	206	228	223	230	...	31.1	30.1	29.4	29.8	31.7	383
3832	Radio,television etc..	55	53	56	58	...	9.1	8.8	9.0	9.9	11.2	3832
384	Transport equipment	283	308	316	294	...	40.7	41.8	42.4	40.6	40.0	384
3841	Shipbuilding, repair..	101	109	112	108	...	22.9	23.5	24.3	23.1	22.1	3841
3843	Motor vehicles	131	146	149	138	...	9.9	10.0	9.5	9.4	9.6	3843
385	Professional goods	72	83	92	88	...	4.5	4.7	4.6	5.0	5.3	385
390	Other industries	117	123	114	107	...	4.9	5.1	4.7	5.2	4.9	390
3	Manufacturing	7082	7557	7493	7412	...	533.8	523.6	513.2	506.5	500.3	3
410	Electricity,gas,steam ..	449	437	441	438	...	24.4	25.6	25.5	25.7	25.7	410
4101	Electricity	347	377	378	374	...	22.2	25.0	24.9	25.0	25.1	4101
420	Water works and supply .	86	86	86	85	...	2.4	2.4	2.4	2.6	2.4	420
4	Electricity,gas etc	535	523	527	523	...	26.8	28.0	27.9	28.3	28.1	4
2-4	All industry	7727	8194	8134	8049	...	568.2	559.3	548.5	541.7	535.2	2-4

a/ Establishments with 5 or more persons engaged.

ISIC	INDUSTRY	3. AVERAGE NUMBER OF EMPLOYEES a/ (THOUSANDS) 1981	1982	1983	1984	*1985	4. WAGES AND SALARIES OF EMPLOYEES a/ (MILLION MARKS) 1981	1982	1983	1984	*1985	ISIC
210	Coal mining	-	-	-	-	-	-	-	-	-	-	210
220	Petroleum and gas	-	-	-	-	-	-	-	-	-	-	220
230	Metal ore mining	4.6	4.3	4.2	3.8	3.7	295	313	325	333	349	230
290	Other mining	3.0	3.4	3.1	3.1	3.0	146	178	193	199	223	290
2	Mining, quarrying .	7.6	7.7	7.3	6.9	6.7	441	491	518	532	572	2
311/2	Food products	53.5	52.9	52.4	51.7	51.2	2562	2797	3022	3257	3502	311/2
313	Beverages	5.6	5.4	5.2	5.1	5.0	304	320	342	354	385	313
314	Tobacco	1.7	1.4	1.3	1.3	1.3	92	91	91	101	108	314
321	Textiles	22.1	20.6	18.7	17.3	15.8	893	933	949	961	943	321
3211	Spinning,weaving etc..	8.7	8.0	7.2	6.6	5.7	364	375	389	396	372	3211
322	Wearing apparel	32.9	31.7	30.8	30.7	29.4	1194	1298	1349	1438	1536	322
323	Leather and products ...	2.7	2.6	2.6	2.6	2.5	104	110	123	131	136	323
324	Footwear	8.1	8.1	7.4	7.2	7.4	306	339	333	354	392	324
331	Wood products	44.4	39.8	38.8	37.7	36.0	1917	1869	2028	2178	2214	331
332	Furniture, fixtures	13.1	13.1	12.9	12.4	11.8	548	610	646	686	707	332
341	Paper and products	50.2	47.0	45.1	44.5	43.7	3097	3191	3363	3717	3909	341
3411	Pulp,paper etc.	40.6	38.5	36.0	35.1	33.7	2561	2676	2754	3023	3117	3411
342	Printing,publishing	36.6	37.2	37.3	38.6	38.9	2028	2289	2557	2916	3197	342
351	Industrial chemicals ...	14.3	14.1	14.6	14.3	14.1	819	886	1008	1103	1185	351
3511	Basic excl fertilizers	5.1	5.0	5.3	5.6	5.3	316	337	392	451	470	3511
3513	Synthetic resins etc .	7.2	7.1	7.2	6.7	6.5	381	420	464	485	516	3513
352	Other chemical products.	10.6	10.4	10.4	10.5	10.6	556	600	671	730	811	352
3522	Drugs and medicines ..	2.9	2.9	3.2	3.6	3.5	150	164	197	247	274	3522
353	Petroleum refineries ...	2.6	2.7	2.7	2.9	2.7	184	204	221	267	272	353
354	Petroleum,coal products.	0.9	1.0	1.0	0.9	0.9	47	54	63	63	69	354
355	Rubber products	4.8	4.6	4.6	4.3	4.0	214	236	252	266	273	355
356	Plastic products n.e.c..	6.8	7.0	6.8	6.8	7.7	320	368	400	432	514	356
361	Pottery,china etc	1.4	1.5	1.5	1.5	1.4	70	77	88	93	95	361
362	Glass and products	3.9	3.8	3.7	3.4	3.2	203	208	221	231	230	362
369	Non-metal products n.e.c	15.7	15.8	16.3	16.4	16.3	791	879	995	1072	1163	369
371	Iron and steel	14.8	14.0	13.6	13.6	13.6	851	898	977	1062	1170	371
372	Non-ferrous metals	5.2	5.1	5.1	5.0	4.9	305	339	361	391	414	372
381	Metal products	31.3	33.4	34.9	34.1	33.8	1555	1835	2090	2202	2385	381
382	Machinery n.e.c.	66.0	65.4	60.8	60.0	59.2	3621	3955	4024	4426	4894	382
3825	Office,computing etc..	2.7	2.9	3.5	3.8	4.1	177	216	277	323	413	3825
383	Electrical machinery ...	31.1	30.0	29.4	29.7	31.7	1616	1737	1843	2007	2349	383
3832	Radio,television etc..	9.1	8.8	9.0	9.9	11.1	460	502	556	674	828	3832
384	Transport equipment	40.5	41.5	42.2	40.4	39.8	2244	2540	2816	2920	3059	384
3841	Shipbuilding, repair..	22.8	23.5	24.3	23.1	22.1	1315	1509	1665	1700	1715	3841
3843	Motor vehicles	9.8	9.9	9.4	9.3	9.5	501	552	583	633	712	3843
385	Professional goods	4.5	4.6	4.5	4.9	5.3	237	273	287	353	398	385
390	Other industries	4.8	5.1	4.7	4.9	4.8	205	232	258	279	314	390
3	Manufacturing	530.1	519.8	509.3	502.7	497.0	26883	29168	31378	33990	36624	3
410	Electricity,gas,steam ..	24.4	25.6	25.5	25.7	25.7	1410	1624	1796	2022	2196	410
4101	Electricity	22.2	25.0	24.9	25.0	25.1	1267	1588	1756	1977	2146	4101
420	Water works and supply .	2.4	2.4	2.4	2.6	2.4	138	146	157	179	188	420
4	Electricity,gas etc	26.8	28.0	27.9	28.3	28.1	1548	1770	1953	2201	2384	4
2-4	All industry	564.5	555.5	544.5	537.9	531.8	28872	31429	33849	36723	39580	2-4

a/ Establishments with 5 or more persons engaged.

ISIC	INDUSTRY	5. SUPPLEMENTS TO WAGES AND SALARIES a/ (MILLION MARKS)					6. AVERAGE NUMBER OF OPERATIVES a/ (THOUSANDS)					ISIC
		1981	1982	1983	1984	*1985	1981	1982	1983	1984	*1985	
210	Coal mining	-	-	-	-	-	-	-	-	-	-	210
220	Petroleum and gas	-	-	-	-	-	-	-	-	-	-	220
230	Metal ore mining	66	69	68	71	75	3.3	3.1	2.9	2.7	2.6	230
290	Other mining	37	43	43	42	47	2.3	2.5	2.4	2.2	2.1	290
2	Mining, quarrying .	103	112	111	113	122	5.6	5.6	5.3	4.9	4.7	2
311/2	Food products	617	658	674	727	785	40.9	40.1	39.8	39.0	38.3	311/2
313	Beverages	63	67	71	73	80	3.8	3.7	3.5	3.4	3.3	313
314	Tobacco	23	20	21	23	25	1.2	0.9	0.8	0.8	0.7	314
321	Textiles	207	218	205	213	209	18.1	16.9	15.2	14.0	12.7	321
3211	Spinning,weaving etc..	84	89	84	87	82	7.1	6.5	5.9	5.3	4.6	3211
322	Wearing apparel	276	297	301	316	338	28.1	26.9	26.1	25.9	25.0	322
323	Leather and products ...	25	26	27	28	29	2.3	2.2	2.2	2.2	2.1	323
324	Footwear	79	92	82	88	98	7.2	7.1	6.5	6.4	6.6	324
331	Wood products	494	475	493	532	543	38.1	33.7	32.6	31.6	29.9	331
332	Furniture, fixtures	131	148	146	161	166	10.7	10.6	10.5	10.0	9.5	332
341	Paper and products	749	768	778	864	907	38.6	35.9	34.5	34.1	33.2	341
3411	Pulp,paper etc.	623	647	643	714	632	30.8	29.2	27.3	26.6	25.4	3411
342	Printing,publishing	446	499	539	614	675	24.0	24.0	23.9	24.6	24.5	342
351	Industrial chemicals ...	195	204	224	244	261	9.6	9.3	9.6	9.3	9.0	351
3511	Basic excl fertilizers	75	78	88	100	104	3.4	3.3	3.4	3.5	3.3	3511
3513	Synthetic resins etc .	91	94	102	108	114	5.1	5.0	5.0	4.7	4.5	3513
352	Other chemical products.	140	140	150	164	182	5.7	5.4	5.3	5.3	5.2	352
3522	Drugs and medicines ..	37	40	47	60	67	1.2	1.2	1.2	1.3	1.3	3522
353	Petroleum refineries ...	36	45	49	52	53	1.4	1.4	1.4	1.3	1.3	353
354	Petroleum,coal products.	11	13	15	17	19	0.6	0.6	0.6	0.6	0.6	354
355	Rubber products	50	56	55	58	60	3.9	3.7	3.5	3.4	3.1	355
356	Plastic products n.e.c..	77	89	89	101	120	5.3	5.3	5.2	5.2	5.8	356
361	Pottery,china etc	14	17	18	19	19	1.1	1.2	1.2	1.1	1.1	361
362	Glass and products	47	49	52	57	57	3.1	3.0	2.9	2.7	2.5	362
369	Non-metal products n.e.c	198	216	229	247	267	12.0	12.1	12.6	12.5	12.3	369
371	Iron and steel	203	212	232	244	268	10.9	10.2	9.8	9.8	9.8	371
372	Non-ferrous metals	75	80	81	87	92	3.8	3.7	3.7	3.6	3.5	372
381	Metal products	367	427	476	505	545	24.5	26.0	26.5	25.8	25.5	381
382	Machinery n.e.c.	842	891	891	980	1088	46.2	45.3	41.2	40.1	38.9	382
3825	Office,computing etc..	40	49	58	70	90	1.4	1.6	1.6	1.8	1.7	3825
383	Electrical machinery ...	359	390	402	450	527	20.7	19.9	19.0	19.2	20.1	383
3832	Radio,television etc..	102	108	117	138	170	5.8	5.4	5.3	5.9	6.4	3832
384	Transport equipment	465	479	520	546	573	30.1	31.1	31.6	29.8	28.9	384
3841	Shipbuilding, repair..	247	241	251	259	262	16.7	17.4	17.9	16.6	15.5	3841
3843	Motor vehicles	109	116	121	132	148	7.4	7.5	7.3	7.1	7.3	3843
385	Professional goods	56	60	66	83	94	2.7	2.7	2.3	2.6	2.8	385
390	Other industries	48	52	53	59	76	3.9	4.1	4.1	4.2	3.9	390
3	Manufacturing	6293	6688	6939	7552	8156	398.5	387.0	376.1	368.5	360.1	3
410	Electricity,gas,steam ..	337	378	415	461	502	14.5	15.4	15.2	15.2	15.0	410
4101	Electricity	303	370	407	452	493	12.8	14.9	14.8	14.7	14.6	4101
420	Water works and supply .	29	33	34	40	39	1.6	1.5	1.5	1.7	1.6	420
4	Electricity,gas etc	366	411	449	501	541	16.1	16.9	16.7	16.9	16.6	4
2-4	All industry	6762	7211	7499	8166	8819	420.2	409.5	398.1	390.3	381.4	2-4

a/ Establishments with 5 or more persons engaged.

ISIC	INDUSTRY	7. WAGES AND SALARIES OF OPERATIVES a/ (MILLION MARKS)					8. HOURS WORKED BY OPERATIVES a/ (MILLIONS)					ISIC
		1981	1982	1983	1984	*1985	1981	1982	1983	1984	*1985	
210	Coal mining	-	-	-	-	-	-	-	-	-	-	210
220	Petroleum and gas	-	-	-	-	-	-	-	-	-	-	220
230	Metal ore mining	191	200	206	214	224	5.5	5.2	4.8	4.5	4.3	230
290	Other mining	102	125	130	133	149	4.1	4.6	4.3	3.8	3.9	290
2	Mining, quarrying .	293	325	336	347	373	9.6	9.8	9.1	8.3	8.2	2
311/2	Food products	1760	1905	2051	2197	2316	73.1	71.5	69.8	68.2	67.1	311/2
313	Beverages	182	189	201	203	220	6.7	6.3	6.0	5.9	5.8	313
314	Tobacco	55	50	46	48	49	2.1	1.6	1.4	1.3	1.2	314
321	Textiles	645	674	681	688	671	30.5	28.3	25.0	23.3	21.3	321
3211	Spinning,weaving etc..	263	270	283	284	263	11.9	10.9	9.6	8.9	7.6	3211
322	Wearing apparel	913	990	1026	1085	1174	48.0	45.1	43.5	42.3	40.8	322
323	Leather and products ...	78	82	91	98	101	3.8	3.6	3.6	3.6	3.5	323
324	Footwear	249	272	264	283	317	12.4	12.0	10.9	10.8	11.1	324
331	Wood products	1525	1453	1558	1673	1664	63.7	55.1	54.5	52.9	49.4	331
332	Furniture, fixtures	404	445	477	508	518	18.7	18.7	18.2	17.5	16.3	332
341	Paper and products	2207	2253	2378	2650	2756	64.6	58.8	56.8	57.2	54.3	341
3411	Pulp,paper etc.	1807	1877	1934	2143	2187	51.4	47.6	44.7	44.5	41.4	3411
342	Printing,publishing	1115	1226	1353	1539	1653	38.6	38.1	37.6	38.1	37.9	342
351	Industrial chemicals ...	485	518	585	631	668	16.7	16.0	16.4	15.9	15.3	351
3511	Basic excl fertilizers	192	203	230	259	264	6.0	5.7	5.9	5.9	5.5	3511
3513	Synthetic resins etc .	235	256	286	297	312	8.8	8.5	8.6	8.2	7.8	3513
352	Other chemical products.	234	243	264	283	311	10.0	9.3	9.1	9.0	9.0	352
3522	Drugs and medicines ..	46	48	54	66	76	2.1	2.0	2.1	2.2	2.3	3522
353	Petroleum refineries ...	82	93	99	108	111	2.6	2.8	2.6	2.5	2.3	353
354	Petroleum,coal products.	26	29	34	33	36	1.1	1.1	1.1	1.0	1.0	354
355	Rubber products	153	168	176	184	190	6.3	5.9	5.6	5.4	5.1	355
356	Plastic products n.e.c..	217	240	267	284	331	9.2	9.1	9.0	9.0	9.9	356
361	Pottery,china etc	50	54	61	64	64	1.9	2.0	2.0	1.8	1.7	361
362	Glass and products	147	150	158	161	161	5.3	5.1	4.9	4.6	4.3	362
369	Non-metal products n.e.c	546	607	692	729	779	21.4	21.7	22.0	21.6	20.9	369
371	Iron and steel	570	598	650	707	774	18.3	17.2	16.4	16.8	16.6	371
372	Non-ferrous metals	207	229	245	265	279	6.3	6.4	6.2	6.1	6.0	372
381	Metal products	1105	1299	1324	1491	1615	42.2	44.3	45.1	43.5	43.3	381
382	Machinery n.e.c.	2261	2423	2388	2623	2848	80.7	77.5	70.2	69.2	68.8	382
3825	Office,computing etc..	88	109	111	135	145	3.0	3.0	2.9	3.2	3.0	3825
383	Electrical machinery ...	906	977	1002	1086	1225	35.4	34.5	32.4	32.9	34.4	383
3832	Radio,television etc..	236	241	265	313	354	9.8	9.0	9.0	10.1	10.8	3832
384	Transport equipment	1539	1749	1931	1952	2006	51.4	52.9	52.8	49.6	46.8	384
3841	Shipbuilding, repair..	886	1024	1116	1095	1076	28.4	29.6	29.5	27.4	24.6	3841
3843	Motor vehicles	345	382	416	445	494	12.7	12.6	12.6	12.2	12.7	3843
385	Professional goods	119	131	133	152	170	4.6	4.6	4.3	4.6	4.8	385
390	Other industries	146	165	181	201	207	6.5	6.7	6.9	6.9	7.1	390
3	Manufacturing	17926	19212	20316	21926	23214	682.1	656.2	634.3	621.5	606.0	3
410	Electricity,gas,steam ..	756	888	961	1072	1148	25.3	26.5	26.2	26.3	25.5	410
4101	Electricity	654	864	935	1044	1115	22.4	25.8	25.5	25.5	24.8	4101
420	Water works and supply .	88	90	99	112	116	2.7	2.6	2.6	2.6	2.5	420
4	Electricity,gas etc	844	978	1060	1184	1264	28.0	29.1	28.8	28.9	28.0	4
2-4	All industry	19063	20515	21712	23457	24851	719.7	695.1	672.2	658.7	642.2	2-4

a/ Establishments with 5 or more persons engaged.

ISIC	INDUSTRY	9. QUANTITY OF ELECTRICITY CONSUMED a/ (MILLION KWH)					10. OUTPUT IN FACTOR VALUES a/ (BILLION MARKS)					ISIC
		1981	1982	1983	1984	*1985	1981	1982	1983	1984	*1985	
210	Coal mining	-	-	-	-	-	-	-	-	-	-	210
220	Petroleum and gas	-	-	-	-	-	-	-	-	-	-	220
230	Metal ore mining	494	471	441	421	420	0.89	0.84	0.92	1.05	1.12	230
290	Other mining	197	211	263	274	295	0.71	1.02	1.02	1.05	1.20	290
2	Mining, quarrying .	691	682	704	695	715	1.60	1.86	1.94	2.10	2.32	2
311/2	Food products	827	861	913	878	908	28.05	30.97	33.63	36.04	37.88	311/2
313	Beverages	94	97	97	98	101	1.98	2.13	2.23	2.49	2.75	313
314	Tobacco	12	12	12	15	15	0.56	0.49	0.59	0.64	0.68	314
321	Textiles	262	261	248	252	238	3.89	3.91	3.94	4.19	4.04	321
3211	Spinning,weaving etc..	156	154	148	147	137	1.64	1.60	1.66	1.76	1.60	3211
322	Wearing apparel	87	92	88	83	84	4.29	4.39	4.33	4.69	5.10	322
323	Leather and products ...	18	18	23	23	24	0.46	0.50	0.58	0.71	0.68	323
324	Footwear	27	32	27	29	29	1.30	1.34	1.23	1.41	1.52	324
331	Wood products	971	889	1130	935	944	10.53	9.86	11.83	12.84	12.19	331
332	Furniture, fixtures	103	106	120	108	116	2.08	2.30	2.48	2.56	2.58	332
341	Paper and products	11770	11300	12196	13748	13191	29.51	28.83	31.74	38.95	38.77	341
3411	Pulp,paper etc.	11577	11129	12005	13537	12897	25.18	25.12	27.46	33.90	33.52	3411
342	Printing,publishing	177	182	204	200	213	8.36	9.31	10.50	11.87	12.96	342
351	Industrial chemicals ...	2587	2281	2515	2738	2867	7.94	8.09	9.20	10.58	10.98	351
3511	Basic excl fertilizers	2055	1740	1926	2089	2208	3.53	3.55	3.89	4.73	4.92	3511
3513	Synthetic resins etc .	435	452	495	514	516	2.86	2.94	3.42	3.69	3.64	3513
352	Other chemical products.	81	88	94	98	110	3.46	3.30	3.60	3.87	4.19	352
3522	Drugs and medicines ..	28	30	35	37	42	0.94	0.97	1.08	1.23	1.42	3522
353	Petroleum refineries ...	383	341	390	390	434	13.92	13.05	14.77	14.88	15.63	353
354	Petroleum,coal products.	18	23	21	19	18	0.52	0.74	0.82	0.88	0.86	354
355	Rubber products	66	68	69	69	74	0.76	0.83	0.84	0.87	0.94	355
356	Plastic products n.e.c..	129	132	156	153	175	1.53	1.63	1.83	1.97	2.30	356
361	Pottery,china etc	18	19	19	17	18	0.25	0.29	0.33	0.32	0.31	361
362	Glass and products	105	97	97	97	88	0.78	0.79	0.84	0.85	0.88	362
369	Non-metal products n.e.c	489	531	595	571	522	3.82	4.62	5.19	4.98	5.21	369
371	Iron and steel	1362	1312	1390	1433	1788	7.11	8.33	8.68	9.91	10.61	371
372	Non-ferrous metals	985	1038	1127	1150	918	3.47	3.66	4.62	5.32	5.40	372
381	Metal products	269	326	355	317	355	6.32	7.74	8.48	8.67	9.40	381
382	Machinery n.e.c.	555	551	495	481	525	13.57	14.67	14.16	16.19	18.90	382
3825	Office,computing etc..	7	9	10	12	19	0.54	0.68	0.79	1.16	1.35	3825
383	Electrical machinery ...	295	257	270	284	348	6.01	6.34	6.93	7.57	9.47	383
3832	Radio,television etc..	34	40	50	59	71	1.73	2.05	2.45	2.86	3.95	3832
384	Transport equipment	337	330	365	359	353	8.22	10.32	11.14	11.27	11.94	384
3841	Shipbuilding, repair..	214	196	227	231	224	4.74	6.38	6.79	6.67	6.72	3841
3843	Motor vehicles	66	72	73	67	58	2.32	2.56	2.91	3.12	3.81	3843
385	Professional goods	21	20	22	23	25	0.84	0.95	1.05	1.35	1.44	385
390	Other industries	26	29	32	34	30	0.79	0.88	0.93	1.04	1.18	390
3	Manufacturing	22074	21293	23070	24602	24511	170.32	180.26	196.49	216.91	228.79	3
410	Electricity,gas,steam ..	2455	2548	2310	2673	3047	20.36	22.86	23.61	25.13	28.68	410
4101	Electricity	1874	1941	2245	2606	2971	18.01	22.49	23.16	24.64	28.09	4101
420	Water works and supply .	143	143	140	141	143	0.45	0.49	0.56	0.61	0.67	420
4	Electricity,gas etc	2598	2691	2450	2814	3190	20.81	23.35	24.17	25.74	29.35	4
2-4	All industry	25363	24666	26224	28111	28416	192.73	205.47	222.60	244.75	260.46	2-4

a/ Establishments with 5 or more persons engaged.

ISIC	INDUSTRY	11. VALUE ADDED IN FACTOR VALUES a/ (BILLION MARKS) 1981	1982	1983	1984	*1985	12. GROSS FIXED CAPITAL FORMATION TOTAL a/ (MILLION MARKS) 1981	1982	1983	1984	1985	ISIC
210	Coal mining	-	-	-	-	-	-	-	-	-	...	210
220	Petroleum and gas	-	-	-	-	-	-	-	-	-	...	220
230	Metal ore mining	0.53	0.47	0.56	0.71	0.76	50	92	28	67	...	230
290	Other mining	0.40	0.61	0.61	0.63	0.74	164	232	177	93	...	290
2	Mining, quarrying .	0.93	1.08	1.17	1.34	1.50	214	324	205	160	...	2
311/2	Food products	6.18	6.93	7.46	8.34	8.86	945	1320	1369	1068	...	311/2
313	Beverages	0.92	1.03	1.12	1.26	1.43	106	108	91	101	...	313
314	Tobacco	0.24	0.23	0.31	0.33	0.36	26	26	28	17	...	314
321	Textiles	1.88	1.84	1.82	1.90	1.87	201	276	148	134	...	321
3211	Spinning,weaving etc..	0.71	0.62	0.67	0.70	0.62	64	131	59	47	...	3211
322	Wearing apparel	2.24	2.32	2.28	2.43	2.81	89	133	151	130	...	322
323	Leather and products ...	0.20	0.19	0.21	0.25	0.25	14	29	30	16	...	323
324	Footwear	0.58	0.65	0.57	0.62	0.65	67	51	33	59	...	324
331	Wood products	3.65	3.19	4.26	4.67	3.95	792	549	578	514	...	331
332	Furniture, fixtures	1.12	1.21	1.28	1.31	1.33	90	156	204	216	...	332
341	Paper and products	8.47	7.71	8.99	11.96	11.00	2566	2843	2135	2836	...	341
3411	Pulp,paper etc.	6.71	6.09	7.27	9.89	8.98	2386	2695	1914	2514	...	3411
342	Printing,publishing	4.71	5.29	6.10	6.88	7.55	473	493	875	913	...	342
351	Industrial chemicals ...	2.11	2.15	2.71	3.30	3.40	851	633	605	803	...	351
3511	Basic excl fertilizers	0.78	0.80	0.94	1.40	1.37	496	322	288	490	...	3511
3513	Synthetic resins etc .	0.86	0.87	1.11	1.20	1.26	261	268	186	174	...	3513
352	Other chemical products.	1.68	1.72	1.88	2.15	2.28	315	388	464	315	...	352
3522	Drugs and medicines ..	0.58	0.61	0.67	0.79	0.89	137	203	245	171	...	3522
353	Petroleum refineries ...	1.90	1.80	2.15	1.97	2.38	186	297	140	331	...	353
354	Petroleum,coal products.	0.18	0.25	0.21	0.30	0.29	14	32	22	17	...	354
355	Rubber products	0.43	0.46	0.46	0.48	0.51	47	45	27	68	...	355
356	Plastic products n.e.c..	0.75	0.82	0.90	0.95	1.12	122	86	156	146	...	356
361	Pottery,china etc	0.19	0.23	0.26	0.25	0.24	16	15	13	16	...	361
362	Glass and products	0.39	0.41	0.43	0.45	0.48	44	41	26	55	...	362
369	Non-metal products n.e.c	1.82	2.30	2.68	2.55	2.68	346	541	440	747	...	369
371	Iron and steel	1.65	2.00	2.44	2.85	2.82	480	320	296	356	...	371
372	Non-ferrous metals	0.53	0.45	0.46	0.69	0.70	204	203	128	90	...	372
381	Metal products	3.22	4.00	4.51	4.51	4.86	344	461	502	517	...	381
382	Machinery n.e.c.	6.63	7.65	7.48	8.77	10.00	708	878	698	766	...	382
3825	Office,computing etc..	0.38	0.48	0.54	0.77	0.90	25	26	48	104	...	3825
383	Electrical machinery ...	3.00	3.50	3.79	4.02	4.95	406	382	455	615	...	383
3832	Radio,television etc..	0.78	1.09	1.27	1.36	2.00	83	95	178	336	...	3832
384	Transport equipment	3.50	4.47	4.73	4.98	5.03	352	515	664	618	...	384
3841	Shipbuilding, repair..	1.99	2.76	2.85	2.95	2.86	168	359	435	293	...	3841
3843	Motor vehicles	1.04	1.00	1.11	1.23	1.44	106	97	143	102	...	3843
385	Professional goods	0.57	0.62	0.72	0.97	0.94	49	86	72	88	...	385
390	Other industries	0.44	0.50	0.51	0.63	0.70	30	43	42	45	...	390
3	Manufacturing	59.18	63.92	70.72	79.77	83.44	9883	10950	10392	11597	...	3
410	Electricity,gas,steam ..	6.72	8.01	8.46	8.92	9.55	2171	3406	3191	3096	...	410
4101	Electricity	6.57	7.92	8.34	8.79	9.40	1812	3309	2951	2791	...	4101
420	Water works and supply .	0.34	0.38	0.45	0.47	0.52	242	256	238	253	...	420
4	Electricity,gas etc	7.06	8.39	8.91	9.39	10.07	2413	3662	3429	3349	...	4
2-4	All industry	67.17	73.39	80.80	90.50	95.01	12510	14936	14026	15106	...	2-4

a/ Establishments with 5 or more persons engaged.

ISIC	INDUSTRY	13. GROSS FIXED CAPITAL FORMATION MACHINERY AND EQUIPMENT a/ (MILLION MARKS) 1981	1982	1983	1984	1985	14. VALUE OF STOCKS AT END OF PERIOD TOTAL a/ (MILLION MARKS) 1981	1982	1983	1984	1985	ISIC
210	Coal mining	-	-	-	-	...	-	-	-	-	...	210
220	Petroleum and gas	-	-	-	-	...	-	-	-	-	...	220
230	Metal ore mining	37	56	8	40	...	866	943	983	1142	...	230
290	Other mining	110	166	136	75	...	110	290	282	309	...	290
2	Mining, quarrying .	147	222	144	115	...	976	1233	1265	1451	...	2
311/2	Food products	657	866	811	808	...	3062	3610	3628	4301	...	311/2
313	Beverages	76	84	59	75	...	452	523	576	548	...	313
314	Tobacco	23	24	20	20	...	148	221	181	178	...	314
321	Textiles	158	198	147	110	...	1114	1209	1265	1212	...	321
3211	Spinning,weaving etc..	61	103	61	30	...	478	537	549	769	...	3211
322	Wearing apparel	67	82	79	92	...	946	998	1021	1163	...	322
323	Leather and products ...	9	21	20	9	...	134	136	186	211	...	323
324	Footwear	38	41	24	38	...	307	328	317	342	...	324
331	Wood products	508	387	406	382	...	3247	3571	3207	3613	...	331
332	Furniture, fixtures	67	95	107	101	...	430	464	543	549	...	332
341	Paper and products	2180	2286	1935	2249	...	2636	3258	3229	3871	...	341
3411	Pulp,paper etc.	2027	2146	1764	1990	...	2244	2857	2758	3269	...	3411
342	Printing,publishing	390	337	599	655	...	859	898	968	1072	...	342
351	Industrial chemicals ...	745	492	488	658	...	1268	1205	1367	1516	...	351
3511	Basic excl fertilizers	449	267	242	411	...	452	441	551	656	...	3511
3513	Synthetic resins etc .	219	197	143	144	...	571	543	602	595	...	3513
352	Other chemical products.	187	182	237	203	...	817	900	966	967	...	352
3522	Drugs and medicines ..	76	93	121	107	...	284	326	330	342	...	3522
353	Petroleum refineries ...	186	240	82	251	...	4605	5155	5278	4740	...	353
354	Petroleum,coal products.	9	20	12	13	...	148	226	258	239	...	354
355	Rubber products	32	37	26	52	...	253	291	318	284	...	355
356	Plastic products n.e.c..	87	72	109	107	...	252	247	331	311	...	356
361	Pottery,china etc	12	10	7	10	...	90	119	129	122	...	361
362	Glass and products	38	27	17	43	...	202	186	196	313	...	362
369	Non-metal products n.e.c	239	409	314	591	...	582	604	747	753	...	369
371	Iron and steel	357	259	262	297	...	955	1188	1257	1373	...	371
372	Non-ferrous metals	148	169	107	82	...	48	46	87	76	...	372
381	Metal products	222	319	340	322	...	1531	1830	2257	2054	...	381
382	Machinery n.e.c.	489	510	467	572	...	4261	4803	4442	4518	...	382
3825	Office,computing etc..	25	25	46	68	...	165	172	268	317	...	3825
383	Electrical machinery ...	338	325	349	441	...	1693	1780	1931	2113	...	383
3832	Radio,television etc..	77	90	124	224	...	558	646	706	874	...	3832
384	Transport equipment	213	224	341	372	...	4967	6486	6425	5709	...	384
3841	Shipbuilding, repair..	106	140	202	156	...	4162	5609	5491	4725	...	3841
3843	Motor vehicles	53	54	70	98	...	498	535	532	563	...	3843
385	Professional goods	29	39	48	63	...	338	433	388	447	...	385
390	Other industries	19	24	30	31	...	279	314	317	347	...	390
3	Manufacturing	7523	7779	7443	8647	...	35624	41029	41815	42942	...	3
410	Electricity,gas,steam ..	875	1654	1541	1549	...	2893	3597	3621	3990	...	410
4101	Electricity	708	1613	1417	1388	...	2452	3581	3608	3976	...	4101
420	Water works and supply .	14	20	19	25	...	12	12	15	14	...	420
4	Electricity,gas etc	889	1674	1560	1574	...	2905	3609	3636	4004	...	4
2-4	All industry	8559	9675	9147	10336	...	39505	45871	46716	48397	...	2-4

a/ Establishments with 5 or more persons engaged.

15. INDEX NUMBERS OF INDUSTRIAL PRODUCTION (1980 = 100)

ISIC	INDUSTRY	1976	1977	1978	1979	1981	1982	1983	1984	1985	a/ RATE	ISIC
210	Coal mining	...	...	...	...	...	...	...	...	...	...	210
220	Petroleum and gas	...	...	...	...	...	...	...	...	...	...	220
230	Metal ore mining	90	98	99	103	106	103	102	106	112	2.5	230
290	Other mining	66	70	77	86	98	133	134	139	154	9.9	290
2	Mining, quarrying .	79	85	89	96	103	115	115	112	108	3.5	2
311/2	Food products	82	82	89	94	104	106	109	109	111	3.4	311/2
313	Beverages	91	84	83	84	100	102	101	106	108	1.9	313
314	Tobacco	91	87	88	98	138	96	96	96	94	0.4	314
321	Textiles	95	92	89	99	94	89	85	84	79	-2.0	321
3211	Spinning,weaving etc..	...	...	...	...	...	...	...	...	...	...	3211
322	Wearing apparel	92	89	90	99	109	108	101	102	107	1.7	322
323	Leather and products ...	84	72	82	89	96	97	103	110	107	2.7	323
324	Footwear	67	63	67	78	113	109	96	104	113	6.0	324
331	Wood products	66	70	76	91	90	82	90	92	89	3.4	331
332	Furniture, fixtures	74	74	79	90	104	110	115	113	109	4.4	332
341	Paper and products	74	73	83	94	101	95	104	114	113	4.8	341
3411	Pulp,paper etc.	...	...	...	...	...	...	...	...	...	...	3411
342	Printing,publishing	85	84	87	95	106	110	116	123	125	4.4	342
351	Industrial chemicals ...	81	75	86	95	97	98	108	114	115	4.0	351
3511	Basic excl fertilizers	...	...	...	...	...	...	...	...	...	...	3511
3513	Synthetic resins etc .	...	...	...	...	...	...	...	...	...	...	3513
352	Other chemical products.	72	74	76	84	112	100	103	108	115	5.3	352
3522	Drugs and medicines ..	...	...	...	...	...	...	...	...	...	...	3522
353	Petroleum refineries ...	94	106	104	114	92	85	92	93	96	0.2	353
354	Petroleum,coal products.	85	90	85	87	100	130	140	144	137	5.4	354
355	Rubber products	75	77	82	93	94	98	96	96	101	3.4	355
356	Plastic products n.e.c..	66	72	88	100	108	115	123	127	144	9.1	356
361	Pottery,china etc	87	76	74	90	102	108	109	103	103	1.9	361
362	Glass and products	72	65	74	78	101	98	97	94	93	2.9	362
369	Non-metal products n.e.c	80	84	81	94	101	113	120	112	114	4.0	369
371	Iron and steel	58	72	89	98	97	100	104	111	116	8.0	371
372	Non-ferrous metals	75	85	84	96	98	110	120	135	134	6.7	372
381	Metal products	71	75	76	88	106	121	129	128	137	7.6	381
382	Machinery n.e.c.	80	80	79	88	114	117	109	120	134	5.9	382
3825	Office,computing etc..	...	...	...	...	...	...	...	...	...	...	3825
383	Electrical machinery ...	84	81	79	85	102	104	108	114	137	5.6	383
3832	Radio,television etc..	...	...	...	...	...	...	...	...	...	...	3832
384	Transport equipment	118	93	84	89	105	119	119	114	112	-0.6	384
3841	Shipbuilding, repair..	...	...	...	...	...	...	...	...	...	...	3841
3843	Motor vehicles	...	...	...	...	...	...	...	...	...	...	3843
385	Professional goods	65	64	78	91	122	131	135	175	182	12.1	385
390	Other industries	76	82	89	94	103	110	108	113	113	4.5	390
3	Manufacturing	80	79	83	92	103	104	107	112	118	4.4	3
410	Electricity,gas,steam ..	74	83	89	96	101	100	104	112	121	5.6	410
4101	Electricity	...	...	...	...	...	...	...	...	...	...	4101
420	Water works and supply .	121	113	109	102	99	99	102	102	104	-1.7	420
4	Electricity,gas etc	75	84	89	96	101	99	104	112	119	5.3	4
2-4	All industry	79	80	84	92	103	104	107	112	116	4.4	2-4

a/ Annual growth rate 1976-1985.

FRANCE

The information on industrial activity is based on the reply to the United Nations Questionnaire on General Industrial Statistics from the Institut national de la statistique et des etudes economiques (INSEE), Paris. The concepts, definitions and classification by branches of industry are generally in accordance with United Nations standards.

The estimates of employment, gross output, value added and fixed capital formation are derived from national accounts calculations and relate to total industry as defined by the national accounting concept. It should be noted that manufacture of wine (ISIC 313) is excluded as that industry is classified under agriculture in the national scheme. The industry classification is based on the national scheme "Nomenclatures d'activites et de produits 1973" but, except for fixed capital formation, the data have been arranged to correspond to the ISIC classification. For fixed capital formation, the industry groups are those used in the national accounts calculations.

The employment figures relate to the population actively engaged. The estimates are based on the results of population censuses and various other indicators, such as annual statistics obtained from the Union nationale interprofessionnelle pour l'emploi dans l'industrie et le commerce (UNEDIC), quarterly inquiries of the Ministere du travail, statistics of large nationalized enterprises and information collected by INSEE in employment inquiries. The estimates refer to annual averages.

The estimates of electricity consumption are compiled by Electricite de France (EDF) and cover the consumption of all producers, including those producing for their own use. The classification of industrial activity is according to the classification followed by EDF.

The estimates of output, value added and gross fixed capital formation are taken from the national accounts estimates based on the year 1971.

The indexes of industrial production are compiled by INSEE and provided in response to the United Nations Questionnaire on Indexes of Industrial Production. In principle, the indexes cover all industrial establishments except handicrafts.

Related national publications:

<u>Rapport sur les comptes de la nation, les Collections de l'INSEE, Serie C, Comptes et planification</u> (annual); <u>Annuaire statistique de la France</u>; <u>Bulletin mensuel de statistique</u>, all published by the Institut national de la statistique et des etudes economiques, Paris. <u>Statistiques de la production et de la consommation</u> (annual), published by Electricite de France.

ISIC	INDUSTRY	1. AVERAGE NUMBER OF PERSONS ENGAGED (THOUSANDS)					2. AVERAGE NUMBER OF EMPLOYEES (THOUSANDS)					ISIC
		1981	1982	1983	1984	1985	1981	1982	1983	1984	1985	
210	Coal mining	58	57	55	52	47	57	57	55	52	47	210
220	Petroleum and gas	8	8	8	8	8	8	8	8	8	8	220
230	Metal ore mining	11	10	10	8	7	11	10	9	8	7	230
290	Other mining	60	59	55	53	52	56	55	52	50	49	290
2	Mining, quarrying .	137	134	128	121	114	132	130	124	118	111	2
311/2	Food products	536	543	548	551	548	451	458	461	463	458	311/2
313	Beverages	55	53	53	53	52	53	51	51	51	50	313
314	Tobacco	10	9	9	8	8	10	9	9	8	8	314
321	Textiles	278	268	259	246	237	272	263	254	241	233	321
3211	Spinning,weaving etc..	...	...	...	...	...	...	...	...	...	...	3211
322	Wearing apparel	249	244	235	226	217	227	223	215	207	199	322
323	Leather and products ...	36	36	35	32	30	33	33	32	29	27	323
324	Footwear	69	66	64	62	60	67	64	62	60	58	324
331	Wood products	109	107	103	98	94	97	95	92	88	85	331
332	Furniture, fixtures	136	134	130	120	113	112	110	107	98	91	332
341	Paper and products	115	112	111	109	106	114	111	110	108	105	341
3411	Pulp,paper etc.	...	...	...	...	...	...	...	...	...	...	3411
342	Printing,publishing	214	214	214	214	214	197	196	197	197	196	342
351	Industrial chemicals ...	136	133	130	128	126	136	132	130	128	125	351
3511	Basic excl fertilizers	...	...	...	...	...	...	...	...	...	...	3511
3513	Synthetic resins etc .	...	...	...	...	...	...	...	...	...	...	3513
352	Other chemical products.	196	193	194	197	197	195	191	193	196	196	352
3522	Drugs and medicines ..	...	...	...	...	...	...	...	...	...	...	3522
353	Petroleum refineries ...	30	29	28	27	26	30	29	28	26	26	353
354	Petroleum,coal products.	1	1	1	1	1	1	1	1	1	1	354
355	Rubber products	107	104	103	95	89	106	104	102	94	88	355
356	Plastic products n.e.c..	105	104	102	105	105	103	102	100	103	103	356
361	Pottery,china etc	43	41	39	34	32	41	39	37	33	30	361
362	Glass and products	68	66	62	60	58	66	65	61	59	57	362
369	Non-metal products n.e.c	98	95	89	84	80	94	91	85	80	76	369
371	Iron and steel	249	243	232	217	206	243	237	227	211	201	371
372	Non-ferrous metals	82	78	76	72	69	81	78	75	71	68	372
381	Metal products	271	262	253	242	234	263	254	245	235	227	381
382	Machinery n.e.c.	623	621	598	578	562	594	592	569	550	534	382
3825	Office,computing etc..	...	...	...	...	...	...	...	...	...	...	3825
383	Electrical machinery ...	498	498	498	491	479	492	492	492	486	474	383
3832	Radio,television etc..	...	...	...	...	...	...	...	...	...	...	3832
384	Transport equipment	641	635	613	590	560	638	632	610	587	558	384
3841	Shipbuilding, repair..	...	...	...	...	...	...	...	...	...	...	3841
3843	Motor vehicles	...	...	...	...	...	...	...	...	...	...	3843
385	Professional goods	84	82	79	78	78	78	75	72	71	71	385
390	Other industries	112	109	106	104	102	98	95	93	91	85	390
3	Manufacturing	5151	5080	4964	4822	4683	4892	4822	4710	4572	4430	3
410	Electricity,gas,steam ..	168	176	180	182	182	168	176	180	182	182	410
4101	Electricity	...	...	...	...	...	...	...	...	...	...	4101
420	Water works and supply .	29	29	30	30	30	29	29	30	30	30	420
4	Electricity,gas etc	197	205	210	212	212	197	205	210	212	212	4
2-4	All industry	5485	5419	5302	5155	5009	5221	5157	5044	4902	4753	2-4

Note. For description of classification, see country note.

ISIC	INDUSTRY	3. QUANTITY OF ELECTRICITY CONSUMED (BILLION KWH) 1981	1982	1983	1984	1985	4. OUTPUT IN PRODUCERS' PRICES a/ (BILLION FRANCS) 1981	1982	1983	1984	1985	ISIC
210	Coal mining	2.14	2.09	2.07	...	...	19.5	19.9	19.2	20.8	20.7	210
220	Petroleum and gas	b/	b/	b/	...	...	10.1	11.2	11.9	13.2	13.7	220
230	Metal ore mining	[2.57	2.50	2.50]	...	...	1.8	1.9	1.8	2.2	2.3	230
290	Other mining				...	...	17.5	18.1	19.2	19.8	20.9	290
2	Mining, quarrying .	b/ 4.71	b/ 4.59	b/ 4.57	...	...	48.9	51.1	52.1	56.0	57.6	2
311/2	Food products	[		]	...	...	328.4	375.2	406.7	445.5	465.5	311/2
313	Beverages	9.00	9.64	9.98	...	...	38.9	43.1	48.8	53.2	56.5	313
314	Tobacco				...	...	12.6	15.2	17.4	19.0	20.9	314
321	Textiles	3.15	3.03	2.90	...	...	66.0	72.1	78.2	88.2	93.5	321
3211	Spinning,weaving etc..	...	...	...	...	...	...	...	...	...	...	3211
322	Wearing apparel	[		]	...	...	41.5	46.9	51.2	53.6	57.8	322
323	Leather and products ...				...	...	8.1	8.9	9.7	10.4	11.0	323
324	Footwear	c/ 5.21	c/ 5.34	c/ 5.54	...	...	11.8	13.7	15.0	14.9	15.8	324
331	Wood products				...	...	24.9	25.3	25.9	26.7	28.3	331
332	Furniture, fixtures				...	...	24.9	28.5	29.5	27.6	28.1	332
341	Paper and products	5.69	5.78	5.09	...	...	53.3	59.7	64.0	76.4	80.0	341
3411	Pulp,paper etc.	...	...	...	...	...	...	...	...	...	...	3411
342	Printing,publishing	c/	c/	c/	...	...	49.6	60.9	66.9	75.9	80.3	342
351	Industrial chemicals ...	d/ 18.89	d/ 18.69	d/ 18.40	...	...	108.9	119.7	136.8	155.5	165.3	351
3511	Basic excl fertilizers	...	...	...	...	...	...	...	...	...	...	3511
3513	Synthetic resins etc .	...	...	...	...	...	...	...	...	...	...	3513
352	Other chemical products.	d/	d/	d/	...	...	88.1	100.2	112.6	127.9	141.0	352
3522	Drugs and medicines ..	...	...	...	...	...	...	...	...	...	...	3522
353	Petroleum refineries ...	b/ 4.38	b/ 4.32	b/ 4.27	...	...	219.7	233.2	243.5	274.6	288.7	353
354	Petroleum,coal products.	e/	e/	e/	...	...	1.1	1.2	1.3	1.7	1.6	354
355	Rubber products	1.75	1.71	1.75	...	...	23.8	25.1	27.1	29.0	30.7	355
356	Plastic products n.e.c..	...	...	...	...	...	36.3	41.9	48.0	54.2	59.1	356
361	Pottery,china etc	f/	f/	f/	...	...	6.2	6.2	6.2	6.5	7.1	361
362	Glass and products	1.65	1.71	1.84	...	...	16.4	17.9	20.5	21.6	21.8	362
369	Non-metal products n.e.c	f/ 4.37	f/ 4.02	f/ 3.85	...	...	37.0	38.6	39.9	40.6	41.1	369
371	Iron and steel	11.33	10.60	9.15	...	...	100.7	107.4	105.8	119.8	128.9	371
372	Non-ferrous metals	11.49	10.43	10.13	...	...	44.0	45.6	55.6	59.0	56.8	372
381	Metal products	6.89	6.92	6.91	...	...	65.9	75.8	78.7	84.2	89.0	381
382	Machinery n.e.c.	1.17	1.14	1.10	...	...	205.4	234.6	247.4	269.6	286.9	382
3825	Office,computing etc..	...	...	...	...	...	...	...	...	...	...	3825
383	Electrical machinery ...	2.61	2.72	2.78	...	...	125.5	140.1	152.3	170.6	180.8	383
3832	Radio,television etc..	...	...	...	...	...	...	...	...	...	...	3832
384	Transport equipment	5.45	5.71	5.88	...	...	231.1	261.8	288.7	296.1	312.1	384
3841	Shipbuilding, repair..	0.49	0.49	0.50	...	...	...	...	...	...	...	3841
3843	Motor vehicles	4.27	4.48	4.60	...	...	...	...	...	...	...	3843
385	Professional goods	0.83	0.86	0.89	...	...	14.8	16.9	18.7	21.3	23.5	385
390	Other industries	c/	c/	c/	...	...	19.4	23.2	25.3	25.7	26.9	390
3	Manufacturing	b/e/g/ 93.86	b/e/g/ 92.62	b/e/g/ 90.46	...	...	2004.2	2239.0	2421.7	2649.3	2799.0	3
410	Electricity,gas,steam .. h/i/	21.61	20.00	...	...	...	...	...	...	...	...	410
4101	Electricity .... h/	20.65	18.96	...	...	...	...	...	...	...	...	4101
420	Water works and supply .	...	...	...	...	...	...	...	...	...	...	420
4	Electricity,gas etc	e/j/ 23.77	e/j/ 22.28	...	...	...	129.5	149.8	172.3	195.2	218.1	4
2-4	All industry	g/ 122.34	g/ 119.49	...	...	...	2182.6	2439.9	2646.4	2900.5	3074.7	2-4

Note. For description of classification, see country note.

a/ Excluding value-added tax.
b/ Major group 220 is included in 353.
c/ Major groups 342 and 390 are included in 322 to 332 combined.
d/ Major group 352 is included in 351.
e/ Major group 354 is included in the total for major division 4.
f/ Major group 361 is included in 369.
g/ Excluding major group 356.
h/ Establishments providing services related to the production and distribution of electricity are included in the total for major division 4 only.
i/ Steam is included in the total for major division 4 only.
j/ Major group 420 is included in the total for major division 4.

ISIC	INDUSTRY	5. VALUE ADDED IN PRODUCERS' PRICES a/b/ (BILLION FRANCS) 1981	1982	1983	1984	1985	6. GROSS FIXED CAPITAL FORMATION TOTAL (BILLION FRANCS) 1981	1982	1983	1984	1985	ISIC
210	Coal mining	9.7	9.9	9.9	10.6	10.8	c/ 2.7	c/ 3.3	c/ 3.3	c/ 2.6	c/ 2.3	210
220	Petroleum and gas	7.8	8.7	9.1	9.8	10.1	d/	d/	d/	d/	d/	220
230	Metal ore mining	1.2	1.2	1.1	1.4	1.5	e/f/	e/f/	e/f/	e/f/	...	230
290	Other mining	8.3	8.5	9.0	9.3	9.8	g/	g/	g/	g/	g/	290
2	Mining, quarrying .	27.0	28.3	29.1	31.1	32.2	...	...	...	...	...	2
311/2	Food products	103.9	117.6	133.6	152.6	160.5	[				]	311/2
313	Beverages	20.7	22.9	26.4	28.9	31.2	15.7	17.5	19.3	23.4	23.5	313
314	Tobacco	9.0	10.8	12.7	13.7	14.7	]				]	314
321	Textiles	27.5	30.0	33.1	36.2	39.1	h/ 2.7	h/ 3.8	h/ 4.7	h/ 5.2	h/ 5.8	321
3211	Spinning,weaving etc..	...	...	...	...	...	...	...	...	...	...	3211
322	Wearing apparel	17.8	19.7	22.2	24.2	26.4	h/	h/	h/	h/	h/	322
323	Leather and products ...	3.7	4.3	4.9	5.0	5.2	[0.5	0.7	0.8	0.8	0.9]	323
324	Footwear	6.6	7.7	8.1	7.4	8.0						324
331	Wood products	8.2	9.3	8.1	7.8	8.0	[i/ 6.4	i/ 7.5	i/ 7.8	i/ 8.8	i/ 9.6]	331
332	Furniture, fixtures	8.0	9.7	10.2	8.8	8.7						332
341	Paper and products	19.1	22.0	24.1	27.2	31.2	2.5	2.9	3.2	4.3	5.9	341
3411	Pulp,paper etc.	...	...	...	...	...	...	...	...	...	...	3411
342	Printing,publishing	19.4	24.9	27.2	29.6	31.6	2.1	2.6	2.7	2.9	2.6	342
351	Industrial chemicals ...	41.8	46.8	53.7	61.3	66.1	6.1	5.0	5.6	7.5	9.7	351
3511	Basic excl fertilizers	...	...	...	...	...	...	...	...	...	...	3511
3513	Synthetic resins etc .	...	...	...	...	...	...	...	...	...	...	3513
352	Other chemical products.	27.3	31.0	32.0	34.0	37.7	2.9	3.5	3.8	4.0	5.0	352
3522	Drugs and medicines ..	...	...	...	...	...	...	...	...	...	...	3522
353	Petroleum refineries ...	34.3	42.5	57.3	67.5	89.1	d/ 9.6	d/ 9.6	d/ 7.8	d/ 8.4	d/ 10.4	353
354	Petroleum,coal products.	0.5	0.5	0.6	0.8	0.7	c/	c/	c/	c/	c/	354
355	Rubber products	13.4	14.3	15.3	15.9	16.8	[3.3	3.2	3.5	4.2	5.5]	355
356	Plastic products n.e.c..	13.7	16.3	17.9	19.7	22.5						356
361	Pottery,china etc	2.9	2.9	3.0	3.1	3.3	g/	g/	g/	g/	g/	361
362	Glass and products	9.5	10.3	11.8	12.2	12.0	1.3	1.6	1.5	1.8	1.7	362
369	Non-metal products n.e.c	18.0	18.6	19.5	19.4	19.7	g/ 5.9	g/ 4.9	g/ 5.0	g/ 5.2	g/ 6.3	369
371	Iron and steel	36.8	43.2	44.4	51.2	56.8	e/ 3.1	e/ 3.3	e/ 3.6	e/ 5.0	e/ 5.1	371
372	Non-ferrous metals	14.5	14.8	18.3	18.9	19.3	f/ 6.2	f/ 5.1	f/ 5.9	f/ 7.7	f/ 10.0	372
381	Metal products	39.1	45.3	47.1	50.7	52.1	5.9	6.3	6.5	7.0	8.5	381
382	Machinery n.e.c.	111.6	128.5	136.5	148.0	157.7	j/ 7.4	j/ 7.2	j/ 7.6	j/ 8.3	j/ 9.9	382
3825	Office,computing etc..	...	...	...	...	...	...	...	...	...	...	3825
383	Electrical machinery ...	61.5	69.0	74.7	83.2	89.3	13.5	14.8	15.8	18.6	21.6	383
3832	Radio,television etc..	...	...	...	...	...	...	...	...	...	...	3832
384	Transport equipment	100.1	112.9	125.2	131.7	141.2	12.5	13.4	13.1	14.1	17.8	384
3841	Shipbuilding, repair..	...	...	...	...	...	...	...	...	...	...	3841
3843	Motor vehicles	...	...	...	...	...	...	...	...	...	...	3843
385	Professional goods	8.1	9.3	10.2	11.5	12.7	j/	j/	j/	j/	j/	385
390	Other industries	10.6	12.9	13.9	13.8	14.4	i/	i/	i/	i/	i/	390
3	Manufacturing	787.8	898.3	992.2	1084.3	1176.2	k/ 107.6	k/ 112.9	k/ 118.2	k/ 137.2	k/ 159.8	3
410	Electricity,gas,steam ..	...	...	...	...	...	...	...	...	...	...	410
4101	Electricity	...	...	...	...	...	...	...	...	...	...	4101
420	Water works and supply .	...	...	...	...	...	...	...	...	...	...	420
4	Electricity,gas etc	67.7	77.2	97.0	109.8	120.5	47.2	54.5	57.2	54.2	55.2	4
2-4	All industry	876.5	1003.8	1118.3	1225.2	1328.9	157.5	170.7	178.7	194.0	217.3	2-4

Note. For description of classification, see country note.

a/ Contributions to the gross domestic product.
b/ Excluding value-added tax.
c/ Major group 354 is included in 210.
d/ Major group 220 is included in 353.
e/ Iron ore mining is included in major group 371.
f/ Non-ferrous metal ore mining is included in major group 372.
g/ Major groups 290 and 361 are included in 369.
h/ Major group 322 is included in 321.
i/ Major group 390 is included in 331 and 332 combined.
j/ Major group 385 is included in 382.
k/ Including mining.

7. GROSS FIXED CAPITAL FORMATION
MACHINERY AND EQUIPMENT
(BILLION FRANCS)

ISIC	INDUSTRY		1981	1982	1983	1984	1985	ISIC
210	Coal mining	a/	2.3	2.9	3.0	2.4	2.1	210
220	Petroleum and gas	b/	...	...	...	...	...	220
230	Metal ore mining		...	...	...	...	...	230
290	Other mining	c/	...	...	...	...	...	290
2	Mining, quarrying .		...	...	...	...	...	2
311/2	Food products							311/2
313	Beverages		[12.4	14.1	15.9	20.0	20.1]	313
314	Tobacco							314
321	Textiles	d/	2.4	3.3	4.0	4.3	4.8	321
3211	Spinning,weaving etc..		...	...	...	...	...	3211
322	Wearing apparel	d/	...	...	...	...	...	322
323	Leather and products ...		[0.5	0.6	0.7	0.6	0.7]	323
324	Footwear							324
331	Wood products	e/	[5.3	6.2	6.4	7.4	8.3]	331
332	Furniture, fixtures							332
341	Paper and products		2.2	2.5	2.9	3.9	5.5	341
3411	Pulp,paper etc.		...	...	...	...	...	3411
342	Printing,publishing		1.8	2.1	2.3	2.4	2.0	342
351	Industrial chemicals ...		6.0	4.8	5.3	7.4	8.0	351
3511	Basic excl fertilizers		...	...	...	...	...	3511
3513	Synthetic resins etc .		...	...	...	...	...	3513
352	Other chemical products.		2.1	2.6	3.0	3.1	4.1	352
3522	Drugs and medicines ..		...	...	...	...	...	3522
353	Petroleum refineries ...	b/	6.3	6.3	4.6	5.3	7.3	353
354	Petroleum,coal products.	a/	...	...	...	...	...	354
355	Rubber products		[2.8	2.9	3.2	3.8	5.1]	355
356	Plastic products n.e.c..							356
361	Pottery,china etc	c/	...	...	...	...	...	361
362	Glass and products		1.2	1.5	1.4	1.6	1.5	362
369	Non-metal products n.e.c	c/	4.9	4.0	4.1	4.4	5.5	369
371	Iron and steel	f/	1.6	1.9	3.4	4.4	4.6	371
372	Non-ferrous metals	g/	4.8	3.4	4.4	6.3	8.6	372
381	Metal products		5.2	5.6	5.7	5.9	7.3	381
382	Machinery n.e.c.	h/	5.8	5.8	6.1	6.6	8.3	382
3825	Office,computing etc..		...	...	...	...	...	3825
383	Electrical machinery ...		11.9	13.1	13.9	16.9	19.9	383
3832	Radio,television etc..		...	...	...	...	...	3832
384	Transport equipment		8.7	9.6	10.3	11.2	15.2	384
3841	Shipbuilding, repair..		...	...	...	...	...	3841
3843	Motor vehicles		...	...	...	...	...	3843
385	Professional goods	h/	...	...	...	...	...	385
390	Other industries	e/	...	...	...	...	...	390
3	Manufacturing	i/	85.9	90.3	97.6	115.5	136.8	3
410	Electricity,gas,steam ..		...	...	...	...	...	410
4101	Electricity		...	...	...	...	...	4101
420	Water works and supply .		...	...	...	...	...	420
4	Electricity,gas etc		22.2	26.1	26.8	24.4	24.4	4
2-4	All industry		110.4	119.3	127.4	142.3	163.3	2-4

Note. For description of classification, see country note.

a/ Major group 354 is included in 210.
b/ Major group 220 is included in 353.
c/ Major groups 290 and 361 are included in 369.
d/ Major group 322 is included in 321.
e/ Major group 390 is included in 331 and 332 combined.
f/ Iron ore mining is included in major group 371.
g/ Non-ferrous metal ore mining is included in major group 372.
h/ Major group 385 is included in 382.
i/ Including mining.

8. INDEX NUMBERS OF INDUSTRIAL PRODUCTION (1980 = 100)

ISIC	INDUSTRY	1976	1977	1978	1979	1981	1982	1983	1984	1985	a/ RATE	ISIC
210	Coal mining	125	119	111	106	101	93	93	90	82	-4.6	210
220	Petroleum and gas	93	98	100	100	97	92	92	92	88	-0.6	220
230	Metal ore mining .... b/c/	112	105	100	99	86	79	70	69	64	-6.0	230
290	Other mining	90	90	91	96	95	88	88	84	83	-0.9	290
2	Mining, quarrying .	103	101	99	100	96	89	88	85	81	-2.6	2
311/2	Food products	91	93	97	99	101	102	103	106	107	1.8	311/2
313	Beverages	94	95	102	104	100	98	101	103	105	1.2	313
314	Tobacco	120	112	111	105	89	88	84	80	90	-3.1	314
321	Textiles	108	104	101	104	93	92	90	90	90	-2.0	321
3211	Spinning,weaving etc..	...	...	...	...	...	...	...	...	...	...	3211
322	Wearing apparel	...	...	...	...	...	...	...	...	...	...	322
323	Leather and products ...	146	127	123	116	100	101	95	91	86	-5.7	323
324	Footwear	113	113	106	106	102	106	105	102	104	-0.9	324
331	Wood products	124	124	94	101	93	84	84	80	78	-5.0	331
332	Furniture, fixtures	...	...	...	...	...	...	...	...	...	...	332
341	Paper and products	91	93	98	102	99	100	103	110	107	1.8	341
3411	Pulp,paper etc.	...	...	...	...	...	...	...	...	...	...	3411
342	Printing,publishing	83	88	92	98	100	103	106	109	108	3.0	342
351	Industrial chemicals ... d/	87	91	95	102	102	103	109	115	117	3.3	351
3511	Basic excl fertilizers	...	...	...	...	...	...	...	...	...	...	3511
3513	Synthetic resins etc .	...	...	...	...	...	...	...	...	...	...	3513
352	Other chemical products. d/	...	...	...	...	...	...	...	...	...	...	352
3522	Drugs and medicines ..	...	...	...	...	...	...	...	...	...	...	3522
353	Petroleum refineries ...	107	104	103	112	86	73	67	67	67	-5.1	353
354	Petroleum,coal products.	102	97	96	105	96	89	78	81	78	-2.9	354
355	Rubber products	90	92	92	98	89	83	82	84	83	-0.9	355
356	Plastic products n.e.c..	87	91	90	98	96	103	109	111	116	3.2	356
361	Pottery,china etc	99	98	92	95	96	93	88	85	83	-1.9	361
362	Glass and products	73	77	84	94	95	96	99	99	97	3.2	362
369	Non-metal products n.e.c	99	97	96	99	93	87	81	77	75	-3.0	369
371	Iron and steel	98	94	98	101	93	83	76	79	79	-2.4	371
372	Non-ferrous metals ..... c/	88	92	92	97	95	97	103	100	94	0.7	372
381	Metal products	94	92	92	100	94	94	94	92	93	-0.1	381
382	Machinery n.e.c.	92	90	94	98	106	102	97	95	96	0.5	382
3825	Office,computing etc..	...	...	...	...	...	...	...	...	...	...	3825
383	Electrical machinery ...	87	91	94	96	101	105	106	112	114	3.0	383
3832	Radio,television etc..	...	...	...	...	...	...	...	...	...	...	3832
384	Transport equipment	99	102	101	104	95	96	99	94	90	-1.1	384
3841	Shipbuilding, repair..	...	...	...	...	...	...	...	...	...	...	3841
3843	Motor vehicles	...	...	...	...	...	...	...	...	...	...	3843
385	Professional goods	87	98	99	100	102	102	101	105	110	2.6	385
390	Other industries	...	...	...	...	...	...	...	...	...	...	390
3	Manufacturing ..... e/	93	94	96	101	98	97	97	98	95	0.2	3
410	Electricity,gas,steam ..	78	82	88	94	107	107	113	123	131	5.9	410
4101	Electricity	...	...	...	...	...	...	...	...	...	...	4101
420	Water works and supply .	.	.	.	.	.	.	.	.	...	.	420
4	Electricity,gas etc	...	...	...	...	...	...	...	...	...	...	4
2-4	All industry e/	92	94	96	100	98	97	98	99	98	0.7	2-4

a/ Annual growth rate 1976-1985.
b/ Iron ore only.
c/ Non-ferrous metal mining is included in major group 372.
d/ Major group 352 is included in 351.
e/ Excluding clothing.

GAMBIA

The information in the tables is based on the reply to the United Nations Questionnaire on General Industrial Statistics from the Central Statistics Department, Ministry of Economic Planning and Industrial Development, Banjul. The concepts, definitions and classification by branches of industry are generally in accordance with United Nations standards.

The estimates in the tables are based on the statistics collected for the estimation of domestic product by industrial activity in relation to the compilation of national accounts. The data relate to reporting establishments employing 5 or more persons, and no estimate has been made for non-response.

The reference period is the fiscal year 1 July to 30 June. In the tables, the period referred to is the fiscal year ending in the year indicated.

The concepts and definitions of the items for which data are presented are principally in conformity with United Nations standards. It should be noted that payments to homeworkes are included in the estimates of wages and salaries. The valuation of output and value added is in producers' prices.

ISIC	INDUSTRY	1. NUMBER OF ESTABLISHMENTS a/b/ (NUMBER)					2. AVERAGE NUMBER OF PERSONS ENGAGED a/b/ (NUMBER)					ISIC
		1981	1982	1983	1984	1985	1981	1982	1983	1984	1985	
210	Coal mining	...	...	...	...	...	...	...	...	...	...	210
220	Petroleum and gas	...	...	...	...	...	...	...	...	...	...	220
230	Metal ore mining	...	...	...	...	...	...	...	...	...	...	230
290	Other mining	...	...	...	...	...	...	...	...	...	...	290
2	Mining, quarrying .	...	...	...	...	...	...	...	...	...	...	2
311/2	Food products	15	10	...	...	...	1041	1472	...	...	...	311/2
313	Beverages	5	3	...	...	...	145	141	...	...	...	313
314	Tobacco	...	...	...	...	...	...	...	...	...	...	314
321	Textiles	1	1	...	...	...	28	54	...	...	...	321
3211	Spinning,weaving etc..	1	1	...	...	...	28	54	...	...	...	3211
322	Wearing apparel	...	...	...	...	...	...	...	...	...	...	322
323	Leather and products ...	1	1	...	...	...	12	12	...	...	...	323
324	Footwear	...	...	...	...	...	...	...	...	...	...	324
331	Wood products	...	...	...	...	...	...	...	...	...	...	331
332	Furniture, fixtures	2	...	...	...	...	304	...	...	...	...	332
341	Paper and products	...	...	...	...	...	...	...	...	...	...	341
3411	Pulp,paper etc.	...	...	...	...	...	...	...	...	...	...	3411
342	Printing,publishing	1	1	...	...	...	42	42	...	...	...	342
351	Industrial chemicals ...	...	...	...	...	...	...	...	...	...	...	351
3511	Basic excl fertilizers	...	...	...	...	...	...	...	...	...	...	3511
3513	Synthetic resins etc .	...	...	...	...	...	...	...	...	...	...	3513
352	Other chemical products.	3	3	...	...	...	62	55	...	...	...	352
3522	Drugs and medicines ..	...	...	...	...	...	...	...	...	...	...	3522
353	Petroleum refineries ...	...	...	...	...	...	...	...	...	...	...	353
354	Petroleum,coal products.	...	...	...	...	...	...	...	...	...	...	354
355	Rubber products	...	...	...	...	...	...	...	...	...	...	355
356	Plastic products n.e.c..	...	...	...	...	...	...	...	...	...	...	356
361	Pottery,china etc	...	...	...	...	...	...	...	...	...	...	361
362	Glass and products	...	...	...	...	...	...	...	...	...	...	362
369	Non-metal products n.e.c	2	2	...	...	...	14	23	...	...	...	369
371	Iron and steel	...	...	...	...	...	...	...	...	...	...	371
372	Non-ferrous metals	...	...	...	...	...	...	...	...	...	...	372
381	Metal products	1	...	...	...	...	83	...	...	...	...	381
382	Machinery n.e.c.	...	...	...	...	...	...	...	...	...	...	382
3825	Office,computing etc..	...	...	...	...	...	...	...	...	...	...	3825
383	Electrical machinery ...	...	...	...	...	...	...	...	...	...	...	383
3832	Radio,television etc..	...	...	...	...	...	...	...	...	...	...	3832
384	Transport equipment	...	...	...	...	...	...	...	...	...	...	384
3841	Shipbuilding, repair..	...	...	...	...	...	...	...	...	...	...	3841
3843	Motor vehicles	...	...	...	...	...	...	...	...	...	...	3843
385	Professional goods	...	...	...	...	...	...	...	...	...	...	385
390	Other industries	4	6	...	...	...	110	89	...	...	...	390
3	Manufacturing ..... c/	35	27	...	...	...	1841	1888	...	...	...	3
410	Electricity,gas,steam ..	...	...	...	...	...	...	...	...	...	...	410
4101	Electricity	1	1	...	...	...	351	423	...	...	...	4101
420	Water works and supply .	1	1	...	...	...	263	199	...	...	...	420
4	Electricity,gas etc	...	...	...	...	...	...	...	...	...	...	4
2-4	All industry	...	...	...	...	...	...	...	...	...	...	2-4

a/ Twelve months ending 30 June of the year indicated.
b/ Manufacturing: establishments employing 5 or more persons.
c/ Total relates only to industries for which data are available.

ISIC	INDUSTRY	3. AVERAGE NUMBER OF EMPLOYEES a/c/ (NUMBER)					4. WAGES AND SALARIES OF EMPLOYEES a/b/c/ (THOUSAND DALASIS)					ISIC
		1981	1982	1983	1984	1985	1981	1982	1983	1984	1985	
210	Coal mining	...	...	...	...	...	...	...	...	...	...	210
220	Petroleum and gas	...	...	...	...	...	...	...	...	...	...	220
230	Metal ore mining	...	...	...	...	...	...	...	...	...	...	230
290	Other mining	...	...	...	...	...	...	...	...	...	...	290
2	Mining, quarrying .	...	...	...	...	...	...	...	...	...	...	2
311/2	Food products	1032	1465	...	...	...	2935	3474	...	...	...	311/2
313	Beverages	143	141	...	...	...	284	697	...	...	...	313
314	Tobacco	...	...	...	...	...	...	...	...	...	...	314
321	Textiles	28	54	...	...	...	153	294	...	...	...	321
3211	Spinning,weaving etc..	28	54	...	...	...	153	294	...	...	...	3211
322	Wearing apparel	...	...	...	...	...	...	...	...	...	...	322
323	Leather and products ...	11	11	...	...	...	12	12	...	...	...	323
324	Footwear	...	...	...	...	...	...	...	...	...	...	324
331	Wood products	...	...	...	...	...	...	...	...	...	...	331
332	Furniture, fixtures	299	...	...	...	...	569	...	...	...	...	332
341	Paper and products	...	...	...	...	...	...	...	...	...	...	341
3411	Pulp,paper etc.	...	...	...	...	...	...	...	...	...	...	3411
342	Printing,publishing	42	42	...	...	...	273	207	...	...	...	342
351	Industrial chemicals ...	...	...	...	...	...	...	...	...	...	...	351
3511	Basic excl fertilizers	...	...	...	...	...	...	...	...	...	...	3511
3513	Synthetic resins etc .	...	...	...	...	...	...	...	...	...	...	3513
352	Other chemical products.	61	53	...	...	...	180	155	...	...	...	352
3522	Drugs and medicines ..	...	...	...	...	...	...	...	...	...	...	3522
353	Petroleum refineries ...	...	...	...	...	...	...	...	...	...	...	353
354	Petroleum,coal products.	...	...	...	...	...	...	...	...	...	...	354
355	Rubber products	...	...	...	...	...	...	...	...	...	...	355
356	Plastic products n.e.c..	...	...	...	...	...	...	...	...	...	...	356
361	Pottery,china etc	...	...	...	...	...	...	...	...	...	...	361
362	Glass and products	...	...	...	...	...	...	...	...	...	...	362
369	Non-metal products n.e.c	13	22	...	...	...	15	104	...	...	...	369
371	Iron and steel	...	...	...	...	...	...	...	...	...	...	371
372	Non-ferrous metals	...	...	...	...	...	...	...	...	...	...	372
381	Metal products	83	...	...	...	...	256	...	...	...	...	381
382	Machinery n.e.c.	...	...	...	...	...	...	...	...	...	...	382
3825	Office,computing etc..	...	...	...	...	...	...	...	...	...	...	3825
383	Electrical machinery ...	...	...	...	...	...	...	...	...	...	...	383
3832	Radio,television etc..	...	...	...	...	...	...	...	...	...	...	3832
384	Transport equipment	...	...	...	...	...	...	...	...	...	...	384
3841	Shipbuilding, repair..	...	...	...	...	...	...	...	...	...	...	3841
3843	Motor vehicles	...	...	...	...	...	...	...	...	...	...	3843
385	Professional goods	...	...	...	...	...	...	...	...	...	...	385
390	Other industries	102	89	...	...	...	350	442	...	...	...	390
3	Manufacturing ..... d/	1814	1877	...	...	...	5027	5385	...	...	...	3
410	Electricity,gas,steam ..	...	...	...	...	...	...	...	...	...	...	410
4101	Electricity	351	423	...	...	...	1136	2574	...	...	...	4101
420	Water works and supply .	263	199	...	...	...	612	1549	...	...	...	420
4	Electricity,gas etc	...	...	...	...	...	...	...	...	...	...	4
2-4	All industry	...	...	...	...	...	...	...	...	...	...	2-4

a/ Twelve months ending 30 June of the year indicated.
b/ Including payments to homeworkers.
c/ Manufacturing: establishments employing 5 or more persons.
d/ Total relates only to industries for which data are available.

ISIC	INDUSTRY	5. AVERAGE NUMBER OF OPERATIVES a/b/ (NUMBER)					6. WAGES AND SALARIES OF OPERATIVES a/b/ (THOUSAND DALASIS)					ISIC
		1981	1982	1983	1984	1985	1981	1982	1983	1984	1985	
210	Coal mining	...	...	...	...	...	...	...	...	...	...	210
220	Petroleum and gas	...	...	...	...	...	...	...	...	...	...	220
230	Metal ore mining	...	...	...	...	...	...	...	...	...	...	230
290	Other mining	...	...	...	...	...	...	...	...	...	...	290
2	Mining, quarrying .	...	...	...	...	...	...	...	...	...	...	2
311/2	Food products	821	1205	...	...	...	2040	2321	...	...	...	311/2
313	Beverages	97	108	...	...	...	138	366	...	...	...	313
314	Tobacco	...	...	...	...	...	...	...	...	...	...	314
321	Textiles	15	21	...	...	...	48	67	...	...	...	321
3211	Spinning,weaving etc..	15	21	...	...	...	48	67	...	...	...	3211
322	Wearing apparel	...	...	...	...	...	...	...	...	...	...	322
323	Leather and products ...	11	11	...	...	...	12	12	...	...	...	323
324	Footwear	...	...	...	...	...	...	...	...	...	...	324
331	Wood products	...	...	...	...	...	...	...	...	...	...	331
332	Furniture, fixtures	277	...	...	...	...	484	...	...	...	...	332
341	Paper and products	...	...	...	...	...	...	...	...	...	...	341
3411	Pulp,paper etc.	...	...	...	...	...	...	...	...	...	...	3411
342	Printing,publishing	31	31	...	...	...	143	128	...	...	...	342
351	Industrial chemicals ...	...	...	...	...	...	...	...	...	...	...	351
3511	Basic excl fertilizers	...	...	...	...	...	...	...	...	...	...	3511
3513	Synthetic resins etc .	...	...	...	...	...	...	...	...	...	...	3513
352	Other chemical products.	34	29	...	...	...	91	70	...	...	...	352
3522	Drugs and medicines ..	...	...	...	...	...	...	...	...	...	...	3522
353	Petroleum refineries ...	...	...	...	...	...	...	...	...	...	...	353
354	Petroleum,coal products.	...	...	...	...	...	...	...	...	...	...	354
355	Rubber products	...	...	...	...	...	...	...	...	...	...	355
356	Plastic products n.e.c..	...	...	...	...	...	...	...	...	...	...	356
361	Pottery,china etc	...	...	...	...	...	...	...	...	...	...	361
362	Glass and products	...	...	...	...	...	...	...	...	...	...	362
369	Non-metal products n.e.c	11	16	...	...	...	11	36	...	...	...	369
371	Iron and steel	...	...	...	...	...	...	...	...	...	...	371
372	Non-ferrous metals	...	...	...	...	...	...	...	...	...	...	372
381	Metal products	66	...	...	...	...	130	...	...	...	...	381
382	Machinery n.e.c.	...	...	...	...	...	...	...	...	...	...	382
3825	Office,computing etc..	...	...	...	...	...	...	...	...	...	...	3825
383	Electrical machinery ...	...	...	...	...	...	...	...	...	...	...	383
3832	Radio,television etc..	...	...	...	...	...	...	...	...	...	...	3832
384	Transport equipment	...	...	...	...	...	...	...	...	...	...	384
3841	Shipbuilding, repair..	...	...	...	...	...	...	...	...	...	...	3841
3843	Motor vehicles	...	...	...	...	...	...	...	...	...	...	3843
385	Professional goods	...	...	...	...	...	...	...	...	...	...	385
390	Other industries	62	61	...	...	...	130	205	...	...	...	390
3	Manufacturing ..... c/	1425	1482	...	...	...	3227	3205	...	...	...	3
410	Electricity,gas,steam ..	...	...	...	...	...	...	...	...	...	...	410
4101	Electricity	222	423	...	...	...	690	2574	...	...	...	4101
420	Water works and supply .	250	199	...	...	...	554	1549	...	...	...	420
4	Electricity,gas etc	...	...	...	...	...	...	...	...	...	...	4
2-4	All industry	...	...	...	...	...	...	...	...	...	...	2-4

a/ Twelve months ending 30 June of the year indicated. b/ Manufacturing: establishments employing 5 or more persons.
c/ Total relates only to industries for which data are available.

ISIC	INDUSTRY	7. OUTPUT IN PRODUCERS' PRICES a/b/ (THOUSAND DALASIS)					8. VALUE ADDED IN PRODUCERS' PRICES a/b/ (THOUSAND DALASIS)					ISIC
		1981	1982	1983	1984	1985	1981	1982	1983	1984	1985	
210	Coal mining	...	...	...	...	...	...	...	...	...	...	210
220	Petroleum and gas	...	...	...	...	...	...	...	...	...	...	220
230	Metal ore mining	...	...	...	...	...	...	...	...	...	...	230
290	Other mining	...	...	...	...	...	...	...	...	...	...	290
2	Mining, quarrying .	...	...	...	...	...	...	...	...	...	...	2
311/2	Food products	44307	62878	...	...	...	7365	9948	...	...	...	311/2
313	Beverages	6821	10546	...	...	...	2045	4052	...	...	...	313
314	Tobacco	...	...	...	...	...	...	...	...	...	...	314
321	Textiles	2323	3252	...	...	...	231	637	...	...	...	321
3211	Spinning,weaving etc..	2323	3252	...	...	...	231	637	...	...	...	3211
322	Wearing apparel	...	...	...	...	...	...	...	...	...	...	322
323	Leather and products ...	113	150	...	...	...	38	33	...	...	...	323
324	Footwear	...	...	...	...	...	...	...	...	...	...	324
331	Wood products	...	...	...	...	...	...	...	...	...	...	331
332	Furniture, fixtures	650	...	...	...	...	c/ 65	...	...	...	...	332
341	Paper and products	...	...	...	...	...	...	...	...	...	...	341
3411	Pulp,paper etc.	...	...	...	...	...	...	...	...	...	...	3411
342	Printing,publishing	837	358	...	...	...	637	...	...	...	...	342
351	Industrial chemicals ...	...	...	...	...	...	...	...	...	...	...	351
3511	Basic excl fertilizers	...	...	...	...	...	...	...	...	...	...	3511
3513	Synthetic resins etc .	...	...	...	...	...	...	...	...	...	...	3513
352	Other chemical products.	1415	1031	...	...	...	502	322	...	...	...	352
3522	Drugs and medicines ..	...	...	...	...	...	...	...	...	...	...	3522
353	Petroleum refineries ...	...	...	...	...	...	...	...	...	...	...	353
354	Petroleum,coal products.	...	...	...	...	...	...	...	...	...	...	354
355	Rubber products	...	...	...	...	...	...	...	...	...	...	355
356	Plastic products n.e.c..	...	...	...	...	...	...	...	...	...	...	356
361	Pottery,china etc	...	...	...	...	...	...	...	...	...	...	361
362	Glass and products	...	...	...	...	...	...	...	...	...	...	362
369	Non-metal products n.e.c	152	922	...	...	...	73	-115	...	...	...	369
371	Iron and steel	...	...	...	...	...	...	...	...	...	...	371
372	Non-ferrous metals	...	...	...	...	...	...	...	...	...	...	372
381	Metal products	1116	...	...	...	...	455	...	...	...	...	381
382	Machinery n.e.c.	...	...	...	...	...	...	...	...	...	...	382
3825	Office,computing etc..	...	...	...	...	...	...	...	...	...	...	3825
383	Electrical machinery ...	...	...	...	...	...	...	...	...	...	...	383
3832	Radio,television etc..	...	...	...	...	...	...	...	...	...	...	3832
384	Transport equipment	...	...	...	...	...	...	...	...	...	...	384
3841	Shipbuilding, repair..	...	...	...	...	...	...	...	...	...	...	3841
3843	Motor vehicles	...	...	...	...	...	...	...	...	...	...	3843
385	Professional goods	...	...	...	...	...	...	...	...	...	...	385
390	Other industries	17071	5872	...	...	...	8731	3946	...	...	...	390
3	Manufacturing ..... d/	74805	85009	...	...	...	20142	18823	...	...	...	3
410	Electricity,gas,steam ..	...	...	...	...	...	...	...	...	...	...	410
4101	Electricity	7266	10025	...	...	...	-1088	-17	...	...	...	4101
420	Water works and supply .	2614	3803	...	...	...	761	1293	...	...	...	420
4	Electricity,gas etc	...	...	...	...	...	...	...	...	...	...	4
2-4	All industry	...	...	...	...	...	...	...	...	...	...	2-4

a/ Twelve months ending 30 June of the year indicated. b/ Manufacturing: establishments employing 5 or more persons.
c/ Value added is less than corresponding wages and salaries due to operating losses.
d/ Total relates only to industries for which data are available.

9. GROSS FIXED CAPITAL FORMATION
TOTAL a/b/
(THOUSAND DALASIS)

ISIC	INDUSTRY	1981	1982	1983	1984	1985	ISIC
210	Coal mining	...	...	...	...	...	210
220	Petroleum and gas	...	...	...	...	...	220
230	Metal ore mining	...	...	...	...	...	230
290	Other mining	...	...	...	...	...	290
2	Mining, quarrying .	...	...	...	...	...	2
311/2	Food products	177	2259	...	...	...	311/2
313	Beverages	...	310	...	...	...	313
314	Tobacco	...	...	...	...	...	314
321	Textiles	-	-	...	...	...	321
3211	Spinning,weaving etc..	-	-	...	...	...	3211
322	Wearing apparel	...	...	...	...	...	322
323	Leather and products ...	-	9	...	...	...	323
324	Footwear	...	...	...	...	...	324
331	Wood products	...	...	...	...	...	331
332	Furniture, fixtures	7	...	...	...	...	332
341	Paper and products	...	...	...	...	...	341
3411	Pulp,paper etc.	...	...	...	...	...	3411
342	Printing,publishing	-	-	...	...	...	342
351	Industrial chemicals ...	...	...	...	...	...	351
3511	Basic excl fertilizers	...	...	...	...	...	3511
3513	Synthetic resins etc .	...	...	...	...	...	3513
352	Other chemical products.	18	69	...	...	...	352
3522	Drugs and medicines ..	...	...	...	...	...	3522
353	Petroleum refineries ...	...	...	...	...	...	353
354	Petroleum,coal products.	...	...	...	...	...	354
355	Rubber products	...	...	...	...	...	355
356	Plastic products n.e.c..	...	...	...	...	...	356
361	Pottery,china etc	...	...	...	...	...	361
362	Glass and products	...	...	...	...	...	362
369	Non-metal products n.e.c	17	-	...	...	...	369
371	Iron and steel	...	...	...	...	...	371
372	Non-ferrous metals	...	...	...	...	...	372
381	Metal products	10	...	...	...	...	381
382	Machinery n.e.c.	...	...	...	...	...	382
3825	Office,computing etc..	...	...	...	...	...	3825
383	Electrical machinery ...	...	...	...	...	...	383
3832	Radio,television etc..	...	...	...	...	...	3832
384	Transport equipment	...	...	...	...	...	384
3841	Shipbuilding, repair..	...	...	...	...	...	3841
3843	Motor vehicles	...	...	...	...	...	3843
385	Professional goods	...	...	...	...	...	385
390	Other industries	99	-	...	...	...	390
3	Manufacturing ..... c/	328	2647	...	...	...	3
410	Electricity,gas,steam ..	...	...	...	...	...	410
4101	Electricity	841	23110	...	...	...	4101
420	Water works and supply .	7390	949	...	...	...	420
4	Electricity,gas etc	...	...	...	...	...	4
2-4	All industry	...	...	...	...	...	2-4

a/ Twelve months ending 30 June of the year indicated.
b/ Manufacturing: establishments employing 5 or more persons.
c/ Total relates only to industries for which data are available.

GERMAN DEMOCRATIC REPUBLIC

The information on industrial activity is based on the reply to the United Nations Questionnaire on General Industrial Statistics from the Staatliche Zentralverwaltung fur Statistik, Berlin. The concepts and definitions are generally in accordance with United Nations standards. The estimates are presented according to broad groupings of the national classification of enterprises.

The estimates cover activities in mining, manufacturing, electricity, gas and water in the industrial sector. The industrial sector comprises socialist industry (State enterprises and co-operatives), and semi-State and private industrial enterprises; handicrafts are excluded. All enterprises in which the main activity is industrial production are covered. Enterprises carrying on industrial production subsidiary to another major activity are not counted as industrial.

The number of enterprises at 31 December of each year is given in table 1. The figures relate to the number of all legally independent enterprises, plus the number of enterprises forming parts of public combines, allocated to branches according to the specific product of the individual enterprise.

The employment estimates refer to the number of production workers and other employees employed by the enterprise in accordance with labour legislation. Included are homeworkers and persons working reduced hours under terms of a labour contract. Persons working under apprenticeship or training contracts for the purpose of attaining professional qualifications are not counted. The estimates relate to annual averages.

The estimates of wages and salaries relate to the average monthly income per employee and per operative in socialist industry.

The output for 1981 is at the constant planned prices of 1980, based on factory prices of 1 January 1980. Beginning 1982, estimates are at current prices. Output comprises the value of (a) all industrial products completed and intended for the market (including goods made available to employees free of charge or at a reduced rate), (b) all material services of an industrial nature provided to others (contract labour, repairs, installation etc.), (c) finished products and material services of an industrial nature intended for purposes of investment or capital repairs and (d) changes in stocks as a result of uncompleted production. It does not include articles produced in the enterprise which are further processed in the same enterprise, current repairs, articles produced for use in the enterprise and used up within a year, general research and development services; rejects and waste,. commercial articles and packing materials included in the price of the product and non-industrial products and services (construction, transport services etc.).

The estimates of gross fixed capital formation relate to investments valued on the price basis for 1980. Capital repairs are not included.

The indexes of industrial production are compiled by the State Central Administration for Statistics and provided in response to the United Nations Questionnaire on Indexes of Industrial Production. In principle, the indexes cover all industrial establishments.

The data include the relevant data relating to Berlin for which separate data have not been supplied. This is without prejudice to any question of status which may be involved.

Related national publications:
<u>Statistisches Jahrbuch der Deutschen Democratischen Republic</u>; <u>Statistical Pocket Book of the German Democratic Republic</u>, both published by the Staatliche Zentralverwaltung fur Statistik, Berlin.

ISIC	INDUSTRY		1. NUMBER OF ENTERPRISES (NUMBER) 1981	1982	1983	1984	1985	2. AVERAGE NUMBER OF EMPLOYEES a/ (THOUSANDS) 1981	1982	1983	1984	1985	ISIC
210	Coal mining	b/	51	50	50	51	49	215	218	222	224	225	210
220	Petroleum and gas	c/	...	...	...	...	...	...	...	...	...	...	220
230	Metal ore mining	d/	...	...	...	...	...	...	...	...	...	...	230
290	Other mining	e/	...	...	...	...	...	...	...	...	...	...	290
2	Mining, quarrying .		...	...	...	...	...	...	...	...	...	...	2
311/2	Food products												311/2
313	Beverages		600	595	572	558	557	275	276	277	276	278	313
314	Tobacco												314
321	Textiles		254	205	186	181	174	226	224	219	222	221	321
3211	Spinning,weaving etc..		...	...	...	...	...	...	...	...	...	...	3211
322	Wearing apparel												322
323	Leather and products ...												323
324	Footwear												324
331	Wood products	f/	1059	933	875	806	774	490	492	495	498	495	331
332	Furniture, fixtures												332
341	Paper and products												341
3411	Pulp,paper etc.		...	...	...	...	...	...	...	...	...	...	3411
342	Printing,publishing	f/	...	...	...	...	...	...	...	...	...	...	342
351	Industrial chemicals ...	c/e/g/	308	309	292	283	260	339	341	341	343	344	351
3511	Basic excl fertilizers		...	...	...	...	...	...	...	...	...	...	3511
3513	Synthetic resins etc .		...	...	...	...	...	...	...	...	...	...	3513
352	Other chemical products.	c/	...	...	...	...	...	...	...	...	...	...	352
3522	Drugs and medicines ..		...	...	...	...	...	...	...	...	...	...	3522
353	Petroleum refineries ...	c/	...	...	...	...	...	...	...	...	...	...	353
354	Petroleum,coal products.	c/	...	...	...	...	...	...	...	...	...	...	354
355	Rubber products	c/	...	...	...	...	...	...	...	...	...	...	355
356	Plastic products n.e.c..	c/	...	...	...	...	...	...	...	...	...	...	356
361	Pottery,china etc	f/	...	...	...	...	...	...	...	...	...	...	361
362	Glass and products	f/	...	...	...	...	...	...	...	...	...	...	362
369	Non-metal products n.e.c	e/	196	168	156	148	145	95	93	93	94	94	369
371	Iron and steel												371
372	Non-ferrous metals	d/	44	43	43	43	43	137	137	137	138	139	372
381	Metal products												381
382	Machinery n.e.c.	h/ i/	1438	1351	1299	1238	1193	936	942	953	958	973	382
3825	Office,computing etc..	i/	...	...	...	...	...	...	...	...	...	...	3825
383	Electrical machinery ...	i/j/	366	359	347	329	315	436	444	451	463	467	383
3832	Radio,television etc..		...	...	...	...	...	...	...	...	...	...	3832
384	Transport equipment	h/	...	...	...	...	...	...	...	...	...	...	384
3841	Shipbuilding, repair..		...	...	...	...	...	...	...	...	...	...	3841
3843	Motor vehicles		...	...	...	...	...	...	...	...	...	...	3843
385	Professional goods	j/	...	...	...	...	...	...	...	...	...	...	385
390	Other industries	f/	...	...	...	...	...	...	...	...	...	...	390
3	Manufacturing		...	...	...	...	...	...	...	...	...	...	3
410	Electricity,gas,steam ..	g/	...	...	...	...	...	...	...	...	...	...	410
4101	Electricity	b/	...	...	...	...	...	...	...	...	...	...	4101
420	Water works and supply .		16	16	16	16	16	23	24	24	24	25	420
4	Electricity,gas etc	b/g/	...	...	...	...	...	...	...	...	...	...	4
2-4	All industry		4332	4029	3836	3653	3526	3171	3190	3212	3240	3261	2-4

a/ Including homeworkers.
b/ Electricity is included in major group 210.
c/ Major groups 220 and 352 to 356 are included in 351.
d/ Major group 230 is included in 371 and 372 combined.
e/ Part of major group 290 is included in 351 and part in 369.
f/ Major groups 342, 361, 362 and 390 are included in 322 to 341 combined.
g/ Gas manufacture and distribution is included in major group 351.
h/ Major group 384 is included in 381 and 382 combined.
i/ Manufacture of office, computing and accounting machinery is included in major group 383.
j/ Major group 385 is included in 383.

ISIC	INDUSTRY		3. WAGES AND SALARIES OF EMPLOYEES a/ (MARKS) 1981	1982	1983	1984	1985	4. AVERAGE NUMBER OF OPERATIVES b/ (THOUSANDS) 1981	1982	1983	1984	1985	ISIC
210	Coal mining	c/	1193	1207	1216	1229	1258	134	137	140	142	143	210
220	Petroleum and gas	d/	...	...	...	...	...	...	...	...	...	...	220
230	Metal ore mining	e/	...	...	...	...	...	...	...	...	...	...	230
290	Other mining	f/	...	...	...	...	...	...	...	...	...	...	290
2	Mining, quarrying .		...	...	...	...	...	...	...	...	...	...	2
311/2	Food products												311/2
313	Beverages		1005	1026	1040	1068	1095	174	173	174	172	173	313
314	Tobacco												314
321	Textiles		938	957	970	997	1019	166	165	161	162	160	321
3211	Spinning,weaving etc..		...	...	...	...	...	...	...	...	...	...	3211
322	Wearing apparel												322
323	Leather and products ...												323
324	Footwear	g/	960	985	1000	1027	1053	351	352	353	351	348	324
331	Wood products												331
332	Furniture, fixtures												332
341	Paper and products												341
3411	Pulp,paper etc.		...	...	...	...	...	...	...	...	...	...	3411
342	Printing,publishing	g/	...	...	...	...	...	...	...	...	...	...	342
351	Industrial chemicals ...	d/f/h/	1110	1117	1131	1148	1174	198	199	200	201	200	351
3511	Basic excl fertilizers		...	...	...	...	...	...	...	...	...	...	3511
3513	Synthetic resins etc .		...	...	...	...	...	...	...	...	...	...	3513
352	Other chemical products.	d/	...	...	...	...	...	...	...	...	...	...	352
3522	Drugs and medicines ..		...	...	...	...	...	...	...	...	...	...	3522
353	Petroleum refineries ...	d/	...	...	...	...	...	...	...	...	...	...	353
354	Petroleum,coal products.	d/	...	...	...	...	...	...	...	...	...	...	354
355	Rubber products	d/	...	...	...	...	...	...	...	...	...	...	355
356	Plastic products n.e.c..	d/	...	...	...	...	...	...	...	...	...	...	356
361	Pottery,china etc	g/	...	...	...	...	...	...	...	...	...	...	361
362	Glass and products	g/	...	...	...	...	...	...	...	...	...	...	362
369	Non-metal products n.e.c	f/	1045	1067	1077	1096	1115	67	66	66	66	66	369
371	Iron and steel	e/	1162	1175	1183	1197	1222	86	87	87	87	89	371
372	Non-ferrous metals												372
381	Metal products	i/	1096	1117	1128	1150	1176	553	557	562	561	567	381
382	Machinery n.e.c.	j/											382
3825	Office,computing etc..	j/	...	...	...	...	...	...	...	...	...	...	3825
383	Electrical machinery ...	j/k/	1081	1111	1121	1146	1169	250	254	258	264	264	383
3832	Radio,television etc..		...	...	...	...	...	...	...	...	...	...	3832
384	Transport equipment	i/	...	...	...	...	...	...	...	...	...	...	384
3841	Shipbuilding, repair..		...	...	...	...	...	...	...	...	...	...	3841
3843	Motor vehicles		...	...	...	...	...	...	...	...	...	...	3843
385	Professional goods	k/	...	...	...	...	...	...	...	...	...	...	385
390	Other industries	g/	...	...	...	...	...	...	...	...	...	...	390
3	Manufacturing		...	...	...	...	...	...	...	...	...	...	3
410	Electricity,gas,steam ..	h/	...	...	...	...	...	...	...	...	...	...	410
4101	Electricity	c/	...	...	...	...	...	...	...	...	...	...	4101
420	Water works and supply .		973	995	1003	1034	1039	14	15	15	15	15	420
4	Electricity,gas etc	c/h/	...	...	...	...	...	...	...	...	...	...	4
2-4	All industry		1064	1085	1097	1120	1145	1993	2005	2016	2021	2025	2-4

a/ Monthly average per employee. Estimates relate to socialist industry.
b/ Including homeworkers.
c/ Electricity is included in major group 210.
d/ Major groups 220 and 352 to 356 are included in 351.
e/ Major group 230 is included in 371 and 372 combined.
f/ Part of major group 290 is included in 351 and part in 369.
g/ Major groups 342, 361, 362 and 390 are included in 322 to 341 combined.
h/ Gas manufacture and distribution is included in major group 351.
i/ Major group 384 is included in 381 and 382 combined.
j/ Manufacture of office, computing and accounting machinery is included in major group 383.
k/ Major group 385 is included in 383.

ISIC	INDUSTRY		5. WAGES AND SALARIES OF OPERATIVES a/ (MARKS) 1981	1982	1983	1984	1985	6. QUANTITY OF ELECTRICITY CONSUMED (MILLION KWH) 1981	1982	1983	1984	1985	ISIC
210	Coal mining	b/	1189	1201	1205	1217	1241	18088	18743	19076	19669	20417	210
220	Petroleum and gas	c/	...	...	...	...	...	...	...	...	...	...	220
230	Metal ore mining	d/	...	...	...	...	...	...	...	...	...	...	230
290	Other mining	e/	...	...	...	...	...	...	...	...	...	...	290
2	Mining, quarrying .		...	...	...	...	...	...	...	...	...	...	2
311/2	Food products												311/2
313	Beverages		1016	1030	1048	1070	1097	2434	2451	2456	2490	2630	313
314	Tobacco												314
321	Textiles		915	936	950	974	993	1564	1571	1556	1572	1584	321
3211	Spinning,weaving etc..		...	...	...	...	...	...	...	...	...	...	3211
322	Wearing apparel												322
323	Leather and products ...												323
324	Footwear	f/	933	960	978	1002	1025	3987	4016	4089	4244	4383	324
331	Wood products												331
332	Furniture, fixtures												332
341	Paper and products												341
3411	Pulp,paper etc.		...	...	...	...	...	...	...	...	...	...	3411
342	Printing,publishing	f/	...	...	...	...	...	...	...	...	...	...	342
351	Industrial chemicals ...	c/e/g/	1079	1085	1096	1114	1139	20540	20757	20999	21004	21063	351
3511	Basic excl fertilizers		...	...	...	...	...	...	...	...	...	...	3511
3513	Synthetic resins etc .		...	...	...	...	...	...	...	...	...	...	3513
352	Other chemical products.	c/	...	...	...	...	...	...	...	...	...	...	352
3522	Drugs and medicines ..		...	...	...	...	...	...	...	...	...	...	3522
353	Petroleum refineries ...	c/	...	...	...	...	...	...	...	...	...	...	353
354	Petroleum,coal products.	c/	...	...	...	...	...	...	...	...	...	...	354
355	Rubber products	c/	...	...	...	...	...	...	...	...	...	...	355
356	Plastic products n.e.c..	c/	...	...	...	...	...	...	...	...	...	...	356
361	Pottery,china etc	f/	...	...	...	...	...	...	...	...	...	...	361
362	Glass and products	f/	...	...	...	...	...	...	...	...	...	...	362
369	Non-metal products n.e.c	e/	1053	1070	1078	1091	1111	2404	2310	2391	2414	2424	369
371	Iron and steel	d/	1162	1174	1183	1193	1211	6310	6293	6341	6568	6681	371
372	Non-ferrous metals												372
381	Metal products	h/	1081	1096	1111	1133	1155	5466	5529	5625	5853	6036	381
382	Machinery n.e.c.	i/											382
3825	Office,computing etc..	i/	...	...	...	...	...	...	...	...	...	...	3825
383	Electrical machinery ...	i/j/	1025	1055	1063	1085	1106	1735	1798	1882	2005	2099	383
3832	Radio,television etc..		...	...	...	...	...	...	...	...	...	...	3832
384	Transport equipment	h/	...	...	...	...	...	...	...	...	...	...	384
3841	Shipbuilding, repair..		...	...	...	...	...	...	...	...	...	...	3841
3843	Motor vehicles		...	...	...	...	...	...	...	...	...	...	3843
385	Professional goods	j/	...	...	...	...	...	...	...	...	...	...	385
390	Other industries	f/	...	...	...	...	...	...	...	...	...	...	390
3	Manufacturing		...	...	...	...	...	...	...	...	...	...	3
410	Electricity,gas,steam ..	g/	...	...	...	...	...	...	...	...	...	...	410
4101	Electricity	b/	...	...	...	...	...	...	...	...	...	...	4101
420	Water works and supply .		940	949	950	981	998	1112	1187	1210	1209	1265	420
4	Electricity,gas etc	b/g/	...	...	...	...	...	...	...	...	...	...	4
2-4	All industry		1041	1059	1072	1093	1116	k/ 63640	k/ 64655	k/ 65625	k/ 67028	k/ 68582	2-4

a/ Monthly average per operative. Estimates relate to socialist industry.
b/ Electricity is included in major group 210.
c/ Major groups 220 and 352 to 356 are included in 351.
d/ Major group 230 is included in 371 and 372 combined.
e/ Part of major group 290 is included in 351 and part in 369.
f/ Major groups 342, 361, 362 and 390 are included in 322 to 341 combined.
g/ Gas manufacture and distribution is included in major group 351.
h/ Major group 384 is included in 381 and 382 combined.
i/ Manufacture of office, computing and accounting machinery is included in major group 383.
j/ Major group 385 is included in 383.
k/ Including consumption for own use of the power stations.

ISIC	INDUSTRY		7. OUTPUT (BILLION MARKS) a/ 1981	b/ 1982	b/ 1983	b/ 1984	b/ 1985	8. GROSS FIXED CAPITAL FORMATION TOTAL a/ (MILLION MARKS) 1981	1982	1983	1984	1985	ISIC
210	Coal mining	c/	37.0	41.0	43.6	59.6	63.9	6799	6843	6542	6434	7104	210
220	Petroleum and gas	d/	...	...	...	...	...	...	...	...	...	...	220
230	Metal ore mining	e/	...	...	...	...	...	...	...	...	...	...	230
290	Other mining	f/	...	...	...	...	...	...	...	...	...	...	290
2	Mining, quarrying .		...	...	...	...	...	...	...	...	...	...	2
311/2	Food products												311/2
313	Beverages		49.5	58.8	61.3	65.9	70.6	1739	1809	1791	1661	1394	313
314	Tobacco												314
321	Textiles		19.7	25.5	25.6	28.8	30.5	739	697	639	922	1226	321
3211	Spinning,weaving etc..		...	...	...	...	...	...	...	...	...	...	3211
322	Wearing apparel												322
323	Leather and products ...												323
324	Footwear	g/	33.3	40.4	42.9	45.5	49.9	1944	1994	2430	2462	2059	324
331	Wood products												331
332	Furniture, fixtures												332
341	Paper and products												341
3411	Pulp,paper etc.		...	...	...	...	...	...	...	...	...	...	3411
342	Printing,publishing	g/	...	...	...	...	...	...	...	...	...	...	342
351	Industrial chemicals ...	d/f/h/	54.4	85.3	88.8	91.5	103.6	4838	5037	4907	5437	5946	351
3511	Basic excl fertilizers		...	...	...	...	...	...	...	...	...	...	3511
3513	Synthetic resins etc .		...	...	...	...	...	...	...	...	...	...	3513
352	Other chemical products.	d/	...	...	...	...	...	...	...	...	...	...	352
3522	Drugs and medicines ..		...	...	...	...	...	...	...	...	...	...	3522
353	Petroleum refineries ...	d/	...	...	...	...	...	...	...	...	...	...	353
354	Petroleum,coal products.	d/	...	...	...	...	...	...	...	...	...	...	354
355	Rubber products	d/	...	...	...	...	...	...	...	...	...	...	355
356	Plastic products n.e.c..	d/	...	...	...	...	...	...	...	...	...	...	356
361	Pottery,china etc	g/	...	...	...	...	...	...	...	...	...	...	361
362	Glass and products	g/	...	...	...	...	...	...	...	...	...	...	362
369	Non-metal products n.e.c	f/	6.6	6.4	8.0	8.5	10.3	1093	704	597	628	524	369
371	Iron and steel	e/	29.3	32.9	33.2	33.7	49.4	3025	3518	4859	1810	1690	371
372	Non-ferrous metals												372
381	Metal products	i/	78.2	86.5	88.7	90.2	99.2	5742	5403	5237	5256	5510	381
382	Machinery n.e.c.	j/											382
3825	Office,computing etc..	j/	...	...	...	...	...	...	...	...	...	...	3825
383	Electrical machinery ...	j/k/	32.9	37.0	39.1	39.9	44.4	2702	2330	2548	2416	2220	383
3832	Radio,television etc..		...	...	...	...	...	...	...	...	...	...	3832
384	Transport equipment	i/	...	...	...	...	...	...	...	...	...	...	384
3841	Shipbuilding, repair..		...	...	...	...	...	...	...	...	...	...	3841
3843	Motor vehicles		...	...	...	...	...	...	...	...	...	...	3843
385	Professional goods	k/	...	...	...	...	...	...	...	...	...	...	385
390	Other industries	g/	...	...	...	...	...	...	...	...	...	...	390
3	Manufacturing		...	...	...	...	...	...	...	...	...	...	3
410	Electricity,gas,steam ..	h/	...	...	...	...	...	...	...	...	...	...	410
4101	Electricity	c/	...	...	...	...	...	...	...	...	...	...	4101
420	Water works and supply .		2.1	2.3	2.3	3.0	3.1	1658	1495	1471	1627	1663	420
4	Electricity,gas etc	c/h/	...	...	...	...	...	...	...	...	...	...	4
2-4	All industry		343.0	416.1	433.5	466.6	524.9	30279	29830	31021	28653	29336	2-4

a/ At prices of 1980.
b/ At current prices.
c/ Electricity is included in major group 210.
d/ Major groups 220 and 352 to 356 are included in 351.
e/ Major group 230 is included in 371 and 372 combined.
f/ Part of major group 290 is included in 351 and part in 369.
g/ Major groups 342, 361, 362 and 390 are included in 322 to 341 combined.
h/ Gas manufacture and distribution is included in major group 351.
i/ Major group 384 is included in 381 and 382 combined.
j/ Manufacture of office, computing and accounting machinery is included in major group 383.
k/ Major group 385 is included in 383.

9. INDEX NUMBERS OF INDUSTRIAL PRODUCTION (1980 = 100)

ISIC	INDUSTRY	1976	1977	1978	1979	1981	1982	1983	1984	1985	a/ RATE	ISIC
210	Coal mining	89	92	92	94	106	110	115	120	124	3.8	210
220	Petroleum and gas	...	...	...	...	...	...	...	...	...	...	220
230	Metal ore mining	...	...	...	...	...	...	...	...	...	...	230
290	Other mining	...	...	...	...	...	...	...	...	...	...	290
2	Mining, quarrying .	90	92	93	95	105	108	112	116	119	3.2	2
311/2	Food products	90	93	95	98	102	102	105	108	111	2.4	311/2
313	Beverages											313
314	Tobacco											314
321	Textiles	87	90	94	96	102	105	107	111	113	2.9	321
3211	Spinning,weaving etc..	...	...	...	...	...	...	...	...	...	...	3211
322	Wearing apparel	90	91	93	98	100	105	113	109	110	2.3	322
323	Leather and products ...	85	90	92	96	103	105	107	108	111	3.0	323
324	Footwear											324
331	Wood products	87	92	97	100	101	104	110	117	120	3.6	331
332	Furniture, fixtures											332
341	Paper and products	84	88	93	96	102	105	109	116	118	3.8	341
3411	Pulp,paper etc.	...	...	...	...	...	...	...	...	...	...	3411
342	Printing,publishing	...	...	...	...	...	...	...	...	...	...	342
351	Industrial chemicals ... b/	84	88	93	97	102	108	112	117	121	4.1	351
3511	Basic excl fertilizers	...	...	...	...	...	...	...	...	...	...	3511
3513	Synthetic resins etc .	...	...	...	...	...	...	...	...	...	...	3513
352	Other chemical products. b/	...	...	...	...	...	...	...	...	...	...	352
3522	Drugs and medicines ..	...	...	...	...	...	...	...	...	...	...	3522
353	Petroleum refineries ...	86	90	93	97	100	112	113	116	121	3.9	353
354	Petroleum,coal products.											354
355	Rubber products	84	88	94	98	104	106	112	119	123	4.3	355
356	Plastic products n.e.c..	84	88	94	99	104	109	113	121	123	4.3	356
361	Pottery,china etc	83	86	91	96	105	110	109	117	130	5.1	361
362	Glass and products											362
369	Non-metal products n.e.c	94	98	102	101	100	97	99	101	104	1.1	369
371	Iron and steel	87	91	94	96	107	109	112	116	120	3.6	371
372	Non-ferrous metals											372
381	Metal products	82	87	91	96	104	108	108	113	116	3.9	381
382	Machinery n.e.c.	79	84	88	93	106	111	115	119	126	5.3	382
3825	Office,computing etc..	...	...	...	...	...	...	...	...	...	...	3825
383	Electrical machinery ... c/	72	78	84	92	111	118	129	140	155	8.9	383
3832	Radio,television etc..	...	...	...	...	...	...	...	...	...	...	3832
384	Transport equipment .... c/	...	...	...	...	...	...	...	...	...	...	384
3841	Shipbuilding, repair..	...	...	...	...	...	...	...	...	...	...	3841
3843	Motor vehicles	...	...	...	...	...	...	...	...	...	...	3843
385	Professional goods ..... c/	...	...	...	...	...	...	...	...	...	...	385
390	Other industries	...	...	...	...	...	...	...	...	...	...	390
3	Manufacturing ..... d/	83	87	91	95	105	109	113	118	123	4.5	3
410	Electricity,gas,steam .. e/	82	85	91	97	103	104	109	114	118	4.1	410
4101	Electricity	...	...	...	...	...	...	...	...	...	...	4101
420	Water works and supply .	...	...	...	...	...	...	...	...	...	...	420
4	Electricity,gas etc	82	86	92	97	104	105	110	113	124	4.7	4
2-4	All industry d/e/f/	83	87	91	95	105	108	113	117	122	4.4	2-4

a/ Annual growth rate 1976-1985.
c/ Major groups 384 and 385 are included in 383.
e/ Excluding gas manufacture and distribution.

b/ Major group 352 is included in 351.
d/ Excluding publishing.
f/ Including fishing.

GERMANY, FEDERAL REPUBLIC OF

The information on industrial activity is based on the reply to the United Nations Questionnaire on General Industrial Statistics from the Statistisches Bundesamt, Wiesbaden. The concepts, definitions and classification by branches of industry are generally in accordance with United Nations standards.

In general, the estimates for mining and manufacturing are derived from the monthly industry inquiry carried out by the Statistisches Bundesamt. The inquiry covers, on a complete enumeration basis, local units of enterprises with 20 or more persons engaged, including non-industrial activities of the units and licensed handicrafts as well. The estimates for electricity, gas and water are obtained from annual surveys with all enterprises with 20 or more persons engaged.

The estimates, which are based on the national classification scheme (Systematik der Wirtschaftszweige, Fassung fur die Statistik im Produzierenden Gewerbe-SYPRO), have been adjusted to the present version of ISIC, in so far as details permit. The differences between the national scheme and ISIC are set out in the following paragraph.

Prefabricated building manufacturing, classified as construction under the national scheme, is not generally included; publishing (ISIC 342) is not surveyed; manufacture of natural stone products (ISIC 369) is included in ISIC 290; manufacture of mattresses (ISIC 332) in ISIC 321; manufacture of umbrellas (ISIC 390) in ISIC 322; manufacture of fur wearing apparel (ISIC 322) in ISIC 323; bookbinding (ISIC 342) in ISIC 341; manufacture of mixed lubricating oils and greases (ISIC 353, 354) in ISIC 351 and 352 combined; manufacture of unprocessed plastic pipes and tubes (ISIC 351) in ISIC 356; founding and casting of non-ferrous metals (ISIC 372) and surface refinement and hardening plants (ISIC 381) in ISIC 371; manufacture of drawn steel wire and forged steel chains (ISIC 371), washing machines (ISIC 382), railroad equipment (ISIC 3842) and assembly and repair of ventilation, heating and sanitary systems (ISIC major division 5) in ISIC 381; manufacture of lighting glassware (ISIC 362), recording of master tapes and records (ISIC major division 9) and manufacture of electric and electronic measuring instruments and meters (ISIC 385) in ISIC 383. The estimates of value added are generally compiled in the same manner as those for the inquiries but quarrying is included in ISIC 369, prefabricated building manufacturing is excluded for all years, erection of structural steel is included in ISIC 381 and the difference in respect of assembly and repair of ventilation, heating and sanitary systems has been adjusted.

The employment figures, in all cases, are annual averages. The number of persons engaged includes working proprietors and unpaid family workers if they are actively engaged for at least one third of the usual working time. Apprentices are included; all tables shown for operatives include data relating to industrial apprentices. Operatives are defined as persons engaged who are subject to obligatory insurance in the workers' old age insurance funds. Homeworkers are not included in the estimates.

The quantity of electricity consumed shown for the electricity industry relates only to own consumption of power generating plants and does not include other power consumption of public power supply enterprises.

The figures of output relate to turnover from own production, including proceeds from non-industrial activities, such as the sale of goods sold in the same condition as received and the sale of waste, power and similar items. The value of shipments effected inside an enterprise consisting of several local units is not recorded. The valuation is based on invoice values and includes excise duties and costs for freight, packing, postage and other charges. The value-added tax is not included.

The estimates of value added are derived from national accounts calculations; they cover industrial enterprises and include industrial activities of licensed handicrafts. The calculations are generally based on the gross value of production comprising the value of current sales of goods and services, including goods sold as purchased and the consumption of entrepreneurs, changes in stocks of semi-finished and finished goods from own production and own-account construction. Value added in producers' prices is obtained by subtracting from the gross value of production the cost of intermediate goods and services. These are goods and services, including goods sold as purchased, received from other economic units and used for production purposes. The value-added estimates do not fully measure the contribution of the industries to gross domestic product because they are valued exclusive of the value added tax and other taxes or duties linked to imports, and they include imputed bank service charges.

The estimates of gross fixed capital formation and value of stocks are derived from annual surveys of enterprises with 20 or more persons engaged. For gross fixed capital formation, the figures shown represent gross increases in new and used fixed assets during each year, excluding capitalized research and development expenditure and advance payments on investment goods not yet supplied.

The indexes of industrial production are compiled by the Statistisches Bundesamt and provided in response to the United Nations Questionnaire on Indexes of Industrial Production. The indexes cover all local units of enterprises with, in general, 20 or more persons engaged, including production handicrafts.

The data include the relevant data relating to Berlin for which separate data have not been supplied. This is without prejudice to any question of status which may be involved.

Related national publications:
Fachserie 4, Reihe 4.1.1, Beschaftigung, Umsatz und Energieversorgung der Unternehmen und Betriebe im Bergbau und im Verarbeitenden Gewerbe (monthly/annual); Fachserie 18, Volkswirtschaftliche Gesamtrechnungen, Reihe 1, Konten und Standardtabellen; Wirtschaft und Statistik (monthly); Statistisches Jahrbuch fur die Bundesrepublik Deutschland, all published by the Statistisches Bundesamt, Wiesbaden.

ISIC	INDUSTRY	1. NUMBER OF ESTABLISHMENTS a/b/ (NUMBER) 1981	1982	1983 c/	1984	1985	2. AVERAGE NUMBER OF PERSONS ENGAGED a/b/ (THOUSANDS) 1981	1982	1983 c/	1984	1985	ISIC
210	Coal mining	150	149	144	139	134	211	209	204	194	189	210
220	Petroleum and gas	48	49	47	46	47	7	7	7	7	7	220
230	Metal ore mining	10	10	9	8	7	2	2	2	2	2	230
290	Other mining	1444	1418	1216	1244	1250	48	46	37	37	37	290
2	Mining, quarrying .	1652	1626	1416	1437	1438	268	264	250	240	235	2
311/2	Food products	3553	3489	3485	3449	3376	360	349	336	334	335	311/2
313	Beverages	1145	1088	1049	1032	994	106	102	98	95	92	313
314	Tobacco	82	76	70	63	60	23	22	20	20	19	314
321	Textiles	2333	2223	2178	2106	2048	296	273	256	249	246	321
3211	Spinning,weaving etc..	...	...	...	...	...	...	...	...	...	...	3211
322	Wearing apparel	2669	2482	2279	2191	2117	211	191	175	174	170	322
323	Leather and products ...	526	475	434	409	382	34	31	28	26	25	323
324	Footwear	431	401	373	361	338	52	49	47	47	45	324
331 332	Wood products .... Furniture, fixtures .... d/	[4792	4598	4460	4344	4203	277	253	242	239	230]	331 332
341	Paper and products	1117	1100	1057	1019	1015	165	159	151	148	150	341
3411	Pulp,paper etc.	180	176	177	174	173	52	50	49	48	49	3411
342	Printing,publishing	2028	1999	1944	1901	1905	181	174	165	162	162	342
351	Industrial chemicals ... e/	1616	1605	1591	1572	1564	567	561	551	553	559	351
3511	Basic excl fertilizers	...	...	...	...	...	...	...	...	...	...	3511
3513	Synthetic resins etc .	...	...	...	...	...	...	...	...	...	...	3513
352	Other chemical products. e/	...	...	...	...	...	...	...	...	...	...	352
3522	Drugs and medicines ..	...	...	...	...	...	...	...	...	...	...	3522
353 354	Petroleum refineries ... Petroleum,coal products.	[89	91	88	84	82	34	34	32	31	29]	353 354
355	Rubber products	277	271	263	262	263	101	97	93	93	95	355
356	Plastic products n.e.c..	1994	1988	1950	1965	1971	201	197	194	202	209	356
361	Pottery,china etc	178	176	167	165	163	41	39	37	37	36	361
362	Glass and products	361	360	347	335	330	74	70	67	65	65	362
369	Non-metal products n.e.c d/	2534	2485	2560	2605	2552	168	157	157	156	146	369
371	Iron and steel	1810	1765	517	507	501	496	470	321	301	296	371
372	Non-ferrous metals	458	455	448	435	434	107	101	102	102	106	372
381	Metal products	4383	4308	5338	5248	5212	504	484	566	562	571	381
382	Machinery n.e.c.	5479	5471	5472	5407	5421	1096	1068	1037	1017	1044	382
3825	Office,computing etc..	127	125	123	128	137	72	69	71	77	83	3825
383	Electrical machinery ...	2870	2859	3205	3178	3237	897	860	871	875	920	383
3832	Radio,television etc..	...	...	...	...	...	...	...	...	...	...	3832
384	Transport equipment	1059	1068	1051	1039	1032	848	853	840	843	870	384
3841	Shipbuilding, repair..	131	124	121	119	119	57	57	53	45	44	3841
3843	Motor vehicles	...	...	...	...	...	...	...	...	...	...	3843
385	Professional goods	1486	1467	1432	1359	1400	161	155	140	138	144	385
390	Other industries	751	707	673	645	622	56	53	50	50	50	390
3	Manufacturing ..... d/	44021	43007	42431	41681	41222	7056	6802	6576	6519	6614	3
410	Electricity,gas,steam ..	585	582	582	581	...	254	255	256	256	...	410
4101	Electricity	462	461	452	459	...	229	230	229	232	...	4101
420	Water works and supply .	159	162	157	158	...	17	17	17	18	...	420
4	Electricity,gas etc	744	744	739	739	...	271	272	273	274	...	4
2-4	All industry	...	...	...	...	...	...	...	...	...	...	2-4

Note. For description of classification, see country note.

a/ Mining and manufacturing: local units of enterprises with 20 or more persons engaged; including production handicrafts.
b/ Electricity, gas and water supply: enterprises with 20 or more persons engaged.
c/ Beginning 1983, data for certain major groups are not fully comparable with those for previous years owing to changes in classification.
d/ Excluding manufacture of prefabricated building parts and structures.
e/ Major group 352 is included in 351.

ISIC	INDUSTRY	3. WAGES AND SALARIES OF EMPLOYEES a/b/ (BILLION MARKS)					4. SUPPLEMENTS TO WAGES AND SALARIES a/b/ (BILLION MARKS)					ISIC
		1981	1982	c/ 1983	1984	1985	1981	1982	c/ 1983	1984	1985	
210	Coal mining	8.36	8.68	8.45	8.38	8.56	3.14	3.14	3.13	3.55	...	210
220	Petroleum and gas	0.32	0.37	0.38	0.40	0.42	[0.08	0.08	0.09	0.15]	...	220
230	Metal ore mining	0.08	0.08	0.08	0.08	0.09					...	230
290	Other mining	1.71	1.65	1.43	1.49	1.52	d/ 0.29	d/ 0.29	d/ 0.30	d/ 0.32	...	290
2	Mining, quarrying	10.47	10.78	10.34	10.35	10.59	d/ 3.51	d/ 3.51	d/ 3.52	d/ 4.02	...	2
311/2	Food products	10.78	10.93	10.87	11.07	11.39	2.42	2.48	2.54	2.73	...	311/2
313	Beverages	3.88	3.94	3.93	3.91	3.89	0.88	0.90	1.00	1.00	...	313
314	Tobacco	0.80	0.87	0.87	0.91	0.86	0.39	0.35	0.30	0.32	...	314
321	Textiles	7.88	7.60	7.47	7.56	7.77	1.60	1.56	1.59	1.67	...	321
3211	Spinning,weaving etc.	...	...	...	...	...	0.90	0.87	0.88	0.95	...	3211
322	Wearing apparel	4.43	4.21	4.06	4.17	4.22	0.82	0.78	0.79	0.83	...	322
323	Leather and products	0.80	0.76	0.74	0.73	0.70	0.16	0.15	0.15	0.15	...	323
324	Footwear	1.27	1.27	1.26	1.30	1.29	0.24	0.23	0.24	0.24	...	324
331	Wood products	[e/ 8.62	e/ 8.11	e/ 8.19	e/ 8.35	e/ 8.17]	0.75	0.69	0.73	0.74	...	331
332	Furniture, fixtures						0.97	0.93	0.94	0.96	...	332
341	Paper and products	5.50	5.50	5.49	5.62	5.90	1.16	1.14	1.24	1.36	...	341
3411	Pulp,paper etc.	2.01	2.01	2.05	2.11	2.21	0.46	0.45	0.50	0.60	...	3411
342	Printing,publishing	6.68	6.73	6.69	6.75	7.03	1.01	1.04	1.06	1.13	...	342
351	Industrial chemicals	f/ 24.45	f/ 25.35	f/ 25.84	f/ 27.15	f/ 28.73	d/ 3.42	d/ 3.72	d/ 4.67	d/ 5.01	...	351
3511	Basic excl fertilizers	...	...	...	...	...	3.25	3.54	4.45	4.79	...	3511
3513	Synthetic resins etc	...	...	...	...	...	0.17	0.18	0.22	0.22	...	3513
352	Other chemical products	f/	f/	f/	f/	f/	d/ 2.59	d/ 2.62	d/ 3.01	d/ 3.15	...	352
3522	Drugs and medicines	...	...	...	...	...	0.96	0.97	1.13	1.18	...	3522
353	Petroleum refineries	[1.87	1.96	1.90	1.93	1.95	0.81	0.83	0.97	1.10]	...	353
354	Petroleum,coal products										...	354
355	Rubber products	3.46	3.49	3.52	3.67	3.89	0.80	0.78	0.87	0.92	...	355
356	Plastic products n.e.c.	6.24	6.39	6.58	7.09	7.57	1.16	1.20	1.27	1.38	...	356
361	Pottery,china etc	1.09	1.07	1.07	1.10	1.11	0.23	0.22	0.23	0.24	...	361
362	Glass and products	2.45	2.45	2.46	2.50	2.57	0.55	0.57	0.59	0.59	...	362
369	Non-metal products n.e.c	e/ 5.99	e/ 5.78	e/ 6.01	e/ 6.17	e/ 5.91	1.48	1.46	1.60	1.59	...	369
371	Iron and steel	17.94	17.48	12.38	12.53	12.79	3.47	3.73	3.63	3.89	...	371
372	Non-ferrous metals	3.88	3.86	3.97	4.14	4.46	0.75	0.75	0.84	0.91	...	372
381	Metal products	17.34	17.30	20.84	21.33	22.37	4.03	4.16	4.07	4.23	...	381
382	Machinery n.e.c.	41.45	41.93	42.02	43.26	46.41	8.79	9.02	9.30	9.81	...	382
3825	Office,computing etc.	3.26	3.38	3.58	3.97	4.39	0.96	0.97	1.03	1.16	...	3825
383	Electrical machinery	31.97	32.21	34.14	35.27	38.43	7.34	8.78	9.26	9.58	...	383
3832	Radio,television etc.	...	...	...	...	...	3.46	4.49	5.09	4.91	...	3832
384	Transport equipment	34.53	35.87	36.78	37.35	40.55	7.53	7.96	9.00	9.25	...	384
3841	Shipbuilding, repair	2.16	2.17	1.97	1.71	1.81	0.46	0.48	0.46	0.41	...	3841
3843	Motor vehicles	...	...	...	...	...	6.40	6.82	7.81	8.10	...	3843
385	Professional goods	5.25	5.22	4.87	5.00	5.45	g/ 1.06	g/ 1.01	g/ 1.05	g/ 1.02	...	385
390	Other industries	1.54	1.53	1.49	1.52	1.59	0.29	0.30	0.30	0.32	...	390
3	Manufacturing	e/ 250.09	e/ 251.81	e/ 253.44	e/ 260.38	e/ 275.00	d/g/ 54.70	d/g/ 57.36	d/g/ 61.25	d/g/ 64.12	...	3
410	Electricity,gas,steam	10.60	11.11	11.52	11.99	...	3.69	3.78	4.28	4.24	...	410
4101	Electricity	9.56	10.05	10.32	10.83	...	3.35	3.46	3.89	3.87	...	4101
420	Water works and supply	0.66	0.70	0.70	0.75	...	0.22	0.23	0.24	0.26	...	420
4	Electricity,gas etc	11.26	11.81	12.22	12.74	...	3.91	4.01	4.52	4.50	...	4
2-4	All industry	...	...	...	...	...	...	...	...	...	...	2-4

Note. For description of classification, see country note.

a/ Mining and manufacturing: local units of enterprises with 20 or more persons engaged; including production handicrafts.
b/ Electricity, gas and water supply: enterprises with 20 or more persons engaged.
c/ Beginning 1983, data for certain major groups are not fully comparable with those for previous years owing to changes in classification.
d/ Parts of group 3512 are included in major groups 290 and 352.
e/ Excluding manufacture of prefabricated building parts and structures.
f/ Major group 352 is included in 351.
g/ Excluding repair of professional goods.

ISIC	INDUSTRY	5. AVERAGE NUMBER OF OPERATIVES a/b/ (THOUSANDS) 1981	1982	c/ 1983	1984	1985	6. WAGES AND SALARIES OF OPERATIVES a/b/ (BILLION MARKS) 1981	1982	c/ 1983	1984	1985	ISIC
210	Coal mining	173	172	167	159	154	6.12	6.33	6.11	6.00	6.16	210
220	Petroleum and gas	4	4	3	3	3	0.14	0.15	0.16	0.16	0.17	220
230	Metal ore mining	2	2	2	2	2	0.06	0.06	0.06	0.06	0.07	230
290	Other mining	37	35	28	28	27	1.20	1.15	0.97	1.01	1.02	290
2	Mining, quarrying .	216	213	200	192	186	7.52	7.69	7.30	7.23	7.42	2
311/2	Food products	240	232	222	222	222	6.29	6.34	6.31	6.45	6.60	311/2
313	Beverages	68	65	62	60	58	2.19	2.21	2.18	2.16	2.14	313
314	Tobacco	15	14	12	12	11	0.42	0.43	0.42	0.41	0.40	314
321	Textiles	226	207	193	188	186	5.24	5.00	4.89	4.97	5.11	321
3211	Spinning,weaving etc..	...	...	...	...	...	...	...	...	...	...	3211
322	Wearing apparel	172	155	142	140	137	3.13	2.94	2.81	2.89	2.91	322
323	Leather and products ...	26	24	21	20	19	0.55	0.51	0.49	0.49	0.47	323
324	Footwear	43	41	39	38	36	0.95	0.94	0.92	0.95	0.93	324
331	Wood products .... d/	[215	195	186	184	177	6.24	5.78	5.84	5.95	6.75]	331
332	Furniture, fixtures											332
341	Paper and products	125	119	112	110	111	3.67	3.61	3.58	3.67	3.85	341
3411	Pulp,paper etc.	40	39	38	37	37	1.41	1.39	1.41	1.45	1.52	3411
342	Printing,publishing	130	123	115	113	113	4.38	4.31	4.24	4.28	4.44	342
351	Industrial chemicals ... e/	308	301	292	292	295	10.64	10.74	10.83	11.31	11.87	351
3511	Basic excl fertilizers	...	...	...	...	...	...	...	...	...	...	3511
3513	Synthetic resins etc .	...	...	...	...	...	...	...	...	...	...	3513
352	Other chemical products. e/	...	...	...	...	...	...	...	...	...	...	352
3522	Drugs and medicines ..	...	...	...	...	...	...	...	...	...	...	3522
353	Petroleum refineries ...	[17	17	16	15	74	0.76	0.79	0.75	0.73	0.73]	353
354	Petroleum,coal products.											354
355	Rubber products	75	71	68	69	70	2.26	2.25	2.26	2.36	2.51	355
356	Plastic products n.e.c..	148	144	143	149	155	3.99	4.05	4.18	4.53	4.85	356
361	Pottery,china etc	34	32	30	30	30	0.82	0.80	0.79	0.81	0.82	361
362	Glass and products	57	54	51	50	50	1.72	1.70	1.70	1.73	1.79	362
369	Non-metal products n.e.c d/	125	115	116	114	106	4.08	3.84	4.00	4.08	3.82	369
371	Iron and steel	385	363	246	229	227	12.64	12.13	8.48	8.62	8.89	371
372	Non-ferrous metals	81	76	76	76	80	2.64	2.60	2.65	2.79	3.01	372
381	Metal products	369	351	415	413	422	11.28	11.07	13.50	13.84	14.62	381
382	Machinery n.e.c.	692	667	638	622	640	22.16	21.88	21.27	21.85	23.67	382
3825	Office,computing etc..	30	27	27	29	32	0.89	0.86	0.85	0.93	1.05	3825
383	Electrical machinery ...	563	531	534	538	571	15.61	15.38	16.14	16.67	18.29	383
3832	Radio,television etc..	...	...	...	...	...	...	...	...	...	...	3832
384	Transport equipment	645	647	634	636	659	23.35	24.05	24.43	24.57	27.04	384
3841	Shipbuilding, repair..	44	44	41	35	34	1.55	1.54	1.36	1.16	1.25	3841
3843	Motor vehicles	...	...	...	...	...	...	...	...	...	...	3843
385	Professional goods	109	103	93	91	95	2.92	2.86	2.62	2.70	2.95	385
390	Other industries	41	39	37	36	37	0.99	0.98	0.93	0.96	1.01	390
3	Manufacturing ..... d/	4909	4686	4493	4447	4521	148.92	147.19	146.21	149.77	159.47	3
410	Electricity,gas,steam ..	140	140	139	138	...	5.39	5.50	5.67	5.81	...	410
4101	Electricity	127	127	125	126	...	4.93	5.03	5.13	5.33	...	4101
420	Water works and supply .	10	10	10	10	...	0.37	0.37	0.36	0.39	...	420
4	Electricity,gas etc	150	150	149	148	...	5.76	5.87	6.03	6.20	...	4
2-4	All industry	...	...	...	...	...	...	...	...	...	...	2-4

Note. For description of classification, see country note.

a/ Mining and manufacturing: local units of enterprises with 20 or more persons engaged; including production handicrafts.
b/ Electricity, gas and water supply: enterprises with 20 or more persons engaged.
c/ Beginning 1983, data for certain major groups are not fully comparable with those for previous years owing to changes in classification.
d/ Excluding manufacture of prefabricated building parts and structures.
e/ Major group 352 is included in 351.

ISIC	INDUSTRY	7. HOURS WORKED BY OPERATIVES a/b/ (MILLIONS)					8. QUANTITY OF ELECTRICITY CONSUMED a/ (BILLION KWH)					ISIC
		1981	1982	c/ 1983	1984	1985	1981	1982	c/ 1983	1984	1985	
210	Coal mining	261	261	242	224	223	12.78	13.00	13.04	13.09	13.40	210
220	Petroleum and gas	6	6	6	6	6	0.44	0.45	0.45	0.46	0.49	220
230	Metal ore mining	3	3	3	3	3	0.14	0.13	0.13	0.14	0.15	230
290	Other mining	70	65	53	52	51	1.96	1.78	1.82	1.93	1.95	290
2	Mining, quarrying .	340	335	304	285	283	15.32	15.36	15.44	15.62	15.99	2
311/2	Food products	443	427	411	409	405	6.05	6.15	6.10	6.27	6.47	311/2
313	Beverages	130	125	118	113	108	1.46	1.46	1.47	1.42	1.44	313
314	Tobacco	23	22	21	20	19	0.21	0.21	0.21	0.22	0.23	314
321	Textiles	362	333	316	311	306	4.04	3.99	3.99	4.15	4.30	321
3211	Spinning,weaving etc..	...	...	...	...	...	...	...	...	...	...	3211
322	Wearing apparel	257	233	218	217	209	0.29	0.28	0.27	0.27	0.28	322
323	Leather and products ...	42	37	35	33	31	0.13	0.13	0.13	0.13	0.13	323
324	Footwear	69	66	63	63	60	0.12	0.11	0.12	0.12	0.72	324
331	Wood products .... d/	[367	330	326	322	302	2.59	2.44	2.51	2.59	2.60]	331
332	Furniture, fixtures											332
341	Paper and products	217	205	197	195	194	9.87	9.94	10.40	10.93	11.10	341
3411	Pulp,paper etc.	73	70	68	67	67	8.45	8.49	8.93	9.40	9.54	3411
342	Printing,publishing	222	210	199	193	188	1.26	1.29	1.33	1.39	1.43	342
351	Industrial chemicals ... e/	517	502	491	490	491	41.10	38.30	40.63	42.89	38.44	351
3511	Basic excl fertilizers	...	...	...	...	...	...	...	...	...	...	3511
3513	Synthetic resins etc .	...	...	...	...	...	...	...	...	...	...	3513
352	Other chemical products. e/	...	...	...	...	...	...	...	...	...	...	352
3522	Drugs and medicines ..	...	...	...	...	...	...	...	...	...	...	3522
353	Petroleum refineries ...	[30	30	28	25	23	5.52	5.16	5.26	5.37	5.43]	353
354	Petroleum,coal products.											354
355	Rubber products	120	117	114	115	117	1.58	1.59	1.61	1.66	1.76	355
356	Plastic products n.e.c..	250	244	245	255	262	3.45	3.56	3.82	4.14	4.38	356
361	Pottery,china etc	56	53	50	49	48	0.31	0.30	0.30	0.30	0.30	361
362	Glass and products	94	90	86	85	86	2.12	2.14	2.21	2.32	2.46	362
369	Non-metal products n.e.c d/	227	205	210	205	185	6.17	5.85	6.11	6.09	5.61	369
371	Iron and steel	637	584	382	377	369	23.93	22.00	19.92	21.53	21.82	371
372	Non-ferrous metals	136	128	129	131	134	16.89	16.68	17.41	18.08	17.94	372
381	Metal products	636	601	716	717	723	3.37	3.28	4.96	5.32	5.52	381
382	Machinery n.e.c.	1173	1113	1057	1057	1085	6.36	6.28	6.28	6.61	7.11	382
3825	Office,computing etc..	49	44	44	47	50	0.68	0.74	0.77	0.83	0.90	3825
383	Electrical machinery ...	895	847	865	873	917	5.40	5.33	5.44	5.71	6.19	383
3832	Radio,television etc..	...	...	...	...	...	...	...	...	...	...	3832
384	Transport equipment	1041	1035	1021	990	1054	9.14	9.27	9.63	9.79	10.68	384
3841	Shipbuilding, repair..	77	76	63	55	56	0.46	0.43	0.37	0.35	0.36	3841
3843	Motor vehicles	...	...	...	...	...	...	...	...	...	...	3843
385	Professional goods	179	169	152	151	158	0.52	0.53	0.52	0.55	0.60	385
390	Other industries	66	62	58	59	59	0.21	0.20	0.20	0.21	0.23	390
3	Manufacturing ..... d/	8189	7768	7508	7455	7533	152.09	146.47	150.83	158.06	156.57	3
410	Electricity,gas,steam ..	233	231	231	229	...	...	...	...	...	...	410
4101	Electricity	211	210	207	209	...	17.73	18.30	18.75	19.95	20.93	4101
420	Water works and supply .	17	17	16	16	...	...	...	...	...	...	420
4	Electricity,gas etc	250	248	247	245	...	...	...	...	...	...	4
2-4	All industry	...	...	...	...	...	...	...	...	...	...	2-4

Note. For description of classification, see country note.

a/ Mining and manufacturing: local units of enterprises with 20 or more persons engaged; including production handicrafts.
b/ Electricity, gas and water supply: enterprises with 20 or more persons engaged.
c/ Beginning 1983, data for certain major groups are not fully comparable with those for previous years owing to changes in classification.
d/ Excluding manufacture of prefabricated building parts and structures.
e/ Major group 352 is included in 351.

ISIC	INDUSTRY	9. OUTPUT IN PRODUCERS' PRICES a/b/d/e/ (BILLION MARKS) 1981	1982	f/ 1983	1984	1985	10. VALUE ADDED IN PRODUCERS' PRICES c/ (BILLION MARKS) 1981	1982	f/ 1983	1984	1985	ISIC
210	Coal mining	26.1	27.1	26.3	28.7	29.2	12.60	13.87	14.58	14.52	...	210
220	Petroleum and gas	4.3	4.2	3.8	3.7	4.1					...	220
230	Metal ore mining	0.1	0.1	0.1	0.2	-	[g/ 2.20	g/ 2.62	g/ 2.84	g/ 3.03]	...	230
290	Other mining	6.6	6.6	6.0	6.5	6.6					...	290
2	Mining, quarrying .	37.1	38.0	36.2	39.1	39.9	g/ 14.80	g/ 16.49	g/ 17.42	g/ 17.55	g/ 18.52	2
311/2	Food products	113.5	118.3	120.4	124.8	127.0	32.54	35.33	36.14	36.64	...	311/2
313	Beverages	26.5	27.7	27.8	27.2	27.5	12.44	13.08	13.09	12.88	...	313
314	Tobacco	16.4	16.7	18.4	19.6	21.1	12.87	13.19	14.68	14.97	...	314
321	Textiles	34.5	34.3	34.8	36.7	38.7	12.09	12.04	12.34	12.66	...	321
3211	Spinning,weaving etc..	...	...	...	...	...	...	...	...	...	...	3211
322	Wearing apparel	18.1	17.6	17.8	19.1	19.6	8.74	8.52	8.67	8.89	...	322
323	Leather and products ...	3.8	3.6	3.8	3.9	3.9	[3.86	3.74	3.67	3.49]	...	323
324	Footwear	5.5	5.6	5.9	6.3	6.3					...	324
331	Wood products	[h/ 36.2	h/ 33.7	h/ 35.6	h/ 36.2	h/ 34.8	17.64	16.95	17.56	17.55]	...	331
332	Furniture, fixtures										...	332
341	Paper and products	29.3	30.1	30.8	34.0	36.3	9.75	9.72	10.63	11.45	...	341
3411	Pulp,paper etc.	12.6	12.8	13.4	15.4	16.3	3.65	3.65	4.09	4.63	...	3411
342	Printing,publishing	21.1	21.4	21.8	23.1	24.3	i/ 11.09	i/ 11.03	i/ 11.62	i/ 12.84	...	342
351	Industrial chemicals ...	j/ 138.4	j/ 141.9	j/ 154.3	j/ 170.2	j/ 178.5	k/ 44.59	k/ 45.28	k/ 53.31	k/ 56.98	...	351
3511	Basic excl fertilizers	...	...	...	...	...	...	...	...	...	...	3511
3513	Synthetic resins etc .	...	...	...	...	...	...	...	...	...	...	3513
352	Other chemical. products.	j/	j/	j/	j/	j/	k/	k/	k/	k/	...	352
3522	Drugs and medicines ..	...	...	...	...	...	...	...	...	...	...	3522
353	Petroleum refineries ...	[107.5	108.7	99.2	106.7	111.8]	25.51	25.80	25.41	26.75	...	353
354	Petroleum,coal products.						k/	k/	k/	k/	...	354
355	Rubber products	13.5	13.9	14.1	14.6	16.1	5.80	6.18	6.73	6.80	...	355
356	Plastic products n.e.c..	26.0	26.9	29.1	32.4	34.4	11.04	11.41	12.39	13.64	...	356
361	Pottery,china etc	2.6	2.6	2.6	2.7	2.8	2.38	2.30	2.36	2.41	...	361
362	Glass and products	8.8	8.7	9.0	9.4	10.2	4.22	4.13	4.22	4.28	...	362
369	Non-metal products n.e.c	h/ 26.1	h/ 25.6	h/ 27.7	h/ 27.7	h/ 25.8	g/ 13.70	g/ 13.48	g/ 14.53	g/ 14.83	...	369
371	Iron and steel	74.3	72.1	52.7	59.6	64.8	l/ 33.18	l/ 32.28	l/ 32.03	l/ 33.78	...	371
372	Non-ferrous metals	26.0	24.2	27.0	30.0	30.2	l/ 4.67	l/ 4.67	l/ 4.48	l/ 5.46	...	372
381	Metal products	61.4	62.2	75.4	80.1	85.0	m/n/ 26.92	m/n/ 27.80	m/n/ 27.87	m/n/ 28.47	...	381
382	Machinery n.e.c.	134.7	140.5	143.8	156.6	177.1	64.78	66.53	67.41	70.99	...	382
3825	Office,computing etc..	9.1	9.6	11.5	15.3	15.1	6.86	7.92	8.50	9.40	...	3825
383	Electrical machinery ...	112.8	116.3	126.7	133.5	151.1	56.05	59.37	61.98	65.89	...	383
3832	Radio,television etc..	...	...	...	...	...	...	...	...	...	...	3832
384	Transport equipment	141.6	152.7	163.3	169.8	190.9	m/ 60.61	m/ 65.10	m/ 69.49	m/ 70.94	...	384
3841	Shipbuilding, repair..	6.7	7.7	8.6	8.2	7.3	2.54	2.87	2.16	2.66	...	3841
3843	Motor vehicles .... o/	...	...	...	...	...	54.26	58.53	63.21	64.10	...	3843
385	Professional goods	15.6	15.2	14.8	15.7	18.3	11.71	10.88	10.64	10.69	...	385
390	Other industries	6.0	6.5	5.7	5.9	6.2	3.55	4.04	3.68	3.71	...	390
3	Manufacturing	h/ 1200.2	h/ 1227.0	h/ 1262.5	h/ 1345.8	h/ 1442.7	g/i/ 489.73	g/i/ 502.85	g/i/ 524.93	g/i/ 546.99	g/i/ 593.62	3
410	Electricity,gas,steam ..	115.7	129.4	134.2	147.2	...	35.23	39.17	41.99	44.24	...	410
4101	Electricity	85.9	96.0	100.7	110.6	...	p/ 31.70	p/ 35.07	p/ 37.43	p/ 39.54	...	4101
420	Water works and supply .	3.2	3.5	3.6	3.8	...	3.02	3.11	3.28	3.53	...	420
4	Electricity,gas etc	118.9	132.9	137.8	151.0	...	38.25	42.28	45.27	47.77	...	4
2-4	All industry i/	...	...	...	...	...	542.78	561.62	587.62	612.31	663.82	2-4

Note. For description of classification, see country note.

a/ Mining and manufacturing: local units of enterprises with 20 or more persons engaged; including production handicrafts.
b/ Excluding value-added tax.
c/ National accounts estimates.
d/ Electricity, gas and water supply: enterprises with 20 or more persons engaged.
e/ Total turnover.
f/ Beginning 1983, data for certain major groups are not fully comparable with those for previous years owing to changes in classification.
g/ Quarrying is included in major group 369.
h/ Excluding manufacture of prefabricated building parts and structures.
i/ Excluding publishing.
j/ Major group 352 is included in 351.
k/ Major groups 352 and 354 are included in 351.
l/ Founding and casting of non-ferrous metals is included in major group 371.
m/ Railroad equipment (group 3842) is included in major group 381.
n/ Including structural steel erection.
o/ Including motorcycles and bicycles.
p/ Including production and distribution of steam and hot water for heating.

ISIC	INDUSTRY	11. GROSS FIXED CAPITAL FORMATION TOTAL a/b/ (MILLION MARKS)					12. GROSS FIXED CAPITAL FORMATION MACHINERY AND EQUIPMENT a/b/ (MILLION MARKS)					ISIC
		1981	1982	1983	1984	1985	1981	1982	1983	1984	1985	
210	Coal mining	...	...	...	...	...	...	...	...	...	...	210
220	Petroleum and gas	...	580	425	...	...	...	326	250	...	...	220
230	Metal ore mining	...	...	...	...	...	...	...	...	...	...	230
290	Other mining	...	...	588	580	...	...	...	460	441	...	290
2	Mining, quarrying	3597	c/ 4249	c/ 4053	c/ 3288	...	2729	...	3120	c/ 2476	...	2
311/2	Food products	3229	3126	3334	3258	...	2530	2497	...	2492	...	311/2
313	Beverages	1738	1722	1966	1784	...	1356	1364	...	1323	...	313
314	Tobacco	313	280	321	321	...	256	208	293	307	...	314
321	Textiles	1059	1078	1416	1389	...	d/ 1081	906	...	...	...	321
3211	Spinning,weaving etc.	578	...	...	891	...	...	...	...	722	...	3211
322	Wearing apparel	231	252	274	320	...	d/	181	199	216	...	322
323	Leather and products	85	...	86	92	...	d/	...	...	...	...	323
324	Footwear	101	96	114	100	...	72	73	82	72	...	324
331	Wood products e/	647	510	630	649	...	475	394	509	497	...	331
332	Furniture, fixtures	478	392	504	509	...	332	292	375	...	...	332
341	Paper and products	1693	1385	1333	1379	...	1359	1154	1149	1167	...	341
3411	Pulp,paper etc.	809	700	542	666	...	680	588	483	568	...	3411
342	Printing,publishing	1089	990	1365	1140	...	885	814	1118	948	...	342
351	Industrial chemicals	4563	4281	3924	...	...	3763	3646	3395	...	...	351
3511	Basic excl fertilizers	...	...	...	...	...	...	...	...	...	...	3511
3513	Synthetic resins etc	...	...	...	...	...	...	...	...	...	...	3513
352	Other chemical products.	2030	2039	2200	2367	...	1507	1548	1650	1761	...	352
3522	Drugs and medicines	663	710	818	866	...	447	486	535	599	...	3522
353	Petroleum refineries	[1563	1920	2089	1259]	...	[1376	1763	1903	1030]	...	353
354	Petroleum,coal products.					...					...	354
355	Rubber products	634	588	549	653	...	528	487	498	569	...	355
356	Plastic products n.e.c.	1272	1229	1478	1685	...	1012	1000	1225	1377	...	356
361	Pottery,china etc	122	108	146	132	...	91	81	115	89	...	361
362	Glass and products	584	567	627	659	...	459	482	546	540	...	362
369	Non-metal products n.e.c f/	1846	1401	1539	1645	...	1476	1126	...	1310	...	369
371	Iron and steel	3861	2693	2741	2809	...	3263	2330	2114	2430	...	371
372	Non-ferrous metals	993	986	762	...	...	853	829	626	...	...	372
381	Metal products	2078	2532	2667	...	...	[6921]	...	...	[5398]	...	381
382	Machinery n.e.c.	g/	6283	6610	6678	...		...	...		...	382
3825	Office,computing etc.	1701	1659	1668	1766	...	1449	...	...	1424	...	3825
383	Electrical machinery	4729	4710	5294	6162	...	4088	4089	4555	...	...	383
3832	Radio,television etc.	2337	2264	2568	3092	...	2042	2022	2258	2771	...	3832
384	Transport equipment	g/ 15126	9789	9519	...	...	6720	7949	8190	...	...	384
3841	Shipbuilding, repair.	183	239	244	142	...	139	...	157	91	...	3841
3843	Motor vehicles	7779	9036	8743	7425	...	7779	7451	7630	6435	...	3843
385	Professional goods	[845]	590	652	682	...	[654]	475	510	540	...	385
390	Other industries		...	206	185	...		...	165	163	...	390
3	Manufacturing e/f/	50909	c/ 49803	52346	c/ 51693	...	41057	c/ 40945	c/ 43445	c/ 42634	...	3
410	Electricity,gas,steam	13894	15717	15709	17253	...	12304	13919	13956	15546	...	410
4101	Electricity	12247	14372	14215	15889	...	10747	12664	12552	14269	...	4101
420	Water works and supply	1111	939	878	990	...	849	718	721	718	...	420
4	Electricity,gas etc	15005	16656	16587	18243	...	13153	14637	14677	16264	...	4
2-4	All industry e/f/	69511	c/ 70708	c/ 72986	c/ 73224	...	56939	...	c/ 61242	c/ 61374	...	2-4

Note. For description of classification, see country note.

a/ The value of sales is not deducted.
b/ Enterprises with 20 or more persons engaged; including handicrafts.
c/ Including data for industries not shown at the major group level.
d/ Major groups 322 and 323 are included in 321.
e/ Excluding prefabricated building parts (SYPRO 7237 AND 7751).
f/ Excluding prefabricated building parts (SYPRO 7233).
g/ Major group 382 is included in 384.

13. VALUE OF STOCKS AT END OF PERIOD
TOTAL a/
(BILLION MARKS)

ISIC	INDUSTRY	1981	1982	1983	1984	1985	ISIC
210	Coal mining	...	...	...	...	...	210
220	Petroleum and gas	...	0.09	0.08	...	...	220
230	Metal ore mining	...	...	...	...	...	230
290	Other mining	...	...	...	0.45	...	290
2	Mining, quarrying	3.78	b/ 5.11	b/ 5.07	b/ 3.91	...	2
311/2	Food products	11.42	11.38	11.60	11.40	...	311/2
313	Beverages	2.69	2.74	2.61	2.63	...	313
314	Tobacco	2.65	2.83	2.84	3.02	...	314
321	Textiles	7.28	6.86	6.92	...	...	321
3211	Spinning,weaving etc.	3.79	3.94	4.07	...	...	3211
322	Wearing apparel	3.01	2.85	2.77	3.02	...	322
323	Leather and products	0.82	0.78	0.79	...	...	323
324	Footwear	0.76	0.79	0.81	0.86	...	324
331	Wood products c/	2.93	2.69	2.72	2.69	...	331
332	Furniture, fixtures	2.42	2.34	2.32	2.34	...	332
341	Paper and products	3.93	3.75	3.94	4.25	...	341
3411	Pulp,paper etc.	1.76	1.78	1.81	1.89	...	3411
342	Printing,publishing	1.45	1.39	1.41	1.60	...	342
351	Industrial chemicals	12.67	11.89	11.74	...	...	351
3511	Basic excl fertilizers	...	...	...	...	...	3511
3513	Synthetic resins etc	...	...	...	...	...	3513
352	Other chemical products.	2.10	9.00	9.24	10.15	...	352
3522	Drugs and medicines	3.23	3.34	3.47	3.72	...	3522
353	Petroleum refineries	[13.25	11.01	9.64	9.64]	...	353
354	Petroleum,coal products.					...	354
355	Rubber products	2.23	2.18	2.11	2.24	...	355
356	Plastic products n.e.c.	3.48	3.46	3.67	3.96	...	356
361	Pottery,china etc	0.36	0.37	0.40	0.41	...	361
362	Glass and products	1.39	1.40	1.38	1.48	...	362
369	Non-metal products n.e.c d/	3.97	3.78	3.82	3.91	...	369
371	Iron and steel	13.10	10.26	9.47	10.76	...	371
372	Non-ferrous metals	4.44	4.41	4.57	...	...	372
381	Metal products	17.17	17.75	18.30	19.10	...	381
382	Machinery n.e.c.	44.05	46.73	46.58	47.83	...	382
3825	Office,computing etc.	2.33	2.44	2.70	3.58	...	3825
383	Electrical machinery	28.31	28.64	28.37	31.20	...	383
3832	Radio,television etc.	14.70	14.41	13.88	15.48	...	3832
384	Transport equipment	26.18	27.96	26.65	24.74	...	384
3841	Shipbuilding, repair.	5.09	6.74	5.50	3.44	...	3841
3843	Motor vehicles	15.99	16.45	16.62	16.91	...	3843
385	Professional goods	3.64	3.50	3.26	3.34	...	385
390	Other industries	1.46	1.47	1.46	1.54	...	390
3	Manufacturing c/d/	224.16	222.21	219.39	b/ 227.78	...	3
410	Electricity,gas,steam	7.86	8.34	9.09	9.16	...	410
4101	Electricity	7.02	7.40	8.08	8.21	...	4101
420	Water works and supply	0.12	0.11	0.11	0.11	...	420
4	Electricity,gas etc	7.98	8.45	9.20	9.27	...	4
2-4	All industry c/d/	235.92	b/ 235.77	b/ 233.66	b/ 240.96	...	2-4

Note. For description of classification, see country note.

a/ Enterprises with 20 or more persons engaged; including handicrafts.
b/ Including data for industries not shown at the major group level.
c/ Excluding prefabricated building parts (SYPRO 7237 AND 7751). d/ Excluding prefabricated building parts (SYPRO 7233).

14. INDEX NUMBERS OF INDUSTRIAL PRODUCTION (1980 = 100)

ISIC	INDUSTRY	1976	1977	1978	1979	1981	1982	1983	1984	1985	a/ RATE	ISIC
210	Coal mining	105	97	93	97	101	99	90	86	90	-1.7	210
220	Petroleum and gas	105	106	109	108	100	90	92	95	91	-1.6	220
230	Metal ore mining	148	146	101	96	96	93	88	89	90	-5.4	230
290	Other mining .... b/	86	94	100	108	92	84	85	92	89	0.4	290
2	Mining, quarrying . b/	102	96	95	99	99	96	89	88	90	-1.4	2
311/2	Food products	86	90	93	97	101	100	100	104	109	2.7	311/2
313	Beverages	101	97	99	100	101	101	100	98	98	-0.3	313
314	Tobacco	94	91	96	99	102	92	96	99	103	1.0	314
321	Textiles .... c/	104	101	100	102	94	89	89	91	95	-1.0	321
3211	Spinning,weaving etc..	108	104	102	103	94	92	93	98	102	-0.6	3211
322	Wearing apparel .... c/	108	107	106	104	92	84	82	83	82	-3.0	322
323	Leather and products ...	104	102	103	104	91	83	82	78	73	-3.9	323
324	Footwear	100	99	103	103	96	91	86	89	85	-1.8	324
331	Wood products	84	90	97	102	87	80	83	87	84	0.0	331
332	Furniture, fixtures	88	95	102	102	91	81	83	81	75	-1.8	332
341	Paper and products	81	87	91	97	101	101	104	110	113	3.8	341
3411	Pulp,paper etc.	83	89	93	99	104	103	109	120	120	4.2	3411
342	Printing,publishing	84	89	92	99	98	95	94	98	100	2.0	342
351	Industrial chemicals ...	95	96	100	107	98	91	102	108	109	1.5	351
3511	Basic excl fertilizers	...	...	...	...	...	...	...	...	...	...	3511
3513	Synthetic resins etc .	106	97	100	104	104	97	103	107	110	0.4	3513
352	Other chemical products.	89	92	96	100	101	101	104	109	113	2.7	352
3522	Drugs and medicines ..	89	91	98	98	102	102	105	108	111	2.5	3522
353	Petroleum refineries ...	[98	98	97	109	88	85	81	81	79	-2.4]	353
354	Petroleum,coal products.											354
355	Rubber products .... d/	107	101	103	104	94	97	99	104	112	0.5	355
356	Plastic products n.e.c..	82	87	92	100	97	97	104	111	117	4.0	356
361	Pottery,china etc	91	97	98	101	98	92	91	92	93	0.2	361
362	Glass and products	83	90	90	98	93	89	92	94	100	2.1	362
369	Non-metal products n.e.c b/d/	86	86	91	100	92	85	88	85	78	-1.1	369
371	Iron and steel	97	92	96	105	96	84	82	89	93	-0.5	371
372	Non-ferrous metals	91	92	94	101	98	97	104	108	112	2.3	372
381	Metal products	87	89	92	98	95	91	90	90	94	0.9	381
382	Machinery n.e.c.	88	90	92	96	100	98	97	101	111	2.6	382
3825	Office,computing etc.	55	73	80	90	112	116	133	171	212	16.2	3825
383	Electrical machinery ...	89	90	93	96	98	98	99	107	120	3.4	383
3832	Radio,television etc..	82	88	91	94	98	98	102	115	136	5.8	3832
384	Transport equipment	86	93	95	101	108	110	110	108	121	3.9	384
3841	Shipbuilding, repair..	124	117	93	86	111	114	95	83	87	-3.9	3841
3843	Motor vehicles	84	92	95	102	108	109	111	110	123	4.3	3843
385	Professional goods	87	94	95	97	95	88	87	90	99	1.4	385
390	Other industries	111	122	124	119	96	93	91	92	94	-1.8	390
3	Manufacturing ..... b/	91	92	95	100	98	95	96	99	104	1.5	3
410	Electricity,gas,steam .. e/	88	89	95	100	101	100	102	108	113	2.8	410
4101	Electricity	...	...	...	...	...	...	...	...	...	...	4101
420	Water works and supply .	...	...	...	...	...	...	...	...	...	...	420
4	Electricity,gas etc	...	...	...	...	...	...	...	...	...	...	4
2-4	All industry f/	91	92	95	100	98	95	96	99	104	1.5	2-4

a/ Annual growth rate 1976-1985.
b/ Stone quarrying, clay and sand pits are included in major group 369.
c/ Made-up textile goods except wearing apparel are included in major group 322.
d/ Asbestos products are included in major group 355. e/ Excluding steam.
f/ Excluding steam, water works and supply.

GHANA

The information in the tables is based on the reply to the United Nations Questionnaire on General Industrial Statistics from the Central Bureau of Statistics, Accra. The concepts, definitions and classification by branches of industry are generally in accordance with United Nations standards.

The estimates are derived from the industrial statistics inquiry conducted annually and quarterly by the Central Bureau of Statistics. The estimates relate to operating establishments with 30 or more persons engaged. The following industrial activities are not covered: (a) Stone quarrying, clay and sand pits, since the establishments which are engaged in this activity are usually ancillary units of construction enterprises and do not keep separate records and (b) Akpeteshie (raw local gin) manufacturing, since the production units of this industry are organized on a loose co-operative basis and, in most cases, do not keep records of their economic activities. It should be noted that bakeries with an average annual output of 50 thousand cedis or more are included even if they engage less than 30 persons, because the output of these bakeries is quite high. It should also be noted that the activity of diamond mining is usually carried out by very small units and is out of the scope of inquiry. Identification and location of industrial establishments are based mainly on information obtained from the 1962 Industrial Census, but the statistical directory is updated every year with information obtained from various sources. The collection of data is carried out by the field staff of the regional offices of the Central Bureau of Statistics. The estimates are based on the national classification system which follows the present version of ISIC.

Table 2 relates to the average number of persons engaged, including homeworkers, as of the last working day of each month during the reference year. Wages and salaries include payments made to homeworkers when they are reported in the number of persons engaged.

The concept of output generally conforms to the United Nations standards. However, the value of work in progress is not taken into account, except in cases such as boat-yards, where it is considered that the exclusion of this item from the value of output of the establishment would be a significant omission. Value added represents the value arrived at by deducting the following costs from the value of output: (a) cost of materials and supplies consumed, (b) cost of fuels and lubricants consumed, (c) cost of contract and commission work done by others, (d) cost of repairs and maintenance done by others and (e) cost of electricity purchased. The valuation of output and value added is in producers' prices.

Related national publications:
Industrial Statistics (annual); Statistical Year Book; Statistical Handbook (annual), all published by the Central Bureau of Statistics, Accra.

ISIC	INDUSTRY	1. NUMBER OF ESTABLISHMENTS a/ (NUMBER)					2. AVERAGE NUMBER OF PERSONS ENGAGED a/b/ (NUMBER)					ISIC
		1981	1982	1983	1984	1985	1981	1982	1983	1984	1985	
210	Coal mining	-	-	-	...	...	-	-	-	...	...	210
220	Petroleum and gas	-	-	-	...	...	-	-	-	...	...	220
230	Metal ore mining	7	7	7	...	...	21679	21545	21977	...	...	230
290	Other mining .... c/	3	2	2	...	...	2752	2882	2370	...	...	290
2	Mining, quarrying . c/	10	9	9	...	...	24431	24427	24347	...	...	2
311/2	Food products	49	46	49	...	...	11492	9022	6846	...	...	311/2
313	Beverages .... d/	12	17	22	...	...	4511	4934	4771	...	...	313
314	Tobacco	3	3	3	...	...	1201	1290	1291	...	...	314
321	Textiles	37	33	22	...	...	15431	11395	9264	...	...	321
3211	Spinning,weaving etc..	...	...	...	...	...	12569	9303	7698	...	...	3211
322	Wearing apparel	23	23	16	...	...	1629	1289	1161	...	...	322
323	Leather and products ...	15	13	12	...	...	391	355	288	...	...	323
324	Footwear	7	6	5	...	...	723	562	489	...	...	324
331	Wood products	72	75	73	...	...	16045	14020	13749	...	...	331
332	Furniture, fixtures	18	22	19	...	...	1180	1170	1002	...	...	332
341	Paper and products	6	6	7	...	...	593	678	748	...	...	341
3411	Pulp,paper etc.	-	-	-	...	...	-	-	-	...	...	3411
342	Printing,publishing	16	17	19	...	...	4481	4365	3262	...	...	342
351	Industrial chemicals ...	8	7	8	...	...	691	515	524	...	...	351
3511	Basic excl fertilizers	2	2	2	...	...	193	193	152	...	...	3511
3513	Synthetic resins etc .	-	-	-	...	...	-	-	-	...	...	3513
352	Other chemical products.	26	24	24	...	...	3197	3091	2861	...	...	352
3522	Drugs and medicines ..	12	11	11	...	...	1530	1582	1392	...	...	3522
353	Petroleum refineries ...	1	1	1	...	...	658	612	626	...	...	353
354	Petroleum,coal products.	-	-	-	...	...	-	-	-	...	...	354
355	Rubber products	5	5	5	...	...	1678	1388	1269	...	...	355
356	Plastic products n.e.c..	9	11	8	...	...	721	705	460	...	...	356
361	Pottery,china etc	2	2	2	...	...	373	506	422	...	...	361
362	Glass and products	2	2	1	...	...	148	127	102	...	...	362
369	Non-metal products n.e.c	12	11	9	...	...	1901	2111	1642	...	...	369
371	Iron and steel	2	2	1	...	...	515	666	413	...	...	371
372	Non-ferrous metals	1	1	1	...	...	2547	2520	2024	...	...	372
381	Metal products	30	29	24	...	...	3086	2631	2070	...	...	381
382	Machinery n.e.c.	2	2	1	...	...	92	201	61	...	...	382
3825	Office,computing etc..	-	-	-	...	...	-	-	-	...	...	3825
383	Electrical machinery ...	10	11	11	...	...	1102	953	765	...	...	383
3832	Radio,television etc..	...	...	...	...	...	702	568	528	...	...	3832
384	Transport equipment	9	9	11	...	...	2351	2003	1708	...	...	384
3841	Shipbuilding, repair..	...	...	...	...	...	449	443	535	...	...	3841
3843	Motor vehicles	...	...	...	...	...	1784	1450	1053	...	...	3843
385	Professional goods	3	3	3	...	...	662	368	331	...	...	385
390	Other industries	6	6	4	...	...	166	184	129	...	...	390
3	Manufacturing ..... d/	386	387	361	...	...	77565	67661	58278	...	...	3
410	Electricity,gas,steam .. e/	40	40	40	...	...	8230	7334	7581	...	...	410
4101	Electricity	40	40	40	...	...	8230	7334	7581	...	...	4101
420	Water works and supply .	190	189	192	...	...	7597	7295	7295	...	...	420
4	Electricity,gas etc e/	230	229	232	...	...	15827	14629	14876	...	...	4
2-4	All industry e/	626	625	602	...	...	117823	106717	97501	...	...	2-4

a/ Establishments with 30 or more persons engaged.
b/ Including homeworkers.
c/ Excluding stone quarrying, clay and sand pits.
d/ Excluding manufacture of raw gin.
e/ Excluding gas and steam.

ISIC	INDUSTRY	3. WAGES AND SALARIES OF EMPLOYEES a/b/ (MILLION CEDIS) 1981	1982	1983	1984	1985	4. AVERAGE NUMBER OF OPERATIVES b/ (NUMBER) 1981	1982	1983	1984	1985	ISIC
210	Coal mining	-	-	-	...	...	-	-	-	...	...	210
220	Petroleum and gas	-	-	-	...	...	-	-	-	...	...	220
230	Metal ore mining	165.6	249.4	367.5	...	...	15990	14888	16865	...	...	230
290	Other mining .... c/	23.0	23.4	36.7	...	...	2393	2303	1794	...	...	290
2	Mining, quarrying . c/	188.6	272.8	404.2	...	...	18383	17191	18659	...	...	2
311/2	Food products	88.9	81.2	108.5	...	...	8430	6375	4697	...	...	311/2
313	Beverages .... d/	48.6	65.2	106.3	...	...	2661	2872	2522	...	...	313
314	Tobacco	16.7	18.5	26.3	...	...	645	830	730	...	...	314
321	Textiles	113.7	104.6	104.9	...	...	12473	9064	7328	...	...	321
3211	Spinning,weaving etc..	97.7	90.5	90.9	...	...	10565	7637	6369	...	...	3211
322	Wearing apparel	8.2	7.8	11.5	...	...	1529	1092	1012	...	...	322
323	Leather and products ...	1.4	1.9	2.3	...	...	311	270	217	...	...	323
324	Footwear	7.0	5.4	4.4	...	...	541	395	222	...	...	324
331	Wood products	90.6	112.2	151.5	...	...	13450	11404	11288	...	...	331
332	Furniture, fixtures	5.7	9.0	10.6	...	...	947	891	702	...	...	332
341	Paper and products	4.9	6.0	8.2	...	...	324	374	416	...	...	341
3411	Pulp,paper etc.	-	-	-	...	...	-	-	-	...	...	3411
342	Printing,publishing	30.1	32.6	45.5	...	...	2599	2508	1612	...	...	342
351	Industrial chemicals ...	8.1	10.0	7.8	...	...	408	304	272	...	...	351
3511	Basic excl fertilizers	5.8	7.0	3.4	...	...	128	126	53	...	...	3511
3513	Synthetic resins etc .	-	-	-	...	...	-	-	-	...	...	3513
352	Other chemical products.	25.7	31.3	46.9	...	...	2165	2016	1794	...	...	352
3522	Drugs and medicines ..	9.5	14.9	21.1	...	...	1054	936	668	...	...	3522
353	Petroleum refineries ...	18.5	18.8	43.6	...	...	300	255	363	...	...	353
354	Petroleum,coal products.	-	-	-	...	...	-	-	-	...	...	354
355	Rubber products	13.5	12.1	15.1	...	...	1258	924	751	...	...	355
356	Plastic products n.e.c..	3.2	6.2	7.9	...	...	547	544	361	...	...	356
361	Pottery,china etc	2.5	3.0	5.1	...	...	362	343	341	...	...	361
362	Glass and products	0.8	1.7	1.1	...	...	94	90	80	...	...	362
369	Non-metal products n.e.c	16.1	22.1	54.5	...	...	1557	1609	1127	...	...	369
371	Iron and steel	3.4	6.3	7.6	...	...	334	544	329	...	...	371
372	Non-ferrous metals	71.8	98.1	441.5	...	...	956	922	652	...	...	372
381	Metal products	23.7	23.4	31.5	...	...	2316	1849	1457	...	...	381
382	Machinery n.e.c.	0.5	1.2	0.3	...	...	78	173	29	...	...	382
3825	Office,computing etc..	-	-	-	...	...	-	-	-	...	...	3825
383	Electrical machinery ...	9.0	10.7	10.2	...	...	663	603	489	...	...	383
3832	Radio,television etc..	5.8	6.9	7.3	...	...	364	323	316	...	...	3832
384	Transport equipment	16.3	23.8	27.4	...	...	1648	1508	1281	...	...	384
3841	Shipbuilding, repair..	3.8	4.3	6.2	...	...	318	290	385	...	...	3841
3843	Motor vehicles	11.2	18.8	20.1	...	...	1249	1145	818	...	...	3843
385	Professional goods	2.7	2.1	5.2	...	...	591	275	269	...	...	385
390	Other industries	0.9	1.1	1.3	...	...	118	131	95	...	...	390
3	Manufacturing ..... d/	632.5	716.3	1287.0	...	...	57305	48165	40436	...	...	3
410	Electricity,gas,steam .. e/	90.5	81.7	117.6	...	...	...	...	...	...	...	410
4101	Electricity	90.5	81.7	117.6	...	...	...	...	...	...	...	4101
420	Water works and supply .	84.9	97.1	102.3	...	...	...	...	...	...	...	420
4	Electricity,gas etc e/	175.4	178.8	219.9	...	...	...	...	...	...	...	4
2-4	All industry e/	996.5	1167.9	1911.1	...	...	...	...	...	...	...	2-4

a/ Including payments to homeworkers.
b/ Establishments with 30 or more persons engaged.
c/ Excluding stone quarrying, clay and sand pits.
d/ Excluding manufacture of raw gin.
e/ Excluding gas and steam.

ISIC	INDUSTRY	5. WAGES AND SALARIES OF OPERATIVES a/ (THOUSAND CEDIS)					6. OUTPUT IN PRODUCERS' PRICES a/ (MILLION CEDIS)					ISIC
		1981	1982	1983	1984	1985	1981	1982	1983	1984	1985	
210	Coal mining	-	-	-	...	...	-	-	-	...	...	210
220	Petroleum and gas	-	-	-	...	...	-	-	-	...	...	220
230	Metal ore mining	82180	113374	211742	...	...	520	429	2360	...	...	230
290	Other mining .... b/	12263	9403	18776	...	...	60	40	59	...	...	290
2	Mining, quarrying . b/	94443	122777	230518	...	...	580	469	2419	...	...	2
311/2	Food products	53557	48848	65499	...	...	774	715	1200	...	...	311/2
313	Beverages .... c/	20263	28245	50464	...	...	599	453	1192	...	...	313
314	Tobacco	7342	8554	9629	...	...	1077	902	1444	...	...	314
321	Textiles	74125	60612	73488	...	...	489	372	411	...	...	321
3211	Spinning,weaving etc..	65664	52120	64978	...	...	419	323	363	...	...	3211
322	Wearing apparel	6564	6095	7957	...	...	39	29	49	...	...	322
323	Leather and products ...	989	1398	1341	...	...	10	7	20	...	...	323
324	Footwear	3289	2035	1498	...	...	26	11	15	...	...	324
331	Wood products	59439	80668	105735	...	...	396	443	768	...	...	331
332	Furniture, fixtures	3848	5642	8004	...	...	34	41	40	...	...	332
341	Paper and products	1734	3174	4161	...	...	19	28	33	...	...	341
3411	Pulp,paper etc.	-	-	-	...	...	-	-	-	...	...	3411
342	Printing,publishing	15813	19119	19022	...	...	68	97	169	...	...	342
351	Industrial chemicals ...	2011	1991	3090	...	...	29	34	44	...	...	351
3511	Basic excl fertilizers	1154	1385	1387	...	...	16	17	27	...	...	3511
3513	Synthetic resins etc .	-	-	-	...	...	-	-	-	...	...	3513
352	Other chemical products.	13099	15123	24852	...	...	226	187	335	...	...	352
3522	Drugs and medicines ..	4496	7275	10417	...	...	86	64	118	...	...	3522
353	Petroleum refineries ...	8335	8213	19098	...	...	1386	1333	1892	...	...	353
354	Petroleum,coal products.	-	-	-	...	...	-	-	-	...	...	354
355	Rubber products	7523	7586	10128	...	...	99	73	125	...	...	355
356	Plastic products n.e.c..	2065	4506	5590	...	...	36	55	86	...	...	356
361	Pottery,china etc	1569	1883	3444	...	...	8	10	6	...	...	361
362	Glass and products	641	1301	763	...	...	6	8	2	...	...	362
369	Non-metal products n.e.c	11189	15171	19532	...	...	226	172	585	...	...	369
371	Iron and steel	1358	2613	2416	...	...	48	45	39	...	...	371
372	Non-ferrous metals	44423	61856	221250	...	...	484	440	1273	...	...	372
381	Metal products	13686	14187	19698	...	...	153	139	162	...	...	381
382	Machinery n.e.c.	323	565	120	...	...	2	5	4	...	...	382
3825	Office,computing etc..	-	-	-	...	...	-	-	-	...	...	3825
383	Electrical machinery ...	4498	4830	4576	...	...	40	39	30	...	...	383
3832	Radio,television etc..	2996	3036	2907	...	...	14	14	10	...	...	3832
384	Transport equipment	8129	14377	19278	...	...	82	106	146	...	...	384
3841	Shipbuilding, repair..	2568	2985	4259	...	...	5	6	21	...	...	3841
3843	Motor vehicles	4754	10981	14384	...	...	71	99	122	...	...	3843
385	Professional goods	1680	1401	4059	...	...	26	15	31	...	...	385
390	Other industries	562	661	844	...	...	6	7	6	...	...	390
3	Manufacturing ..... c/	368054	420654	705536	...	...	6388	5766	10107	...	...	3
410	Electricity,gas,steam .. d/	...	...	...	...	...	366	398	289	...	...	410
4101	Electricity	...	...	...	...	...	366	398	289	...	...	4101
420	Water works and supply .	...	...	...	...	...	49	63	91	...	...	420
4	Electricity,gas etc d/	...	...	...	...	...	415	461	380	...	...	4
2-4	All industry d/	...	...	...	...	...	7383	6696	12906	...	...	2-4

a/ Establishments with 30 or more persons engaged.
b/ Excluding stone quarrying, clay and sand pits.
c/ Excluding manufacture of raw gin.
d/ Excluding gas and steam.

7. VALUE ADDED IN PRODUCERS' PRICES a/ (MILLION CEDIS)

ISIC	INDUSTRY	1981	1982	1983	1984	1985	ISIC
210	Coal mining	-	-	-	...	...	210
220	Petroleum and gas	-	-	-	...	...	220
230	Metal ore mining	382.7	310.5	1847.0	...	...	230
290	Other mining .... b/	51.8	24.0	43.0	...	...	290
2	Mining, quarrying . b/	434.5	334.5	1890.0	...	...	2
311/2	Food products	323.7	305.3	640.7	...	...	311/2
313	Beverages .... c/	492.7	333.5	985.7	...	...	313
314	Tobacco	998.8	793.9	1334.7	...	...	314
321	Textiles	270.8	221.1	265.3	...	...	321
3211	Spinning,weaving etc..	220.1	187.5	232.7	...	...	3211
322	Wearing apparel	26.5	14.2	31.2	...	...	322
323	Leather and products ...	5.7	4.7	16.0	...	...	323
324	Footwear	12.9	d/ 4.1	6.9	...	...	324
331	Wood products	206.8	240.2	408.9	...	...	331
332	Furniture, fixtures	22.1	21.0	23.3	...	...	332
341	Paper and products	5.3	16.7	22.0	...	...	341
3411	Pulp,paper etc.	-	-	-	...	...	3411
342	Printing,publishing	47.8	68.8	128.5	...	...	342
351	Industrial chemicals ...	20.3	24.2	29.8	...	...	351
3511	Basic excl fertilizers	12.7	13.2	19.9	...	...	3511
3513	Synthetic resins etc .	-	-	-	...	...	3513
352	Other chemical products.	143.7	108.3	210.8	...	...	352
3522	Drugs and medicines ..	61.7	43.8	77.6	...	...	3522
353	Petroleum refineries ...	382.2	475.5	439.0	...	...	353
354	Petroleum,coal products.	-	-	-	...	...	354
355	Rubber products	52.1	22.7	59.6	...	...	355
356	Plastic products n.e.c..	19.0	36.3	46.2	...	...	356
361	Pottery,china etc	6.9	8.3	4.1	...	...	361
362	Glass and products	1.4	2.4	1.2	...	...	362
369	Non-metal products n.e.c	120.6	94.6	327.3	...	...	369
371	Iron and steel	25.7	19.7	16.5	...	...	371
372	Non-ferrous metals	271.9	192.7	358.1	...	...	372
381	Metal products	83.8	81.5	102.4	...	...	381
382	Machinery n.e.c.	0.8	3.4	2.8	...	...	382
3825	Office,computing etc..	-	-	-	...	...	3825
383	Electrical machinery ...	21.1	21.0	21.5	...	...	383
3832	Radio,television etc..	7.6	8.7	6.6	...	...	3832
384	Transport equipment	36.5	48.9	75.1	...	...	384
3841	Shipbuilding, repair..	d/ 2.5	d/ 2.6	14.9	...	...	3841
3843	Motor vehicles	31.7	45.6	59.6	...	...	3843
385	Professional goods	13.0	9.8	9.7	...	...	385
390	Other industries	3.3	5.1	4.4	...	...	390
3	Manufacturing ..... c/	3615.4	3177.9	5571.7	...	...	3
410	Electricity,gas,steam .. e/	308.0	347.8	226.4	...	...	410
4101	Electricity	308.0	347.8	226.4	...	...	4101
420	Water works and supply .	9.6	31.1	40.8	...	...	420
4	Electricity,gas etc e/	317.6	378.9	267.2	...	...	4
2-4	All industry e/	4367.5	3891.3	7728.9	...	...	2-4

a/ Establishments with 30 or more persons engaged.
b/ Excluding stone quarrying, clay and sand pits.
c/ Excluding manufacture of raw gin.
d/ Value added is less than corresponding wages and salaries due to operating losses.
e/ Excluding gas and steam.

The information on industrial activity is based on the reply to the United Nations Questionnaire on General Industrial Statistics from the National Statistical Service of Greece, Athens. The concepts, definitions and classification by branches of industry are generally in accordance with United Nations standards.

The estimates are derived from the annual statistical survey of mines, quarries and salterns, the annual industrial survey, and annual surveys of electricity and gas, all conducted by the National Statistical Service of Greece. The mining survey covers all establishments on a complete enumeration basis, except for quarrying of crude stone, gravel, sand and marble, where establishments with fewer than 20 persons engaged are covered by sampling methods. Because of the lack of adequate records for reporting purposes, the results presented exclude emery mines. For the industrial survey, manufacturing establishments with 10 or more persons engaged are covered on the basis of a complete enumeration of establishments with 20 or more persons engaged and a stratified random sample of establishments with 10 to 19 persons. Government establishments are not included in the industrial survey. The electricity and gas surveys cover the two enterprises engaged in production and distribution for public use. Steam and water supply are not covered. The statistical unit is the establishment except for electricity and gas where the enterprise is used.

The estimates are based on the national classification, generally following the preceding version of ISIC, but have been adjusted to the present version as far as possible. As stated above, the estimates for mining exclude emery mines (ISIC 290).

The estimates of employment relate to annual averages based on enumerations in every other month of the year. Unpaid family workers are included in numbers engaged if they work for at least 3 hours a day. Employees cover salaried employees, defined as persons receiving a monthly salary on a contractual basis irrespective of the amount of the remuneration, and wage earners, defined as persons receiving a daily pay or paid on a piece-work basis either in cash or in kind. The estimates shown for operatives relate to wage earners defined in this way. Wages and salaries cover wages, salaries, payments for overtime work and regular leave, bonuses, allowances, dismissal compensation and the value of receipts in kind.

The concept of output comprises the value of finished goods produced, receipts from contract work on account of others, receipts from repair work, receipts from the sale of goods sold in the same condition as purchased and other receipts (sales of self-produced steam, electric energy, processing waste etc.; subsidies and reimbursements for re-export of products). The valuation is at ex-factory selling price, exclusive of taxes. Value added is calculated as the value of output less the cost of materials and supplies, purchased fuels and electricity consumed, the purchase value of goods sold in the same condition as purchased, and payments for contract work done by others and for repair work.

Gross fixed capital formation represents current expenditure on new and used fixed assets less sales and write-offs owing to obsolescence. Own-account construction of fixed assets is included. The estimates for mining exclude salterns and the value of sales (insignificant) is not generally deducted.

The indexes of industrial production are compiled by the National Statistical Service of Greece and provided in response to the United Nations Questionnaire on Indexes of Industrial Production. In principle, the indexes cover all industrial establishments except handicrafts.

Related national publications:
<u>Annual Statistical Survey on Mines, Quarries and Salterns</u>; <u>Annual Industrial Survey</u>; <u>Statistical Yearbook</u>; <u>Monthly Statistical Bulletin</u>, all published by the National Statistical Service of Greece, Athens.

ISIC	INDUSTRY	1. NUMBER OF ESTABLISHMENTS a/ (NUMBER) 1981	1982	1983	1984	1985	2. AVERAGE NUMBER OF PERSONS ENGAGED (THOUSANDS) 1981	1982	1983	1984	1985	ISIC
210	Coal mining	32	...	...	...	...	5.41	...	...	...	...	210
220	Petroleum and gas	6	...	...	...	...	0.54	...	...	...	...	220
230	Metal ore mining	61	...	...	...	...	4.03	...	...	...	...	230
290	Other mining	1141	...	...	...	...	14.33	...	...	...	...	290
2	Mining, quarrying .	1240	...	...	...	...	24.31	...	...	...	...	2
311/2	Food products	1189	...	...	...	...	47.85	...	...	...	...	311/2
313	Beverages	199	...	...	...	...	10.96	...	...	...	...	313
314	Tobacco	80	...	...	...	...	8.44	...	...	...	...	314
321	Textiles	1038	...	...	...	...	66.79	...	...	...	...	321
3211	Spinning,weaving etc..	538	...	...	...	...	42.81	...	...	...	...	3211
322	Wearing apparel	1030	...	...	...	...	35.84	...	...	...	...	322
323	Leather and products ...	268	...	...	...	...	4.88	...	...	...	...	323
324	Footwear	302	...	...	...	...	8.62	...	...	...	...	324
331	Wood products	306	...	...	...	...	9.11	...	...	...	...	331
332	Furniture, fixtures	334	...	...	...	...	5.81	...	...	...	...	332
341	Paper and products	125	...	...	...	...	8.65	...	...	...	...	341
3411	Pulp,paper etc.	26	...	...	...	...	3.19	...	...	...	...	3411
342	Printing,publishing	283	...	...	...	...	9.74	...	...	...	...	342
351	Industrial chemicals ...	61	...	...	...	...	6.71	...	...	...	...	351
3511	Basic excl fertilizers	28	...	...	...	...	1.59	...	...	...	...	3511
3513	Synthetic resins etc .	23	...	...	...	...	1.08	...	...	...	...	3513
352	Other chemical products.	262	...	...	...	...	14.49	...	...	...	...	352
3522	Drugs and medicines ..	93	...	...	...	...	6.16	...	...	...	...	3522
353	Petroleum refineries ...	14	...	...	...	...	3.22	...	...	...	...	353
354	Petroleum,coal products.	37	...	...	...	...	1.21	...	...	...	...	354
355	Rubber products	49	...	...	...	...	2.95	...	...	...	...	355
356	Plastic products n.e.c..	294	...	...	...	...	11.50	...	...	...	...	356
361	Pottery,china etc	64	...	...	...	...	3.78	...	...	...	...	361
362	Glass and products	37	...	...	...	...	2.52	...	...	...	...	362
369	Non-metal products n.e.c	541	...	...	...	...	18.64	...	...	...	...	369
371	Iron and steel	56	...	...	...	...	7.35	...	...	...	...	371
372	Non-ferrous metals	33	...	...	...	...	5.27	...	...	...	...	372
381	Metal products	623	...	...	...	...	25.05	...	...	...	...	381
382	Machinery n.e.c.	413	...	...	...	...	9.31	...	...	...	...	382
3825	Office,computing etc..	5	...	...	...	...	0.14	...	...	...	...	3825
383	Electrical machinery ...	334	...	...	...	...	17.82	...	...	...	...	383
3832	Radio,television etc..	50	...	...	...	...	3.19	...	...	...	...	3832
384	Transport equipment	279	...	...	...	...	29.90	...	...	...	...	384
3841	Shipbuilding, repair..	170	...	...	...	...	15.98	...	...	...	...	3841
3843	Motor vehicles	83	...	...	...	...	5.55	...	...	...	...	3843
385	Professional goods	22	...	...	...	...	0.62	...	...	...	...	385
390	Other industries	123	...	...	...	...	2.87	...	...	...	...	390
3	Manufacturing	8396	...	...	...	...	379.90	...	...	...	...	3
410	Electricity,gas,steam ..	2	2	...	...	...	22.15	22.54	...	...	...	410
4101	Electricity	1	1	...	...	...	21.75	22.15	...	...	...	4101
420	Water works and supply .	.	.	...	...	...	.	.	...	...	...	420
4	Electricity,gas etc	2	2	...	...	...	22.15	22.54	...	...	...	4
2-4	All industry	...	...	...	...	...	426.36	...	...	...	...	2-4

a/ Electricity and gas: number of enterprises.

ISIC	INDUSTRY	3. AVERAGE NUMBER OF EMPLOYEES (THOUSANDS)					4. WAGES AND SALARIES OF EMPLOYEES (MILLION DRACHMAS)					ISIC
		1981	1982	1983	1984	1985	1981	1982	1983	1984	1985	
210	Coal mining	5.39	...	...	...	...	3889	...	...	...	...	210
220	Petroleum and gas	0.54	...	...	...	...	514	...	...	...	...	220
230	Metal ore mining	4.02	...	...	...	...	1828	...	...	...	...	230
290	Other mining	13.26	...	...	...	...	5112	...	...	...	...	290
2	Mining, quarrying .	23.21	...	...	...	...	11343	...	...	...	...	2
311/2	Food products	46.56	...	...	...	...	14400	...	...	...	...	311/2
313	Beverages	10.72	...	...	...	...	4288	...	...	...	...	313
314	Tobacco	8.42	...	...	...	...	2793	...	...	...	...	314
321	Textiles	65.56	...	...	...	...	20295	...	...	...	...	321
3211	Spinning,weaving etc..	42.24	...	...	...	...	14001	...	...	...	...	3211
322	Wearing apparel	34.19	...	...	...	...	7342	...	...	...	...	322
323	Leather and products ...	4.37	...	...	...	...	1176	...	...	...	...	323
324	Footwear	8.09	...	...	...	...	2400	...	...	...	...	324
331	Wood products	8.65	...	...	...	...	2617	...	...	...	...	331
332	Furniture, fixtures	5.19	...	...	...	...	1307	...	...	...	...	332
341	Paper and products	8.51	...	...	...	...	3381	...	...	...	...	341
3411	Pulp,paper etc.	3.18	...	...	...	...	1331	...	...	...	...	3411
342	Printing,publishing	9.39	...	...	...	...	4367	...	...	...	...	342
351	Industrial chemicals ...	6.69	...	...	...	...	4357	...	...	...	...	351
3511	Basic excl fertilizers	1.58	...	...	...	...	1056	...	...	...	...	3511
3513	Synthetic resins etc .	1.07	...	...	...	...	447	...	...	...	...	3513
352	Other chemical products.	14.39	...	...	...	...	5592	...	...	...	...	352
3522	Drugs and medicines ..	6.13	...	...	...	...	2385	...	...	...	...	3522
353	Petroleum refineries ...	3.22	...	...	...	...	2031	...	...	...	...	353
354	Petroleum,coal products.	1.19	...	...	...	...	680	...	...	...	...	354
355	Rubber products	2.90	...	...	...	...	1270	...	...	...	...	355
356	Plastic products n.e.c..	11.15	...	...	...	...	3730	...	...	...	...	356
361	Pottery,china etc	3.69	...	...	...	...	1395	...	...	...	...	361
362	Glass and products	2.47	...	...	...	...	1106	...	...	...	...	362
369	Non-metal products n.e.c	17.93	...	...	...	...	7853	...	...	...	...	369
371	Iron and steel	7.31	...	...	...	...	3694	...	...	...	...	371
372	Non-ferrous metals	5.26	...	...	...	...	3728	...	...	...	...	372
381	Metal products	24.19	...	...	...	...	8759	...	...	...	...	381
382	Machinery n.e.c.	8.74	...	...	...	...	2968	...	...	...	...	382
3825	Office,computing etc..	0.14	...	...	...	...	57	...	...	...	...	3825
383	Electrical machinery ...	17.47	...	...	...	...	6543	...	...	...	...	383
3832	Radio,television etc..	3.15	...	...	...	...	1197	...	...	...	...	3832
384	Transport equipment	29.62	...	...	...	...	14544	...	...	...	...	384
3841	Shipbuilding, repair..	15.79	...	...	...	...	7865	...	...	...	...	3841
3843	Motor vehicles	5.46	...	...	...	...	2128	...	...	...	...	3843
385	Professional goods	0.60	...	...	...	...	183	...	...	...	...	385
390	Other industries	2.67	...	...	...	...	692	...	...	...	...	390
3	Manufacturing	369.14	...	...	...	...	133491	...	...	...	...	3
410	Electricity,gas,steam ..	22.15	22.54	...	...	...	15967	19672	...	...	...	410
4101	Electricity	21.75	22.15	...	...	...	15676	19373	...	...	...	4101
420	Water works and supply .	.	.	...	...	...	.	.	...	...	...	420
4	Electricity,gas etc	22.15	22.54	...	...	...	15967	19672	...	...	...	4
2-4	All industry	414.50	...	...	...	...	160801	...	...	...	...	2-4

ISIC	INDUSTRY	5. SUPPLEMENTS TO WAGES AND SALARIES a/ (MILLION DRACHMAS)					6. AVERAGE NUMBER OF OPERATIVES (THOUSANDS)					ISIC
		1981	1982	1983	1984	1985	1981	1982	1983	1984	1985	
210	Coal mining	1433	...	...	...	...	0.20	...	...	...	...	210
220	Petroleum and gas	44	...	...	...	...	0.01	...	...	...	...	220
230	Metal ore mining	361	...	...	...	...	1.73	...	...	...	...	230
290	Other mining	989	...	...	...	...	8.06	...	...	...	...	290
2	Mining, quarrying .	2827	...	...	...	...	10.00	...	...	...	...	2
311/2	Food products	2541	...	...	...	...	33.25	...	...	...	...	311/2
313	Beverages	953	...	...	...	...	6.07	...	...	...	...	313
314	Tobacco	526	...	...	...	...	7.01	...	...	...	...	314
321	Textiles	4118	...	...	...	...	54.35	...	...	...	...	321
3211	Spinning,weaving etc..	2905	...	...	...	...	34.24	...	...	...	...	3211
322	Wearing apparel	1243	...	...	...	...	30.94	...	...	...	...	322
323	Leather and products ...	200	...	...	...	...	4.02	...	...	...	...	323
324	Footwear	534	...	...	...	...	7.54	...	...	...	...	324
331	Wood products	517	...	...	...	...	6.88	...	...	...	...	331
332	Furniture, fixtures	279	...	...	...	...	4.63	...	...	...	...	332
341	Paper and products	608	...	...	...	...	5.72	...	...	...	...	341
3411	Pulp,paper etc.	219	...	...	...	...	1.87	...	...	...	...	3411
342	Printing,publishing	542	...	...	...	...	5.10	...	...	...	...	342
351	Industrial chemicals ...	960	...	...	...	...	1.93	...	...	...	...	351
3511	Basic excl fertilizers	208	...	...	...	...	0.21	...	...	...	...	3511
3513	Synthetic resins etc .	99	...	...	...	...	0.59	...	...	...	...	3513
352	Other chemical products.	1111	...	...	...	...	6.64	...	...	...	...	352
3522	Drugs and medicines ..	494	...	...	...	...	2.49	...	...	...	...	3522
353	Petroleum refineries ...	430	...	...	...	...	0.33	...	...	...	...	353
354	Petroleum,coal products.	158	...	...	...	...	0.34	...	...	...	...	354
355	Rubber products	255	...	...	...	...	2.09	...	...	...	...	355
356	Plastic products n.e.c..	736	...	...	...	...	8.27	...	...	...	...	356
361	Pottery,china etc	272	...	...	...	...	2.88	...	...	...	...	361
362	Glass and products	255	...	...	...	...	1.89	...	...	...	...	362
369	Non-metal products n.e.c	1543	...	...	...	...	10.03	...	...	...	...	369
371	Iron and steel	728	...	...	...	...	5.06	...	...	...	...	371
372	Non-ferrous metals	647	...	...	...	...	2.90	...	...	...	...	372
381	Metal products	1950	...	...	...	...	18.23	...	...	...	...	381
382	Machinery n.e.c.	655	...	...	...	...	6.51	...	...	...	...	382
3825	Office,computing etc..	11	...	...	...	...	0.05	...	...	...	...	3825
383	Electrical machinery ...	1325	...	...	...	...	11.70	...	...	...	...	383
3832	Radio,television etc..	244	...	...	...	...	1.76	...	...	...	...	3832
384	Transport equipment	2689	...	...	...	...	19.75	...	...	...	...	384
3841	Shipbuilding, repair..	1419	...	...	...	...	12.47	...	...	...	...	3841
3843	Motor vehicles	440	...	...	...	...	4.09	...	...	...	...	3843
385	Professional goods	38	...	...	...	...	0.43	...	...	...	...	385
390	Other industries	134	...	...	...	...	2.16	...	...	...	...	390
3	Manufacturing	25947	...	...	...	...	266.65	...	...	...	...	3
410	Electricity,gas,steam ..	...	...	...	...	...	...	...	...	...	...	410
4101	Electricity	...	...	...	...	...	...	...	...	...	...	4101
420	Water works and supply .	...	...	...	...	...	...	...	...	...	...	420
4	Electricity,gas etc	...	...	...	...	...	...	...	...	...	...	4
2-4	All industry	...	...	...	...	...	...	...	...	...	...	2-4

a/ Employers' contributions to social security schemes on behalf of employees and wage earners.

ISIC	INDUSTRY	7. WAGES AND SALARIES OF OPERATIVES (MILLION DRACHMAS) 1981	1982	1983	1984	1985	8. QUANTITY OF ELECTRICITY CONSUMED a/ (MILLION KWH) 1981	1982	1983	1984	1985	ISIC
210	Coal mining	55	...	...	...	...	6	...	...	...	...	210
220	Petroleum and gas	37	...	...	...	...	8	...	...	...	...	220
230	Metal ore mining	660	...	...	...	...	25	...	...	...	...	230
290	Other mining	2603	...	...	...	...	222	...	...	...	...	290
2	Mining, quarrying .	3355	...	...	...	...	261	...	...	...	...	2
311/2	Food products	8188	...	...	...	...	392	...	...	...	...	311/2
313	Beverages	1883	...	...	...	...	83	...	...	...	...	313
314	Tobacco	2033	...	...	...	...	25	...	...	...	...	314
321	Textiles	15120	...	...	...	...	1064	...	...	...	...	321
3211	Spinning,weaving etc..	10168	...	...	...	...	959	...	...	...	...	3211
322	Wearing apparel	6220	...	...	...	...	50	...	...	...	...	322
323	Leather and products ...	1006	...	...	...	...	19	...	...	...	...	323
324	Footwear	2164	...	...	...	...	16	...	...	...	...	324
331	Wood products	1837	...	...	...	...	116	...	...	...	...	331
332	Furniture, fixtures	1106	...	...	...	...	18	...	...	...	...	332
341	Paper and products	1950	...	...	...	...	402	...	...	...	...	341
3411	Pulp,paper etc.	666	...	...	...	...	234	...	...	...	...	3411
342	Printing,publishing	2214	...	...	...	...	31	...	...	...	...	342
351	Industrial chemicals ...	867	...	...	...	...	938	...	...	...	...	351
3511	Basic excl fertilizers	84	...	...	...	...	328	...	...	...	...	3511
3513	Synthetic resins etc .	195	...	...	...	...	48	...	...	...	...	3513
352	Other chemical products.	1962	...	...	...	...	55	...	...	...	...	352
3522	Drugs and medicines ..	719	...	...	...	...	19	...	...	...	...	3522
353	Petroleum refineries ...	112	...	...	...	...	286	...	...	...	...	353
354	Petroleum,coal products.	146	...	...	...	...	4	...	...	...	...	354
355	Rubber products	783	...	...	...	...	33	...	...	...	...	355
356	Plastic products n.e.c..	2385	...	...	...	...	193	...	...	...	...	356
361	Pottery,china etc	995	...	...	...	...	53	...	...	...	...	361
362	Glass and products	811	...	...	...	...	73	...	...	...	...	362
369	Non-metal products n.e.c	3696	...	...	...	...	1417	...	...	...	...	369
371	Iron and steel	2307	...	...	...	...	696	...	...	...	...	371
372	Non-ferrous metals	1640	...	...	...	...	3015	...	...	...	...	372
381	Metal products	5837	...	...	...	...	179	...	...	...	...	381
382	Machinery n.e.c.	2011	...	...	...	...	28	...	...	...	...	382
3825	Office,computing etc..	15	...	...	...	...	...	...	...	...	...	3825
383	Electrical machinery ...	3586	...	...	...	...	102	...	...	...	...	383
3832	Radio,television etc..	506	...	...	...	...	9	...	...	...	...	3832
384	Transport equipment	7917	...	...	...	...	128	...	...	...	...	384
3841	Shipbuilding, repair..	5783	...	...	...	...	70	...	...	...	...	3841
3843	Motor vehicles	1388	...	...	...	...	21	...	...	...	...	3843
385	Professional goods	115	...	...	...	...	4	...	...	...	...	385
390	Other industries	496	...	...	...	...	10	...	...	...	...	390
3	Manufacturing	79387	...	...	...	...	9430	...	...	...	...	3
410	Electricity,gas,steam ..	...	...	...	...	...	...	...	...	...	...	410
4101	Electricity	...	...	...	...	...	...	...	...	...	...	4101
420	Water works and supply .	...	...	...	...	...	...	...	...	...	...	420
4	Electricity,gas etc	...	...	...	...	...	...	...	...	...	...	4
2-4	All industry	...	...	...	...	...	...	...	...	...	...	2-4

a/ Purchased electricity only.

ISIC	INDUSTRY	9. OUTPUT IN FACTOR VALUES (BILLION DRACHMAS)					10. VALUE ADDED IN FACTOR VALUES (BILLION DRACHMAS)					ISIC
		1981	1982	1983	1984	1985	1981	1982	1983	1984	1985	
210	Coal mining	7.7	...	...	...	...	6.60	...	...	...	...	210
220	Petroleum and gas	3.1	...	...	...	...	2.80	...	...	...	...	220
230	Metal ore mining	5.7	...	...	...	...	4.30	...	...	...	...	230
290	Other mining	15.8	...	...	...	...	9.30	...	...	...	...	290
2	Mining, quarrying .	32.3	...	...	...	...	23.00	...	...	...	...	2
311/2	Food products	180.9	...	...	...	...	40.74	...	...	...	...	311/2
313	Beverages	36.3	...	...	...	...	12.47	...	...	...	...	313
314	Tobacco	30.0	...	...	...	...	7.35	...	...	...	...	314
321	Textiles	131.6	...	...	...	...	45.54	...	...	...	...	321
3211	Spinning,weaving etc..	95.3	...	...	...	...	30.95	...	...	...	...	3211
322	Wearing apparel	32.8	...	...	...	...	14.33	...	...	...	...	322
323	Leather and products ...	7.6	...	...	...	...	2.67	...	...	...	...	323
324	Footwear	10.7	...	...	...	...	4.37	...	...	...	...	324
331	Wood products	18.3	...	...	...	...	6.10	...	...	...	...	331
332	Furniture, fixtures	5.6	...	...	...	...	2.72	...	...	...	...	332
341	Paper and products	26.1	...	...	...	...	7.90	...	...	...	...	341
3411	Pulp,paper etc.	6.6	...	...	...	...	1.08	...	...	...	...	3411
342	Printing,publishing	14.5	...	...	...	...	7.25	...	...	...	...	342
351	Industrial chemicals ...	37.2	...	...	...	...	10.03	...	...	...	...	351
3511	Basic excl fertilizers	12.0	...	...	...	...	3.32	...	...	...	...	3511
3513	Synthetic resins etc .	6.3	...	...	...	...	1.23	...	...	...	...	3513
352	Other chemical products.	42.8	...	...	...	...	16.31	...	...	...	...	352
3522	Drugs and medicines ..	12.8	...	...	...	...	5.47	...	...	...	...	3522
353	Petroleum refineries ...	198.8	...	...	...	...	6.38	...	...	...	...	353
354	Petroleum,coal products.	6.2	...	...	...	...	1.72	...	...	...	...	354
355	Rubber products	8.4	...	...	...	...	3.42	...	...	...	...	355
356	Plastic products n.e.c..	25.5	...	...	...	...	9.67	...	...	...	...	356
361	Pottery,china etc	5.3	...	...	...	...	3.04	...	...	...	...	361
362	Glass and products	5.3	...	...	...	...	2.66	...	...	...	...	362
369	Non-metal products n.e.c	57.9	...	...	...	...	21.27	...	...	...	...	369
371	Iron and steel	45.4	...	...	...	...	10.08	...	...	...	...	371
372	Non-ferrous metals	33.6	...	...	...	...	9.75	...	...	...	...	372
381	Metal products	56.1	...	...	...	...	19.61	...	...	...	...	381
382	Machinery n.e.c.	15.2	...	...	...	...	6.37	...	...	...	...	382
3825	Office,computing etc..	0.2	...	...	...	...	0.07	...	...	...	...	3825
383	Electrical machinery ...	45.3	...	...	...	...	16.10	...	...	...	...	383
3832	Radio,television etc..	9.2	...	...	...	...	3.21	...	...	...	...	3832
384	Transport equipment	49.2	...	...	...	...	25.95	...	...	...	...	384
3841	Shipbuilding, repair..	24.1	...	...	...	...	15.03	...	...	...	...	3841
3843	Motor vehicles	17.1	...	...	...	...	5.45	...	...	...	...	3843
385	Professional goods	0.7	...	...	...	...	0.34	...	...	...	...	385
390	Other industries	3.7	...	...	...	...	1.63	...	...	...	...	390
3	Manufacturing	1131.0	...	...	...	...	315.77	...	...	...	...	3
410	Electricity,gas,steam ..	70.3	88.6	...	...	...	37.45	51.89	...	...	...	410
4101	Electricity	70.1	88.4	...	...	...	37.47	52.05	...	...	...	4101
420	Water works and supply .	.	.	...	...	...	.	.	...	...	...	420
4	Electricity,gas etc	70.3	88.6	...	...	...	37.45	51.89	...	...	...	4
2-4	All industry	1131.0	...	...	...	...	376.22	...	...	...	...	2-4

ISIC	INDUSTRY	11. GROSS FIXED CAPITAL FORMATION TOTAL (MILLION DRACHMAS) 1981	1982	1983	1984	1985	12. GROSS FIXED CAPITAL FORMATION MACHINERY AND EQUIPMENT (MILLION DRACHMAS) 1981	1982	1983	1984	1985	ISIC
210	Coal mining	5475	...	...	...	...	3206	...	...	...	...	210
220	Petroleum and gas	22461	...	...	...	...	164	...	...	...	...	220
230	Metal ore mining	1281	...	...	...	...	831	...	...	...	...	230
290	Other mining .... a/	5690	...	...	...	...	2865	...	...	...	...	290
2	Mining, quarrying . a/	34907	...	...	...	...	7066	...	...	...	...	2
311/2	Food products	8649	...	...	...	...	4979	...	...	...	...	311/2
313	Beverages	7358	...	...	...	...	3793	...	...	...	...	313
314	Tobacco	906	...	...	...	...	636	...	...	...	...	314
321	Textiles	9967	...	...	...	...	6875	...	...	...	...	321
3211	Spinning,weaving etc..	7854	...	...	...	...	5468	...	...	...	...	3211
322	Wearing apparel	1241	...	...	...	...	640	...	...	...	...	322
323	Leather and products ...	347	...	...	...	...	227	...	...	...	...	323
324	Footwear	360	...	...	...	...	242	...	...	...	...	324
331	Wood products	1374	...	...	...	...	734	...	...	...	...	331
332	Furniture, fixtures	205	...	...	...	...	139	...	...	...	...	332
341	Paper and products	1774	...	...	...	...	1107	...	...	...	...	341
3411	Pulp,paper etc.	908	...	...	...	...	433	...	...	...	...	3411
342	Printing,publishing	788	...	...	...	...	563	...	...	...	...	342
351	Industrial chemicals ...	1574	...	...	...	...	1138	...	...	...	...	351
3511	Basic excl fertilizers	368	...	...	...	...	193	...	...	...	...	3511
3513	Synthetic resins etc .	525	...	...	...	...	485	...	...	...	...	3513
352	Other chemical products.	1334	...	...	...	...	924	...	...	...	...	352
3522	Drugs and medicines ..	406	...	...	...	...	247	...	...	...	...	3522
353	Petroleum refineries ...	2746	...	...	...	...	1141	...	...	...	...	353
354	Petroleum,coal products.	217	...	...	...	...	156	...	...	...	...	354
355	Rubber products	443	...	...	...	...	277	...	...	...	...	355
356	Plastic products n.e.c..	2032	...	...	...	...	1382	...	...	...	...	356
361	Pottery,china etc	413	...	...	...	...	259	...	...	...	...	361
362	Glass and products	1122	...	...	...	...	890	...	...	...	...	362
369	Non-metal products n.e.c	13829	...	...	...	...	7378	...	...	...	...	369
371	Iron and steel	7821	...	...	...	...	5662	...	...	...	...	371
372	Non-ferrous metals	2429	...	...	...	...	1538	...	...	...	...	372
381	Metal products	3096	...	...	...	...	1815	...	...	...	...	381
382	Machinery n.e.c.	628	...	...	...	...	432	...	...	...	...	382
3825	Office,computing etc..	10	...	...	...	...	10	...	...	...	...	3825
383	Electrical machinery ...	1583	...	...	...	...	870	...	...	...	...	383
3832	Radio,television etc..	205	...	...	...	...	101	...	...	...	...	3832
384	Transport equipment	10500	...	...	...	...	1464	...	...	...	...	384
3841	Shipbuilding, repair..	905	...	...	...	...	491	...	...	...	...	3841
3843	Motor vehicles	593	...	...	...	...	392	...	...	...	...	3843
385	Professional goods	125	...	...	...	...	52	...	...	...	...	385
390	Other industries	161	...	...	...	...	85	...	...	...	...	390
3	Manufacturing	83022	...	...	...	...	45398	...	...	...	...	3
410	Electricity,gas,steam ..	...	...	...	...	...	...	...	...	...	...	410
4101	Electricity	...	...	...	...	...	...	...	...	...	...	4101
420	Water works and supply .	...	...	...	...	...	...	...	...	...	...	420
4	Electricity,gas etc	...	...	...	...	...	...	...	...	...	...	4
2-4	All industry	...	...	...	...	...	...	...	...	...	...	2-4

a/ Excluding salterns.

13. VALUE OF STOCKS AT END OF PERIOD
TOTAL
(MILLION DRACHMAS)

ISIC	INDUSTRY	1981	1982	1983	1984	1985	ISIC
210	Coal mining	142	...	...	...	...	210
220	Petroleum and gas	626	...	...	...	...	220
230	Metal ore mining	2791	...	...	...	...	230
290	Other mining	4032	...	...	...	...	290
2	Mining, quarrying . a/	7591	...	...	...	...	2
311/2	Food products	54990	...	...	...	...	311/2
313	Beverages	11028	...	...	...	...	313
314	Tobacco	17747	...	...	...	...	314
321	Textiles	39367	...	...	...	...	321
3211	Spinning,weaving etc..	28573	...	...	...	...	3211
322	Wearing apparel	8421	...	...	...	...	322
323	Leather and products ...	2122	...	...	...	...	323
324	Footwear	1999	...	...	...	...	324
331	Wood products	6152	...	...	...	...	331
332	Furniture, fixtures	1680	...	...	...	...	332
341	Paper and products	4875	...	...	...	...	341
3411	Pulp,paper etc.	2146	...	...	...	...	3411
342	Printing,publishing	1815	...	...	...	...	342
351	Industrial chemicals ...	5557	...	...	...	...	351
3511	Basic excl fertilizers	1589	...	...	...	...	3511
3513	Synthetic resins etc .	1301	...	...	...	...	3513
352	Other chemical products.	10345	...	...	...	...	352
3522	Drugs and medicines ..	3251	...	...	...	...	3522
353	Petroleum refineries ...	30639	...	...	...	...	353
354	Petroleum,coal products.	393	...	...	...	...	354
355	Rubber products	1556	...	...	...	...	355
356	Plastic products n.e.c..	5956	...	...	...	...	356
361	Pottery,china etc	1687	...	...	...	...	361
362	Glass and products	1372	...	...	...	...	362
369	Non-metal products n.e.c	9844	...	...	...	...	369
371	Iron and steel	15094	...	...	...	...	371
372	Non-ferrous metals	12327	...	...	...	...	372
381	Metal products	12915	...	...	...	...	381
382	Machinery n.e.c.	4587	...	...	...	...	382
3825	Office,computing etc..	64	...	...	...	...	3825
383	Electrical machinery ...	10827	...	...	...	...	383
3832	Radio,television etc..	1832	...	...	...	...	3832
384	Transport equipment	13705	...	...	...	...	384
3841	Shipbuilding, repair..	5751	...	...	...	...	3841
3843	Motor vehicles	4792	...	...	...	...	3843
385	Professional goods	230	...	...	...	...	385
390	Other industries	1151	...	...	...	...	390
3	Manufacturing	288381	...	...	...	...	3
410	Electricity,gas,steam ..	...	...	...	...	...	410
4101	Electricity	...	...	...	...	...	4101
420	Water works and supply .	...	...	...	...	...	420
4	Electricity,gas etc	...	...	...	...	...	4
2-4	All industry	...	...	...	...	...	2-4

a/ Excluding major group 220 and extraction of miscellaneous minerals.

14. INDEX NUMBERS OF INDUSTRIAL PRODUCTION (1980 = 100)

ISIC	INDUSTRY	1976	1977	1978	1979	1981	1982	1983	1984	1985	RATE a/	ISIC
210	Coal mining	97	103	102	104	119	122	124	140	162	5.9	210
220	Petroleum and gas	...	...	...	...	...	...	...	...	...	...	220
230	Metal ore mining	91	99	89	93	98	82	80	89	97	0.7	230
290	Other mining	93	95	93	103	90	86	85	98	92	-0.1	290
2	Mining, quarrying . b/c/	94	97	95	102	101	148	161	178	183	7.7	2
311/2	Food products	82	82	98	102	99	99	100	110	112	3.5	311/2
313	Beverages	65	79	84	95	103	104	104	110	124	7.4	313
314	Tobacco	90	98	94	99	95	106	115	108	120	3.2	314
321	Textiles	91	89	94	101	100	94	92	92	95	0.5	321
3211	Spinning,weaving etc.	...	...	...	...	...	...	...	...	...	...	3211
322	Wearing apparel	82	92	94	97	88	88	80	79	79	-0.4	322
323	Leather and products	130	118	107	107	97	78	77	72	71	-6.5	323
324	Footwear	123	104	98	128	108	84	80	79	108	-1.4	324
331	Wood products	86	91	92	106	83	81	80	70	62	-3.6	331
332	Furniture, fixtures	125	128	138	121	101	111	64	56	78	-5.1	332
341	Paper and products	60	63	84	100	96	95	106	118	137	9.6	341
3411	Pulp,paper etc.	...	...	...	...	...	...	...	...	...	...	3411
342	Printing,publishing	93	92	95	95	101	102	102	109	117	2.6	342
351	Industrial chemicals	79	86	96	97	94	98	108	113	117	4.5	351
3511	Basic excl fertilizers	...	...	...	...	...	...	...	...	...	...	3511
3513	Synthetic resins etc	...	...	...	...	...	...	...	...	...	...	3513
352	Other chemical products.	89	89	100	99	104	102	108	119	129	4.2	352
3522	Drugs and medicines	...	...	...	...	...	...	...	...	...	...	3522
353	Petroleum refineries	71	70	81	102	109	102	100	98	97	3.5	353
354	Petroleum,coal products.	119	101	89	90	66	57	58	63	61	-7.2	354
355	Rubber products	85	85	93	97	101	100	97	97	102	2.0	355
356	Plastic products n.e.c.	99	110	114	114	105	110	118	116	123	2.4	356
361	Pottery,china etc	80	83	91	98	91	78	80	77	67	-2.0	361
362	Glass and products	95	92	105	92	112	98	91	76	80	-1.9	362
369	Non-metal products n.e.c c/	68	81	86	95	97	99	96	100	98	4.1	369
371	Iron and steel	79	77	95	101	93	94	85	95	91	1.6	371
372	Non-ferrous metals	97	76	97	98	88	75	85	87	86	-1.3	372
381	Metal products	82	98	86	94	101	103	106	101	93	1.4	381
382	Machinery n.e.c.	144	138	125	119	103	105	95	84	91	-5.0	382
3825	Office,computing etc.	...	...	...	...	...	...	...	...	...	...	3825
383	Electrical machinery	79	79	81	86	103	100	95	88	102	2.9	383
3832	Radio,television etc.	...	...	...	...	...	...	...	...	...	...	3832
384	Transport equipment	88	89	81	90	103	100	84	78	62	-3.8	384
3841	Shipbuilding, repair.	...	...	...	...	...	...	...	...	...	...	3841
3843	Motor vehicles	...	...	...	...	...	...	...	...	...	...	3843
385	Professional goods	95	109	84	85	92	90	89	100	76	-2.4	385
390	Other industries	104	127	136	108	84	105	109	138	62	-5.6	390
3	Manufacturing ..... c/	85	87	93	99	101	99	97	98	101	1.9	3
410	Electricity,gas,steam	78	83	92	97	103	103	105	109	123	5.2	410
4101	Electricity	...	...	...	...	...	...	...	...	...	...	4101
420	Water works and supply	.	.	.	.	.	.	.	.	.	.	420
4	Electricity,gas etc	...	...	...	...	...	...	...	...	...	...	4
2-4	All industry b/	85	87	93	99	101	102	101	104	107	2.6	2-4

a/ Annual growth rate 1976-1985.
b/ Excluding crude petroleum and natural gas.
c/ Magnesite roasting is included in mining.

GUATEMALA

The information in the tables is based on the reply to the United Nations Questionnaire on General Industrial Statistics from the Instituto Nacional de Estadistica, Ministerio de Economia, Guatemala. The concepts, definitions and classification by branches of industry are generally in accordance with United Nations standards.

The data in the tables are derived from the annual survey of manufacturing industries conducted since 1969 by the Instituto Nacional de Estadistica on a sample basis. The data shown in the tables relate to establishments with 5 or more persons engaged. The tabulation of data is based on the national classification, which is generally comparable with the present ISIC.

Employment numbers refer to averages during the reference year. Homeworkers are excluded. Wages and salaries relate to all payments, in cash and in kind, made by the employer during the reference year for work done by employees. They include bonuses, cost-of-living allowances, wages and salaries paid during regular leave, dismissal compensations, taxes and employees' contributions to social insurance and other funds.

Output comprises the value of (a) goods produced, (b) work performed for others, (c) goods sold without transformation, (d) electricity sold and (e) other receipts. The valuation of output and value added is in producers' prices.

Related national publications:
<u>Encuesta Industrial</u> (annual), published by the Instituto Nacional de Estadistica, Guatemala; <u>Boletin Estadistico</u> (quarterly), published by the Banco de Guatemala, Guatemala.

GUATEMALA

ISIC	INDUSTRY	1. NUMBER OF ESTABLISHMENTS a/ (NUMBER)					2. AVERAGE NUMBER OF PERSONS ENGAGED a/ (NUMBER)					ISIC
		1981	1982	1983	*1984	1985	1981	1982	1983	*1984	1985	
210	Coal mining	...	...	...	...	...	...	...	...	...	...	210
220	Petroleum and gas	...	...	...	...	...	...	...	...	...	...	220
230	Metal ore mining	...	...	...	...	...	...	...	...	...	...	230
290	Other mining	...	...	...	...	...	...	...	...	...	...	290
2	Mining, quarrying .	...	...	...	...	...	...	...	...	...	...	2
311/2	Food products	502	570	496	551	...	23110	23697	23939	24089	...	311/2
313	Beverages	22	22	21	23	...	4000	4229	3664	3662	...	313
314	Tobacco	5	4	4	3	...	904	887	931	810	...	314
321	Textiles	102	95	94	108	...	9581	8417	8684	8614	...	321
3211	Spinning,weaving etc..	54	55	54	66	...	7354	6459	6936	6905	...	3211
322	Wearing apparel	169	150	151	180	...	3099	3123	2821	3389	...	322
323	Leather and products ...	27	26	27	31	...	633	529	685	602	...	323
324	Footwear	48	60	60	69	...	2445	1988	2106	2322	...	324
331	Wood products	126	116	116	118	...	2659	2455	2266	2169	...	331
332	Furniture, fixtures	55	63	61	27	...	950	1139	1115	1128	...	332
341	Paper and products	19	19	20	22	...	1794	1517	1408	1309	...	341
3411	Pulp,paper etc.	6	5	6	6	...	1044	588	667	467	...	3411
342	Printing,publishing	123	127	130	141	...	3050	3197	3207	3700	...	342
351	Industrial chemicals ...	20	20	20	18	...	1295	1293	1151	1129	...	351
3511	Basic excl fertilizers	8	9	9	6	...	273	288	286	226	...	3511
3513	Synthetic resins etc .	2	3	3	4	...	29	61	61	65	...	3513
352	Other chemical products.	102	106	110	122	...	6254	6137	5859	6258	...	352
3522	Drugs and medicines ..	33	38	39	43	...	2202	2265	2352	2415	...	3522
353	Petroleum refineries ...	2	2	2	4	...	138	136	130	153	...	353
354	Petroleum,coal products.	2	2	2	2	...	59	52	51	48	...	354
355	Rubber products	16	18	18	15	...	1576	3052	3008	2021	...	355
356	Plastic products n.e.c..	44	63	64	76	...	1841	2586	2547	2897	...	356
361	Pottery,china etc	7	7	7	6	...	215	184	179	194	...	361
362	Glass and products	9	9	10	12	...	1299	915	802	887	...	362
369	Non-metal products n.e.c	129	131	130	150	...	4438	4247	3964	3686	...	369
371	Iron and steel	12	13	12	14	...	1137	1173	1123	990	...	371
372	Non-ferrous metals	5	3	3	4	...	124	69	72	75	...	372
381	Metal products	90	108	119	107	...	3467	3263	3001	2564	...	381
382	Machinery n.e.c.	17	19	19	20	...	778	546	550	534	...	382
3825	Office,computing etc..	1	1	1	1	...	60	35	40	41	...	3825
383	Electrical machinery ...	28	30	31	29	...	1423	1289	1053	1027	...	383
3832	Radio,television etc..	9	9	10	12	...	532	436	331	388	...	3832
384	Transport equipment	23	22	22	22	...	1133	898	853	858	...	384
3841	Shipbuilding, repair..	1	-	-	1	...	18	-	-	9	...	3841
3843	Motor vehicles	18	18	18	18	...	613	573	584	601	...	3843
385	Professional goods	10	11	12	12	...	167	166	180	165	...	385
390	Other industries	30	28	29	29	...	525	463	430	447	...	390
3	Manufacturing	1744	1844	1790	1915	...	78094	77647	75779	75727	...	3
410	Electricity,gas,steam ..	...	...	...	...	...	...	...	...	...	...	410
4101	Electricity	...	...	...	...	...	...	...	...	...	...	4101
420	Water works and supply .	...	...	...	...	...	...	...	...	...	...	420
4	Electricity,gas etc	...	...	...	...	...	...	...	...	...	...	4
2-4	All industry	...	...	...	...	...	...	...	...	...	...	2-4

a/ Establishments with 5 or more persons engaged.

ISIC	INDUSTRY	3. AVERAGE NUMBER OF EMPLOYEES a/ (NUMBER)					4. WAGES AND SALARIES OF EMPLOYEES a/ (THOUSAND QUETZALES)					ISIC
		1981	1982	1983	*1984	1985	1981	1982	1983	*1984	1985	
210	Coal mining	...	...	...	...	...	...	...	...	...	...	210
220	Petroleum and gas	...	...	...	...	...	...	...	...	...	...	220
230	Metal ore mining	...	...	...	...	...	...	...	...	...	...	230
290	Other mining	...	...	...	...	...	...	...	...	...	...	290
2	Mining, quarrying .	...	...	...	...	...	...	...	...	...	...	2
311/2	Food products	22180	23215	23478	23398	...	49147	49636	50253	54516	...	311/2
313	Beverages	3998	4227	3663	3658	...	14804	17062	14810	15198	...	313
314	Tobacco	899	885	929	809	...	4026	4806	5300	4769	...	314
321	Textiles	9467	8338	8608	8529	...	19390	17110	18303	18331	...	321
3211	Spinning,weaving etc..	7277	6414	6898	6864	...	15056	13307	14400	14504	...	3211
322	Wearing apparel	2941	2935	2643	3196	...	5278	5489	5579	6247	...	322
323	Leather and products ...	611	503	660	570	...	1043	879	1000	988	...	323
324	Footwear	2392	1929	2040	2260	...	4442	3452	3920	4697	...	324
331	Wood products	2536	2318	2123	2013	...	3730	3626	3313	3535	...	331
332	Furniture, fixtures	891	1067	1048	1017	...	1875	2016	1858	1883	...	332
341	Paper and products	1786	1507	1395	1297	...	5575	5271	4782	4917	...	341
3411	Pulp,paper etc.	1040	585	663	463	...	2926	2046	2230	1788	...	3411
342	Printing,publishing	2939	3080	3097	3475	...	7811	7720	7979	9507	...	342
351	Industrial chemicals ...	1294	1289	1147	1126	...	5981	6196	5440	5848	...	351
3511	Basic excl fertilizers	273	285	283	226	...	828	814	809	678	...	3511
3513	Synthetic resins etc .	28	60	60	62	...	87	317	317	336	...	3513
352	Other chemical products.	6219	6076	5791	6183	...	24120	25870	26811	29428	...	352
3522	Drugs and medicines ..	2193	2252	2333	2393	...	10953	11989	13125	14084	...	3522
353	Petroleum refineries ...	137	135	129	152	...	1135	1337	1433	1615	...	353
354	Petroleum,coal products.	59	52	51	48	...	140	136	137	129	...	354
355	Rubber products	1564	3042	2999	2015	...	5735	7473	7564	7432	...	355
356	Plastic products n.e.c..	1803	2549	2499	2856	...	4937	7339	7806	9245	...	356
361	Pottery,china etc	205	175	168	182	...	520	592	642	599	...	361
362	Glass and products	1294	909	793	874	...	5341	4235	4197	4291	...	362
369	Non-metal products n.e.c	4316	4152	3840	3496	...	10812	10974	9815	9453	...	369
371	Iron and steel	1127	1169	1120	986	...	2958	2801	2868	2977	...	371
372	Non-ferrous metals	118	65	68	71	...	238	187	224	218	...	372
381	Metal products	3395	3178	2908	2422	...	8444	7905	7147	6921	...	381
382	Machinery n.e.c.	767	531	530	514	...	2419	1787	1788	1804	...	382
3825	Office,computing etc..	60	35	40	41	...	249	156	190	186	...	3825
383	Electrical machinery ...	1404	1261	1025	1006	...	4607	4727	4208	4084	...	383
3832	Radio,television etc..	528	426	321	377	...	1313	1372	1131	1241	...	3832
384	Transport equipment	1116	879	836	839	...	1948	1722	1626	1781	...	384
3841	Shipbuilding, repair..	17	-	-	7	...	79	-	-	23	...	3841
3843	Motor vehicles	597	556	567	584	...	1013	918	947	1025	...	3843
385	Professional goods	140	159	175	150	...	324	485	474	443	...	385
390	Other industries	500	439	406	416	...	1360	1153	1096	1100	...	390
3	Manufacturing	76098	76064	74169	73558	...	198140	201986	200373	211956	...	3
410	Electricity,gas,steam ..	...	...	...	...	...	...	...	...	...	...	410
4101	Electricity	...	...	...	...	...	...	...	...	...	...	4101
420	Water works and supply .	...	...	...	...	...	...	...	...	...	...	420
4	Electricity,gas etc	...	...	...	...	...	...	...	...	...	...	4
2-4	All industry	...	...	...	...	...	...	...	...	...	...	2-4

a/ Establishments with 5 or more persons engaged.

ISIC	INDUSTRY	5. AVERAGE NUMBER OF OPERATIVES a/ (NUMBER)					6. WAGES AND SALARIES OF OPERATIVES a/ (THOUSAND QUETZALES)					ISIC
		1981	1982	1983	*1984	1985	1981	1982	1983	*1984	1985	
210	Coal mining	...	...	...	...	...	...	...	...	...	...	210
220	Petroleum and gas	...	...	...	...	...	...	...	...	...	...	220
230	Metal ore mining	...	...	...	...	...	...	...	...	...	...	230
290	Other mining	...	...	...	...	...	...	...	...	...	...	290
2	Mining, quarrying .	...	...	...	...	...	...	...	...	...	...	2
311/2	Food products	17441	17926	18274	18122	...	27244	25661	26593	28540	...	311/2
313	Beverages	2448	2441	1585	1483	...	6900	7037	4814	4632	...	313
314	Tobacco	476	439	483	373	...	893	1174	1086	1060	...	314
321	Textiles	8283	7284	7570	7498	...	14523	12823	13982	13934	...	321
3211	Spinning,weaving etc..	6428	5720	6182	6145	...	11712	10414	11476	11540	...	3211
322	Wearing apparel	2495	2336	2051	2565	...	3771	3540	3396	3871	...	322
323	Leather and products ...	492	387	530	451	...	710	566	640	649	...	323
324	Footwear	1957	1570	1676	1826	...	2936	2070	2361	2766	...	324
331	Wood products	2255	1960	1774	1740	...	2807	2530	2299	2514	...	331
332	Furniture, fixtures	751	919	904	891	...	1355	1518	1437	1409	...	332
341	Paper and products	1233	976	953	916	...	3178	2506	2497	2425	...	341
3411	Pulp,paper etc.	660	318	400	309	...	1646	905	1109	830	...	3411
342	Printing,publishing	2177	2333	2329	2582	...	4452	4818	4965	5893	...	342
351	Industrial chemicals ...	792	774	640	658	...	2331	2506	2052	2438	...	351
3511	Basic excl fertilizers	90	101	99	54	...	243	212	220	141	...	3511
3513	Synthetic resins etc .	22	41	41	39	...	31	159	159	162	...	3513
352	Other chemical products.	3397	3333	3287	3485	...	7225	7110	7452	8149	...	352
3522	Drugs and medicines ..	1066	1084	1098	1136	...	2366	2595	2849	2976	...	3522
353	Petroleum refineries ...	105	102	95	106	...	675	853	907	1004	...	353
354	Petroleum,coal products.	50	45	44	41	...	93	100	106	98	...	354
355	Rubber products	1211	2434	2373	1556	...	3444	4784	4536	4538	...	355
356	Plastic products n.e.c..	1451	1967	1889	2154	...	2833	4026	4108	4838	...	356
361	Pottery,china etc	149	124	113	125	...	275	291	295	267	...	361
362	Glass and products	1025	670	597	669	...	3246	2420	2601	2635	...	362
369	Non-metal products n.e.c	3452	3244	2973	2706	...	6331	6458	5570	5236	...	369
371	Iron and steel	951	982	940	802	...	2004	1814	1881	1897	...	371
372	Non-ferrous metals	106	56	58	56	...	168	126	138	131	...	372
381	Metal products	2791	2551	2341	1887	...	5246	4623	4227	3886	...	381
382	Machinery n.e.c.	629	421	420	383	...	1499	1062	1065	1016	...	382
3825	Office,computing etc..	27	13	13	10	...	68	44	37	27	...	3825
383	Electrical machinery ...	1128	974	738	690	...	3274	3126	2551	2312	...	383
3832	Radio,television etc..	365	265	155	192	...	622	556	330	386	...	3832
384	Transport equipment	905	658	640	641	...	1296	992	1004	1030	...	384
3841	Shipbuilding, repair..	16	-	-	4	...	77	-	-	10	...	3841
3843	Motor vehicles	499	432	463	477	...	688	570	653	686	...	3843
385	Professional goods	88	99	109	98	...	173	238	247	234	...	385
390	Other industries	371	333	306	308	...	761	683	604	591	...	390
3	Manufacturing	58609	57338	55692	54812	...	109643	105455	103414	107993	...	3
410	Electricity,gas,steam ..	...	...	...	...	...	...	...	...	...	...	410
4101	Electricity	...	...	...	...	...	...	...	...	...	...	4101
420	Water works and supply .	...	...	...	...	...	...	...	...	...	...	420
4	Electricity,gas etc	...	...	...	...	...	...	...	...	...	...	4
2-4	All industry	...	...	...	...	...	...	...	...	...	...	2-4

a/ Establishments with 5 or more persons engaged.

ISIC	INDUSTRY	7. HOURS WORKED BY OPERATIVES a/ (THOUSANDS)					8. QUANTITY OF ELECTRICITY CONSUMED a/ (MILLION KWH)					ISIC
		1981	1982	1983	*1984	1985	1981	1982	1983	*1984	1985	
210	Coal mining	...	...	...	...	...	...	...	...	...	...	210
220	Petroleum and gas	...	...	...	...	...	...	...	...	...	...	220
230	Metal ore mining	...	...	...	...	...	...	...	...	...	...	230
290	Other mining	...	...	...	...	...	...	...	...	...	...	290
2	Mining, quarrying	...	...	...	...	...	...	...	...	...	...	2
311/2	Food products	37522	38122	38296	39680	...	100	90	82	87	...	311/2
313	Beverages	5561	5445	3647	3369	...	23	23	20	23	...	313
314	Tobacco	1045	1057	1179	867	...	4	3	4	3	...	314
321	Textiles	18293	16123	16687	16457	...	60	45	51	59	...	321
3211	Spinning, weaving etc.	14211	12614	13571	13442	...	53	39	46	55	...	3211
322	Wearing apparel	5519	5154	4597	5671	...	2	3	2	3	...	322
323	Leather and products	1127	864	1198	1005	...	2	1	2	1	...	323
324	Footwear	4312	3429	3834	4110	...	4	3	3	3	...	324
331	Wood products	4730	4298	3918	3861	...	2	3	3	4	...	331
332	Furniture, fixtures	1634	2026	1985	1974	...	1	1	1	1	...	332
341	Paper and products	2859	2178	2138	2075	...	29	21	26	15	...	341
3411	Pulp, paper etc.	1544	673	883	687	...	27	18	24	12	...	3411
342	Printing, publishing	4955	5212	5249	5733	...	4	4	4	4	...	342
351	Industrial chemicals	1726	1694	1419	1452	...	10	9	9	8	...	351
3511	Basic excl fertilizers	205	222	221	120	...	6	5	5	4	...	3511
3513	Synthetic resins etc	49	91	91	86	...	-	-	-	-	...	3513
352	Other chemical products	7508	7427	7400	7714	...	16	12	13	14	...	352
3522	Drugs and medicines	2357	2416	2445	2515	...	5	5	5	5	...	3522
353	Petroleum refineries	234	235	215	235	...	8	8	7	7	...	353
354	Petroleum, coal products	112	100	97	92	...	-	-	-	-	...	354
355	Rubber products	2666	5383	5266	3370	...	16	17	16	14	...	355
356	Plastic products n.e.c.	3244	4369	4173	4791	...	20	22	24	27	...	356
361	Pottery, china etc	336	275	273	299	...	1	1	1	1	...	361
362	Glass and products	2257	1413	1319	1481	...	12	13	15	15	...	362
369	Non-metal products n.e.c	7621	7322	6627	5888	...	93	84	69	...	...	369
371	Iron and steel	2089	2260	2079	1773	...	25	16	11	9	...	371
372	Non-ferrous metals	236	129	128	125	...	1	1	1	1	...	372
381	Metal products	6194	5598	5201	4199	...	6	5	5	5	...	381
382	Machinery n.e.c.	1378	947	926	851	...	2	1	1	1	...	382
3825	Office, computing etc.	58	30	30	22	...	-	-	-	-	...	3825
383	Electrical machinery	2478	2151	1614	1539	...	4	4	3	3	...	383
3832	Radio, television etc.	807	628	345	428	...	1	1	1	1	...	3832
384	Transport equipment	2017	1483	1427	1428	...	1	1	1	1	...	384
3841	Shipbuilding, repair	33	-	-	9	...	...	-	-	-	...	3841
3843	Motor vehicles	1118	981	1035	1063	...	-	-	-	-	...	3843
385	Professional goods	203	229	244	220	...	-	-	-	-	...	385
390	Other industries	828	727	680	688	...	2	1	1	1	...	390
3	Manufacturing	128684	125650	121816	120947	...	448	392	375	b/ 310	...	3
410	Electricity, gas, steam	...	...	...	...	...	...	...	...	...	...	410
4101	Electricity	...	...	...	...	...	...	...	...	...	...	4101
420	Water works and supply	...	...	...	...	...	...	...	...	...	...	420
4	Electricity, gas etc	...	...	...	...	...	...	...	...	...	...	4
2-4	All industry	...	...	...	...	...	...	...	...	...	...	2-4

a/ Establishments with 5 or more persons engaged.

b/ Excluding major group 369

ISIC	INDUSTRY	9. OUTPUT IN PRODUCERS' PRICES a/ (MILLION QUETZALES)					10. VALUE ADDED IN PRODUCERS' PRICES a/ (MILLION QUETZALES)					ISIC
		1981	1982	1983	*1984	1985	1981	1982	1983	*1984	1985	
210	Coal mining	...	...	...	...	...	...	...	...	...	...	210
220	Petroleum and gas	...	...	...	...	...	...	...	...	...	...	220
230	Metal ore mining	...	...	...	...	...	...	...	...	...	...	230
290	Other mining	...	...	...	...	...	...	...	...	...	...	290
2	Mining, quarrying .	...	...	...	...	...	...	...	...	...	...	2
311/2	Food products	727	706	666	732	...	256	190	264	248	...	311/2
313	Beverages	143	159	140	140	...	99	106	89	80	...	313
314	Tobacco	25	28	29	28	...	16	16	18	13	...	314
321	Textiles	146	117	123	140	...	52	40	51	63	...	321
3211	Spinning,weaving etc..	121	96	101	115	...	41	30	40	50	...	3211
322	Wearing apparel	32	34	35	39	...	16	17	18	22	...	322
323	Leather and products ...	10	7	9	10	...	2	2	3	3	...	323
324	Footwear	24	18	19	25	...	12	10	10	15	...	324
331	Wood products	19	20	17	29	...	8	12	10	11	...	331
332	Furniture, fixtures	8	9	7	8	...	5	5	4	4	...	332
341	Paper and products	67	53	50	53	...	23	16	18	17	...	341
3411	Pulp,paper etc.	31	19	23	22	...	12	6	9	7	...	3411
342	Printing,publishing	32	32	39	40	...	26	27	33	31	...	342
351	Industrial chemicals ...	78	70	52	87	...	39	32	19	41	...	351
3511	Basic excl fertilizers	4	5	4	3	...	3	2	2	2	...	3511
3513	Synthetic resins etc .	1	1	1	1	...	-	-	-	1	...	3513
352	Other chemical products.	191	183	209	224	...	106	103	119	121	...	352
3522	Drugs and medicines ..	85	82	98	96	...	53	52	62	62	...	3522
353	Petroleum refineries ...	224	183	169	180	...	31	15	12	16	...	353
354	Petroleum,coal products.	1	1	1	1	...	1	1	1	1	...	354
355	Rubber products	58	56	59	55	...	26	24	29	26	...	355
356	Plastic products n.e.c..	51	61	66	82	...	19	25	29	36	...	356
361	Pottery,china etc	5	4	4	4	...	4	3	3	3	...	361
362	Glass and products	52	34	39	33	...	23	17	24	14	...	362
369	Non-metal products n.e.c	97	86	81	80	...	48	46	45	43	...	369
371	Iron and steel	56	53	49	48	...	15	14	15	19	...	371
372	Non-ferrous metals	3	3	2	2	...	1	1	1	1	...	372
381	Metal products	52	38	36	37	...	29	23	21	21	...	381
382	Machinery n.e.c.	13	6	9	9	...	8	5	5	4	...	382
3825	Office,computing etc..	...	-	-	-	...	1	-	-	-	...	3825
383	Electrical machinery ...	44	42	34	31	...	24	21	18	16	...	383
3832	Radio,television etc..	13	15	11	10	...	9	11	8	6	...	3832
384	Transport equipment	19	12	10	11	...	8	5	5	6	...	384
3841	Shipbuilding, repair..	1	-	-	-	...	-	-	-	-	...	3841
3843	Motor vehicles	8	6	5	5	...	3	3	3	3	...	3843
385	Professional goods	1	2	2	2	...	1	1	1	1	...	385
390	Other industries	10	6	7	7	...	5	3	5	4	...	390
3	Manufacturing	2188	2023	1963	2137	...	903	780	870	880	...	3
410	Electricity,gas,steam ..	...	...	...	...	...	...	...	...	...	...	410
4101	Electricity	...	...	...	...	...	...	...	...	...	...	4101
420	Water works and supply .	...	...	...	...	...	...	...	...	...	...	420
4	Electricity,gas etc	...	...	...	...	...	...	...	...	...	...	4
2-4	All industry	...	...	...	...	...	...	...	...	...	...	2-4

a/ Establishments with 5 or more persons engaged.

11. GROSS FIXED CAPITAL FORMATION
TOTAL a/
(THOUSAND QUETZALES)

ISIC	INDUSTRY	1981	1982	1983	*1984	1985	ISIC
210	Coal mining	...	...	...	...	...	210
220	Petroleum and gas	...	...	...	...	...	220
230	Metal ore mining	...	...	...	...	...	230
290	Other mining	...	...	...	...	...	290
2	Mining, quarrying .	...	...	...	...	...	2
311/2	Food products	15040	18700	11449	13536	...	311/2
313	Beverages	5634	6997	1931	301	...	313
314	Tobacco	868	936	594	692	...	314
321	Textiles	7139	6062	3142	2647	...	321
3211	Spinning,weaving etc..	4874	4023	2938	2865	...	3211
322	Wearing apparel	558	297	837	888	...	322
323	Leather and products ...	479	205	220	114	...	323
324	Footwear	225	176	530	482	...	324
331	Wood products	345	493	581	551	...	331
332	Furniture, fixtures	304	273	244	344	...	332
341	Paper and products	504	1013	3623	1505	...	341
3411	Pulp,paper etc.	257	848	1073	464	...	3411
342	Printing,publishing	743	862	798	1300	...	342
351	Industrial chemicals ...	3854	2354	737	811	...	351
3511	Basic excl fertilizers	1624	632	654	247	...	3511
3513	Synthetic resins etc .	-	484	51	14	...	3513
352	Other chemical products.	6116	3572	5169	4015	...	352
3522	Drugs and medicines ..	2838	1587	2911	2090	...	3522
353	Petroleum refineries ...	2098	597	387	672	...	353
354	Petroleum,coal products.	90	3	-	-	...	354
355	Rubber products	988	256	2123	1974	...	355
356	Plastic products n.e.c..	3450	3441	2897	5448	...	356
361	Pottery,china etc	268	149	37	124	...	361
362	Glass and products	875	732	282	436	...	362
369	Non-metal products n.e.c	24161	1677	-	2861	...	369
371	Iron and steel	6284	1172	173	38	...	371
372	Non-ferrous metals	31	30	17	41	...	372
381	Metal products	1859	989	974	600	...	381
382	Machinery n.e.c.	74	22	62	103	...	382
3825	Office,computing etc..	40	2	8	12	...	3825
383	Electrical machinery ...	751	553	260	223	...	383
3832	Radio,television etc..	252	255	278	104	...	3832
384	Transport equipment	841	434	134	200	...	384
3841	Shipbuilding, repair..	-	-	-	2	...	3841
3843	Motor vehicles	128	274	117	189	...	3843
385	Professional goods	119	133	60	67	...	385
390	Other industries	277	222	53	143	...	390
3	Manufacturing	83975	52350	37314	40116	...	3
410	Electricity,gas,steam ..	...	...	...	...	...	410
4101	Electricity	...	...	...	...	...	4101
420	Water works and supply .	...	...	...	...	...	420
4	Electricity,gas etc	...	...	...	...	...	4
2-4	All industry	...	...	...	...	...	2-4

a/ Establishments with 5 or more persons engaged.

HAITI

The information in the tables is based on the reply to the United Nations Questionnaire on General Industrial Statistics from the Institut haitien de statistique et d'informatique, Port-au-Prince. The concepts, definitions and classification by branches of industry are generally in accordance with United Nations standards.

Data on numbers of establishments and employees and wages and salaries of employees are derived from official administrative records of the Office d'assurance accident du travail, maladie et maternite. These data relate to the establishments registered with that office. Estimates of value added are derived from national accounts calculations made by the Institut haitien de statistique et d'informatique and cover all establishments including handicraft and artisan activities. It should be noted that the estimates relate to value added at constant prices of 1975/76 and that data for ISIC 323 cover manufacture of goat skin only.

The reference period is the fiscal year from 1 October to 30 September; in the tables the period referred to is the fiscal year ending in the year indicated.

Related national publications:
Bulletin de statistique, Supplement annuel; Guide economique de la Republique d'Haiti (irregular), both published by the Institut haitien de statistique et d'informatique, Port-au-Prince.

ISIC	INDUSTRY	1. NUMBER OF ESTABLISHMENTS a/b/ (NUMBER)					2. AVERAGE NUMBER OF EMPLOYEES a/b/ (NUMBER)					ISIC
		1981	1982	1983	1984	1985	1981	1982	1983	1984	1985	
210	Coal mining	-	-	-	-	-	-	-	-	-	-	210
220	Petroleum and gas	-	-	-	-	-	-	-	-	-	-	220
230	Metal ore mining	2	3	3	3	2	213	221	219	39	29	230
290	Other mining	-	-	-	-	-	-	-	-	-	-	290
2	Mining, quarrying	2	3	3	3	2	213	221	219	39	29	2
311/2	Food products	286	273	320	326	257	5927	5708	5937	6130	6379	311/2
313	Beverages	195	151	230	223	214	1047	1015	1306	1278	1376	313
314	Tobacco	1	1	2	1	1	300	350	376	350	350	314
321	Textiles	38	35	32	33	31	2062	2092	2193	2468	1842	321
3211	Spinning,weaving etc.	...	...	...	...	...	...	...	...	...	...	3211
322	Wearing apparel	81	77	65	80	77	3685	4456	3392	4223	5003	322
323	Leather and products	18	17	16	15	11	1869	589	660	644	750	323
324	Footwear	8	8	7	10	7	158	1068	1827	1173	1209	324
331	Wood products	3	6	7	9	10	130	116	128	132	142	331
332	Furniture, fixtures	27	34	49	36	39	393	400	414	681	440	332
341	Paper and products	6	4	8	5	6	105	78	208	63	88	341
3411	Pulp,paper etc.	-	-	-	-	-	-	-	-	-	-	3411
342	Printing,publishing	11	12	13	14	21	188	115	310	295	344	342
351	Industrial chemicals	c/ 34	c/ 33	36	c/ 30	c/ 31	c/ 627	c/ 656	624	c/ 572	c/ 473	351
3511	Basic excl fertilizers	...	...	...	...	...	...	...	...	...	...	3511
3513	Synthetic resins etc	...	...	...	...	...	...	...	...	...	...	3513
352	Other chemical products	c/	c/	1	c/	c/	c/	c/	90	c/	c/	352
3522	Drugs and medicines	...	...	...	...	...	...	...	...	...	...	3522
353	Petroleum refineries	-	-	-	-	-	-	-	-	-	-	353
354	Petroleum,coal products	-	-	-	-	-	-	-	-	-	-	354
355	Rubber products	2	2	2	1	1	236	208	208	196	196	355
356	Plastic products n.e.c.	3	3	2	2	2	40	62	42	42	42	356
361	Pottery,china etc	-	-	-	-	-	-	-	-	-	-	361
362	Glass and products	-	-	1	1	3	-	-	19	9	30	362
369	Non-metal products n.e.c	36	35	33	33	31	761	800	929	835	892	369
371	Iron and steel	8	5	6	4	5	223	363	305	305	305	371
372	Non-ferrous metals	-	-	-	-	-	-	-	-	-	-	372
381	Metal products	11	18	12	23	18	399	570	493	1111	691	381
382	Machinery n.e.c. d/	22	33	35	30	33	1680	2927	3243	3461	3426	382
3825	Office,computing etc.	...	...	...	...	...	...	...	...	...	...	3825
383	Electrical machinery d/	...	...	...	...	...	...	...	...	...	...	383
3832	Radio,television etc.	...	...	...	...	...	...	...	...	...	...	3832
384	Transport equipment e/	4	3	2	2	1	14	49	44	22	10	384
3841	Shipbuilding, repair	...	...	...	...	...	...	...	...	...	...	3841
3843	Motor vehicles	...	...	...	...	...	...	...	...	...	...	3843
385	Professional goods	-	-	-	-	-	-	-	-	-	-	385
390	Other industries	107	51	79	31	56	5853	5069	7339	3724	4425	390
3	Manufacturing e/f/	901	801	958	909	855	25697	26691	30087	27714	28413	3
410	Electricity,gas,steam	...	...	...	...	...	...	...	...	...	...	410
4101	Electricity	...	...	...	...	...	...	...	...	...	...	4101
420	Water works and supply	...	...	...	...	...	...	...	...	...	...	420
4	Electricity,gas etc g/	7	11	10	10	8	858	894	894	906	890	4
2-4	All industry e/f/g/	910	815	971	922	865	26768	27806	31200	28659	29332	2-4

a/ Establishments registered with the Office d'assurance accident du travail, maladie et maternite.
b/ Twelve months ending 30 September of the year indicated.
c/ Major group 352 is included in 351.
d/ Major group 383 is included in 382.
e/ Major group 384; incomplete coverage.
f/ Including repair services.
g/ Excluding gas and steam.

ISIC	INDUSTRY	3. WAGES AND SALARIES OF EMPLOYEES a/b/ (THOUSAND GOURDES) 1981	1982	1983	1984	1985	4. VALUE ADDED IN PRODUCERS' PRICES b/c/d/e/ (MILLION GOURDES) 1981	1982	1983	1984	1985	ISIC
210	Coal mining	-	-	-	-	-	-	-	-	-	-	210
220	Petroleum and gas	-	-	-	-	-	-	-	-	-	-	220
230	Metal ore mining	7385	7673	8787	206	149	57.0	70.5	4.8	4.9	5.9	230
290	Other mining	-	-	-	-	-	-	-	-	-	-	290
2	Mining, quarrying	7385	7673	8787	206	149	57.0	70.5	4.8	4.9	5.9	2
311/2	Food products	36042	41247	47981	51698	46879	286.7	247.8	312.8	272.9	283.3	311/2
313	Beverages	7588	8946	10935	10644	11627	20.3	20.6	22.7	20.9	20.7	313
314	Tobacco	3792	4584	5964	6854	7582	37.0	34.2	33.0	32.3	27.9	314
321	Textiles	9282	10198	11968	15665	11352	f/ 124.8	f/ 117.4	f/ 123.0	f/ 120.4	f/ 117.9	321
3211	Spinning, weaving etc.	...	...	...	...	...	...	...	...	...	...	3211
322	Wearing apparel	18946	22222	20257	25474	30056	f/	f/	f/	f/	f/	322
323	Leather and products	9307	5287	6213	4824	6200	f/g/	f/g/	f/g/	f/g/	f/g/	323
324	Footwear	1168	13949	16038	10333	15236	f/	f/	f/	f/	f/	324
331	Wood products	769	755	863	633	735	...	...	...	...	...	331
332	Furniture, fixtures	1440	2088	1774	3123	1884	...	...	...	...	...	332
341	Paper and products	1006	425	1181	539	977	-	-	-	-	-	341
3411	Pulp, paper etc.	-	-	-	-	-	-	-	-	-	-	3411
342	Printing, publishing	1610	618	3153	3011	3360	h/	h/	h/	h/	h/	342
351	Industrial chemicals	i/ 3109	i/ 3422	3401	i/ 3357	i/ 3339	j/ 54.1	j/ 66.2	j/ 63.8	j/ 51.3	j/ 26.5	351
3511	Basic excl fertilizers	...	...	...	...	...	...	...	...	...	...	3511
3513	Synthetic resins etc	...	...	...	...	...	...	...	...	...	...	3513
352	Other chemical products	i/	i/	1447	i/	i/	j/	j/	j/	j/	j/	352
3522	Drugs and medicines	...	...	...	...	...	...	...	...	...	...	3522
353	Petroleum refineries	-	-	-	-	-	-	-	-	-	-	353
354	Petroleum, coal products	-	-	-	-	-	-	-	-	-	-	354
355	Rubber products	1931	2411	2714	2660	2000	j/	j/	j/	j/	j/	355
356	Plastic products n.e.c.	147	222	156	160	146	j/	j/	j/	j/	j/	356
361	Pottery, china etc	-	-	-	-	-	-	-	-	-	-	361
362	Glass and products	-	-	110	58	227	-	-	-	-	-	362
369	Non-metal products n.e.c	9797	11513	12836	13898	15786	36.1	30.9	33.0	35.2	40.8	369
371	Iron and steel	3065	2930	3562	3697	4048	...	...	...	...	...	371
372	Non-ferrous metals	-	-	-	-	-	-	-	-	-	-	372
381	Metal products	3083	4408	3941	6399	6140	[k/	k/	k/	k/	k/]	381
382	Machinery n.e.c.	l/ 12578	l/ 26961	l/ 20071	l/ 22739	l/ 27582	[197.8	211.0	178.2	173.3	182.8]	382
3825	Office, computing etc.	...	...	...	...	...	...	...	...	...	...	3825
383	Electrical machinery	l/	l/	l/	l/	l/	k/	k/	k/	k/	k/	383
3832	Radio, television etc.	...	...	...	...	...	...	...	...	...	...	3832
384	Transport equipment	m/ 183	m/ 558	m/ 173	m/ 168	...	k/	k/	k/	k/	k/	384
3841	Shipbuilding, repair	...	...	...	...	...	...	...	...	...	...	3841
3843	Motor vehicles	...	...	...	...	...	...	...	...	...	...	3843
385	Professional goods	-	-	-	-	-	-	-	-	-	-	385
390	Other industries	29530	26973	32251	16266	22199	h/ 99.0	h/ 113.9	h/ 121.2	h/ 129.7	h/ 112.1	390
3	Manufacturing n/	m/ 154373	m/ 189717	m/ 206989	m/ 202200	o/ 217355	p/q/ 855.8	p/q/ 842.0	p/q/ 887.7	p/q/ 836.0	p/q/ 812.0	3
410	Electricity, gas, steam	...	...	...	...	...	...	...	...	...	...	410
4101	Electricity	...	...	...	...	...	...	...	...	...	...	4101
420	Water works and supply	...	...	...	...	...	...	...	...	...	...	420
4	Electricity, gas etc r/	17079	17605	17460	27739	27903	38.0	40.5	42.0	44.6	43.9	4
2-4	All industry n/r/	m/ 178837	m/ 214995	m/ 233236	m/ 230145	o/ 245407	p/q/ 950.8	p/q/ 953.0	p/q/ 934.5	p/q/ 885.5	p/q/ 861.8	2-4

a/ Establishments registered with the Office d'assurance accident du travail, maladie et maternite.
b/ Twelve months ending 30 September of the year indicated.
c/ Contributions to the gross domestic product.
d/ All establishments including handicrafts.
e/ At prices of 1975/76.
f/ Major groups 322 to 324 are included in 321.
g/ Goat skin industry only.
h/ Major group 342 is included in 390.
i/ Major group 352 is included in 351.
j/ Major groups 352, 355 and 356 are included in 351.
k/ Major groups 383 and 384 are included in 381 and 382 combined.
l/ Major group 383 is included in 382.
m/ Major group 384; incomplete coverage.
n/ Including repair services.
o/ Excluding major group 384.
p/ Excluding industries for major group 323 other than goat skin industry.
q/ Excluding major groups 331, 332 and 371.
r/ Excluding gas and steam.

HONG KONG

The information in the tables is based on the reply to the United Nations Questionnaire on General Industrial Statistics from the Census and Statistics Department, Hong Kong. The concepts, definitions and classification by branches of industry are generally in accordance with United Nations standards.

The data for number of establishments, persons engaged and operatives are derived from the Quarterly Survey of Employment, Vacancies and Payroll conducted in December each year with the last full working day of December as the survey reference data. The figures cover all industrial establishments in operation during the enumeration period. The data for wages and salaries of employees and operatives, hours worked by operatives, output, value added and fixed capital formation are derived from the Annual Survey of Industrial Production which has been conducted since 1978. The figures cover establishments in operation during the enumeration period and, in addition, contain an estimate of the contribution of units which were in operation for all or part of the reference period but which ceased operation during the survey period.

The estimates in the tables are based on the Hong Kong industrial classification system which follows the present version of ISIC. Homeworkers are not included in the employment count. Wages and salaries relate to cash payments only.

Output, prior to 1984, is defined as the sum of the value of (a) sales of goods produced, (b) machinery produced for own use, (c) goods sold in the same condition as purchased, (d) work performed or industrial services rendered to others, and (e) changes in stocks of work in progress and finished products. Value added is obtained by deducting from the value of output the value of materials, supplies, fuels, water and electricity consumed and industrial services (repair, maintenance, contract and commission work) rendered by others. Beginning 1984, output conforms to the definition of gross output and comprises the following: the sum of (a) sales of goods produced, (b) machinery produced for own use, (c) resale margin of goods sold in the same condition as purchased, (d) work performed or industrial services rendered to others, (e) changes in stocks of work in progress and finished products, (f) rents received, and (g) income from other sources. Value added refers to the contribution to the gross domestic product and is obtained by deducting from the value of gross output (a) the stock appreciation of work-in-progress, finished products and goods for resale, (b) consumption of materials supplies and industrial services, (c) stock appreciation of materials/supplies, (d) rents and rates, (e) rentals for hiring machinery and equipment, and (f) other operating expenses. The valuation of output and value added is in producers' prices.

Related national publications:
Hong Kong Annual Report; Hong Kong Monthly Digest of Statistics; Report on the Survey of Industrial Production (annual); Report of Employment, Vacancies and Payroll Statistics (quarterly), all published by the Census and Statistics Department, Hong Kong.

ISIC	INDUSTRY	1. NUMBER OF ESTABLISHMENTS a/ (NUMBER) 1981	1982	1983	1984	1985	2. AVERAGE NUMBER OF PERSONS ENGAGED a/ (THOUSANDS) 1981	1982	1983	1984	1985	ISIC
210	Coal mining	-	-	-	-	-	-	-	-	-	-	210
220	Petroleum and gas	-	-	-	-	-	-	-	-	-	-	220
230	Metal ore mining	-	-	-	-	-	-	-	-	-	-	230
290	Other mining	18	18	11	10	9	0.9	0.9	0.8	0.6	0.6	290
2	Mining, quarrying .	18	18	11	10	9	0.9	0.9	0.8	0.6	0.6	2
311/2	Food products	1127	1124	971	974	924	17.3	18.4	16.7	17.1	18.0	311/2
313	Beverages	23	28	32	30	29	4.2	4.3	4.5	4.4	4.3	313
314	Tobacco	3	3	3	3	3	0.9	0.9	0.9	1.1	1.2	314
321	Textiles	4865	4854	4737	4971	4554	122.6	111.9	111.3	117.4	110.6	321
3211	Spinning,weaving etc..	1702	1611	1717	...	...	57.0	51.6	53.9	...	...	3211
322	Wearing apparel	9805	9107	9004	9396	8559	259.7	257.3	253.3	268.9	264.6	322
323	Leather and products ...	251	220	203	215	238	3.6	3.0	3.1	3.4	3.3	323
324	Footwear	560	542	530	504	456	8.1	7.4	7.3	7.5	7.5	324
331	Wood products	1222	1152	1039	1012	958	7.0	6.3	5.7	5.4	4.8	331
332	Furniture, fixtures	1521	1489	1281	1369	1261	10.7	9.4	8.1	8.3	8.0	332
341	Paper and products	1308	1341	1288	1384	1394	11.7	12.4	12.0	12.9	13.5	341
3411	Pulp,paper etc.	112	116	105	...	...	1.6	1.7	1.7	...	...	3411
342	Printing,publishing	2874	2930	2809	3102	3246	28.5	28.5	27.4	29.6	30.8	342
351	Industrial chemicals ...	210	223	256	b/ 822	b/ 818	2.0	2.0	2.3	b/ 8.6	b/ 8.1	351
3511	Basic excl fertilizers	59	61	53	...	...	1.0	0.9	0.9	...	...	3511
3513	Synthetic resins etc .	148	160	201	220	235	1.0	1.0	1.3	1.6	1.4	3513
352	Other chemical products.	483	488	505	b/	b/	5.9	5.6	5.9	b/	b/	352
3522	Drugs and medicines ..	275	289	301	...	...	2.3	2.3	2.5	...	...	3522
353	Petroleum refineries ...	-	1	-	[5	6]	-	-	-	[0.2	0.2]	353
354	Petroleum,coal products.	6	6	6			0.3	0.3	0.2			354
355	Rubber products	416	348	322	313	268	4.6	3.8	2.8	3.2	2.4	355
356	Plastic products n.e.c..	5431	5021	5041	5336	5031	89.1	80.7	81.1	90.6	82.5	356
361	Pottery,china etc	79	80	85	[376	358]	0.8	0.6	0.7	[4.2	4.2]	361
362	Glass and products	169	161	143			1.9	1.5	1.6			362
369	Non-metal products n.e.c	150	157	147			2.2	2.5	2.6			369
371	Iron and steel	153	143	101	[264	254]	3.1	2.6	1.6	[3.5	3.7]	371
372	Non-ferrous metals	148	143	144			1.6	1.6	1.8			372
381	Metal products	7747	7119	6458	6715	6360	82.4	70.8	66.1	66.7	61.8	381
382	Machinery n.e.c.	2230	2403	3123	3526	3806	16.3	14.1	17.9	20.9	21.9	382
3825	Office,computing etc..	13	9	14	...	...	0.2	0.1	0.2	...	...	3825
383	Electrical machinery ...	2331	2378	2273	2392	1972	124.8	113.1	131.6	135.3	111.2	383
3832	Radio,television etc..	1352	1375	1383	...	...	93.8	86.3	101.5	...	...	3832
384	Transport equipment	452	489	521	546	557	17.1	17.2	14.5	13.3	12.6	384
3841	Shipbuilding, repair..	116	97	88	82	70	9.4	9.0	6.5	5.7	5.2	3841
3843	Motor vehicles	51	44	30	42	52	0.5	0.5	0.2	0.3	0.4	3843
385	Professional goods	1415	1489	1571	1540	1629	46.5	43.4	45.5	46.2	42.1	385
390	Other industries	3017	3008	2984	3243	3234	33.1	27.7	28.9	30.3	30.4	390
3	Manufacturing	47996	46447	45577	48038	45915	906.0	847.3	855.4	899.0	847.7	3
410	Electricity,gas,steam ..	4	4	4	3	3	10.6	11.5	10.7	10.5	11.0	410
4101	Electricity	3	3	3	2	2	9.4	10.1	9.2	8.9	9.2	4101
420	Water works and supply .	1	1	1	1	1	4.1	4.3	4.4	4.6	4.8	420
4	Electricity,gas etc	5	5	5	4	4	14.7	15.8	15.1	15.1	15.8	4
2-4	All industry	48019	46470	45593	48052	45928	921.6	864.0	871.3	914.7	864.1	2-4

a/ In December of the year indicated.

b/ Major group 352 is included in 351.

ISIC	INDUSTRY	3. WAGES AND SALARIES OF EMPLOYEES a/ (MILLION DOLLARS) 1981	1982	1983	1984	1985	4. AVERAGE NUMBER OF OPERATIVES b/ (THOUSANDS) 1981	1982	1983	1984	1985	ISIC
210	Coal mining	-	-	-	-	...	-	-	-	-	-	210
220	Petroleum and gas	-	-	-	-	...	-	-	-	-	-	220
230	Metal ore mining	-	-	-	-	...	-	-	-	-	-	230
290	Other mining	48	55	53	52	...	0.8	0.8	0.7	0.6	0.6	290
2	Mining, quarrying .	48	55	53	52	...	0.8	0.8	0.7	0.6	0.6	2
311/2	Food products	394	489	544	645	...	13.4	14.6	13.5	13.8	14.2	311/2
313	Beverages	174	201	223	246	...	1.7	1.9	1.9	1.6	1.5	313
314	Tobacco	32	37	42	54	...	0.6	0.5	0.5	0.7	0.7	314
321	Textiles	3014	2943	3552	3922	...	107.1	96.7	96.8	101.4	94.9	321
3211	Spinning,weaving etc..	1649	1589	1840	2038	...	49.0	44.0	46.6	...	...	3211
322	Wearing apparel	6381	6745	7741	9095	...	233.7	231.4	228.6	241.2	236.4	322
323	Leather and products ...	119	115	131	177	...	3.2	2.7	2.8	3.0	2.8	323
324	Footwear	224	184	234	308	...	7.4	6.8	6.7	6.8	6.8	324
331	Wood products	172	147	154	163	...	6.3	5.8	5.3	4.9	4.3	331
332	Furniture, fixtures	263	201	214	294	...	9.8	8.7	7.5	7.6	7.2	332
341	Paper and products	290	296	313	403	...	10.1	10.5	10.2	11.1	11.4	341
3411	Pulp,paper etc.	70	57	66	85	...	1.3	1.4	1.4	...	...	3411
342	Printing,publishing	902	936	1081	1268	...	22.6	22.0	20.8	22.4	23.4	342
351	Industrial chemicals ...	57	72	97	81	...	1.4	1.4	1.7	c/ 6.4	c/ 5.8	351
3511	Basic excl fertilizers	28	31	36	39	...	0.6	0.6	0.5	...	...	3511
3513	Synthetic resins etc .	28	40	62	41	...	0.8	0.8	1.1	1.3	1.2	3513
352	Other chemical products.	167	165	197	242	...	4.5	4.3	4.3	c/	c/	352
3522	Drugs and medicines ..	64	61	49	70	...	1.8	1.7	1.9	...	...	3522
353	Petroleum refineries ...	-	-	-	-	...	-	-	-	[0.1	0.2]	353
354	Petroleum,coal products.	-	-	-	-	...	0.2	0.3	0.2			354
355	Rubber products	86	113	76	73	...	4.0	3.3	2.5	2.8	2.1	355
356	Plastic products n.e.c..	1823	1870	2028	2719	...	77.0	70.3	70.6	79.1	70.5	356
361	Pottery,china etc	13	15	23	34	...	0.7	0.6	0.6			361
362	Glass and products	45	42	63	95	...	1.7	1.3	1.4	[3.5	3.4]	362
369	Non-metal products n.e.c	78	85	158	159	...	1.7	2.0	2.1			369
371	Iron and steel	118	105	116	96	...	2.6	2.3	1.4	[3.0	3.1]	371
372	Non-ferrous metals	68	77	89	95	...	1.4	1.4	1.6			372
381	Metal products	1794	1651	1955	2012	...	73.8	62.8	58.7	59.1	54.3	381
382	Machinery n.e.c.	418	431	510	673	...	14.3	12.2	15.7	18.1	19.3	382
3825	Office,computing etc..	109	134	291	477	...	0.2	0.1	0.1	...	...	3825
383	Electrical machinery ...	2808	2970	3634	4412	...	104.8	92.6	108.6	108.1	87.7	383
3832	Radio,television etc..	1751	1916	2247	2597	...	78.3	69.9	82.7	...	...	3832
384	Transport equipment	643	766	752	768	...	14.2	14.0	11.9	10.8	10.3	384
3841	Shipbuilding, repair..	465	570	503	479	...	7.7	7.2	5.1	4.6	4.1	3841
3843	Motor vehicles	14	11	18	33	...	0.4	0.4	0.2	0.3	0.4	3843
385	Professional goods	1269	1209	1273	1341	...	39.8	36.7	38.6	39.2	36.0	385
390	Other industries	793	762	912	1037	...	27.7	23.5	24.6	25.3	24.8	390
3	Manufacturing	22145	22627	26112	30412	...	785.7	730.6	739.1	770.0	721.1	3
410	Electricity,gas,steam ..	449	596	643	700	...	5.2	5.6	5.5	5.3	5.7	410
4101	Electricity	...	...	...	...	...	4.5	4.9	4.7	4.5	4.8	4101
420	Water works and supply .	199	236	244	280	...	2.0	2.1	2.1	2.2	2.2	420
4	Electricity,gas etc	648	832	887	980	...	7.2	7.7	7.6	7.5	7.9	4
2-4	All industry	22841	23514	27052	31444	...	793.7	739.1	747.4	778.1	729.6	2-4

a/ Excluding payments in kind.
b/ In December of the year indicated.
c/ Major group 352 is included in 351.

ISIC	INDUSTRY	5. WAGES AND SALARIES OF OPERATIVES a/ (MILLION DOLLARS) 1981	1982	1983	1984	1985	6. HOURS WORKED BY OPERATIVES (MILLIONS) 1981	1982	1983	1984	1985	ISIC
210	Coal mining	-	-	...	...	...	-	-	-	-	...	210
220	Petroleum and gas	-	-	...	...	...	-	-	-	-	...	220
230	Metal ore mining	-	-	...	...	...	-	-	-	-	...	230
290	Other mining	40	44	...	...	...	3	3	3	2	...	290
2	Mining, quarrying .	40	44	...	...	...	3	3	3	2	...	2
311/2	Food products	276	336	...	...	...	30	31	33	34	...	311/2
313	Beverages	47	54	...	...	...	5	5	6	5	...	313
314	Tobacco	15	18	...	...	...	1	1	1	2	...	314
321	Textiles	2402	2292	...	...	...	262	226	239	235	...	321
3211	Spinning,weaving etc..	1281	1225	...	...	...	134	117	120	119	...	3211
322	Wearing apparel	5427	5748	...	...	...	628	593	604	623	...	322
323	Leather and products ...	99	92	...	...	...	12	10	10	12	...	323
324	Footwear	199	163	...	...	...	20	15	19	21	...	324
331	Wood products	153	127	...	...	...	15	12	11	11	...	331
332	Furniture, fixtures	230	173	...	...	...	23	16	15	19	...	332
341	Paper and products	235	237	...	...	...	25	23	21	25	...	341
3411	Pulp,paper etc.	54	44	...	...	...	5	4	4	4	...	3411
342	Printing,publishing	641	623	...	...	...	65	55	59	60	...	342
351	Industrial chemicals ...	29	44	...	...	...	3	4	5	3	...	351
3511	Basic excl fertilizers	11	13	...	...	...	1	1	1	1	...	3511
3513	Synthetic resins etc .	18	30	...	...	...	2	3	4	2	...	3513
352	Other chemical products.	101	93	...	...	...	12	10	10	11	...	352
3522	Drugs and medicines ..	40	33	...	...	...	5	4	3	4	...	3522
353	Petroleum refineries ...	-	-	...	...	...	-	-	-	-	...	353
354	Petroleum,coal products.	-	-	...	...	...	-	-	-	-	...	354
355	Rubber products	71	98	...	...	...	8	9	6	5	...	355
356	Plastic products n.e.c..	1443	1460	...	...	...	184	167	167	181	...	356
361	Pottery,china etc	12	13	...	...	...	1	1	2	2	...	361
362	Glass and products	37	34	...	...	...	3	3	5	6	...	362
369	Non-metal products n.e.c	49	59	...	...	...	5	4	7	6	...	369
371	Iron and steel	92	81	...	...	...	8	6	6	4	...	371
372	Non-ferrous metals	51	52	...	...	...	5	5	5	4	...	372
381	Metal products	1453	1361	...	...	...	171	144	152	136	...	381
382	Machinery n.e.c.	351	354	...	...	...	37	30	35	38	...	382
3825	Office,computing etc..	6	2	...	...	...	9	9	18	27	...	3825
383	Electrical machinery ...	2118	2170	...	...	...	267	239	264	277	...	383
3832	Radio,television etc..	1291	1391	...	...	...	165	153	162	160	...	3832
384	Transport equipment	511	601	...	...	...	42	41	35	30	...	384
3841	Shipbuilding, repair..	334	409	...	...	...	30	30	26	22	...	3841
3843	Motor vehicles	13	9	...	...	...	1	1	1	2	...	3843
385	Professional goods	1005	920	...	...	...	117	98	93	81	...	385
390	Other industries	631	587	...	...	...	67	55	65	61	...	390
3	Manufacturing	17678	17790	...	...	...	2016	1803	1875	1892	...	3
410	Electricity,gas,steam ..	179	227	...	...	...	15	16	16	15	...	410
4101	Electricity	...	...	...	...	...	...	...	...	...	...	4101
420	Water works and supply .	124	146	...	...	...	10	10	9	10	...	420
4	Electricity,gas etc	303	373	...	...	...	25	26	25	25	...	4
2-4	All industry	18021	18207	...	...	...	2044	1832	1903	1919	...	2-4

a/ Excluding payments in kind.

ISIC	INDUSTRY	7. OUTPUT IN PRODUCERS' PRICES (MILLION DOLLARS)					8. VALUE ADDED IN PRODUCERS' PRICES (MILLION DOLLARS)					ISIC
		1981	1982	1983	a/ 1984	1985	1981	1982	1983	b/ 1984	1985	
210	Coal mining	-	-	-	-	...	-	-	-	-	...	210
220	Petroleum and gas	-	-	-	-	...	-	-	-	-	...	220
230	Metal ore mining	-	-	-	-	...	-	-	-	-	...	230
290	Other mining	409	520	584	500	...	279	348	365	272	...	290
2	Mining, quarrying .	409	520	584	500	...	279	348	365	272	...	2
311/2	Food products	3333	4722	5027	5498	...	937	1251	1446	1317	...	311/2
313	Beverages	1182	1323	1634	1831	...	597	672	886	711	...	313
314	Tobacco	736	812	1091	1328	...	424	483	526	790	...	314
321	Textiles	21189	20086	28502	29076	...	5610	5591	7920	7294	...	321
3211	Spinning,weaving etc..	12468	11677	15745	16052	...	2972	3015	4227	3866	...	3211
322	Wearing apparel	30415	29423	36006	41309	...	10825	11411	13310	13171	...	322
323	Leather and products ...	815	653	924	1118	...	213	204	272	273	...	323
324	Footwear	821	598	924	1129	...	324	280	385	401	...	324
331	Wood products	1292	1042	1583	1157	...	387	304	375	279	...	331
332	Furniture, fixtures	1070	893	1010	1186	...	468	390	415	402	...	332
341	Paper and products	1826	1774	2243	2956	...	587	631	766	700	...	341
3411	Pulp,paper etc.	527	434	626	906	...	127	118	180	170	...	3411
342	Printing,publishing	4588	4353	5493	6786	...	2133	2085	2471	2458	...	342
351	Industrial chemicals ...	1021	934	1136	1026	...	214	223	285	240	...	351
3511	Basic excl fertilizers	262	241	305	313	...	107	98	129	143	...	3511
3513	Synthetic resins etc .	745	685	831	708	...	103	122	156	96	...	3513
352	Other chemical products.	1270	1140	1471	1860	...	480	455	606	626	...	352
3522	Drugs and medicines ..	368	358	261	419	...	165	181	140	161	...	3522
353	Petroleum refineries ...	-	-	-	-	...	-	-	-	-	...	353
354	Petroleum,coal products.	-	-	-	-	...	-	-	-	-	...	354
355	Rubber products	369	441	334	335	...	141	176	137	117	...	355
356	Plastic products n.e.c..	9351	9098	11915	16864	...	3659	3645	4170	4809	...	356
361	Pottery,china etc	34	49	88	129	...	19	25	49	51	...	361
362	Glass and products	223	220	404	542	...	89	80	133	170	...	362
369	Non-metal products n.e.c	1654	1594	2650	2254	...	348	290	469	327	...	369
371	Iron and steel	1005	891	1121	811	...	214	170	211	132	...	371
372	Non-ferrous metals	728	770	1152	1125	...	161	193	234	209	...	372
381	Metal products	8729	7952	10498	10650	...	3381	3134	3979	3450	...	381
382	Machinery n.e.c.	1918	1892	2353	2866	...	842	807	1085	1060	...	382
3825	Office,computing etc..	1175	1267	3135	4745	...	489	536	1160	1162	...	3825
383	Electrical machinery ...	25173	24370	31166	35815	...	7397	7527	9435	8912	...	383
3832	Radio,television etc..	16805	16711	19900	21559	...	4520	4709	5595	5194	...	3832
384	Transport equipment	1806	2264	2468	2167	...	1095	1383	1224	1171	...	384
3841	Shipbuilding, repair..	1291	1692	1434	1239	...	717	944	627	588	...	3841
3843	Motor vehicles	60	38	246	206	...	27	18	48	52	...	3843
385	Professional goods	11571	10533	13814	12574	...	2349	2179	2691	2303	...	385
390	Other industries	4727	4712	5987	7855	...	1612	1539	1993	2004	...	390
3	Manufacturing	136846	132539	170994	190247	...	44506	45128	55473	53377	...	3
410	Electricity,gas,steam ..	6859	7454	9087	9759	...	2579	3530	5105	5466	...	410
4101	Electricity	...	...	...	...	...	...	...	...	...	...	4101
420	Water works and supply .	502	600	766	611	...	c/ -52	c/ 137	240	276	...	420
4	Electricity,gas etc	7361	8054	9853	10370	...	2527	3667	5345	5742	...	4
2-4	All industry	144616	141113	181431	201117	...	47312	49143	61183	59391	...	2-4

a/ Gross output (i.e. including non-industrial services). b/ Contribution to the gross domestic product.
c/ Value added is less than corresponding wages and salaries due to a drastic increase in input costs of desalting plants.

9. GROSS FIXED CAPITAL FORMATION
TOTAL
(MILLION DOLLARS)

ISIC	INDUSTRY	1981	1982	1983	1984	1985	ISIC
210	Coal mining	-	-	-	-	...	210
220	Petroleum and gas	-	-	-	-	...	220
230	Metal ore mining	-	-	-	-	...	230
290	Other mining	45	-	16	11	...	290
2	Mining, quarrying .	45	-	16	11	...	2
311/2	Food products	91	135	104	158	...	311/2
313	Beverages	98	192	325	43	...	313
314	Tobacco	26	7	5	92	...	314
321	Textiles	557	312	728	631	...	321
3211	Spinning,weaving etc..	255	148	478	341	...	3211
322	Wearing apparel	987	589	611	625	...	322
323	Leather and products ...	7	-	19	30	...	323
324	Footwear	26	17	22	21	...	324
331	Wood products	18	12	5	9	...	331
332	Furniture, fixtures	36	12	29	22	...	332
341	Paper and products	85	53	8	69	...	341
3411	Pulp,paper etc.	57	19	8	16	...	3411
342	Printing,publishing	361	314	225	328	...	342
351	Industrial chemicals ...	65	85	33	96	...	351
3511	Basic excl fertilizers	59	44	8	75	...	3511
3513	Synthetic resins etc .	6	40	25	21	...	3513
352	Other chemical products.	54	28	17	42	...	352
3522	Drugs and medicines ..	5	12	9	19	...	3522
353	Petroleum refineries ...	-	-	-	-	...	353
354	Petroleum,coal products.	-	-	-	-	...	354
355	Rubber products	7	14	7	14	...	355
356	Plastic products n.e.c..	350	410	492	747	...	356
361	Pottery,china etc	-	3	3	1	...	361
362	Glass and products	7	16	15	24	...	362
369	Non-metal products n.e.c	247	207	321	-249	...	369
371	Iron and steel	15	23	11	10	...	371
372	Non-ferrous metals	7	32	62	78	...	372
381	Metal products	399	361	283	332	...	381
382	Machinery n.e.c.	85	69	94	158	...	382
3825	Office,computing etc..	24	14	85	149	...	3825
383	Electrical machinery ...	729	771	994	1561	...	383
3832	Radio,television etc..	392	553	620	929	...	3832
384	Transport equipment	179	199	39	19	...	384
3841	Shipbuilding, repair..	143	172	35	8	...	3841
3843	Motor vehicles	2	1	1	7	...	3843
385	Professional goods	214	196	197	240	...	385
390	Other industries	107	78	113	153	...	390
3	Manufacturing	4757	4135	4762	5254	...	3
410	Electricity,gas,steam ..	5257	3885	4391	4526	...	410
4101	Electricity	...	...	...	...	...	4101
420	Water works and supply .	51	50	55	669	...	420
4	Electricity,gas etc	5308	3935	4446	5195	...	4
2-4	All industry	10110	8070	9224	10460	...	2-4

HUNGARY

The information on industrial activity is based on the reply to the United Nations Questionnaire on General Industrial Statistics from the Hungarian Central Statistical Office, Budapest. The concepts, definitions and classification by branches of industry have been adjusted as far as possible to comply with United Nations standards.

The estimates are derived from the annual industrial inquiry carried out by the Hungarian Central Statistical Office. The figures given in the tables relate to the socialist sector, covering all State-owned industrial enterprises and industrial co-operatives. The socialist sector of industry accounted for 98.6 per cent and 96.6 per cent of the output and employment, respectively, of the industrial sector as a whole in 1985.

The estimates are based on the national classification scheme which is generally comparable to the present version of ISIC. It should be noted that adjustments have not been made for the following: publishing, water works and supply are not covered; manufacture of made-up textile goods except wearing apparel (ISIC 321) is included in ISIC 322; and repair services for the general public are included in related manufacturing industries.

The estimates of total employment refer to the average number of workers and other employees, including persons engaged in the social and cultural institutions of the enterprise. Gainfully occupied pensioners working without stopping their pension are included. Working proprietors and unpaid family workers are not found in the socialist sector.

Wages and salaries relate to total annual wages, including payments in kind, but excluding non-wage payments. These non-wage payments cover such items as (a) employee's share in profits, sick pay and rewards and (b) amounts paid by the employer as social insurance contributions, welfare fund contributions, invention and innovation fees, certain subsidies and family allowances. Payments of employee's share in profits are also included in wages and salaries.

The estimates of operatives relate to all manual workers, whether or not directly engaged in production activities of the enterprises. Apprentices are not included in this category.

Output is defined as the value of finished production plus the value of industrial services provided and own-account construction, adjusted for changes in work in progress between the beginning and the end of the year. The value of goods shipped in the same condition as received is not included, nor are receipts from such activities as canteen services and transport. The valuation is net of turnover taxes and includes price supplements granted by the State on individual products. Value added is the value of output less material costs.

The estimates of gross fixed capital formation relate to actual expenditure incurred during the year on new fixed assets, regardless of whether put into operation or not. The cost of the acquisition of used fixed assets and the corresponding value of sales is not covered.

The indexes of industrial production are compiled by the Hungarian Central Statistical Office and provided in response to the United Nations Questionnaire on Indexes of Industrial Production. In principle, the indexes cover all State-owned enterprises and co-operatives.

Related national publication:
Statisztikai Evkonyv (Statistical Yearbook), published by the Hungarian Central Statistical Office, Budapest.

ISIC	INDUSTRY	1. NUMBER OF ENTERPRISES (NUMBER)					2. AVERAGE NUMBER OF PERSONS ENGAGED a/ (THOUSANDS)					ISIC
		1981	1982	1983	1984	1985	1981	1982	1983	1984	1985	
210	Coal mining	12	12	13	12	14	80	80	80	78	81	210
220	Petroleum and gas	6	6	7	7	7	15	14	14	15	15	220
230	Metal ore mining	5	5	5	5	6	16	15	16	16	16	230
290	Other mining	5	4	4	4	5	9	9	8	8	8	290
2	Mining, quarrying .	28	27	29	28	32	120	118	118	117	120	2
311/2	Food products	164	163	162	166	171	164	163	163	167	170	311/2
313	Beverages	22	23	22	21	22	26	26	26	27	26	313
314	Tobacco	7	7	7	6	6	6	5	5	5	5	314
321	Textiles	53	54	54	55	67	114	111	107	105	104	321
3211	Spinning,weaving etc..	30	29	29	30	30	84	82	78	77	75	3211
322	Wearing apparel	128	131	130	131	146	77	73	71	68	67	322
323	Leather and products ...	26	20	17	16	30	13	13	12	12	12	323
324	Footwear	58	59	60	60	62	36	36	36	36	36	324
331	Wood products	31	25	27	27	44	17	12	12	12	12	331
332	Furniture, fixtures	75	67	63	58	83	30	29	28	27	29	332
341	Paper and products	7	7	6	6	9	15	14	14	14	15	341
3411	Pulp,paper etc.	...	...	...	...	...	...	...	...	...	...	3411
342	Printing,publishing	35	35	34	33	48	19	19	19	19	19	342
351	Industrial chemicals ...	31	31	32	32	38	41	41	40	41	42	351
3511	Basic excl fertilizers	...	...	...	...	...	...	...	...	...	...	3511
3513	Synthetic resins etc .	...	...	...	...	...	...	...	...	...	...	3513
352	Other chemical products.	20	19	18	19	21	26	25	25	25	26	352
3522	Drugs and medicines ..	16	17	16	17	17	23	22	23	23	24	3522
353	Petroleum refineries ...	4	4	4	4	4	6	6	6	6	6	353
354	Petroleum,coal products.	-	-	-	-	-	-	-	-	-	-	354
355	Rubber products	2	2	2	2	2	11	11	11	11	11	355
356	Plastic products n.e.c..	23	23	23	23	46	13	13	13	13	13	356
361	Pottery,china etc	6	12	11	11	13	15	14	11	12	12	361
362	Glass and products	7	6	6	6	7	17	17	17	17	17	362
369	Non-metal products n.e.c	28	26	26	27	30	39	38	37	37	36	369
371	Iron and steel	17	16	13	15	24	74	68	64	63	64	371
372	Non-ferrous metals	13	13	13	14	18	18	19	18	19	20	372
381	Metal products	64	60	61	60	96	57	52	52	52	52	381
382	Machinery n.e.c.	116	121	121	126	218	128	131	127	123	125	382
3825	Office,computing etc..	...	...	...	...	...	...	...	...	...	...	3825
383	Electrical machinery ...	59	62	64	65	180	158	156	151	150	154	383
3832	Radio,television etc..	24	23	24	25	115	98	97	93	93	96	3832
384	Transport equipment	41	42	36	39	125	101	99	87	88	95	384
3841	Shipbuilding, repair..	1	1	1	1	2	8	8	8	8	9	3841
3843	Motor vehicles	7	7	6	6	8	43	42	41	41	41	3843
385	Professional goods	48	45	42	40	77	57	57	54	52	53	385
390	Other industries	219	211	206	202	212	74	71	63	60	57	390
3	Manufacturing ..... b/	1304	1284	1260	1264	1799	1352	1319	1269	1261	1278	3
410	Electricity,gas,steam ..	27	27	28	28	28	47	47	49	51	51	410
4101	Electricity	21	21	22	22	22	35	35	38	39	39	4101
420	Water works and supply .	.	.	.	.	.	.	.	.	.	.	420
4	Electricity,gas etc	27	27	28	28	28	47	47	49	51	51	4
2-4	All industry b/	1359	1338	1317	1320	1859	1519	1484	1436	1429	1449	2-4

Note. For certain deviations in classification, see country note.

a/ Working proprietors and unpaid family workers are not found in socialist industry.
b/ Including repair services for the general public.

ISIC	INDUSTRY	3. AVERAGE NUMBER OF EMPLOYEES (THOUSANDS)					4. WAGES AND SALARIES OF EMPLOYEES a/ (MILLION FORINTS)					ISIC
		1981	1982	1983	1984	1985	1981	1982	1983	1984	1985	
210	Coal mining	80	80	80	78	81	6588	7009	7216	7725	8772	210
220	Petroleum and gas	15	14	14	15	15	1005	1059	1143	1351	1674	220
230	Metal ore mining	16	15	16	16	16	1236	1289	1376	1535	1719	230
290	Other mining	9	9	8	8	8	519	506	520	554	518	290
2	Mining, quarrying .	120	118	118	117	120	9348	9863	10255	11165	12683	2
311/2	Food products	164	163	163	167	170	8375	8923	9315	10825	11931	311/2
313	Beverages	26	26	26	27	26	1245	1361	1413	1589	1758	313
314	Tobacco	6	5	5	5	5	260	276	286	317	352	314
321	Textiles	114	111	107	105	104	5481	5585	5578	6173	6588	321
3211	Spinning,weaving etc..	84	82	78	77	75	4129	4220	4191	4623	4928	3211
322	Wearing apparel	77	73	71	68	67	3202	3199	3196	3563	3708	322
323	Leather and products ...	13	13	12	12	12	636	659	646	658	777	323
324	Footwear	36	36	36	36	36	1624	1688	1777	2010	2177	324
331	Wood products	17	12	12	12	12	821	603	612	675	767	331
332	Furniture, fixtures	30	29	28	27	29	1380	1372	1388	1513	1756	332
341	Paper and products	15	14	14	14	15	824	853	944	1143	1239	341
3411	Pulp,paper etc.	...	...	...	...	...	...	...	...	...	...	3411
342	Printing,publishing	19	19	19	19	19	994	1061	1114	1244	1414	342
351	Industrial chemicals ...	41	41	40	41	42	2358	2472	2587	3053	3405	351
3511	Basic excl fertilizers	...	...	...	...	...	...	...	...	...	...	3511
3513	Synthetic resins etc .	...	...	...	...	...	...	...	...	...	...	3513
352	Other chemical products.	26	25	25	25	26	1488	1504	1598	1930	2221	352
3522	Drugs and medicines ..	23	22	23	23	24	1304	1395	1490	1806	2077	3522
353	Petroleum refineries ...	6	6	6	6	6	403	426	458	561	695	353
354	Petroleum,coal products.	-	-	-	-	-	-	-	-	-	-	354
355	Rubber products	11	11	11	11	11	606	641	714	827	911	355
356	Plastic products n.e.c..	13	13	13	13	13	644	690	715	814	968	356
361	Pottery,china etc	15	14	11	12	12	735	753	615	716	773	361
362	Glass and products	17	17	17	17	17	859	903	960	1131	1217	362
369	Non-metal products n.e.c	39	38	37	37	36	2035	2093	2149	2418	2486	369
371	Iron and steel	74	68	64	63	64	4436	4321	4204	4776	5248	371
372	Non-ferrous metals	18	19	18	19	20	1201	1259	1277	1502	1766	372
381	Metal products	57	52	52	52	52	2790	2739	2872	3153	3530	381
382	Machinery n.e.c.	128	131	127	123	125	6675	7310	7397	8079	9012	382
3825	Office,computing etc..	...	...	...	...	...	...	...	...	...	...	3825
383	Electrical machinery ...	158	156	151	150	154	7933	8253	8389	9556	10728	383
3832	Radio,television etc..	98	97	93	93	96	4906	5109	5197	5991	6829	3832
384	Transport equipment	101	99	87	88	95	5443	5655	5378	6204	7226	384
3841	Shipbuilding, repair..	8	8	8	8	9	499	526	529	568	683	3841
3843	Motor vehicles	43	42	41	41	41	2339	2431	2546	2936	3274	3843
385	Professional goods	57	57	54	52	53	2960	3108	3143	3413	3891	385
390	Other industries	74	71	63	60	57	3215	3264	3056	3393	3344	390
3	Manufacturing ..... b/	1352	1319	1269	1261	1278	68623	70971	71781	81236	89888	3
410	Electricity,gas,steam ..	47	47	49	51	51	2632	2792	3123	3619	4213	410
4101	Electricity	35	35	38	39	39	1989	2123	2415	2812	3238	4101
420	Water works and supply .	.	.	.	.	.	.	.	.	.	.	420
4	Electricity,gas etc	47	47	49	51	51	2632	2792	3123	3619	4213	4
2-4	All industry b/	1519	1484	1436	1429	1449	80603	83626	85159	96020	106784	2-4

Note. For certain deviations in classification, see country note.

a/ For concept, see country note.

b/ Including repair services for the general public.

ISIC	INDUSTRY	5. AVERAGE NUMBER OF OPERATIVES (THOUSANDS)					6. WAGES AND SALARIES OF OPERATIVES a/ (MILLION FORINTS)					ISIC
		1981	1982	1983	1984	1985	1981	1982	1983	1984	1985	
210	Coal mining	67	67	67	65	67	5321	5671	5798	6195	6972	210
220	Petroleum and gas	11	11	10	11	11	726	766	822	975	1178	220
230	Metal ore mining	13	13	13	13	13	986	1026	1096	1185	1301	230
290	Other mining	8	7	7	7	7	410	398	406	467	453	290
2	Mining, quarrying .	99	98	97	96	98	7443	7861	8122	8822	9904	2
311/2	Food products	131	130	130	134	136	6311	6715	7002	8123	8881	311/2
313	Beverages	20	20	20	20	20	899	977	1004	1128	1232	313
314	Tobacco	4	4	4	4	4	195	205	213	240	265	314
321	Textiles	96	92	89	87	86	4340	4380	4357	4812	5076	321
3211	Spinning,weaving etc..	70	67	65	63	62	3249	3292	3262	3593	3793	3211
322	Wearing apparel	66	64	60	58	57	2568	2589	2520	2812	2905	322
323	Leather and products ...	11	9	9	10	10	487	458	489	485	577	323
324	Footwear	31	31	31	31	31	1322	1365	1427	1608	1732	324
331	Wood products	14	10	9	9	10	623	455	458	504	573	331
332	Furniture, fixtures	25	24	23	23	23	1058	1037	1041	1135	1308	332
341	Paper and products	12	12	12	12	12	660	683	749	899	959	341
3411	Pulp,paper etc.	...	...	...	...	...	...	...	...	...	...	3411
342	Printing,publishing	16	16	16	15	16	781	835	873	972	1086	342
351	Industrial chemicals ...	31	31	31	31	31	1699	1768	1837	2157	2391	351
3511	Basic excl fertilizers	...	...	...	...	...	...	...	...	...	...	3511
3513	Synthetic resins etc .	...	...	...	...	...	...	...	...	...	...	3513
352	Other chemical products.	19	18	18	18	19	1015	1024	1072	1289	1474	352
3522	Drugs and medicines ..	17	17	17	17	18	891	947	997	1204	1376	3522
353	Petroleum refineries ...	5	5	5	5	5	288	304	328	402	484	353
354	Petroleum,coal products.	-	-	-	-	-	-	-	-	-	-	354
355	Rubber products	8	8	8	8	8	428	441	486	564	618	355
356	Plastic products n.e.c..	10	10	10	10	10	455	490	503	570	653	356
361	Pottery,china etc	12	12	9	10	10	579	590	489	564	604	361
362	Glass and products	14	14	14	14	14	694	730	767	904	963	362
369	Non-metal products n.e.c	31	30	30	30	29	1558	1593	1624	1811	1881	369
371	Iron and steel	61	56	53	53	54	3485	3403	3368	3835	4205	371
372	Non-ferrous metals	14	14	14	13	15	834	877	883	1033	1204	372
381	Metal products	45	41	41	40	41	2063	2024	2107	2301	2552	381
382	Machinery n.e.c.	94	96	92	90	90	4632	5061	5056	5484	6056	382
3825	Office,computing etc..	...	...	...	...	...	...	...	...	...	...	3825
383	Electrical machinery ...	117	115	111	110	112	5441	5661	5730	6474	7156	383
3832	Radio,television etc..	72	71	69	68	70	3355	3505	3538	4039	4509	3832
384	Transport equipment	75	74	65	65	71	3904	4038	3798	4348	5054	384
3841	Shipbuilding, repair..	6	6	5	5	6	339	355	354	374	450	3841
3843	Motor vehicles	33	32	31	31	31	1735	1791	1872	2123	2339	3843
385	Professional goods	41	40	39	37	38	1954	2037	2051	2204	2500	385
390	Other industries	61	58	51	50	46	2435	2445	2271	2498	2421	390
3	Manufacturing ..... b/	1064	1034	994	987	998	50708	52185	52503	59156	64810	3
410	Electricity,gas,steam ..	34	34	36	37	37	1790	1897	2121	2449	2788	410
4101	Electricity	26	25	27	28	28	1348	1442	1642	1904	2142	4101
420	Water works and supply .	.	.	.	.	.	.	.	.	.	.	420
4	Electricity,gas etc	34	34	36	37	37	1790	1897	2121	2449	2788	4
2-4	All industry b/	1197	1166	1127	1120	1133	59941	61943	62746	70427	77502	2-4

Note. For certain deviations in classification, see country note.

a/ For concept, see country note.

b/ Including repair services for the general public.

ISIC	INDUSTRY	7. HOURS WORKED BY OPERATIVES (MILLIONS)					8. QUANTITY OF ELECTRICITY CONSUMED (MILLION KWH)					ISIC
		1981	1982	1983	1984	1985	1981	1982	1983	1984	1985	
210	Coal mining	127	123	120	115	117	855	874	894	919	1008	210
220	Petroleum and gas	21	20	20	19	19	220	235	240	250	261	220
230	Metal ore mining	23	22	22	22	22	378	372	360	369	363	230
290	Other mining	15	13	12	12	11	111	108	113	102	100	290
2	Mining, quarrying .	186	178	174	168	169	1564	1589	1607	1640	1732	2
311/2	Food products	248	237	233	231	230	987	1051	1091	1118	1133	311/2
313	Beverages	38	37	36	35	34	174	191	200	204	211	313
314	Tobacco	8	8	8	7	7	20	22	22	23	23	314
321	Textiles	173	160	152	144	140	759	738	741	741	742	321
3211	Spinning,weaving etc..	125	117	111	105	102	676	659	662	660	660	3211
322	Wearing apparel	120	109	103	96	92	73	70	71	73	71	322
323	Leather and products ...	19	18	17	16	16	55	53	53	52	54	323
324	Footwear	58	53	53	52	51	53	53	54	55	56	324
331	Wood products	25	17	16	15	16	117	82	86	90	84	331
332	Furniture, fixtures	47	42	40	38	39	74	72	75	68	80	332
341	Paper and products	22	21	21	21	20	456	462	463	510	506	341
3411	Pulp,paper etc.	...	...	...	...	...	...	...	...	...	...	3411
342	Printing,publishing	28	26	26	25	25	64	64	66	68	68	342
351	Industrial chemicals ...	57	56	54	53	53	2616	2600	2724	2774	2830	351
3511	Basic excl fertilizers	...	...	...	...	...	...	...	...	...	...	3511
3513	Synthetic resins etc .	...	...	...	...	...	...	...	...	...	...	3513
352	Other chemical products.	35	32	31	31	32	187	190	206	226	239	352
3522	Drugs and medicines ..	30	29	29	29	29	173	182	198	216	229	3522
353	Petroleum refineries ...	9	8	8	8	8	344	337	359	407	442	353
354	Petroleum,coal products.	-	-	-	-	-	-	-	-	-	-	354
355	Rubber products	15	14	14	14	14	107	106	108	111	115	355
356	Plastic products n.e.c..	17	17	16	15	16	106	115	122	128	131	356
361	Pottery,china etc	23	21	17	17	16	77	78	69	69	70	361
362	Glass and products	26	25	25	25	24	196	193	215	232	239	362
369	Non-metal products n.e.c	60	56	54	51	49	804	784	783	790	750	369
371	Iron and steel	112	100	96	92	92	1971	2007	2032	2112	2153	371
372	Non-ferrous metals	26	25	24	23	25	1885	1879	1873	1894	1910	372
381	Metal products	83	72	71	66	67	259	247	265	262	266	381
382	Machinery n.e.c.	178	175	166	153	152	403	424	424	426	439	382
3825	Office,computing etc..	...	...	...	...	...	...	...	...	...	...	3825
383	Electrical machinery ...	223	207	197	188	189	567	553	557	577	595	383
3832	Radio,television etc..	139	129	122	117	118	310	300	302	314	327	3832
384	Transport equipment	143	133	115	111	120	513	505	505	532	525	384
3841	Shipbuilding, repair..	11	10	9	9	10	27	28	27	29	32	3841
3843	Motor vehicles	62	58	57	54	54	320	307	316	325	327	3843
385	Professional goods	77	72	68	61	62	107	110	111	108	115	385
390	Other industries	105	95	85	79	71	142	137	81	83	79	390
3	Manufacturing ..... a/	1975	1836	1746	1667	1660	13116	13123	13356	13733	13926	3
410	Electricity,gas,steam ..	64	62	64	62	62	133	145	212	245	268	410
4101	Electricity	49	47	49	48	47	108	119	188	222	246	4101
420	Water works and supply .	.	.	.	.	.	.	.	.	.	.	420
4	Electricity,gas etc	64	62	64	62	62	133	145	212	245	268	4
2-4	All industry a/	2225	2076	1984	1897	1891	14813	14857	15175	15618	15926	2-4

Note. For certain deviations in classification, see country note.

a/ Including repair services for the general public.

ISIC	INDUSTRY	9. OUTPUT a/b/ (BILLION FORINTS) 1981	1982	1983	1984	1985	10. VALUE ADDED a/ (BILLION FORINTS) 1981	1982	1983	1984	1985	ISIC
210	Coal mining	22.7	26.0	27.9	29.1	34.0	12.17	13.85	14.34	14.15	15.39	210
220	Petroleum and gas	38.8	47.0	49.1	50.0	53.1	33.23	40.59	41.71	42.39	43.74	220
230	Metal ore mining	5.2	4.9	5.1	5.4	5.4	2.70	2.17	2.23	2.21	2.06	230
290	Other mining	3.5	3.5	3.6	3.7	3.9	1.53	1.63	1.53	1.73	1.88	290
2	Mining, quarrying .	70.2	81.4	85.7	88.2	96.4	49.63	58.24	59.81	60.48	63.07	2
311/2	Food products	161.8	167.9	177.5	190.9	186.6	20.23	19.58	18.64	17.82	14.10	311/2
313	Beverages	17.6	21.1	21.6	21.7	23.6	4.30	4.58	4.82	5.04	5.35	313
314	Tobacco	5.6	5.9	6.0	6.6	7.0	1.09	1.08	1.15	1.34	1.42	314
321	Textiles	46.5	45.8	47.6	51.9	55.1	13.36	13.44	13.70	15.01	16.31	321
3211	Spinning,weaving etc..	34.6	34.2	35.2	38.3	40.3	9.73	9.87	9.91	11.03	11.73	3211
322	Wearing apparel	19.2	19.0	19.0	20.8	22.5	6.60	6.50	6.62	7.30	7.91	322
323	Leather and products ...	7.5	7.4	7.7	8.8	8.2	1.84	1.80	1.73	1.75	1.93	323
324	Footwear	12.5	12.7	13.9	15.2	17.3	3.29	3.53	3.98	3.94	4.25	324
331	Wood products	8.6	6.5	6.6	6.9	7.4	2.54	1.68	1.69	1.82	2.13	331
332	Furniture, fixtures	12.4	11.9	12.1	12.9	14.3	3.53	3.53	3.54	3.80	4.60	332
341	Paper and products	13.1	14.1	15.1	16.8	17.7	3.30	3.85	4.45	4.71	5.30	341
3411	Pulp,paper etc.	...	...	...	...	...	...	...	...	...	...	3411
342	Printing,publishing	9.4	9.9	10.6	11.5	12.8	3.15	3.48	3.79	4.12	4.69	342
351	Industrial chemicals ...	59.0	62.6	67.4	74.2	75.9	13.21	12.34	12.56	15.53	16.03	351
3511	Basic excl fertilizers	...	...	...	...	...	...	...	...	...	...	3511
3513	Synthetic resins etc .	...	...	...	...	...	...	...	...	...	...	3513
352	Other chemical products.	29.1	27.5	31.1	35.3	39.5	10.11	10.71	11.92	13.78	15.17	352
3522	Drugs and medicines ..	23.2	25.0	28.3	32.1	36.0	8.57	10.00	11.12	12.96	14.19	3522
353	Petroleum refineries ...	79.7	87.9	94.0	98.0	100.7	4.45	4.64	4.49	8.06	9.75	353
354	Petroleum,coal products.	-	-	-	-	-	-	-	-	-	-	354
355	Rubber products	8.3	8.4	9.1	9.9	10.8	2.19	2.55	2.77	3.08	3.56	355
356	Plastic products n.e.c..	8.1	9.5	10.1	11.3	12.3	2.41	2.97	3.12	3.57	3.99	356
361	Pottery,china etc	4.0	4.2	3.9	4.1	4.4	2.09	2.23	1.99	2.16	2.30	361
362	Glass and products	7.2	7.4	7.7	8.5	9.1	2.67	2.80	2.98	3.31	3.57	362
369	Non-metal products n.e.c	20.1	21.2	23.2	24.9	24.0	6.83	7.11	7.66	8.85	8.05	369
371	Iron and steel	61.5	64.2	65.2	67.1	71.8	9.27	9.37	8.81	10.86	10.01	371
372	Non-ferrous metals	28.2	28.0	26.9	31.3	33.3	5.51	4.61	2.40	3.22	2.69	372
381	Metal products	24.6	23.0	25.5	27.3	30.2	7.26	7.46	8.35	9.21	10.80	381
382	Machinery n.e.c.	51.1	59.1	62.9	66.0	71.3	18.51	21.87	23.40	25.46	28.53	382
3825	Office,computing etc..	...	...	...	...	...	...	...	...	...	...	3825
383	Electrical machinery ...	68.4	72.5	76.9	85.3	95.5	24.69	27.26	30.03	32.61	38.01	383
3832	Radio,television etc..	35.2	37.2	41.2	46.8	54.4	15.35	16.57	19.23	21.52	25.79	3832
384	Transport equipment	63.0	69.3	71.9	77.4	86.8	17.69	20.07	20.22	22.36	25.42	384
3841	Shipbuilding, repair..	4.4	4.9	5.0	4.4	5.1	1.49	1.76	1.52	0.93	1.36	3841
3843	Motor vehicles	41.0	44.9	49.0	53.2	59.2	9.90	10.87	12.52	13.84	15.08	3843
385	Professional goods	20.8	22.2	23.7	24.7	28.8	10.06	11.09	11.63	12.38	14.37	385
390	Other industries	21.7	21.1	19.0	20.4	20.2	8.60	8.33	7.51	7.98	8.22	390
3	Manufacturing ..... c/	869.0	910.3	956.2	1029.7	1087.1	208.78	218.46	223.95	249.07	268.46	3
410	Electricity,gas,steam ..	63.5	75.2	84.3	88.9	101.3	17.18	18.83	22.37	21.72	26.88	410
4101	Electricity	46.2	53.2	60.3	63.5	72.6	14.57	15.78	17.96	17.40	21.61	4101
420	Water works and supply .	.	.	.	.	.	.	.	.	.	.	420
4	Electricity,gas etc	63.5	75.2	84.3	88.9	101.3	17.18	18.83	22.37	21.72	26.88	4
2-4	All industry c/	1002.7	1066.9	1126.2	1206.8	1284.8	275.59	295.53	306.13	331.27	358.41	2-4

Note. For certain deviations in classification, see country note.

a/ Net of turnover taxes. b/ For concept, see country note.
c/ Including repair services for the general public.

ISIC	INDUSTRY	11. GROSS FIXED CAPITAL FORMATION TOTAL a/ (MILLION FORINTS)					12. GROSS FIXED CAPITAL FORMATION MACHINERY AND EQUIPMENT a/ (MILLION FORINTS)					ISIC
		1981	1982	1983	1984	1985	1981	1982	1983	1984	1985	
210	Coal mining	4317	4250	5548	7112	9117	2359	2181	2593	3341	5138	210
220	Petroleum and gas	3573	4139	4946	5463	6411	1317	1721	1781	2251	2056	220
230	Metal ore mining	1566	1503	1501	1492	1412	642	564	544	560	524	230
290	Other mining	277	94	99	32	119	198	55	66	25	101	290
2	Mining, quarrying .	9733	9986	12094	14099	17059	4516	4521	4984	6177	7819	2
311/2	Food products	6580	6457	5876	6556	7116	3582	3525	3462	3976	3775	311/2
313	Beverages	1518	1158	1156	1251	1420	821	763	604	772	781	313
314	Tobacco	95	126	98	145	120	61	76	60	77	89	314
321	Textiles	1497	1811	1585	1360	1525	1192	1371	1114	1035	1169	321
3211	Spinning,weaving etc..	1088	1334	1190	1036	1060	850	997	799	785	806	3211
322	Wearing apparel	528	555	405	401	271	262	270	177	238	135	322
323	Leather and products ...	283	296	208	185	84	131	177	106	105	47	323
324	Footwear	250	291	334	457	268	149	176	209	242	108	324
331	Wood products	198	175	443	447	182	76	71	303	249	107	331
332	Furniture, fixtures	445	479	474	370	316	219	251	242	206	199	332
341	Paper and products	912	2408	1354	1303	1501	402	1827	646	546	1175	341
3411	Pulp,paper etc.	...	...	...	...	...	...	...	...	...	...	3411
342	Printing,publishing	739	743	466	547	386	448	480	265	488	315	342
351	Industrial chemicals ...	3609	4080	3893	3431	5989	2311	2669	2621	2085	4153	351
3511	Basic excl fertilizers	...	...	...	...	...	...	...	...	...	...	3511
3513	Synthetic resins etc .	...	...	...	...	...	...	...	...	...	...	3513
352	Other chemical products.	1842	2126	2171	2584	2867	1119	1160	1226	1569	1591	352
3522	Drugs and medicines ..	1682	2035	2056	2440	2625	990	1109	1194	1516	1452	3522
353	Petroleum refineries ...	1584	3089	2996	1864	1707	1074	2161	2008	828	1168	353
354	Petroleum,coal products.	-	-	-	-	-	-	-	-	-	-	354
355	Rubber products	281	158	394	727	370	199	96	273	514	256	355
356	Plastic products n.e.c..	593	616	465	520	668	401	383	275	325	511	356
361	Pottery,china etc	343	319	251	279	282	199	146	127	130	124	361
362	Glass and products	360	436	463	354	809	176	280	226	223	635	362
369	Non-metal products n.e.c	1533	1472	1859	1882	1974	826	868	979	979	1077	369
371	Iron and steel	4998	3982	4689	5036	3386	2960	2092	2643	2758	2115	371
372	Non-ferrous metals	2295	1567	1273	830	981	1340	706	726	471	619	372
381	Metal products	1228	1189	1192	1297	1125	849	771	703	1005	815	381
382	Machinery n.e.c.	2698	2215	1922	1940	1542	1730	1337	1176	1282	1075	382
3825	Office,computing etc..	...	...	...	...	...	...	...	...	...	...	3825
383	Electrical machinery ...	2509	3055	3428	3979	3219	1591	2073	2410	3104	2367	383
3832	Radio,television etc..	1260	1834	2523	3037	2099	838	1337	1841	2428	1627	3832
384	Transport equipment	3412	3671	3719	2634	2632	1949	2030	2203	1536	1585	384
3841	Shipbuilding, repair..	...	...	...	...	...	...	...	...	...	...	3841
3843	Motor vehicles	...	...	...	...	...	...	...	...	...	...	3843
385	Professional goods	781	1056	1162	1176	912	435	660	647	772	616	385
390	Other industries	1232	1161	904	671	575	626	492	387	287	256	390
3	Manufacturing ..... b/	42343	44691	43180	42226	42227	25128	26911	25818	25802	26863	3
410	Electricity,gas,steam ..	13801	14494	16696	17264	17569	6142	6463	6420	6623	7124	410
4101	Electricity	12856	13511	15542	15668	15682	5912	6292	6280	6451	6871	4101
420	Water works and supply .	.	.	.	.	.	.	.	.	.	.	420
4	Electricity,gas etc	13801	14494	16696	17264	17569	6142	6463	6420	6623	7124	4
2-4	All industry b/	65877	69171	71970	73589	76855	35786	37895	37222	38602	41806	2-4

Note. For certain deviations in classification, see country note.

a/ Data relate to expenditure on new fixed assets only.

b/ Including repair services for the general public.

13. VALUE OF STOCKS AT END OF PERIOD
TOTAL
(BILLION FORINTS)

ISIC	INDUSTRY	1981	1982	1983	1984	1985	ISIC
210	Coal mining	3.97	4.31	4.58	4.79	5.55	210
220	Petroleum and gas	2.11	2.30	2.02	2.23	2.88	220
230	Metal ore mining	1.25	1.24	1.29	1.24	1.53	230
290	Other mining	0.64	0.69	0.67	0.69	0.68	290
2	Mining, quarrying	7.97	8.54	8.56	8.95	10.64	2
311/2	Food products	46.00	47.84	49.87	54.65	58.74	311/2
313	Beverages	7.27	8.98	9.49	9.03	9.42	313
314	Tobacco	2.08	2.31	2.33	2.14	2.26	314
321	Textiles	13.31	13.65	13.88	14.30	14.41	321
3211	Spinning,weaving etc.	10.49	10.76	10.82	11.03	11.01	3211
322	Wearing apparel	3.98	4.23	4.50	4.77	5.31	322
323	Leather and products	2.72	2.38	2.63	2.58	2.44	323
324	Footwear	2.58	2.63	2.86	3.32	3.69	324
331	Wood products	1.94	1.59	1.61	1.62	1.93	331
332	Furniture, fixtures	2.67	2.74	2.76	2.94	2.81	332
341	Paper and products	2.94	3.12	3.66	3.90	4.00	341
3411	Pulp,paper etc.	...	...	...	...	...	3411
342	Printing,publishing	1.79	1.95	1.94	2.04	2.05	342
351	Industrial chemicals	10.58	11.97	12.11	12.98	13.29	351
3511	Basic excl fertilizers	...	...	...	...	...	3511
3513	Synthetic resins etc	...	...	...	...	...	3513
352	Other chemical products	7.26	7.26	7.83	8.65	9.79	352
3522	Drugs and medicines	6.11	6.81	7.24	8.11	9.20	3522
353	Petroleum refineries	7.31	6.43	6.87	7.45	5.95	353
354	Petroleum,coal products	-	-	-	-	-	354
355	Rubber products	1.89	2.08	2.14	2.16	2.16	355
356	Plastic products n.e.c.	1.65	2.06	2.01	2.15	2.22	356
361	Pottery,china etc	1.10	1.12	0.90	0.92	0.95	361
362	Glass and products	1.59	1.71	1.84	1.83	2.08	362
369	Non-metal products n.e.c	5.06	5.17	5.26	5.56	6.10	369
371	Iron and steel	15.49	14.86	15.97	15.71	17.11	371
372	Non-ferrous metals	5.82	7.05	6.65	6.68	7.37	372
381	Metal products	7.18	6.93	7.34	7.72	8.18	381
382	Machinery n.e.c.	17.07	19.59	19.45	19.94	20.23	382
3825	Office,computing etc.	...	...	...	...	...	3825
383	Electrical machinery	25.32	26.70	28.81	30.70	33.70	383
3832	Radio,television etc.	14.39	15.71	16.76	18.93	21.07	3832
384	Transport equipment	19.22	19.99	20.62	22.21	21.86	384
3841	Shipbuilding, repair	1.67	1.88	1.87	1.83	2.03	3841
3843	Motor vehicles	10.93	11.22	11.22	12.48	12.49	3843
385	Professional goods	8.83	9.62	9.80	10.29	10.98	385
390	Other industries	4.02	4.07	3.68	3.92	3.85	390
3	Manufacturing a/	226.67	238.03	245.81	260.16	272.88	3
410	Electricity,gas,steam	7.89	9.51	10.93	10.74	14.15	410
4101	Electricity	5.62	6.98	8.25	7.91	10.86	4101
420	Water works and supply	.	.	.	.	.	420
4	Electricity,gas etc	7.89	9.51	10.93	10.74	14.15	4
2-4	All industry a/	242.53	256.08	265.30	279.85	297.67	2-4

a/ Including repair services for the general public.

14. INDEX NUMBERS OF INDUSTRIAL PRODUCTION (1980 = 100)

ISIC	INDUSTRY		1976	1977	1978	1979	1981	1982	1983	1984	1985	a/ RATE	ISIC
210	Coal mining		104	102	102	101	101	103	102	100	98	-0.7	210
220	Petroleum and gas		115	121	124	103	98	103	99	99	106	-0.9	220
230	Metal ore mining		104	107	107	102	99	96	98	95	94	-1.1	230
290	Other mining	b/	102	108	114	116	99	95	87	83	75	-3.4	290
2	Mining, quarrying .	b/c/	97	101	104	106	97	100	97	97	99	0.2	2
311/2	Food products												311/2
313	Beverages		85	93	96	98	102	106	108	111	109	2.8	313
314	Tobacco												314
321	Textiles		98	101	102	99	100	98	98	100	101	0.3	321
3211	Spinning,weaving etc..		...	...	...	...	...	...	...	...	...	...	3211
322	Wearing apparel		98	97	95	94	102	99	94	97	95	-0.3	322
323	Leather and products ...		103	111	115	110	102	101	101	101	101	-0.2	323
324	Footwear		107	107	109	103	103	104	110	118	123	1.6	324
331	Wood products		115	118	120	109	96	94	95	95	102	-1.3	331
332	Furniture, fixtures		93	94	98	100	100	97	99	104	104	1.2	332
341	Paper and products		88	98	103	101	106	108	113	121	117	3.2	341
3411	Pulp,paper etc.		...	...	...	...	...	...	...	...	...	...	3411
342	Printing,publishing	d/	76	82	89	94	108	111	116	120	124	5.6	342
351	Industrial chemicals ...		...	...	...	...	...	...	...	...	...	...	351
3511	Basic excl fertilizers		...	...	...	...	...	...	...	...	...	...	3511
3513	Synthetic resins etc .		...	...	...	...	...	...	...	...	...	...	3513
352	Other chemical products.		86	90	99	98	110	116	125	135	145	6.0	352
3522	Drugs and medicines ..		...	...	...	...	...	...	...	...	...	...	3522
353	Petroleum refineries ...		88	87	94	102	96	96	94	94	94	0.7	353
354	Petroleum,coal products.		...	...	...	...	...	...	...	...	...	...	354
355	Rubber products		88	96	101	99	106	113	118	126	129	4.3	355
356	Plastic products n.e.c..												356
361	Pottery,china etc		76	87	90	97	103	106	108	110	113	4.5	361
362	Glass and products		84	87	92	93	99	102	103	110	110	3.0	362
369	Non-metal products n.e.c		98	99	100	100	98	100	105	105	99	0.1	369
371	Iron and steel		98	102	105	105	101	102	100	100	98	0.0	371
372	Non-ferrous metals		91	96	98	97	104	108	109	116	121	3.2	372
381	Metal products		118	110	111	113	98	92	97	96	98	-2.0	381
382	Machinery n.e.c.		109	109	108	103	105	113	112	111	113	0.4	382
3825	Office,computing etc..		...	...	...	...	...	...	...	...	...	...	3825
383	Electrical machinery ...		76	88	97	102	107	112	114	120	127	5.9	383
3832	Radio,television etc..		...	...	...	...	...	...	...	...	...	...	3832
384	Transport equipment		80	85	95	101	104	110	109	112	114	4.0	384
3841	Shipbuilding, repair..		...	...	...	...	...	...	...	...	...	...	3841
3843	Motor vehicles		...	...	...	...	...	...	...	...	...	...	3843
385	Professional goods		78	88	96	102	113	119	126	127	135	6.3	385
390	Other industries		87	94	102	106	106	106	100	105	98	1.3	390
3	Manufacturing	b/c/d/	89	95	99	102	103	106	107	110	110	2.4	3
410	Electricity,gas,steam ..		79	84	92	94	105	109	112	117	120	4.8	410
4101	Electricity		89	93	100	100	102	106	109	115	117	3.1	4101
420	Water works and supply .		.	.	.	.	.	.	.	.	.	.	420
4	Electricity,gas etc		...	...	...	...	...	...	...	...	...	...	4
2-4	All industry	d/	89	95	99	102	103	105	106	109	110	2.4	2-4

a/ Annual growth rate 1976-1985.
b/ Stone quarrying, clay and sand pits are included in manufacturing.
c/ Coal briquetting is included in mining.
d/ Excluding publishing.

ICELAND

The information in the tables is based on the reply to the United Nations Questionnaire on General Industrial Statistics from the Statistical Bureau of Iceland, Reykjavik. The concepts, definitions and classification by branches of industry are generally in accordance with United Nations standards.

The estimates are derived from annual industrial statistics which are compiled by the National Economic Institute. The figures cover estimates for operating accounts of enterprises on a sample basis and data from administrative records.

The national classification is based on the preceding version of ISIC but the estimates have been adjusted as far as possible to reflect the present version of ISIC.

The employment figures are expressed in terms of man-years, based on the number of weeks worked, where one man-year is equal to 52 weeks.

Wages and salaries comprise all payments, whether in cash or in kind, made to employees during the year. Included are bonuses, compensations, etc.

The estimates of output for manufacturing represent the ex-factory value of goods produced and services rendered. Also included are receipts for contract and commission work and receipts from renting of machinery and buildings. The valuation is in producers' prices, where indirect taxes are included and subsidies are excluded.

Value added for manufacturing is the value of output less the cost of raw materials and all other intermediate consumption as defined in national accounts.

The estimates of cost of goods and industrial services consumed, materials and supplies consumed, purchased fuels and electricity consumed are based on the operating accounts of enterprises.

Related national publications:

Atvinnuvegskyrslur (Industrial Statistics of Iceland), published by the National Economic Institute, Reykjavik; Tolfraedihandbok 1984 (Statistical Abstract of Iceland 1984), published by the Statistical Bureau of Iceland, Reykjavik.

ISIC	INDUSTRY	1. NUMBER OF ESTABLISHMENTS (NUMBER)					2. AVERAGE NUMBER OF PERSONS ENGAGED a/ (NUMBER)					ISIC
		1981	1982	1983	1984	1985	1981	1982	1983	1984	1985	
210	Coal mining	-	-	-	-	...	-	-	-	-	...	210
220	Petroleum and gas	-	-	-	-	...	-	-	-	-	...	220
230	Metal ore mining	-	-	-	-	...	-	-	-	-	...	230
290	Other mining	-	-	-	-	...	-	-	-	-	...	290
2	Mining, quarrying .	-	-	-	-	...	-	-	-	-	...	2
311/2	Food products	782	784	818	896	...	13383	13158	13588	13802	...	311/2
313	Beverages	4	5	5	4	...	354	374	364	351	...	313
314	Tobacco	2	1	1	1	...	2	2	3	2	...	314
321	Textiles	86	96	93	93	...	1188	1149	1169	1280	...	321
3211	Spinning,weaving etc..	6	5	4	4	...	408	420	434	466	...	3211
322	Wearing apparel	140	120	112	128	...	1117	1051	960	1021	...	322
323	Leather and products ...	28	26	26	29	...	203	203	249	283	...	323
324	Footwear	3	4	4	3	...	39	40	42	48	...	324
331	Wood products	47	47	49	51	...	35	42	42	48	...	331
332	Furniture, fixtures	423	379	347	321	...	1753	1643	1579	1538	...	332
341	Paper and products	7	7	10	13	...	190	163	174	205	...	341
3411	Pulp,paper etc.	-	-	-	-	...	-	-	-	-	...	3411
342	Printing,publishing	269	295	300	318	...	1573	1694	1746	1809	...	342
351	Industrial chemicals ...	6	6	6	5	...	298	309	323	328	...	351
3511	Basic excl fertilizers	5	5	5	4	...	106	108	113	112	...	3511
3513	Synthetic resins etc .	-	-	-	-	...	-	-	-	-	...	3513
352	Other chemical products.	15	17	16	14	...	285	286	290	285	...	352
3522	Drugs and medicines ..	-	-	-	-	...	-	-	-	-	...	3522
353	Petroleum refineries ...	-	-	-	-	...	-	-	-	-	...	353
354	Petroleum,coal products.	2	2	3	2	...	1	5	7	6	...	354
355	Rubber products	-	-	-	-	...	-	-	-	-	...	355
356	Plastic products n.e.c..	47	61	51	57	...	429	445	450	442	...	356
361	Pottery,china etc	33	30	37	36	...	37	36	38	43	...	361
362	Glass and products	15	18	18	22	...	103	109	109	118	...	362
369	Non-metal products n.e.c	67	68	66	67	...	685	748	747	838	...	369
371	Iron and steel	1	1	1	1	...	163	165	173	193	...	371
372	Non-ferrous metals	1	1	1	1	...	730	731	666	661	...	372
381	Metal products	[412	400	445	441]	...	[2495	2528	2448	2537]	...	381
382	Machinery n.e.c.					...					...	382
3825	Office,computing etc..	-	-	-	-	...	-	-	-	-	...	3825
383	Electrical machinery ...	-	-	-	-	...	-	-	-	-	...	383
3832	Radio,television etc..	-	-	-	-	...	-	-	-	-	...	3832
384	Transport equipment	62	63	67	62	...	992	1043	1005	902	...	384
3841	Shipbuilding, repair..	62	63	67	62	...	992	1043	1005	902	...	3841
3843	Motor vehicles	-	-	-	-	...	-	-	-	-	...	3843
385	Professional goods	-	-	-	-	...	-	-	-	-	...	385
390	Other industries	127	129	136	125	...	334	399	440	443	...	390
3	Manufacturing	2579	2560	2612	2690	...	26389	26323	26612	27183	...	3
410	Electricity,gas,steam ..	48	48	46	41	...	983	993	1024	1083	...	410
4101	Electricity	25	25	24	22	...	871	889	910	935	...	4101
420	Water works and supply .	11	10	10	4	...	15	14	18	21	...	420
4	Electricity,gas etc	59	58	56	45	...	998	1007	1042	1104	...	4
2-4	All industry	2638	2618	2668	2735	...	27387	27330	27654	28287	...	2-4

a/ Number of man-years.

ISIC	INDUSTRY	3. WAGES AND SALARIES OF EMPLOYEES (MILLION KRONUR)					4. OUTPUT IN FACTOR VALUES (MILLION KRONUR)					ISIC
		1981	1982	1983	1984	1985	1981	1982	1983	1984	1985	
210	Coal mining	-	-	-	-	...	-	-	-	-	...	210
220	Petroleum and gas	-	-	-	-	...	-	-	-	-	...	220
230	Metal ore mining	-	-	-	-	...	-	-	-	-	...	230
290	Other mining	-	-	-	-	...	-	-	-	-	...	290
2	Mining, quarrying .	-	-	-	-	...	-	-	-	-	...	2
311/2	Food products	1367	2057	3278	4117	...	7794	11876	18795	25939	...	311/2
313	Beverages	37	61	87	110	...	129	242	338	468	...	313
314	Tobacco	-	-	-	1	...	-	-	-	-	...	314
321	Textiles	126	187	300	402	...	524	769	1150	1830	...	321
3211	Spinning,weaving etc..	51	74	130	170	...	248	364	376	638	...	3211
322	Wearing apparel	71	102	149	201	...	241	354	684	760	...	322
323	Leather and products ...	20	30	57	76	...	105	177	285	392	...	323
324	Footwear	4	6	-	1	...	9	18	33	43	...	324
331	Wood products	1	2	3	4	...	7	14	27	31	...	331
332	Furniture, fixtures	158	240	344	414	...	499	827	1231	1752	...	332
341	Paper and products	21	28	49	78	...	85	159	315	358	...	341
3411	Pulp,paper etc.	-	-	-	-	...	-	-	-	-	...	3411
342	Printing,publishing	161	279	446	598	...	462	738	1528	2033	...	342
351	Industrial chemicals ...	37	61	95	123	...	230	380	781	1018	...	351
3511	Basic excl fertilizers	...	...	...	...	...	42	85	239	285	...	3511
3513	Synthetic resins etc .	-	-	-	-	...	-	-	-	-	...	3513
352	Other chemical products.	22	39	57	72	...	190	239	434	545	...	352
3522	Drugs and medicines ..	-	-	-	-	...	-	-	-	-	...	3522
353	Petroleum refineries ...	-	-	-	-	...	-	-	-	-	...	353
354	Petroleum,coal products.	1	1	2	3	...	3	4	13	13	...	354
355	Rubber products	-	-	-	-	...	-	-	-	-	...	355
356	Plastic products n.e.c..	43	65	105	141	...	196	400	540	761	...	356
361	Pottery,china etc	2	3	5	7	...	9	11	23	34	...	361
362	Glass and products	11	18	32	38	...	45	75	123	169	...	362
369	Non-metal products n.e.c	68	118	191	267	...	401	845	1184	1657	...	369
371	Iron and steel	25	39	62	87	...	136	221	667	1159	...	371
372	Non-ferrous metals	118	199	263	339	...	727	1128	2667	3481	...	372
381	Metal products	[269	429	629	799]	...	[893	1193	1805	2467]	...	381
382	Machinery n.e.c.					...					...	382
3825	Office,computing etc..	-	-	-	-	...	-	-	-	-	...	3825
383	Electrical machinery ...	-	-	-	-	...	-	-	-	-	...	383
3832	Radio,television etc..	-	-	-	-	...	-	-	-	-	...	3832
384	Transport equipment	124	193	289	326	...	266	462	653	684	...	384
3841	Shipbuilding, repair..	124	193	289	326	...	266	462	653	684	...	3841
3843	Motor vehicles	-	-	-	-	...	-	-	-	-	...	3843
385	Professional goods	-	-	-	-	...	-	-	-	-	...	385
390	Other industries	37	75	119	155	...	164	340	666	865	...	390
3	Manufacturing	2723	4232	6562	8359	...	13115	20472	33942	46459	...	3
410	Electricity,gas,steam ..	155	249	395	536	...	1242	2284	5486	7576	...	410
4101	Electricity	139	225	355	455	...	969	1857	4441	6032	...	4101
420	Water works and supply .	2	3	6	1	...	62	96	174	237	...	420
4	Electricity,gas etc	157	252	401	537	...	1304	2380	5660	7813	...	4
2-4	All industry	2880	4484	6963	8896	...	14419	22852	39602	54272	...	2-4

5. VALUE ADDED IN FACTOR VALUES

(MILLION KRONUR)

ISIC	INDUSTRY	1981	1982	1983	1984	1985	ISIC
210	Coal mining	-	-	-	-	...	210
220	Petroleum and gas	-	-	-	-	...	220
230	Metal ore mining	-	-	-	-	...	230
290	Other mining	-	-	-	-	...	290
2	Mining, quarrying .	-	-	-	-	...	2
311/2	Food products	2433	3817	5540	7150	...	311/2
313	Beverages	48	100	140	199	...	313
314	Tobacco	-	-	-	-	...	314
321	Textiles	193	343	463	688	...	321
3211	Spinning,weaving etc..	75	141	157	231	...	3211
322	Wearing apparel	98	143	263	290	...	322
323	Leather and products ...	41	77	124	159	...	323
324	Footwear	4	8	16	17	...	324
331	Wood products	3	6	8	10	...	331
332	Furniture, fixtures	241	415	562	741	...	332
341	Paper and products	33	67	124	120	...	341
3411	Pulp,paper etc.	-	-	-	-	...	3411
342	Printing,publishing	257	400	656	968	...	342
351	Industrial chemicals ...	78	173	250	350	...	351
3511	Basic excl fertilizers	16	34	67	62	...	3511
3513	Synthetic resins etc .	-	-	-	-	...	3513
352	Other chemical products.	53	80	123	172	...	352
3522	Drugs and medicines ..	-	-	-	-	...	3522
353	Petroleum refineries ...	-	-	-	-	...	353
354	Petroleum,coal products.	1	1	5	4	...	354
355	Rubber products	-	-	-	-	...	355
356	Plastic products n.e.c..	71	142	197	246	...	356
361	Pottery,china etc	5	6	11	16	...	361
362	Glass and products	16	28	45	66	...	362
369	Non-metal products n.e.c	133	294	403	575	...	369
371	Iron and steel	40	39	200	503	...	371
372	Non-ferrous metals	164	272	736	950	...	372
381	Metal products	[428	601	968	1172]	...	381
382	Machinery n.e.c.					...	382
3825	Office,computing etc..	-	-	-	-	...	3825
383	Electrical machinery ...	-	-	-	-	...	383
3832	Radio,television etc..	-	-	-	-	...	3832
384	Transport equipment	163	277	369	392	...	384
3841	Shipbuilding, repair..	163	277	369	392	...	3841
3843	Motor vehicles	-	-	-	-	...	3843
385	Professional goods	-	-	-	-	...	385
390	Other industries	82	117	223	275	...	390
3	Manufacturing	4585	7406	11426	15063	...	3
410	Electricity,gas,steam ..	675	1252	3201	4603	...	410
4101	Electricity	455	945	2364	3381	...	4101
420	Water works and supply .	46	69	121	171	...	420
4	Electricity,gas etc	721	1321	3322	4774	...	4
2-4	All industry	5306	8727	14748	19837	...	2-4

INDIA

The information in the tables, except for the indexes, is based on the reply to the United Nations Questionnaire on General Industrial Statistics from the Department of Statistics, Ministry of Planning, New Delhi. The concepts, definitions and classification by branches of industry are generally in accordance with United Nations standards.

Mining data are derived from periodical returns collected by the Indian Bureau of Mines, the Coal Controller, Oil and Natural Gas Commission, Oil India Limited and the Chief Inspector of Mines. These data relate to all working mines, excluding those which extract the minerals declared as "prescribed minerals" under the Atomic Energy Act 1962. The data for manufacturing, electricity, gas and water are derived from the annual survey of industries. Except for electricity, the data in the tables relate to factories employing 10 or more workers with the aid of power or 20 or more workers without the aid of power. For operational purposes of the survey, the registered industrial establishments are divided into two sectors. The large-scale establishments, employing 50 or more workers, and using power, or, 100 or more workers without using power, constitute the census sector. These establishments, together with factories located in relatively less industrialized States, are completely enumerated every year. Other registered establishments, employing 10 to 49 workers and using power, or 20 to 99 workers and not using power constitute the non-census sector which is covered in two years on the basis of a complementary 50 per cent sample in alternate years. The field work is carried out by the Field Operations Division of the National Sample Survey Organisation, New Delhi. The term "worker" employed in these definitions of coverage stands for persons employed, whether for wages or not, in any manufacturing process or any other incidental or connected work, but excludes persons holding positions of supervision or management or employed in a confidential position. For electricity, inquiries are made as part of the census sector and cover all units of electricity undertakings on a complete enumeration basis. An electricity undertaking is defined as a State electricity board, an electricity department of the government of a State or Union territory, or an electric licensee or a sanction holder under the Indian Electricity Act engaging in the business of electric supply, including non-licensed undertakings registered as factories. Data shown in the tables relate to the entire sector.

The estimates in the tables are based on a classification which follows the preceding version of ISIC and are shown against the most applicable category of the present version. It should be noted, however, that manufacture of inedible oils (ISIC 3115), is included in ISIC 352, manufacture of prime movers, boilers etc.(ISIC 3813) is included in ISIC 382 and manufacture of electronic computers etc. (ISIC 3825) is included in ISIC 383.

The reference period is the financial year from 1 April to 31 March. In the tables, the estimates relate to aggregates of returns covering a 12-month period ending anywhere between 1 April of the year indicated and 31 March of the following year.

The average number of persons engaged is derived by dividing the person-days worked by the number of days on which the manufacturing process (other than the repairs and maintenance) was carried on. The number of person-days worked for each category is obtained by summing up the number of persons attending in each shift over all the shifts worked on all days (working and non-working). Wages and salaries of employees refer to all payments made in cash and in kind as compensation for work done during the reference year for all persons on the pay-roll. Payments to labour contractors are included but cover only the amounts payable to the contract labourers. The average number of operatives and wages and salaries of operatives refer to all workers engaged directly in the production process, including persons employed through labour contractors. Wages and salaries of operatives exclude imputed value of benefits in kind. The information in the table for days worked by operatives relates to all employees.

Output represents the sum of (a) ex-factory value of all finished products and by-products, (b) net balance of semi-finished goods, (c) value of industrial services rendered to others, (d) value of goods sold in the same condition as purchased and (e) value of capital assets produced by the establishment for its own use. Value added is obtained by deducting from the value of output (a) the total purchase value of raw materials, supplies, fuels, oils, electricity and water, (b) the cost of repair and maintenance of fixed capital assets, (c) the purchase value of goods sold in the same condition as purchased and (d) the cost of industrial and non-industrial services. The valuation of output and value added is in factor values.

The indexes of industrial production are compiled by the Department of Statistics, Ministry of Planning and provided in response to the United Nations Questionnaire on Indexes of Industrial Production. In principle, the indexes cover, for mining and electricity, all establishments. In case of manufacturing industries, the coverage of units differs from source to source supplying the data; some sources cover all units irrespective of size and some sources cover establishments employing plant and machinery worth one million rupees or more (recently, changed to two million rupees or more).

Related national publications:

Annual Survey of Industries (summary results for census and factory sectors and supplement to summary results; detailed results in 10 volumes); Statistical Abstract, India (annual); Monthly Statistics of the Production of Selected Industries of India, all published by the Department of Statistics, Ministry of Planning, New Delhi.

ISIC	INDUSTRY	1. NUMBER OF ESTABLISHMENTS a/b/ (NUMBER) 1981	1982	*1983	1984	1985	2. AVERAGE NUMBER OF PERSONS ENGAGED a/b/c/ (THOUSANDS) 1981	1982	1983	1984	1985	ISIC
210	Coal mining	462	478	496	...	...	733	...	...	...	...	210
220	Petroleum and gas	...	...	...	...	...	35	38	...	...	...	220
230	Metal ore mining	730	714	728	...	...	...	...	...	...	...	230
290	Other mining .... d/	2733	2901	2957	...	...	...	...	...	...	...	290
2	Mining, quarrying .	...	...	...	...	...	...	...	...	...	...	2
311/2	Food products	18351	17111	...	...	...	1325	1266	...	...	...	311/2
313	Beverages	374	400	...	...	...	39	40	...	...	...	313
314	Tobacco	9194	8086	...	...	...	402	415	...	...	...	314
321	Textiles	13286	11578	...	...	...	1554	1631	...	...	...	321
3211	Spinning,weaving etc..	11520	10055	...	...	...	1500	1579	...	...	...	3211
322	Wearing apparel	1215	1001	...	...	...	51	52	...	...	...	322
323	Leather and products ...	662	671	...	...	...	34	34	...	...	...	323
324	Footwear	199	176	...	...	...	26	28	...	...	...	324
331	Wood products	3775	3302	...	...	...	74	75	...	...	...	331
332	Furniture, fixtures	319	316	...	...	...	8	9	...	...	...	332
341	Paper and products	1470	1424	...	...	...	133	143	...	...	...	341
3411	Pulp,paper etc.	676	637	...	...	...	110	121	...	...	...	3411
342	Printing,publishing	3420	3147	...	...	...	161	165	...	...	...	342
351	Industrial chemicals ...	2058	1559	...	...	...	183	187	...	...	...	351
3511	Basic excl fertilizers	1223	934	...	...	...	72	76	...	...	...	3511
3513	Synthetic resins etc .	217	183	...	...	...	40	38	...	...	...	3513
352	Other chemical products.	4776	3791	...	...	...	314	313	...	...	...	352
3522	Drugs and medicines ..	1434	1131	...	...	...	112	113	...	...	...	3522
353	Petroleum refineries ...	17	17	...	...	...	20	39	...	...	...	353
354	Petroleum,coal products.	423	331	...	...	...	28	29	...	...	...	354
355	Rubber products	1656	1483	...	...	...	88	85	...	...	...	355
356	Plastic products n.e.c..	1768	1683	...	...	...	45	48	...	...	...	356
361	Pottery,china etc	493	443	...	...	...	31	33	...	...	...	361
362	Glass and products	674	607	...	...	...	63	67	...	...	...	362
369	Non-metal products n.e.c	6527	5613	...	...	...	281	319	...	...	...	369
371	Iron and steel	5081	4635	...	...	...	540	558	...	...	...	371
372	Non-ferrous metals	932	874	...	...	...	56	54	...	...	...	372
381	Metal products	6563	5884	...	...	...	199	203	...	...	...	381
382	Machinery n.e.c.	7876	7207	...	...	...	425	442	...	...	...	382
3825	Office,computing etc..	111	122	...	...	...	8	8	...	...	...	3825
383	Electrical machinery ...	4229	3641	...	...	...	314	340	...	...	...	383
3832	Radio,television etc..	819	732	...	...	...	55	82	...	...	...	3832
384	Transport equipment	3339	2816	...	...	...	501	509	...	...	...	384
3841	Shipbuilding, repair..	180	148	...	...	...	47	50	...	...	...	3841
3843	Motor vehicles	1565	1334	...	...	...	174	186	...	...	...	3843
385	Professional goods	978	680	...	...	...	39	41	...	...	...	385
390	Other industries	1405	795	...	...	...	30	30	...	...	...	390
3	Manufacturing ..... e/	101060	89271	...	...	...	6964	7155	...	...	...	3
410	Electricity,gas,steam ..	244	240	...	...	...	735	777	...	...	...	410
4101	Electricity	184	208	...	...	...	731	775	...	...	...	4101
420	Water works and supply .	211	193	...	...	...	14	13	...	...	...	420
4	Electricity,gas etc	455	433	...	...	...	749	790	...	...	...	4
2-4	All industry	...	...	...	...	...	...	...	...	...	...	2-4

a/ Mining: all working mines excluding those extracting minerals prescribed under the Atomic Energy Act.
b/ Manufacturing, gas and water: establishments with 10 or more workers using power, or 20 or more workers not using power. Electricity: all units of electricity undertakings.
c/ Twelve months beginning 1 April of the year indicated. d/ Excluding minor minerals.
e/ For certain deviations in classification, see country note.

ISIC	INDUSTRY	3. AVERAGE NUMBER OF EMPLOYEES a/b/c/ (THOUSANDS) 1981	1982	1983	1984	1985	4. WAGES AND SALARIES OF EMPLOYEES a/b/c/ (MILLION RUPEES) 1981	1982	1983	1984	1985	ISIC
210	Coal mining	733	...	...	...	...	10910	...	...	...	...	210
220	Petroleum and gas	...	...	...	...	...	d/ 645	d/ 862	...	...	...	220
230	Metal ore mining	...	...	...	...	...	...	...	...	...	...	230
290	Other mining	...	...	...	...	...	...	...	...	...	...	290
2	Mining, quarrying .	...	...	...	...	...	...	...	...	...	...	2
311/2	Food products	1302	1235	...	...	...	4346	5635	...	...	...	311/2
313	Beverages	38	39	...	...	...	284	314	...	...	...	313
314	Tobacco	393	404	...	...	...	961	1770	...	...	...	314
321	Textiles	1546	1616	...	...	...	12700	14453	...	...	...	321
3211	Spinning,weaving etc..	1495	1566	...	...	...	12347	14066	...	...	...	3211
322	Wearing apparel	50	51	...	...	...	271	306	...	...	...	322
323	Leather and products ...	34	32	...	...	...	211	230	...	...	...	323
324	Footwear	26	28	...	...	...	220	250	...	...	...	324
331	Wood products	69	69	...	...	...	287	367	...	...	...	331
332	Furniture, fixtures	8	9	...	...	...	50	58	...	...	...	332
341	Paper and products	131	142	...	...	...	1264	1347	...	...	...	341
3411	Pulp,paper etc.	109	120	...	...	...	1098	1168	...	...	...	3411
342	Printing,publishing	158	161	...	...	...	1667	1814	...	...	...	342
351	Industrial chemicals ...	182	186	...	...	...	3047	3247	...	...	...	351
3511	Basic excl fertilizers	71	75	...	...	...	1036	1327	...	...	...	3511
3513	Synthetic resins etc .	39	38	...	...	...	794	643	...	...	...	3513
352	Other chemical products.	299	308	...	...	...	3324	3980	...	...	...	352
3522	Drugs and medicines ..	111	112	...	...	...	1705	2023	...	...	...	3522
353	Petroleum refineries ...	20	39	...	...	...	259	589	...	...	...	353
354	Petroleum,coal products.	28	29	...	...	...	342	402	...	...	...	354
355	Rubber products	86	84	...	...	...	906	1039	...	...	...	355
356	Plastic products n.e.c..	44	46	...	...	...	313	375	...	...	...	356
361	Pottery,china etc	31	33	...	...	...	228	246	...	...	...	361
362	Glass and products	62	66	...	...	...	389	433	...	...	...	362
369	Non-metal products n.e.c	273	307	...	...	...	1747	2450	...	...	...	369
371	Iron and steel	535	551	...	...	...	6670	7788	...	...	...	371
372	Non-ferrous metals	55	53	...	...	...	716	784	...	...	...	372
381	Metal products	191	196	...	...	...	1719	1814	...	...	...	381
382	Machinery n.e.c.	416	432	...	...	...	4793	5596	...	...	...	382
3825	Office,computing etc..	7	8	...	...	...	86	107	...	...	...	3825
383	Electrical machinery ...	310	337	...	...	...	3877	5051	...	...	...	383
3832	Radio,television etc..	55	81	...	...	...	606	1098	...	...	...	3832
384	Transport equipment	498	506	...	...	...	6520	7398	...	...	...	384
3841	Shipbuilding, repair..	47	50	...	...	...	793	849	...	...	...	3841
3843	Motor vehicles	173	185	...	...	...	2557	3118	...	...	...	3843
385	Professional goods	38	41	...	...	...	363	467	...	...	...	385
390	Other industries	28	28	...	...	...	244	280	...	...	...	390
3	Manufacturing ..... e/	6851	7028	...	...	...	57718	68483	...	...	...	3
410	Electricity,gas,steam ..	735	777	...	...	...	8265	9823	...	...	...	410
4101	Electricity	731	775	...	...	...	8230	9796	...	...	...	4101
420	Water works and supply .	14	13	...	...	...	103	118	...	...	...	420
4	Electricity,gas etc	749	790	...	...	...	8368	9941	...	...	...	4
2-4	All industry	...	...	...	...	...	...	...	...	...	...	2-4

a/ Twelve months beginning 1 April of the year indicated.
b/ Manufacturing, gas and water: establishments with 10 or more workers using power, or 20 or more workers not using power. Electricity: all units of electricity undertakings.
c/ Mining: all working mines excluding those extracting minerals prescribed under the Atomic Energy Act.
d/ Total emoluments paid to all persons engaged.
e/ For certain deviations in classification, see country note.

ISIC	INDUSTRY	5. AVERAGE NUMBER OF OPERATIVES a/b/c/ (THOUSANDS)					6. WAGES AND SALARIES OF OPERATIVES a/c/d/ (MILLION RUPEES)					ISIC
		1981	1982	*1983	1984	1985	1981	1982	1983	1984	1985	
210	Coal mining	513	530	530	...	...	...	...	...	...	...	210
220	Petroleum and gas	...	...	...	...	...	...	...	...	...	...	220
230	Metal ore mining	110	116	107	...	...	...	...	...	...	...	230
290	Other mining .... e/	112	118	116	...	...	...	...	...	...	...	290
2	Mining, quarrying .	...	...	...	...	...	...	...	...	...	...	2
311/2	Food products	1025	985	...	...	...	2756	3471	...	...	...	311/2
313	Beverages	27	29	...	...	...	163	188	...	...	...	313
314	Tobacco	369	381	...	...	...	784	889	...	...	...	314
321	Textiles	1347	1411	...	...	...	10253	11454	...	...	...	321
3211	Spinning,weaving etc..	1305	1370	...	...	...	10005	11191	...	...	...	3211
322	Wearing apparel	42	42	...	...	...	186	206	...	...	...	322
323	Leather and products ...	28	27	...	...	...	155	165	...	...	...	323
324	Footwear	22	24	...	...	...	163	179	...	...	...	324
331	Wood products	57	57	...	...	...	204	246	...	...	...	331
332	Furniture, fixtures	6	7	...	...	...	35	41	...	...	...	332
341	Paper and products	102	110	...	...	...	805	854	...	...	...	341
3411	Pulp,paper etc.	85	92	...	...	...	699	739	...	...	...	3411
342	Printing,publishing	120	122	...	...	...	1030	1181	...	...	...	342
351	Industrial chemicals ...	121	124	...	...	...	1572	1624	...	...	...	351
3511	Basic excl fertilizers	48	50	...	...	...	514	601	...	...	...	3511
3513	Synthetic resins etc .	27	26	...	...	...	416	339	...	...	...	3513
352	Other chemical products.	212	220	...	...	...	1679	2028	...	...	...	352
3522	Drugs and medicines ..	70	70	...	...	...	794	981	...	...	...	3522
353	Petroleum refineries ...	12	34	...	...	...	129	399	...	...	...	353
354	Petroleum,coal products.	21	22	...	...	...	207	250	...	...	...	354
355	Rubber products	65	64	...	...	...	560	643	...	...	...	355
356	Plastic products n.e.c..	33	35	...	...	...	182	225	...	...	...	356
361	Pottery,china etc	25	27	...	...	...	158	171	...	...	...	361
362	Glass and products	52	52	...	...	...	269	292	...	...	...	362
369	Non-metal products n.e.c	230	259	...	...	...	1196	1486	...	...	...	369
371	Iron and steel	406	416	...	...	...	4418	5144	...	...	...	371
372	Non-ferrous metals	41	39	...	...	...	434	477	...	...	...	372
381	Metal products	151	153	...	...	...	1108	1160	...	...	...	381
382	Machinery n.e.c.	293	303	...	...	...	2676	3173	...	...	...	382
3825	Office,computing etc..	5	6	...	...	...	49	70	...	...	...	3825
383	Electrical machinery ...	210	231	...	...	...	2078	2777	...	...	...	383
3832	Radio,television etc..	39	58	...	...	...	324	641	...	...	...	3832
384	Transport equipment	381	382	...	...	...	4281	4841	...	...	...	384
3841	Shipbuilding, repair..	38	39	...	...	...	510	585	...	...	...	3841
3843	Motor vehicles	124	130	...	...	...	1515	1817	...	...	...	3843
385	Professional goods	28	30	...	...	...	207	280	...	...	...	385
390	Other industries	22	23	...	...	...	157	189	...	...	...	390
3	Manufacturing ..... f/	5448	5609	...	...	...	37845	44033	...	...	...	3
410	Electricity,gas,steam ..	500	538	...	...	...	4773	5855	...	...	...	410
4101	Electricity	497	536	...	...	...	4752	5839	...	...	...	4101
420	Water works and supply	11	11	...	...	...	79	89	...	...	...	420
4	Electricity,gas etc	511	549	...	...	...	4852	5944	...	...	...	4
2-4	All industry	...	...	...	...	...	...	...	...	...	...	2-4

a/ Twelve months beginning 1 April of the year indicated.
b/ Mining: all working mines excluding those extracting minerals prescribed under the Atomic Energy Act.
c/ Manufacturing, gas and water: establishments with 10 or more workers using power, or 20 or more workers not using power. Electricity: all units of electricity undertakings.
d/ Excluding imputed value of benefits in kind.
e/ Excluding minor minerals.
f/ For certain deviations in classification, see country note.

ISIC	INDUSTRY	7. DAYS WORKED BY OPERATIVES a/b/d/ (MILLIONS)					8. OUTPUT IN FACTOR VALUES a/b/c/ (MILLION RUPEES)					ISIC
		1981	1982	1983	1984	1985	1981	1982	1983	1984	1985	
210	Coal mining	...	...	...	...	...	18716	22008	25298	31429	...	210
220	Petroleum and gas	...	...	...	...	...	15278	24695	29677	34420	...	220
230	Metal ore mining	...	...	...	...	...	2700	3273	3967	4608	...	230
290	Other mining	...	...	...	...	...	3761	4830	5677	5936	...	290
2	Mining, quarrying	...	...	...	...	...	40455	54806	64619	76393	...	2
311/2	Food products	171	185	...	...	...	96723	118801	...	...	...	311/2
313	Beverages	8	8	...	...	...	4029	3983	...	...	...	313
314	Tobacco	83	93	...	...	...	9608	10188	...	...	...	314
321	Textiles	392	415	...	...	...	93517	103242	...	...	...	321
3211	Spinning,weaving etc.	380	403	...	...	...	87493	97042	...	...	...	3211
322	Wearing apparel	12	13	...	...	...	3935	4827	...	...	...	322
323	Leather and products	8	8	...	...	...	4368	4248	...	...	...	323
324	Footwear	6	6	...	...	...	1459	1880	...	...	...	324
331	Wood products	16	16	...	...	...	3060	3462	...	...	...	331
332	Furniture, fixtures	2	2	...	...	...	307	389	...	...	...	332
341	Paper and products	33	33	...	...	...	12565	12534	...	...	...	341
3411	Pulp,paper etc.	28	28	...	...	...	10353	10275	...	...	...	3411
342	Printing,publishing	36	37	...	...	...	7983	9300	...	...	...	342
351	Industrial chemicals	39	40	...	...	...	52584	57604	...	...	...	351
3511	Basic excl fertilizers	16	17	...	...	...	15242	16993	...	...	...	3511
3513	Synthetic resins etc	9	8	...	...	...	9264	8268	...	...	...	3513
352	Other chemical products.	61	65	...	...	...	45819	52279	...	...	...	352
3522	Drugs and medicines	21	22	...	...	...	15551	18493	...	...	...	3522
353	Petroleum refineries	2	12	...	...	...	50359	68995	...	...	...	353
354	Petroleum,coal products.	7	7	...	...	...	8597	10111	...	...	...	354
355	Rubber products	19	19	...	...	...	13127	16480	...	...	...	355
356	Plastic products n.e.c.	10	10	...	...	...	4793	5654	...	...	...	356
361	Pottery,china etc	8	9	...	...	...	1294	1339	...	...	...	361
362	Glass and products	13	13	...	...	...	2832	3115	...	...	...	362
369	Non-metal products n.e.c	63	70	...	...	...	16516	22851	...	...	...	369
371	Iron and steel	128	132	...	...	...	82248	94773	...	...	...	371
372	Non-ferrous metals	13	13	...	...	...	10185	11921	...	...	...	372
381	Metal products	44	44	...	...	...	16522	17585	...	...	...	381
382	Machinery n.e.c.	87	92	...	...	...	42577	48099	...	...	...	382
3825	Office,computing etc.	1	2	...	...	...	410	494	...	...	...	3825
383	Electrical machinery	61	70	...	...	...	39183	47406	...	...	...	383
3832	Radio,television etc.	11	17	...	...	...	4066	7566	...	...	...	3832
384	Transport equipment	116	114	...	...	...	42407	47692	...	...	...	384
3841	Shipbuilding, repair.	11	11	...	...	...	3109	4144	...	...	...	3841
3843	Motor vehicles	37	39	...	...	...	24044	27740	...	...	...	3843
385	Professional goods	8	9	...	...	...	2695	3378	...	...	...	385
390	Other industries	6	7	...	...	...	1999	2414	...	...	...	390
3	Manufacturing e/	1452	1542	...	...	...	671291	784550	...	...	...	3
410	Electricity,gas,steam	182	196	...	...	...	55931	66407	...	...	...	410
4101	Electricity	181	195	...	...	...	55581	66094	...	...	...	4101
420	Water works and supply	4	4	...	...	...	893	839	...	...	...	420
4	Electricity,gas etc	186	200	...	...	...	56824	67246	...	...	...	4
2-4	All industry	...	...	...	...	...	768570	906602	...	...	...	2-4

a/ Twelve months beginning 1 April of the year indicated.
b/ Manufacturing, gas and water: establishments with 10 or more workers using power, or 20 or more workers not using power. Electricity: all units of electricity undertakings.
c/ Mining: all working mines excluding those extracting minerals prescribed under the Atomic Energy Act.
d/ Data relate to paid employees.
e/ For certain deviations in classification, see country note.

ISIC	INDUSTRY	9. VALUE ADDED IN FACTOR VALUES a/b/c/d/ (MILLION RUPEES)					10. GROSS FIXED CAPITAL FORMATION TOTAL a/b/c/ (MILLION RUPEES)					ISIC
		1981	1982	1983	1984	1985	1981	1982	1983	1984	1985	
210	Coal mining	12270	14409	16508	20467	...	...	...	...	...	...	210
220	Petroleum and gas	13695	21519	26015	30169	...	...	...	...	...	...	220
230	Metal ore mining	2052	2573	3080	3554	...	...	...	...	...	...	230
290	Other mining	2931	4179	4803	5086	...	...	...	...	...	...	290
2	Mining, quarrying .	30948	42680	50406	59276	...	14976	26598	27640	...	...	2
311/2	Food products	9364	11884	...	...	...	2476	3046	...	...	...	311/2
313	Beverages	843	927	...	...	...	237	256	...	...	...	313
314	Tobacco	1680	1692	...	...	...	103	96	...	...	...	314
321	Textiles	20153	20275	...	...	...	5332	7022	...	...	...	321
3211	Spinning,weaving etc..	19242	19269	...	...	...	5209	6847	...	...	...	3211
322	Wearing apparel	573	659	...	...	...	66	159	...	...	...	322
323	Leather and products ...	404	445	...	...	...	106	188	...	...	...	323
324	Footwear	317	385	...	...	...	38	81	...	...	...	324
331	Wood products	648	685	...	...	...	98	120	...	...	...	331
332	Furniture, fixtures	78	98	...	...	...	5	8	...	...	...	332
341	Paper and products	2744	1921	...	...	...	1692	2218	...	...	...	341
3411	Pulp,paper etc.	2371	1562	...	...	...	1625	2127	...	...	...	3411
342	Printing,publishing	2614	3009	...	...	...	659	-4	...	...	...	342
351	Industrial chemicals ...	9103	10521	...	...	...	5242	4202	...	...	...	351
3511	Basic excl fertilizers	3570	3874	...	...	...	1499	2298	...	...	...	3511
3513	Synthetic resins etc .	1921	1519	...	...	...	547	614	...	...	...	3513
352	Other chemical products.	8251	9936	...	...	...	1855	1800	...	...	...	352
3522	Drugs and medicines ..	3717	4759	...	...	...	666	709	...	...	...	3522
353	Petroleum refineries ...	2223	4128	...	...	...	3664	2969	...	...	...	353
354	Petroleum,coal products.	1137	1407	...	...	...	148	412	...	...	...	354
355	Rubber products	1909	3036	...	...	...	501	739	...	...	...	355
356	Plastic products n.e.c..	756	952	...	...	...	290	433	...	...	...	356
361	Pottery,china etc	490	513	...	...	...	117	80	...	...	...	361
362	Glass and products	687	682	...	...	...	228	417	...	...	...	362
369	Non-metal products n.e.c	3656	6189	...	...	...	2369	2317	...	...	...	369
371	Iron and steel	16555	16490	...	...	...	12188	11603	...	...	...	371
372	Non-ferrous metals	1013	1548	...	...	...	1056	952	...	...	...	372
381	Metal products	3648	3812	...	...	...	698	754	...	...	...	381
382	Machinery n.e.c.	10498	11906	...	...	...	2523	2509	...	...	...	382
3825	Office,computing etc..	148	192	...	...	...	15	22	...	...	...	3825
383	Electrical machinery ...	8990	11973	...	...	...	2217	2512	...	...	...	383
3832	Radio,television etc..	1056	2114	...	...	...	290	613	...	...	...	3832
384	Transport equipment	11031	13091	...	...	...	2704	4792	...	...	...	384
3841	Shipbuilding, repair..	1105	1191	...	...	...	497	1282	...	...	...	3841
3843	Motor vehicles	6173	7326	...	...	...	1559	2127	...	...	...	3843
385	Professional goods	790	1156	...	...	...	229	163	...	...	...	385
390	Other industries	463	496	...	...	...	58	80	...	...	...	390
3	Manufacturing ..... e/	120618	139816	...	...	...	46899	49924	...	...	...	3
410	Electricity,gas,steam ..	22632	24272	...	...	...	25261	27973	...	...	...	410
4101	Electricity	22572	24125	...	...	...	25253	27928	...	...	...	4101
420	Water works and supply .	258	150	...	...	...	17	116	...	...	...	420
4	Electricity,gas etc	22890	24422	...	...	...	25278	28089	...	...	...	4
2-4	All industry	174456	206918	...	...	...	87153	104611	...	...	...	2-4

a/ Twelve months beginning 1 April of the year indicated.
b/ Mining: all working mines excluding those extracting minerals prescribed under the Atomic Energy Act.
c/ Manufacturing, gas and water: establishments with 10 or more workers using power, or 20 or more workers not using power. Electricity: all units of electricity undertakings.
d/ Net of non-industrial costs.
e/ For certain deviations in classification, see country note.

11. INDEX NUMBERS OF INDUSTRIAL PRODUCTION (1980 = 100)

ISIC	INDUSTRY	1976	1977	1978	1979	1981	1982	1983	1984	1985	RATE a/	ISIC
210	Coal mining	92	92	92	95	114	119	125	134	138	4.6	210
220	Petroleum and gas	69	80	89	102	117	155	197	218	234	14.5	220
230	Metal ore mining	109	109	99	103	101	106	113	124	129	1.9	230
290	Other mining	100	104	108	108	107	112	122	138	139	3.7	290
2	Mining, quarrying .	94	96	99	104	118	130	147	158	166	6.5	2
311/2	Food products	86	94	111	101	110	132	132	124	128	4.5	311/2
313	Beverages	[87	100	96	98	125	154	144	144	142	5.6]	313
314	Tobacco											314
321	Textiles	92	90	100	95	101	89	94	96	102	1.2	321
3211	Spinning,weaving etc..	...	...	...	...	...	...	...	...	...	...	3211
322	Wearing apparel .... b/	129	114	104	108	122	110	126	131	137	0.7	322
323	Leather and products ...	99	69	73	70	90	82	76	75	...	-3.4 d/	323
324	Footwear .... b/	...	...	...	...	...	...	...	...	...	...	324
331	Wood products	95	105	114	106	72	88	170	173	...	7.8 d/	331
332	Furniture, fixtures	...	...	...	...	...	...	...	...	...	...	332
341	Paper and products	85	90	97	95	113	117	110	131	142	5.9	341
3411	Pulp,paper etc.	...	...	...	...	...	...	...	...	...	...	3411
342	Printing,publishing	...	...	...	...	...	...	...	...	...	...	342
351	Industrial chemicals ...	81	92	100	101	116	124	127	146	158	7.7	351
3511	Basic excl fertilizers	...	...	...	...	...	...	...	...	...	...	3511
3513	Synthetic resins etc .	...	...	...	...	...	...	...	...	...	...	3513
352	Other chemical products.	91	96	105	102	110	112	118	120	115	2.6	352
3522	Drugs and medicines ..	103	107	107	107	109	105	113	113	96	-0.8	3522
353	Petroleum refineries ...	91	97	101	112	117	127	137	139	162	6.6	353
354	Petroleum,coal products.	...	...	...	...	...	...	...	...	...	...	354
355	Rubber products	81	86	94	95	102	109	119	129	132	5.6	355
356	Plastic products n.e.c..	...	...	...	...	...	...	...	...	...	...	356
361	Pottery,china etc	124	124	122	114	83	91	131	172	...	4.2 d/	361
362	Glass and products	71	77	88	94	101	102	106	110	...	5.6 d/	362
369	Non-metal products n.e.c	90	93	95	99	108	115	113	119	172	7.5	369
371	Iron and steel	107	109	109	104	111	118	120	121	131	2.3	371
372	Non-ferrous metals	94	94	103	106	111	118	128	159	160	6.1	372
381	Metal products	88	92	102	108	100	105	105	110	109	2.4	381
382	Machinery n.e.c.	75	83	93	93	106	109	121	130	131	6.4	382
3825	Office,computing etc..	...	...	...	...	...	...	...	...	...	...	3825
383	Electrical machinery ...	76	86	90	96	106	106	104	110	118	5.0	383
3832	Radio,television etc..	...	...	...	...	...	...	...	...	...	...	3832
384	Transport equipment	100	96	95	96	110	109	136	148	162	5.5	384
3841	Shipbuilding, repair..	...	...	...	...	...	...	...	...	...	...	3841
3843	Motor vehicles	...	...	...	...	...	...	...	...	...	...	3843
385	Professional goods	58	68	88	89	91	82	79	112	131	9.5	385
390	Other industries	86	112	122	133	85	75	62	60	48	-6.3	390
3	Manufacturing	88	92	100	99	108	111	115	122	130	4.4	3
410	Electricity,gas,steam ..	...	...	...	...	...	...	...	...	...	...	410
4101	Electricity	81	84	93	98	112	120	124	142	153	7.3	4101
420	Water works and supply .	.	.	.	.	.	.	.	.	.	.	420
4	Electricity,gas etc	...	...	...	...	...	...	...	...	...	...	4
2-4	All industry c/	88	92	99	99	109	114	119	128	136	5.0	2-4

a/ Annual growth rate 1976-1985.
b/ Major group 324 is included in 322.
c/ Excluding gas and steam.
d/ Annual growth rate 1976-1984.

INDONESIA

The information in the tables, except for the indexes, is based on the reply to the United Nations Questionnaire on General Industrial Statistics from the Central Bureau of Statistics, Jakarta. The concepts, definitions and classification by branches of industry are generally in accordance with United Nations standards.

The data for mining and quarrying are derived from the administrative records kept by the Department of Mining. The data for manufacturing are derived from the annual industrial survey conducted by the Central Bureau of Statistics. The survey covers large-and medium-scale establishments. Large-scale establishments cover those with 100 or more persons engaged and medium-scale establishments cover those with 20-99 persons engaged. The inquiry is made on a complete enumeration basis regardless of large-scale or medium-scale establishments. For a certain number of provinces where establishments are concentrated, the inquiry is carried out by field enumerators through direct interview and in the remaining regions with more or less scattered establishments, the inquiry is made by mail. The survey does not cover petroleum manufacturing activities (ISIC 353 and 354) and manufacturing activities on agricultural estates of tea, tobacco and rubber. The data for electricity and gas cover all establishments of the State Electricity Enterprise and the State Gas Enterprise. Data on water supply cover government and private establishments engaged in purification and distribution of drinking water. The data in the tables are based on the present version of ISIC.

Wages and salaries represent employment costs which include employers' contributions to pension and health insurance schemes. The estimates of output and value added for manufacturing industries are defined as follows. Output comprises (a) the value of all products of the establishment, (b) the net change in the value of semi-finished goods and work in progress during the year, (c) receipts from industrial and non-industrial services rendered to others, (d) the value of goods shipped in the same condition as received and (e) the value of electricity sold. Value added is the difference between output and the cost of the following inputs: raw materials, auxiliary materials, packing materials, oils, fuels, gas and electricity consumed and industrial and non-industrial services rendered by others. For manufacturing industries, the valuation of output is in producers' prices and that of value added is in factor values. In the case of electricity industry, output represents the value of electric power sold. For gas manufacturing, output estimates refer to the value of goods produced, gross income from resale and receipts from non-industrial services rendered. For water supply, output is defined as the value of potable water supplied, electric power sold and other income from non-industrial services. Value-added estimates for electricity, gas and water supply is the difference between the value of output and the input costs (expenditures for the purchase of fuels, electricity, spare parts, office supplies, repairs and maintenance, rental of buildings and machines and non-industrial services). The estimates of output and value added for electricity, gas and water supply are valued in producers' prices.

Gross fixed capital formation represents the value of acquisitions of new and used fixed assets; sales are not taken into account.

The indexes of industrial production are compiled by the Central Bureau of Statistics and provided in response to the United Nations Questionnaire on Indexes of Industrial Production.

Related national publication:

<u>Industrial Statistics (Survey of Manufacturing Industries)</u> Volumes I and II (annual), published by the Central Bureau of Statistics, Jakarta.

ISIC	INDUSTRY	1. NUMBER OF ESTABLISHMENTS a/ (NUMBER)					2. AVERAGE NUMBER OF PERSONS ENGAGED a/ (THOUSANDS)					ISIC
		1981	1982	1983	1984	1985	1981	1982	1983	1984	1985	
210	Coal mining	2	2	6	6	6	3.0	3.0	...	...	...	210
220	Petroleum and gas	50	53	59	59	37	...	26.0	...	...	...	220
230	Metal ore mining	17	20	19	19	19	...	40.0	...	...	...	230
290	Other mining	5	4	8	8	8	...	2.0	...	...	...	290
2	Mining, quarrying .	74	79	92	92	70	...	71.0	...	...	...	2
311/2	Food products	1648	1594	1586	1671	...	155.8	155.0	162.4	165.6	...	311/2
313	Beverages	94	99	105	107	...	7.4	7.4	8.3	8.6	...	313
314	Tobacco	599	575	577	578	...	157.7	161.1	168.0	167.8	...	314
321	Textiles	1892	1822	1755	1669	...	234.8	233.1	226.5	240.4	...	321
3211	Spinning,weaving etc.. b/	73	80	78	78	...	44.1	47.4	43.6	52.1	...	3211
322	Wearing apparel	157	169	190	207	...	20.2	24.0	29.4	35.9	...	322
323	Leather and products ...	40	41	42	42	...	2.8	2.9	3.1	3.2	...	323
324	Footwear	64	56	55	61	...	7.5	6.3	6.3	6.8	...	324
331	Wood products	510	573	573	563	...	65.9	91.4	113.0	166.3	...	331
332	Furniture, fixtures	137	132	139	136	...	5.3	5.5	5.9	5.7	...	332
341	Paper and products	86	85	82	78	...	13.2	14.5	14.3	13.8	...	341
3411	Pulp,paper etc.	55	52	48	43	...	9.8	10.6	10.7	9.8	...	3411
342	Printing,publishing	280	293	295	297	...	21.2	22.8	22.7	21.9	...	342
351	Industrial chemicals ...	99	114	124	130	...	16.6	20.5	20.9	23.1	...	351
3511	Basic excl fertilizers	56	63	73	79	...	5.2	7.6	7.2	9.0	...	3511
3513	Synthetic resins etc .	13	14	13	13	...	0.4	0.4	0.4	0.4	...	3513
352	Other chemical products.	314	327	336	337	...	45.7	49.6	52.2	52.7	...	352
3522	Drugs and medicines ..	135	141	147	151	...	21.7	22.3	25.0	26.4	...	3522
353	Petroleum refineries ...	.	.	.	.	...	.	.	.	.	...	353
354	Petroleum,coal products.	.	.	.	.	...	.	.	.	.	...	354
355	Rubber products	211	203	211	212	...	38.4	38.1	38.4	40.0	...	355
356	Plastic products n.e.c..	227	276	289	294	...	20.5	24.3	29.3	31.1	...	356
361	Pottery,china etc	22	25	28	29	...	7.4	8.2	9.4	10.3	...	361
362	Glass and products	46	44	37	34	...	9.5	10.2	10.1	9.8	...	362
369	Non-metal products n.e.c	597	635	635	613	...	33.4	34.7	36.5	35.6	...	369
371	Iron and steel	22	23	24	26	...	9.5	10.1	12.9	14.0	...	371
372	Non-ferrous metals	-	-	-	-	...	-	-	-	-	...	372
381	Metal products	355	360	366	353	...	44.0	44.3	45.3	43.1	...	381
382	Machinery n.e.c.	128	131	132	131	...	12.7	13.0	12.7	12.8	...	382
3825	Office,computing etc..	-	-	-	-	...	-	-	-	-	...	3825
383	Electrical machinery ...	115	118	121	115	...	38.8	36.9	37.2	36.6	...	383
3832	Radio,television etc..	36	36	36	34	...	16.1	15.3	15.4	14.7	...	3832
384	Transport equipment	188	204	203	195	...	35.9	44.5	46.1	42.9	...	384
3841	Shipbuilding, repair..	46	54	53	49	...	7.3	8.1	8.0	7.5	...	3841
3843	Motor vehicles .... c/	52	55	55	51	...	21.1	21.8	23.3	20.2	...	3843
385	Professional goods	27	26	27	29	...	1.0	1.0	1.0	1.5	...	385
390	Other industries	84	95	95	99	...	6.6	7.6	7.9	8.6	...	390
3	Manufacturing	7942	8020	8027	8006	...	1011.8	1067.0	1119.8	1198.1	...	3
410	Electricity,gas,steam ..	27	27	27	27	27	...	...	...	...	...	410
4101	Electricity	18	18	18	18	18	...	...	...	...	...	4101
420	Water works and supply .	203	214	235	254	...	...	...	...	...	...	420
4	Electricity,gas etc	230	241	262	281	...	...	...	...	...	...	4
2-4	All industry	8246	8340	8381	8379	...	...	...	...	...	...	2-4

a/ Manufacturing: establishments with 20 or more persons engaged. b/ Manufacture of yarns and threads only.
c/ Including manufacture of motorcycles (ISIC 3844).

ISIC	INDUSTRY	3. AVERAGE NUMBER OF EMPLOYEES b/ (THOUSANDS)					4. WAGES AND SALARIES OF EMPLOYEES a/b/ (BILLION RUPIAHS)					ISIC
		1981	1982	1983	1984	1985	1981	1982	1983	1984	1985	
210	Coal mining	...	...	...	...	...	...	4	...	...	...	210
220	Petroleum and gas	...	...	...	...	...	...	160	...	...	...	220
230	Metal ore mining	...	...	...	...	...	...	81	...	...	...	230
290	Other mining	...	...	...	...	...	...	2	...	...	...	290
2	Mining, quarrying .	...	...	...	...	...	...	247	...	...	...	2
311/2	Food products	154.2	153.4	160.9	164.0	...	87	107	130	150	...	311/2
313	Beverages	7.3	7.3	8.2	8.5	...	9	9	12	14	...	313
314	Tobacco	157.0	160.4	167.2	167.0	...	39	58	73	86	...	314
321	Textiles	232.6	231.0	224.4	238.3	...	98	110	126	145	...	321
3211	Spinning,weaving etc.. c/	44.0	47.3	43.5	52.1	...	22	27	32	37	...	3211
322	Wearing apparel	20.0	23.9	29.2	35.7	...	8	12	17	25	...	322
323	Leather and products ...	2.8	2.9	3.1	3.2	...	1	2	2	3	...	323
324	Footwear	7.5	6.3	6.2	6.8	...	6	6	7	9	...	324
331	Wood products	65.5	91.0	112.5	165.9	...	38	72	94	118	...	331
332	Furniture, fixtures	5.1	5.3	5.6	5.4	...	2	3	4	4	...	332
341	Paper and products	13.2	14.4	14.2	13.7	...	11	13	14	15	...	341
3411	Pulp,paper etc.	9.0	10.6	10.7	9.0	...	8	10	10	11	...	3411
342	Printing,publishing	21.1	22.6	22.5	21.7	...	15	19	22	27	...	342
351	Industrial chemicals ...	16.6	20.5	20.8	23.0	...	22	33	43	50	...	351
3511	Basic excl fertilizers	5.2	7.6	7.2	8.9	...	4	6	9	11	...	3511
3513	Synthetic resins etc .	0.4	0.4	0.4	0.4	...	-	-	-	-	...	3513
352	Other chemical products.	45.5	49.4	52.1	52.6	...	45	63	76	86	...	352
3522	Drugs and medicines ..	21.6	22.3	25.0	26.4	...	25	34	43	54	...	3522
353	Petroleum refineries ...	.	.	.	.	...	.	.	.	.	...	353
354	Petroleum,coal products.	.	.	.	.	...	.	.	.	.	...	354
355	Rubber products	38.3	38.0	38.4	39.9	...	24	29	34	44	...	355
356	Plastic products n.e.c..	20.3	24.1	29.1	30.9	...	9	12	16	20	...	356
361	Pottery,china etc	7.4	8.2	9.4	10.3	...	4	5	6	7	...	361
362	Glass and products	9.5	10.2	10.1	9.7	...	9	12	14	15	...	362
369	Non-metal products n.e.c	32.9	34.2	36.0	35.0	...	24	31	37	43	...	369
371	Iron and steel	9.5	10.1	12.9	14.0	...	9	11	20	27	...	371
372	Non-ferrous metals	-	-	-	-	...	-	-	-	-	...	372
381	Metal products	43.8	44.1	45.0	42.8	...	28	35	42	44	...	381
382	Machinery n.e.c.	12.6	12.9	12.6	12.7	...	10	11	13	15	...	382
3825	Office,computing etc..	-	-	-	-	...	-	-	-	-	...	3825
383	Electrical machinery ...	38.8	36.9	37.2	36.6	...	29	34	40	47	...	383
3832	Radio,television etc..	16.1	15.3	15.4	14.7	...	11	11	15	15	...	3832
384	Transport equipment	35.9	44.4	46.0	42.8	...	38	57	69	73	...	384
3841	Shipbuilding, repair..	7.2	8.1	8.0	7.4	...	7	10	11	12	...	3841
3843	Motor vehicles .... d/	21.1	21.8	23.3	20.2	...	26	34	42	43	...	3843
385	Professional goods	1.0	0.9	1.0	1.4	...	-	-	-	1	...	385
390	Other industries	6.5	7.4	7.8	8.5	...	3	4	4	6	...	390
3	Manufacturing	1004.9	1059.8	1112.4	1190.4	...	568	748	915	1074	...	3
410	Electricity,gas,steam ..	29.4	39.8	37.2	40.4	...	49	52	80	91	...	410
4101	Electricity	28.6	38.9	36.4	39.5	...	48	51	79	89	...	4101
420	Water works and supply .	12.1	13.1	14.3	16.0	...	10	11	14	17	...	420
4	Electricity,gas etc	41.5	52.9	51.5	56.4	...	59	63	94	108	...	4
2-4	All industry	...	...	...	...	...	...	1058	...	...	...	2-4

a/ Including employers' contributions to pension and health insurance schemes.
b/ Manufacturing: establishments with 20 or more persons engaged. c/ Manufacture of yarns and threads only.
d/ Including manufacture of motorcycles (ISIC 3844).

ISIC	INDUSTRY	5. AVERAGE NUMBER OF OPERATIVES a/ (THOUSANDS)					6. QUANTITY OF ELECTRICITY CONSUMED a/ (MILLION KWH)					ISIC
		1981	1982	1983	1984	1985	1981	1982	1983	1984	1985	
210	Coal mining	...	2.0	...	...	...	...	32	...	...	...	210
220	Petroleum and gas	...	17.0	...	...	...	...	1195	...	...	...	220
230	Metal ore mining	...	23.0	...	...	...	...	1052	...	...	...	230
290	Other mining	...	1.0	...	...	...	...	9	...	...	...	290
2	Mining, quarrying .	...	43.0	...	...	...	...	2288	...	...	...	2
311/2	Food products	105.6	110.3	116.6	116.5	...	624	722	666	856	...	311/2
313	Beverages	4.8	4.8	5.3	5.3	...	31	26	32	37	...	313
314	Tobacco	140.4	147.5	151.0	149.9	...	48	44	55	59	...	314
321	Textiles	205.7	204.3	198.2	209.5	...	1327	1209	1147	4176	...	321
3211	Spinning,weaving etc.. b/	38.0	41.5	37.4	45.0	...	552	527	480	3300	...	3211
322	Wearing apparel	17.9	21.5	26.4	32.0	...	11	20	17	89	...	322
323	Leather and products ...	2.3	2.4	2.6	2.7	...	5	7	7	22	...	323
324	Footwear	6.4	5.3	5.1	5.6	...	10	10	12	21	...	324
331	Wood products	53.6	76.8	93.9	141.2	...	197	431	562	829	...	331
332	Furniture, fixtures	4.3	4.5	4.9	4.7	...	7	7	11	9	...	332
341	Paper and products	10.5	10.9	10.3	10.2	...	209	233	202	275	...	341
3411	Pulp,paper etc.	8.4	8.0	7.8	7.2	...	204	221	191	257	...	3411
342	Printing,publishing	16.6	17.4	17.4	16.7	...	40	45	44	51	....	342
351	Industrial chemicals ...	10.7	11.6	12.9	14.3	...	213	422	667	662	...	351
3511	Basic excl fertilizers	3.6	5.0	4.2	5.0	...	76	77	121	164	...	3511
3513	Synthetic resins etc .	0.2	0.3	0.3	0.3	...	1	1	1	2	...	3513
352	Other chemical products.	32.1	36.7	38.4	38.7	...	159	169	191	263	...	352
3522	Drugs and medicines ..	15.5	15.0	16.9	17.5	...	52	99	74	186	...	3522
353	Petroleum refineries ...	.	.	.	.	...	.	.	.	.	...	353
354	Petroleum,coal products.	.	.	.	.	...	.	.	.	.	...	354
355	Rubber products	33.1	32.8	32.2	33.0	...	245	250	180	2206	...	355
356	Plastic products n.e.c..	17.6	21.0	25.6	26.9	...	165	148	156	197	...	356
361	Pottery,china etc	6.6	7.2	8.3	9.2	...	21	74	36	39	...	361
362	Glass and products	7.6	8.4	8.1	7.6	...	67	87	74	131	...	362
369	Non-metal products n.e.c	26.2	27.8	28.9	27.6	...	543	746	973	1000	...	369
371	Iron and steel	7.0	7.4	9.6	9.6	...	202	217	336	1344	...	371
372	Non-ferrous metals	-	-	-	-	...	-	-	-	-	...	372
381	Metal products	37.1	36.7	37.8	35.5	...	155	189	171	173	...	381
382	Machinery n.e.c.	9.5	9.9	9.5	9.2	...	24	27	23	22	...	382
3825	Office,computing etc..	-	-	-	-	...	-	-	-	-	...	3825
383	Electrical machinery ...	31.7	29.5	30.4	29.4	...	99	124	123	123	...	383
3832	Radio,television etc..	13.2	12.5	12.6	11.8	...	27	22	26	24	...	3832
384	Transport equipment	28.2	34.0	34.1	32.4	...	107	166	124	134	...	384
3841	Shipbuilding, repair..	5.2	5.9	5.6	5.7	...	17	39	25	22	...	3841
3843	Motor vehicles .... c/	16.6	17.0	17.3	15.3	...	77	104	78	89	...	3843
385	Professional goods	0.8	0.8	0.8	1.3	...	1	1	1	1	...	385
390	Other industries	5.8	6.7	7.1	7.6	...	4	8	11	21	...	390
3	Manufacturing	822.1	876.2	915.4	976.6	...	4514	5382	5821	12740	...	3
410	Electricity,gas,steam ..	17.9	25.3	20.6	24.5	...	2	2	2	2	...	410
4101	Electricity	17.4	24.9	20.2	24.1	...	.	.	.	.	...	4101
420	Water works and supply .	6.3	6.9	7.3	7.7	...	97	132	160	163	...	420
4	Electricity,gas etc	24.2	32.2	27.9	32.2	...	99	134	162	165	...	4
2-4	All industry	...	951.4	...	...	...	...	7804	...	...	...	2-4

a/ Manufacturing: establishments with 20 or more persons engaged. b/ Manufacture of yarns and threads only.
c/ Including manufacture of motorcycles (ISIC 3844).

ISIC	INDUSTRY	7. OUTPUT IN PRODUCERS' PRICES c/ (BILLION RUPIAHS) 1981	1982	1983	1984	1985	8. VALUE ADDED IN FACTOR VALUES a/b/c/ (BILLION RUPIAHS) 1981	1982	1983	1984	1985	ISIC
210	Coal mining	7	9	...	...	...	4	5	...	...	...	210
220	Petroleum and gas	...	11687	...	...	...	...	10841	...	...	...	220
230	Metal ore mining	507	429	...	...	...	299	258	...	...	...	230
290	Other mining	16	27	...	...	...	13	21	...	...	...	290
2	Mining, quarrying .	...	12152	...	...	...	...	11125	...	...	...	2
311/2	Food products	1257	1416	1812	2140	...	342	352	403	478	...	311/2
313	Beverages	97	125	157	178	...	39	53	78	79	...	313
314	Tobacco	1548	1720	1974	2396	...	474	499	565	712	...	314
321	Textiles	939	1005	1139	1660	...	288	339	349	566	...	321
3211	Spinning,weaving etc.. d/	306	312	366	524	...	86	92	108	164	...	3211
322	Wearing apparel	49	79	115	169	...	16	32	44	71	...	322
323	Leather and products ...	21	24	28	46	...	5	8	10	17	...	323
324	Footwear	32	34	46	57	...	10	12	22	24	...	324
331	Wood products	503	690	882	1101	...	201	243	290	313	...	331
332	Furniture, fixtures	10	12	16	19	...	4	5	6	7	...	332
341	Paper and products	111	136	130	179	...	20	30	25	40	...	341
3411	Pulp,paper etc.	89	104	160	139	...	16	20	19	32	...	3411
342	Printing,publishing	94	114	132	147	...	36	46	48	59	...	342
351	Industrial chemicals ...	433	509	601	733	...	189	209	206	249	...	351
3511	Basic excl fertilizers	47	55	88	116	...	17	17	29	37	...	3511
3513	Synthetic resins etc .	3	3	3	4	...	1	1	1	1	...	3513
352	Other chemical products.	464	544	630	721	...	168	188	194	275	...	352
3522	Drugs and medicines ..	200	219	270	323	...	83	77	83	109	...	3522
353	Petroleum refineries ...	.	.	.	.	...	.	.	.	.	...	353
354	Petroleum,coal products.	.	.	.	.	...	.	.	.	.	...	354
355	Rubber products	507	401	664	829	...	91	92	123	133	...	355
356	Plastic products n.e.c..	100	113	152	237	...	18	24	37	67	...	356
361	Pottery,china etc	15	24	30	37	...	7	9	12	14	...	361
362	Glass and products	78	88	113	123	...	43	39	45	48	...	362
369	Non-metal products n.e.c	270	322	433	477	...	141	136	161	177	...	369
371	Iron and steel	249	276	613	980	...	79	68	201	493	...	371
372	Non-ferrous metals	-	-	-	-	...	-	-	-	-	...	372
381	Metal products	339	462	521	629	...	86	135	154	175	...	381
382	Machinery n.e.c.	110	124	124	144	...	43	52	49	61	...	382
3825	Office,computing etc..	-	-	-	-	...	-	-	-	-	...	3825
383	Electrical machinery ...	443	509	564	706	...	126	161	134	150	...	383
3832	Radio,television etc..	230	227	231	268	...	46	54	54	56	...	3832
384	Transport equipment	605	747	745	838	...	278	227	213	248	...	384
3841	Shipbuilding, repair..	44	63	97	65	...	27	27	50	34	...	3841
3843	Motor vehicles .... e/	527	596	559	656	...	239	170	138	171	...	3843
385	Professional goods	2	3	3	4	...	1	1	1	2	...	385
390	Other industries	22	28	33	64	...	8	10	9	16	...	390
3	Manufacturing	8298	9505	11657	14614	...	2713	2970	3379	4474	...	3
410	Electricity,gas,steam ..	313	474	751	1093	...	154	160	209	226	...	410
4101	Electricity	310	469	742	1080	...	152	157	203	220	...	4101
420	Water works and supply .	34	39	55	84	...	22	25	34	54	...	420
4	Electricity,gas etc	347	513	806	1177	...	176	185	243	280	...	4
2-4	All industry	...	22170	...	...	...	...	14280	...	...	...	2-4

a/ Net of non-industrial costs.
b/ Electricity, gas and water supply: in producers' prices.
c/ Manufacturing: establishments with 20 or more persons engaged.
d/ Manufacture of yarns and threads only.
e/ Including manufacture of motorcycles (ISIC 3844).

9. GROSS FIXED CAPITAL FORMATION
TOTAL a/b/
(BILLION RUPIAHS)

ISIC	INDUSTRY	1981	1982	1983	1984	1985	ISIC
210	Coal mining	-	5	...	...	...	210
220	Petroleum and gas	...	183	...	...	...	220
230	Metal ore mining	23	42	...	...	...	230
290	Other mining	-	11	...	...	...	290
2	Mining, quarrying .	...	241	...	...	...	2
311/2	Food products	45	82	107	159	...	311/2
313	Beverages	4	16	20	29	...	313
314	Tobacco	13	39	36	40	...	314
321	Textiles	106	119	182	171	...	321
3211	Spinning,weaving etc.. c/	31	43	78	86	...	3211
322	Wearing apparel	5	7	10	11	...	322
323	Leather and products ...	2	2	2	2	...	323
324	Footwear	3	3	5	4	...	324
331	Wood products	44	122	111	241	...	331
332	Furniture, fixtures	1	1	3	3	...	332
341	Paper and products	51	23	9	155	...	341
3411	Pulp,paper etc.	50	21	6	140	...	3411
342	Printing,publishing	12	16	27	21	...	342
351	Industrial chemicals ...	20	30	70	28	...	351
3511	Basic excl fertilizers	8	14	50	13	...	3511
3513	Synthetic resins etc .	-	-	-	-	...	3513
352	Other chemical products.	34	54	54	40	...	352
3522	Drugs and medicines ..	13	24	31	19	...	3522
353	Petroleum refineries ...	.	.	.	.	...	353
354	Petroleum,coal products.	.	.	.	.	...	354
355	Rubber products	34	85	64	43	...	355
356	Plastic products n.e.c..	12	14	22	20	...	356
361	Pottery,china etc	9	16	31	25	...	361
362	Glass and products	31	10	4	7	...	362
369	Non-metal products n.e.c	66	172	149	35	...	369
371	Iron and steel	5	33	86	40	...	371
372	Non-ferrous metals	-	-	-	-	...	372
381	Metal products	18	45	41	36	...	381
382	Machinery n.e.c.	10	7	10	11	...	382
3825	Office,computing etc..	-	-	-	-	...	3825
383	Electrical machinery ...	24	29	39	53	...	383
3832	Radio,television etc..	9	9	13	12	...	3832
384	Transport equipment	24	94	111	86	...	384
3841	Shipbuilding, repair..	2	10	16	13	...	3841
3843	Motor vehicles .... d/	13	41	48	43	...	3843
385	Professional goods	-	-	1	-	...	385
390	Other industries	-	2	5	1	...	390
3	Manufacturing	573	1021	1199	1261	...	3
410	Electricity,gas,steam ..	293	220	214	302	...	410
4101	Electricity	291	220	214	301	...	4101
420	Water works and supply .	15	17	28	19	...	420
4	Electricity,gas etc	308	237	242	321	...	4
2-4	All industry	...	1499	...	...	...	2-4

a/ The value of sales is not deducted.
b/ Manufacturing: establishments with 20 or more persons engaged.
c/ Manufacture of yarns and threads only.
d/ Including manufacture of motorcycles (ISIC 3844).

10. INDEX NUMBERS OF INDUSTRIAL PRODUCTION (1980 = 100)

ISIC	INDUSTRY	1976	1977	1978	1979	1981	1982	1983	1984	1985	RATE a/	ISIC
210	Coal mining	...	...	...	...	...	...	...	...	...	...	210
220	Petroleum and gas	...	...	...	...	...	...	...	...	...	...	220
230	Metal ore mining	...	...	...	...	...	...	...	...	...	...	230
290	Other mining	...	...	...	...	...	...	...	...	...	...	290
2	Mining, quarrying	95	106	102	100	102	85	84	91	84	-1.4	2
311/2	Food products	63	74	74	86	98	102	111	94	88	3.8	311/2
313	Beverages	73	80	81	92	114	132	111	83	92	2.6	313
314	Tobacco	71	82	82	83	115	117	124	138	151	8.7	314
321	Textiles	89	87	92	96	107	102	96	100	98	1.1	321
3211	Spinning,weaving etc.	89	86	91	96	107	102	97	105	93	0.5	3211
322	Wearing apparel	...	...	...	...	...	...	...	...	...	...	322
323	Leather and products	...	...	...	...	...	...	...	...	...	...	323
324	Footwear	88	88	92	86	95	95	118	138	133	4.7	324
331	Wood products	30	50	56	56	120	108	112	107	99	14.2	331
332	Furniture, fixtures	...	...	...	...	...	...	...	...	...	...	332
341	Paper and products	64	70	88	99	99	97	84	107	119	7.1	341
3411	Pulp,paper etc.	...	...	...	...	...	...	...	...	...	...	3411
342	Printing,publishing	...	...	...	...	...	...	...	...	...	...	342
351	Industrial chemicals	34	46	60	79	104	105	116	141	164	19.1	351
3511	Basic excl fertilizers	76	76	68	97	99	102	103	115	117	4.9	3511
3513	Synthetic resins etc	...	...	...	...	...	...	...	...	...	...	3513
352	Other chemical products.	81	78	85	84	134	144	132	147	160	7.9	352
3522	Drugs and medicines	...	...	...	...	...	...	...	...	...	...	3522
353	Petroleum refineries	...	...	...	...	...	...	...	...	...	...	353
354	Petroleum,coal products.	...	...	...	...	...	...	...	...	...	...	354
355	Rubber products	53	65	79	88	117	114	117	117	121	9.6	355
356	Plastic products n.e.c.	...	...	...	...	...	...	...	...	...	...	356
361	Pottery,china etc	...	...	...	...	...	...	...	...	...	...	361
362	Glass and products	45	67	77	82	124	100	109	119	121	11.6	362
369	Non-metal products n.e.c	34	48	70	86	108	114	125	168	187	20.9	369
371	Iron and steel	13	14	17	43	121	94	111	113	112	27.0	371
372	Non-ferrous metals	...	...	...	...	...	...	...	...	...	...	372
381	Metal products	63	77	90	90	109	114	118	115	124	7.8	381
382	Machinery n.e.c.	...	...	...	...	...	...	...	...	...	...	382
3825	Office,computing etc.	...	...	...	...	...	...	...	...	...	...	3825
383	Electrical machinery	40	56	69	70	102	102	112	95	89	9.3	383
3832	Radio,television etc.	37	53	68	68	102	98	103	82	72	7.7	3832
384	Transport equipment	75	66	77	65	140	158	113	83	89	1.9	384
3841	Shipbuilding, repair.	...	...	...	...	...	...	...	...	...	...	3841
3843	Motor vehicles	56	63	70	60	132	116	102	92	95	6.0	3843
385	Professional goods	...	...	...	...	...	...	...	...	...	...	385
390	Other industries	...	...	...	...	...	...	...	...	...	...	390
3	Manufacturing	56	64	75	81	109	110	113	123	133	10.1	3
410	Electricity,gas,steam	...	...	...	...	...	...	...	...	...	...	410
4101	Electricity	...	...	...	...	...	...	...	...	...	...	4101
420	Water works and supply	...	...	...	...	...	...	...	...	...	...	420
4	Electricity,gas etc	...	...	...	...	...	...	...	...	...	...	4
2-4	All industry	...	...	...	...	...	...	...	...	...	...	2-4

a/ Annual growth rate 1976-1985.

IRAN (ISLAMIC REPUBLIC OF)

The information in the tables, except for the indexes, is based on the reply to the United Nations Questionnaire on General Industrial Statistics from the Statistical Centre of Iran, Plan and Budget Organization, Teheran. The concepts, definitions and classification by branches of industry are generally in accordance with United Nations standards.

The data in the tables are derived from the annual survey of industrial establishments conducted by field enumeration by the Statistics Division, Ministry of Industry and Mines, Teheran. The survey covers establishments with 10 or more persons engaged on a complete enumeration basis. The industrial establishment is defined as a place where an accumulation of capital and manpower is invested for producing one or more products under a single management and accounting system. The period of reference of the data is the Iranian year beginning 21 March of the year indicated. The data in the tables are based on the national classification, which is comparable with the present version of ISIC.

The number of establishments relates to those in operation during the reference year. Employment numbers relate to averages of quarterly counts. Wages and salaries include employers' contributions to social insurance schemes and also the establishments' 20 per cent special net profit which is distributed among workers.

Output is the sum of the value of products, electricity and water sold, contract work done for others, goods shipped in the same condition as received, work in progress and own-account construction. Value added is the difference between the value of output and the cost of materials and supplies, fuels, electricity and water, value of contract and repair work done by others and the cost of goods purchased for resale without transformation.

The estimates of gross fixed capital formation represent the value of purchases of new and used fixed assets, capital repairs and own-account construction during the year less the value of corresponding sales and disposals. The estimates do not cover new establishments not yet in operation during the reference year and also do not include progress payments made for fixed assets on order but not yet completed at the end of the reference year.

The indexes of industrial production are compiled by the Statistics Division, Ministry of Industry and Mines. The indexes provided by the national authorities are compiled according to the preceding version of ISIC. Wherever possible, adjustments have been incorporated to convert the data to the present version; owing to lack of detail, the conversion is not complete for all industries.

Related national publication:

Large-scale Industrial Establishments (annual), available only in the national language), published by the Statistical Centre of Iran, Teheran.

ISIC	INDUSTRY	1. NUMBER OF ESTABLISHMENTS a/b/ (NUMBER)					2. AVERAGE NUMBER OF EMPLOYEES a/b/ (THOUSANDS)					ISIC
		1981	1982	1983	1984	1985	1981	1982	1983	1984	1985	
210	Coal mining	...	...	...	...	...	...	...	...	...	...	210
220	Petroleum and gas	...	...	...	...	...	...	...	...	...	...	220
230	Metal ore mining	...	...	...	...	...	...	...	...	...	...	230
290	Other mining	...	...	...	...	...	...	...	...	...	...	290
2	Mining, quarrying .	...	...	...	...	...	...	...	...	...	...	2
311/2	Food products	842	966	939	922	...	58.10	67.33	69.86	69.80	...	311/2
313	Beverages	26	30	30	30	...	9.64	10.31	11.13	10.81	...	313
314	Tobacco	1	1	1	1	...	7.58	7.38	7.33	7.52	...	314
321	Textiles	795	810	804	790	...	116.09	125.41	120.22	124.77	...	321
3211	Spinning,weaving etc..	...	...	480	473	...	...	...	104.33	106.58	...	3211
322	Wearing apparel	232	207	196	192	...	5.21	5.10	5.53	5.43	...	322
323	Leather and products ...	118	111	109	107	...	3.83	4.22	4.86	4.11	...	323
324	Footwear	261	95	91	87	...	10.74	9.61	10.49	10.78	...	324
331	Wood products	141	122	119	117	...	4.81	9.85	10.87	10.76	...	331
332	Furniture, fixtures	198	77	72	71	...	3.87	3.72	3.02	3.04	...	332
341	Paper and products	83	101	103	100	...	9.67	8.71	10.16	10.35	...	341
3411	Pulp,paper etc.	...	...	16	15	...	...	...	0.62	0.68	...	3411
342	Printing,publishing	202	135	134	133	...	6.53	6.09	5.53	5.53	...	342
351	Industrial chemicals ...	49	62	61	61	...	3.16	9.23	6.63	9.86	...	351
3511	Basic excl fertilizers	...	...	48	47	...	...	...	1.96	2.07	...	3511
3513	Synthetic resins etc .	...	...	3	4	...	...	...	2.75	3.32	...	3513
352	Other chemical products.	136	167	166	159	...	15.96	16.58	18.47	18.78	...	352
3522	Drugs and medicines ..	...	...	40	40	...	...	...	8.24	8.28	...	3522
353	Petroleum refineries ...	12	7	7	7	...	5.53	1.40	1.49	1.50	...	353
354	Petroleum,coal products.	20	24	23	25	...	0.58	0.91	0.74	0.80	...	354
355	Rubber products	36	40	39	39	...	6.30	7.07	8.21	8.20	...	355
356	Plastic products n.e.c..	273	252	249	237	...	12.62	11.43	12.75	12.95	...	356
361	Pottery,china etc	17	17	17	16	...	2.68	3.43	3.55	4.96	...	361
362	Glass and products	64	59	58	49	...	6.25	6.25	7.71	7.29	...	362
369	Non-metal products n.e.c	2672	2582	2494	2406	...	70.42	88.84	86.17	84.78	...	369
371	Iron and steel	26	26	26	27	...	19.27	22.20	27.78	33.31	...	371
372	Non-ferrous metals	33	43	45	45	...	3.64	4.33	4.79	5.89	...	372
381	Metal products	513	486	474	464	...	22.02	24.41	25.35	26.24	...	381
382	Machinery n.e.c.	149	226	229	221	...	21.49	24.18	28.10	32.54	...	382
3825	Office,computing etc..	...	...	...	...	...	...	...	...	...	...	3825
383	Electrical machinery ...	111	145	144	144	...	25.13	28.17	31.55	34.42	...	383
3832	Radio,television etc..	...	...	23	23	...	...	...	...	8.01	...	3832
384	Transport equipment	73	97	96	96	...	32.82	36.00	41.44	45.50	...	384
3841	Shipbuilding, repair..	...	...	11	11	...	...	...	1.42	1.48	...	3841
3843	Motor vehicles	...	...	74	73	...	...	...	37.61	40.30	...	3843
385	Professional goods	12	19	19	19	...	1.68	1.97	2.15	2.32	...	385
390	Other industries	36	31	30	31	...	0.80	0.97	1.16	1.19	...	390
3	Manufacturing	7131	6938	6775	6596	...	486.42	545.10	567.04	593.43	...	3
410	Electricity,gas,steam ..	...	...	...	...	...	...	...	...	...	...	410
4101	Electricity	...	...	...	...	...	...	...	...	...	...	4101
420	Water works and supply .	...	...	...	...	...	...	...	...	...	...	420
4	Electricity,gas etc	...	...	...	...	...	...	...	...	...	...	4
2-4	All industry	...	...	...	...	...	...	...	...	...	...	2-4

a/ Twelve months beginning 21 March of the year indicated. b/ Establishments with 10 or more persons engaged.

ISIC	INDUSTRY	3. WAGES AND SALARIES OF EMPLOYEES a/b/c/ (MILLION RIALS)					4. AVERAGE NUMBER OF OPERATIVES b/c/ (THOUSANDS)					ISIC
		1981	1982	1983	1984	1985	1981	1982	1983	1984	1985	
210	Coal mining	...	...	...	...	...	...	...	...	...	...	210
220	Petroleum and gas	...	...	...	...	...	...	...	...	...	...	220
230	Metal ore mining	...	...	...	...	...	...	...	...	...	...	230
290	Other mining	...	...	...	...	...	...	...	...	...	...	290
2	Mining, quarrying	...	...	...	...	...	...	...	...	...	...	2
311/2	Food products	39313	48388	55810	60284	...	50.20	58.26	60.84	60.67	...	311/2
313	Beverages	7949	8909	9706	10045	...	8.80	9.45	10.18	9.82	...	313
314	Tobacco	5574	6906	8258	8381	...	3.78	3.58	3.53	3.73	...	314
321	Textiles	80686	91536	103029	116198	...	107.39	111.71	113.56	117.31	...	321
3211	Spinning,weaving etc.	...	...	89359	99724	...	...	...	98.23	100.38	...	3211
322	Wearing apparel	2312	2584	3313	3618	...	4.83	4.67	5.13	5.03	...	322
323	Leather and products	2613	2868	3767	3447	...	3.41	3.71	4.15	3.53	...	323
324	Footwear	7233	6467	7755	8629	...	9.82	8.79	9.40	9.67	...	324
331	Wood products	2872	7152	8353	8806	...	4.37	8.66	9.39	9.05	...	331
332	Furniture, fixtures	2126	2457	2630	2607	...	3.58	3.39	2.69	2.73	...	332
341	Paper and products	7973	7522	10236	11590	...	8.06	7.33	8.32	8.55	...	341
3411	Pulp,paper etc.	...	...	577	679	...	...	...	0.55	0.62	...	3411
342	Printing,publishing	4132	5285	5348	5399	...	5.50	4.74	4.32	3.94	...	342
351	Industrial chemicals	2906	10029	7249	12118	...	2.23	6.61	4.77	6.63	...	351
3511	Basic excl fertilizers	...	...	1900	2338	...	...	...	1.42	1.57	...	3511
3513	Synthetic resins etc	...	...	3430	4015	...	...	...	2.16	2.07	...	3513
352	Other chemical products.	13049	14379	17040	19285	...	12.83	13.19	14.71	15.04	...	352
3522	Drugs and medicines	...	...	7073	7866	...	...	...	6.23	6.44	...	3522
353	Petroleum refineries	7085	1424	1633	1935	...	3.04	1.04	1.06	1.04	...	353
354	Petroleum,coal products.	354	671	568	584	...	0.49	0.75	0.66	0.73	...	354
355	Rubber products	5247	6871	8651	9131	...	5.11	5.63	6.62	6.49	...	355
356	Plastic products n.e.c.	8811	8066	10427	11544	...	11.44	10.26	11.27	11.43	...	356
361	Pottery,china etc	1987	2595	3199	3510	...	2.32	2.97	3.04	4.41	...	361
362	Glass and products	5078	5737	7607	7572	...	5.66	5.72	6.63	6.78	...	362
369	Non-metal products n.e.c	44068	57553	67238	72505	...	65.09	82.60	80.52	79.09	...	369
371	Iron and steel	16576	19980	26185	34122	...	17.53	20.08	25.02	28.55	...	371
372	Non-ferrous metals	2635	3679	4321	5242	...	2.90	3.68	4.03	4.89	...	372
381	Metal products	15298	18616	21976	24718	...	19.41	21.24	22.00	22.86	...	381
382	Machinery n.e.c.	16702	19114	24491	29684	...	17.17	19.29	22.53	25.89	...	382
3825	Office,computing etc.	...	...	...	...	...	...	...	...	...	...	3825
383	Electrical machinery	20807	23298	30041	34114	...	21.14	23.78	26.26	29.20	...	383
3832	Radio,television etc.	...	...	6848	7375	...	...	...	5.57	6.40	...	3832
384	Transport equipment	27674	32007	45449	52989	...	27.95	30.93	35.04	38.47	...	384
3841	Shipbuilding, repair.	...	...	1308	1328	...	...	...	1.31	1.36	...	3841
3843	Motor vehicles	...	...	42220	48094	...	...	...	32.31	34.45	...	3843
385	Professional goods	1425	1776	2293	2532	...	1.47	1.74	1.81	2.05	...	385
390	Other industries	406	562	784	743	...	0.74	0.88	1.04	1.08	...	390
3	Manufacturing	352891	416431	497357	561332	...	426.26	474.68	498.52	518.66	...	3
410	Electricity,gas,steam	...	...	...	...	...	...	...	...	...	...	410
4101	Electricity	...	...	...	...	...	...	...	...	...	...	4101
420	Water works and supply	...	...	...	...	...	...	...	...	...	...	420
4	Electricity,gas etc	...	...	...	...	...	...	...	...	...	...	4
2-4	All industry	...	...	...	...	...	...	...	...	...	...	2-4

a/ Including employers' contributions to insurance schemes. b/ Twelve months beginning 21 March of the year indicated.
c/ Establishments with 10 or more persons engaged.

ISIC	INDUSTRY	5. WAGES AND SALARIES OF OPERATIVES a/b/c/ (MILLION RIALS)					6. OUTPUT IN PRODUCERS' PRICES b/c/ (BILLION RIALS)					ISIC
		1981	1982	1983	1984	1985	1981	1982	1983	1984	1985	
210	Coal mining	...	...	...	...	...	...	...	...	...	...	210
220	Petroleum and gas	...	...	...	...	...	...	...	...	...	...	220
230	Metal ore mining	...	...	...	...	...	...	...	...	...	...	230
290	Other mining	...	...	...	...	...	...	...	...	...	...	290
2	Mining, quarrying	...	...	...	...	...	...	...	...	...	...	2
311/2	Food products	31849	39906	47079	50906	...	227.3	304.2	316.8	300.3	...	311/2
313	Beverages	7064	8016	8614	8930	...	24.3	28.3	26.9	36.7	...	313
314	Tobacco	3963	4272	5150	5196	...	22.2	24.7	28.6	15.6	...	314
321	Textiles	72596	83693	94959	107249	...	253.4	305.1	340.9	362.8	...	321
3211	Spinning,weaving etc.	...	...	82482	92190	...	...	...	275.0	290.2	...	3211
322	Wearing apparel	2055	2290	3001	3215	...	8.1	9.6	12.0	14.0	...	322
323	Leather and products	2133	2331	3063	2752	...	19.3	19.4	19.2	22.6	...	323
324	Footwear	6234	5679	6753	7439	...	20.9	23.0	28.9	30.6	...	324
331	Wood products	2521	6012	6683	6796	...	9.6	16.9	17.4	20.2	...	331
332	Furniture, fixtures	1902	2155	2277	2246	...	7.0	7.4	8.6	8.0	...	332
341	Paper and products	6166	5829	7957	8960	...	26.7	36.2	43.4	46.6	...	341
3411	Pulp,paper etc.	...	...	502	593	...	...	...	2.3	2.7	...	3411
342	Printing,publishing	3333	3975	3960	3717	...	15.2	15.8	16.7	15.5	...	342
351	Industrial chemicals	1879	6359	4887	7444	...	9.7	24.0	31.4	39.6	...	351
3511	Basic excl fertilizers	...	...	1294	1607	...	...	...	9.8	13.1	...	3511
3513	Synthetic resins etc	...	...	2440	2395	...	...	...	15.2	18.8	...	3513
352	Other chemical products.	9328	10410	12687	14464	...	61.0	76.0	100.1	110.8	...	352
3522	Drugs and medicines	...	...	4952	5702	...	...	...	36.0	43.6	...	3522
353	Petroleum refineries	3236	840	1022	1177	...	207.9	8.0	10.2	11.3	...	353
354	Petroleum,coal products.	279	500	502	531	...	1.5	2.7	2.6	2.4	...	354
355	Rubber products	3822	4972	6405	6588	...	18.3	24.1	28.6	28.9	...	355
356	Plastic products n.e.c.	7559	6978	8926	9761	...	45.5	42.2	55.8	53.7	...	356
361	Pottery,china etc	1611	2049	2603	2881	...	4.4	5.9	7.2	7.7	...	361
362	Glass and products	4362	5059	6783	6841	...	14.1	18.3	22.2	25.6	...	362
369	Non-metal products n.e.c	39350	52054	61399	65664	...	116.1	139.2	161.0	173.9	...	369
371	Iron and steel	15051	17838	23226	28892	...	61.1	99.1	119.2	157.9	...	371
372	Non-ferrous metals	1963	2961	3387	4180	...	18.8	18.9	28.5	39.8	...	372
381	Metal products	12806	15586	18435	20841	...	55.9	74.4	84.7	92.1	...	381
382	Machinery n.e.c.	12124	13879	18588	23127	...	63.2	77.0	111.6	153.9	...	382
3825	Office,computing etc.	...	...	...	...	...	...	...	...	...	...	3825
383	Electrical machinery	16324	18231	23349	27352	...	72.7	94.7	119.9	125.5	...	383
3832	Radio,television etc.	...	...	4952	5284	...	...	...	30.4	30.2	...	3832
384	Transport equipment	22927	26701	38055	41748	...	119.8	140.8	200.5	243.2	...	384
3841	Shipbuilding, repair.	...	...	1112	1124	...	...	...	2.3	2.9	...	3841
3843	Motor vehicles	...	...	35913	38163	...	...	...	185.1	224.9	...	3843
385	Professional goods	1129	1448	1885	2064	...	4.2	5.4	6.6	8.6	...	385
390	Other industries	366	486	652	647	...	1.6	2.4	3.6	3.9	...	390
3	Manufacturing	293932	350509	422287	471608	...	1509.8	1643.7	1953.1	2151.7	...	3
410	Electricity,gas,steam	...	...	...	...	...	...	...	...	...	...	410
4101	Electricity	...	...	...	...	...	...	...	...	...	...	4101
420	Water works and supply	...	...	...	...	...	...	...	...	...	...	420
4	Electricity,gas etc	...	...	...	...	...	...	...	...	...	...	4
2-4	All industry	...	...	...	...	...	...	...	...	...	...	2-4

a/ Including employers' contributions to insurance schemes. b/ Twelve months beginning 21 March of the year indicated.
c/ Establishments with 10 or more persons engaged.

7. VALUE ADDED IN PRODUCERS' PRICES a/b/ (BILLION RIALS)

ISIC	INDUSTRY	1981	1982	1983	1984	1985	ISIC
210	Coal mining	...	...	...	..	...	210
220	Petroleum and gas	...	...	...	..	...	220
230	Metal ore mining	...	...	...	...	...	230
290	Other mining	...	...	...	...	...	290
2	Mining, quarrying	...	...	...	...	...	2
311/2	Food products	79.5	89.5	95.6	101.1	...	311/2
313	Beverages	14.7	19.2	16.0	22.0	...	313
314	Tobacco	17.6	19.9	23.9	...	...	314
321	Textiles	131.5	171.6	184.8	191.0	...	321
3211	Spinning,weaving etc.	...	...	153.8	155.1	...	3211
322	Wearing apparel	4.6	4.7	5.8	6.9	...	322
323	Leather and products	6.0	5.3	6.0	6.7	...	323
324	Footwear	10.5	11.2	15.4	15.1	...	324
331	Wood products	4.4	8.3	9.0	10.8	...	331
332	Furniture, fixtures	3.4	4.6	4.7	4.0	...	332
341	Paper and products	11.3	16.2	20.8	22.7	...	341
3411	Pulp,paper etc.	...	...	1.1	1.3	...	3411
342	Printing,publishing	7.3	8.3	7.9	9.1	...	342
351	Industrial chemicals	5.4	11.0	14.9	20.1	...	351
3511	Basic excl fertilizers	...	...	4.0	7.0	...	3511
3513	Synthetic resins etc	...	...	7.3	9.6	...	3513
352	Other chemical products.	26.4	34.6	46.0	55.7	...	352
3522	Drugs and medicines	...	...	21.0	27.4	...	3522
353	Petroleum refineries	169.9	3.6	4.5	5.8	...	353
354	Petroleum,coal products.	0.8	1.4	1.3	1.1	...	354
355	Rubber products	9.1	12.2	16.0	15.9	...	355
356	Plastic products n.e.c.	19.5	18.5	24.7	24.5	...	356
361	Pottery,china etc	3.3	4.7	5.6	5.8	...	361
362	Glass and products	9.0	12.2	14.4	17.0	...	362
369	Non-metal products n.e.c	81.1	96.8	111.1	116.7	...	369
371	Iron and steel	21.1	26.1	33.7	58.6	...	371
372	Non-ferrous metals	10.4	7.5	11.9	18.0	...	372
381	Metal products	25.3	37.0	44.0	47.9	...	381
382	Machinery n.e.c.	24.9	32.4	49.1	64.0	...	382
3825	Office,computing etc.	...	...	...	...	...	3825
383	Electrical machinery	35.7	49.8	61.9	66.0	...	383
3832	Radio,television etc.	...	...	19.5	18.7	...	3832
384	Transport equipment	47.0	59.5	81.5	97.9	...	384
3841	Shipbuilding, repair.	...	...	1.6	1.9	...	3841
3843	Motor vehicles	...	...	76.3	91.7	...	3843
385	Professional goods	2.6	3.4	4.0	5.5	...	385
390	Other industries	0.7	1.2	2.0	2.3	...	390
3	Manufacturing	783.0	770.7	916.5	c/ 1012.2	...	3
410	Electricity,gas,steam	...	...	...	...	...	410
4101	Electricity	...	...	...	...	...	4101
420	Water works and supply	...	...	...	...	...	420
4	Electricity,gas etc	...	...	...	...	...	4
2-4	All industry	...	...	...	...	...	2-4

a/ Twelve months beginning 21 March of the year indicated. b/ Establishments with 10 or more persons engaged.
c/ Excluding major group 314.

8. INDEX NUMBERS OF INDUSTRIAL PRODUCTION (1980 = 100) a/

ISIC	INDUSTRY	1976	1977	1978	1979	1981	1982	1983	1984	1985	b/ RATE	ISIC
210	Coal mining	...	...	...	...	...	...	...	...	...	...	210
220	Petroleum and gas	...	...	...	...	...	...	...	...	...	...	220
230	Metal ore mining	...	...	...	...	...	...	...	...	...	...	230
290	Other mining	...	...	...	...	...	...	...	...	...	...	290
2	Mining, quarrying .	...	...	...	...	...	...	...	...	...	...	2
311/2	Food products	115	119	117	109	101	104	120	122	126	1.0	311/2
313	Beverages	90	111	129	97	103	90	108	102	111	2.4	313
314	Tobacco	...	...	...	...	...	...	...	...	...	...	314
321	Textiles	76	81	91	82	112	126	154	146	148	7.7	321
3211	Spinning,weaving etc..	...	...	...	...	...	...	...	...	...	...	3211
322	Wearing apparel .... c/	92	82	92	81	114	126	155	186	182	7.9	322
323	Leather and products ...	101	109	121	104	116	125	136	181	197	7.7	323
324	Footwear .... c/	...	...	...	...	...	...	...	...	...	...	324
331	Wood products	[74	82	100	84	103	142	180	160	156	8.6]	331
332	Furniture, fixtures											332
341	Paper and products	...	...	...	...	...	...	...	...	...	...	341
3411	Pulp,paper etc.	...	...	...	...	...	...	...	...	...	...	3411
342	Printing,publishing	...	...	...	...	...	...	...	...	...	...	342
351	Industrial chemicals ... d/	66	122	121	82	82	98	131	140	141	8.8	351
3511	Basic excl fertilizers	...	...	...	...	...	...	...	...	...	...	3511
3513	Synthetic resins etc .	...	...	...	...	...	...	...	...	...	...	3513
352	Other chemical products. d/	...	...	...	...	...	...	...	...	...	...	352
3522	Drugs and medicines ..	...	...	...	...	...	...	...	...	...	...	3522
353	Petroleum refineries ...	...	...	...	...	...	...	...	...	...	...	353
354	Petroleum,coal products.	...	...	...	...	...	...	...	...	...	...	354
355	Rubber products	73	122	134	100	108	127	169	147	145	7.9	355
356	Plastic products n.e.c..	...	...	...	...	...	...	...	...	...	...	356
361	Pottery,china etc											361
362	Glass and products	[81	84	96	82	106	125	137	141	145	6.7]	362
369	Non-metal products n.e.c											369
371	Iron and steel	...	...	...	...	...	...	...	...	...	...	371
372	Non-ferrous metals	...	...	...	...	...	...	...	...	...	...	372
381	Metal products	130	128	146	91	107	117	139	133	123	-0.6	381
382	Machinery n.e.c.	140	147	146	94	123	158	196	271	250	6.7	382
3825	Office,computing etc..	...	...	...	...	...	...	...	...	...	...	3825
383	Electrical machinery ...	116	106	137	88	114	124	161	168	152	3.0	383
3832	Radio,television etc..	...	...	...	...	...	...	...	...	...	...	3832
384	Transport equipment	188	174	183	78	109	117	164	194	175	-0.8	384
3841	Shipbuilding, repair..	...	...	...	...	...	...	...	...	...	...	3841
3843	Motor vehicles	...	...	...	...	...	...	...	...	...	...	3843
385	Professional goods	...	...	...	...	...	...	...	...	...	...	385
390	Other industries	...	...	...	...	...	...	...	...	...	...	390
3	Manufacturing ..... e/	101	106	116	88	107	120	146	151	...	f/ 5.2	3
410	Electricity,gas,steam ..	...	...	...	...	...	...	...	...	...	...	410
4101	Electricity	...	...	...	...	...	...	...	...	...	...	4101
420	Water works and supply .	...	...	...	...	...	...	...	...	...	...	420
4	Electricity,gas etc	...	...	...	...	...	...	...	...	...	...	4
2-4	All industry	...	...	...	...	...	...	...	...	...	...	2-4

a/ Twelve months beginning 21 March of the year indicated.
b/ Annual growth rate 1976-1985.
c/ Major group 324 is included in 322.
d/ Major group 352 is included in 351.
e/ Excluding tobacco and petroleum refineries.
f/ Annual growth rate 1976-1984.

IRAQ

The information in the tables is based on the reply to the United Nations Questionnaire on General Industrial Statistics from the Central Statistical Organization, Ministry of Planning, Baghdad. The concepts, definitions and classification by branches of industry are generally in accordance with United Nations standards.

The estimates are derived from the quarterly industrial survey undertaken by the Central Statistical Organization. The inquiry covers all establishments with 10 or more employees in the public and private sectors, and is carried out through personal interview by permanent enumerators. The industry of cutting, rolling and making hand-made cigarettes is excluded from tobacco manufactures (ISIC 314).

The estimates in the tables are based on the national classification, which is not strictly comparable with ISIC. The data shown in the tables have been adjusted to the present version of ISIC as far as possible, by the Central Statistical Organization. It should be noted that ISIC 321 includes medical cotton manufacturing (ISIC 3851) and ISIC 381 includes founding and casting (part of ISIC 372). Establishments specializing in repair work are classified in manufacturing industries according to the type of product repaired. The numbers of establishments and employment relate to quarterly averages and cover establishments which are actually in operation.

Related national publications:
<u>Annual Abstract of Statistics</u>; <u>Results of the Industrial Survey</u> (annual), both published by the Central Statistical Organization, Ministry of Planning, Baghdad.

ISIC	INDUSTRY	1. NUMBER OF ESTABLISHMENTS a/ (NUMBER) 1981	1982	1983	1984	1985	2. AVERAGE NUMBER OF EMPLOYEES a/ (THOUSANDS) 1981	1982	1983	1984	1985	ISIC
210	Coal mining	...	...	...	...	...	...	...	...	...	...	210
220	Petroleum and gas	...	...	...	...	...	...	...	...	...	...	220
230	Metal ore mining	...	...	...	...	...	...	...	...	...	...	230
290	Other mining	...	...	...	...	...	...	...	...	...	...	290
2	Mining, quarrying	...	...	...	...	...	...	...	...	...	...	2
311/2	Food products	266	242	104	...	...	28.00	27.73	26.21	...	...	311/2
313	Beverages	19	18	11	...	...	6.05	6.14	6.57	...	...	313
314	Tobacco	2	2	2	...	...	5.85	5.34	4.81	...	...	314
321	Textiles b/	252	232	88	...	...	30.46	29.09	23.90	...	...	321
3211	Spinning,weaving etc.	...	...	...	...	...	...	...	...	...	...	3211
322	Wearing apparel b/	...	...	...	...	...	...	...	...	...	...	322
323	Leather and products	13	9	2	...	...	0.21	0.16	0.11	...	...	323
324	Footwear	14	11	6	...	...	5.64	5.76	5.01	...	...	324
331	Wood products	[29	28	19]	...	...	[1.93	2.00	1.55]	...	...	331
332	Furniture, fixtures				...	...				...	...	332
341	Paper and products c/	52	46	39	...	...	9.01	9.03	8.47	...	...	341
3411	Pulp,paper etc.	...	...	...	...	...	...	...	...	...	...	3411
342	Printing,publishing c/	...	...	...	...	...	...	...	...	...	...	342
351	Industrial chemicals	d/ 187	d/ 183	d/ 120	...	...	e/ 23.35	e/ 23.02	e/ 25.74	...	...	351
3511	Basic excl fertilizers	...	...	...	...	...	...	...	...	...	...	3511
3513	Synthetic resins etc	...	...	...	...	...	...	...	...	...	...	3513
352	Other chemical products. e/	...	...	...	...	...	...	...	...	...	...	352
3522	Drugs and medicines	...	...	...	...	...	...	...	...	...	...	3522
353	Petroleum refineries	d/	d/	d/	...	...	e/	e/	e/	...	...	353
354	Petroleum,coal products. e/	...	...	...	...	...	...	...	...	...	...	354
355	Rubber products e/	...	...	...	...	...	...	...	...	...	...	355
356	Plastic products n.e.c.. e/	...	...	...	...	...	...	...	...	...	...	356
361	Pottery,china etc				...	...				...	...	361
362	Glass and products	[365	329	231]	...	...	[33.86	33.18	31.76]	...	...	362
369	Non-metal products n.e.c				...	...				...	...	369
371	Iron and steel	...	...	...	...	...	...	...	...	...	...	371
372	Non-ferrous metals	...	...	...	...	...	...	...	...	...	...	372
381	Metal products	27	19	27	...	...	2.48	2.20	1.55	...	...	381
382	Machinery n.e.c.	...	...	...	...	...	...	...	...	...	...	382
3825	Office,computing etc.	...	...	...	...	...	...	...	...	...	...	3825
383	Electrical machinery	17	18	13	...	...	9.20	9.06	9.06	...	...	383
3832	Radio,television etc.	...	...	...	...	...	...	...	...	...	...	3832
384	Transport equipment	13	11	5	...	...	2.02	1.90	1.59	...	...	384
3841	Shipbuilding, repair.	...	...	...	...	...	...	...	...	...	...	3841
3843	Motor vehicles	...	...	...	...	...	...	...	...	...	...	3843
385	Professional goods	...	...	...	...	...	...	...	...	...	...	385
390	Other industries	4	5	1	...	...	0.08	0.08	0.03	...	...	390
3	Manufacturing	...	...	...	...	...	...	...	...	...	...	3
410	Electricity,gas,steam	...	...	...	...	...	...	...	...	...	...	410
4101	Electricity	...	...	...	...	...	...	...	...	...	...	4101
420	Water works and supply	...	...	...	...	...	...	...	...	...	...	420
4	Electricity,gas etc	...	...	...	...	...	...	...	...	...	...	4
2-4	All industry	...	...	...	...	...	...	...	...	...	...	2-4

a/ Mining and manufacturing: establishments with 10 or more employees.
b/ Major group 322 is included in 321.
c/ Major group 342 is included in 341.
d/ Major group 353 is included in 351.
e/ Major groups 352 to 356 are included in 351.

3. WAGES AND SALARIES OF EMPLOYEES a/ (THOUSAND DINARS)

ISIC	INDUSTRY		1981	1982	1983	1984	1985	ISIC
210	Coal mining		...	...	...	...	...	210
220	Petroleum and gas		...	...	...	...	...	220
230	Metal ore mining		...	...	...	...	...	230
290	Other mining		...	...	...	...	...	290
2	Mining, quarrying .		...	...	...	...	...	2
311/2	Food products		35182	35525	37735	...	...	311/2
313	Beverages		10434	11662	10855	...	...	313
314	Tobacco		7050	7248	7770	...	...	314
321	Textiles	b/	37649	42448	32635	...	...	321
3211	Spinning,weaving etc..		...	...	...	...	...	3211
322	Wearing apparel	b/	...	...	...	...	...	322
323	Leather and products ...		293	279	225	...	...	323
324	Footwear		7120	7787	7130	...	...	324
331	Wood products		[2232	2513	1929]	...	...	331
332	Furniture, fixtures					...	...	332
341	Paper and products	c/	12426	11571	9474	...	...	341
3411	Pulp,paper etc.		...	...	...	...	...	3411
342	Printing,publishing	c/	...	...	...	...	...	342
351	Industrial chemicals ...	d/	36854	39516	44402	...	...	351
3511	Basic excl fertilizers		...	...	...	...	...	3511
3513	Synthetic resins etc .		...	...	...	...	...	3513
352	Other chemical products.	d/	...	...	...	...	...	352
3522	Drugs and medicines ..		...	...	...	...	...	3522
353	Petroleum refineries ...	d/	...	...	...	...	...	353
354	Petroleum,coal products.	d/	...	...	...	...	...	354
355	Rubber products	d/	...	...	...	...	...	355
356	Plastic products n.e.c..	d/	...	...	...	...	...	356
361	Pottery,china etc		[		]	...	...	361
362	Glass and products		44092	51216	48804	...	...	362
369	Non-metal products n.e.c					...	...	369
371	Iron and steel		...	...	...	...	...	371
372	Non-ferrous metals		...	...	...	...	...	372
381	Metal products		4146	4324	2396	...	...	381
382	Machinery n.e.c.		...	...	...	...	...	382
3825	Office,computing etc..		...	...	...	...	...	3825
383	Electrical machinery ...		12368	11824	11491	...	...	383
3832	Radio,television etc..		...	...	...	...	...	3832
384	Transport equipment		2695	3092	2339	...	...	384
3841	Shipbuilding, repair..		...	...	...	...	...	3841
3843	Motor vehicles		...	...	...	...	...	3843
385	Professional goods		...	...	...	...	...	385
390	Other industries		88	107	44	...	...	390
3	Manufacturing		...	...	...	...	...	3
410	Electricity,gas,steam ..		...	...	...	...	...	410
4101	Electricity		...	...	...	...	...	4101
420	Water works and supply .		...	...	...	...	...	420
4	Electricity,gas etc		...	...	...	...	...	4
2-4	All industry		...	...	...	...	...	2-4

a/ Mining and manufacturing: establishments with 10 or more employees.
b/ Major group 322 is included in 321.
c/ Major group 342 is included in 341.
d/ Major groups 352 to 356 are included in 351.

IRELAND

The information on industrial activity is based on the reply to the United Nations Questionnaire on General Industrial Statistics from the Central Statistics Office, Dublin. The concepts, definitions and classification by branches of industry are generally in accordance with United Nations standards; any significant departures from these standards are noted in the following paragraphs.

The estimates are derived from the results of the annual census of industrial production which covers all industrial establishments with 3 or more persons engaged. However, it should be noted that the figures shown are not fully comparable with those formerly published for the years prior to 1979. Commencing with 1979, the scope of the census has been extended to include two additional activities, namely poultry processing (part of ISIC 311/2) and photographic laboratories (part of ISIC 390). Coverage has also been improved to include a number of small firms not identified previously. The overall effect of the extended coverage is to add some 700 establishments to the census coverage of ISIC 2-4. They accounted for 4.2 per cent of total employment and 3.0 per cent of the value of output in 1979; of this, the two additional industrial activities accounted for 0.7 per cent of both employment and output. Further information including estimates for the main census variables for the years 1973 to 1978 on the basis of the extended coverage of the 1979 census can be obtained from the Central Statistics Office, Dublin.

The classification used in compiling the estimates is the General Industrial Classification of Economic Activities within the European Communities (NACE). In the tables, the NACE industries are arranged under the most appropriate category of ISIC.

The employment figures refer to the numbers in a week in September. Homeworkers are excluded and payments to homeworkers are not included in wages and salaries. Wages and salaries cover cash payments only, i.e. housing allowances, family allowances and payments in kind are excluded.

The estimates of output are compiled on the "production" basis representing the net selling value of all goods produced in the year, whether sold or added to stock, together with the value of industrial services rendered to other establishments. Goods sold in the same condition as bought are not included. The value of fixed assets produced by the establishment for its own use is included only in the electricity industry (ISIC 4101) and in the turf (peat) production industry (part of ISIC 290). Valuation is in factor values excluding contributions from local authorities to make up deficiencies in the income of water works.

Value added is the difference between the value of output and the cost of fuels, materials and industrial services. The cost of materials is the actual cost of materials used during the year, whether purchased or taken from stock, used in production or repair work; packaging materials are included. Industrial services comprise the cost of work done on commission or contract by others (including earnings of home workers) together with payments for repair work done by others. Deductible value added tax is excluded.

The estimates of gross fixed capital formation represent the net additions to capital assets during the year, i.e. additions less disposals. Own account construction of capital assets is included. Where possible, investment in establishments not yet in production is included.

The estimates of the value of stocks at the end of the period are, in general, based on the accounting conventions used by the respondents themselves in their own accounts (i.e. they are book values). Stocks of goods purchased for resale without further processing are included.

The indexes of industrial production are compiled by the Central Statistics Office and provided in response to the United Nations Questionnaire on Indexes of Industrial Production. In principle, the indexes cover all industrial establishments with 3 or more persons engaged.

Related national publications:
<u>Statistical Abstract of Ireland</u> (annual); <u>Irish Statistical Bulletin</u> (quarterly); <u>Census of Industrial Production</u> (annual), all published by the Central Statistics Office, Dublin.

ISIC	INDUSTRY	1. NUMBER OF ESTABLISHMENTS a/ (NUMBER) 1981	1982	1983	1984	1985	2. AVERAGE NUMBER OF PERSONS ENGAGED a/b/ (THOUSANDS) 1981	1982	1983	c/ 1984	c/ 1985	ISIC
210	Coal mining	5	6	6	...	...	0.3	0.3	0.4	...	...	210
220	Petroleum and gas ...... d/	...	...	...	...	...	...	...	...	...	...	220
230	Metal ore mining	5	4	2	...	...	1.7	1.0	1.0	...	...	230
290	Other mining	143	135	123	...	...	10.5	9.2	8.9	9.5	8.3	290
2	Mining, quarrying . d/	153	145	131	...	...	12.5	10.5	10.3	9.5	8.3	2
311/2	Food products	871	864	841	...	...	46.3	44.7	43.0	42.5	39.1	311/2
313	Beverages	82	84	83	...	...	8.3	7.6	6.9	6.8	6.4	313
314	Tobacco	9	9	9	...	...	2.2	2.2	2.1	1.9	1.9	314
321	Textiles	280	276	266	...	...	16.7	14.7	12.8	...	...	321
3211	Spinning,weaving etc..	...	...	...	...	...	...	...	...	...	...	3211
322	Wearing apparel	353	330	310	...	...	13.6	13.0	12.3	11.7	11.7	322
323	Leather and products ...	60	61	64	...	...	1.6	1.5	1.2	1.2	0.8	323
324	Footwear	27	29	28	...	...	3.1	3.1	2.8	2.3	1.4	324
331	Wood products	346	343	336	...	...	5.6	5.3	4.8	4.8	4.8	331
332	Furniture, fixtures	316	331	328	...	...	4.4	4.3	4.2	4.2	4.0	332
341	Paper and products	77	80	73	...	...	4.6	4.0	3.5	3.5	3.3	341
3411	Pulp,paper etc.	...	...	...	...	...	...	...	...	...	...	3411
342	Printing,publishing	325	322	316	...	...	11.5	10.8	10.6	9.6	9.8	342
351	Industrial chemicals ... e/	199	204	202	...	...	12.3	11.5	11.8	11.8	11.8	351
3511	Basic excl fertilizers	...	...	...	...	...	...	...	...	...	...	3511
3513	Synthetic resins etc .	...	...	...	...	...	...	...	...	...	...	3513
352	Other chemical products. e/	...	...	...	...	...	...	...	...	...	...	352
3522	Drugs and medicines ..	...	...	...	...	...	...	...	...	...	...	3522
353	Petroleum refineries ...	[9	9	9]	...	...	[0.4	0.4	0.4	0.4	0.4]	353
354	Petroleum,coal products.				...	...						354
355	Rubber products	36	39	41	...	...	3.0	3.0	2.8	2.1	2.1	355
356	Plastic products n.e.c..	157	171	174	...	...	5.0	5.0	5.0	5.2	5.4	356
361	Pottery,china etc	20	20	19	...	...	1.7	[6.3	5.6	5.5	5.3]	361
362	Glass and products	54	55	55	...	...	5.3					362
369	Non-metal products n.e.c	294	291	284	...	...	8.6	8.3	7.6	7.1	7.3	369
371	Iron and steel	27	26	24	...	...	1.7	[2.3	1.9	1.5	1.6]	371
372	Non-ferrous metals	14	13	13	...	...	0.7					372
381	Metal products	691	722	712	...	...	16.7	15.9	13.9	13.8	13.0	381
382	Machinery n.e.c.	271	276	296	...	...	13.2	13.1	13.5	13.5	13.9	382
3825	Office,computing etc..	35	40	49	...	...	5.0	5.3	5.9	6.2	6.1	3825
383	Electrical machinery ...	218	229	244	...	...	15.9	16.6	16.2	16.8	17.1	383
3832	Radio,television etc..	84	93	100	...	...	6.9	7.1	7.2	7.9	7.7	3832
384	Transport equipment	172	168	153	...	...	11.5	11.1	9.8	7.8	6.6	384
3841	Shipbuilding, repair..	38	41	37	...	...	1.8	1.8	1.2	...	...	3841
3843	Motor vehicles	122	115	105	...	...	6.0	5.6	5.2	3.3	2.9	3843
385	Professional goods	81	84	85	...	...	6.4	7.0	7.1	6.7	6.5	385
390	Other industries	106	107	108	...	...	3.0	3.1	3.0	3.1	2.2	390
3	Manufacturing	5095	5143	5073	...	...	223.3	f/ 214.8	f/ 202.8	196.8	189.2	3
410	Electricity,gas,steam .. d/	37	37	39	...	...	14.7	14.8	14.7	169.8	...	410
4101	Electricity	28	28	28	...	...	13.1	13.1	13.1	...	...	4101
420	Water works and supply .	66	64	66	...	...	2.3	2.3	2.3	...	...	420
4	Electricity,gas etc d/	103	101	105	...	...	17.0	17.1	17.0	...	...	4
2-4	All industry	5351	5389	5309	...	...	252.8	242.4	230.1	...	...	2-4

Note. For description of classification, see country note.

a/ Establishments with 3 or more persons engaged.
b/ For a week in the middle of September.
c/ Estimates derived from the results of quarterly sample surveys.
d/ Major group 220 is included in 410.
e/ Major group 352 is included in 351.
f/ Including industries not shown separately.

ISIC	INDUSTRY	3. AVERAGE NUMBER OF EMPLOYEES a/b/ (THOUSANDS) 1981	1982	1983	1984	1985	4. WAGES AND SALARIES OF EMPLOYEES a/c/ (MILLION POUNDS) 1981	1982	1983	1984	1985	ISIC
210	Coal mining	0.3	0.3	0.4	...	...	2.0	2.3	3.1	...	...	210
220	Petroleum and gas ...... d/	...	...	...	...	...	...	...	...	...	...	220
230	Metal ore mining	1.7	1.0	1.0	...	...	12.0	13.4	15.8	...	...	230
290	Other mining	10.4	9.2	8.9	...	...	74.7	78.8	82.1	...	...	290
2	Mining, quarrying . d/	12.5	10.5	10.3	...	...	88.7	94.5	101.0	...	...	2
311/2	Food products	45.9	44.4	42.6	...	...	291.7	325.6	349.6	...	...	311/2
313	Beverages	8.3	7.5	6.9	...	...	70.0	74.3	81.1	...	...	313
314	Tobacco	2.2	2.2	2.1	...	...	17.2	20.8	22.0	...	...	314
321	Textiles	16.6	14.6	12.7	...	...	85.9	85.6	82.9	...	...	321
3211	Spinning,weaving etc..	...	...	...	...	...	...	...	...	...	...	3211
322	Wearing apparel	13.4	12.9	12.2	...	...	51.6	55.0	57.6	...	...	322
323	Leather and products ...	1.6	1.5	1.2	...	...	8.4	8.8	8.1	...	...	323
324	Footwear	3.1	3.1	2.8	...	...	13.6	15.4	15.3	...	...	324
331	Wood products	5.4	5.0	4.7	...	...	26.1	27.0	27.5	...	...	331
332	Furniture, fixtures	4.2	4.1	4.0	...	...	18.2	20.3	21.3	...	...	332
341	Paper and products	4.5	4.0	3.5	...	...	32.3	32.4	29.8	...	...	341
3411	Pulp,paper etc.	...	...	...	...	...	...	...	...	...	...	3411
342	Printing,publishing	11.4	10.7	10.5	...	...	82.9	91.3	96.3	...	...	342
351	Industrial chemicals ... e/	12.3	11.5	11.8	...	...	97.8	108.6	129.0	...	...	351
3511	Basic excl fertilizers	...	...	...	...	...	...	...	...	...	...	3511
3513	Synthetic resins etc .	...	...	...	...	...	...	...	...	...	...	3513
352	Other chemical products. e/	...	...	...	...	...	...	...	...	...	...	352
3522	Drugs and medicines ..	...	...	...	...	...	...	...	...	...	...	3522
353	Petroleum refineries ...	[0.4	0.4	0.4]	...	...	[3.7	4.0	4.7]	...	...	353
354	Petroleum,coal products.				...	...				...	...	354
355	Rubber products	3.0	3.0	2.8	...	...	20.8	23.7	22.3	...	...	355
356	Plastic products n.e.c..	5.0	5.0	5.0	...	...	30.4	34.5	38.7	...	...	356
361	Pottery,china etc	1.7	1.3	0.9	...	...	10.0	8.1	6.8	...	...	361
362	Glass and products	5.3	5.0	4.7	...	...	38.0	43.2	45.0	...	...	362
369	Non-metal products n.e.c	8.5	8.2	7.5	...	...	63.3	68.2	70.6	...	...	369
371	Iron and steel	1.7	1.7	1.6	...	...	11.0	13.4	15.3	...	...	371
372	Non-ferrous metals	0.7	0.6	0.3	...	...	4.1	3.6	2.4	...	...	372
381	Metal products	16.4	15.7	13.6	...	...	93.9	99.5	98.6	...	...	381
382	Machinery n.e.c.	13.1	13.0	13.4	...	...	77.2	91.0	109.5	...	...	382
3825	Office,computing etc..	5.0	5.3	5.9	...	...	31.8	39.9	54.4	...	...	3825
383	Electrical machinery ...	15.9	16.6	16.2	...	...	90.2	107.0	120.4	...	...	383
3832	Radio,television etc..	6.9	7.1	7.2	...	...	40.6	46.1	54.9	...	...	3832
384	Transport equipment	11.4	11.1	9.8	...	...	87.7	91.2	90.9	...	...	384
3841	Shipbuilding, repair..	1.8	1.7	1.1	...	...	12.0	11.3	10.1	...	...	3841
3843	Motor vehicles	5.9	5.6	5.1	...	...	43.7	44.1	43.6	...	...	3843
385	Professional goods	6.4	7.0	7.1	...	...	39.0	46.8	57.7	...	...	385
390	Other industries	3.0	3.0	3.0	...	...	15.6	17.7	20.2	...	...	390
3	Manufacturing	221.4	213.1	201.3	...	...	1380.6	1517.0	1623.6	...	...	3
410	Electricity,gas,steam .. d/	14.7	14.8	14.7	...	...	131.5	147.4	163.9	...	...	410
4101	Electricity	13.1	13.1	13.1	...	...	119.2	132.0	145.8	...	...	4101
420	Water works and supply .	2.3	2.3	2.3	...	...	12.2	14.4	16.9	...	...	420
4	Electricity,gas etc d/	17.0	17.1	17.0	...	...	143.7	161.8	180.8	...	...	4
2-4	All industry	250.9	240.7	228.6	...	...	1613.0	1773.3	1905.4	...	...	2-4

Note. For description of classification, see country note.

a/ Establishments with 3 or more persons engaged.
b/ For a week in the middle of September.
c/ Excluding housing and family allowances paid directly by the employer and also excluding payments in kind.
d/ Major group 220 is included in 410.
e/ Major group 352 is included in 351.

ISIC	INDUSTRY	5. AVERAGE NUMBER OF OPERATIVES a/b/c/ (THOUSANDS)					6. WAGES AND SALARIES OF OPERATIVES a/ (MILLION POUNDS)					ISIC
		1981	1982	1983	1984	1985	1981	1982	1983	1984	1985	
210	Coal mining	0.3	0.3	0.4	...	...	1.8	2.0	2.8	...	...	210
220	Petroleum and gas ...... d/	...	...	...	...	...	...	...	...	...	...	220
230	Metal ore mining	1.4	0.8	0.8	...	...	8.8	10.0	12.1	...	...	230
290	Other mining	9.1	7.9	7.7	...	...	59.8	62.0	64.8	...	...	290
2	Mining, quarrying . d/	10.8	9.0	8.9	...	...	70.4	74.0	79.7	...	...	2
311/2	Food products	37.1	35.7	34.2	...	...	223.1	247.4	263.9	...	...	311/2
313	Beverages	5.9	5.7	5.0	...	...	46.5	52.6	56.7	...	...	313
314	Tobacco	1.5	1.5	1.4	...	...	10.6	12.3	12.7	...	...	314
321	Textiles	14.1	12.4	10.7	...	...	68.6	67.6	65.7	...	...	321
3211	Spinning,weaving etc..	...	...	...	...	...	...	...	...	...	...	3211
322	Wearing apparel	12.1	11.6	11.0	...	...	42.8	46.1	48.4	...	...	322
323	Leather and products ...	1.4	1.3	1.0	...	...	7.2	7.5	7.0	...	...	323
324	Footwear	2.7	2.7	2.5	...	...	11.1	12.1	12.0	...	...	324
331	Wood products	4.5	4.2	3.8	...	...	20.3	20.7	21.0	...	...	331
332	Furniture, fixtures	3.6	3.5	3.4	...	...	14.8	16.5	17.3	...	...	332
341	Paper and products	3.6	3.2	2.7	...	...	24.3	24.4	21.9	...	...	341
3411	Pulp,paper etc.	...	...	...	...	...	...	...	...	...	...	3411
342	Printing,publishing	7.7	7.1	6.9	...	...	52.6	56.4	58.9	...	...	342
351	Industrial chemicals ... e/	8.3	7.7	7.9	...	...	60.8	68.8	79.6	...	...	351
3511	Basic excl fertilizers	...	...	...	...	...	...	...	...	...	...	3511
3513	Synthetic resins etc .	...	...	...	...	...	...	...	...	...	...	3513
352	Other chemical products. e/	...	...	...	...	...	...	...	...	...	...	352
3522	Drugs and medicines ..	...	...	...	...	...	...	...	...	...	...	3522
353	Petroleum refineries ...	[0.3	0.2	0.3]	...	...	[2.3	2.6	3.1]	...	...	353
354	Petroleum,coal products.				...	...				...	...	354
355	Rubber products	2.5	2.5	2.3	...	...	15.5	18.1	17.3	...	...	355
356	Plastic products n.e.c..	3.9	3.9	3.9	...	...	21.7	24.6	27.8	...	...	356
361	Pottery,china etc	1.5	1.1	0.7	...	...	8.5	6.3	5.1	...	...	361
362	Glass and products	4.7	4.6	4.2	...	...	32.7	38.0	38.8	...	...	362
369	Non-metal products n.e.c	6.6	6.3	5.7	...	...	46.0	47.8	48.7	...	...	369
371	Iron and steel	1.4	1.3	1.3	...	...	8.1	9.9	10.9	...	...	371
372	Non-ferrous metals	0.6	0.5	0.2	...	...	3.3	2.6	1.5	...	...	372
381	Metal products	13.4	12.6	11.0	...	...	72.6	75.8	75.3	...	...	381
382	Machinery n.e.c.	9.4	9.2	9.4	...	...	47.8	56.6	67.4	...	...	382
3825	Office,computing etc..	3.0	3.2	3.5	...	...	15.0	19.7	27.6	...	...	3825
383	Electrical machinery ...	12.7	13.1	12.8	...	...	63.2	74.1	83.7	...	...	383
3832	Radio,television etc..	5.4	5.4	5.6	...	...	27.5	30.2	37.6	...	...	3832
384	Transport equipment	9.5	9.2	8.1	...	...	69.9	71.8	71.1	...	...	384
3841	Shipbuilding, repair..	1.5	1.4	0.9	...	...	9.0	8.3	7.3	...	...	3841
3843	Motor vehicles	4.9	4.6	4.2	...	...	34.4	34.0	33.2	...	...	3843
385	Professional goods	5.0	5.4	5.7	...	...	27.7	32.4	39.5	...	...	385
390	Other industries	2.4	2.4	2.3	...	...	11.5	12.1	13.3	...	...	390
3	Manufacturing	176.4	168.9	158.4	...	...	1013.5	1105.1	1168.6	...	...	3
410	Electricity,gas,steam .. d/	10.0	9.9	10.0	...	...	85.0	90.8	97.5	...	...	410
4101	Electricity	9.0	8.9	9.0	...	...	77.1	81.7	86.3	...	...	4101
420	Water works and supply .	1.9	1.9	1.9	...	...	9.5	11.4	13.3	...	...	420
4	Electricity,gas etc d/	11.9	11.8	11.9	...	...	94.5	102.2	110.8	...	...	4
2-4	All industry	199.1	189.7	179.2	...	...	1178.4	1281.3	1359.1	...	...	2-4

Note. For description of classification, see country note.

a/ Establishments with 3 or more persons engaged.
b/ For a week in the middle of September.
c/ Excluding housing and family allowances paid directly by the employer and also excluding payments in kind.
d/ Major group 220 is included in 410.
e/ Major group 352 is included in 351.

ISIC	INDUSTRY	7. OUTPUT IN FACTOR VALUES a/ (MILLION POUNDS) 1981	1982	1983	1984	1985	8. VALUE ADDED IN FACTOR VALUES a/ (MILLION POUNDS) 1981	1982	1983	1984	1985	ISIC
210	Coal mining	3	3	5	...	...	2.7	2.6	3.4	...	...	210
220	Petroleum and gas ...... b/	...	...	...	...	...	...	...	...	...	...	220
230	Metal ore mining	52	65	76	...	...	34.9	44.5	54.5	...	...	230
290	Other mining	203	202	222	...	...	151.8	153.6	169.8	...	...	290
2	Mining, quarrying . b/	258	270	303	...	...	189.4	200.7	227.7	...	...	2
311/2	Food products	3143	3558	4052	...	...	708.6	820.2	950.6	...	...	311/2
313	Beverages	346	423	434	...	...	191.0	239.9	243.6	...	...	313
314	Tobacco	85	99	110	...	...	50.3	58.5	66.7	...	...	314
321	Textiles	456	465	444	...	...	155.6	172.8	153.7	...	...	321
3211	Spinning,weaving etc..	...	...	...	...	...	...	...	...	...	...	3211
322	Wearing apparel	168	182	193	...	...	83.3	90.2	94.7	...	...	322
323	Leather and products ...	47	44	54	...	...	15.0	11.3	12.6	...	...	323
324	Footwear	46	51	48	...	...	23.3	25.8	24.6	...	...	324
331	Wood products	121	120	125	...	...	50.4	51.2	53.4	...	...	331
332	Furniture, fixtures	78	84	84	...	...	35.7	37.0	37.5	...	...	332
341	Paper and products	155	151	156	...	...	56.6	57.1	59.5	...	...	341
3411	Pulp,paper etc.	...	...	...	...	...	...	...	...	...	...	3411
342	Printing,publishing	224	244	259	...	...	144.1	159.6	169.5	...	...	342
351	Industrial chemicals ... c/	959	1047	1283	...	...	513.0	565.9	731.6	...	...	351
3511	Basic excl fertilizers	...	...	...	...	...	...	...	...	...	...	3511
3513	Synthetic resins etc .	...	...	...	...	...	...	...	...	...	...	3513
352	Other chemical products. c/	...	...	...	...	...	...	...	...	...	...	352
3522	Drugs and medicines ..	...	...	...	...	...	...	...	...	...	...	3522
353	Petroleum refineries ...	[140	127	266]	...	...	[9.0	14.3	14.8]	...	...	353
354	Petroleum,coal products.				...	...				...	...	354
355	Rubber products	78	91	91	...	...	33.1	45.1	44.6	...	...	355
356	Plastic products n.e.c..	154	172	209	...	...	65.2	74.2	92.3	...	...	356
361	Pottery,china etc	46	36	26	...	...	20.9	16.4	10.5	...	...	361
362	Glass and products	97	108	125	...	...	58.4	67.1	78.0	...	...	362
369	Non-metal products n.e.c	418	411	476	...	...	181.7	174.5	210.2	...	...	369
371	Iron and steel	41	57	68	...	...	13.7	21.3	24.5	...	...	371
372	Non-ferrous metals	28	25	25	...	...	6.6	6.4	5.8	...	...	372
381	Metal products	384	407	413	...	...	173.9	179.9	183.5	...	...	381
382	Machinery n.e.c.	728	912	1353	...	...	298.2	364.2	562.0	...	...	382
3825	Office,computing etc..	520	675	1087	...	...	199.8	257.0	433.5	...	...	3825
383	Electrical machinery ...	448	583	730	...	...	206.3	278.8	349.0	...	...	383
3832	Radio,television etc..	238	337	462	...	...	108.5	162.4	230.2	...	...	3832
384	Transport equipment	315	324	344	...	...	105.2	113.8	116.1	...	...	384
3841	Shipbuilding, repair..	54	52	67	...	...	14.4	14.4	16.4	...	...	3841
3843	Motor vehicles	202	205	189	...	...	50.0	54.2	49.9	...	...	3843
385	Professional goods	200	255	332	...	...	108.0	140.9	182.4	...	...	385
390	Other industries	94	96	126	...	...	45.6	42.9	55.4	...	...	390
3	Manufacturing	8999	10072	11826	...	...	3352.7	3829.3	4527.1	...	...	3
410	Electricity,gas,steam .. b/	697	811	914	...	...	370.1	473.8	543.9	...	...	410
4101	Electricity	602	665	739	...	...	300.4	353.6	388.0	...	...	4101
420	Water works and supply .	19	23	32	...	...	7.0	8.3	16.7	...	...	420
4	Electricity,gas etc b/	716	834	946	...	...	377.1	482.1	560.6	...	...	4
2-4	All industry	9973	11176	13075	...	...	3919.2	4512.1	5315.4	...	...	2-4

Note. For description of classification, see country note.

a/ Establishments with 3 or more persons engaged.
b/ Major group 220 is included in 410.
c/ Major group 352 is included in 351.

ISIC	INDUSTRY	9. GROSS FIXED CAPITAL FORMATION TOTAL a/ (MILLION POUNDS) 1981	1982	1983	1984	1985	10. GROSS FIXED CAPITAL FORMATION MACHINERY AND EQUIPMENT a/ (MILLION POUNDS) 1981	1982	1983	1984	1985	ISIC
210	Coal mining	0.3	0.6	0.9	...	...	0.3	0.2	0.9	...	...	210
220	Petroleum and gas ...... b/	...	...	...	...	...	...	...	...	...	...	220
230	Metal ore mining	1.1	-0.4	1.9	...	...	0.9	0.3	1.1	...	...	230
290	Other mining	30.7	20.9	24.9	...	...	20.3	13.1	16.3	...	...	290
2	Mining, quarrying . b/	32.1	21.1	27.7	...	...	21.5	13.6	18.3	...	...	2
311/2	Food products	99.3	98.7	111.4	...	...	72.1	67.1	79.7	...	...	311/2
313	Beverages	29.2	35.2	27.3	...	...	17.6	17.5	17.6	...	...	313
314	Tobacco	3.1	3.2	2.3	...	...	2.3	2.6	1.9	...	...	314
321	Textiles	8.6	5.2	9.6	...	...	5.9	3.3	6.4	...	...	321
3211	Spinning,weaving etc..	...	...	...	...	...	...	...	...	...	...	3211
322	Wearing apparel	6.3	2.0	4.8	...	...	3.3	1.7	2.7	...	...	322
323	Leather and products ...	0.6	0.4	0.7	...	...	0.3	0.3	0.5	...	...	323
324	Footwear	0.9	1.1	0.7	...	...	0.6	0.9	0.5	...	...	324
331	Wood products	7.8	5.2	4.1	...	...	5.0	3.5	2.5	...	...	331
332	Furniture, fixtures	3.6	4.7	2.4	...	...	1.6	1.8	1.4	...	...	332
341	Paper and products	4.3	4.5	3.8	...	...	3.4	3.6	2.8	...	...	341
3411	Pulp,paper etc.	...	...	...	...	...	...	...	...	...	...	3411
342	Printing,publishing	10.8	5.7	8.4	...	...	7.5	5.0	5.9	...	...	342
351	Industrial chemicals ... c/	50.7	34.6	42.6	...	...	24.9	21.3	23.7	...	...	351
3511	Basic excl fertilizers	...	...	...	...	...	...	...	...	...	...	3511
3513	Synthetic resins etc .	...	...	...	...	...	...	...	...	...	...	3513
352	Other chemical products. c/	...	...	...	...	...	...	...	...	...	...	352
3522	Drugs and medicines ..	...	...	...	...	...	...	...	...	...	...	3522
353	Petroleum refineries ...	[0.5	0.8	1.1]	...	...	[0.4	0.8	0.9]	...	...	353
354	Petroleum,coal products.				...	...				...	...	354
355	Rubber products	1.0	5.0	2.8	...	...	1.6	4.3	2.1	...	...	355
356	Plastic products n.e.c..	10.7	11.0	9.1	...	...	6.5	8.8	7.6	...	...	356
361	Pottery,china etc	1.2	0.9	0.4	...	...	1.1	0.8	0.4	...	...	361
362	Glass and products	3.9	5.0	3.3	...	...	2.3	3.5	2.9	...	...	362
369	Non-metal products n.e.c	77.4	76.4	36.0	...	...	70.0	59.8	32.8	...	...	369
371	Iron and steel	1.1	63.9	1.3	...	...	0.6	44.9	0.9	...	...	371
372	Non-ferrous metals	0.3	-0.2	0.7	...	...	0.1	0.4	0.4	...	...	372
381	Metal products	23.1	16.6	8.7	...	...	14.1	11.5	7.2	...	...	381
382	Machinery n.e.c.	42.5	58.5	48.3	...	...	19.1	31.6	29.0	...	...	382
3825	Office,computing etc..	30.0	40.3	39.5	...	...	12.0	18.7	22.2	...	...	3825
383	Electrical machinery ...	28.7	38.0	32.3	...	...	17.0	27.7	23.1	...	...	383
3832	Radio,television etc..	17.1	21.5	20.0	...	...	9.8	17.3	14.9	...	...	3832
384	Transport equipment	10.1	8.3	6.4	...	...	4.6	7.1	2.8	...	...	384
3841	Shipbuilding, repair..	1.4	0.4	0.3	...	...	0.8	0.3	0.1	...	...	3841
3843	Motor vehicles	5.2	6.4	4.9	...	...	2.2	5.6	1.7	...	...	3843
385	Professional goods	12.6	24.3	15.1	...	...	6.3	10.4	12.5	...	...	385
390	Other industries	3.7	6.4	3.4	...	...	2.5	3.8	2.4	...	...	390
3	Manufacturing	442.0	515.4	387.0	...	...	290.7	343.2	270.6	...	...	3
410	Electricity,gas,steam .. b/	214.8	285.8	236.2	...	...	149.8	172.6	180.8	...	...	410
4101	Electricity	208.6	240.2	226.8	...	...	148.4	170.1	176.8	...	...	4101
420	Water works and supply .	13.2	17.5	17.7	...	...	2.3	4.1	3.9	...	...	420
4	Electricity,gas etc b/	228.0	303.3	253.9	...	...	152.1	176.7	184.7	...	...	4
2-4	All industry	702.1	839.8	668.6	...	...	464.3	533.5	473.6	...	...	2-4

Note. For description of classification, see country note.

a/ Establishments with 3 or more persons engaged.
b/ Major group 220 is included in 410.
c/ Major group 352 is included in 351.

11. VALUE OF STOCKS AT END OF PERIOD
TOTAL a/
(MILLION POUNDS)

ISIC	INDUSTRY	b/ 1981	b/ 1982	b/ 1983	1984	1985	ISIC
210	Coal mining	0.1	0.2	0.4	...	...	210
220	Petroleum and gas ...... c/	...	...	...	...	...	220
230	Metal ore mining	8.6	5.2	5.0	...	...	230
290	Other mining	41.4	44.3	47.9	...	...	290
2	Mining, quarrying . c/	50.1	49.7	53.3	...	...	2
311/2	Food products	293.1	309.3	332.0	...	...	311/2
313	Beverages	99.4	111.6	124.0	...	...	313
314	Tobacco	25.8	32.8	31.6	...	...	314
321	Textiles	88.5	83.3	80.1	...	...	321
3211	Spinning,weaving etc..	...	...	...	...	...	3211
322	Wearing apparel	34.6	35.8	35.5	...	...	322
323	Leather and products ...	8.4	7.9	8.7	...	...	323
324	Footwear	8.9	9.8	8.6	...	...	324
331	Wood products	26.0	23.5	22.1	...	...	331
332	Furniture, fixtures	16.6	16.4	17.3	...	...	332
341	Paper and products	22.4	21.1	21.7	...	...	341
3411	Pulp,paper etc.	...	...	...	...	...	3411
342	Printing,publishing	22.3	24.0	19.4	...	...	342
351	Industrial chemicals ... d/	228.6	239.1	256.0	...	...	351
3511	Basic excl fertilizers	...	...	...	...	...	3511
3513	Synthetic resins etc .	...	...	...	...	...	3513
352	Other chemical products. d/	...	...	...	...	...	352
3522	Drugs and medicines ..	...	...	...	...	...	3522
353	Petroleum refineries ...	[23.9	42.4	40.5]	...	...	353
354	Petroleum,coal products.				...	...	354
355	Rubber products	18.9	17.5	17.6	...	...	355
356	Plastic products n.e.c..	30.7	29.9	35.8	...	...	356
361	Pottery,china etc	13.5	11.4	8.2	...	...	361
362	Glass and products	27.1	33.9	38.4	...	...	362
369	Non-metal products n.e.c	75.8	91.3	98.3	...	...	369
371	Iron and steel	12.8	19.2	18.0	...	...	371
372	Non-ferrous metals	4.3	3.6	3.9	...	...	372
381	Metal products	75.6	69.7	71.2	...	...	381
382	Machinery n.e.c.	170.0	224.9	291.1	...	...	382
3825	Office,computing etc..	103.6	155.5	222.6	...	...	3825
383	Electrical machinery ...	97.4	103.6	121.5	...	...	383
3832	Radio,television etc..	51.4	54.3	67.3	...	...	3832
384	Transport equipment	159.8	171.9	162.6	...	...	384
3841	Shipbuilding, repair..	17.8	40.1	20.8	...	...	3841
3843	Motor vehicles	103.3	85.4	91.9	...	...	3843
385	Professional goods	45.6	62.0	77.5	...	...	385
390	Other industries	18.9	26.3	20.9	...	...	390
3	Manufacturing	1648.9	1822.2	1962.5	...	...	3
410	Electricity,gas,steam .. c/	158.8	172.5	163.4	...	...	410
4101	Electricity	151.9	166.5	158.4	...	...	4101
420	Water works and supply .	1.1	1.1	1.3	...	...	420
4	Electricity,gas etc c/	159.9	173.6	164.7	...	...	4
2-4	All industry	1858.9	2045.5	2180.5	...	...	2-4

Note. For description of classification, see country note.

a/ Establishments with 3 or more persons engaged.
b/ Including goods purchased for resale.
c/ Major group 220 is included in 410.
d/ Major group 352 is included in 351.

12. INDEX NUMBERS OF INDUSTRIAL PRODUCTION (1980 = 100)

ISIC	INDUSTRY	1976	1977	1978	1979	1981	1982	1983	1984	1985	a/ RATE	ISIC
210	Coal mining	83	73	42	65	101	84	98	90	75	-1.1	210
220	Petroleum and gas	...	...	...	...	...	...	...	...	...	...	220
230	Metal ore mining	42	62	87	103	59	65	69	77	71	6.0	230
290	Other mining	85	91	93	101	103	100	98	111	77	-1.1	290
2	Mining, quarrying .	67	78	90	101	85	90	88	99	74	1.1	2
311/2	Food products	87	94	100	103	100	103	110	114	119	3.5	311/2
313	Beverages	84	85	92	97	102	103	104	106	110	3.0	313
314	Tobacco	94	95	94	94	98	94	84	83	89	-0.6	314
321	Textiles	102	110	114	114	107	102	94	93	87	-1.8	321
3211	Spinning,weaving etc..	...	...	...	...	...	...	...	...	...	...	3211
322	Wearing apparel	101	102	101	104	101	106	100	100	100	-0.1	322
323	Leather and products ...	126	123	127	109	95	89	83	80	64	-7.2	323
324	Footwear	...	...	...	...	...	...	...	...	...	...	324
331	Wood products	[107	109	113	113	98	92	89	84	89	-2.0]	331
332	Furniture, fixtures											332
341	Paper and products	94	102	101	102	99	81	80	77	78	-2.1	341
3411	Pulp,paper etc.	...	...	...	...	...	...	...	...	...	...	3411
342	Printing,publishing	78	82	86	94	100	94	94	93	92	1.9	342
351	Industrial chemicals ... b/	62	70	91	105	115	110	128	158	162	11.3	351
3511	Basic excl fertilizers	...	...	...	...	...	...	...	...	...	...	3511
3513	Synthetic resins etc .	...	...	...	...	...	...	...	...	...	...	3513
352	Other chemical products. b/	...	...	...	...	...	...	...	...	...	...	352
3522	Drugs and medicines ..	...	...	...	...	...	...	...	...	...	...	3522
353	Petroleum refineries ...	...	...	...	...	...	...	...	...	...	...	353
354	Petroleum,coal products.	...	...	...	...	...	...	...	...	...	...	354
355	Rubber products	101	110	97	111	107	113	109	104	111	1.1	355
356	Plastic products n.e.c..	86	100	95	115	110	118	140	158	170	7.9	356
361	Pottery,china etc											361
362	Glass and products	[84	89	99	106	101	88	88	93	98	1.7]	362
369	Non-metal products n.e.c											369
371	Iron and steel	[120	108	105	112	102	102	111	120	128	0.7]	371
372	Non-ferrous metals											372
381	Metal products	70	81	89	103	91	83	76	77	79	1.4	381
382	Machinery n.e.c.	58	64	73	88	134	139	176	243	258	18.0	382
3825	Office,computing etc..	34	42	45	65	174	190	269	415	430	32.6	3825
383	Electrical machinery ...	71	78	81	84	111	120	135	177	183	11.1	383
3832	Radio,television etc..	...	...	...	...	...	...	...	...	...	...	3832
384	Transport equipment	105	113	105	118	102	95	91	93	82	-2.7	384
3841	Shipbuilding, repair..	145	110	98	105	87	66	51	34	...	e/ -16.6	3841
3843	Motor vehicles	93	110	105	98	97	89	76	61	45	-7.7	3843
385	Professional goods	91	100	113	115	122	128	159	186	189	8.5	385
390	Other industries	32	44	48	71	94	85	99	77	56	6.4	390
3	Manufacturing ..... c/	80	86	94	101	103	102	113	127	130	5.5	3
410	Electricity,gas,steam ..	...	...	...	...	...	...	...	...	...	...	410
4101	Electricity	...	...	...	...	...	...	...	...	...	...	4101
420	Water works and supply .	.	.	.	.	.	.	.	.	.	.	420
4	Electricity,gas etc	...	...	...	...	...	...	...	...	...	...	4
2-4	All industry d/	80	86	94	101	102	102	111	125	127	5.3	2-4

a/ Annual growth rate 1976-1985.
c/ Excluding petroleum refineries.
e/ Annual growth rate 1976-1984.

b/ Major group 352 is included in 351.
d/ Excluding petroleum refineries electricity, gas and steam.

ISRAEL

The information on industrial activity is based on the reply to the United Nations Questionnaire on General Industrial Statistics from the Central Bureau of Statistics, Jerusalem. The concepts, definitions and classification by branches of industry are generally in accordance with United Nations standards.

The estimates are generally derived from the annual industry and crafts survey carried out by the Central Bureau of Statistics. The survey covers mining and manufacturing and is conducted by sampling methods. The survey population comprises all establishments operating during the survey year, or part of it, which on the average engage 5 persons or more, except (a) non-profit establishments (such as workshops for training or rehabilitation purposes), (b) auxiliary industrial units in kibbutz establishments where the bulk of production is consumed by the kibbutz itself and (c) establishments that are being set-up or run-in throughout the survey year, and do not currently contribute to the output. The establishments surveyed cover about 95 per cent of all employees in industry. The diamond industry (ISIC 390) is excluded from the scope of inquiry because of the special nature of the establishments in the industry.

The reference period for the survey is the financial year from 1 April to 31 March, which coincides with the financial year of most establishments. Other establishments are allowed to report for different periods, provided that their returns cover at least six months of the financial year.

As the results of the 1984/85 and 1985/86 surveys are not yet available, figures shown in the tables for 1984 and 1985 are obtained from the results of a monthly sample survey of industrial production. These data cover establishments with one employee or more and relate to the calendar year.

The estimates are based on the national classification of 1970 which, in principle, follows the present version of ISIC. It should be noted that manufacture of knitted goods, except fabrics (ISIC 321) is included in ISIC 322 and for the estimates other than those obtained from the industry and crafts survey, ISIC group 3513 is included in ISIC 321. Beginning 1983, valuation of estimates has been changed by using June prices of the year instead of current prices.

The unit of investigation which is also the unit of tabulation is the establishment, defined as an economic unit producing or manufacturing products and/or supplying industrial services, generally located at one site and engaged in a single economic activity. In the case of establishments engaged in different economic activities, the book-keeping practices of the departments involved determine which units can be treated as separate establishments. Departments operating as auxiliary units for the sole purpose of serving the establishment are not treated separately.

The employment figures are annual averages of the number of paid employees and members of co-operative societies in four selected months of the reference year plus, for persons engaged, the number of working proprietors and unpaid family workers for one period. Homeworkers are not included. Unsalaried kibbutz members are considered to be in the category of working proprietors. For 1984 and 1985, the estimates of employees are averages of 12 monthly figures.

Wages and salaries cover all payments appearing on the pay-roll on which income tax is due (before deduction of taxes), including basic salary, cost-of-living and other allowances (except employees' child allowance), premiums, bonuses, payments for overtime, leave, sickness etc., bus fare, professional literature, "13th" month salary, maintenance of vehicles, telephone, clothing, lodging and payments in kind (meals, presents, housing etc.).

Supplements to wages and salaries refer to labour expenses of the establishment which do not appear on the pay-roll and include payments to national insurance and other insurance funds (provident, army reserve, pension and severance), sick fund, employers' tax, pension and severance paid by employers, transportation of staff and expenditure for maintaining restaurants etc.

The estimates of days worked refer to operatives, defined as all employees directly associated with the production process, the physical handling of materials and products and the maintenance of equipment, regardless of basis of remuneration. These data are obtained from the production survey mentioned above. Overtime is included and converted into work-days by dividing the overtime hours worked by the normal number of hours worked per day in the establishment (usually 8).

The estimates of electricity consumed are obtained from the Israel Electric Corporation and from industrial establishments with power stations having a registered capacity of 300 or more kilowatts. The estimates cover the consumption of all establishments and relate to calendar years. The classification is by broad groupings of the classification followed by the Israel Electric Corporation.

The estimates of output relate to gross revenue adjusted for changes in the value of stocks of finished goods. Gross revenue is defined as the ex-factory value of sales made or work done of an industrial nature excluding income from non-industrial activities, such as the sale of goods sold in the same condition as received and income from business sources (interest, rent etc.). The value of fixed assets produced by the establishment for its own use is included. Valuation is in producers' prices.

Value added is the difference between output as defined above and expenditures on materials, fuels and electricity purchased, work contracted out and maintenance and repairs; adjustments are made for changes in the value of stocks of materials and work in progress.

The estimates of gross fixed capital formation relate to the gross value of new and used assets acquired, except land. No deduction is made for revenue derived from sales. Progress payments made for fixed assets on order but not yet completed are not included, nor is fixed capital formation in new establishments not yet in operation. The latter is the subject of a special inquiry.

The indexes of industrial production are compiled by the Central Bureau of Statistics and provided in response to the United Nations Questionnaire on Indexes of Industrial Production. In principle, the indexes cover all industrial establishments and workshops with at least one employee.

Related national publications:

<u>Industry and Crafts Survey</u> (annual); <u>Statistical Abstract of Israel</u> (annual); <u>Monthly Bulletin of Statistics</u>, all published by the Central Bureau of Statistics, Jerusalem.

ISIC	INDUSTRY	1. NUMBER OF ESTABLISHMENTS a/b/ (NUMBER)					2. AVERAGE NUMBER OF PERSONS ENGAGED a/b/ (THOUSANDS)					ISIC
		1981	1982	1983	c/d/ 1984	c/d/ 1985	1981	1982	1983	c/d/ 1984	c/d/ 1985	
210	Coal mining	...	...	...	...	...	-	-	-	-	-	210
220	Petroleum and gas	...	...	...	...	...	...	...	...	...	...	220
230	Metal ore mining	...	...	...	...	...	...	...	...	...	...	230
290	Other mining	...	...	...	...	...	...	...	...	...	...	290
2	Mining, quarrying	61	61	53	69	37	5.7	4.9	4.8	5.1	4.3	2
311/2	Food products	690	684	655	[	]	36.8	37.6	40.3	[	]	311/2
313	Beverages	40	33	33	1027	977	2.8	2.9	3.0	45.4	44.3	313
314	Tobacco	3	3	3	[	]	0.7	0.7	0.7	[	]	314
321	Textiles	328	343	364	467	414	20.4	19.1	18.7	18.3	16.7	321
3211	Spinning,weaving etc.	178	163	179	...	...	16.4	14.9	14.7	...	...	3211
322	Wearing apparel	667	745	719	1209	1109	25.2	28.2	27.5	28.5	29.0	322
323	Leather and products	77	54	67	[281	285]	1.1	0.8	0.8	[3.5	3.8]	323
324	Footwear	109	93	88			2.4	2.6	2.6			324
331	Wood products	239	215	171	[1534	1373]	5.8	5.8	5.4	[14.5	13.5]	331
332	Furniture, fixtures	413	402	359			7.4	7.0	6.6			332
341	Paper and products	125	108	136	209	202	5.7	4.9	6.0	6.3	6.5	341
3411	Pulp,paper etc.	11	8	7	...	...	1.8	0.8	1.7	...	...	3411
342	Printing,publishing	541	555	591	971	987	10.1	10.5	11.4	13.9	13.2	342
351	Industrial chemicals	e/ 74	e/ 60	e/ 66	f/ 239	f/ 239	e/ 9.8	e/ 8.6	e/ 8.6	f/ 18.4	f/ 18.7	351
3511	Basic excl fertilizers	...	...	...	...	...	...	...	...	...	...	3511
3513	Synthetic resins etc	...	...	...	...	...	...	...	...	...	...	3513
352	Other chemical products	124	164	172	f/	f/	7.9	8.3	8.9	f/	f/	352
3522	Drugs and medicines	20	29	29	...	...	2.6	2.7	3.1	...	...	3522
353	Petroleum refineries	e/	e/	e/	f/	f/	e/	e/	e/	f/	f/	353
354	Petroleum,coal products	e/	e/	e/	f/	f/	e/	e/	e/	f/	f/	354
355	Rubber products	55	46	65	[524	526]	4.2	3.8	3.9	[12.5	12.8]	355
356	Plastic products n.e.c.	272	291	305			7.2	7.3	7.5			356
361	Pottery,china etc	47	46	34	[	]	1.6	1.6	1.4	[	]	361
362	Glass and products	14	14	13	486	447	1.0	0.9	0.9	11.2	9.5	362
369	Non-metal products n.e.c	257	253	311	[	]	8.4	8.2	8.5	[	]	369
371	Iron and steel	54	86	61	[158	144]	4.1	3.7	3.4	[5.8	5.7]	371
372	Non-ferrous metals	64	59	54			1.8	1.6	1.6			372
381	Metal products	1148	1143	1184	2334	2327	39.2	40.1	40.7	45.8	45.2	381
382	Machinery n.e.c.	230	249	250	299	274	9.4	10.0	10.4	10.5	10.4	382
3825	Office,computing etc.	55	60	51	...	...	3.3	3.7	4.0	...	...	3825
383	Electrical machinery	436	420	434	497	460	30.6	38.7	40.5	36.2	37.1	383
3832	Radio,television etc.	146	147	146	...	...	21.9	29.7	31.5	...	...	3832
384	Transport equipment	101	104	95	88	91	20.6	20.3	19.9	19.8	19.6	384
3841	Shipbuilding, repair.	34	39	39	...	...	2.0	1.7	1.5	...	...	3841
3843	Motor vehicles	53	49	41	...	...	3.0	2.9	2.9	...	...	3843
385	Professional goods	75	60	56	[392	400]	2.8	2.7	3.2	[7.3	7.4]	385
390	Other industries	148	172	160			3.6	3.6	3.6			390
3	Manufacturing	6331	6402	6446	10715	10255	269.6	279.4	286.0	297.9	293.4	3
410	Electricity,gas,steam	...	...	...	...	...	...	...	...	...	...	410
4101	Electricity	...	...	...	...	...	...	...	...	...	...	4101
420	Water works and supply	...	...	...	...	...	...	...	...	...	...	420
4	Electricity,gas etc	...	...	...	...	...	...	...	...	...	...	4
2-4	All industry	...	...	...	...	...	...	...	...	...	...	2-4

Note. For certain differences in classification, see country note.

a/ Twelve months beginning 1 April of the year indicated.
b/ Establishments with 5 or more persons engaged.
c/ Establishments with at least one employee.
d/ Twelve months beginning 1 January.
e/ Major groups 353 and 354 are included in 351.
f/ Major groups 352 to 354 are included in 351.

ISIC	INDUSTRY	3. AVERAGE NUMBER OF EMPLOYEES a/b/ (THOUSANDS) 1981	1982	1983	c/d/ 1984	c/d/ 1985	4. WAGES AND SALARIES OF EMPLOYEES a/b/ (MILLION SHEKELS) 1981	1982	e/ 1983	c/d/ 1984	c/d/ 1985	ISIC
210	Coal mining	-	-	-	-	-	-	-	-	-	-	210
220	Petroleum and gas	...	...	...	...	...	...	...	...	...	...	220
230	Metal ore mining	...	...	...	...	...	...	150	1	...	...	230
290	Other mining	...	...	...	...	...	...	2841	8	...	...	290
2	Mining, quarrying .	5.7	4.9	4.8	5.0	4.2	1396	2991	9	16	59	2
311/2	Food products	36.3	37.1	39.9			4029	10102	31			311/2
313	Beverages	2.8	2.9	3.0	[44.1	43.0]	364	911	3	[61	276]	313
314	Tobacco	0.7	0.7	0.7			119	297	1			314
321	Textiles	20.3	19.0	18.6	18.0	16.4	2397	5399	15	24	98	321
3211	Spinning,weaving etc..	16.4	14.8	14.6	...	...	2058	4275	12	...	...	3211
322	Wearing apparel	24.7	27.6	27.0	27.6	28.1	1776	4490	12	23	108	322
323	Leather and products ...	1.0	0.8	0.8	[3.2	3.5]	107	174	-	[4	23]	323
324	Footwear	2.3	2.5	2.5			316	932	2			324
331	Wood products	5.5	5.7	5.4	[12.5	12.0]	728	1701	5	[18	84]	331
332	Furniture, fixtures	7.0	6.6	6.2			736	1524	4			332
341	Paper and products	5.7	4.8	5.9	5.8	6.0	943	2124	6	11	50	341
3411	Pulp,paper etc.	1.8	0.8	1.7	...	...	304	704	2	...	...	3411
342	Printing,publishing	9.7	10.0	11.0	13.0	12.3	1357	3483	11	23	41	342
351	Industrial chemicals ...	f/ 8.8	f/ 8.6	f/ 8.6	g/ 18.1	g/ 18.4	f/ 2177	f/ 5035	f/ 15	g/ 49	g/ 224	351
3511	Basic excl fertilizers	...	...	...	...	...	...	...	...	...	...	3511
3513	Synthetic resins etc .	...	...	...	...	...	...	...	...	...	...	3513
352	Other chemical products.	7.8	8.3	8.8	g/	g/	1320	3164	10	g/	g/	352
3522	Drugs and medicines ..	2.6	2.7	3.1	...	...	424	1070	3	...	...	3522
353	Petroleum refineries ...	f/	f/	f/	g/	g/	f/	f/	f/	g/	g/	353
354	Petroleum,coal products.	f/	f/	f/	g/	g/	f/	f/	f/	g/	g/	354
355	Rubber products	4.2	3.8	3.9	[9.7	9.8]	637	1442	4	[16	75]	355
356	Plastic products n.e.c..	7.0	7.2	7.3			845	1942	6			356
361	Pottery,china etc	1.5	1.6	1.4			199	442	1			361
362	Glass and products	1.0	0.9	0.9	[10.7	9.0]	207	440	1	[20	77]	362
369	Non-metal products n.e.c	8.3	8.1	8.3			1337	3042	9			369
371	Iron and steel	4.1	3.7	3.3	[5.6	5.6]	912	1785	5	[12	57]	371
372	Non-ferrous metals	1.7	1.6	1.6			232	470	1			372
381	Metal products	38.7	39.5	40.0	42.6	41.9	6416	15151	44	89	411	381
382	Machinery n.e.c.	9.3	9.9	10.3	9.9	9.7	1518	3698	11	21	97	382
3825	Office,computing etc..	3.3	3.7	4.0	...	...	563	1379	4	...	...	3825
383	Electrical machinery ...	30.5	38.5	40.5	35.4	36.4	6155	17684	56	105	519	383
3832	Radio,television etc..	21.9	29.7	31.5	...	...	4866	14792	47	...	...	3832
384	Transport equipment	20.6	20.2	19.9	19.7	19.5	4933	12226	35	69	320	384
3841	Shipbuilding, repair..	1.9	1.7	1.4	...	...	317	683	2	...	...	3841
3843	Motor vehicles	3.0	2.9	2.9	...	...	448	1026	3	...	...	3843
385	Professional goods	2.7	2.7	3.1	[6.5	6.6]	595	1216	6	[12	61]	385
390	Other industries	3.5	3.5	3.5			362	840	3			390
3	Manufacturing	265.7	275.8	282.4	282.4	278.2	40717	99715	296	559	2578	3
410	Electricity,gas,steam ..	...	...	...	...	...	...	...	...	...	...	410
4101	Electricity	...	...	...	...	...	...	...	...	...	...	4101
420	Water works and supply .	...	...	...	...	...	...	...	...	...	...	420
4	Electricity,gas etc	...	...	...	...	...	...	...	...	...	...	4
2-4	All industry	...	...	...	...	...	...	...	...	...	...	2-4

Note. For certain differences in classification, see country note.

a/ Twelve months beginning 1 April of the year indicated.
b/ Establishments with 5 or more persons engaged.
c/ Establishments with at least one employee.
d/ Twelve months beginning 1 January.
e/ Effective 1 January 1986, a new currency was introduced by which 1,000 "old" shekels became equivalent to one "new" shekel. Data are reported in new curreny beginning 1983.
f/ Major groups 353 and 354 are included in 351.
g/ Major groups 352 to 354 are included in 351.

ISIC	INDUSTRY	5. DAYS WORKED BY OPERATIVES (MILLIONS)					6. QUANTITY OF ELECTRICITY CONSUMED a/b/ (MILLION KWH)					ISIC
		c/d/ 1981	c/d/ 1982	c/d/ 1983	b/e/ 1984	b/e/ 1985	1981	1982	1983	1984	1985	
210	Coal mining	-	-	-	-	-	-	-	-	-	...	210
220	Petroleum and gas	...	...	...	...	...	...	...	...	...	...	220
230	Metal ore mining	...	...	...	...	...	...	...	...	...	...	230
290	Other mining	...	...	...	...	...	...	...	...	...	...	290
2	Mining, quarrying	1.47	1.21	1.23	1.15	0.99	308	363	416	455	444	2
311/2	Food products	8.81	9.22	9.91								311/2
313	Beverages	0.68	0.68	0.70	10.77	10.68	454	471	513	545	569	313
314	Tobacco	0.18	0.18	0.20								314
321	Textiles	5.27	4.83	4.77	4.58	4.21	335	331	328	322	320	321
3211	Spinning,weaving etc.	4.32	3.81	3.80	...	...	...	...	...	...	...	3211
322	Wearing apparel	6.06	6.79	6.62	6.94	6.92	21	24	28	29	31	322
323	Leather and products	0.27	0.21	0.21	0.81	0.90	11	10	10	10	12	323
324	Footwear	0.58	0.66	0.67								324
331	Wood products	1.35	1.33	1.28	3.18	3.05	73	76	81	75	81	331
332	Furniture, fixtures	1.73	1.65	1.64								332
341	Paper and products	1.48	1.28	1.56	1.55	1.60	125	114	108	112	110	341
3411	Pulp,paper etc.	0.47	0.22	0.44	...	...	...	...	...	...	...	3411
342	Printing,publishing	2.57	2.71	3.03	3.53	3.34	28	29	33	36	34	342
351	Industrial chemicals	f/ 2.43	f/ 2.28	f/ 2.38	g/ 4.60	g/ 4.64	g/ 897	g/ 891	g/ 983	g/ 1137	g/ 1174	351
3511	Basic excl fertilizers	...	...	...	...	...	...	...	...	...	...	3511
3513	Synthetic resins etc	...	...	...	...	...	...	...	...	...	...	3513
352	Other chemical products	2.01	2.07	2.23	g/	g/	g/	g/	g/	g/	g/	352
3522	Drugs and medicines	0.71	0.74	0.83	...	...	...	...	...	...	...	3522
353	Petroleum refineries	f/	f/	f/	g/	g/	g/	g/	g/	g/	g/	353
354	Petroleum,coal products	f/	f/	f/	g/	g/	g/	g/	g/	g/	g/	354
355	Rubber products	1.02	0.95	0.96	2.49	2.52	175	188	200	189	194	355
356	Plastic products n.e.c.	1.80	1.82	1.88								356
361	Pottery,china etc	0.37	0.36	0.34								361
362	Glass and products	0.26	0.23	0.21	2.55	2.25	268	281	323	289	281	362
369	Non-metal products n.e.c	2.10	2.04	2.18								369
371	Iron and steel	1.06	0.90	0.80	1.43	1.36	188	165	167	169	171	371
372	Non-ferrous metals	0.44	0.38	0.39								372
381	Metal products	9.43	9.57	10.03	10.76	10.19	302	316	351	362	402	381
382	Machinery n.e.c.	2.39	2.44	2.54	2.45	2.41	44	45	48	42	48	382
3825	Office,computing etc.	0.84	0.91	0.92	...	...	...	...	...	...	...	3825
383	Electrical machinery	7.47	9.56	9.82	8.60	9.05	114	127	145	174	208	383
3832	Radio,television etc.	5.24	7.35	7.65	...	...	...	...	...	...	...	3832
384	Transport equipment	4.75	4.43	4.58	4.69	4.87	137	150	145	166	180	384
3841	Shipbuilding, repair	0.46	0.29	0.32	...	...	...	...	...	...	...	3841
3843	Motor vehicles	0.72	0.67	0.69	...	...	...	...	...	...	...	3843
385	Professional goods	0.66	0.67	0.78	1.61	1.67	93	79	94	97	114	385
390	Other industries	0.85	0.89	0.89								390
3	Manufacturing	66.02	68.13	70.60	70.54	70.76	3265	3297	3557	3754	3929	3
410	Electricity,gas,steam	...	...	...	...	...	...	...	...	...	...	410
4101	Electricity	...	...	...	...	...	...	...	...	...	...	4101
420	Water works and supply	...	...	...	...	...	...	...	...	...	...	420
4	Electricity,gas etc	...	...	...	...	...	...	...	...	...	...	4
2-4	All industry	...	...	...	...	...	...	...	...	...	...	2-4

a/ For description, see country note.
b/ Twelve months beginning 1 January.
c/ Twelve months beginning 1 April of the year indicated.
d/ Establishments with 5 or more persons engaged.
e/ Establishments with at least one employee.
f/ Major groups 353 and 354 are included in 351.
g/ Major groups 352 to 354 are included in 351.

ISIC	INDUSTRY	7. OUTPUT IN PRODUCERS' PRICES a/b/ (MILLION SHEKELS) 1981	1982	c/ 1983	d/e/f/ 1984	d/e/f/ 1985	8. VALUE ADDED IN PRODUCERS' PRICES a/b/ (MILLION SHEKELS) 1981	1982	c/ 1983	1984	1985	ISIC
210	Coal mining	-	-	-	-	...	...	...	...	...	...	210
220	Petroleum and gas	...	...	...	...	...	...	...	...	...	...	220
230	Metal ore mining	...	300	1	...	...	...	124	-	...	...	230
290	Other mining	...	13500	41	...	...	...	8349	25	...	...	290
2	Mining, quarrying	6383	13800	42	114	440	3537	8473	25	...	...	2
311/2	Food products	30919	71700	220			8533	17016	52	...	...	311/2
313	Beverages	1674	4800	14	742	3663	878	2359	5	...	...	313
314	Tobacco	554	1600	6			174	59	1	...	...	314
321	Textiles	11400	23000	63	203	903	4438	6156	12	...	...	321
3211	Spinning, weaving etc.	8932	16600	50	...	...	3612	3874	7	...	...	3211
322	Wearing apparel	7210	16100	38	117	644	3574	6590	14	...	...	322
323	Leather and products	588	900	2	26	158	228	280	1	...	...	323
324	Footwear	1016	2600	7			556	1293	3	...	...	324
331	Wood products	2910	5800	15	103	512	1271	2255	6	...	...	331
332	Furniture, fixtures	2639	5400	14			1250	2070	5	...	...	332
341	Paper and products	4384	9600	28	104	520	1802	3398	9	...	...	341
3411	Pulp, paper etc.	1401	3000	8	...	...	467	856	2	...	...	3411
342	Printing, publishing	4422	11300	35	115	537	2340	6034	19	...	...	342
351	Industrial chemicals	g/ 12828	g/ 27100	g/ 88	h/ 390	h/ 1905	g/ 4791	g/ 10114	g/ 34	...	...	351
3511	Basic excl fertilizers	...	...	...	...	...	...	...	...	...	...	3511
3513	Synthetic resins etc	...	...	...	...	...	...	...	...	...	...	3513
352	Other chemical products	6187	12900	40	h/	h/	3240	5526	17	...	...	352
3522	Drugs and medicines	1984	4100	13	...	...	981	1624	5	...	...	3522
353	Petroleum refineries	g/	g/	g/	h/	h/	g/	g/	g/	...	...	353
354	Petroleum, coal products	g/	g/	g/	h/	h/	g/	g/	g/	...	...	354
355	Rubber products	2652	5300	13	176	850	1063	1702	4	...	...	355
356	Plastic products n.e.c.	5395	11800	37			2664	4941	16	...	...	356
361	Pottery, china etc	497	900	2			323	455	1	...	...	361
362	Glass and products	612	1000	2	149	660	357	490	1	...	...	362
369	Non-metal products n.e.c	7058	15000	45			2665	5693	18	...	...	369
371	Iron and steel	3844	7400	21	101	467	1548	2690	6	...	...	371
372	Non-ferrous metals	1199	2300	9			573	871	3	...	...	372
381	Metal products	22728	47700	151	426	1977	13021	23213	72	...	...	381
382	Machinery n.e.c.	5160	10800	32	104	524	2872	5252	15	...	...	382
3825	Office, computing etc.	2325	4600	13	...	...	1262	2037	6	...	...	3825
383	Electrical machinery	17903	46200	146	451	2262	11172	25737	79	...	...	383
3832	Radio, television etc.	13026	36900	120	...	...	8560	21619	68	...	...	3832
384	Transport equipment	11201	19200	55	190	996	7292	10542	31	...	...	384
3841	Shipbuilding, repair	667	500	2	...	...	420	213	1	...	...	3841
3843	Motor vehicles	1712	3600	10	...	...	757	1320	3	...	...	3843
385	Professional goods	1340	2900	15	72	433	909	1494	6	...	...	385
390	Other industries	2084	4600	14			714	1288	4	...	...	390
3	Manufacturing	168404	368100	1111	3469	17012	78248	147518	435	...	...	3
410	Electricity, gas, steam	...	...	...	...	...	...	...	...	...	...	410
4101	Electricity	...	...	...	...	...	...	...	...	...	...	4101
420	Water works and supply	...	...	...	...	...	...	...	...	...	...	420
4	Electricity, gas etc	...	...	...	...	...	...	...	...	...	...	4
2-4	All industry	...	...	...	...	...	...	...	...	...	...	2-4

Note. For certain differences in classification, see country note.

a/ Twelve months beginning 1 April of the year indicated.
b/ Establishments with 5 or more persons engaged.
c/ Effective 1 January 1986, a new currency was introduced by which 1,000 "old" shekels became equivalent to one "new" shekel. Data are reported in new curreny beginning 1983.
d/ Establishments with at least one employee.
e/ Twelve months beginning 1 January.
f/ Gross revenue including value added tax at June prices of the year indicated.
g/ Major groups 353 and 354 are included in 351.
h/ Major groups 352 to 354 are included in 351.

ISIC	INDUSTRY	9. GROSS FIXED CAPITAL FORMATION TOTAL a/b/c/ (MILLION SHEKELS) 1981	1982	e/ 1983	1984	1985	10. GROSS FIXED CAPITAL FORMATION MACHINERY AND EQUIPMENT a/b/d/ (MILLION SHEKELS) 1981	1982	e/ 1983	1984	1985	ISIC
210	Coal mining	...	...	...	...	...	...	...	...	...	...	210
220	Petroleum and gas	...	...	...	...	...	...	...	...	...	...	220
230	Metal ore mining	...	233	-	...	...	...	123	-	...	...	230
290	Other mining	...	1294	3	...	...	...	1071	2	...	...	290
2	Mining, quarrying .	1010	1527	3	...	...	719	1194	2	...	...	2
311/2	Food products	1041	3034	10	...	...	783	2468	8	...	...	311/2
313	Beverages	83	167	1	...	...	77	156	1	...	...	313
314	Tobacco	24	152	-	...	...	24	151	-	...	...	314
321	Textiles	397	1357	3	...	...	340	906	2	...	...	321
3211	Spinning,weaving etc..	311	1232	2	...	...	264	798	2	...	...	3211
322	Wearing apparel	183	622	3	...	...	156	505	2	...	...	322
323	Leather and products ...	6	15	-	...	...	6	15	-	...	...	323
324	Footwear	32	165	-	...	...	27	156	-	...	...	324
331	Wood products	59	118	1	...	...	45	108	1	...	...	331
332	Furniture, fixtures	105	214	1	...	...	82	189	1	...	...	332
341	Paper and products	193	480	5	...	...	179	447	4	...	...	341
3411	Pulp,paper etc.	66	85	1	...	...	66	64	1	...	...	3411
342	Printing,publishing	160	831	1	...	...	149	754	1	...	...	342
351	Industrial chemicals ... f/	713	2115	8	...	...	605	1990	8	...	...	351
3511	Basic excl fertilizers	...	...	...	...	...	...	...	...	...	...	3511
3513	Synthetic resins etc .	...	...	...	...	...	...	...	...	...	...	3513
352	Other chemical products.	477	1380	3	...	...	275	952	2	...	...	352
3522	Drugs and medicines ..	51	930	1	...	...	29	634	1	...	...	3522
353	Petroleum refineries ... f/	...	...	...	...	...	...	...	...	...	...	353
354	Petroleum,coal products. f/	...	...	...	...	...	...	...	...	...	...	354
355	Rubber products	69	150	1	...	...	60	140	1	...	...	355
356	Plastic products n.e.c..	361	1482	4	...	...	322	1274	3	...	...	356
361	Pottery,china etc	20	273	-	...	...	16	270	-	...	...	361
362	Glass and products	177	170	1	...	...	173	165	1	...	...	362
369	Non-metal products n.e.c	326	1397	3	...	...	296	1309	3	...	...	369
371	Iron and steel	109	198	2	...	...	95	180	2	...	...	371
372	Non-ferrous metals	24	41	-	...	...	18	40	-	...	...	372
381	Metal products	1244	2992	8	...	...	970	2439	7	...	...	381
382	Machinery n.e.c.	244	670	2	...	...	180	579	2	...	...	382
3825	Office,computing etc..	116	207	1	...	...	85	194	1	...	...	3825
383	Electrical machinery ...	955	2753	12	...	...	693	2340	9	...	...	383
3832	Radio,television etc..	797	2353	11	...	...	568	2010	8	...	...	3832
384	Transport equipment	411	1467	7	...	...	266	1101	5	...	...	384
3841	Shipbuilding, repair..	14	53	1	...	...	12	53	-	...	...	3841
3843	Motor vehicles	21	117	1	...	...	16	108	-	...	...	3843
385	Professional goods	190	537	1	...	...	174	335	1	...	...	385
390	Other industries	50	143	1	...	...	42	136	1	...	...	390
3	Manufacturing	7653	22924	79	...	...	6053	19105	64	...	...	3
410	Electricity,gas,steam ..	...	...	...	...	...	...	...	...	...	...	410
4101	Electricity	...	...	...	...	...	...	...	...	...	...	4101
420	Water works and supply .	...	...	...	...	...	...	...	...	...	...	420
4	Electricity,gas etc	...	...	...	...	...	...	...	...	...	...	4
2-4	All industry	...	...	...	...	...	...	...	...	...	...	2-4

Note. For certain differences in classification, see country note.

a/ Twelve months beginning 1 April of the year indicated.
b/ Establishments with 5 or more persons engaged.
c/ Excluding land. The value of sales is not deducted.
d/ The value of sales is not deducted.
e/ Effective 1 January 1986, a new currency was introduced by which 1,000 "old" shekels became equivalent to one "new" shekel. Data are reported in new curreny beginning 1983.
f/ Major groups 353 and 354 are included in 351.

11. VALUE OF STOCKS AT END OF PERIOD
TOTAL a/b/
(MILLION SHEKELS)

ISIC	INDUSTRY	1981	1982	1983 c/	1984	1985	ISIC
210	Coal mining	...	...	...	...	...	210
220	Petroleum and gas	...	...	...	...	...	220
230	Metal ore mining	...	83	-	...	...	230
290	Other mining	...	1656	4	...	...	290
2	Mining, quarrying .	1237	1739	4	...	...	2
311/2	Food products	3891	6361	18	...	...	311/2
313	Beverages	287	560	1	...	...	313
314	Tobacco	277	715	2	...	...	314
321	Textiles	3652	6771	20	...	...	321
3211	Spinning,weaving etc..	3252	5802	18	...	...	3211
322	Wearing apparel	1622	3092	8	...	...	322
323	Leather and products ...	148	117	-	...	...	323
324	Footwear	180	343	1	...	...	324
331	Wood products	612	1012	3	...	...	331
332	Furniture, fixtures	635	785	2	...	...	332
341	Paper and products	760	1092	5	...	...	341
3411	Pulp,paper etc.	268	376	1	...	...	3411
342	Printing,publishing	419	611	1	...	...	342
351	Industrial chemicals ... d/	2637	4062	11	...	...	351
3511	Basic excl fertilizers	...	...	...	...	...	3511
3513	Synthetic resins etc .	...	...	...	...	...	3513
352	Other chemical products.	1765	2845	8	...	...	352
3522	Drugs and medicines ..	557	874	3	...	...	3522
353	Petroleum refineries ... d/	...	...	...	...	...	353
354	Petroleum,coal products. d/	...	...	...	...	...	354
355	Rubber products	554	849	2	...	...	355
356	Plastic products n.e.c..	978	1678	5	...	...	356
361	Pottery,china etc	134	251	1	...	...	361
362	Glass and products	186	262	1	...	...	362
369	Non-metal products n.e.c	1247	1300	3	...	...	369
371	Iron and steel	895	1505	3	...	...	371
372	Non-ferrous metals	227	384	1	...	...	372
381	Metal products	7468	11776	30	...	...	381
382	Machinery n.e.c.	1498	2465	6	...	...	382
3825	Office,computing etc..	759	1134	3	...	...	3825
383	Electrical machinery ...	5454	10281	31	...	...	383
3832	Radio,television etc..	4341	8464	26	...	...	3832
384	Transport equipment	4241	6797	16	...	...	384
3841	Shipbuilding, repair..	459	373	-	...	...	3841
3843	Motor vehicles	558	919	3	...	...	3843
385	Professional goods	433	1100	5	...	...	385
390	Other industries	417	604	2	...	...	390
3	Manufacturing	40617	67620	186	...	...	3
410	Electricity,gas,steam ..	...	...	...	...	...	410
4101	Electricity	...	...	...	...	...	4101
420	Water works and supply .	...	...	...	...	...	420
4	Electricity,gas etc	...	...	...	...	...	4
2-4	All industry	...	...	...	...	...	2-4

Note. For certain differences in classification, see country note.

a/ Establishments with 5 or more persons engaged. b/ At 31 March of the following year.
c/ Effective 1 January 1986, a new currency was introduced by which 1,000 "old" shekels became equivalent to one "new" shekel. Data are reported in new curreny beginning 1983.
d/ Major groups 353 and 354 are included in 351.

12. INDEX NUMBERS OF INDUSTRIAL PRODUCTION (1980 = 100)

ISIC	INDUSTRY		1976	1977	1978	1979	1981	1982	1983	1984	1985	a/ RATE	ISIC
210	Coal mining		...	...	...	...	...	...	...	...	...	...	210
220	Petroleum and gas		...	...	...	...	...	...	...	...	...	...	220
230	Metal ore mining		...	...	...	...	...	...	...	...	...	...	230
290	Other mining		78	79	86	94	105	107	99	104	...	f/ 3.7	290
2	Mining, quarrying		77	78	86	93	104	107	98	102	...	f/ 3.6	2
311/2	Food products												311/2
313	Beverages		81	87	94	104	110	113	123	128	...	f/ 5.9	313
314	Tobacco												314
321	Textiles		89	97	104	107	100	106	103	103	...	f/ 1.8	321
3211	Spinning,weaving etc.		...	...	...	...	...	...	...	...	...	...	3211
322	Wearing apparel	b/	81	88	96	96	110	109	102	93	...	f/ 1.7	322
323	Leather and products		104	112	118	102	104	112	101	101	...	f/ -0.4	323
324	Footwear	b/	...	...	...	...	...	...	...	...	...	...	324
331	Wood products		102	101	114	115	110	117	112	108	...	f/ 0.7	331
332	Furniture, fixtures												332
341	Paper and products		92	96	103	110	104	105	107	110	...	f/ 2.3	341
3411	Pulp,paper etc.		...	...	...	...	...	...	...	...	...	...	3411
342	Printing,publishing		67	77	88	90	107	98	110	109	...	f/ 6.3	342
351	Industrial chemicals	c/	86	94	99	103	104	106	118	128	...	f/ 5.1	351
3511	Basic excl fertilizers		...	...	...	...	...	...	...	...	...	...	3511
3513	Synthetic resins etc		...	...	...	...	...	...	...	...	...	...	3513
352	Other chemical products.	c/	...	...	...	...	...	...	...	...	...	...	352
3522	Drugs and medicines		...	...	...	...	...	...	...	...	...	...	3522
353	Petroleum refineries	c/	...	...	...	...	...	...	...	...	...	...	353
354	Petroleum,coal products.	c/	...	...	...	...	...	...	...	...	...	...	354
355	Rubber products		92	99	108	103	105	108	119	129	...	f/ 4.3	355
356	Plastic products n.e.c.												356
361	Pottery,china etc												361
362	Glass and products		105	98	97	100	107	99	96	93	...	f/ -1.5	362
369	Non-metal products n.e.c												369
371	Iron and steel		95	98	108	108	103	88	87	99	...	f/ 0.5	371
372	Non-ferrous metals												372
381	Metal products		89	90	96	106	102	106	112	118	...	f/ 3.6	381
382	Machinery n.e.c.		75	85	101	100	108	112	123	127	...	f/ 6.8	382
3825	Office,computing etc.		...	...	...	...	...	...	...	...	...	...	3825
383	Electrical machinery		88	90	99	102	109	114	118	128	...	f/ 4.8	383
3832	Radio,television etc.		...	...	...	...	...	...	...	...	...	...	3832
384	Transport equipment		83	90	90	107	100	95	96	98	...	f/ 2.1	384
3841	Shipbuilding, repair.		...	...	...	...	...	...	...	...	...	...	3841
3843	Motor vehicles		...	...	...	...	...	...	...	...	...	...	3843
385	Professional goods		...	...	...	...	...	...	...	...	...	...	385
390	Other industries		111	124	106	116	102	100	117	139	...	f/ 2.9	390
3	Manufacturing		88	93	99	103	106	107	111	117	...	f/ 3.6	3
410	Electricity,gas,steam		...	...	...	...	...	...	...	...	...	...	410
4101	Electricity	d/	83	89	95	99	105	110	116	119	...	f/ 4.6	4101
420	Water works and supply		.	.	.	.	.	.	.	.	...	.	420
4	Electricity,gas etc		...	...	...	...	...	...	...	...	...	...	4
2-4	All industry	e/	87	93	98	103	106	107	111	116	...	f/ 3.7	2-4

a/ Annual growth rate 1976-1985.
c/ Major groups 352 to 354 are included in 351.
e/ Excluding electricity, gas and steam.
b/ Major group 324 is included in 322.
d/ Calculated from output of electricity in kWh.
f/ Annual growth rate 1976-1984.

ITALY

The information on industrial activity is based on the reply to the United Nations Questionnaire on General Industrial Statistics from the Central Institute of Statistics, Rome. The concepts, definitions and classification by branches of industry are generally in accordance with United Nations standards.

The estimates are primarily obtained from annual inquiries into gross product and capital investments of the industrial sector conducted by the Central Institute of Statistics. The inquiries are based on a register of all enterprises with 20 or more persons engaged in the 1971 general census, updated annually by information obtained from various sources. The enterprises included account for about 90 per cent of the total contribution of industry to the gross domestic product. The coverage of persons engaged in 1971 represented 68 per cent of the total recorded in industry in the general census of that year.

The statistical unit employed in the survey is the enterprise. However, in order to obtain more homogeneous industrial groupings, multi-unit enterprises with more than 250 persons engaged are required to provide separate data for each functional unit. The information set out in the tables is classified according to activities of the functional units of the enterprises obtained in this way.

The estimates are compiled by industrial groupings of the national classification, which are not fully convertible to ISIC. The following differences should be noted: peat cutting and digging (ISIC 290) is included in ISIC 210; extraction of pyrites (ISIC 290) in ISIC 230; manufacture of olive oil, margarine, compound cooking fats etc. (ISIC 311/2) in ISIC 351-352 combined; asbestos spinning and weaving (ISIC 369) in ISIC 321; made-up textile goods, except wearing apparel, (ISIC 321) in ISIC 322; repair of footwear (ISIC major division 9) in ISIC 324; industrial furnaces and ovens, cooking ranges and ovens, tanks, small arms, ordnance and artillery (ISIC 382) in ISIC 381; laboratory equipment (ISIC 385) in ISIC 381; invalid and baby carriages (ISIC 384) in ISIC 381; aircraft engines (ISIC 384) in ISIC 382; typewriters, calculators, cash registers and scales (ISIC 382) in ISIC 385; electric lamps and tubes (ISIC 383) in ISIC 390; jewellery and related articles (ISIC 390) in ISIC 385. The following activities are excluded: superficially treating and electro-galvanizing metals, repair of agricultural and other machinery, repair, painting and caulking of floating equipment, and repair of scientific and professional equipment.

The employment numbers are annual averages. Wages and salaries relate to the gross earnings of employees (before deduction of taxes and social insurance contributions payable by the employee) and include basic pay, cost-of-living allowances, overtime and vacation pay, bonuses and payments in kind. The estimates of supplements to wages and salaries represent employers' contributions to social security and provident funds etc.; outlays for social, cultural and recreational purposes are excluded. The number of operatives and wages and salaries of operatives refer to enterprises with 50 or more persons engaged.

The estimates of electricity consumption are compiled by the Ente Nazionale per la Energia Elettrica and cover all industrial enterprises. Consumption for lighting purposes is excluded.

The value of output is calculated as the sum of the following items: (a) value of sales of products of the enterprise, (b) value of goods shipped in the same condition as received, (c) receipts for work done for others, (d) receipts for non-industrial services rendered, and (e) value of fixed assets produced for own use. Adjustments are made for changes in the value of work in progress and stocks of finished goods between the beginning and the end of the year. The valuation is net of indirect taxes; subsidies, however, are not taken into account.

The estimates of value added are derived as the difference between the value of output as defined above and the cost of the following inputs: materials and supplies purchased (adjusted for changes in stocks), goods shipped in the same condition as received and industrial work done by others. The estimates presented are gross of the cost of non-industrial services which is deducted in the national concept.

The estimates of gross fixed capital formation relate to the acquisition of new and used fixed assets, including investments of a social nature. Sales are not deducted. In the case of this inquiry, the coverage is extended to include new enterprises not yet in operation.

The indexes of industrial production are compiled by the Central Institute of Statistics and provided in response to the United Nations Questionnaire on Indexes of Industrial Production. In principle, the indexes cover all industrial establishments.

Related national publications:
Annuario Statistico Italiano; *Annuario di Statistiche Industriali*; *Compendio Statistico Italiano* (annual); *Bolletino Mensile di Statistica*; *Supplemento Straordinario al Bolletino Mensile di Statistica* (selected issues), all published by the Central Institute of Statistics, Rome.

ISIC	INDUSTRY	1. NUMBER OF ENTERPRISES a/b/ (NUMBER)					2. AVERAGE NUMBER OF PERSONS ENGAGED a/ (THOUSANDS)					ISIC
		1981	1982	1983	1984	1985	1981	1982	1983	1984	1985	
210	Coal mining	-	-	...	...	...	-	-	...	...	...	210
220	Petroleum and gas	7	8	...	...	...	7	8	...	...	...	220
230	Metal ore mining	14	11	...	...	...	6	6	...	...	...	230
290	Other mining	301	275	...	...	...	18	15	...	...	...	290
2	Mining, quarrying	322	294	...	...	...	31	29	...	...	...	2
311/2	Food products	1607	1646	...	...	...	172	167	...	...	...	311/2
313	Beverages	376	380	...	...	...	32	32	...	...	...	313
314	Tobacco	28	30	...	...	...	19	19	...	...	...	314
321	Textiles	2935	2783	...	...	...	275	247	...	...	...	321
3211	Spinning,weaving etc.	...	...	...	...	...	...	...	...	...	...	3211
322	Wearing apparel	1729	1657	...	...	...	165	154	...	...	...	322
323	Leather and products	457	428	...	...	...	27	24	...	...	...	323
324	Footwear	1157	1105	...	...	...	77	72	...	...	...	324
331	Wood products	974	942	...	...	...	48	44	...	...	...	331
332	Furniture, fixtures	1292	1243	...	...	...	71	66	...	...	...	332
341	Paper and products	607	678	...	...	...	64	66	...	...	...	341
3411	Pulp,paper etc.	...	...	...	...	...	...	...	...	...	...	3411
342	Printing,publishing	776	726	...	...	...	85	79	...	...	...	342
351	Industrial chemicals	c/ 1037	c/ 1016	...	...	...	d/ 244	d/ 211	...	...	...	351
3511	Basic excl fertilizers	...	...	...	...	...	...	...	...	...	...	3511
3513	Synthetic resins etc	...	...	...	...	...	...	...	...	...	...	3513
352	Other chemical products.	c/	c/	...	...	...	d/	d/	...	...	...	352
3522	Drugs and medicines	...	...	...	...	...	...	...	...	...	...	3522
353	Petroleum refineries	59	53	...	...	...	[20	20]	...	...	...	353
354	Petroleum,coal products.	c/	c/	...	...	...			...	...	...	354
355	Rubber products	266	265	...	...	...	63	58	...	...	...	355
356	Plastic products n.e.c.	916	911	...	...	...	71	69	...	...	...	356
361	Pottery,china etc			...	...	...			...	...	...	361
362	Glass and products	[2427	2363]	...	...	...	[207	198]	...	...	...	362
369	Non-metal products n.e.c			...	...	...			...	...	...	369
371	Iron and steel	872	848	...	...	...	236	223	...	...	...	371
372	Non-ferrous metals	462	477	...	...	...	47	45	...	...	...	372
381	Metal products	2379	2202	...	...	...	197	176	...	...	...	381
382	Machinery n.e.c.	2484	2420	...	...	...	299	283	...	...	...	382
3825	Office,computing etc.	...	...	...	...	...	...	...	...	...	...	3825
383	Electrical machinery	1145	1127	...	...	...	310	295	...	...	...	383
3832	Radio,television etc.	...	...	...	...	...	...	...	...	...	...	3832
384	Transport equipment	730	810	...	...	...	402	387	...	...	...	384
3841	Shipbuilding, repair.	...	...	...	...	...	...	...	...	...	...	3841
3843	Motor vehicles	...	...	...	...	...	...	...	...	...	...	3843
385	Professional goods	385	341	...	...	...	63	58	...	...	...	385
390	Other industries	485	488	...	...	...	34	32	...	...	...	390
3	Manufacturing	25585	24939	...	...	...	3228	3025	...	...	...	3
410	Electricity,gas,steam	126	123	...	...	...	149	149	...	...	...	410
4101	Electricity	49	49	...	...	...	129	129	...	...	...	4101
420	Water works and supply	66	66	...	...	...	12	12	...	...	...	420
4	Electricity,gas etc	192	189	...	...	...	161	161	...	...	...	4
2-4	All industry	26099	25422	...	...	...	3420	3215	...	...	...	2-4

Note. For description of classification, see country note.

a/ Enterprises with 20 or more persons engaged.
b/ Number of functional units.
c/ Major groups 352 and 354 are included in 351.
d/ Major group 352 is included in 351.

ISIC	INDUSTRY	3. AVERAGE NUMBER OF EMPLOYEES a/ (THOUSANDS) 1981	1982	1983	1984	1985	4. WAGES AND SALARIES OF EMPLOYEES a/ (BILLION LIRE) 1981	1982	1983	1984	1985	ISIC
210	Coal mining	-	-	...	...	...	-	-	...	...	...	210
220	Petroleum and gas	7	8	...	...	...	125	150	...	...	...	220
230	Metal ore mining	6	6	...	...	...	71	74	...	...	...	230
290	Other mining	18	15	...	...	...	210	213	...	...	...	290
2	Mining, quarrying .	31	29	...	...	...	406	437	...	...	...	2
311/2	Food products	169	166	...	...	...	2010	2345	...	...	...	311/2
313	Beverages	31	31	...	...	...	418	490	...	...	...	313
314	Tobacco	19	19	...	...	...	220	237	...	...	...	314
321	Textiles	271	245	...	...	...	2583	2700	...	...	...	321
3211	Spinning,weaving etc..	...	...	...	...	...	...	...	...	...	...	3211
322	Wearing apparel	162	153	...	...	...	1351	1512	...	...	...	322
323	Leather and products ...	26	24	...	...	...	252	260	...	...	...	323
324	Footwear	75	71	...	...	...	611	686	...	...	...	324
331	Wood products	46	43	...	...	...	428	456	...	...	...	331
332	Furniture, fixtures	69	64	...	...	...	650	709	...	...	...	332
341	Paper and products	63	65	...	...	...	755	880	...	...	...	341
3411	Pulp,paper etc.	...	...	...	...	...	...	...	...	...	...	3411
342	Printing,publishing	84	79	...	...	...	1190	1335	...	...	...	342
351	Industrial chemicals ... b/	243	211	...	...	...	3356	3455	...	...	...	351
3511	Basic excl fertilizers	...	...	...	...	...	...	...	...	...	...	3511
3513	Synthetic resins etc .	...	...	...	...	...	...	...	...	...	...	3513
352	Other chemical products. b/	...	...	...	...	...	...	...	...	...	...	352
3522	Drugs and medicines ..	...	...	...	...	...	...	...	...	...	...	3522
353	Petroleum refineries ...	[20	20]	...	...	...	[320	374]	...	...	...	353
354	Petroleum,coal products.			...	...	...			...	...	...	354
355	Rubber products	62	58	...	...	...	766	822	...	...	...	355
356	Plastic products n.e.c..	70	68	...	...	...	773	887	...	...	...	356
361	Pottery,china etc			...	...	...			...	...	...	361
362	Glass and products	[204	197]	...	...	...	[2220	2442]	...	...	...	362
369	Non-metal products n.e.c			...	...	...			...	...	...	369
371	Iron and steel	234	222	...	...	...	2926	3143	...	...	...	371
372	Non-ferrous metals	47	44	...	...	...	523	538	...	...	...	372
381	Metal products	194	174	...	...	...	2154	2200	...	...	...	381
382	Machinery n.e.c.	295	280	...	...	...	3551	3787	...	...	...	382
3825	Office,computing etc..	...	...	...	...	...	...	...	...	...	...	3825
383	Electrical machinery ...	308	294	...	...	...	3444	3838	...	...	...	383
3832	Radio,television etc..	...	...	...	...	...	...	...	...	...	...	3832
384	Transport equipment	401	386	...	...	...	4393	4733	...	...	...	384
3841	Shipbuilding, repair..	...	...	...	...	...	...	...	...	...	...	3841
3843	Motor vehicles	...	...	...	...	...	...	...	...	...	...	3843
385	Professional goods	62	57	...	...	...	771	844	...	...	...	385
390	Other industries	33	31	...	...	...	310	352	...	...	...	390
3	Manufacturing	3188	3002	...	...	...	35975	39025	...	...	...	3
410	Electricity,gas,steam ..	149	149	...	...	...	2392	2729	...	...	...	410
4101	Electricity	129	129	...	...	...	2103	2409	...	...	...	4101
420	Water works and supply .	12	12	...	...	...	187	221	...	...	...	420
4	Electricity,gas etc	161	161	...	...	...	2579	2950	...	...	...	4
2-4	All industry	3380	3192	...	...	...	38960	42412	...	...	...	2-4

Note. For description of classification, see country note.

a/ Enterprises with 20 or more persons engaged.

b/ Major group 352 is included in 351.

ISIC	INDUSTRY	5. SUPPLEMENTS TO WAGES AND SALARIES a/ (BILLION LIRE)					6. AVERAGE NUMBER OF OPERATIVES b/ (THOUSANDS)					ISIC
		1981	1982	1983	1984	1985	1981	1982	1983	1984	1985	
210	Coal mining	-	-	...	..	...	-	-	...	...	...	210
220	Petroleum and gas	57	65	...	..	...	4	4	...	...	...	220
230	Metal ore mining	35	37	...	...	...	5	4	...	...	...	230
290	Other mining	91	100	...	...	...	10	9	...	...	...	290
2	Mining, quarrying .	183	202	...	...	...	19	17	...	...	...	2
311/2	Food products	794	1000	...	...	...	103	99	...	...	...	311/2
313	Beverages	176	225	...	...	...	18	17	...	...	...	313
314	Tobacco	26	29	...	...	...	15	15	...	...	...	314
321	Textiles	1002	1135	...	...	...	191	169	...	...	...	321
3211	Spinning,weaving etc..	...	...	...	...	...	...	...	...	...	...	3211
322	Wearing apparel	458	548	...	...	...	112	105	...	...	...	322
323	Leather and products ...	95	113	...	...	...	14	12	...	...	...	323
324	Footwear	216	268	...	...	...	46	43	...	...	...	324
331	Wood products	180	212	...	...	...	24	21	...	...	...	331
332	Furniture, fixtures	272	322	...	...	...	36	33	...	...	...	332
341	Paper and products	306	395	...	...	...	42	41	...	...	...	341
3411	Pulp,paper etc.	...	...	...	...	...	...	...	...	...	...	3411
342	Printing,publishing	528	658	...	...	...	42	39	...	...	...	342
351	Industrial chemicals ... c/	1240	1380	...	...	...	134	130	...	...	...	351
3511	Basic excl fertilizers	...	...	...	...	...	...	...	...	...	...	3511
3513	Synthetic resins etc .	...	...	...	...	...	...	...	...	...	...	3513
352	Other chemical products. c/	...	...	...	...	...	...	...	...	...	...	352
3522	Drugs and medicines ..	...	...	...	...	...	...	...	...	...	...	3522
353	Petroleum refineries ...	[140	168]	...	...	...	[11	11]	...	...	...	353
354	Petroleum,coal products.			...	...	...			...	...	...	354
355	Rubber products	327	352	...	...	...	46	43	...	...	...	355
356	Plastic products n.e.c..	306	373	...	...	...	41	40	...	...	...	356
361	Pottery,china etc			...	...	...			...	...	...	361
362	Glass and products	[911	1101]	...	...	...	[128	123]	...	...	...	362
369	Non-metal products n.e.c			...	...	...			...	...	...	369
371	Iron and steel	1270	1383	...	...	...	174	163	...	...	...	371
372	Non-ferrous metals	240	267	...	...	...	33	30	...	...	...	372
381	Metal products	880	982	...	...	...	114	102	...	...	...	381
382	Machinery n.e.c.	1548	1740	...	...	...	175	164	...	...	...	382
3825	Office,computing etc..	...	...	...	...	...	...	...	...	...	...	3825
383	Electrical machinery ...	1346	1587	...	...	...	204	190	...	...	...	383
3832	Radio,television etc..	...	...	...	...	...	...	...	...	...	...	3832
384	Transport equipment	1818	2063	...	...	...	309	295	...	...	...	384
3841	Shipbuilding, repair..	...	...	...	...	...	...	...	...	...	...	3841
3843	Motor vehicles	...	...	...	...	...	...	...	...	...	...	3843
385	Professional goods	314	344	...	...	...	33	32	...	...	...	385
390	Other industries	125	154	...	...	...	20	19	...	...	...	390
3	Manufacturing	14518	16799	...	...	...	2065	1936	...	...	...	3
410	Electricity,gas,steam ..	1370	1540	...	...	...	81	80	...	...	...	410
4101	Electricity	1226	1378	...	...	...	72	72	...	...	...	4101
420	Water works and supply .	79	104	...	...	...	5	5	...	...	...	420
4	Electricity,gas etc	1449	1644	...	...	...	86	85	...	...	...	4
2-4	All industry	16150	18645	...	...	...	2170	2038	...	...	...	2-4

Note. For description of classification, see country note.

a/ Enterprises with 20 or more persons engaged.
b/ Enterprises with 50 or more persons engaged.
c/ Major group 352 is included in 351.

ISIC	INDUSTRY	7. WAGES AND SALARIES OF OPERATIVES a/ (BILLION LIRE) 1981	1982	1983	1984	1985	8. HOURS WORKED BY OPERATIVES b/ (MILLIONS) 1981	1982	1983	1984	1985	ISIC
210	Coal mining	-	-	...	...	...	-	-	...	...	...	210
220	Petroleum and gas	61	72	...	...	...	8	9	...	...	...	220
230	Metal ore mining	51	52	...	...	...	6	6	...	...	...	230
290	Other mining	114	114	...	...	...	25	23	...	...	...	290
2	Mining, quarrying .	226	238	...	...	...	39	38	...	...	...	2
311/2	Food products	1125	1299	...	...	...	222	210	...	...	...	311/2
313	Beverages	205	235	...	...	...	36	36	...	...	...	313
314	Tobacco	169	181	...	...	...	24	24	...	...	...	314
321	Textiles	1666	1712	...	...	...	359	318	...	...	...	321
3211	Spinning,weaving etc..	...	...	...	...	...	...	...	...	...	...	3211
322	Wearing apparel	884	976	...	...	...	212	196	...	...	...	322
323	Leather and products ...	132	150	...	...	...	38	33	...	...	...	323
324	Footwear	358	411	...	...	...	107	100	...	...	...	324
331	Wood products	216	223	...	...	...	65	58	...	...	...	331
332	Furniture, fixtures	329	352	...	...	...	99	88	...	...	...	332
341	Paper and products	466	530	...	...	...	83	82	...	...	...	341
3411	Pulp,paper etc.	...	...	...	...	...	...	...	...	...	...	3411
342	Printing,publishing	528	574	...	...	...	93	82	...	...	...	342
351	Industrial chemicals ... c/	1553	1660	...	...	...	236	213	...	...	...	351
3511	Basic excl fertilizers	...	...	...	...	...	...	...	...	...	...	3511
3513	Synthetic resins etc .	...	...	...	...	...	...	...	...	...	...	3513
352	Other chemical products. c/	...	...	...	...	...	...	...	...	...	...	352
3522	Drugs and medicines ..	...	...	...	...	...	...	...	...	...	...	3522
353	Petroleum refineries ...	[154	177]	...	...	...	[19	19]	...	...	...	353
354	Petroleum,coal products.			...	...	...			...	...	...	354
355	Rubber products	516	549	...	...	...	77	69	...	...	...	355
356	Plastic products n.e.c..	418	479	...	...	...	90	87	...	...	...	356
361	Pottery,china etc			...	...	...			...	...	...	361
362	Glass and products	[1307	1422]	...	...	...	[285	260]	...	...	...	362
369	Non-metal products n.e.c			...	...	...			...	...	...	369
371	Iron and steel	1983	2118	...	...	...	294	269	...	...	...	371
372	Non-ferrous metals	337	332	...	...	...	59	52	...	...	...	372
381	Metal products	1159	1178	...	...	...	243	216	...	...	...	381
382	Machinery n.e.c.	1881	1952	...	...	...	349	313	...	...	...	382
3825	Office,computing etc..	...	...	...	...	...	...	...	...	...	...	3825
383	Electrical machinery ...	1912	2085	...	...	...	310	293	...	...	...	383
3832	Radio,television etc..	...	...	...	...	...	...	...	...	...	...	3832
384	Transport equipment	2998	3205	...	...	...	463	426	...	...	...	384
3841	Shipbuilding, repair..	...	...	...	...	...	...	...	...	...	...	3841
3843	Motor vehicles	...	...	...	...	...	...	...	...	...	...	3843
385	Professional goods	328	331	...	...	...	61	58	...	...	...	385
390	Other industries	174	191	...	...	...	42	42	...	...	...	390
3	Manufacturing	20798	22322	...	...	...	3866	3544	...	...	...	3
410	Electricity,gas,steam ..	1218	1373	...	...	...	142	137	...	...	...	410
4101	Electricity	1083	1231	...	...	...	123	122	...	...	...	4101
420	Water works and supply .	74	86	...	...	...	11	11	...	...	...	420
4	Electricity,gas etc	1292	1459	...	...	...	153	148	...	...	...	4
2-4	All industry	22316	24019	...	...	...	4058	3730	...	...	...	2-4

Note. For description of classification, see country note.

a/ Enterprises with 50 or more persons engaged.
c/ Major group 352 is included in 351.

b/ Enterprises with 20 or more persons engaged.

ISIC	INDUSTRY	9. QUANTITY OF ELECTRICITY CONSUMED a/ (MILLION KWH) 1981	1982	1983	1984	1985	10. OUTPUT b/c/ (BILLION LIRE) 1981	1982	1983	1984	1985	ISIC
210	Coal mining	71	65	52	...	...	-	-	...	...	...	210
220	Petroleum and gas	209	220	166	...	...	2964	3420	...	...	...	220
230	Metal ore mining	182	176	172	...	...	183	217	...	...	...	230
290	Other mining	1064	1041	1028	...	...	941	866	...	...	...	290
2	Mining, quarrying .	1526	1502	1418	...	...	4088	4503	...	...	...	2
311/2	Food products	[		]	...	...	25962	29108	...	...	...	311/2
313	Beverages	5242	5322	5398	...	...	3790	4558	...	...	...	313
314	Tobacco	[		]	...	...	1061	1453	...	...	...	314
321	Textiles	5451	5488	5394	...	...	14792	16147	...	...	...	321
3211	Spinning,weaving etc..	...	...	...	...	...	...	...	...	...	...	3211
322	Wearing apparel	561	585	570	...	...	6624	8026	...	...	...	322
323	Leather and products ...	445	485	500	...	...	2118	2384	...	...	...	323
324	Footwear	321	347	360	...	...	3304	3879	...	...	...	324
331	Wood products	1268	1244	1254	...	...	2962	2896	...	...	...	331
332	Furniture, fixtures	842	839	837	...	...	3971	4162	...	...	...	332
341	Paper and products	4996	4695	4608	...	...	5696	6513	...	...	...	341
3411	Pulp,paper etc.	...	...	...	...	...	...	...	...	...	...	3411
342	Printing,publishing	628	644	658	...	...	5455	6059	...	...	...	342
351	Industrial chemicals ... d/	15741	16534	16973	...	...	28733	29899	...	...	...	351
3511	Basic excl fertilizers	...	...	...	...	...	...	...	...	...	...	3511
3513	Synthetic resins etc . e/	1520	1684	1663	...	...	...	...	...	...	...	3513
352	Other chemical products. d/	...	...	...	...	...	...	...	...	...	...	352
3522	Drugs and medicines ..	...	...	...	...	...	...	...	...	...	...	3522
353	Petroleum refineries ...	2295	2277	2419	...	...	[18514	19098]	...	...	...	353
354	Petroleum,coal products.	122	219	186	...	...			...	...	...	354
355	Rubber products	958	932	899	...	...	3461	3753	...	...	...	355
356	Plastic products n.e.c..	2460	2620	2736	...	...	4745	5569	...	...	...	356
361	Pottery,china etc	[2903	2774	2864]	...	...	[	]	...	...	...	361
362	Glass and products				...	...	14227	15024	...	...	...	362
369	Non-metal products n.e.c	7254	6969	6882	...	...	[	]	...	...	...	369
371	Iron and steel	18223	17875	16424	...	...	20850	23878	...	...	...	371
372	Non-ferrous metals	6602	5800	5089	...	...	2478	2568	...	...	...	372
381	Metal products	[f/ 8147	f/ 8067	f/ 7933]	...	...	12153	12839	...	...	...	381
382	Machinery n.e.c.				...	...	20835	21838	...	...	...	382
3825	Office,computing etc..	...	...	...	...	...	...	...	...	...	...	3825
383	Electrical machinery ...	1857	1868	1904	...	...	16608	19612	...	...	...	383
3832	Radio,television etc..	...	...	...	...	...	...	...	...	...	...	3832
384	Transport equipment	2922	2881	2968	...	...	23731	26761	...	...	...	384
3841	Shipbuilding, repair..	255	241	234	...	...	...	...	...	...	...	3841
3843	Motor vehicles	2430	2372	2467	...	...	...	...	...	...	...	3843
385	Professional goods	f/	f/	f/	...	...	4269	4722	...	...	...	385
390	Other industries	f/ 410	f/ 390	f/ 415	...	...	1896	2339	...	...	...	390
3	Manufacturing	89648	88855	87271	...	...	248235	273085	...	...	...	3
410	Electricity,gas,steam ..	514	514	532	...	...	22467	25414	...	...	...	410
4101	Electricity	380	394	414	...	...	15231	17108	...	...	...	4101
420	Water works and supply .	2858	3062	3204	...	...	641	841	...	...	...	420
4	Electricity,gas etc	3372	3576	3736	...	...	23108	26255	...	...	...	4
2-4	All industry	94546	93933	92425	...	...	275431	303843	...	...	...	2-4

Note. For description of classification, see country note.

a/ All enterprises.
b/ Enterprises with 20 or more persons engaged.
c/ Net of indirect taxes and subsidies.
d/ Major group 352 is included in 351.
e/ Manufacture of artificial and synthetic fibres.
f/ Part of major group 385 is included in 381 and 382 combined and part in 390.

ISIC	INDUSTRY	11. VALUE ADDED a/b/ (BILLION LIRE) 1981	1982	1983	1984	1985	12. GROSS FIXED CAPITAL FORMATION TOTAL a/c/ (BILLION LIRE) 1981	1982	1983	1984	1985	ISIC
210	Coal mining	-	-	...	...	...	-	-	...	...	...	210
220	Petroleum and gas	2460	2856	...	...	...	363	609	...	...	...	220
230	Metal ore mining	106	131	...	...	...	105	126	...	...	...	230
290	Other mining	536	520	...	...	...	96	101	...	...	...	290
2	Mining, quarrying	3102	3507	...	...	...	564	836	...	...	...	2
311/2	Food products	6424	3308	...	...	...	831	914	...	...	...	311/2
313	Beverages	1708	2000	...	...	...	224	243	...	...	...	313
314	Tobacco	302	475	...	...	...	35	43	...	...	...	314
321	Textiles	6348	6797	...	...	...	764	716	...	...	...	321
3211	Spinning, weaving etc.	...	...	...	...	...	...	...	...	...	...	3211
322	Wearing apparel	3157	3678	...	...	...	151	187	...	...	...	322
323	Leather and products	741	668	...	...	...	93	88	...	...	...	323
324	Footwear	1397	1643	...	...	...	76	87	...	...	...	324
331	Wood products	1186	1208	...	...	...	172	127	...	...	...	331
332	Furniture, fixtures	1877	1999	...	...	...	135	147	...	...	...	332
341	Paper and products	2030	2443	...	...	...	314	305	...	...	...	341
3411	Pulp, paper etc.	...	...	...	...	...	...	...	...	...	...	3411
342	Printing, publishing	3075	3400	...	...	...	252	246	...	...	...	342
351	Industrial chemicals ... d/	10128	10982	...	...	...	1274	1260	...	...	...	351
3511	Basic excl fertilizers	...	...	...	...	...	...	...	...	...	...	3511
3513	Synthetic resins etc	...	...	...	...	...	...	...	...	...	...	3513
352	Other chemical products. d/	...	...	...	...	...	...	...	...	...	...	352
3522	Drugs and medicines	...	...	...	...	...	...	...	...	...	...	3522
353	Petroleum refineries	[1523	1451]	...	...	...	[406	438]	...	...	...	353
354	Petroleum, coal products.			...	...	...			...	...	...	354
355	Rubber products	1749	1855	...	...	...	175	205	...	...	...	355
356	Plastic products n.e.c.	2090	2447	...	...	...	258	300	...	...	...	356
361	Pottery, china etc	[6767	7515]	...	...	...	[1163	1225]	...	...	...	361
362	Glass and products			...	...	...			...	...	...	362
369	Non-metal products n.e.c			...	...	...			...	...	...	369
371	Iron and steel	6702	7321	...	...	...	1196	1284	...	...	...	371
372	Non-ferrous metals	1231	1266	...	...	...	138	126	...	...	...	372
381	Metal products	5734	6132	...	...	...	552	632	...	...	...	381
382	Machinery n.e.c.	9777	10558	...	...	...	854	818	...	...	...	382
3825	Office, computing etc.	...	...	...	...	...	...	...	...	...	...	3825
383	Electrical machinery	8249	9398	...	...	...	703	744	...	...	...	383
3832	Radio, television etc.	...	...	...	...	...	...	...	...	...	...	3832
384	Transport equipment	10388	11687	...	...	...	1156	1880	...	...	...	384
3841	Shipbuilding, repair	...	...	...	...	...	...	...	...	...	...	3841
3843	Motor vehicles	...	...	...	...	...	...	...	...	...	...	3843
385	Professional goods	2027	2365	...	...	...	237	203	...	...	...	385
390	Other industries	816	947	...	...	...	59	72	...	...	...	390
3	Manufacturing	95426	101543	...	...	...	11218	12290	...	...	...	3
410	Electricity, gas, steam	7320	9285	...	...	...	4339	4576	...	...	...	410
4101	Electricity	6187	7887	...	...	...	3589	3744	...	...	...	4101
420	Water works and supply	274	399	...	...	...	282	289	...	...	...	420
4	Electricity, gas etc	7594	9684	...	...	...	4621	4865	...	...	...	4
2-4	All industry	106122	114734	...	...	...	16403	17991	...	...	...	2-4

Note. For description of classification, see country note.

a/ Enterprises with 20 or more persons engaged.
b/ Net of indirect taxes and subsidies.
c/ The value of sales is not deducted.
d/ Major group 352 is included in 351.

13. GROSS FIXED CAPITAL FORMATION MACHINERY AND EQUIPMENT a/b/ (BILLION LIRE)

ISIC	INDUSTRY	1981	1982	1983	1984	1985	ISIC
210	Coal mining	-	-	...	...	...	210
220	Petroleum and gas	47	78	...	...	...	220
230	Metal ore mining	66	86	...	...	...	230
290	Other mining	83	71	...	...	...	290
2	Mining, quarrying	196	235	...	...	...	2
311/2	Food products	631	716	...	...	...	311/2
313	Beverages	185	193	...	...	...	313
314	Tobacco	27	27	...	...	...	314
321	Textiles	631	602	...	...	...	321
3211	Spinning,weaving etc.	...	...	...	...	...	3211
322	Wearing apparel	101	124	...	...	...	322
323	Leather and products	57	66	...	...	...	323
324	Footwear	53	51	...	...	...	324
331	Wood products	137	98	...	...	...	331
332	Furniture, fixtures	103	98	...	...	...	332
341	Paper and products	264	265	...	...	...	341
3411	Pulp,paper etc.	...	...	...	...	...	3411
342	Printing,publishing	185	179	...	...	...	342
351	Industrial chemicals ... c/	957	1023	...	...	...	351
3511	Basic excl fertilizers	...	...	...	...	...	3511
3513	Synthetic resins etc	...	...	...	...	...	3513
352	Other chemical products. c/	...	...	...	...	...	352
3522	Drugs and medicines	...	...	...	...	...	3522
353	Petroleum refineries	[355	403]	...	...	...	353
354	Petroleum,coal products.			...	...	...	354
355	Rubber products	149	175	...	...	...	355
356	Plastic products n.e.c.	213	238	...	...	...	356
361	Pottery,china etc	[	]	...	...	...	361
362	Glass and products	938	945	...	...	...	362
369	Non-metal products n.e.c			...	...	...	369
371	Iron and steel	998	1051	...	...	...	371
372	Non-ferrous metals	117	112	...	...	...	372
381	Metal products	412	477	...	...	...	381
382	Machinery n.e.c.	664	630	...	...	...	382
3825	Office,computing etc.	...	...	...	...	...	3825
383	Electrical machinery	549	598	...	...	...	383
3832	Radio,television etc.	...	...	...	...	...	3832
384	Transport equipment	914	1557	...	...	...	384
3841	Shipbuilding, repair	...	...	...	...	...	3841
3843	Motor vehicles	...	...	...	...	...	3843
385	Professional goods	177	140	...	...	...	385
390	Other industries	45	54	...	...	...	390
3	Manufacturing	8862	9822	...	...	...	3
410	Electricity,gas,steam	1426	1564	...	...	...	410
4101	Electricity	1306	1412	...	...	...	4101
420	Water works and supply	21	50	...	...	...	420
4	Electricity,gas etc	1447	1614	...	...	...	4
2-4	All industry	10505	11671	...	...	...	2-4

Note. For description of classification, see country note.

a/ Enterprises with 20 or more persons engaged.
b/ The value of sales is not deducted.
c/ Major group 352 is included in 351.

14. INDEX NUMBERS OF INDUSTRIAL PRODUCTION (1980 = 100)

ISIC	INDUSTRY	1976	1977	1978	1979	1981	1982	1983	1984	1985	a/ RATE	ISIC
210	Coal mining	104	95	97	109	101	99	90	94	89	-1.7	210
220	Petroleum and gas	119	105	107	110	106	113	107	113	115	-0.4	220
230	Metal ore mining	183	136	125	110	81	59	61	58	45	-14.4	230
290	Other mining	83	88	88	99	107	98	99	100	103	2.4	290
2	Mining, quarrying .	102	97	97	104	104	98	97	99	100	-0.2	2
311/2	Food products	87	84	89	97	102	101	102	101	105	2.1	311/2
313	Beverages											313
314	Tobacco	102	104	99	94	99	110	112	109	107	0.5	314
321	Textiles	91	88	84	95	100	98	89	96	97	0.7	321
3211	Spinning,weaving etc..	101	96	93	101	97	96	89	95	...	b/ -0.8	3211
322	Wearing apparel	...	...	...	...	...	...	...	...	...	...	322
323	Leather and products ...	107	101	100	112	103	107	105	112	116	0.9	323
324	Footwear	94	95	91	100	98	104	96	90	86	-1.0	324
331	Wood products	93	98	91	95	101	96	89	95	81	-1.5	331
332	Furniture, fixtures	71	80	77	90	95	84	79	83	87	2.3	332
341	Paper and products	88	86	93	100	98	96	95	104	100	1.4	341
3411	Pulp,paper etc.	85	84	92	102	99	93	87	102	...	b/ 2.3	3411
342	Printing,publishing	...	...	...	...	...	...	...	...	...	...	342
351	Industrial chemicals ...	95	95	99	103	91	83	85	94	95	0.0	351
3511	Basic excl fertilizers	112	109	104	106	88	78	78	82	...	b/ -3.8	3511
3513	Synthetic resins etc .	105	100	102	106	94	92	100	106	107	0.2	3513
352	Other chemical products.	...	...	...	...	...	...	...	...	...	...	352
3522	Drugs and medicines ..	67	70	83	89	109	122	125	135	...	b/ 9.2	3522
353	Petroleum refineries ...	114	112	118	118	98	91	84	81	78	-4.1	353
354	Petroleum,coal products.											354
355	Rubber products	94	96	93	100	93	88	83	90	97	0.3	355
356	Plastic products n.e.c..	...	...	...	...	...	...	...	...	...	...	356
361	Pottery,china etc											361
362	Glass and products	83	86	85	90	95	90	86	90	87	0.5	362
369	Non-metal products n.e.c											369
371	Iron and steel	89	90	91	94	97	91	85	92	92	0.4	371
372	Non-ferrous metals	90	93	94	93	93	90	88	92	98	1.0	372
381	Metal products	...	...	...	...	...	...	...	...	...	...	381
382	Machinery n.e.c.	75	79	83	91	97	89	86	88	98	3.0	382
3825	Office,computing etc..	49	52	71	94	105	124	152	160	...	b/ 15.9	3825
383	Electrical machinery ...	84	87	89	90	95	103	104	108	109	2.9	383
3832	Radio,television etc..	70	73	80	87	84	106	110	119	...	b/ 6.9	3832
384	Transport equipment	78	81	86	88	103	99	103	102	100	2.8	384
3841	Shipbuilding, repair..	226	150	105	88	109	91	71	52	...	b/ -16.8	3841
3843	Motor vehicles	83	87	94	95	94	88	92	91	...	b/ 1.2	3843
385	Professional goods	90	88	85	87	94	72	64	78	91	0.1	385
390	Other industries	...	...	...	...	...	...	...	...	...	...	390
3	Manufacturing	86	87	88	94	98	95	92	95	96	1.2	3
410	Electricity,gas,steam ..	89	90	94	98	113	99	98	100	103	1.6	410
4101	Electricity	88	90	94	98	98	99	98	101	104	1.9	4101
420	Water works and supply .	.	.	.	.	.	.	.	.	.	.	420
4	Electricity,gas etc	...	...	...	...	...	...	...	...	...	...	4
2-4	All industry	86	87	89	95	98	95	92	95	96	1.2	2-4

a/ Annual growth rate 1976-1985.

b/ Annual growth rate 1976-1984.

JAPAN

The information on industrial activity is based on the reply to the United Nations Questionnaire on General Industrial Statistics from the Statistical Standards Department, Statistics Bureau, Management and Coordination Agency, Tokyo. The concepts, definitions and classification by branches of industry are generally in accordance with United Nations standards.

The estimates are derived from the Japan mining survey, the current survey of production, the census of manufactures, the current survey of production in gas utility industry, all of which are undertaken by the Ministry of International Trade and Industry, and periodical returns on electricity. The mining survey covers all private establishments engaged in mining activities other than salt mining, stone quarrying for construction use and sand pit operations. The census of manufactures is carried out annually on a complete enumeration basis, covering all private establishments except those engaged in slaughtering through 1980 and establishments with 4 or more persons or belonging to specific industries beginning 1981. A separate schedule is used and certain items of data are not collected for the smaller establishments, defined as establishments with fewer than 30 persons engaged. The estimates in the tables refer to all establishments unless otherwise footnoted and, in most cases, supplementary information has been incorporated for tobacco manufacturing which had been exclusively carried out in government establishments until March 1985. The tobacco manufacturing public corporation transformed into a private enterprise in April 1985. Consequently, supplementary information ceased to be published in view of protection of privacy. For electricity, the estimates in the tables relate to 9 large electric power enterprises only, but these produce approximately 90 per cent of the total electricity for public supply. The gas survey covers all licensed enterprises engaged in gas manufacture and distribution. Steam and hot water supply are not surveyed. The estimates cover selected items for water works and supply; the data shown for this industry refer to the collection and purification of water and its diversion to industrial channels (under the direction of the Ministry of Health and Welfare), and exclude industrial distribution (under the direction of the Ministry of International Trade and Industry).

The estimates, which are based on the national classification scheme, have generally been adjusted as far as possible to the present version of ISIC. It should be noted that the estimates for mining, as stated in the preceding paragraph, exclude certain activities owing to the scope of the inquiry. Also, pyrites mining (ISIC 290) is included in ISIC 230. The figures shown for manufacture of motor vehicles, ISIC 3843, include three-wheeled vehicles and motorcycles (ISIC 3844).

The statistical unit is the establishment, defined as a physical location where chiefly mining, manufacturing or processing activities are carried on. Establishments are classified by their principal activity. The figures shown are the numbers at 31 December of the reference year.

The employment figures generally relate to the numbers at the end of the reference period but the figures for the tobacco industry are averages of four periods during the year. Persons engaged comprise employees, working proprietors, unpaid family workers and, in the case of mining, contract workers. Apprentices are included in the estimates of employees, as are temporary workers if the time worked meets minimum requirements. Other temporary or daily workers are not counted, although the remuneration of these workers is included in wages and salaries of employees.

Wages and salaries relate to total cash payments during the year, including basic wages, bonuses and other premiums and allowances. Payments to contract workers are included for mining. For manufacturing, the estimates for employees include retirement and termination allowances; these payments are not included in the data for operatives.

The estimates of electricity consumed are derived from the Survey of Oil Consumption in Commerce, Mining and Manufacturing, which is compiled by the Research and Statistics Department of the Ministry of International Trade and Industry. The estimates for manufacturing cover establishments with 30 or more persons engaged.

The estimates of output, in the case of mining, represent the value of production and other receipts and, in the case of manufacturing, the value of shipments of finished products (adjusted for changes in stocks of finished goods and work in progress), including shipments to other establishments of the same enterprise; receipts for contract and repair and maintenance work; shipments of scrap and salable waste and other receipts (for cold storage, installation work, advertising, sale of power etc.). The value of goods shipped in the same condition as received is not included. The valuation for mining is at mine prices, excluding indirect taxes and subsidies. Estimates for manufacturing also exclude subsidies but indirect taxes are included. For electricity, total revenue is shown. Value added is the difference between output and the cost of materials and fuels consumed, electricity purchased and, for manufacturing, contract work and indirect taxes. The estimates for electricity and gas include indirect taxes.

The estimates of gross fixed capital formation for manufacturing relate to the value of acquisitions of new and used fixed assets, adjusted by increases or decreases in construction accounts and decreased by the value of assets liquidated. The estimates for machinery and equipment relate to the value of acquisitions of new machinery and equipment only. For electricity, the estimates are calculated by deducting the value at the end of the previous year from the value at the end of the year surveyed; increases in construction accounts are included.

The indexes of industrial production are compiled by the Ministry of International Trade and Industry and provided in response to the United Nations Questionnaire on Indexes of Industrial Production. In principle, the indexes cover all privately owned establishments, irrespective of size.

Related national publications:

Honpo Kogyo no Susei (Mining Yearbook of Japan) (annual) (in Japanese only); Census of Manufactures (annual); The Survey of Oil Consumption in Commerce, Mining and Manufacturing (annual) (in Japanese only); Report of Electric Industry (annual) (in Japanese only); Yearbook of Gas Industry (in Japanese only), all published by the Ministry of International Trade and Industry, Tokyo. Japan Statistical Yearbook; Monthly Statistics of Japan, both published by the Statistics Bureau, Management and Coordination Agency, Tokyo.

ISIC	INDUSTRY	1. NUMBER OF ESTABLISHMENTS a/c/ (NUMBER) 1981	1982	1983	1984	1985	2. AVERAGE NUMBER OF PERSONS ENGAGED b/c/ (THOUSANDS) 1981	1982	1983	1984	1985	ISIC
210	Coal mining	33	31	32	30	...	28	26	25	24	...	210
220	Petroleum and gas	54	52	53	62	...	3	3	3	3	...	220
230	Metal ore mining	58	57	54	54	...	8	8	7	7	...	230
290	Other mining	775	778	748	750	...	17	17	16	15	...	290
2	Mining, quarrying .	920	918	887	896	...	56	54	51	49	...	2
311/2	Food products	48617	47970	50276	48204	...	1018	1024	1046	1041	...	311/2
313	Beverages	3564	3451	3416	3333	...	96	93	92	89	...	313
314	Tobacco .... d/	560	557	557	...	...	39	38	37	...	...	314
321	Textiles	47651	46500	46654	44420	...	765	749	733	711	...	321
3211	Spinning,weaving etc..	27205	26107	25677	24416	...	457	439	423	406	...	3211
322	Wearing apparel	24018	23764	24805	23786	...	456	459	457	454	...	322
323	Leather and products ...	4173	4040	3899	3823	...	46	44	42	41	...	323
324	Footwear	1863	1766	1704	1612	...	35	34	32	32	...	324
331	Wood products	34944	33396	33179	30986	...	406	384	369	347	...	331
332	Furniture, fixtures	10548	10444	10357	9836	...	172	171	167	155	...	332
341	Paper and products	12168	11829	12364	11808	...	284	276	278	276	...	341
3411	Pulp,paper etc.	925	851	831	790	...	80	76	74	71	...	3411
342	Printing,publishing	28487	28076	30431	28753	...	493	494	508	503	...	342
351	Industrial chemicals ...	1789	1790	1826	1810	...	206	199	196	190	...	351
3511	Basic excl fertilizers	1241	1243	1256	1264	...	110	105	101	100	...	3511
3513	Synthetic resins etc .	228	240	247	241	...	76	75	77	74	...	3513
352	Other chemical products.	3649	3666	3798	3732	...	206	210	210	210	...	352
3522	Drugs and medicines ..	1123	1150	1170	1162	...	96	100	99	98	...	3522
353	Petroleum refineries ...	164	166	168	171	...	28	27	26	25	...	353
354	Petroleum,coal products.	792	804	839	818	...	16	17	16	13	...	354
355	Rubber products	3599	3607	3801	3699	...	133	132	136	137	...	355
356	Plastic products n.e.c..	18117	18102	19635	19387	...	351	353	378	393	...	356
361	Pottery,china etc	4366	4277	4241	4180	...	81	79	78	77	...	361
362	Glass and products	1355	1310	1351	1344	...	64	61	62	65	...	362
369	Non-metal products n.e.c	16484	16193	16410	15634	...	356	347	337	326	...	369
371	Iron and steel	7173	7054	7050	6758	...	422	417	407	396	...	371
372	Non-ferrous metals	3701	3608	3686	3580	...	145	137	137	136	...	372
381	Metal products	51310	49568	52555	49680	...	807	797	811	794	...	381
382	Machinery n.e.c.	41731	41381	45121	44107	...	1157	1166	1212	1246	...	382
3825	Office,computing etc..	3242	3287	3910	4104	...	164	171	206	236	...	3825
383	Electrical machinery ...	29639	29515	31629	32044	...	1450	1465	1574	1720	...	383
3832	Radio,television etc..	13847	13740	14762	15124	...	822	843	915	1031	...	3832
384	Transport equipment	14721	14600	15119	14534	...	905	898	888	911	...	384
3841	Shipbuilding, repair..	3015	2906	2892	2695	...	139	137	125	125	...	3841
3843	Motor vehicles .... e/	10007	10109	10580	10272	...	700	696	699	722	...	3843
385	Professional goods	7221	6776	6938	6614	...	247	232	233	227	...	385
390	Other industries	14619	14345	15510	14345	...	222	218	226	221	...	390
3	Manufacturing	437023	428555	446762	f/ 428998	...	10522	10521	10651	f/ 10736	...	3
410	Electricity,gas,steam ..	258	257	...	...	...	221	221	...	...	...	410
4101	Electricity .... d/	9	9	...	...	...	177	177	...	...	...	4101
420	Water works and supply . d/	18086	17943	17779	17619	...	g/ 83	g/ 84	g/ 84	g/ 83	...	420
4	Electricity,gas etc	18344	18200	...	...	...	304	305	...	...	...	4
2-4	All industry	...	...	...	...	...	10882	10880	...	...	...	2-4

a/ Electricity and gas: number of enterprises.
b/ Except for major group 314, at the end of the reference period.
c/ Manufacturing: establishments with 4 or more persons engaged.
d/ Twelve months beginning 1 April of the year indicated.
e/ Including three-wheeled vehicles and motorcycles.
f/ Excluding major group 314.
g/ Number of employees.

ISIC	INDUSTRY	3. AVERAGE NUMBER OF EMPLOYEES a/c/ (THOUSANDS)					4. WAGES AND SALARIES OF EMPLOYEES b/c/ (BILLION YEN)					ISIC
		1981	1982	1983	1984	1985	1981	1982	1983	1984	1985	
210	Coal mining	...	...	...	...	...	124	127	123	115	...	210
220	Petroleum and gas	...	...	...	...	...	12	12	11	11	...	220
230	Metal ore mining	...	...	...	...	...	31	31	31	28	...	230
290	Other mining	...	...	...	...	...	55	55	52	50	...	290
2	Mining, quarrying .	...	...	...	...	...	222	225	217	204	...	2
311/2	Food products	980	988	1007	1006	...	2095	2185	2291	2365	...	311/2
313	Beverages	95	92	91	89	...	263	270	278	283	...	313
314	Tobacco .... d/	39	38	...	...	...	197	207	...	...	...	314
321	Textiles	722	708	692	673	...	1487	1517	1543	1563	...	321
3211	Spinning,weaving etc..	430	414	397	383	...	957	960	965	972	...	3211
322	Wearing apparel	438	441	438	436	...	635	658	675	692	...	322
323	Leather and products ...	42	40	39	37	...	92	89	90	90	...	323
324	Footwear	34	33	31	30	...	74	74	73	74	...	324
331	Wood products	381	360	345	325	...	833	817	806	791	...	331
332	Furniture, fixtures	165	164	160	148	...	374	390	399	383	...	332
341	Paper and products	278	270	272	270	...	790	808	839	869	...	341
3411	Pulp,paper etc.	79	75	73	71	...	281	282	287	292	...	3411
342	Printing,publishing	482	484	495	493	...	1654	1747	1843	1919	...	342
351	Industrial chemicals ...	206	199	195	190	...	806	824	841	854	...	351
3511	Basic excl fertilizers	110	105	101	99	...	440	449	441	461	...	3511
3513	Synthetic resins etc .	76	75	77	74	...	288	301	331	327	...	3513
352	Other chemical products.	205	209	209	209	...	727	781	832	854	...	352
3522	Drugs and medicines ..	96	100	99	98	...	340	374	398	402	...	3522
353	Petroleum refineries ...	28	27	26	25	...	132	134	132	137	...	353
354	Petroleum,coal products.	16	17	16	13	...	56	59	57	49	...	354
355	Rubber products	131	130	134	135	...	387	408	428	447	...	355
356	Plastic products n.e.c..	340	343	366	382	...	864	920	999	1082	...	356
361	Pottery,china etc	76	74	74	73	...	170	175	181	178	...	361
362	Glass and products	63	60	61	64	...	209	215	216	239	...	362
369	Non-metal products n.e.c	349	340	331	320	...	944	963	973	979	...	369
371	Iron and steel	420	415	405	395	...	1683	1731	1754	1755	...	371
372	Non-ferrous metals	142	136	139	134	...	480	489	492	504	...	372
381	Metal products	782	773	784	770	...	2168	2249	2356	2383	...	381
382	Machinery n.e.c.	1141	1152	1195	1231	...	3731	3989	4209	4484	...	382
3825	Office,computing etc..	163	170	205	235	...	466	514	627	717	...	3825
383	Electrical machinery ...	1438	1454	1557	1709	...	3745	4024	4363	4947	...	383
3832	Radio,television etc..	817	838	905	1026	...	1980	2161	2361	2780	...	3832
384	Transport equipment	898	891	881	905	...	3050	3180	3302	3547	...	384
3841	Shipbuilding, repair..	138	136	123	124	...	474	479	462	502	...	3841
3843	Motor vehicles .... e/	695	692	693	718	...	2356	2472	2602	2800	...	3843
385	Professional goods	244	229	230	224	...	642	639	656	672	...	385
390	Other industries	213	210	217	212	...	507	520	556	567	...	390
3	Manufacturing	10348	10277	f/ 10390	f/ 10498	...	28783	30062	f/ 31184	f/ 32707	...	3
410	Electricity,gas,steam ..	220	219	...	...	...	868	919	...	...	...	410
4101	Electricity .... d/	176	176	...	...	...	692	733	...	...	...	4101
420	Water works and supply . d/	83	84	...	...	...	348	360	372	390	...	420
4	Electricity,gas etc	303	303	...	...	...	1216	1279	...	...	...	4
2-4	All industry	...	...	...	...	...	30221	31566	...	...	...	2-4

a/ Except for major group 314, at the end of the reference period.
b/ Excluding payments in kind.
c/ Manufacturing: establishments with 4 or more persons engaged.
d/ Twelve months beginning 1 April of the year indicated.
e/ Including three-wheeled vehicles and motorcycles.
f/ Excluding major group 314.

ISIC	INDUSTRY	5. AVERAGE NUMBER OF OPERATIVES a/b/ (THOUSANDS) d/ 1981	1982	1983	d/ 1984	1985	6. WAGES AND SALARIES OF OPERATIVES a/c/ (BILLION YEN) d/ 1981	1982	1983	d/ 1984	1985	ISIC
210	Coal mining	...	...	...	...	...	...	...	...	...	...	210
220	Petroleum and gas	...	...	...	...	...	...	...	...	...	...	220
230	Metal ore mining	...	...	...	...	...	...	...	...	...	...	230
290	Other mining	...	...	...	...	...	...	...	...	...	...	290
2	Mining, quarrying	...	...	...	...	...	...	...	...	...	...	2
311/2	Food products	452	...	...	473	...	898	...	...	1033	...	311/2
313	Beverages	44	...	...	40	...	126	...	...	130	...	313
314	Tobacco	...	...	...	...	...	...	...	...	...	...	314
321	Textiles	329	...	...	303	...	640	...	...	677	...	321
3211	Spinning,weaving etc.	210	...	...	185	...	446	...	...	457	...	3211
322	Wearing apparel	213	...	...	212	...	280	...	...	312	...	322
323	Leather and products	11	...	...	9	...	22	...	...	20	...	323
324	Footwear	16	...	...	14	...	32	...	...	32	...	324
331	Wood products	90	...	...	74	...	201	...	...	185	...	331
332	Furniture, fixtures	65	...	...	56	...	135	...	...	136	...	332
341	Paper and products	132	...	...	125	...	378	...	...	413	...	341
3411	Pulp,paper etc.	54	...	...	49	...	181	...	...	192	...	3411
342	Printing,publishing	147	...	...	153	...	536	...	...	651	...	342
351	Industrial chemicals	118	...	...	106	...	424	...	...	452	...	351
3511	Basic excl fertilizers	58	...	...	51	...	215	...	...	230	...	3511
3513	Synthetic resins etc	49	...	...	47	...	171	...	...	191	...	3513
352	Other chemical products.	101	...	...	100	...	322	...	...	376	...	352
3522	Drugs and medicines	51	...	...	51	...	155	...	...	190	...	3522
353	Petroleum refineries	16	...	...	14	...	72	...	...	75	...	353
354	Petroleum,coal products.	6	...	...	4	...	24	...	...	16	...	354
355	Rubber products	75	...	...	78	...	220	...	...	258	...	355
356	Plastic products n.e.c.	136	...	...	156	...	335	...	...	427	...	356
361	Pottery,china etc	39	...	...	39	...	86	...	...	93	...	361
362	Glass and products	42	...	...	42	...	133	...	...	149	...	362
369	Non-metal products n.e.c	142	...	...	123	...	391	...	...	387	...	369
371	Iron and steel	275	...	...	256	...	1043	...	...	1116	...	371
372	Non-ferrous metals	83	...	...	77	...	274	...	...	283	...	372
381	Metal products	268	...	...	265	...	735	...	...	805	...	381
382	Machinery n.e.c.	500	...	...	533	...	1559	...	...	1834	...	382
3825	Office,computing etc.	79	...	...	116	...	183	...	...	294	...	3825
383	Electrical machinery	800	...	...	986	...	1803	...	...	2425	...	383
3832	Radio,television etc.	483	...	...	632	...	981	...	...	1408	...	3832
384	Transport equipment	557	...	...	553	...	1842	...	...	2127	...	384
3841	Shipbuilding, repair.	75	...	...	68	...	255	...	...	269	...	3841
3843	Motor vehicles e/	448	...	...	454	...	1480	...	...	1743	...	3843
385	Professional goods	136	...	...	121	...	324	...	...	329	...	385
390	Other industries	75	...	...	75	...	173	...	...	195	...	390
3	Manufacturing f/	4868	...	...	4987	...	13008	...	...	14936	...	3
410	Electricity,gas,steam	...	...	...	...	...	...	...	...	...	...	410
4101	Electricity g/	83	83	...	...	...	374	396	...	...	...	4101
420	Water works and supply	...	...	...	...	...	...	...	...	...	...	420
4	Electricity,gas etc	...	...	...	...	...	...	...	...	...	...	4
2-4	All industry	...	...	...	...	...	...	...	...	...	...	2-4

a/ Manufacturing: establishments with 20 or more persons engaged.
b/ At the end of the reference period.
c/ Excluding payments in kind.
d/ Manufacturing: establishments with 30 or more persons engaged.
e/ Including three-wheeled vehicles and motorcycles.
f/ Excluding major group 314.
g/ Twelve months beginning 1 April of the year indicated.

ISIC	INDUSTRY	7. QUANTITY OF ELECTRICITY CONSUMED (BILLION KWH) 1981	1982	1983	1984	1985	8. OUTPUT a/b/ (BILLION YEN) 1981	1982	1983	1984	1985	ISIC
210	Coal mining	1.45	1.48	1.41	...	...	272	287	280	274	...	210
220	Petroleum and gas	0.30	0.31	0.31	...	...	104	110	118	125	...	220
230	Metal ore mining	0.57	0.49	0.47	...	...	84	82	83	79	...	230
290	Other mining	0.74	0.65	0.62	...	...	214	214	207	208	...	290
2	Mining, quarrying .	3.09	2.93	2.81	...	...	674	693	688	686	...	2
311/2	Food products	9.24	11.98	9.92	...	...	19883	20695	21541	22426	...	311/2
313	Beverages	1.19	1.23	1.30	...	...	4289	4516	4747	4841	...	313
314	Tobacco .... c/	...	...	...	...	...	2423	2470	2722	...	...	314
321	Textiles	8.34	8.29	8.16	...	...	8874	9059	8951	9130	...	321
3211	Spinning,weaving etc..	6.03	5.91	5.76	...	...	5461	5550	5417	5519	...	3211
322	Wearing apparel	0.38	0.41	0.44	...	...	2491	2528	2552	2602	...	322
323	Leather and products ...	0.07	0.07	0.09	...	...	579	542	555	557	...	323
324	Footwear	0.05	0.05	0.05	...	...	418	410	392	410	...	324
331	Wood products	1.66	1.58	1.60	...	...	5005	4893	4724	4550	...	331
332	Furniture, fixtures	0.48	0.49	0.51	...	...	1948	1994	2047	1944	...	332
341	Paper and products	23.90	23.82	24.41	...	...	6799	6896	7066	7402	...	341
3411	Pulp,paper etc.	21.95	22.08	22.60	...	...	2906	2942	3005	3145	...	3411
342	Printing,publishing	1.66	1.74	1.91	...	...	7363	7781	8196	8490	...	342
351	Industrial chemicals ...	39.58	38.35	38.07	...	...	10973	10894	11057	11898	...	351
3511	Basic excl fertilizers	24.56	24.27	23.31	...	...	6590	6589	6248	6790	...	3511
3513	Synthetic resins etc .	13.48	12.62	13.66	...	...	3477	3437	3950	4258	...	3513
352	Other chemical products.	3.96	4.05	4.43	...	...	7155	7643	8154	8384	...	352
3522	Drugs and medicines ..	1.85	1.88	1.97	...	...	3168	3444	3640	3671	...	3522
353	Petroleum refineries ...	6.02	5.89	5.84	...	...	14396	14386	12854	12526	...	353
354	Petroleum,coal products.	1.50	1.55	1.43	...	...	1497	1501	1341	1068	...	354
355	Rubber products	2.47	2.40	2.59	...	...	2320	2305	2464	2596	...	355
356	Plastic products n.e.c..	5.34	5.72	6.27	...	...	6146	6385	6969	7804	...	356
361	Pottery,china etc	0.75	0.77	0.83	...	...	619	627	665	715	...	361
362	Glass and products	3.17	3.26	3.53	...	...	1322	1364	1486	1651	...	362
369	Non-metal products n.e.c	15.22	14.41	14.18	...	...	6648	6491	6360	6362	...	369
371	Iron and steel	65.87	64.68	63.57	...	...	17237	17492	16002	17367	...	371
372	Non-ferrous metals	22.17	15.43	14.61	...	...	5578	5000	5229	5467	...	372
381	Metal products	4.46	4.62	4.84	...	...	11917	12132	12242	12625	...	381
382	Machinery n.e.c.	8.35	8.30	9.23	...	...	21691	22801	23588	26807	...	382
3825	Office,computing etc..	0.79	0.96	1.91	...	...	3481	3955	5258	6675	...	3825
383	Electrical machinery ...	10.62	11.45	13.16	...	...	26053	27362	30312	37531	...	383
3832	Radio,television etc..	5.94	6.84	8.09	...	...	14761	15635	18031	23434	...	3832
384	Transport equipment	14.73	14.01	14.54	...	...	28085	28586	29334	31921	...	384
3841	Shipbuilding, repair..	1.23	1.18	1.06	...	...	3056	3141	2688	2930	...	3841
3843	Motor vehicles	13.12	12.48	13.11	...	...	d/ 23834	d/ 24247	d/ 25488	d/ 27709	...	3843
385	Professional goods	0.99	1.10	1.16	...	...	3442	3234	3308	3517	...	385
390	Other industries	0.64	0.67	0.72	...	...	2938	3018	3290	3469	...	390
3	Manufacturing	e/ 252.81	e/ 246.32	e/ 247.39	...	...	228089	233005	235426	e/ 254060	...	3
410	Electricity,gas,steam ..	...	...	...	...	...	12360	...	...	...	...	410
4101	Electricity	19.28	19.49	...	...	...	c/ 10770	c/ 11036	...	...	...	4101
420	Water works and supply .	...	...	...	...	...	...	...	...	...	...	420
4	Electricity,gas etc	...	...	...	...	...	...	...	...	...	...	4
2-4	All industry	...	...	...	...	...	...	...	...	...	...	2-4

a/ Excluding subsidies. Manufacturing, electricity and gas: including indirect taxes.
b/ Manufacturing: establishments with 4 or more persons engaged. c/ Twelve months beginning 1 April of the year indicated.
d/ Including three-wheeled vehicles and motorcycles. e/ Excluding major group 314.

ISIC	INDUSTRY	11. GROSS FIXED CAPITAL FORMATION MACHINERY AND EQUIPMENT a/b/ (BILLION YEN) 1981	1982	1983	1984	1985	12. VALUE OF STOCKS AT END OF PERIOD TOTAL b/ (BILLION YEN) 1981	1982	1983	1984	1985	ISIC
210	Coal mining	...	...	...	...	...	...	...	...	...	...	210
220	Petroleum and gas	...	...	...	...	...	...	...	...	...	...	220
230	Metal ore mining	...	...	...	...	...	...	...	...	...	...	230
290	Other mining	...	...	...	...	...	...	...	...	...	...	290
2	Mining, quarrying .	...	...	...	...	...	...	...	...	...	...	2
311/2	Food products	298	304	318	342	...	1087	1091	1130	1148	...	311/2
313	Beverages	79	79	90	80	...	466	460	462	492	...	313
314	Tobacco	128	129	...	...	...	c/ 1084	c/ 1113	c/ 1126	...	...	314
321	Textiles	135	154	133	145	...	732	774	754	760	...	321
3211	Spinning,weaving etc..	97	112	94	105	...	482	511	492	488	...	3211
322	Wearing apparel	17	18	16	18	...	148	151	147	148	...	322
323	Leather and products ...	2	2	2	2	...	36	36	36	33	...	323
324	Footwear	2	3	2	2	...	33	33	28	33	...	324
331	Wood products	32	42	37	61	...	289	278	260	256	...	331
332	Furniture, fixtures	16	19	19	18	...	167	173	179	168	...	332
341	Paper and products	218	174	196	266	...	581	538	526	561	...	341
3411	Pulp,paper etc.	150	112	120	186	...	348	315	302	333	...	3411
342	Printing,publishing	126	126	140	150	...	303	309	317	330	...	342
351	Industrial chemicals ...	443	456	508	477	...	1310	1273	1212	1258	...	351
3511	Basic excl fertilizers	260	246	272	244	...	765	738	648	673	...	3511
3513	Synthetic resins etc .	153	165	214	212	...	395	401	426	469	...	3513
352	Other chemical products.	166	195	250	207	...	855	926	938	949	...	352
3522	Drugs and medicines ..	81	100	115	81	...	453	518	503	511	...	3522
353	Petroleum refineries ...	127	114	96	85	...	2280	2256	1675	1700	...	353
354	Petroleum,coal products.	35	49	27	17	...	91	107	89	72	...	354
355	Rubber products	109	88	84	107	...	156	148	150	153	...	355
356	Plastic products n.e.c..	184	178	199	250	...	408	400	419	466	...	356
361	Pottery,china etc	19	16	23	32	...	72	76	79	77	...	361
362	Glass and products	695	724	812	898	...	96	105	75	141	...	362
369	Non-metal products n.e.c	2926	2880	2892	2920	...	266	231	170	174	...	369
371	Iron and steel	5543	5588	4843	5696	...	756	966	1046	938	...	371
372	Non-ferrous metals	1474	1328	1278	1472	...	221	187	214	168	...	372
381	Metal products	5184	5310	5393	5585	...	264	305	240	311	...	381
382	Machinery n.e.c.	9444	10177	10332	11552	...	736	838	831	997	...	382
3825	Office,computing etc..	1449	1684	2195	2608	...	157	194	265	333	...	3825
383	Electrical machinery ...	9937	10924	12183	14718	...	1173	1299	1376	2115	...	383
3832	Radio,television etc..	5555	6139	7063	9039	...	779	875	917	1554	...	3832
384	Transport equipment	8207	8480	9050	9556	...	1343	1393	1203	1134	...	384
3841	Shipbuilding, repair..	1140	1200	1044	1148	...	73	81	107	52	...	3841
3843	Motor vehicles .... e/	6570	6794	7519	7846	...	1235	1285	1068	1046	...	3843
385	Professional goods	1389	1384	1474	1514	...	161	150	137	134	...	385
390	Other industries	1235	1275	1411	1486	...	60	69	64	68	...	390
3	Manufacturing	f/ 78961	f/ 82585	f/ 85775	f/ 93188	...	8239	8709	8530	f/ 9224	...	3
410	Electricity,gas,steam ..	g/ 4728	...	...	...	...	4100	...	...	...	...	410
4101	Electricity .... d/	g/ 4185	g/ 4308	...	...	...	2677	2587	...	...	...	4101
420	Water works and supply .	...	...	...	...	...	...	...	...	...	...	420
4	Electricity,gas etc	...	...	...	...	...	...	...	...	...	...	4
2-4	All industry	...	...	...	...	...	...	...	...	...	...	2-4

a/ Excluding subsidies. Unless otherwise indicated, excluding indirect taxes.
b/ Manufacturing: establishments with 30 or more persons engaged.
c/ Manufacturing: establishments with 4 or more persons engaged.
d/ Twelve months beginning 1 April of the year indicated.
e/ Including three-wheeled vehicles and motorcycles.
f/ Excluding major group 314.
g/ Including indirect taxes.

ISIC	INDUSTRY	9. VALUE ADDED a/c/ (BILLION YEN) 1981	1982	1983	1984	1985	10. GROSS FIXED CAPITAL FORMATION TOTAL b/ (BILLION YEN) 1981	1982	1983	1984	1985	ISIC
210	Coal mining	161	173	142	144	...	...	...	...	...	...	210
220	Petroleum and gas	79	83	82	77	...	...	...	...	...	...	220
230	Metal ore mining	43	41	39	37	...	...	...	...	...	...	230
290	Other mining	104	109	83	82	...	...	...	...	...	...	290
2	Mining, quarrying .	387	406	346	340	...	...	...	...	...	...	2
311/2	Food products	6105	6538	6859	7227	...	418	458	447	497	...	311/2
313	Beverages	1223	1280	1392	1408	...	105	139	97	102	...	313
314	Tobacco .... d/	...	...	...	...	...	401	401	404	...	...	314
321	Textiles	3386	3461	3464	3563	...	175	201	172	195	...	321
3211	Spinning,weaving etc..	2096	2132	2108	2170	...	124	146	116	138	...	3211
322	Wearing apparel	1208	1242	1268	1290	...	34	33	29	33	...	322
323	Leather and products ...	203	196	203	201	...	3	4	4	3	...	323
324	Footwear	156	158	152	149	...	4	5	5	3	...	324
331	Wood products	1722	1740	1729	1657	...	50	52	53	46	...	331
332	Furniture, fixtures	815	855	872	843	...	25	32	29	31	...	332
341	Paper and products	2138	2194	2300	2473	...	256	200	237	333	...	341
3411	Pulp,paper etc.	861	860	896	975	...	169	114	144	217	...	3411
342	Printing,publishing	4078	4298	4447	4569	...	188	183	201	251	...	342
351	Industrial chemicals ...	3002	3126	3467	4021	...	543	603	545	557	...	351
3511	Basic excl fertilizers	1727	1814	1904	2280	...	313	329	265	315	...	3511
3513	Synthetic resins etc .	963	1018	1264	1449	...	194	223	242	195	...	3513
352	Other chemical products.	3750	4051	4423	4513	...	299	312	365	295	...	352
3522	Drugs and medicines ..	2057	2216	2406	2397	...	129	174	185	131	...	3522
353	Petroleum refineries ...	1276	1395	1215	1169	...	244	152	188	197	...	353
354	Petroleum,coal products.	305	250	217	180	...	35	53	37	18	...	354
355	Rubber products	956	988	1049	1100	...	124	91	93	123	...	355
356	Plastic products n.e.c..	2253	2390	2678	3025	...	234	226	237	318	...	356
361	Pottery,china etc	351	353	371	403	...	25	21	31	42	...	361
362	Glass and products	88	84	89	115	...	205	192	197	213	...	362
369	Non-metal products n.e.c	217	198	348	147	...	496	497	459	458	...	369
371	Iron and steel	577	745	905	900	...	2496	2652	2426	2506	...	371
372	Non-ferrous metals	177	204	179	216	...	994	903	832	823	...	372
381	Metal products	196	222	217	240	...	1243	1163	1377	1177	...	381
382	Machinery n.e.c.	563	621	689	761	...	3796	4106	4065	4260	...	382
3825	Office,computing etc..	122	142	210	258	...	514	564	727	918	...	3825
383	Electrical machinery ...	918	1032	1158	1665	...	2919	3007	3041	3751	...	383
3832	Radio,television etc..	603	680	777	1225	...	1614	1727	1739	2287	...	3832
384	Transport equipment	1115	1116	1078	1026	...	2536	2749	2721	2846	...	384
3841	Shipbuilding, repair..	38	57	41	41	...	1138	1208	1110	1180	...	3841
3843	Motor vehicles .... d/	1050	1035	1018	959	...	930	1009	1075	1101	...	3843
385	Professional goods	124	120	118	115	...	409	393	355	384	...	385
390	Other industries	44	48	50	55	...	233	239	265	284	...	390
3	Manufacturing	6108	6507	e/ 7086	e/ 7580	...	25425	26041	25265	e/ 25306	...	3
410	Electricity,gas,steam ..	...	...	...	...	...	...	...	...	...	...	410
4101	Electricity .... f/	1147	1072	...	...	...	...	...	...	...	...	4101
420	Water works and supply .	...	...	...	...	...	...	...	...	...	...	420
4	Electricity,gas etc	...	...	...	...	...	...	...	...	...	...	4
2-4	All industry	...	...	...	...	...	...	...	...	...	...	2-4

a/ Manufacturing: excluding used fixed assets.
c/ At 31 March of the following year.
e/ Excluding major group 314.
b/ Manufacturing: establishments with 30 or more persons engaged.
d/ Including three-wheeled vehicles and motorcycles.
f/ Twelve months beginning 1 April of the year indicated.

13. INDEX NUMBERS OF INDUSTRIAL PRODUCTION (1980 = 100)

ISIC	INDUSTRY	1976	1977	1978	1979	1981	1982	1983	1984	1985	a/ RATE	ISIC
210	Coal mining	102	101	105	98	98	98	95	92	91	-1.3	210
220	Petroleum and gas	117	129	121	110	95	93	96	97	106	-1.1	220
230	Metal ore mining	121	126	120	104	102	107	106	107	109	-1.2	230
290	Other mining	79	82	92	98	95	91	93	93	91	1.6	290
2	Mining, quarrying .	102	105	107	101	97	96	96	95	96	-0.7	2
311/2	Food products	[90	93	98	101	101	101	103	101	101	1.3]	311/2
313	Beverages											313
314	Tobacco	96	100	103	102	105	103	104	104	101	0.6	314
321	Textiles	100	98	100	101	98	97	97	99	98	-0.2	321
3211	Spinning,weaving etc..	...	...	...	...	...	...	...	...	...	...	3211
322	Wearing apparel	101	101	102	103	101	101	99	100	...	c/ -0.1	322
323	Leather and products ...	103	102	103	106	103	99	97	99	...	c/ -0.5	323
324	Footwear	98	99	102	106	102	100	96	99	...	c/ 0.1	324
331	Wood products	105	103	107	108	91	87	85	81	79	-3.1	331
332	Furniture, fixtures	...	...	...	...	...	...	...	...	...	...	332
341	Paper and products	84	86	92	100	94	97	103	108	113	3.3	341
3411	Pulp,paper etc.	...	...	...	...	...	...	...	...	...	...	3411
342	Printing,publishing	...	...	...	...	...	...	...	...	...	...	342
351	Industrial chemicals ...	88	90	98	106	94	92	96	105	106	2.1	351
3511	Basic excl fertilizers	...	...	...	...	...	...	...	...	...	...	3511
3513	Synthetic resins etc .	...	...	...	...	...	...	...	...	...	...	3513
352	Other chemical products.	73	78	90	98	103	108	116	126	122	5.9	352
3522	Drugs and medicines ..	...	...	...	...	...	...	...	...	...	...	3522
353	Petroleum refineries ...	101	104	105	107	93	88	85	88	83	-2.2	353
354	Petroleum,coal products.	97	96	86	91	100	98	92	101	102	0.6	354
355	Rubber products	76	78	83	91	98	93	100	106	109	4.1	355
356	Plastic products n.e.c..	84	87	94	103	97	100	106	113	116	3.7	356
361	Pottery,china etc											361
362	Glass and products	[83	87	92	98	94	92	93	96	96	1.6]	362
369	Non-metal products n.e.c											369
371	Iron and steel	88	86	89	98	94	91	89	98	100	1.4	371
372	Non-ferrous metals	85	89	96	100	96	93	96	100	100	1.8	372
381	Metal products	86	92	100	102	96	99	94	98	99	1.6	381
382	Machinery n.e.c.	67	72	80	91	104	105	108	124	135	8.1	382
3825	Office,computing etc..	...	...	...	...	...	...	...	...	...	...	3825
383	Electrical machinery ...	65	68	77	86	114	123	147	193	213	14.1	383
3832	Radio,television etc..	...	...	...	...	...	...	...	...	...	...	3832
384	Transport equipment	79	82	81	83	106	99	95	104	108	3.5	384
3841	Shipbuilding, repair..	...	...	...	...	...	...	...	...	...	...	3841
3843	Motor vehicles	...	...	...	...	...	...	...	...	...	...	3843
385	Professional goods	44	58	67	78	111	103	111	130	152	14.8	385
390	Other industries	85	87	91	95	99	99	94	97	95	1.2	390
3	Manufacturing ..... b/	80	84	89	96	101	101	105	117	122	4.8	3
410	Electricity,gas,steam ..	84	88	94	98	102	103	108	115	119	3.9	410
4101	Electricity	...	...	...	...	...	...	...	...	...	...	4101
420	Water works and supply .	.	.	.	.	.	.	.	.	.	.	420
4	Electricity,gas etc	...	...	...	...	...	...	...	...	...	...	4
2-4	All industry b/	80	84	89	96	101	101	105	116	122	4.8	2-4

a/ Annual growth rate 1976-1985.
c/ Annual growth rate 1976-1984.

b/ Excluding printing and publishing.

JORDAN

The information in the tables is based on the reply to the United Nations Questionnaire on General Industrial Statistics from the Department of Statistics, Amman. The concepts, definitions and classification by branches of industry are generally in accordance with United Nations standards.

The data in the tables refer to all establishments in principle and, except for electricity, are derived from the annual survey of mining and manufacturing establishments undertaken by the Department of Statistics. The survey is conducted on the basis of a complete enumeration of all establishments but excludes household industries. The estimates for electricity are derived from information obtained directly from electricity companies and municipal electricity undertakings. The data shown in the tables relate to the East Bank only.

The data in the tables are based on the national classification, but are arranged to represent the present version of ISIC as far as details permit. It should be noted, however, that included in ISIC 390 are establishments specializing in repair services for the general public, bakeries located in rural areas and establishments engaging in both manufacturing and repair activities (mainly observed in the case of ISIC 322, 381 and 383) in addition to other manufacturing industries defined in ISIC.

The number of establishments relates to the establishments in operation during the year. Data on employment refer, for mining and manufacturing, to the number at the end of June of the reference year and, for electricity, to the average of the number of persons at the end of June and December.

Output is the sum of the value of goods produced, value of goods sold in the same condition as purchased and receipts for industrial services rendered to others. Value added is the difference between the value of output and the cost of materials, supplies, fuels, water and electricity consumed, cost of work done by others and cost of non-industrial services purchased. Valuation of output is in producers' prices and value added is in factor values.

Related national publications:
Industry Survey (annual); *Statistical Yearbook*, both published by the Department of Statistics, Amman.

ISIC	INDUSTRY	1. NUMBER OF ESTABLISHMENTS b/ (NUMBER)					2. AVERAGE NUMBER OF PERSONS ENGAGED a/b/ (NUMBER)					ISIC
		1981	1982	1983	1984	1985	1981	1982	1983	1984	1985	
210	Coal mining	-	-	-	-	...	-	-	-	-	...	210
220	Petroleum and gas	-	-	-	-	...	-	-	-	-	...	220
230	Metal ore mining	-	-	-	-	...	-	-	-	-	...	230
290	Other mining	195	191	192	161	...	6051	6061	5869	5534	...	290
2	Mining, quarrying .	195	191	192	161	...	6051	6061	5869	5534	...	2
311/2	Food products	557	615	620	726	...	4031	4174	4404	5545	...	311/2
313	Beverages	12	15	16	16	...	946	768	931	866	...	313
314	Tobacco	3	3	4	4	...	691	598	642	730	...	314
321	Textiles	72	77	77	117	...	1276	1203	1161	1162	...	321
3211	Spinning,weaving etc..	...	...	...	...	...	...	...	...	...	...	3211
322	Wearing apparel	383	385	389	728	...	1740	2054	2630	2701	...	322
323	Leather and products ...	12	12	20	31	...	195	203	243	247	...	323
324	Footwear	69	69	102	101	...	548	624	752	699	...	324
331	Wood products	[720	720	720	1100]	...	[2266	2440	2484	4533]	...	331
332	Furniture, fixtures					...					...	332
341	Paper and products	13	14	16	16	...	1098	1177	1178	899	...	341
3411	Pulp,paper etc.	...	...	...	...	...	...	...	...	...	...	3411
342	Printing,publishing	71	101	146	100	...	920	1042	1346	1664	...	342
351	Industrial chemicals ... c/	32	37	46	61	...	1784	2965	3212	3401	...	351
3511	Basic excl fertilizers	...	...	...	...	...	...	...	...	...	...	3511
3513	Synthetic resins etc .	...	...	...	...	...	...	...	...	...	...	3513
352	Other chemical products. c/	...	...	...	...	...	...	...	...	...	...	352
3522	Drugs and medicines ..	...	...	...	...	...	...	...	...	...	...	3522
353	Petroleum refineries ...	1	1	1	1	...	2415	2482	2456	2615	...	353
354	Petroleum,coal products.	-	-	-	-	...	-	-	-	-	...	354
355	Rubber products	3	3	3	4	...	89	92	24	10	...	355
356	Plastic products n.e.c..	44	47	49	54	...	1216	1335	1117	1467	...	356
361	Pottery,china etc					...					...	361
362	Glass and products	[538	539	539	848]	...	[5349	5737	6050	6369]	...	362
369	Non-metal products n.e.c					...					...	369
371	Iron and steel	[10	12	13	30]	...	[654	691	857	1030]	...	371
372	Non-ferrous metals					...					...	372
381	Metal products	[805	805	805	1260]	...	[4284	4185	4095	5599]	...	381
382	Machinery n.e.c.					...					...	382
3825	Office,computing etc..	...	...	...	...	...	...	...	...	...	...	3825
383	Electrical machinery ...	5	5	6	12	...	246	232	256	295	...	383
3832	Radio,television etc..	...	...	...	...	...	...	...	...	...	...	3832
384	Transport equipment	13	13	14	4	...	289	171	177	80	...	384
3841	Shipbuilding, repair..	...	...	...	...	...	...	...	...	...	...	3841
3843	Motor vehicles	...	...	...	...	...	...	...	...	...	...	3843
385	Professional goods	-	-	-	-	...	-	-	-	-	...	385
390	Other industries .... d/	2778	2778	2943	3156	...	7038	7052	6789	7648	...	390
3	Manufacturing ..... e/	6141	6251	6529	8369	...	37075	39225	40804	47560	...	3
410	Electricity,gas,steam ..	...	...	...	...	...	...	...	...	...	...	410
4101	Electricity	3	3	3	3	...	3241	3434	3844	3757	...	4101
420	Water works and supply .	...	...	...	...	...	...	...	...	...	...	420
4	Electricity,gas etc	...	...	...	...	...	...	...	...	...	...	4
2-4	All industry	...	...	...	...	...	...	...	...	...	...	2-4

For certain differences in classification, see country note.

a/ Mining and manufacturing: at 30 June of the year indicated. b/ Data relate to the East Bank only.
c/ Major group 352 is included in 351.
d/ Including repair services, bakeries in rural areas and manufacture-repair activities.
e/ Including repair services for the general public.

ISIC	INDUSTRY	3. AVERAGE NUMBER OF EMPLOYEES a/b/ (NUMBER) 1981	1982	1983	1984	1985	4. WAGES AND SALARIES OF EMPLOYEES b/ (THOUSAND DINARS) 1981	1982	1983	1984	1985	ISIC
210	Coal mining	-	-	-	-	...	-	-	-	-	...	210
220	Petroleum and gas	-	-	-	-	...	-	-	-	-	...	220
230	Metal ore mining	-	-	-	-	...	-	-	-	-	...	230
290	Other mining	5892	5743	5537	5393	...	13110	15010	15610	17685	...	290
2	Mining, quarrying .	5892	5743	5537	5393	...	13110	15010	15610	17685	...	2
311/2	Food products	3641	3352	3630	4691	...	3851	4092	4365	5887	...	311/2
313	Beverages	946	761	927	846	...	1411	1384	1735	1781	...	313
314	Tobacco	691	598	642	729	...	1920	2242	2217	2325	...	314
321	Textiles	1112	1091	1085	1038	...	1240	1263	1343	1504	...	321
3211	Spinning,weaving etc..	...	...	...	...	...	...	...	...	...	...	3211
322	Wearing apparel	1283	1572	2318	1895	...	1361	1827	2268	2079	...	322
323	Leather and products ...	178	188	190	199	...	254	258	241	335	...	323
324	Footwear	492	584	647	589	...	777	853	915	956	...	324
331	Wood products	[1666	1752	1782	3276]	...	[1683	2068	2098	4389]	...	331
332	Furniture, fixtures					...					...	332
341	Paper and products	1098	1072	1171	891	...	2037	2163	2140	1666	...	341
3411	Pulp,paper etc.	...	...	...	...	...	...	...	...	...	...	3411
342	Printing,publishing	876	912	1247	1557	...	1322	1476	2121	3138	...	342
351	Industrial chemicals ... c/	1765	2798	3203	3367	...	4670	5696	7756	8431	...	351
3511	Basic excl fertilizers	...	...	...	...	...	...	...	...	...	...	3511
3513	Synthetic resins etc .	...	...	...	...	...	...	...	...	...	...	3513
352	Other chemical products. c/	...	...	...	...	...	...	...	...	...	...	352
3522	Drugs and medicines ..	...	...	...	...	...	...	...	...	...	...	3522
353	Petroleum refineries ...	2415	2482	2456	2615	...	6844	8907	9624	10026	...	353
354	Petroleum,coal products.	-	-	-	-	...	-	-	-	-	...	354
355	Rubber products	86	90	22	3	...	135	138	30	2	...	355
356	Plastic products n.e.c..	1102	1209	1081	1416	...	1016	1268	1589	2141	...	356
361	Pottery,china etc					...					...	361
362	Glass and products	[5067	5467	5582	5529]	...	[8090	9054	10665	9281]	...	362
369	Non-metal products n.e.c					...					...	369
371	Iron and steel	[653	687	851	1001]	...	[1190	1147	1425	1836]	...	371
372	Non-ferrous metals					...					...	372
381	Metal products	[3755	3263	3621	4095]	...	[5037	4847	4514	5476]	...	381
382	Machinery n.e.c.					...					...	382
3825	Office,computing etc..	...	...	...	...	...	...	...	...	...	...	3825
383	Electrical machinery ...	246	232	256	284	...	360	328	296	416	...	383
3832	Radio,television etc..	...	...	...	...	...	...	...	...	...	...	3832
384	Transport equipment	280	156	158	71	...	376	206	216	115	...	384
3841	Shipbuilding, repair..	...	...	...	...	...	...	...	...	...	...	3841
3843	Motor vehicles	...	...	...	...	...	...	...	...	...	...	3843
385	Professional goods	-	-	-	-	...	-	-	-	-	...	385
390	Other industries .... d/	4615	4603	4140	4213	...	3271	3313	3174	3381	...	390
3	Manufacturing ..... e/	31967	32869	35009	38305	...	46845	52530	58732	65165	...	3
410	Electricity,gas,steam ..	...	...	...	...	...	...	...	...	...	...	410
4101	Electricity	3241	3434	3844	3757	...	7340	8625	9169	10018	...	4101
420	Water works and supply .	...	...	...	...	...	...	...	...	...	...	420
4	Electricity,gas etc	...	...	...	...	...	...	...	...	...	...	4
2-4	All industry	...	...	...	...	...	...	...	...	...	...	2-4

For certain differences in classification, see country note.

a/ Mining and manufacturing: at 30 June of the year indicated. b/ Data relate to the East Bank only.
c/ Major group 352 is included in 351.
d/ Including repair services, bakeries in rural areas and manufacture-repair activities.
e/ Including repair services for the general public.

ISIC	INDUSTRY	5. OUTPUT IN PRODUCERS' PRICES a/ (THOUSAND DINARS) 1981	1982	1983	1984	1985	6. VALUE ADDED IN FACTOR VALUES a/b/ (THOUSAND DINARS) 1981	1982	1983	1984	a/ 1985	ISIC
210	Coal mining	-	-	-	-	...	-	-	-	-	...	210
220	Petroleum and gas	-	-	-	-	...	-	-	-	-	...	220
230	Metal ore mining	-	-	-	-	...	-	-	-	-	...	230
290	Other mining	80545	81750	84616	104051	...	43344	45462	37966	51562	...	290
2	Mining, quarrying	80545	81750	84616	104051	...	43344	45462	37966	51562	...	2
311/2	Food products	46703	51603	48542	69774	...	11055	11371	13047	17052	...	311/2
313	Beverages	11140	14740	16270	17197	...	5848	7191	7994	8819	...	313
314	Tobacco	27037	32216	39316	43459	...	16982	21490	29409	32908	...	314
321	Textiles	10173	10156	9925	13153	...	3701	2776	3095	4986	...	321
3211	Spinning,weaving etc.	...	...	...	...	...	...	...	...	...	...	3211
322	Wearing apparel	5846	7968	9960	11020	...	3128	3894	4123	4301	...	322
323	Leather and products	1295	1339	1893	1743	...	406	506	655	579	...	323
324	Footwear	4839	5401	5434	4954	...	3087	3260	3182	2322	...	324
331	Wood products	12643	13759	13746	28342	...	6459	6563	6478	5906	...	331
332	Furniture, fixtures					...					...	332
341	Paper and products	16162	17551	17209	13911	...	4021	4741	4122	3610	...	341
3411	Pulp,paper etc.	...	...	...	...	...	...	...	...	...	...	3411
342	Printing,publishing	5468	6497	7997	12657	...	2564	2459	3721	5320	...	342
351	Industrial chemicals c/	34888	51322	69881	161287	...	11510	16023	17865	22107	...	351
3511	Basic excl fertilizers	...	...	...	...	...	...	...	...	...	...	3511
3513	Synthetic resins etc	...	...	...	...	...	...	...	...	...	...	3513
352	Other chemical products. c/	...	...	...	...	...	...	...	...	...	...	352
3522	Drugs and medicines	...	...	...	...	...	...	...	...	...	...	3522
353	Petroleum refineries	206390	263198	239809	272126	...	26590	28215	26327	29552	...	353
354	Petroleum,coal products.	-	-	-	-	...	-	-	-	-	...	354
355	Rubber products	740	774	134	24	...	202	211	52	18	...	355
356	Plastic products n.e.c.	12222	13076	12763	19383	...	5130	5113	5364	5985	...	356
361	Pottery,china etc	79732	90667	78965	88821	...	34380	38959	41972	46823	...	361
362	Glass and products					...					...	362
369	Non-metal products n.e.c					...					...	369
371	Iron and steel	25442	26877	32464	33854	...	5104	4535	5984	5686	...	371
372	Non-ferrous metals					...					...	372
381	Metal products	35366	33632	31923	29846	...	13674	13673	13822	11211	...	381
382	Machinery n.e.c.					...					...	382
3825	Office,computing etc.	...	...	...	...	...	...	...	...	...	...	3825
383	Electrical machinery	1352	1347	1204	1783	...	738	623	562	840	...	383
3832	Radio,television etc.	...	...	...	...	...	...	...	...	...	...	3832
384	Transport equipment	2110	1302	763	353	...	647	540	374	204	...	384
3841	Shipbuilding, repair.	...	...	...	...	...	...	...	...	...	...	3841
3843	Motor vehicles	...	...	...	...	...	...	...	...	...	...	3843
385	Professional goods	-	-	-	-	...	-	-	-	-	...	385
390	Other industries d/	14207	15095	14383	13774	...	10042	10669	12042	10006	...	390
3	Manufacturing e/	553755	658520	652581	837461	...	165268	182812	200190	218235	...	3
410	Electricity,gas,steam	...	...	...	...	...	...	...	...	...	...	410
4101	Electricity	35109	45147	52142	59051	...	13018	13779	16177	20366	...	4101
420	Water works and supply	...	...	...	...	...	...	...	...	...	...	420
4	Electricity,gas etc	...	...	...	...	...	...	...	...	...	...	4
2-4	All industry	...	...	...	...	...	...	...	...	...	...	2-4

For certain differences in classification, see country note.

a/ Data relate to the East Bank only.
b/ Net of non-industrial costs.
c/ Major group 352 is included in 351.
d/ Including repair services, bakeries in rural areas and manufacture-repair activities.
e/ Including repair services for the general public.

7. GROSS FIXED CAPITAL FORMATION TOTAL a/ (THOUSAND DINARS)

ISIC	INDUSTRY	1981	1982	1983	1964	1985	ISIC
210	Coal mining	-	-	-	-	...	210
220	Petroleum and gas	-	-	-	-	...	220
230	Metal ore mining	-	-	-	-	...	230
290	Other mining	47747	154096	151678	185628	...	290
2	Mining, quarrying .	47747	154096	151678	185628	...	2
311/2	Food products	18080	18126	15245	39671	...	311/2
313	Beverages	11761	13198	14283	18782	...	313
314	Tobacco	3238	2877	2680	6150	...	314
321	Textiles	7455	4784	4599	10145	...	321
3211	Spinning,weaving etc..	...	...	...	...	...	3211
322	Wearing apparel	1442	1409	2140	2975	...	322
323	Leather and products ...	967	702	641	1349	...	323
324	Footwear	1076	838	937	1550	...	324
331	Wood products	[4680	4706	4687	25483]	...	331
332	Furniture, fixtures					...	332
341	Paper and products	6281	11544	11799	13014	...	341
3411	Pulp,paper etc.	...	...	...	...	...	3411
342	Printing,publishing	3117	3364	4315	8543	...	342
351	Industrial chemicals ... b/	14757	118350	129065	169260	...	351
3511	Basic excl fertilizers	...	...	...	...	...	3511
3513	Synthetic resins etc .	...	...	...	...	...	3513
352	Other chemical products. b/	...	...	...	...	...	352
3522	Drugs and medicines ..	...	...	...	...	...	3522
353	Petroleum refineries ...	57010	72838	67202	120799	...	353
354	Petroleum,coal products.	-	-	-	-	...	354
355	Rubber products	306	397	121	18	...	355
356	Plastic products n.e.c..	6502	10752	14007	18234	...	356
361	Pottery,china etc					...	361
362	Glass and products	[58086	70149	133065	234758]	...	362
369	Non-metal products n.e.c					...	369
371	Iron and steel	[12531	13340	16609	25321]	...	371
372	Non-ferrous metals					...	372
381	Metal products	[13600	14111	19215	18455]	...	381
382	Machinery n.e.c.					...	382
3825	Office,computing etc..	...	...	...	...	...	3825
383	Electrical machinery ...	969	1516	2870	3335	...	383
3832	Radio,television etc..	...	...	...	...	...	3832
384	Transport equipment	1117	1201	841	1056	...	384
3841	Shipbuilding, repair..	...	...	...	...	...	3841
3843	Motor vehicles	...	...	...	...	...	3843
385	Professional goods	-	-	-	-	...	385
390	Other industries .... c/	4124	4138	3726	5677	...	390
3	Manufacturing ..... d/	227099	368340	448047	724575	...	3
410	Electricity,gas,steam ..	...	...	...	...	...	410
4101	Electricity	102976	121458	147720	198322	...	4101
420	Water works and supply .	...	...	...	...	...	420
4	Electricity,gas etc	...	...	...	...	...	4
2-4	All industry	...	...	...	...	...	2-4

For certain differences in classification, see country note.

a/ Data relate to the East Bank only.
b/ Major group 352 is included in 351.
c/ Including repair services, bakeries in rural areas and manufacture-repair activities.
d/ Including repair services for the general public.

KENYA

The information in the tables, except for the indexes, is based on the reply to the United Nations Questionnaire on General Industrial Statistics from the Central Bureau of Statistics, Ministry of Finance and Planning, Nairobi. The concepts, definitions and classification by branches of industry are generally in accordance with United Nations standards.

The data in the tables are derived from the survey of industrial production undertaken annually since 1964 by the Central Bureau of Statistics, mainly on the basis of a mail inquiry. The survey covers firms with 50 or more employees in both the public and private sectors, except for mining where the private sector only is covered. The unit of enumeration is the firm rather than the establishment. However, in cases where a firm is split by economic activity, the responding unit is often of an establishment nature. The value of production of the units covered by the survey accounts for 70 to 80 per cent of total industrial production. In the tables, figures include estimates for non-response. It should be noted that many of the figures published in official reports are revised in subsequent reports in the light of more complete information based on later surveys.

The data in the tables are based on the national classification which is comparable with the present ISIC. It should be noted, however, that the manufacture of metal furniture and fixtures (ISIC 381) is classified under ISIC 332.

The reference period is the calendar year, but returns are accepted for the accounting year (12 months beginning 1 July of the year indicated).

The number of persons engaged refers to averages of the numbers at the beginning and at the end of the reporting year. Wages and salaries include, in addition to regular wages and salaries, overtime payments, bonuses, cash allowances for rations and housing, payments in kind and employers' contributions to pension, health and other similar schemes.

Output is the sum of (a) the value of sales of all products of the establishment, adjusted for annual changes in stocks of finished and semi-finished goods produced, (b) receipts for industrial work done for or services rendered to others, (c) value of goods sold in the same condition as purchased, (d) value of fixed assets produced by the establishment for its own use, (e) rents received for non-residential property and (f) other income, minus excise duty, sales tax and any other indirect taxes. Value added is the value of output less the value of input. The input comprises the cost of materials, supplies, fuels and electricity purchased, cost of goods sold in the same condition as purchased and payments for industrial services rendered by others. Output and value added are compiled in factor values.

The unit of currency in Kenya is the Kenyan shilling, but the Kenyan pound is employed as the monetary unit in the tables. One Kenyan pound equals 20 Kenyan shillings.

The indexes of industrial production are compiled by the Central Bureau of Statistics, Ministry of Finance and Planning and provided in response to the United Nations Questionnaire on Indexes of Industrial Production.

Related national publication:
<u>Statistical Abstract</u> (annual), published by the Central Bureau of Statistics, Ministry of Economic Planning and Development, Nairobi.

KENYA

ISIC	INDUSTRY	1. NUMBER OF ESTABLISHMENTS a/ (NUMBER) *1981	*1982	1983	1984	1985	2. AVERAGE NUMBER OF PERSONS ENGAGED a/ (NUMBER) *1981	*1982	1983	1984	1985	ISIC
210	Coal mining	-	-	...	...	...	-	-	...	...	...	210
220	Petroleum and gas	-	-	...	...	...	-	-	...	...	...	220
230	Metal ore mining	1	1	...	...	...	76	72	...	...	...	230
290	Other mining	20	18	...	...	...	3131	2901	...	...	...	290
2	Mining, quarrying .	21	19	...	...	...	3207	2973	...	...	...	2
311/2	Food products	93	113	...	...	...	32952	32256	...	...	...	311/2
313	Beverages	8	12	...	...	...	3930	5104	...	...	...	313
314	Tobacco	1	1	...	...	...	1150	1196	...	...	...	314
321	Textiles	46	56	...	...	...	22098	23037	...	...	...	321
3211	Spinning,weaving etc..	12	16	...	...	...	10764	10955	...	...	...	3211
322	Wearing apparel	38	41	...	...	...	4280	4920	...	...	...	322
323	Leather and products ...	5	6	...	...	...	1409	970	...	...	...	323
324	Footwear	2	2	...	...	...	2220	2125	...	...	...	324
331	Wood products	54	57	...	...	...	9112	9026	...	...	...	331
332	Furniture, fixtures .... b/	14	17	...	...	...	1764	1506	...	...	...	332
341	Paper and products	13	14	...	...	...	3496	3448	...	...	...	341
3411	Pulp,paper etc.	3	3	...	...	...	1648	1679	...	...	...	3411
342	Printing,publishing	18	19	...	...	...	2404	2777	...	...	...	342
351	Industrial chemicals ...	13	11	...	...	...	2855	2773	...	...	...	351
3511	Basic excl fertilizers	[7	6]	...	...	...	[751	644]	...	...	...	3511
3513	Synthetic resins etc .			...	...	...			...	...	...	3513
352	Other chemical products.	38	38	...	...	...	6236	6131	...	...	...	352
3522	Drugs and medicines ..	12	10	...	...	...	1287	1278	...	...	...	3522
353	Petroleum refineries ...	1	1	...	...	...	348	345	...	...	...	353
354	Petroleum,coal products.	-	-	...	...	...	-	-	...	...	...	354
355	Rubber products	7	7	...	...	...	1872	1552	...	...	...	355
356	Plastic products n.e.c..	12	14	...	...	...	1563	1620	...	...	...	356
361	Pottery,china etc	1	1	...	...	...	155	132	...	...	...	361
362	Glass and products	2	3	...	...	...	1029	1204	...	...	...	362
369	Non-metal products n.e.c	8	14	...	...	...	4295	5037	...	...	...	369
371	Iron and steel	[9	10]	...	...	...	[1722	1706]	...	...	...	371
372	Non-ferrous metals			...	...	...			...	...	...	372
381	Metal products .... b/	42	48	...	...	...	9501	8214	...	...	...	381
382	Machinery n.e.c.	7	9	...	...	...	662	539	...	...	...	382
3825	Office,computing etc..	...	...	...	...	...	...	...	...	...	...	3825
383	Electrical machinery ...	11	16	...	...	...	6056	6472	...	...	...	383
3832	Radio,television etc..	...	...	...	...	...	...	...	...	...	...	3832
384	Transport equipment	22	24	...	...	...	17617	18258	...	...	...	384
3841	Shipbuilding, repair..	2	4	...	...	...	1027	1080	...	...	...	3841
3843	Motor vehicles	15	15	...	...	...	3437	3047	...	...	...	3843
385	Professional goods	1	1	...	...	...	[1908	1104]	...	...	...	385
390	Other industries	9	10	...	...	...			...	...	...	390
3	Manufacturing	475	545	...	...	...	140634	141452	...	...	...	3
410	Electricity,gas,steam ..	...	...	...	...	...	...	...	...	...	...	410
4101	Electricity	...	...	...	...	...	...	...	...	...	...	4101
420	Water works and supply .	...	...	...	...	...	...	...	...	...	...	420
4	Electricity,gas etc	...	...	...	...	...	...	...	...	...	...	4
2-4	All industry	...	...	...	...	...	...	...	...	...	...	2-4

a/ In general, firms with 50 or more employees.
b/ Manufacture of metal furniture and fixtures is included in major group 332.

ISIC	INDUSTRY	3. WAGES AND SALARIES OF EMPLOYEES a/b/ (THOUSAND POUNDS)					4. OUTPUT IN FACTOR VALUES b/ (MILLION POUNDS)					ISIC
		*1981	*1982	1983	1984	1985	*1981	*1982	1983	1984	1985	
210	Coal mining	-	-	...	...	...	-	-	...	...	...	210
220	Petroleum and gas	-	-	...	...	...	-	-	...	...	...	220
230	Metal ore mining	31	35	...	...	...	0.1	0.1	...	...	...	230
290	Other mining	2613	2941	...	...	...	26.0	30.7	...	...	...	290
2	Mining, quarrying .	2644	2976	...	...	...	26.1	30.8	...	...	...	2
311/2	Food products	27717	34308	...	...	...	570.6	616.1	...	...	...	311/2
313	Beverages	8284	9294	...	...	...	59.7	65.3	...	...	...	313
314	Tobacco	2505	2450	...	...	...	21.8	25.1	...	...	...	314
321	Textiles	14130	16012	...	...	...	85.2	86.5	...	...	...	321
3211	Spinning,weaving etc..	7703	8660	...	...	...	40.6	39.8	...	...	...	3211
322	Wearing apparel	3517	3533	...	...	...	25.1	20.7	...	...	...	322
323	Leather and products ...	1135	985	...	...	...	5.9	5.8	...	...	...	323
324	Footwear	2363	2426	...	...	...	13.7	13.4	...	...	...	324
331	Wood products	4098	5700	...	...	...	19.5	20.9	...	...	...	331
332	Furniture, fixtures .... c/	1479	1473	...	...	...	11.9	11.0	...	...	...	332
341	Paper and products	4636	5400	...	...	...	40.4	47.9	...	...	...	341
3411	Pulp,paper etc.	1741	1762	...	...	...	19.3	22.8	...	...	...	3411
342	Printing,publishing	6418	6663	...	...	...	29.7	36.6	...	...	...	342
351	Industrial chemicals ...	4356	4332	...	...	...	42.5	55.9	...	...	...	351
3511	Basic excl fertilizers	[2057	1974]	...	...	...	[19.0	25.0]	...	...	...	3511
3513	Synthetic resins etc .			...	...	...			...	...	...	3513
352	Other chemical products.	8943	10768	...	...	...	89.9	106.9	...	...	...	352
3522	Drugs and medicines ..	2564	3511	...	...	...	11.2	13.3	...	...	...	3522
353	Petroleum refineries ...	1542	1453	...	...	...	187.5	222.9	...	...	...	353
354	Petroleum,coal products.	-	-	...	...	...	-	-	...	...	...	354
355	Rubber products	3120	3552	...	...	...	33.3	40.0	...	...	...	355
356	Plastic products n.e.c..	1319	1631	...	...	...	12.1	15.3	...	...	...	356
361	Pottery,china etc	171	166	...	...	...	[6.0	6.6]	...	...	...	361
362	Glass and products	832	982	...	...	...			...	...	...	362
369	Non-metal products n.e.c	3722	3456	...	...	...	42.8	51.6	...	...	...	369
371	Iron and steel	[2399	2500]	...	...	...	[36.1	36.1]	...	...	...	371
372	Non-ferrous metals			...	...	...			...	...	...	372
381	Metal products .... c/	8284	8792	...	...	...	68.7	68.7	...	...	...	381
382	Machinery n.e.c.	726	697	...	...	...	9.7	8.7	...	...	...	382
3825	Office,computing etc..	...	...	...	...	...	...	...	...	...	...	3825
383	Electrical machinery ...	11023	11720	...	...	...	52.1	69.4	...	...	...	383
3832	Radio,television etc..	...	...	...	...	...	...	...	...	...	...	3832
384	Transport equipment	10529	12427	...	...	...	77.5	81.8	...	...	...	384
3841	Shipbuilding, repair..	947	621	...	...	...	15.8	11.5	...	...	...	3841
3843	Motor vehicles	2270	2263	...	...	...	41.8	45.5	...	...	...	3843
385	Professional goods	[1433	1702]	...	...	...	[6.4	7.3]	...	...	...	385
390	Other industries			...	...	...			...	...	...	390
3	Manufacturing	134681	152422	...	...	...	1548.1	1720.5	...	...	...	3
410	Electricity,gas,steam ..	...	...	...	...	...	...	...	...	...	...	410
4101	Electricity	...	...	...	...	...	...	...	...	...	...	4101
420	Water works and supply .	...	...	...	...	...	...	...	...	...	...	420
4	Electricity,gas etc	...	...	...	...	...	...	...	...	...	...	4
2-4	All industry	...	...	...	...	...	...	...	...	...	...	2-4

a/ Including employers' contributions to the social security fund.
b/ In general, firms with 50 or more employees.
c/ Manufacture of metal furniture and fixtures is included in major group 332.

5. VALUE ADDED IN FACTOR VALUES a/ (MILLION POUNDS)

ISIC	INDUSTRY	*1981	*1982	1983	1984	1985	ISIC
210	Coal mining	-	-	...	...	...	210
220	Petroleum and gas	-	-	...	...	...	220
230	Metal ore mining	0.05	0.05	...	...	...	230
290	Other mining	5.39	5.99	...	...	...	290
2	Mining, quarrying .	5.44	6.04	...	...	...	2
311/2	Food products	71.33	87.05	...	...	...	311/2
313	Beverages	[36.32]	30.83	...	...	...	313
314	Tobacco		10.42	...	...	...	314
321	Textiles	24.95	30.11	...	...	...	321
3211	Spinning,weaving etc..	13.85	16.54	...	...	...	3211
322	Wearing apparel	6.62	6.65	...	...	...	322
323	Leather and products ...	[5.30]	1.66	...	...	...	323
324	Footwear		3.47	...	...	...	324
331	Wood products	6.55	8.90	...	...	...	331
332	Furniture, fixtures .... b/	2.74	2.72	...	...	...	332
341	Paper and products	15.78	17.90	...	...	...	341
3411	Pulp,paper etc.	7.89	7.98	...	...	...	3411
342	Printing,publishing	8.51	8.85	...	...	...	342
351	Industrial chemicals ...	10.42	10.44	...	...	...	351
3511	Basic excl fertilizers	[3.78	3.63]	...	...	...	3511
3513	Synthetic resins etc .			...	...	...	3513
352	Other chemical products.	19.93	23.85	...	...	...	352
3522	Drugs and medicines ..	5.12	7.01	...	...	...	3522
353	Petroleum refineries ...	2.85	2.69	...	...	...	353
354	Petroleum,coal products.	-	-	...	...	...	354
355	Rubber products	9.21	10.49	...	...	...	355
356	Plastic products n.e.c..	2.97	3.67	...	...	...	356
361	Pottery,china etc	[1.64]	0.23	...	...	...	361
362	Glass and products		1.66	...	...	...	362
369	Non-metal products n.e.c	8.23	7.57	...	...	...	369
371	Iron and steel	[4.60	4.80]	...	...	...	371
372	Non-ferrous metals			...	...	...	372
381	Metal products .... b/	13.52	14.22	...	...	...	381
382	Machinery n.e.c.	1.29	1.24	...	...	...	382
3825	Office,computing etc..	...	...	...	...	...	3825
383	Electrical machinery ...	23.92	25.44	...	...	...	383
3832	Radio,television etc..	...	...	...	...	...	3832
384	Transport equipment	17.59	18.69	...	...	...	384
3841	Shipbuilding, repair..	4.50	2.95	...	...	...	3841
3843	Motor vehicles	4.52	4.50	...	...	...	3843
385	Professional goods	[1.56	1.86]	...	...	...	385
390	Other industries			...	...	...	390
3	Manufacturing	295.83	335.41	...	...	...	3
410	Electricity,gas,steam ..	...	...	...	...	...	410
4101	Electricity	...	...	...	...	...	4101
420	Water works and supply .	...	...	...	...	...	420
4	Electricity,gas etc	...	...	...	...	...	4
2-4	All industry	...	...	...	...	...	2-4

a/ In general, firms with 50 or more employees.
b/ Manufacture of metal furniture and fixtures is included in major group 332.

6. INDEX NUMBERS OF INDUSTRIAL PRODUCTION (1980 = 100)

ISIC	INDUSTRY	1976	1977	1978	1979	1981	1982	1983	1984	1985	a/ RATE	ISIC
210	Coal mining	...	...	...	...	...	...	...	...	...	...	210
220	Petroleum and gas	...	...	...	...	...	...	...	...	...	...	220
230	Metal ore mining	30	109	164	193	14	17	117	38	32	0.7	230
290	Other mining	112	226	204	182	81	80	95	100	96	-1.7	290
2	Mining, quarrying .	81	96	88	119	165	153	181	171	...	b/ 9.8	2
311/2	Food products	93	101	98	102	101	105	111	119	126	3.4	311/2
313	Beverages	70	82	94	96	99	89	82	89	99	3.9	313
314	Tobacco	81	86	101	101	109	115	140	130	122	4.7	314
321	Textiles	62	80	87	95	105	83	91	103	108	6.4	321
3211	Spinning,weaving etc..	...	...	...	...	...	...	...	...	...	...	3211
322	Wearing apparel	36	60	75	85	138	141	148	134	128	15.1	322
323	Leather and products ...	[106	101	122	107	118	98	99	86	85	-2.4]	323
324	Footwear											324
331	Wood products	74	84	90	96	93	98	81	68	49	-4.5	331
332	Furniture, fixtures	130	147	123	76	101	84	88	91	93	-3.7	332
341	Paper and products	64	75	93	100	87	91	83	88	94	4.4	341
3411	Pulp,paper etc.	...	...	...	...	...	...	...	...	...	...	3411
342	Printing,publishing	54	69	85	116	132	145	154	172	179	14.2	342
351	Industrial chemicals ...	57	59	73	84	91	95	86	96	94	5.7	351
3511	Basic excl fertilizers	...	...	...	...	...	...	...	...	...	...	3511
3513	Synthetic resins etc .	...	...	...	...	...	...	...	...	...	...	3513
352	Other chemical products.	...	...	...	...	...	...	...	...	...	...	352
3522	Drugs and medicines ..	...	...	...	...	...	...	...	...	...	...	3522
353	Petroleum refineries ...	[51	55	54	70	106	96	101	126	132	11.1]	353
354	Petroleum,coal products.											354
355	Rubber products	52	62	64	95	106	79	101	118	128	10.5	355
356	Plastic products n.e.c..	48	65	86	95	85	79	97	90	95	7.9	356
361	Pottery,china etc	...	...	...	...	...	...	...	...	...	...	361
362	Glass and products	34	76	82	85	68	63	75	97	100	12.7	362
369	Non-metal products n.e.c	79	93	89	91	100	99	97	86	96	2.2	369
371	Iron and steel	...	...	...	...	...	...	...	...	...	...	371
372	Non-ferrous metals	...	...	...	...	...	...	...	...	...	...	372
381	Metal products	77	86	96	104	91	69	75	69	73	-0.6	381
382	Machinery n.e.c.	81	79	81	79	83	79	81	83	88	0.9	382
3825	Office,computing etc..	...	...	...	...	...	...	...	...	...	...	3825
383	Electrical machinery ...	63	76	101	97	90	88	88	93	98	5.0	383
3832	Radio,television etc..	...	...	...	...	...	...	...	...	...	...	3832
384	Transport equipment	15	32	87	98	120	118	137	118	102	23.7	384
3841	Shipbuilding, repair..	...	...	...	...	...	...	...	...	...	...	3841
3843	Motor vehicles	...	...	...	...	...	...	...	...	...	...	3843
385	Professional goods	...	...	...	...	...	...	...	...	...	...	385
390	Other industries	73	84	71	90	107	78	86	115	147	8.1	390
3	Manufacturing	68	78	88	95	105	106	111	115	...	b/ 6.8	3
410	Electricity,gas,steam ..	...	...	...	...	...	...	...	...	...	...	410
4101	Electricity	...	...	...	...	...	...	...	...	...	...	4101
420	Water works and supply .	...	...	...	...	...	...	...	...	...	...	420
4	Electricity,gas etc	...	...	...	...	...	...	...	...	...	...	4
2-4	All industry	...	...	...	...	...	...	...	...	...	...	2-4

a/ Annual growth rate 1976-1985.

b/ Annual growth rate 1976-1984.

KOREA, REPUBLIC OF

The information in the tables, except for the indexes, is based on the reply to the United Nations Questionnaire on General Industrial Statistics from the National Bureau of Statistics, Economic Planning Board, Seoul. The concepts, definitions and classification by branches of industry are generally in accordance with United Nations standards.

The data, other than those for hours worked by employees and quantity of electricity consumed, are derived from the annual survey of mining and manufacturing conducted by the National Bureau of Statistics. The inquiry is carried out by field enumeration. The data in the tables cover establishments with 5 or more persons engaged, but the following establishments are not covered: (a) establishments under construction as of 31 December, (b) establishments operated directly by the armed forces of the Republic of Korea and by allied forces, (c) workshops operated by public occupation guidance centres and (d) experimental stations or laboratories attached to public organizations and schools. Data on hours worked by employees are derived from labour statistics compiled by the Labour Office, Seoul, and relate to the regular workers of the Establishment Labour Conditions Survey which is carried out 30 April of every year. Data for the quantity of electricity consumed are derived from the records kept by the Korea Electric Power Corporation, a monopolized government-operating enterprise. The data in the tables are based on the national classification which is comparable with the present version of ISIC.

Numbers of persons engaged and employees refer to averages during the year. Homeworkers are included in the count of employees. It should be noted that the number of operatives refers to 31 December of each year and is not comparable with the average number of employees. Wages and salaries relate to the gross payments in cash and in kind made to all employees on the pay-roll of the establishments surveyed. These payments include all forms of compensation for employees' labour such as salaries, wages, bonuses, allowances and subsidies, but exclude payments to the retired, long-term absentees and members of armed forces. The number of hours worked by operatives refers to the hours worked by employees of establishments with 10 or more persons engaged modified on the basis of the Establishment Labour Conditions Survey which is taken 30 April each year.

Output is the total value of products shipped and industrial services rendered to others by the establishments plus net additions of inventories of finished goods, semi-finished goods and work in progress. Value added is derived by subtracting the cost of materials, fuels, purchased electricity and water, contract and repair and maintenance work from the value of output. Valuation of output and value added is in producers' prices.

Gross fixed capital formation relates to expenditure for the acquisition, installation, expansion and capitalized repair of new and used fixed assets. For fixed assets constructed by the establishment's own labour force for its own use, the expenditure actually made during the year is included. The annual disposal of fixed assets is not taken into account.

The indexes of industrial production are compiled by the Bank of Korea and provided in response to the United Nations Questionnaire on Indexes of Industrial Production. The indexes cover, in principle, all establishments with 5 or more persons engaged.

Related national publications:

Report on Mining and Manufacturing Survey (annual); Korea Statistical Yearbook, both published by the Economic Planning Board, Seoul. Economic Statistics Yearbook; Monthly Economic Statistics, both published by the Bank of Korea, Seoul.

ISIC	INDUSTRY	1. NUMBER OF ESTABLISHMENTS a/ (NUMBER)					2. AVERAGE NUMBER OF PERSONS ENGAGED a/b/ (THOUSANDS)					ISIC
		1981	1982	1983	1984	1985	1981	1982	1983	1984	1985	
210	Coal mining	220	275	296	297	...	60.9	59.5	59.0	60.5	...	210
220	Petroleum and gas	-	-	-	-	...	-	-	-	-	...	220
230	Metal ore mining	64	53	53	50	...	7.3	6.2	5.7	5.4	...	230
290	Other mining	1642	1620	1496	1532	...	21.8	22.1	20.1	21.9	...	290
2	Mining, quarrying .	1926	1948	1845	1879	...	90.0	87.8	84.8	87.8	...	2
311/2	Food products	3475	3353	3424	3523	...	131.2	133.5	146.8	154.1	...	311/2
313	Beverages	1124	1069	1019	1009	...	27.9	28.6	27.6	27.2	...	313
314	Tobacco	22	23	22	22	...	13.4	13.1	13.5	11.6	...	314
321	Textiles	4920	5325	5598	5745	...	392.6	383.5	382.5	374.6	...	321
3211	Spinning,weaving etc..	3095	3168	c/ 3248	c/ 3380	...	299.2	287.4	c/ 291.3	c/ 286.4	...	3211
322	Wearing apparel	2811	3077	3468	3668	...	212.1	216.4	223.3	241.2	...	322
323	Leather and products ...	429	571	688	725	...	22.7	25.7	29.3	28.1	...	323
324	Footwear	308	431	506	435	...	26.3	36.9	40.9	30.8	...	324
331	Wood products	1543	1672	1669	1672	...	45.9	41.8	42.0	39.7	...	331
332	Furniture, fixtures	751	887	910	985	...	16.9	20.5	23.5	26.9	...	332
341	Paper and products	1092	1206	1189	1249	...	45.6	46.3	47.3	49.7	...	341
3411	Pulp,paper etc.	384	364	294	305	...	...	20.7	18.9	20.2	...	3411
342	Printing,publishing	1495	1735	1856	1914	...	45.3	49.6	51.2	53.9	...	342
351	Industrial chemicals ...	726	797	747	704	...	38.9	42.5	40.0	37.6	...	351
3511	Basic excl fertilizers	368	362	d/ 328	d/ 319	...	16.2	16.0	d/ 15.1	d/ 14.6	...	3511
3513	Synthetic resins etc ..	288	366	269	220	...	13.8	19.3	15.3	15.0	...	3513
352	Other chemical products.	659	653	683	715	...	49.7	53.5	54.9	55.3	...	352
3522	Drugs and medicines ..	227	220	239	263	...	26.1	27.9	28.5	28.0	...	3522
353	Petroleum refineries ...	45	41	16	18	...	5.8	5.8	4.0	4.3	...	353
354	Petroleum,coal products.	262	265	296	297	...	11.4	11.6	12.2	12.0	...	354
355	Rubber products	388	505	599	679	...	100.6	106.7	121.1	130.1	...	355
356	Plastic products n.e.c..	1151	1375	1507	1785	...	55.3	56.0	49.3	53.7	...	356
361	Pottery,china etc	298	295	307	309	...	18.0	19.0	17.0	16.7	...	361
362	Glass and products	177	183	178	203	...	18.3	18.1	17.8	21.2	...	362
369	Non-metal products n.e.c	2151	2120	2324	2422	...	56.1	58.0	65.0	70.4	...	369
371	Iron and steel	568	610	621	630	...	67.1	65.6	72.1	74.2	...	371
372	Non-ferrous metals	393	399	434	475	...	20.7	22.0	22.9	25.4	...	372
381	Metal products	2364	2765	2975	3212	...	92.5	106.0	117.0	121.7	...	381
382	Machinery n.e.c.	1910	2311	2532	2814	...	83.8	87.7	100.8	114.1	...	382
3825	Office,computing etc..	59	58	81	95	...	3.1	2.8	6.9	11.1	...	3825
383	Electrical machinery ...	1757	2059	2292	2629	...	213.0	207.1	235.9	276.4	...	383
3832	Radio,television etc..	889	1039	775	920	...	151.7	145.0	99.9	122.2	...	3832
384	Transport equipment	1009	1115	1193	1287	...	126.2	133.0	143.2	161.7	...	384
3841	Shipbuilding, repair..	380	399	410	433	...	56.5	70.2	73.4	84.7	...	3841
3843	Motor vehicles	448	531	613	670	...	56.2	50.8	58.7	64.6	...	3843
385	Professional goods	393	466	481	545	...	28.4	30.0	28.6	34.8	...	385
390	Other industries	1210	1491	1709	1878	...	78.5	80.6	86.2	96.0	...	390
3	Manufacturing	33431	36799	39243	41549	...	2044.2	2099.1	2215.9	2343.4	...	3
410	Electricity,gas,steam ..	...	...	88	...	...	...	...	25.3	...	...	410
4101	Electricity	...	...	74	...	...	...	...	24.5	...	...	4101
420	Water works and supply .	...	...	341	...	...	...	...	10.8	...	...	420
4	Electricity,gas etc	...	...	429	...	...	...	...	36.1	...	...	4
2-4	All industry	...	...	41517	...	...	...	...	2336.8	...	...	2-4

a/ Establishments with 5 or more persons engaged.
c/ Including ISIC 3212 and 3213.

b/ Manufacturing: including homeworkers.
d/ Including ISIC 3514.

ISIC	INDUSTRY	3. AVERAGE NUMBER OF EMPLOYEES a/b/ (THOUSANDS) 1981	1982	1983	1984	1985	4. WAGES AND SALARIES OF EMPLOYEES b/ (BILLION WON) 1981	1982	1983	1984	1985	ISIC
210	Coal mining	60.7	59.3	58.7	60.2	...	171.2	193.4	201.3	225.2	...	210
220	Petroleum and gas	-	-	-	-	...	-	-	-	-	...	220
230	Metal ore mining	7.3	6.2	5.6	5.4	...	22.5	19.7	20.9	20.1	...	230
290	Other mining	19.8	20.2	18.4	20.2	...	36.0	38.0	31.7	49.9	...	290
2	Mining, quarrying .	87.8	85.7	82.7	85.8	...	229.7	251.1	253.9	295.2	...	2
311/2	Food products	126.8	129.4	142.7	149.8	...	252.0	288.1	342.9	366.2	...	311/2
313	Beverages	26.4	27.2	26.2	25.9	...	71.5	86.8	90.9	91.4	...	313
314	Tobacco	13.4	13.1	13.5	11.6	...	34.2	41.0	48.4	49.5	...	314
321	Textiles	387.6	378.0	376.8	368.7	...	661.0	725.2	762.0	871.2	...	321
3211	Spinning,weaving etc..	296.1	284.3	c/ 288.2	c/ 283.1	...	515.9	554.6	c/ 592.5	c/ 678.0	...	3211
322	Wearing apparel	209.1	213.1	219.6	237.3	...	298.6	347.4	385.0	482.1	...	322
323	Leather and products ...	22.3	25.2	28.6	27.4	...	38.3	49.5	61.3	67.0	...	323
324	Footwear	26.0	36.5	40.5	30.4	...	39.7	66.0	81.5	69.2	...	324
331	Wood products	44.3	40.0	40.3	38.0	...	82.2	82.2	91.5	100.7	...	331
332	Furniture, fixtures	16.1	19.5	22.5	25.8	...	30.0	38.7	52.0	65.8	...	332
341	Paper and products	44.6	45.2	46.2	48.5	...	98.5	110.1	127.3	144.0	...	341
3411	Pulp,paper etc.	22.1	20.3	18.7	19.9	...	46.5	53.3	56.0	65.8	...	3411
342	Printing,publishing	43.9	47.8	49.4	52.1	...	134.2	150.2	175.0	182.1	...	342
351	Industrial chemicals ...	38.4	42.0	39.1	37.1	...	123.7	142.1	150.7	158.8	...	351
3511	Basic excl fertilizers	16.0	15.8	d/ 14.8	d/ 14.4	...	51.0	54.9	d/ 61.0	d/ 64.9	...	3511
3513	Synthetic resins etc .	13.5	19.0	15.1	14.4	...	43.2	58.1	56.2	62.8	...	3513
352	Other chemical products.	49.3	53.1	54.5	54.9	...	132.8	170.3	189.8	203.9	...	352
3522	Drugs and medicines ..	26.1	27.8	28.5	27.9	...	74.3	97.1	103.1	108.6	...	3522
353	Petroleum refineries ...	5.8	5.8	4.0	4.3	...	33.1	33.1	31.2	33.0	...	353
354	Petroleum,coal products.	11.0	11.4	12.0	11.9	...	30.1	33.9	40.4	41.3	...	354
355	Rubber products	100.2	106.2	120.5	129.4	...	171.7	205.4	237.4	288.7	...	355
356	Plastic products n.e.c..	54.2	54.5	47.9	52.1	...	97.8	114.4	111.6	142.5	...	356
361	Pottery,china etc	17.7	18.6	16.6	16.4	...	27.9	34.0	32.2	35.7	...	361
362	Glass and products	18.1	18.0	17.7	21.1	...	46.3	47.5	51.5	65.7	...	362
369	Non-metal products n.e.c	53.8	55.8	62.6	67.8	...	124.7	145.3	186.7	218.4	...	369
371	Iron and steel	66.7	65.2	71.6	73.7	...	190.4	175.7	235.2	297.4	...	371
372	Non-ferrous metals	20.4	21.7	22.6	25.0	...	54.1	59.8	68.6	88.6	...	372
381	Metal products	90.3	103.3	114.3	118.7	...	195.0	249.5	320.2	364.0	...	381
382	Machinery n.e.c.	82.1	85.6	98.6	111.6	...	191.0	224.5	286.2	368.9	...	382
3825	Office,computing etc..	3.0	2.7	6.8	11.1	...	6.2	6.0	16.9	34.0	...	3825
383	Electrical machinery ...	211.8	205.6	234.3	274.4	...	420.8	465.0	562.0	760.8	...	383
3832	Radio,television etc..	151.1	144.3	99.4	121.6	...	285.8	317.2	230.8	334.8	...	3832
384	Transport equipment	125.3	132.0	142.2	160.7	...	373.8	457.1	547.5	645.3	...	384
3841	Shipbuilding, repair..	56.1	69.8	73.0	84.3	...	197.5	273.0	313.0	364.2	...	3841
3843	Motor vehicles	55.9	50.3	58.2	64.1	...	142.3	148.8	200.2	240.0	...	3843
385	Professional goods	28.1	29.3	28.2	34.4	...	50.0	62.1	60.7	86.9	...	385
390	Other industries	77.3	79.2	84.5	94.0	...	130.1	149.2	169.9	206.0	...	390
3	Manufacturing	2011.0	2062.3	2177.5	2303.0	...	4133.5	4754.1	5499.6	6495.1	...	3
410	Electricity,gas,steam ..	...	...	...	...	...	...	...	138.9	...	...	410
4101	Electricity	...	...	...	...	...	...	...	134.2	...	...	4101
420	Water works and supply .	...	...	...	...	...	...	...	38.7	...	...	420
4	Electricity,gas etc	...	...	...	...	...	...	...	177.6	...	...	4
2-4	All industry	...	...	...	...	...	...	...	5931.1	...	...	2-4

a/ Manufacturing: including homeworkers.
c/ Including ISIC 3212 and 3213.
b/ Establishments with 5 or more persons engaged.
d/ Including ISIC 3514.

ISIC	INDUSTRY	5. AVERAGE NUMBER OF OPERATIVES a/b/c/ (THOUSANDS)					6. WAGES AND SALARIES OF OPERATIVES c/ (BILLION WON)					ISIC
		1981	1982	1983	1984	1985	1981	1982	1983	1984	1985	
210	Coal mining	53.7	50.4	48.9	52.4	...	143.6	161.1	166.9	194.3	...	210
220	Petroleum and gas	-	-	-	-	...	-	-	-	-	...	220
230	Metal ore mining	6.0	4.8	4.7	4.4	...	17.7	14.9	17.3	15.5	...	230
290	Other mining	9.1	10.0	16.7	17.9	...	30.7	31.7	31.1	41.8	...	290
2	Mining, quarrying .	68.8	65.2	70.3	74.7	...	192.0	207.7	215.3	251.6	...	2
311/2	Food products	89.9	88.7	108.7	115.0	...	164.0	185.3	216.0	226.1	...	311/2
313	Beverages	16.0	14.7	15.0	15.5	...	37.2	37.5	43.8	47.4	...	313
314	Tobacco	13.1	10.7	11.1	9.6	...	29.0	34.3	38.6	39.8	...	314
321	Textiles	348.1	337.4	333.6	324.5	...	542.2	585.1	623.9	716.8	...	321
3211	Spinning,weaving etc..	267.3	254.6	d/ 256.2	d/ 250.5	...	429.3	451.0	d/ 491.4	d/ 566.2	...	3211
322	Wearing apparel	191.9	192.2	195.8	211.4	...	243.5	281.8	313.7	391.0	...	322
323	Leather and products ...	19.2	21.8	24.2	22.9	...	27.3	37.2	46.5	49.9	...	323
324	Footwear	22.9	33.1	35.4	25.2	...	30.3	53.0	65.8	52.3	...	324
331	Wood products	34.9	33.1	33.5	30.4	...	61.7	62.1	70.1	74.7	...	331
332	Furniture, fixtures	14.0	17.2	19.2	22.2	...	23.1	30.6	41.3	51.7	...	332
341	Paper and products	35.7	35.1	36.1	37.8	...	70.3	76.5	90.4	101.1	...	341
3411	Pulp,paper etc.	16.2	15.9	14.8	15.6	...	33.6	38.4	41.5	46.5	...	3411
342	Printing,publishing	29.5	32.6	33.5	32.7	...	72.4	87.8	104.4	100.4	...	342
351	Industrial chemicals ...	26.0	30.0	28.3	25.8	...	81.6	94.1	101.5	101.1	...	351
3511	Basic excl fertilizers	11.1	10.8	e/ 10.4	e/ 9.9	...	33.5	34.4	e/ 40.7	e/ 40.7	...	3511
3513	Synthetic resins etc .	9.8	14.7	11.5	9.5	...	29.7	39.8	40.3	38.4	...	3513
352	Other chemical products.	28.6	30.6	31.5	31.1	...	63.2	76.3	88.8	97.2	...	352
3522	Drugs and medicines ..	13.8	13.8	14.9	14.8	...	30.4	36.6	40.9	44.9	...	3522
353	Petroleum refineries ...	3.8	3.9	2.6	2.9	...	22.4	20.4	21.9	21.2	...	353
354	Petroleum,coal products.	7.6	7.9	7.5	7.7	...	17.8	20.6	21.8	24.0	...	354
355	Rubber products	92.5	95.9	110.3	118.6	...	140.7	171.3	200.4	243.3	...	355
356	Plastic products n.e.c..	42.5	48.1	38.7	41.4	...	74.0	86.6	80.2	102.1	...	356
361	Pottery,china etc	15.7	21.1	15.1	14.7	...	23.5	28.0	27.2	30.6	...	361
362	Glass and products	14.4	14.5	14.3	17.3	...	35.5	35.9	38.3	50.6	...	362
369	Non-metal products n.e.c	38.9	42.0	50.1	54.3	...	93.3	108.6	139.5	161.6	...	369
371	Iron and steel	56.2	54.3	57.0	58.3	...	150.7	130.2	176.7	220.5	...	371
372	Non-ferrous metals	15.7	17.4	16.5	19.4	...	39.6	44.9	47.2	62.6	...	372
381	Metal products	73.9	83.4	90.3	95.3	...	139.6	175.3	239.9	271.8	...	381
382	Machinery n.e.c.	65.3	66.1	76.4	84.3	...	133.1	157.6	203.1	254.2	...	382
3825	Office,computing etc..	2.5	2.2	5.6	8.5	...	4.1	4.1	11.4	19.8	...	3825
383	Electrical machinery ...	173.0	166.4	188.9	219.1	...	295.8	318.4	395.1	540.8	...	383
3832	Radio,television etc..	124.9	118.4	78.1	94.1	...	202.0	217.4	153.4	231.9	...	3832
384	Transport equipment	99.8	103.6	105.0	122.5	...	253.5	323.9	374.2	452.8	...	384
3841	Shipbuilding, repair..	47.7	56.3	55.5	64.2	...	143.5	198.4	224.4	258.9	...	3841
3843	Motor vehicles	41.2	38.4	41.0	49.1	...	84.8	100.3	127.0	167.0	...	3843
385	Professional goods	23.8	24.1	23.2	28.2	...	35.8	43.7	45.3	62.4	...	385
390	Other industries	68.0	68.5	72.6	81.4	...	99.5	113.1	132.9	159.2	...	390
3	Manufacturing	1660.9	1694.4	1774.4	1869.5	...	3000.6	3420.1	3988.5	4707.2	...	3
410	Electricity,gas,steam ..	...	...	...	...	...	...	...	...	...	...	410
4101	Electricity	...	...	...	...	...	...	...	...	...	...	4101
420	Water works and supply .	...	...	...	...	...	...	...	...	...	...	420
4	Electricity,gas etc	...	...	...	...	...	...	...	...	...	...	4
2-4	All industry	...	...	...	...	...	...	...	...	...	...	2-4

a/ Manufacturing: including homeworkers.
b/ At 31 December of the year indicated.
c/ Establishments with 5 or more persons engaged.
d/ Including ISIC 3212 and 3213.
e/ Including ISIC 3514.

ISIC	INDUSTRY	7. HOURS WORKED BY OPERATIVES a/ (MILLIONS) 1981	1982	1983	1984	1985	8. QUANTITY OF ELECTRICITY CONSUMED b/ (MILLION KWH) 1981	1982	1983	1984	1985	ISIC
210	Coal mining	106.5	108.4	112.8	114.0	'13.0	474	494	525	563	622	210
220	Petroleum and gas	-	-	-	-	-	-	-	-	-	-	220
230	Metal ore mining	21.2	13.9	14.4	14.7	14.7	177	166	163	174	172	230
290	Other mining	20.3	24.4	22.2	24.8	27.3	64	61	80	94	113	290
2	Mining, quarrying .	148.0	146.7	149.4	153.5	155.0	715	721	768	831	907	2
311/2	Food products	264.1	264.5	284.2	299.3	290.2	800	836	1482	1603	1726	311/2
313	Beverages	57.5	59.6	57.5	59.5	54.5	214	203	208	242	235	313
314	Tobacco	...	...	...	...	...	61	60	66	66	64	314
321	Textiles	1059.7	1039.9	1037.8	1020.8	936.5	4601	4919	5378	5889	5982	321
3211	Spinning,weaving etc..	...	...	...	...	...	...	...	...	...	...	3211
322	Wearing apparel	589.6	596.4	567.2	551.4	510.0	149	165	180	200	189	322
323	Leather and products ...	70.1	72.5	78.9	80.9	77.3	78	81	96	107	122	323
324	Footwear	140.7	169.5	205.3	191.3	197.6	26	39	64	77	98	324
331	Wood products	104.2	92.7	94.6	86.9	73.4	321	293	312	305	251	331
332	Furniture, fixtures	44.5	46.6	53.6	50.4	49.1	26	23	39	53	95	332
341	Paper and products	109.4	106.5	111.9	110.3	107.1	1496	1495	1657	1744	1887	341
3411	Pulp,paper etc.	...	...	...	...	...	...	...	...	...	...	3411
342	Printing,publishing	102.4	111.6	107.4	103.4	98.7	94	103	119	145	155	342
351	Industrial chemicals ...	101.9	92.8	92.9	89.2	90.4	3004	2900	3212	3313	3454	351
3511	Basic excl fertilizers	...	...	...	...	...	...	...	...	...	...	3511
3513	Synthetic resins etc .	...	...	...	...	...	...	...	...	...	...	3513
352	Other chemical products.	148.5	151.3	158.3	166.7	166.5	461	550	630	778	881	352
3522	Drugs and medicines ..	...	...	...	...	...	...	...	...	...	...	3522
353	Petroleum refineries ...	19.1	17.6	16.8	18.8	19.1	196	218	233	248	284	353
354	Petroleum,coal products.	27.8	28.4	26.8	28.4	28.9	89	75	76	87	96	354
355	Rubber products	218.1	254.3	267.7	293.2	296.6	477	466	507	556	566	355
356	Plastic products n.e.c..	102.9	119.0	142.1	132.5	128.7	290	357	423	471	450	356
361	Pottery,china etc	50.5	49.6	42.5	43.7	42.0	85	79	93	105	94	361
362	Glass and products	45.5	42.7	44.8	51.6	50.3	198	193	239	290	322	362
369	Non-metal products n.e.c	118.2	122.9	140.5	155.3	156.0	2359	2651	2989	2970	3083	369
371	Iron and steel	141.6	119.0	105.6	126.0	124.1	3559	3798	4126	4509	4542	371
372	Non-ferrous metals	26.6	23.2	22.1	25.1	25.7	1386	1294	1384	1508	1544	372
381	Metal products	276.8	318.2	356.5	353.2	347.3	635	677	789	952	1002	381
382	Machinery n.e.c.	252.5	257.1	273.5	281.4	268.6	394	383	431	466	515	382
3825	Office,computing etc..	...	...	...	...	...	...	...	...	...	...	3825
383	Electrical machinery ...	540.5	549.9	655.2	732.3	694.8	831	889	1141	1487	1798	383
3832	Radio,television etc..	...	...	...	...	...	...	...	...	...	...	3832
384	Transport equipment	258.6	323.3	381.4	409.7	430.1	723	855	999	1006	1424	384
3841	Shipbuilding, repair..	...	...	...	...	...	...	...	...	...	...	3841
3843	Motor vehicles	...	...	...	...	...	...	...	...	...	...	3843
385	Professional goods	70.1	76.7	70.6	79.2	73.6	[314	248	254	289	328]	385
390	Other industries	195.0	210.1	213.1	282.4	223.3						390
3	Manufacturing	c/ 5136.4	c/ 5315.9	c/ 5608.8	c/ 5822.9	c/ 5560.4	22867	23850	27127	29466	31187	3
410	Electricity,gas,steam ..	53.0	58.8	59.1	60.8	62.7	45	151	106	130	226	410
4101	Electricity	...	...	...	...	...	45	151	106	130	226	4101
420	Water works and supply .	...	...	...	...	...	1280	1393	1501	1669	1745	420
4	Electricity,gas etc	...	...	...	...	...	1325	1544	1607	1799	1971	4
2-4	All industry	...	...	...	...	...	24907	26115	29502	32096	34065	2-4

a/ Hours worked by employees of establishments with 10 or more persons engaged.
b/ Data derived from the Korea Electric Power Corporation c/ Excluding major group 314.

ISIC	INDUSTRY	9. OUTPUT IN PRODUCERS' PRICES a/ (BILLION WON) 1981	1982	1983	1984	1985	10. VALUE ADDED IN PRODUCERS' PRICES a/ (BILLION WON) 1981	1982	1983	1984	1985	ISIC
210	Coal mining	520	564	560	651	...	366	447	445	499	...	210
220	Petroleum and gas	-	-	-	-	...	-	-	-	-	...	220
230	Metal ore mining	84	66	61	66	...	57	38	38	42	...	230
290	Other mining	161	172	162	275	...	106	116	118	166	...	290
2	Mining, quarrying .	765	802	783	992	...	529	601	601	707	...	2
311/2	Food products	3948	4547	5328	5966	...	1083	1280	1493	1651	...	311/2
313	Beverages	993	1127	1203	1272	...	474	534	600	619	...	313
314	Tobacco	1224	1546	1632	1676	...	876	1060	1214	1277	...	314
321	Textiles	5601	5679	6087	6978	...	2021	2005	2234	2625	...	321
3211	Spinning,weaving etc..	4556	4587	b/ 4990	b/ 5642	...	1633	1613	b/ 1770	b/ 2122	...	3211
322	Wearing apparel	1974	1973	2208	2704	...	792	803	896	1111	...	322
323	Leather and products ...	447	507	624	761	...	148	141	165	192	...	323
324	Footwear	249	340	459	447	...	91	135	183	176	...	324
331	Wood products	812	820	854	870	...	162	242	242	233	...	331
332	Furniture, fixtures	158	217	313	399	...	69	87	133	162	...	332
341	Paper and products	1211	1264	1549	1819	...	332	358	494	551	...	341
3411	Pulp,paper etc.	690	755	869	1003	...	183	197	285	310	...	3411
342	Printing,publishing	595	744	940	1088	...	309	398	527	588	...	342
351	Industrial chemicals ...	3022	3137	3494	3936	...	767	785	938	1038	...	351
3511	Basic excl fertilizers	1112	1051	c/ 1977	c/ 2230	...	294	257	c/ 460	c/ 524	...	3511
3513	Synthetic resins etc .	1183	1390	1493	1782	...	292	378	389	465	...	3513
352	Other chemical products.	1444	1786	2143	2365	...	681	849	1011	1133	...	352
3522	Drugs and medicines ..	657	804	919	1087	...	370	452	541	624	...	3522
353	Petroleum refineries ...	5542	5831	6200	6594	...	765	776	841	903	...	353
354	Petroleum,coal products.	666	740	851	995	...	162	172	192	210	...	354
355	Rubber products	1107	1150	1358	1820	...	417	420	515	669	...	355
356	Plastic products n.e.c..	861	910	1104	1505	...	286	301	367	520	...	356
361	Pottery,china etc	114	118	127	138	...	70	68	83	85	...	361
362	Glass and products	286	297	355	525	...	129	143	170	248	...	362
369	Non-metal products n.e.c	1380	1579	2034	2257	...	568	535	768	862	...	369
371	Iron and steel	3800	4161	4821	5568	...	1107	1310	1449	1714	...	371
372	Non-ferrous metals ....,	704	772	985	1121	...	189	174	244	276	...	372
381	Metal products	1430	1708	2052	2337	...	559	702	859	953	...	381
382	Machinery n.e.c.	1234	1502	2037	2664	...	517	602	858	1102	...	382
3825	Office,computing etc..	48	42	139	278	...	15	13	56	111	...	3825
383	Electrical machinery ...	3732	4113	5690	7866	...	1319	1521	2104	2943	...	383
3832	Radio,television etc..	2542	2713	2830	4123	...	893	1005	1050	1642	...	3832
384	Transport equipment	3057	3911	4770	5921	...	1070	1402	1752	2105	...	384
3841	Shipbuilding, repair..	1417	1959	2210	3038	...	556	694	859	1104	...	3841
3843	Motor vehicles	1405	1703	2235	2497	...	445	613	767	832	...	3843
385	Professional goods	364	383	400	586	...	135	152	160	236	...	385
390	Other industries	761	789	929	1130	...	314	351	420	474	...	390
3	Manufacturing	46716	51651	60547	71308	...	15412	17306	20912	24656	...	3
410	Electricity,gas,steam ..	...	...	3121	...	...	...	...	1371	...	...	410
4101	Electricity	...	...	3102	...	...	...	...	1361	...	...	4101
420	Water works and supply .	...	...	306	...	...	...	...	163	...	...	420
4	Electricity,gas etc	...	...	3427	...	...	...	...	1534	...	...	4
2-4	All industry	...	...	64757	...	...	...	...	23047	...	...	2-4

a/ Establishments with 5 or more persons engaged.
b/ Including ISIC 3212 and 3213.
c/ Including ISIC 3514.

11. GROSS FIXED CAPITAL FORMATION TOTAL a/b/ (BILLION WON)

ISIC	INDUSTRY	1981	1982	1983	1984	1985	ISIC
210	Coal mining	70.8	69.1	93.9	90.8	...	210
220	Petroleum and gas	-	-	-	-	...	220
230	Metal ore mining	8.8	7.1	6.0	5.5	...	230
290	Other mining	12.0	19.6	15.8	32.8	...	290
2	Mining, quarrying .	91.6	95.8	115.7	129.1	...	2
311/2	Food products	198.8	247.6	389.3	364.2	...	311/2
313	Beverages	103.6	73.7	73.9	111.1	...	313
314	Tobacco	23.9	12.1	73.9	33.7	...	314
321	Textiles	392.7	349.4	396.6	552.0	...	321
3211	Spinning,weaving etc..	346.7	300.4	c/ 345.3	c/ 494.8	...	3211
322	Wearing apparel	61.2	54.6	69.5	80.9	...	322
323	Leather and products ...	17.8	17.4	23.4	27.3	...	323
324	Footwear	16.0	16.5	19.5	13.7	...	324
331	Wood products	48.8	26.2	33.0	44.7	...	331
332	Furniture, fixtures	10.8	22.8	15.6	25.5	...	332
341	Paper and products	60.3	114.1	103.3	124.5	...	341
3411	Pulp,paper etc.	32.6	81.0	59.9	65.9	...	3411
342	Printing,publishing	30.8	54.7	53.0	142.5	...	342
351	Industrial chemicals ...	403.7	357.3	227.2	319.3	...	351
3511 .	Basic excl fertilizers	140.7	153.9	d/ 72.4	d/ 155.4	...	3511
3513	Synthetic resins etc .	249.9	175.9	128.7	208.3	...	3513
352	Other chemical products.	78.5	71.7	137.4	164.1	...	352
3522	Drugs and medicines ..	33.6	39.8	53.4	97.8	...	3522
353	Petroleum refineries ...	137.7	44.6	75.2	32.5	...	353
354	Petroleum,coal products.	18.4	15.8	29.9	17.7	...	354
355	Rubber products	68.5	98.4	66.3	80.2	...	355
356	Plastic products n.e.c..	67.9	42.7	99.2	181.4	...	356
361	Pottery,china etc	6.6	9.4	7.2	17.3	...	361
362	Glass and products	71.4	22.9	97.2	53.9	...	362
369	Non-metal products n.e.c	140.8	135.5	168.7	244.8	...	369
371	Iron and steel	724.3	1337.0	436.6	354.0	...	371
372	Non-ferrous metals	28.9	48.0	48.0	58.0	...	372
381	Metal products	105.0	230.7	182.4	181.5	...	381
382	Machinery n.e.c.	257.3	159.6	187.8	259.8	...	382
3825	Office,computing etc..	10.4	4.7	11.6	44.9	...	3825
383	Electrical machinery ...	263.6	286.7	413.1	914.3	...	383
3832	Radio,television etc..	191.3	212.3	187.7	421.5	...	3832
384	Transport equipment	415.2	459.7	345.5	576.4	...	384
3841	Shipbuilding, repair..	235.4	345.4	186.3	374.6	...	3841
3843	Motor vehicles	116.8	70.1	133.0	177.8	...	3843
385	Professional goods	19.1	16.8	27.4	41.3	...	385
390	Other industries	32.8	39.5	51.5	72.1	...	390
3	Manufacturing	3804.4	4365.4	3851.6	5088.7	...	3
410	Electricity,gas,steam ..	...	...	...	...	...	410
4101	Electricity	...	...	...	...	...	4101
420	Water works and supply .	...	...	...	...	...	420
4	Electricity,gas etc	...	...	...	...	...	4
2-4	All industry	...	...	...	...	...	2-4

a/ Establishments with 5 or more persons engaged.
b/ The value of sales is not deducted.
c/ Including ISIC 3212 and 3213.
d/ Including ISIC 3514.

12. INDEX NUMBERS OF INDUSTRIAL PRODUCTION (1980 = 100)

ISIC	INDUSTRY	1976	1977	1978	1979	1981	1982	1983	1984	1985	a/ RATE	ISIC
210	Coal mining	88	93	97	98	99	95	89	97	111	2.6	210
220	Petroleum and gas	...	...	...	...	...	...	...	...	...	...	220
230	Metal ore mining	106	117	109	101	106	98	101	105	99	-0.8	230
290	Other mining .... b/	84	99	106	109	115	104	127	133	138	5.7	290
2	Mining, quarrying . b/	91	99	101	101	103	97	98	105	115	2.6	2
311/2	Food products	55	71	85	105	106	119	139	150	165	13.0	311/2
313	Beverages	53	69	89	105	103	110	110	120	121	9.6	313
314	Tobacco	68	76	87	91	103	104	110	114	110	5.5	314
321	Textiles	66	71	81	91	111	114	119	124	124	7.3	321
3211	Spinning,weaving etc..	...	...	...	...	...	...	...	...	...	...	3211
322	Wearing apparel	73	82	102	98	126	123	139	150	154	8.6	322
323	Leather and products ...	85	106	123	102	138	142	165	177	167	7.8	323
324	Footwear	74	108	159	107	111	113	122	133	127	6.2	324
331	Wood products	117	133	154	143	108	102	125	120	113	-0.4	331
332	Furniture, fixtures	46	64	96	110	120	156	199	238	216	18.7	332
341	Paper and products	56	70	82	92	111	118	136	142	144	11.1	341
3411	Pulp,paper etc.	...	...	...	...	...	...	...	...	...	...	3411
342	Printing,publishing	61	68	80	91	104	102	102	104	112	7.0	342
351	Industrial chemicals ...	60	71	87	97	104	102	116	126	129	8.9	351
3511	Basic excl fertilizers	...	...	...	...	...	...	...	...	...	...	3511
3513	Synthetic resins etc .	...	...	...	...	...	...	...	...	...	...	3513
352	Other chemical products.	56	72	92	108	106	122	142	161	172	13.3	352
3522	Drugs and medicines ..	...	...	...	...	...	...	...	...	...	...	3522
353	Petroleum refineries ...	74	85	94	101	98	97	114	118	124	5.9	353
354	Petroleum,coal products.	54	66	68	92	120	118	120	138	144	11.5	354
355	Rubber products	51	62	75	89	99	99	120	158	158	13.4	355
356	Plastic products n.e.c..	58	98	139	128	92	93	124	145	154	11.5	356
361	Pottery,china etc	33	50	56	74	120	115	128	124	122	15.6	361
362	Glass and products	62	79	97	108	105	102	135	160	171	11.9	362
369	Non-metal products n.e.c	65	82	93	101	97	107	136	147	148	9.6	369
371	Iron and steel	45	55	70	93	129	136	152	169	175	16.3	371
372	Non-ferrous metals	40	50	75	92	150	175	216	234	251	22.6	372
381	Metal products	55	76	100	100	122	134	162	181	193	15.0	381
382	Machinery n.e.c.	82	87	133	133	126	141	203	252	288	15.0	382
3825	Office,computing etc..	...	...	...	...	...	...	...	...	...	...	3825
383	Electrical machinery ...	56	71	99	117	121	128	180	235	255	18.3	383
3832	Radio,television etc..	...	...	...	...	...	...	...	...	...	...	3832
384	Transport equipment	53	74	111	128	149	163	158	265	265	19.6	384
3841	Shipbuilding, repair..	...	...	...	...	...	...	...	...	...	...	3841
3843	Motor vehicles	...	...	...	...	...	...	...	...	...	...	3843
385	Professional goods	61	71	92	98	100	101	111	127	126	8.4	385
390	Other industries	96	117	99	96	103	105	122	150	149	5.0	390
3	Manufacturing	61	73	91	102	113	119	139	161	167	11.8	3
410	Electricity,gas,steam ..	...	...	...	...	...	...	...	...	...	...	410
4101	Electricity	62	71	85	96	108	116	131	144	156	10.8	4101
420	Water works and supply .	.	.	.	.	.	.	.	.	.	.	420
4	Electricity,gas etc	...	...	...	...	...	...	...	...	...	...	4
2-4	All industry b/c/	62	74	91	102	113	118	137	158	164	11.4	2-4

a/ Annual growth rate 1976-1985.
b/ Excluding saltern operations.
c/ Excluding gas and steam.

The information in the tables is based on the reply to the United Nations Questionnaire on General Industrial Statistics from the Central Statistical Office, Ministry of Planning, Safat. The concepts, definitions and classification by branches of industry are generally in accordance with United Nations standards.

The data in the tables are derived from the industrial survey taken annually by the Central Statistical Office. The survey covers all industrial establishments in the private and public sectors, including joint (private and public) ownership, engaged in the exploration and production of crude petroleum and natural gas, other mining and quarrying and manufacturing. The establishments are covered on a census-cum-sample basis as follows: (a) census coverage of all establishments with 10 or more employees as well as establishments in those activities (as defined by a 5-digit code based on ISIC) containing less than 20 establishments; (b) sample coverage of all establishments not covered by the census. These establishments are divided into two groups according to employment size 5-9 and 1-4 and samples are taken from both groups. The period of reference is the calendar year. However, where data are available only on the basis of an accounting year different from the calendar year, the data are incorporated in the calendar year in which the major part of the accounting year falls. For establishments in the petroleum sector, estimates for the calendar year are made on the basis of the average of the two fiscal years. The data in the tables are based on the International Standard Industrial Classification (ISIC).

The value of output comprises (a) the value of all products of the establishment, (b) receipts for industrial work done for or services rendered to others, (c) the value of goods shipped in the same condition as received, less the cost of these goods, (d) the value of fixed assets produced by the establishment for its own use and (e) changes in stocks of finished goods. Value added is estimated by subtracting the cost of materials, fuels, electricity and water consumed and the cost of industrial services rendered by others from the value of output. Valuation of output and value added is in producers' prices.

Related national publication:
Annual Survey of Industries and Statistical Abstract (annual), both published by the Central Statistical Office, Ministry of Planning, Kuwait City.

ISIC	INDUSTRY	1. NUMBER OF ESTABLISHMENTS (NUMBER) 1981	1982	1983	1984	1985	2. AVERAGE NUMBER OF PERSONS ENGAGED (NUMBER) 1981	1982	1983	1984	1985	ISIC
210	Coal mining	-	-	-	-	...	-	-	-	-	...	210
220	Petroleum and gas	4	3	2	2	...	6029	5356	4844	4687	...	220
230	Metal ore mining	-	-	-	-	...	-	-	-	-	...	230
290	Other mining	14	14	14	9	...	714	748	775	443	...	290
2	Mining, quarrying .	18	17	16	11	...	6743	6104	5619	5130	...	2
311/2	Food products	406	480	470	398	...	5754	6868	8820	6971	...	311/2
313	Beverages	11	8	9	8	...	1560	1481	1590	1429	...	313
314	Tobacco	-	-	-	-	...	-	-	-	-	...	314
321	Textiles	100	112	187	183	...	483	557	1055	902	...	321
3211	Spinning,weaving etc..	-	-	-	-	...	-	-	-	-	...	3211
322	Wearing apparel	1784	1830	1848	1967	...	6771	7308	7470	7720	...	322
323	Leather and products ...	-	-	-	-	...	-	-	-	-	...	323
324	Footwear	-	-	-	-	...	-	-	-	-	...	324
331	Wood products	74	57	50	51	...	1446	1229	1025	1322	...	331
332	Furniture, fixtures	350	363	319	289	...	2280	2680	2399	2362	...	332
341	Paper and products	5	7	10	12	...	286	511	568	631	...	341
3411	Pulp,paper etc.	-	-	-	-	...	-	-	-	-	...	3411
342	Printing,publishing	40	39	40	40	...	2857	3012	2915	3148	...	342
351	Industrial chemicals ...	7	7	7	7	...	2055	2240	2041	1982	...	351
3511	Basic excl fertilizers	5	5	5	5	...	...	452	298	194	...	3511
3513	Synthetic resins etc .	-	-	-	-	...	-	-	-	-	...	3513
352	Other chemical products.	a/ 9	8	9	11	...	a/ 395	441	453	568	...	352
3522	Drugs and medicines ..	-	-	-	-	...	-	-	-	-	...	3522
353	Petroleum refineries ...	1	1	1	1	...	3518	3956	3911	4588	...	353
354	Petroleum,coal products.	a/	2	2	2	...	a/	58	60	30	...	354
355	Rubber products	6	6	5	4	...	214	313	321	232	...	355
356	Plastic products n.e.c..	22	20	22	19	...	1460	1541	1662	1207	...	356
361	Pottery,china etc	1	1	1	-	...	261	163	145	-	...	361
362	Glass and products	5	10	17	16	...	84	58	135	133	...	362
369	Non-metal products n.e.c	143	102	120	113	...	4707	5643	5505	5276	...	369
371	Iron and steel	5	4	3	2	...	615	738	385	322	...	371
372	Non-ferrous metals	-	-	-	-	...	-	-	-	-	...	372
381	Metal products	599	590	592	620	...	5958	5774	6058	7278	...	381
382	Machinery n.e.c.	13	13	13	14	...	586	1776	1904	776	...	382
3825	Office,computing etc..	-	-	-	-	...	-	-	-	-	...	3825
383	Electrical machinery ...	28	25	24	25	...	581	624	577	567	...	383
3832	Radio,television etc..	-	-	-	-	...	-	-	-	-	...	3832
384	Transport equipment	40	35	35	33	...	1807	1670	1686	1465	...	384
3841	Shipbuilding, repair..	8	6	7	8	...	676	626	647	794	...	3841
3843	Motor vehicles	32	29	28	25	...	1131	1044	1039	671	...	3843
385	Professional goods	-	-	-	-	...	-	-	-	-	...	385
390	Other industries	75	74	75	75	...	344	331	346	321	...	390
3	Manufacturing	3724	3794	3859	3890	...	44022	48972	51031	49230	...	3
410	Electricity,gas,steam ..	...	...	...	...	...	...	...	...	...	...	410
4101	Electricity	...	...	...	...	...	...	...	...	...	...	4101
420	Water works and supply .	...	...	...	...	...	...	...	...	...	...	420
4	Electricity,gas etc	...	...	...	...	...	...	...	...	...	...	4
2-4	All industry	...	...	...	...	...	...	...	...	...	...	2-4

a/ Major group 354 is included in 352.

ISIC	INDUSTRY	3. AVERAGE NUMBER OF EMPLOYEES (NUMBER)					4. WAGES AND SALARIES OF EMPLOYEES (THOUSAND DINARS)					ISIC
		1981	1982	1983	1984	1985	1981	1982	1983	1984	1985	
210	Coal mining	-	-	-	-	...	-	-	-	-	...	210
220	Petroleum and gas	6029	5356	4844	4687	...	44108	43966	45262	46849	...	220
230	Metal ore mining	-	-	-	-	...	-	-	-	-	...	230
290	Other mining	714	727	754	431	...	1731	2387	2218	1260	...	290
2	Mining, quarrying .	6743	6083	5598	5118	...	45839	46353	47480	48109	...	2
311/2	Food products	5754	6308	6727	6597	...	11651	12679	14467	15481	...	311/2
313	Beverages	1560	1480	1588	1429	...	2714	3192	3419	2717	...	313
314	Tobacco	-	-	-	-	...	-	-	-	-	...	314
321	Textiles	483	439	855	720	...	686	872	1438	1437	...	321
3211	Spinning,weaving etc..	-	-	-	-	...	-	-	-	-	...	3211
322	Wearing apparel	6771	5422	5612	5826	...	8644	10037	10469	10249	...	322
323	Leather and products ...	-	-	-	-	...	-	-	-	-	...	323
324	Footwear	-	-	-	-	...	-	-	-	-	...	324
331	Wood products	1446	1162	971	1283	...	3590	3012	2541	3032	...	331
332	Furniture, fixtures	2280	2269	2038	2081	...	4710	5311	4991	4918	...	332
341	Paper and products	286	506	563	625	...	562	1266	1521	1867	...	341
3411	Pulp,paper etc.	-	-	-	-	...	-	-	-	-	...	3411
342	Printing,publishing	2857	2965	2878	3113	...	6039	7765	8049	9666	...	342
351	Industrial chemicals ...	2055	2235	2034	1981	...	12089	16502	15263	15371	...	351
3511	Basic excl fertilizers	...	449	293	193	...	...	2012	787	688	...	3511
3513	Synthetic resins etc .	-	-	-	-	...	-	-	-	-	...	3513
352	Other chemical products.	a/ 395	436	450	567	...	a/ 1061	1268	1471	1942	...	352
3522	Drugs and medicines ..	-	-	-	-	...	-	-	-	-	...	3522
353	Petroleum refineries ...	3518	3956	3911	4588	...	25363	30885	37482	41637	...	353
354	Petroleum,coal products.	a/	57	59	29	...	a/	146	167	86	...	354
355	Rubber products	214	304	313	229	...	469	440	460	374	...	355
356	Plastic products n.e.c..	1460	1528	1649	1195	...	3025	3704	4515	3512	...	356
361	Pottery,china etc	261	163	145	-	...	512	456	425	-	...	361
362	Glass and products	84	48	116	116	...	223	98	303	275	...	362
369	Non-metal products n.e.c	4707	5545	5400	5184	...	10659	13561	14313	12421	...	369
371	Iron and steel	615	736	382	321	...	1253	1596	717	821	...	371
372	Non-ferrous metals	-	-	-	-	...	-	-	-	-	...	372
381	Metal products	5958	5065	5339	6682	...	13923	13268	14398	19175	...	381
382	Machinery n.e.c.	586	1762	1889	765	...	1540	4146	4569	1729	...	382
3825	Office,computing etc..	-	-	-	-	...	-	-	-	-	...	3825
383	Electrical machinery ...	581	597	550	546	...	1225	1408	1536	1426	...	383
3832	Radio,television etc..	-	-	-	-	...	-	-	-	-	...	3832
384	Transport equipment	1807	1622	1642	1438	...	4322	5293	4080	4247	...	384
3841	Shipbuilding, repair..	676	618	640	788	...	1909	2243	1806	2263	...	3841
3843	Motor vehicles	1131	1004	1002	650	...	2413	3050	2274	1984	...	3843
385	Professional goods	-	-	-	-	...	-	-	-	-	...	385
390	Other industries	344	248	257	218	...	563	561	581	509	...	390
3	Manufacturing	44022	44853	45368	45533	...	114823	137466	147175	152892	...	3
410	Electricity,gas,steam ..	...	...	...	...	...	...	...	...	...	...	410
4101	Electricity	...	...	...	...	...	...	...	...	...	...	4101
420	Water works and supply .	...	...	...	...	...	...	...	...	...	...	420
4	Electricity,gas etc	...	...	...	...	...	...	...	...	...	...	4
2-4	All industry	...	...	...	...	...	...	...	...	...	...	2-4

a/ Major group 354 is included in 352.

ISIC	INDUSTRY	5. AVERAGE NUMBER OF OPERATIVES (NUMBER)					6. WAGES AND SALARIES OF OPERATIVES (THOUSAND DINARS)					ISIC
		1981	1982	1983	1984	1985	1981	1982	1983 a/	1984 a/	1985	
210	Coal mining	...	...	-	-	...	...	...	-	-	...	210
220	Petroleum and gas	...	...	3406	3232	...	...	...	27241	27068	...	220
230	Metal ore mining	...	...	-	-	...	...	...	-	-	...	230
290	Other mining	...	...	673	371	...	...	...	1818	999	...	290
2	Mining, quarrying	...	...	4079	3603	...	...	...	29059	28067	...	2
311/2	Food products	...	...	5875	5417	...	...	...	11848	11610	...	311/2
313	Beverages	...	...	607	421	...	...	...	1169	701	...	313
314	Tobacco	...	...	-	-	...	...	...	-	-	...	314
321	Textiles	...	...	769	650	...	...	...	1213	1222	...	321
3211	Spinning,weaving etc.	...	...	-	-	...	...	...	-	-	...	3211
322	Wearing apparel	...	...	5584	5785	...	...	...	10092	10158	...	322
323	Leather and products	...	...	-	-	...	...	...	-	-	...	323
324	Footwear	...	...	-	-	...	...	...	-	-	...	324
331	Wood products	...	...	832	1081	...	...	...	1891	2321	...	331
332	Furniture, fixtures	...	...	1874	1863	...	...	...	4363	4051	...	332
341	Paper and products	...	...	432	477	...	...	...	872	1181	...	341
3411	Pulp,paper etc.	...	...	-	-	...	...	...	-	-	...	3411
342	Printing,publishing	...	...	1776	2084	...	...	...	5173	5954	...	342
351	Industrial chemicals	...	...	1300	1320	...	...	...	7747	9118	...	351
3511	Basic excl fertilizers	...	...	145	87	...	...	...	285	265	...	3511
3513	Synthetic resins etc	...	...	-	-	...	...	...	-	-	...	3513
352	Other chemical products	...	...	286	355	...	...	...	670	1022	...	352
3522	Drugs and medicines	...	...	-	-	...	...	...	-	-	...	3522
353	Petroleum refineries	...	...	3168	3800	...	...	...	24807	29617	...	353
354	Petroleum,coal products	...	...	32	21	...	...	...	85	57	...	354
355	Rubber products	...	...	282	186	...	...	...	265	263	...	355
356	Plastic products n.e.c.	...	...	1325	916	...	...	...	3119	2130	...	356
361	Pottery,china etc	...	...	110	-	...	...	...	252	-	...	361
362	Glass and products	...	...	100	101	...	...	...	247	231	...	362
369	Non-metal products n.e.c	...	...	4258	3919	...	...	...	8813	7627	...	369
371	Iron and steel	...	...	341	280	...	...	...	561	663	...	371
372	Non-ferrous metals	...	...	-	-	...	...	...	-	-	...	372
381	Metal products	...	...	4498	5674	...	...	...	10311	13915	...	381
382	Machinery n.e.c.	...	...	1696	560	...	...	...	3620	925	...	382
3825	Office,computing etc.	...	...	-	-	...	...	...	-	-	...	3825
383	Electrical machinery	...	...	444	452	...	...	...	936	952	...	383
3832	Radio,television etc.	...	...	-	-	...	...	...	-	-	...	3832
384	Transport equipment	...	...	1337	1187	...	...	...	2851	2815	...	384
3841	Shipbuilding, repair	...	...	504	649	...	...	...	1230	1502	...	3841
3843	Motor vehicles	...	...	833	538	...	...	...	1621	1313	...	3843
385	Professional goods	...	...	-	-	...	...	...	-	-	...	385
390	Other industries	...	...	247	211	...	...	...	550	477	...	390
3	Manufacturing	...	...	37173	36760	...	...	...	101455	107010	...	3
410	Electricity,gas,steam	...	...	...	...	...	...	...	...	...	...	410
4101	Electricity	...	...	...	...	...	...	...	...	...	...	4101
420	Water works and supply	...	...	...	...	...	...	...	...	...	...	420
4	Electricity,gas etc	...	...	...	...	...	...	...	...	...	...	4
2-4	All industry	...	...	...	...	...	...	...	...	...	...	2-4

a/ Excluding payments in kind.

ISIC	INDUSTRY	7. OUTPUT IN PRODUCERS' PRICES (MILLION DINARS)					8. VALUE ADDED IN PRODUCERS' PRICES (MILLION DINARS)					ISIC
		1981	1982	1983	1984	1985	1981	1982	1983	1984	1985	
210	Coal mining	-	-	-	-	...	-	-	-	-	...	210
220	Petroleum and gas	4151.1	2848.8	3090.5	3444.5	...	4121.8	2816.0	3056.4	3404.4	...	220
230	Metal ore mining	-	-	-	-	...	-	-	-	-	...	230
290	Other mining	11.9	18.6	17.9	8.3	...	7.4	8.4	7.2	3.5	...	290
2	Mining, quarrying	4163.0	2867.4	3108.4	3452.8	...	4129.2	2824.4	3063.6	3407.9	...	2
311/2	Food products	61.1	71.5	71.5	76.4	...	23.8	21.8	29.3	33.4	...	311/2
313	Beverages	17.7	20.5	22.0	16.6	...	8.4	9.0	10.1	7.7	...	313
314	Tobacco	-	-	-	-	...	-	-	-	-	...	314
321	Textiles	3.9	5.7	7.7	7.7	...	1.7	2.5	3.7	3.5	...	321
3211	Spinning, weaving etc.	-	-	-	-	...	...	...	-	-	...	3211
322	Wearing apparel	26.7	29.1	30.9	31.0	...	21.7	23.5	24.5	24.7	...	322
323	Leather and products	-	-	-	-	...	-	-	-	-	...	323
324	Footwear	-	-	-	-	...	-	-	-	-	...	324
331	Wood products	26.6	17.9	10.3	13.2	...	13.1	7.5	4.9	7.2	...	331
332	Furniture, fixtures	18.7	21.3	20.8	20.0	...	11.0	12.3	12.0	10.7	...	332
341	Paper and products	4.6	6.5	7.3	10.0	...	1.5	1.6	3.1	4.3	...	341
3411	Pulp, paper etc.	-	-	-	-	...	-	-	-	-	...	3411
342	Printing, publishing	23.3	25.4	18.6	14.4	...	13.7	15.0	8.6	6.5	...	342
351	Industrial chemicals	42.2	35.8	30.7	41.8	...	28.3	21.9	16.8	30.2	...	351
3511	Basic excl fertilizers	...	6.2	3.4	3.0	...	...	4.5	2.0	1.8	...	3511
3513	Synthetic resins etc	-	-	-	-	...	-	-	-	-	...	3513
352	Other chemical products	a/ 12.1	11.6	12.1	14.5	...	a/ 4.6	4.6	5.0	5.6	...	352
3522	Drugs and medicines	-	-	-	-	...	-	-	-	-	...	3522
353	Petroleum refineries	1225.1	1642.0	1604.7	1563.0	...	169.6	176.6	159.4	92.0	...	353
354	Petroleum, coal products	a/	1.1	1.2	0.9	...	a/	0.4	0.6	0.5	...	354
355	Rubber products	3.1	4.2	4.8	3.2	...	1.8	2.1	2.1	1.1	...	355
356	Plastic products n.e.c.	20.0	21.6	22.2	19.6	...	9.2	9.4	11.3	11.3	...	356
361	Pottery, china etc	1.7	1.2	0.2	-	...	1.0	0.9	-	-	...	361
362	Glass and products	1.0	0.5	1.4	0.4	...	0.5	0.3	0.9	0.1	...	362
369	Non-metal products n.e.c	91.6	105.2	93.1	86.4	...	32.9	42.2	39.3	40.5	...	369
371	Iron and steel	5.6	6.3	2.5	2.7	...	2.5	5.0	1.8	1.8	...	371
372	Non-ferrous metals	-	-	-	-	...	-	-	-	-	...	372
381	Metal products	76.6	75.8	74.5	74.1	...	42.1	35.8	33.9	38.7	...	381
382	Machinery n.e.c.	7.3	9.5	11.3	7.7	...	4.5	7.3	7.2	4.0	...	382
3825	Office, computing etc.	-	-	-	-	...	-	-	-	-	...	3825
383	Electrical machinery	21.5	25.3	22.1	14.1	...	9.3	13.4	11.7	4.8	...	383
3832	Radio, television etc.	-	-	-	-	...	-	-	-	-	...	3832
384	Transport equipment	29.3	22.7	13.3	8.5	...	13.8	10.2	5.1	3.1	...	384
3841	Shipbuilding, repair	5.1	3.6	4.4	2.1	...	4.8	1.8	1.8	0.5	...	3841
3843	Motor vehicles	24.2	19.0	8.9	6.4	...	9.0	8.4	3.3	2.6	...	3843
385	Professional goods	-	-	-	-	...	-	-	-	-	...	385
390	Other industries	1.5	2.1	2.0	2.3	...	1.4	1.4	1.5	1.4	...	390
3	Manufacturing	1721.2	2162.8	2085.2	2028.5	...	416.4	424.7	392.8	333.1	...	3
410	Electricity, gas, steam	...	...	...	...	...	...	...	...	...	...	410
4101	Electricity	...	...	...	...	...	...	...	...	...	...	4101
420	Water works and supply	...	...	...	...	...	...	...	...	...	...	420
4	Electricity, gas etc	...	...	...	...	...	...	...	...	...	...	4
2-4	All industry	...	...	...	...	...	...	...	...	...	...	2-4

a/ Major group 354 is included in 352.

9. GROSS FIXED CAPITAL FORMATION
TOTAL
(THOUSAND DINARS)

ISIC	INDUSTRY	1981	1982	1983	1984	1985	ISIC
210	Coal mining	-	-	-	-	...	210
220	Petroleum and gas	47069	83928	115701	93623	...	220
230	Metal ore mining	-	-	-	-	...	230
290	Other mining	951	1618	739	571	...	290
2	Mining, quarrying .	48020	85546	116440	94194	...	2
311/2	Food products	8216	10580	7161	6448	...	311/2
313	Beverages	1296	1524	2076	3519	...	313
314	Tobacco	-	-	-	-	...	314
321	Textiles	268	453	384	699	...	321
3211	Spinning,weaving etc..	-	-	-	-	...	3211
322	Wearing apparel	413	30	12	21	...	322
323	Leather and products ...	-	-	-	-	...	323
324	Footwear	-	-	-	-	...	324
331	Wood products	194	135	256	749	...	331
332	Furniture, fixtures	22	69	230	839	...	332
341	Paper and products	140	2412	434	396	...	341
3411	Pulp,paper etc.	-	-	-	-	...	3411
342	Printing,publishing	4193	3285	3136	1403	...	342
351	Industrial chemicals ...	13491	19495	17194	23721	...	351
3511	Basic excl fertilizers	...	1470	1038	201	...	3511
3513	Synthetic resins etc .	-	-	-	-	...	3513
352	Other chemical products.	a/ 108	138	216	352	...	352
3522	Drugs and medicines ..	-	-	-	-	...	3522
353	Petroleum refineries ...	36472	15220	195990	226669	...	353
354	Petroleum,coal products.	a/	1565	-	1	...	354
355	Rubber products	102	19	-17	153	...	355
356	Plastic products n.e.c..	3590	2672	2724	1412	...	356
361	Pottery,china etc	-	4	-48	-	...	361
362	Glass and products	-	-	-	-	...	362
369	Non-metal products n.e.c	5341	4899	6034	6245	...	369
371	Iron and steel	1002	2810	852	-	...	371
372	Non-ferrous metals	-	-	-	-	...	372
381	Metal products	2119	3206	2142	1749	...	381
382	Machinery n.e.c.	94	143	238	128	...	382
3825	Office,computing etc..	-	-	-	-	...	3825
383	Electrical machinery ...	298	209	1197	548	...	383
3832	Radio,television etc..	-	-	-	-	...	3832
384	Transport equipment	88	1042	2571	397	...	384
3841	Shipbuilding, repair..	2	599	315	424	...	3841
3843	Motor vehicles	86	443	2256	-27	...	3843
385	Professional goods	-	-	-	-	...	385
390	Other industries	-	9	39	5	...	390
3	Manufacturing	77447	69919	242821	275454	...	3
410	Electricity,gas,steam ..	...	...	...	...	...	410
4101	Electricity	...	...	...	...	...	4101
420	Water works and supply .	...	...	...	...	...	420
4	Electricity,gas etc	...	...	...	...	...	4
2-4	All industry	...	...	...	...	...	2-4

a/ Major group 354 is included in 352.

LUXEMBOURG

The information on industrial activity is based on the reply to the United Nations Questionnaire on General Industrial Statistics from the Service central de la statistique et des etudes economiques, Luxembourg. The concepts, definitions and classification by branches of industry are generally in accordance with United Nations standards.

The estimates are derived from the annual survey of industrial production undertaken by the Service central de la statistique et des etudes economiques. The estimates presented cover enterprises with an average of 20 or more persons engaged during the year.

The estimates are based on the national classification of industry which follows the General Industrial Classification of Economic Activities within the European Communities (NACE). The figures shown in the tables have been arranged as far as possible to represent the present version of ISIC. Among the residual differences, it should be noted that production of Thomas slag (ISIC 371) is included in ISIC 351 and for gross fixed capital formation, iron foundries (ISIC 371) and two non-ferrous metal establishments (ISIC 372) are included in ISIC 381 to 384 combined. It should also be noted that combined information is shown for a number of industries in order not to divulge confidential information.

The estimates of persons engaged relate to the average number of working proprietors, unpaid family workers, wage earners and other employees. Homeworkers, whose contribution is considered negligible, are not covered. The distinction between wage earners and other employees is based on method of payment and affiliation with the different branches of social security. The estimates shown for operatives relate to workers paid by the hour or on a piece-work basis.

Wages and salaries include, in addition to regular and overtime wage and salary payments, production bonuses and gratuities, and payments in kind. Supplements to wages and salaries represent employers' legal and voluntary contributions to social insurance schemes, covering sickness, old age, unemployment, family allowances etc.

The estimates of output relate to the value of sales effected during the year, adjusted for changes in the value of stocks of finished goods and work in progress, and receipts for services rendered. The value of work done for own account and the value of goods provided to employees as payments in kind are included. For goods sold in the same condition as received, the gross margin is used. The valuation is calculated in factor values. The estimates of value added relate to the value of output less the cost of materials and supplies, and services purchased for use in the production process; adjustments are made for changes in the value of stocks of materials.

The estimates of gross fixed capital formation represent the acquisition of new and used fixed assets, less sales, including own-account investment work and fixed capital formation in new establishments not yet in operation. Investments of a social nature are included. Transactions are recorded at the time of delivery except for large-scale projects where the value of work put in place is recorded.

The indexes of industrial production are compiled by the Service central de la statistique et des etudes economiques and provided in response to the United Nations Questionnaire on Indexes of Industrial Production. In principle, the indexes cover all establishments except handicrafts.

Related national publication:
<u>Annuaire statistique</u>, published by the Service central de la statistique et des etudes economiques, Luxembourg.

ISIC	INDUSTRY		1. NUMBER OF ENTERPRISES a/ (NUMBER)					2. AVERAGE NUMBER OF PERSONS ENGAGED a/ (NUMBER)					ISIC
			1981	1982	1983	1984	1985	1981	1982	1983	1984	1985	
210	Coal mining		-	-	-	...	...	-	-	-	...	...	210
220	Petroleum and gas		-	-	-	...	...	-	-	-	...	...	220
230	Metal ore mining		1	-	-	...	...	...	...	...	...	...	230
290	Other mining		4	3	3	...	...	...	...	...	...	...	290
2	Mining, quarrying .		5	3	3	...	...	602	183	181	...	...	2
311/2	Food products		19	21	20	...	...	1400	1450	1465	...	...	311/2
313	Beverages		[12	12	11]	...	...	[985	935	906]	...	...	313
314	Tobacco					...	...				...	...	314
321	Textiles		5	5	4	...	...	340	333	304	...	...	321
3211	Spinning,weaving etc..		...	...	...	...	...	...	...	...	...	...	3211
322	Wearing apparel		6	5	5	...	...	456	429	447	...	...	322
323	Leather and products ...		-	-	-	...	...	-	-	-	...	...	323
324	Footwear		-	-	-	...	...	-	-	-	...	...	324
331	Wood products		[7	4	5]	...	...	[259	183	200]	...	...	331
332	Furniture, fixtures					...	...				...	...	332
341	Paper and products	b/	...	...	...	...	...	...	...	...	...	...	341
3411	Pulp,paper etc.		...	...	...	...	...	...	...	...	...	...	3411
342	Printing,publishing	b/	12	14	12	...	...	1215	1256	1197	...	...	342
351	Industrial chemicals ...	c/	d/ 17	e/ 21	e/ 22	...	...	d/ 4631	e/ 4726	e/ 4805	...	...	351
3511	Basic excl fertilizers		...	...	...	...	...	...	...	...	...	...	3511
3513	Synthetic resins etc .		...	...	...	...	...	...	...	...	...	...	3513
352	Other chemical products.		3	e/	e/	...	...	92	e/	e/	...	...	352
3522	Drugs and medicines ..		...	...	...	...	...	...	...	...	...	...	3522
353	Petroleum refineries ...		-	-	-	...	...	-	-	-	...	...	353
354	Petroleum,coal products.		d/	e/	e/	...	...	d/	e/	e/	...	...	354
355	Rubber products		d/	e/	e/	...	...	d/	e/	e/	...	...	355
356	Plastic products n.e.c..		d/	e/	e/	...	...	d/	e/	e/	...	...	356
361	Pottery,china etc					...	...				...	...	361
362	Glass and products	f/	[13	13	13]	...	...	[2355	2510	2593]	...	...	362
369	Non-metal products n.e.c					...	...				...	...	369
371	Iron and steel	c/	10	11	12	...	...	18742	18213	17108	...	...	371
372	Non-ferrous metals		4	4	5	...	...	741	770	842	...	...	372
381	Metal products		17	18	20	...	...	991	980	1089	...	...	381
382	Machinery n.e.c.		16	16	17	...	...	3699	3566	3393	...	...	382
3825	Office,computing etc..		...	...	...	...	...	...	...	...	...	...	3825
383	Electrical machinery ...		9	7	7	...	...	636	582	582	...	...	383
3832	Radio,television etc..		...	...	...	...	...	...	...	...	...	...	3832
384	Transport equipment	g/	9	10	9	...	...	896	932	912	...	...	384
3841	Shipbuilding, repair..		...	...	...	...	...	...	...	...	...	...	3841
3843	Motor vehicles		...	...	...	...	...	...	...	...	...	...	3843
385	Professional goods	g/	...	...	...	...	...	...	...	...	...	...	385
390	Other industries	f/	...	...	...	...	...	...	...	...	...	...	390
3	Manufacturing		159	161	162	...	...	37438	36865	35843	...	...	3
410	Electricity,gas,steam ..		...	...	...	...	...	...	...	...	...	...	410
4101	Electricity		6	6	6	...	...	961	980	940	...	...	4101
420	Water works and supply .		...	...	...	...	...	...	...	...	...	...	420
4	Electricity,gas etc		12	12	12	...	...	1255	1267	1230	...	...	4
2-4	All industry		176	176	177	...	...	39295	38315	37254	...	...	2-4

Note. For description of classification, see country note.

a/ Enterprises with 20 or more persons engaged.
b/ Major group 341 is included in 342.
c/ Production of Thomas slag is included in major group 351.
d/ Major groups 354, 355 and 356 are included in 351.
e/ Major groups 352 and 354 to 356 are included in 351.
f/ Major group 390 is included in 361 to 369 combined.
g/ Major group 385 is included in 384.

ISIC	INDUSTRY	3. AVERAGE NUMBER OF EMPLOYEES a/ (NUMBER) 1981	1982	1983	1984	1985	4. WAGES AND SALARIES OF EMPLOYEES a/ (MILLION FRANCS) 1981	1982	1983	1984	1985	ISIC
210	Coal mining	-	-	-	...	...	-	-	-	...	...	210
220	Petroleum and gas	-	-	-	...	...	-	-	-	...	...	220
230	Metal ore mining	...	...	...	...	...	...	...	...	...	...	230
290	Other mining	...	...	...	...	...	...	...	...	...	...	290
2	Mining, quarrying .	597	180	178	...	...	329	82	87	...	...	2
311/2	Food products	1385	1429	1448	...	...	601	667	722	...	...	311/2
313	Beverages	[978	930	903]	...	...	[569	592	625]	...	...	313
314	Tobacco				...	...				...	...	314
321	Textiles	337	331	303	...	...	231	245	255	...	...	321
3211	Spinning,weaving etc..	...	...	...	...	...	...	...	...	...	...	3211
322	Wearing apparel	451	425	445	...	...	129	127	147	...	...	322
323	Leather and products ...	-	-	-	...	...	-	-	-	...	...	323
324	Footwear	-	-	-	...	...	-	-	-	...	...	324
331	Wood products	[249	177	192]	...	...	[101	77	92]	...	...	331
332	Furniture, fixtures				...	...				...	...	332
341	Paper and products ..... b/	...	...	...	...	...	...	...	...	...	...	341
3411	Pulp,paper etc.	...	...	...	...	...	...	...	...	...	...	3411
342	Printing,publishing .... b/	1211	1250	1192	...	...	669	728	785	...	...	342
351	Industrial chemicals ... c/	d/ 4629	e/ 4723	e/ 4802	...	...	d/ 3077	e/ 3331	e/ 3713	...	...	351
3511	Basic excl fertilizers	...	...	...	...	...	...	...	...	...	...	3511
3513	Synthetic resins etc .	...	...	...	...	...	...	...	...	...	...	3513
352	Other chemical products.	91	e/	e/	...	...	58	e/	e/	...	...	352
3522	Drugs and medicines ..	...	...	...	...	...	...	...	...	...	...	3522
353	Petroleum refineries ...	-	-	-	...	...	-	-	-	...	...	353
354	Petroleum,coal products.	d/	e/	e/	...	...	d/	e/	e/	...	...	354
355	Rubber products	d/	e/	e/	...	...	d/	e/	e/	...	...	355
356	Plastic products n.e.c..	d/	e/	e/	...	...	d/	e/	e/	...	...	356
361	Pottery,china etc	[2351	2506	2590]	...	...	[1186	1359	1494]	...	...	361
362	Glass and products ..... f/				...	...				...	...	362
369	Non-metal products n.e.c				...	...				...	...	369
371	Iron and steel .... c/	18742	18212	17107	...	...	12720	13264	12608	...	...	371
372	Non-ferrous metals	741	770	842	...	...	473	522	625	...	...	372
381	Metal products	971	962	1072	...	...	462	503	610	...	...	381
382	Machinery n.e.c.	3694	3562	3388	...	...	2114	2406	2385	...	...	382
3825	Office,computing etc..	...	...	...	...	...	...	...	...	...	...	3825
383	Electrical machinery ...	628	579	580	...	...	362	360	374	...	...	383
3832	Radio,television etc..	...	...	...	...	...	...	...	...	...	...	3832
384	Transport equipment .... g/	887	923	904	...	...	360	387	394	...	...	384
3841	Shipbuilding, repair..	...	...	...	...	...	...	...	...	...	...	3841
3843	Motor vehicles	...	...	...	...	...	...	...	...	...	...	3843
385	Professional goods ..... g/	...	...	...	...	...	...	...	...	...	...	385
390	Other industries .... f/	...	...	...	...	...	...	...	...	...	...	390
3	Manufacturing	37345	36779	35768	...	...	23112	24568	24829	...	...	3
410	Electricity,gas,steam ..	...	...	...	...	...	...	...	...	...	...	410
4101	Electricity	961	980	940	...	...	767	816	867	...	...	4101
420	Water works and supply .	...	...	...	...	...	...	...	...	...	...	420
4	Electricity,gas etc	1255	1267	1230	...	...	970	1039	1107	...	...	4
2-4	All industry	39197	38226	37176	...	...	24411	25689	26023	...	...	2-4

Note. For description of classification, see country note.

a/ Enterprises with 20 or more persons engaged.
b/ Major group 341 is included in 342.
c/ Production of Thomas slag is included in major group 351.
d/ Major groups 354, 355 and 356 are included in 351.
e/ Major groups 352 and 354 to 356 are included in 351.
f/ Major group 390 is included in 361 to 369 combined.
g/ Major group 385 is included in 384.

ISIC	INDUSTRY		5. SUPPLEMENTS TO WAGES AND SALARIES a/ (MILLION FRANCS) 1981	1982	1983	1984	1985	6. AVERAGE NUMBER OF OPERATIVES a/ (NUMBER) 1981	1982	1983	1984	1985	ISIC
210	Coal mining		-	-	-	...	...	-	-	-	...	...	210
220	Petroleum and gas		-	-	-	...	...	-	-	-	...	...	220
230	Metal ore mining		...	...	...	...	...	...	...	...	...	...	230
290	Other mining		...	...	...	...	...	...	...	...	...	...	290
2	Mining, quarrying .		69	19	20	...	...	514	154	151	...	...	2
311/2	Food products		96	108	114	...	...	1147	1187	1194	...	...	311/2
313	Beverages		[108	118	121]	...	...	[692	655	645]	...	...	313
314	Tobacco					...	...				...	...	314
321	Textiles		34	35	34	...	...	232	229	203	...	...	321
3211	Spinning,weaving etc..		...	...	...	...	...	...	...	...	...	...	3211
322	Wearing apparel		20	19	22	...	...	417	396	417	...	...	322
323	Leather and products ...		-	-	-	...	...	-	-	-	...	...	323
324	Footwear		-	-	-	...	...	-	-	-	...	...	324
331	Wood products		[18	14	16]	...	...	[212	148	162]	...	...	331
332	Furniture, fixtures					...	...				...	...	332
341	Paper and products	b/	...	...	...	...	...	...	...	...	...	...	341
3411	Pulp,paper etc.		...	...	...	...	...	...	...	...	...	...	3411
342	Printing,publishing	b/	94	104	111	...	...	834	859	815	...	...	342
351	Industrial chemicals ...	c/	d/ 486	e/ 519	e/ 541	...	...	d/ 3610	e/ 3661	e/ 3717	...	...	351
3511	Basic excl fertilizers		...	...	...	...	...	...	...	...	...	...	3511
3513	Synthetic resins etc .		...	...	...	...	...	...	...	...	...	...	3513
352	Other chemical products.		8	e/	e/	...	...	50	e/	e/	...	...	352
3522	Drugs and medicines ..		...	...	...	...	...	...	...	...	...	...	3522
353	Petroleum refineries ...		-	-	-	...	...	-	-	-	...	...	353
354	Petroleum,coal products.		d/	e/	e/	...	...	d/	e/	e/	...	...	354
355	Rubber products		d/	e/	e/	...	...	d/	e/	e/	...	...	355
356	Plastic products n.e.c..		d/	e/	e/	...	...	d/	e/	e/	...	...	356
361	Pottery,china etc					...	...				...	...	361
362	Glass and products	f/	[199	227	260]	...	...	[1955	2095	2165]	...	...	362
369	Non-metal products n.e.c					...	...				...	...	369
371	Iron and steel	c/	2245	2341	2250	...	...	15077	14592	13579	...	...	371
372	Non-ferrous metals		81	89	101	...	...	592	601	654	...	...	372
381	Metal products		76	81	94	...	...	789	758	830	...	...	381
382	Machinery n.e.c.		392	407	380	...	...	2521	2450	2282	...	...	382
3825	Office,computing etc..		...	...	...	...	...	...	...	...	...	...	3825
383	Electrical machinery ...		57	58	59	...	...	482	443	429	...	...	383
3832	Radio,television etc..		...	...	...	...	...	...	...	...	...	...	3832
384	Transport equipment	g/	56	63	64	...	...	748	779	771	...	...	384
3841	Shipbuilding, repair..		...	...	...	...	...	...	...	...	...	...	3841
3843	Motor vehicles		...	...	...	...	...	...	...	...	...	...	3843
385	Professional goods	g/	...	...	...	...	...	...	...	...	...	...	385
390	Other industries	f/	...	...	...	...	...	...	...	...	...	...	390
3	Manufacturing		3970	4183	4167	...	...	29358	28853	27863	...	...	3
410	Electricity,gas,steam ..		...	...	...	...	...	...	...	...	...	...	410
4101	Electricity		147	156	176	...	...	478	499	463	...	...	4101
420	Water works and supply .		...	...	...	...	...	...	...	...	...	...	420
4	Electricity,gas etc		181	207	232	...	...	605	627	588	...	...	4
2-4	All industry		4220	4409	4419	...	...	30477	29634	28602	...	...	2-4

Note. For description of classification, see country note.

a/ Enterprises with 20 or more persons engaged.
b/ Major group 341 is included in 342.
c/ Production of Thomas slag is included in major group 351.
d/ Major groups 354, 355 and 356 are included in 351.
e/ Major groups 352 and 354 to 356 are included in 351.
f/ Major group 390 is included in 361 to 369 combined.
g/ Major group 385 is included in 384.

ISIC	INDUSTRY		7. WAGES AND SALARIES OF OPERATIVES a/ (MILLION FRANCS) 1981	1982	1983	1984	1985	8. HOURS WORKED BY OPERATIVES a/ (THOUSANDS) 1981	1982	1983	1984	1985	ISIC
210	Coal mining		-	-	-	...	...	-	-	-	...	...	210
220	Petroleum and gas		-	-	-	...	...	-	-	-	...	...	220
230	Metal ore mining		...	...	...	...	...	...	...	...	...	...	230
290	Other mining		...	...	...	...	...	...	...	...	...	...	290
2	Mining, quarrying .		263	68	76	...	...	861	270	259	...	...	2
311/2	Food products		444	492	523	...	...	2097	2183	2191	...	...	311/2
313	Beverages		[301	313	327]	...	...	[1249	1167	1129]	...	...	313
314	Tobacco					...	...				...	...	314
321	Textiles		122	133	136	...	...	411	410	368	...	...	321
3211	Spinning,weaving etc..		...	...	...	...	...	...	...	...	...	...	3211
322	Wearing apparel		109	109	127	...	...	717	685	732	...	...	322
323	Leather and products ...		-	-	-	...	...	-	-	-	...	...	323
324	Footwear		-	-	-	...	...	-	-	-	...	...	324
331	Wood products		[79	59	71]	...	...	[376	258	279]	...	...	331
332	Furniture, fixtures					...	...				...	...	332
341	Paper and products	b/	...	...	...	...	...	...	...	...	...	...	341
3411	Pulp,paper etc.		...	...	...	...	...	...	...	...	...	...	3411
342	Printing,publishing	b/	383	414	433	...	...	1360	1381	1326	...	...	342
351	Industrial chemicals ...	c/	d/ 2077	e/ 2225	e/ 2463	...	...	d/ 6260	e/ 6348	e/ 6600	...	...	351
3511	Basic excl fertilizers		...	...	...	...	...	...	...	...	...	...	3511
3513	Synthetic resins etc .		...	...	...	...	...	...	...	...	...	...	3513
352	Other chemical products.		22	e/	e/	...	...	93	e/	e/	...	...	352
3522	Drugs and medicines ..		...	...	...	...	...	...	...	...	...	...	3522
353	Petroleum refineries ...		-	-	-	...	...	-	-	-	...	...	353
354	Petroleum,coal products.		d/	e/	e/	...	...	d/	e/	e/	...	...	354
355	Rubber products		d/	e/	e/	...	...	d/	e/	e/	...	...	355
356	Plastic products n.e.c..		d/	e/	e/	...	...	d/	e/	e/	...	...	356
361	Pottery,china etc					...	...				...	...	361
362	Glass and products	f/	[858	973	1078]	...	...	[3349	3564	3697]	...	...	362
369	Non-metal products n.e.c					...	...				...	...	369
371	Iron and steel	c/	8602	8916	8363	...	...	25246	24387	22393	...	...	371
372	Non-ferrous metals		334	358	424	...	...	1023	1021	1141	...	...	372
381	Metal products		331	342	401	...	...	1415	1363	1461	...	...	381
382	Machinery n.e.c.		1245	1372	1286	...	...	4341	4267	3771	...	...	382
3825	Office,computing etc..		...	...	...	...	...	...	...	...	...	...	3825
383	Electrical machinery ...		239	235	235	...	...	863	777	732	...	...	383
3832	Radio,television etc..		...	...	...	...	...	...	...	...	...	...	3832
384	Transport equipment	g/	263	281	287	...	...	1334	1326	1299	...	...	384
3841	Shipbuilding, repair..		...	...	...	...	...	...	...	...	...	...	3841
3843	Motor vehicles		...	...	...	...	...	...	...	...	...	...	3843
385	Professional goods	g/	...	...	...	...	...	...	...	...	...	...	385
390	Other industries	f/	...	...	...	...	...	...	...	...	...	...	390
3	Manufacturing		15409	16222	16154	...	...	50134	49137	47119	...	...	3
410	Electricity,gas,steam ..		...	...	...	...	...	...	...	...	...	...	410
4101	Electricity		318	335	341	...	...	838	848	803	...	...	4101
420	Water works and supply .		...	...	...	...	...	...	...	...	...	...	420
4	Electricity,gas etc		393	417	429	...	...	1063	1066	1019	...	...	4
2-4	All industry		16065	16707	16654	...	...	52058	50473	48397	...	...	2-4

Note. For description of classification, see country note.

a/ Enterprises with 20 or more persons engaged.
b/ Major group 341 is included in 342.
c/ Production of Thomas slag is included in major group 351.
d/ Major groups 354, 355 and 356 are included in 351.
e/ Major groups 352 and 354 to 356 are included in 351.
f/ Major group 390 is included in 361 to 369 combined.
g/ Major group 385 is included in 384.

ISIC	INDUSTRY	9. OUTPUT IN FACTOR VALUES a/ (MILLION FRANCS)					10. VALUE ADDED IN FACTOR VALUES a/b/ (MILLION FRANCS)					ISIC
		1981	1982	1983	1984	1985	1981	1982	1983	1984	1985	
210	Coal mining	-	-	-	...	...	-	-	...	...	...	210
220	Petroleum and gas	-	-	-	...	...	-	-	...	...	...	220
230	Metal ore mining	...	...	...	...	...	...	...	...	...	...	230
290	Other mining	...	...	...	...	...	...	...	...	...	...	290
2	Mining, quarrying .	657	235	253	...	...	427	135	144	...	...	2
311/2	Food products	5750	7143	7606	...	...	1017	1063	1116	...	...	311/2
313	Beverages	[2702	3349	3838]	...	...	[1265	1567	1773]	...	...	313
314	Tobacco				...	...				...	...	314
321	Textiles	1496	1650	1754	...	...	729	703	761	...	...	321
3211	Spinning,weaving etc..	...	...	...	...	...	...	...	...	...	...	3211
322	Wearing apparel	240	213	272	...	...	172	147	174	...	...	322
323	Leather and products ...	-	-	-	...	...	-	-	...	...	...	323
324	Footwear	-	-	-	...	...	-	-	...	...	...	324
331	Wood products	[350	281	314]	...	...	[148	118	134]	...	...	331
332	Furniture, fixtures				...	...				...	...	332
341	Paper and products ..... c/	...	...	...	...	...	...	...	...	...	...	341
3411	Pulp,paper etc.	...	...	...	...	...	...	...	...	...	...	3411
342	Printing,publishing .... c/	2159	2303	2510	...	...	1085	1156	1228	...	...	342
351	Industrial chemicals ... d/	e/ 16344	f/ 20635	f/ 25100	...	...	e/ 5657	f/ 7146	f/ 8253	...	...	351
3511	Basic excl fertilizers	...	...	...	...	...	...	...	...	...	...	3511
3513	Synthetic resins etc .	...	...	...	...	...	...	...	...	...	...	3513
352	Other chemical products.	202	f/	f/	...	...	102	f/	f/	...	...	352
3522	Drugs and medicines ..	...	...	...	...	...	...	...	...	...	...	3522
353	Petroleum refineries ...	-	-	-	...	...	-	-	...	...	...	353
354	Petroleum,coal products.	e/	f/	f/	...	...	e/	f/	f/	...	...	354
355	Rubber products	e/	f/	f/	...	...	e/	f/	f/	...	...	355
356	Plastic products n.e.c..	e/	f/	f/	...	...	e/	f/	f/	...	...	356
361	Pottery,china etc	[		]	...	...	[		]	...	...	361
362	Glass and products ..... g/	4828	6431	7254	...	...	2131	2905	3184	...	...	362
369	Non-metal products n.e.c	[		]	...	...	[		]	...	...	369
371	Iron and steel .... d/	47883	56340	53752	...	...	h/ 16637	h/ 20588	h/ 19677	...	...	371
372	Non-ferrous metals	4719	4303	5454	...	...	1006	1003	1361	...	...	372
381	Metal products	1521	1740	3505	...	...	756	759	1056	...	...	381
382	Machinery n.e.c.	7824	8811	8343	...	...	3396	3623	3261	...	...	382
3825	Office,computing etc..	...	...	...	...	...	...	...	...	...	...	3825
383	Electrical machinery ...	1162	1211	1592	...	...	555	577	617	...	...	383
3832	Radio,television etc..	...	...	...	...	...	...	...	...	...	...	3832
384	Transport equipment .... i/	1233	1406	1482	...	...	552	646	687	...	...	384
3841	Shipbuilding, repair..	...	...	...	...	...	...	...	...	...	...	3841
3843	Motor vehicles	...	...	...	...	...	...	...	...	...	...	3843
385	Professional goods ..... i/	...	...	...	...	...	...	...	...	...	...	385
390	Other industries .... g/	...	...	...	...	...	...	...	...	...	...	390
3	Manufacturing	98413	115816	122776	...	...	35208	42001	43282	...	...	3
410	Electricity,gas,steam ..	...	...	...	...	...	...	...	...	...	...	410
4101	Electricity	4247	4355	4378	...	...	2914	3068	3026	...	...	4101
420	Water works and supply .	...	...	...	...	...	...	...	...	...	...	420
4	Electricity,gas etc	4893	5219	5332	...	...	3362	3724	3757	...	...	4
2-4	All industry	103963	121270	128361	...	...	38997	45860	47183	...	...	2-4

Note. For description of classification, see country note.

a/ Enterprises with 20 or more persons engaged.
b/ Net of non-industrial costs.
c/ Major group 341 is included in 342.
d/ Production of Thomas slag is included in major group 351.
e/ Major groups 354, 355 and 356 are included in 351.
f/ Major groups 352 and 354 to 356 are included in 351.
g/ Major group 390 is included in 361 to 369 combined.
h/ Data for establishments belonging to the integrated iron and steel industry are included in major group 371.
i/ Major group 385 is included in 384.

ISIC	INDUSTRY	11. GROSS FIXED CAPITAL FORMATION TOTAL a/ (MILLION FRANCS) 1981	1982	1983	1984	1985	12. GROSS FIXED CAPITAL FORMATION MACHINERY AND EQUIPMENT a/ (MILLION FRANCS) 1981	1982	1983	1984	1985	ISIC
210	Coal mining	-	-	-	-	...	-	-	-	-	...	210
220	Petroleum and gas	-	-	-	-	...	-	-	-	-	...	220
230	Metal ore mining	-	-	-	-	...	-	-	-	-	...	230
290	Other mining	3	9	9	3	...	1	7	5	2	...	290
2	Mining, quarrying	3	9	9	3	b/	1	7	5	2	b/	2
311/2	Food products	222	206	195	252	394	198	200	184	170	237	311/2
313	Beverages	[195	123	264	291	335	174	99	185	243	267]	313
314	Tobacco											314
321	Textiles c/	33	80	26	17	177	27	75	22	15	91	321
3211	Spinning,weaving etc.	...	...	...	...	...	...	...	...	...	...	3211
322	Wearing apparel c/	...	...	...	...	...	...	...	...	...	...	322
323	Leather and products	-	-	-	-	-	-	-	-	-	-	323
324	Footwear	-	-	-	-	-	-	-	-	-	-	324
331	Wood products d/	[8	12	8	6	3	6	6	8	3	3]	331
332	Furniture, fixtures											332
341	Paper and products e/	...	...	...	...	...	...	...	...	...	...	341
3411	Pulp,paper etc.	...	...	...	...	...	...	...	...	...	...	3411
342	Printing,publishing e/	128	158	114	155	103	112	128	82	136	79	342
351	Industrial chemicals f/g/	770	1398	1641	1627	1989	585	1103	1247	1489	936	351
3511	Basic excl fertilizers	...	...	...	...	...	...	...	...	...	...	3511
3513	Synthetic resins etc	...	...	...	...	...	...	...	...	...	...	3513
352	Other chemical products f/	...	...	...	...	...	...	...	...	...	...	352
3522	Drugs and medicines	...	...	...	...	...	...	...	...	...	...	3522
353	Petroleum refineries	-	-	-	-	-	-	-	-	-	-	353
354	Petroleum,coal products f/	...	...	...	...	...	...	...	...	...	...	354
355	Rubber products f/	...	...	...	...	...	...	...	...	...	...	355
356	Plastic products n.e.c. f/	...	...	...	...	...	...	...	...	...	...	356
361	Pottery,china etc	[1887	288	640	204]	[b/	[1457	161	501	122]	[b/	361
362	Glass and products					638					560	362
369	Non-metal products n.e.c	263	192	170,	206	]	211	148	120	160	]	369
371	Iron and steel g/	[h/ 3436	h/ 3452	h/ 3376	h/ 3218	3292	h/ 2760	h/ 2972	h/ 3578	h/ 2897	3199]	371
372	Non-ferrous metals											372
381	Metal products	831	786	120	231	150	656	447	87	168	140	381
382	Machinery n.e.c. i/	346	278	421	508	552	285	244	316	395	403	382
3825	Office,computing etc.	...	...	...	...	...	...	...	...	...	...	3825
383	Electrical machinery i/	...	...	...	...	...	...	...	...	...	...	383
3832	Radio,television etc.	...	...	...	...	...	...	...	...	...	...	3832
384	Transport equipment i/	...	...	...	...	...	...	...	...	...	...	384
3841	Shipbuilding, repair	...	...	...	...	...	...	...	...	...	...	3841
3843	Motor vehicles	...	...	...	...	...	...	...	...	...	...	3843
385	Professional goods i/	...	...	...	...	...	...	...	...	...	...	385
390	Other industries d/	...	...	...	...	...	...	...	...	...	...	390
3	Manufacturing	8119	6973	6975	6715	j/ 7633	6471	5583	6330	5798	j/ 5915	3
410	Electricity,gas,steam	...	...	...	...	...	...	...	...	...	...	410
4101	Electricity	772	738	868	755	770	130	101	182	176	171	4101
420	Water works and supply	...	...	...	...	...	...	...	...	...	...	420
4	Electricity,gas etc	979	921	1052	972	1014	149	116	202	190	193	4
2-4	All industry	9101	7903	8036	7690	8647	6619	5706	6537	5990	6108	2-4

Note. For description of classification, see country note.

a/ Enterprises with 20 or more persons engaged.
b/ Mining is included in major group 369.
c/ Major group 322 is included in 321.
d/ Major group 390 is included in 331 and 332 combined.
e/ Major group 341 is included in 342.
f/ Major groups 352 and 354 to 356 are included in 351.
g/ Production of Thomas slag is included in major group 351.
h/ Data for establishments belonging to the integrated iron and steel industry are included in major group 371.
i/ Major groups 383, 384, and 385 are included in 382.
j/ Including mining.

13. VALUE OF STOCKS AT END OF PERIOD
TOTAL a/
(MILLION FRANCS)

ISIC	INDUSTRY		1981	1982	1983	1984	1985	ISIC
210	Coal mining		-	-	-	...	...	210
220	Petroleum and gas		-	-	-	...	...	220
230	Metal ore mining		...	...	...	...	...	230
290	Other mining		...	...	...	...	...	290
2	Mining, quarrying		28	7	8	...	...	2
311/2	Food products		263	357	332	...	...	311/2
313	Beverages		[981	1284	1670]	...	...	313
314	Tobacco					...	...	314
321	Textiles		99	131	147	...	...	321
3211	Spinning, weaving etc.		...	...	...	...	...	3211
322	Wearing apparel		75	60	43	...	...	322
323	Leather and products		-	-	-	...	...	323
324	Footwear		-	-	-	...	...	324
331	Wood products		[62	49	56]	...	...	331
332	Furniture, fixtures					...	...	332
341	Paper and products	b/	...	...	...	...	...	341
3411	Pulp, paper etc.		...	...	...	...	...	3411
342	Printing, publishing	b/	161	182	179	...	...	342
351	Industrial chemicals	c/	d/ 1807	e/ 2143	e/ 2314	...	...	351
3511	Basic excl fertilizers		...	...	...	...	...	3511
3513	Synthetic resins etc		...	...	...	...	...	3513
352	Other chemical products		27	e/	e/	...	...	352
3522	Drugs and medicines		...	...	...	...	...	3522
353	Petroleum refineries		-	-	-	...	...	353
354	Petroleum, coal products		d/	e/	e/	...	...	354
355	Rubber products		d/	e/	e/	...	...	355
356	Plastic products n.e.c.		d/	e/	e/	...	...	356
361	Pottery, china etc		[		]	...	...	361
362	Glass and products	f/	719	855	882	...	...	362
369	Non-metal products n.e.c					...	...	369
371	Iron and steel	c/	6948	6879	6375	...	...	371
372	Non-ferrous metals		955	1108	c/ 1052	...	...	372
381	Metal products		229	262	609	...	...	381
382	Machinery n.e.c.		1125	1231	1305	...	...	382
3825	Office, computing etc.		...	...	...	...	...	3825
383	Electrical machinery		277	308	337	...	...	383
3832	Radio, television etc.		...	...	...	...	...	3832
384	Transport equipment	g/	164	176	177	...	...	384
3841	Shipbuilding, repair		...	...	...	...	...	3841
3843	Motor vehicles		...	...	...	...	...	3843
385	Professional goods	g/	...	...	...	...	...	385
390	Other industries	f/	...	...	...	...	...	390
3	Manufacturing		13892	15024	15478	...	...	3
410	Electricity, gas, steam		...	...	...	...	...	410
4101	Electricity		671	683	624	...	...	4101
420	Water works and supply		...	...	...	...	...	420
4	Electricity, gas etc		693	692	649	...	...	4
2-4	All industry		14613	15723	16135	...	...	2-4

Note. For description of classification, see country note.

a/ Enterprises with 20 or more persons engaged.
b/ Major group 341 is included in 342.
c/ Production of Thomas slag is included in major group 351.
d/ Major groups 354, 355 and 356 are included in 351.
e/ Major groups 352 and 354 to 356 are included in 351.
f/ Major group 390 is included in 361 to 369 combined.
g/ Major group 385 is included in 384.

14. INDEX NUMBERS OF INDUSTRIAL PRODUCTION (1980 = 100)

ISIC	INDUSTRY		1976	1977	1978	1979	1981	1982	1983	1984	1985	a/ RATE	ISIC
210	Coal mining		...	...	...	...	...	...	...	...	...	...	210
220	Petroleum and gas		...	...	...	...	...	...	...	...	...	...	220
230	Metal ore mining		...	...	...	...	...	...	...	...	...	...	230
290	Other mining		97	91	100	102	90	90	89	75	70	-3.6	290
2	Mining, quarrying .		234	183	124	106	77	46	42	32	29	-20.7	2
311/2	Food products		91	94	94	95	98	102	108	110	109	2.0	311/2
313	Beverages		[107	98	92	98	96	120	148	138	153	4.1]	313
314	Tobacco												314
321	Textiles		...	...	...	...	...	...	...	...	...	...	321
3211	Spinning,weaving etc..		...	...	...	...	...	...	...	...	...	...	3211
322	Wearing apparel	b/	124	107	92	111	100	101	110	101	108	-1.5	322
323	Leather and products ...		...	...	...	...	...	...	...	...	...	...	323
324	Footwear	b/	...	...	...	...	...	...	...	...	...	...	324
331	Wood products		[83	88	87	95	104	110	115	108	107	2.9]	331
332	Furniture, fixtures												332
341	Paper and products		...	...	...	...	...	...	...	...	...	...	341
3411	Pulp,paper etc.		...	...	...	...	...	...	...	...	...	...	3411
342	Printing,publishing		91	102	101	100	100	100	101	109	115	2.6	342
351	Industrial chemicals ...	c/	96	102	103	110	94	92	101	118	143	4.5	351
3511	Basic excl fertilizers		...	...	...	...	...	...	...	...	...	...	3511
3513	Synthetic resins etc .		...	...	...	...	...	...	...	...	...	...	3513
352	Other chemical products.	c/	...	...	...	...	...	...	...	...	...	...	352
3522	Drugs and medicines ..		...	...	...	...	...	...	...	...	...	...	3522
353	Petroleum refineries ...		...	...	...	...	...	...	...	...	...	...	353
354	Petroleum,coal products.		...	...	...	...	...	...	...	...	...	...	354
355	Rubber products		76	86	85	94	102	100	112	125	126	5.8	355
356	Plastic products n.e.c..		...	...	...	...	110	122	138	142	146	f/ 7.9	356
361	Pottery,china etc		[									]	361
362	Glass and products		82	82	86	90	105	133	143	144	142	6.3	362
369	Non-metal products n.e.c											]	369
371	Iron and steel		93	92	101	104	86	82	80	94	102	1.0	371
372	Non-ferrous metals		...	...	...	...	...	...	...	...	...	...	372
381	Metal products	d/	[94	97	97	99	94	94	102	139	151	5.4]	381
382	Machinery n.e.c.												382
3825	Office,computing etc..		...	...	...	...	...	...	...	...	...	...	3825
383	Electrical machinery ...	d/	...	...	...	...	...	...	...	...	...	...	383
3832	Radio,television etc..		...	...	...	...	...	...	...	...	...	...	3832
384	Transport equipment	d/	...	...	...	...	...	...	...	...	...	...	384
3841	Shipbuilding, repair..		...	...	...	...	...	...	...	...	...	...	3841
3843	Motor vehicles		...	...	...	...	...	...	...	...	...	...	3843
385	Professional goods		...	...	...	...	...	...	...	...	...	...	385
390	Other industries		...	...	...	...	...	...	...	...	...	...	390
3	Manufacturing	e/	94	95	99	102	93	90	90	114	122	2.9	3
410	Electricity,gas,steam ..		117	105	113	111	107	90	85	121	126	0.8	410
4101	Electricity		...	...	...	...	...	...	...	...	...	...	4101
420	Water works and supply .		.	.	.	.	.	.	.	.	.	.	420
4	Electricity,gas etc		...	...	...	...	...	...	...	...	...	...	4
2-4	All industry	e/	97	96	100	103	94	90	90	114	121	2.5	2-4

a/ Annual growth rate 1976-1985.
b/ Major group 324 is included in 322.
c/ Major group 352 is included in 351.
d/ Major groups 383 and 384 are included in 381 and 382 combined.
e/ Excluding major group 341.
f/ Annual growth rate 1980-1985.

MACAU

The information in the tables is based on the reply to the United Nations Questionnaire on General Industrial Statistics from the Direccao de Servicos de Estatistica e Censos, Macau. The concepts, definitions and classification by branches of industry are generally in accordance with United Nations standards.

The data in the tables are derived from the industrial census taken annually since 1978 covering all legal establishments. The inquiry is carried out through field interview by enumerators. The establishment is defined as an economic unit which, under a single ownership or control, engages exclusively or principally in one kind of industrial activity at the same location.

The data are compiled according to the national classification system which basically follows the present version of ISIC. The period of reference is the calendar year.

Employment numbers relate to quarterly averages. Persons engaged refer to all persons engaged including working proprietors, active business partners and unpaid family workers. Homeworkers are excluded. Employees refer to administrative and clerical personnel and operatives. Operatives are defined as all the persons directly engaged in the production process and other supporting activities of the establishment. The data on number of persons engaged, employees and wages and salaries of employees cover, for administrative and clerical personnel, establishments with 5 or more persons engaged and, for operatives, all establishments. It should be noted that the data for hours worked by operatives, and for gross fixed capital formation prior to 1984, relate to establishments with 5 or more persons engaged. Wages and salaries relate to payments made in cash and in kind during the reference year.

Output, prior to 1984, is the sum of the value of finished products in ex-factory prices, value of fixed assets produced by the establishment for its own use, receipts for industrial services rendered to others, value of sales of waste, value of electricity sold and the net change in the value of work in progress during the year. Value added is calculated as the difference between the value of output and the value of input (i.e. the value of materials, energy and water consumed, value of contract, commission, repair and maintenance work done by others, value of non-industrial services rendered by others and other expenses). Beginning 1984, the definitions of output and value added conform to the concepts of census output and census value added as outlined in the international recommendations.

Gross fixed capital formation refers to the value of new and used fixed assets purchased and own-account construction of fixed assets less the value of fixed assets sold during the year.

Related national publication:
    Inquerito Industrial (annual), published by the Direccao de Servicos de Estatistica e Censos, Macau.

ISIC	INDUSTRY	1. NUMBER OF ESTABLISHMENTS (NUMBER) 1981	1982	1983	1984	1985	2. AVERAGE NUMBER OF PERSONS ENGAGED a/ (NUMBER) 1981	1982	1983	1984	1985	ISIC
210	Coal mining	-	-	-	-	...	-	-	-	-	...	210
220	Petroleum and gas	-	-	-	-	...	-	-	-	-	...	220
230	Metal ore mining	-	-	-	-	...	-	-	-	-	...	230
290	Other mining	1	1	1	1	...	62	64	64	47	...	290
2	Mining, quarrying .	1	1	1	1	...	62	64	64	47	...	2
311/2	Food products	86	82	83	78	...	693	715	945	967	...	311/2
313	Beverages	20	18	18	17	...	170	184	183	198	...	313
314	Tobacco	2	1	1	1	...	38	63	59	58	...	314
321	Textiles	123	129	130	124	...	10063	10549	9806	8825	...	321
3211	Spinning,weaving etc..	...	...	...	24	...	...	...	...	1832	...	3211
322	Wearing apparel	371	388	389	410	...	28409	29968	30624	28693	...	322
323	Leather and products ...	18	19	18	18	...	1462	1490	1594	1537	...	323
324	Footwear	10	8	9	10	...	169	63	106	158	...	324
331	Wood products	54	50	43	35	...	331	346	266	248	...	331
332	Furniture, fixtures	45	46	47	46	...	799	770	735	783	...	332
341	Paper and products	29	34	34	34	...	266	386	450	476	...	341
3411	Pulp,paper etc.	...	...	...	3	...	...	...	...	70	...	3411
342	Printing,publishing	74	54	53	51	...	1621	816	837	910	...	342
351	Industrial chemicals ...	-	-	-	-	...	-	-	-	-	...	351
3511	Basic excl fertilizers	-	-	-	-	...	-	-	-	-	...	3511
3513	Synthetic resins etc .	-	-	-	-	...	-	-	-	-	...	3513
352	Other chemical products.	15	16	13	12	...	346	390	329	531	...	352
3522	Drugs and medicines ..	...	...	...	4	...	...	...	...	32	...	3522
353	Petroleum refineries ...	-	-	-	-	...	-	-	-	-	...	353
354	Petroleum,coal products.	-	-	-	-	...	-	-	-	-	...	354
355	Rubber products	2	1	1	1	...	31	32	32	32	...	355
356	Plastic products n.e.c..	35	50	53	56	...	2748	5281	6293	4999	...	356
361	Pottery,china etc	1	19	17	15	...	26	746	665	642	...	361
362	Glass and products	3	4	4	5	...	15	17	16	14	...	362
369	Non-metal products n.e.c	3	3	4	4	...	61	50	221	190	...	369
371	Iron and steel	-	-	-	-	...	-	-	-	-	...	371
372	Non-ferrous metals	-	-	-	-	...	-	-	-	-	...	372
381	Metal products	79	83	83	78	...	373	444	535	2224	...	381
382	Machinery n.e.c.	11	13	12	19	...	49	56	58	769	...	382
3825	Office,computing etc..	...	...	...	3	...	...	...	...	682	...	3825
383	Electrical machinery ...	27	34	33	30	...	1542	2461	3025	2217	...	383
3832	Radio,television etc..	...	...	...	19	...	...	...	...	1790	...	3832
384	Transport equipment	13	37	32	32	...	257	593	634	501	...	384
3841	Shipbuilding, repair..	...	...	...	31	...	...	...	...	498	...	3841
3843	Motor vehicles	...	...	...	-	...	...	...	...	-	...	3843
385	Professional goods	7	8	8	10	...	967	961	782	938	...	385
390	Other industries	78	84	87	81	...	3245	3610	3856	3091	...	390
3	Manufacturing	1106	1181	1172	1167	...	53681	59991	62051	59001	...	3
410	Electricity,gas,steam ..	3	3	1	1	...	797	746	771	792	...	410
4101	Electricity	3	3	1	1	...	797	746	771	792	...	4101
420	Water works and supply .	2	2	1	1	...	233	244	242	247	...	420
4	Electricity,gas etc	5	5	2	2	...	1030	990	1013	1039	...	4
2-4	All industry	1112	1187	1175	1170	...	54773	61045	63128	60087	...	2-4

a/ For employees other than operatives, data cover establishments with 5 or more persons engaged only.

ISIC	INDUSTRY	3. AVERAGE NUMBER OF EMPLOYEES a/ (NUMBER)					4. WAGES AND SALARIES OF EMPLOYEES a/ (THOUSAND PATACAS)					ISIC
		1981	1982	1983	1984	1985	1981	1982	1983	1984	1985	
210	Coal mining	-	-	-	-	...	-	-	-	-	...	210
220	Petroleum and gas	-	-	-	-	...	-	-	-	-	...	220
230	Metal ore mining	-	-	-	-	...	-	-	-	-	...	230
290	Other mining	62	64	64	47	...	1864	2457	2762	2308	...	290
2	Mining, quarrying .	62	64	64	47	...	1864	2457	2762	2308	...	2
311/2	Food products	635	654	894	860	...	5931	6740	10065	11320	...	311/2
313	Beverages	165	179	179	182	...	1614	2112	2386	2691	...	313
314	Tobacco	38	63	59	58	...	264	508	567	658	...	314
321	Textiles	10006	10479	9755	8745	...	95959	107806	122074	143922	...	321
3211	Spinning,weaving etc..	...	...	...	1820	...	...	...	...	34894	...	3211
322	Wearing apparel	28259	29788	30427	28433	...	250760	292023	342098	406259	...	322
323	Leather and products ...	1457	1486	1591	1532	...	11761	15479	19047	25755	...	323
324	Footwear	167	60	103	148	...	1102	483	886	2268	...	324
331	Wood products	310	326	252	208	...	2207	2995	2700	2992	...	331
332	Furniture, fixtures	771	748	703	737	...	7633	8663	9470	12512	...	332
341	Paper and products	257	371	434	443	...	2565	4272	5750	7321	...	341
3411	Pulp,paper etc.	...	...	...	69	...	...	...	...	1260	...	3411
342	Printing,publishing	1578	766	789	869	...	19700	12589	12709	16522	...	342
351	Industrial chemicals ...	-	-	-	-	...	-	-	-	-	...	351
3511	Basic excl fertilizers	-	-	-	-	...	-	-	-	-	...	3511
3513	Synthetic resins etc .	-	-	-	-	...	-	-	-	-	...	3513
352	Other chemical products.	346	390	329	529	...	1909	2930	2970	6035	...	352
3522	Drugs and medicines ..	...	...	...	31	...	...	...	...	543	...	3522
353	Petroleum refineries ...	-	-	-	-	...	-	-	-	-	...	353
354	Petroleum,coal products.	-	-	-	-	...	-	-	-	-	...	354
355	Rubber products	30	31	32	32	...	284	294	341	377	...	355
356	Plastic products n.e.c..	2722	5247	6256	4966	...	15633	39085	60618	76667	...	356
361	Pottery,china etc	25	734	656	629	...	209	8115	7933	12839	...	361
362	Glass and products	13	15	14	9	...	124	137	221	161	...	362
369	Non-metal products n.e.c	59	49	218	188	...	690	626	1775	5605	...	369
371	Iron and steel	-	-	-	-	...	-	-	-	-	...	371
372	Non-ferrous metals	-	-	-	-	...	-	-	-	-	...	372
381	Metal products	348	410	503	2169	...	3520	4777	6466	34835	...	381
382	Machinery n.e.c.	42	54	57	751	...	445	639	910	11938	...	382
3825	Office,computing etc..	...	...	...	681	...	...	...	...	10648	...	3825
383	Electrical machinery ...	1527	2441	3015	2211	...	11175	19313	28244	27119	...	383
3832	Radio,television etc..	...	...	...	1789	...	...	...	...	22101	...	3832
384	Transport equipment	251	560	607	473	...	4863	11879	19315	14027	...	384
3841	Shipbuilding, repair..	...	...	...	471	...	...	...	...	13993	...	3841
3843	Motor vehicles	...	...	...	-	...	...	...	...	-	...	3843
385	Professional goods	967	960	780	936	...	8690	9878	9603	13619	...	385
390	Other industries	3178	3555	3795	3019	...	25715	31091	39998	44008	...	390
3	Manufacturing	53151	59366	61448	58127	...	472753	582434	706146	879454	...	3
410	Electricity,gas,steam ..	797	746	771	792	...	30762	39308	43416	54412	...	410
4101	Electricity	797	746	771	792	...	30762	39308	43416	54412	...	4101
420	Water works and supply .	233	244	242	247	...	6234	7363	8045	9722	...	420
4	Electricity,gas etc	1030	990	1013	1039	...	36996	46671	51461	64134	...	4
2-4	All industry	54243	60420	62525	59213	...	511613	631562	760369	945896	...	2-4

a/ For employees other than operatives, data cover establishments with 5 or more persons engaged only.

ISIC	INDUSTRY	5. AVERAGE NUMBER OF OPERATIVES (NUMBER)					6. WAGES AND SALARIES OF OPERATIVES (THOUSAND PATACAS)					ISIC
		1981	1982	1983	1984	1985	1981	1982	1983	1984	1985	
210	Coal mining	-	-	-	-	...	-	-	-	-	...	210
220	Petroleum and gas	-	-	-	-	...	-	-	-	-	...	220
230	Metal ore mining	-	-	-	-	...	-	-	-	-	...	230
290	Other mining	52	50	51	36	...	1550	1894	1913	1216	...	290
2	Mining, quarrying .	52	50	51	36	...	1550	1894	1913	1216	...	2
311/2	Food products	571	575	811	774	...	4780	5548	8565	9322	...	311/2
313	Beverages	135	147	143	162	...	987	1500	1621	1923	...	313
314	Tobacco	31	56	53	49	...	207	424	472	520	...	314
321	Textiles	8892	9294	8491	7555	...	73450	77693	86253	102830	...	321
3211	Spinning,weaving etc..	...	...	...	1535	...	...	...	...	21274	...	3211
322	Wearing apparel	25102	26499	27087	24694	...	203623	235585	275310	323365	...	322
323	Leather and products ...	1310	1313	1375	1357	...	9282	11608	14242	20226	...	323
324	Footwear	157	57	96	135	...	960	441	800	1863	...	324
331	Wood products	302	314	228	201	...	2109	2814	2235	2559	...	331
332	Furniture, fixtures	711	680	642	678	...	6519	7287	8358	10856	...	332
341	Paper and products	226	312	376	398	...	2068	3360	4721	5981	...	341
3411	Pulp,paper etc.	...	...	...	59	...	...	...	...	1020	...	3411
342	Printing,publishing	1284	561	571	642	...	15226	8425	8639	11314	...	342
351	Industrial chemicals ...	-	-	-	-	...	-	-	-	-	...	351
3511	Basic excl fertilizers	-	-	-	-	...	-	-	-	-	...	3511
3513	Synthetic resins etc .	-	-	-	-	...	-	-	-	-	...	3513
352	Other chemical products.	318	356	296	467	...	1567	2402	2349	4775	...	352
3522	Drugs and medicines ..	...	...	...	24	...	...	...	...	345	...	3522
353	Petroleum refineries ...	-	-	-	-	...	-	-	-	-	...	353
354	Petroleum,coal products.	-	-	-	-	...	-	-	-	-	...	354
355	Rubber products	28	28	28	27	...	258	263	286	294	...	355
356	Plastic products n.e.c..	2483	4825	5673	4446	...	11845	30811	46246	63416	...	356
361	Pottery,china etc	25	672	585	556	...	209	7151	6830	11098	...	361
362	Glass and products	13	15	14	14	...	124	137	221	161	...	362
369	Non-metal products n.e.c	41	35	166	150	...	427	410	1091	3627	...	369
371	Iron and steel	-	-	-	-	...	-	-	-	-	...	371
372	Non-ferrous metals	-	-	-	-	...	-	-	-	-	...	372
381	Metal products	330	387	466	2000	...	3319	4434	5854	29024	...	381
382	Machinery n.e.c.	40	51	53	723	...	427	504	815	10197	...	382
3825	Office,computing etc..	...	...	...	650	...	...	...	...	9019	...	3825
383	Electrical machinery ...	1402	2246	2777	2000	...	9153	15717	22388	21865	...	383
3832	Radio,television etc..	...	...	...	1633	...	...	...	...	17919	...	3832
384	Transport equipment	242	549	600	460	...	4424	11399	18893	13224	...	384
3841	Shipbuilding, repair..	...	...	...	457	...	...	...	...	13190	...	3841
3843	Motor vehicles	...	...	...	-	...	...	...	...	-	...	3843
385	Professional goods	870	842	698	838	...	6655	7426	7116	10846	...	385
390	Other industries	2917	3237	3428	2684	...	22056	25458	32614	36366	...	390
3	Manufacturing	47430	53051	54657	51010	...	379675	460797	555919	695652	...	3
410	Electricity,gas,steam ..	413	432	466	473	...	13012	17234	24483	29739	...	410
4101	Electricity	413	432	466	473	...	13012	17234	24483	29739	...	4101
420	Water works and supply .	123	124	117	117	...	3030	3601	3546	4251	...	420
4	Electricity,gas etc	536	556	583	590	...	16042	20835	28029	33990	...	4
2-4	All industry	48018	53657	55291	51636	...	397267	483526	585861	730854	...	2-4

ISIC	INDUSTRY	7. HOURS WORKED BY OPERATIVES (THOUSANDS) a/ 1981	a/ 1982	a/ 1983	a/ 1984	1985	8. OUTPUT IN PRODUCERS' PRICES (MILLION PATACAS) 1981	1982	1983	1984	1985	ISIC
210	Coal mining	-	-	-	-	...	-	-	-	-	...	210
220	Petroleum and gas	-	-	-	-	...	-	-	-	-	...	220
230	Metal ore mining	-	-	-	-	...	-	-	-	-	...	230
290	Other mining	193	176	188	110	...	18.7	26.3	28.7	16.0	...	290
2	Mining, quarrying .	193	176	188	110	...	18.7	26.3	28.7	16.0	...	2
311/2	Food products	1268	1302	2011	1897	...	56.7	60.5	150.6	111.2	...	311/2
313	Beverages	216	254	255	311	...	9.9	10.7	12.3	16.2	...	313
314	Tobacco	56	117	111	102	...	2.1	2.2	2.4	2.7	...	314
321	Textiles	25075	25684	23382	20262	...	988.8	979.8	1182.1	1269.5	...	321
3211	Spinning,weaving etc..	...	...	...	4270	...	...	...	...	413.7	...	3211
322	Wearing apparel	67641	71629	79143	67213	...	1626.3	1900.2	2282.1	2820.3	...	322
323	Leather and products ...	3574	3701	4122	3904	...	55.0	71.2	104.0	125.0	...	323
324	Footwear	316	110	201	302	...	6.8	2.3	3.0	6.7	...	324
331	Wood products	563	671	443	406	...	8.0	10.0	9.1	12.2	...	331
332	Furniture, fixtures	1568	1526	1577	1661	...	23.5	25.0	29.2	42.1	...	332
341	Paper and products	513	889	936	965	...	21.4	33.0	44.2	57.1	...	341
3411	Pulp,paper etc.	...	...	...	146	...	...	...	...	11.8	...	3411
342	Printing,publishing	3360	1275	1257	1496	...	51.3	24.2	27.4	47.8	...	342
351	Industrial chemicals ...	-	-	-	-	...	-	-	-	-	...	351
3511	Basic excl fertilizers	-	-	-	-	...	-	-	-	-	...	3511
3513	Synthetic resins etc .	-	-	-	-	...	-	-	-	-	...	3513
352	Other chemical products.	777	946	789	1166	...	6.0	16.7	19.8	17.5	...	352
3522	Drugs and medicines ..	...	...	...	43	...	...	...	...	1.9	...	3522
353	Petroleum refineries ...	-	-	-	-	...	-	-	-	-	...	353
354	Petroleum,coal products.	-	-	-	-	...	-	-	-	-	...	354
355	Rubber products	62	67	67	72	...	2.0	2.3	2.5	2.4	...	355
356	Plastic products n.e.c..	4831	13135	17355	14291	...	134.1	306.9	469.8	452.0	...	356
361	Pottery,china etc	70	1814	1576	1441	...	0.2	29.1	31.8	45.4	...	361
362	Glass and products	15	10	10	...	...	0.4	0.6	0.8	1.0	...	362
369	Non-metal products n.e.c	69	35	106	346	...	4.2	4.9	13.1	81.7	...	369
371	Iron and steel	-	-	-	-	...	-	-	-	-	...	371
372	Non-ferrous metals	-	-	-	-	...	-	-	-	-	...	372
381	Metal products	449	565	818	4941	...	13.1	15.0	23.2	219.7	...	381
382	Machinery n.e.c.	41	64	75	1903	...	1.0	1.6	2.0	66.1	...	382
3825	Office,computing etc..	...	...	...	1772	...	...	...	...	62.7	...	3825
383	Electrical machinery ...	3120	5070	6852	4991	...	71.5	128.0	194.7	160.4	...	383
3832	Radio,television etc..	...	...	...	4065	...	...	...	...	146.1	...	3832
384	Transport equipment	446	1036	1233	907	...	15.5	46.5	50.4	36.2	...	384
3841	Shipbuilding, repair..	...	...	...	907	...	...	...	...	36.0	...	3841
3843	Motor vehicles	...	...	...	-	...	...	...	...	-	...	3843
385	Professional goods	2000	2022	1643	1983	...	46.8	44.2	43.5	61.9	...	385
390	Other industries	7135	8842	9643	7296	...	149.9	171.7	244.9	290.4	...	390
3	Manufacturing	123165	140764	153605	137856	...	3294.5	3886.6	4942.9	5945.5	...	3
410	Electricity,gas,steam ..	949	1261	1225	1087	...	244.7	310.7	344.7	413.4	...	410
4101	Electricity	949	1261	1225	1087	...	244.7	310.7	344.7	413.4	...	4101
420	Water works and supply .	282	359	342	362	...	21.5	22.3	35.6	66.7	...	420
4	Electricity,gas etc	1231	1620	1567	1450	...	266.2	333.0	380.3	480.1	...	4
2-4	All industry	124589	142560	155360	139416	...	3579.4	4245.9	5351.9	6441.6	...	2-4

a/ Establishments with 5 or more persons engaged.

ISIC	INDUSTRY	9. VALUE ADDED IN PRODUCERS' PRICES (MILLION PATACAS)					10. GROSS FIXED CAPITAL FORMATION TOTAL b/ (THOUSAND PATACAS)					ISIC
		a/ 1981	a/ 1982	a/ 1983	1984	1985	1981	1982	1983	1984	1985	
210	Coal mining	-	-	-	-	...	-	-	-	-	...	210
220	Petroleum and gas	-	-	-	-	...	-	-	-	-	...	220
230	Metal ore mining	-	-	-	-	...	-	-	-	-	...	230
290	Other mining	10.6	18.9	20.4	11.0	...	471	-	128	-	...	290
2	Mining, quarrying	10.6	18.9	20.4	11.0	...	471	-	128	-	...	2
311/2	Food products	8.1	13.2	12.8	18.6	...	640	531	1596	21596	...	311/2
313	Beverages	3.4	3.8	4.0	6.0	...	359	289	609	325	...	313
314	Tobacco	0.4	0.7	0.8	0.9	...	-	18	-	-	...	314
321	Textiles	214.5	216.3	249.0	330.0	...	46913	37838	16345	36294	...	321
3211	Spinning,weaving etc.	...	...	...	66.7	...	...	...	...	16757	...	3211
322	Wearing apparel	362.1	441.8	509.1	777.9	...	34419	50809	47728	74757	...	322
323	Leather and products	17.6	23.9	36.9	52.7	...	4356	6750	84420	2863	...	323
324	Footwear	2.2	0.8	1.2	2.2	...	420	947	23	1606	...	324
331	Wood products	3.6	4.4	4.0	6.5	...	17	602	50	833	...	331
332	Furniture, fixtures	12.1	10.8	12.6	18.8	...	5679	603	340	2133	...	332
341	Paper and products	4.3	7.7	9.8	15.0	...	424	3921	718	1496	...	341
3411	Pulp,paper etc.	...	...	...	3.1	...	...	...	...	35	...	3411
342	Printing,publishing	c/ 18.5	c/ 7.7	c/ 8.1	22.0	...	2849	2696	1805	4235	...	342
351	Industrial chemicals	-	-	-	-	...	-	-	-	-	...	351
3511	Basic excl fertilizers	-	-	-	-	...	-	-	-	-	...	3511
3513	Synthetic resins etc	-	-	-	-	...	-	-	-	-	...	3513
352	Other chemical products	2.5	7.9	6.0	6.5	...	180	343	-	4924	...	352
3522	Drugs and medicines	...	...	...	0.8	...	...	...	-	-	...	3522
353	Petroleum refineries	-	-	-	-	...	-	-	-	-	...	353
354	Petroleum,coal products	-	-	-	-	...	-	-	-	-	...	354
355	Rubber products	0.4	0.5	0.5	0.5	...	-	-	-	-	...	355
356	Plastic products n.e.c.	38.4	97.9	136.5	162.6	...	28723	57727	38025	37064	...	356
361	Pottery,china etc	c/ 0.2	12.3	12.0	24.9	...	2	52	697	1317	...	361
362	Glass and products	0.1	0.2	0.3	0.3	...	-	-	-	-	...	362
369	Non-metal products n.e.c	1.1	0.6	-0.2	3.3	...	330	60	169085	18415	...	369
371	Iron and steel	-	-	-	-	...	-	-	-	-	...	371
372	Non-ferrous metals	-	-	-	-	...	-	-	-	-	...	372
381	Metal products	4.8	5.9	8.3	79.4	...	995	731	275	28245	...	381
382	Machinery n.e.c.	0.6	0.9	1.2	35.8	...	6	11	-	5653	...	382
3825	Office,computing etc.	...	...	...	33.7	...	...	...	-	5653	...	3825
383	Electrical machinery	15.4	29.1	46.8	34.9	...	5582	9457	16700	745	...	383
3832	Radio,television etc.	...	...	...	28.1	...	...	...	...	-186	...	3832
384	Transport equipment	6.9	19.8	19.8	17.3	...	92	1877	2985	1688	...	384
3841	Shipbuilding, repair	...	...	...	17.2	...	...	...	...	1688	...	3841
3843	Motor vehicles	...	...	...	-	...	...	...	...	-	...	3843
385	Professional goods	14.9	25.9	13.2	24.4	...	889	801	605	4412	...	385
390	Other industries	50.3	54.5	78.0	94.1	...	7028	15292	9394	6803	...	390
3	Manufacturing	782.4	986.6	1170.7	1734.6	...	139903	191355	391400	255404	...	3
410	Electricity,gas,steam	79.3	102.6	111.6	155.0	...	28061	29327	274185	75640	...	410
4101	Electricity	79.3	102.6	111.6	155.0	...	28061	29327	274185	75640	...	4101
420	Water works and supply	c/ 4.8	c/ 1.0	8.6	21.4	...	5285	4134	5210	6069	...	420
4	Electricity,gas etc	84.1	103.6	120.2	176.4	...	33346	33461	279395	81709	...	4
2-4	All industry	877.1	1109.1	1311.3	1922.0	...	173720	224816	670923	337113	...	2-4

a/ Net of non-industrial costs. b/ Establishments with 5 or more persons engaged.
c/ Value added is less than corresponding wages and salaries due to operating losses.

MADAGASCAR

The information in the tables is based on the reply to the United Nations Questionnaire on General Industrial Statistics from the Institut national de la statistique et de la recherche economique, Antananarivo. The concepts, definitions and classification by branches of industry are generally in accordance with United Nations standards.

The data in the tables are derived from the annual industrial survey conducted since 1967 by the Institut national de la statistique et de la recherche economique. The inquiry covers all establishments engaged in industrial activities except handicrafts. Production of the establishments included represents more than 85 per cent of total production.

The data are compiled according to the national classification scheme, which is comparable with the preceding version of ISIC, but have been arranged to represent the present version. It should be noted, however, that repair of motor vehicles (ISIC major division 9) is included in ISIC 384 and manufacture of made-up textile goods except wearing apparel (ISIC 321), manufacture of metal furniture and fixtures (ISIC 381) and plastic products (ISIC 356) are included in ISIC 322, 332 and 390 respectively.

The employment numbers are as of 2 January of the reference year. Temporary and seasonal workers are included in the count of persons engaged and employees by converting the number of days actually worked during the year into full-time equivalent numbers, on the basis of 300 days per year. Wages and salaries are the payments made to permanent and temporary employees.

Estimates of hours worked relate to employees who participate directly in production or other related activities of the establishment (excluding supervisory personnel) and are calculated on the basis of the average number of hours worked per day.

Output refers to the value of products sold only. Value added represents the value of products sold minus the cost of materials, fuels and electricity consumed.

Related national publication:

<u>Recensement Industriel</u> (annual), published by the Institut national de la statistique et de la recherche economique, Antananarivo.

ISIC	INDUSTRY		1. NUMBER OF ESTABLISHMENTS (NUMBER) 1981	1982	1983	1984	1985	2. AVERAGE NUMBER OF PERSONS ENGAGED a/ (NUMBER) 1981	1982	1983	1984	1985	ISIC
210	Coal mining		...	...	...	...	...	...	...	...	...	...	210
220	Petroleum and gas		...	...	...	...	...	...	...	...	...	...	220
230	Metal ore mining		...	...	...	...	...	...	...	...	...	...	230
290	Other mining		13	13	14	14	...	1936	1805	2646	2591	...	290
2	Mining, quarrying		...	...	...	...	...	...	...	...	...	...	2
311/2	Food products		83	82	100	100	...	16268	15518	19780	20730	...	311/2
313	Beverages		10	10	23	24	...	1428	1226	2693	3316	...	313
314	Tobacco		6	6	6	6	...	1009	1032	931	879	...	314
321	Textiles	b/	22	22	21	21	...	11310	11478	11370	11549	...	321
3211	Spinning, weaving etc.		...	...	...	...	...	...	...	...	...	...	3211
322	Wearing apparel	b/	14	14	26	27	...	1676	1502	3128	3041	...	322
323	Leather and products		1	1	2	2	...	50	39	295	303	...	323
324	Footwear		8	8	6	6	...	1040	1015	875	819	...	324
331	Wood products	c/	[30	29	29	30]	...	[1278	1177	1792	1838]	...	331
332	Furniture, fixtures	c/					...					...	332
341	Paper and products		3	3	3	3	...	959	910	944	950	...	341
3411	Pulp, paper etc.		...	...	...	...	...	...	...	...	...	...	3411
342	Printing, publishing		29	29	34	34	...	1300	1290	1316	1285	...	342
351	Industrial chemicals	d/	22	22	...	...	...	1601	1471	...	...	...	351
3511	Basic excl fertilizers		...	...	...	...	...	...	...	...	...	...	3511
3513	Synthetic resins etc		...	...	...	...	...	...	...	...	...	...	3513
352	Other chemical products	d/	...	...	...	...	...	...	...	...	...	...	352
3522	Drugs and medicines		...	...	...	...	...	...	...	...	...	...	3522
353	Petroleum refineries		1	1	1	1	...	306	369	...	...	...	353
354	Petroleum, coal products		-	-	-	-	...	-	-	-	-	...	354
355	Rubber products		2	2	3	3	...	77	48	166	167	...	355
356	Plastic products n.e.c.	e/	...	...	...	...	...	...	...	...	...	...	356
361	Pottery, china etc		-	-	-	-	...	-	-	-	-	...	361
362	Glass and products		3	3	3	3	...	331	348	368	352	...	362
369	Non-metal products n.e.c		...	...	...	...	...	1007	994	...	...	...	369
371	Iron and steel		-	-	-	-	...	-	-	-	-	...	371
372	Non-ferrous metals		-	-	-	-	...	-	-	-	-	...	372
381	Metal products	c/	...	...	19	19	...	1380	1409	2351	2298	...	381
382	Machinery n.e.c.		-	-	-	-	...	-	-	-	-	...	382
3825	Office, computing etc.		-	-	-	-	...	-	-	-	-	...	3825
383	Electrical machinery		10	10	9	9	...	848	735	673	632	...	383
3832	Radio, television etc.		...	...	...	...	...	...	...	...	...	...	3832
384	Transport equipment	f/	...	...	10	11	...	411	345	474	497	...	384
3841	Shipbuilding, repair		...	...	...	...	...	...	...	...	...	...	3841
3843	Motor vehicles		...	...	...	...	...	...	...	...	...	...	3843
385	Professional goods		-	-	-	-	...	-	-	-	-	...	385
390	Other industries	e/	...	...	9	9	...	602	509	580	651	...	390
3	Manufacturing	f/	g/ 244	g/ 242	h/ 304	h/ 308	...	42881	41415	i/ 47736	i/ 49307	...	3
410	Electricity, gas, steam		...	...	...	...	...	...	...	...	...	...	410
4101	Electricity		...	...	...	...	...	...	...	...	...	...	4101
420	Water works and supply		...	...	...	...	...	...	...	...	...	...	420
4	Electricity, gas etc	j/	1	1	1	1	...	4580	4422	4790	4829	...	4
2-4	All industry		...	...	...	...	...	...	...	...	...	...	2-4

a/ At 2 January of the year indicated.
b/ Manufacture of made-up textile goods except wearing apparel is included in major group 322.
c/ Manufacture of metal furniture and fixtures is included in major groups 331 and 332 combined.
d/ Major group 352 is included in 351.
e/ Major group 356 is included in 390.
f/ Including repair of motor vehicles.
g/ Excluding major groups 369, 381, 384 and 390.
h/ Excluding major groups 351, 352 and 369.
i/ Excluding major groups 351, 352, 353 and 369.
j/ Excluding gas.

ISIC	INDUSTRY	3. AVERAGE NUMBER OF EMPLOYEES a/ (NUMBER) 1981	1982	1983	1984	1985	4. WAGES AND SALARIES OF EMPLOYEES b/ (MILLION FRANCS) 1981	1982	1983	1984	1985	ISIC
210	Coal mining	...	...	...	...	...	...	...	...	...	...	210
220	Petroleum and gas	...	...	...	...	...	...	...	...	...	...	220
230	Metal ore mining	...	...	...	...	...	...	...	...	...	...	230
290	Other mining	1933	1802	2641	2586	...	937	916	1606	1862	...	290
2	Mining, quarrying	...	...	...	...	...	...	...	...	...	...	2
311/2	Food products	16268	15518	19692	20631	...	6039	6432	8377	9363	...	311/2
313	Beverages	1424	1221	2680	3307	...	1979	1958	1543	2191	...	313
314	Tobacco	1009	1030	928	876	...	471	521	553	565	...	314
321	Textiles c/	11302	11478	11364	11546	...	6458	7312	7005	8652	...	321
3211	Spinning,weaving etc.	...	...	...	...	...	...	...	...	...	...	3211
322	Wearing apparel c/	3259	2993	3116	3027	...	1754	1738	1642	1792	...	322
323	Leather and products	50	39	294	302	...	210	195	153	154	...	323
324	Footwear	1035	1010	875	819	...	803	917	996	1066	...	324
331	Wood products d/	[1260	1154	1771	1812]	...	[380	450	730	774]	...	331
332	Furniture, fixtures					...					...	332
341	Paper and products	959	910	944	950	...	745	741	836	951	...	341
3411	Pulp,paper etc.	...	...	...	...	...	...	...	...	...	...	3411
342	Printing,publishing	1225	1191	1295	1264	...	704	725	923	986	...	342
351	Industrial chemicals e/	1469	1466	...	...	...	854	2583	...	...	...	351
3511	Basic excl fertilizers	...	...	...	...	...	...	...	...	...	...	3511
3513	Synthetic resins etc	...	...	...	...	...	...	...	...	...	...	3513
352	Other chemical products. e/	...	...	...	...	...	...	...	...	...	...	352
3522	Drugs and medicines	...	...	...	...	...	...	...	...	...	...	3522
353	Petroleum refineries	306	369	...	...	...	358	421	...	...	...	353
354	Petroleum,coal products.	-	-	-	-	...	-	-	-	-	...	354
355	Rubber products	77	48	164	165	...	47	27	97	106	...	355
356	Plastic products n.e.c. f/	...	...	...	...	...	...	...	...	...	...	356
361	Pottery,china etc	-	-	-	-	...	-	-	-	-	...	361
362	Glass and products	331	348	367	351	...	225	256	307	329	...	362
369	Non-metal products n.e.c	1007	994	...	...	...	356	472	...	...	...	369
371	Iron and steel	-	-	-	-	...	-	-	-	-	...	371
372	Non-ferrous metals	-	-	-	-	...	-	-	-	-	...	372
381	Metal products d/	1371	1396	2342	2288	...	1053	1105	1598	1843	...	381
382	Machinery n.e.c.	-	-	-	-	...	-	-	-	-	...	382
3825	Office,computing etc.	-	-	-	-	...	-	-	-	-	...	3825
383	Electrical machinery	847	734	673	632	...	595	537	482	640	...	383
3832	Radio,television etc.	...	...	...	...	...	...	...	...	...	...	3832
384	Transport equipment g/	409	343	471	493	...	263	191	...	...	...	384
3841	Shipbuilding, repair	...	...	...	...	...	...	...	...	...	...	3841
3843	Motor vehicles	...	...	...	...	...	...	...	...	...	...	3843
385	Professional goods	-	-	-	-	...	-	-	-	-	...	385
390	Other industries f/	601	508	579	650	...	357	332	411	476	...	390
3	Manufacturing g/	44209	42750	h/ 47555	h/ 49113	...	23651	26913	h/ 25653	h/ 29888	...	3
410	Electricity,gas,steam	...	...	...	...	...	...	...	...	...	...	410
4101	Electricity	...	...	...	...	...	...	...	...	...	...	4101
420	Water works and supply	...	...	...	...	...	...	...	...	...	...	420
4	Electricity,gas etc i/	4580	4421	4790	4829	...	3111	4230	3381	3988	...	4
2-4	All industry	...	...	...	...	...	...	...	...	...	...	2-4

a/ At 2 January of the year indicated.
b/ Excluding payments in kind.
c/ Manufacture of made-up textile goods except wearing apparel is included in major group 322.
d/ Manufacture of metal furniture and fixtures is included in major groups 331 and 332 combined.
e/ Major group 352 is included in 351.
f/ Major group 356 is included in 390.
g/ Including repair of motor vehicles.
h/ Excluding major groups 351, 352, 353 and 369.
i/ Excluding gas.

ISIC	INDUSTRY		5. AVERAGE NUMBER OF OPERATIVES a/ (NUMBER) 1981	1982	1983	1984	1985	6. WAGES AND SALARIES OF OPERATIVES b/ (MILLION FRANCS) 1981	1982	1983	1984	1985	ISIC
210	Coal mining		...	...	...	...	...	...	...	...	...	...	210
220	Petroleum and gas		...	...	...	...	...	...	...	...	...	...	220
230	Metal ore mining		...	...	...	...	...	...	...	...	...	...	230
290	Other mining		1520	1511	2022	1905	...	490	483	731	740	...	290
2	Mining, quarrying		...	...	...	...	...	...	...	...	...	...	2
311/2	Food products		7951	7650	12308	10488	...	3820	4091	3936	4270	...	311/2
313	Beverages		871	849	1759	2268	...	735	642	790	1045	...	313
314	Tobacco		833	842	727	691	...	228	253	244	257	...	314
321	Textiles	c/	9155	9241	7914	7937	...	3284	3320	3086	3297	...	321
3211	Spinning,weaving etc.		...	...	...	...	...	...	...	...	...	...	3211
322	Wearing apparel	c/	3028	2721	2415	2352	...	919	894	804	902	...	322
323	Leather and products		340	303	237	236	...	70	66	73	70	...	323
324	Footwear		897	877	511	503	...	252	185	334	354	...	324
331	Wood products	d/	[947	967	1346	1364]	...	[267	284	367	403]	...	331
332	Furniture, fixtures						...					...	332
341	Paper and products		759	709	757	754	...	266	265	388	373	...	341
3411	Pulp,paper etc.		...	...	...	...	...	...	...	...	...	...	3411
342	Printing,publishing		967	956	870	861	...	342	364	383	403	...	342
351	Industrial chemicals	e/	965	974	...	...	...	340	328	...	...	...	351
3511	Basic excl fertilizers		...	...	...	...	...	...	...	...	...	...	3511
3513	Synthetic resins etc		...	...	...	...	...	...	...	...	...	...	3513
352	Other chemical products.	e/	...	...	...	...	...	...	...	...	...	...	352
3522	Drugs and medicines		...	...	...	...	...	...	...	...	...	...	3522
353	Petroleum refineries		228	260	...	...	...	215	258	...	...	...	353
354	Petroleum,coal products.		-	-	-	-	...	-	-	-	-	...	354
355	Rubber products		46	32	128	133	...	15	13	35	43	...	355
356	Plastic products n.e.c..	f/	...	...	...	...	...	...	...	...	...	...	356
361	Pottery,china etc		-	-	-	-	...	-	-	-	-	...	361
362	Glass and products		232	231	297	279	...	77	81	121	117	...	362
369	Non-metal products n.e.c		843	840	888	848	...	265	289	172	200	...	369
371	Iron and steel		-	-	-	-	...	-	-	-	-	...	371
372	Non-ferrous metals		-	-	-	-	...	-	-	-	-	...	372
381	Metal products	d/	1098	1136	1070	1031	...	498	528	507	511	...	381
382	Machinery n.e.c.		-	-	-	-	...	-	-	-	-	...	382
3825	Office,computing etc..		-	-	-	-	...	-	-	-	-	...	3825
383	Electrical machinery		517	416	462	414	...	241	219	168	195	...	383
3832	Radio,television etc..		...	...	...	...	...	...	...	...	...	...	3832
384	Transport equipment	g/	335	280	335	342	...	128	103	108	130	...	384
3841	Shipbuilding, repair..		...	...	...	...	...	...	...	...	...	...	3841
3843	Motor vehicles		...	...	...	...	...	...	...	...	...	...	3843
385	Professional goods		-	-	-	-	...	-	-	-	-	...	385
390	Other industries	f/	488	408	379	428	...	148	127	132	163	...	390
3	Manufacturing	g/	30500	29692	h/ 32403	h/ 30929	...	12110	12310	h/ 11648	h/ 12733	...	3
410	Electricity,gas,steam		...	...	...	...	...	...	...	...	...	...	410
4101	Electricity		...	...	...	...	...	...	...	...	...	...	4101
420	Water works and supply		...	...	...	...	...	...	...	...	...	...	420
4	Electricity,gas etc	i/	3247	3144	1425	1248	...	1403	1415	539	513	...	4
2-4	All industry		...	...	...	...	...	...	...	...	...	...	2-4

a/ At 2 January of the year indicated.
b/ Excluding payments in kind.
c/ Manufacture of made-up textile goods except wearing apparel is included in major group 322.
d/ Manufacture of metal furniture and fixtures is included in major groups 331 and 332 combined.
e/ Major group 352 is included in 351.
f/ Major group 356 is included in 390.
g/ Including repair of motor vehicles.
h/ Excluding major groups 351, 352 and 353.
i/ Excluding gas.

ISIC	INDUSTRY		7. HOURS WORKED BY OPERATIVES a/ (THOUSANDS)					8. OUTPUT IN PRODUCERS' PRICES b/ (MILLION FRANCS)					ISIC
			1981	1982	1983	1984	1985	1981	1982	1983	1984	1985	
210	Coal mining		...	...	...	...	...	...	...	...	...	...	210
220	Petroleum and gas		...	...	...	...	...	...	...	...	...	...	220
230	Metal ore mining		...	...	...	...	...	...	...	...	...	...	230
290	Other mining		2874	2938	4112	3943	...	3501	4015	6537	8280	...	290
2	Mining, quarrying .		...	...	...	...	...	...	...	...	...	...	2
311/2	Food products		24047	23412	29826	28378	...	19704	22061	46703	67710	...	311/2
313	Beverages		1674	1627	3712	4836	...	11438	9991	14254	16588	...	313
314	Tobacco		1596	1619	1409	1327	...	3333	3858	3922	4394	...	314
321	Textiles	c/	19552	19770	18018	18159	...	40227	45475	43067	55798	...	321
3211	Spinning,weaving etc..		...	...	...	...	...	...	...	...	...	...	3211
322	Wearing apparel	c/	5823	5181	5417	4691	...	9660	9038	15244	15753	...	322
323	Leather and products ...		84	63	...	...	...	138	42	1118	1600	...	323
324	Footwear		1744	1716	1057	966	...	3829	4204	...	...	...	324
331	Wood products	d/	[2100	2369	2665	2733]	...	[1758	1737	2638	2843]	...	331
332	Furniture, fixtures						...					...	332
341	Paper and products		1457	1362	1372	1448	...	3657	4046	5294	7109	...	341
3411	Pulp,paper etc.		...	...	...	...	...	...	...	...	...	...	3411
342	Printing,publishing		1979	1938	1699	1700	...	3463	3481	4504	5647	...	342
351	Industrial chemicals ...	e/	2003	1925	...	...	...	8668	8309	...	...	...	351
3511	Basic excl fertilizers		...	...	...	...	...	...	...	...	...	...	3511
3513	Synthetic resins etc .		...	...	...	...	...	...	...	...	...	...	3513
352	Other chemical products.	e/	...	...	...	...	...	...	...	...	...	...	352
3522	Drugs and medicines ..		...	...	...	...	...	...	...	...	...	...	3522
353	Petroleum refineries ...		459	524	...	...	...	...	...	...	...	...	353
354	Petroleum,coal products.		-	-	-	-	...	-	-	-	-	...	354
355	Rubber products		88	61	250	255	...	349	291	1189	1073	...	355
356	Plastic products n.e.c..	f/	...	...	...	...	...	...	...	...	...	...	356
361	Pottery,china etc		-	-	-	-	...	-	-	-	-	...	361
362	Glass and products		463	460	474	536	...	1073	1227	...	...	...	362
369	Non-metal products n.e.c		1656	1650	1977	1986	...	764	1445	...	...	...	369
371	Iron and steel		-	-	-	-	...	-	-	-	-	...	371
372	Non-ferrous metals		-	-	-	-	...	-	-	-	-	...	372
381	Metal products	d/	2112	2158	2332	2258	...	5854	4492	5344	6483	...	381
382	Machinery n.e.c.		-	-	-	-	...	-	-	-	-	...	382
3825	Office,computing etc..		-	-	-	-	...	-	-	-	-	...	3825
383	Electrical machinery ...		1039	901	804	798	...	3429	2455	2956	3714	...	383
3832	Radio,television etc..		...	...	...	...	...	...	...	...	...	...	3832
384	Transport equipment	g/	677	537	640	654	...	984	958	1509	2072	...	384
3841	Shipbuilding, repair..		...	...	...	...	...	...	...	...	...	...	3841
3843	Motor vehicles		...	...	...	...	...	...	...	...	...	...	3843
385	Professional goods		-	-	-	-	...	-	-	-	-	...	385
390	Other industries	f/	944	811	731	823	...	2045	1762	2613	3606	...	390
3	Manufacturing	g/	69497	68084	h/ 72383	h/ 71548	...	i/ 120373	i/ 124872	...	...	...	3
410	Electricity,gas,steam ..		...	...	...	...	...	...	...	...	...	...	410
4101	Electricity		...	...	...	...	...	...	...	...	...	...	4101
420	Water works and supply .		...	...	...	...	...	...	...	...	...	...	420
4	Electricity,gas etc	j/	6234	6036	2817	2517	...	13122	16272	19821	20273	...	4
2-4	All industry		...	...	...	...	...	...	...	...	...	...	2-4

a/ For concept, see country note.
b/ Value of products sold.
c/ Manufacture of made-up textile goods except wearing apparel is included in major group 322.
d/ Manufacture of metal furniture and fixtures is included in major groups 331 and 332 combined.
e/ Major group 352 is included in 351.
f/ Major group 356 is included in 390.
g/ Including repair of motor vehicles.
h/ Excluding major groups 351, 352 and 353.
i/ Excluding major group 353.
j/ Excluding gas.

9. VALUE ADDED IN PRODUCERS' PRICES a/ (MILLION FRANCS)

ISIC	INDUSTRY		1981	1982	1983	1984	1985	ISIC
210	Coal mining		...	...	...	...	...	210
220	Petroleum and gas		...	...	...	...	...	220
230	Metal ore mining		...	...	...	...	...	230
290	Other mining		1967	1370	3065	3721	...	290
2	Mining, quarrying		...	...	...	...	...	2
311/2	Food products		8921	8550	14417	20605	...	311/2
313	Beverages		4810	4762	8050	8737	...	313
314	Tobacco		667	926	821	923	...	314
321	Textiles	b/	17279	21524	22956	32720	...	321
3211	Spinning,weaving etc.		...	...	...	...	...	3211
322	Wearing apparel	b/	2046	1912	3681	4392	...	322
323	Leather and products		580	424	231	608	...	323
324	Footwear		1929	2058	2728	2828	...	324
331	Wood products	c/	[861	749	1270	1352]	...	331
332	Furniture, fixtures						...	332
341	Paper and products		1006	1481	2087	2876	...	341
3411	Pulp,paper etc.		...	...	...	...	...	3411
342	Printing,publishing		1490	1426	1554	2073	...	342
351	Industrial chemicals	d/	2989	2671	...	...	...	351
3511	Basic excl fertilizers		...	...	...	...	...	3511
3513	Synthetic resins etc		...	...	...	...	...	3513
352	Other chemical products	d/	...	...	...	...	...	352
3522	Drugs and medicines		...	...	...	...	...	3522
353	Petroleum refineries		...	...	...	...	...	353
354	Petroleum,coal products		-	-	-	-	...	354
355	Rubber products		141	147	600	291	...	355
356	Plastic products n.e.c.	e/	...	...	...	...	...	356
361	Pottery,china etc		-	-	-	-	...	361
362	Glass and products		237	620	536	...	...	362
369	Non-metal products n.e.c		...	...	...	...	...	369
371	Iron and steel		-	-	-	-	...	371
372	Non-ferrous metals		-	-	-	-	...	372
381	Metal products	c/	1919	1674	2320	2686	...	381
382	Machinery n.e.c.		-	-	-	-	...	382
3825	Office,computing etc.		-	-	-	-	...	3825
383	Electrical machinery		1045	788	1362	1355	...	383
3832	Radio,television etc.		...	...	...	...	...	3832
384	Transport equipment	f/	293	343	596	927	...	384
3841	Shipbuilding, repair		...	...	...	...	...	3841
3843	Motor vehicles		...	...	...	...	...	3843
385	Professional goods		-	-	...	...	...	385
390	Other industries	e/	912	940	1502	1881	...	390
3	Manufacturing	f/	g/ 47125	g/ 50995	h/ 64711	...	...	3
410	Electricity,gas,steam		...	...	...	...	...	410
4101	Electricity		...	...	...	...	...	4101
420	Water works and supply		...	...	...	...	...	420
4	Electricity,gas etc	i/	6290	11141	12285	12235	...	4
2-4	All industry		...	...	...	...	...	2-4

a/ For concept, see country note.
b/ Manufacture of made-up textile goods except wearing apparel is included in major group 322.
c/ Manufacture of metal furniture and fixtures is included in major groups 331 and 332 combined.
d/ Major group 352 is included in 351.
e/ Major group 356 is included in 390.
f/ Including repair of motor vehicles.
g/ Excluding major groups 353 and 369.
h/ Excluding major groups 351, 352, 353 and 369.
i/ Excluding gas.

MALAWI

The information in the tables, except for the indexes, is based on the reply to the United Nations Questionnaire on General Industrial Statistics from the National Statistical Office, Ministry of Finance, Zomba. The concepts, definitions and classification by branches of industry are generally in accordance with United Nations standards.

The data in the tables are derived from the annual economic survey undertaken by the National Statistical Office since 1967. The inquiry is carried out by mail and followed up by field visit of the trained personnel. The survey covers enterprises with a turnover exceeding 100 thousand kwacha. For manufacturing, Forestry Department sawmills are included. Enterprises are requested to report separately for each of their establishments. However, where an enterprise has two or more establishments engaged in the same activity, a combined return is acceptable if this is more convenient. Data for electricity and water supply relate to the Blantyre Water Board, the Lilongwe Water Board, the Electricity Supply Commission of Malawi and water supply operations undertaken directly by the Ministry of Works and Supplies; electricity generation by private enterprises is excluded. The data in the tables include adjustments for non-response. The tabulation of data is based on the present version of ISIC.

The indexes of industrial production are compiled by the National Statistical Office and provided in response to the United Nations Questionnaire on Indexes of Industrial Production.

Related national publication:
Annual Economic Survey (larger establishments), published by the National Statistical Office, Zomba.

ISIC	INDUSTRY	1. NUMBER OF ENTERPRISES a/ (NUMBER) 1981	1982	1983	1984	1985	2. AVERAGE NUMBER OF EMPLOYEES a/ (NUMBER) 1981	1982	1983	1984	1985	ISIC
210	Coal mining	-	-	-	...	...	-	-	-	...	...	210
220	Petroleum and gas	-	-	-	...	...	-	-	-	...	...	220
230	Metal ore mining	-	-	-	...	...	-	-	-	...	...	230
290	Other mining	2	2	2	...	...	232	251	245	...	...	290
2	Mining, quarrying	2	2	2	...	...	232	251	245	...	...	2
311/2	Food products	27	27	27	...	...	14700	12900	15500	...	...	311/2
313	Beverages	4	4	4	...	...	1800	1800	1500	...	...	313
314	Tobacco	6	6	6	...	...	5234	5100	3300	...	...	314
321	Textiles	8	8	8	...	...	4231	4500	4700	...	...	321
3211	Spinning,weaving etc.	3	3	3	...	...	3416	3432	3611	...	...	3211
322	Wearing apparel	12	12	12	...	...	1675	2658	1865	...	...	322
323	Leather and products	-	-	-	...	...	-	-	-	...	...	323
324	Footwear	2	2	2	...	...	372	369	350	...	...	324
331	Wood products	4	4	4	...	...	1565	1641	1590	...	...	331
332	Furniture, fixtures	3	3	3	...	...	563	386	370	...	...	332
341	Paper and products	2	2	2	...	...	256	275	265	...	...	341
3411	Pulp,paper etc.	...	...	...	...	...	...	...	...	...	...	3411
342	Printing,publishing	7	7	7	...	...	1024	1036	1016	...	...	342
351	Industrial chemicals	3	3	3	...	...	339	323	300	...	...	351
3511	Basic excl fertilizers	2	2	2	...	...	87	99	102	...	...	3511
3513	Synthetic resins etc	...	...	...	...	...	...	...	...	...	...	3513
352	Other chemical products.	8	8	8	...	...	932	942	800	...	...	352
3522	Drugs and medicines	...	...	...	...	...	...	...	...	...	...	3522
353	Petroleum refineries	-	-	-	...	...	-	-	-	...	...	353
354	Petroleum,coal products.	-	-	-	...	...	-	-	-	...	...	354
355	Rubber products	2	2	2	...	...	161	149	137	...	...	355
356	Plastic products n.e.c.	5	5	5	...	...	371	394	395	...	...	356
361	Pottery,china etc	-	-	-	...	...	-	-	-	...	...	361
362	Glass and products	-	-	-	...	...	-	-	-	...	...	362
369	Non-metal products n.e.c	4	4	4	...	...	1941	1859	1600	...	...	369
371	Iron and steel	-	-	-	...	...	-	-	-	...	...	371
372	Non-ferrous metals	-	-	-	...	...	-	-	-	...	...	372
381	Metal products	12	12	12	...	...	1300	1399	1300	...	...	381
382	Machinery n.e.c.	-	-	-	...	...	-	-	-	...	...	382
3825	Office,computing etc.	-	-	-	...	...	-	-	-	...	...	3825
383	Electrical machinery	4	4	4	...	...	472	406	389	...	...	383
3832	Radio,television etc.	-	-	-	...	...	-	-	-	...	...	3832
384	Transport equipment	2	2	2	...	...	223	212	197	...	...	384
3841	Shipbuilding, repair.	-	-	-	...	...	-	-	-	...	...	3841
3843	Motor vehicles	2	2	2	...	...	223	212	197	...	...	3843
385	Professional goods	-	-	-	...	...	-	-	-	...	...	385
390	Other industries	-	-	-	...	...	-	-	-	...	...	390
3	Manufacturing	115	115	115	...	...	37159	36349	35574	...	...	3
410	Electricity,gas,steam	...	...	...	...	...	...	...	...	...	...	410
4101	Electricity	...	...	...	...	...	...	...	...	...	...	4101
420	Water works and supply	...	...	...	...	...	...	...	...	...	...	420
4	Electricity,gas etc b/	3	3	3	...	...	3351	3500	3500	...	...	4
2-4	All industry b/	120	120	120	...	...	40742	40100	39319	...	...	2-4

a/ Enterprises with a turnover in excess of 100 thousand kwacha. b/ Excluding gas and steam.

ISIC	INDUSTRY	3. WAGES AND SALARIES OF EMPLOYEES a/ (THOUSAND KWACHA)					4. OUTPUT IN FACTOR VALUES a/ (THOUSAND KWACHA)					ISIC
		1981	1982	1983	1984	1985	1981	1982	1983	1984	1985	
210	Coal mining	-	-	-	...	...	-	-	-	...	...	210
220	Petroleum and gas	-	-	-	...	...	-	-	-	...	...	220
230	Metal ore mining	-	-	-	...	...	-	-	-	...	...	230
290	Other mining	188	137	172	...	...	765	1110	1194	...	...	290
2	Mining, quarrying .	188	137	172	...	...	765	1110	1194	...	...	2
311/2	Food products	13100	12700	15700	...	...	83100	72300	63700	...	...	311/2
313	Beverages	2406	3000	2200	...	...	31048	37700	41900	...	...	313
314	Tobacco	5048	5200	4400	...	...	27654	30700	25400	...	...	314
321	Textiles	4264	5000	5300	...	...	44000	41200	38500	...	...	321
3211	Spinning,weaving etc..	3706	4395	4848	...	...	33797	33857	34542	...	...	3211
322	Wearing apparel	1074	1890	1377	...	...	8297	9614	10048	...	...	322
323	Leather and products ...	-	-	-	...	...	-	-	-	...	...	323
324	Footwear	514	468	594	...	...	2366	2129	2881	...	...	324
331	Wood products	895	1052	1531	...	...	7300	8619	7792	...	...	331
332	Furniture, fixtures	618	585	578	...	...	4047	4331	4543	...	...	332
341	Paper and products	254	322	435	...	...	5336	7209	9452	...	...	341
3411	Pulp,paper etc.	...	...	...	...	...	...	...	...	...	...	3411
342	Printing,publishing	1655	2004	2093	...	...	23783	15346	17448	...	...	342
351	Industrial chemicals ...	600	700	800	...	...	30007	22800	21300	...	...	351
3511	Basic excl fertilizers	323	380	447	...	...	5732	8960	9437	...	...	3511
3513	Synthetic resins etc .	...	...	...	...	...	...	...	...	...	...	3513
352	Other chemical products.	2200	2500	3000	...	...	30517	32100	40200	...	...	352
3522	Drugs and medicines ..	...	...	...	...	...	...	...	...	...	...	3522
353	Petroleum refineries ...	-	-	-	...	...	-	-	-	...	...	353
354	Petroleum,coal products.	-	-	-	...	...	-	-	-	...	...	354
355	Rubber products	267	263	254	...	...	1883	2134	2207	...	...	355
356	Plastic products n.e.c..	580	734	805	...	...	6713	7526	7893	...	...	356
361	Pottery,china etc	-	-	-	...	...	-	-	-	...	...	361
362	Glass and products	-	-	-	...	...	-	-	-	...	...	362
369	Non-metal products n.e.c	1349	1400	1400	...	...	11745	11700	13500	...	...	369
371	Iron and steel	-	-	-	...	...	-	-	-	...	...	371
372	Non-ferrous metals	-	-	-	...	...	-	-	-	...	...	372
381	Metal products	2900	2200	2500	...	...	13100	19613	18000	...	...	381
382	Machinery n.e.c.	-	-	-	...	...	-	-	-	...	...	382
3825	Office,computing etc..	-	-	-	...	...	-	-	-	...	...	3825
383	Electrical machinery ...	517	699	610	...	...	5993	9672	5364	...	...	383
3832	Radio,television etc..	-	-	-	...	...	-	-	-	...	...	3832
384	Transport equipment	571	646	679	...	...	5114	3597	4982	...	...	384
3841	Shipbuilding, repair..	-	-	-	...	...	-	-	-	...	...	3841
3843	Motor vehicles	571	646	679	...	...	5114	3597	4982	...	...	3843
385	Professional goods	-	-	-	...	...	-	-	-	...	...	385
390	Other industries	-	-	-	...	...	-	-	-	...	...	390
3	Manufacturing	38812	41363	44256	...	...	342003	338290	335110	...	...	3
410	Electricity,gas,steam ..	...	...	...	...	...	...	...	...	...	...	410
4101	Electricity	...	...	...	...	...	...	...	...	...	...	4101
420	Water works and supply	...	...	...	...	...	...	...	...	...	...	420
4	Electricity,gas etc b/	3559	4900	5100	...	...	24707	27323	32031	...	...	4
2-4	All industry b/	42559	46400	49528	...	...	367475	366723	368335	...	...	2-4

a/ Enterprises with a turnover in excess of 100 thousand kwacha. b/ Excluding gas and steam.

MALAWI

ISIC	INDUSTRY	5. VALUE ADDED IN FACTOR VALUES a/c/ (THOUSAND KWACHA) 1981	1982	1983	1984	1985	6. GROSS FIXED CAPITAL FORMATION TOTAL b/c/ (THOUSAND KWACHA) 1981	1982	1983	1984	1985	ISIC
210	Coal mining	-	-	-	...	...	-	-	-	...	...	210
220	Petroleum and gas	-	-	-	...	...	-	-	-	...	...	220
230	Metal ore mining	-	-	-	...	...	-	-	-	...	...	230
290	Other mining	279	265	...	...	...	64	31	14	...	...	290
2	Mining, quarrying	279	265	...	...	...	64	31	14	...	...	2
311/2	Food products	35910	34266	...	...	...	11300	3177	2517	...	...	311/2
313	Beverages	7774	7774	9400	...	...	927	3759	2585	...	...	313
314	Tobacco	8593	7920	5200	...	...	862	1690	3303	...	...	314
321	Textiles	13540	15914	14600	...	...	1252	3983	16712	...	...	321
3211	Spinning, weaving etc.	13017	13552	10711	...	...	350	2090	16542	...	...	3211
322	Wearing apparel	2343	3339	2857	...	...	184	277	125	...	...	322
323	Leather and products	-	-	-	...	...	-	-	-	...	...	323
324	Footwear	-1537	575	-1727	...	...	251	244	276	...	...	324
331	Wood products	4205	3622	4054	...	...	200	155	5332	...	...	331
332	Furniture, fixtures	1031	885	1259	...	...	44	97	50	...	...	332
341	Paper and products	466	1233	2504	...	...	167	241	399	...	...	341
3411	Pulp, paper etc.	...	...	...	...	...	...	...	...	...	...	3411
342	Printing, publishing	5366	-404	7035	...	...	728	902	781	...	...	342
351	Industrial chemicals	4000	3882	3600	...	...	985	198	252	...	...	351
3511	Basic excl fertilizers	2014	1770	1913	...	...	960	194	240	...	...	3511
3513	Synthetic resins etc	...	...	...	...	...	...	...	...	...	...	3513
352	Other chemical products	3700	7069	9706	...	...	500	877	1062	...	...	352
3522	Drugs and medicines	...	...	...	...	...	...	...	...	...	...	3522
353	Petroleum refineries	-	-	-	...	...	-	-	-	...	...	353
354	Petroleum, coal products	-	-	-	...	...	-	-	-	...	...	354
355	Rubber products	496	838	928	...	...	21	20	64	...	...	355
356	Plastic products n.e.c.	2259	3268	2796	...	...	400	595	603	...	...	356
361	Pottery, china etc	-	-	-	...	...	-	-	-	...	...	361
362	Glass and products	-	-	-	...	...	-	-	-	...	...	362
369	Non-metal products n.e.c	11700	1669	4244	...	...	869	329	387	...	...	369
371	Iron and steel	-	-	-	...	...	-	-	-	...	...	371
372	Non-ferrous metals	-	-	-	...	...	-	-	-	...	...	372
381	Metal products	13100	4367	6338	...	...	200	418	869	...	...	381
382	Machinery n.e.c.	-	-	-	...	...	-	-	-	...	...	382
3825	Office, computing etc.	-	-	-	...	...	-	-	-	...	...	3825
383	Electrical machinery	737	1096	885	...	...	169	171	153	...	...	383
3832	Radio, television etc.	-	-	-	...	...	-	-	-	...	...	3832
384	Transport equipment	330	1887	925	...	...	369	112	141	...	...	384
3841	Shipbuilding, repair	-	-	-	...	...	-	-	-	...	...	3841
3843	Motor vehicles	330	1887	925	...	...	369	112	141	...	...	3843
385	Professional goods	-	-	-	...	...	-	-	-	...	...	385
390	Other industries	-	-	-	...	...	-	-	-	...	...	390
3	Manufacturing	114013	99200	d/ 74604	...	...	19428	17245	35611	...	...	3
410	Electricity, gas, steam	...	...	...	...	...	...	...	...	...	...	410
4101	Electricity	...	...	...	...	...	...	...	...	...	...	4101
420	Water works and supply	...	...	...	...	...	...	...	...	...	...	420
4	Electricity, gas etc e/	15672	17363	21374	...	...	20182	12689	10006	...	...	4
2-4	All industry e/	129964	116828	...	...	...	39674	29965	45631	...	...	2-4

a/ Net of non-industrial costs and interest paid.
b/ Sales and disposals are not deducted.
c/ Enterprises with a turnover in excess of 100 thousand kwacha.
d/ Excluding major group 311/2.
e/ Excluding gas and steam.

7. INDEX NUMBERS OF INDUSTRIAL PRODUCTION (1980 = 100)

ISIC	INDUSTRY	1976	1977	1978	1979	1981	1982	1983	1984	1985	a/ RATE	ISIC
210	Coal mining	...	...	...	...	...	...	...	...	...	...	210
220	Petroleum and gas	...	...	...	...	...	...	...	...	...	...	220
230	Metal ore mining	...	...	...	...	...	...	...	...	...	...	230
290	Other mining	...	...	...	...	...	...	...	...	...	...	290
2	Mining, quarrying .	...	...	...	...	...	...	...	...	...	...	2
311/2	Food products											311/2
313	Beverages	82	89	94	94	128	126	146	138	139	6.0	313
314	Tobacco											314
321	Textiles .... b/	74	84	99	113	114	121	125	117	122	5.7	321
3211	Spinning,weaving etc..	...	...	...	...	...	...	...	...	...	...	3211
322	Wearing apparel .... b/	...	...	...	...	...	...	...	...	...	...	322
323	Leather and products ...	...	...	...	...	...	...	...	...	...	...	323
324	Footwear .... b/	...	...	...	...	...	...	...	...	...	...	324
331	Wood products	...	...	...	...	...	...	...	...	...	...	331
332	Furniture, fixtures .... c/ d/	68	73	90	79	105	70	110	97	92	3.4	332
341	Paper and products											341
3411	Pulp,paper etc.	...	...	...	...	...	...	...	...	...	...	3411
342	Printing,publishing .... d/	...	...	...	...	...	...	...	...	...	...	342
351	Industrial chemicals ...	...	...	...	...	...	...	...	...	...	...	351
3511	Basic excl fertilizers	...	...	...	...	...	...	...	...	...	...	3511
3513	Synthetic resins etc .	...	...	...	...	...	...	...	...	...	...	3513
352	Other chemical products.	...	...	...	...	...	...	...	...	...	...	352
3522	Drugs and medicines ..	...	...	...	...	...	...	...	...	...	...	3522
353	Petroleum refineries ...	...	...	...	...	...	...	...	...	...	...	353
354	Petroleum,coal products.	...	...	...	...	...	...	...	...	...	...	354
355	Rubber products	...	...	...	...	...	...	...	...	...	...	355
356	Plastic products n.e.c..	...	...	...	...	...	...	...	...	...	...	356
361	Pottery,china etc	...	...	...	...	...	...	...	...	...	...	361
362	Glass and products	...	...	...	...	...	...	...	...	...	...	362
369	Non-metal products n.e.c e/	92	102	112	122	84	58	76	74	67	-3.5	369
371	Iron and steel	...	...	...	...	...	...	...	...	...	...	371
372	Non-ferrous metals	...	...	...	...	...	...	...	...	...	...	372
381	Metal products	...	...	...	...	...	...	...	...	...	...	381
382	Machinery n.e.c.	...	...	...	...	...	...	...	...	...	...	382
3825	Office,computing etc..	...	...	...	...	...	...	...	...	...	...	3825
383	Electrical machinery ...	...	...	...	...	...	...	...	...	...	...	383
3832	Radio,television etc..	...	...	...	...	...	...	...	...	...	...	3832
384	Transport equipment	...	...	...	...	...	...	...	...	...	...	384
3841	Shipbuilding, repair..	...	...	...	...	...	...	...	...	...	...	3841
3843	Motor vehicles	...	...	...	...	...	...	...	...	...	...	3843
385	Professional goods	...	...	...	...	...	...	...	...	...	...	385
390	Other industries	...	...	...	...	...	...	...	...	...	...	390
3	Manufacturing	80	89	98	99	110	104	120	117	118	4.4	3
410	Electricity,gas,steam ..	...	...	...	...	...	...	...	...	...	...	410
4101	Electricity	...	...	...	...	...	...	...	...	...	...	4101
420	Water works and supply .	...	...	...	...	...	...	...	...	...	...	420
4	Electricity,gas etc	...	...	...	...	...	...	...	...	...	...	4
2-4	All industry	...	...	...	...	...	...	...	...	...	...	2-4

a/ Annual growth rate 1976-1985.
b/ Major groups 322 and 324 are included in 321.
c/ Including soaps and detergents and matches.
d/ Major group 342 is included in 332 and 341 combined.
e/ Including sawn timber, metal doors, frames and windows.

MALAYSIA

The information in the tables, except for the indexes, is based on the reply to the United Nations Questionnaire on General Industrial Statistics from the Jabatan Perangkaan (Department of Statistics), Kuala Lumpur. The concepts, definitions and classification by branches of industry are generally in accordance with United Nations standards.

The data for mining are derived from the census of mining industries undertaken annually by the Department of Statistics. It covers all establishments engaged in iron-ore mining, tin-ore mining, gold mining, bauxite mining, amang treatment antimony mining, copper mining, crude petroleum and natural gas mining, and mining management services. The data for manufacturing are derived from the Annual Survey of Manufacturing Industries conducted by the Department of Statistics. The data in the tables are based on the revised national classification which is comparable with the present ISIC. The survey covers all establishments registered under the Industrial Co-ordination Act (I.C.A.) 1975. A complete coverage or a census of all manufacturing industries was conducted for reference year 1981. The coverage of the survey data for reference year 1982 is based on the results of the census for reference year 1973, while that for 1983 and 1984 is based on the census for reference year 1981. The coverage of the annual survey is reviewed after a census to ensure that the survey design covers about the same percentage of the output value, value added and employment of the total manufacturing sector in any one year. The coverage of the annual survey represents the major output of the total manufacturing sector in Malaysia. Both the mining and manufacturing inquiries are carried out on the basis of a complete enumeration by mail and field contact. The period of reference is basically the calendar year. However, the figures include data for accounting years not coinciding with the calendar year.

Numbers of persons engaged and employees relate to 31 December or the last pay period of the reference year. The number of employees refers to full-time and part-time paid employees (full-time employees are those who normally work at least 6 hours a day and at least 20 days a month). Persons employed through labour contractors are also included. Wages and salaries represent all payments made during the year to all persons engaged other than working proprietors and unpaid family workers. Employers' contributions to provident funds and payments to homeworkers are excluded. Data on number of operatives and wages and salaries of operatives cover workers directly employed (excluding managerial, technical, supervisory, clerical and general workers) and workers employed through labour contractors.

Output refers to the value of products manufactured by the establishment, plus receipts from industrial services rendered to others, value of stock changes of finished and semi-finished goods and value of goods sold in the same condition as purchased. Value added is derived as the difference between the value of output and the cost of materials, supplies and fuels consumed, electricity purchased, work done by others and goods sold in the same condition as purchased. Gross fixed capital formation represents the value of purchases of new and used fixed assets and own-account construction of fixed assets during the year less the value of corresponding sales.

The indexes of industrial production are compiled by the Department of Statistics and provided in response to the United Nations Questionnaire on Indexes of Industrial Production.

Related national publications:

Census of Mining Industries (annual); Survey of Manufacturing Industries (annual); Industrial Surveys, Malaysia; Annual Statistical Bulletin, Malaysia; Monthly Statistical Bulletin, all published by the Jabatan Perangkaan (Department of Statistics), Kuala Lumpur.

ISIC	INDUSTRY	1. NUMBER OF ESTABLISHMENTS a/ (NUMBER)					2. AVERAGE NUMBER OF PERSONS ENGAGED a/b/ (THOUSANDS)					ISIC
		c/ 1981	1982	1983	1984	1985	c/ 1981	1982	1983	1984	1985	
210	Coal mining	...	...	...	...	...	...	...	...	...	...	210
220	Petroleum and gas	4	...	4	5	...	3.2	...	4.6	5.6	...	220
230	Metal ore mining	977	...	847	785	...	41.8	...	31.1	28.4	...	230
290	Other mining	250	...	239	244	...	9.3	...	10.1	10.5	...	290
2	Mining, quarrying .	...	...	...	...	...	...	...	...	...	...	2
311/2	Food products	3707	1582	1232	1243	...	73.5	65.6	62.4	61.9	...	311/2
313	Beverages	116	85	65	64	...	6.6	6.4	5.8	5.9	...	313
314	Tobacco	218	159	22	19	...	11.7	11.6	5.5	3.8	...	314
321	Textiles	480	335	211	202	...	39.9	37.1	33.1	31.0	...	321
3211	Spinning,weaving etc..	172	167	98	95	...	28.0	26.0	23.0	20.7	...	3211
322	Wearing apparel	2624	295	213	217	...	33.0	25.1	27.7	31.0	...	322
323	Leather and products ...	65	23	22	22	...	0.9	0.6	0.6	0.6	...	323
324	Footwear	144	26	13	10	...	3.7	1.4	1.3	1.3	...	324
331	Wood products	1694	1150	723	708	...	79.0	74.3	63.6	60.0	...	331
332	Furniture, fixtures	1711	601	321	361	...	13.9	10.8	8.1	8.6	...	332
341	Paper and products	239	127	103	109	...	6.7	6.4	6.6	6.9	...	341
3411	Pulp,paper etc.	14	13	7	10	...	0.8	1.3	0.8	0.8	...	3411
342	Printing,publishing	810	493	255	265	...	25.9	23.5	19.8	21.7	...	342
351	Industrial chemicals ...	127	107	76	77	...	5.2	5.2	5.4	5.5	...	351
3511	Basic excl fertilizers	67	45	34	38	...	2.5	2.2	2.8	2.9	...	3511
3513	Synthetic resins etc .	17	20	12	9	...	0.5	0.7	0.6	0.5	...	3513
352	Other chemical products.	352	185	135	139	...	12.2	11.7	9.8	9.5	...	352
3522	Drugs and medicines ..	83	38	29	29	...	2.6	2.3	2.0	1.8	...	3522
353	Petroleum refineries ...	6	7	8	10	...	0.7	0.8	0.9	1.4	...	353
354	Petroleum,coal products.	10	13	15	17	...	0.2	0.3	0.7	0.7	...	354
355	Rubber products	597	384	239	240	...	34.2	33.1	30.1	30.0	...	355
356	Plastic products n.e.c..	658	337	246	247	...	18.3	15.4	15.1	15.6	...	356
361	Pottery,china etc	58	27	19	18	...	2.1	2.3	1.9	2.0	...	361
362	Glass and products	54	11	15	19	...	2.5	2.2	2.3	2.4	...	362
369	Non-metal products n.e.c	789	471	348	381	...	25.2	23.5	21.9	22.8	...	369
371	Iron and steel	408	179	133	142	...	10.7	10.0	10.0	11.0	...	371
372	Non-ferrous metals	23	19	15	20	...	3.1	3.1	3.2	3.2	...	372
381	Metal products	2666	618	463	519	...	33.5	24.1	21.8	22.4	...	381
382	Machinery n.e.c.	1519	498	445	433	...	22.4	16.4	14.6	14.4	...	382
3825	Office,computing etc..	8	2	6	5	...	0.1	0.1	0.1	0.1	..	3825
383	Electrical machinery ...	318	254	207	230	...	81.1	78.4	87.0	93.1	...	383
3832	Radio,television etc..	119	105	98	107	...	70.7	68.2	75.7	81.6	...	3832
384	Transport equipment	419	252	220	225	...	21.3	21.7	21.1	20.3	...	384
3841	Shipbuilding, repair..	132	64	57	64	...	6.2	6.6	6.0	5.2	...	3841
3843	Motor vehicles	232	143	121	114	...	12.5	12.1	11.9	11.8	...	3843
385	Professional goods	40	18	20	16	...	4.9	4.2	5.6	4.8	...	385
390	Other industries	579	87	115	127	...	7.6	5.8	7.3	7.2	...	390
3	Manufacturing	20431	8343	5899	6080	...	580.0	521.0	493.2	499.0	...	3
410	Electricity,gas,steam ..	...	...	...	...	...	...	...	...	...	...	410
4101	Electricity	...	...	...	...	...	...	...	...	...	...	4101
420	Water works and supply .	...	...	...	...	...	...	...	...	...	...	420
4	Electricity,gas etc	...	...	...	...	...	...	...	...	...	...	4
2-4	All industry	...	...	...	...	...	...	...	...	...	...	2-4

a/ Manufacturing: selected industries; for coverage, see country note.
b/ At 31 December or last pay period of the year indicated.
c/ Data obtained from the 1981 industrial census covering all establishments.

ISIC	INDUSTRY	3. AVERAGE NUMBER OF EMPLOYEES a/b/ (THOUSANDS)					4. WAGES AND SALARIES OF EMPLOYEES b/ (MILLION RINGGITS)					ISIC
		1981 c/	1982	1983	1984	1985	1981 c/	1982	1983	1984	1985	
210	Coal mining	...	...	...	...	...	...	...	...	...	...	210
220	Petroleum and gas	3.2	...	4.6	5.6	...	143	...	218	327	...	220
230	Metal ore mining	41.5	...	30.5	28.1	...	268	...	210	210	...	230
290	Other mining	9.3	...	10.1	10.4	...	64	...	79	91	...	290
2	Mining, quarrying	...	...	...	...	...	...	...	...	...	...	2
311/2	Food products	68.4	64.1	61.3	60.9	...	339	360	362	401	...	311/2
313	Beverages	6.5	6.3	5.8	5.9	...	46	51	56	60	...	313
314	Tobacco	11.3	11.3	5.5	3.8	...	43	48	43	45	...	314
321	Textiles	39.5	36.9	33.0	30.9	...	181	167	165	176	...	321
3211	Spinning,weaving etc.	27.9	25.9	23.0	20.7	...	143	124	124	124	...	3211
322	Wearing apparel	29.7	24.9	27.6	30.9	...	93	84	108	132	...	322
323	Leather and products	0.8	0.6	0.6	0.6	...	3	2	2	3	...	323
324	Footwear	3.5	1.4	1.3	1.3	...	13	6	6	6	...	324
331	Wood products	77.7	73.8	63.4	59.8	...	397	419	371	369	...	331
332	Furniture, fixtures	11.9	10.1	7.7	8.3	...	48	49	39	47	...	332
341	Paper and products	6.5	6.4	6.6	6.9	...	29	33	37	44	...	341
3411	Pulp,paper etc.	0.8	1.3	0.8	0.8	...	4	7	5	6	...	3411
342	Printing,publishing	25.3	23.3	19.7	21.6	...	149	177	183	201	...	342
351	Industrial chemicals	5.2	5.2	5.4	5.5	...	41	49	77	91	...	351
3511	Basic excl fertilizers	2.5	2.2	2.8	2.9	...	18	22	50	62	...	3511
3513	Synthetic resins etc	0.5	0.7	0.6	0.5	...	3	5	5	5	...	3513
352	Other chemical products.	11.9	11.6	9.8	9.5	...	79	88	88	96	...	352
3522	Drugs and medicines	2.5	2.3	1.9	1.8	...	14	16	14	16	...	3522
353	Petroleum refineries	0.7	0.8	0.9	1.4	...	15	20	22	27	...	353
354	Petroleum,coal products.	0.2	0.3	0.6	0.7	...	1	2	5	5	...	354
355	Rubber products	33.7	32.9	30.0	30.0	...	170	182	194	210	...	355
356	Plastic products n.e.c.	17.7	15.2	15.1	15.5	...	66	65	71	91	...	356
361	Pottery,china etc	2.1	2.3	1.9	2.0	...	9	10	10	11	...	361
362	Glass and products	2.5	2.2	2.3	2.3	...	17	18	21	24	...	362
369	Non-metal products n.e.c	24.5	23.2	21.7	22.6	...	130	148	156	178	...	369
371	Iron and steel	10.2	9.9	9.9	10.9	...	73	76	89	94	...	371
372	Non-ferrous metals	3.0	3.1	3.2	3.2	...	23	27	31	33	...	372
381	Metal products	30.5	23.6	21.5	22.1	...	152	144	144	157	...	381
382	Machinery n.e.c.	20.7	15.9	14.2	14.0	...	114	106	111	118	...	382
3825	Office,computing etc.	0.1	0.1	0.1	0.1	...	1	1	1	1	...	3825
383	Electrical machinery	81.0	78.3	86.9	93.1	...	390	460	548	639	...	383
3832	Radio,television etc.	70.7	68.2	75.7	81.6	...	327	387	463	543	...	3832
384	Transport equipment	21.0	21.5	21.0	20.1	...	152	167	172	187	...	384
3841	Shipbuilding, repair.	6.1	6.5	6.0	5.1	...	57	63	52	59	...	3841
3843	Motor vehicles	12.3	12.0	11.8	11.7	...	81	87	100	109	...	3843
385	Professional goods	4.9	4.2	5.6	4.8	...	28	24	30	26	...	385
390	Other industries	6.9	5.8	7.3	7.2	...	26	25	34	38	...	390
3	Manufacturing	557.8	515.1	489.8	495.8	...	2827	3007	3175	3509	...	3
410	Electricity,gas,steam	...	...	...	...	...	...	...	...	...	...	410
4101	Electricity	...	...	...	...	...	...	...	...	...	...	4101
420	Water works and supply	...	...	...	...	...	...	...	...	...	...	420
4	Electricity,gas etc	...	...	...	...	...	...	...	...	...	...	4
2-4	All industry	...	...	...	...	...	...	...	...	...	...	2-4

a/ At 31 December or last pay period of the year indicated.
b/ Manufacturing: selected industries; for coverage, see country note.
c/ Data obtained from the 1981 industrial census covering all establishments.

ISIC	INDUSTRY	5. OUTPUT IN FACTOR VALUES a/ (MILLION RINGGITS) 1981 b/	1982	1983	1984	1985	6. VALUE ADDED IN FACTOR VALUES a/ (MILLION RINGGITS) 1981 b/	1982	1983	1984	1985	ISIC
210	Coal mining	...	...	...	...	...	...	...	...	...	...	210
220	Petroleum and gas	7131	...	8210	10043	...	6871	...	7567	9522	...	220
230	Metal ore mining	1596	...	1316	1258	...	825	...	727	682	...	230
290	Other mining	...	...	493	...	...	...	...	270	...	...	290
2	Mining, quarrying .	...	...	...	...	...	...	...	...	...	...	2
311/2	Food products	9427	9342	10237	12574	...	1555	1423	1475	2006	...	311/2
313	Beverages	586	569	572	546	...	305	293	287	284	...	313
314	Tobacco	732	835	993	979	...	271	312	383	352	...	314
321	Textiles	1401	1334	1291	1290	...	408	371	346	419	...	321
3211	Spinning,weaving etc..	1119	1050	1004	1001	...	312	266	251	320	...	3211
322	Wearing apparel	575	469	550	663	...	200	162	190	235	...	322
323	Leather and products ...	25	21	19	19	...	7	6	7	7	...	323
324	Footwear	108	26	26	21	...	31	10	10	8	...	324
331	Wood products	2620	2626	2480	2248	...	871	886	771	709	...	331
332	Furniture, fixtures	275	222	190	203	...	101	90	75	80	...	332
341	Paper and products	314	315	332	367	...	94	102	113	125	...	341
3411	Pulp,paper etc.	45	68	42	44	...	12	23	13	14	...	3411
342	Printing,publishing	870	895	880	985	...	414	431	434	535	...	342
351	Industrial chemicals ...	747	769	1877	3006	...	167	204	811	1440	...	351
3511	Basic excl fertilizers	209	236	1365	2466	...	68	102	716	1364	...	3511
3513	Synthetic resins etc .	77	86	95	76	...	24	25	17	16	...	3513
352	Other chemical products.	782	814	881	840	...	295	319	370	348	...	352
3522	Drugs and medicines ..	84	86	97	102	...	41	40	43	51	...	3522
353	Petroleum refineries ...	4083	3494	3666	3724	...	539	219	249	233	...	353
354	Petroleum,coal products.	17	30	54	71	...	6	10	21	17	...	354
355	Rubber products	2761	2539	2824	2833	...	636	618	734	662	...	355
356	Plastic products n.e.c..	565	513	581	581	...	179	176	196	186	...	356
361	Pottery,china etc	48	43	54	47	...	28	21	30	26	...	361
362	Glass and products	165	158	170	167	...	66	63	63	66	...	362
369	Non-metal products n.e.c	1226	1308	1340	1509	...	487	598	584	743	...	369
371	Iron and steel	839	925	1222	1408	...	196	245	329	303	...	371
372	Non-ferrous metals	1946	2034	1480	1550	...	117	80	110	109	...	372
381	Metal products	1285	1145	1319	1192	...	388	352	409	357	...	381
382	Machinery n.e.c.	928	832	874	796	...	330	292	309	314	...	382
3825	Office,computing etc..	9	8	8	9	...	4	3	3	4	...	3825
383	Electrical machinery ...	4369	4740	5759	6894	...	1235	1420	1614	2021	...	383
3832	Radio,television etc..	3771	4048	4959	6051	...	1066	1218	1363	1789	...	3832
384	Transport equipment	1224	1184	1402	1368	...	441	421	502	569	...	384
3841	Shipbuilding, repair..	409	280	268	264	...	197	113	93	147	...	3841
3843	Motor vehicles	665	731	872	850	...	193	257	330	364	...	3843
385	Professional goods	155	154	186	148	...	56	60	77	59	...	385
390	Other industries	207	152	214	225	...	67	62	88	86	...	390
3	Manufacturing	38280	37488	41473	46254	...	9490	9246	10587	12299	...	3
410	Electricity,gas,steam ..	...	...	...	...	...	...	...	...	...	...	410
4101	Electricity	...	...	...	...	...	...	...	...	...	...	4101
420	Water works and supply .	...	...	...	...	...	...	...	...	...	...	420
4	Electricity,gas etc	...	...	...	...	...	...	...	...	...	...	4
2-4	All industry	...	...	...	...	...	...	...	...	...	...	2-4

a/ Manufacturing: selected industries; for coverage, see country note.
b/ Data obtained from the 1981 industrial census covering all establishments.

7. GROSS FIXED CAPITAL FORMATION
TOTAL a/
(MILLION RINGGITS)

ISIC	INDUSTRY	1981	1982	1983	1984	1985	ISIC
210	Coal mining	...	...	...	...	...	210
220	Petroleum and gas	...	...	1246	...	...	220
230	Metal ore mining	...	...	167	...	...	230
290	Other mining	...	...	44	...	...	290
2	Mining, quarrying	...	...	...	...	...	2
311/2	Food products	...	...	360	...	...	311/2
313	Beverages	...	...	54	...	...	313
314	Tobacco	...	...	51	...	...	314
321	Textiles	...	...	50	...	...	321
3211	Spinning,weaving etc.	...	...	36	...	...	3211
322	Wearing apparel	...	...	28	...	...	322
323	Leather and products	...	...	1	...	...	323
324	Footwear	...	...	-	...	...	324
331	Wood products	...	...	116	...	...	331
332	Furniture, fixtures	...	...	4	...	...	332
341	Paper and products	...	...	71	...	...	341
3411	Pulp,paper etc.	...	...	1	...	...	3411
342	Printing,publishing	...	...	34	...	...	342
351	Industrial chemicals	...	...	198	...	...	351
3511	Basic excl fertilizers	...	...	180	...	...	3511
3513	Synthetic resins etc	...	...	11	...	...	3513
352	Other chemical products	...	...	27	...	...	352
3522	Drugs and medicines	...	...	3	...	...	3522
353	Petroleum refineries	...	...	34	...	...	353
354	Petroleum,coal products	...	...	5	...	...	354
355	Rubber products	...	...	123	...	...	355
356	Plastic products n.e.c.	...	...	38	...	...	356
361	Pottery,china etc	...	...	8	...	...	361
362	Glass and products	...	...	26	...	...	362
369	Non-metal products n.e.c	...	...	130	...	...	369
371	Iron and steel	...	...	149	...	...	371
372	Non-ferrous metals	...	...	65	...	...	372
381	Metal products	...	...	69	...	...	381
382	Machinery n.e.c.	...	...	54	...	...	382
3825	Office,computing etc.	...	...	-	...	...	3825
383	Electrical machinery	...	...	342	...	...	383
3832	Radio,television etc.	...	...	315	...	...	3832
384	Transport equipment	...	...	74	...	...	384
3841	Shipbuilding, repair.	...	...	21	...	...	3841
3843	Motor vehicles	...	...	46	...	...	3843
385	Professional goods	...	...	9	...	...	385
390	Other industries	...	...	15	...	...	390
3	Manufacturing	...	...	2135	...	...	3
410	Electricity,gas,steam	...	...	...	...	...	410
4101	Electricity	...	...	...	...	...	4101
420	Water works and supply	...	...	...	...	...	420
4	Electricity,gas etc	...	...	...	...	...	4
2-4	All industry	...	...	...	...	...	2-4

a/ Manufacturing: selected industries; for coverage, see country note.

8. INDEX NUMBERS OF INDUSTRIAL PRODUCTION (1980 = 100)

ISIC	INDUSTRY	1976	1977	1978	1979	1981	1982	1983	1984	1985	a/ RATE	ISIC
210	Coal mining	...	...	...	...	...	...	...	...	...	...	210
220	Petroleum and gas	...	...	...	...	...	...	...	...	...	...	220
230	Metal ore mining	...	...	...	...	...	...	...	...	...	...	230
290	Other mining	...	...	...	...	...	...	...	...	...	...	290
2	Mining, quarrying .	103	95	102	103	98	104	130	162	163	5.2	2
311/2	Food products	84	87	92	96	98	107	107	120	132	5.1	311/2
313	Beverages	57	66	77	92	93	88	78	77	81	4.0	313
314	Tobacco	84	91	92	100	101	111	106	115	108	2.8	314
321	Textiles	...	...	...	...	...	...	...	...	...	...	321
3211	Spinning,weaving etc..	...	...	...	...	...	...	...	...	...	...	3211
322	Wearing apparel	80	84	98	97	102	106	105	132	128	5.4	322
323	Leather and products ...	...	...	...	...	...	...	...	...	...	...	323
324	Footwear	...	...	...	...	...	...	...	...	...	...	324
331	Wood products	...	...	...	...	...	...	...	...	...	...	331
332	Furniture, fixtures	...	...	...	...	...	...	...	...	...	...	332
341	Paper and products	...	...	...	...	...	...	...	...	...	...	341
3411	Pulp,paper etc.	...	...	...	...	...	...	...	...	...	...	3411
342	Printing,publishing	...	...	...	...	...	...	...	...	...	...	342
351	Industrial chemicals ...	70	72	81	94	104	90	92	105	111	5.3	351
3511	Basic excl fertilizers	...	...	...	...	...	...	...	...	...	...	3511
3513	Synthetic resins etc .	...	...	...	...	...	...	...	...	...	...	3513
352	Other chemical products.	...	...	...	...	...	...	...	...	...	...	352
3522	Drugs and medicines ..	...	...	...	...	...	...	...	...	...	...	3522
353	Petroleum refineries ...	...	...	...	...	...	...	...	...	...	...	353
354	Petroleum,coal products.	...	...	...	...	...	...	...	...	...	...	354
355	Rubber products	91	96	95	96	109	116	118	130	123	3.4	355
356	Plastic products n.e.c..	...	...	...	...	...	...	...	...	...	...	356
361	Pottery,china etc	[									]	361
362	Glass and products	68	70	88	93	116	110	116	129	115	6.0	362
369	Non-metal products n.e.c	[									]	369
371	Iron and steel	68	79	88	88	100	105	124	165	131	7.6	371
372	Non-ferrous metals	...	...	...	...	...	...	...	...	...	...	372
381	Metal products	64	72	90	92	118	119	107	160	154	10.2	381
382	Machinery n.e.c.	...	...	...	...	...	...	...	...	...	...	382
3825	Office,computing etc..	...	...	...	...	...	...	...	...	...	...	3825
383	Electrical machinery ...	69	89	96	99	105	133	156	211	159	9.7	383
3832	Radio,television etc..	...	...	...	...	...	...	...	...	...	...	3832
384	Transport equipment	49	56	67	72	100	96	111	120	121	10.6	384
3841	Shipbuilding, repair..	...	...	...	...	...	...	...	...	...	...	3841
3843	Motor vehicles	...	...	...	...	...	...	...	...	...	...	3843
385	Professional goods	[69	77	84	95	96	89	90	90	93	3.4]	385
390	Other industries											390
3	Manufacturing ..... b/	71	78	86	94	103	109	116	129	121	6.1	3
410	Electricity,gas,steam ..	...	...	...	...	...	...	...	...	...	...	410
4101	Electricity	67	74	82	91	106	110	123	132	143	8.8	4101
420	Water works and supply .	...	...	...	...	...	...	...	...	...	...	420
4	Electricity,gas etc	...	...	...	...	...	...	...	...	...	...	4
2-4	All industry b/c/	73	79	87	94	103	109	122	142	137	7.2	2-4

a/ Annual growth rate 1976-1985.
b/ Excluding other wearing apparel and made-up textiles; leather, fur and leather products; footwear; furniture and fixture; printing and publishing; non-electrical machinery and miscellaneous industries.
c/ Excluding gas, steam and water works and supply.

MALTA

The information in the tables, except for the indexes, is based on the reply to the United Nations Questionnaire on General Industrial Statistics from the Central Office of Statistics, Valletta. The concepts, definitions and classification by branches of industry are generally in accordance with United Nations standards.

Mining and manufacturing data are derived from the census of production taken annually by the Central Office of Statistics, covering all establishments in mining and manufacturing industries. The inquiry is carried out by mail with a response rate of about 98 per cent. It should be noted that data concerning ship-repairing activities are excluded because of disclosure rules imposed by law. The data are compiled according to the national classification system which is in line with the present version of ISIC.

The data on persons engaged represent the monthly average of persons engaged on a full-time or part-time basis. Homeworkers are excluded. The numbers of employees and operatives relate to the average number of persons on the pay-roll during the last week of each month of the year.

Wages and salaries cover cash earnings of employees, including overtime payments, bonuses and commissions whether paid regularly or not, and excluding insurance contributions paid by employees. It should be noted, however, that wages and salaries of employees include employers' contributions to the national insurance scheme.

Output represents the value of sales and the net change between the beginning and the end of the year in the value of stocks of goods produced. The valuation is at the establishment price, excluding any discounts, commissions or rebates, but including charges for delivery. Value added is the difference between the value of output defined above and the cost of materials and fuels used, transport expenses, payments to homeworkers and the value of work given out. The estimates exclude value added from sales of goods shipped in the same condition as received. The valuation of output is in producers' prices and value added in factor values.

The data on gross fixed capital formation refer to acquisitions less disposals of land, buildings, plant, machinery and vehicles during the reference year, valued before the addition of legal charges, stamp duties, agent's fees etc.

The indexes of industrial production are compiled by the Central Office of Statistics and provided in response to the United Nations Questionnaire on Indexes of Industrial Production. The indexes cover, in principle, all industrial establishments.

Related national publications:
<u>Census of Production Report</u> (annual); <u>Annual Abstract of Statistics</u>, both published by the Central Office of Statistics, Valletta.

ISIC	INDUSTRY	1. NUMBER OF ESTABLISHMENTS (NUMBER) 1981	1982	1983	1984	1985	2. AVERAGE NUMBER OF PERSONS ENGAGED (NUMBER) 1981	1982	1983	1984	1985	ISIC
210	Coal mining	-	-	-	...	...	-	-	-	...	...	210
220	Petroleum and gas	-	-	-	...	...	-	-	-	...	...	220
230	Metal ore mining	-	-	-	...	...	-	-	-	...	...	230
290	Other mining	63	67	59	...	...	377	453	347	...	...	290
2	Mining, quarrying .	63	67	59	...	...	377	453	347	...	...	2
311/2	Food products	353	336	322	...	...	2132	2064	2056	...	...	311/2
313	Beverages	34	31	30	...	...	1211	1156	1154	...	...	313
314	Tobacco	6	6	5	...	...	833	765	695	...	...	314
321	Textiles	31	29	24	...	...	1974	1547	1195	...	...	321
3211	Spinning,weaving etc..	...	...	...	...	...	...	...	...	...	...	3211
322	Wearing apparel	184	160	140	...	...	8682	7202	7213	...	...	322
323	Leather and products ...	12	11	7	...	...	264	189	93	...	...	323
324	Footwear	23	21	21	...	...	1078	1102	1118	...	...	324
331	Wood products	137	113	109	...	...	355	294	293	...	...	331
332	Furniture, fixtures	349	304	286	...	...	2160	1920	1616	...	...	332
341	Paper and products	11	10	10	...	...	225	220	218	...	...	341
3411	Pulp,paper etc.	...	...	...	...	...	...	...	...	...	...	3411
342	Printing,publishing	73	69	63	...	...	1444	1411	1281	...	...	342
351	Industrial chemicals ...	5	4	4	...	...	95	87	85	...	...	351
3511	Basic excl fertilizers	...	...	...	...	...	...	...	...	...	...	3511
3513	Synthetic resins etc .	...	...	...	...	...	...	...	...	...	...	3513
352	Other chemical products. a/	32	27	24	...	...	387	348	359	...	...	352
3522	Drugs and medicines ..	...	...	...	...	...	...	...	...	...	...	3522
353	Petroleum refineries ...	-	-	-	...	...	-	-	-	...	...	353
354	Petroleum,coal products. a/	...	...	...	...	...	...	...	...	...	...	354
355	Rubber products	9	8	8	...	...	794	673	558	...	...	355
356	Plastic products n.e.c..	14	13	14	...	...	400	441	356	...	...	356
361	Pottery,china etc	9	8	8	...	...	115	64	71	...	...	361
362	Glass and products	5	5	5	...	...	126	104	92	...	...	362
369	Non-metal products n.e.c	68	68	65	...	...	688	617	693	...	...	369
371	Iron and steel	-	-	-	...	...	-	-	-	...	...	371
372	Non-ferrous metals	-	-	-	...	...	-	-	-	...	...	372
381	Metal products	162	144	146	...	...	1601	1213	1239	...	...	381
382	Machinery n.e.c.	22	18	17	...	...	728	676	583	...	...	382
3825	Office,computing etc..	...	...	...	...	...	...	...	...	...	...	3825
383	Electrical machinery ...	38	37	35	...	...	1653	1926	1767	...	...	383
3832	Radio,television etc..	...	...	...	...	...	...	...	...	...	...	3832
384	Transport equipment .... b/	36	32	34	...	...	758	557	594	...	...	384
3841	Shipbuilding, repair..	...	...	...	...	...	...	...	...	...	...	3841
3843	Motor vehicles	...	...	...	...	...	...	...	...	...	...	3843
385	Professional goods	9	9	10	...	...	1039	1123	1135	...	...	385
390	Other industries	106	95	86	...	...	850	737	718	...	...	390
3	Manufacturing ..... b/	1728	1558	1473	...	...	29592	26436	25182	...	...	3
410	Electricity,gas,steam ..	...	...	...	...	...	...	...	...	...	...	410
4101	Electricity	...	...	...	...	...	...	...	...	...	...	4101
420	Water works and supply .	...	...	...	...	...	...	...	...	...	...	420
4	Electricity,gas etc	...	...	...	...	...	...	...	...	...	...	4
2-4	All industry	...	...	...	...	...	...	...	...	...	...	2-4

a/ Major group 354 is included in 352.

b/ Excluding data for the Malta Drydocks.

ISIC	INDUSTRY	3. AVERAGE NUMBER OF EMPLOYEES (NUMBER) 1981	1982	1983	1984	1985	4. WAGES AND SALARIES OF EMPLOYEES a/ (THOUSAND POUNDS) 1981	1982	1983	1984	1985	ISIC
210	Coal mining	-	-	-	...	...	-	-	-	...	...	210
220	Petroleum and gas	-	-	-	...	...	-	-	-	...	...	220
230	Metal ore mining	-	-	-	...	...	-	-	-	...	...	230
290	Other mining	279	357	259	...	...	444	474	483	...	...	290
2	Mining, quarrying	279	357	259	...	...	444	474	483	...	...	2
311/2	Food products	1677	1640	1662	...	...	3158	3650	3776	...	...	311/2
313	Beverages	1188	1138	1136	...	...	3123	3423	3418	...	...	313
314	Tobacco	831	761	692	...	...	1862	1889	1791	...	...	314
321	Textiles	1963	1536	1189	...	...	3848	3315	2531	...	...	321
3211	Spinning, weaving etc.	...	...	...	...	...	...	...	...	...	...	3211
322	Wearing apparel	8539	7085	7115	...	...	17041	18247	16833	...	...	322
323	Leather and products	259	185	89	...	...	584	392	163	...	...	323
324	Footwear	1064	1094	1110	...	...	1773	2222	2264	...	...	324
331	Wood products	207	177	187	...	...	323	307	352	...	...	331
332	Furniture, fixtures	1773	1603	1328	...	...	3260	3603	3030	...	...	332
341	Paper and products	222	215	215	...	...	446	486	506	...	...	341
3411	Pulp, paper etc.	...	...	...	...	...	...	...	...	...	...	3411
342	Printing, publishing	1387	1360	1240	...	...	3302	3501	3478	...	...	342
351	Industrial chemicals	94	86	85	...	...	191	204	213	...	...	351
3511	Basic excl fertilizers	...	...	...	...	...	...	...	...	...	...	3511
3513	Synthetic resins etc	...	...	...	...	...	...	...	...	...	...	3513
352	Other chemical products. b/	354	322	346	...	...	907	859	957	...	...	352
3522	Drugs and medicines	...	...	...	...	...	...	...	...	...	...	3522
353	Petroleum refineries	-	-	-	...	...	-	-	-	...	...	353
354	Petroleum, coal products. b/	...	...	...	...	...	...	...	...	...	...	354
355	Rubber products	785	663	548	...	...	2432	2021	2001	...	...	355
356	Plastic products n.e.c.	400	440	355	...	...	796	1001	839	...	...	356
361	Pottery, china etc	108	55	65	...	...	156	137	111	...	...	361
362	Glass and products	124	103	91	...	...	266	270	237	...	...	362
369	Non-metal products n.e.c	615	593	633	...	...	984	1069	1377	...	...	369
371	Iron and steel	-	-	-	...	...	-	-	-	...	...	371
372	Non-ferrous metals	-	-	-	...	...	-	-	-	...	...	372
381	Metal products	1441	1085	1114	...	...	2989	2927	2950	...	...	381
382	Machinery n.e.c.	714	665	574	...	...	1406	1557	1447	...	...	382
3825	Office, computing etc.	...	...	...	...	...	...	...	...	...	...	3825
383	Electrical machinery	1629	1917	1758	...	...	3530	4310	4356	...	...	383
3832	Radio, television etc.	...	...	...	...	...	...	...	...	...	...	3832
384	Transport equipment .... c/	724	528	571	...	...	1820	1393	1313	...	...	384
3841	Shipbuilding, repair	...	...	...	...	...	...	...	...	...	...	3841
3843	Motor vehicles	...	...	...	...	...	...	...	...	...	...	3843
385	Professional goods	1037	1121	1133	...	...	2251	2652	2830	...	...	385
390	Other industries	744	657	646	...	...	1321	1413	1463	...	...	390
3	Manufacturing ..... c/	27879	25029	23882	...	...	57769	60848	58236	...	...	3
410	Electricity, gas, steam	...	...	...	...	...	...	...	...	...	...	410
4101	Electricity	...	...	...	...	...	...	...	...	...	...	4101
420	Water works and supply	...	...	...	...	...	...	...	...	...	...	420
4	Electricity, gas etc	...	...	...	...	...	...	...	...	...	...	4
2-4	All industry	...	...	...	...	...	...	...	...	...	...	2-4

a/ Excluding payments in kind and employees' contributions to national insurance schemes. Employers' payments to these schemes are included.
b/ Major group 354 is included in 352.
c/ Excluding data for the Malta Drydocks.

ISIC	INDUSTRY	5. AVERAGE NUMBER OF OPERATIVES (NUMBER) 1981	1982	1983	1984	1985	6. WAGES AND SALARIES OF OPERATIVES a/ (THOUSAND POUNDS) 1981	1982	1983	1984	1985	ISIC
210	Coal mining	-	-	-	...	...	-	-	-	...	...	210
220	Petroleum and gas	-	-	-	...	...	-	-	-	...	...	220
230	Metal ore mining	-	-	-	...	...	-	-	-	...	...	230
290	Other mining	257	342	240	...	...	373	391	394	...	...	290
2	Mining, quarrying .	257	342	240	...	...	373	391	394	...	...	2
311/2	Food products	1357	1300	1321	...	...	2181	2565	2600	...	...	311/2
313	Beverages	888	846	838	...	...	2088	2295	2207	...	...	313
314	Tobacco	706	652	563	...	...	1499	1543	1203	...	...	314
321	Textiles	1752	1347	1035	...	...	2949	2566	1947	...	...	321
3211	Spinning,weaving etc..	...	...	...	...	...	...	...	...	...	...	3211
322	Wearing apparel	7636	6214	6393	...	...	12978	14037	13147	...	...	322
323	Leather and products ...	230	166	83	...	...	460	293	136	...	...	323
324	Footwear	973	976	1001	...	...	1482	1780	1852	...	...	324
331	Wood products	178	159	166	...	...	254	239	282	...	...	331
332	Furniture, fixtures	1519	1358	1116	...	...	2419	2690	2226	...	...	332
341	Paper and products	166	168	128	...	...	274	299	298	...	...	341
3411	Pulp,paper etc.	...	...	...	...	...	...	...	...	...	...	3411
342	Printing,publishing	1000	924	812	...	...	2010	2127	2102	...	...	342
351	Industrial chemicals ...	65	58	55	...	...	107	116	114	...	...	351
3511	Basic excl fertilizers	...	...	...	...	...	...	...	...	...	...	3511
3513	Synthetic resins etc .	...	...	...	...	...	...	...	...	...	...	3513
352	Other chemical products. b/	258	228	245	...	...	534	487	566	...	...	352
3522	Drugs and medicines ..	...	...	...	...	...	...	...	...	...	...	3522
353	Petroleum refineries ...	-	-	-	...	...	-	-	-	...	...	353
354	Petroleum,coal products. b/	...	...	...	...	...	...	...	...	...	...	354
355	Rubber products	553	498	400	...	...	1808	1565	1568	...	...	355
356	Plastic products n.e.c..	317	336	261	...	...	520	676	546	...	...	356
361	Pottery,china etc	88	43	52	...	...	116	106	78	...	...	361
362	Glass and products	96	74	67	...	...	180	170	150	...	...	362
369	Non-metal products n.e.c	539	475	528	...	...	749	780	1039	...	...	369
371	Iron and steel	-	-	-	...	...	-	-	-	...	...	371
372	Non-ferrous metals	-	-	-	...	...	-	-	-	...	...	372
381	Metal products	1209	881	888	...	...	2142	2061	2045	...	...	381
382	Machinery n.e.c.	624	586	473	...	...	1136	1259	1066	...	...	382
3825	Office,computing etc..	...	...	...	...	...	...	...	...	...	...	3825
383	Electrical machinery ...	1268	1483	1317	...	...	2280	2989	2716	...	...	383
3832	Radio,television etc..	...	...	...	...	...	...	...	...	...	...	3832
384	Transport equipment .... c/	591	391	430	...	...	1423	950	863	...	...	384
3841	Shipbuilding, repair..	...	...	...	...	...	...	...	...	...	...	3841
3843	Motor vehicles	...	...	...	...	...	...	...	...	...	...	3843
385	Professional goods	934	996	1010	...	...	1884	2159	2365	...	...	385
390	Other industries	591	534	522	...	...	982	1019	1028	...	...	390
3	Manufacturing ..... c/	23538	20693	19704	...	...	42455	44771	42144	...	...	3
410	Electricity,gas,steam ..	...	...	...	...	...	...	...	...	...	...	410
4101	Electricity	...	...	...	...	...	...	...	...	...	...	4101
420	Water works and supply .	...	...	...	...	...	...	...	...	...	...	420
4	Electricity,gas etc	...	...	...	...	...	...	...	...	...	...	4
2-4	All industry	...	...	...	...	...	...	...	...	...	...	2-4

a/ Excluding payments in kind and employees' contributions to national insurance schemes.
b/ Major group 354 is included in 352.
c/ Excluding data for the Malta Drydocks.

ISIC	INDUSTRY	7. OUTPUT IN PRODUCERS' PRICES (THOUSAND POUNDS) 1981	1982	1983	1984	1985	8. VALUE ADDED IN FACTOR VALUES (THOUSAND POUNDS) 1981	1982	1983	1984	1985	ISIC
210	Coal mining	-	-	-	...	...	-	-	-	...	...	210
220	Petroleum and gas	-	-	-	...	...	-	-	-	...	...	220
230	Metal ore mining	-	-	-	...	...	-	-	-	...	...	230
290	Other mining	1809	1855	1702	...	...	1088	1038	971	...	...	290
2	Mining, quarrying .	1809	1855	1702	...	...	1088	1038	971	...	...	2
311/2	Food products	27792	33542	35760	...	...	7449	9174	9456	...	...	311/2
313	Beverages	16827	16798	16878	...	...	9147	9426	8970	...	...	313
314	Tobacco	14985	15456	15589	...	...	2986	3482	3006	...	...	314
321	Textiles	10026	8408	7383	...	...	5120	4390	4144	...	...	321
3211	Spinning,weaving etc..	...	...	...	...	...	...	...	...	...	...	3211
322	Wearing apparel	66941	63513	56156	...	...	28986	29162	26684	...	...	322
323	Leather and products ...	2498	1277	469	...	...	1087	704	345	...	...	323
324	Footwear	8045	8127	8261	...	...	2988	3198	4020	...	...	324
331	Wood products	1577	1262	1481	...	...	740	642	664	...	...	331
332	Furniture, fixtures	9431	9944	8243	...	...	5134	5824	5075	...	...	332
341	Paper and products	2284	2340	2769	...	...	886	842	1034	...	...	341
3411	Pulp,paper etc.	...	...	...	...	...	...	...	...	...	...	3411
342	Printing,publishing	12938	11535	11359	...	...	7371	6288	6348	...	...	342
351	Industrial chemicals ...	878	866	1065	...	...	501	552	715	...	...	351
3511	Basic excl fertilizers	...	...	...	...	...	...	...	...	...	...	3511
3513	Synthetic resins etc .	...	...	...	...	...	...	...	...	...	...	3513
352	Other chemical products. a/	5562	5368	6492	...	...	2193	1880	2280	...	...	352
3522	Drugs and medicines ..	...	...	...	...	...	...	...	...	...	...	3522
353	Petroleum refineries ...	-	-	-	...	...	-	-	-	...	...	353
354	Petroleum,coal products. a/	...	...	...	...	...	...	...	...	...	...	354
355	Rubber products	4779	4458	5022	...	...	2643	2618	2826	...	...	355
356	Plastic products n.e.c..	3406	2993	2755	...	...	1854	1511	1585	...	...	356
361	Pottery,china etc	303	385	197	...	...	210	226	140	...	...	361
362	Glass and products	974	848	625	...	...	448	452	357	...	...	362
369	Non-metal products n.e.c	6548	9806	11019	...	...	2477	2981	3783	...	...	369
371	Iron and steel	-	-	-	...	...	-	-	-	...	...	371
372	Non-ferrous metals	-	-	-	...	...	-	-	-	...	...	372
381	Metal products	14068	13005	11228	...	...	5987	5319	4673	...	...	381
382	Machinery n.e.c.	2893	3052	3425	...	...	1974	2291	2687	...	...	382
3825	Office,computing etc..	...	...	...	...	...	...	...	...	...	...	3825
383	Electrical machinery ...	19157	23370	26026	...	...	7328	12003	11566	...	...	383
3832	Radio,television etc..	...	...	...	...	...	...	...	...	...	...	3832
384	Transport equipment .... b/	7227	4521	4679	...	...	3434	1999	2141	...	...	384
3841	Shipbuilding, repair..	...	...	...	...	...	...	...	...	...	...	3841
3843	Motor vehicles	...	...	...	...	...	...	...	...	...	...	3843
385	Professional goods	8715	11172	12615	...	...	4383	5410	5724	...	...	385
390	Other industries	4306	4925	5533	...	...	2178	2327	2216	...	...	390
3	Manufacturing ..... b/	252160	256971	255029	...	...	107504	112701	110439	...	...	3
410	Electricity,gas,steam ..	...	...	...	...	...	...	...	...	...	...	410
4101	Electricity	...	...	...	...	...	...	...	...	...	...	4101
420	Water works and supply .	...	...	...	...	...	...	...	...	...	...	420
4	Electricity,gas etc	...	...	...	...	...	...	...	...	...	...	4
2-4	All industry	...	...	...	...	...	...	...	...	...	...	2-4

a/ Major group 354 is included in 352.

b/ Excluding data for the Malta Drydocks.

9. GROSS FIXED CAPITAL FORMATION
TOTAL
(THOUSAND POUNDS)

ISIC	INDUSTRY	1981	1982	1983	1984	1985	ISIC
210	Coal mining	-	-	-	...	...	210
220	Petroleum and gas	-	-	-	...	...	220
230	Metal ore mining	-	-	-	...	...	230
290	Other mining	97	155	73	...	...	290
2	Mining, quarrying .	97	155	73	...	...	2
311/2	Food products	1395	1180	1056	...	...	311/2
313	Beverages	585	735	479	...	...	313
314	Tobacco	759	398	222	...	...	314
321	Textiles	363	338	147	...	...	321
3211	Spinning,weaving etc..	...	...	...	...	...	3211
322	Wearing apparel	1212	1686	767	...	...	322
323	Leather and products ...	25	22	1	...	...	323
324	Footwear	90	106	71	...	...	324
331	Wood products	34	34	26	...	...	331
332	Furniture, fixtures	329	284	183	...	...	332
341	Paper and products	86	25	39	...	...	341
3411	Pulp,paper etc.	...	...	...	...	...	3411
342	Printing,publishing	311	437	276	...	...	342
351	Industrial chemicals ...	148	110	41	...	...	351
3511	Basic excl fertilizers	...	...	...	...	...	3511
3513	Synthetic resins etc .	...	...	...	...	...	3513
352	Other chemical products. a/	435	174	191	...	...	352
3522	Drugs and medicines ..	...	...	...	...	...	3522
353	Petroleum refineries ...	-	-	-	...	...	353
354	Petroleum,coal products. a/	...	...	...	...	...	354
355	Rubber products	181	46	16	...	...	355
356	Plastic products n.e.c..	90	105	156	...	...	356
361	Pottery,china etc	34	3	10	...	...	361
362	Glass and products	28	9	10	...	...	362
369	Non-metal products n.e.c	410	418	227	...	...	369
371	Iron and steel	-	-	-	...	...	371
372	Non-ferrous metals	-	-	-	...	...	372
381	Metal products	271	467	2813	...	...	381
382	Machinery n.e.c.	148	88	108	...	...	382
3825	Office,computing etc..	...	...	...	...	...	3825
383	Electrical machinery ...	1201	2257	2905	...	...	383
3832	Radio,television etc..	...	...	...	...	...	3832
384	Transport equipment .... b/	66	26	71	...	...	384
3841	Shipbuilding, repair..	...	...	...	...	...	3841
3843	Motor vehicles	...	...	...	...	...	3843
385	Professional goods	437	546	265	...	...	385
390	Other industries	143	82	53	...	...	390
3	Manufacturing ..... b/	8781	9576	10133	...	...	3
410	Electricity,gas,steam ..	...	...	...	...	...	410
4101	Electricity	...	...	...	...	...	4101
420	Water works and supply .	...	...	...	...	...	420
4	Electricity,gas etc	...	...	...	...	...	4
2-4	All industry	...	...	...	...	...	2-4

a/ Major group 354 is included in 352.

b/ Excluding data for the Malta Drydocks.

10. INDEX NUMBERS OF INDUSTRIAL PRODUCTION (1980 = 100)

ISIC	INDUSTRY	1976	1977	1978	1979	1981	1982	1983	1984	1985	RATE a/	ISIC
210	Coal mining	...	...	...	...	...	...	...	...	...	...	210
220	Petroleum and gas	...	...	...	...	...	...	...	...	...	...	220
230	Metal ore mining	...	...	...	...	...	...	...	...	...	...	230
290	Other mining	113	109	83	107	113	113	104	86	...	-3.4	290
2	Mining, quarrying	113	109	83	107	113	113	104	...	...	c/ -1.2	2
311/2	Food products	99	100	102	102	111	147	155	177	...	7.5	311/2
313	Beverages	82	92	88	99	130	124	129	123	...	5.2	313
314	Tobacco	82	92	93	98	109	107	108	109	...	3.6	314
321	Textiles	132	107	99	108	94	83	75	...	...	c/ -7.8	321
3211	Spinning,weaving etc.	...	...	...	...	...	...	...	...	...	...	3211
322	Wearing apparel	63	85	84	87	82	78	68	73	...	1.9	322
323	Leather and products	66	87	90	99	91	50	22	25	...	-11.4	323
324	Footwear	26	48	75	80	102	102	103	113	...	20.2	324
331	Wood products	107	101	104	101	109	89	116	91	...	-2.0	331
332	Furniture, fixtures	67	81	94	98	111	116	96	97	...	4.7	332
341	Paper and products	19	28	47	65	87	79	90	123	...	26.3	341
3411	Pulp,paper etc.	...	...	...	...	...	...	...	...	...	...	3411
342	Printing,publishing	43	59	69	61	107	92	96	119	...	13.6	342
351	Industrial chemicals	55	57	68	75	101	97	95	108	...	8.8	351
3511	Basic excl fertilizers	...	...	...	...	...	...	...	...	...	...	3511
3513	Synthetic resins etc	...	...	...	...	...	...	...	...	...	...	3513
352	Other chemical products	37	40	48	92	106	123	155	161	...	20.2	352
3522	Drugs and medicines	...	...	...	...	...	...	...	...	...	...	3522
353	Petroleum refineries	...	...	...	...	...	...	...	...	...	...	353
354	Petroleum,coal products	...	...	...	...	...	...	...	...	...	...	354
355	Rubber products	68	90	88	104	82	69	71	83	...	2.5	355
356	Plastic products n.e.c.	55	78	77	86	83	72	66	69	...	2.9	356
361	Pottery,china etc	[									]	361
362	Glass and products	60	68	67	76	96	121	107	143	...	11.5	362
369	Non-metal products n.e.c	[									]	369
371	Iron and steel	...	...	...	...	...	...	...	...	...	...	371
372	Non-ferrous metals	...	...	...	...	...	...	...	...	...	...	372
381	Metal products	37	41	44	46	113	120	102	105	...	13.9	381
382	Machinery n.e.c.	33	37	51	69	83	82	100	105	...	15.6	382
3825	Office,computing etc.	...	...	...	...	...	...	...	...	...	...	3825
383	Electrical machinery	65	87	81	75	80	89	115	149	...	10.9	383
3832	Radio,television etc.	...	...	...	...	...	...	...	...	...	...	3832
384	Transport equipment	84	95	98	99	110	100	96	...	...	c/ 1.9	384
3841	Shipbuilding, repair	...	...	...	...	...	...	...	...	...	...	3841
3843	Motor vehicles	...	...	...	...	...	...	...	...	...	...	3843
385	Professional goods	7	13	41	42	109	152	167	172	...	49.2	385
390	Other industries	53	57	71	94	83	82	122	...	...	c/ 12.6	390
3	Manufacturing	62	78	83	83	101	103	104	...	...	c/ 7.7	3
410	Electricity,gas,steam	...	...	...	...	...	...	...	...	...	...	410
4101	Electricity	71	80	86	92	106	116	127	125	...	7.3	4101
420	Water works and supply	58	63	75	86	97	98	98	118	...	9.3	420
4	Electricity,gas etc b/	70	79	85	92	105	114	125	...	...	c/ 8.6	4
2-4	All industry b/	64	75	79	84	102	107	110	...	...	c/ 8.0	2-4

a/ Annual growth rate 1976-1984.
c/ Annual growth rate 1976-1983.
b/ Excluding gas and steam.

MAURITIUS

The information in the tables is based on the reply to the United Nations Questionnaire on General Industrial Statistics from the Central Statistical Office, Rose Hill. The concepts, definitions and classification by branches of industry are generally in accordance with United Nations standards.

The data in the tables are derived from the census of industrial production taken annually by the Central Statistical Office, covering mining, quarrying, manufacturing and the production and distribution of electricity. The data cover establishments with 10 or more employees only. Government and semi-government establishments are excluded.

The data are compiled according to the national classification, which follows the preceding version of ISIC, but are arranged to represent the present version as far as details permit. Repair services for the general public (ISIC major division 9), except the repair of motor vehicles, are included in manufacturing according to the type of product repaired.

The reference period is basically the calendar year. However, the estimates in the tables may include those for the accounting year of establishments covered.

Wages and salaries include contributions payable by the employer to insurance and pension schemes. For sugar factories, wages and salaries cover those attributable directly to the manufacturing operation as far as the apportionment of expenses between the plantation and the factory is possible.

Output is defined as the total value of sales and work done for others during the year, adjusted for changes in stocks of finished goods and work in progress. Value added is defined as the difference between output and the cost of materials, electricity and industrial services rendered. Valuation of output and value added is, as a general rule, in producers' prices. However, excise duties are excluded in the case of wine, beer and matches.

Related national publication:
<u>The Census of Industrial Production</u> (infrequent), published by the Central Statistical Office, Rose Hill.

ISIC	INDUSTRY	1. NUMBER OF ESTABLISHMENTS a/ (NUMBER)					2. AVERAGE NUMBER OF PERSONS ENGAGED a/ (NUMBER)					ISIC
		1981	1982	1983	1984	1985	1981	1982	1983	1984	1985	
210	Coal mining	...	...	...	...	...	...	...	...	...	...	210
220	Petroleum and gas	...	...	...	...	...	...	...	...	...	...	220
230	Metal ore mining	...	...	...	...	...	...	...	...	...	...	230
290	Other mining	...	...	...	...	...	...	...	...	...	...	290
2	Mining, quarrying .	...	...	...	...	...	...	...	...	...	...	2
311/2	Food products	162	174	180	184	191	9871	10220	10159	10164	...	311/2
313	Beverages	14	12	12	12	12	1877	1745	1683	1779	...	313
314	Tobacco	1	1	1	1	1	398	388	366	361	...	314
321	Textiles	13	17	14	18	20	2156	2382	1848	2064	...	321
3211	Spinning,weaving etc..	...	...	...	...	...	...	...	...	...	...	3211
322	Wearing apparel	99	109	117	141	207	18718	19395	21324	29186	...	322
323	Leather and products ...	5	5	6	6	6	273	324	374	334	...	323
324	Footwear	9	9	11	12	14	442	420	512	523	...	324
331	Wood products	7	6	7	8	9	443	449	549	610	...	331
332	Furniture, fixtures	17	17	22	20	22	585	621	659	638	...	332
341	Paper and products	3	3	5	6	6	199	231	377	937	...	341
3411	Pulp,paper etc.	...	...	...	...	...	...	...	...	...	...	3411
342	Printing,publishing	41	29	26	23	27	1191	1184	1149	1083	...	342
351	Industrial chemicals ...	4	4	5	5	5	386	386	365	412	...	351
3511	Basic excl fertilizers	...	...	...	...	...	...	...	...	...	...	3511
3513	Synthetic resins etc .	...	...	...	...	...	...	...	...	...	...	3513
352	Other chemical products.	16	16	19	17	19	768	745	708	588	...	352
3522	Drugs and medicines ..	...	...	...	...	...	...	...	...	...	...	3522
353	Petroleum refineries ...	-	-	-	-	-	-	-	-	-	...	353
354	Petroleum,coal products.	-	-	-	-	-	-	-	-	-	...	354
355	Rubber products	9	8	9	10	10	275	255	253	291	...	355
356	Plastic products n.e.c..	11	13	18	18	21	414	435	506	465	...	356
361	Pottery,china etc	1	1	1	1	1	...	13	14	10	...	361
362	Glass and products	1	1	1	1	1	21	30	41	43	...	362
369	Non-metal products n.e.c	27	28	26	27	30	1103	1137	1021	998	...	369
371	Iron and steel										...	371
372	Non-ferrous metals	36	33	32	33	37	1244	1088	1064	1078	...	372
381	Metal products										...	381
382	Machinery n.e.c.	10	11	8	10	10	692	686	601	623	...	382
3825	Office,computing etc..	...	...	...	...	...	...	...	...	...	...	3825
383	Electrical machinery ...	10	11	17	14	15	356	416	536	460	...	383
3832	Radio,television etc..	...	...	...	...	...	...	...	...	...	...	3832
384	Transport equipment	5	7	8	7	7	615	351	344	316	...	384
3841	Shipbuilding, repair..	1	1	1	1	1	330	113	98	100	...	3841
3843	Motor vehicles	4	6	7	6	6	285	238	246	216	...	3843
385	Professional goods	9	9	12	9	9	499	541	734	589	...	385
390	Other industries	19	24	26	30	31	1263	1497	1612	1942	...	390
3	Manufacturing ..... b/	529	548	583	613	711	c/ 43789	44939	46799	55494	...	3
410	Electricity,gas,steam ..	...	...	...	...	...	...	...	...	...	...	410
4101	Electricity	1	1	1	1	...	1864	1821	1807	1755	...	4101
420	Water works and supply .	...	...	...	...	...	...	...	...	...	...	420
4	Electricity,gas etc	...	...	...	...	...	...	...	...	...	...	4
2-4	All industry	...	...	...	...	...	...	...	...	...	...	2-4

a/ Privately-owned establishments with 10 or more employees. b/ Including repair services except repair of motor vehicles.
c/ Excluding major group 361.

ISIC	INDUSTRY	3. WAGES AND SALARIES OF EMPLOYEES a/c/ (THOUSAND RUPEES)					4. OUTPUT IN PRODUCERS' PRICES b/c/ (MILLION RUPEES)					ISIC
		1981	1982	1983	1984	1985	1981	1982	1983	1984	1985	
210	Coal mining	...	...	...	...	...	...	...	...	...	...	210
220	Petroleum and gas	...	...	...	...	...	...	...	...	...	...	220
230	Metal ore mining	...	...	...	...	...	...	...	...	...	...	230
290	Other mining	...	...	...	...	...	...	...	...	...	...	290
2	Mining, quarrying .	...	...	...	...	...	...	...	...	...	...	2
311/2	Food products	223302	245947	257219	272600	...	3048	3622	3690	4174	...	311/2
313	Beverages	36481	35019	41889	42941	...	384	392	409	432	...	313
314	Tobacco	14571	15789	16313	17368	...	158	207	219	222	...	314
321	Textiles	28666	30948	28315	32612	...	318	361	333	384	...	321
3211	Spinning,weaving etc..	...	...	...	...	...	...	...	...	...	...	3211
322	Wearing apparel	146272	165923	205682	332428	...	866	927	1083	1906	...	322
323	Leather and products ...	4152	4883	5584	7920	...	23	31	32	47	...	323
324	Footwear	6454	7022	8489	8100	...	38	45	52	53	...	324
331	Wood products	6157	6903	7368	9187	...	24	24	30	37	...	331
332	Furniture, fixtures	9531	10086	10574	10495	...	38	45	49	48	...	332
341	Paper and products	3197	4341	6278	9429	...	29	34	57	77	...	341
3411	Pulp,paper etc.	...	...	...	...	...	...	...	...	...	...	3411
342	Printing,publishing	24500	27729	29266	29209	...	95	99	102	90	...	342
351	Industrial chemicals ...	9673	10702	11405	12694	...	d/ 271	d/ 310	d/ 334	d/ 356	...	351
3511	Basic excl fertilizers	...	...	...	...	...	...	...	...	...	...	3511
3513	Synthetic resins etc .	...	...	...	...	...	...	...	...	...	...	3513
352	Other chemical products.	13656	15259	15370	16245	...	d/	d/	d/	d/	...	352
3522	Drugs and medicines ..	...	...	...	...	...	...	...	...	...	...	3522
353	Petroleum refineries ...	-	-	-	-	...	-	-	-	-	...	353
354	Petroleum,coal products.	-	-	-	-	...	-	-	-	-	...	354
355	Rubber products	4274	4266	4811	5359	...	31	33	40	48	...	355
356	Plastic products n.e.c..	5668	6441	8002	8389	...	29	39	51	67	...	356
361	Pottery,china etc	21	231	219	129	...	-	-	-	1	...	361
362	Glass and products	251	655	1040	1075	...	2	4	4	5	...	362
369	Non-metal products n.e.c	16331	18070	18158	18988	...	142	137	127	147	...	369
371	Iron and steel	[19606	16243	13686	13756]	...					...	371
372	Non-ferrous metals					...	[228	175	190	210]	...	372
381	Metal products	8178	8319	9764	9738	...					...	381
382	Machinery n.e.c.	20008	17715	17112	18764	...	76	49	43	59	...	382
3825	Office,computing etc..	...	...	...	...	...	...	...	...	...	...	3825
383	Electrical machinery ...	6273	7936	10752	10102	...	39	57	89	79	...	383
3832	Radio,television etc..	...	...	...	...	...	...	...	...	...	...	3832
384	Transport equipment	7114	6507	7207	8032	...	44	26	36	37	...	384
3841	Shipbuilding, repair..	3814	3000	3445	4622	...	12	13	20	21	...	3841
3843	Motor vehicles	3300	3507	3762	3410	...	32	13	16	16	...	3843
385	Professional goods	6358	7379	9555	9459	...	52	66	104	138	...	385
390	Other industries	14263	15812	21592	32245	...	89	125	155	224	...	390
3	Manufacturing ..... e/	634957	690125	765650	937264	...	6024	6808	7229	8841	...	3
410	Electricity,gas,steam ..	...	...	...	...	...	...	...	...	...	...	410
4101	Electricity	...	...	...	...	...	...	...	...	...	...	4101
420	Water works and supply .	...	...	...	...	...	...	...	...	...	...	420
4	Electricity,gas etc	...	...	...	...	...	...	...	...	...	...	4
2-4	All industry	...	...	...	...	...	...	...	...	...	...	2-4

a/ Including employers' contributions to social insurance and pension fund.
b/ Net of excise duties for wine, beer and matches.
c/ Privately-owned establishments with 10 or more employees.
d/ Major group 352 is included in 351.
e/ Including repair services except repair of motor vehicles.

5. VALUE ADDED IN PRODUCERS' PRICES a/b/ (MILLION RUPEES)

ISIC	INDUSTRY	1981	1982	1983	1984	1985	ISIC
210	Coal mining	...	...	...	...	...	210
220	Petroleum and gas	...	...	...	...	...	220
230	Metal ore mining	...	...	...	...	...	230
290	Other mining	...	...	...	...	...	290
2	Mining, quarrying	...	...	...	...	...	2
311/2	Food products	374	449	440	584	...	311/2
313	Beverages	74	76	69	75	...	313
314	Tobacco	15	37	54	55	...	314
321	Textiles	97	96	85	102	...	321
3211	Spinning,weaving etc.	...	...	...	...	...	3211
322	Wearing apparel	289	302	369	620	...	322
323	Leather and products	9	12	13	17	...	323
324	Footwear	20	23	27	22	...	324
331	Wood products	10	12	14	19	...	331
332	Furniture, fixtures	14	19	20	17	...	332
341	Paper and products	9	12	22	23	...	341
3411	Pulp,paper etc.	...	...	...	...	...	3411
342	Printing,publishing	47	46	48	49	...	342
351	Industrial chemicals c/	63	79	65	79	...	351
3511	Basic excl fertilizers	...	...	...	...	...	3511
3513	Synthetic resins etc	...	...	...	...	...	3513
352	Other chemical products. c/	...	...	...	...	...	352
3522	Drugs and medicines	...	...	...	...	...	3522
353	Petroleum refineries	-	-	-	-	...	353
354	Petroleum,coal products.	-	-	-	-	...	354
355	Rubber products	11	11	13	16	...	355
356	Plastic products n.e.c.	13	15	20	23	...	356
361	Pottery,china etc	-	-	-	-	...	361
362	Glass and products	-	-	-	1	...	362
369	Non-metal products n.e.c	52	52	52	52	...	369
371	Iron and steel	[			]	...	371
372	Non-ferrous metals	74	66	63	62	...	372
381	Metal products	[			]	...	381
382	Machinery n.e.c.	24	19	d/ 16	19	...	382
3825	Office,computing etc.	...	...	...	...	...	3825
383	Electrical machinery	14	23	29	23	...	383
3832	Radio,television etc.	...	...	...	...	...	3832
384	Transport equipment	16	13	16	22	...	384
3841	Shipbuilding, repair	7	8	10	17	...	3841
3843	Motor vehicles	9	5	6	5	...	3843
385	Professional goods	18	21	29	36	...	385
390	Other industries	30	43	55	84	...	390
3	Manufacturing e/	1273	1426	1519	2000	...	3
410	Electricity,gas,steam	...	...	...	...	...	410
4101	Electricity	...	...	...	...	...	4101
420	Water works and supply	...	...	...	...	...	420
4	Electricity,gas etc	...	...	...	...	...	4
2-4	All industry	...	...	...	...	...	2-4

a/ Net of excise duties for wine, beer and matches.
b/ Privately-owned establishments with 10 or more employees.
c/ Major group 352 is included in 351.
d/ Value added is less than corresponding wages and salaries due to operating losses.
e/ Including repair services except repair of motor vehicles.

MEXICO

The information in the tables, except for the indexes, is based on the reply to the United Nations Questionnaire on General Industrial Statistics from the Direccion General de Estadistica, Secretaria de Programacion y Presupuesto, Mexico, D.F.. The concepts, definitions and classification by branches of industry are generally in accordance with United Nations standards.

Information on the production of crude petroleum and natural gas is based on administrative records of the Petroleos Mexicanos (PEMEX) which is an enterprise controlling the activities in this field in Mexico and relates to all activities covering extraction, transformation and distribution of petroleum and natural gas and their derivatives. Except for output and value added, the data for manufacturing industries are derived from the industrial survey conducted monthly by the above-mentioned office covering selected manufacturing industries. The scope of the industries surveyed covers 58 industries out of 225 industrial groups of the national industrial classification.

The selected manufacturing industries covered by the monthly industrial survey are listed below.

ISIC 311/312: preparation and preserving of meat; condensed and evaporated milk and milk powder; canning of fruits and vegetables; canning of fish and shellfish; wheat mills; corn flour; tea and instant coffee; chewing gum; biscuits and pastries; yeast, baking powder, starch and similar products; vegetable oils and margarine; prepared foods for animals and fowls.
ISIC 313: malt; beer; soft drinks; carbonated water.
ISIC 314: cigarettes.
ISIC 321: spinning, weaving and finishing of cotton, artificial fibres and henequen; manufacture of yarns; manufacture of cashmere textiles, shawls and similar products; manufacture of wool.
ISIC 331: manufacture of plywood, veneer and lamina.
ISIC 341: manufacture of pulp from fibre, paper and paperboard; manufacture of articles of paperboard, including oil impregnated board.
ISIC 351: manufacture of cellulosic fibres and other artificial fibres; manufacture of fertilizers.
ISIC 3513: manufacture of cellulosic fibres and other artificial fibres.
ISIC 352: manufacture of matches and candles; soap, detergents and other cleaning compounds; paints, varnishes and lacquers; drugs and medicines.
ISIC 3522: manufacture of drugs and medicines.
ISIC 354: manufacture of coke and other coal products; regeneration of lubricating oils including additives.
ISIC 355: manufacture of tires and tubes.
ISIC 362: manufacture of sheet glass (smooth and elaborated), glass fibres and safety glass, glass containers and bulbs, other glass products including glassware and refractory crystal.
ISIC 369: manufacture of hydraulic cement, brick, fire-proof partitions, refractory mortar; manufacture of asbestos products.
ISIC 371: manufacture of iron and steel tubes and rods; founding, casting and rolling of iron and steel.
ISIC 372: founding, refining, casting, extruding and drawing of copper and its alloys; casting, extruding and drawing of aluminium and manufacture of aluminium solders.
ISIC 381: manufacture of furniture and fixtures primarily of metal; manufacture of crown caps and other cast and enamelled metal products; manufacture of containers and other products from tin-plate.
ISIC 382: manufacture and assembly of agricultural machinery and equipment; manufacture and assembly of typing, computing and accounting machinery.
ISIC 3825: manufacture and assembly of typing, computing and accounting machinery.
ISIC 383: manufacture of record-players and receiving sets of radio and television; manufacture of condensers and batteries; manufacture and assembly of electrical apparatus and parts; manufacture of other electronic equipment and apparatus.
ISIC 3832: manufacture of record-players and receiving sets of radio and television; manufacture of other electronic equipment and aparatus.
ISIC 384: industries enumerated under ISIC 3843 and manufacture of railroad equipment.
ISIC 3843: manufacture and assembly of motor vehicles, including tractors for trailers; manufacture of bodies for motor vehicles.

Employment numbers relate to monthly averages. Wages and salaries exclude payments in kind. However, wages and salaries for ISIC 220 include payments in kind, employers' contributions to social insurance schemes and profits distributed to employees.

The estimates of output and value added are derived from national accounts calculations made by the Direccion General de Estadistica. The estimates cover all establishments irrespective of size and are arranged in accordance with the present version of ISIC. The valuation of these estimates is in producers' prices.

The indexes of industrial production are compiled by the Bank of Mexico and provided in response to the United Nations Questionnaire on Indexes of Industrial Production. The indexes cover, in principle, all industrial establishments.

Related national publications:
Estadistica Industrial Anual; Estadistica Industrial Mensual, both published by the Direccion General de Estadistica, Secretaria de Programacion y Presupuesto, Mexico, D.F. Anuario Estadistico, published by the Petroleos Mexicanos (PEMEX), Mexico, D.F.

ISIC	INDUSTRY	1. NUMBER OF ESTABLISHMENTS a/ (NUMBER)					2. AVERAGE NUMBER OF EMPLOYEES a/ (THOUSANDS)					ISIC
		1981	1982	1983	1984	1985	1981	1982	1983	1984	*1985	
210	Coal mining	...	...	...	...	...	...	...	...	...	...	210
220	Petroleum and gas	1	1	1	1	1	b/ 123.00	b/ 134.00	...	...	...	220
230	Metal ore mining	...	...	...	...	...	...	...	...	...	...	230
290	Other mining	...	...	...	...	...	...	...	...	...	...	290
2	Mining, quarrying .	...	...	...	...	...	...	...	...	...	...	2
311/2	Food products	364	371	371	371	330	76.78	78.33	75.02	71.74	71.70	311/2
313	Beverages	96	96	96	96	86	72.24	74.51	70.03	67.62	72.52	313
314	Tobacco	9	9	9	9	8	5.97	6.19	5.50	5.53	6.03	314
321	Textiles	135	136	136	136	133	59.57	57.80	53.46	51.53	52.07	321
3211	Spinning,weaving etc..	109	110	110	110	107	49.25	48.07	44.62	42.78	42.81	3211
322	Wearing apparel	...	...	...	...	...	...	...	...	...	...	322
323	Leather and products ...	...	...	...	...	...	...	...	...	...	...	323
324	Footwear	...	...	...	...	...	...	...	...	...	...	324
331	Wood products	17	17	17	17	15	5.74	5.38	5.37	5.12	5.22	331
332	Furniture, fixtures	...	...	...	...	...	...	...	...	...	...	332
341	Paper and products	96	96	96	96	95	31.53	30.97	29.00	29.14	29.68	341
3411	Pulp,paper etc.	...	...	...	...	...	...	...	...	...	...	3411
342	Printing,publishing	...	...	...	...	...	...	...	...	...	...	342
351	Industrial chemicals ...	30	30	30	30	29	31.76	32.37	30.60	29.86	30.01	351
3511	Basic excl fertilizers	...	...	...	...	...	...	...	...	...	...	3511
3513	Synthetic resins etc .	15	15	15	15	14	21.81	20.35	18.23	17.63	18.01	3513
352	Other chemical products.	176	176	176	176	165	42.96	42.78	40.89	41.36	41.26	352
3522	Drugs and medicines ..	73	73	73	73	69	24.80	24.99	23.86	23.87	23.33	3522
353	Petroleum refineries ...	...	...	...	...	...	...	...	...	...	...	353
354	Petroleum,coal products.	14	14	14	14	14	5.31	5.31	5.11	4.29	5.42	354
355	Rubber products	8	8	8	8	8	11.82	12.12	11.82	11.72	12.41	355
356	Plastic products n.e.c..	...	...	...	...	...	...	...	...	...	...	356
361	Pottery,china etc	...	...	...	...	...	...	...	...	...	...	361
362	Glass and products	21	21	21	21	20	22.73	20.15	20.29	19.49	20.36	362
369	Non-metal products n.e.c	44	44	44	44	44	22.18	23.46	20.70	22.11	22.19	369
371	Iron and steel	89	90	90	90	88	68.16	65.69	63.73	64.18	62.84	371
372	Non-ferrous metals	18	18	18	18	18	17.86	17.72	16.62	17.11	18.76	372
381	Metal products	57	57	57	57	55	30.50	27.04	22.11	20.17	20.82	381
382	Machinery n.e.c.	13	13	13	13	13	6.80	6.46	5.19	5.12	5.55	382
3825	Office,computing etc..	8	8	8	8	8	3.34	3.46	2.90	3.06	3.02	3825
383	Electrical machinery ...	66	66	66	66	63	41.82	39.23	31.44	26.27	27.25	383
3832	Radio,television etc..	27	28	28	28	25	18.99	16.48	12.60	10.69	10.87	3832
384	Transport equipment	34	34	34	34	34	65.84	60.82	48.63	45.15	50.19	384
3841	Shipbuilding, repair..	...	...	...	...	...	...	...	...	...	...	3841
3843	Motor vehicles	30	30	30	30	30	60.31	53.99	43.20	40.31	44.81	3843
385	Professional goods	...	...	...	...	...	...	...	...	...	...	385
390	Other industries	...	...	...	...	...	...	...	...	...	...	390
3	Manufacturing	...	...	...	...	...	...	...	...	...	...	3
410	Electricity,gas,steam ..	...	...	...	...	...	...	...	...	...	...	410
4101	Electricity	...	...	...	...	...	...	...	...	...	...	4101
420	Water works and supply .	...	...	...	...	...	...	...	...	...	...	420
4	Electricity,gas etc	...	...	...	...	...	...	...	...	...	...	4
2-4	All industry	...	...	...	...	...	...	...	...	...	...	2-4

a/ Manufacturing: selected industries; see country note.
b/ Data relate to PEMEX activities including transformation and distribution of crude petroleum and natural gas and their derivatives.

ISIC	INDUSTRY	3. WAGES AND SALARIES OF EMPLOYEES a/b/ (MILLION PESOS)					4. AVERAGE NUMBER OF OPERATIVES b/ (THOUSANDS)					ISIC
		1981	1982	1983	1984	*1985	1981	1982	1983	1984	*1985	
210	Coal mining	...	...	...	...	...	...	...	...	...	...	210
220	Petroleum and gas ...... c/d/	43336	67877	...	...	...	...	...	...	...	...	220
230	Metal ore mining	...	...	...	...	...	...	...	...	...	...	230
290	Other mining	...	...	...	...	...	...	...	...	...	...	290
2	Mining, quarrying .	...	...	...	...	...	...	...	...	...	...	2
311/2	Food products	9807	15320	21953	34654	58624	56.22	56.92	52.14	49.98	50.48	311/2
313	Beverages	10810	17480	24044	37314	58922	50.11	53.25	50.71	48.11	51.57	313
314	Tobacco	1083	1727	2367	3798	7196	3.91	4.06	3.41	3.33	3.61	314
321	Textiles	7972	12425	17307	26230	43446	49.54	47.92	44.08	42.47	42.77	321
3211	Spinning,weaving etc..	6586	10298	14463	21526	35183	41.23	40.20	37.21	35.70	35.63	3211
322	Wearing apparel	...	...	...	...	...	...	...	...	...	...	322
323	Leather and products ...	...	...	...	...	...	...	...	...	...	...	323
324	Footwear	...	...	...	...	...	...	...	...	...	...	324
331	Wood products	674	1005	1497	2206	3507	4.51	4.21	4.23	3.90	3.99	331
332	Furniture, fixtures	...	...	...	...	...	...	...	...	...	...	332
341	Paper and products	5792	9038	12634	20880	33920	23.62	22.97	21.33	21.46	21.89	341
3411	Pulp,paper etc.	...	...	...	...	...	...	...	...	...	...	3411
342	Printing,publishing	...	...	...	...	...	...	...	...	...	...	342
351	Industrial chemicals ...	6136	9297	12315	18471	29985	25.59	25.14	23.94	23.42	23.50	351
3511	Basic excl fertilizers	...	...	...	...	...	...	...	...	...	...	3511
3513	Synthetic resins etc .	4032	5844	7517	11349	19221	16.30	15.15	13.64	13.27	13.58	3513
352	Other chemical products.	8253	12989	19951	33028	53148	22.92	22.36	21.09	21.56	21.32	352
3522	Drugs and medicines ..	5081	7833	11912	19254	30500	11.27	11.00	10.23	10.44	10.23	3522
353	Petroleum refineries ...	...	...	...	...	...	...	...	...	...	...	353
354	Petroleum,coal products.	945	1448	1907	2839	5021	3.93	3.88	3.25	3.07	4.09	354
355	Rubber products	3486	5642	8574	14244	25309	8.28	8.56	8.38	8.29	8.67	355
356	Plastic products n.e.c..	...	...	...	...	...	...	...	...	...	...	356
361	Pottery,china etc	...	...	...	...	...	...	...	...	...	...	361
362	Glass and products	4267	5947	9175	14223	24797	16.93	14.86	15.25	14.67	15.31	362
369	Non-metal products n.e.c	4862	7875	10971	18284	30971	16.18	16.94	14.55	15.95	15.71	369
371	Iron and steel	14555	21991	31688	50328	74016	52.17	50.54	48.77	48.88	47.63	371
372	Non-ferrous metals	3039	4836	6606	11046	20326	12.26	11.92	10.66	11.24	12.28	372
381	Metal products	4269	6296	7668	11043	18113	22.12	20.96	17.03	15.23	15.87	381
382	Machinery n.e.c.	1372	2034	2640	4005	7612	4.21	3.72	2.99	2.91	3.31	382
3825	Office,computing etc..	657	1125	1543	2423	4512	1.98	1.89	1.70	1.77	1.78	3825
383	Electrical machinery ...	6774	9473	11223	15710	25277	28.03	25.56	19.60	16.33	17.57	383
3832	Radio,television etc..	3149	4208	4586	6416	9440	11.67	9.49	7.03	6.12	6.64	3832
384	Transport equipment	14583	19084	20331	31539	56921	49.92	44.05	31.02	32.99	36.92	384
3841	Shipbuilding, repair..	...	...	...	...	...	...	...	...	...	...	3841
3843	Motor vehicles	13144	16871	17731	27629	51311	44.55	38.72	26.85	29.06	32.90	3843
385	Professional goods	...	...	...	...	...	...	...	...	...	...	385
390	Other industries	...	...	...	...	...	...	...	...	...	...	390
3	Manufacturing	...	...	...	...	...	...	...	...	...	...	3
410	Electricity,gas,steam ..	...	...	...	...	...	...	...	...	...	...	410
4101	Electricity	...	...	...	...	...	...	...	...	...	...	4101
420	Water works and supply .	...	...	...	...	...	...	...	...	...	...	420
4	Electricity,gas etc	...	...	...	...	...	...	...	...	...	...	4
2-4	All industry	...	...	...	...	...	...	...	...	...	...	2-4

a/ Excluding payments in kind.

b/ Manufacturing: selected industries; see country note.

c/ Major group 220: including payments in kind and other benefits; see country note.

d/ Data relate to PEMEX activities including transformation and distribution of crude petroleum and natural gas and their derivatives.

ISIC	INDUSTRY	5. WAGES AND SALARIES OF OPERATIVES a/b/ (MILLION PESOS)					6. HOURS WORKED BY OPERATIVES b/c/ (THOUSANDS)					ISIC
		1981	1982	1983	1984	*1985	1981	1982	1983	1984	*1985	
210	Coal mining	...	...	...	...	...	...	...	...	...	...	210
220	Petroleum and gas	...	...	...	...	...	...	...	...	...	...	220
230	Metal ore mining	...	...	...	...	...	...	...	...	...	...	230
290	Other mining	...	...	...	...	...	...	...	...	...	...	290
2	Mining, quarrying .	...	...	...	...	...	...	...	...	...	...	2
311/2	Food products	5508	8797	12467	19715	32867	10370	10399	9705	9587	9879	311/2
313	Beverages	6397	10971	15103	22943	36110	10286	10515	9759	9444	10114	313
314	Tobacco	498	789	981	1498	2678	711	731	619	629	637	314
321	Textiles	6033	9474	13165	19740	32640	9034	8304	7727	7373	7415	321
3211	Spinning,weaving etc..	5053	7947	11206	16581	27241	...	...	...	6149	6219	3211
322	Wearing apparel	...	...	...	...	...	...	...	...	...	...	322
323	Leather and products ...	...	...	...	...	...	...	...	...	...	...	323
324	Footwear	...	...	...	...	...	...	...	...	...	...	324
331	Wood products	447	663	999	1443	2314	928	815	853	787	785	331
332	Furniture, fixtures	...	...	...	...	...	...	...	...	...	...	332
341	Paper and products	3517	5697	7896	12813	21059	4997	4795	4437	4525	4656	341
3411	Pulp,paper etc.	...	...	...	...	...	...	...	...	...	...	3411
342	Printing,publishing	...	...	...	...	...	...	...	...	...	...	342
351	Industrial chemicals ...	3909	6088	8111	11931	19157	4814	4675	4429	4546	4628	351
3511	Basic excl fertilizers	...	...	...	...	...	...	...	...	...	...	3511
3513	Synthetic resins etc .	2404	3601	4725	7048	11709	3178	2915	2518	2643	2801	3513
352	Other chemical products.	2856	4711	7008	11405	18030	3943	4077	3834	3884	3975	352
3522	Drugs and medicines ..	1363	2179	3130	4911	7753	1867	2000	1848	1862	1903	3522
353	Petroleum refineries ...	...	...	...	...	...	...	...	...	...	...	353
354	Petroleum,coal products.	585	892	1170	1647	2914	802	743	628	590	789	354
355	Rubber products	2264	3688	5359	9462	17186	1214	1379	1265	1358	1463	355
356	Plastic products n.e.c..	...	...	...	...	...	...	...	...	...	...	356
361	Pottery,china etc	...	...	...	...	...	...	...	...	...	...	361
362	Glass and products	2346	3249	5127	7784	12664	3680	3068	3228	3111	3294	362
369	Non-metal products n.e.c	2868	4710	6446	10915	18222	3420	3484	2920	3106	3158	369
371	Iron and steel	9724	14558	21063	33323	46370	10184	9865	9589	9562	9013	371
372	Non-ferrous metals	1616	2587	3295	5594	10363	2408	2326	2094	2246	2438	372
381	Metal products	2815	4190	4998	6922	11416	4270	3953	3113	2878	2920	381
382	Machinery n.e.c.	625	874	1165	1721	3041	741	606	522	536	612	382
3825	Office,computing etc..	283	466	687	1108	1722	349	326	310	332	332	3825
383	Electrical machinery ...	3436	4742	5371	7491	12639	4936	4391	3543	2896	3037	383
3832	Radio,television etc..	1302	1691	1781	2653	4348	1931	1644	1269	1095	1142	3832
384	Transport equipment	9322	11955	11482	18382	33726	8747	7256	5051	5803	6762	384
3841	Shipbuilding, repair..	...	...	...	...	...	...	...	...	...	...	3841
3843	Motor vehicles	8203	10255	9538	15560	29730	8866	6366	322	5168	6113	3843
385	Professional goods	...	...	...	...	...	...	...	...	...	...	385
390	Other industries	...	...	...	...	...	...	...	...	...	...	390
3	Manufacturing	...	...	...	...	...	...	...	...	...	...	3
410	Electricity,gas,steam ..	...	...	...	...	...	...	...	...	...	...	410
4101	Electricity	...	...	...	...	...	...	...	...	...	...	4101
420	Water works and supply .	...	...	...	...	...	...	...	...	...	...	420
4	Electricity,gas etc	...	...	...	...	...	...	...	...	...	...	4
2-4	All industry	...	...	...	...	...	...	...	...	...	...	2-4

a/ Excluding payments in kind.
b/ Manufacturing: selected industries; see country note.
c/ Monthly average for persons engaged.

ISIC	INDUSTRY	7. QUANTITY OF ELECTRICITY CONSUMED a/ (MILLION KWH)					8. OUTPUT b/c/d/ (BILLION PESOS)					ISIC
		1981	1982	1983	1984	1985	1981	1982	1983	1984	1985	
210	Coal mining	...	...	...	...	...	4	6	16	33	...	210
220	Petroleum and gas	...	...	...	...	...	374	965	2132	3068	...	220
230	Metal ore mining	...	...	...	...	...	54	90	236	314	...	230
290	Other mining	...	...	...	...	...	37	60	96	159	...	290
2	Mining, quarrying .	...	...	...	...	...	469	1121	2480	3574	...	2
311/2	Food products	1039	959	960	...	...	686	1076	2020	3586	...	311/2
313	Beverages	558	597	589	...	...	158	248	435	759	...	313
314	Tobacco	29	31	29	...	...	27	43	80	145	...	314
321	Textiles	705	664	832	...	...	204	286	604	994	...	321
3211	Spinning,weaving etc..	...	...	...	...	...	137	195	408	678	...	3211
322	Wearing apparel	...	...	...	...	...	85	130	245	370	...	322
323	Leather and products ...	...	...	...	...	...	24	39	72	137	...	323
324	Footwear	...	...	...	...	...	51	78	125	205	...	324
331	Wood products	56	71	72	...	...	60	85	147	279	...	331
332	Furniture, fixtures	...	...	...	...	...	49	74	109	151	...	332
341	Paper and products	1673	2000	1914	...	...	83	122	250	424	...	341
3411	Pulp,paper etc.	...	...	...	...	...	54	79	162	288	...	3411
342	Printing,publishing	...	...	...	...	...	65	105	169	348	...	342
351	Industrial chemicals ...	1846	1366	1435	...	...	162	268	650	1164	...	351
3511	Basic excl fertilizers	...	...	...	...	...	82	138	333	621	...	3511
3513	Synthetic resins etc .	875	836	832	...	...	54	88	226	390	...	3513
352	Other chemical products.	268	276	301	...	...	156	248	514	880	...	352
3522	Drugs and medicines ..	115	131	123	...	...	52	76	148	246	...	3522
353	Petroleum refineries ...	...	...	...	...	...	103	159	618	1051	...	353
354	Petroleum,coal products.	159	170	163	...	...	16	26	56	102	...	354
355	Rubber products	236	254	237	...	...	42	72	167	311	...	355
356	Plastic products n.e.c..	...	...	...	...	...	49	78	144	240	...	356
361	Pottery,china etc	...	...	...	...	...	16	27	52	88	...	361
362	Glass and products	540	479	534	...	...	28	42	85	147	...	362
369	Non-metal products n.e.c	2280	2368	2389	...	...	100	141	230	400	...	369
371	Iron and steel	5315	5242	5386	...	...	179	254	509	1072	...	371
372	Non-ferrous metals	1089	1003	1000	...	...	40	56	117	196	...	372
381	Metal products	132	142	117	...	...	121	181	298	527	...	381
382	Machinery n.e.c.	42	54	48	...	...	131	181	282	447	...	382
3825	Office,computing etc..	12	29	27	...	...	8	13	19	31	...	3825
383	Electrical machinery ...	150	156	151	...	...	118	168	287	494	...	383
3832	Radio,television etc..	44	38	27	...	...	52	69	133	217	...	3832
384	Transport equipment	333	302	274	...	...	278	371	538	1095	...	384
3841	Shipbuilding, repair..	...	...	...	...	...	2	5	9	16	...	3841
3843	Motor vehicles	319	288	257	...	...	261	344	493	1022	...	3843
385	Professional goods	...	...	...	...	...	14	25	57	92	...	385
390	Other industries	...	...	...	...	...	40	62	121	205	...	390
3	Manufacturing	...	...	...	...	...	3085	4645	8981	15909	...	3
410	Electricity,gas,steam ..	...	...	...	...	...	...	...	...	...	...	410
4101	Electricity	...	...	...	...	...	68	102	220	423	...	4101
420	Water works and supply .	...	...	...	...	...	...	...	...	...	...	420
4	Electricity,gas etc	...	...	...	...	...	...	...	...	...	...	4
2-4	All industry	...	...	...	...	...	...	...	...	...	...	2-4

a/ Manufacturing: selected industries; see country note.
c/ All establishments.
b/ In producers' prices.
d/ Estimates derived from national accounts calculations.

ISIC	INDUSTRY	9. VALUE ADDED a/b/c/ (BILLION PESOS)					10. GROSS FIXED CAPITAL FORMATION TOTAL d/ (MILLION PESOS)					ISIC
		1981	1982	1983	1984	1985	1981	1982	1983	1984	1985	
210	Coal mining	3	4	12	26	...	...	...	...	...	...	210
220	Petroleum and gas	302	826	1825	2565	...	581200	e/ 2156	e/ 3045	...	...	220
230	Metal ore mining	29	48	127	161	...	...	...	...	...	...	230
290	Other mining	32	51	78	128	...	...	...	...	...	...	290
2	Mining, quarrying .	366	929	2042	2880	...	...	...	...	...	...	2
311/2	Food products	206	327	597	1046	...	4499	5853	7017	...	...	311/2
313	Beverages	87	140	238	418	...	6951	5277	4874	...	...	313
314	Tobacco	21	33	62	114	...	427	1014	109	...	...	314
321	Textiles	94	134	274	447	...	2780	6017	4398	...	...	321
3211	Spinning,weaving etc..	64	92	185	306	...	...	...	...	...	...	3211
322	Wearing apparel	37	60	113	169	...	...	...	...	...	...	322
323	Leather and products ...	10	17	32	61	...	...	...	...	...	...	323
324	Footwear	26	40	63	102	...	...	...	...	...	...	324
331	Wood products	26	36	63	121	...	119	655	884	...	...	331
332	Furniture, fixtures	25	38	55	77	...	...	...	...	...	...	332
341	Paper and products	34	50	105	179	...	4517	11954	1830	...	...	341
3411	Pulp,paper etc.	24	34	73	128	...	...	...	...	...	...	3411
342	Printing,publishing	35	57	93	189	...	...	...	...	...	...	342
351	Industrial chemicals ...	68	110	275	462	...	3166	1564	4291	...	...	351
3511	Basic excl fertilizers	42	67	162	286	...	...	...	...	...	...	3511
3513	Synthetic resins etc .	18	30	84	139	...	2594	1056	2357	...	...	3513
352	Other chemical products.	71	111	229	393	...	2744	4059	5886	...	...	352
3522	Drugs and medicines ..	28	39	76	125	...	1041	1974	4641	...	...	3522
353	Petroleum refineries ...	55	89	346	667	...	...	...	...	...	...	353
354	Petroleum,coal products.	6	9	17	80	...	628	41	414	...	...	354
355	Rubber products	22	38	88	167	...	904	3220	3443	...	...	355
356	Plastic products n.e.c..	23	38	69	118	...	...	...	...	...	...	356
361	Pottery,china etc	12	20	37	63	...	...	...	...	...	...	361
362	Glass and products	16	24	47	80	...	1681	3863	1326	...	...	362
369	Non-metal products n.e.c	51	72	116	202	...	16132	18018	15100	...	...	369
371	Iron and steel	62	90	176	378	...	6638	14815	14423	...	...	371
372	Non-ferrous metals	16	22	45	77	...	1631	5283	3189	...	...	372
381	Metal products	59	90	151	262	...	528	1423	896	...	...	381
382	Machinery n.e.c.	66	93	144	229	...	410	407	498	...	...	382
3825	Office,computing etc..	5	8	11	16	...	284	292	334	...	...	3825
383	Electrical machinery ...	58	83	140	240	...	1746	788	1106	...	...	383
3832	Radio,television etc..	24	32	62	102	...	387	215	605	...	...	3832
384	Transport equipment	99	135	197	404	...	6299	4886	7455	...	...	384
3841	Shipbuilding, repair..	1	3	6	10	...	...	...	...	...	...	3841
3843	Motor vehicles	90	121	174	368	...	6040	4721	7376	...	...	3843
385	Professional goods	8	15	33	54	...	...	...	...	...	...	385
390	Other industries	22	35	68	116	...	...	...	...	...	...	390
3	Manufacturing	1315	2006	3873	6915	...	...	...	...	...	...	3
410	Electricity,gas,steam ..	...	...	...	...	...	...	...	...	...	...	410
4101	Electricity	52	77	155	277	...	...	...	...	...	...	4101
420	Water works and supply .	...	...	...	...	...	...	...	...	...	...	420
4	Electricity,gas etc	...	...	...	...	...	...	...	...	...	...	4
2-4	All industry	...	...	...	...	...	...	...	...	...	...	2-4

a/ In producers' prices.
b/ All establishments.
c/ Contributions to the gross domestic product.
d/ Manufacturing: selected industries; see country note.
e/ In billion pesos.

11. INDEX NUMBERS OF INDUSTRIAL PRODUCTION (1980 = 100)

ISIC	INDUSTRY		1976	1977	1978	1979	1981	1982	1983	1984	1985	RATE a/	ISIC
210	Coal mining		81	94	97	105	114	108	127	132	137	6.0	210
220	Petroleum and gas		42	50	62	75	119	136	134	137	135	13.9	220
230	Metal ore mining		77	76	82	90	111	109	107	109	108	3.8	230
290	Other mining		110	96	95	100	102	95	87	97	109	-0.1	290
2	Mining, quarrying		58	62	71	82	115	126	123	124	123	8.7	2
311/2	Food products												311/2
313	Beverages		80	82	65	94	105	109	109	111	116	4.2	313
314	Tobacco												314
321	Textiles	b/	79	83	88	97	107	101	93	94	100	2.7	321
3211	Spinning,weaving etc.		...	...	...	...	...	...	...	...	...	...	3211
322	Wearing apparel	b/	...	...	...	...	...	...	...	...	...	...	322
323	Leather and products		...	...	...	...	...	...	...	...	...	...	323
324	Footwear		...	...	...	...	...	...	...	...	...	...	324
331	Wood products		76	79	85	94	104	108	104	107	112	4.4	331
332	Furniture, fixtures												332
341	Paper and products	c/	74	77	82	90	104	106	100	108	118	5.3	341
3411	Pulp,paper etc.		...	...	...	...	...	...	...	...	...	...	3411
342	Printing,publishing	c/	...	...	...	...	...	...	...	...	...	...	342
351	Industrial chemicals	d/	72	76	83	91	108	110	110	116	121	5.9	351
3511	Basic excl fertilizers		...	...	...	...	...	...	...	...	...	...	3511
3513	Synthetic resins etc		...	...	...	...	...	...	...	...	...	...	3513
352	Other chemical products.	d/	...	...	...	...	...	...	...	...	...	...	352
3522	Drugs and medicines		...	...	...	...	...	...	...	...	...	...	3522
353	Petroleum refineries	d/	...	...	...	...	...	...	...	...	...	...	353
354	Petroleum,coal products.	d/	...	...	...	...	...	...	...	...	...	...	354
355	Rubber products	d/	...	...	...	...	...	...	...	...	...	...	355
356	Plastic products n.e.c..	d/	...	...	...	...	...	...	...	...	...	...	356
361	Pottery,china etc												361
362	Glass and products		78	73	83	92	108	101	82	88	96	2.3	362
369	Non-metal products n.e.c												369
371	Iron and steel		71	75	90	97	104	94	88	100	97	3.5	371
372	Non-ferrous metals												372
381	Metal products	e/	66	66	77	90	111	96	72	78	89	3.4	381
382	Machinery n.e.c.												382
3825	Office,computing etc..		...	...	...	...	...	...	...	...	...	...	3825
383	Electrical machinery	e/	...	...	...	...	...	...	...	...	...	...	383
3832	Radio,television etc..		...	...	...	...	...	...	...	...	...	...	3832
384	Transport equipment	e/	...	...	...	...	...	...	...	...	...	...	384
3841	Shipbuilding, repair..		...	...	...	...	...	...	...	...	...	...	3841
3843	Motor vehicles		...	...	...	...	...	...	...	...	...	...	3843
385	Professional goods	e/	...	...	...	...	...	...	...	...	...	...	385
390	Other industries		83	67	93	101	112	105	93	100	107	2.9	390
3	Manufacturing		74	76	84	93	107	104	96	101	108	4.3	3
410	Electricity,gas,steam		...	...	...	...	...	...	...	...	...	...	410
4101	Electricity		71	78	85	93	108	115	116	123	131	7.0	4101
420	Water works and supply		.	.	.	.	.	.	.	.	.	.	420
4	Electricity,gas etc		...	...	...	...	...	...	...	...	...	...	4
2-4	All industry	f/	72	74	82	91	109	107	97	102	107	4.5	2-4

a/ Annual growth rate 1976-1985.
b/ Major group 322 is included in 321.
c/ Major group 342 is included in 341.
d/ Major groups 352 to 356 are included in 351.
e/ Major groups 383 to 385 are included in 381 and 382 combined.
f/ Including construction; excluding gas and steam.

MONGOLIA

The information on industrial activity is compiled by the United Nations Statistical Office from data published by the Central Statistical Board of Mongolia, Ulan-Bator, and the Council for Mutual Economic Assistance (CMEA), Moscow. The concepts, definitions and classification by branches of industry are generally in accordance with United Nations standards.

The estimates are based on regular monthly and annual reports of enterprises. The statistical unit is the industrial enterprise or the industrial unit of the non-industrial enterprise; industrial units of collective farms and small subsidiary industrial enterprises, however, are not covered.

The estimates, which are based on the national classification, are shown in the most appropriate category of ISIC. The national classification includes logging; commercial fishing; repair of motor vehicles, household appliances, furniture and footwear; repair and restoration of knitted goods and apparel; film copying and cleaning and dyeing. The following industries are excluded: (a) prospecting and drilling for minerals, crude petroleum and natural gas, and preparing sites for extraction, (b) publishing, (c) gas distribution and (d) water supply. It should also be noted that the manufacture of fur products (ISIC 322) is included in ISIC 323.

Employment numbers are annual averages of monthly figures and relate to persons engaged in the industrial activities of enterprises classified under mining, manufacturing, electricity and gas. They comprise production workers, apprentices, engineers and technicians, office staff, minor service personnel and guards.

Output relates to the value of the output of industry at constant prices of 1967, excluding turnover tax; the value of resale of commodities without further processing is not included.

The estimates of gross fixed capital formation represent acquisitions of new fixed assets and relate to the "productive" investments of industrial enterprises, valued at current prices; the investments of industrial enterprises in dwellings, public utilities, social facilities and other "non-productive" assets are not included.

The indexes of industrial production are compiled by the Central Statistical Board of Mongolia and the Council for Mutual Economic Assistance (CMEA).

Related publications:

<u>National Economy of Mongolia</u> (annual), published by the Central Statistical Board of Mongolia, Ulan-Bator. <u>Statistical Yearbook</u> (annual), published by the Council for Mutual Economic Assistance (CMEA), Moscow.

ISIC	INDUSTRY		1. NUMBER OF ENTERPRISES (NUMBER) 1981	1982	1983	1984	1985	2. AVERAGE NUMBER OF EMPLOYEES (THOUSANDS) 1981	1982	1983	1984	1985	ISIC
210	Coal mining		15	15	15	15	15	3.3	3.3	4.0	3.6	3.9	210
220	Petroleum and gas		-	-	-	-	-	-	-	-	-	-	220
230	Metal ore mining		4	4	4	5	5	3.8	4.2	4.3	4.5	4.6	230
290	Other mining		...	...	...	...	...	...	...	...	...	...	290
2	Mining, quarrying		...	...	...	...	...	...	...	...	...	...	2
311/2	Food products												311/2
313	Beverages		43	43	43	45	45	12.1	12.6	13.4	14.7	15.7	313
314	Tobacco												314
321	Textiles		11	11	12	12	12	4.4	6.2	6.8	7.5	7.7	321
3211	Spinning,weaving etc.		...	...	...	...	...	...	...	...	...	...	3211
322	Wearing apparel	a/	26	26	26	26	26	10.4	10.7	11.2	11.5	11.6	322
323	Leather and products	a/	16	18	18	18	18	6.7	7.2	7.8	7.9	8.3	323
324	Footwear												324
331	Wood products		51	52	52	53	53	9.2	9.3	9.2	10.1	10.4	331
332	Furniture, fixtures												332
341	Paper and products		-	-	-	-	-	-	-	-	-	-	341
3411	Pulp,paper etc.		-	-	-	-	-	-	-	-	-	-	3411
342	Printing,publishing	b/	28	28	28	28	28	2.0	2.0	2.0	1.9	1.9	342
351	Industrial chemicals	c/	7	8	8	9	9	2.0	2.2	2.4	2.4	2.5	351
3511	Basic excl fertilizers		...	...	...	...	...	...	...	...	...	...	3511
3513	Synthetic resins etc		...	...	...	...	...	...	...	...	...	...	3513
352	Other chemical products	c/	...	...	...	...	...	...	...	...	...	...	352
3522	Drugs and medicines		...	...	...	...	...	...	...	...	...	...	3522
353	Petroleum refineries		-	-	-	-	-	-	-	-	-	-	353
354	Petroleum,coal products		-	-	-	-	-	-	-	-	-	-	354
355	Rubber products		-	-	-	-	-	-	-	-	-	-	355
356	Plastic products n.e.c.		-	-	-	-	-	-	-	-	-	-	356
361	Pottery,china etc		3	3	3	3	3	0.4	0.5	0.5	0.5	0.5	361
362	Glass and products												362
369	Non-metal products n.e.c		-	-	-	-	-	-	-	-	-	-	369
371	Iron and steel		-	-	-	-	-	-	-	-	-	-	371
372	Non-ferrous metals		-	-	-	-	-	-	-	-	-	-	372
381	Metal products	d/	20	20	21	21	21	4.4	4.9	5.3	4.9	5.8	381
382	Machinery n.e.c.												382
3825	Office,computing etc.		...	...	...	...	...	...	...	...	...	...	3825
383	Electrical machinery	d/	...	...	...	...	...	...	...	...	...	...	383
3832	Radio,television etc.		...	...	...	...	...	...	...	...	...	...	3832
384	Transport equipment	d/	...	...	...	...	...	...	...	...	...	...	384
3841	Shipbuilding, repair		...	...	...	...	...	...	...	...	...	...	3841
3843	Motor vehicles		...	...	...	...	...	...	...	...	...	...	3843
385	Professional goods	d/	...	...	...	...	...	...	...	...	...	...	385
390	Other industries		...	...	...	...	...	...	...	...	...	...	390
3	Manufacturing		...	...	...	...	...	...	...	...	...	...	3
410	Electricity,gas,steam	e/	28	28	29	29	29	5.4	5.9	6.1	6.9	7.0	410
4101	Electricity		...	...	...	...	...	...	...	...	...	...	4101
420	Water works and supply		.	.	.	.	.	.	.	.	.	.	420
4	Electricity,gas etc	e/	28	28	29	29	29	5.4	5.9	6.1	6.9	7.0	4
2-4	All industry	b/e/f/g/	285	297	304	310	315	71.8	77.4	82.2	86.9	91.0	2-4

a/ Wearing apparel of fur is included in major group 323.
b/ Excluding publishing.
c/ Major group 352 is included in 351.
d/ Major groups 383 to 385 are included in 381 and 382 combined.
e/ Excluding gas distribution.
f/ Including repair services for the general public.
g/ Total includes industries for which data are not shown separately.

ISIC	INDUSTRY		3. AVERAGE NUMBER OF OPERATIVES (THOUSANDS)					4. OUTPUT a/b/ (MILLION TUGRIKS)					ISIC
			1981	1982	1983	1984	1985	1981	1982	1983	1984	1985	
210	Coal mining		2.6	2.6	3.1	2.8	3.0	176.4	201.7	203.9	222.5	266.8	210
220	Petroleum and gas		-	-	...	...	...	-	-	-	-	-	220
230	Metal ore mining		2.9	3.3	3.4	3.5	3.6	550.2	731.7	808.9	845.4	863.0	230
290	Other mining		...	...	...	...	...	...	...	...	...	...	290
2	Mining, quarrying .		...	...	...	...	...	...	...	...	...	...	2
311/2	Food products												311/2
313	Beverages		8.6	9.1	9.7	10.6	11.4	881.3	912.7	963.0	1055.9	1036.4	313
314	Tobacco												314
321	Textiles		3.6	5.0	5.6	6.1	6.2	342.6	482.6	568.2	651.8	734.9	321
3211	Spinning,weaving etc..		...	...	...	...	...	...	...	...	...	...	3211
322	Wearing apparel	c/	8.2	8.4	8.7	8.9	9.0	339.0	341.1	347.3	356.9	370.1	322
323	Leather and products ...	c/	5.5	5.8	6.3	6.3	6.5	441.0	438.8	502.6	523.8	565.4	323
324	Footwear												324
331	Wood products		6.7	6.8	6.9	7.5	7.8	557.9	567.5	586.1	627.4	650.6	331
332	Furniture, fixtures												332
341	Paper and products		-	-	-	-	-	-	-	-	-	-	341
3411	Pulp,paper etc.		-	-	-	-	-	-	-	-	-	-	3411
342	Printing,publishing	d/	1.3	1.3	1.3	1.3	1.2	43.9	43.9	44.7	46.0	44.1	342
351	Industrial chemicals ...	e/	1.4	1.5	1.7	1.7	1.7	168.7	180.9	193.7	202.2	208.5	351
3511	Basic excl fertilizers		...	...	...	...	...	...	...	...	...	...	3511
3513	Synthetic resins etc .		...	...	...	...	...	...	...	...	...	...	3513
352	Other chemical products.	e/	...	...	...	...	...	...	...	...	...	...	352
3522	Drugs and medicines ..		...	...	...	...	...	...	...	...	...	...	3522
353	Petroleum refineries ...		-	-	-	-	-	-	-	-	-	-	353
354	Petroleum,coal products.		-	-	-	-	-	-	-	-	-	-	354
355	Rubber products		-	-	-	-	-	-	-	-	-	-	355
356	Plastic products n.e.c..		-	-	-	-	-	-	-	-	-	-	356
361	Pottery,china etc		0.3	0.4	0.4	0.4	0.4	18.4	20.2	23.3	23.4	26.3	361
362	Glass and products												362
369	Non-metal products n.e.c		-	-	-	-	-	-	-	-	-	-	369
371	Iron and steel		-	-	-	-	-	-	-	-	-	-	371
372	Non-ferrous metals		-	-	-	-	-	-	-	-	-	-	372
381	Metal products	f/	3.6	4.0	4.3	3.6	4.4	160.5	168.9	187.2	203.7	230.9	381
382	Machinery n.e.c.												382
3825	Office,computing etc..		...	...	...	...	...	...	...	...	...	...	3825
383	Electrical machinery ...	f/	...	...	...	...	...	...	...	...	...	...	383
3832	Radio,television etc..		...	...	...	...	...	...	...	...	...	...	3832
384	Transport equipment	f/	...	...	...	...	...	...	...	...	...	...	384
3841	Shipbuilding, repair..		...	...	...	...	...	...	...	...	...	...	3841
3843	Motor vehicles		...	...	...	...	...	...	...	...	...	...	3843
385	Professional goods	f/	...	...	...	...	...	...	...	...	...	...	385
390	Other industries		...	...	...	...	...	...	...	...	...	...	390
3	Manufacturing		...	...	...	...	...	...	...	...	...	...	3
410	Electricity,gas,steam ..	g/	4.0	4.4	4.4	5.1	5.2	453.3	436.8	493.2	600.5	723.4	410
4101	Electricity		...	...	...	...	...	...	...	...	...	...	4101
420	Water works and supply .		.	.	.	.	.	.	.	.	.	.	420
4	Electricity,gas etc	g/	4.0	4.4	4.4	5.1	5.2	453.3	436.8	493.2	600.5	723.4	4
2-4	All industry	d/g/h/i/	54.6	59.2	62.8	65.9	69.3	4439.2	4895.4	5352.8	5829.1	6263.1	2-4

a/ At prices of 1967.
b/ Excluding turnover tax.
c/ Wearing apparel of fur is included in major group 323.
d/ Excluding publishing.
e/ Major group 352 is included in 351.
f/ Major groups 383 to 385 are included in 381 and 382 combined.
g/ Excluding gas distribution.
h/ Including repair services for the general public.
i/ Total includes industries for which data are not shown separately.

5. GROSS FIXED CAPITAL FORMATION
TOTAL a/
(MILLION TUGRIKS)

ISIC	INDUSTRY		1981	1982	1983	1984	1985	ISIC
210	Coal mining		275.0	333.0	296.0	219.0	105.0	210
220	Petroleum and gas		-	-	-	-	-	220
230	Metal ore mining	b/	-	-	-	-	-	230
290	Other mining		...	...	...	...	...	290
2	Mining, quarrying .		...	...	...	...	...	2
311/2	Food products							311/2
313	Beverages		57.2	145.0	191.0	105.0	110.0	313
314	Tobacco							314
321	Textiles		164.0	86.7	38.0	27.2	23.9	321
3211	Spinning,weaving etc..		...	...	...	...	...	3211
322	Wearing apparel	c/	...	2.4	3.3	2.9	1.0	322
323	Leather and products ...	c/	58.3	29.7	24.0	41.5	43.9	323
324	Footwear							324
331	Wood products		83.1	65.4	74.8	63.7	58.0	331
332	Furniture, fixtures							332
341	Paper and products		-	-	-	-	-	341
3411	Pulp,paper etc.		-	-	-	-	-	3411
342	Printing,publishing	d/	...	...	...	...	1.7	342
351	Industrial chemicals ...	e/	84.0	181.0	172.0	192.0	168.0	351
3511	Basic excl fertilizers		...	...	...	...	...	3511
3513	Synthetic resins etc .		...	...	...	...	...	3513
352	Other chemical products.	e/	...	...	...	...	...	352
3522	Drugs and medicines ..		...	...	...	...	...	3522
353	Petroleum refineries ...		-	-	-	-	-	353
354	Petroleum,coal products.		-	-	-	-	-	354
355	Rubber products		-	-	-	-	-	355
356	Plastic products n.e.c..		-	-	-	-	-	356
361	Pottery,china etc		9.0	1.7	...	...	...	361
362	Glass and products				...	...	...	362
369	Non-metal products n.e.c		525.0	162.0	107.0	190.0	284.0	369
371	Iron and steel		-	-	-	-	-	371
372	Non-ferrous metals	b/	76.7	377.0	55.4	84.6	116.0	372
381	Metal products	f/	15.1	11.2	6.1	14.3	28.9	381
382	Machinery n.e.c.							382
3825	Office,computing etc..		...	...	...	...	...	3825
383	Electrical machinery ...	f/	...	...	...	...	...	383
3832	Radio,television etc..		...	...	...	...	...	3832
384	Transport equipment	f/	...	...	...	...	...	384
3841	Shipbuilding, repair..		...	...	...	...	...	3841
3843	Motor vehicles		...	...	...	...	...	3843
385	Professional goods	f/	...	...	...	...	...	385
390	Other industries		6.6	6.9	12.4	41.8	53.6	390
3	Manufacturing		...	...	...	...	...	3
410	Electricity,gas,steam ..	g/	413.0	616.0	761.0	686.0	589.0	410
4101	Electricity		...	...	...	...	...	4101
420	Water works and supply .		.	.	.	.	.	420
4	Electricity,gas etc	g/	413.0	616.0	761.0	686.0	589.0	4
2-4	All industry	d/g/h/	1767.0	2018.0	1741.0	1668.0	1583.0	2-4

a/ For concept, see country note.
b/ Non-ferrous ore mining is included in major group 372.
c/ Wearing apparel of fur is included in major group 323.
d/ Excluding publishing.
e/ Major group 352 is included in 351.
f/ Major groups 383 to 385 are included in 381 and 382 combined.
g/ Excluding gas distribution.
h/ Including repair services for the general public.

6. INDEX NUMBERS OF INDUSTRIAL PRODUCTION (1980 = 100)

ISIC	INDUSTRY	1976	1977	1978	1979	1981	1982	1983	1984	1985	a/ RATE	ISIC
210	Coal mining .... b/	67	76	87	94	98	112	114	...	...	g/ 7.9	210
220	Petroleum and gas	...	...	...	...	...	...	...	...	...	...	220
230	Metal ore mining	...	...	...	...	...	...	...	...	...	...	230
290	Other mining .... c/	...	...	...	...	...	...	...	...	...	...	290
2	Mining, quarrying .	...	...	...	...	...	...	...	...	...	...	2
311/2	Food products											311/2
313	Beverages	99	96	105	111	118	121	128	...	...	g/ 3.7	313
314	Tobacco											314
321	Textiles	80	85	85	92	105	149	175	...	...	g/ 11.8	321
3211	Spinning,weaving etc..	...	...	...	...	...	...	...	...	...	...	3211
322	Wearing apparel	70	73	79	90	102	103	104	...	...	g/ 5.8	322
323	Leather and products ...	76	79	81	83	106	106	121	...	...	g/ 6.9	323
324	Footwear											324
331	Wood products	77	82	86	93	100	102	105	...	...	g/ 4.5	331
332	Furniture, fixtures											332
341	Paper and products	-	-	-	-	-	-	-	...	...	...	341
3411	Pulp,paper etc.	-	-	-	-	-	-	-	...	...	...	3411
342	Printing,publishing	74	81	87	92	103	103	105	...	...	g/ 5.1	342
351	Industrial chemicals ... d/	60	68	81	93	105	112	120	...	...	g/ 10.4	351
3511	Basic excl fertilizers	...	...	...	...	...	...	...	...	...	...	3511
3513	Synthetic resins etc .	...	...	...	...	...	...	...	...	...	...	3513
352	Other chemical products. d/	...	...	...	...	...	...	...	...	...	...	352
3522	Drugs and medicines ..	...	...	...	...	...	...	...	...	...	...	3522
353	Petroleum refineries ... b/	...	...	...	...	...	...	...	...	...	...	353
354	Petroleum,coal products. b/	...	...	...	...	...	...	...	...	...	...	354
355	Rubber products	-	-	-	-	-	-	-	...	...	...	355
356	Plastic products n.e.c..	-	-	-	-	-	-	-	...	...	...	356
361	Pottery,china etc	107	91	97	100	123	135	...	...	...	h/ 3.9	361
362	Glass and products											362
369	Non-metal products n.e.c c/	66	62	73	88	94	116	130	...	...	g/ 10.2	369
371	Iron and steel	-	-	-	-	-	-	-	...	...	...	371
372	Non-ferrous metals	4	4	3	46	152	202	204	...	...	g/ 75.3	372
381	Metal products	e/ 75	e/ 86	e/ 97	e/ 97	e/ 111	e/ 117	e/ 129	...	...	g/ 8.1	381
382	Machinery n.e.c.											382
3825	Office,computing etc..	...	...	...	...	...	...	...	...	...	...	3825
383	Electrical machinery ... e/	...	...	...	...	...	...	...	...	...	...	383
3832	Radio,television etc..	...	...	...	...	...	...	...	...	...	...	3832
384	Transport equipment .... e/	...	...	...	...	...	...	...	...	...	...	384
3841	Shipbuilding, repair..	...	...	...	...	...	...	...	...	...	...	3841
3843	Motor vehicles	...	...	...	...	...	...	...	...	...	...	3843
385	Professional goods ..... e/	...	...	...	...	...	...	...	...	...	...	385
390	Other industries	86	91	95	100	110	118	121	...	...	g/ 5.0	390
3	Manufacturing	...	...	...	...	...	...	...	...	...	...	3
410	Electricity,gas,steam .. f/	67	75	78	88	110	107	120	...	...	g/ 8.7	410
4101	Electricity	...	...	...	...	...	...	...	...	...	...	4101
420	Water works and supply .	.	.	.	.	.	.	.	...	...	.	420
4	Electricity,gas etc	...	...	...	...	...	...	...	...	...	...	4
2-4	All industry f/	72	75	80	91	110	122	133	...	...	g/ 9.2	2-4

a/ Annual growth rate 1976-1985.
b/ Major groups 353 and 354 are included in 210.
c/ Major group 290 is included in 369.
d/ Major group 352 is included in 351.
e/ Major groups 383 to 385 are included in 381 and 382 combined.
f/ Excluding gas.
g/ Annual growth rate 1976-1983.
h/ Annual growth rate 1976-1982.

NETHERLANDS

The information on industrial activity is based on the reply to the United Nations Questionnaire on General Industrial Statistics from the Netherlands Central Bureau of Statistics, Voorburg. The concepts, definitions and classification by branches of industry are generally in accordance with United Nations standards.

The estimates are derived primarily from the production statistics inquiry and the survey of fixed capital formation, both of which are carried out annually by the Netherlands Central Bureau of Statistics. These inquiries generally cover all kind-of-activity units with 10 or more employees. Except for gross fixed capital formation, the information in the tables has been adjusted to cover all industrial units irrespective of size by the use of supplementary estimates from social security and other sources.

The estimates are based on the national classification which generally follows the present version of ISIC.

The employment data are estimated within the framework of the national accounts. The data are converted into an annual average expressed in terms of person-years. Persons who were not employed throughout the year have been counted only partially on the basis of the number of days or the number of hours worked per day during which they were employed.

The estimates of electricity consumed relate to total industrial consumption. They are based on returns covering all companies with energy consumption of 20 terajoules or more plus estimates for the small companies below this level. The latter are not distributed by industry and in the table are included under other industries, ISIC 390.

The value of output is derived from input-output tables; the valuation is in producers' prices but the value-added tax is not included. The estimates of value added relate to the contribution of each branch of industry to the gross domestic product. Data are shown after the deduction of net indirect taxes.

Estimates of gross fixed capital formation refer to the current value of purchases and own-account construction of fixed assets (net of sales), including fixed capital formation in new establishments not yet in operation; progress payments made for fixed assets on order, but not completed at the end of the year, are not included. The information shown does not cover land. The investments are measured directly and not by the commodity-flow method and are, therefore, not consistent with those in the Netherlands national accounts statistics. The estimates for mining and manufacturing relate to kind-of-activity units with 10 or more employees; all kind-of-activity units are covered for electricity, gas and water.

The indexes of industrial production are compiled by the Central Bureau of Statistics and provided in response to the United Nations Questionnaire on Indexes of Industrial Production. In principle, the indexes cover all establishments including handicrafts.

Related national publications:

Nationale Rekeningen (National Accounts) (annual); Statistiek van de Investeringen in Vaste Activa in de Nijverheid (Statistics on Fixed Capital Formation in Industry) (annual); Produkiestatistieken (for individual industries); Statistiek van de Electriciteitsvoorziening in Nederland; Statistiek van de Gazvoorziening in Nederland; Maandstatistiek van de Industrie, all published by the Central Bureau of Statistics, Voorburg.

ISIC	INDUSTRY	1. AVERAGE NUMBER OF PERSONS ENGAGED a/ (THOUSANDS)					2. AVERAGE NUMBER OF EMPLOYEES a/ (THOUSANDS)					ISIC
		1981	1982	1983	1984	1985	1981	1982	1983	1984	1985	
210	Coal mining .... b/	...	...	...	...	...	...	...	...	...	...	210
220	Petroleum and gas	5	5	6	6	6	5	5	6	6	6	220
230	Metal ore mining	-	-	-	-	-	-	-	-	-	-	230
290	Other mining	3	3	3	3	3	3	3	3	3	3	290
2	Mining, quarrying .	8	8	9	9	9	8	8	9	9	9	2
311/2	Food products	149	145	140	139	139	131	127	123	122	122	311/2
313	Beverages	23	22	22	22	22	22	21	21	21	21	313
314	Tobacco											314
321	Textiles	30	27	24	23	23	29	26	23	22	22	321
3211	Spinning,weaving etc..	...	...	...	...	...	...	...	...	...	...	3211
322	Wearing apparel	18	16	15	14	14	15	13	12	11	11	322
323	Leather and products ...	9	8	8	8	8	8	7	7	7	7	323
324	Footwear											324
331	Wood products	42	38	35	34	34	38	34	31	30	30	331
332	Furniture, fixtures											332
341	Paper and products	25	24	23	23	24	25	24	23	23	24	341
3411	Pulp,paper etc.	...	...	...	...	...	...	...	...	...	...	3411
342	Printing,publishing	83	81	78	77	78	80	78	75	74	75	342
351	Industrial chemicals ... b/	111	109	109	109	112	110	108	108	108	111	351
3511	Basic excl fertilizers	...	...	...	...	...	...	...	...	...	...	3511
3513	Synthetic resins etc .	...	...	...	...	...	...	...	...	...	...	3513
352	Other chemical products. b/	...	...	...	...	...	...	...	...	...	...	352
3522	Drugs and medicines ..	...	...	...	...	...	...	...	...	...	...	3522
353	Petroleum refineries ...	11	11	11	11	11	11	11	11	11	11	353
354	Petroleum,coal products.											354
355	Rubber products .... b/	...	...	...	...	...	...	...	...	...	...	355
356	Plastic products n.e.c.. b/	...	...	...	...	...	...	...	...	...	...	356
361	Pottery,china etc	40	37	34	33	33	39	36	33	32	32	361
362	Glass and products											362
369	Non-metal products n.e.c											369
371	Iron and steel	35	34	33	32	32	35	34	33	32	32	371
372	Non-ferrous metals											372
381	Metal products	184	175	166	162	167	177	168	159	155	160	381
382	Machinery n.e.c.											382
3825	Office,computing etc..	...	...	...	...	...	...	...	...	...	...	3825
383	Electrical machinery ...	109	104	99	97	100	109	104	99	97	100	383
3832	Radio,television etc..	...	...	...	...	...	...	...	...	...	...	3832
384	Transport equipment	74	71	67	64	64	72	69	65	62	62	384
3841	Shipbuilding, repair..	...	...	...	...	...	...	...	...	...	...	3841
3843	Motor vehicles	...	...	...	...	...	...	...	...	...	...	3843
385	Professional goods	20	20	19	18	18	18	18	17	16	16	385
390	Other industries											390
3	Manufacturing	963	922	883	866	880	919	878	840	823	836	3
410	Electricity,gas,steam ..	...	...	...	...	...	...	...	...	...	...	410
4101	Electricity	...	...	...	...	...	...	...	...	...	...	4101
420	Water works and supply .	...	...	...	...	...	...	...	...	...	...	420
4	Electricity,gas etc	47	47	47	46	46	47	47	47	46	46	4
2-4	All industry	1018	977	939	921	935	974	933	896	878	891	2-4

a/ Including homeworkers.

b/ Major groups 210, 352, 355 and 356 are included in 351.

ISIC	INDUSTRY	3. WAGES AND SALARIES OF EMPLOYEES a/ (MILLION GUILDERS) 1981	1982	1983	1984	1985	4. SUPPLEMENTS TO WAGES AND SALARIES b/ (MILLION GUILDERS) 1981	1982	1983	1984	1985	ISIC
210	Coal mining .... c/	...	...	...	...	...	...	...	...	...	...	210
220	Petroleum and gas	286	329	363	...	...	119	136	149	...	...	220
230	Metal ore mining	-	-	-	...	...	-	-	-	...	...	230
290	Other mining	133	140	137	...	...	38	40	42	...	...	290
2	Mining, quarrying .	419	469	500	...	...	157	176	191	...	...	2
311/2	Food products	4708	4904	4918	...	...	1396	1473	1551	...	...	311/2
313	Beverages	504	526	550	...	...	157	164	174	...	...	313
314	Tobacco	329	344	352	...	...	103	104	107	...	...	314
321	Textiles	957	927	880	...	...	264	257	251	...	...	321
3211	Spinning,weaving etc..	...	...	...	...	...	...	...	...	...	...	3211
322	Wearing apparel	433	404	380	...	...	109	100	99	...	...	322
323	Leather and products ...	[240	228	227]	...	...	[63	58	58]	...	...	323
324	Footwear				...	...				...	...	324
331	Wood products	[1196	1142	1083]	...	...	[353	336	320]	...	...	331
332	Furniture, fixtures				...	...				...	...	332
341	Paper and products	974	975	1000	...	...	265	266	275	...	...	341
3411	Pulp,paper etc.	375	364	372	...	...	97	95	98	...	...	3411
342	Printing,publishing	2876	2999	2994	...	...	803	835	853	...	...	342
351	Industrial chemicals ... c/	4782	5033	5181	...	...	1329	1385	1522	...	...	351
3511	Basic excl fertilizers	...	...	...	...	...	...	...	...	...	...	3511
3513	Synthetic resins etc .	...	...	...	...	...	...	...	...	...	...	3513
352	Other chemical products. c/	...	...	...	...	...	...	...	...	...	...	352
3522	Drugs and medicines ..	...	...	...	...	...	...	...	...	...	...	3522
353	Petroleum refineries ...	[551	587	593]	...	...	[214	224	248]	...	...	353
354	Petroleum,coal products.				...	...				...	...	354
355	Rubber products .... c/	...	...	...	...	...	...	...	...	...	...	355
356	Plastic products n.e.c.. c/	...	...	...	...	...	...	...	...	...	...	356
361	Pottery,china etc				...	...				...	...	361
362	Glass and products	[1350	1340	1293]	...	...	[414	406	391]	...	...	362
369	Non-metal products n.e.c				...	...				...	...	369
371	Iron and steel	[1437	1482	1494]	...	...	[446	459	506]	...	...	371
372	Non-ferrous metals				...	...				...	...	372
381	Metal products	3102	3152	2987	...	...	847	853	829	...	...	381
382	Machinery n.e.c.	3261	3359	3315	...	...	887	912	933	...	...	382
3825	Office,computing etc..	...	...	...	...	...	...	...	...	...	...	3825
383	Electrical machinery ...	4569	4643	4623	...	...	1431	1444	1502	...	...	383
3832	Radio,television etc..	...	...	...	...	...	...	...	...	...	...	3832
384	Transport equipment	2601	2744	2557	...	...	733	762	747	...	...	384
3841	Shipbuilding, repair..	...	...	...	...	...	...	...	...	...	...	3841
3843	Motor vehicles	827	859	882	...	...	234	240	259	...	...	3843
385	Professional goods	[624	652	651]	...	...	[174	179	183]	...	...	385
390	Other industries				...	...				...	...	390
3	Manufacturing	34494	35441	35078	...	...	9988	10217	10549	...	...	3
410	Electricity,gas,steam ..	1564	1628	1636	...	...	626	640	672	...	...	410
4101	Electricity	1176	1216	1222	...	...	467	481	505	...	...	4101
420	Water works and supply .	307	287	275	...	...	115	109	112	...	...	420
4	Electricity,gas etc	1871	1915	1911	...	...	741	749	784	...	...	4
2-4	All industry	36784	37825	37489	...	...	10886	11142	11524	...	...	2-4

a/ Including payments to homeworkers.
c/ Major groups 210, 352, 355 and 356 are included in 351.

b/ Including payments in respect of homeworkers.

ISIC	INDUSTRY	5. QUANTITY OF ELECTRICITY CONSUMED (MILLION KWH) 1981	1982	1983	1984	1985	6. OUTPUT IN PRODUCERS' PRICES a/ (BILLION GUILDERS) 1981	1982	1983	1984	1985	ISIC
210	Coal mining	-	-	-	-	-	b/	b/	b/	...	...	210
220	Petroleum and gas	232	217	208	204	202	27.76	28.95	30.23	...	...	220
230	Metal ore mining	-	-	-	-	-	-	-	-	...	...	230
290	Other mining	133	117	125	130	133	1.00	1.10	1.27	...	...	290
2	Mining, quarrying .	365	334	333	334	335	...	...	...	...	...	2
311/2	Food products						55.20	58.41	60.42	...	...	311/2
313	Beverages	[3309	3350	3280	3459	3518]	4.51	4.91	5.05	...	...	313
314	Tobacco						3.46	3.65	3.99	...	...	314
321	Textiles	554	506	472	389	434	5.05	5.11	5.09	...	...	321
3211	Spinning,weaving etc..	...	...	...	...	...	...	...	...	...	...	3211
322	Wearing apparel	36	34	35	21	23	2.25	2.29	2.25	...	...	322
323	Leather and products ...	[36	35	38	25	27	0.86	0.95	0.95]	...	...	323
324	Footwear									...	...	324
331	Wood products	[268	254	255	164	171	4.92	4.70	4.75]	...	...	331
332	Furniture, fixtures									...	...	332
341	Paper and products	1597	1523	1537	1525	1539	5.54	5.69	5.73	...	...	341
3411	Pulp,paper etc.	...	...	...	...	...	2.26	2.26	2.30	...	...	3411
342	Printing,publishing	650	617	606	490	402	11.82	12.03	12.22	...	...	342
351	Industrial chemicals ...	c/ 9086	c/ 8634	c/ 9300	c/ 9983	c/ 10234	b/ 36.70	b/ 36.44	b/ 41.12	...	...	351
3511	Basic excl fertilizers	...	...	...	...	...	...	...	...	...	...	3511
3513	Synthetic resins etc .	...	...	...	...	...	...	...	...	...	...	3513
352	Other chemical products.	c/	c/	c/	c/	c/	b/	b/	b/	...	...	352
3522	Drugs and medicines ..	...	...	...	...	...	...	...	...	...	...	3522
353	Petroleum refineries ...	1117	1267	1262	1335	1287	[33.55	33.93	35.72]	...	...	353
354	Petroleum,coal products.	180	194	185	288	305				...	...	354
355	Rubber products	816	689	940	601	739	b/	b/	b/	...	...	355
356	Plastic products n.e.c..	c/	c/	c/	c/	c/	b/	b/	b/	...	...	356
361	Pottery,china etc									...	...	361
362	Glass and products	[1039	999	1019	1044	1210	5.67	5.52	5.49]	...	...	362
369	Non-metal products n.e.c									...	...	369
371	Iron and steel	1854	1627	1646	1866	1870	[9.18	9.29	9.51]	...	...	371
372	Non-ferrous metals	5114	4899	4663	4912	4853				...	...	372
381	Metal products	[d/ 2658	d/ 2691	d/ 2696	d/ 2631	d/ 2631]	11.68	12.20	11.77	...	...	381
382	Machinery n.e.c.						11.58	11.88	12.33	...	...	382
3825	Office,computing etc..	...	...	...	...	...	...	...	...	...	...	3825
383	Electrical machinery ...	d/	d/	d/	d/	d/	17.75	17.99	18.87	...	...	383
3832	Radio,television etc..	...	...	...	...	...	...	...	...	...	...	3832
384	Transport equipment	d/	d/	d/	d/	d/	12.93	14.15	13.10	...	...	384
3841	Shipbuilding, repair..	...	...	...	...	...	...	...	...	...	...	3841
3843	Motor vehicles	...	...	...	...	...	4.16	4.55	4.75	...	...	3843
385	Professional goods	d/	d/	d/	d/	d/	[3.14	3.23	3.47]	...	...	385
390	Other industries	27	24	27	56	65				...	...	390
3	Manufacturing	28341	27343	27961	28789	29308	e/ 264.55	e/ 272.42	e/ 283.33	...	...	3
410	Electricity,gas,steam ..	f/ 2486	f/ 2388	f/ 2356	f/ 2124	f/ 2133	20.78	21.59	22.08	...	...	410
4101	Electricity	2486	2388	2356	2117	2126	11.36	11.51	11.49	...	...	4101
420	Water works and supply .	370	379	412	420	422	1.44	1.56	1.68	...	...	420
4	Electricity,gas etc	f/ 2856	f/ 2767	f/ 2768	f/ 2544	f/ 2555	22.22	23.15	23.76	...	...	4
2-4	All industry	f/ 31562	f/ 30444	f/ 31062	f/ 31667	f/ 32198	286.77	295.57	307.09	...	...	2-4

a/ Excluding value-added tax.
b/ Major groups 210, 352, 355 and 356 are included in 351.
c/ Major groups 352 and 356 are included in 351.
d/ Major groups 383 to 385 are included in 381 and 382 combined.
e/ Including mining.
f/ Excluding establishments engaged in the distribution of gas.

ISIC	INDUSTRY	7. VALUE ADDED IN FACTOR VALUES a/ (BILLION GUILDERS) 1981	1982	1983	1984	1985	8. GROSS FIXED CAPITAL FORMATION TOTAL b/ (MILLION GUILDERS) 1981	1982	1983	1984	1985	ISIC
210	Coal mining	c/	c/	c/	...	...	-	-	-	-	-	210
220	Petroleum and gas	25.01	25.40	26.71	...	...	d/ 1031	d/ 1336	d/ 1355	d/ 1477	d/ 2168	220
230	Metal ore mining	-	-	-	...	...	-	-	-	-	-	230
290	Other mining	0.51	0.54	0.57	...	...	d/	d/	d/	d/	d/	290
2	Mining, quarrying .	25.52	25.94	27.28	...	...	1031	1336	1355	1477	2168	2
311/2	Food products	8.96	10.10	10.24	...	...	1336	1377	1587	1561	1866	311/2
313	Beverages	1.39	1.47	1.50	...	...	296	142	183	257	266	313
314	Tobacco	0.54	0.62	0.57	...	...	154	121	100	86	98	314
321	Textiles	1.45	1.50	1.47	...	...	117	152	163	187	214	321
3211	Spinning,weaving etc..	...	...	...	...	...	72	73	88	81	101	3211
322	Wearing apparel	0.64	0.69	0.66	...	...	24	21	25	20	35	322
323	Leather and products ...	[0.34	0.37	0.36]	...	...	10	15	12	12	17	323
324	Footwear				...	...	8	11	6	16	16	324
331	Wood products	[1.83	1.73	1.68]	...	...	66	69	54	85	82	331
332	Furniture, fixtures				...	...	46	35	30	43	45	332
341	Paper and products	1.61	1.79	1.78	...	...	288	321	289	348	449	341
3411	Pulp,paper etc.	0.57	0.68	0.67	...	...	211	246	202	156	213	3411
342	Printing,publishing	5.00	5.15	5.38	...	...	498	400	789	601	652	342
351	Industrial chemicals ...	c/ 7.93	c/ 7.96	c/ 9.14	...	...	1204	1372	1523	2007	1713	351
3511	Basic excl fertilizers	...	...	...	...	...	...	...	...	...	...	3511
3513	Synthetic resins etc .	...	...	...	...	...	...	...	...	...	...	3513
352	Other chemical products.	c/	c/	c/	...	...	291	281	328	468	741	352
3522	Drugs and medicines ..	...	...	...	...	...	...	...	...	...	...	3522
353	Petroleum refineries ...	[0.05	1.57	2.37]	...	...	[663	384	563	1300	2041]	353
354	Petroleum,coal products.				...	...						354
355	Rubber products	c/	c/	c/	...	...	50	56	51	80	79	355
356	Plastic products n.e.c..	c/	c/	c/	...	...	156	153	183	234	373	356
361	Pottery,china etc	[2.29	2.18	2.22]	...	...	34	19	19	203	82	361
362	Glass and products				...	...	[255	270	268	396	309]	362
369	Non-metal products n.e.c				...	...						369
371	Iron and steel	[2.35	2.91	2.83]	...	...	347	336	431	496	870	371
372	Non-ferrous metals				...	...	133	85	61	120	105	372
381	Metal products	4.91	5.12	5.04	...	...	391	356	368	439	545	381
382	Machinery n.e.c.	4.81	5.02	5.13	...	...	339	373	344	485	647	382
3825	Office,computing etc..	...	...	...	...	...	57	65	74	101	122	3825
383	Electrical machinery ...	7.95	8.26	8.69	...	...	666	649	754	969	1613	383
3832	Radio,television etc..	...	...	...	...	...	...	...	...	...	...	3832
384	Transport equipment	3.70	4.31	4.16	...	...	394	469	334	512	595	384
3841	Shipbuilding, repair..	...	...	...	...	...	163	252	122	99	123	3841
3843	Motor vehicles	1.12	1.27	1.37	...	...	...	...	...	...	...	3843
385	Professional goods	[1.30	1.35	1.43]	...	...	55	59	29	35	51	385
390	Other industries				...	...	46	37	20	22	20	390
3	Manufacturing	57.05	62.10	64.65	...	...	7867	7569	8114	10982	13524	3
410	Electricity,gas,steam ..	6.40	6.84	6.97	...	...	2655	2152	1941	2073	2087	410
4101	Electricity	4.67	5.06	5.09	...	...	2180	1595	1527	1665	1681	4101
420	Water works and supply .	1.16	1.27	1.39	...	...	423	388	336	372	335	420
4	Electricity,gas etc	7.56	8.11	8.36	...	...	3078	2540	2277	2445	2422	4
2-4	All industry	90.13	96.15	100.29	...	...	11976	11445	11746	14904	18114	2-4

a/ Contributions to the gross domestic product.
c/ Major groups 210, 352, 355 and 356 are included in 351.
b/ Excluding land.
d/ Major group 290 is included in 220.

9. GROSS FIXED CAPITAL FORMATION
MACHINERY AND EQUIPMENT
(MILLION GUILDERS)

ISIC	INDUSTRY	1981	1982	1983	1984	1985		ISIC
210	Coal mining	-	-	-	-	-		210
220	Petroleum and gas ...... a/	947	1253	1230	1425	2014		220
230	Metal ore mining	-	-	-	-	-		230
290	Other mining .... a/	...	...	...	...	...		290
2	Mining, quarrying .	947	1253	1230	1425	2014		2
311/2	Food products	1054	1110	1268	1252	1561		311/2
313	Beverages	215	107	155	222	230		313
314	Tobacco	109	83	86	67	88		314
321	Textiles	100	116	135	154	174		321
3211	Spinning,weaving etc..	61	61	75	68	82		3211
322	Wearing apparel	15	18	19	18	25		322
323	Leather and products ...	7	13	11	10	13		323
324	Footwear	7	10	6	12	9		324
331	Wood products	53	61	45	64	61		331
332	Furniture, fixtures	23	18	23	31	31		332
341	Paper and products	245	274	247	287	380		341
3411	Pulp,paper etc.	180	210	179	131	186		3411
342	Printing,publishing	359	330	318	481	545		342
351	Industrial chemicals ...	1045	1265	1411	1836	1568		351
3511	Basic excl fertilizers	...	...	...	...	...		3511
3513	Synthetic resins etc .	...	...	...	...	...		3513
352	Other chemical products.	205	190	268	390	610		352
3522	Drugs and medicines ..	...	...	...	...	...		3522
353	Petroleum refineries ...	[596	363	531	1245	1984]		353
354	Petroleum,coal products.							354
355	Rubber products	47	52	50	74	70		355
356	Plastic products n.e.c..	128	128	153	195	310		356
361	Pottery,china etc	29	17	18	88	65		361
362	Glass and products	[214	213	236	340	260]		362
369	Non-metal products n.e.c							369
371	Iron and steel	300	301	401	449	797		371
372	Non-ferrous metals	121	66	52	103	84		372
381	Metal products	273	266	256	353	419		381
382	Machinery n.e.c.	249	287	286	382	490		382
3825	Office,computing etc..	47	53	68	80	109		3825
383	Electrical machinery ...	515	509	582	808	1306		383
3832	Radio,television etc..	...	...	...	...	...		3832
384	Transport equipment	221	223	219	400	500		384
3841	Shipbuilding, repair..	82	91	53	58	89		3841
3843	Motor vehicles	...	...	...	...	...		3843
385	Professional goods	35	43	22	31	36		385
390	Other industries	36	25	15	14	18		390
3	Manufacturing	6201	6088	6813	9306	11634		3
410	Electricity,gas,steam ..	883	836	670	907	1073		410
4101	Electricity	816	701	574	807	977		4101
420	Water works and supply .	62	84	66	118	92		420
4	Electricity,gas etc	945	920	736	1025	1165		4
2-4	All industry	8093	8261	8779	11756	14813		2-4

a/ Major group 290 is included in 220.

10. INDEX NUMBERS OF INDUSTRIAL PRODUCTION (1980 = 100)

ISIC	INDUSTRY	1976	1977	1978	1979	1981	1982	1983	1984	1985	a/ RATE	ISIC
210	Coal mining	...	...	...	...	...	...	...	...	...	...	210
220	Petroleum and gas ...... b/	109	108	100	106	91	78	84	85	93	-1.7	220
230	Metal ore mining	...	...	...	...	...	...	...	...	...	...	230
290	Other mining .... b/	...	...	...	...	...	...	...	...	...	...	290
2	Mining, quarrying .	109	108	100	106	91	78	84	85	93	-1.7	2
311/2	Food products	89	90	96	98	103	104	104	109	110	2.4	311/2
313	Beverages	86	86	93	99	105	104	101	100	101	1.8	313
314	Tobacco	104	98	102	105	104	117	117	116	128	2.3	314
321	Textiles	114	108	106	107	96	92	90	94	99	-1.6	321
3211	Spinning,weaving etc..	...	...	...	...	...	...	...	...	...	...	3211
322	Wearing apparel	129	111	108	107	85	84	81	75	72	-6.3	322
323	Leather and products ...	106	106	105	110	104	120	129	144	144	3.5	323
324	Footwear .... c/	111	107	108	100	87	91	84	76	76	-4.1	324
331	Wood products	...	...	...	...	...	...	...	...	...	...	331
332	Furniture, fixtures	...	...	...	...	...	...	...	...	...	...	332
341	Paper and products	87	87	93	100	102	110	109	117	124	4.0	341
3411	Pulp,paper etc.	...	...	...	...	...	...	...	...	...	...	3411
342	Printing,publishing .... d/	89	90	97	100	97	93	91	95	96	0.8	342
351	Industrial chemicals ... e/	91	94	98	103	107	104	120	131	133	4.3	351
3511	Basic excl fertilizers	...	...	...	...	...	...	...	...	...	...	3511
3513	Synthetic resins etc .	...	...	...	...	...	...	...	...	...	...	3513
352	Other chemical products. e/	...	...	...	...	...	...	...	...	...	...	352
3522	Drugs and medicines ..	...	...	...	...	...	...	...	...	...	...	3522
353	Petroleum refineries ...	...	...	...	...	...	...	...	...	...	...	353
354	Petroleum,coal products.	...	...	...	...	...	...	...	...	...	...	354
355	Rubber products .... c/	98	104	102	101	110	114	126	133	137	3.8	355
356	Plastic products n.e.c.. e/	...	...	...	...	...	...	...	...	...	...	356
361	Pottery,china etc											361
362	Glass and products	94	101	99	99	91	85	87	89	96	0.2	362
369	Non-metal products n.e.c											369
371	Iron and steel	94	91	100	103	106	97	95	109	106	1.3	371
372	Non-ferrous metals											372
381	Metal products	96	96	94	98	96	93	88	94	99	0.3	381
382	Machinery n.e.c.	97	99	100	100	100	95	93	99	103	0.7	382
3825	Office,computing etc..	...	...	...	...	...	...	...	...	...	...	3825
383	Electrical machinery ...	82	83	92	96	105	104	107	116	121	4.4	383
3832	Radio,television etc..	...	...	...	...	...	...	...	...	...	...	3832
384	Transport equipment	118	109	96	96	97	109	106	105	102	-1.6	384
3841	Shipbuilding, repair..	...	...	...	...	...	...	...	...	...	...	3841
3843	Motor vehicles	...	...	...	...	...	...	...	...	...	...	3843
385	Professional goods	...	...	...	...	...	...	...	...	...	...	385
390	Other industries	...	...	...	...	...	...	...	...	...	...	390
3	Manufacturing	93	94	96	99	100	99	101	106	109	1.8	3
410	Electricity,gas,steam ..	...	...	...	...	...	...	...	...	...	...	410
4101	Electricity	...	...	...	...	...	...	...	...	...	...	4101
420	Water works and supply .	105	98	99	101	101	104	105	107	108	0.3	420
4	Electricity,gas etc	95	94	99	98	100	103	104	106	107	1.3	4
2-4	All industry	97	97	98	101	98	94	97	101	105	0.9	2-4

a/ Annual growth rate 1976-1985.
b/ Major group 290 is included in 220.
c/ Vulcanized or moulded rubber and plastic footwear is included in major group 324.
d/ Printing only.
e/ Major groups 352 and 356 are included in 351.

NEW ZEALAND

The information on industrial activity is based on the reply to the United Nations Questionnaire on General Industrial Statistics from the Department of Statistics, Wellington. The concepts, definitions and classification by branches of industry are generally in accordance with United Nations standards.

The estimates for mining relate to the Department of Statistics integrated economic census of mining and quarrying which was conducted for the year 1983. This census will be repeated every 5 years. For manufacturing, the data for 1981 and 1983 relate to the integrated census conducted for the year but this census will not be conducted again until 1986. The 1982, 1984 and 1985 data for manufacturing shown in the tables are derived from a series of quarterly sample surveys which obviate the need for an annual census. The sample survey is based on 1 500 firms selected from the 1978/79 census; all manufacturing divisions of the industrial classification are represented. The estimates for electricity are obtained from annual surveys carried out by the New Zealand Electricity Department while the gas industry is surveyed within the framework of the economic census. The integrated census is conducted on an enterprise basis and covers all activity units in all industries (except, prior to the 1983 census, all single-activity unit manufacturing enterprises with an average of fewer than 2 persons engaged full-time during the year). A short form is used for small enterprises defined as those with at least 2 but fewer than 10 persons engaged full-time, and data for some of the tables exclude these units. The electricity survey covers all electric power plants engaged in production and distribution for public use.

The period for which census returns are collected is the year ended 31 March, or the financial year ended prior to that date. The period referred to in the tables is the financial year beginning in the year indicated.

The statistical unit employed in the census is the activity unit (previously known as the establishment). All operatives up to the point of sale of goods or services are covered, including the activities of ancillary activity units which service, or predominantly service, the activity units.

The estimates are compiled according to the national classification which generally follows the present ISIC.

The employment figures refer to the numbers recorded at, or on the nearest pay-day to, 28 February of the following year unless otherwise footnoted. The total number of persons engaged comprises employees, working proprietors or partners, and shareholders actively engaged in the business. Wages and salaries refer to gross earnings during the reference year before taxation and other deductions, covering such items as sick and holiday pay, bonuses, benefit allowances, and payments under piece-rate schemes. Capitalized wages and salaries are included. The estimates of hours worked relate to the total hours worked, including overtime, by all employees.

The data shown for output relate to turnover, defined as the total of all sales and other income except interest, dividends, royalties, patent fees and insurance claims received, plus the value of capital work done by own employees. The estimates for electricity relate to gross revenue.

Value added is defined as the industry contribution to gross domestic product, comprising wages and salaries, employer contributions to superannuation schemes, operating surplus, depreciation and indirect taxes less subsidies.

The estimates of gross fixed capital formation represent the amount spent by establishments and ancillary units in the census on the purchases of fixed assets, less the proceeds received from sales.

Related national publications:
<u>Census of Manufacturing</u> (for years conducted); <u>New Zealand Official Yearbook</u>; <u>Monthly Abstract of Statistics</u>, all published by the Department of Statistics, Wellington.

NEW ZEALAND

ISIC	INDUSTRY	1. NUMBER OF ESTABLISHMENTS a/ (NUMBER) 1981 b/	1982	1983	1984	1985	2. AVERAGE NUMBER OF PERSONS ENGAGED (THOUSANDS) 1981 b/c/	1982	1983 c/	1984	1985	ISIC
210	Coal mining	...	...	72	...	...	...	...	1.80	...	...	210
220	Petroleum and gas	...	...	46	...	...	...	...	1.10	...	...	220
230	Metal ore mining	...	...	62	...	...	...	...	0.40	...	...	230
290	Other mining	...	...	344	...	...	...	...	1.80	...	...	290
2	Mining, quarrying .	...	...	524	...	...	...	...	5.10	...	...	2
311/2	Food products	1365	...	1728	...	...	70.11	...	70.79	...	...	311/2
313	Beverages	[144]	...	[192]	...	...	[5.15]	...	[5.34]	...	...	313
314	Tobacco		...		...	...		...		...	...	314
321	Textiles	487	...	700	...	...	15.16	...	15.75	...	...	321
3211	Spinning,weaving etc..	100	...	120	...	...	4.66	...	5.05	...	...	3211
322	Wearing apparel	770	...	1044	...	...	18.89	...	19.90	...	...	322
323	Leather and products ...	174	...	235	...	...	3.59	...	3.46	...	...	323
324	Footwear	125	...	147	...	...	4.95	...	4.86	...	...	324
331	Wood products	934	...	1294	...	...	15.29	...	16.73	...	...	331
332	Furniture, fixtures	549	...	939	...	...	7.03	...	7.83	...	...	332
341	Paper and products	132	...	160	...	...	10.99	...	12.97	...	...	341
3411	Pulp,paper etc.	13	...	19	...	...	5.66	...	7.53	...	...	3411
342	Printing,publishing	763	...	1024	...	...	17.49	...	18.55	...	...	342
351	Industrial chemicals ...	166	...	225	...	...	5.12	...	4.94	...	...	351
3511	Basic excl fertilizers	33	...	36	...	...	0.52	...	0.69	...	...	3511
3513	Synthetic resins etc .	96	...	114	...	...	3.12	...	2.59	...	...	3513
352	Other chemical products.	319	...	385	...	...	7.53	...	7.65	...	...	352
3522	Drugs and medicines ..	47	...	55	...	...	1.76	...	1.66	...	...	3522
353	Petroleum refineries ...	16	...	24	...	...	0.51	...	0.79	...	...	353
354	Petroleum,coal products.	25	...	33	...	...	0.34	...	0.38	...	...	354
355	Rubber products	148	...	137	...	...	4.75	...	3.81	...	...	355
356	Plastic products n.e.c..	234	...	349	...	...	6.07	...	7.52	...	...	356
361	Pottery,china etc	55	...	161	...	...	1.27	...	1.23	...	...	361
362	Glass and products	93	...	132	...	...	2.37	...	2.37	...	...	362
369	Non-metal products n.e.c	439	...	534	...	...	6.24	...	6.50	...	...	369
371	Iron and steel	54	...	63	...	...	3.29	...	3.75	...	...	371
372	Non-ferrous metals	90	...	102	...	...	3.49	...	3.44	...	...	372
381	Metal products	1472	...	2133	...	...	23.14	...	25.83	...	...	381
382	Machinery n.e.c.	1143	...	1923	...	...	16.77	...	19.00	...	...	382
3825	Office,computing etc..	44	...	68	...	...	0.39	...	0.42	...	...	3825
383	Electrical machinery ...	428	...	612	...	...	15.58	...	15.59	...	...	383
3832	Radio,television etc..	132	...	220	...	...	4.62	...	4.65	...	...	3832
384	Transport equipment	456	...	675	...	...	22.07	...	21.07	...	...	384
3841	Shipbuilding, repair..	153	...	266	...	...	3.16	...	3.65	...	...	3841
3843	Motor vehicles	220	...	324	...	...	10.44	...	11.37	...	...	3843
385	Professional goods	63	...	100	...	...	1.08	...	1.40	...	...	385
390	Other industries	331	...	636	...	...	3.85	...	4.36	...	...	390
3	Manufacturing	d/ 11064	...	15687	...	...	d/ 296.75	...	305.81	...	...	3
410	Electricity,gas,steam .. e/	...	...	18	...	...	...	...	1.05	...	...	410
4101	Electricity	...	...	...	...	...	...	...	...	...	...	4101
420	Water works and supply .	...	...	...	...	...	...	...	...	...	...	420
4	Electricity,gas etc e/	...	...	18	...	...	...	...	1.05	...	...	4
2-4	All industry	...	...	...	...	...	...	...	...	...	...	2-4

a/ Twelve months beginning 1 April of the year indicated.
b/ Manufacturing: excluding single activity unit enterprises with less than 2 persons engaged.
c/ At 28 February of the following year.
d/ Including data for ancillary units servicing more than one major group which are not included at the industry level.
e/ Gas only.

ISIC	INDUSTRY	3. AVERAGE NUMBER OF EMPLOYEES (THOUSANDS) b/c/ 1981	1982	c/ 1983	1984	1985	4. WAGES AND SALARIES OF EMPLOYEES a/ (MILLION DOLLARS) b/ 1981	d/ 1982	1983	d/ 1984	d/ 1985	ISIC
210	Coal mining	...	...	1.70	...	...	...	...	32.9	...	...	210
220	Petroleum and gas	...	...	1.10	...	...	...	...	29.7	...	...	220
230	Metal ore mining	...	...	0.40	...	...	...	...	6.8	...	...	230
290	Other mining	...	...	1.70	...	...	...	...	27.3	...	...	290
2	Mining, quarrying .	...	...	4.90	...	...	...	...	96.7	...	...	2
311/2	Food products	69.03	...	69.35	...	...	952.0		1109.6			311/2
313	Beverages	[5.04]	...	[5.11]	...	...	[67.4]	[1212.1]	[82.7]	[1274.5	1262.6]	313
314	Tobacco		...		...	...						314
321	Textiles	14.63	...	14.69	...	...	170.1	e/ 460.7	191.8	e/ 488.1	e/ 556.7	321
3211	Spinning,weaving etc..	4.60	...	4.97	...	...	62.7	...	73.4	...	...	3211
322	Wearing apparel	18.15	...	18.86	...	...	165.4	e/	193.6	e/	e/	322
323	Leather and products ...	3.41	...	3.20	...	...	35.7	e/	40.7	e/	e/	323
324	Footwear	4.83	...	4.71	...	...	49.2	e/	55.0	e/	e/	324
331	Wood products	14.36	...	15.31	...	...	178.5	[320.7]	228.0	[343.2	401.5]	331
332	Furniture, fixtures	6.34	...	6.64	...	...	70.3		80.0			332
341	Paper and products	10.99	...	12.88	...	...	197.4	f/ 490.0	273.4	f/ 569.7	f/ 697.4	341
3411	Pulp,paper etc.	5.65	...	7.53	...	...	121.1	...	186.6	...	...	3411
342	Printing,publishing	16.63	...	17.32	...	...	235.9	f/	272.7	f/	f/	342
351	Industrial chemicals ...	5.05	...	4.85	...	...	79.4	g/ 387.9	86.2	g/ 428.2	g/ 509.5	351
3511	Basic excl fertilizers	0.51	...	0.68	...	...	7.5	...	13.6	...	...	3511
3513	Synthetic resins etc .	3.07	...	2.54	...	...	45.7	...	40.6	...	...	3513
352	Other chemical products.	7.40	...	7.40	...	...	99.4	g/	114.4	g/	g/	352
3522	Drugs and medicines ..	1.74	...	1.64	...	...	23.4	...	27.0	...	...	3522
353	Petroleum refineries ...	0.51	...	0.79	...	...	9.6	g/	19.7	g/	g/	353
354	Petroleum,coal products.	0.34	...	0.37	...	...	4.6	g/	6.1	g/	g/	354
355	Rubber products	4.71	...	3.74	...	...	75.0	g/	57.7	g/	g/	355
356	Plastic products n.e.c..	5.82	...	7.13	...	...	75.0	g/	100.9	g/	g/	356
361	Pottery,china etc	1.21	...	1.03	...	...	13.9		15.6			361
362	Glass and products	2.25	...	2.20	...	...	37.2	[152.4]	40.4	[145.3	171.6]	362
369	Non-metal products n.e.c	5.97	...	6.11	...	...	82.3		101.3			369
371	Iron and steel	3.26	...	3.71	...	...	60.5	[139.3]	71.9	[161.9	185.2]	371
372	Non-ferrous metals	3.42	...	3.35	...	...	55.0		66.6			372
381	Metal products	21.55	...	23.35	...	...	275.5	[h/ 1062.4]	346.1	[h/ 1149.7	h/ 1322.8]	381
382	Machinery n.e.c.	15.56	...	16.76	...	...	203.5		247.7			382
3825	Office,computing etc..	0.37	...	0.37	...	...	6.2	...	7.6	...	...	3825
383	Electrical machinery ...	15.21	...	14.95	...	...	187.7	h/	214.5	h/	h/	383
3832	Radio,television etc..	4.49	...	4.41	...	...	52.0	...	57.3	...	...	3832
384	Transport equipment	21.63	...	20.35	...	...	300.0	h/	338.1	h/	h/	384
3841	Shipbuilding, repair..	2.98	...	3.32	...	...	41.1	...	53.1	...	...	3841
3843	Motor vehicles	11.04	...	11.05	...	...	141.5	...	154.9	...	...	3843
385	Professional goods	1.02	...	1.32	...	...	11.0	h/	18.8	h/	h/	385
390	Other industries	3.44	...	3.59	...	...	35.0	44.9	42.0	53.5	65.3	390
3	Manufacturing	281.76	...	289.07	...	...	i/ 3798.0	4270.4	4415.5	4614.1	5172.6	3
410	Electricity,gas,steam .. j/	...	...	1.05	...	...	...	...	16.1	...	...	410
4101	Electricity	...	...	...	...	...	...	...	...	...	...	4101
420	Water works and supply .	...	...	...	...	...	...	...	...	...	...	420
4	Electricity,gas etc j/	...	...	1.05	...	...	...	...	16.1	...	...	4
2-4	All industry	...	...	...	...	...	...	...	...	...	...	2-4

a/ Twelve months beginning 1 April of the year indicated.
b/ Manufacturing: excluding single activity unit enterprises with less than 2 persons engaged.
c/ At 28 February of the following year.
d/ Manufacturing: derived from sample survey.
e/ Major groups 322 to 324 are included in 321.
f/ Major group 342 is included in 341.
g/ Major groups 352 to 356 are included in 351.
h/ Major groups 383 to 385 are included in 381 and 382 combined.
i/ Including data for ancillary units servicing more than one major group which are not included at the industry level.
j/ Gas only.

ISIC	INDUSTRY	5. SUPPLEMENTS TO WAGES AND SALARIES a/ (MILLION DOLLARS)					6. HOURS WORKED BY OPERATIVES a/b/c/ (MILLIONS)					ISIC
		d/ 1981	1982	1983	1984	1985	1981	e/ 1982	1983	e/ 1984	e/ 1985	
210	Coal mining	...	...	1.9	...	...	...	...	...	...	...	210
220	Petroleum and gas	...	...	2.3	...	...	...	...	...	...	...	220
230	Metal ore mining	...	...	0.5	...	...	...	...	...	...	...	230
290	Other mining	...	...	0.4	...	...	...	...	...	...	...	290
2	Mining, quarrying .	...	...	5.1	...	...	...	...	...	...	...	2
311/2	Food products	32.5	...	44.3	...	...	...	[	...	[	]	311/2
313	Beverages	[2.6]	...	[2.7]	...	...	...	135.6	...	135.8	128.3	313
314	Tobacco		...		...	...	...	]	...	]		314
321	Textiles	4.4	...	5.3	...	...	...	f/ 73.0	...	f/ 70.9	f/ 74.0	321
3211	Spinning,weaving etc..	1.7	...	2.4	...	...	...	...	...	...	...	3211
322	Wearing apparel	1.6	...	2.2	...	...	...	f/	...	f/	f/	322
323	Leather and products ...	0.9	...	1.3	...	...	...	f/	...	f/	f/	323
324	Footwear	0.9	...	1.2	...	...	...	f/	...	f/	f/	324
331	Wood products	4.5	...	7.0	...	...	...	[43.4]	...	[42.5	43.6]	331
332	Furniture, fixtures	1.2	...	1.4	...	...	...		...			332
341	Paper and products	8.0	...	10.8	...	...	...	g/ 56.6	...	g/ 62.0	g/ 67.1	341
3411	Pulp,paper etc.	4.9	...	6.6	...	...	...	...	...	...	...	3411
342	Printing,publishing	6.0	...	6.0	...	...	...	g/	...	g/	g/	342
351	Industrial chemicals ...	3.0	...	4.1	...	...	...	h/ 48.0	...	h/ 47.7	h/ 49.1	351
3511	Basic excl fertilizers	0.2	...	0.5	...	...	...	...	...	...	...	3511
3513	Synthetic resins etc .	1.4	...	1.4	...	...	...	...	...	...	...	3513
352	Other chemical products.	4.2	...	5.0	...	...	...	h/	...	h/	h/	352
3522	Drugs and medicines ..	1.2	...	1.2	...	...	...	...	...	...	...	3522
353	Petroleum refineries ...	0.9	...	1.2	...	...	...	h/	...	h/	h/	353
354	Petroleum,coal products.	0.2	...	0.3	...	...	...	h/	...	h/	h/	354
355	Rubber products	1.9	...	2.3	...	...	...	h/	...	h/	h/	355
356	Plastic products n.e.c..	1.8	...	2.9	...	...	...	h/	...	h/	h/	356
361	Pottery,china etc	0.3	...	0.5	...	...	...	[	...	[	]	361
362	Glass and products	1.4	...	1.7	...	...	...	18.8	...	17.0	17.5	362
369	Non-metal products n.e.c	2.8	...	4.6	...	...	...	]	...	]		369
371	Iron and steel	4.2	...	5.3	...	...	...	[13.4]	...	[14.7	13.9]	371
372	Non-ferrous metals	2.8	...	3.3	...	...	...		...			372
381	Metal products	6.5	...	10.0	...	...	...	[i/ 137.3]	...	[i/ 140.0	i/ 142.1]	381
382	Machinery n.e.c.	5.0	...	7.4	...	...	...		...			382
3825	Office,computing etc..	0.3	...	0.5	...	...	...	...	...	...	...	3825
383	Electrical machinery ...	6.1	...	7.7	...	...	...	i/	...	i/	i/	383
3832	Radio,television etc..	1.8	...	1.8	...	...	...	...	...	...	...	3832
384	Transport equipment	12.4	...	14.7	...	...	...	i/	...	i/	i/	384
3841	Shipbuilding, repair..	1.3	...	0.9	...	...	...	...	...	...	...	3841
3843	Motor vehicles	5.4	...	6.3	...	...	...	...	...	...	...	3843
385	Professional goods	0.3	...	0.8	...	...	...	i/	...	i/	i/	385
390	Other industries	0.7	...	1.3	...	...	...	7.3	...	7.8	8.2	390
3	Manufacturing	117.1	...	155.3	...	...	...	533.4	...	538.4	543.8	3
410	Electricity,gas,steam ..	...	...	0.7	...	...	...	...	...	...	...	410
4101	Electricity	...	...	...	...	...	...	...	...	...	...	4101
420	Water works and supply .	...	...	...	...	...	...	...	...	...	...	420
4	Electricity,gas etc	...	...	0.7	...	...	...	...	...	...	...	4
2-4	All industry	...	...	...	...	...	...	...	...	...	...	2-4

a/ Twelve months beginning 1 April of the year indicated.
b/ Manufacturing: excluding single activity unit enterprises with less than 2 persons engaged.
c/ Hours worked by all employees.
d/ Excluding single activity enterprises with fewer than 10 employees.
e/ Manufacturing: derived from sample survey.
f/ Major groups 322 to 324 are included in 321.
g/ Major group 342 is included in 341.
h/ Major groups 352 to 356 are included in 351.
i/ Major groups 383 to 385 are included in 381 and 382 combined.

ISIC	INDUSTRY	7. OUTPUT a/ (MILLION DOLLARS) c/d/ 1981	e/ 1982	c/d/f/ 1983	e/ 1984	e/ 1985	8. VALUE ADDED IN PRODUCERS' PRICES a/b/ (MILLION DOLLARS) c/ 1981	1982	1983	1984	1985	ISIC
210	Coal mining	...	...	102	...	...	...	...	37.1	...	...	210
220	Petroleum and gas	...	...	754	...	...	...	...	251.1	...	...	220
230	Metal ore mining	...	...	61	...	...	...	...	19.9	...	...	230
290	Other mining	...	...	155	...	...	...	...	60.7	...	...	290
2	Mining, quarrying .	...	...	1072	...	...	...	...	368.8	...	...	2
311/2	Food products	5503	6494	6087	7415	8110	1373.8	...	1716.3	...	...	311/2
313	Beverages	513		667			166.6	...	203.5	...	...	313
314	Tobacco							...		...	...	314
321	Textiles	813	g/ 1886	1003	g/ 2314	g/ 2532	272.2	...	314.8	...	...	321
3211	Spinning,weaving etc..	302	...	425	...	...	101.6	...	116.6	...	...	3211
322	Wearing apparel	493	g/	635	g/	g/	219.7	...	265.8	...	...	322
323	Leather and products ...	178	g/	228	g/	g/	54.2	...	65.4	...	...	323
324	Footwear	166	g/	188	g/	g/	66.0	...	79.1	...	...	324
331	Wood products	888	1294	1100	1676	1896	289.4	...	357.0	...	...	331
332	Furniture, fixtures	279		352			106.0	...	121.7	...	...	332
341	Paper and products	1231	h/ 2122	1348	h/ 2956	h/ 3274	331.1	...	405.7	...	...	341
3411	Pulp,paper etc.	777	...	855	...	...	192.9	...	257.2	...	...	3411
342	Printing,publishing	728	h/	929	h/	h/	353.5	...	424.9	...	...	342
351	Industrial chemicals ...	632	i/ 2269	751	i/ 3029	i/ 3371	151.3	...	179.8	...	...	351
3511	Basic excl fertilizers	51	...	91	...	...	16.4	...	38.2	...	...	3511
3513	Synthetic resins etc .	300	...	296	...	...	83.6	...	81.2	...	...	3513
352	Other chemical products.	643	i/	781	i/	i/	176.4	...	25.6	...	...	352
3522	Drugs and medicines ..	146	...	170	...	...	36.5	...	47.6	...	...	3522
353	Petroleum refineries ...	112	i/	142	i/	i/	39.8	...	0.4	...	...	353
354	Petroleum,coal products.	36	i/	46	i/	i/	9.7	...	11.3	...	...	354
355	Rubber products	266	i/	229	i/	i/	105.5	...	78.3	...	...	355
356	Plastic products n.e.c..	327	i/	546	i/	i/	123.1	...	184.3	...	...	356
361	Pottery,china etc	33	726	36	833	974	18.4	...	20.0	...	...	361
362	Glass and products	142		163			59.5	...	69.0	...	...	362
369	Non-metal products n.e.c	456		598			148.8	...	254.0	...	...	369
371	Iron and steel	386	831	466	1168	1085	108.5	...	121.9	...	...	371
372	Non-ferrous metals	332		496			105.8	...	173.6	...	...	372
381	Metal products	1314	j/ 4829	1678	j/ 6282	j/ 6795	445.3	...	584.4	...	...	381
382	Machinery n.e.c.	850		1123			295.3	...	377.0	...	...	382
3825	Office,computing etc..	22	...	26	...	...	7.6	...	8.8	...	...	3825
383	Electrical machinery ...	863	j/	1106	j/	j/	293.3	...	344.2	...	...	383
3832	Radio,television etc..	258	...	348	...	...	80.5	...	91.8	...	...	3832
384	Transport equipment	1328	j/	1429	j/	j/	393.1	...	439.7	...	...	384
3841	Shipbuilding, repair..	96	...	131	...	...	47.3	...	61.3	...	...	3841
3843	Motor vehicles	971	...	1020	...	...	209.9	...	215.2	...	...	3843
385	Professional goods	44	j/	85	j/	j/	17.1	...	27.0	...	...	385
390	Other industries	153	210	207	323	368	57.2	...	70.2	...	...	390
3	Manufacturing	f/ 18709	20661	22419	25996	28405	f/ 5878.6	...	7104.9	...	...	3
410	Electricity,gas,steam .. k/	...	...	106	...	...	...	...	33.6	...	...	410
4101	Electricity	...	...	...	...	...	...	...	...	...	...	4101
420	Water works and supply .	...	...	...	...	...	...	...	...	...	...	420
4	Electricity,gas etc k/	...	...	106	...	...	...	...	33.6	...	...	4
2-4	All industry	...	...	...	...	...	...	...	...	...	...	2-4

a/ Twelve months beginning 1 April of the year indicated.
b/ Net of non-industrial costs.
c/ Manufacturing: excluding single activity unit enterprises with less than 2 persons engaged.
d/ Turnover; excluding indirect taxes; including subsidies.
e/ Manufacturing: derived from sample survey; value of sales and other income.
f/ Including data for ancillary units servicing more than one major group which are not included at the industry level.
g/ Major groups 322 to 324 are included in 321.
h/ Major group 342 is included in 341.
i/ Major groups 352 to 356 are included in 351.
j/ Major groups 383 to 385 are included in 381 and 382 combined.
k/ Gas only.

ISIC	INDUSTRY	9. GROSS FIXED CAPITAL FORMATION TOTAL a/ (MILLION DOLLARS)					10. GROSS FIXED CAPITAL FORMATION MACHINERY AND EQUIPMENT a/b/ (MILLION DOLLARS)					ISIC
		c/ 1981	b/ 1982	1983	b/ 1984	b/ 1985	d/ 1981	1982	1983	1984	1985	
210	Coal mining	...	...	25.7	...	...	...	...	12.30	...	...	210
220	Petroleum and gas	...	...	29.4	...	...	...	...	17.30	...	...	220
230	Metal ore mining	...	...	2.5	...	...	...	...	1.60	...	...	230
290	Other mining	...	...	11.5	...	...	...	...	8.50	...	...	290
2	Mining, quarrying .	...	...	69.1	...	...	...	...	39.70	...	...	2
311/2	Food products	385.3		378.4			221.73	...	259.20	...	...	311/2
313	Beverages	[31.1]	[393.8]	[26.2]	[466.5	473.7]	[19.53]	...	[21.20]	...	...	313
314	Tobacco							...		...	...	314
321	Textiles	28.3	e/ 56.3	35.1	e/ 73.3	e/ 87.0	20.75	...	29.90	...	...	321
3211	Spinning,weaving etc..	13.8	...	16.4	...	...	10.16	...	15.10	...	...	3211
322	Wearing apparel	10.6	e/	20.0	e/	e/	4.93	...	14.50	...	...	322
323	Leather and products ...	6.6	e/	7.0	e/	e/	4.52	...	5.60	...	...	323
324	Footwear	2.7	e/	3.7	e/	e/	1.77	...	4.10	...	...	324
331	Wood products	33.8	[46.1]	48.8	[109.2	162.2]	19.26	...	26.80	...	...	331
332	Furniture, fixtures	7.7		8.7			3.81	...	7.00	...	...	332
341	Paper and products	59.6	f/ 149.9	85.3	f/ 195.0	f/ 178.5	48.01	...	68.70	...	...	341
3411	Pulp,paper etc.	40.2	...	69.3	...	...	33.21	...	55.10	...	...	3411
342	Printing,publishing	42.1	f/	56.9	f/	f/	23.64	...	57.20	...	...	342
351	Industrial chemicals ...	78.8	g/ 1158.8	90.7	g/ 691.4	g/ 638.4	27.51	...	84.80	...	...	351
3511	Basic excl fertilizers	58.2	...	63.5	...	...	12.11	...	62.70	...	...	3511
3513	Synthetic resins etc .	10.7	...	10.2	...	...	7.84	...	9.40	...	...	3513
352	Other chemical products.	9.6	g/	14.9	g/	g/	9.56	...	16.50	...	...	352
3522	Drugs and medicines ..	5.4	...	3.1	...	...	2.70	...	3.80	...	...	3522
353	Petroleum refineries ...	80.8	g/	85.9	g/	g/	1.71	...	424.70	...	...	353
354	Petroleum,coal products.	1.8	g/	0.3	g/	g/	1.07	...	0.20	...	...	354
355	Rubber products	8.2	g/	14.6	g/	g/	5.91	...	12.70	...	...	355
356	Plastic products n.e.c..	17.7	g/	36.8	g/	g/	12.71	...	31.70	...	...	356
361	Pottery,china etc	1.8		0.8			1.28	...	0.40	...	...	361
362	Glass and products	4.6	[70.0]	4.3	[49.7	48.4]	3.93	...	3.50	...	...	362
369	Non-metal products n.e.c	47.6		33.8			37.09	...	23.70	...	...	369
371	Iron and steel	23.8	[314.4]	371.0	[172.0	526.7]	17.14	...	18.60	...	...	371
372	Non-ferrous metals	80.2		18.5			38.17	...	16.70	...	...	372
381	Metal products	50.2	[h/ 127.9]	53.6	[h/ 188.3	h/ 265.5]	36.04	...	44.20	...	...	381
382	Machinery n.e.c.	22.3		30.5			11.91	...	27.60	...	...	382
3825	Office,computing etc..	0.9	...	0.5	...	...	0.24	...	0.70	...	...	3825
383	Electrical machinery ...	28.3	h/	32.7	h/	h/	18.08	...	26.70	...	...	383
3832	Radio,television etc..	5.9	...	8.6	...	...	3.76	...	7.30	...	...	3832
384	Transport equipment	44.9	h/	27.5	h/	h/	27.89	...	23.60	...	...	384
3841	Shipbuilding, repair..	1.7	...	3.1	...	...	0.43	...	2.10	...	...	3841
3843	Motor vehicles	20.8	...	13.3	...	...	14.66	...	16.00	...	...	3843
385	Professional goods	1.0	h/	3.5	h/	h/	0.56	...	1.70	...	...	385
390	Other industries	4.2	6.7	7.9	10.8	13.5	1.85	...	6.20	...	...	390
3	Manufacturing	i/ 1248.1	2323.9	1497.4	1956.2	2393.9	620.36	...	257.70	...	...	3
410	Electricity,gas,steam .. j/	...	...	19.1	...	...	...	...	0.60	...	...	410
4101	Electricity	...	...	...	...	...	...	...	...	...	...	4101
420	Water works and supply .	...	...	...	...	...	...	...	...	...	...	420
4	Electricity,gas etc j/	...	...	19.1	...	...	...	...	0.60	...	...	4
2-4	All industry	...	...	...	...	...	...	...	...	...	...	2-4

a/ Twelve months beginning 1 April of the year indicated.
b/ The value of sales is not deducted.
c/ Manufacturing: excluding single activity unit enterprises with less than 2 persons engaged.
d/ Manufacturing: excluding single activity unit enterprises with fewer than 10 employees.
e/ Major groups 322 to 324 are included in 321.
f/ Major group 342 is included in 341.
g/ Major groups 352 to 356 are included in 351.
h/ Major groups 383 to 385 are included in 381 and 382 combined.
i/ Including data for ancillary units servicing more than one major group which are not included at the industry level.
j/ Gas only.

11. VALUE OF STOCKS AT END OF PERIOD
TOTAL a/
(MILLION DOLLARS)

ISIC	INDUSTRY	1981	b/ 1982	1983	b/ 1984	b/ 1985	ISIC
210	Coal mining	...	...	61.0	...	...	210
220	Petroleum and gas	...	...	37.9	...	...	220
230	Metal ore mining	...	...	3.2	...	...	230
290	Other mining	...	...	12.1	...	...	290
2	Mining, quarrying .	...	...	114.2	...	...	2
311/2	Food products	536.6	[	549.1	[	]	311/2
313	Beverages	[139.7]	762.2]	[174.4]	891.4	831.0]	313
314	Tobacco						314
321	Textiles	156.2	c/ 359.9	181.5	c/ 488.8	c/ 509.4	321
3211	Spinning,weaving etc..	62.7	...	70.7	...	...	3211
322	Wearing apparel	86.0	c/	115.6	c/	c/	322
323	Leather and products ...	40.5	c/	53.7	c/	c/	323
324	Footwear	25.8	c/	31.8	c/	c/	324
331	Wood products	144.6	[229.9]	188.1	[239.2	284.2]	331
332	Furniture, fixtures	33.4		44.5			332
341	Paper and products	170.8	d/ 303.7	228.0	d/ 390.3	d/ 437.5	341
3411	Pulp,paper etc.	84.3	...	143.9	...	...	3411
342	Printing,publishing	88.9	d/	106.8	d/	d/	342
351	Industrial chemicals ...	142.7	e/ 499.4	143.4	e/ 621.7	e/ 764.6	351
3511	Basic excl fertilizers	10.7	...	11.3	...	...	3511
3513	Synthetic resins etc .	54.0	...	49.0	...	...	3513
352	Other chemical products.	156.6	e/	178.6	e/	e/	352
3522	Drugs and medicines ..	45.6	...	51.7	...	...	3522
353	Petroleum refineries ...	24.9	e/	24.9	e/	e/	353
354	Petroleum,coal products.	4.8	e/	6.7	e/	e/	354
355	Rubber products	61.9	e/	36.8	e/	e/	355
356	Plastic products n.e.c..	57.1	e/	93.5	e/	e/	356
361	Pottery,china etc	7.5	[	8.1	[	]	361
362	Glass and products	27.4	97.2]	28.9	101.0	104.1]	362
369	Non-metal products n.e.c	52.9		70.3			369
371	Iron and steel	83.3	[159.8]	106.2	[229.2	204.9]	371
372	Non-ferrous metals	77.0		79.1			372
381	Metal products	234.6	f/ [1100.5]	291.7	f/ [1420.0	f/ 1498.0]	381
382	Machinery n.e.c.	186.5		171.9			382
3825	Office,computing etc..	10.1	...	207.4	...	...	3825
383	Electrical machinery ...	210.0	f/	235.2	f/	f/	383
3832	Radio,television etc..	66.0	...	70.8	...	...	3832
384	Transport equipment	300.5	f/	313.3	f/	f/	384
3841	Shipbuilding, repair..	9.6	...	19.2	...	...	3841
3843	Motor vehicles	185.7	...	196.0	...	...	3843
385	Professional goods	9.9	f/	21.0	f/	f/	385
390	Other industries	31.5	47.2	43.5	68.3	84.2	390
3	Manufacturing	3097.9	3559.8	3562.1	4449.9	4717.9	3
410	Electricity,gas,steam .. g/	...	...	6.7	...	...	410
4101	Electricity	...	...	...	...	...	4101
420	Water works and supply .	...	...	...	...	...	420
4	Electricity,gas etc g/	...	...	6.7	...	...	4
2-4	All industry	...	...	...	...	...	2-4

a/ At 31 March of the following year.
b/ Manufacturing: derived from sample survey.
c/ Major groups 322 to 324 are included in 321.
d/ Major group 342 is included in 341.
e/ Major groups 352 to 356 are included in 351.
f/ Major groups 383 to 385 are included in 381 and 382 combined.
g/ Gas only.

NICARAGUA

The information in the tables is based on the reply to the United Nations Questionnaire on General Industrial Statistics from the Instituto Nacional de Estadisticas y Censos, Managua and the official publication of the Banco Central de Nicaragua, Managua. The concepts, definitions and classification by branches of industry are generally in accordance with United Nations standards.

The data are derived from the annual manufacturing survey recently initiated by the Instituto Nacional de Estadisticas and cover establishments with 30 or more persons engaged. It should be noted that for 1981 the estimates include data for 173 establishments with less than 30 persons engaged, and in 1982 100 of these establishments are included in the tabulations. The data are compiled according to the national classification system which generally follows the present version of ISIC.

Wages and salaries of employees include employers' contributions to the Instituto Nicaraguense de Seguridad Social (INSS) on behalf of their employees. Output is the sum of the following values: (a) all goods sold, (b) changes in stock of finished products and work in progress, (c) losses, donations, internal consumption of finished products and work in progress and (d) own-account construction and excess of indirect taxes over subsidies. Value added is calculated as the difference between the output obtained above and the value of intermediate consumption (total of the costs of primary materials and supplies, electricity, fuels, oils and other goods and services required for manufacturing process). Gross fixed capital formation is the value of purchases and own-account construction of fixed assets during the year less the value of corresponding sales.

Related national publications:
<u>Compendio Estadistico</u> (occasional), published jointly by the Banco Central de Nicaragua and the Ministerio de Economia, Industria y Comercio, Managua.

ISIC	INDUSTRY	1. NUMBER OF ENTERPRISES a/b/ (NUMBER) 1981	1982	1983	1984	1985	2. AVERAGE NUMBER OF EMPLOYEES a/b/ (NUMBER) 1981	1982	1983	1984	1985	ISIC
210	Coal mining	...	...	...	...	...	...	...	...	...	...	210
220	Petroleum and gas	...	...	...	...	...	...	...	...	...	...	220
230	Metal ore mining	...	...	...	...	...	...	...	...	...	...	230
290	Other mining	...	...	...	...	...	...	...	...	...	...	290
2	Mining, quarrying .	...	...	...	...	...	...	...	...	...	...	2
311/2	Food products	126	91	66	73	...	14246	15481	13208	16365	...	311/2
313	Beverages	9	9	9	9	...	4025	4543	4587	4379	...	313
314	Tobacco	3	2	2	2	...	771	460	516	513	...	314
321	Textiles	34	34	19	32	...	4058	4793	4386	5652	...	321
3211	Spinning,weaving etc..	25	25	10	21	...	2736	3482	2773	3713	...	3211
322	Wearing apparel	26	16	16	15	...	1262	1457	1428	1615	...	322
323	Leather and products ...	10	9	8	7	...	516	478	452	388	...	323
324	Footwear	14	6	5	5	...	1051	992	945	1040	...	324
331	Wood products	22	13	12	8	...	1602	1415	1378	1149	...	331
332	Furniture, fixtures	20	5	5	5	...	582	277	319	288	...	332
341	Paper and products	3	3	4	3	...	151	171	213	136	...	341
3411	Pulp,paper etc.	-	-	-	-	...	-	-	-	-	...	3411
342	Printing,publishing	25	20	21	14	...	1437	1460	1940	1577	...	342
351	Industrial chemicals ...	17	16	14	15	...	1768	1293	1009	1710	...	351
3511	Basic excl fertilizers	6	6	5	5	...	861	522	486	492	...	3511
3513	Synthetic resins etc .	1	1	1	1	...	419	397	294	901	...	3513
352	Other chemical products.	35	29	31	33	...	2157	2114	2274	2469	...	352
3522	Drugs and medicines ..	10	9	9	9	...	670	691	692	760	...	3522
353	Petroleum refineries ...	1	1	1	1	...	96	96	56	54	...	353
354	Petroleum,coal products.	-	1	1	1	...	-	11	11	9	...	354
355	Rubber products	4	6	6	4	...	166	211	201	170	...	355
356	Plastic products n.e.c..	10	9	7	6	...	1055	937	1000	1117	...	356
361	Pottery,china etc	2	2	2	2	...	99	79	88	80	...	361
362	Glass and products	3	3	2	3	...	83	75	51	84	...	362
369	Non-metal products n.e.c	16	12	12	10	...	1548	1235	1553	1616	...	369
371	Iron and steel	3	3	4	3	...	95	77	125	72	...	371
372	Non-ferrous metals	-	-	-	-	...	-	-	-	-	...	372
381	Metal products	26	23	23	21	...	1882	1795	2215	2321	...	381
382	Machinery n.e.c.	3	3	3	3	...	209	193	197	220	...	382
3825	Office,computing etc..	-	-	-	-	...	-	-	-	-	...	3825
383	Electrical machinery ...	9	9	9	8	...	323	325	345	287	...	383
3832	Radio,television etc..	2	2	2	2	...	55	61	48	24	...	3832
384	Transport equipment	5	5	3	4	...	188	188	246	391	...	384
3841	Shipbuilding, repair..	2	2	1	2	...	120	86	196	364	...	3841
3843	Motor vehicles	2	2	2	2	...	41	51	50	27	...	3843
385	Professional goods	3	3	2	2	...	326	319	306	344	...	385
390	Other industries	2	1	1	1	...	93	72	62	47	...	390
3	Manufacturing	431	334	288	290	...	39789	40547	39111	44093	...	3
410	Electricity,gas,steam ..	...	...	...	...	...	...	...	...	...	...	410
4101	Electricity	...	...	...	...	...	...	...	...	...	...	4101
420	Water works and supply .	...	...	...	...	...	...	...	...	...	...	420
4	Electricity,gas etc	...	...	...	...	...	...	...	...	...	...	4
2-4	All industry	...	...	...	...	...	...	...	...	...	...	2-4

a/ Establishments with 30 or more persons engaged.
b/ Including certain establishments with less than 30 persons engaged.

ISIC	INDUSTRY	3. WAGES AND SALARIES OF EMPLOYEES a/b/c/ (MILLION CORDOBAS) 1981	1982	1983	1984	1985	4. OUTPUT IN PRODUCERS' PRICES a/c/ (MILLION CORDOBAS) 1981	1982	1983	1984	1985	ISIC
210	Coal mining	...	...	...	...	...	...	...	...	...	...	210
220	Petroleum and gas	...	...	...	...	...	...	...	...	...	...	220
230	Metal ore mining	...	...	...	...	...	...	...	...	...	...	230
290	Other mining	...	...	...	...	...	...	...	...	...	...	290
2	Mining, quarrying .	...	...	...	...	...	...	...	...	...	...	2
311/2	Food products	500.3	574.1	541.7	949.6	...	3429	5022	4885	7054	...	311/2
313	Beverages	177.8	209.1	245.5	305.5	...	1493	1990	2570	4363	...	313
314	Tobacco	29.9	31.1	52.0	64.1	...	613	1210	1428	1101	...	314
321	Textiles	122.9	155.2	179.6	261.8	...	486	812	989	1435	...	321
3211	Spinning,weaving etc..	86.2	116.0	119.7	168.6	...	322	581	608	890	...	3211
322	Wearing apparel	26.7	41.9	64.2	70.2	...	131	215	384	469	...	322
323	Leather and products ...	16.1	16.6	17.5	23.0	...	116	117	140	214	...	323
324	Footwear	37.4	43.5	69.4	77.3	...	199	266	392	534	...	324
331	Wood products	42.6	55.7	53.3	40.6	...	129	166	222	250	...	331
332	Furniture, fixtures	16.9	12.9	13.2	16.0	...	58	45	58	94	...	332
341	Paper and products	5.7	6.8	11.4	12.4	...	38	59	99	116	...	341
3411	Pulp,paper etc.	-	-	-	-	...	-	-	-	-	...	3411
342	Printing,publishing	63.0	88.7	85.6	128.6	...	217	272	371	582	...	342
351	Industrial chemicals ...	81.5	69.3	73.3	105.8	...	712	756	856	1053	...	351
3511	Basic excl fertilizers	40.9	34.1	36.9	51.8	...	232	244	270	281	...	3511
3513	Synthetic resins etc .	19.8	17.6	18.7	21.2	...	190	196	207	270	...	3513
352	Other chemical products.	102.7	106.0	133.8	165.6	...	738	910	1315	1624	...	352
3522	Drugs and medicines ..	34.5	33.3	44.6	60.8	...	130	149	191	249	...	3522
353	Petroleum refineries ...	16.1	16.0	16.7	16.8	...	2333	2189	1495	2559	...	353
354	Petroleum,coal products.	-	1.6	2.1	1.9	...	-	90	71	82	...	354
355	Rubber products	7.9	9.2	12.6	13.3	...	43	59	77	115	...	355
356	Plastic products n.e.c..	41.3	37.8	43.0	59.8	...	217	277	339	604	...	356
361	Pottery,china etc	2.7	5.4	4.6	5.7	...	14	24	28	31	...	361
362	Glass and products	3.4	3.7	2.7	6.0	...	15	17	17	34	...	362
369	Non-metal products n.e.c	54.5	46.2	64.1	85.0	...	330	343	483	572	...	369
371	Iron and steel	3.4	2.8	5.9	5.9	...	16	9	22	21	...	371
372	Non-ferrous metals	-	-	-	-	...	-	-	-	-	...	372
381	Metal products	69.0	67.9	90.8	118.3	...	398	585	758	1270	...	381
382	Machinery n.e.c.	9.6	7.7	10.6	12.4	...	48	35	37	56	...	382
3825	Office,computing etc..	-	-	-	-	...	-	-	-	-	...	3825
383	Electrical machinery ...	15.0	15.0	20.8	24.3	...	97	116	142	141	...	383
3832	Radio,television etc..	1.9	2.2	2.3	1.1	...	17	27	27	14	...	3832
384	Transport equipment	6.7	9.5	12.7	29.1	...	33	53	50	109	...	384
3841	Shipbuilding, repair..	2.9	4.0	7.1	21.3	...	8	22	26	75	...	3841
3843	Motor vehicles	2.2	3.9	5.5	7.8	...	10	13	24	34	...	3843
385	Professional goods	10.9	11.6	11.6	14.8	...	42	52	44	51	...	385
390	Other industries	4.0	2.8	3.8	3.2	...	9	9	15	17	...	390
3	Manufacturing	1468.0	1648.1	1842.5	2617.0	...	11954	15698	17287	24551	...	3
410	Electricity,gas,steam ..	...	...	...	...	...	...	...	...	...	...	410
4101	Electricity	...	...	...	...	...	...	...	...	...	...	4101
420	Water works and supply .	...	...	...	...	...	...	...	...	...	...	420
4	Electricity,gas etc	...	...	...	...	...	...	...	...	...	...	4
2-4	All industry	...	...	...	...	...	...	...	...	...	...	2-4

a/ Establishments with 30 or more persons engaged. b/ Including employers' contributions to insurance schemes.
c/ Including certain establishments with less than 30 persons engaged.

ISIC	INDUSTRY	5. VALUE ADDED IN PRODUCERS' PRICES a/b/ (MILLION CORDOBAS)					6. GROSS FIXED CAPITAL FORMATION TOTAL a/b/ (THOUSAND CORDOBAS)					ISIC
		1981	1982	1983	1984	1985	1981	1982	1983	1984	1985	
210	Coal mining	...	...	...	...	...	...	...	...	...	...	210
220	Petroleum and gas	...	...	...	...	...	...	...	...	...	...	220
230	Metal ore mining	...	...	...	...	...	...	...	...	...	...	230
290	Other mining	...	...	...	...	...	...	...	...	...	...	290
2	Mining, quarrying .	...	...	...	...	...	...	...	...	...	...	2
311/2	Food products	1079	1623	1576	2675	...	92971	204181	75268	253349	...	311/2
313	Beverages	1042	1293	1836	3044	...	82958	31420	33246	54474	...	313
314	Tobacco	508	1111	1314	966	...	32500	12626	6426	9434	...	314
321	Textiles	262	442	594	880	...	17019	17477	17556	80280	...	321
3211	Spinning,weaving etc..	182	323	358	269	...	15443	14982	11653	16200	...	3211
322	Wearing apparel	49	133	226	275	...	1538	1406	1736	11668	...	322
323	Leather and products ...	57	56	67	99	...	3918	1151	5095	3067	...	323
324	Footwear	101	152	236	381	...	11706	6248	20491	11396	...	324
331	Wood products	56	92	108	100	...	6678	4459	5189	17301	...	331
332	Furniture, fixtures	33	29	37	54	...	1872	4260	1703	2809	...	332
341	Paper and products	13	23	40	48	...	579	673	379	1378	...	341
3411	Pulp,paper etc.	-	-	-	-	...	-	-	-	-	...	3411
342	Printing,publishing	114	156	209	329	...	21238	14084	12863	39757	...	342
351	Industrial chemicals ...	191	291	307	372	...	10833	123102	8660	29084	...	351
3511	Basic excl fertilizers	52	98	100	99	...	3159	14383	7282	22533	...	3511
3513	Synthetic resins etc .	60	121	95	112	...	160	106429	118	9475	...	3513
352	Other chemical products.	329	458	671	887	...	12895	19070	38237	60821	...	352
3522	Drugs and medicines ..	78	89	122	164	...	4244	2279	13752	17714	...	3522
353	Petroleum refineries ...	445	562	204	1417	...	3350	3499	3080	7537	...	353
354	Petroleum,coal products.	-	31	28	43	...	-	67	279	17	...	354
355	Rubber products	24	33	44	76	...	403	525	778	3528	...	355
356	Plastic products n.e.c..	99	142	188	398	...	3024	1552	2358	24045	...	356
361	Pottery,china etc	4	12	12	18	...	155	1525	17	1546	...	361
362	Glass and products	6	9	12	22	...	241	162	414	129	...	362
369	Non-metal products n.e.c	130	131	202	201	...	11557	15267	124676	19037	...	369
371	Iron and steel	8	5	14	11	...	210	-	1036	310	...	371
372	Non-ferrous metals	-	-	-	-	...	-	-	-	-	...	372
381	Metal products	159	270	350	790	...	7396	16389	25083	16393	...	381
382	Machinery n.e.c.	22	16	21	35	...	1685	2462	3048	5089	...	382
3825	Office,computing etc..	-	-	-	-	...	-	-	-	-	...	3825
383	Electrical machinery ...	54	67	98	88	...	4031	2622	3177	2646	...	383
3832	Radio,television etc..	10	19	22	11	...	3044	577	74	-	...	3832
384	Transport equipment	14	31	27	58	...	189	410	-	13274	...	384
3841	Shipbuilding, repair..	2	10	10	31	...	-	368	-	13051	...	3841
3843	Motor vehicles	6	9	17	27	...	71	-	-	223	...	3843
385	Professional goods	22	26	18	24	...	377	1070	1386	4415	...	385
390	Other industries	7	7	12	14	...	229	226	-	349	...	390
3	Manufacturing	4828	7201	8451	13305	...	329552	485933	392181	673133	...	3
410	Electricity,gas,steam ..	...	...	...	...	...	...	...	...	...	...	410
4101	Electricity	...	...	...	...	...	...	...	...	...	...	4101
420	Water works and supply .	...	...	...	...	...	...	...	...	...	...	420
4	Electricity,gas etc	...	...	...	...	...	...	...	...	...	...	4
2-4	All industry	...	...	...	...	...	...	...	...	...	...	2-4

a/ Establishments with 30 or more persons engaged.
b/ Including certain establishments with less than 30 persons engaged.

NIGERIA

The information in the tables is based on the national publications of the Federal Office of Statistics, Lagos. The concepts, definitions and classification by branches of industry are generally in accordance with United Nations standards.

The data in the tables are derived from the annual industrial survey of Nigeria conducted jointly by the Federal Office of Statistics and the regional Ministries of Economic Planning; the survey covers manufacturing establishments with 10 or more employees listed in the directory compiled by the Federal Office of Statistics. It should be noted that the number of reporting establishments varies from year to year, however, estimates for non-responding establishments are included in the data shown in the tables. The data in the tables are based on the national classification system which follows the present version of ISIC.

The employment data relate to an average calculated from the number of persons reported for the four periods of March, June, September and December. Employees are defined as all persons on the pay-roll of the establishment whether they are part-time, casual or full-time workers; homeworkers are excluded. Wages and salaries exclude payments in kind.

Output is the sum of the value of sales of products plus receipts for goods sold in the same condition as purchased, receipts for contract work done for others, value of fixed assets produced by own employees for own use and net change in the value of stocks of finished goods and work in progress. Value added is the difference between the output and industrial costs. Industrial costs include costs of materials, fuels, electricity, goods bought and resold without further processing, contract work done by others on own materials and repair and maintenance work done by others. Valuation of output and value added is in producers' prices.

Gross fixed capital formation is the sum of the cost of new or used capital equipment and the value of assets produced by own employees, less proceeds from sales of fixed assets already held by the establishment.

Related national publications:

Industrial Survey of Nigeria 1980-1983 published by the Federal Office of Statistics, Lagos.

ISIC	INDUSTRY	1. NUMBER OF ESTABLISHMENTS a/ (NUMBER)					2. AVERAGE NUMBER OF PERSONS ENGAGED a/ (THOUSANDS)					ISIC
		1981	1982	1983	1984	1985	1981	1982	1983	1984	1985	
210	Coal mining	1	1	1	1	1	2.95	2.85	2.75	1.98	...	210
220	Petroleum and gas	11	11	11	11	11	...	...	...	...	...	220
230	Metal ore mining	1	1	1	1	1	33.22	31.32	27.82	18.20	...	230
290	Other mining	...	...	...	...	...	...	...	...	...	...	290
2	Mining, quarrying .	...	...	...	...	...	...	...	...	...	...	2
311/2	Food products	579	665	627	...	...	48.14	54.27	42.69	...	...	311/2
313	Beverages	41	44	49	...	...	24.88	16.69	19.31	...	...	313
314	Tobacco	-	-	-	...	...	-	-	-	...	...	314
321	Textiles	110	83	90	...	...	82.59	59.20	59.09	...	...	321
3211	Spinning,weaving etc..	66	43	43	...	...	70.00	44.13	45.80	...	...	3211
322	Wearing apparel	61	30	29	...	...	3.30	2.53	3.40	...	...	322
323	Leather and products ...	16	16	17	...	...	13.59	4.57	3.54	...	...	323
324	Footwear	16	17	16	...	...	9.96	9.57	4.32	...	...	324
331	Wood products	276 b/	187	186	...	...	16.86 b/	12.03	19.73	...	...	331
332	Furniture, fixtures	218 b/	173	175	...	...	18.77 b/	13.27	13.18	...	...	332
341	Paper and products	35	43	37	...	...	11.08	7.22	5.66	...	...	341
3411	Pulp,paper etc.	-	...	-	...	...	-	...	-	...	...	3411
342	Printing,publishing	182	168	167	...	...	16.23	25.84	21.08	...	...	342
351	Industrial chemicals ...	11	5	4	...	...	2.89	0.76	0.71	...	...	351
3511	Basic excl fertilizers	...	...	...	...	...	...	...	...	...	...	3511
3513	Synthetic resins etc .	-	-	-	...	...	-	-	-	...	...	3513
352	Other chemical products.	70	60	64	...	...	25.16	13.60	18.14	...	...	352
3522	Drugs and medicines ..	20	19	19	...	...	3.21	2.81	3.06	...	...	3522
353	Petroleum refineries ...	7	6	6	...	...	5.01	4.72	4.63	...	...	353
354	Petroleum,coal products.	-	-	-	...	...	-	-	-	...	...	354
355	Rubber products	17	15	12	...	...	15.61	5.77	4.97	...	...	355
356	Plastic products n.e.c..	81	74	86	...	...	24.48	8.91	10.33	...	...	356
361	Pottery,china etc	5	4	4	...	...	0.29	0.14	0.12	...	...	361
362	Glass and products	11	7	7	...	...	2.14	2.18	1.98	...	...	362
369	Non-metal products n.e.c	285	260	261	...	...	29.67	11.84	17.54	...	...	369
371	Iron and steel	4	10	10	...	...	1.33	10.55	20.19	...	...	371
372	Non-ferrous metals	-	-	-	...	...	-	-	-	...	...	372
381	Metal products	202	169	177	...	...	54.74	40.11	31.91	...	...	381
382	Machinery n.e.c.	19	11	13	...	...	5.18	4.08	4.11	...	...	382
3825	Office,computing etc..	-	-	-	...	...	-	-	-	...	...	3825
383	Electrical machinery ...	35	32	33	...	...	12.07	11.34	8.65	...	...	383
3832	Radio,television etc..	19	15	16	...	...	6.22	5.11	2.44	...	...	3832
384	Transport equipment	30	27	27	...	...	26.91	14.17	12.79	...	...	384
3841	Shipbuilding, repair..	7	4	4	...	...	0.79	0.32	0.31	...	...	3841
3843	Motor vehicles	19	18	18	...	...	24.70	13.05	11.66	...	...	3843
385	Professional goods	-	5	4	...	...	-	0.14	0.13	...	...	385
390	Other industries	31	9	11	...	...	3.08	0.98	0.90	...	...	390
3	Manufacturing	2342	2120	2112	...	...	453.96	334.48	329.10	...	...	3
410	Electricity,gas,steam ..	3	3	4	4	4	...	...	...	...	...	410
4101	Electricity	...	...	...	...	...	...	...	...	...	...	4101
420	Water works and supply .	...	...	...	...	...	...	...	...	...	...	420
4	Electricity,gas etc	...	...	...	...	...	...	...	...	...	...	4
2-4	All industry	...	...	...	...	...	...	...	...	...	...	2-4

a/ Establishments with 10 or more employees.

b/ ISIC 3319 is included in 332.

ISIC	INDUSTRY	3. AVERAGE NUMBER OF EMPLOYEES a/ (THOUSANDS)					4. WAGES AND SALARIES OF EMPLOYEES a/b/ (MILLION NAIRA)					ISIC
		1981	1982	1983	1984	1985	1981	1982	1983	1984	1985	
210	Coal mining	2.95	2.85	2.75	1.98	...	...	...	...	...	...	210
220	Petroleum and gas	...	...	...	...	...	...	...	...	...	...	220
230	Metal ore mining	33.22	31.32	27.82	18.20	...	...	...	...	...	...	230
290	Other mining	...	...	...	...	...	...	...	...	...	...	290
2	Mining, quarrying	...	...	...	...	...	...	...	...	...	...	2
311/2	Food products	46.04	52.30	40.21	...	...	145	155	116	...	...	311/2
313	Beverages	24.87	16.69	19.28	...	...	88	71	78	...	...	313
314	Tobacco	-	-	-	...	...	-	-	-	...	...	314
321	Textiles	82.51	59.14	59.03	...	...	256	187	204	...	...	321
3211	Spinning,weaving etc.	69.97	44.10	45.77	...	...	221	135	159	...	...	3211
322	Wearing apparel	3.10	2.44	3.24	...	...	3	4	7	...	...	322
323	Leather and products	13.59	4.55	3.53	...	...	53	14	11	...	...	323
324	Footwear	9.95	9.56	4.31	...	...	25	25	11	...	...	324
331	Wood products	c/ 16.53	11.75	19.37	...	...	c/ 46	39	68	...	...	331
332	Furniture, fixtures	c/ 17.97	12.74	11.86	...	...	c/ 38	32	30	...	...	332
341	Paper and products	11.07	7.19	5.62	...	...	33	25	19	...	...	341
3411	Pulp,paper etc.	-	...	-	...	...	-	...	-	...	...	3411
342	Printing,publishing	15.90	25.27	20.73	...	...	50	69	55	...	...	342
351	Industrial chemicals	2.89	0.76	0.71	...	...	15	3	3	...	...	351
3511	Basic excl fertilizers	...	...	...	...	...	...	...	...	...	...	3511
3513	Synthetic resins etc	-	-	-	...	...	-	-	-	...	...	3513
352	Other chemical products	25.11	13.58	18.10	...	...	95	49	59	...	...	352
3522	Drugs and medicines	3.19	2.79	3.04	...	...	17	17	21	...	...	3522
353	Petroleum refineries	5.01	4.71	4.63	...	...	29	30	32	...	...	353
354	Petroleum,coal products	-	-	-	...	...	-	-	-	...	...	354
355	Rubber products	15.61	5.75	4.95	...	...	35	21	21	...	...	355
356	Plastic products n.e.c.	24.38	8.91	10.23	...	...	91	28	38	...	...	356
361	Pottery,china etc	0.26	0.08	0.07	...	...	-	-	-	...	...	361
362	Glass and products	2.13	2.18	1.98	...	...	8	8	8	...	...	362
369	Non-metal products n.e.c	29.35	11.55	16.76	...	...	99	37	59	...	...	369
371	Iron and steel	1.33	10.54	20.19	...	...	5	38	26	...	...	371
372	Non-ferrous metals	-	-	-	...	...	-	-	-	...	...	372
381	Metal products	54.38	39.95	31.73	...	...	176	160	128	...	...	381
382	Machinery n.e.c.	5.17	4.07	4.09	...	...	18	13	16	...	...	382
3825	Office,computing etc.	-	-	-	...	...	-	-	-	...	...	3825
383	Electrical machinery	12.07	10.77	8.00	...	...	38	41	33	...	...	383
3832	Radio,television etc.	6.22	5.10	2.43	...	...	17	18	9	...	...	3832
384	Transport equipment	26.83	14.14	12.77	...	...	90	43	43	...	...	384
3841	Shipbuilding, repair.	0.78	0.32	0.31	...	...	3	1	2	...	...	3841
3843	Motor vehicles	24.63	13.01	11.64	...	...	82	38	38	...	...	3843
385	Professional goods	-	0.13	0.11	...	...	-	-	-	...	...	385
390	Other industries	3.05	0.97	0.90	...	...	10	4	4	...	...	390
3	Manufacturing	449.10	329.72	322.40	...	...	1446	1096	1069	...	...	3
410	Electricity,gas,steam	...	...	...	...	...	...	...	...	...	...	410
4101	Electricity	...	...	...	...	...	...	...	...	...	...	4101
420	Water works and supply	...	...	...	...	...	...	...	...	...	...	420
4	Electricity,gas etc	...	...	...	...	...	...	...	...	...	...	4
2-4	All industry	...	...	...	...	...	...	...	...	...	...	2-4

a/ Establishments with 10 or more employees.
b/ Excluding payments in kind.
c/ ISIC 3319 is included in 332.

ISIC	INDUSTRY	5. AVERAGE NUMBER OF OPERATIVES a/ (THOUSANDS)					6. OUTPUT IN PRODUCERS' PRICES a/ (MILLION NAIRA)					ISIC
		1981	1982	1983	1984	1985	1981	1982	1983	1984	1985	
210	Coal mining	...	...	...	...	...	...	...	...	...	...	210
220	Petroleum and gas	...	...	...	...	...	...	...	...	...	...	220
230	Metal ore mining	...	...	...	...	...	...	...	...	...	...	230
290	Other mining	...	...	...	...	...	...	...	...	...	...	290
2	Mining, quarrying .	...	...	...	...	...	...	...	...	...	...	2
311/2	Food products	35.66	40.47	29.36	...	...	1788	1397	1339	...	...	311/2
313	Beverages	19.70	9.84	10.02	...	...	904	708	998	...	...	313
314	Tobacco	-	-	-	...	...	-	-	-	...	...	314
321	Textiles	71.60	51.75	50.38	...	...	1115	972	1158	...	...	321
3211	Spinning,weaving etc..	60.82	38.71	39.24	...	...	907	721	836	...	...	3211
322	Wearing apparel	2.08	2.09	2.71	...	...	14	28	30	...	...	322
323	Leather and products ...	12.02	3.84	2.90	...	...	264	74	54	...	...	323
324	Footwear	7.36	7.72	3.46	...	...	98	127	59	...	...	324
331	Wood products	b/ 13.29	9.80	16.46	...	...	b/ 181	157	315	...	...	331
332	Furniture, fixtures	b/ 13.11	9.38	8.71	...	...	b/ 264	165	169	...	...	332
341	Paper and products	7.65	3.43	3.92	...	...	238	154	138	...	...	341
3411	Pulp,paper etc.	-	...	-	...	...	-	...	-	...	...	3411
342	Printing,publishing	10.35	9.95	5.96	...	...	232	170	236	...	...	342
351	Industrial chemicals ...	1.42	0.37	0.32	...	...	91	24	17	...	...	351
3511	Basic excl fertilizers	...	...	...	...	...	...	...	...	...	...	3511
3513	Synthetic resins etc .	-	-	-	...	...	-	-	-	...	...	3513
352	Other chemical products.	17.12	8.44	11.15	...	...	1206	542	938	...	...	352
3522	Drugs and medicines ..	1.87	1.62	1.59	...	...	137	57	202	...	...	3522
353	Petroleum refineries ...	1.42	2.38	2.27	...	...	1017	1125	1130	...	...	353
354	Petroleum,coal products.	-	-	-	...	...	-	-	-	...	...	354
355	Rubber products	14.30	4.54	3.81	...	...	113	96	109	...	...	355
356	Plastic products n.e.c..	19.36	7.21	8.32	...	...	546	228	289	...	...	356
361	Pottery,china etc	0.12	0.03	0.03	...	...	-	-	-	...	...	361
362	Glass and products	1.46	1.69	1.52	...	...	39	42	40	...	...	362
369	Non-metal products n.e.c	21.28	8.64	11.59	...	...	706	294	496	...	...	369
371	Iron and steel	0.71	6.91	14.44	...	...	22	153	147	...	...	371
372	Non-ferrous metals	-	-	-	...	...	-	-	-	...	...	372
381	Metal products	44.03	31.63	24.79	...	...	1157	1062	793	...	...	381
382	Machinery n.e.c.	3.97	2.79	2.59	...	...	226	151	129	...	...	382
3825	Office,computing etc..	-	-	-	...	...	-	-	-	...	...	3825
383	Electrical machinery ...	9.49	7.36	5.67	...	...	398	278	202	...	...	383
3832	Radio,television etc..	4.73	3.32	1.62	...	...	216	97	48	...	...	3832
384	Transport equipment	20.81	10.82	9.74	...	...	1956	914	1351	...	...	384
3841	Shipbuilding, repair..	0.55	0.22	0.22	...	...	5	3	3	...	...	3841
3843	Motor vehicles	19.29	9.95	8.96	...	...	1840	839	1296	...	...	3843
385	Professional goods	-	0.08	0.07	...	...	-	5	2	...	...	385
390	Other industries	2.16	0.83	0.74	...	...	44	19	17	...	...	390
3	Manufacturing	350.47	241.99	230.93	...	...	12619	8885	10156	...	...	3
410	Electricity,gas,steam ..	...	...	...	...	...	...	...	...	...	...	410
4101	Electricity	...	...	...	...	...	...	...	...	...	...	4101
420	Water works and supply .	...	...	...	...	...	...	...	...	...	...	420
4	Electricity,gas etc	...	...	...	...	...	...	...	...	...	...	4
2-4	All industry	...	...	...	...	...	...	...	...	...	...	2-4

a/ Establishments with 10 or more employees.

b/ ISIC 3319 is included in 332.

ISIC	INDUSTRY	7. VALUE ADDED IN PRODUCERS' PRICES a/ (MILLION NAIRA)					8. GROSS FIXED CAPITAL FORMATION TOTAL a/ (MILLION NAIRA)					ISIC
		1981	1982	1983	1984	1985	1981	1982	1983	1984	1985	
210	Coal mining	...	...	...	...	...	...	...	...	...	...	210
220	Petroleum and gas	...	...	...	...	...	...	...	...	...	...	220
230	Metal ore mining	...	...	...	...	...	...	...	...	...	...	230
290	Other mining	...	...	...	...	...	...	...	...	...	...	290
2	Mining, quarrying .	...	...	...	...	...	...	...	...	...	...	2
311/2	Food products	476.1	553.7	654.5	...	...	229.0	191.3	85.5	...	...	311/2
313	Beverages	556.7	517.5	768.2	...	...	344.0	208.1	176.7	...	...	313
314	Tobacco	-	-	-	...	...	-	-	-	...	...	314
321	Textiles	432.5	319.5	538.6	...	...	150.1	200.9	101.8	...	...	321
3211	Spinning,weaving etc..	360.9	216.8	383.5	...	...	145.7	62.9	38.3	...	...	3211
322	Wearing apparel	8.8	10.4	12.1	...	...	5.9	6.3	10.9	...	...	322
323	Leather and products ...	165.7	33.3	31.3	...	...	19.9	17.5	5.0	...	...	323
324	Footwear	30.5	69.2	12.3	...	...	3.0	2.9	-0.2	...	...	324
331	Wood products	b/ 61.5	64.3	146.5	...	...	b/ 20.5	16.6	11.3	...	...	331
332	Furniture, fixtures	b/ 115.3	70.7	56.4	...	...	b/ 57.9	27.1	23.8	...	...	332
341	Paper and products	86.0	39.5	38.4	...	...	13.3	28.7	17.6	...	...	341
3411	Pulp,paper etc.	-	...	-	...	...	-	...	-	...	...	3411
342	Printing,publishing	82.1	49.4	153.3	...	...	30.0	53.7	78.6	...	...	342
351	Industrial chemicals ...	51.5	12.8	6.9	...	...	8.8	2.1	1.9	...	...	351
3511	Basic excl fertilizers	...	...	...	...	...	...	...	...	...	...	3511
3513	Synthetic resins etc .	-	-	-	...	...	-	-	-	...	...	3513
352	Other chemical products.	570.8	244.7	458.1	...	...	103.5	41.2	72.3	...	...	352
3522	Drugs and medicines ..	59.9	24.2	95.0	...	...	7.4	14.9	0.7	...	...	3522
353	Petroleum refineries ...	357.3	681.4	687.0	...	...	54.1	485.0	27.4	...	...	353
354	Petroleum,coal products.	-	-	-	...	...	-	-	-	...	...	354
355	Rubber products	64.0	48.7	62.5	...	...	6.9	7.1	4.3	...	...	355
356	Plastic products n.e.c..	275.0	87.1	99.2	...	...	146.1	36.0	36.4	...	...	356
361	Pottery,china etc	0.1	-	-	...	...	-	-	-	...	...	361
362	Glass and products	15.5	22.0	21.1	...	...	2.0	11.4	13.4	...	...	362
369	Non-metal products n.e.c	419.1	172.1	206.6	...	...	86.2	21.9	32.2	...	...	369
371	Iron and steel	7.8	-1.8	-12.2	...	...	6.8	735.0	84.9	...	...	371
372	Non-ferrous metals	-	-	-	...	...	-	-	-	...	...	372
381	Metal products	375.4	512.1	369.4	...	...	105.8	86.2	64.8	...	...	381
382	Machinery n.e.c.	61.2	52.0	60.5	...	...	35.5	23.1	11.3	...	...	382
3825	Office,computing etc..	-	-	-	...	...	-	-	-	...	...	3825
383	Electrical machinery ...	161.6	79.8	93.3	...	...	25.1	14.3	11.7	...	...	383
3832	Radio,television etc..	57.8	-1.0	19.9	...	...	10.9	6.8	2.2	...	...	3832
384	Transport equipment	415.5	313.8	754.2	...	...	116.3	40.3	34.3	...	...	384
3841	Shipbuilding, repair..	0.3	1.2	1.8	...	...	1.5	0.2	-0.1	...	...	3841
3843	Motor vehicles	394.2	294.2	734.4	...	...	97.8	38.6	29.7	...	...	3843
385	Professional goods	-	1.0	-	...	...	-	-	-	...	...	385
390	Other industries	20.3	3.8	7.3	...	...	12.7	2.4	0.2	...	...	390
3	Manufacturing	4810.3	3957.0	5225.5	...	...	1583.4	2259.1	906.1	...	...	3
410	Electricity,gas,steam ..	...	...	...	...	...	...	...	...	...	...	410
4101	Electricity	...	...	...	...	...	...	...	...	...	...	4101
420	Water works and supply .	...	...	...	...	...	...	...	...	...	...	420
4	Electricity,gas etc	...	...	...	...	...	...	...	...	...	...	4
2-4	All industry	...	...	...	...	...	...	...	...	...	...	2-4

a/ Establishments with 10 or more employees.

b/ ISIC 3319 is included in 332.

The information on industrial activity is based on the reply to the United Nations Questionnaire on General Industrial Statistics from the Central Bureau of Statistics, Oslo. The concepts, definitions and classification by branches of industry are generally in accordance with United Nations standards.

The estimates are derived from the annual industrial statistics inquiry and the annual electricity statistics inquiry. Complete annual reports are collected from all large establishments. From small establishments only reports on persons engaged and sales etc. are collected. The definition of a large establishment differs slightly according to industries: in general, large establishments are those with at least 5 persons engaged but for some groups of industrial activity, a lower limit of 3 persons is used; all establishments are covered for coal mining, crude petroleum and natural gas production, metal mining, manufacture of dairy products (except ice cream), margarine, fish oils and fish meal, tobacco products, petroleum refining and manufacture of oil and gas well machinery and tools. The estimates for mining and manufacturing shown in the tables generally relate to large establishments defined in this way; in 1985 these accounted for 96 per cent of the total number of persons engaged and 98 per cent of the total value added in all establishments surveyed. The electricity statistics inquiry covers public supply plants with an installed generating capacity of 100 kW or more and, in the case of those producing for their own use, electricity plants with an installed capacity of 500 kW; all gas undertakings are covered. Steam and water supply are not surveyed.

The estimates are based on the national classification which corresponds very closely to the present version of ISIC. It should be noted that in the figures shown, manufacture of motorcycles and bicycles (ISIC 3844) is included in ISIC 3843.

The number of persons engaged represents the average during the year of employees, working proprietors and unpaid family workers. Homeworkers are not included.

Wages and salaries comprise all payments, whether in cash or in kind, made by the employer for work done to all persons included in the count of employees and to employed homeworkers. Included are bonuses, production awards, holiday allowances, wages and salaries paid during periods of sickness, military leave or other absence, and commissions earned by salesmen and representatives. The estimates of supplements to wages and salaries comprise all supplemental labour costs payable by the employer, both obligatory under law and voluntary.

The concept of output for mining and manufacturing relates to the gross value of production comprising (a) the sales value of goods produced on own account, adjusted for changes in work in progress between the beginning and end of the year, (b) receipts for repair work, (c) receipts for mounting or installation of own products, (d) receipts for contract work, (e) the gross profit on goods sold in the same condition as received, (f) receipts for other work (commissions, consulting services, canteen sales, transport services rendered to others etc.), (g) receipts from renting of machinery and buildings and (h) the value of investment and repair work executed by the employees of the establishment. Indirect taxes, other than the value-added tax, are included and subsidies are excluded. The sales value of production on own account is stated at ex-factory prices, including the value of packing materials and any price additions for distribution with the establishments' own labour and equipment.

Value added for mining and manufacturing is the value of output as defined above, less the cost of raw materials and certain other inputs, excluding value-added tax. The inputs deducted include (a) raw and auxiliary materials and components used as direct input in the manufacturing process, (b) fuels and electricity consumed, (c) consumption of purchased ready-made containers and packaging material, as well as raw materials for the manufacture thereof, (d) other inputs consumed during the year (operating supplies, materials for own-account investment, repair and maintenance work, office supplies, foods for company operated canteens etc.), (e) cost of repair work done by others, (f) cost of contract work done by others (including payments to homeworkers not employed by the establishment), (g) rental outlays, (h) other working expenses (advertising, telephone charges, postal expenses, subsistence allowances etc.), (i) cost of own-account repair work, (j) investment levy not already included in any of the above-mentioned items.

The estimates for electricity and gas are similarly compiled. For electricity, the following definitions describe the concepts. Gross output - the sum of (a) sales of electric power to own establishments, to other consumers (both firm and occasional power), and to other electricity plants, (b) exports, (c) transit and transformer income, (d) receipts for mounting, installation and repair work, (e) value of own-account investment and repair work and (f) receipts from renting of buildings, plant, machinery etc. Intermediate consumption - the sum of (a) electric energy purchased from other electricity plants, (b) imports, (c) transmission expenditure, (d) value of own-account repair work, (e) cost of fuel, lubricating oil, grease etc. and other materials consumed, (g) cost of repair work, (h) renting of buildings, plant, machinery etc. and (i) working expenses. Value added is equal to the value of gross output less intermediate consumption. Data are compiled exclusive of the value-added tax.

Gross fixed capital formation is calculated as the value of the acquisition of new and used fixed assets, including own-account investment work. The value of sales is deducted for the total estimates but not for the data on machinery and equipment. The value is stated at actual costs incurred during the year, irrespective of time of payment. The investment levy is included. Fixed capital formation in new establishments not yet in operation and progress payments are included.

The estimates of total value of stocks comprise stocks of materials, fuels and supplies valued at purchase prices, work in progress valued at cost plus expected profit, and stocks of finished goods and goods for resale in the same condition as received valued at sales prices. The value-added tax is excluded in each category. The figures include stocks of unsold goods located abroad.

The indexes of industrial production are compiled by the Central Bureau of Statistics and provided in response to the United Nations Questionnaire on Indexes of Industrial Production. In principle, the indexes cover all establishments, irrespective of size.

Related national publications:
Industristatistikk (annual); Elektrisitetsstatistikk (annual); Produksjonsstatistikk, all published by the Central Bureau of Statistics, Oslo.

ISIC	INDUSTRY	1. NUMBER OF ESTABLISHMENTS a/ (NUMBER) 1981	1982	1983	1984	1985	2. AVERAGE NUMBER OF PERSONS ENGAGED a/ (THOUSANDS) 1981	1982	1983	1984	1985	ISIC
210	Coal mining	1	1	1	1	1	0.8	0.8	0.8	0.8	0.8	210
220	Petroleum and gas	6	7	7	7	8	7.9	8.3	9.2	11.2	12.8	220
230	Metal ore mining	14	13	13	14	14	3.9	3.7	3.2	3.4	3.2	230
290	Other mining	281	257	240	243	235	3.1	2.9	2.8	2.8	2.8	290
2	Mining, quarrying .	302	278	261	265	258	15.7	15.7	16.0	18.2	19.6	2
311/2	Food products	1723	1693	1603	1577	1575	49.3	48.9	47.2	47.4	47.8	311/2
313	Beverages	54	54	50	49	50	5.1	4.9	4.4	4.3	4.3	313
314	Tobacco	6	6	6	6	4	1.1	1.1	1.0	0.9	0.9	314
321	Textiles	288	266	236	227	218	11.0	9.9	8.5	7.9	8.0	321
3211	Spinning,weaving etc..	57	55	51	48	46	3.4	3.2	2.7	2.5	2.6	3211
322	Wearing apparel	220	198	150	139	143	6.2	5.6	4.5	4.4	4.3	322
323	Leather and products ...	45	46	37	34	32	1.1	1.0	0.8	0.8	0.8	323
324	Footwear	32	30	26	26	25	1.2	1.0	0.8	0.7	0.7	324
331	Wood products	920	879	827	818	803	22.3	21.6	19.5	18.5	18.2	331
332	Furniture, fixtures	292	285	266	254	247	8.8	8.5	8.1	7.7	8.1	332
341	Paper and products	143	133	119	114	111	16.2	15.4	14.4	13.9	13.6	341
3411	Pulp,paper etc.	69	63	57	54	53	11.6	11.0	10.4	9.9	9.7	3411
342	Printing,publishing	795	779	761	782	808	33.6	33.1	31.7	31.1	32.0	342
351	Industrial chemicals ...	57	56	53	54	56	9.6	9.6	8.8	8.8	9.0	351
3511	Basic excl fertilizers	38	38	36	38	40	3.6	3.5	3.4	3.6	3.7	3511
3513	Synthetic resins etc .	12	12	11	11	11	2.4	2.3	1.9	1.9	2.0	3513
352	Other chemical products.	104	101	99	101	96	7.5	7.1	6.9	7.1	6.0	352
3522	Drugs and medicines ..	12	12	13	12	12	1.5	1.5	1.5	1.7	1.7	3522
353	Petroleum refineries ...	3	3	3	3	3	0.9	0.9	0.9	0.9	0.9	353
354	Petroleum,coal products.	45	40	30	34	38	1.9	1.7	1.8	1.7	1.6	354
355	Rubber products	44	42	35	33	35	1.9	1.7	1.6	1.6	1.6	355
356	Plastic products n.e.c..	206	204	197	204	203	6.6	6.5	6.1	6.1	6.3	356
361	Pottery,china etc	6	5	4	4	5	1.1	1.1	1.1	1.1	1.0	361
362	Glass and products	41	37	35	33	34	2.4	2.2	1.9	1.9	1.9	362
369	Non-metal products n.e.c	393	381	354	347	341	8.2	7.8	7.6	7.3	7.4	369
371	Iron and steel	51	51	48	46	48	13.1	12.2	11.2	10.8	9.9	371
372	Non-ferrous metals	51	51	48	44	43	14.1	13.1	12.4	12.7	12.7	372
381	Metal products	807	819	755	767	756	25.4	24.8	22.7	22.8	23.2	381
382	Machinery n.e.c.	599	581	559	556	596	33.7	33.6	33.5	35.1	39.9	382
3825	Office,computing etc..	17	17	20	19	18	1.5	1.7	1.9	2.2	2.6	3825
383	Electrical machinery ...	246	238	239	243	251	21.0	21.3	20.8	19.9	20.2	383
3832	Radio,television etc..	86	84	85	89	93	10.0	10.2	9.9	9.2	9.2	3832
384	Transport equipment	594	595	542	517	485	43.0	41.5	34.0	32.3	29.6	384
3841	Shipbuilding, repair..	465	468	418	394	363	34.2	32.5	25.2	23.4	20.7	3841
3843	Motor vehicles .... b/	90	91	86	87	86	3.9	3.9	3.5	3.7	3.8	3843
385	Professional goods	31	33	31	32	31	1.2	1.2	1.2	1.2	1.3	385
390	Other industries	120	108	98	91	95	2.8	2.6	2.4	2.4	2.5	390
3	Manufacturing	7916	7714	7211	7135	7132	350.3	339.9	315.8	311.3	313.7	3
410	Electricity,gas,steam ..	453	447	438	426	423	17.0	17.3	17.8	17.9	18.3	410
4101	Electricity	452	446	437	425	423	17.0	17.3	17.8	17.9	18.3	4101
420	Water works and supply .	.	.	.	.	.	.	.	.	.	.	420
4	Electricity,gas etc	453	447	438	426	423	17.0	17.3	17.8	17.9	18.3	4
2-4	All industry	8671	8439	7910	7826	7813	383.0	372.9	349.6	347.4	351.6	2-4

a/ Mining and manufacturing: large establishments, generally with 5 or more persons engaged.
b/ Including motorcycles and bicycles.

NORWAY

ISIC	INDUSTRY	3. AVERAGE NUMBER OF EMPLOYEES a/ (THOUSANDS)					4. WAGES AND SALARIES OF EMPLOYEES a/ (MILLION KRONER)					ISIC
		1981	1982	1983	1984	1985	1981	1982	1983	1984	1985	
210	Coal mining	0.8	0.8	0.8	0.7	0.8	85	107	116	109	117	210
220	Petroleum and gas	7.9	8.3	9.2	11.2	12.8	1787	2066	2401	3131	3967	220
230	Metal ore mining	3.9	3.7	3.2	3.4	3.2	365	371	362	423	429	230
290	Other mining	3.0	2.9	2.8	2.8	2.8	269	276	300	320	348	290
2	Mining, quarrying .	15.6	15.7	16.0	18.1	19.6	2506	2820	3179	3983	4861	2
311/2	Food products	48.6	48.2	46.6	46.8	47.2	3698	4025	4340	4669	5043	311/2
313	Beverages	5.1	4.9	4.4	4.3	4.3	445	483	509	531	597	313
314	Tobacco	1.1	1.1	1.0	0.9	0.9	90	95	94	95	110	314
321	Textiles	10.9	9.8	8.5	7.9	7.9	720	701	656	676	748	321
3211	Spinning,weaving etc..	3.4	3.2	2.7	2.5	2.6	233	233	217	222	258	3211
322	Wearing apparel	6.1	5.5	4.5	4.3	4.3	368	359	324	337	361	322
323	Leather and products ...	1.0	1.0	0.8	0.8	0.7	65	65	61	66	68	323
324	Footwear	1.2	1.0	0.8	0.7	0.7	75	69	61	59	59	324
331	Wood products	21.9	21.3	19.1	18.2	17.9	1780	1868	1821	1880	1984	331
332	Furniture, fixtures	8.7	8.4	8.0	7.7	8.1	669	684	722	768	895	332
341	Paper and products	16.2	15.4	14.3	13.9	13.6	1466	1452	1512	1627	1753	341
3411	Pulp,paper etc.	11.6	11.0	10.4	9.9	9.7	1075	1059	1101	1174	1265	3411
342	Printing,publishing	33.4	33.0	31.6	30.9	31.9	2497	2663	3083	3414	3903	342
351	Industrial chemicals ...	9.6	9.6	8.8	8.8	9.0	1051	1119	1112	1243	1349	351
3511	Basic excl fertilizers	3.6	3.5	3.4	3.6	3.7	394	404	416	492	541	3511
3513	Synthetic resins etc .	2.4	2.3	1.9	1.9	2.0	261	274	258	280	327	3513
352	Other chemical products.	7.5	7.1	6.9	7.1	6.0	689	709	788	874	822	352
3522	Drugs and medicines ..	1.5	1.5	1.5	1.7	1.7	134	151	169	197	241	3522
353	Petroleum refineries ...	0.9	0.9	0.9	0.9	0.9	117	.141	159	161	175	353
354	Petroleum,coal products.	1.9	1.7	1.8	1.7	1.6	173	182	202	208	222	354
355	Rubber products	1.9	1.7	1.6	1.6	1.6	158	150	155	167	191	355
356	Plastic products n.e.c..	6.6	6.5	6.1	6.1	6.3	532	582	594	654	713	356
361	Pottery,china etc	1.1	1.1	1.1	1.1	1.0	93	97	93	106	110	361
362	Glass and products	2.4	2.2	1.9	1.9	1.9	200	206	193	211	240	362
369	Non-metal products n.e.c	8.0	7.8	7.4	7.2	7.3	754	796	844	873	992	369
371	Iron and steel	13.1	12.2	11.2	10.8	9.9	1279	1265	1279	1398	1388	371
372	Non-ferrous metals	14.1	13.0	12.4	12.7	12.7	1411	1409	1463	1663	1847	372
381	Metal products	25.1	24.4	22.5	22.6	23.1	2178	2306	2320	2518	2804	381
382	Machinery n.e.c.	33.6	33.5	33.4	35.0	39.9	3485	3769	4162	4777	6042	382
3825	Office,computing etc..	1.5	1.7	1.9	2.2	2.6	185	225	281	365	395	3825
383	Electrical machinery ...	21.0	21.3	20.8	19.9	20.2	2093	2368	2544	2688	2958	383
3832	Radio,television etc..	10.0	10.2	9.9	9.2	9.2	1012	1157	1242	1290	1389	3832
384	Transport equipment	42.8	41.4	33.9	32.9	29.5	4033	4309	3785	3906	3840	384
3841	Shipbuilding, repair..	34.1	32.4	25.1	23.4	20.6	3226	3396	2774	2799	2618	3841
3843	Motor vehicles .... b/	3.9	3.9	2.5	3.6	3.8	315	346	334	374	438	3843
385	Professional goods	1.2	1.2	1.2	1.2	1.3	107	115	127	154	185	385
390	Other industries	2.7	2.5	2.4	2.3	2.4	210	212	215	228	268	390
3	Manufacturing	347.7	337.7	313.9	309.5	312.1	30436	32199	33218	35951	39667	3
410	Electricity,gas,steam ..	17.0	17.3	17.8	17.9	18.3	1719	1964	2104	2302	2565	410
4101	Electricity	17.0	17.3	17.8	17.9	18.3	1714	1958	2097	2302	2565	4101
420	Water works and supply .	.	.	.	.	.	.	.	.	.	.	420
4	Electricity,gas etc	17.0	17.3	17.8	17.9	18.3	1719	1964	2104	2302	2565	4
2-4	All industry	380.3	370.7	347.7	345.5	350.0	34661	36983	38501	42236	47093	2-4

a/ Mining and manufacturing: large establishments, generally with 5 or more persons engaged.
b/ Including motorcycles and bicycles.

ISIC	INDUSTRY	5. SUPPLEMENTS TO WAGES AND SALARIES a/ (MILLION KRONER)					6. AVERAGE NUMBER OF OPERATIVES a/ (THOUSANDS)					ISIC
		1981	1982	1983	1984	1985	1981	1982	1983	1984	1985	
210	Coal mining	19	20	16	12	12	0.6	0.7	...	...	...	210
220	Petroleum and gas	414	525	577	897	1059	2.2	2.4	...	...	...	220
230	Metal ore mining	83	72	59	66	64	3.1	2.8	...	...	...	230
290	Other mining	48	48	55	63	68	2.5	2.4	...	...	...	290
2	Mining, quarrying	564	665	707	1038	1203	8.4	8.3	...	...	...	2
311/2	Food products	705	772	832	881	945	39.5	38.9	...	...	...	311/2
313	Beverages	99	111	128	137	143	3.7	3.4	...	...	...	313
314	Tobacco	30	25	18	19	22	0.6	0.6	...	...	...	314
321	Textiles	136	132	125	130	138	8.9	8.0	...	...	...	321
3211	Spinning,weaving etc.	43	42	40	42	48	2.6	2.5	...	...	...	3211
322	Wearing apparel	65	63	59	63	65	5.1	4.6	...	...	...	322
323	Leather and products	11	11	11	13	13	0.9	0.9	...	...	...	323
324	Footwear	13	12	11	11	11	1.1	0.9	...	...	...	324
331	Wood products	313	338	334	342	363	17.2	16.5	...	...	...	331
332	Furniture, fixtures	116	119	136	143	164	7.0	6.7	...	...	...	332
341	Paper and products	302	295	323	349	384	12.4	11.7	...	...	...	341
3411	Pulp,paper etc.	218	212	229	249	283	8.9	8.4	...	...	...	3411
342	Printing,publishing	522	538	657	726	844	20.8	20.3	...	...	...	342
351	Industrial chemicals	282	304	315	337	362	5.5	5.5	...	...	...	351
3511	Basic excl fertilizers	94	96	96	113	128	2.5	2.5	...	...	...	3511
3513	Synthetic resins etc	62	66	64	69	77	1.0	1.0	...	...	...	3513
352	Other chemical products.	162	172	192	211	203	4.2	3.9	...	...	...	352
3522	Drugs and medicines	34	38	44	54	62	0.6	0.6	...	...	...	3522
353	Petroleum refineries	38	34	33	36	39	0.5	0.5	...	...	...	353
354	Petroleum,coal products.	34	37	43	42	43	1.3	1.1	...	...	...	354
355	Rubber products	29	33	33	37	40	1.5	1.4	...	...	...	355
356	Plastic products n.e.c.	101	114	119	125	134	5.0	4.9	...	...	...	356
361	Pottery,china etc	19	21	19	23	24	0.9	0.9	...	...	...	361
362	Glass and products	43	44	43	44	52	1.8	1.7	...	...	...	362
369	Non-metal products n.e.c	138	146	167	190	202	6.2	5.9	...	...	...	369
371	Iron and steel	251	247	263	286	294	10.0	9.2	...	...	...	371
372	Non-ferrous metals	334	327	318	393	439	10.3	9.3	...	...	...	372
381	Metal products	427	454	463	483	560	19.6	19.0	...	...	...	381
382	Machinery n.e.c.	714	799	896	981	1228	22.8	22.1	...	...	...	382
3825	Office,computing etc.	40	47	78	75	101	0.2	0.3	...	...	...	3825
383	Electrical machinery	450	562	568	624	689	12.8	12.6	...	...	...	383
3832	Radio,television etc.	220	284	263	290	318	5.5	5.3	...	...	...	3832
384	Transport equipment	779	814	728	744	734	34.5	33.2	...	...	...	384
3841	Shipbuilding, repair.	600	611	509	512	473	27.3	26.0	...	...	...	3841
3843	Motor vehicles b/	59	68	65	68	83	3.2	3.2	...	...	...	3843
385	Professional goods	22	25	27	32	42	0.9	0.9	...	...	...	385
390	Other industries	38	38	41	41	53	2.1	1.9	...	...	...	390
3	Manufacturing	6173	6587	6902	7443	8230	257.1	246.5	...	...	...	3
410	Electricity,gas,steam	370	422	470	516	562	...	...	...	...	...	410
4101	Electricity	369	421	469	516	562	...	...	...	...	...	4101
420	Water works and supply	.	.	.	.	.	.	.	...	...	...	420
4	Electricity,gas etc	370	422	470	516	562	...	...	...	...	...	4
2-4	All industry	7007	7674	8079	8997	9995	...	...	...	...	...	2-4

a/ Mining and manufacturing: large establishments, generally with 5 or more persons engaged.
b/ Including motorcycles and bicycles.

ISIC	INDUSTRY	7. WAGES AND SALARIES OF OPERATIVES a/ (MILLION KRONER)					8. HOURS WORKED BY OPERATIVES a/ (MILLIONS)					ISIC
		1981	1982	1983	1984	1985	1981	1982	1983	1984	1985	
210	Coal mining	63	85	...	...	...	1.2	1.3	...	...	...	210
220	Petroleum and gas	434	527	...	...	...	3.9	4.3	...	...	...	220
230	Metal ore mining	280	278	...	...	...	4.6	4.2	...	...	...	230
290	Other mining	215	222	...	...	...	4.1	4.0	...	...	...	290
2	Mining, quarrying .	992	1112	...	...	...	13.8	13.8	...	...	...	2
311/2	Food products	2796	3013	...	...	...	63.0	62.9	...	...	...	311/2
313	Beverages	294	316	...	...	...	5.8	5.7	...	...	...	313
314	Tobacco	46	46	...	...	...	0.9	0.9	...	...	...	314
321	Textiles	526	504	...	...	...	13.2	11.5	...	...	...	321
3211	Spinning,weaving etc..	163	161	...	...	...	3.9	3.4	...	...	...	3211
322	Wearing apparel	281	274	...	...	...	7.5	6.8	...	...	...	322
323	Leather and products ...	51	52	...	...	...	1.3	1.3	...	...	...	323
324	Footwear	61	55	...	...	...	1.6	1.4	...	...	...	324
331	Wood products	1313	1349	...	...	...	28.6	27.3	...	...	...	331
332	Furniture, fixtures	506	508	...	...	...	11.2	10.7	...	...	...	332
341	Paper and products	1031	1001	...	...	...	20.3	18.5	...	...	...	341
3411	Pulp,paper etc.	758	733	...	...	...	14.6	13.2	...	...	...	3411
342	Printing,publishing	1276	1317	...	...	...	24.1	24.0	...	...	...	342
351	Industrial chemicals ...	516	550	...	...	...	9.1	8.9	...	...	...	351
3511	Basic excl fertilizers	246	258	...	...	...	4.2	4.1	...	...	...	3511
3513	Synthetic resins etc .	88	89	...	...	...	1.7	1.6	...	...	...	3513
352	Other chemical products.	336	333	...	...	...	7.1	6.4	...	...	...	352
3522	Drugs and medicines ..	43	49	...	...	...	1.0	1.0	...	...	...	3522
353	Petroleum refineries ...	71	85	...	...	...	1.0	1.0	...	...	...	353
354	Petroleum,coal products.	111	110	...	...	...	2.1	1.9	...	...	...	354
355	Rubber products	112	107	...	...	...	2.4	2.3	...	...	...	355
356	Plastic products n.e.c..	368	393	...	...	...	8.1	8.1	...	...	...	356
361	Pottery,china etc	66	69	...	...	...	1.4	1.3	...	...	...	361
362	Glass and products	135	138	...	...	...	2.8	2.6	...	...	...	362
369	Non-metal products n.e.c	530	559	...	...	...	10.3	9.8	...	...	...	369
371	Iron and steel	904	860	...	...	...	16.1	14.2	...	...	...	371
372	Non-ferrous metals	918	901	...	...	...	16.7	15.5	...	...	...	372
381	Metal products	1576	1629	...	...	...	31.6	30.6	...	...	...	381
382	Machinery n.e.c.	2166	2273	...	...	...	38.1	37.1	...	...	...	382
3825	Office,computing etc..	20	25	...	...	...	0.4	0.5	...	...	...	3825
383	Electrical machinery ...	1087	1172	...	...	...	20.3	19.9	...	...	...	383
3832	Radio,television etc..	447	472	...	...	...	8.5	8.2	...	...	...	3832
384	Transport equipment	3065	3267	...	...	...	57.3	54.5	...	...	...	384
3841	Shipbuilding, repair..	2434	2572	...	...	...	45.6	42.7	...	...	...	3841
3843	Motor vehicles .... b/	244	262	...	...	...	5.2	5.2	...	...	...	3843
385	Professional goods	72	78	...	...	...	1.5	1.5	...	...	...	385
390	Other industries	145	145	...	...	...	3.4	3.1	...	...	...	390
3	Manufacturing	20359	21104	...	...	...	406.8	389.7	...	...	...	3
410	Electricity,gas,steam ..	...	...	...	...	...	...	...	...	...	...	410
4101	Electricity	...	...	...	...	...	...	...	...	...	...	4101
420	Water works and supply .	.	.	...	...	...	.	.	...	...	...	420
4	Electricity,gas etc	...	...	...	...	...	...	...	...	...	...	4
2-4	All industry	...	...	...	...	...	...	...	...	...	...	2-4

a/ Mining and manufacturing: large establishments, generally with 5 or more persons engaged.
b/ Including motorcycles and bicycles.

ISIC	INDUSTRY	9. QUANTITY OF ELECTRICITY CONSUMED a/ (MILLION KWH)					10. OUTPUT a/b/ (BILLION KRONER)					ISIC
		1981	1982	1983	1984	1985	1981	1982	1983	1984	1985	
210	Coal mining	18	21	24	29	23	0.20	0.20	0.19	0.19	0.24	210
220	Petroleum and gas	-	2	11	-	-	56.73	64.13	76.29	92.44	105.21	220
230	Metal ore mining	720	680	738	725	665	1.40	1.26	1.40	1.56	1.67	230
290	Other mining	157	138	174	170	181	1.20	1.28	1.41	1.58	1.66	290
2	Mining, quarrying .	895	841	947	925	869	59.52	66.87	79.29	95.77	108.78	2
311/2	Food products	1579	1588	1700	1744	1753	33.81	36.97	39.47	42.89	46.20	311/2
313	Beverages	196	161	170	166	166	2.64	2.95	3.22	3.54	3.95	313
314	Tobacco	13	13	15	16	14	1.36	1.68	1.85	2.00	2.31	314
321	Textiles	178	181	181	127	145	2.87	2.68	2.56	2.67	2.98	321
3211	Spinning,weaving etc..	...	...	...	...	...	0.90	0.82	0.79	0.85	1.02	3211
322	Wearing apparel	40	32	29	28	30	1.28	1.25	0.97	1.13	1.33	322
323	Leather and products ...	10	9	12	20	14	0.25	0.25	0.23	0.25	0.26	323
324	Footwear	8	7	5	5	5	0.25	0.22	0.19	0.20	0.20	324
331	Wood products	529	531	494	540	567	9.74	10.01	9.39	9.67	10.38	331
332	Furniture, fixtures	129	120	130	132	129	2.75	2.87	3.22	3.43	4.00	332
341	Paper and products	4454	4270	5077	6080	5858	10.46	10.17	10.30	12.09	13.26	341
3411	Pulp,paper etc.	...	...	...	...	...	8.41	8.10	8.16	9.72	10.62	3411
342	Printing,publishing	205	238	252	240	381	8.89	9.56	10.91	12.32	13.97	342
351	Industrial chemicals ...	5724	5406	6152	6462	5813	8.72	8.74	10.21	12.07	12.72	351
3511	Basic excl fertilizers	...	...	...	...	...	3.95	4.07	4.57	5.40	5.75	3511
3513	Synthetic resins etc .	...	...	...	...	...	2.17	2.11	2.55	2.88	3.06	3513
352	Other chemical products.	187	199	223	228	167	3.57	3.96	4.14	4.69	4.80	352
3522	Drugs and medicines ..	...	...	...	...	...	0.66	0.74	0.82	1.01	1.34	3522
353	Petroleum refineries ...	190	199	197	220	226	12.04	12.37	13.32	15.00	15.78	353
354	Petroleum,coal products.	241	240	223	283	318	1.44	1.46	1.47	1.65	1.84	354
355	Rubber products	84	66	110	106	110	0.58	0.55	0.54	0.62	0.75	355
356	Plastic products n.e.c..	246	217	240	244	289	2.57	2.67	2.86	3.13	3.58	356
361	Pottery,china etc	38	37	39	36	38	0.23	0.25	0.23	0.25	0.27	361
362	Glass and products	177	182	162	171	195	0.82	0.79	0.80	0.85	0.98	362
369	Non-metal products n.e.c	441	529	440	445	492	4.25	4.47	4.63	4.68	5.33	369
371	Iron and steel	7788	7317	8900	9508	9538	5.83	5.68	6.42	8.00	9.07	371
372	Non-ferrous metals	14308	13885	14341	16042	15451	10.58	9.46	12.18	16.26	15.83	372
381	Metal products	606	562	505	548	560	7.40	8.11	8.59	8.61	9.98	381
382	Machinery n.e.c.	505	552	586	662	941	18.83	19.10	18.28	23.00	36.21	382
3825	Office,computing etc..	...	...	...	...	...	0.88	1.12	1.37	2.05	2.52	3825
383	Electrical machinery ...	302	349	337	333	339	7.56	8.42	8.77	9.39	10.27	383
3832	Radio,television etc..	...	...	...	...	...	3.19	3.74	3.94	4.19	4.51	3832
384	Transport equipment	594	581	511	514	591	14.99	16.53	13.69	13.85	14.37	384
3841	Shipbuilding, repair..	...	...	...	...	...	12.30	13.54	10.44	10.25	10.29	3841
3843	Motor vehicles .... c/	...	...	...	...	...	1.39	1.50	1.46	1.67	1.99	3843
385	Professional goods	9	11	10	20	25	0.37	0.38	0.43	0.55	0.72	385
390	Other industries	33	31	27	24	30	0.68	0.70	0.73	0.78	0.91	390
3	Manufacturing	38814	37513	41067	44944	44185	174.76	182.25	189.60	213.57	242.25	3
410	Electricity,gas,steam ..	...	...	...	...	...	19.96	25.01	28.93	33.67	39.47	410
4101	Electricity	...	...	...	...	...	19.95	25.00	28.92	33.66	39.47	4101
420	Water works and supply .	.	...	...	...	...	.	.	.	.	.	420
4	Electricity,gas etc	...	...	...	...	...	19.96	25.01	28.93	33.67	39.47	4
2-4	All industry	...	...	...	...	45054	254.25	274.13	297.82	343.01	390.50	2-4

a/ Mining and manufacturing: large establishments, generally with 5 or more persons engaged.
b/ In producers' prices but the value-added tax is not included. c/ Including motorcycles and bicycles.

ISIC	INDUSTRY	11. VALUE ADDED a/b/ (BILLION KRONER)					12. GROSS FIXED CAPITAL FORMATION TOTAL a/ (MILLION KRONER)					ISIC
		1981	1982	1983	1984	1985	1981	1982	1983	1984	1985	
210	Coal mining	0.07	0.05	0.07	0.07	0.11	123	35	40	36	61	210
220	Petroleum and gas	50.70	57.02	67.84	82.72	91.01	17561	11143	15042	28040	19734	220
230	Metal ore mining	0.48	0.41	0.48	0.46	0.40	300	202	106	97	100	230
290	Other mining	0.57	0.62	0.71	0.74	0.74	209	174	167	161	192	290
2	Mining, quarrying .	51.82	58.10	69.10	83.99	92.26	18193	11554	15355	28334	20087	2
311/2	Food products	2.92	3.83	4.36	4.78	5.44	1591	1559	1458	1545	1493	311/2
313	Beverages	1.65	1.91	2.03	2.31	2.55	292	144	278	208	254	313
314	Tobacco	1.10	1.41	1.55	1.62	1.89	25	18	39	18	18	314
321	Textiles	1.07	0.95	0.94	0.99	1.08	128	96	43	84	120	321
3211	Spinning,weaving etc..	0.35	0.30	0.29	0.32	0.37	49	34	7	29	44	3211
322	Wearing apparel	0.53	0.51	0.42	0.46	0.51	37	49	23	20	17	322
323	Leather and products ...	0.09	0.09	0.08	0.09	0.08	20	19	10	3	8	323
324	Footwear	0.11	0.09	0.08	0.08	0.08	9	6	11	2	4	324
331	Wood products	3.00	3.04	2.94	2.91	3.14	608	522	524	588	472	331
332	Furniture, fixtures	1.04	1.11	1.15	1.22	1.41	97	106	122	115	180	332
341	Paper and products	2.52	2.51	2.84	3.49	3.44	1515	456	359	542	595	341
3411	Pulp,paper etc.	1.88	1.84	2.17	2.70	2.63	1416	366	257	407	484	3411
342	Printing,publishing	3.66	3.94	4.80	5.32	6.16	430	351	503	648	746	342
351	Industrial chemicals ...	2.14	1.97	2.68	3.82	3.63	524	472	442	574	678	351
3511	Basic excl fertilizers	1.13	1.10	1.29	1.73	1.64	236	175	119	160	251	3511
3513	Synthetic resins etc .	0.35	0.25	0.50	0.64	0.65	65	53	84	86	64	3513
352	Other chemical products.	1.27	1.43	1.52	1.66	1.58	190	216	227	234	257	352
3522	Drugs and medicines ..	0.29	0.32	0.35	0.42	0.50	43	61	74	71	115	3522
353	Petroleum refineries ...	-0.15	0.28	-	0.06	0.21	144	269	222	61	497	353
354	Petroleum,coal products.	0.30	0.28	0.34	0.41	0.50	63	41	27	38	46	354
355	Rubber products	0.24	0.24	0.25	0.28	0.33	39	28	16	22	29	355
356	Plastic products n.e.c..	0.87	0.90	0.93	1.03	1.26	167	112	131	198	213	356
361	Pottery,china etc	0.14	0.15	0.13	0.14	0.15	17	15	3	6	7	361
362	Glass and products	0.31	0.32	0.35	0.36	0.43	61	36	30	49	69	362
369	Non-metal products n.e.c	1.55	1.63	1.75	1.74	1.85	409	335	221	303	493	369
371	Iron and steel	1.81	1.69	1.99	2.66	2.37	651	497	351	691	862	371
372	Non-ferrous metals	2.56	2.13	3.95	5.49	4.73	1291	1093	595	540	1145	372
381	Metal products	3.19	3.29	3.28	3.53	4.00	360	395	298	342	471	381
382	Machinery n.e.c.	5.55	6.13	6.09	7.07	9.28	582	565	330	772	1195	382
3825	Office,computing etc..	0.36	0.48	0.57	0.76	0.91	55	44	55	196	286	3825
383	Electrical machinery ...	3.49	3.67	3.85	4.03	4.28	388	382	462	452	578	383
3832	Radio,television etc..	1.48	1.68	1.80	1.90	1.92	180	134	200	225	211	3832
384	Transport equipment	5.27	5.61	4.95	5.00	4.77	654	518	416	334	311	384
3841	Shipbuilding, repair..	3.99	4.23	3.50	3.47	3.09	479	387	307	206	138	3841
3843	Motor vehicles .... c/	0.50	0.55	0.53	0.55	0.63	82	23	66	52	79	3843
385	Professional goods	0.18	0.19	0.22	0.26	0.33	13	13	41	17	22	385
390	Other industries	0.29	0.28	0.32	0.33	0.36	49	20	29	20	50	390
3	Manufacturing	46.68	49.58	53.79	61.14	65.84	10354	8333	7211	8426	10830	3
410	Electricity,gas,steam ..	9.77	11.37	13.23	15.41	16.98	7199	7390	7517	7332	7160	410
4101	Electricity	9.77	11.37	13.23	15.41	16.98	7199	7390	7517	7332	7160	4101
420	Water works and supply .	.	.	.	.	.	.	.	.	.	.	420
4	Electricity,gas etc	9.77	11.37	13.23	15.41	16.98	7199	7390	7517	7332	7160	4
2-4	All industry	108.27	119.05	136.12	160.54	175.08	35746	27277	30083	44092	38077	2-4

a/ Mining and manufacturing: large establishments, generally with 5 or more persons engaged.
b/ In producers' prices but the value-added tax is not included. c/ Including motorcycles and bicycles.

ISIC	INDUSTRY	13. GROSS FIXED CAPITAL FORMATION MACHINERY AND EQUIPMENT a/b/ (MILLION KRONER)					14. VALUE OF STOCKS AT END OF PERIOD TOTAL a/ (MILLION KRONER)					ISIC
		1981	1982	1983	1984	1985	1981	1982	1983	1984	1985	
210	Coal mining	8	11	5	11	15	65	88	91	61	83	210
220	Petroleum and gas	11858	3453	6450	17410	8420	328	797	916	687	651	220
230	Metal ore mining	247	150	81	89	84	250	370	267	298	244	230
290	Other mining	161	157	120	136	144	95	104	136	142	126	290
2	Mining, quarrying .	12274	3771	6656	17646	8663	738	1359	1410	1188	1104	2
311/2	Food products	927	989	895	1000	1053	3344	3867	3985	4122	4101	311/2
313	Beverages	150	105	165	122	187	214	244	227	211	207	313
314	Tobacco	17	17	14	7	9	251	354	381	411	430	314
321	Textiles	91	73	46	75	83	749	703	635	703	690	321
3211	Spinning,weaving etc..	...	...	...	...	...	234	225	203	251	268	3211
322	Wearing apparel	22	28	15	17	23	256	246	194	193	212	322
323	Leather and products ...	7	7	7	5	6	45	36	36	41	39	323
324	Footwear	5	5	5	3	4	70	60	42	49	43	324
331	Wood products	380	359	325	349	334	1834	1830	1851	1811	1823	331
332	Furniture, fixtures	58	61	71	79	114	484	467	518	547	634	332
341	Paper and products	1166	430	353	490	459	1642	1768	1413	1443	1403	341
3411	Pulp,paper etc.	...	...	...	...	...	1413	1534	1170	1162	1111	3411
342	Printing,publishing	322	291	331	485	617	907	928	498	1117	1252	342
351	Industrial chemicals ...	388	357	378	411	461	1247	1253	1173	1486	1535	351
3511	Basic excl fertilizers	...	...	...	...	...	461	524	456	550	634	3511
3513	Synthetic resins etc .	...	...	...	...	...	316	312	363	404	437	3513
352	Other chemical products.	126	165	170	175	203	736	827	873	956	864	352
3522	Drugs and medicines ..	...	...	...	...	...	121	141	149	179	225	3522
353	Petroleum refineries ...	129	250	179	51	115	1777	2518	1781	1877	1830	353
354	Petroleum,coal products.	44	37	18	32	52	268	312	271	260	236	354
355	Rubber products	23	25	19	17	36	101	97	100	105	118	355
356	Plastic products n.e.c..	118	103	103	149	183	423	455	487	488	505	356
361	Pottery,china etc	11	6	3	6	7	66	76	71	70	82	361
362	Glass and products	38	29	18	27	54	155	153	130	129	128	362
369	Non-metal products n.e.c	307	264	180	227	322	521	595	553	695	518	369
371	Iron and steel	505	406	230	399	610	1569	1458	1329	1344	1411	371
372	Non-ferrous metals	627	718	388	472	744	3051	2599	2077	2655	2377	372
381	Metal products	257	294	196	269	358	1535	2313	1558	1532	1648	381
382	Machinery n.e.c.	363	385	408	484	742	4835	10257	13025	12920	25294	382
3825	Office,computing etc..	...	...	...	...	...	233	254	325	592	629	3825
383	Electrical machinery ...	273	267	293	328	412	2495	2832	2722	2584	2690	383
3832	Radio,television etc..	...	...	...	...	...	1101	1359	1266	1250	1388	3832
384	Transport equipment	342	326	247	237	263	5597	5347	3696	3446	3322	384
3841	Shipbuilding, repair..	...	...	...	...	...	5094	4677	2947	2551	2279	3841
3843	Motor vehicles .... c/	...	...	...	...	...	246	242	258	289	287	3843
385	Professional goods	7	8	12	14	19	76	78	83	108	154	385
390	Other industries	16	15	26	25	46	175	178	163	173	172	390
3	Manufacturing	6719	6020	5095	5955	7516	34423	41851	39872	41476	53718	3
410	Electricity,gas,steam ..	2043	2453	2361	2580	2855	...	...	...	...	...	410
4101	Electricity	2043	2453	2361	2580	2855	...	...	...	...	...	4101
420	Water works and supply .				...	.	.	.	.	...	...	420
4	Electricity,gas etc	2043	2453	2361	2580	2855	...	...	...	...	...	4
2-4	All industry	21036	12244	14112	26181	19034	...	...	...	...	...	2-4

a/ Mining and manufacturing: large establishments, generally with 5 or more persons engaged.
b/ The value of sales is not deducted.
c/ Including motorcycles and bicycles.

15. INDEX NUMBERS OF INDUSTRIAL PRODUCTION (1980 = 100)

ISIC	INDUSTRY	1976	1977	1978	1979	1981	1982	1983	1984	1985	RATE a/	ISIC
210	Coal mining	318	260	235	156	114	131	219	208	279	-1.4	210
220	Petroleum and gas	35	38	65	80	96	97	114	127	134	16.1	220
230	Metal ore mining	112	109	111	120	129	107	123	124	116	0.4	230
290	Other mining	88	94	96	100	86	93	104	108	115	3.0	290
2	Mining, quarrying .	39	42	68	81	96	97	114	127	134	14.7	2
311/2	Food products	104	110	108	110	83	80	74	71	64	-5.3	311/2
313	Beverages	83	86	91	91	92	93	89	90	92	1.2	313
314	Tobacco	98	97	95	97	98	97	96	96	105	0.8	314
321	Textiles	94	100	90	91	93	75	72	72	76	-2.3	321
3211	Spinning,weaving etc..	...	...	...	...	...	...	...	...	...	...	3211
322	Wearing apparel	114	112	105	99	96	95	83	81	82	-3.6	322
323	Leather and products ...	143	126	109	108	112	107	104	105	104	-3.5	323
324	Footwear	129	127	108	96	81	60	54	51	48	-10.4	324
331	Wood products	100	105	106	103	95	93	88	86	87	-1.5	331
332	Furniture, fixtures	95	98	94	98	100	89	81	84	86	-1.1	332
341	Paper and products	83	84	87	97	105	101	106	118	122	4.4	341
3411	Pulp,paper etc.	...	...	...	...	...	...	...	...	...	...	3411
342	Printing,publishing	114	111	110	107	101	98	100	101	103	-1.1	342
351	Industrial chemicals ...	74	77	78	99	109	110	126	139	135	6.9	351
3511	Basic excl fertilizers	...	...	...	...	...	...	...	...	...	...	3511
3513	Synthetic resins etc .	...	...	...	...	...	...	...	...	...	...	3513
352	Other chemical products.	96	96	90	90	107	108	106	110	114	1.9	352
3522	Drugs and medicines ..	...	...	...	...	...	...	...	...	...	...	3522
353	Petroleum refineries ...	109	114	108	109	149	209	226	234	243	9.3	353
354	Petroleum,coal products.	171	151	154	155	69	104	102	105	106	-5.2	354
355	Rubber products	114	107	91	90	85	83	84	98	105	-0.9	355
356	Plastic products n.e.c..	117	120	113	109	95	104	107	108	114	-0.3	356
361	Pottery,china etc	116	113	106	96	93	87	74	74	66	-6.1	361
362	Glass and products	85	92	90	88	97	102	100	94	96	1.4	362
369	Non-metal products n.e.c	107	101	98	101	96	93	92	87	95	-1.3	369
371	Iron and steel	125	104	106	123	127	111	134	150	151	2.1	371
372	Non-ferrous metals	108	108	105	112	86	91	117	130	127	1.8	372
381	Metal products	93	96	95	93	96	94	84	87	91	-0.2	381
382	Machinery n.e.c.	89	87	86	95	105	105	94	98	105	1.9	382
3825	Office,computing etc..	...	...	...	...	...	...	...	...	...	...	3825
383	Electrical machinery ...	119	120	115	108	110	113	113	118	127	0.7	383
3832	Radio,television etc..	...	...	...	...	...	...	...	...	...	...	3832
384	Transport equipment	121	110	108	99	95	95	82	78	75	-5.2	384
3841	Shipbuilding, repair..	...	...	...	...	...	...	...	...	...	...	3841
3843	Motor vehicles	...	...	...	...	...	...	...	...	...	...	3843
385	Professional goods	122	141	151	133	110	113	125	126	131	0.8	385
390	Other industries	154	160	164	158	102	105	106	104	112	-3.5	390
3	Manufacturing	103	101	99	102	99	99	98	100	103	0.0	3
410	Electricity,gas,steam ..	94	86	96	106	110	112	127	128	124	3.1	410
4101	Electricity	...	...	...	...	...	...	...	...	...	...	4101
420	Water works and supply .	.	.	.	.	.	.	.	.	.	.	420
4	Electricity,gas etc	...	...	...	...	...	...	...	...	...	...	4
2-4	All industry	81	81	89	96	99	99	108	115	119	4.4	2-4

a/ Annual growth rate 1976-1985.

PAKISTAN

The information in the tables is based on the reply to the United Nations Questionnaire on General Industrial Statistics from the Statistics Division, Ministry of Planning and Development, Karachi. The concepts, definitions and classification by branches of industry are generally in accordance with United Nations standards.

The data in the tables are derived from the censuses of mining industries and manufacturing industries carried out by the Statistics Division in co-operation with the provincial Directorates of Industries. The census of mining industries enumerates completely all mining and quarrying establishments with a lease or license in the name of one leasee or licensee. The manufacturing census covers all registered manufacturing establishments; establishments working under the Ministry of Defence and government establishments engaged in manufacturing activities are excluded. The census is conducted through mail inquiry supplemented by field visits. The data in the tables reflect only reporting establishments as no adjustment is made for non-response.

The data are compiled according to the national classification which follows the present version of ISIC. The reference period is the fiscal year 1 July - 30 June; in the tables, the period referred to is the fiscal year ending in the year indicated.

The number of employees relates to average daily employment during the reference year. In the case of manufacturing, the data refer to the number of part-time and full-time employees, excluding homeworkers and including persons employed through labour contractors. Wages and salaries include payments to labour contractors.

Output is calculated as the sum of (a) the value of products and by-products, including industrial waste, (b) receipts from sale of electricity, (c) receipts from industrial work done or services rendered to others and (d) net change in the value of work in progress between the beginning and the end of the year. Value added is the difference between output and the value of input, comprising the cost of materials, fuels and electricity consumed, payments to others for work done on the establishment's materials (including payments to homeworkers) and payments to others for repair and maintenance work. Valuation of output and value added is in producers' prices.

Related national publication:
Census of Manufacturing Industries Report (occasional), published by the Statistics Division, Ministry of Planning and Development, Karachi.

ISIC	INDUSTRY	1. NUMBER OF ESTABLISHMENTS a/b/ (NUMBER)					2. AVERAGE NUMBER OF PERSONS ENGAGED a/ (THOUSANDS)					ISIC
		c/ 1981	1982	1983	1984	1985	b/ 1981	b/ 1982	1983	1984	1985	
210	Coal mining	264	...	...	...	...	...	...	...	...	...	210
220	Petroleum and gas	22	...	...	...	...	...	...	...	...	...	220
230	Metal ore mining	86	...	...	...	...	...	...	...	...	...	230
290	Other mining	315	...	...	...	...	...	...	...	...	...	290
2	Mining, quarrying .	687	...	...	...	...	...	...	...	...	...	2
311/2	Food products	494	581	...	...	...	52.5	59.6	...	...	...	311/2
313	Beverages	35	40	...	...	...	4.0	4.3	...	...	...	313
314	Tobacco	20	19	...	...	...	13.1	10.0	...	...	...	314
321	Textiles	1175	1161	...	...	...	200.6	203.0	...	...	...	321
3211	Spinning,weaving etc..	960	930	...	...	...	194.2	...	...	...	...	3211
322	Wearing apparel	56	55	...	...	...	4.3	4.4	...	...	...	322
323	Leather and products ...	61	71	...	...	...	4.6	3.8	...	...	...	323
324	Footwear	19	18	...	...	...	5.1	2.0	...	...	...	324
331	Wood products	22	28	...	...	...	1.8	1.8	...	...	...	331
332	Furniture, fixtures	35	36	...	...	...	1.0	0.9	...	...	...	332
341	Paper and products	38	33	...	...	...	8.3	7.0	...	...	...	341
3411	Pulp,paper etc.	13	19	...	...	...	7.0	4.5	...	...	...	3411
342	Printing,publishing	139	136	...	...	...	8.5	9.9	...	...	...	342
351	Industrial chemicals ...	80	86	...	...	...	12.8	13.9	...	...	...	351
3511	Basic excl fertilizers	59	33	...	...	...	5.0	3.9	...	...	...	3511
3513	Synthetic resins etc .	4	7	...	...	...	2.0	1.9	...	...	...	3513
352	Other chemical products.	251	241	...	...	...	20.4	19.8	...	...	...	352
3522	Drugs and medicines ..	103	104	...	...	...	11.2	12.4	...	...	...	3522
353	Petroleum refineries ...	3	3	...	...	...	2.8	2.6	...	...	...	353
354	Petroleum,coal products.	12	14	...	...	...	0.8	0.6	...	...	...	354
355	Rubber products	52	53	...	...	...	5.6	9.2	...	...	...	355
356	Plastic products n.e.c..	31	38	...	...	...	2.0	2.5	...	...	...	356
361	Pottery,china etc	17	18	...	...	...	2.0	2.0	...	...	...	361
362	Glass and products	28	22	...	...	...	3.2	3.7	...	...	...	362
369	Non-metal products n.e.c	69	71	...	...	...	11.8	13.1	...	...	...	369
371	Iron and steel	197	193	...	...	...	18.2	34.1	...	...	...	371
372	Non-ferrous metals	14	8	...	...	...	0.5	0.2	...	...	...	372
381	Metal products	272	272	...	...	...	10.3	10.0	...	...	...	381
382	Machinery n.e.c.	273	295	...	...	...	13.8	15.2	...	...	...	382
3825	Office,computing etc..	...	...	...	...	...	...	...	...	...	...	3825
383	Electrical machinery ...	185	178	...	...	...	16.8	17.6	...	...	...	383
3832	Radio,television etc..	9	8	...	...	...	0.8	0.9	...	...	...	3832
384	Transport equipment	122	103	...	...	...	22.7	18.6	...	...	...	384
3841	Shipbuilding, repair..	7	8	...	...	...	6.3	5.2	...	...	...	3841
3843	Motor vehicles	36	28	...	...	...	10.5	...	...	...	...	3843
385	Professional goods	52	44	...	...	...	2.8	2.5	...	...	...	385
390	Other industries	63	65	...	...	...	2.9	2.5	...	...	...	390
3	Manufacturing	3815	3882	...	...	...	453.2	474.8	...	...	...	3
410	Electricity,gas,steam ..	24	24	...	...	...	...	...	...	...	...	410
4101	Electricity	11	11	...	...	...	...	...	...	...	...	4101
420	Water works and supply .	...	...	...	...	...	...	...	...	...	...	420
4	Electricity,gas etc	...	...	...	...	...	...	...	...	...	...	4
2-4	All industry	...	...	...	...	...	...	...	...	...	...	2-4

a/ Manufacturing: establishments with 10 or more workers.
c/ Mining: licensed establishments submitting returns.
b/ Twelve months ending 30 June of the year indicated.

ISIC	INDUSTRY	3. AVERAGE NUMBER OF EMPLOYEES a/b/c/ (THOUSANDS)					4. WAGES AND SALARIES OF EMPLOYEES b/c/ (MILLION RUPEES)					ISIC
		d/ 1981	1982	1983	1984	1985	d/ 1981	1982	1983	1984	1985	
210	Coal mining	16.4	...	...	...	...	167.9	...	...	...	...	210
220	Petroleum and gas	3.3	...	...	...	...	55.1	...	...	...	...	220
230	Metal ore mining	0.1	...	...	...	...	2.4	...	...	...	...	230
290	Other mining	8.7	...	...	...	...	95.3	...	...	...	...	290
2	Mining, quarrying .	28.5	...	...	...	...	320.7	...	...	...	...	2
311/2	Food products	52.4	59.6	...	...	...	725.5	1014.1	...	...	...	311/2
313	Beverages	3.8	4.3	...	...	...	55.3	79.8	...	...	...	313
314	Tobacco	13.1	9.9	...	...	...	136.3	155.7	...	...	...	314
321	Textiles	200.1	202.3	...	...	...	1858.7	2077.4	...	...	...	321
3211	Spinning,weaving etc..	192.0	190.5	...	...	...	1764.0	1931.7	...	...	...	3211
322	Wearing apparel	4.2	4.5	...	...	...	60.3	66.5	...	...	...	322
323	Leather and products ...	4.6	3.8	...	...	...	41.0	49.2	...	...	...	323
324	Footwear	5.1	1.7	...	...	...	66.5	17.0	...	...	...	324
331	Wood products	1.7	1.9	...	...	...	18.6	25.1	...	...	...	331
332	Furniture, fixtures	0.9	0.9	...	...	...	12.4	11.6	...	...	...	332
341	Paper and products	8.3	7.0	...	...	...	129.0	121.2	...	...	...	341
3411	Pulp,paper etc.	7.0	4.5	...	...	...	105.5	86.0	...	...	...	3411
342	Printing,publishing	8.4	9.9	...	...	...	85.3	155.0	...	...	...	342
351	Industrial chemicals ...	12.8	14.0	...	...	...	305.4	409.6	...	...	...	351
3511	Basic excl fertilizers	5.0	3.8	...	...	...	157.2	102.0	...	...	...	3511
3513	Synthetic resins etc .	2.0	1.9	...	...	...	47.1	49.0	...	...	...	3513
352	Other chemical products.	20.3	19.8	...	...	...	370.6	455.5	...	...	...	352
3522	Drugs and medicines ..	11.0	12.4	...	...	...	228.9	305.2	...	...	...	3522
353	Petroleum refineries ...	2.8	2.7	...	...	...	64.2	74.8	...	...	...	353
354	Petroleum,coal products.	0.8	0.6	...	...	...	12.6	14.8	...	...	...	354
355	Rubber products	5.7	9.3	...	...	...	68.0	148.0	...	...	...	355
356	Plastic products n.e.c..	2.0	2.5	...	...	...	29.1	52.5	...	...	...	356
361	Pottery,china etc	2.0	2.0	...	...	...	21.2	22.0	...	...	...	361
362	Glass and products	3.2	3.7	...	...	...	33.5	47.1	...	...	...	362
369	Non-metal products n.e.c	11.8	13.2	...	...	...	205.4	328.3	...	...	...	369
371	Iron and steel	18.2	34.1	...	...	...	257.6	280.2	...	...	...	371
372	Non-ferrous metals	0.5	0.2	...	...	...	6.9	1.4	...	...	...	372
381	Metal products	10.2	9.9	...	...	...	128.1	128.4	...	...	...	381
382	Machinery n.e.c.	13.7	15.2	...	...	...	201.4	247.8	...	...	...	382
3825	Office,computing etc..	...	...	...	...	...	...	...	...	...	...	3825
383	Electrical machinery ...	16.7	17.7	...	...	...	254.9	292.0	...	...	...	383
3832	Radio,television etc..	1.0	1.0	...	...	...	18.4	24.6	...	...	...	3832
384	Transport equipment	22.7	18.6	...	...	...	412.8	413.2	...	...	...	384
3841	Shipbuilding, repair..	6.0	5.3	...	...	...	87.3	96.5	...	...	...	3841
3843	Motor vehicles	10.0	7.4	...	...	...	266.4	263.8	...	...	...	3843
385	Professional goods	2.8	2.6	...	...	...	30.3	31.1	...	...	...	385
390	Other industries	2.9	2.4	...	...	...	32.9	27.3	...	...	...	390
3	Manufacturing	451.7	474.3	...	...	...	5623.8	6746.6	...	...	...	3
410	Electricity,gas,steam ..	84.8	1070.0	1073.0	...	...	1014.7	1281.7	1483.3	...	...	410
4101	Electricity	...	...	...	...	...	...	...	...	...	...	4101
420	Water works and supply .	...	...	...	...	...	...	...	...	...	...	420
4	Electricity,gas etc	...	...	...	...	...	...	...	...	...	...	4
2-4	All industry	...	...	...	...	...	...	...	...	...	...	2-4

a/ Average daily employment, excluding working proprietors, unpaid family workers and homeworkers.
b/ Manufacturing: establishments with 10 or more workers. c/ Twelve months ending 30 June of the year indicated.
d/ Mining: licensed establishments submitting returns.

ISIC	INDUSTRY	5. AVERAGE NUMBER OF OPERATIVES a/b/ (THOUSANDS)					6. WAGES AND SALARIES OF OPERATIVES a/b/ (MILLION RUPEES)					ISIC
		1981	1982	1983	1984	1985	1981	1982	1983	1984	1985	
210	Coal mining	...	...	...	...	...	...	...	...	...	...	210
220	Petroleum and gas	...	...	...	...	...	...	...	...	...	...	220
230	Metal ore mining	...	...	...	...	...	...	...	...	...	...	230
290	Other mining	...	...	...	...	...	...	...	...	...	...	290
2	Mining, quarrying .	...	...	...	...	...	...	...	...	...	...	2
311/2	Food products	35.5	39.1	...	...	...	528.0	654.9	...	...	...	311/2
313	Beverages	1.7	2.0	...	...	...	22.9	33.8	...	...	...	313
314	Tobacco	9.8	7.6	...	...	...	102.8	108.2	...	...	...	314
321	Textiles	166.2	169.9	...	...	...	1507.9	1728.4	...	...	...	321
3211	Spinning,weaving etc..	154.5	160.1	...	...	...	1221.4	1540.2	...	...	...	3211
322	Wearing apparel	3.6	3.8	...	...	...	49.2	53.8	...	...	...	322
323	Leather and products ...	3.6	3.2	...	...	...	31.2	38.5	...	...	...	323
324	Footwear	3.9	1.3	...	...	...	51.0	13.0	...	...	...	324
331	Wood products	1.2	1.4	...	...	...	14.0	19.7	...	...	...	331
332	Furniture, fixtures	0.8	0.7	...	...	...	10.2	9.1	...	...	...	332
341	Paper and products	6.4	5.0	...	...	...	96.1	92.2	...	...	...	341
3411	Pulp,paper etc.	2.6	3.0	...	...	...	20.0	66.0	...	...	...	3411
342	Printing,publishing	6.4	7.7	...	...	...	59.8	109.4	...	...	...	342
351	Industrial chemicals ...	8.7	9.9	...	...	...	198.0	265.5	...	...	...	351
3511	Basic excl fertilizers	3.0	2.7	...	...	...	49.0	73.3	...	...	...	3511
3513	Synthetic resins etc .	...	1.2	...	...	...	...	24.9	...	...	...	3513
352	Other chemical products.	12.9	12.3	...	...	...	200.8	229.3	...	...	...	352
3522	Drugs and medicines ..	6.6	7.3	...	...	...	115.3	147.8	...	...	...	3522
353	Petroleum refineries ...	1.3	1.8	...	...	...	46.8	48.1	...	...	...	353
354	Petroleum,coal products.	0.5	0.3	...	...	...	7.3	8.2	...	...	...	354
355	Rubber products	4.8	7.5	...	...	...	54.8	117.9	...	...	...	355
356	Plastic products n.e.c..	1.5	1.9	...	...	...	21.9	40.0	...	...	...	356
361	Pottery,china etc	1.4	1.6	...	...	...	15.7	18.7	...	...	...	361
362	Glass and products	2.6	2.9	...	...	...	26.1	37.9	...	...	...	362
369	Non-metal products n.e.c	8.6	10.0	...	...	...	141.4	230.6	...	...	...	369
371	Iron and steel	14.5	22.5	...	...	...	208.7	214.1	...	...	...	371
372	Non-ferrous metals	0.4	0.1	...	...	...	5.3	1.1	...	...	...	372
381	Metal products	8.4	7.8	...	...	...	97.8	100.0	...	...	...	381
382	Machinery n.e.c.	10.4	11.8	...	...	...	134.2	170.5	...	...	...	382
3825	Office,computing etc..	...	...	...	...	...	...	...	...	...	...	3825
383	Electrical machinery ...	12.6	12.1	...	...	...	186.6	163.8	...	...	...	383
3832	Radio,television etc..	0.6	0.6	...	...	...	8.4	13.7	...	...	...	3832
384	Transport equipment	15.8	13.1	...	...	...	282.3	272.3	...	...	...	384
3841	Shipbuilding, repair..	4.1	3.6	...	...	...	64.4	66.8	...	...	...	3841
3843	Motor vehicles	7.0	4.6	...	...	...	176.5	163.6	...	...	...	3843
385	Professional goods	2.1	2.2	...	...	...	17.6	21.4	...	...	...	385
390	Other industries	...	2.0	...	...	...	25.2	19.9	...	...	...	390
3	Manufacturing	c/ 345.6	361.5	...	...	...	4143.6	4820.3	...	...	...	3
410	Electricity,gas,steam ..	...	...	...	...	...	...	...	...	...	...	410
4101	Electricity	...	...	...	...	...	...	...	...	...	...	4101
420	Water works and supply .	...	...	...	...	...	...	...	...	...	...	420
4	Electricity,gas etc	...	...	...	...	...	...	...	...	...	...	4
2-4	All industry	...	...	...	...	...	...	...	...	...	...	2-4

a/ Manufacturing: establishments with 10 or more workers.
b/ Twelve months ending 30 June of the year indicated.
c/ Excluding major group 390.

ISIC	INDUSTRY	7. QUANTITY OF ELECTRICITY CONSUMED a/b/ (MILLION KWH)					8. OUTPUT IN PRODUCERS' PRICES a/b/ (MILLION RUPEES)					ISIC
		1981	1982	1983	1984	1985	c/ 1981	1982	1983	1984	1985	
210	Coal mining	...	...	...	...	...	387	...	...	...	...	210
220	Petroleum and gas	...	...	...	...	...	418	...	...	...	...	220
230	Metal ore mining	...	...	...	...	...	5	...	...	...	...	230
290	Other mining	...	...	...	...	...	245	...	...	...	...	290
2	Mining, quarrying	...	...	...	...	...	1055	...	...	...	...	2
311/2	Food products	390	498	...	...	...	17532	23538	...	...	...	311/2
313	Beverages	15	20	...	...	...	994	1382	...	...	...	313
314	Tobacco	18	17	...	...	...	4850	4988	...	...	...	314
321	Textiles	1081	1127	...	...	...	20317	23417	...	...	...	321
3211	Spinning, weaving etc.	1061	1019	...	...	...	18918	21140	...	...	...	3211
322	Wearing apparel	5	5	...	...	...	608	705	...	...	...	322
323	Leather and products	13	17	...	...	...	1195	1338	...	...	...	323
324	Footwear	10	2	...	...	...	558	142	...	...	...	324
331	Wood products	20	27	...	...	...	200	208	...	...	...	331
332	Furniture, fixtures	2	2	...	...	...	85	79	...	...	...	332
341	Paper and products	142	99	...	...	...	1109	1048	...	...	...	341
3411	Pulp, paper etc.	60	54	...	...	...	875	536	...	...	...	3411
342	Printing, publishing	10	66	...	...	...	555	799	...	...	...	342
351	Industrial chemicals	465	500	...	...	...	3290	4056	...	...	...	351
3511	Basic excl fertilizers	280	133	...	...	...	1107	918	...	...	...	3511
3513	Synthetic resins etc	20	49	...	...	...	277	403	...	...	...	3513
352	Other chemical products	67	59	...	...	...	4650	5185	...	...	...	352
3522	Drugs and medicines	46	39	...	...	...	2655	3162	...	...	...	3522
353	Petroleum refineries	82	73	...	...	...	12505	15681	...	...	...	353
354	Petroleum, coal products	1	1	...	...	...	481	777	...	...	...	354
355	Rubber products	21	31	...	...	...	789	1263	...	...	...	355
356	Plastic products n.e.c.	8	37	...	...	...	225	503	...	...	...	356
361	Pottery, china etc	4	5	...	...	...	102	127	...	...	...	361
362	Glass and products	18	20	...	...	...	196	403	...	...	...	362
369	Non-metal products n.e.c	337	345	...	...	...	2738	3458	...	...	...	369
371	Iron and steel	250	467	...	...	...	3309	5569	...	...	...	371
372	Non-ferrous metals	1	1	...	...	...	56	13	...	...	...	372
381	Metal products	22	31	...	...	...	924	992	...	...	...	381
382	Machinery n.e.c.	28	37	...	...	...	1424	2048	...	...	...	382
3825	Office, computing etc.	...	...	...	...	...	...	...	...	...	...	3825
383	Electrical machinery	36	44	...	...	...	2656	3118	...	...	...	383
3832	Radio, television etc.	1	2	...	...	...	361	470	...	...	...	3832
384	Transport equipment	27	27	...	...	...	2419	2623	...	...	...	384
3841	Shipbuilding, repair	11	11	...	...	...	284	328	...	...	...	3841
3843	Motor vehicles	8	9	...	...	...	1545	1918	...	...	...	3843
385	Professional goods	5	4	...	...	...	221	196	...	...	...	385
390	Other industries	43	4	...	...	...	301	200	...	...	...	390
3	Manufacturing	3121	3566	...	...	...	84289	103856	...	...	...	3
410	Electricity, gas, steam	...	...	...	...	...	5796	8076	9022	...	...	410
4101	Electricity	...	...	...	...	...	...	...	...	...	...	4101
420	Water works and supply	...	...	...	...	...	...	...	...	...	...	420
4	Electricity, gas etc	...	...	...	...	...	...	...	...	...	...	4
2-4	All industry	...	...	...	...	...	...	...	...	...	...	2-4

a/ Manufacturing: establishments with 10 or more workers.
c/ Mining: licensed establishments submitting returns.
b/ Twelve months ending 30 June of the year indicated.

9. VALUE ADDED IN PRODUCERS' PRICES a/b/ (MILLION RUPEES)

ISIC	INDUSTRY	1981 c/	1982	1983	1984	1985	ISIC
210	Coal mining	306	...	...	...	...	210
220	Petroleum and gas	386	...	...	...	...	220
230	Metal ore mining	5	...	...	...	...	230
290	Other mining	198	...	...	...	...	290
2	Mining, quarrying	895	...	...	...	...	2
311/2	Food products	5772	7081	...	...	...	311/2
313	Beverages	523	762	...	...	...	313
314	Tobacco	3805	3914	...	...	...	314
321	Textiles	5335	5988	...	...	...	321
3211	Spinning,weaving etc..	4898	5329	...	...	...	3211
322	Wearing apparel	255	278	...	...	...	322
323	Leather and products	305	424	...	...	...	323
324	Footwear	228	35	...	...	...	324
331	Wood products	79	83	...	...	...	331
332	Furniture, fixtures	44	30	...	...	...	332
341	Paper and products	425	408	...	...	...	341
3411	Pulp,paper etc.	355	315	...	...	...	3411
342	Printing,publishing	216	327	...	...	...	342
351	Industrial chemicals	1589	1870	...	...	...	351
3511	Basic excl fertilizers	501	475	...	...	...	3511
3513	Synthetic resins etc	134	179	...	...	...	3513
352	Other chemical products.	1943	2281	...	...	...	352
3522	Drugs and medicines	1236	1428	...	...	...	3522
353	Petroleum refineries	1972	2187	...	...	...	353
354	Petroleum,coal products.	146	167	...	...	...	354
355	Rubber products	277	498	...	...	...	355
356	Plastic products n.e.c..	86	165	...	...	...	356
361	Pottery,china etc	55	62	...	...	...	361
362	Glass and products	96	208	...	...	...	362
369	Non-metal products n.e.c	1697	2095	...	...	...	369
371	Iron and steel	1143	2714	...	...	...	371
372	Non-ferrous metals	14	4	...	...	...	372
381	Metal products	303	355	...	...	...	381
382	Machinery n.e.c.	491	631	...	...	...	382
3825	Office,computing etc..	...	...	...	...	...	3825
383	Electrical machinery	995	1119	...	...	...	383
3832	Radio,television etc..	121	126	...	...	...	3832
384	Transport equipment	708	741	...	...	...	384
3841	Shipbuilding, repair..	111	171	...	...	...	3841
3843	Motor vehicles	440	450	...	...	...	3843
385	Professional goods	84	64	...	...	...	385
390	Other industries	106	63	...	...	...	390
3	Manufacturing	28692	34554	...	...	...	3
410	Electricity,gas,steam	4568	6013	6080	...	...	410
4101	Electricity	...	...	...	...	...	4101
420	Water works and supply	...	...	...	...	...	420
4	Electricity,gas etc	...	...	...	...	...	4
2-4	All industry	...	...	...	...	...	2-4

a/ Manufacturing: establishments with 10 or more workers.
b/ Twelve months ending 30 June of the year indicated.
c/ Mining: licensed establishments submitting returns.

PANAMA

The information in the tables, except for the indexes, is based on the reply to the United Nations Questionnaire on General Industrial Statistics from the Direccion de Estadistica y Censo, Contraloria General de la Republica, Panama. The concepts, definitions and classification by branches of industry are generally in accordance with United Nations standards.

The data in the tables are derived from the survey of manufacturing industries and the survey of production and distribution of electricity, both of which are undertaken annually by the Direccion de Estadistica y Censo. The manufacturing inquiry is carried out through field interviews by enumerators and covers establishments with 5 or more persons engaged. The response rate is reported to be more than 90 per cent; in the tables, adjustments have been made for non-response. The data for electricity relate to all enterprises engaged in the production and distribution of electricity for public use.

The data in the tables are based on the national classification system which follows the present version of ISIC. It should be noted that, except for the number of establishments, ISIC 390 includes industries for which data cannot be divulged because of disclosure rules.

The period of reference is the calendar year; in cases where the establishment uses a period other than the calendar year, necessary adjustments have been made to maintain the consistency of estimates.

The number of persons engaged refers to annual averages of employees on the last day of February, May, August and November, plus the number of working proprietors, unpaid family workers and other unpaid workers reported for 31 August. Employees are defined as those receiving regular wages or salaries or commissions and included on the pay-roll at the pay period nearest the end of each month. Homeworkers are excluded. Wages and salaries represent all payments in cash and in kind which employees receive in respect of their work. However, bonuses, profits distributed to employees and lay-off payments and social security contributions and the like payable by the employer are excluded. Data on electricity consumed relate to the quantity of electricity purchased and self-generated. No adjustment has been made for the quantity sold to others.

Output is calculated as the sum of the following components: (a) value of sales of all products, (b) value of work and services done for others, (c) value of goods sold in the same condition as purchased, (d) net change in the value of stocks of finished goods and work in progress between the beginning and the end of the year, (e) value of electricity sold and (f) value of fixed assets produced on own account. Value added is obtained as the difference between output and the cost of (a) materials, supplies and fuels, (b) goods sold in the same condition as purchased, (c) industrial services purchased from others and (d) electricity purchased. Valuation of output and value added is in producers' prices.

Gross fixed capital formation refers to the gross increment in fixed assets in each year obtained as the sum of the value of new and used fixed assets acquired and construction on own account, less the value of sales of fixed assets. Fixed assets consist of land, buildings and other construction work, vehicles, machinery and other equipment.

The indexes of industrial production are compiled by the Direccion de Estadistica y Censo and provided in response to the United Nations Questionnaire on Indexes of Industrial Production. The indexes cover, in principle, all industrial establishments with 5 or more persons engaged.

Related national publication:
<u>Estadistica Panamena: Situacion Economica, Industria (Encuesta)</u> (annual), published by the Direccion de Estadistica y Censo, Panama.

ISIC	INDUSTRY	1. NUMBER OF ESTABLISHMENTS a/ (NUMBER) 1981	1982	*1983	*1984	1985	2. AVERAGE NUMBER OF PERSONS ENGAGED a/ (NUMBER) 1981	1982	*1983	*1984	1985	ISIC
210	Coal mining	...	...	...	...	...	...	...	...	...	...	210
220	Petroleum and gas	...	...	...	...	...	...	...	...	...	...	220
230	Metal ore mining	...	...	...	...	...	...	...	...	...	...	230
290	Other mining	...	...	...	...	...	...	...	...	...	...	290
2	Mining, quarrying .	...	...	...	...	...	...	...	...	...	...	2
311/2	Food products	238	...	300	304	...	10615	...	13226	13419	...	311/2
313	Beverages	19	...	19	18	...	1896	...	1802	1881	...	313
314	Tobacco	2	...	2	2	...	474	...	432	438	...	314
321	Textiles	6	...	7	7	...	387	...	450	373	...	321
3211	Spinning,weaving etc..	...	...	...	...	...	...	...	...	...	...	3211
322	Wearing apparel	66	...	64	61	...	4886	...	4357	4044	...	322
323	Leather and products ...	8	...	8	7	...	301	...	320	331	...	323
324	Footwear	15	...	16	16	...	1098	...	990	1000	...	324
331	Wood products	22	...	27	28	...	1041	...	973	991	...	331
332	Furniture, fixtures	47	...	63	65	...	1315	...	1377	1414	...	332
341	Paper and products	20	...	21	27	...	1155	...	1077	1155	...	341
3411	Pulp,paper etc.	1	...	1	1	...	...	...	...	...	...	3411
342	Printing,publishing	52	...	71	69	...	2110	...	2216	2116	...	342
351	Industrial chemicals ...	7	...	7	9	...	240	...	221	265	...	351
3511	Basic excl fertilizers	7	...	7	5	...	240	...	221	204	...	3511
3513	Synthetic resins etc .	-	...	-	-	...	-	...	-	-	...	3513
352	Other chemical products.	34	...	39	45	...	1393	...	1474	1584	...	352
3522	Drugs and medicines ..	7	...	6	8	...	317	...	289	293	...	3522
353	Petroleum refineries ...	1	...	1	1	...	b/	...	...	...	...	353
354	Petroleum,coal products.	2	...	4	3	...	b/	...	83	66	...	354
355	Rubber products	7	...	7	9	...	119	...	231	216	...	355
356	Plastic products n.e.c..	20	...	25	29	...	988	...	1042	1195	...	356
361	Pottery,china etc	1	...	6	4	...	c/	...	49	38	...	361
362	Glass and products	6	...	7	8	...	296	...	257	263	...	362
369	Non-metal products n.e.c	37	...	44	45	...	c/ 2223	...	1947	2317	...	369
371	Iron and steel	4	...	3	3	...	392	...	274	279	...	371
372	Non-ferrous metals	3	...	6	5	...	146	...	168	166	...	372
381	Metal products	48	...	62	61	...	1423	...	1460	1427	...	381
382	Machinery n.e.c.	11	...	9	8	...	141	...	119	90	...	382
3825	Office,computing etc..	-	...	-	-	...	-	...	-	-	...	3825
383	Electrical machinery ...	8	...	12	13	...	226	...	278	311	...	383
3832	Radio,television etc..	2	...	3	4	...	46	...	90	118	...	3832
384	Transport equipment	8	...	12	15	...	269	...	277	280	...	384
3841	Shipbuilding, repair..	6	...	9	9	...	269	...	249	225	...	3841
3843	Motor vehicles	2	...	3	6	...	...	...	28	55	...	3843
385	Professional goods	5	...	5	6	...	80	...	59	77	...	385
390	Other industries	18	...	20	23	...	b/ 1063	...	946	1001	...	390
3	Manufacturing	715	809	867	891	...	34277	...	36105	36737	...	3
410	Electricity,gas,steam ..	...	...	...	...	...	...	...	...	...	...	410
4101	Electricity	d/ 7	d/ 3	d/ 3	d/ 3	d/ 3	5321	5324	5279	5365	5355	4101
420	Water works and supply .	...	...	...	...	...	...	...	...	...	...	420
4	Electricity,gas etc	...	...	...	...	...	...	...	...	...	...	4
2-4	All industry	...	...	...	...	...	...	...	...	...	...	2-4

a/ Manufacturing: establishments with 5 or more persons engaged.
b/ Major groups 353 and 354 are included in 390.
c/ Major group 361 is included in 369.
d/ Number of enterprises.

ISIC	INDUSTRY	3. AVERAGE NUMBER OF EMPLOYEES a/ (NUMBER) 1981	1982	*1983	*1984	1985	4. WAGES AND SALARIES OF EMPLOYEES a/ (THOUSAND BALBOAS) 1981	1982	*1983	1984	1985	ISIC
210	Coal mining	...	...	...	...	...	...	...	...	...	...	210
220	Petroleum and gas	...	...	...	...	...	...	...	...	...	...	220
230	Metal ore mining	...	...	...	...	...	...	...	...	...	...	230
290	Other mining	...	...	...	...	...	...	...	...	...	...	290
2	Mining, quarrying .	...	...	...	...	...	...	...	...	...	...	2
311/2	Food products	10573	...	13130	12785	...	42619	...	58405	...	...	311/2
313	Beverages	1896	...	1802	1833	...	9425	...	11087	...	...	313
314	Tobacco	474	...	432	420	...	4030	...	4792	...	...	314
321	Textiles	387	...	450	352	...	1664	...	1640	...	...	321
3211	Spinning,weaving etc..	...	...	...	...	...	...	...	...	...	...	3211
322	Wearing apparel	4879	...	4344	4013	...	15679	...	15318	...	...	322
323	Leather and products ...	300	...	318	329	...	1355	...	1343	...	...	323
324	Footwear	1094	...	985	974	...	3854	...	4053	...	...	324
331	Wood products	1041	...	960	977	...	3378	...	3555	...	...	331
332	Furniture, fixtures	1304	...	1350	1377	...	4755	...	5001	...	...	332
341	Paper and products	1155	...	1075	1136	...	6155	...	6890	...	...	341
3411	Pulp,paper etc.	...	...	...	...	...	...	...	...	...	...	3411
342	Printing,publishing	2109	...	2209	2090	...	9764	...	12845	...	...	342
351	Industrial chemicals ...	240	...	221	260	...	1270	...	1485	...	...	351
3511	Basic excl fertilizers	240	...	221	200	...	1270	...	1485	...	...	3511
3513	Synthetic resins etc .	-	...	-	-	...	-	...	-	...	...	3513
352	Other chemical products.	1392	...	1471	1509	...	7717	...	9920	...	...	352
3522	Drugs and medicines ..	286	...	289	268	...	1919	...	2371	...	...	3522
353	Petroleum refineries ...	b/	...	c/	c/	...	b/	...	c/	...	...	353
354	Petroleum,coal products.	b/	...	83	63	...	b/	...	453	...	...	354
355	Rubber products	119	...	231	213	...	587	...	983	...	...	355
356	Plastic products n.e.c..	984	...	1036	1163	...	4597	...	5490	...	...	356
361	Pottery,china etc	d/	...	40	36	...	d/	...	91	...	...	361
362	Glass and products	296	...	257	262	...	1354	...	1709	...	...	362
369	Non-metal products n.e.c	d/ 2221	...	...	2200	...	d/ 10314	...	12222	...	...	369
371	Iron and steel	392	...	274	277	...	1571	...	1617	...	...	371
372	Non-ferrous metals	146	...	168	163	...	936	...	1160	...	...	372
381	Metal products	1419	...	1444	1377	...	6073	...	6954	...	...	381
382	Machinery n.e.c.	141	...	116	82	...	518	...	482	...	...	382
3825	Office,computing etc..	-	...	-	-	...	-	...	-	...	...	3825
383	Electrical machinery ...	226	...	278	299	...	967	...	1030	...	...	383
3832	Radio,television etc..	46	...	79	45	...	...	...	...	...	...	3832
384	Transport equipment	269	...	275	275	...	1686	...	2212	...	...	384
3841	Shipbuilding, repair..	269	...	247	220	...	1686	...	2087	...	...	3841
3843	Motor vehicles	...	...	28	50	...	...	...	125	...	...	3843
385	Professional goods	80	...	59	74	...	415	...	319	...	...	385
390	Other industries	b/ 1060	...	c/ 943	c/ 940	...	b/ 11054	...	c/ 13171	...	...	390
3	Manufacturing	34197	...	e/ 33951	35479	...	151737	...	184227	...	...	3
410	Electricity,gas,steam ..	...	...	...	...	...	...	...	...	...	...	410
4101	Electricity	5321	5324	5279	5365	5355	43014	53471	58437	59015	64355	4101
420	Water works and supply .	...	...	...	...	...	...	...	...	...	...	420
4	Electricity,gas etc	...	...	...	...	...	...	...	...	...	...	4
2-4	All industry	...	...	...	...	...	...	...	...	...	...	2-4

a/ Manufacturing: establishments with 5 or more persons engaged.
b/ Major groups 353 and 354 are included in 390.
c/ Major group 353 is included in 390.
d/ Major group 361 is included in 369.
e/ Excluding major grup 369.

ISIC	INDUSTRY	5. AVERAGE NUMBER OF OPERATIVES a/ (NUMBER)					6. WAGES AND SALARIES OF OPERATIVES a/ (THOUSAND BALBOAS)					ISIC
		1981	1982	*1983	*1984	1985	1981	1982	1983	1984	1985	
210	Coal mining	...	...	...	...	...	...	...	...	...	...	210
220	Petroleum and gas	...	...	...	...	...	...	...	...	...	...	220
230	Metal ore mining	...	...	...	...	...	...	...	...	...	...	230
290	Other mining	...	...	...	...	...	...	...	...	...	...	290
2	Mining, quarrying .	...	...	...	...	...	...	...	...	...	...	2
311/2	Food products	7847	...	9598	9419	...	23528	...	...	...	...	311/2
313	Beverages	1331	...	1286	1203	...	4707	...	...	...	...	313
314	Tobacco	152	...	144	149	...	797	...	...	...	...	314
321	Textiles	305	...	369	297	...	934	...	...	...	...	321
3211	Spinning,weaving etc..	...	...	...	...	...	...	...	...	...	...	3211
322	Wearing apparel	4374	...	3875	3581	...	11246	...	...	...	...	322
323	Leather and products ...	268	...	280	300	...	816	...	...	...	...	323
324	Footwear	996	...	881	882	...	2889	...	...	...	...	324
331	Wood products	903	...	811	884	...	2341	...	...	...	...	331
332	Furniture, fixtures	1158	...	1182	1220	...	3561	...	...	...	...	332
341	Paper and products	926	...	829	874	...	3891	...	...	...	...	341
3411	Pulp,paper etc.	...	...	58	...	...	...	...	...	...	...	3411
342	Printing,publishing	1491	...	1549	1448	...	6112	...	...	...	...	342
351	Industrial chemicals ...	167	...	167	166	...	529	...	...	...	...	351
3511	Basic excl fertilizers	167	...	167	116	...	529	...	...	...	...	3511
3513	Synthetic resins etc .	-	...	-	-	...	-	...	...	...	...	3513
352	Other chemical products.	925	...	953	1034	...	3030	...	...	...	...	352
3522	Drugs and medicines ..	155	...	149	146	...	557	...	...	...	...	3522
353	Petroleum refineries ...	b/	...	c/	c/	...	b/	...	...	...	...	353
354	Petroleum,coal products.	b/	...	59	46	...	b/	...	...	...	...	354
355	Rubber products	88	...	179	169	...	297	...	...	...	...	355
356	Plastic products n.e.c..	756	...	797	904	...	2519	...	...	...	...	356
361	Pottery,china etc	d/	...	26	28	...	d/	...	...	...	...	361
362	Glass and products	253	...	213	218	...	730	...	...	...	...	362
369	Non-metal products n.e.c	d/ 1788	...	1978	1860	...	d/ 6807	...	...	...	...	369
371	Iron and steel	330	...	219	222	...	977	...	...	...	...	371
372	Non-ferrous metals	113	...	128	136	...	545	...	...	...	...	372
381	Metal products	1165	...	1144	1099	...	3898	...	...	...	...	381
382	Machinery n.e.c.	120	...	94	70	...	353	...	...	...	...	382
3825	Office,computing etc..	-	...	-	-	...	-	...	...	...	...	3825
383	Electrical machinery ...	160	...	183	209	...	476	...	...	...	...	383
3832	Radio,television etc..	...	...	50	16	...	...	...	...	...	...	3832
384	Transport equipment	219	...	208	234	...	1053	...	...	...	...	384
3841	Shipbuilding, repair..	219	...	188	195	...	1053	...	...	...	...	3841
3843	Motor vehicles	...	...	20	36	...	...	...	...	...	...	3843
385	Professional goods	52	...	40	57	...	184	...	...	...	...	385
390	Other industries	b/ 809	...	c/ 670	c/ 721	...	b/ 5373	...	...	...	...	390
3	Manufacturing	26696	...	27862	27430	...	87593	...	...	...	...	3
410	Electricity,gas,steam ..	...	...	...	...	...	...	...	...	...	...	410
4101	Electricity	3491	3519	3485	3585	3583	27580	...	...	...	...	4101
420	Water works and supply .	...	...	...	...	...	...	...	...	...	...	420
4	Electricity,gas etc	...	...	...	...	...	...	...	...	...	...	4
2-4	All industry	...	...	...	...	...	...	...	...	...	...	2-4

a/ Manufacturing: establishments with 5 or more persons engaged.
b/ Major groups 353 and 354 are included in 390.
c/ Major group 353 is included in 390.
d/ Major group 361 is included in 369.

ISIC	INDUSTRY	7. HOURS WORKED BY OPERATIVES a/ (THOUSANDS)					8. QUANTITY OF ELECTRICITY CONSUMED a/b/ (MILLION KWH)					ISIC
		1981	1982	*1983	*1984	1985	1981	1982	1983	1984	1985	
210	Coal mining	...	...	...	...	...	...	...	...	...	...	210
220	Petroleum and gas	...	...	...	...	...	...	...	...	...	...	220
230	Metal ore mining	...	...	...	...	...	...	...	...	...	...	230
290	Other mining	...	...	...	...	...	...	...	...	...	...	290
2	Mining, quarrying .	...	...	...	...	...	...	...	...	...	...	2
311/2	Food products	17811	...	20231	19219	...	123.15	...	...	...	...	311/2
313	Beverages	2968	...	3104	2745	...	23.04	...	...	...	...	313
314	Tobacco	329	...	236	318	...	2.20	...	...	...	...	314
321	Textiles	612	...	1652	700	...	1.95	...	...	...	...	321
3211	Spinning,weaving etc..	...	...	...	...	...	...	...	...	...	...	3211
322	Wearing apparel	8681	...	9452	7189	...	10.44	...	...	...	...	322
323	Leather and products ...	596	...	626	662	...	1.87	...	...	...	...	323
324	Footwear	2118	...	1985	1945	...	2.22	...	...	...	...	324
331	Wood products	2050	...	1999	2025	...	5.10	...	...	...	...	331
332	Furniture, fixtures	2481	...	2546	2602	...	2.19	...	...	...	...	332
341	Paper and products	2089	...	2235	1705	...	20.27	...	...	...	...	341
3411	Pulp,paper etc.	...	...	...	...	...	...	...	...	...	...	3411
342	Printing,publishing	3317	...	3189	2877	...	8.50	...	...	...	...	342
351	Industrial chemicals ...	413	...	361	366	...	5.95	...	...	...	...	351
3511	Basic excl fertilizers	413	...	361	259	...	5.95	...	...	...	...	3511
3513	Synthetic resins etc .	-	...	-	-	...	-	...	...	...	...	3513
352	Other chemical products.	2032	...	1614	1996	...	7.67	...	...	...	...	352
3522	Drugs and medicines ..	325	...	400	305	...	2.19	...	...	...	...	3522
353	Petroleum refineries ...	c/	...	d/	d/	...	c/	...	...	...	...	353
354	Petroleum,coal products.	c/	...	126	113	...	c/	...	...	...	...	354
355	Rubber products	192	...	394	202	...	0.72	...	...	...	...	355
356	Plastic products n.e.c..	1589	...	1625	1895	...	13.42	...	...	...	...	356
361	Pottery,china etc	e/	...	51	60	...	e/	...	...	...	...	361
362	Glass and products	566	...	212	498	...	5.79	...	...	...	...	362
369	Non-metal products n.e.c	e/ 4293	...	4522	3859	...	e/ 48.94	...	...	...	...	369
371	Iron and steel	794	...	524	558	...	5.74	...	...	...	...	371
372	Non-ferrous metals	222	...	258	275	...	0.24	...	...	...	...	372
381	Metal products	2445	...	2393	2318	...	5.20	...	...	...	...	381
382	Machinery n.e.c.	276	...	184	151	...	0.40	...	...	...	...	382
3825	Office,computing etc..	-	...	-	-	...	-	...	...	...	...	3825
383	Electrical machinery ...	325	...	394	450	...	1.62	...	...	...	...	383
3832	Radio,television etc..	...	...	...	...	...	...	...	...	...	...	3832
384	Transport equipment	497	...	453	510	...	0.66	...	...	...	...	384
3841	Shipbuilding, repair..	497	...	405	434	...	0.66	...	...	...	...	3841
3843	Motor vehicles	...	...	48	69	...	...	...	...	...	...	3843
385	Professional goods	98	...	88	125	...	0.33	...	...	...	...	385
390	Other industries	c/ 1546	...	d/ 1258	d/ 1336	...	c/ 26.13	...	...	...	...	390
3	Manufacturing	58340	...	61712	56699	...	323.74	...	...	...	...	3
410	Electricity,gas,steam ..	...	...	...	...	...	...	...	...	...	...	410
4101	Electricity	8933	9048	8972	9115	9827	72.04	61.02	...	...	...	4101
420	Water works and supply .	...	...	...	...	...	...	...	...	...	...	420
4	Electricity,gas etc	...	...	...	...	...	...	...	...	...	...	4
2-4	All industry	...	...	...	...	...	...	...	...	...	...	2-4

a/ Manufacturing: establishments with 5 or more persons engaged.
b/ The quantity of electricity sold is not deducted.
c/ Major groups 353 and 354 are included in 390.
d/ Major group 353 is included in 390.
e/ Major group 361 is included in 369.

ISIC	INDUSTRY	9. OUTPUT IN PRODUCERS' PRICES a/ (MILLION BALBOAS)					10. VALUE ADDED IN PRODUCERS' PRICES a/ (MILLION BALBOAS)					ISIC
		1981	1982	*1983	*1984	1985	1981	1982	*1983	*1984	1985	
210	Coal mining	...	...	...	...	...	...	...	...	...	...	210
220	Petroleum and gas	...	...	...	...	...	...	...	...	...	...	220
230	Metal ore mining	...	...	...	...	...	...	...	...	...	...	230
290	Other mining	...	...	...	...	...	...	...	...	...	...	290
2	Mining, quarrying .	...	...	...	...	...	...	...	...	...	...	2
311/2	Food products	533.3	...	615.1	645.2	...	175.2	...	174.3	211.1	...	311/2
313	Beverages	109.5	...	115.1	123.9	...	54.5	...	63.3	62.6	...	313
314	Tobacco	37.8	...	39.7	37.4	...	29.2	...	29.8	28.0	...	314
321	Textiles	9.5	...	7.9	6.7	...	4.0	...	3.8	2.8	...	321
3211	Spinning,weaving etc..	...	...	...	...	...	...	...	...	...	...	3211
322	Wearing apparel	66.9	...	59.3	56.3	...	32.6	...	28.7	25.4	...	322
323	Leather and products ...	7.2	...	10.2	13.2	...	3.1	...	3.7	6.9	...	323
324	Footwear	19.6	...	18.2	19.8	...	7.3	...	7.0	7.1	...	324
331	Wood products	17.5	...	21.3	21.0	...	8.4	...	8.6	9.1	...	331
332	Furniture, fixtures	18.7	...	22.1	22.3	...	9.0	...	9.4	9.4	...	332
341	Paper and products	66.4	...	58.4	64.2	...	21.6	...	22.2	22.6	...	341
3411	Pulp,paper etc.	...	...	...	...	...	...	...	...	...	...	3411
342	Printing,publishing	38.5	...	59.6	62.5	...	23.7	...	38.6	39.1	...	342
351	Industrial chemicals ...	26.3	...	25.4	26.3	...	5.5	...	6.2	8.7	...	351
3511	Basic excl fertilizers	26.3	...	25.4	19.2	...	5.5	...	6.2	5.9	...	3511
3513	Synthetic resins etc .	-	...	-	-	...	-	...	-	-	...	3513
352	Other chemical products.	67.8	...	74.5	85.0	...	28.2	...	32.2	35.0	...	352
3522	Drugs and medicines ..	14.5	...	12.6	13.2	...	7.5	...	6.3	6.7	...	3522
353	Petroleum refineries ...	b/	...	c/	c/	...	b/	...	c/	c/	...	353
354	Petroleum,coal products.	b/	...	8.8	9.7	...	b/	...	2.6	2.3	...	354
355	Rubber products	3.6	...	4.8	3.8	...	1.9	...	2.0	1.4	...	355
356	Plastic products n.e.c..	35.7	...	43.8	48.8	...	14.1	...	18.9	18.1	...	356
361	Pottery,china etc	d/	...	0.4	0.5	...	d/	...	0.2	0.2	...	361
362	Glass and products	10.7	...	10.0	12.2	...	4.8	...	3.2	6.7	...	362
369	Non-metal products n.e.c	d/ 77.7	...	79.8	71.0	...	d/ 32.0	...	34.2	31.8	...	369
371	Iron and steel	17.1	...	9.1	9.1	...	6.0	...	4.5	4.5	...	371
372	Non-ferrous metals	5.9	...	8.0	8.7	...	3.0	...	3.4	3.9	...	372
381	Metal products	51.9	...	53.1	56.1	...	22.1	...	19.5	21.2	...	381
382	Machinery n.e.c.	2.0	...	1.9	1.2	...	1.0	...	1.0	0.9	...	382
3825	Office,computing etc..	-	...	-	-	...	-	...	-	-	...	3825
383	Electrical machinery ...	9.0	...	16.9	15.8	...	3.4	...	8.9	8.2	...	383
3832	Radio,television etc..	9.0	...	1.1	1.0	...	3.4	...	...	0.6	...	3832
384	Transport equipment	7.4	...	7.2	7.1	...	5.5	...	5.1	4.9	...	384
3841	Shipbuilding, repair..	7.4	...	6.6	5.8	...	5.5	...	4.7	4.1	...	3841
3843	Motor vehicles	...	...	0.6	1.3	...	...	...	0.4	0.6	...	3843
385	Professional goods	2.8	...	2.5	3.8	...	1.5	...	1.4	2.2	...	385
390	Other industries	b/ 456.6	...	c/ 433.8	c/ 394.1	...	b/ 28.4	...	c/ 45.3	c/ 28.7	...	390
3	Manufacturing	1699.4	...	1806.9	1825.7	...	526.0	...	578.0	602.8	...	3
410	Electricity,gas,steam ..	...	...	...	...	...	...	...	...	...	...	410
4101	Electricity	167.0	192.0	232.8	229.3	235.8	55.6	47.4	...	...	...	4101
420	Water works and supply .	...	...	...	...	...	...	...	...	...	...	420
4	Electricity,gas etc	...	...	...	...	...	...	...	...	...	...	4
2-4	All industry	...	...	...	...	...	...	...	...	...	...	2-4

a/ Manufacturing: establishments with 5 or more persons engaged. b/ Major groups 353 and 354 are included in 390.
c/ Major group 353 is included in 390. d/ Major group 361 is included in 369.

11. GROSS FIXED CAPITAL FORMATION
TOTAL a/
(THOUSAND BALBOAS)

ISIC	INDUSTRY	1981	1982	1983	1984	1985	ISIC
210	Coal mining	...	...	...	...	...	210
220	Petroleum and gas	...	...	...	...	...	220
230	Metal ore mining	...	...	...	...	...	230
290	Other mining	...	...	...	...	...	290
2	Mining, quarrying	...	...	...	...	...	2
311/2	Food products	55768	...	...	...	...	311/2
313	Beverages	5085	...	...	...	...	313
314	Tobacco	665	...	...	...	...	314
321	Textiles	577	...	...	...	...	321
3211	Spinning,weaving etc.	...	...	...	...	...	3211
322	Wearing apparel	1201	...	...	...	...	322
323	Leather and products	426	...	...	...	...	323
324	Footwear	195	...	...	...	...	324
331	Wood products	1048	...	...	...	...	331
332	Furniture, fixtures	1817	...	...	...	...	332
341	Paper and products	4795	...	...	...	...	341
3411	Pulp,paper etc.	...	...	...	...	...	3411
342	Printing,publishing	3228	...	...	...	...	342
351	Industrial chemicals	1731	...	...	...	...	351
3511	Basic excl fertilizers	1731	...	...	...	...	3511
3513	Synthetic resins etc	-	...	...	...	...	3513
352	Other chemical products	6291	...	...	...	...	352
3522	Drugs and medicines	286	...	...	...	...	3522
353	Petroleum refineries ... b/	...	...	...	...	...	353
354	Petroleum,coal products. b/	...	...	...	...	...	354
355	Rubber products	165	...	...	...	...	355
356	Plastic products n.e.c.	3090	...	...	...	...	356
361	Pottery,china etc ...... c/	...	...	...	...	...	361
362	Glass and products	4	...	...	...	...	362
369	Non-metal products n.e.c c/	14900	...	...	...	...	369
371	Iron and steel	5525	...	...	...	...	371
372	Non-ferrous metals	106	...	...	...	...	372
381	Metal products	1422	...	...	...	...	381
382	Machinery n.e.c.	285	...	...	...	...	382
3825	Office,computing etc.	-	...	...	...	...	3825
383	Electrical machinery	291	...	...	...	...	383
3832	Radio,television etc.	...	...	...	...	...	3832
384	Transport equipment	544	...	...	...	...	384
3841	Shipbuilding, repair	544	...	...	...	...	3841
3843	Motor vehicles	...	...	...	...	...	3843
385	Professional goods	47	...	...	...	...	385
390	Other industries .... b/	4945	...	...	...	...	390
3	Manufacturing	114151	...	...	...	...	3
410	Electricity,gas,steam	...	...	...	...	...	410
4101	Electricity	84702	51860	87477	...	50302	4101
420	Water works and supply	...	...	...	...	...	420
4	Electricity,gas etc	...	...	...	...	...	4
2-4	All industry	...	...	...	...	...	2-4

a/ Manufacturing: establishments with 5 or more persons engaged. b/ Major groups 353 and 354 are included in 390.
c/ Major group 361 is included in 369.

12. INDEX NUMBERS OF INDUSTRIAL PRODUCTION (1980 = 100)

ISIC	INDUSTRY	1976	1977	1978	1979	1981	1982	1983	1984	1985	a/ RATE	ISIC
210	Coal mining	...	...	...	...	...	...	...	...	...	...	210
220	Petroleum and gas	...	...	...	...	...	...	...	...	...	...	220
230	Metal ore mining	...	...	...	...	...	...	...	...	...	...	230
290	Other mining	...	...	...	...	...	...	...	...	...	...	290
2	Mining, quarrying	...	...	...	...	...	...	...	...	...	...	2
311/2	Food products	79	86	91	99	106	113	116	105	112	4.0	311/2
313	Beverages	73	76	85	97	108	108	107	112	113	5.0	313
314	Tobacco	98	91	100	98	97	96	93	85	83	-1.8	314
321	Textiles	86	76	79	92	86	86	76	74	61	-3.7	321
3211	Spinning,weaving etc.	...	...	...	...	...	...	...	...	...	...	3211
322	Wearing apparel	79	80	87	93	111	119	104	90	94	2.0	322
323	Leather and products	111	129	122	163	139	140	148	257	281	10.9	323
324	Footwear	68	62	84	97	97	93	89	98	112	5.7	324
331	Wood products	82	92	87	103	95	102	93	107	101	2.3	331
332	Furniture, fixtures	75	62	79	97	91	94	103	93	96	2.8	332
341	Paper and products	67	66	84	89	101	101	107	108	114	6.1	341
3411	Pulp,paper etc.	...	...	...	...	...	...	...	...	...	...	3411
342	Printing,publishing	81	86	98	99	109	87	97	94	92	1.4	342
351	Industrial chemicals	59	76	83	83	127	134	136	159	162	11.9	351
3511	Basic excl fertilizers	...	...	...	...	...	...	...	...	...	...	3511
3513	Synthetic resins etc	...	...	...	...	...	...	...	...	...	...	3513
352	Other chemical products	75	74	83	93	103	108	117	112	118	5.2	352
3522	Drugs and medicines	...	...	...	...	...	...	...	...	...	...	3522
353	Petroleum refineries	151	149	124	116	76	86	87	82	68	-8.5	353
354	Petroleum,coal products											354
355	Rubber products	80	84	101	100	92	98	151	63	54	-4.3	355
356	Plastic products n.e.c.	67	84	86	93	110	127	128	137	129	7.5	356
361	Pottery,china etc	...	...	...	...	...	...	...	...	...	...	361
362	Glass and products	17	15	16	16	125	132	154	146	143	26.7	362
369	Non-metal products n.e.c	91	80	84	100	113	117	104	81	79	-1.6	369
371	Iron and steel	48	60	66	85	92	83	62	58	62	2.9	371
372	Non-ferrous metals											372
381	Metal products	94	80	82	97	86	88	91	81	78	-2.1	381
382	Machinery n.e.c.	170	141	118	129	199	203	230	223	132	-2.8	382
3825	Office,computing etc.	...	...	...	...	...	...	...	...	...	...	3825
383	Electrical machinery	67	73	83	97	114	120	201	215	212	13.7	383
3832	Radio,television etc.	...	...	...	...	...	...	...	...	...	...	3832
384	Transport equipment	115	93	101	79	159	134	119	114	92	-2.4	384
3841	Shipbuilding, repair	...	...	...	...	...	...	...	...	...	...	3841
3843	Motor vehicles	...	...	...	...	...	...	...	...	...	...	3843
385	Professional goods	80	86	84	95	91	86	78	118	121	4.7	385
390	Other industries	104	103	113	130	174	116	176	162	162	5.0	390
3	Manufacturing	79	82	86	96	74	75	77	73	74	-0.7	3
410	Electricity,gas,steam	...	...	...	...	...	...	...	...	...	...	410
4101	Electricity	...	...	...	...	...	...	...	...	...	...	4101
420	Water works and supply	...	...	...	...	...	...	...	...	...	...	420
4	Electricity,gas etc	...	...	...	...	...	...	...	...	...	...	4
2-4	All industry	...	...	...	...	...	...	...	...	...	...	2-4

a/ Annual growth rate 1976-1985.

PAPUA NEW GUINEA

The information in the tables is based on the reply to the United Nations Questionnare on General Industrial Statistics from the National Statistical Office, Port Moresby. The concepts and definitions are generally in accordance with United Nations standards.

The data for manufacturing are derived from compulsory returns furnished annually by factories under the Statistics Act. The data in the tables cover establishments with 4 or more persons engaged or using power other than manual. Government-owned factories and workshops are also included. Electricity data cover all establishments engaged in the production and distribution of electricity for public use.

The data are compiled in accordance with the revised national classification system which is comparable with the present version of ISIC. The reference period is the calendar year.

The number of establishments relates to those in operation during the period of reference. Employment numbers are annual averages. Output is the ex-factory selling value (excluding excise duties and all delivery costs and charges) of goods manufactured, treated or worked up during the year, plus the value of work done for others. Value added is estimated by deducting from the value of output the cost of materials, fuels, lubricating oils, electricity and water consumed, tools replaced and repairs to buildings and plant. Valuation of output and value added is in factor values.

Related national publication:
Secondary Industries (annual), published by the National Statistical Office, Port Moresby.

ISIC	INDUSTRY	1. NUMBER OF ESTABLISHMENTS a/ (NUMBER)					2. AVERAGE NUMBER OF PERSONS ENGAGED a/ (NUMBER)					ISIC
		1981	1982	1983	1984	1985	1981	1982	1983	1984	1985	
210	Coal mining	...	...	...	...	...	...	...	...	...	...	210
220	Petroleum and gas	...	...	...	...	...	...	...	...	...	...	220
230	Metal ore mining	...	...	...	...	...	...	...	...	...	...	230
290	Other mining	...	...	...	...	...	...	...	...	...	...	290
2	Mining, quarrying	...	...	...	...	...	...	...	...	...	...	2
311/2	Food products	132	136	130	...	...	5073	9222	8198	...	...	311/2
313	Beverages	17	16	15	...	...	1346	1432	1619	...	...	313
314	Tobacco	5	5	5	...	...	663	669	611	...	...	314
321	Textiles	5	9	12	...	...	55	90	31	...	...	321
3211	Spinning,weaving etc.	1	2	-	...	...	...	...	-	...	...	3211
322	Wearing apparel	4	3	3	...	...	[173	159	318]	...	...	322
323	Leather and products	-	-	1	...	...				...	...	323
324	Footwear	-	-	-	...	...	-	-	-	...	...	324
331	Wood products	59	49	46	...	...	4190	4354	3875	...	...	331
332	Furniture, fixtures	49	48	54	...	...	982	998	1094	...	...	332
341	Paper and products	5	5	5	...	...	186	167	199	...	...	341
3411	Pulp,paper etc.	2	2	2	...	...	...	...	...	...	...	3411
342	Printing,publishing	26	22	20	...	...	1070	870	813	...	...	342
351	Industrial chemicals	10	11	6	...	...	b/ 215	b/ 191	b/ 150	...	...	351
3511	Basic excl fertilizers	7	6	5	...	...	...	...	...	...	...	3511
3513	Synthetic resins etc	2	4	1	...	...	...	...	...	...	...	3513
352	Other chemical products	7	7	7	...	...	179	188	199	...	...	352
3522	Drugs and medicines	...	...	...	...	...	...	...	...	...	...	3522
353	Petroleum refineries	-	-	-	...	...	-	-	-	...	...	353
354	Petroleum,coal products	-	-	-	...	...	-	-	-	...	...	354
355	Rubber products	2	2	3	...	...	12	11	144	...	...	355
356	Plastic products n.e.c.	3	2	6	...	...	b/	b/	b/	...	...	356
361	Pottery,china etc	-	-	-	...	...	-	-	-	...	...	361
362	Glass and products	4	5	5	...	...	[717	711	549]	...	...	362
369	Non-metal products n.e.c	17	16	13	...	...				...	...	369
371	Iron and steel	4	4	3	...	...	c/ 361	c/ 301	c/ 90	...	...	371
372	Non-ferrous metals	-	-	-	...	...	-	-	-	...	...	372
381	Metal products	47	45	41	...	...	1975	1785	...	...	...	381
382	Machinery n.e.c.	21	20	20	...	...	1260	1229	1726	...	...	382
3825	Office,computing etc.	...	...	...	...	...	...	...	...	...	...	3825
383	Electrical machinery	6	7	14	...	...	78	80	109	...	...	383
3832	Radio,television etc.	1	1	8	...	...	...	...	...	...	...	3832
384	Transport equipment	58	53	49	...	...	1332	1258	1024	...	...	384
3841	Shipbuilding, repair	26	24	25	...	...	507	487	404	...	...	3841
3843	Motor vehicles	11	10	7	...	...	...	...	...	...	...	3843
385	Professional goods	1	1	1	...	...	c/	c/	c/	...	...	385
390	Other industries	2	2	2	...	...	101	166	...	...	...	390
3	Manufacturing	484	468	461	...	...	19968	23881	d/ 20749	...	...	3
410	Electricity,gas,steam	...	...	...	...	...	...	...	...	...	...	410
4101	Electricity	26	...	...	...	...	467	...	...	...	...	4101
420	Water works and supply	...	...	...	...	...	...	...	...	...	...	420
4	Electricity,gas etc	...	...	...	...	...	...	...	...	...	...	4
2-4	All industry	...	...	...	...	...	...	...	...	...	...	2-4

a/ Establishments with 4 or more persons engaged or using power other than manual.
b/ Major group 356 is included in 351. c/ Major group 385 is included in 371.
d/ Excluding major groups 381 and 390.

ISIC	INDUSTRY	3. AVERAGE NUMBER OF EMPLOYEES a/ (NUMBER) 1981	1982	1983	1984	1985	4. WAGES AND SALARIES OF EMPLOYEES a/ (THOUSAND KINA) 1981	1982	1983	1984	1985	ISIC
210	Coal mining	...	...	...	...	...	...	...	...	...	...	210
220	Petroleum and gas	...	...	...	...	...	...	...	...	...	...	220
230	Metal ore mining	...	...	...	...	...	...	...	...	...	...	230
290	Other mining	...	...	...	...	...	...	...	...	...	...	290
2	Mining, quarrying .	...	...	...	...	...	...	...	...	...	...	2
311/2	Food products	5004	7049	8145	...	...	12130	17994	20596	...	...	311/2
313	Beverages	1338	1426	1618	...	...	5575	6061	8495	...	...	313
314	Tobacco	663	669	611	...	...	1668	1808	1753	...	...	314
321	Textiles	50	84	27	...	...	84	135	49	...	...	321
3211	Spinning,weaving etc..	...	...	-	...	...	...	...	-	...	...	3211
322	Wearing apparel	[170	156	312]	...	...	[397	399	855]	...	...	322
323	Leather and products ...				...	...				...	...	323
324	Footwear	-	-	-	...	...	-	-	-	...	...	324
331	Wood products	4168	4332	3858	...	...	10758	10221	10409	...	...	331
332	Furniture, fixtures	942	956	1047	...	...	2614	3352	3269	...	...	332
341	Paper and products	185	166	199	...	...	639	767	834	...	...	341
3411	Pulp,paper etc.	...	...	...	...	...	...	...	...	...	...	3411
342	Printing,publishing	1060	864	797	...	...	3509	3133	3179	...	...	342
351	Industrial chemicals ...	b/ 213	b/ 190	b/ 150	...	...	902	931	801	...	...	351
3511	Basic excl fertilizers	...	...	...	...	...	...	...	...	...	...	3511
3513	Synthetic resins etc .	...	...	...	...	...	...	...	...	...	...	3513
352	Other chemical products.	178	187	197	...	...	780	937	1016	...	...	352
3522	Drugs and medicines ..	...	...	...	...	...	...	...	...	...	...	3522
353	Petroleum refineries ...	-	-	-	...	...	-	-	-	...	...	353
354	Petroleum,coal products.	-	-	-	...	...	-	-	-	...	...	354
355	Rubber products	12	11	...	...	...	[244	144	647]	...	...	355
356	Plastic products n.e.c..	b/	b/	b/	...	...				...	...	356
361	Pottery,china etc	-	-	-	...	...	-	-	-	...	...	361
362	Glass and products	[710	704	542]	...	...	[2415	2603	2489]	...	...	362
369	Non-metal products n.e.c				...	...				...	...	369
371	Iron and steel	c/ 361	c/ 301	c/ 90	...	...	d/ 1824	d/ 1665	...	...	...	371
372	Non-ferrous metals	-	-	-	...	...	-	-	-	...	...	372
381	Metal products	1957	1770	1697	...	...	8669	8708	9142	...	...	381
382	Machinery n.e.c.	1257	1226	1071	...	...	6893	10314	10610	...	...	382
3825	Office,computing etc..	...	...	...	...	...	...	...	...	...	...	3825
383	Electrical machinery ...	75	77	97	...	...	320	395	490	...	...	383
3832	Radio,television etc..	...	...	...	...	...	...	...	...	...	...	3832
384	Transport equipment	1276	1220	1000	...	...	6608	6556	7876	...	...	384
3841	Shipbuilding, repair..	494	474	392	...	...	1887	1918	1676	...	...	3841
3843	Motor vehicles	...	...	...	...	...	...	...	...	...	...	3843
385	Professional goods	c/	c/	c/	...	...	d/	d/	...	...	...	385
390	Other industries	96	161	150	...	...	d/	d/	247	...	...	390
3	Manufacturing	19715	21549	e/ 21608	...	...	66029	76123	f/ 82757	...	...	3
410	Electricity,gas,steam ..	...	...	...	...	...	...	...	...	...	...	410
4101	Electricity	467	...	...	...	...	3448	...	...	...	...	4101
420	Water works and supply .	...	...	...	...	...	...	...	...	...	...	420
4	Electricity,gas etc	...	...	...	...	...	...	...	...	...	...	4
2-4	All industry	...	...	...	...	...	...	...	...	...	...	2-4

a/ Establishments with 4 or more persons engaged or using power other than manual.
b/ Major group 356 is included in 351.
c/ Major group 385 is included in 371.
d/ Major groups 385 and 390 are included in 371.
e/ Excluding major group 355.
f/ Excluding major groups 371 and 385.

ISIC	INDUSTRY	5. AVERAGE NUMBER OF OPERATIVES a/ (NUMBER) 1981	1982	1983	1984	1985	6. WAGES AND SALARIES OF OPERATIVES a/ (THOUSAND KINA) 1981	1982	1983	1984	1985	ISIC
210	Coal mining	...	...	...	...	...	...	...	...	...	...	210
220	Petroleum and gas	...	...	...	...	...	...	...	...	...	...	220
230	Metal ore mining	...	...	...	...	...	...	...	...	...	...	230
290	Other mining	...	...	...	...	...	...	...	...	...	...	290
2	Mining, quarrying .	...	...	...	...	...	...	...	...	...	...	2
311/2	Food products	4478	5597	6476	...	...	8775	11676	12984	...	...	311/2
313	Beverages	718	821	1102	...	...	1910	2437	4138	...	...	313
314	Tobacco	595	595	526	...	...	1310	1375	1307	...	...	314
321	Textiles	49	80	26	...	...	82	113	49	...	...	321
3211	Spinning,weaving etc..	...	...	-	...	...	...	...	-	...	...	3211
322	Wearing apparel	[169	150	272]	...	...	[395	336	765]	...	...	322
323	Leather and products ...				...	...				...	...	323
324	Footwear	-	-	-	...	...	-	-	-	...	...	324
331	Wood products	3862	4065	2598	...	...	8491	8368	8519	...	...	331
332	Furniture, fixtures	864	843	959	...	...	2188	2736	2765	...	...	332
341	Paper and products	143	123	151	...	...	298	371	477	...	...	341
3411	Pulp,paper etc.	...	...	...	...	...	...	...	...	...	...	3411
342	Printing,publishing	729	615	586	...	...	2074	1944	2036	...	...	342
351	Industrial chemicals ...	155	140	91	...	...	584	499	301	...	...	351
3511	Basic excl fertilizers	...	...	...	...	...	...	...	...	...	...	3511
3513	Synthetic resins etc .	...	...	...	...	...	...	...	...	...	...	3513
352	Other chemical products.	141	139	128	...	...	381	443	408	...	...	352
3522	Drugs and medicines ..	...	...	...	...	...	...	...	...	...	...	3522
353	Petroleum refineries ...	-	-	-	...	...	-	-	-	...	...	353
354	Petroleum,coal products.	-	-	-	...	...	-	-	-	...	...	354
355	Rubber products	[46	34	114]	...	...	[178	90	432]	...	...	355
356	Plastic products n.e.c..				...	...				...	...	356
361	Pottery,china etc	-	-	-	...	...	-	-	-	...	...	361
362	Glass and products	[626	632	473]	...	...	[1727	1961	1771]	...	...	362
369	Non-metal products n.e.c				...	...				...	...	369
371	Iron and steel	b/ 407	b/ 423	84	...	...	b/ 1433	b/ 1280	b/ 197	...	...	371
372	Non-ferrous metals	-	-	-	...	...	-	-	-	...	...	372
381	Metal products	1713	1537	1476	...	...	6266	6484	6887	...	...	381
382	Machinery n.e.c.	1067	1059	861	...	...	5596	8959	8983	...	...	382
3825	Office,computing etc..	...	...	...	...	...	...	...	...	...	...	3825
383	Electrical machinery ...	61	66	71	...	...	213	313	359	...	...	383
3832	Radio,television etc..	...	...	...	...	...	...	...	...	...	...	3832
384	Transport equipment	1138	1058	872	...	...	5259	5339	6822	...	...	384
3841	Shipbuilding, repair..	445	407	323	...	...	1466	1572	1225	...	...	3841
3843	Motor vehicles	...	...	...	...	...	...	...	...	...	...	3843
385	Professional goods ..... b/	...	...	...	...	...	...	...	...	...	...	385
390	Other industries	b/	b/	84	...	...	b/	b/	b/	...	...	390
3	Manufacturing	16961	17977	16950	...	...	47160	54724	59200	...	...	3
410	Electricity,gas,steam ..	...	...	...	...	...	...	...	...	...	...	410
4101	Electricity	464	...	...	...	...	3364	...	...	...	...	4101
420	Water works and supply .	...	...	...	...	...	...	...	...	...	...	420
4	Electricity,gas etc	...	...	...	...	...	...	...	...	...	...	4
2-4	All industry	...	...	...	...	...	...	...	...	...	...	2-4

a/ Establishments with 4 or more persons engaged or using power other than manual.
b/ Major groups 385 and 390 are included in 371.

ISIC	INDUSTRY	7. OUTPUT IN FACTOR VALUES a/ (THOUSAND KINA) 1981	1982	1983	1984	1985	8. VALUE ADDED IN FACTOR VALUES a/ (THOUSAND KINA) 1981	1982	1983	1984	1985	ISIC
210	Coal mining	...	...	...	...	...	...	...	...	...	...	210
220	Petroleum and gas	...	...	...	...	...	...	...	...	...	...	220
230	Metal ore mining	...	...	...	...	...	...	...	...	...	...	230
290	Other mining	...	...	...	...	...	...	...	...	...	...	290
2	Mining, quarrying .	...	...	...	...	...	...	...	...	...	...	2
311/2	Food products	162529	179202	228649	...	...	50088	70171	89551	...	...	311/2
313	Beverages	68524	53755	62177	...	...	41584	24503	30116	...	...	313
314	Tobacco	16715	19700	17612	...	...	4067	6781	5219	...	...	314
321	Textiles	501	628	307	...	...	311	362	184	...	...	321
3211	Spinning,weaving etc..	...	...	-	...	...	...	...	-	...	...	3211
322	Wearing apparel	[2023	1232	2304]	...	...	[1105	586	1022]	...	...	322
323	Leather and products ...				...	...				...	...	323
324	Footwear	-	-	-	...	...	-	-	-	...	...	324
331	Wood products	53013	59596	57349	...	...	29082	35441	31224	...	...	331
332	Furniture, fixtures	9905	10897	13437	...	...	4741	5263	5492	...	...	332
341	Paper and products	5490	6368	8567	...	...	2642	2549	4625	...	...	341
3411	Pulp,paper etc.	...	...	...	...	...	...	...	...	...	...	3411
342	Printing,publishing	10736	10915	8310	...	...	5535	6824	4787	...	...	342
351	Industrial chemicals ...	6560	7595	5161	...	...	4225	...	2718	...	...	351
3511	Basic excl fertilizers	...	...	...	...	...	...	...	...	...	...	3511
3513	Synthetic resins etc .	...	...	...	...	...	...	...	...	...	...	3513
352	Other chemical products.	7850	7484	8318	...	...	3388	3740	3774	...	...	352
3522	Drugs and medicines ..	...	...	...	...	...	...	...	...	...	...	3522
353	Petroleum refineries ...	-	-	-	...	...	-	-	-	...	...	353
354	Petroleum,coal products.	-	-	-	...	...	-	-	-	...	...	354
355	Rubber products	[2088	953]	...	...	...	[1008	538]	...	...	...	355
356	Plastic products n.e.c..			...	...	...			...	...	...	356
361	Pottery,china etc	-	-	-	...	...	-	-	-	...	...	361
362	Glass and products	[17035	15006	11018]	...	...	[7585	6451	6040]	...	...	362
369	Non-metal products n.e.c				...	...				...	...	369
371	Iron and steel .... b/	7013	6662	5034	...	...	3463	3264	2274	...	...	371
372	Non-ferrous metals	-	-	-	...	...	-	-	-	...	...	372
381	Metal products	41105	33444	42739	...	...	15591	12569	15900	...	...	381
382	Machinery n.e.c.	29704	27723	27449	...	...	13621	10394	10693	...	...	382
3825	Office,computing etc..	...	...	...	...	...	...	...	...	...	....	3825
383	Electrical machinery ...	1287	1281	1826	...	...	700	538	1020	...	...	383
3832	Radio,television etc..	...	...	...	...	...	...	...	...	...	...	3832
384	Transport equipment	18024	17221	15909	...	...	8432	8044	7161	...	...	384
3841	Shipbuilding, repair..	6018	5986	6028	...	...	3217	3210	3455	...	...	3841
3843	Motor vehicles	...	...	...	...	...	...	...	...	...	...	3843
385	Professional goods ..... b/	...	...	...	...	...	...	...	...	...	...	385
390	Other industries .... b/	...	...	...	...	...	...	...	...	...	...	390
3	Manufacturing	460102	459662	c/ 516166	...	...	197168	d/ 198018	c/ 221800	...	...	3
410	Electricity,gas,steam ..	...	...	...	...	...	...	...	...	...	...	410
4101	Electricity	51918	...	...	...	...	14716	...	...	...	...	4101
420	Water works and supply .	...	...	...	...	...	...	...	...	...	...	420
4	Electricity,gas etc	...	...	...	...	...	...	...	...	...	...	4
2-4	All industry	...	...	...	...	...	...	...	...	...	...	2-4

a/ Establishments with 4 or more persons engaged or using power other than manual.
b/ Major groups 385 and 390 are included in 371.
c/ Excluding major groups 355 and 356.
d/ Excluding major group 351.

The information in the tables, except for the indexes, is based on the reply to the United Nations Questionnaire on General Industrial Statistics from the Instituto Nacional de Estadistica, Lima. The concepts, definitions and classification by branches of industry are generally in accordance with United Nations standards.

The data shown in the tables are compiled by the office mentioned above. The data for manufacturing are derived from the survey of manufacturing industries and relate to establishments with 5 or more persons engaged. Estimates of output and value added are derived from national accounts calculations and cover all establishments including handicrafts.

The data in the tables are based on the national classification which is comparable with the present version of ISIC. The following industries are omitted from the scope of manufacturing: canning, preserving and processing of fish and crustacea; extraction of fish and other marine animal oils; production of fish meal.

The reference period is the calendar year. When the establishment uses a financial year different from the calendar year, the data are adjusted to a calendar-year basis.

The number of establishments refers to those operated during the whole or part of the year under review. Wages and salaries relate to payments in cash and in kind during the year, excluding bonuses. The estimates of value added represent the contribution of each branch of industry to the gross domestic product. Valuation of output and value added is in producers' prices.

The indexes of industrial production are compiled by the Ministerio de Industria, Turismo e Integracion and provided in response to the United Nations Questionnaire on Indexes of Industrial Production. The indexes cover, in principle, all industrial establishments.

Related national publication:
Cuentas Nacionales del Peru, published by the Instituto Nacional de Estadistica, Lima.

ISIC	INDUSTRY	1. NUMBER OF ESTABLISHMENTS a/ (NUMBER) 1981	1982	1983	1984	1985	2. AVERAGE NUMBER OF PERSONS ENGAGED a/ (THOUSANDS) 1981	1982	1983	1984	1985	ISIC
210	Coal mining	...	...	...	...	...	...	...	...	...	...	210
220	Petroleum and gas	...	...	...	...	...	...	...	...	...	...	220
230	Metal ore mining	...	...	...	...	...	...	...	...	...	...	230
290	Other mining	...	...	...	...	...	...	...	...	...	...	290
2	Mining, quarrying .	...	...	...	...	...	...	...	...	...	...	2
311/2	Food products .... b/	1807	1852	...	...	...	33.2	41.5	...	...	...	311/2
313	Beverages	522	527	...	...	...	10.9	13.6	...	...	...	313
314	Tobacco	3	2	...	...	...	1.0	0.8	...	...	...	314
321	Textiles	841	879	...	...	...	31.1	36.5	...	...	...	321
3211	Spinning,weaving etc..	353	382	...	...	...	23.4	26.9	...	...	...	3211
322	Wearing apparel	937	1017	...	...	...	10.8	17.1	...	...	...	322
323	Leather and products ...	210	216	...	...	...	3.2	4.0	...	...	...	323
324	Footwear	357	382	...	...	...	6.3	7.9	...	...	...	324
331	Wood products	635	657	...	...	...	6.8	10.9	...	...	...	331
332	Furniture, fixtures	505	538	...	...	...	4.5	6.5	...	...	...	332
341	Paper and products	121	128	...	...	...	7.1	7.8	...	...	...	341
3411	Pulp,paper etc.	16	23	...	...	...	3.6	3.8	...	...	...	3411
342	Printing,publishing	560	593	...	...	...	8.6	12.1	...	...	...	342
351	Industrial chemicals ...	193	197	...	...	...	7.8	8.5	...	...	...	351
3511	Basic excl fertilizers	136	138	...	...	...	2.8	3.5	...	...	...	3511
3513	Synthetic resins etc .	29	29	...	...	...	3.6	3.5	...	...	...	3513
352	Other chemical products.	496	514	...	...	...	16.4	18.4	...	...	...	352
3522	Drugs and medicines ..	103	106	...	...	...	7.4	7.1	...	...	...	3522
353	Petroleum refineries ...	12	14	...	...	...	2.6	3.3	...	...	...	353
354	Petroleum,coal products.	9	10	...	...	...	0.1	0.1	...	...	...	354
355	Rubber products	62	63	...	...	...	3.4	3.6	...	...	...	355
356	Plastic products n.e.c..	266	279	...	...	...	7.8	9.4	...	...	...	356
361	Pottery,china etc	35	40	...	...	...	1.6	2.1	...	...	...	361
362	Glass and products	84	90	...	...	...	4.1	4.5	...	...	...	362
369	Non-metal products n.e.c	490	500	...	...	...	8.2	10.6	...	...	...	369
371	Iron and steel	71	70	...	...	...	7.5	7.6	...	...	...	371
372	Non-ferrous metals	57	67	...	...	...	3.9	4.6	...	...	...	372
381	Metal products	966	1033	...	...	...	14.5	19.9	...	...	...	381
382	Machinery n.e.c.	390	419	...	...	...	8.4	11.6	...	...	...	382
3825	Office,computing etc..	19	18	...	...	...	0.2	0.3	...	...	...	3825
383	Electrical machinery ...	325	329	...	...	...	9.3	10.7	...	...	...	383
3832	Radio,television etc..	99	102	...	...	...	3.0	3.3	...	...	...	3832
384	Transport equipment	366	375	...	...	...	10.2	11.9	...	...	...	384
3841	Shipbuilding, repair..	58	59	...	...	...	1.2	1.9	...	...	...	3841
3843	Motor vehicles	271	279	...	...	...	8.2	8.9	...	...	...	3843
385	Professional goods	78	85	...	...	...	1.2	1.6	...	...	...	385
390	Other industries	372	379	...	...	...	3.5	5.0	...	...	...	390
3	Manufacturing ..... b/	10770	11255	...	...	...	234.0	292.1	...	...	...	3
410	Electricity,gas,steam ..	...	...	...	...	...	...	...	...	...	...	410
4101	Electricity	...	...	...	...	...	...	...	...	...	...	4101
420	Water works and supply .	...	...	...	...	...	...	...	...	...	...	420
4	Electricity,gas etc	...	...	...	...	...	...	...	...	...	...	4
2-4	All industry	...	...	...	...	...	...	...	...	...	...	2-4

a/ Establishments with 5 or more persons engaged.
b/ Excluding canning, preserving and processing of fish and crustacea, extraction of fish and other marine animal oils, production of fish meal.

ISIC	INDUSTRY	3. WAGES AND SALARIES OF EMPLOYEES a/ (MILLION SOLES)					4. AVERAGE NUMBER OF OPERATIVES a/ (THOUSANDS)					ISIC
		1981	1982	1983	1984	1985	1981	1982	1983	1984	1985	
210	Coal mining	...	...	...	...	...	...	...	...	...	...	210
220	Petroleum and gas	...	...	...	...	...	...	...	...	...	...	220
230	Metal ore mining	...	...	...	...	...	...	...	...	...	...	230
290	Other mining	...	...	...	...	...	...	...	...	...	...	290
2	Mining, quarrying .	...	...	...	...	...	...	...	...	...	...	2
311/2	Food products .... b/	50809	99211	...	...	...	23.5	27.7	...	...	...	311/2
313	Beverages	22196	38775	...	...	...	6.9	8.3	...	...	...	313
314	Tobacco	2080	3114	...	...	...	0.7	1.0	...	...	...	314
321	Textiles	41739	76019	...	...	...	23.6	27.1	...	...	...	321
3211	Spinning,weaving etc..	32670	21472	...	...	...	18.4	20.9	...	...	...	3211
322	Wearing apparel	10288	20694	...	...	...	8.2	12.7	...	...	...	322
323	Leather and products ...	3723	6937	...	...	...	2.3	2.8	...	...	...	323
324	Footwear	7298	11542	...	...	...	4.6	5.7	...	...	...	324
331	Wood products	7254	15861	...	...	...	5.2	8.1	...	...	...	331
332	Furniture, fixtures	5443	10009	...	...	...	3.3	4.6	...	...	...	332
341	Paper and products	13443	47542	...	...	...	4.6	4.9	...	...	...	341
3411	Pulp,paper etc.	7769	13810	...	...	...	2.2	2.2	...	...	...	3411
342	Printing,publishing	15399	29613	...	...	...	4.8	6.1	...	...	...	342
351	Industrial chemicals ...	16076	29273	...	...	...	4.8	5.1	...	...	...	351
3511	Basic excl fertilizers	5759	11380	...	...	...	1.6	1.9	...	...	...	3511
3513	Synthetic resins etc .	6654	11594	...	...	...	2.5	2.4	...	...	...	3513
352	Other chemical products.	29483	51347	...	...	...	7.8	9.0	...	...	...	352
3522	Drugs and medicines ..	13114	21840	...	...	...	3.2	3.3	...	...	...	3522
353	Petroleum refineries ...	15578	35311	...	...	...	0.7	0.7	...	...	...	353
354	Petroleum,coal products.	152	165	...	...	...	-	0.1	...	...	...	354
355	Rubber products	6415	11976	...	...	...	2.2	2.2	...	...	...	355
356	Plastic products n.e.c..	11587	20923	...	...	...	5.4	6.3	...	...	...	356
361	Pottery,china etc	2334	4941	...	...	...	1.3	1.7	...	...	...	361
362	Glass and products	4800	9781	...	...	...	3.3	3.5	...	...	...	362
369	Non-metal products n.e.c	11738	25799	...	...	...	6.3	7.6	...	...	...	369
371	Iron and steel	19610	32084	...	...	...	4.3	4.3	...	...	...	371
372	Non-ferrous metals	6601	11529	...	...	...	3.2	3.8	...	...	...	372
381	Metal products	19339	41561	...	...	...	10.8	13.9	...	...	...	381
382	Machinery n.e.c.	13151	26733	...	...	...	5.6	7.6	...	...	...	382
3825	Office,computing etc..	175	448	...	...	...	0.1	0.2	...	...	...	3825
383	Electrical machinery ...	15355	30460	...	...	...	5.6	6.2	...	...	...	383
3832	Radio,television etc..	4902	8734	...	...	...	1.7	1.7	...	...	...	3832
384	Transport equipment	16242	30617	...	...	...	6.5	7.4	...	...	...	384
3841	Shipbuilding, repair..	1641	4491	...	...	...	0.7	1.2	...	...	...	3841
3843	Motor vehicles	13610	24411	...	...	...	5.3	5.5	...	...	...	3843
385	Professional goods	1708	3503	...	...	...	0.7	1.0	...	...	...	385
390	Other industries	4250	8765	...	...	...	1.9	2.8	...	...	...	390
3	Manufacturing ..... b/	374091	734085	...	...	...	158.1	192.2	...	...	...	3
410	Electricity,gas,steam ..	...	...	...	...	...	...	...	...	...	...	410
4101	Electricity	...	...	...	...	...	...	...	...	...	...	4101
420	Water works and supply .	...	...	...	...	...	...	...	...	...	...	420
4	Electricity,gas etc	...	...	...	...	...	...	...	...	...	...	4
2-4	All industry	...	...	...	...	...	...	...	...	...	...	2-4

a/ Establishments with 5 or more persons engaged.
b/ Excluding canning, preserving and processing of fish and crustacea, extraction of fish and other marine animal oils, production of fish meal.

ISIC	INDUSTRY	5. WAGES AND SALARIES OF OPERATIVES a/ (MILLION SOLES) 1981	1982	1983	1984	1985	6. OUTPUT IN PRODUCERS' PRICES b/ (BILLION SOLES) 1981	1982	1983	1984	1985	ISIC
210	Coal mining	...	...	...	...	...	...	...	...	...	...	210
220	Petroleum and gas	...	...	...	...	...	...	...	...	...	...	220
230	Metal ore mining	...	...	...	...	...	...	...	...	...	...	230
290	Other mining	...	...	...	...	...	...	...	...	...	...	290
2	Mining, quarrying	...	...	...	...	...	...	...	...	...	...	2
311/2	Food products c/	29237	56844	...	...	...	962.4	1429.3	...	...	...	311/2
313	Beverages	9625	16795	...	...	...	297.2	558.9	...	...	...	313
314	Tobacco	981	1566	...	...	...	51.0	78.1	...	...	...	314
321	Textiles	26017	47422	...	...	...	356.2	635.3	...	...	...	321
3211	Spinning,weaving etc.	20543	...	...	...	...	271.8	484.7	...	...	...	3211
322	Wearing apparel	6745	13044	...	...	...	83.5	165.6	...	...	...	322
323	Leather and products	2350	4135	...	...	...	31.3	50.4	...	...	...	323
324	Footwear	5325	7845	...	...	...	40.4	86.1	...	...	...	324
331	Wood products	4950	10357	...	...	...	57.0	115.9	...	...	...	331
332	Furniture, fixtures	3399	6314	...	...	...	58.7	63.2	...	...	...	332
341	Paper and products	6915	12320	...	...	...	160.3	211.9	...	...	...	341
3411	Pulp,paper etc.	3623	6313	...	...	...	92.7	117.4	...	...	...	3411
342	Printing,publishing	8006	13086	...	...	...	105.5	207.0	...	...	...	342
351	Industrial chemicals	7774	13942	...	...	...	165.6	308.4	...	...	...	351
3511	Basic excl fertilizers	2644	5019	...	...	...	61.3	145.2	...	...	...	3511
3513	Synthetic resins etc	3774	6832	...	...	...	63.9	106.8	...	...	...	3513
352	Other chemical products.	8927	15605	...	...	...	384.7	498.3	...	...	...	352
3522	Drugs and medicines	3610	5977	...	...	...	113.8	154.9	...	...	...	3522
353	Petroleum refineries	2315	6112	...	...	...	533.3	1165.3	...	...	...	353
354	Petroleum,coal products.	101	57	...	...	...	2.1	1.6	...	...	...	354
355	Rubber products	3252	5952	...	...	...	59.4	85.5	...	...	...	355
356	Plastic products n.e.c.	6189	11384	...	...	...	117.4	195.9	...	...	...	356
361	Pottery,china etc	1806	3440	...	...	...	13.0	29.8	...	...	...	361
362	Glass and products	3484	6542	...	...	...	31.8	73.1	...	...	...	362
369	Non-metal products n.e.c	7158	14889	...	...	...	105.8	254.2	...	...	...	369
371	Iron and steel	9146	16346	...	...	...	145.3	236.0	...	...	...	371
372	Non-ferrous metals	4947	8171	...	...	...	309.6	392.3	...	...	...	372
381	Metal products	11518	24149	...	...	...	170.3	387.7	...	...	...	381
382	Machinery n.e.c.	7475	15271	...	...	...	96.4	285.4	...	...	...	382
3825	Office,computing etc.	89	270	...	...	...	1.4	2.9	...	...	...	3825
383	Electrical machinery	7108	13843	...	...	...	165.1	336.0	...	...	...	383
3832	Radio,television etc.	2238	3640	...	...	...	60.7	91.1	...	...	...	3832
384	Transport equipment	7724	14266	...	...	...	233.3	380.5	...	...	...	384
3841	Shipbuilding, repair.	708	1927	...	...	...	11.5	84.5	...	...	...	3841
3843	Motor vehicles	6592	11547	...	...	...	210.8	281.0	...	...	...	3843
385	Professional goods	628	1474	...	...	...	13.4	26.4	...	...	...	385
390	Other industries	1681	3653	...	...	...	d/ 39.2	d/ 91.4	...	...	...	390
3	Manufacturing c/	194783	364824	...	...	...	4789.2	8349.5	...	...	...	3
410	Electricity,gas,steam	...	...	...	...	...	...	...	...	...	...	410
4101	Electricity	...	...	...	...	...	...	...	...	...	...	4101
420	Water works and supply	...	...	...	...	...	...	...	...	...	...	420
4	Electricity,gas etc	...	...	...	...	...	...	...	...	...	...	4
2-4	All industry	...	...	...	...	...	...	...	...	...	...	2-4

a/ Establishments with 5 or more persons engaged.
b/ Estimates derived from national accounts calculations.
c/ Excluding canning, preserving and processing of fish and crustacea, extraction of fish and other marine animal oils, production of fish meal.
d/ Including handicraft activities.

ISIC	INDUSTRY	7. VALUE ADDED IN PRODUCERS' PRICES a/ (BILLION SOLES)					8. GROSS FIXED CAPITAL FORMATION TOTAL b/ (BILLION SOLES)					ISIC
		1981	1982	1983	1984	1985	1981	1982	1983	1984	1985	
210	Coal mining	...	...	...	...	...	...	...	...	...	...	210
220	Petroleum and gas	...	...	...	...	...	...	...	...	...	...	220
230	Metal ore mining	...	...	...	...	...	...	...	...	...	...	230
290	Other mining	...	...	...	...	...	...	...	...	...	...	290
2	Mining, quarrying .	...	...	...	...	...	...	...	...	...	...	2
311/2	Food products .... c/	280.9	403.3	...	...	...	116.0	138.6	...	...	...	311/2
313	Beverages	172.4	319.6	...	...	...	59.4	102.8	...	...	...	313
314	Tobacco	39.9	58.3	...	...	...	4.9	3.8	...	...	...	314
321	Textiles	142.6	247.9	...	...	...	64.3	127.2	...	...	...	321
3211	Spinning,weaving etc..	112.9	194.9	...	...	...	53.9	97.4	...	...	...	3211
322	Wearing apparel	32.4	72.0	...	...	...	9.1	24.9	...	...	...	322
323	Leather and products ...	10.7	18.3	...	...	...	5.5	10.5	...	...	...	323
324	Footwear	23.0	42.3	...	...	...	7.0	9.2	...	...	...	324
331	Wood products	20.7	46.9	...	...	...	7.3	23.4	...	...	...	331
332	Furniture, fixtures	28.2	27.8	...	...	...	9.9	13.8	...	...	...	332
341	Paper and products	52.9	55.4	...	...	...	29.0	35.7	...	...	...	341
3411	Pulp,paper etc.	29.0	29.5	...	...	...	16.7	17.0	...	...	...	3411
342	Printing,publishing	51.8	89.0	...	...	...	18.3	32.2	...	...	...	342
351	Industrial chemicals ...	79.9	135.9	...	...	...	40.9	47.9	...	...	...	351
3511	Basic excl fertilizers	30.4	72.4	...	...	...	16.3	14.3	...	...	...	3511
3513	Synthetic resins etc .	24.6	34.4	...	...	...	19.4	23.4	...	...	...	3513
352	Other chemical products.	168.8	187.5	...	...	...	36.1	61.7	...	...	...	352
3522	Drugs and medicines ..	45.9	60.5	...	...	...	13.9	23.1	...	...	...	3522
353	Petroleum refineries ...	109.8	503.2	...	...	...	27.2	53.3	...	...	...	353
354	Petroleum,coal products.	0.8	0.6	...	...	...	0.2	0.5	...	...	...	354
355	Rubber products	27.7	45.2	...	...	...	6.6	15.9	...	...	...	355
356	Plastic products n.e.c..	47.1	81.9	...	...	...	22.7	30.7	...	...	...	356
361	Pottery,china etc	7.7	15.4	...	...	...	2.5	9.1	...	...	...	361
362	Glass and products	13.6	29.0	...	...	...	9.3	20.7	...	...	...	362
369	Non-metal products n.e.c	40.6	110.0	...	...	...	10.9	38.6	...	...	...	369
371	Iron and steel	64.9	95.0	...	...	...	46.4	56.7	...	...	...	371
372	Non-ferrous metals	90.3	123.2	...	...	...	-4.1	53.0	...	...	...	372
381	Metal products	63.1	163.4	...	...	...	30.8	55.1	...	...	...	381
382	Machinery n.e.c.	44.6	155.6	...	...	...	14.1	-393.4	...	...	...	382
3825	Office,computing etc..	0.6	1.3	...	...	...	0.4	0.2	...	...	...	3825
383	Electrical machinery ...	71.8	123.4	...	...	...	21.7	30.0	...	...	...	383
3832	Radio,television etc..	26.5	34.1	...	...	...	5.7	8.2	...	...	...	3832
384	Transport equipment	68.4	169.3	...	...	...	28.8	56.0	...	...	...	384
3841	Shipbuilding, repair..	3.3	49.2	...	...	...	3.6	11.8	...	...	...	3841
3843	Motor vehicles	61.8	114.9	...	...	...	23.2	43.3	...	...	...	3843
385	Professional goods	5.6	10.6	...	...	...	2.0	6.5	...	...	...	385
390	Other industries	d/ 15.9	d/ 36.7	...	...	...	8.7	16.4	...	...	...	390
3	Manufacturing ..... c/	1776.1	3366.7	...	...	...	635.4	680.8	...	...	...	3
410	Electricity,gas,steam ..	...	...	...	...	...	...	...	...	...	...	410
4101	Electricity	...	...	...	...	...	...	...	...	...	...	4101
420	Water works and supply .	...	...	...	...	...	...	...	...	...	...	420
4	Electricity,gas etc	...	...	...	...	...	...	...	...	...	...	4
2-4	All industry	...	...	...	...	...	...	...	...	...	...	2-4

a/ Contributions to the gross domestic product.
b/ Establishments with 5 or more persons engaged.
c/ Excluding canning, preserving and processing of fish and crustacea, extraction of fish and other marine animal oils, production of fish meal.
d/ Including handicraft activities.

9. INDEX NUMBERS OF INDUSTRIAL PRODUCTION (1980 = 100)

ISIC	INDUSTRY	1976	1977	1978	1979	1981	1982	1983	1984	1985	a/ RATE	ISIC
210	Coal mining	...	...	...	...	...	...	...	...	...	...	210
220	Petroleum and gas	...	...	...	...	...	...	...	...	...	...	220
230	Metal ore mining	...	...	...	...	...	...	...	...	...	...	230
290	Other mining	...	...	...	...	...	...	...	...	...	...	290
2	Mining, quarrying .	...	...	...	...	...	...	...	...	...	...	2
311/2	Food products	80	83	86	91	95	81	67	86	79	-0.1	311/2
313	Beverages	102	93	83	90	99	101	100	91	97	-0.6	313
314	Tobacco	91	90	82	90	106	108	93	93	82	-1.2	314
321	Textiles	102	90	98	105	100	93	96	103	112	1.0	321
3211	Spinning,weaving etc..	...	...	...	...	...	...	...	...	...	...	3211
322	Wearing apparel	142	128	102	94	72	...	...	...	...	b/ -12.7	322
323	Leather and products ...	117	89	87	83	94	78	75	70	63	-6.6	323
324	Footwear	153	98	92	87	89	69	52	51	48	-12.1	324
331	Wood products	125	115	113	109	101	...	...	...	...	b/ -4.2	331
332	Furniture, fixtures	136	110	94	88	77	...	...	...	...	b/ -10.8	332
341	Paper and products	97	100	87	82	93	67	58	58	54	-6.3	341
3411	Pulp,paper etc.	...	...	...	...	...	...	...	...	...	...	3411
342	Printing,publishing	142	115	106	84	118	119	...	...	...	c/ -2.9	342
351	Industrial chemicals ...	77	84	91	95	100	108	77	96	94	2.2	351
3511	Basic excl fertilizers	...	...	...	...	...	...	...	...	...	...	3511
3513	Synthetic resins etc .	...	...	...	...	...	...	...	...	...	...	3513
352	Other chemical products.	104	91	90	82	104	110	74	60	65	-5.1	352
3522	Drugs and medicines ..	...	...	...	...	...	...	...	...	...	...	3522
353 354	Petroleum refineries ... Petroleum,coal products.	[84	85	84	97	102	104	102	113	113	3.3]	353 354
355	Rubber products	106	88	76	82	98	93	74	82	84	-2.6	355
356	Plastic products n.e.c..	97	87	80	91	109	113	84	85	92	-0.6	356
361	Pottery,china etc	117	130	87	100	120	117	...	...	...	c/ 0.0	361
362	Glass and products	114	103	82	97	100	112	87	77	74	-4.7	362
369	Non-metal products n.e.c	102	90	89	88	102	90	76	65	64	-5.0	369
371	Iron and steel	67	79	84	89	90	72	49	59	64	-0.5	371
372	Non-ferrous metals	53	80	91	106	95	99	90	99	104	7.8	372
381	Metal products	99	94	88	83	91	86	54	59	59	-5.6	381
382	Machinery n.e.c.	93	93	75	82	108	84	50	42	46	-7.5	382
3825	Office,computing etc..	...	...	...	...	...	...	...	...	...	...	3825
383	Electrical machinery ...	108	104	93	85	113	90	68	72	78	-3.6	383
3832	Radio,television etc..	...	...	...	...	...	...	...	...	...	...	3832
384	Transport equipment	163	108	57	65	94	88	35	37	45	-13.3	384
3841	Shipbuilding, repair..	...	...	...	...	...	...	...	...	...	...	3841
3843	Motor vehicles	...	...	...	...	...	...	...	...	...	...	3843
385	Professional goods	115	99	102	89	126	...	...	...	...	b/ 1.8	385
390	Other industries	170	141	138	106	64	93	109	...	...	d/ -6.1	390
3	Manufacturing	99	95	92	95	100	97	81	85	88	-1.3	3
410	Electricity,gas,steam ..	...	...	...	...	...	...	...	...	...	...	410
4101	Electricity	...	...	...	...	...	...	...	...	...	...	4101
420	Water works and supply .	...	...	...	...	...	...	...	...	...	...	420
4	Electricity,gas etc	...	...	...	...	...	...	...	...	...	...	4
2-4	All industry	...	...	...	...	...	...	...	...	...	...	2-4

a/ Annual growth rate 1976-1985.
b/ Annual growth rate 1976-1981.
c/ Annual growth rate 1976-1982.
d/ Annual growth rate 1976-1983.

The information in the tables, except for the indexes, is based on the reply to the United Nations Questionnaire on General Industrial Statistics from the National Census and Statistics Office, National Economic and Development Authority, Manila. The concepts, definitions and classification by branches of industry are generally in accordance with United Nations standards.

The data in the tables are derived from the annual surveys of mining, manufacturing, electricity, gas and water supply carried out by the National Census and Statistics Office, by personal delivery of questionnaires. As a rule, the survey of mining and the survey of electricity, gas and water supply cover all establishments. The survey of manufactures covers establishments with 20 or more workers on a complete enumeration basis and smaller establishments on a probability sampling basis. Prior to 1983, the data shown in the tables relate to all establishments with one or more workers. Beginning 1983, the data relate to establishments with 10 or more workers engaged.

The data shown in the tables are based on the national classification system which generally follows the present version of ISIC. It should be noted, however, that manufacture of electric household refrigerators (ISIC 3829) is classified under ISIC 383.

The employment numbers are averages of the four pay-roll periods ending nearest the 15th of February, May, August and November. The difference between the number of employees and persons engaged is attributed simply to working proprietors not on the regular pay-roll and unpaid family workers.

Output is the sum of (a) the value of shipments adjusted for change in inventories of finished products and work in progress, (b) receipts from contract and other industrial work done for others by the establishment, (c) the value of goods shipped in the same condition as received and (d) the value of electricity sold. Value added is the difference between output and the value of input, comprising the cost of raw materials used, containers, fuels consumed, electric energy purchased, contract work done by others and the cost of goods shipped in the same condition as received. Valuation of output and value added is in producers' prices.

Gross fixed capital formation represents, prior to 1983, expenditures on new and used fixed assets during the reference year, plus the value of fixed assets produced by the establishment for its own use less the value of sales. Beginning 1983, the data include an estimate for alterations and improvements to existing fixed assets.

The indexes of industrial production are compiled by the Central Bank of the Philippines and provided in response to the United Nations Questionnaire on Indexes of Industrial Production. The indexes for mining cover approximately 100 per cent of total mineral production in 1965, whereas the indexes for manufacturing are based on data obtained from a sample of firms.

Related national publications:

Annual Survey of Manufactures (annual), published by the National Census and Statistics Office, National Economic and Development Authority, Manila. Statistical Bulletin (quarterly), published by the Central Bank of the Philippines, Manila.

ISIC	INDUSTRY	1. NUMBER OF ESTABLISHMENTS (NUMBER)					2. AVERAGE NUMBER OF PERSONS ENGAGED (THOUSANDS)					ISIC
		a/ 1981	a/ 1982	b/ 1983	b/ *1984	1985	a/ 1981	a/ 1982	b/ 1983	b/ *1984	1985	
210	Coal mining	11	10	13	12	...	1.6	1.8	3.1	6.2	...	210
220	Petroleum and gas	27	26	19	10	...	0.6	0.5	0.8	0.6	...	220
230	Metal ore mining	100	63	56	44	...	52.7	49.0	52.5	43.6	...	230
290	Other mining	1035	981	401	137	...	16.0	10.6	7.2	5.1	...	290
2	Mining, quarrying .	1173	1080	489	203	...	70.9	61.9	63.6	55.5	...	2
311/2	Food products	29287	29044	1506	1427	...	235.1	237.4	132.0	118.4	...	311/2
313	Beverages	1082	1076	91	89	...	35.2	31.5	27.9	27.2	...	313
314	Tobacco	40	40	29	25	...	16.7	18.6	18.0	15.8	...	314
321	Textiles	4471	4361	323	300	...	135.5	145.6	85.8	65.7	...	321
3211	Spinning,weaving etc..	2017	1958	...	115	...	105.1	120.8	...	40.0	...	3211
322	Wearing apparel	28184	26864	438	406	...	153.5	145.3	75.5	88.1	...	322
323	Leather and products ...	252	250	47	53	...	3.9	4.2	3.6	2.8	...	323
324	Footwear	1375	1363	141	135	...	13.8	14.7	8.6	7.4	...	324
331	Wood products	2438	2369	347	298	...	75.9	65.9	60.0	47.5	...	331
332	Furniture, fixtures	3459	3438	301	289	...	37.2	36.4	19.3	19.6	...	332
341	Paper and products	246	244	98	94	...	18.0	20.2	13.4	11.3	...	341
3411	Pulp,paper etc.........	...	...	...	27	...	...	...	...	5.4	...	3411
342	Printing,publishing	1366	1384	353	350	...	23.2	24.6	15.1	13.3	...	342
351	Industrial chemicals ...	146	145	95	85	...	14.2	11.8	10.4	8.7	...	351
3511	Basic excl fertilizers	...	...	...	51	...	...	...	...	3.6	...	3511
3513	Synthetic resins etc .	...	...	...	20	...	...	...	...	2.5	...	3513
352	Other chemical products.	355	357	191	196	...	29.7	30.9	24.4	22.8	...	352
3522	Drugs and medicines ..	87	88	58	55	...	12.6	15.6	11.0	10.5	...	3522
353	Petroleum refineries ...	4	4	3	3	...	1.7	2.5	1.7	1.6	...	353
354	Petroleum,coal products.	12	11	8	7	...	0.3	0.4	0.5	0.3	...	354
355	Rubber products	772	768	107	102	...	32.4	31.1	17.5	17.4	...	355
356	Plastic products n.e.c..	286	300	143	144	...	20.9	21.3	16.8	10.4	...	356
361	Pottery,china etc	724	713	19	18	...	7.1	6.6	2.3	3.1	...	361
362	Glass and products	84	79	27	24	...	9.5	7.7	7.2	5.4	...	362
369	Non-metal products n.e.c	1678	1685	184	175	...	19.0	19.2	12.2	10.9	...	369
371	Iron and steel	256	253	119	97	...	17.5	16.8	17.4	15.7	...	371
372	Non-ferrous metals	63	68	33	40	...	4.5	5.6	3.6	2.9	...	372
381	Metal products	4743	4675	291	282	...	41.0	41.0	19.4	18.9	...	381
382	Machinery n.e.c. .... c/	1236	1224	322	307	...	27.8	26.8	16.5	13.0	...	382
3825	Office,computing etc..	...	...	...	7	...	...	...	...	0.3	...	3825
383	Electrical machinery ... c/	296	295	152	139	...	60.3	55.1	53.0	50.5	...	383
3832	Radio,television etc..	...	...	...	...	...	...	...	...	39.2	...	3832
384	Transport equipment	890	792	178	162	...	33.2	35.0	22.3	13.9	...	384
3841	Shipbuilding, repair..	...	...	...	36	...	...	...	...	4.9	...	3841
3843	Motor vehicles	...	...	...	21	...	...	...	...	4.3	...	3843
385	Professional goods	33	29	10	9	...	3.3	1.9	0.9	3.7	...	385
390	Other industries	1360	1349	132	134	...	15.9	20.0	8.7	14.6	...	390
3	Manufacturing	85138	83180	5688	5390	...	1086.3	1078.1	694.0	630.9	...	3
410	Electricity,gas,steam ..	230	219	152	161	...	33.0	35.0	36.4	36.4	...	410
4101	Electricity	229	218	150	158	...	32.7	34.7	35.4	35.5	...	4101
420	Water works and supply .	304	305	260	109	...	8.2	8.9	9.5	9.2	...	420
4	Electricity,gas etc	534	524	412	270	...	41.2	43.9	45.9	45.6	...	4
2-4	All industry	86845	84784	6589	5863	...	1198.4	1183.9	803.5	732.0	...	2-4

a/ Manufacturing: establishments with one or more workers engaged.
b/ Manufacturing: establishments with 10 or more workers engaged.
c/ Electric household refrigerators are included in major group 383.

ISIC	INDUSTRY	3. AVERAGE NUMBER OF EMPLOYEES (THOUSANDS) a/ 1981	a/ 1982	b/ 1983	b/ *1984	1985	4. WAGES AND SALARIES OF EMPLOYEES (MILLION PESOS) a/ 1981	a/ 1982	b/ 1983	b/ *1984	1985	ISIC
210	Coal mining	1.6	1.7	3.1	6.2	...	11	14	45	129	...	210
220	Petroleum and gas	0.6	0.5	0.8	0.6	...	29	28	53	69	...	220
230	Metal ore mining	52.7	49.0	52.5	43.6	...	553	544	1056	919	...	230
290	Other mining	14.6	9.6	5.8	5.0	...	99	64	55	39	...	290
2	Mining, quarrying .	69.5	60.8	62.2	55.4	...	692	650	1209	1156	...	2
311/2	Food products	194.1	198.1	129.5	115.9	...	1887	2005	1909	2284	...	311/2
313	Beverages	33.4	30.2	27.9	27.2	...	400	455	542	726	...	313
314	Tobacco	16.7	18.6	18.0	15.8	...	209	229	254	309	...	314
321	Textiles	128.3	139.0	85.7	65.5	...	964	1236	963	920	...	321
3211	Spinning,weaving etc..	102.4	118.6	...	40.0	...	780	1062	...	554	...	3211
322	Wearing apparel	114.6	107.5	74.9	87.5	...	810	974	795	1345	...	322
323	Leather and products ...	3.6	3.8	3.6	2.7	...	22	30	32	33	...	323
324	Footwear	11.5	12.5	8.3	7.1	...	64	103	71	82	...	324
331	Wood products	72.4	63.2	59.4	47.2	...	624	562	663	715	...	331
332	Furniture, fixtures	32.7	31.7	18.9	19.1	...	200	218	156	228	...	332
341	Paper and products	17.9	20.1	13.4	11.3	...	216	276	225	269	...	341
3411	Pulp,paper etc.	...	...	...	5.4	...	...	...	...	127	...	3411
342	Printing,publishing	21.6	23.0	14.8	13.0	...	228	253	234	266	...	342
351	Industrial chemicals ...	14.2	11.8	10.3	8.6	...	221	203	267	266	...	351
3511	Basic excl fertilizers	...	...	...	3.6	...	...	...	...	92	...	3511
3513	Synthetic resins etc .	...	...	...	2.5	...	...	...	...	79	...	3513
352	Other chemical products.	29.5	30.7	24.4	22.7	...	589	719	804	934	...	352
3522	Drugs and medicines ..	12.5	15.6	11.0	10.5	...	287	382	385	487	...	3522
353	Petroleum refineries ...	1.7	2.5	1.7	1.6	...	70	133	112	128	...	353
354	Petroleum,coal products.	0.3	0.4	0.5	0.3	...	3	5	6	7	...	354
355	Rubber products	30.9	30.0	17.4	17.3	...	318	321	255	338	...	355
356	Plastic products n.e.c..	20.8	21.2	16.7	10.3	...	210	215	226	188	...	356
361	Pottery,china etc	5.9	5.2	2.2	3.1	...	64	69	34	55	...	361
362	Glass and products	9.4	7.7	7.2	5.4	...	100	117	130	221	...	362
369	Non-metal products n.e.c	17.6	18.0	11.9	10.7	...	146	180	151	188	...	369
371	Iron and steel	17.4	16.6	17.3	15.7	...	216	229	349	403	...	371
372	Non-ferrous metals	4.4	5.5	3.6	2.9	...	60	87	85	60	...	372
381	Metal products	35.6	35.5	19.1	18.7	...	333	371	257	319	...	381
382	Machinery n.e.c. .... c/	26.8	26.7	16.3	12.8	...	271	310	200	232	...	382
3825	Office,computing etc..	...	...	...	0.3	...	...	...	...	6	...	3825
383	Electrical machinery ... c/	60.1	55.0	52.9	50.4	...	651	816	941	1216	...	383
3832	Radio,television etc..	...	...	...	39.2	...	...	...	...	963	...	3832
384	Transport equipment	32.3	34.3	22.2	13.8	...	510	455	487	314	...	384
3841	Shipbuilding, repair..	...	...	...	4.9	...	...	...	...	92	...	3841
3843	Motor vehicles	...	...	...	4.3	...	...	...	...	124	...	3843
385	Professional goods	3.2	1.9	0.9	3.7	...	49	13	9	45	...	385
390	Other industries	13.6	17.9	8.6	14.4	...	109	175	102	221	...	390
3	Manufacturing	970.5	968.6	687.6	624.7	...	9544	10759	10259	12312	...	3
410	Electricity,gas,steam ..	32.9	35.0	36.4	36.4	...	639	796	1038	1242	...	410
4101	Electricity	32.7	34.7	35.4	35.5	...	635	793	1008	1200	...	4101
420	Water works and supply .	8.2	8.8	9.5	9.2	...	82	88	135	175	...	420
4	Electricity,gas etc	41.1	43.8	45.9	45.6	...	721	884	1173	1417	...	4
2-4	All industry	1081.1	1073.2	795.7	725.7	...	10957	12293	12641	14885	...	2-4

a/ Manufacturing: establishments with one or more workers engaged.
b/ Manufacturing: establishments with 10 or more workers engaged.
c/ Electric household refrigerators are included in major group 383.

ISIC	INDUSTRY	5. AVERAGE NUMBER OF OPERATIVES (THOUSANDS) a/ 1981	a/ 1982	b/ 1983	b/ *1984	1985	6. WAGES AND SALARIES OF OPERATIVES (MILLION PESOS) a/c/ 1981	a/ 1982	b/ 1983	b/ *1984	1985	ISIC
210	Coal mining	1.4	1.5	2.8	4.6	...	7.7	10.8	37.6	74.6	...	210
220	Petroleum and gas	0.2	0.2	0.5	0.2	...	1.9	2.8	14.1	18.3	...	220
230	Metal ore mining	33.2	32.5	31.8	27.2	...	287.1	320.1	578.7	498.6	...	230
290	Other mining	11.3	8.0	4.8	4.2	...	58.9	43.4	28.2	26.2	...	290
2	Mining, quarrying	46.1	42.2	39.9	36.2	...	355.6	377.1	658.6	617.7	...	2
311/2	Food products	158.2	158.4	92.5	80.1	...	1146.5	1259.1	1066.5	1201.4	...	311/2
313	Beverages	18.3	16.8	13.5	13.6	...	199.6	171.8	173.8	256.3	...	313
314	Tobacco	13.5	15.1	14.8	14.1	...	134.7	135.4	148.8	237.7	...	314
321	Textiles	114.7	117.8	72.7	55.3	...	742.8	935.1	657.9	630.8	...	321
3211	Spinning,weaving etc.	91.6	99.9	...	33.9	...	603.8	810.8	...	368.2	...	3211
322	Wearing apparel	104.1	95.8	67.3	78.6	...	661.1	790.8	638.6	1105.8	...	322
323	Leather and products	3.1	3.1	3.0	2.2	...	15.6	20.6	22.3	20.6	...	323
324	Footwear	10.6	11.6	7.4	6.1	...	50.1	85.5	55.7	63.9	...	324
331	Wood products	60.3	50.3	47.6	36.5	...	455.0	381.0	481.7	505.1	...	331
332	Furniture, fixtures	29.0	26.9	16.4	16.5	...	158.5	163.4	114.2	169.2	...	332
341	Paper and products	14.5	15.6	10.1	8.2	...	141.7	174.5	127.8	154.6	...	341
3411	Pulp,paper etc.	...	...	...	4.0	...	...	...	...	81.4	...	3411
342	Printing,publishing	15.8	16.9	10.7	8.7	...	134.6	155.5	130.7	132.2	...	342
351	Industrial chemicals	8.4	7.4	5.0	3.9	...	90.3	91.2	89.2	79.7	...	351
3511	Basic excl fertilizers	...	...	...	1.4	...	...	...	...	25.1	...	3511
3513	Synthetic resins etc	...	...	...	1.5	...	...	...	...	34.8	...	3513
352	Other chemical products	16.4	15.7	12.8	9.6	...	230.7	262.6	294.4	260.9	...	352
3522	Drugs and medicines	5.7	6.5	5.2	3.3	...	90.0	107.8	127.3	110.7	...	3522
353	Petroleum refineries	0.7	0.6	0.6	0.5	...	20.2	24.0	29.4	34.5	...	353
354	Petroleum,coal products	0.2	0.2	0.3	0.2	...	1.4	1.7	3.0	3.7	...	354
355	Rubber products	23.0	21.9	11.9	12.2	...	190.3	192.8	150.6	183.6	...	355
356	Plastic products n.e.c.	16.5	17.5	13.4	7.8	...	123.1	142.7	137.4	111.3	...	356
361	Pottery,china etc	5.0	4.0	1.7	2.5	...	41.1	44.4	18.5	33.3	...	361
362	Glass and products	7.2	6.0	5.2	3.9	...	65.6	69.0	68.5	125.2	...	362
369	Non-metal products n.e.c	14.3	14.5	9.3	7.3	...	86.7	117.1	88.1	97.7	...	369
371	Iron and steel	14.3	13.8	12.8	9.6	...	146.5	157.3	208.2	181.2	...	371
372	Non-ferrous metals	3.0	4.7	2.7	2.3	...	29.2	58.0	47.9	35.4	...	372
381	Metal products	29.3	29.7	14.9	14.8	...	216.5	251.3	151.6	182.5	...	381
382	Machinery n.e.c. d/	21.4	21.0	12.9	9.3	...	172.3	200.4	122.2	125.5	...	382
3825	Office,computing etc.	...	...	...	0.2	...	...	...	...	2.8	...	3825
383	Electrical machinery d/	50.7	46.1	42.7	38.9	...	423.8	577.2	596.3	742.8	...	383
3832	Radio,television etc.	...	...	...	30.7	...	...	...	...	606.1	...	3832
384	Transport equipment	25.2	24.1	15.3	9.1	...	230.3	249.4	234.9	144.4	...	384
3841	Shipbuilding, repair	...	...	...	3.7	...	...	...	...	65.8	...	3841
3843	Motor vehicles	...	...	...	2.7	...	...	...	...	43.4	...	3843
385	Professional goods	2.4	1.6	0.8	3.0	...	23.6	7.6	5.9	31.0	...	385
390	Other industries	11.5	14.4	6.6	12.0	...	73.1	108.9	62.0	163.9	...	390
3	Manufacturing	791.6	771.5	524.9	466.8	...	6004.9	6828.3	5926.1	7014.2	...	3
410	Electricity,gas,steam	27.3	28.2	28.9	24.3	...	416.4	532.9	738.9	713.1	...	410
4101	Electricity	27.1	28.0	28.3	23.7	...	414.7	531.1	722.3	688.7	...	4101
420	Water works and supply	6.4	7.2	6.8	6.1	...	57.2	65.2	96.1	115.4	...	420
4	Electricity,gas etc	33.7	35.4	35.7	30.4	...	473.6	598.1	835.0	828.5	...	4
2-4	All industry	871.4	849.1	600.5	533.4	...	6834.1	7803.5	7419.7	8460.4	...	2-4

a/ Manufacturing: establishments with one or more workers engaged.
b/ Manufacturing: establishments with 10 or more workers engaged. c/ Mining: including employers' contributions to pension schemes.
d/ Electric household refrigerators are included in major group 383.

ISIC	INDUSTRY	7. HOURS WORKED BY OPERATIVES (MILLIONS)					8. QUANTITY OF ELECTRICITY CONSUMED (MILLION KWH)					ISIC
		a/ 1981	a/ 1982	b/ 1983	b/ *1984	1985	a/ 1981	a/ 1982	1983	1984	1985	
210	Coal mining	3.4	3.6	6.6	12.0	...	4	2343	...	...	...	210
220	Petroleum and gas	0.4	0.4	1.2	0.7	...	2	1	...	...	...	220
230	Metal ore mining	67.1	70.1	80.7	68.4	...	1962	1374	...	...	...	230
290	Other mining	24.9	14.8	9.7	5.3	...	313	13	...	...	...	290
2	Mining, quarrying .	95.8	88.9	98.2	86.4	...	2281	3731	...	...	...	2
311/2	Food products	403.3	399.8	217.7	187.2	...	1262	1349	...	...	...	311/2
313	Beverages	46.9	39.4	37.5	35.9	...	145	179	...	...	...	313
314	Tobacco	38.9	40.0	41.2	40.6	...	82	54	...	...	...	314
321	Textiles	277.5	302.5	171.9	125.6	...	940	1400	...	...	...	321
3211	Spinning,weaving etc..	222.9	257.1	...	73.5	...	858	874	...	...	...	3211
322	Wearing apparel	249.2	247.3	160.6	188.9	...	126	317	...	...	...	322
323	Leather and products ...	7.3	7.6	6.9	4.5	...	8	9	...	...	...	323
324	Footwear	25.2	28.2	17.3	18.9	...	9	11	...	...	...	324
331	Wood products	145.0	131.0	113.0	90.0	...	370	383	...	...	...	331
332	Furniture, fixtures	83.9	69.6	39.5	40.3	...	29	35	...	...	...	332
341	Paper and products	40.4	37.8	24.8	25.2	...	484	447	...	...	...	341
3411	Pulp,paper etc.	...	...	...	12.6	...	...	...	...	...	...	3411
342	Printing,publishing	41.9	48.9	25.7	22.3	...	42	42	...	...	...	342
351	Industrial chemicals ...	20.9	19.0	12.7	10.3	...	697	509	...	...	...	351
3511	Basic excl fertilizers	...	...	...	4.3	...	...	...	...	...	...	3511
3513	Synthetic resins etc .	...	...	...	3.5	...	...	...	...	...	...	3513
352	Other chemical products.	42.9	40.7	32.1	23.0	...	142	142	...	...	...	352
3522	Drugs and medicines ..	14.8	16.6	12.6	7.8	...	48	63	...	...	...	3522
353	Petroleum refineries ...	1.7	1.6	1.4	1.4	...	55	36	...	...	...	353
354	Petroleum,coal products.	0.5	0.5	0.7	0.5	...	2	8	...	...	...	354
355	Rubber products	57.8	53.8	27.6	29.6	...	131	149	...	...	...	355
356	Plastic products n.e.c..	40.2	44.2	37.0	21.2	...	134	215	...	...	...	356
361	Pottery,china etc	12.7	9.7	4.0	5.6	...	26	34	...	...	...	361
362	Glass and products	17.6	15.3	10.9	10.2	...	113	74	...	...	...	362
369	Non-metal products n.e.c	35.1	35.0	24.9	18.1	...	125	348	...	...	...	369
371	Iron and steel	35.8	33.8	32.3	24.9	...	568	437	...	...	...	371
372	Non-ferrous metals	7.0	11.5	7.3	5.9	...	57	71	...	...	...	372
381	Metal products	71.5	75.4	37.4	36.1	...	100	107	...	...	...	381
382	Machinery n.e.c. .... c/	50.1	51.5	31.9	20.7	...	76	191	...	...	...	382
3825	Office,computing etc..	...	...	...	0.5	...	...	...	...	...	...	3825
383	Electrical machinery ... c/	105.4	111.9	98.1	84.0	...	177	180	...	...	...	383
3832	Radio,television etc..	...	...	...	64.8	...	...	...	...	...	...	3832
384	Transport equipment	59.7	59.1	37.8	20.0	...	232	92	...	...	...	384
3841	Shipbuilding, repair..	...	...	...	7.7	...	...	...	...	...	...	3841
3843	Motor vehicles	...	...	...	5.6	...	...	...	...	...	...	3843
385	Professional goods	5.9	4.6	1.5	6.3	...	7	3	...	...	...	385
390	Other industries	34.2	46.5	15.3	24.4	...	22	37	...	...	...	390
3	Manufacturing	1958.6	1966.2	1269.0	1121.6	...	6161	6859	...	...	...	3
410	Electricity,gas,steam ..	64.7	68.9	70.6	59.9	...	...	...	...	...	...	410
4101	Electricity	64.2	68.5	69.2	58.7	...	...	...	...	...	...	4101
420	Water works and supply .	15.4	17.8	16.3	15.9	...	...	...	...	...	...	420
4	Electricity,gas etc	80.1	86.7	86.9	75.8	...	...	...	...	...	...	4
2-4	All industry	2134.5	2141.8	1454.1	1283.8	...	...	...	...	...	...	2-4

a/ Manufacturing: establishments with one or more workers engaged.
b/ Manufacturing: establishments with 10 or more workers engaged.
c/ Electric household refrigerators are included in major group 383.

ISIC	INDUSTRY	9. OUTPUT IN PRODUCERS' PRICES (MILLION PESOS) a/ 1981	a/ 1982	b/ 1983	b/ *1984	1985	10. VALUE ADDED IN PRODUCERS' PRICES (MILLION PESOS) a/ 1981	a/ 1982	b/ 1983	b/ *1984	1985	ISIC
210	Coal mining	39	58	173	1708	...	27	42	-251	610	...	210
220	Petroleum and gas	58	155	532	1586	...	36	129	357	1364	...	220
230	Metal ore mining	9113	8816	10752	10675	...	5039	5281	7187	4820	...	230
290	Other mining	2227	410	319	273	...	1472	272	200	196	...	290
2	Mining, quarrying .	11437	9439	11776	14242	...	6574	5724	7493	6990	...	2
311/2	Food products	31246	34686	36429	52207	...	7314	10070	10263	13056	...	311/2
313	Beverages	7192	7243	7535	14305	...	3191	3215	4279	8757	...	313
314	Tobacco	5829	6643	7287	10587	...	2360	2831	2060	2143	...	314
321	Textiles	9724	9600	8482	10454	...	3156	2935	3234	4206	...	321
3211	Spinning,weaving etc..	8096	8127	...	7096	...	2598	2531	...	3001	...	3211
322	Wearing apparel	4998	4405	3769	4652	...	2129	1935	1541	2228	...	322
323	Leather and products ...	168	182	207	213	...	48	53	89	92	...	323
324	Footwear	639	604	456	408	...	278	229	263	168	...	324
331	Wood products	5148	4571	5425	5391	...	1700	1796	2224	2188	...	331
332	Furniture, fixtures	1109	1378	844	1153	...	461	453	417	553	...	332
341	Paper and products	3513	3820	3978	5963	...	869	1044	1407	1858	...	341
3411	Pulp,paper etc.	...	...	...	3358	...	...	...	...	1064	...	3411
342	Printing,publishing	1854	1920	1716	2081	...	722	687	744	811	...	342
351	Industrial chemicals ...	6260	3965	5565	6949	...	2281	1423	1927	2297	...	351
3511	Basic excl fertilizers	...	...	...	1920	...	...	...	...	586	...	3511
3513	Synthetic resins etc .	...	...	...	1738	...	...	...	...	715	...	3513
352	Other chemical products.	8350	10697	10529	13820	...	2589	4004	4252	5397	...	352
3522	Drugs and medicines ..	3409	4920	3951	4905	...	1333	2147	1741	2210	...	3522
353	Petroleum refineries ...	22279	32832	29486	35900	...	3154	4700	7376	4815	...	353
354	Petroleum,coal products.	73	519	154	204	...	18	26	30	43	...	354
355	Rubber products	2620	2841	2168	2878	...	1107	1307	968	1259	...	355
356	Plastic products n.e.c..	1835	2351	2376	2663	...	646	609	889	946	...	356
361	Pottery,china etc	438	407	242	371	...	210	127	138	225	...	361
362	Glass and products	1226	970	1152	1987	...	425	415	399	788	...	362
369	Non-metal products n.e.c	940	1070	1173	1704	...	459	470	462	914	...	369
371	Iron and steel	4054	3320	9498	11198	...	649	695	4321	4621	...	371
372	Non-ferrous metals	683	1160	964	1075	...	152	460	319	503	...	372
381	Metal products	3378	3658	2915	4525	...	415	1190	1010	1580	...	381
382	Machinery n.e.c. .... c/	1643	2152	1062	1441	...	689	958	501	717	...	382
3825	Office,computing etc..	...	...	...	25	...	...	...	...	11	...	3825
383	Electrical machinery ... c/	4721	6997	8597	11348	...	1435	3012	3327	4894	...	383
3832	Radio,television etc..	...	...	...	8437	...	...	...	...	3776	...	3832
384	Transport equipment	4674	6051	6098	3004	...	1013	1811	1688	964	...	384
3841	Shipbuilding, repair..	...	...	...	355	...	...	...	...	215	...	3841
3843	Motor vehicles	...	...	...	1629	...	...	...	...	388	...	3843
385	Professional goods	170	94	106	246	...	93	28	29	148	...	385
390	Other industries	708	1079	619	906	...	297	385	303	492	...	390
3	Manufacturing	135472	155215	158832	207633	...	37860	46868	54460	66663	...	3
410	Electricity,gas,steam ..	14693	16445	20861	29162	...	3490	3892	5801	6124	...	410
4101	Electricity	14526	16300	20351	28539	...	3474	3868	5523	5801	...	4101
420	Water works and supply .	582	756	813	1993	...	223	520	641	1717	...	420
4	Electricity,gas etc	15275	17201	21674	31155	...	3713	4412	6442	7841	...	4
2-4	All industry	162184	181855	192282	253030	...	48147	57004	68395	81494	...	2-4

a/ Manufacturing: establishments with one or more workers engaged.
b/ Manufacturing: establishments with 10 or more workers engaged.
c/ Electric household refrigerators are included in major group 383.

11. GROSS FIXED CAPITAL FORMATION
TOTAL
(MILLION PESOS)

ISIC	INDUSTRY	a/b/ 1981	a/b/ 1982	c/ 1983	c/ *1984	1985	ISIC
210	Coal mining	4	3	432	1848	...	210
220	Petroleum and gas	97	87	77	104	...	220
230	Metal ore mining	1126	799	5438	1896	...	230
290	Other mining	55	17	49	13	...	290
2	Mining, quarrying .	1282	906	5996	3861	...	2
311/2	Food products	1149	1557	2061	1493	...	311/2
313	Beverages	374	508	639	1010	...	313
314	Tobacco	152	330	885	154	...	314
321	Textiles	666	568	419	216	...	321
3211	Spinning,weaving etc..	567	529	...	145	...	3211
322	Wearing apparel	367	83	113	125	...	322
323	Leather and products ...	4	4	2	5	...	323
324	Footwear	4	33	12	27	...	324
331	Wood products	646	194	252	413	...	331
332	Furniture, fixtures	49	62	48	40	...	332
341	Paper and products	250	136	112	259	...	341
3411	Pulp,paper etc.	...	...	...	237	...	3411
342	Printing,publishing	67	84	66	47	...	342
351	Industrial chemicals ...	739	305	245	227	...	351
3511	Basic excl fertilizers	...	...	...	58	...	3511
3513	Synthetic resins etc .	...	...	...	145	...	3513
352	Other chemical products.	264	292	252	377	...	352
3522	Drugs and medicines ..	99	127	117	110	...	3522
353	Petroleum refineries ...	138	212	113	210	...	353
354	Petroleum,coal products.	1	1	3	1	...	354
355	Rubber products	106	108	53	93	...	355
356	Plastic products n.e.c..	82	100	96	207	...	356
361	Pottery,china etc	131	16	7	16	...	361
362	Glass and products	158	153	183	90	...	362
369	Non-metal products n.e.c	85	56	46	47	...	369
371	Iron and steel	1059	1057	253	619	...	371
372	Non-ferrous metals	88	38	51	-51	...	372
381	Metal products	111	156	94	150	...	381
382	Machinery n.e.c. .... d/	66	55	44	44	...	382
3825	Office,computing etc..	...	...	...	...	...	3825
383	Electrical machinery ... d/	419	379	641	1076	...	383
3832	Radio,television etc..	...	...	...	1003	...	3832
384	Transport equipment	176	126	201	55	...	384
3841	Shipbuilding, repair..	...	...	...	23	...	3841
3843	Motor vehicles	...	...	...	11	...	3843
385	Professional goods	2	2	9	6	...	385
390	Other industries	10	29	27	49	...	390
3	Manufacturing	7363	6644	6927	7005	...	3
410	Electricity,gas,steam ..	4196	5323	10009	14072	...	410
4101	Electricity	4195	5322	9947	13931	...	4101
420	Water works and supply .	401	705	2454	942	...	420
4	Electricity,gas etc	4597	6028	12463	15014	...	4
2-4	All industry	13242	13578	25386	25880	...	2-4

a/ Manufacturing: establishments with one or more workers engaged.
b/ Excluding alterations and improvements.
c/ Manufacturing: establishments with 10 or more workers engaged.
d/ Electric household refrigerators are included in major group 383.

12. INDEX NUMBERS OF INDUSTRIAL PRODUCTION (1980 = 100)

ISIC	INDUSTRY	1976	1977	1978	1979	1981	1982	1983	1984	1985	a/ RATE	ISIC
210	Coal mining	...	...	...	...	...	...	...	...	...	...	210
220	Petroleum and gas	...	...	...	...	...	...	...	...	...	...	220
230	Metal ore mining	72	88	84	91	95	86	77	67	82	1.5	230
290	Other mining	...	...	...	...	...	...	...	...	...	...	290
2	Mining, quarrying .	69	83	83	91	96	91	84	75	85	2.3	2
311/2	Food products	63	64	68	82	120	142	151	229	265	17.3	311/2
313	Beverages	54	65	64	81	124	141	172	267	312	21.5	313
314	Tobacco	55	54	62	79	118	148	216	378	698	32.6	314
321	Textiles	55	62	70	83	120	134	184	214	234	17.5	321
3211	Spinning,weaving etc..	...	...	...	...	...	...	...	...	...	...	3211
322	Wearing apparel .... b/	47	49	54	73	138	162	210	242	233	19.5	322
323	Leather and products ...	60	68	63	78	115	125	132	128	132	9.2	323
324	Footwear .... b/	...	...	...	...	...	...	...	...	...	...	324
331	Wood products	58	66	62	88	118	128	140	153	157	11.7	331
332	Furniture, fixtures	85	76	83	94	116	125	214	240	174	8.3	332
341	Paper and products	67	71	79	91	110	110	119	166	170	10.9	341
3411	Pulp,paper etc.	...	...	...	...	...	...	...	...	...	...	3411
342	Printing,publishing	83	72	79	84	122	141	148	190	270	14.0	342
351	Industrial chemicals ...	50	57	62	80	102	110	145	178	161	13.9	351
3511	Basic excl fertilizers	...	...	...	...	...	...	...	...	...	...	3511
3513	Synthetic resins etc .	...	...	...	...	...	...	...	...	...	...	3513
352	Other chemical products.	...	...	...	...	...	...	...	...	...	...	352
3522	Drugs and medicines ..	...	...	...	...	...	...	...	...	...	...	3522
353	Petroleum refineries ...	...	...	...	...	...	...	...	...	...	...	353
354	Petroleum,coal products.	39	50	48	63	112	132	115	187	182	18.7	354
355	Rubber products	73	59	65	71	107	126	75	109	120	5.7	355
356	Plastic products n.e.c..	...	...	...	...	...	...	...	...	...	...	356
361	Pottery,china etc											361
362	Glass and products	57	58	63	75	115	128	147	126	120	8.6	362
369	Non-metal products n.e.c											369
371	Iron and steel	...	...	...	...	...	...	...	...	...	...	371
372	Non-ferrous metals	...	...	...	...	...	...	...	...	...	...	372
381	Metal products	63	60	70	88	113	129	145	337	629	29.1	381
382	Machinery n.e.c.	56	59	66	84	112	118	137	190	302	20.6	382
3825	Office,computing etc..	...	...	...	...	...	...	...	...	...	...	3825
383	Electrical machinery ...	45	42	58	78	122	142	165	231	277	22.4	383
3832	Radio,television etc..	...	...	...	...	...	...	...	...	...	...	3832
384	Transport equipment	61	62	72	85	108	120	128	196	240	16.4	384
3841	Shipbuilding, repair..	...	...	...	...	...	...	...	...	...	...	3841
3843	Motor vehicles	...	...	...	...	...	...	...	...	...	...	3843
385	Professional goods	...	...	...	...	...	...	...	...	...	...	385
390	Other industries	52	64	76	91	113	130	147	243	289	21.0	390
3	Manufacturing ..... c/	82	83	63	79	116	133	152	212	256	13.5	3
410	Electricity,gas,steam ..	...	...	...	...	...	...	...	...	...	...	410
4101	Electricity	69	75	82	92	106	117	126	125	124	6.7	4101
420	Water works and supply .	.	.	.	.	.	.	.	.	.	.	420
4	Electricity,gas etc	...	...	...	...	...	...	...	...	...	...	4
2-4	All industry c/d/	80	83	66	80	113	128	142	193	231	12.5	2-4

a/ Annual growth rate 1976-1985.
b/ Major group 324 is included in 322.
c/ Excluding basic metals.
d/ Excluding gas and steam.

POLAND

The information on industrial activity is based on the reply to the United Nations Questionnaire on General Industrial Statistics from the Central Statistical Office, Warsaw. The concepts, definitions and classification by branches of industry have been adjusted as far as possible to comply with United Nations standards. The data are derived from annual statistical reports collected regularly by the Central Statistical Office from all enterprises in socialized industry. Socialized industry comprises industrial enterprises (state-owned, co-operative and of social organizations), industrial establishments belonging to non-industrial co-operatives (i.e. consumer, horticulture co-operatives) and to budgetary units.

The data in table 1 are compiled according to the establishment method, and tables 3, 6 and 8 according to the enterprise method. The data in tables 4, 7 and 13 are compiled according to the enterprise method. The data in table 9 are compiled on the basis on the establishment method up to 1982, since 1983 according to the enterprise method (1982 is counted by both methods). Since 1982 output includes the whole operational activity. An industrial enterprise is an economic organizational unit possessing legal status and balancing independently of which its main operational activity is manufacturing industrial production, rendering industrial services or running auxiliary activities and which was assigned a basic statistical number in the sector "Industry". An industrial establishment (technical and local unit) is understood as an object or complex of objects located within premises equipped with means and objects of labour, being an independent enterprise or organizational part of an enterprise meant for industrial production, assuming that this production should be characterized by a technological link, similarity of raw material processed or similarity of product and service destination. Reporting is compulsory for all statistical units.

The data on persons engaged relate to total industry, i.e. socialized and non-socialized, in other tables on employment, the data relate to socialized industry only. The employment figures are annual averages of full- and part-time employees. In the case of part-time employees, the figures have been converted to represent full-time equivalent numbers. The data of wages and salaries relate to average monthly earnings of full- and part-time workers. They comprise all cash payments and benefits in kind due to employees under employment contracts, including payments for overtime, holidays and occasional leave, value of allowances in kind and uniforms. Data are shown after deduction of the payroll tax and contributions to the pension fund.

The estimates of electricity consumed are presented by broad groupings of the national classification, unadjusted for classification differences. Comparisons with other items of data should be made with caution.

Output comprises the value of finished products and industrial services, and the net change in value of uncompleted production and semi-finished and non-durable goods of own production. Data are shown at constant factory prices: for 1981 at prices of 1 January 1979, since 1982 at prices of 1982. Value added at current prices, in the national concept, relates to net output and is calculated as the value of output less the costs of materials and fuels, electricity, transport and other services from outside the enterprise, and depreciation allowances. The estimates shown, however, have been adjusted to include depreciation allowances in accordance with the international recommendations. The data on gross fixed capital formation relate to total investment outlays in socialized industry at current prices, i.e. outlays increasing value of fixed assets, outlays on working assets (i.e. primary equipment of newly completed objects) and outlays on non-productive investment (i.e. training of staff). They exclude outlays on capital repairs.

The indexes of industrial production are compiled by the Central Statistical Office of Poland and provided in response to the United Nations Questionnaire on Indexes of Industrial Production.

Related national publications:
<u>Rocznik Statystyczny Przemyslu</u> (Statistical Yearbook of Industry); <u>Rocznik Statystyczny</u> (Statistical Yearbook); <u>Concise Statistical Yearbook of Poland</u>, all published by the Central Statistical Office, Warsaw.

ISIC	INDUSTRY	1. NUMBER OF ESTABLISHMENTS a/b/ (NUMBER) 1981	1982	1983	1984	1985	2. AVERAGE NUMBER OF PERSONS ENGAGED c/d/ (THOUSANDS) 1981	1982	1983	1984	1985	ISIC
210	Coal mining	84	85	93	94	94	405	425	433	438	439	210
220	Petroleum and gas	81	83	91	92	92	4	5	5	5	5	220
230	Metal ore mining	20	21	19	18	18	31	31	30	29	29	230
290	Other mining	454	448	449	440	442	57	54	54	53	52	290
2	Mining, quarrying .	639	637	652	644	646	497	515	522	525	525	2
311/2	Food products	9582	9533	9427	9349	9297	504	493	502	505	512	311/2
313	Beverages	1300	1293	1290	1292	1294	53	51	52	53	53	313
314	Tobacco	15	15	15	15	15	9	10	10	10	10	314
321	Textiles	2149	2040	1973	1991	1963	440	390	373	371	373	321
3211	Spinning,weaving etc..	411	391	383	379	374	266	230	213	205	203	3211
322	Wearing apparel	4165	3786	3464	3358	3272	249	239	242	251	255	322
323	Leather and products ...	849	825	778	758	740	46	43	45	45	45	323
324	Footwear	2502	2412	2202	2025	1837	111	106	107	110	113	324
331	Wood products	965	931	903	899	862	118	114	114	109	109	331
332	Furniture, fixtures	2218	2065	2012	2038	2062	119	114	115	121	122	332
341	Paper and products	323	325	315	296	292	55	52	51	50	49	341
3411	Pulp,paper etc.	56	56	56	54	53	30	29	28	27	27	3411
342	Printing,publishing	602	570	561	597	602	49	45	45	46	47	342
351	Industrial chemicals ...	172	175	167	169	171	123	116	113	110	107	351
3511	Basic excl fertilizers	139	143	135	136	136	57	52	51	49	47	3511
3513	Synthetic resins etc .	15	15	15	15	15	41	38	37	36	35	3513
352	Other chemical products.	341	349	348	348	338	64	64	63	65	67	352
3522	Drugs and medicines ..	107	108	110	109	110	27	26	25	25	26	3522
353	Petroleum refineries ...	18	18	16	16	14	16	15	15	14	14	353
354	Petroleum,coal products.	34	34	34	34	33	22	21	21	20	20	354
355	Rubber products	282	270	260	264	252	52	48	47	48	46	355
356	Plastic products n.e.c..	422	435	432	423	407	63	62	66	70	68	356
361	Pottery,china etc	89	89	89	85	86	32	30	30	30	30	361
362	Glass and products	745	694	679	653	625	67	65	64	63	62	362
369	Non-metal products n.e.c	1098	1078	1071	1063	1045	152	147	148	149	148	369
371	Iron and steel	55	56	57	60	62	180	167	162	157	155	371
372	Non-ferrous metals	28	28	28	28	28	37	34	34	34	33	372
381	Metal products	1194	1199	1241	1204	1172	268	249	237	225	217	381
382	Machinery n.e.c.	1103	1095	1111	1136	1139	559	530	519	513	512	382
3825	Office,computing etc..	16	15	16	16	17	15	15	14	14	16	3825
383	Electrical machinery ...	718	746	735	739	747	332	315	310	297	294	383
3832	Radio,television etc..	253	265	260	269	275	119	111	113	113	114	3832
384	Transport equipment	727	733	711	700	689	362	335	326	319	311	384
3841	Shipbuilding, repair..	81	81	81	84	78	84	77	75	73	71	3841
3843	Motor vehicles	514	519	501	484	476	156	142	140	128	129	3843
385	Professional goods	259	260	246	298	298	51	50	48	49	47	385
390	Other industries	1024	1019	924	896	855	153	143	161	174	181	390
3	Manufacturing	32979	32073	31089	30734	30197	4286	4048	4020	4008	4000	3
410	Electricity,gas,steam ..	1021	1033	1044	1052	1070	126	130	134	138	144	410
4101	Electricity	...	...	...	...	...	...	...	...	...	...	4101
420	Water works and supply .	.	.	.	.	.	.	.	.	.	.	420
4	Electricity,gas etc	1021	1033	1044	1052	1070	126	130	134	138	144	4
2-4	All industry	34639	33743	32785	32430	31913	4909	4693	4676	4671	4669	2-4

a/ At 31 December of the year indicated. b/ Socialized industry only.
c/ Including persons engaged in private industry other than handicrafts.
d/ Socialized and non-socialized industry.

ISIC	INDUSTRY	3. AVERAGE NUMBER OF EMPLOYEES a/ (THOUSANDS) 1981	1982	1983	1984	1985	4. WAGES AND SALARIES OF EMPLOYEES a/b/ (ZLOTYS) 1981 c/	1982	1983	1984	1985	ISIC
210	Coal mining	415	435	445	450	452	14187	24556	30375	35148	43084	210
220	Petroleum and gas	4	6	6	7	7	7498	11633	15137	18108	21250	220
230	Metal ore mining	26	31	31	31	33	13015	21521	28928	33575	39069	230
290	Other mining	63	60	59	58	56	8007	12789	16050	19124	22882	290
2	Mining, quarrying .	508	532	541	546	548	13310	22912	28547	33153	40484	2
311/2	Food products	508	496	501	498	501	7125	11085	13318	15491	18200	311/2
313	Beverages	38	36	37	36	36	6854	11029	13376	15744	18492	313
314	Tobacco	10	11	11	11	12	7119	11066	13911	17654	21088	314
321	Textiles	431	378	357	352	352	6781	9747	13400	16048	19064	321
3211	Spinning,weaving etc..	271	235	219	213	211	7937	9871	13676	16413	19437	3211
322	Wearing apparel	215	201	200	202	200	6145	9354	12738	14822	17228	322
323	Leather and products ...	37	34	34	34	34	6833	10403	13851	15763	18747	323
324	Footwear	104	96	97	98	99	6445	9910	13385	15351	17970	324
331	Wood products	94	89	88	84	83	7009	10763	13223	15406	18467	331
332	Furniture, fixtures	108	101	100	100	99	6783	10496	13374	15311	18141	332
341	Paper and products	54	51	51	49	48	7029	10660	13303	15643	18600	341
3411	Pulp,paper etc.	36	35	34	36	36	7283	10899	13477	15908	19060	3411
342	Printing,publishing	48	44	44	45	46	6902	10180	13245	16822	20170	342
351	Industrial chemicals ...	132	125	121	119	117	7433	11283	14610	17307	20518	351
3511	Basic excl fertilizers	51	48	46	45	44	7589	11482	14600	17152	20397	3511
3513	Synthetic resins etc .	47	43	42	41	40	7212	10832	14592	17597	20557	3513
352	Other chemical products.	66	64	65	63	63	6708	10603	14022	16540	20037	352
3522	Drugs and medicines ..	28	27	26	26	26	6550	10164	13849	16473	20415	3522
353	Petroleum refineries ...	17	17	16	16	16	7417	11102	14741	17900	21858	353
354	Petroleum,coal products.	13	13	13	13	12	9468	14104	18157	21321	24799	354
355	Rubber products	47	43	42	43	40	6749	10367	14340	16780	19622	355
356	Plastic products n.e.c..	58	54	53	52	51	6651	10536	13986	16141	18771	356
361	Pottery,china etc	29	27	26	26	26	6775	9837	13104	15675	18905	361
362	Glass and products	62	59	57	56	55	7457	10826	13856	16471	19223	362
369	Non-metal products n.e.c	138	133	131	129	124	7481	11040	13716	16072	18823	369
371	Iron and steel	184	169	165	161	160	9455	13775	18591	22272	26477	371
372	Non-ferrous metals	42	34	34	34	34	9690	13703	18332	21829	25621	372
381	Metal products	287	263	255	250	243	6872	10308	13522	15896	18786	381
382	Machinery n.e.c.	564	531	519	513	509	7509	11293	14909	17904	21636	382
3825	Office,computing etc..	15	14	14	13	13	6547	10276	13784	16318	20304	3825
383	Electrical machinery ...	302	285	279	276	275	6630	10248	13407	16001	19564	383
3832	Radio,television etc..	142	133	132	131	132	6476	9834	13073	15678	19097	3832
384	Transport equipment	385	356	347	343	335	7509	11278	14803	17684	21400	384
3841	Shipbuilding, repair..	60	54	52	52	50	8951	13312	16970	20196	25575	3841
3843	Motor vehicles	143	131	127	124	121	6758	10391	13738	16404	19832	3843
385	Professional goods	49	46	45	47	45	7014	10689	14143	16635	20183	385
390	Other industries	73	69	81	85	87	7102	11005	14774	17648	20821	390
3	Manufacturing	4095	3825	3769	3735	3702	7184	10832	14113	16704	19895	3
410	Electricity,gas,steam ..	106	109	113	118	123	8841	13240	16529	19540	23251	410
4101	Electricity	...	...	...	...	...	...	...	...	...	...	4101
420	Water works and supply .	.	.	.	.	.	.	.	.	.	.	420
4	Electricity,gas etc	106	109	113	118	123	8841	13240	16529	19540	23251	4
2-4	All industry	4709	4466	4423	4399	4373	7882	12330	15941	18819	22568	2-4

a/ Socialized industry only.
b/ Monthly average per employee.
c/ Since 1981 - including compensations for increase of prices.

ISIC	INDUSTRY	5. AVERAGE NUMBER OF OPERATIVES a/ (THOUSANDS)					6. WAGES AND SALARIES OF OPERATIVES a/b/ (ZLOTYS)					ISIC
		1981	1982	1983	1984	1985	1981 c/	1982	1983	1984	1985	
210	Coal mining	331	349	354	358	358	14555	25022	30852	35831	43909	210
220	Petroleum and gas	3	4	4	4	4	7464	11449	13861	16182	19102	220
230	Metal ore mining	21	25	25	24	25	13191	21973	29071	33414	39236	230
290	Other mining	45	43	42	41	40	8004	12734	15891	18962	22501	290
2	Mining, quarrying .	400	421	425	427	427	13696	23459	29126	33916	41415	2
311/2	Food products	346	336	337	334	335	7275	11056	13233	15412	18089	311/2
313	Beverages	24	23	24	24	24	6584	10591	12834	15121	17719	313
314	Tobacco	8	8	8	8	9	7034	10845	13748	17584	20974	314
321	Textiles	343	298	280	275	276	6569	9446	13145	15783	18712	321
3211	Spinning,weaving etc..	215	184	170	165	164	6706	9587	13845	16230	19169	3211
322	Wearing apparel	176	164	163	164	163	5948	9075	12401	14477	16781	322
323	Leather and products ...	29	27	26	26	26	6719	10212	13680	15575	18526	323
324	Footwear	86	79	79	80	82	6206	9670	13129	15060	17559	324
331	Wood products	71	66	65	62	61	7005	10743	13168	15328	18271	331
332	Furniture, fixtures	83	77	75	75	75	6709	10296	13166	15082	17832	332
341	Paper and products	40	38	39	37	37	6885	10447	13039	15353	18291	341
3411	Pulp,paper etc.	26	25	26	28	27	7176	10762	13288	15708	18836	3411
342	Printing,publishing	39	35	35	36	36	6694	9818	12741	16251	19380	342
351	Industrial chemicals ...	96	90	87	85	83	7310	11085	14461	17212	20344	351
3511	Basic excl fertilizers	36	34	33	32	31	7528	11328	14492	17119	20366	3511
3513	Synthetic resins etc .	36	33	32	31	31	7044	10607	14908	17425	20318	3513
352	Other chemical products.	44	42	43	42	42	6455	10259	13572	16086	19436	352
3522	Drugs and medicines ..	18	18	17	17	17	6299	9842	13497	16027	19899	3522
353	Petroleum refineries ...	12	12	11	11	11	7233	10826	14544	17857	21607	353
354	Petroleum,coal products.	10	10	10	10	9	9542	14108	18247	21451	25109	354
355	Rubber products	36	33	32	32	30	6641	10220	14309	16793	19694	355
356	Plastic products n.e.c..	42	39	37	37	36	6505	10266	13590	15791	18310	356
361	Pottery,china etc	23	22	21	21	21	6681	9659	12925	15482	18696	361
362	Glass and products	50	48	46	46	44	7484	10730	13786	16486	19230	362
369	Non-metal products n.e.c	103	98	96	94	91	7482	10993	13684	16115	18852	369
371	Iron and steel	142	129	124	121	119	9570	13871	18863	22780	27183	371
372	Non-ferrous metals	32	26	25	26	25	9805	13698	18413	21983	25846	372
381	Metal products	206	187	179	176	169	6864	10266	13462	15924	18777	381
382	Machinery n.e.c.	393	366	357	353	349	7705	11384	15131	18288	22113	382
3825	Office,computing etc..	10	9	9	8	8	6239	9895	13337	15836	19814	3825
383	Electrical machinery ...	219	203	198	195	194	6448	9883	13044	15584	19039	383
3832	Radio,television etc..	105	96	95	95	95	6149	9332	12539	15032	18295	3832
384	Transport equipment	281	254	245	240	235	7346	11302	14839	17764	21549	384
3841	Shipbuilding, repair..	42	38	36	36	35	9043	13421	17113	20493	25956	3841
3843	Motor vehicles	106	95	91	89	86	6729	10384	13769	16483	19991	3843
385	Professional goods	34	32	31	32	31	6838	10377	13851	16365	19806	385
390	Other industries	36	34	33	32	32	6428	9851	13004	15098	17624	390
3	Manufacturing	3004	2776	2706	2674	2645	7119	10681	13979	16593	19737	3
410	Electricity,gas,steam ..	71	74	77	80	82	8891	13084	16316	19278	22888	410
4101	Electricity	...	...	...	...	...	...	...	...	...	...	4101
420	Water works and supply .	.	.	.	.	.	.	.	.	.	.	420
4	Electricity,gas etc	71	74	77	80	82	8891	13084	16316	19278	22888	4
2-4	All industry	3475	3271	3208	3181	3154	7912	12379	16041	18988	22754	2-4

a/ Socialized industry only.
b/ Monthly average per operative.
c/ Since 1981 - including compensations for increase of prices.

ISIC	INDUSTRY	7. HOURS WORKED BY OPERATIVES a/ (MILLIONS) 1981	1982	1983	1984	1985	8. QUANTITY OF ELECTRICITY CONSUMED a/ (MILLION KWH) 1981	1982	1983	1984	1985	ISIC
210	Coal mining	609	702	708	713	714	8354	8519	8765	9511	9951	210
220	Petroleum and gas	6	10	8	8	8	...	...	20	24	25	220
230	Metal ore mining	37	45	45	45	47	b/	b/	2011	2085	2130	230
290	Other mining	81	78	77	76	75	...	...	1076	1119	1123	290
2	Mining, quarrying .	733	835	838	842	844	c/ 8354	c/ 8519	11872	12739	13229	2
311/2	Food products	649	628	631	629	638			2805	3082	3183	311/2
313	Beverages	47	44	44	44	45	[3005	2899]	312	325	341	313
314	Tobacco	14	15	15	15	16			34	34	35	314
321	Textiles	575	510	491	484	486	2635	2514	2450	2506	2584	321
3211	Spinning,weaving etc..	361	317	300	293	290	...	...	...	1956	2011	3211
322	Wearing apparel	305	293	290	292	288	166	172	196	201	245	322
323	Leather and products ...	49	45	46	46	45	[223	275]	100	100	86	323
324	Footwear	144	138	144	144	145			214	192	179	324
331	Wood products	129	120	120	114	114	[1133	1066]	961	953	933	331
332	Furniture, fixtures	147	141	139	137	136			324	336	325	332
341	Paper and products	71	68	71	67	67	1922	1848	1806	1824	2088	341
3411	Pulp,paper etc.	47	46	49	51	51	...	...	...	1786	2048	3411
342	Printing,publishing	61	55	57	59	59	97	93	99	110	118	342
351	Industrial chemicals ...	166	154	150	149	148	d/ 12401	d/ 12351	10195	10501	10453	351
3511	Basic excl fertilizers	63	59	57	56	56	...	...	...	2857	2836	3511
3513	Synthetic resins etc .	60	54	53	55	53	...	...	...	2651	2634	3513
352	Other chemical products.	79	73	76	74	76	d/	d/	524	560	578	352
3522	Drugs and medicines ..	33	31	31	30	32	...	...	...	170	194	3522
353	Petroleum refineries ...	22	21	20	19	19	[1868	2272]	1396	1390	1512	353
354	Petroleum,coal products.	18	18	18	17	16			529	521	506	354
355	Rubber products	63	57	58	56	54	d/	d/	447	494	476	355
356	Plastic products n.e.c..	72	67	65	65	64	d/	d/	368	324	325	356
361	Pottery,china etc	41	38	38	38	38	179	164	156	161	159	361
362	Glass and products	84	79	78	77	75	500	458	504	511	522	362
369	Non-metal products n.e.c	188	189	182	179	173	3053	3001	2874	2823	2731	369
371	Iron and steel	261	240	233	227	226	7856	7768	8193	8389	8389	371
372	Non-ferrous metals	56	46	45	46	45	b/ 4917	b/ 4795	2897	2923	2986	372
381	Metal products	363	334	327	319	309	2299	2017	1679	1759	1660	381
382	Machinery n.e.c.	699	666	668	655	654	2744	2622	3104	3240	3440	382
3825	Office,computing etc..	17	16	15	15	15	...	...	...	24	25	3825
383	Electrical machinery ...	385	357	355	350	351	1507	1500	1319	1342	1286	383
3832	Radio,television etc..	182	168	170	169	171	...	...	...	515	484	3832
384	Transport equipment	491	458	452	445	441	2309	1919	2038	2159	2248	384
3841	Shipbuilding, repair..	76	71	69	69	69	...	...	...	283	292	3841
3843	Motor vehicles	183	168	166	163	160	...	...	...	1087	1108	3843
385	Professional goods	61	58	57	60	57	158	201	119	123	125	385
390	Other industries	65	61	62	58	58	271	222	340	367	345	390
3	Manufacturing	5305	4973	4932	4865	4843	49243	48157	45983	47250	47862	3
410	Electricity,gas,steam ..	138	142	150	154	159	10172	10751	12792	13614	14316	410
4101	Electricity	...	...	...	...	...	...	...	...	...	...	4101
420	Water works and supply .	.	.	.	.	.	.	.	.	.	.	420
4	Electricity,gas etc	138	142	150	154	159	10172	10751	12792	13614	14316	4
2-4	All industry	6176	5950	5920	5861	5846	c/ 67769	c/ 67427	70647	73603	75407	2-4

a/ Socialized industry only.
c/ Excluding major groups 220, 230 and 290.
b/ Major group 230 is included in 372.
d/ Major groups 352, 355 and 356 are included in 351.

ISIC	INDUSTRY	9. OUTPUT a/ (BILLION ZLOTYS) 1981 b/	1982 c/d/	1983 c/d/	1984	1985	10. VALUE ADDED a/ (BILLION ZLOTYS) 1981	1982	1983	1984	1985	ISIC
210	Coal mining	77.1	473.4	493.7	503.6	506.6	46.8	174.2	236.6	254.2	287.8	210
220	Petroleum and gas	0.9	7.1	7.7	8.1	9.2	1.0	5.5	5.1	18.7	24.4	220
230	Metal ore mining	3.6	47.9	52.9	50.8	53.5	11.6	21.9	25.9	41.0	42.7	230
290	Other mining	21.1	74.9	73.8	79.1	80.3	20.6	37.2	51.8	50.4	54.2	290
2	Mining, quarrying .	102.7	603.3	628.1	641.6	649.6	80.0	238.8	319.4	364.3	409.1	2
311/2	Food products	425.8	1450.6	1536.6	1650.4	1721.6	-143.3	77.2	54.7	81.8	80.5	311/2
313	Beverages	34.5	135.8	142.7	100.7	108.8	154.0	334.3	460.8	484.2	530.7	313
314	Tobacco	15.0	44.7	42.3	34.7	36.4	4.6	5.6	6.7	9.3	10.9	314
321	Textiles	165.4	346.6	352.5	377.0	399.6	120.5	175.2	215.2	286.4	359.6	321
3211	Spinning,weaving etc..	103.4	228.5	231.3	252.5	271.4	69.0	110.3	127.1	164.5	201.0	3211
322	Wearing apparel	82.7	153.1	160.3	173.6	183.3	30.9	60.1	84.6	102.1	117.9	322
323	Leather and products ...	16.3	41.2	42.6	47.3	47.8	7.0	15.3	21.3	25.1	31.5	323
324	Footwear	26.8	67.5	76.5	79.7	85.8	17.9	30.6	42.1	49.8	63.2	324
331	Wood products	42.8	112.5	121.0	128.4	135.3	19.4	41.1	44.7	51.4	64.1	331
332	Furniture, fixtures	41.6	91.8	102.5	106.8	112.1	22.9	37.7	45.3	62.6	73.6	332
341	Paper and products	28.0	80.0	87.7	88.7	90.3	9.6	25.7	23.6	27.5	39.6	341
3411	Pulp,paper etc.	13.2	57.1	61.8	66.5	67.3	5.1	17.5	15.1	20.3	30.8	3411
342	Printing,publishing	8.6	33.0	40.8	46.4	52.1	6.6	13.0	17.3	24.3	30.6	342
351	Industrial chemicals ...	87.9	248.5	268.6	278.8	285.7	33.1	67.6	78.1	89.8	108.0	351
3511	Basic excl fertilizers	36.0	97.7	102.9	105.4	110.3	12.8	33.2	31.0	35.2	39.0	3511
3513	Synthetic resins etc .	26.0	66.1	70.1	72.3	71.3	11.4	20.2	31.6	37.4	57.2	3513
352	Other chemical products.	54.5	144.4	156.1	167.7	182.9	39.8	56.5	60.9	73.6	94.8	352
3522	Drugs and medicines ..	19.7	46.7	53.3	65.5	75.5	23.5	23.3	26.6	32.6	44.2	3522
353	Petroleum refineries ...	44.8	229.4	235.4	235.4	239.2	54.4	111.6	159.6	179.6	182.3	353
354	Petroleum,coal products.	19.7	74.1	73.4	63.8	59.3	1.8	9.3	8.4	8.3	8.8	354
355	Rubber products	24.9	54.1	58.5	63.1	60.2	11.8	23.7	29.6	39.0	50.2	355
356	Plastic products n.e.c..	29.9	63.8	71.3	73.2	73.3	15.9	28.7	31.5	38.9	43.6	356
361	Pottery,china etc	7.2	14.3	16.1	17.5	18.4	4.5	10.4	13.7	18.1	21.5	361
362	Glass and products	18.2	44.9	48.1	50.7	50.9	12.4	25.6	31.8	38.7	41.5	362
369	Non-metal products n.e.c	51.8	159.5	171.1	173.6	168.8	11.4	68.2	73.6	84.9	93.3	369
371	Iron and steel	134.5	370.9	394.8	404.3	397.8	29.4	86.4	104.8	140.7	170.8	371
372	Non-ferrous metals	79.1	169.0	179.7	193.3	198.0	19.7	24.7	34.8	41.3	49.5	372
381	Metal products	92.7	233.1	244.0	256.0	271.1	57.7	111.2	130.7	166.8	198.2	381
382	Machinery n.e.c.	255.6	536.8	577.3	618.4	670.9	152.8	275.4	318.6	390.4	494.4	382
3825	Office,computing etc..	12.9	18.6	20.6	21.6	26.6	5.7	12.5	13.1	14.8	20.8	3825
383	Electrical machinery ...	160.1	284.5	311.0	345.0	376.7	69.7	143.5	170.0	213.6	265.0	383
3832	Radio,television etc..	58.9	126.7	139.2	158.3	177.8	30.3	66.4	82.6	106.9	130.2	3832
384	Transport equipment	196.7	439.2	462.9	487.7	508.9	100.8	210.6	237.4	282.5	331.8	384
3841	Shipbuilding, repair..	45.1	72.0	68.6	67.2	73.1	14.9	32.0	21.9	26.1	42.2	3841
3843	Motor vehicles	98.7	200.0	220.1	233.8	241.8	44.3	100.4	121.8	144.7	152.4	3843
385	Professional goods	16.8	30.6	34.0	37.3	40.2	14.2	20.4	22.4	29.0	36.9	385
390	Other industries	21.6	63.7	70.9	79.9	87.3	15.2	30.4	41.7	54.3	64.4	390
3	Manufacturing	2183.5	5717.6	6078.7	6379.4	6662.7	894.7	2120.0	2563.9	3094.0	3657.2	3
410	Electricity,gas,steam ..	88.6	287.9	308.8	340.9	354.1	22.0	79.6	90.1	124.4	143.6	410
4101	Electricity	...	...	...	...	...	13.2	5.2	...	...	...	4101
420	Water works and supply .	.	.	.	.	.	.	.	.	.	.	420
4	Electricity,gas etc	88.6	287.9	308.8	340.9	354.1	22.0	79.6	90.1	124.4	143.6	4
2-4	All industry	2374.8	6608.8	7015.6	7361.9	7666.4	996.7	2438.4	2973.4	3582.7	4209.9	2-4

a/ Socialized industry only.
b/ At prices of 1 January 1979.
c/ At prices of 1982.
d/ Beginning 1982, output computed by the enterprise method; prior to 1982 by the establishment method.

ISIC	INDUSTRY	11. GROSS FIXED CAPITAL FORMATION TOTAL a/ (BILLION ZLOTYS)					12. GROSS FIXED CAPITAL FORMATION MACHINERY AND EQUIPMENT a/ (BILLION ZLOTYS)					ISIC
		1981	1982	1983	1984	1985	1981	1982	1983	1984	1985	
210	Coal mining	28.23	64.58	66.42	73.33	95.17	15.34	32.49	30.39	30.55	43.18	210
220	Petroleum and gas	0.29	0.95	2.05	3.30	2.60	0.06	0.16	0.11	0.59	0.69	220
230	Metal ore mining	2.35	5.05	7.13	8.65	11.22	0.89	1.61	2.34	3.39	4.04	230
290	Other mining	2.92	6.00	8.25	11.30	12.07	1.38	2.19	2.75	3.55	3.55	290
2	Mining, quarrying .	33.79	76.58	83.85	96.58	121.06	17.67	36.45	35.59	38.08	51.46	2
311/2	Food products	16.45	35.64	40.15	52.51	71.11	9.03	14.85	15.42	20.84	27.74	311/2
313	Beverages	1.64	2.68	3.90	4.29	4.61	0.90	1.18	1.70	1.87	1.98	313
314	Tobacco	0.10	0.23	0.31	0.97	1.69	0.08	0.15	0.15	0.70	1.14	314
321	Textiles	4.32	7.25	9.14	16.23	25.59	3.44	4.40	6.00	11.36	18.76	321
3211	Spinning,weaving etc..	3.29	4.51	5.68	10.80	17.21	2.68	2.96	3.91	7.99	12.85	3211
322	Wearing apparel	1.12	2.36	3.55	4.99	6.07	0.58	0.96	1.67	1.95	2.50	322
323	Leather and products ...	0.21	0.61	0.75	1.05	1.58	0.17	0.29	0.33	0.42	0.70	323
324	Footwear	0.47	1.09	1.73	2.90	5.10	0.32	0.57	0.97	1.59	3.23	324
331	Wood products	1.65	3.11	3.39	4.43	5.57	1.11	1.23	1.73	2.43	2.86	331
332	Furniture, fixtures	1.08	2.45	3.00	4.02	5.03	0.53	0.91	1.06	1.64	2.24	332
341	Paper and products	2.82	4.38	5.01	7.40	9.14	1.64	1.49	2.11	2.91	3.56	341
3411	Pulp,paper etc.	2.64	4.04	4.68	7.12	8.01	1.54	1.24	1.89	2.75	2.75	3411
342	Printing,publishing	0.52	1.15	2.60	2.55	4.85	0.35	0.67	2.10	1.67	3.68	342
351	Industrial chemicals ...	8.55	13.76	17.94	26.16	31.24	5.05	5.68	6.28	7.67	9.25	351
3511	Basic excl fertilizers	2.71	2.83	3.58	5.05	5.97	1.81	1.29	1.71	2.55	2.74	3511
3513	Synthetic resins etc .	2.15	4.79	5.48	7.45	9.24	1.20	1.97	2.10	1.64	2.23	3513
352	Other chemical products.	2.85	5.95	6.84	8.62	10.88	1.89	3.01	2.53	3.69	4.72	352
3522	Drugs and medicines ..	1.83	3.96	4.57	5.94	7.47	1.31	2.06	1.67	2.65	3.34	3522
353	Petroleum refineries ...	0.49	1.22	1.49	1.87	2.88	0.26	0.58	0.66	0.69	0.87	353
354	Petroleum,coal products.	1.65	1.47	1.72	9.33	26.13	1.25	0.35	0.25	0.67	3.94	354
355	Rubber products	1.61	3.25	3.44	4.13	6.00	1.33	2.04	1.81	1.73	2.80	355
356	Plastic products n.e.c..	1.08	1.89	3.12	4.75	5.74	0.76	1.04	1.15	2.00	2.54	356
361	Pottery,china etc	0.52	1.05	1.31	1.54	3.09	0.21	0.50	0.43	0.47	0.99	361
362	Glass and products	0.62	1.26	1.46	2.14	3.23	0.37	0.58	0.55	0.88	1.77	362
369	Non-metal products n.e.c	2.50	6.02	7.97	12.12	14.69	1.40	1.78	3.09	4.27	5.54	369
371	Iron and steel	9.46	9.32	8.09	15.48	23.73	7.26	5.01	2.57	4.27	7.49	371
372	Non-ferrous metals	0.96	1.52	2.85	4.63	5.52	0.45	0.60	0.99	1.76	2.09	372
381	Metal products	4.86	12.22	14.26	17.28	20.22	2.96	4.90	5.63	7.72	10.43	381
382	Machinery n.e.c.	21.36	30.02	38.11	49.44	56.12	17.21	16.22	20.99	27.45	31.34	382
3825	Office,computing etc..	0.11	0.10	0.60	0.94	1.56	0.09	0.08	0.43	0.46	1.04	3825
383	Electrical machinery ...	7.30	8.41	12.49	15.85	23.51	5.76	5.16	6.11	7.55	13.68	383
3832	Radio,television etc..	3.70	3.97	5.80	7.15	12.04	2.75	2.12	2.82	3.15	7.52	3832
384	Transport equipment	7.08	11.31	16.65	22.73	30.71	4.49	5.54	7.65	10.37	14.14	384
3841	Shipbuilding, repair..	0.94	1.75	2.80	3.14	3.66	0.37	0.80	1.43	1.43	1.66	3841
3843	Motor vehicles	2.08	3.13	5.11	7.60	8.66	1.64	1.56	2.26	4.01	3.90	3843
385	Professional goods	0.85	2.02	2.38	3.41	2.74	0.58	1.26	1.19	1.95	1.45	385
390	Other industries	0.53	1.16	2.39	3.33	4.80	0.25	0.55	1.24	1.51	2.40	390
3	Manufacturing	b/ 105.31	172.80	216.04	304.15	411.57	b/ 72.59	81.50	96.36	132.03	183.83	3
410	Electricity,gas,steam ..	21.26	54.54	63.22	82.08	101.13	9.16	14.89	17.41	20.89	27.47	410
4101	Electricity	17.75	42.37	44.91	54.83	64.07	8.22	11.92	13.41	15.50	20.51	4101
420	Water works and supply .	.	.	.	.	.	.	.	.	.	.	420
4	Electricity,gas etc	21.26	54.54	63.22	82.08	101.13	9.16	14.89	17.41	20.89	27.47	4
2-4	All industry	b/ 160.36	303.92	363.11	482.81	633.76	b/ 99.42	132.84	149.36	191.00	262.76	2-4

a/ Socialized industry only.
b/ Total includes industries other than those for which separate data are shown.

13. INDEX NUMBERS OF INDUSTRIAL PRODUCTION (1980 = 100)

ISIC	INDUSTRY	1976	1977	1978	1979	1981	1982	1983	1984	1985	RATE a/	ISIC
210	Coal mining	94	98	101	105	85	99	103	105	106	1.3	210
220	Petroleum and gas	150	108	100	98	94	84	91	95	108	-3.6	220
230	Metal ore mining	57	56	55	64	55	60	66	64	67	1.8	230
290	Other mining	88	94	98	100	90	88	86	93	94	0.7	290
2	Mining, quarrying .	97	101	102	106	85	97	102	104	104	0.8	2
311/2	Food products	93	96	101	103	93	83	88	95	99	0.7	311/2
313	Beverages	90	98	100	104	87	83	88	62	67	-3.2	313
314	Tobacco	103	115	102	100	95	107	102	83	87	-1.9	314
321	Textiles	93	98	101	100	88	78	80	85	90	-0.4	321
3211	Spinning,weaving etc..	...	...	...	...	...	...	...	...	...	...	3211
322	Wearing apparel	89	95	97	96	94	89	93	101	107	2.1	322
323	Leather and products ...	92	94	95	99	91	90	93	103	104	1.4	323
324	Footwear	87	90	95	98	90	92	104	108	117	3.3	324
331	Wood products	98	102	104	99	87	84	90	96	101	0.3	331
332	Furniture, fixtures	79	91	98	96	91	90	101	105	110	3.7	332
341	Paper and products	94	99	102	96	87	91	99	100	102	0.9	341
3411	Pulp,paper etc.	...	...	...	...	...	...	...	...	...	...	3411
342	Printing,publishing	86	99	100	103	90	103	127	144	162	7.3	342
351	Industrial chemicals ...	95	101	103	100	89	88	95	99	101	0.7	351
3511	Basic excl fertilizers	...	...	...	...	...	...	...	...	...	...	3511
3513	Synthetic resins etc .	...	...	...	...	...	...	...	...	...	...	3513
352	Other chemical products.	84	88	93	101	88	90	97	104	114	3.5	352
3522	Drugs and medicines ..	...	...	...	...	...	...	...	...	...	...	3522
353	Petroleum refineries ...	90	98	105	103	86	88	90	90	92	0.2	353
354	Petroleum,coal products.	126	108	106	105	94	92	91	79	73	-5.9	354
355	Rubber products	83	88	91	94	84	82	89	96	91	1.0	355
356	Plastic products n.e.c..	90	94	99	103	92	94	105	108	108	2.0	356
361	Pottery,china etc	70	78	87	94	98	104	116	126	133	7.4	361
362	Glass and products	73	80	88	96	91	92	99	104	104	4.0	362
369	Non-metal products n.e.c	102	106	108	101	83	86	92	93	91	-1.3	369
371	Iron and steel	88	94	100	100	82	78	83	85	84	-0.5	371
372	Non-ferrous metals	93	98	104	103	86	88	93	100	103	1.1	372
381	Metal products	85	94	97	99	86	82	86	91	96	1.4	381
382	Machinery n.e.c.	80	90	94	100	91	91	98	105	114	4.0	382
3825	Office,computing etc..	...	...	...	...	...	...	...	...	...	...	3825
383	Electrical machinery ...	76	84	91	99	88	87	95	105	115	4.7	383
3832	Radio,television etc..	...	...	...	...	...	...	...	...	...	...	3832
384	Transport equipment	84	89	95	100	85	85	71	75	78	-0.8	384
3841	Shipbuilding, repair..	...	...	...	...	...	...	...	...	...	...	3841
3843	Motor vehicles	...	...	...	...	...	...	...	...	...	...	3843
385	Professional goods	78	86	94	99	90	92	102	112	121	5.0	385
390	Other industries	79	84	91	106	99	91	101	114	125	5.2	390
3	Manufacturing	90	96	99	101	86	84	89	94	98	1.0	3
410	Electricity,gas,steam ..	...	...	...	...	...	...	...	...	...	...	410
4101	Electricity	84	87	92	95	102	109	118	130	133	5.2	4101
420	Water works and supply .	.	.	.	.	.	.	.	.	.	.	420
4	Electricity,gas etc	...	...	...	...	...	...	...	...	...	...	4
2-4	All industry b/	90	96	99	101	86	85	90	95	99	1.1	2-4

a/ Annual growth rate 1976-1985.

b/ Excluding gas and steam.

PORTUGAL

The information on industrial activity is based on the reply to the United Nations Questionnaire on General Industrial Statistics from the National Statistical Institute, Lisbon. The concepts, definitions and classification by branches of industry are generally in accordance with United Nations standards. Data for the Azores and Madeira islands are included.

The estimates are derived from the annual industrial inquiry carried out by the National Statistical Institute. The inquiry generally covers all mining establishments, irrespective of size, and selected industries in manufacturing. For most of the manufacturing industries included, all establishments are covered but for some the coverage is limited to establishments with 10 or more operatives or meeting other specified criteria. For a few industries, the results are suppressed in conformity with the disclosure rules. A comparison with the 1971 census shows that in that year the annual inquiry covered 31 per cent of the establishments, 70 per cent of employment and 78 per cent of output. For electricity, power stations with a generating capacity of 50 kW or more are included. The data for gas relate to the two operating enterprises, one engaged in production and one engaged in distribution. The industrial activity of steam and water works and supply is not surveyed.

The estimates are compiled according to the national classification which follows the present version of ISIC.

The employment data generally relate to the numbers in the last week of the year. Working proprietors and unpaid family workers are included in the number of persons engaged. Homeworkers are not included in the employment count but payments to homeworkers are included in wages and salaries. Wages and salaries cover all payments made to employees; payments in kind forming part of the basic remuneration are included. Supplements to wages and salaries comprise obligatory and voluntary payments made by the employer in respect of employees, including contributions to social activities and employee facilities. Actual hours worked by operatives are now collected for all industries.

The concept of output for mining is defined as the total ex-establishment value of production and for manufacturing, the total value of products manufactured plus the value of electricity and residues sold and the value of industrial work done for others. Adjustments are made in the value of finished production in respect of changes during the year in work in progress, and the value of own-account capital goods produced is included. The valuation is at ex-establishment price, including indirect taxes and excluding subsidies. Value added is the value of output less the value of materials and energy consumed and for manufacturing, the cost of industrial work done by others, repair and maintenance and non-industrial services.

The estimates of gross fixed capital formation represent the acquisition of new and used fixed assets less sales. Capital work performed by the establishment's own labour force for its own use is included.

The indexes of industrial production are compiled by the Centro de Estudos de Economia Aplicada, Associacao Industrial Portuguesa, and provided in response to the United Nations Questionnaire on Indexes of Industrial Production. In principle, the indexes cover all establishments.

Related national publications:

Estatisticas Industriais: Volume I, Industrias extractivas, Electricidades Gas e Agua; Volume II, Industrias transformadoras (annual); Anuario Estatistico, all published by the National Statistical Institute, Lisbon.

ISIC	INDUSTRY	1. NUMBER OF ESTABLISHMENTS a/ (NUMBER)					2. AVERAGE NUMBER OF PERSONS ENGAGED a/b/ (THOUSANDS)					ISIC
		1981	1982	1983	1984	1985	1981	1982	1983	1984	1985	
210	Coal mining	1	1	1	1	...	1.1	1.1	1.2	1.1	...	210
220	Petroleum and gas	-	-	-	-	...	-	-	-	-	...	220
230	Metal ore mining	38	43	38	35	...	3.9	4.1	3.8	3.7	...	230
290	Other mining	1750	1627	1610	1031	...	12.5	11.7	11.4	10.1	...	290
2	Mining, quarrying .	1789	1671	1649	1067	...	17.5	16.9	16.4	14.9	...	2
311/2	Food products	3329	3200	3229	3217	...	81.9	78.6	78.3	74.7	...	311/2
313	Beverages	241	238	243	231	...	9.5	9.1	9.0	8.7	...	313
314	Tobacco	8	8	8	8	...	1.9	1.9	1.9	2.2	...	314
321	Textiles	1240	1206	1167	1148	...	147.1	141.9	140.3	138.1	...	321
3211	Spinning,weaving etc..	632	615	593	589	...	102.1	96.9	96.1	94.8	...	3211
322	Wearing apparel	464	475	500	516	...	40.9	41.4	43.8	45.5	...	322
323	Leather and products ...	182	178	186	173	...	5.2	5.1	5.0	5.0	...	323
324	Footwear	420	410	417	421	...	18.6	18.6	20.0	21.5	...	324
331	Wood products	2398	2419	2350	2319	...	43.5	42.9	40.2	40.5	...	331
332	Furniture, fixtures	711	643	632	612	...	14.1	13.0	13.0	12.0	...	332
341	Paper and products	230	238	237	230	...	18.7	18.5	18.1	18.4	...	341
3411	Pulp,paper etc.	86	86	88	87	...	12.7	12.6	12.2	12.5	...	3411
342	Printing,publishing	1000	968	980	964	...	25.1	26.0	25.5	24.3	...	342
351	Industrial chemicals ...	166	162	161	160	...	14.9	15.0	13.6	13.0	...	351
3511	Basic excl fertilizers	104	102	102	97	...	6.8	6.9	6.7	6.7	...	3511
3513	Synthetic resins etc .	25	15	26	28	...	4.9	4.9	4.0	3.4	...	3513
352	Other chemical products.	495	507	474	468	...	21.1	21.7	20.8	20.4	...	352
3522	Drugs and medicines ..	88	86	88	87	...	7.9	7.7	7.8	7.9	...	3522
353	Petroleum refineries ...	3	2	2	3	...	2.2	2.2	2.3	2.3	...	353
354	Petroleum,coal products.	2	2	2	2	...	...	...	...	...	...	354
355	Rubber products	165	164	156	149	...	7.6	7.5	7.3	7.0	...	355
356	Plastic products n.e.c..	286	286	299	297	...	15.7	15.2	15.6	14.5	...	356
361	Pottery,china etc	95	126	134	139	...	12.9	13.6	13.8	14.0	...	361
362	Glass and products	116	116	118	113	...	10.5	10.0	9.4	9.2	...	362
369	Non-metal products n.e.c	1114	1032	1001	950	...	36.1	35.4	33.4	30.5	...	369
371	Iron and steel	104	102	99	97	...	17.3	17.0	16.4	15.3	...	371
372	Non-ferrous metals	115	113	101	109	...	4.4	4.3	4.0	3.9	...	372
381	Metal products	698	716	693	695	...	41.7	41.3	40.3	37.8	...	381
382	Machinery n.e.c.	331	352	341	326	...	24.6	25.2	23.7	21.0	...	382
3825	Office,computing etc..	23	22	23	18	...	2.2	2.3	2.3	1.4	...	3825
383	Electrical machinery ...	178	196	203	200	...	32.8	33.0	32.9	32.3	...	383
3832	Radio,television etc..	39	43	48	45	...	15.7	15.7	15.5	15.4	...	3832
384	Transport equipment	260	275	272	254	...	46.5	45.1	42.6	39.0	...	384
3841	Shipbuilding, repair..	86	90	86	79	...	25.0	22.8	20.4	20.5	...	3841
3843	Motor vehicles	133	144	144	136	...	16.4	17.4	16.6	14.6	...	3843
385	Professional goods	33	32	33	30	...	2.9	2.8	2.8	2.7	...	385
390	Other industries	77	76	74	66	...	2.8	2.6	2.5	2.4	...	390
3	Manufacturing	14461	14242	14112	13897	...	700.5 c/	688.9 c/	676.5 c/	656.2 c/	...	3
410	Electricity,gas,steam ..	622	597	576	583	...	27.4	27.7	28.1	27.9	...	410
4101	Electricity	620	595	574	581	...	26.8	27.2	27.5	27.3	...	4101
420	Water works and supply .	-	-	-	-	...	-	-	-	-	...	420
4	Electricity,gas etc	622	597	576	583	...	27.4	27.7	28.1	27.9	...	4
2-4	All industry	16872	16510	16337	15547	...	745.4 c/	733.5 c/	721.0 c/	699.0 c/	...	2-4

a/ Selected industries; for coverage, see country note. b/ In the last week of the year indicated.
c/ Excluding major group 354.

ISIC	INDUSTRY	3. AVERAGE NUMBER OF EMPLOYEES a/b/ (THOUSANDS) 1981	1982	1983	1984	1985	4. WAGES AND SALARIES OF EMPLOYEES a/c/ (MILLION ESCUDOS) 1981	1982	1983	1984	1985	ISIC
210	Coal mining	1.1	1.1	1.2	1.1	...	264	414	501	589	...	210
220	Petroleum and gas	-	-	-	-	...	-	-	-	-	...	220
230	Metal ore mining	3.9	4.1	3.7	3.7	...	1028	1285	1309	1501	...	230
290	Other mining	12.5	11.6	11.3	10.1	...	2400	2723	3275	3426	...	290
2	Mining, quarrying	17.5	16.8	16.2	14.9	...	3692	4442	5085	5516	...	2
311/2	Food products	76.1	74.0	73.8	65.2	...	14522	17151	20736	23560	...	311/2
313	Beverages	9.3	9.1	8.8	8.6	...	2239	2640	3028	3408	...	313
314	Tobacco	1.9	1.9	1.9	2.2	...	649	854	991	1107	...	314
321	Textiles	145.4	141.3	139.8	137.6	...	25183	28561	34242	40046	...	321
3211	Spinning,weaving etc.	101.0	96.7	95.9	94.6	...	17800	19845	23785	27993	...	3211
322	Wearing apparel	40.8	41.2	43.7	45.4	...	6034	7486	9403	11505	...	322
323	Leather and products	5.1	5.0	4.9	4.9	...	949	1090	1354	1681	...	323
324	Footwear	18.3	18.4	19.7	21.3	...	2789	3231	4064	5217	...	324
331	Wood products	40.7	37.9	37.9	38.1	...	6498	7369	8563	10253	...	331
332	Furniture, fixtures	13.3	12.3	12.4	11.5	...	1939	2126	2439	2680	...	332
341	Paper and products	18.6	18.5	18.0	18.4	...	4837	5883	7165	8784	...	341
3411	Pulp,paper etc.	12.7	12.6	12.2	12.4	...	3730	4444	5372	6698	...	3411
342	Printing,publishing	24.6	25.4	25.0	23.8	...	5843	7383	8687	9646	...	342
351	Industrial chemicals	14.9	14.7	13.5	12.9	...	4679	5842	6475	7644	...	351
3511	Basic excl fertilizers	6.7	6.9	6.7	6.7	...	2208	2757	3237	3931	...	3511
3513	Synthetic resins etc	4.9	4.9	3.9	3.4	...	1428	1801	1913	2108	...	3513
352	Other chemical products	20.6	21.1	20.4	20.0	...	5819	7293	8645	10231	...	352
3522	Drugs and medicines	7.9	7.7	7.8	7.9	...	2139	2522	3101	3861	...	3522
353	Petroleum refineries	2.2	2.2	2.3	2.3	...	895	1091	1424	1657	...	353
354	Petroleum,coal products	...	...	...	...	...	...	...	...	...	...	354
355	Rubber products	7.4	7.3	7.1	6.9	...	1717	2109	2482	2889	...	355
356	Plastic products n.e.c.	15.6	15.1	15.6	14.5	...	3341	3928	4694	5272	...	356
361	Pottery,china etc	12.8	13.5	13.7	13.9	...	2773	3422	4173	4945	...	361
362	Glass and products	10.4	9.9	9.3	9.2	...	2891	3233	3802	4426	...	362
369	Non-metal products n.e.c	35.1	34.7	32.8	30.0	...	7452	9046	10468	10973	...	369
371	Iron and steel	17.2	17.0	16.3	15.3	...	5008	6399	7171	8110	...	371
372	Non-ferrous metals	4.4	4.2	3.9	3.8	...	964	1128	1292	1416	...	372
381	Metal products	41.4	41.2	40.1	37.6	...	9492	11072	12704	14293	...	381
382	Machinery n.e.c.	24.5	25.1	23.6	20.9	...	6132	7447	8254	8717	...	382
3825	Office,computing etc.	2.2	2.3	2.3	1.4	...	556	660	775	746	...	3825
383	Electrical machinery	31.6	33.0	32.9	32.3	...	8479	10274	12394	15326	...	383
3832	Radio,television etc.	15.7	15.7	15.5	15.4	...	3937	4590	5592	6809	...	3832
384	Transport equipment	46.2	45.0	42.3	38.9	...	14915	17160	18505	19611	...	384
3841	Shipbuilding, repair.	25.0	22.7	20.4	20.4	...	9232	9714	9962	11139	...	3841
3843	Motor vehicles	16.3	17.4	16.5	14.5	...	4514	5854	7047	6962	...	3843
385	Professional goods	2.9	2.8	2.8	2.7	...	608	760	902	1092	...	385
390	Other industries	2.8	2.5	2.5	2.4	...	497	539	601	686	...	390
3	Manufacturing d/	684.1	674.3	665.0	640.6	...	147144	174517	204658	235175	...	3
410	Electricity,gas,steam	27.4	27.7	28.1	27.9	...	9756	12208	15164	18269	...	410
4101	Electricity	26.8	27.2	27.5	27.4	...	9541	11937	14842	17899	...	4101
420	Water works and supply	-	-	-	-	...	-	-	-	-	...	420
4	Electricity,gas etc	27.4	27.7	28.1	27.9	...	9756	12208	15164	18269	...	4
2-4	All industry d/	729.0	718.8	709.3	683.4	...	160592	191167	224907	258960	...	2-4

a/ Selected industries; for coverage, see country note.
b/ In the last week of the year indicated.
c/ Including payments to homeworkers.
d/ Excluding major group 354.

ISIC	INDUSTRY	5. SUPPLEMENTS TO WAGES AND SALARIES a/ (MILLION ESCUDOS) 1981	1982	1983	1984	1985	6. AVERAGE NUMBER OF OPERATIVES a/b/ (THOUSANDS) 1981	1982	1983	1984	1985	ISIC
210	Coal mining	84	128	159	193	...	1.0	1.0	1.0	1.0	...	210
220	Petroleum and gas	-	-	-	-	...	-	-	-	-	...	220
230	Metal ore mining	283	392	428	515	...	3.5	3.6	3.3	3.2	...	230
290	Other mining	121	124	158	186	...	11.8	10.9	10.6	9.0	...	290
2	Mining, quarrying .	488	644	745	894	...	16.3	15.5	14.9	13.2	...	2
311/2	Food products	3945	4689	6096	7140	...	62.4	60.9	59.2	57.4	...	311/2
313	Beverages	687	825	1017	1145	...	7.4	7.0	7.0	6.8	...	313
314	Tobacco	177	208	255	307	...	1.5	1.4	1.4	1.6	...	314
321	Textiles	6226	7419	9122	10999	...	133.3	129.4	128.0	126.1	...	321
3211	Spinning,weaving etc..	4445	5321	6404	7697	...	93.1	89.1	88.3	87.1	...	3211
322	Wearing apparel	1480	1865	2545	3166	...	37.3	38.0	40.3	41.7	...	322
323	Leather and products ...	244	292	372	467	...	4.4	4.3	4.2	4.2	...	323
324	Footwear	691	809	1090	1303	...	16.8	16.8	18.3	19.6	...	324
331	Wood products	1779	2068	2548	3168	...	36.3	33.8	33.7	33.8	...	331
332	Furniture, fixtures	536	614	689	772	...	11.8	10.9	10.9	10.0	...	332
341	Paper and products	1386	1669	2204	2829	...	15.3	15.1	14.8	15.1	...	341
3411	Pulp,paper etc.	1027	1223	1623	2099	...	10.6	10.4	10.1	10.3	...	3411
342	Printing,publishing	1483	1877	2399	2798	...	17.3	17.4	17.3	16.2	...	342
351	Industrial chemicals ...	1536	2026	2335	2791	...	11.3	11.3	9.9	9.4	...	351
3511	Basic excl fertilizers	687	931	1155	1374	...	4.7	4.6	4.5	4.5	...	3511
3513	Synthetic resins etc .	444	611	674	744	...	3.9	3.0	3.2	2.6	...	3513
352	Other chemical products.	1957	2499	2993	3650	...	12.6	13.1	12.2	12.8	...	352
3522	Drugs and medicines ..	751	926	1144	1476	...	4.6	4.4	4.3	4.3	...	3522
353	Petroleum refineries ...	452	527	719	860	...	1.7	1.7	1.7	1.7	...	353
354	Petroleum,coal products.	...	...	...	...	...	...	...	...	...	...	354
355	Rubber products	610	641	803	960	...	6.3	6.2	6.0	5.8	...	355
356	Plastic products n.e.c..	902	1111	1399	1656	...	13.2	12.7	13.0	12.0	...	356
361	Pottery,china etc	744	962	1258	1465	...	11.4	11.9	12.2	11.9	...	361
362	Glass and products	845	930	1139	1366	...	9.0	8.6	8.0	7.9	...	362
369	Non-metal products n.e.c	2235	2735	3403	3643	...	30.8	30.0	28.3	25.6	...	369
371	Iron and steel	1465	1766	2194	2554	...	15.1	15.0	14.4	11.8	...	371
372	Non-ferrous metals	250	309	363	414	...	3.8	3.7	3.4	3.3	...	372
381	Metal products	2665	3359	3983	4793	...	34.9	34.2	33.2	31.1	...	381
382	Machinery n.e.c.	1570	2266	2610	2841	...	19.9	20.2	18.7	16.3	...	382
3825	Office,computing etc..	141	198	241	238	...	1.8	1.8	1.8	1.0	...	3825
383	Electrical machinery ...	2645	3414	4448	5412	...	25.4	25.9	26.4	26.0	...	383
3832	Radio,television etc..	1224	1580	1973	2577	...	12.8	12.7	13.1	13.0	...	3832
384	Transport equipment	4303	5412	6282	7367	...	38.8	38.0	35.8	32.2	...	384
3841	Shipbuilding, repair..	2483	3044	3403	4178	...	20.6	19.2	18.2	17.0	...	3841
3843	Motor vehicles	1531	2022	2445	2730	...	14.0	14.7	13.9	11.9	...	3843
385	Professional goods	162	196	272	319	...	2.6	2.5	2.4	2.4	...	385
390	Other industries	148	142	168	206	...	2.3	2.1	2.0	1.9	...	390
3	Manufacturing ..... c/	41123	50632	62706	74391	...	582.9	572.1	562.7	544.6	...	3
410	Electricity,gas,steam ..	3231	4162	6002	7794	...	16.4	15.9	15.7	15.5	...	410
4101	Electricity	3032	3906	5656	7387	...	16.1	15.6	15.4	15.2	...	4101
420	Water works and supply .	-	-	-	-	...	-	-	-	-	...	420
4	Electricity,gas etc	3231	4162	6002	7794	...	16.4	15.9	15.7	15.5	...	4
2-4	All industry c/	44842	55438	69453	83079	...	615.6	603.5	593.3	577.3	...	2-4

a/ Selected industries; for coverage, see country note. b/ In the last week of the year indicated.
c/ Excluding major group 354.

ISIC	INDUSTRY	7. WAGES AND SALARIES OF OPERATIVES a/ (MILLION ESCUDOS)					8. HOURS WORKED BY OPERATIVES a/ (MILLIONS)					ISIC
		1981	1982	1983	1984	1985	1981	1982	1983	1984	1985	
210	Coal mining	233	369	446	519	...	1.6	1.7	1.7	1.7	...	210
220	Petroleum and gas	-	-	-	-	...	-	-	-	-	...	220
230	Metal ore mining	849	1065	1067	1230	...	6.1	6.5	5.9	5.9	...	230
290	Other mining	2227	2477	3012	3023	...	20.6	19.2	18.7	16.4	...	290
2	Mining, quarrying .	3309	3911	4525	4772	...	28.3	27.4	26.3	24.0	...	2
311/2	Food products	11323	12886	15668	16192	...	141.2	126.2	126.6	119.6	...	311/2
313	Beverages	1670	1921	2198	2479	...	16.3	16.1	15.6	15.2	...	313
314	Tobacco	473	598	693	677	...	2.9	2.9	2.8	3.3	...	314
321	Textiles	21503	24204	28832	33621	...	263.1	260.3	253.2	247.7	...	321
3211	Spinning,weaving etc..	15602	17160	20497	24015	...	184.1	181.2	174.0	170.2	...	3211
322	Wearing apparel	5118	6313	7966	9763	...	71.3	73.7	76.1	80.8	...	322
323	Leather and products ...	764	859	1069	1330	...	9.1	9.3	8.5	8.6	...	323
324	Footwear	2363	2724	3401	4477	...	33.9	33.3	35.7	38.1	...	324
331	Wood products	5463	6122	7182	8581	...	73.2	68.9	69.4	70.1	...	331
332	Furniture, fixtures	1615	1684	1997	2195	...	25.6	22.3	22.5	20.3	...	332
341	Paper and products	4201	4521	5520	6714	...	31.8	31.5	31.0	31.2	...	341
3411	Pulp,paper etc.	3343	3462	5199	5193	...	22.3	21.5	21.1	21.2	...	3411
342	Printing,publishing	3535	4422	5086	5517	...	35.6	37.5	36.1	33.9	...	342
351	Industrial chemicals ...	3142	3829	4249	4918	...	22.2	22.5	20.4	18.7	...	351
3511	Basic excl fertilizers	1305	1582	1874	2284	...	9.6	9.4	8.9	8.8	...	3511
3513	Synthetic resins etc .	1022	1352	1365	1429	...	7.3	7.8	6.8	5.4	...	3513
352	Other chemical products.	2976	3772	4307	4978	...	24.8	25.6	23.8	23.7	...	352
3522	Drugs and medicines ..	988	1159	1335	1608	...	8.5	8.1	7.9	7.8	...	3522
353	Petroleum refineries ...	670	820	1039	1211	...	3.1	3.3	3.6	3.7	...	353
354	Petroleum,coal products.	...	...	...	...	...	...	...	...	...	...	354
355	Rubber products	1468	1663	1940	2267	...	12.1	11.7	11.3	10.8	...	355
356	Plastic products n.e.c..	2582	3042	3648	3972	...	26.3	25.8	26.8	25.1	...	356
361	Pottery,china etc	2359	2845	3466	4131	...	24.9	24.4	26.3	27.2	...	361
362	Glass and products	2419	2639	3072	3621	...	20.0	16.8	16.4	15.8	...	362
369	Non-metal products n.e.c	6093	7353	8568	8881	...	64.1	62.4	58.5	53.2	...	369
371	Iron and steel	4176	5260	5893	5546	...	28.6	28.9	27.2	23.0	...	371
372	Non-ferrous metals	787	915	1048	1137	...	7.8	7.5	6.9	6.8	...	372
381	Metal products	7181	8536	9712	10884	...	61.5	70.2	68.6	64.9	...	381
382	Machinery n.e.c.	4524	5144	5979	6105	...	40.9	41.7	39.4	33.2	...	382
3825	Office,computing etc..	346	483	552	449	...	3.5	4.1	4.1	1.7	...	3825
383	Electrical machinery ...	6127	7290	8881	10875	...	48.1	51.5	60.0	49.5	...	383
3832	Radio,television etc..	2872	3368	4255	5186	...	23.0	25.7	24.9	23.5	...	3832
384	Transport equipment	12143	13716	14695	15220	...	76.4	77.3	64.5	56.8	...	384
3841	Shipbuilding, repair..	7714	8163	8154	8923	...	40.2	35.2	31.0	27.9	...	3841
3843	Motor vehicles	3531	4545	5429	5201	...	27.6	28.8	25.9	22.1	...	3843
385	Professional goods	509	630	739	900	...	5.1	5.1	5.1	5.2	...	385
390	Other industries	370	386	422	482	...	4.8	4.3	4.2	4.2	...	390
3	Manufacturing ..... b/	115554	134094	157270	176674	...	1174.7	1161.0	1140.5	1090.6	...	3
410	Electricity,gas,steam ..	5525	6597	8069	9365	...	34.3	30.8	30.1	29.1	...	410
4101	Electricity	5412	6456	7897	9172	...	33.7	30.3	29.6	28.6	...	4101
420	Water works and supply .	-	-	-	-	...	-	-	-	-	...	420
4	Electricity,gas etc	5525	6597	8069	9365	...	34.3	30.8	30.1	29.1	...	4
2-4	All industry b/	124388	144602	169864	190811	...	1237.3	1219.2	1196.9	1143.7	...	2-4

a/ Selected industries; for coverage, see country note. b/ Excluding major group 354.

ISIC	INDUSTRY	9. QUANTITY OF ELECTRICITY CONSUMED a/ (MILLION KWH)					10. OUTPUT IN PRODUCERS' PRICES a/ (BILLION ESCUDOS)					ISIC
		1981	1982	1983	1984	1985	1981	1982	1983	1984	1985	
210	Coal mining	5	6	6	6	...	0.5	0.6	0.9	1.3	...	210
220	Petroleum and gas	-	-	-	-	...	-	-	-	-	...	220
230	Metal ore mining	47	52	48	51	...	2.5	2.9	3.3	4.1	...	230
290	Other mining	66	74	81	79	...	8.6	9.6	11.1	12.5	...	290
2	Mining, quarrying .	118	132	135	136	...	11.6	13.1	15.3	17.9	...	2
311/2	Food products	552	530	554	510	...	187.4	218.6	325.0	427.2	...	311/2
313	Beverages	80	79	82	81	...	18.8	21.5	27.9	34.5	...	313
314	Tobacco	17	17	15	16	...	7.4	10.9	15.0	18.5	...	314
321	Textiles	1316	1257	1175	1243	...	132.7	152.2	201.9	235.2	...	321
3211	Spinning,weaving etc..	1166	1108	1032	1089	...	91.6	106.2	141.6	191.6	...	3211
322	Wearing apparel	39	49	54	56	...	30.8	38.6	50.2	68.8	...	322
323	Leather and products ...	21	30	28	26	...	8.0	10.3	15.1	21.8	...	323
324	Footwear	20	25	21	27	...	14.2	17.0	23.2	36.0	...	324
331	Wood products	285	306	263	290	...	41.9	43.6	54.1	69.7	...	331
332	Furniture, fixtures	56	25	32	34	...	9.3	9.6	11.2	12.0	...	332
341	Paper and products	923	875	956	912	...	45.4	51.2	67.9	108.1	...	341
3411	Pulp,paper etc.	823	842	917	869	...	36.0	39.8	53.6	86.7	...	3411
342	Printing,publishing	47	47	54	57	...	20.4	30.2	35.5	42.8	...	342
351	Industrial chemicals ...	949	1324	1113	1176	...	50.1	90.3	118.5	179.7	...	351
3511	Basic excl fertilizers	622	802	694	801	...	20.6	45.9	57.7	89.2	...	3511
3513	Synthetic resins etc .	211	348	291	308	...	16.9	26.9	41.1	61.0	...	3513
352	Other chemical products.	61	84	64	62	...	38.3	62.8	66.3	81.7	...	352
3522	Drugs and medicines ..	21	17	19	19	...	13.0	14.4	19.1	23.7	...	3522
353	Petroleum refineries ...	269	259	291	262	...	158.4	198.8	260.6	298.8	...	353
354	Petroleum,coal products.	...	...	...	...	...	...	...	...	...	...	354
355	Rubber products	62	64	66	72	...	9.7	10.6	13.0	18.4	...	355
356	Plastic products n.e.c..	424	209	200	181	...	22.5	23.0	30.7	37.9	...	356
361	Pottery,china etc	132	149	151	165	...	9.9	12.6	15.7	20.4	...	361
362	Glass and products	135	113	114	122	...	10.7	11.8	14.7	19.2	...	362
369	Non-metal products n.e.c	910	944	965	960	...	46.7	58.5	71.0	78.6	...	369
371	Iron and steel	892	1038	1004	1078	...	36.4	49.7	55.4	63.5	...	371
372	Non-ferrous metals	51	59	65	68	...	7.5	8.5	11.7	14.8	...	372
381	Metal products	203	223	208	214	...	46.1	55.3	64.4	72.4	...	381
382	Machinery n.e.c.	61	68	51	62	...	26.8	33.8	40.8	48.4	...	382
3825	Office,computing etc..	2	4	8	4	...	3.6	4.1	6.5	9.5	...	3825
383	Electrical machinery ...	130	139	144	150	...	49.0	62.5	87.2	113.1	...	383
3832	Radio,television etc..	49	46	54	59	...	22.7	31.2	44.7	61.8	...	3832
384	Transport equipment	173	201	184	188	...	63.0	72.6	85.1	88.6	...	384
3841	Shipbuilding, repair..	105	108	78	73	...	17.3	17.7	19.2	22.7	...	3841
3843	Motor vehicles	49	71	83	89	...	41.3	51.4	59.3	60.5	...	3843
385	Professional goods	11	9	8	7	...	2.0	2.8	3.7	4.8	...	385
390	Other industries	10	10	11	10	...	1.9	2.0	2.4	3.3	...	390
3	Manufacturing ..... b/	7829	8133	7873	8029	...	1095.4	1359.3	1768.2	2218.2	...	3
410	Electricity,gas,steam ..	709	693	851	812	...	c/ 1.8	c/ 2.1	c/ 2.9	c/ 4.1	...	410
4101	Electricity	678	664	814	781	...	...	...	...	...	...	4101
420	Water works and supply .	-	-	-	-	...	...	...	...	...	...	420
4	Electricity,gas etc	709	693	851	812	...	...	...	...	...	...	4
2-4	All industry b/	8656	8958	8859	8977	...	...	...	...	...	...	2-4

a/ Selected industries; for coverage, see country note.
b/ Excluding major group 354.
c/ Gas only.

ISIC	INDUSTRY	11. VALUE ADDED IN PRODUCERS' PRICES a/b/ (BILLION ESCUDOS)					12. GROSS FIXED CAPITAL FORMATION TOTAL a/ (MILLION ESCUDOS)					ISIC
		1981	1982	1983	1984	1985	1981	1982	1983	1984	1985	
210	Coal mining	0.49	0.60	0.86	1.22	...	...	...	...	...	...	210
220	Petroleum and gas	-	-	-	-	...	...	...	...	...	...	220
230	Metal ore mining	2.20	2.48	2.82	3.43	...	...	...	...	...	...	230
290	Other mining	7.12	7.53	8.64	11.82	...	...	...	...	...	...	290
2	Mining, quarrying	9.81	10.61	12.32	17.47	...	...	...	...	...	...	2
311/2	Food products	35.19	40.23	58.77	77.04	...	9749	8590	8645	10571	...	311/2
313	Beverages	9.79	9.98	14.07	16.35	...	2161	1855	1993	1410	...	313
314	Tobacco	4.12	6.83	8.86	11.83	...	540	669	952	742	...	314
321	Textiles	48.83	55.47	66.88	92.48	...	13472	12667	8904	10373	...	321
3211	Spinning,weaving etc..	34.68	38.32	47.21	68.32	...	11044	10031	5936	7457	...	3211
322	Wearing apparel	11.15	14.85	19.08	25.96	...	1092	1576	2184	2403	...	322
323	Leather and products	2.63	2.85	4.11	6.30	...	424	325	552	397	...	323
324	Footwear	5.68	6.38	8.04	12.17	...	912	1046	1265	1799	...	324
331	Wood products	14.14	14.90	19.18	22.86	...	2560	2280	3012	3324	...	331
332	Furniture, fixtures	4.50	4.06	4.64	4.97	...	564	620	648	481	...	332
341	Paper and products	17.57	17.56	23.22	43.28	...	5707	6213	26482	11863	...	341
3411	Pulp,paper etc.	14.47	13.84	19.35	37.65	...	5096	4979	25503	11095	...	3411
342	Printing,publishing	12.36	15.34	17.88	20.52	...	1574	2232	2246	1646	...	342
351	Industrial chemicals	6.90	6.48	16.70	27.51	...	11597	18893	11659	12932	...	351
3511	Basic excl fertilizers	3.89	1.11	7.70	15.04	...	7684	13471	10691	11631	...	3511
3513	Synthetic resins etc	4.47	5.53	7.15	10.77	...	2965	4824	982	860	...	3513
352	Other chemical products.	13.51	16.68	19.89	25.26	...	1607	2621	2414	2564	...	352
3522	Drugs and medicines	4.67	5.14	6.37	8.45	...	520	948	852	979	...	3522
353	Petroleum refineries	105.57	8.55	7.07	16.40	...	303	458	252	184	...	353
354	Petroleum,coal products.	...	...	...	...	...	...	...	...	...	...	354
355	Rubber products	3.70	3.63	4.15	6.20	...	1053	597	585	1123	...	355
356	Plastic products n.e.c..	8.13	7.69	9.39	12.59	...	1983	2213	1589	1518	...	356
361	Pottery,china etc	5.49	6.80	7.81	10.14	...	1315	2743	2263	2390	...	361
362	Glass and products	4.94	5.16	5.93	7.74	...	769	1533	1192	1085	...	362
369	Non-metal products n.e.c	18.44	21.20	28.20	32.22	...	4942	12325	7658	5400	...	369
371	Iron and steel	12.10	17.86	16.65	14.60	...	5139	12353	9135	6382	...	371
372	Non-ferrous metals	2.02	2.64	3.00	3.94	...	2255	1209	615	493	...	372
381	Metal products	17.91	22.78	26.78	27.98	...	3580	4556	3710	4830	...	381
382	Machinery n.e.c.	11.58	13.97	15.99	18.52	...	2175	2828	1955	2863	...	382
3825	Office,computing etc..	1.11	1.18	1.82	2.30	...	34	87	180	206	...	3825
383	Electrical machinery	18.70	24.53	33.70	44.58	...	3377	4511	5444	5626	...	383
3832	Radio,television etc..	7.34	11.20	15.18	22.89	...	1480	1946	2937	3086	...	3832
384	Transport equipment	19.11	23.23	27.37	26.75	...	5237	8432	5919	4402	...	384
3841	Shipbuilding, repair..	8.40	9.39	11.24	12.89	...	1612	1352	935	1058	...	3841
3843	Motor vehicles	9.43	11.67	14.02	12.67	...	3303	8122	4703	3208	...	3843
385	Professional goods	1.00	1.53	1.91	2.88	...	139	222	218	278	...	385
390	Other industries	0.96	0.91	1.00	1.59	...	89	133	152	133	...	390
3	Manufacturing c/	416.02	371.49	470.27	612.66	...	84315	113700	111643	97212	...	3
410	Electricity,gas,steam d/	0.81	0.83	1.38	2.08	...	133	114	88	147	...	410
4101	Electricity	...	...	...	...	...	...	...	...	...	...	4101
420	Water works and supply	...	...	...	...	...	...	...	...	...	...	420
4	Electricity,gas etc	...	...	...	...	...	...	...	...	...	...	4
2-4	All industry	...	...	...	...	...	...	...	...	...	...	2-4

a/ Selected industries; for coverage, see country note.
b/ Manufacturing: net of non-industrial costs.
c/ Excluding major group 354.
d/ Gas only.

ISIC	INDUSTRY	13. GROSS FIXED CAPITAL FORMATION MACHINERY AND EQUIPMENT a/ (MILLION ESCUDOS)					14. VALUE OF STOCKS AT END OF PERIOD TOTAL a/ (BILLION ESCUDOS)					ISIC
		1981	1982	1983	1984	1985	1981	1982	1983	1984	1985	
210	Coal mining	...	...	...	...	...	...	...	...	...	...	210
220	Petroleum and gas	...	...	...	...	...	...	...	...	...	...	220
230	Metal ore mining	...	...	...	...	...	...	...	...	...	...	230
290	Other mining	...	...	...	...	...	...	...	...	...	...	290
2	Mining, quarrying .	...	...	...	...	...	...	...	...	...	...	2
311/2	Food products	5712	5180	5010	6092	...	24.89	29.73	36.91	53.45	...	311/2
313	Beverages	1766	1371	1679	1268	...	3.10	5.31	5.54	7.51	...	313
314	Tobacco	149	429	791	604	...	3.93	5.15	7.02	8.93	...	314
321	Textiles	11455	9992	6943	8520	...	43.45	52.65	62.48	79.81	...	321
3211	Spinning,weaving etc..	9401	8083	4734	6268	...	31.05	38.49	45.62	58.74	...	3211
322	Wearing apparel	807	935	1195	1603	...	8.65	11.08	13.86	17.39	...	322
323	Leather and products ...	319	252	390	301	...	1.93	3.06	4.12	5.85	...	323
324	Footwear	644	704	822	1230	...	2.96	4.02	5.44	8.37	...	324
331	Wood products	1875	1755	1922	2165	...	14.78	16.34	18.42	22.17	...	331
332	Furniture, fixtures	461	447	353	283	...	3.27	4.38	4.92	5.69	...	332
341	Paper and products	4437	3887	23029	9881	...	10.18	11.49	11.89	20.76	...	341
3411	Pulp,paper etc.	4056	2999	22389	9324	...	8.84	9.80	9.72	17.99	...	3411
342	Printing,publishing	1372	2014	1663	1248	...	4.73	5.26	6.35	8.53	...	342
351	Industrial chemicals ...	8961	15566	9352	9233	...	13.73	16.38	20.00	22.44	...	351
3511	Basic excl fertilizers	5749	11087	8652	8219	...	6.40	7.66	9.82	10.19	...	3511
3513	Synthetic resins etc .	2820	4008	416	667	...	3.77	4.44	5.39	6.51	...	3513
352	Other chemical products.	1231	1689	1341	1472	...	11.37	14.38	16.21	19.30	...	352
3522	Drugs and medicines ..	360	484	445	551	...	4.65	5.26	5.93	6.39	...	3522
353	Petroleum refineries ...	304	458	254	185	...	38.21	47.51	49.27	67.59	...	353
354	Petroleum,coal products.	...	...	...	...	...	...	...	...	...	...	354
355	Rubber products	655	524	484	920	...	2.56	2.84	3.21	3.78	...	355
356	Plastic products n.e.c..	1655	1771	1226	1200	...	4.86	5.12	6.43	7.04	...	356
361	Pottery,china etc	993	2107	1680	1720	...	2.22	3.10	4.27	5.85	...	361
362	Glass and products	589	1268	972	942	...	3.05	3.77	4.63	5.52	...	362
369	Non-metal products n.e.c	4120	9955	5214	3398	...	7.56	10.09	12.76	14.32	...	369
371	Iron and steel	3841	10969	8742	5910	...	15.87	18.08	18.11	20.94	...	371
372	Non-ferrous metals	2218	863	533	417	...	2.08	2.08	2.58	2.69	...	372
381	Metal products	2651	3284	2573	3669	...	16.34	19.69	22.93	25.48	...	381
382	Machinery n.e.c.	1531	1793	984	1816	...	15.97	21.63	27.12	35.30	...	382
3825	Office,computing etc..	33	27	19	66	...	0.84	1.15	1.55	2.14	...	3825
383	Electrical machinery ...	2597	3424	4402	4707	...	15.35	19.64	26.07	28.47	...	383
3832	Radio,television etc..	1176	1746	2567	2802	...	6.71	8.29	11.86	13.38	...	3832
384	Transport equipment	1960	7274	4072	2694	...	25.45	33.65	34.33	37.50	...	384
3841	Shipbuilding, repair..	657	1052	538	498	...	13.89	18.04	15.82	21.47	...	3841
3843	Motor vehicles	1065	6002	3296	2091	...	9.46	13.17	14.79	13.22	...	3843
385	Professional goods	110	174	164	212	...	0.51	0.72	0.95	1.43	...	385
390	Other industries	78	113	138	84	...	0.65	0.72	0.82	0.78	...	390
3	Manufacturing ..... b/	62491	88198	85928	71774	...	297.65	367.87	426.64	536.89	...	3
410	Electricity,gas,steam ..	c/ 133	c/ 114	c/ 88	c/ 147	...	d/ 0.03	d/ 0.03	d/ 0.05	d/ 0.04	...	410
4101	Electricity	...	...	...	...	...	...	...	...	...	...	4101
420	Water works and supply .	...	...	...	...	...	...	...	...	...	...	420
4	Electricity,gas etc	...	...	...	...	...	...	...	...	...	...	4
2-4	All industry	...	...	...	...	...	...	...	...	...	...	2-4

a/ Selected industries; for coverage, see country note.
b/ Excluding major group 354.
c/ Gas only.
d/ Gas production only.

15. INDEX NUMBERS OF INDUSTRIAL PRODUCTION (1980 = 100)

ISIC	INDUSTRY	1976	1977	1978	1979	1981	1982	1983	1984	1985	a/ RATE	ISIC
210	Coal mining	109	110	102	101	104	101	104	107	134	2.3	210
220	Petroleum and gas	...	...	...	...	...	...	...	...	...	...	220
230	Metal ore mining	86	69	74	91	89	90	79	102	111	2.9	230
290	Other mining	88	85	78	93	84	80	82	101	95	0.9	290
2	Mining, quarrying .	88	75	76	92	88	87	81	97	109	2.4	2
311/2	Food products	81	88	94	96	104	100	105	98	97	2.0	311/2
313	Beverages	81	83	100	105	110	105	105	97	98	2.1	313
314	Tobacco	96	99	102	102	103	104	119	112	117	2.2	314
321	Textiles .... b/	80	77	78	92	97	99	102	106	118	4.4	321
3211	Spinning,weaving etc..	...	...	...	...	...	...	...	...	...	...	3211
322	Wearing apparel .... b/	...	...	...	...	...	...	...	...	...	...	322
323	Leather and products ...	80	87	96	96	103	112	124	119	112	3.8	323
324	Footwear .... b/	...	...	...	...	...	...	...	...	...	...	324
331	Wood products	[76	85	88	96	96	92	105	100	106	3.8]	331
332	Furniture, fixtures											332
341	Paper and products	70	81	78	89	105	108	117	124	143	8.3	341
3411	Pulp,paper etc.	...	...	...	...	...	...	...	...	...	...	3411
342	Printing,publishing	...	...	...	...	...	...	...	...	...	...	342
351	Industrial chemicals ... c/	76	83	90	100	98	110	105	112	120	5.2	351
3511	Basic excl fertilizers	...	...	...	...	...	...	...	...	...	...	3511
3513	Synthetic resins etc .	...	...	...	...	...	...	...	...	...	...	3513
352	Other chemical products. c/	...	...	...	...	...	...	...	...	...	...	352
3522	Drugs and medicines ..	...	...	...	...	...	...	...	...	...	...	3522
353	Petroleum refineries ...	[73	74	78	97	104	100	106	94	109	4.6]	353
354	Petroleum,coal products.											354
355	Rubber products	77	96	97	98	104	102	101	108	111	4.1	355
356	Plastic products n.e.c..	...	...	...	...	...	...	...	...	...	...	356
361	Pottery,china etc	[									]	361
362	Glass and products	72	82	90	91	106	110	114	115	118	5.6	362
369	Non-metal products n.e.c											369
371	Iron and steel	[57	74	91	89	95	112	102	107	104	6.9]	371
372	Non-ferrous metals											372
381	Metal products	71	84	92	88	94	100	92	87	78	1.1	381
382	Machinery n.e.c.	73	95	88	96	114	140	126	95	90	2.4	382
3825	Office,computing etc..	...	...	...	...	...	...	...	...	...	...	3825
383	Electrical machinery ...	56	68	76	86	101	116	119	108	116	8.4	383
3832	Radio,television etc..	...	...	...	...	...	...	...	...	...	...	3832
384	Transport equipment	71	90	83	77	110	106	79	63	63	-1.3	384
3841	Shipbuilding, repair..	...	...	...	...	...	...	...	...	...	...	3841
3843	Motor vehicles	...	...	...	...	...	...	...	...	...	...	3843
385	Professional goods	...	...	...	...	...	...	...	...	...	...	385
390	Other industries	62	76	79	90	97	105	96	92	97	5.1	390
3	Manufacturing ..... d/	74	82	88	93	101	105	106	105	117	5.2	3
410	Electricity,gas,steam ..	...	...	...	...	...	...	...	...	...	...	410
4101	Electricity	67	90	94	108	91	102	117	126	127	7.4	4101
420	Water works and supply .	.	.	.	.	.	.	.	.	.	.	420
4	Electricity,gas etc	...	...	...	...	...	...	...	...	...	...	4
2-4	All industry d/	73	83	88	95	100	105	107	106	118	5.5	2-4

a/ Annual growth rate 1976-1985.
b/ Major groups 322 and 324 are included in 321.
c/ Major group 352 is included in 351.
d/ Excluding printing and publishing.

PUERTO RICO

The information in the tables is based on the reply to the United Nations Questionnaire on General Industrial Statistics from the Puerto Rico Planning Board, Puerto Rico. The concepts, definitions and classification by branches of industry are generally in accordance with United Nations standards.

The data in the tables are derived from the census of employment in the manufacturing industries, which is undertaken annually by the Puerto Rico Department of Labor and Human Resources. For 1981, the inquiry covers establishments with at least one paid employee operating during a specified week of October. The information is obtained by means of a canvass of these establishments by the field force of the Bureau of Labor Statistics. In 1982, no census was taken and, therefore, the estimates are based on the results of the monthly survey. Beginning 1983, the census is conducted in March of each year.

The data are compiled according to an updated industrial classification scheme of the United States Bureau of the Budget. In the tables, the data have been adjusted to represent the present version of ISIC. The following difference should be noted: manufacture of ordnance and accessories (ISIC 382) is included in ISIC 381.

Numbers of employees, for 1981, refer to persons who worked during, or received pay for all or any part of the pay period ending nearest the 15th of October of the year under review. The estimates for 1982 are based on the results of the monthly survey, and beginning 1983, the data refer to a period in March of the year indicated. Data on operatives relate to production and related workers. These workers are defined as working foremen and all non-supervisory workers (including trainees and apprentices) engaged in fabricating, processing, assembling, inspecting, receiving, storing, handling, packing, warehousing, repair and maintenance of machinery and building, production for plant's own use (for example, power plant), record keeping and other services closely associated with the above production operations.

Wages and salaries of operatives represent average weekly earnings of production and related workers. Estimates are obtained by multiplying the weekly hours worked by these workers by the average hourly earnings. Payments for sick leave, paid holidays and paid vacations are included, but payments for vacations not taken, retroactive pay not earned during the period reported, value of payments in kind and irregular bonuses and commissions are excluded.

Estimates of hours worked by operatives are calculated by multiplying the number of production and related workers by the average weekly hours worked or paid for. Time spent on stand-by or reporting, vacation, sick leave and holidays is included. Overtime hours are excluded.

Related national publication:

<u>Census of Manufacturing Industries of Puerto Rico</u> (annual), published by the Puerto Rico Department of Labor and Human Resources, Puerto Rico.

ISIC	INDUSTRY	1. NUMBER OF ESTABLISHMENTS (NUMBER) 1981	1982	1983	1984	1985	2. AVERAGE NUMBER OF EMPLOYEES (THOUSANDS) a/ 1981	b/ 1982	c/ 1983	c/ 1984	c/ 1985	ISIC
210	Coal mining	...	...	...	...	...	...	...	...	...	...	210
220	Petroleum and gas	...	...	...	...	...	...	...	...	...	...	220
230	Metal ore mining	...	...	...	...	...	...	...	...	...	...	230
290	Other mining	...	...	...	...	...	...	...	...	...	...	290
2	Mining, quarrying .	...	...	...	...	...	...	...	...	...	...	2
311/2	Food products	[379]	...	[358	320	277	21.79]	17.86	[22.66	22.96	23.20]	311/2
313	Beverages		...					3.79				313
314	Tobacco	15	...	11	10	10	1.67	1.23	1.08	0.96	0.80	314
321	Textiles	26	...	25	24	22	3.23	2.46	2.64	2.63	2.79	321
3211	Spinning,weaving etc..	...	...	...	...	...	...	...	...	...	...	3211
322	Wearing apparel	304	...	293	286	269	33.63	30.29	30.15	33.03	30.08	322
323	Leather and products ...	[38]	...	[41	36	34	5.20]	1.71	[5.40	5.46	4.85]	323
324	Footwear		...					3.43				324
331	Wood products	[244]	...	[211	209	208	3.39]	0.86	[2.64	3.03	3.13]	331
332	Furniture, fixtures		...					2.17				332
341	Paper and products	d/ 157	...	d/ 154	d/ 156	d/ 155	d/ 4.88	1.50	d/ 4.79	d/ 4.87	d/ 4.68	341
3411	Pulp,paper etc.	...	...	...	...	...	...	...	...	...	...	3411
342	Printing,publishing	d/	...	d/	d/	d/	d/	3.09	d/	d/	d/	342
351	Industrial chemicals ...	e/ 166	...	e/ 162	e/ 164	e/ 174	e/ 15.83	f/ 1.34	e/ 15.95	e/ 15.99	e/ 17.15	351
3511	Basic excl fertilizers	...	...	...	...	...	...	...	...	...	...	3511
3513	Synthetic resins etc .	...	...	...	...	...	...	...	...	...	...	3513
352	Other chemical products.	e/	...	e/	e/	e/	e/	f/ 14.08	e/	e/	e/	352
3522	Drugs and medicines ..	...	...	...	...	...	11.75	11.83	12.33	...	...	3522
353	Petroleum refineries ...	[92]	...	[92	90	93	6.90]	[1.57]	[5.97	6.60	6.73]	353
354	Petroleum,coal products.		...									354
355	Rubber products		...					1.96				355
356	Plastic products n.e.c..		...					1.17				356
361	Pottery,china etc	[170]	...	[153	154	148	4.31]	g/ 0.74	[3.83	3.85	3.82]	361
362	Glass and products		...					0.94				362
369	Non-metal products n.e.c		...					g/ 2.02				369
371	Iron and steel	[h/ 248]	...	[h/ 223	h/ 220	h/ 210	h/ 4.77]	[0.84]	[h/ 3.99	h/ 4.24	h/ 4.48]	371
372	Non-ferrous metals		...									372
381	Metal products		...					h/ 3.31				381
382	Machinery n.e.c. .... h/	i/ 105	...	i/ 102	i/ 107	i/ 93	i/ 9.57	8.41	i/ 10.06	i/ 10.12	i/ 7.59	382
3825	Office,computing etc..	...	...	...	...	...	...	...	...	...	...	3825
383	Electrical machinery ...	135	...	141	136	148	19.77	17.21	18.27	22.86	22.88	383
3832	Radio,television etc..	...	...	...	...	...	4.09	3.82	4.76	...	...	3832
384	Transport equipment	i/	...	i/	i/	i/	i/	0.65	i/	i/	i/	384
3841	Shipbuilding, repair..	...	...	...	...	...	...	...	...	...	...	3841
3843	Motor vehicles	...	...	...	...	...	...	...	...	...	...	3843
385	Professional goods	93	...	87	87	93	13.11	12.98	12.17	12.87	13.75	385
390	Other industries	83	...	78	71	70	3.63	3.32	3.16	3.15	2.85	390
3	Manufacturing	2255	...	2131	2070	2004	151.68	138.93	142.76	152.62	148.78	3
410	Electricity,gas,steam ..	...	...	...	...	...	...	...	...	...	...	410
4101	Electricity	...	...	...	...	...	...	...	...	...	...	4101
420	Water works and supply .	...	...	...	...	...	...	...	...	...	...	420
4	Electricity,gas etc	...	...	...	...	...	...	...	...	...	...	4
2-4	All industry	...	...	...	...	...	...	...	...	...	...	2-4

a/ In a pay period of October of the year indicated.
b/ Based on estimates from the monthly survey.
c/ In a pay period in March of the year indicated.
d/ Major group 342 is included in 341.
e/ Major group 352 is included in 351.
f/ Manufacture of agricultural chemicals is included in major group 352.
g/ Manufacture of structural clay products and Portland cement is included in major group 361.
h/ Manufacture of ordnance and accessories is included in major group 381.
i/ Major group 384 is included in 382.

ISIC	INDUSTRY	3. AVERAGE NUMBER OF OPERATIVES (THOUSANDS)					4. WAGES AND SALARIES OF OPERATIVES a/ (THOUSAND DOLLARS)					ISIC
		b/ 1981	c/ 1982	d/ 1983	d/ 1984	d/ 1985	1981	c/ 1982	1983	1984	1985	
210	Coal mining	...	...	...	...	...	...	...	...	...	...	210
220	Petroleum and gas	...	...	...	...	...	...	...	...	...	...	220
230	Metal ore mining	...	...	...	...	...	...	...	...	...	...	230
290	Other mining	...	...	...	...	...	...	...	...	...	...	290
2	Mining, quarrying	...	...	...	...	...	...	...	...	...	...	2
311/2	Food products	[14.26]	12.93	[15.66	16.16	16.54]	2377]	2198	[2693	2988	3255]	311/2
313	Beverages	[	1.58	[				330	[			313
314	Tobacco	1.50	1.07	0.93	0.80	0.67	255	194	127	159	140	314
321	Textiles	2.94	2.22	2.42	2.41	2.53	438	309	334	386	406	321
3211	Spinning, weaving etc.	...	...	...	...	...	...	...	...	...	...	3211
322	Wearing apparel	31.51	28.07	28.06	31.08	28.21	4220	3658	3834	4397	3832	322
323	Leather and products	[4.86]	1.60	[5.04	5.13	4.49]	671]	235	[743	745	706]	323
324	Footwear	[	3.22	[				452	[			324
331	Wood products	[2.65]	0.69	[2.01	2.39	2.45]	337]	87	[270	339	351]	331
332	Furniture, fixtures	[	1.78	[				228	[			332
341	Paper and products	e/ 2.91	1.02	e/ 2.85	e/ 2.78	e/ 2.68	e/ 528	172	e/ 554	e/ 569	e/ 562	341
3411	Pulp, paper etc.	...	...	...	...	...	...	...	...	...	...	3411
342	Printing, publishing	e/	1.49	e/	e/	e/	e/	293	e/	e/	e/	342
351	Industrial chemicals	f/ 10.41	g/ 0.72	f/ 10.67	f/ 10.79	f/ 11.49	f/ 2543	g/ 284	f/ 3093	f/ 3175	f/ 3471	351
3511	Basic excl fertilizers	...	...	...	...	...	...	...	...	...	...	3511
3513	Synthetic resins etc	...	...	...	...	...	...	...	...	...	...	3513
352	Other chemical products	f/	g/ 9.40	f/	f/	f/	f/	g/ 2435	f/	f/	f/	352
3522	Drugs and medicines	7.92	8.01	8.40	...	...	1974	2167	2371	...	...	3522
353	Petroleum refineries	[	[0.86]	[				[341]	[			353
354	Petroleum, coal products	[4.93]		[4.57	5.03	5.29	986]		[942	1063	1139]	354
355	Rubber products	[	1.71	[				278	[			355
356	Plastic products n.e.c.	[	0.88	[				183	[			356
361	Pottery, china etc	[	h/ 0.47	[				h/ 113	[			361
362	Glass and products	[3.12]	0.76	[2.78	2.83	2.85	543]	148	[526	570	582]	362
369	Non-metal products n.e.c	[	h/ 1.48	[				h/ 247	[			369
371	Iron and steel	[	[0.63]	[				[131]	[			371
372	Non-ferrous metals	[i/ 3.69]		[i/ 3.01	i/ 3.24	i/ 3.46	i/ 702]		[i/ 620	i/ 684	i/ 721]	372
381	Metal products	[	i/ 2.58	[				i/ 485	[			381
382	Machinery n.e.c. i/	j/ 7.33	6.32	j/ 7.61	j/ 7.87	j/ 5.95	j/ 1437	1294	j/ 1575	j/ 1647	j/ 1281	382
3825	Office, computing etc.	...	...	...	...	...	...	...	...	...	...	3825
383	Electrical machinery	17.24	14.63	15.31	19.33	18.86	3156	2872	3022	4304	4120	383
3832	Radio, television etc.	3.62	3.31	3.86	...	...	574	604	726	...	...	3832
384	Transport equipment	j/	0.53	j/	j/	j/	j/	80	j/	j/	j/	384
3841	Shipbuilding, repair	...	...	...	...	...	...	...	...	...	...	3841
3843	Motor vehicles	...	...	...	...	...	...	...	...	...	...	3843
385	Professional goods	11.05	10.88	10.32	10.88	11.32	1998	2145	2104	2300	2636	385
390	Other industries	3.15	2.85	2.74	2.67	2.39	561	500	528	532	427	390
3	Manufacturing	121.55	110.37	113.98	123.39	119.18	20752	19692	20965	23858	23629	3
410	Electricity, gas, steam	...	...	...	...	...	...	...	...	...	...	410
4101	Electricity	...	...	...	...	...	...	...	...	...	...	4101
420	Water works and supply	...	...	...	...	...	...	...	...	...	...	420
4	Electricity, gas etc	...	...	...	...	...	...	...	...	...	...	4
2-4	All industry	...	...	...	...	...	...	...	...	...	...	2-4

a/ Weekly average. Excluding payments in kind.
b/ In a pay period of October of the year indicated.
c/ Based on estimates from the monthly survey.
d/ In a pay period in March of the year indicated.
e/ Major group 342 is included in 341.
f/ Major group 352 is included in 351.
g/ Manufacture of agricultural chemicals is included in major group 352.
h/ Manufacture of structural clay products and Portland cement is included in major group 361.
i/ Manufacture of ordnance and accessories is included in major group 381.
j/ Major group 384 is included in 382.

5. HOURS WORKED BY OPERATIVES a/ (THOUSANDS)

ISIC	INDUSTRY	1981	1982 b/	1983	1984	1985	ISIC
210	Coal mining	...	...	...	...	...	210
220	Petroleum and gas	...	...	...	...	...	220
230	Metal ore mining	...	...	...	...	...	230
290	Other mining	...	...	...	...	...	290
2	Mining, quarrying .	...	...	...	...	...	2
311/2	Food products	538	483	586	612	628	311/2
313	Beverages		61				313
314	Tobacco	57	42	24	31	26	314
321	Textiles	110	75	81	94	92	321
3211	Spinning,weaving etc..	...	...	...	...	...	3211
322	Wearing apparel	1135	973	993	1119	972	322
323	Leather and products ...	182	59	190	187	170	323
324	Footwear		118				324
331	Wood products	93	24	72	88	90	331
332	Furniture, fixtures		59				332
341	Paper and products	c/ 115	37	c/ 107	c/ 111	c/ 106	341
3411	Pulp,paper etc.	...	...	...	...	...	3411
342	Printing,publishing	c/	56	c/	c/	c/	342
351	Industrial chemicals ...	d/ 436	e/ 30	d/ 454	d/ 453	d/ 487	351
3511	Basic excl fertilizers	...	...	...	...	...	3511
3513	Synthetic resins etc .	...	...	...	...	...	3513
352	Other chemical products.	d/	e/ 392	d/	d/	d/	352
3522	Drugs and medicines ..	340	341	357	...	...	3522
353	Petroleum refineries ...		36				353
354	Petroleum,coal products.	178		177	198	198	354
355	Rubber products		66				355
356	Plastic products n.e.c..		35				356
361	Pottery,china etc		f/ 20				361
362	Glass and products	120	30	109	115	115	362
369	Non-metal products n.e.c		f/ 53				369
371	Iron and steel		29				371
372	Non-ferrous metals	g/ 138		g/ 119	g/ 129	g/ 136	372
381	Metal products		g/ 96				381
382	Machinery n.e.c. .... g/	h/ 301	248	h/ 315	h/ 332	h/ 248	382
3825	Office,computing etc..	...	...	...	...	...	3825
383	Electrical machinery ...	685	595	617	798	760	383
3832	Radio,television etc..	144	145	158	...	...	3832
384	Transport equipment	h/	18	h/	h/	h/	384
3841	Shipbuilding, repair..	...	...	...	...	...	3841
3843	Motor vehicles	...	...	...	...	...	3843
385	Professional goods	443	445	416	445	476	385
390	Other industries	125	108	106	107	88	390
3	Manufacturing	4656	4188	4366	4819	4592	3
410	Electricity,gas,steam ..	...	...	...	...	...	410
4101	Electricity	...	...	...	...	...	4101
420	Water works and supply .	...	...	...	...	...	420
4	Electricity,gas etc	...	...	...	...	...	4
2-4	All industry	...	...	...	...	...	2-4

a/ Weekly average. Excluding overtime.
b/ Based on estimates from the monthly survey.
c/ Major group 342 is included in 341.
d/ Major group 352 is included in 351.
e/ Manufacture of agricultural chemicals is included in major group 352.
f/ Manufacture of structural clay products and Portland cement is included in major group 361.
g/ Manufacture of ordnance and accessories is included in major group 381.
h/ Major group 384 is included in 382.

The information on industrial activity is based on the reply to the United Nations Questionnaire on General Industrial Statistics from the Central Statistical Office, Bucharest. The concepts, definitions and classification by branches of industry are in keeping with national methodology.

The estimates are generally derived from statistical reports collected regularly by the Central Statistical Office from enterprises in the socialist sector. The socialist sector of industry comprises State enterprises under the direction of the central Government and local authorities, as well as industrial co-operatives. Estimates covering State enterprises under the direction of the central Government only are annotated in the tables. The classification by branches of industry is generally based on the output of the enterprise in accordance with prevalent activities of enterprises. However, where output covers several branches, as in the case of local industry and co-operatives, individual units are classified under different branches.

The estimates are based on the national classification. The figures do not include information on publishing, gas and water distribution. Owing to the lack of detail, adjustments have not been made for the following activities: manufacture of wearing apparel of leather and fur (ISIC 322) is included in ISIC 323; cellulose manufacturing (ISIC 351) is included in ISIC 341; maching building industry (ISIC 381-385) is included in ISIC 381-382 combined. Repair services are included in the following industries for all years: manufacture of textiles (ISIC 321), wearing apparel (ISIC 322), leather and leather products and footwear (ISIC 323-324 combined).

The employment estimates relate to the average annual registered number of employees in the socialist sector, excluding employees of industrial units attached to enterprises whose basic activity is non-industrial. Working proprietors and unpaid family workers are not found in the socialist sector. Persons engaged in artisan's shops and small-scale private industry not covered by these estimates account for less than 2 per cent of total employment in industry.

The data for wages and salaries are available as monthly averages per employee and operative for all industry only as follows (in lei):

	1981	1982	1983	1984	1985
Monthly average per employee	2 342	2 540	2 621	2 812	2 824
Monthly average per operative	2 277	2 481	2 560	2 749	2 769

The estimates of gross fixed capital formation are also obtained from statistical reports. Data relate to investments from State, co-operative and other funds for building and putting into operation new fixed productive and non-productive assets, as well as investments for expanding, rebuilding and re-equipping existing enterprises.

The indexes of industrial production are compiled by the Central Statistical Office and provided in response to the United Nations Questionnaire on Indexes of Industrial Production. In principle, the indexes cover all industrial establishments.

Related national publication:
Anuarul Statistic al Republicii Socialiste Romania published by the Central Statistical Office, Bucharest.

ISIC	INDUSTRY		1. NUMBER OF ENTERPRISES a/ (NUMBER) 1981	1982	1983	1984	1985	2. AVERAGE NUMBER OF EMPLOYEES a/ (THOUSANDS) 1981	1982	1983	1984	1985	ISIC
210	Coal mining	b/	45	45	66	68	70	138	132	157	168	178	210
220	Petroleum and gas												220
230	Metal ore mining	c/	...	...	...	...	...	...	...	...	...	...	230
290	Other mining	d/	...	...	...	...	...	...	...	...	...	...	290
2	Mining, quarrying .		...	...	...	...	...	...	...	...	...	...	2
311/2	Food products												311/2
313	Beverages		298	291	298	299	301	189	187	191	191	186	313
314	Tobacco												314
321	Textiles		180	185	187	188	188	325	337	342	338	336	321
3211	Spinning,weaving etc..		...	...	...	...	...	...	...	...	...	...	3211
322	Wearing apparel		...	...	...	...	...	...	...	...	...	...	322
323	Leather and products ...		39	40	39	39	39	83	88	88	89	89	323
324	Footwear												324
331	Wood products		80	80	80	79	78	274	280	279	279	273	331
332	Furniture, fixtures												332
341	Paper and products		18	18	18	18	14	32	32	33	34	33	341
3411	Pulp,paper etc.		...	...	...	...	...	...	...	...	...	...	3411
342	Printing,publishing		17	17	17	17	16	18	18	18	18	17	342
351	Industrial chemicals ...	e/	82	85	87	91	88	201	220	209	213	210	351
3511	Basic excl fertilizers		...	...	...	...	...	...	...	...	...	...	3511
3513	Synthetic resins etc .		...	...	...	...	...	...	...	...	...	...	3513
352	Other chemical products.	e/	...	...	...	...	...	...	...	...	...	...	352
3522	Drugs and medicines ..		...	...	...	...	...	...	...	...	...	...	3522
353	Petroleum refineries ...	b/	...	...	...	...	...	...	...	...	...	...	353
354	Petroleum,coal products.	b/	...	...	...	...	...	...	...	...	...	...	354
355	Rubber products	e/	...	...	...	...	...	...	...	...	...	...	355
356	Plastic products n.e.c..	e/	...	...	...	...	...	...	...	...	...	...	356
361	Pottery,china etc		30	31	32	31	30	55	57	58	57	57	361
362	Glass and products												362
369	Non-metal products n.e.c	d/	64	64	64	64	59	102	100	96	96	93	369
371	Iron and steel	c/	29	31	31	31	30	151	153	160	164	170	371
372	Non-ferrous metals	c/	20	20	21	21	22	85	85	86	87	93	372
381	Metal products	f/	320	325	329	335	331	1099	1117	1200	1161	1187	381
382	Machinery n.e.c.												382
3825	Office,computing etc..		...	...	...	...	...	...	...	...	...	...	3825
383	Electrical machinery ...	f/	...	...	...	...	...	...	...	...	...	...	383
3832	Radio,television etc..		...	...	...	...	...	...	...	...	...	...	3832
384	Transport equipment	f/	...	...	...	...	...	...	...	...	...	...	384
3841	Shipbuilding, repair..		...	...	...	...	...	...	...	...	...	...	3841
3843	Motor vehicles		...	...	...	...	...	...	...	...	...	...	3843
385	Professional goods	f/	...	...	...	...	...	...	...	...	...	...	385
390	Other industries		...	...	...	...	...	...	...	...	...	...	390
3	Manufacturing		...	...	...	...	...	...	...	...	...	...	3
410	Electricity,gas,steam ..		...	...	...	...	...	...	...	...	...	...	410
4101	Electricity		...	...	...	...	...	...	...	...	...	...	4101
420	Water works and supply .		...	...	...	...	...	...	...	...	...	...	420
4	Electricity,gas etc		...	...	...	...	...	...	...	...	...	...	4
2-4	All industry	g/	1793	1820	1896	1909	1913	3266	3330	3455	3446	3504	2-4

Note: For certain deviations in classification, see country note.

a/ Estimates relate to state enterprises under the direction of the central government.
b/ Major groups 353 and 354 are included in 210 and 220 combined. c/ Part of major group 230 is included in 371 and part in 372.
d/ Major group 290 is included in 369. e/ Major groups 352, 355 and 356 are included in 351.
f/ Major groups 383 to 385 are included in 381 and 382 combined.
g/ For industry as a whole, all enterprises of national economy are included.

ISIC	INDUSTRY		3. AVERAGE NUMBER OF OPERATIVES a/ (THOUSANDS) 1981	1982	1983	1984	1985	4. QUANTITY OF ELECTRICITY CONSUMED a/b/ (KWH) 1981	1982	1983	1984	1985	ISIC
210	Coal mining	c/	125	117	140	148	157	48473	40103	46737	47591	45762	210
220	Petroleum and gas												220
230	Metal ore mining	d/	...	...	...	...	...	...	...	...	...	...	230
290	Other mining	e/	...	...	...	...	...	...	...	...	...	...	290
2	Mining, quarrying		...	...	...	...	...	...	...	...	...	...	2
311/2	Food products		171	168	171	169	163	7618	7654	7657	9022	8556	311/2
313	Beverages												313
314	Tobacco												314
321	Textiles		303	312	315	309	308	5586	5186	5438	5458	5362	321
3211	Spinning,weaving etc.		...	...	...	...	...	...	...	...	...	...	3211
322	Wearing apparel		...	...	...	...	...	...	...	...	...	...	322
323	Leather and products		78	82	82	82	82	1668	1601	1493	1539	1520	323
324	Footwear												324
331	Wood products		255	257	255	253	246	4553	4623	4347	4558	4540	331
332	Furniture, fixtures												332
341	Paper and products		29	29	30	31	30	59512	57923	56052	57670	48198	341
3411	Pulp,paper etc.		...	...	...	...	...	...	...	...	...	...	3411
342	Printing,publishing		17	16	16	16	15	2265	2294	2270	2316	1866	342
351	Industrial chemicals	f/	181	196	185	186	182	51225	56642	51500	53657	55444	351
3511	Basic excl fertilizers		...	...	...	...	...	...	...	...	...	...	3511
3513	Synthetic resins etc		...	...	...	...	...	...	...	...	...	...	3513
352	Other chemical products.	f/	...	...	...	...	...	...	...	...	...	...	352
3522	Drugs and medicines		...	...	...	...	...	...	...	...	...	...	3522
353	Petroleum refineries	c/	...	...	...	...	...	...	...	...	...	...	353
354	Petroleum,coal products.	c/	...	...	...	...	...	...	...	...	...	...	354
355	Rubber products	f/	...	...	...	...	...	...	...	...	...	...	355
356	Plastic products n.e.c..	f/	...	...	...	...	...	...	...	...	...	...	356
361	Pottery,china etc		50	52	52	51	51	6669	6744	6596	6794	6617	361
362	Glass and products												362
369	Non-metal products n.e.c	e/	92	89	85	85	82	25019	26114	26304	26505	25149	369
371	Iron and steel	d/	138	139	144	146	152	53490	54397	53286	56876	54915	371
372	Non-ferrous metals	d/	77	77	77	77	83	68363	60479	65246	70485	67714	372
381	Metal products	g/	970	976	989	997	1014	6256	6225	6259	6601	6693	381
382	Machinery n.e.c.												382
3825	Office,computing etc..		...	...	...	...	...	...	...	...	...	...	3825
383	Electrical machinery	g/	...	...	...	...	...	...	...	...	...	...	383
3832	Radio,television etc..		...	...	...	...	...	...	...	...	...	...	3832
384	Transport equipment	g/	...	...	...	...	...	...	...	...	...	...	384
3841	Shipbuilding, repair..		...	...	...	...	...	...	...	...	...	...	3841
3843	Motor vehicles		...	...	...	...	...	...	...	...	...	...	3843
385	Professional goods	g/	...	...	...	...	...	...	...	...	...	...	385
390	Other industries		...	...	...	...	...	...	...	...	...	...	390
3	Manufacturing		...	...	...	...	...	...	...	...	...	...	3
410	Electricity,gas,steam		...	...	...	...	...	...	...	...	...	...	410
4101	Electricity		...	...	...	...	...	...	...	...	...	...	4101
420	Water works and supply		...	...	...	...	...	...	...	...	...	...	420
4	Electricity,gas etc		...	...	...	...	...	...	...	...	...	...	4
2-4	All industry	h/	2961	2997	3040	3059	3100	16739	16594	16664	17593	17374	2-4

Note: For certain deviations in classification, see country note.

a/ Estimates relate to state enterprises under the direction of the central government.
b/ Electricity consumed per operative. Including the technological consumption of electric power stations.
c/ Major groups 353 and 354 are included in 210 and 220 combined. d/ Part of major group 230 is included in 371 and part in 372.
e/ Major group 290 is included in 369. f/ Major groups 352, 355 and 356 are included in 351.
g/ Major groups 383 to 385 are included in 381 and 382 combined.
h/ For industry as a whole, all enterprises of national economy are included.

5. GROSS FIXED CAPITAL FORMATION
TOTAL a/
(MILLION LEI)

ISIC	INDUSTRY		1981	1982	1983	1984	1985	ISIC
210	Coal mining		5427	6144	8182	8788	9844	210
220	Petroleum and gas	b/	1275	1611	1845	1577	2060	220
230	Metal ore mining		...	...	...	...	...	230
290	Other mining		554	272	775	1474	1240	290
2	Mining, quarrying .		...	...	...	...	...	2
311/2	Food products		[5833	6822	8070	8164	5890]	311/2
313	Beverages							313
314	Tobacco							314
321	Textiles		3497	2440	2107	2255	1593	321
3211	Spinning,weaving etc..		...	...	...	...	...	3211
322	Wearing apparel		246	340	385	435	613	322
323	Leather and products ...		[305	290	294	239	322]	323
324	Footwear							324
331	Wood products		[2040	2375	2571	2977	2750]	331
332	Furniture, fixtures							332
341	Paper and products		1112	971	1691	1632	1546	341
3411	Pulp,paper etc.		...	...	...	...	...	3411
342	Printing,publishing		144	91	50	70	94	342
351	Industrial chemicals ...	c/	15554	13002	12555	12862	11340	351
3511	Basic excl fertilizers		...	...	...	...	...	3511
3513	Synthetic resins etc .		...	...	...	...	...	3513
352	Other chemical products.		9	18	25	114	68	352
3522	Drugs and medicines ..		...	...	...	...	...	3522
353	Petroleum refineries ...	d/	8448	10121	10794	13018	12621	353
354	Petroleum,coal products.		1177	973	1136	1651	1178	354
355	Rubber products	c/	...	...	...	...	...	355
356	Plastic products n.e.c..	c/	...	...	...	...	...	356
361	Pottery,china etc		[497	391	361	371	339]	361
362	Glass and products							362
369	Non-metal products n.e.c		3521	2877	2402	2314	2184	369
371	Iron and steel	d/	10089	8700	8186	9043	7738	371
372	Non-ferrous metals	d/	2475	2813	3339	4170	4103	372
381	Metal products	e/	[27346	21373	23257	25686	23900]	381
382	Machinery n.e.c.							382
3825	Office,computing etc..		...	...	...	...	...	3825
383	Electrical machinery ...	e/	...	...	...	...	...	383
3832	Radio,television etc..		...	...	...	...	...	3832
384	Transport equipment	e/	...	...	...	...	...	384
3841	Shipbuilding, repair..		...	...	...	...	...	3841
3843	Motor vehicles		...	...	...	...	...	3843
385	Professional goods	e/	...	...	...	...	...	385
390	Other industries		1661	1434	1335	1227	1397	390
3	Manufacturing		...	...	...	...	...	3
410	Electricity,gas,steam ..	f/	14280	18487	22324	26027	28301	410
4101	Electricity		...	...	...	...	...	4101
420	Water works and supply .		.	...	...	...	...	420
4	Electricity,gas etc	f/	14280	18487	22324	26027	28301	4
2-4	All industry		105490	101545	111684	124094	119121	2-4

a/ At current prices.
b/ Gas methane mining.
c/ Major groups 355 and 356 are included in 351.
d/ Including mining.
e/ Major groups 383 to 385 are included in 381 and 382 combined.
f/ Excluding gas manufacture and distribution.

6. INDEX NUMBERS OF INDUSTRIAL PRODUCTION (1980 = 100)

ISIC	INDUSTRY		1976	1977	1978	1979	1981	1982	1983	1984	1985	a/ RATE	ISIC
210	Coal mining		76	81	85	93	98	99	110	114	113	4.5	210
220	Petroleum and gas		111	114	110	103	105	107	110	111	107	-0.4	220
230	Metal ore mining		75	85	92	98	104	102	104	114	113	4.7	230
290	Other mining	b/c/	70	78	82	88	110	121	137	154	167	10.1	290
2	Mining, quarrying .	d/	87	92	95	97	102	104	109	112	114	3.0	2
311/2	Food products												311/2
313	Beverages	c/	82	91	92	98	99	97	102	107	112	3.5	313
314	Tobacco											.	314
321	Textiles		70	78	84	91	106	109	111	110	116	5.8	321
3211	Spinning,weaving etc..		...	...	...	...	...	...	...	...	...	...	3211
322	Wearing apparel		74	80	85	92	106	108	115	126	160	8.9	322
323	Leather and products ...		72	80	85	92	105	108	119	127	133	7.1	323
324	Footwear												324
331	Wood products		75	83	89	94	102	105	109	112	115	4.9	331
332	Furniture, fixtures												332
341	Paper and products		78	87	91	95	101	100	104	109	111	4.0	341
3411	Pulp,paper etc.		...	...	...	...	...	...	...	...	...	...	3411
342	Printing,publishing	e/	82	88	92	96	99	101	103	99	115	3.8	342
351	Industrial chemicals ...		74	84	92	94	104	106	111	120	121	5.6	351
3511	Basic excl fertilizers		...	...	...	...	...	...	...	...	...	...	3511
3513	Synthetic resins etc .		...	...	...	...	...	...	...	...	...	...	3513
352	Other chemical products.	f/	70	83	91	94	90	85	102	92	99	3.9	352
3522	Drugs and medicines ..		...	...	...	...	...	...	...	...	...	...	3522
353	Petroleum refineries ...		88	91	98	100	97	91	97	101	102	1.7	353
354	Petroleum,coal products.	g/	81	103	112	99	95	113	135	149	143	6.5	354
355	Rubber products		...	...	...	...	...	...	...	...	...	...	355
356	Plastic products n.e.c..		...	...	...	...	...	...	...	...	...	...	356
361	Pottery,china etc		69	76	84	91	110	114	116	122	125	6.8	361
362	Glass and products												362
369	Non-metal products n.e.c	b/	63	73	85	96	100	102	104	110	108	6.2	369
371	Iron and steel		72	84	91	99	104	104	106	119	117	5.5	371
372	Non-ferrous metals		...	...	...	...	...	...	...	...	...	...	372
381	Metal products		64	74	86	91	104	108	112	125	138	8.9	381
382	Machinery n.e.c.	h/	63	72	82	91	101	106	112	121	129	8.3	382
3825	Office,computing etc..		...	...	...	...	...	...	...	...	...	...	3825
383	Electrical machinery ...		59	68	78	89	102	99	100	107	116	7.8	383
3832	Radio,television etc..		...	...	...	...	...	...	...	...	...	...	3832
384	Transport equipment	h/	...	...	...	...	...	...	...	...	...	...	384
3841	Shipbuilding, repair..		...	...	...	...	...	...	...	...	...	...	3841
3843	Motor vehicles		...	...	...	...	...	...	...	...	...	...	3843
385	Professional goods		...	...	...	...	...	...	...	...	...	...	385
390	Other industries		...	...	...	...	...	...	...	...	...	...	390
3	Manufacturing	d/e/	70	79	86	94	103	104	109	116	123	6.5	3
410	Electricity,gas,steam ..	i/	87	91	97	98	104	102	106	112	114	3.0	410
4101	Electricity		...	...	...	...	...	...	...	...	...	...	4101
420	Water works and supply .		.	.	.	.	.	.	.	.	.	.	420
4	Electricity,gas etc		...	...	...	...	...	...	...	...	...	...	4
2-4	All industry	e/i/	71	80	87	94	103	104	109	116	122	6.2	2-4

a/ Annual growth rate 1976-1985.
b/ Stone quarrying, clay and sand pits are included in major group 369.
c/ Salt mining is included in major groups 311/2 to 314 combined.
d/ Other mining is included in manufacturing.
e/ Excluding publishing.
f/ Soap and cosmetics only.
g/ Coke manufacturing only.
h/ Major group 384 is included in 382.
i/ Excluding gas manufacture and distribution.

SENEGAL

The information in the tables is based on the reply to the United Nations Questionnaire on General Industrial Statistics from the Direction de la statistique, Ministere de l'economie et des finances, Dakar. The concepts and definitions are generally in accordance with United Nations standards.

The data in the tables are derived from the survey of industrial activities conducted by the Direction de la statistique and labour statistics compiled by the Division des statistiques du travail. The data cover all establishments excluding handicrafts.

The national industrial classification system on which the data are based is not strictly comparable with ISIC. The figures in the tables are shown in the most appropriate category of ISIC. It should be noted that the data for food products (ISIC 311/2) excludes the processing of fish.

The employment data cover regular and seasonal workers. Output represents the total value of turnover adjusted for changes in the value of stocks of finished goods and work in progress. Value added is the balance remaining from output after deduction of the value of purchases of goods and services, adjusted for the net change in the value of stocks of input items between the beginning and end of the year. Valuation of output and value added is in producers' prices.

The indexes of industrial production are compiled by the Ministere de l'economie et des finances and provided in response to the United Nations Questionnaire on Indexes of Industrial Production.

Related national publicaton:
<u>Comptes economiques</u> (annual), published by the Direction de la statistique, Ministere de l'economie et des finances, Dakar.

ISIC	INDUSTRY	1. NUMBER OF ESTABLISHMENTS (NUMBER) 1981	1982	1983	*1984	1985	2. AVERAGE NUMBER OF EMPLOYEES (THOUSANDS) 1981	1982	1983	*1984	1985	ISIC
210	Coal mining	...	...	...	...	...	...	...	...	...	...	210
220	Petroleum and gas	...	...	...	...	...	...	...	...	...	...	220
230	Metal ore mining	...	...	...	...	...	...	...	...	...	...	230
290	Other mining	...	...	...	...	...	...	...	...	...	...	290
2	Mining, quarrying .	5	7	9	11	...	2.6	2.5	1.9	2.5	...	2
311/2	Food products .... a/	[46	45	35	49]	...	[11.5	22.0	10.5	18.0]	...	311/2
313	Beverages					...					...	313
314	Tobacco	2	2	3	3	...	0.5	0.7	0.5	0.5	...	314
321	Textiles .... b/	29	29	29	26	...	4.9	3.9	4.0	4.9	...	321
3211	Spinning,weaving etc..	...	...	...	...	...	...	...	...	...	...	3211
322	Wearing apparel .... b/	...	...	...	...	...	...	...	...	...	...	322
323	Leather and products ...	[3	3	4	7]	...	[1.0	1.0	0.9	0.9]	...	323
324	Footwear					...					...	324
331	Wood products	[11	12	13	12]	...	[0.4	0.3	0.3	0.3]	...	331
332	Furniture, fixtures					...					...	332
341	Paper and products	4	5	4	5	...	0.3	0.4	0.2	0.2	...	341
3411	Pulp,paper etc.	4	5	4	5	...	0.3	0.4	0.2	0.2	...	3411
342	Printing,publishing	15	18	16	13	...	0.5	0.4	0.8	0.6	...	342
351	Industrial chemicals ... c/	36	37	33	42	...	4.0	3.7	2.4	3.8	...	351
3511	Basic excl fertilizers	...	...	...	...	...	...	...	...	...	...	3511
3513	Synthetic resins etc .	...	...	...	...	...	...	...	...	...	...	3513
352	Other chemical products. c/	...	...	...	...	...	...	...	...	...	...	352
3522	Drugs and medicines ..	...	...	...	...	...	...	...	...	...	...	3522
353	Petroleum refineries ... c/	...	...	...	...	...	...	...	...	...	...	353
354	Petroleum,coal products. c/	...	...	...	...	...	...	...	...	...	...	354
355	Rubber products .... c/	...	...	...	...	...	...	...	...	...	...	355
356	Plastic products n.e.c.. c/	...	...	...	...	...	...	...	...	...	...	356
361	Pottery,china etc					...			[		...	361
362	Glass and products	[4	6	5	5]	...	[0.7	0.8]		[0.7]	...	362
369	Non-metal products n.e.c					...					...	369
371	Iron and steel					...			d/ 3.3		...	371
372	Non-ferrous metals	[e/ 27	e/ 38	e/ 40	e/ 40]	...	[e/ 2.8	e/ 3.5]		[e/ 4.8]	...	372
381	Metal products					...					...	381
382	Machinery n.e.c.					...			]		...	382
3825	Office,computing etc..	...	...	...	...	...	...	...	...	...	...	3825
383	Electrical machinery ...	e/	e/	e/	e/	...	e/	e/	d/	e/	...	383
3832	Radio,television etc..	...	...	...	...	...	...	...	...	...	...	3832
384	Transport equipment	e/	e/	e/	e/	...	e/	e/	d/	e/	...	384
3841	Shipbuilding, repair..	...	...	...	...	...	...	...	...	...	...	3841
3843	Motor vehicles	...	...	...	...	...	...	...	...	...	...	3843
385	Professional goods	e/	e/	e/	e/	...	e/	e/	[d/]	e/	...	385
390	Other industries	e/	e/	e/	e/	...	e/	e/		e/	...	390
3	Manufacturing ..... a/	177	195	182	202	...	26.6	36.7	22.9	34.7	...	3
410	Electricity,gas,steam ..	...	...	...	...	...	...	...	...	...	...	410
4101	Electricity	...	...	...	...	...	...	...	...	...	...	4101
420	Water works and supply .	...	...	...	...	...	...	...	...	...	...	420
4	Electricity,gas etc	5	4	6	3	...	3.7	3.5	3.3	9.2	...	4
2-4	All industry a/	187	206	197	221	...	32.9	42.7	28.1	46.4	...	2-4

a/ Excluding processing of fish.
b/ Major group 322 is included in 321.
c/ Major groups 352 to 356 are included in 351.
d/ Major groups 383 to 390 are included in 361 to 382 combined.
e/ Major groups 383 to 390 are included in 371 to 382 combined.

SENEGAL

ISIC	INDUSTRY		3. WAGES AND SALARIES OF EMPLOYEES (MILLION FRANCS) 1981	1982	1983	*1984	1985	4. AVERAGE NUMBER OF OPERATIVES (NUMBER) 1981	1982	1983	1984	1985	ISIC
210	Coal mining		...	...	...	...	...	...	...	...	...	...	210
220	Petroleum and gas		...	...	...	...	...	...	...	...	...	...	220
230	Metal ore mining		...	...	...	...	...	...	...	...	...	...	230
290	Other mining		...	...	...	...	...	...	...	...	...	...	290
2	Mining, quarrying .		2933	3907	4140	4328	...	...	1350	...	...	...	2
311/2	Food products	a/	[10262	12289	17603	14759]	...	...	[8450]	...	...	...	311/2
313	Beverages						...	...		...	...	...	313
314	Tobacco		684	660	1016	850	...	...	398	...	...	...	314
321	Textiles	b/	3922	3514	5946	5538	...	...	3075	...	...	...	321
3211	Spinning,weaving etc..		...	...	...	...	...	...	...	...	...	...	3211
322	Wearing apparel	b/	...	...	...	...	...	...	...	...	...	...	322
323	Leather and products ...		[1035	1153	1688	1358]	...	...	[550]	...	...	...	323
324	Footwear						...	...		...	...	...	324
331	Wood products		[269	263	306	292]	...	...	[179]	...	...	...	331
332	Furniture, fixtures						...	...		...	...	...	332
341	Paper and products		313	505	495	402	...	...	330	...	...	...	341
3411	Pulp,paper etc.		313	505	495	402	...	...	330	...	...	...	3411
342	Printing,publishing		531	409	1233	730	...	...	237	...	...	...	342
351	Industrial chemicals ...	c/	4203	4671	4371	6798	...	...	2432	...	...	...	351
3511	Basic excl fertilizers		...	...	...	...	...	...	...	...	...	...	3511
3513	Synthetic resins etc .		...	...	...	...	...	...	...	...	...	...	3513
352	Other chemical products.	c/	...	...	...	...	...	...	...	...	...	...	352
3522	Drugs and medicines ..		...	...	...	...	...	...	...	...	...	...	3522
353	Petroleum refineries ...	c/	...	...	...	...	...	...	...	...	...	...	353
354	Petroleum,coal products.	c/	...	...	...	...	...	...	...	...	...	...	354
355	Rubber products	c/	...	...	...	...	...	...	...	...	...	...	355
356	Plastic products n.e.c..	c/	...	...	...	...	...	...	...	...	...	...	356
361	Pottery,china etc		[	]	[	[	...	...	[	...	...	...	361
362	Glass and products		874	1120		1319	...	...	613	...	...	...	362
369	Non-metal products n.e.c		]	]		]	...	...	]	...	...	...	369
371	Iron and steel		[	]	d/ 5682	[	...	...	[	...	...	...	371
372	Non-ferrous metals		e/ 2947	e/ 3977		e/ 6602	...	...	e/ 2263	...	...	...	372
381	Metal products						...	...		...	...	...	381
382	Machinery n.e.c.		]	]	]	]	...	...	]	...	...	...	382
3825	Office,computing etc..		...	...	...	...	...	...	...	...	...	...	3825
383	Electrical machinery ...		e/	e/	d/	e/	...	...	e/	...	...	...	383
3832	Radio,television etc..		...	...	...	...	...	...	...	...	...	...	3832
384	Transport equipment		e/	e/	d/	e/	...	...	e/	...	...	...	384
3841	Shipbuilding, repair..		...	...	...	...	...	...	...	...	...	...	3841
3843	Motor vehicles		...	...	...	...	...	...	...	...	...	...	3843
385	Professional goods		e/	e/	[d/]	e/	...	...	e/	...	...	...	385
390	Other industries		e/	e/		e/	...	...	e/	...	...	...	390
3	Manufacturing	a/	25040	28561	38340	38648	...	...	18527	...	...	...	3
410	Electricity,gas,steam ..		...	...	...	...	...	...	...	...	...	...	410
4101	Electricity		...	...	...	...	...	...	...	...	...	...	4101
420	Water works and supply .		...	...	...	...	...	...	...	...	...	...	420
4	Electricity,gas etc		5223	5366	7408	6596	...	...	2097	...	...	...	4
2-4	All industry	a/	33196	37834	49888	49572	...	...	21974	...	...	...	2-4

a/ Excluding processing of fish.
b/ Major group 322 is included in 321.
c/ Major groups 352 to 356 are included in 351.
d/ Major groups 383 to 390 are included in 361 to 382 combined.
e/ Major groups 383 to 390 are included in 371 to 382 combined.

ISIC	INDUSTRY		5. WAGES AND SALARIES OF OPERATIVES (MILLION FRANCS) 1981	1982	1983	1984	1985	6. OUTPUT IN PRODUCERS' PRICES (MILLION FRANCS) 1981	1982	1983	*1984	1985	ISIC
210	Coal mining		...	...	...	...	...	...	...	...	...	...	210
220	Petroleum and gas		...	...	...	...	...	...	...	...	...	...	220
230	Metal ore mining		...	...	...	...	...	...	...	...	...	...	230
290	Other mining		...	...	...	...	...	...	...	...	...	...	290
2	Mining, quarrying .		...	1299	...	...	...	25396	28685	29642	41368	...	2
311/2	Food products	a/	...	[5378]	...	...	...	[93095	135880	172402	155988]	...	311/2
313	Beverages		...		...	...	...					...	313
314	Tobacco		...	306	...	...	...	3617	4210	6751	9133	...	314
321	Textiles	b/	...	1905	...	...	...	30967	36770	49017	40149	...	321
3211	Spinning,weaving etc..		...	...	...	...	...	...	...	...	...	...	3211
322	Wearing apparel	b/	...	...	...	...	...	...	...	...	...	...	322
323	Leather and products ...		...	[544]	...	...	...	[3294	4283	5012	5075]	...	323
324	Footwear		...		...	...	...					...	324
331	Wood products		...	[107]	...	...	...	[2120	2567	2234	1828]	...	331
332	Furniture, fixtures		...		...	...	...					...	332
341	Paper and products		...	224	...	...	...	3568	3140	3938	3602	...	341
3411	Pulp,paper etc.		...	224	...	...	...	3568	3140	3938	3602	...	3411
342	Printing,publishing		...	156	...	...	...	3416	3858	6528	5038	...	342
351	Industrial chemicals ...	c/	...	1756	...	...	...	86003	77375	81244	83018	...	351
3511	Basic excl fertilizers		...	...	...	...	...	...	...	...	...	...	3511
3513	Synthetic resins etc .		...	...	...	...	...	...	...	...	...	...	3513
352	Other chemical products.	c/	...	...	...	...	...	...	...	...	...	...	352
3522	Drugs and medicines ..		...	...	...	...	...	...	...	...	...	...	3522
353	Petroleum refineries ...	c/	...	...	...	...	...	...	...	...	...	...	353
354	Petroleum,coal products.	c/	...	...	...	...	...	...	...	...	...	...	354
355	Rubber products	c/	...	...	...	...	...	...	...	...	...	...	355
356	Plastic products n.e.c..	c/	...	...	...	...	...	...	...	...	...	...	356
361	Pottery,china etc		...	[	...	...	...	[		[	[	...	361
362	Glass and products		...	524]	...	...	...	8877	11093]		15381]	...	362
369	Non-metal products n.e.c		...		...	...	...					...	369
371	Iron and steel		...	[	...	...	...	[		d/ 27626	[	...	371
372	Non-ferrous metals		...	e/ 1536	...	...	...	e/ 15000	e/ 29927		e/ 26010	...	372
381	Metal products		...		...	...	...					...	381
382	Machinery n.e.c.		...	]	...	...	...		]	]	]	...	382
3825	Office,computing etc..		...	...	...	...	...	...	...	...	...	...	3825
383	Electrical machinery ...		...	e/	...	...	...	e/	e/	d/	e/	...	383
3832	Radio,television etc..		...	...	...	...	...	...	...	...	...	...	3832
384	Transport equipment		...	e/	...	...	...	e/	e/	d/	e/	...	384
3841	Shipbuilding, repair..		...	...	...	...	...	...	...	...	...	...	3841
3843	Motor vehicles		...	...	...	...	...	...	...	...	...	...	3843
385	Professional goods		...	e/	...	...	...	e/	e/	[d/]	e/	...	385
390	Other industries		...	e/	...	...	...	e/	e/		e/	...	390
3	Manufacturing	a/	...	12436	...	...	...	249957	309103	354752	345222	...	3
410	Electricity,gas,steam ..		...	...	...	...	...	...	...	...	...	...	410
4101	Electricity		...	...	...	...	...	...	...	...	...	...	4101
420	Water works and supply .		...	...	...	...	...	...	...	...	...	...	420
4	Electricity,gas etc		...	2563	...	...	...	31223	33498	45415	54571	...	4
2-4	All industry	a/	...	16298	...	...	...	306576	371286	429809	441161	...	2-4

a/ Excluding processing of fish.
b/ Major group 322 is included in 321.
c/ Major groups 352 to 356 are included in 351.
d/ Major groups 383 to 390 are included in 361 to 382 combined.
e/ Major groups 383 to 390 are included in 371 to 382 combined.

ISIC	INDUSTRY		7. VALUE ADDED IN PRODUCERS' PRICES (MILLION FRANCS) 1981	1982	1983	*1984	1985	8. GROSS FIXED CAPITAL FORMATION TOTAL (MILLION FRANCS) 1981	1982	1983	*1984	1985	ISIC
210	Coal mining		...	...	...	...	...	...	...	...	...	...	210
220	Petroleum and gas		...	...	...	...	...	...	...	...	...	...	220
230	Metal ore mining		...	...	...	...	...	...	...	...	...	...	230
290	Other mining		...	...	...	...	...	...	...	...	...	...	290
2	Mining, quarrying .		11590	8892	12303	18839	...	3434	2691	6979	8592	...	2
311/2	Food products	a/	[23210	28608	40212	39998]	...	[19574	9339	13871	11046]	...	311/2
313	Beverages						...					...	313
314	Tobacco		1444	1737	4188	3122	...	627	170	212	675	...	314
321	Textiles	b/	6752	7766	10522	12854	...	1813	1426	1535	1406	...	321
3211	Spinning,weaving etc..		...	...	...	...	...	...	...	...	...	...	3211
322	Wearing apparel	b/	...	...	...	...	...	...	...	...	...	...	322
323	Leather and products ...		[-137	1588	1695	1403]	...	[-	338	307	240]	...	323
324	Footwear						...					...	324
331	Wood products		[583	589	886	522]	...	[31	37	66	27]	...	331
332	Furniture, fixtures						...					...	332
341	Paper and products		814	839	1778	782	...	23	156	77	83	...	341
3411	Pulp,paper etc.		814	839	1778	782	...	23	156	77	83	...	3411
342	Printing,publishing		1638	1257	2558	1941	...	108	33	334	247	...	342
351	Industrial chemicals ...	c/	7279	8508	13508	10544	...	3111	10031	4484	12458	...	351
3511	Basic excl fertilizers		...	...	...	...	...	...	...	...	...	...	3511
3513	Synthetic resins etc .		...	...	...	...	...	...	...	...	...	...	3513
352	Other chemical products.	c/	...	...	...	...	...	...	...	...	...	...	352
3522	Drugs and medicines ..		...	...	...	...	...	...	...	...	...	...	3522
353	Petroleum refineries ...	c/	...	...	...	...	...	...	...	...	...	...	353
354	Petroleum,coal products.	c/	...	...	...	...	...	...	...	...	...	...	354
355	Rubber products	c/	...	...	...	...	...	...	...	...	...	...	355
356	Plastic products n.e.c..	c/	...	...	...	...	...	...	...	...	...	...	356
361	Pottery,china etc		[	]	[	[	...	[	]	[	[	...	361
362	Glass and products		3513	4578		6294	...	92	946		1362	...	362
369	Non-metal products n.e.c		]	]		]	...	]	]		]	...	369
371	Iron and steel		[		d/ 15284	[	...	[		d/ 1618	[	...	371
372	Non-ferrous metals		e/ 4223	e/ 8864		e/ 11922	...	e/ 1649	e/ 775		e/ 1126	...	372
381	Metal products						...					...	381
382	Machinery n.e.c.		]	]	]	]	...	]	]	]	]	...	382
3825	Office,computing etc..		...	...	...	...	...	...	...	...	...	...	3825
383	Electrical machinery ...		e/	e/	d/	e/	...	e/	e/	d/	e/	...	383
3832	Radio,television etc..		...	...	...	...	...	...	...	...	...	...	3832
384	Transport equipment		e/	e/	d/	e/	...	e/	e/	d/	e/	...	384
3841	Shipbuilding, repair..		...	...	...	...	...	...	...	...	...	...	3841
3843	Motor vehicles		...	...	...	...	...	...	...	...	...	...	3843
385	Professional goods		e/	e/	[d/]	e/	...	e/	e/	[d/]	e/	...	385
390	Other industries		e/	e/		e/	...	e/	e/		e/	...	390
3	Manufacturing	a/	49319	64334	90631	89382	...	27028	23251	22504	28670	...	3
410	Electricity,gas,steam ..		...	...	...	...	...	...	...	...	...	...	410
4101	Electricity		...	...	...	...	...	...	...	...	...	...	4101
420	Water works and supply .		...	...	...	...	...	...	...	...	...	...	420
4	Electricity,gas etc		7146	10155	15661	17524	...	237	7007	7339	9291	...	4
2-4	All industry	a/	68055	83381	118595	125745	...	30699	32949	36822	46553	...	2-4

a/ Excluding processing of fish.
b/ Major group 322 is included in 321.
c/ Major groups 352 to 356 are included in 351.
d/ Major groups 383 to 390 are included in 361 to 382 combined.
e/ Major groups 383 to 390 are included in 371 to 382 combined.

9. INDEX NUMBERS OF INDUSTRIAL PRODUCTION (1980 = 100)

ISIC	INDUSTRY	1976	1977	1978	1979	1981	1982	1983	1984	1985	a/ RATE	ISIC
210	Coal mining	...	...	...	...	...	...	...	...	...	...	210
220	Petroleum and gas	...	...	...	...	...	...	...	...	...	...	220
230	Metal ore mining	...	...	...	...	...	...	...	...	...	...	230
290	Other mining	111	105	107	113	120	76	94	120	130	1.8	290
2	Mining, quarrying .	111	105	107	113	120	76	94	120	125	1.3	2
311/2	Food products	177	180	98	160	68	135	145	108	101	-6.0	311/2
313	Beverages	85	104	107	130	91	85	82	72	77	-1.1	313
314	Tobacco	98	100	112	113	97	97	112	89	99	0.1	314
321	Textiles	96	127	105	99	123	159	153	125	131	3.5	321
3211	Spinning,weaving etc..	...	...	...	...	...	...	...	...	...	...	3211
322	Wearing apparel	...	...	...	...	...	...	...	...	...	...	322
323	Leather and products ...	187	183	127	113	105	126	87	188	93	-7.5	323
324	Footwear	...	...	...	...	...	...	...	...	...	...	324
331	Wood products	72	78	80	102	100	104	96	91	83	1.6	331
332	Furniture, fixtures	...	...	...	...	...	...	...	...	...	...	332
341	Paper and products	84	83	96	99	112	111	116	118	115	3.6	341
3411	Pulp,paper etc.	...	...	...	...	...	...	...	...	...	...	3411
342	Printing,publishing	...	...	...	...	...	...	...	...	...	...	342
351	Industrial chemicals ... b/	110	112	114	115	115	87	80	79	72	-4.6	351
3511	Basic excl fertilizers	...	...	...	...	...	...	...	...	...	...	3511
3513	Synthetic resins etc .	...	...	...	...	...	...	...	...	...	...	3513
352	Other chemical products. b/	...	...	...	...	...	...	...	...	...	...	352
3522	Drugs and medicines ..	...	...	...	...	...	...	...	...	...	...	3522
353	Petroleum refineries ... b/	...	...	...	...	...	...	...	...	...	...	353
354	Petroleum,coal products. b/	...	...	...	...	...	...	...	...	...	...	354
355	Rubber products .... b/	...	...	...	...	...	...	...	...	...	...	355
356	Plastic products n.e.c.. b/	...	...	...	...	...	...	...	...	...	...	356
361	Pottery,china etc	...	...	...	...	...	...	...	...	...	...	361
362	Glass and products	...	...	...	...	...	...	...	...	...	...	362
369	Non-metal products n.e.c	107	94	111	102	99	99	138	124	102	-0.5	369
371	Iron and steel	...	...	...	...	...	...	...	...	...	...	371
372	Non-ferrous metals	...	...	...	...	...	...	...	...	...	...	372
381	Metal products	92	105	119	121	73	104	128	126	135	4.4	381
382	Machinery n.e.c.	...	...	...	...	...	...	...	...	...	...	382
3825	Office,computing etc..	...	...	...	...	...	...	...	...	...	...	3825
383	Electrical machinery ...	76	96	100	126	108	143	166	197	272	15.2	383
3832	Radio,television etc..	...	...	...	...	...	...	...	...	...	...	3832
384	Transport equipment	405	689	344	264	104	103	138	190	156	-10.1	384
3841	Shipbuilding, repair..	...	...	...	...	...	...	...	...	...	...	3841
3843	Motor vehicles	...	...	...	...	...	...	...	...	...	...	3843
385	Professional goods	...	...	...	...	...	...	...	...	...	...	385
390	Other industries	...	...	...	...	...	...	...	...	...	...	390
3	Manufacturing	112	125	109	124	108	120	134	113	115	0.3	3
410	Electricity,gas,steam ..	...	...	...	...	...	...	...	...	...	...	410
4101	Electricity	72	80	91	100	96	99	111	108	116	5.4	4101
420	Water works and supply .	84	95	97	102	115	122	119	132	120	4.0	420
4	Electricity,gas etc c/	77	86	94	101	104	109	115	118	120	5.1	4
2-4	All industry c/	110	120	108	121	109	113	118	115	118	0.8	2-4

a/ Annual growth rate 1976-1985.
c/ Excluding gas and steam.
b/ Major groups 352 to 356 are included in 351.

SEYCHELLES

The information in the tables is based on the reply to the United Nations Questionnaire on General Industrial Statistics from the Statistics Division, Department of Finance and Industry, President's Office, Victoria. The concepts, definitions and classification by branches of industry are generally in accordance with United Nations standards.

The data in the tables are derived from various sources, that is (a) annual national accounts inquiry of manufacturing establishments conducted by the Statistics Division, (b) annual report of the Accountant General, (c) monthly information on employment and earnings supplied by government agencies and (d) social security records. Casual workers such as persons employed on daily contract and paid daily are excluded.

The data are compiled according to the present version of ISIC. In the tables, however, the data are presented only by broad groupings of industries owing to disclosure rules imposed by law. It should be noted that ISIC 290 relates to guano mining, ISIC 321, 322, 323 and 324 combined relate mainly to the manufacture of clothing and footwear, ISIC 351-356 combined mostly to the manufacture of paints, plastic materials, detergents and reinforced plastic products and ISIC 381 to the manufacture of steel and aluminium products.

ISIC	INDUSTRY		1. NUMBER OF ESTABLISHMENTS (NUMBER) 1981	1982	1983	1984	1985	2. AVERAGE NUMBER OF PERSONS ENGAGED (NUMBER) 1981	1982	1983	1984	1985	ISIC
210	Coal mining		-	-	-	-	...	-	-	-	-	...	210
220	Petroleum and gas		-	-	-	-	...	-	-	-	-	...	220
230	Metal ore mining		-	-	-	-	...	-	-	-	-	...	230
290	Other mining		1	-	-	-	...	a/ 32	-	-	-	...	290
2	Mining, quarrying .		1	-	-	-	...	32	-	-	-	...	2
311/2	Food products		[			]	...	[			]	...	311/2
313	Beverages		12	13	14	14	...	361	385	438	456	...	313
314	Tobacco						...					...	314
321	Textiles	b/	3	2	2	2	...	28	27	26	26	...	321
3211	Spinning,weaving etc..		...	...	...	...	...	...	...	...	...	...	3211
322	Wearing apparel	b/	...	...	...	...	...	...	...	...	...	...	322
323	Leather and products ...	b/	...	...	...	...	...	...	...	...	...	...	323
324	Footwear	b/	...	...	...	...	...	...	...	...	...	...	324
331	Wood products		[5	3	3	3]	...	[132	118	115	116]	...	331
332	Furniture, fixtures						...					...	332
341	Paper and products	c/	4	4	4	3	...	148	156	150	134	...	341
3411	Pulp,paper etc.		...	...	...	...	...	...	...	...	...	...	3411
342	Printing,publishing	c/	...	...	...	...	...	...	...	...	...	...	342
351	Industrial chemicals ...	d/	5	5	5	4	...	25	33	31	33	...	351
3511	Basic excl fertilizers		...	...	...	...	...	...	...	...	...	...	3511
3513	Synthetic resins etc .		...	...	...	...	...	...	...	...	...	...	3513
352	Other chemical products.	d/	...	...	...	...	...	...	...	...	...	...	352
3522	Drugs and medicines ..		...	...	...	...	...	...	...	...	...	...	3522
353	Petroleum refineries ...	d/	...	...	...	...	...	...	...	...	...	...	353
354	Petroleum,coal products.	d/	...	...	...	...	...	...	...	...	...	...	354
355	Rubber products	d/	...	...	...	...	...	...	...	...	...	...	355
356	Plastic products n.e.c..	d/	...	...	...	...	...	...	...	...	...	...	356
361	Pottery,china etc		[			]	...	[			]	...	361
362	Glass and products		2	2	1	1	...	102	67	48	28	...	362
369	Non-metal products n.e.c						...					...	369
371	Iron and steel		-	-	-	...	...	-	-	-	-	...	371
372	Non-ferrous metals		-	-	-	...	...	-	-	-	-	...	372
381	Metal products		3	3	3	3	...	76	59	55	49	...	381
382	Machinery n.e.c.		-	-	-	-	...	-	-	-	-	...	382
3825	Office,computing etc..		-	-	-	-	...	-	-	-	-	...	3825
383	Electrical machinery ...		-	-	-	-	...	-	-	-	-	...	383
3832	Radio,television etc..		-	-	-	-	...	-	-	-	-	...	3832
384	Transport equipment		-	-	-	-	...	-	-	-	-	...	384
3841	Shipbuilding, repair..		-	-	-	-	...	-	-	-	-	...	3841
3843	Motor vehicles		-	-	-	-	...	-	-	-	-	...	3843
385	Professional goods		-	-	-	-	...	-	-	-	-	...	385
390	Other industries		-	-	-	-	...	-	-	-	-	...	390
3	Manufacturing		34	32	32	30	...	872	845	863	842	...	3
410	Electricity,gas,steam ..	e/	1	1	1	1	...	371	358	351	342	...	410
4101	Electricity		1	1	1	1	...	371	358	351	342	...	4101
420	Water works and supply .		1	1	1	1	...	457	436	416	417	...	420
4	Electricity,gas etc	e/	2	2	2	2	...	828	794	767	759	...	4
2-4	All industry	e/	37	34	34	32	...	1732	1639	1630	1601	...	2-4

a/ Average for January to July 1981 due to discontinued operation.
b/ Major groups 322 to 324 are included in 321.
c/ Major group 342 is included in 341.
d/ Major groups 352 to 356 are included in 351.
e/ Excluding gas and steam.

ISIC	INDUSTRY	3. AVERAGE NUMBER OF EMPLOYEES (NUMBER) 1981	1982	1983	1984	1985	4. WAGES AND SALARIES OF EMPLOYEES (THOUSAND RUPEES) 1981	1982	1983	1984	1985	ISIC
210	Coal mining	-	-	-	-	...	-	-	-	-	...	210
220	Petroleum and gas	-	-	-	-	...	-	-	-	-	...	220
230	Metal ore mining	-	-	-	-	...	-	-	-	-	...	230
290	Other mining	a/ 32	-	-	-	...	b/ 330	-	-	-	...	290
2	Mining, quarrying	32	-	-	-	...	330	-	-	-	...	2
311/2	Food products	[			]	...	[			]	...	311/2
313	Beverages	358	378	436	454	...	9756	11454	15993	16282	...	313
314	Tobacco					...					...	314
321	Textiles c/	28	27	26	26	...	829	892	683	685	...	321
3211	Spinning, weaving etc.	...	...	...	...	...	...	...	...	...	...	3211
322	Wearing apparel c/	...	...	...	...	...	...	...	...	...	...	322
323	Leather and products c/	...	...	...	...	...	...	...	...	...	...	323
324	Footwear c/	...	...	...	...	...	...	...	...	...	...	324
331	Wood products	[132	118	115	116]	...	[2734	2556	2706	2904]	...	331
332	Furniture, fixtures					...					...	332
341	Paper and products d/	148	156	150	134	...	3956	4456	4074	3823	...	341
3411	Pulp, paper etc.	...	...	...	...	...	...	...	...	...	...	3411
342	Printing, publishing d/	...	...	...	...	...	...	...	...	...	...	342
351	Industrial chemicals e/	25	33	31	33	...	588	816	981	923	...	351
3511	Basic excl fertilizers	...	...	...	...	...	...	...	...	...	...	3511
3513	Synthetic resins etc	...	...	...	...	...	...	...	...	...	...	3513
352	Other chemical products. e/	...	...	...	...	...	...	...	...	...	...	352
3522	Drugs and medicines	...	...	...	...	...	...	...	...	...	...	3522
353	Petroleum refineries e/	...	...	...	...	...	...	...	...	...	...	353
354	Petroleum, coal products. e/	...	...	...	...	...	...	...	...	...	...	354
355	Rubber products e/	...	...	...	...	...	...	...	...	...	...	355
356	Plastic products n.e.c. e/	...	...	...	...	...	...	...	...	...	...	356
361	Pottery, china etc	[			]	...	[			]	...	361
362	Glass and products	102	67	48	28	...	2733	1814	1323	1072	...	362
369	Non-metal products n.e.c					...					...	369
371	Iron and steel	-	-	-	-	...	-	-	-	-	...	371
372	Non-ferrous metals	-	-	-	-	...	-	-	-	-	...	372
381	Metal products	73	59	55	49	...	1521	1626	1543	1492	...	381
382	Machinery n.e.c.	-	-	-	-	...	-	-	-	-	...	382
3825	Office, computing etc.	-	-	-	-	...	-	-	-	-	...	3825
383	Electrical machinery	-	-	-	-	...	-	-	-	-	...	383
3832	Radio, television etc.	-	-	-	-	...	-	-	-	-	...	3832
384	Transport equipment	-	-	-	-	...	-	-	-	-	...	384
3841	Shipbuilding, repair	-	-	-	-	...	-	-	-	-	...	3841
3843	Motor vehicles	-	-	-	-	...	-	-	-	-	...	3843
385	Professional goods	-	-	-	-	...	-	-	-	-	...	385
390	Other industries	-	-	-	-	...	-	-	-	-	...	390
3	Manufacturing	866	838	861	840	...	22117	23614	27303	27181	...	3
410	Electricity, gas, steam f/	371	358	351	342	...	8504	7088	9399	9617	...	410
4101	Electricity	371	358	351	342	...	8504	7088	9399	9617	...	4101
420	Water works and supply	457	436	416	417	...	4434	5137	8652	8579	...	420
4	Electricity, gas etc f/	828	794	767	759	...	12938	12225	18051	18196	...	4
2-4	All industry f/	1726	1632	1628	1599	...	35385	35839	45354	45377	...	2-4

a/ Average for January to July 1981 due to discontinued operation.
b/ For the period January to July 1981 due to discontinued operation.
c/ Major groups 322 to 324 are included in 321.
d/ Major group 342 is included in 341.
e/ Major groups 352 to 356 are included in 351.
f/ Excluding gas and steam.

ISIC	INDUSTRY	5. OUTPUT (THOUSAND RUPEES) 1981	1982	1983	1984	1985	6. VALUE ADDED (THOUSAND RUPEES) 1981	1982	1983	1984	1985	ISIC
210	Coal mining	-	-	-	-	...	-	-	-	-	...	210
220	Petroleum and gas	-	-	-	-	...	-	-	-	-	...	220
230	Metal ore mining	-	-	-	-	...	-	-	-	-	...	230
290	Other mining	406	-	-	-	...	244	-	-	-	...	290
2	Mining, quarrying .	406	-	-	-	...	244	-	-	-	...	2
311/2	Food products	[			]	...	[			]	...	311/2
313	Beverages	101500	105050	117403	121607	...	55858	58515	72490	70853	...	313
314	Tobacco	[			]	...	[			]	...	314
321	Textiles .... a/	2845	3444	2904	2897	...	1685	2015	1832	1829	...	321
3211	Spinning,weaving etc..	...	...	...	...	...	...	...	...	...	...	3211
322	Wearing apparel .... a/	...	...	...	...	...	...	...	...	...	...	322
323	Leather and products ... a/	...	...	...	...	...	...	...	...	...	...	323
324	Footwear .... a/	...	...	...	...	...	...	...	...	...	...	324
331	Wood products	[9088	6889	8072	7182]	...	[3649	3225	4314	3371]	...	331
332	Furniture, fixtures					...					...	332
341	Paper and products ..... b/	7563	12510	11761	12477	...	c/ 3457	5441	4669	4838	...	341
3411	Pulp,paper etc.	...	...	...	...	...	...	...	...	...	...	3411
342	Printing,publishing .... b/	...	...	...	...	...	...	...	...	...	...	342
351	Industrial chemicals ... d/	5100	5879	6210	7735	...	925	1381	2219	2542	...	351
3511	Basic excl fertilizers	...	...	...	...	...	...	...	...	...	...	3511
3513	Synthetic resins etc .	...	...	...	...	...	...	...	...	...	...	3513
352	Other chemical products. d/	...	...	...	...	...	...	...	...	...	...	352
3522	Drugs and medicines ..	...	...	...	...	...	...	...	...	...	...	3522
353	Petroleum refineries ... d/	...	...	...	...	...	...	...	...	...	...	353
354	Petroleum,coal products. d/	...	...	...	...	...	...	...	...	...	...	354
355	Rubber products .... d/	...	...	...	...	...	...	...	...	...	...	355
356	Plastic products n.e.c.. d/	...	...	...	...	...	...	...	...	...	...	356
361	Pottery,china etc	[			]	...	[			]	...	361
362	Glass and products	16457	10377	7280	7399	...	6316	2110	1696	3469	...	362
369	Non-metal products n.e.c	[			]	...	[			]	...	369
371	Iron and steel	-	-	-	-	...	-	-	-	-	...	371
372	Non-ferrous metals	-	-	-	-	...	-	-	-	-	...	372
381	Metal products	7424	6305	8937	7864	...	2232	2201	2789	2697	...	381
382	Machinery n.e.c.	-	-	-	-	...	-	-	-	-	...	382
3825	Office,computing etc..	-	-	-	-	...	-	-	-	-	...	3825
383	Electrical machinery ...	-	-	-	-	...	-	-	-	-	...	383
3832	Radio,television etc..	-	-	-	-	...	-	-	-	-	...	3832
384	Transport equipment	-	-	-	-	...	-	-	-	-	...	384
3841	Shipbuilding, repair..	-	-	-	-	...	-	-	-	-	...	3841
3843	Motor vehicles	-	-	-	-	...	-	-	-	-	...	3843
385	Professional goods	-	-	-	-	...	-	-	-	-	...	385
390	Other industries	-	-	-	-	...	-	-	-	-	...	390
3	Manufacturing	149977	150454	162567	167161	...	74122	74888	90009	89599	...	3
410	Electricity,gas,steam .. e/	58298	58689	60909	62858	...	7711	9281	11310	12494	...	410
4101	Electricity	58290	58689	60909	62858	...	7711	9281	11310	12494	...	4101
420	Water works and supply .	9449	9370	13273	17074	...	3335	3349	3549	6733	...	420
4	Electricity,gas etc e/	67747	68059	74182	79932	...	11046	12630	14859	19227	...	4
2-4	All industry e/	218130	218513	236749	247093	...	85412	87518	104868	108826	...	2-4

a/ Major groups 322 to 324 are included in 321.
b/ Major group 342 is included in 341.
c/ Value added is less than corresponding wages and salaries due to operating losses.
d/ Major groups 352 to 356 are included in 351.
e/ Excluding gas and steam.

The information in the tables, except for the indexes, is based on the reply to the United Nations Questionnaire on General Industrial Statistics from the Department of Statistics, Singapore. The concepts, definitions and classification by branches of industry are generally in accordance with United Nations standards.

The data in the tables relate to establishments in the private sector with 10 or more persons engaged and are derived from the census of industrial production undertaken annually by the Department of Statistics. The activities covered by the census are granite quarrying and manufacturing. The census is primarily conducted by mail, but field enumerators customarily visit establishments to assist in the completion and return of the questionnaire. The response rate is 99 per cent. Rubber processing and rubber packing on plantations (ISIC major division 1) are included in the manufacture of rubber products (ISIC 355).

The data in the tables are based on the national classification scheme, which generally follows the present version of ISIC. The reference period is the calendar year, but establishments with financial years ending on or before 31 March are allowed to report on a financial year basis.

The numbers of persons engaged and employees relate to the number on or at the pay period nearest to 30 June of the reference year. Data on wages and salaries include employers' contributions to the provident fund, pension and other funds and the value of other benefits such as food, lodging, transport and medical care.

The estimates of output relate to the total value of all commodities produced (including by-products) and industrial services rendered to others. The valuation of commodities is at ex-factory price, excluding transport charges. For industries producing commodities such as alcoholic drinks and cigarettes, where excise duties are payable, the duties paid are excluded from the total value of output. In cases where proper records of production are not available, the value of output is calculated from the value of sales after adjusting for changes in stocks during the year.

Value added is estimated as the value of output less the cost of materials, electricity, fuel, water and transport and the cost of work given out. Valuation is in factor values.

The estimates of gross fixed capital formation relate to the total expenditure incurred by the establishment during the reference year on land, buildings and structures, machinery and equipment, vehicles and office equipment.

The indexes of industrial production are compiled by the Department of Statistics and provided in response to the United Nations Questionnaire on Indexes of Industrial Production. In principle, the indexes cover all industrial establishments with 10 or more persons engaged.

Related national publications:

Report on the Census of Industrial Production (annual) and Yearbook of Statistics, Singapore, both published by the Department of Statistics, Singapore.

ISIC	INDUSTRY	1. NUMBER OF ESTABLISHMENTS a/ (NUMBER)					2. AVERAGE NUMBER OF PERSONS ENGAGED a/b/ (THOUSANDS)					ISIC
		1981	1982	1983	1984	1985	1981	1982	1983	1984	1985	
210	Coal mining	...	...	...	...	...	...	...	...	...	...	210
220	Petroleum and gas	...	...	...	...	...	...	...	...	...	...	220
230	Metal ore mining	...	...	...	...	...	...	...	...	...	...	230
290	Other mining .... c/	20	20	17	19	18	1.01	1.05	1.14	1.15	0.78	290
2	Mining, quarrying .	...	...	...	...	...	...	...	...	...	...	2
311/2	Food products	274	283	289	301	284	10.08	10.21	10.31	10.28	9.69	311/2
313	Beverages	17	16	16	14	14	2.74	2.59	2.49	2.40	2.27	313
314	Tobacco	6	6	6	4	4	0.98	0.88	0.87	0.81	0.75	314
321	Textiles	94	95	87	80	62	7.91	6.36	4.62	3.96	2.74	321
3211	Spinning,weaving etc..	36	37	35	31	23	4.76	3.69	2.51	2.12	1.46	3211
322	Wearing apparel	374	406	391	387	370	27.87	28.61	27.23	25.71	24.78	322
323	Leather and products ...	40	43	37	38	28	1.19	1.15	0.97	0.95	0.65	323
324	Footwear	57	53	51	57	49	1.43	1.41	1.25	1.23	0.87	324
331	Wood products	132	119	110	104	109	8.29	7.19	5.95	4.95	4.12	331
332	Furniture, fixtures	117	125	127	142	145	6.56	6.71	6.86	7.48	7.08	332
341	Paper and products	95	92	88	86	81	4.50	4.45	3.79	3.59	3.36	341
3411	Pulp,paper etc.	...	...	...	...	...	...	...	...	...	...	3411
342	Printing,publishing	295	319	321	326	305	12.49	13.45	13.81	14.21	13.22	342
351	Industrial chemicals ...	44	48	50	56	55	2.06	2.27	2.28	3.22	3.14	351
3511	Basic excl fertilizers	...	...	...	...	...	...	...	...	...	...	3511
3513	Synthetic resins etc .	...	...	...	...	...	...	...	...	...	...	3513
352	Other chemical products.	86	84	85	90	90	4.29	4.51	4.57	4.60	4.62	352
3522	Drugs and medicines ..	...	...	...	...	...	...	...	...	...	...	3522
353	Petroleum refineries ...	[11	11	11	12	12	3.51	3.79	3.76	3.61	3.49]	353
354	Petroleum,coal products.											354
355	Rubber products	47	45	46	46	38	3.34	2.75	2.44	2.14	1.70	355
356	Plastic products n.e.c..	209	214	215	224	221	9.12	8.89	8.56	8.56	8.47	356
361	Pottery,china etc	[13	11	10	13	12	1.13	1.05	0.99	1.01	0.35]	361
362	Glass and products											362
369	Non-metal products n.e.c	76	77	90	96	98	3.93	4.61	6.56	7.18	6.85	369
371	Iron and steel	17	16	15	15	15	1.92	1.72	1.65	1.61	1.51	371
372	Non-ferrous metals	11	16	18	20	18	0.45	0.66	0.64	0.73	0.69	372
381	Metal products	371	413	426	435	435	19.48	21.55	21.16	20.75	19.45	381
382	Machinery n.e.c.	319	314	341	349	349	23.96	23.80	22.43	21.41	19.69	382
3825	Office,computing etc..	...	...	...	...	...	...	...	...	...	...	3825
383	Electrical machinery ...	298	300	315	324	322	85.50	75.17	81.30	89.05	82.63	383
3832	Radio,television etc..	176	172	172	173	168	65.78	54.97	54.63	56.66	52.35	3832
384	Transport equipment	261	295	291	252	220	28.49	30.75	27.04	24.79	21.77	384
3841	Shipbuilding, repair..	211	240	231	197	168	23.62	25.11	21.25	18.40	15.50	3841
3843	Motor vehicles	26	29	31	27	27	1.69	1.87	1.70	1.92	1.83	3843
385	Professional goods	52	48	46	46	41	5.42	5.77	5.20	5.36	5.07	385
390	Other industries	135	148	144	139	134	6.88	6.46	5.39	5.51	5.06	390
3	Manufacturing	3451	3597	3626	3656	3511	283.52	276.76	272.12	275.10	254.02	3
410	Electricity,gas,steam ..	...	...	...	...	...	...	...	...	...	...	410
4101	Electricity	...	...	...	...	...	...	...	...	...	...	4101
420	Water works and supply .	...	...	...	...	...	...	...	...	...	...	420
4	Electricity,gas etc	...	...	...	...	...	...	...	...	...	...	4
2-4	All industry	...	...	...	...	...	...	...	...	...	...	2-4

a/ Private establishments with 10 or more persons engaged. b/ At 30 June of the year indicated.
c/ Granite quarrying only.

ISIC	INDUSTRY	3. AVERAGE NUMBER OF EMPLOYEES a/b/ (THOUSANDS)					4. WAGES AND SALARIES OF EMPLOYEES b/c/ (MILLION DOLLARS)					ISIC
		1981	1982	1983	1984	1985	1981	1982	1983	1984	1985	
210	Coal mining	...	...	...	...	...	...	...	...	...	...	210
220	Petroleum and gas	...	...	...	...	...	...	...	...	...	...	220
230	Metal ore mining	...	...	...	...	...	...	...	...	...	...	230
290	Other mining .... d/	1.00	1.04	1.13	1.14	0.77	15.3	15.7	17.7	19.3	14.3	290
2	Mining, quarrying .	...	...	...	...	...	...	...	...	...	...	2
311/2	Food products	9.76	9.90	10.04	10.02	9.44	103.4	115.2	129.7	148.3	156.8	311/2
313	Beverages	2.74	2.59	2.49	2.40	2.27	40.0	35.3	36.5	40.6	44.1	313
314	Tobacco	0.97	0.88	0.86	0.81	0.75	15.6	17.3	19.2	21.1	20.8	314
321	Textiles	7.87	6.31	4.59	3.93	2.73	68.8	60.4	49.9	47.1	34.6	321
3211	Spinning,weaving etc..	4.75	3.67	2.50	2.11	1.46	43.6	36.5	27.5	24.1	18.0	3211
322	Wearing apparel	27.55	28.26	26.92	25.42	24.52	179.3	203.4	216.1	236.9	227.3	322
323	Leather and products ...	1.14	1.10	0.94	0.92	0.62	8.0	8.5	8.2	8.7	6.9	323
324	Footwear	1.36	1.34	1.19	1.16	0.81	10.1	10.7	10.3	10.9	7.0	324
331	Wood products	8.19	7.10	5.88	4.88	4.06	77.4	69.0	64.8	56.4	48.2	331
332	Furniture, fixtures	6.47	6.58	6.74	7.35	6.95	54.8	58.3	63.7	73.5	74.3	332
341	Paper and products	4.45	4.41	3.74	3.56	3.33	44.2	51.4	51.5	52.0	53.2	341
3411	Pulp,paper etc.	...	...	...	...	...	...	...	...	...	...	3411
342	Printing,publishing	12.25	13.21	13.58	13.99	13.02	140.5	171.9	196.5	234.7	217.9	342
351	Industrial chemicals ...	2.06	2.27	2.28	3.21	3.14	33.4	41.1	43.2	85.7	93.9	351
3511	Basic excl fertilizers	...	...	...	...	...	...	...	...	...	...	3511
3513	Synthetic resins etc .	...	...	...	...	...	...	...	...	...	...	3513
352	Other chemical products.	4.27	4.49	4.54	4.58	4.61	62.5	76.4	90.5	99.4	107.4	352
3522	Drugs and medicines ..	...	...	...	...	...	...	...	...	...	...	3522
353	Petroleum refineries ...	[3.51	3.79	3.76	3.61	3.49	114.7	138.6	148.0	151.4	154.6]	353
354	Petroleum,coal products.											354
355	Rubber products	3.33	2.74	2.42	2.13	1.69	33.1	32.4	33.9	30.9	27.0	355
356	Plastic products n.e.c..	9.05	8.83	8.50	8.49	8.41	71.8	79.9	86.5	98.5	103.0	356
361	Pottery,china etc	[1.13	1.05	0.99	1.00	0.34	13.5	14.4	16.3	17.8	5.9]	361
362	Glass and products											362
369	Non-metal products n.e.c	3.90	4.59	6.53	7.14	6.81	55.5	70.1	105.0	117.2	117.7	369
371	Iron and steel	1.91	1.71	1.64	1.60	1.50	30.2	32.5	36.3	38.8	38.8	371
372	Non-ferrous metals	0.45	0.65	0.63	0.72	0.68	7.4	10.1	10.7	12.9	12.2	372
381	Metal products	19.27	21.32	20.93	20.53	19.25	202.0	259.1	276.5	303.1	307.4	381
382	Machinery n.e.c.	23.82	23.63	22.25	21.24	19.54	323.8	346.5	365.3	393.5	399.3	382
3825	Office,computing etc..	...	...	...	...	...	...	...	...	...	...	3825
383	Electrical machinery ...	85.47	75.12	81.25	89.00	82.58	731.5	788.9	945.6	1167.8	1210.6	383
3832	Radio,television etc..	65.77	54.95	54.62	56.64	52.33	536.7	554.7	632.5	756.7	770.4	3832
384	Transport equipment	28.34	30.57	26.89	24.68	21.69	433.2	486.9	467.7	476.7	443.2	384
3841	Shipbuilding, repair..	23.49	24.96	21.12	18.31	15.44	368.6	399.7	367.8	354.9	309.8	3841
3843	Motor vehicles	1.68	1.85	1.68	1.90	1.82	17.3	21.4	23.2	26.6	29.6	3843
385	Professional goods	5.42	5.76	5.19	5.36	5.07	47.3	53.9	59.9	68.7	68.9	385
390	Other industries	6.80	6.39	5.32	5.44	5.00	54.3	54.6	55.1	61.7	62.2	390
3	Manufacturing	281.48	274.59	270.09	273.17	252.30	2956.3	3286.8	3586.9	4054.3	4043.2	3
410	Electricity,gas,steam ..	...	...	...	...	...	...	...	...	...	...	410
4101	Electricity	...	...	...	...	...	...	...	...	...	...	4101
420	Water works and supply .	...	...	...	...	...	...	...	...	...	...	420
4	Electricity,gas etc	...	...	...	...	...	...	...	...	...	...	4
2-4	All industry	...	...	...	...	...	...	...	...	...	...	2-4

a/ At 30 June of the year indicated.
c/ Including employers' contributions to provident funds.
b/ Private establishments with 10 or more persons engaged.
d/ Granite quarrying only.

ISIC	INDUSTRY	5. QUANTITY OF ELECTRICITY CONSUMED a/ (MILLION KWH) 1981	1982	1983	1984	1985	6. OUTPUT IN FACTOR VALUES a/ (MILLION DOLLARS) 1981	1982	1983	1984	1985	ISIC
210	Coal mining	...	...	...	...	...	...	...	...	...	...	210
220	Petroleum and gas	...	...	...	...	...	...	...	...	...	...	220
230	Metal ore mining	...	...	...	...	...	...	...	...	...	...	230
290	Other mining .... b/	12.5	9.3	19.1	24.6	17.8	134	179	238	224	163	290
2	Mining, quarrying .	...	...	...	...	...	...	...	...	...	...	2
311/2	Food products	112.7	100.8	119.3	126.8	132.0	1693	1806	1936	2241	2312	311/2
313	Beverages	20.9	21.1	23.8	22.6	23.7	327	317	318	309	319	313
314	Tobacco	5.8	5.7	5.9	6.0	5.9	194	219	207	184	188	314
321	Textiles	129.5	104.0	78.6	67.6	48.7	422	324	272	252	193	321
3211	Spinning,weaving etc..	110.1	87.0	63.0	54.2	40.1	233	172	136	120	104	3211
322	Wearing apparel	48.4	50.3	51.4	52.9	51.2	925	929	939	1085	1035	322
323	Leather and products ...	1.5	1.5	1.6	1.5	1.0	50	47	41	40	36	323
324	Footwear	3.8	3.6	3.9	4.1	2.8	55	45	44	47	34	324
331	Wood products	87.8	72.2	61.1	47.6	39.2	641	532	468	399	339	331
332	Furniture, fixtures	24.3	24.4	27.6	29.4	31.2	277	260	282	353	363	332
341	Paper and products	40.2	58.5	46.7	47.9	44.0	302	326	331	372	386	341
3411	Pulp,paper etc.	...	...	...	...	...	...	...	...	...	...	3411
342	Printing,publishing	42.3	46.7	54.1	59.7	61.8	674	727	833	938	931	342
351	Industrial chemicals ...	129.4	126.9	126.1	362.4	564.9	364	384	383	1072	1506	351
3511	Basic excl fertilizers	...	...	...	...	...	...	...	...	...	...	3511
3513	Synthetic resins etc .	...	...	...	...	...	...	...	...	...	...	3513
352	Other chemical products.	41.3	48.6	58.7	66.5	73.9	663	704	885	1104	1070	352
3522	Drugs and medicines ..	...	...	...	...	...	...	...	...	...	...	3522
353	Petroleum refineries ...	[704.4	778.1	828.4	892.8	879.4	14454	14641	13164	12449	11031]	353
354	Petroleum,coal products.											354
355	Rubber products	25.8	20.7	19.1	18.8	19.4	877	595	531	507	251	355
356	Plastic products n.e.c..	120.6	119.9	132.1	176.0	143.4	519	505	547	635	589	356
361	Pottery,china etc	[22.7	23.2	25.0	24.0	6.8	90	81	94	81	30]	361
362	Glass and products											362
369	Non-metal products n.e.c	124.1	150.6	199.7	194.6	144.7	784	951	1238	1120	896	369
371	Iron and steel	282.4	283.7	255.2	293.9	309.6	343	357	333	333	337	371
372	Non-ferrous metals	6.8	12.2	13.2	15.2	17.7	131	156	154	212	236	372
381	Metal products	138.4	165.1	184.7	195.7	184.0	1493	1673	1815	1952	1753	381
382	Machinery n.e.c.	144.3	146.5	140.1	141.5	147.7	2484	2322	2050	1943	1805	382
3825	Office,computing etc..	...	...	...	...	...	...	...	...	...	...	3825
383	Electrical machinery ...	456.7	443.1	521.6	597.8	634.7	6779	6293	8219	11107	10475	383
3832	Radio,television etc..	314.5	297.6	341.5	382.8	419.4	5344	4647	5261	6540	6065	3832
384	Transport equipment	202.0	194.5	214.2	213.0	190.7	2224	2076	1866	1957	1790	384
3841	Shipbuilding, repair..	169.7	156.8	162.4	157.6	127.8	1868	1657	1348	1353	1020	3841
3843	Motor vehicles	3.9	4.0	4.8	7.5	13.9	95	90	85	108	109	3843
385	Professional goods	29.1	31.4	36.9	41.4	40.3	291	284	269	300	326	385
390	Other industries	30.3	23.3	26.3	23.8	23.7	505	408	430	489	433	390
3	Manufacturing	2975.5	3056.6	3255.3	3723.5	3822.4	37561	36962	37649	41481	38664	3
410	Electricity,gas,steam ..	...	...	...	...	...	...	...	...	...	...	410
4101	Electricity	...	...	...	...	...	...	...	...	...	...	4101
420	Water works and supply .	...	...	...	...	...	...	...	...	...	...	420
4	Electricity,gas etc	...	...	...	...	...	...	...	...	...	...	4
2-4	All industry	...	...	...	...	...	...	...	...	...	...	2-4

a/ Private establishments with 10 or more persons engaged. b/ Granite quarrying only.

ISIC	INDUSTRY	7. VALUE ADDED IN FACTOR VALUES a/ (MILLION DOLLARS) 1981	1982	1983	1984	1985	8. GROSS FIXED CAPITAL FORMATION TOTAL a/b/ (MILLION DOLLARS) 1981	1982	1983	1984	1985	ISIC
210	Coal mining	...	...	...	...	...	...	...	...	...	...	210
220	Petroleum and gas	...	...	...	...	...	...	...	...	...	...	220
230	Metal ore mining	...	...	...	...	...	...	...	...	...	...	230
290	Other mining .... c/	109	122	157	146	103	42.8	18.9	7.0	6.7	3.9	290
2	Mining, quarrying .	...	...	...	...	...	...	...	...	...	...	2
311/2	Food products	356	326	354	380	396	83.6	78.0	88.7	125.1	67.3	311/2
313	Beverages	140	141	148	152	167	15.9	26.3	21.6	43.1	30.9	313
314	Tobacco	68	91	89	79	78	3.9	6.7	19.3	34.9	8.2	314
321	Textiles	135	106	94	83	62	27.2	9.4	9.3	8.5	4.9	321
3211	Spinning,weaving etc..	82	59	50	40	33	21.3	4.2	5.4	6.2	3.2	3211
322	Wearing apparel	308	326	333	365	346	34.9	32.3	34.8	44.2	23.7	322
323	Leather and products ...	14	14	13	14	11	1.2	3.0	1.0	1.5	0.2	323
324	Footwear	19	17	18	19	12	5.8	3.7	4.9	1.4	1.0	324
331	Wood products	175	136	139	116	95	28.7	29.1	12.1	13.7	10.2	331
332	Furniture, fixtures	102	102	111	131	134	16.0	20.4	13.9	24.1	17.1	332
341	Paper and products	104	123	146	164	179	90.0	57.0	34.4	31.4	37.2	341
3411	Pulp,paper etc.	...	...	...	...	...	...	...	...	...	...	3411
342	Printing,publishing	342	380	459	531	503	92.7	89.7	119.3	91.4	124.4	342
351	Industrial chemicals ...	119	140	142	257	304	87.2	34.9	29.5	138.5	197.9	351
3511	Basic excl fertilizers	...	...	...	...	...	...	...	...	...	...	3511
3513	Synthetic resins etc .	...	...	...	...	...	...	...	...	...	...	3513
352	Other chemical products.	341	361	496	644	588	37.1	134.7	55.7	68.5	36.4	352
3522	Drugs and medicines ..	...	...	...	...	...	...	...	...	...	...	3522
353 354	Petroleum refineries ... Petroleum,coal products.	[1707	1618	1383	956	874	376.4	314.0	230.1	145.6	181.0]	353 354
355	Rubber products	75	66	73	60	46	8.7	19.2	24.4	22.2	6.2	355
356	Plastic products n.e.c..	185	181	195	228	225	54.8	72.9	64.3	55.2	45.0	356
361 362	Pottery,china etc ...... Glass and products	[37	28	34	35	11	5.5	15.9	5.7	1.6	2.5]	361 362
369	Non-metal products n.e.c	240	286	383	364	308	32.5	79.7	143.7	57.0	55.1	369
371	Iron and steel	138	136	123	122	106	12.9	33.7	49.7	46.7	5.4	371
372	Non-ferrous metals	25	25	33	44	38	10.6	11.2	10.8	5.6	5.6	372
381	Metal products	538	657	692	753	656	152.6	190.3	224.4	164.0	94.8	381
382	Machinery n.e.c.	1141	1012	870	889	814	215.0	221.2	185.9	134.6	164.7	382
3825	Office,computing etc..	...	...	...	...	...	...	...	...	...	...	3825
383	Electrical machinery ...	2014	1872	2357	3440	3384	404.8	443.4	475.2	742.3	753.1	383
3832	Radio,television etc..	1458	1228	1348	1850	1724	262.8	271.4	282.5	531.3	502.1	3832
384	Transport equipment	1181	1006	929	1009	1034	120.1	236.2	200.7	136.1	67.8	384
3841	Shipbuilding, repair..	957	729	573	583	466	81.1	194.5	166.9	83.8	31.9	3841
3843	Motor vehicles	31	32	36	47	57	6.4	5.8	5.3	7.9	6.8	3843
385	Professional goods	110	119	120	164	196	31.5	52.2	36.5	23.3	20.7	385
390	Other industries	143	114	121	125	128	20.3	19.5	29.5	24.0	17.2	390
3	Manufacturing	9757	9383	9855	11124	10695	1969.9	2234.6	2125.4	2184.5	1978.5	3
410	Electricity,gas,steam ..	...	...	...	...	...	...	...	...	...	...	410
4101	Electricity	...	...	...	...	...	...	...	...	...	...	4101
420	Water works and supply .	...	...	...	...	...	...	...	...	...	...	420
4	Electricity,gas etc	...	...	...	...	...	...	...	...	...	...	4
2-4	All industry	...	...	...	...	...	...	...	...	...	...	2-4

a/ Private establishments with 10 or more persons engaged. b/ The value of sales is not deducted.
c/ Granite quarrying only.

9. INDEX NUMBERS OF INDUSTRIAL PRODUCTION (1980 = 100)

ISIC	INDUSTRY	1976	1977	1978	1979	1981	1982	1983	1984	1985	RATE a/	ISIC
210	Coal mining	...	...	...	...	...	...	...	...	...	...	210
220	Petroleum and gas	...	...	...	...	...	...	...	...	...	...	220
230	Metal ore mining	...	...	...	...	...	...	...	...	...	...	230
290	Other mining	...	...	...	...	...	...	...	...	...	...	290
2	Mining, quarrying	...	...	...	...	...	...	...	...	...	...	2
311/2	Food products	72	88	89	97	96	93	86	85	85	1.9	311/2
313	Beverages	68	75	89	90	107	97	101	90	92	3.4	313
314	Tobacco	98	104	105	104	102	121	101	97	118	2.1	314
321	Textiles	108	109	97	96	89	66	50	42	30	-13.3	321
3211	Spinning,weaving etc.	...	...	...	...	...	...	...	...	...	...	3211
322	Wearing apparel	90	84	100	104	93	92	96	108	102	1.4	322
323	Leather and products	124	155	114	112	96	67	50	71	50	-9.6	323
324	Footwear	147	105	91	106	109	78	72	72	46	-12.1	324
331	Wood products	131	89	130	118	94	80	61	50	40	-12.3	331
332	Furniture, fixtures	45	53	77	94	128	119	126	131	121	11.6	332
341	Paper and products	69	78	85	91	103	95	68	61	56	-2.3	341
3411	Pulp,paper etc.	...	...	...	...	...	...	...	...	...	...	3411
342	Printing,publishing	62	71	80	82	110	111	118	133	135	9.0	342
351	Industrial chemicals	74	76	91	100	114	119	113	229	310	17.3	351
3511	Basic excl fertilizers	...	...	...	...	...	...	...	...	...	...	3511
3513	Synthetic resins etc	...	...	...	...	...	...	...	...	...	...	3513
352	Other chemical products	61	75	84	83	105	110	125	127	143	9.9	352
3522	Drugs and medicines	...	...	...	...	...	...	...	...	...	...	3522
353	Petroleum refineries	81	92	99	104	117	120	122	131	118	4.3	353
354	Petroleum,coal products											354
355	Rubber products	80	88	95	92	93	85	68	76	73	-1.0	355
356	Plastic products n.e.c.	91	92	107	100	99	100	103	105	86	-0.6	356
361	Pottery,china etc	68	70	98	112	132	140	119	124	34	-7.4	361
362	Glass and products											362
369	Non-metal products n.e.c	88	108	97	110	112	115	117	94	72	-2.2	369
371	Iron and steel	68	69	87	98	109	142	134	129	128	7.3	371
372	Non-ferrous metals	64	64	67	94	86	72	74	93	84	3.1	372
381	Metal products	73	80	88	98	108	98	89	104	97	3.2	381
382	Machinery n.e.c.	45	52	63	82	112	116	130	125	105	9.9	382
3825	Office,computing etc.	...	...	...	...	...	...	...	...	...	...	3825
383	Electrical machinery	43	52	61	80	105	93	106	125	109	10.9	383
3832	Radio,television etc.	...	...	...	...	...	...	...	...	...	...	3832
384	Transport equipment	60	55	63	79	126	112	104	112	93	5.0	384
3841	Shipbuilding, repair	...	...	...	...	...	...	...	...	...	...	3841
3843	Motor vehicles	...	...	...	...	...	...	...	...	...	...	3843
385	Professional goods	...	...	...	...	...	...	...	...	...	...	385
390	Other industries	80	99	87	98	85	64	57	69	63	-2.6	390
3	Manufacturing	63	69	77	89	110	104	106	116	107	6.1	3
410	Electricity,gas,steam	...	...	...	...	...	...	...	...	...	...	410
4101	Electricity	...	...	...	...	...	...	...	...	...	...	4101
420	Water works and supply	...	...	...	...	...	...	...	...	...	...	420
4	Electricity,gas etc	...	...	...	...	...	...	...	...	...	...	4
2-4	All industry	...	...	...	...	...	...	...	...	...	...	2-4

a/ Annual growth rate 1976-1985.

The information on industrial activity is based on the reply to the United Nations Questionnaire on General Industrial Statistics from the Central Statistical Services, Pretoria, and on data obtained from national publications. The concepts, definitions and classification by branches of industry are generally in accordance with United Nations standards.

The estimates are derived, in the case of mining, from inquiries carried out by the Department of Mineral and Energy Affairs and for other industries, from periodic censuses and monthly sample surveys conducted by the Central Statistical Services. The censuses are conducted. infrequently, for manufacturing with an interval of three years. The estimates for mining cover all mining establishments and for manufacturing, except as noted below, all private manufacturing establishments. The estimates for electricity, gas and steam cover all establishments where the main activity is the generation and/or distribution of these commodities.

The estimates are based on the national classification which follows the present version of ISIC. However, certain activities are excluded from the scope of manufacturing: manufacture mainly for consumption on premises; grain mills and sawmills operated by farmers for and at their own convenience, and custom milling by retail stores.

For employment and wages and salaries, the manufacturing data include the following government establishments: government sawmills and wood preservation installations of the Department of Environmental Affairs; the Government Printer: the South African Mint; municipal abattoirs and those of the Abattoir Corporation; beer breweries of the Development Boards; and sheltered employment factories of the Department of Manpower.

The employment figures represent the average for June of each year for mining and the numbers at 30 June for other industries. Wages and salaries include employers' contributions to pension or provident and holiday and medical aid funds. Employers' contributions to other funds, such as unemployment insurance and workmen's compensation, are not included. Payments in kind are excluded.

The estimates of gross fixed capital formation are compiled by the South African Reserve Bank.

The indexes of industrial production for mining and manufacturing are compiled by the Central Statistical Services and provided in response to the United Nations Questionnaire on Indexes of Industrial Production. In principle, the indexes cover all establishments. The indexes for electricity are calculated by the United Nations Statistical Office on the basis of the output of electricity in kWh.

Related national publications:

South African Statistics (biennial); Bulletin of Statistics (quarterly); both published by the Central Statistical Services, Pretoria.

ISIC	INDUSTRY	1. AVERAGE NUMBER OF EMPLOYEES (THOUSANDS) 1981	1982	1983	1984	1985	2. WAGES AND SALARIES OF EMPLOYEES a/ (MILLION RAND) 1981	1982	1983	1984	1985	ISIC
210	Coal mining	101	104	97	93	99	450	551	584	593	734	210
220	Petroleum and gas	-	-	-	-	-	-	-	-	-	-	220
230	Metal ore mining	517	509	518	532	536	b/ 1883	b/ 2210	b/ 2537	b/ 2957	b/ 3353	230
290	Other mining	110	95	92	87	89	b/ 487	b/ 485	b/ 526	b/ 584	b/ 685	290
2	Mining, quarrying .	728	708	707	712	724	2820	3246	3647	4134	4772	2
311/2	Food products	176	181	172	173	171	710	865	974	1124	1265	311/2
313	Beverages	35	37	37	36	36	190	242	277	316	357	313
314	Tobacco	5	5	5	4	4	34	40	46	50	56	314
321	Textiles	115	115	106	104	102	421	508	526	596	657	321
3211	Spinning, weaving etc..	...	...	...	...	...	...	...	...	...	...	3211
322	Wearing apparel	118	119	114	115	112	309	385	436	495	524	322
323	Leather and products ...	10	10	10	9	9	33	38	41	45	48	323
324	Footwear	29	28	27	28	26	101	115	127	147	154	324
331	Wood products	54	55	54	53	51	142	159	179	203	212	331
332	Furniture, fixtures	31	31	31	31	29	136	166	190	206	221	332
341	Paper and products	37	38	36	37	36	229	272	308	352	394	341
3411	Pulp, paper etc.	...	...	...	...	...	...	...	...	...	...	3411
342	Printing, publishing	43	45	44	45	45	330	390	442	527	570	342
351	Industrial chemicals ... c/	100	103	98	98	95	786	954	1065	1208	1351	351
3511	Basic excl fertilizers	...	...	...	...	...	...	...	...	...	...	3511
3513	Synthetic resins etc .	...	...	...	...	...	...	...	...	...	...	3513
352	Other chemical products. c/	...	...	...	...	...	...	...	...	...	...	352
3522	Drugs and medicines ..	...	...	...	...	...	...	...	...	...	...	3522
353	Petroleum refineries ... c/	...	...	...	...	...	...	...	...	...	...	353
354	Petroleum, coal products. c/	...	...	...	...	...	...	...	...	...	...	354
355	Rubber products	20	20	18	18	18	134	151	164	192	213	355
356	Plastic products n.e.c..	27	27	25	25	23	162	188	188	218	233	356
361	Pottery, china etc											361
362	Glass and products	86	86	83	86	79	404	488	535	615	646	362
369	Non-metal products n.e.c											369
371	Iron and steel	123	121	108	111	109	1008	1153	1144	1317	1436	371
372	Non-ferrous metals											372
381	Metal products	138	134	128	131	123	853	990	1084	1224	1303	381
382	Machinery n.e.c.	86	79	73	71	68	724	809	846	898	954	382
3825	Office, computing etc..	...	...	...	...	...	...	...	...	...	...	3825
383	Electrical machinery ...	77	76	70	72	67	548	649	692	782	822	383
3832	Radio, television etc..	...	...	...	...	...	...	...	...	...	...	3832
384	Transport equipment	115	119	109	108	100	830	1005	1081	1185	1234	384
3841	Shipbuilding, repair..	...	...	...	...	...	...	...	...	...	...	3841
3843	Motor vehicles	...	...	...	...	...	...	...	...	...	...	3843
385	Professional goods	5	5	5	5	5	27	33	38	43	49	385
390	Other industries	21	21	20	21	20	104	118	129	146	156	390
3	Manufacturing	1451	1455	1373	1381	1328	8215	9718	10512	11889	12855	3
410	Electricity, gas, steam ..	49	55	60	63	66	358	486	592	656	773	410
4101	Electricity	...	...	...	...	...	...	...	...	...	...	4101
420	Water works and supply .	...	...	...	...	...	...	...	...	...	...	420
4	Electricity, gas etc	...	...	...	...	...	...	...	...	...	...	4
2-4	All industry	...	...	...	...	...	...	...	...	...	...	2-4

a/ Including employers' contributions to pension or provident and holiday and medical aid funds; excluding payments in kind.
b/ Metal mining other than chrome, gold, iron, manganese and tin is included in major group 290.
c/ Major groups 352 to 354 are included in 351.

ISIC	INDUSTRY	3. VALUE ADDED IN FACTOR VALUES a/ (MILLION RAND) 1981	1982	1983	1984	1985	4. GROSS FIXED CAPITAL FORMATION TOTAL b/ (MILLION RAND) 1981	1982	1983	1984	1985	ISIC
210	Coal mining	1245	1524	1560	1576	2244	...	...	...	...	...	210
220	Petroleum and gas	-	-	-	-	-	...	...	...	...	...	220
230	Metal ore mining	[9180	8863	10533	11506	15451]	...	...	...	...	...	230
290	Other mining						...	...	...	...	...	290
2	Mining, quarrying .	10425	10387	12093	13082	17695	229.0	227.1	217.3	255.9	328.8	2
311/2	Food products	1572	1782	2003	2271	2761	...	...	...	...	...	311/2
313	Beverages	475	630	722	817	1009	...	...	...	...	...	313
314	Tobacco	116	117	137	194	274	...	...	...	...	...	314
321	Textiles	853	869	843	1028	980	...	...	...	...	...	321
3211	Spinning,weaving etc..	...	...	...	...	...	...	...	...	...	...	3211
322	Wearing apparel	452	503	534	613	622	...	...	...	...	...	322
323	Leather and products ...	37	45	63	79	83	...	...	...	...	...	323
324	Footwear	150	162	177	219	226	...	...	...	...	...	324
331	Wood products	211	247	275	307	317	...	...	...	...	...	331
332	Furniture, fixtures	195	217	216	270	237	...	...	...	...	...	332
341	Paper and products	529	564	576	730	731	...	...	...	...	...	341
3411	Pulp,paper etc.	...	...	...	...	...	...	...	...	...	...	3411
342	Printing,publishing	542	606	763	820	795	...	...	...	...	...	342
351	Industrial chemicals ...	814	916	1094	1042	1287	...	...	...	...	...	351
3511	Basic excl fertilizers	...	...	...	...	...	...	...	...	...	...	3511
3513	Synthetic resins etc .	...	...	...	...	...	...	...	...	...	...	3513
352	Other chemical products. c/	1449	1862	2358	3148	3911	...	...	...	...	...	352
3522	Drugs and medicines ..	...	...	...	...	...	...	...	...	...	...	3522
353	Petroleum refineries ... c/	...	...	...	...	...	...	...	...	...	...	353
354	Petroleum,coal products. c/	...	...	...	...	...	...	...	...	...	...	354
355	Rubber products	287	288	291	369	372	...	...	...	...	...	355
356	Plastic products n.e.c..	366	382	413	486	515	...	...	...	...	...	356
361	Pottery,china etc	28	34	32	34	29	...	...	...	...	...	361
362	Glass and products	193	214	226	291	293	...	...	...	...	...	362
369	Non-metal products n.e.c	704	777	964	1122	1125	...	...	...	...	...	369
371	Iron and steel	1792	1766	1818	2645	2435	...	...	...	...	...	371
372	Non-ferrous metals	478	531	646	811	1162	...	...	...	...	...	372
381	Metal products	1457	1629	1775	1865	1956	...	...	...	...	...	381
382	Machinery n.e.c.	1204	1298	1211	1249	1326	...	...	...	...	...	382
3825	Office,computing etc..	...	...	...	...	...	...	...	...	...	...	3825
383	Electrical machinery ...	1132	1285	1461	1513	1461	...	...	...	...	...	383
3832	Radio,television etc..	...	...	...	...	...	...	...	...	...	...	3832
384	Transport equipment	1268	1306	1230	1287	939	...	...	...	...	...	384
3841	Shipbuilding, repair..	...	...	...	...	...	...	...	...	...	...	3841
3843	Motor vehicles	1060	1139	997	1062	686	...	...	...	...	...	3843
385	Professional goods	41	47	57	64	66	...	...	...	...	...	385
390	Other industries	403	494	532	619	665	...	...	...	...	...	390
3	Manufacturing	d/ 15644	d/ 16944	d/ 19412	d/ 22705	d/ 24391	475.0	495.1	414.8	385.8	429.9	3
410	Electricity,gas,steam ..	1924	2334	2864	3452	3886	...	...	...	...	...	410
4101	Electricity	1908	2314	2844	3433	3865	...	...	...	...	...	4101
420	Water works and supply .	236	260	272	316	380	...	...	...	...	...	420
4	Electricity,gas etc	2160	2594	3136	3768	4265	230.9	303.7	362.9	434.8	498.6	4
2-4	All industry	28229	29925	34641	39555	46351	934.9	1025.9	995.0	1076.5	1257.3	2-4

a/ Mining, electricity, gas and water and all industry: contributions to the gross domestic product.
b/ Mining, electricity, gas and water and all industry: estimates derived from national accounts calculations.
c/ Major groups 353 and 354 are included in 352.
d/ Net of stock evaluation adjustment.

5. INDEX NUMBERS OF INDUSTRIAL PRODUCTION (1980 = 100)

ISIC	INDUSTRY	1976	1977	1978	1979	1981	1982	1983	1984	1985	a/ RATE	ISIC
210	Coal mining	66	75	78	91	114	117	119	137	148	9.4	210
220	Petroleum and gas	...	...	...	...	...	...	...	...	...	...	220
230	Metal ore mining	99	100	100	102	98	96	97	99	98	-0.1	230
290	Other mining	92	94	91	99	104	91	96	95	94	0.2	290
2	Mining, quarrying	96	97	98	101	100	99	100	103	104	0.9	2
311/2	Food products	96	94	89	94	105	108	103	107	111	1.6	311/2
313	Beverages	71	68	71	78	112	107	108	115	115	5.5	313
314	Tobacco	88	85	83	93	101	110	106	108	105	2.0	314
321	Textiles	86	79	80	83	114	105	88	84	82	-0.5	321
3211	Spinning,weaving etc.	...	...	...	...	...	...	...	...	...	...	3211
322	Wearing apparel	85	78	80	85	113	111	96	95	82	-0.4	322
323	Leather and products	120	95	106	100	94	85	88	91	84	-3.9	323
324	Footwear	95	88	95	97	99	92	91	97	93	-0.2	324
331	Wood products	84	65	70	81	101	98	92	79	74	-1.4	331
332	Furniture, fixtures	78	80	82	89	107	105	91	81	75	-0.4	332
341	Paper and products	97	92	96	102	107	107	108	121	124	2.8	341
3411	Pulp,paper etc.	...	...	...	...	...	...	...	...	...	...	3411
342	Printing,publishing	92	83	85	88	104	110	114	126	116	2.6	342
351	Industrial chemicals	67	72	78	86	102	102	84	92	92	3.6	351
3511	Basic excl fertilizers	...	...	...	...	...	...	...	...	...	...	3511
3513	Synthetic resins etc	...	...	...	...	...	...	...	...	...	...	3513
352	Other chemical products	87	90	91	96	106	102	104	110	106	2.2	352
3522	Drugs and medicines	...	...	...	...	...	...	...	...	...	...	3522
353	Petroleum refineries	...	...	...	...	...	...	...	...	...	...	353
354	Petroleum,coal products	...	...	...	...	...	...	...	...	...	...	354
355	Rubber products	102	90	88	94	110	102	88	93	87	-1.8	355
356	Plastic products n.e.c.	84	70	81	91	110	108	110	112	124	4.4	356
361	Pottery,china etc	...	...	...	94	105	79	70	69	61	b/ -7.0	361
362	Glass and products	78	70	77	79	118	118	105	125	111	4.0	362
369	Non-metal products n.e.c	100	82	82	84	101	98	97	100	86	-1.7	369
371	Iron and steel	70	68	81	97	98	89	87	92	97	3.7	371
372	Non-ferrous metals	81	83	85	94	109	106	102	116	109	3.4	372
381	Metal products	90	83	94	93	110	104	87	87	85	-0.6	381
382	Machinery n.e.c.	102	87	83	88	101	101	89	96	77	-3.1	382
3825	Office,computing etc.	...	...	...	...	...	...	...	...	...	...	3825
383	Electrical machinery	105	85	87	87	110	110	104	101	90	-1.7	383
3832	Radio,television etc.	...	...	...	...	...	...	...	...	...	...	3832
384	Transport equipment	101	85	89	84	119	114	103	92	65	-4.8	384
3841	Shipbuilding, repair	...	...	...	...	...	...	...	...	...	...	3841
3843	Motor vehicles	107	67	80	77	124	116	107	97	66	-5.2	3843
385	Professional goods	87	83	80	94	112	109	119	122	134	4.9	385
390	Other industries	72	66	78	82	109	98	95	98	101	3.8	390
3	Manufacturing	81	78	83	91	107	104	96	100	94	1.7	3
410	Electricity,gas,steam	...	...	...	...	...	...	...	...	...	...	410
4101	Electricity	...	...	...	...	...	...	...	...	...	...	4101
420	Water works and supply	...	...	...	...	...	...	...	...	...	...	420
4	Electricity,gas etc	...	...	...	...	...	...	...	...	...	...	4
2-4	All industry	...	...	...	...	...	...	...	...	...	...	2-4

a/ Annual growth rate 1976-1985.

b/ Annual growth rate 1979-1985.

The information on industrial activity is based on the reply to the United Nations Questionnaire on General Industrial Statistics from the Instituto Nacional de Estadistica, Madrid. The concepts, definitions and classification by branches of industry are generally in accordance with United Nations standards.

The estimates are compiled by the Instituto Nacional de Estadistica from the results of annual industrial surveys conducted within the framework of the 1978 industrial census. These surveys cover, in general, all establishments irrespective of size in water distribution, manufacture of bakery products and tailoring and dressmaking.

The estimates, which are compiled according to the national classification, have been adjusted to the present version of ISIC as far as practicable. However, it should be noted that custom tailoring (ISIC 322) and manufacture of mattresses except inner spring and foam rubber mattresses are included in ISIC 321; manufacture of canes, umbrellas and fans (ISIC 390) in ISIC 322; orthopaedic footwear (ISIC 385) in ISIC 324; manufacture of wooden blinds and brooms (ISIC 390) in ISIC 331; and inner spring mattresses (ISIC 332) and repairing of farm implements (ISIC 382) in ISIC 381.

The estimates of persons engaged refer to averages of 4 quarters comprising employees, working proprietors and unpaid family workers. Number of employees and operatives (defined as workers directly engaged in production activities) relate to average numbers employed during the reference period. Wages and salaries relate to gross earnings of employees excluding employers' contributions to social security schemes. Hours worked by operatives refer to total number of hours spent by operatives at work during the reference period.

The quantity of electricity consumed refers to the sum of the quantity of electricity purchased and generated less the quantity sold to others.

Output is the sum of (a) the value of goods produced for sale whether they are sold or in stock, (b) receipts for work done for or services rendered to others, (c) value of goods sold in the same condition as purchased, (d) value of electricity sold, (e) net change in the value of finished goods and work in progress, (f) receipts from renting of capital goods, and (g) value of fixed assets produced for own use. The estimates of value added are derived as the value of output less the cost of (a) materials and supplies consumed, (b) purchased fuels and electricity consumed, (c) goods sold in the same condition as purchased, and (d) services rendered by others. The valuation of output and value added is in producers' prices.

Gross fixed capital formation relates to acquisitions of new and used fixed assets less sales of fixed assets during the reference period.

The indexes of industrial production are compiled by the Instituto Nacional de Estadistica and provided in response to the United Nations Questionnaire on Indexes of Industrial Production.

Related national publications:
Estadistica Industrial de Espana (annual); Anuario Estadistico, both published by the Instituto Nacional de Estadistica, Madrid.

ISIC	INDUSTRY	1. NUMBER OF ESTABLISHMENTS (NUMBER)					2. AVERAGE NUMBER OF PERSONS ENGAGED (THOUSANDS)					ISIC
		1981	1982	1983	1984	1985	1981	1982	1983	1984	1985	
210	Coal mining	217	243	248	...	...	52	54	54	...	...	210
220	Petroleum and gas	6	5	5	...	...	...	...	...	...	...	220
230	Metal ore mining	86	89	84	...	...	10	8	9	...	...	230
290	Other mining	3885	3725	3568	...	...	28	27	25	...	...	290
2	Mining, quarrying .	4194	4062	3905	...	...	a/ 90	a/ 89	a/ 88	...	...	2
311/2	Food products	39867	38301	38547	...	...	297	284	279	...	...	311/2
313	Beverages	6482	6040	5814	...	...	69	64	64	...	...	313
314	Tobacco	41	40	38	...	...	12	12	12	...	...	314
321	Textiles	6032	4696	5857	...	...	161	146	144	...	...	321
3211	Spinning,weaving etc..	2016	1517	2502	...	...	75	70	85	...	...	3211
322	Wearing apparel	7032	6172	6307	...	...	106	95	93	...	...	322
323	Leather and products ...	1291	1319	1201	...	...	22	19	18	...	...	323
324	Footwear	2594	2041	1844	...	...	53	45	40	...	...	324
331	Wood products	20814	19882	19439	...	...	100	88	86	...	...	331
332	Furniture, fixtures	12011	11240	11785	...	...	90	79	76	...	...	332
341	Paper and products	1196	1064	1168	...	...	49	44	44	...	...	341
3411	Pulp,paper etc.	194	178	171	...	...	20	19	18	...	...	3411
342	Printing,publishing	5595	5270	5709	...	...	82	79	72	...	...	342
351	Industrial chemicals ...	787	742	566	...	...	54	52	45	...	...	351
3511	Basic excl fertilizers	490	452	301	...	...	23	21	18	...	...	3511
3513	Synthetic resins etc .	112	128	105	...	...	17	18	15	...	...	3513
352	Other chemical products.	1916	1862	2040	...	...	75	74	77	...	...	352
3522	Drugs and medicines ..	397	370	352	...	...	34	34	32	...	...	3522
353	Petroleum refineries ...	10	10	10	...	...	9	9	10	...	...	353
354	Petroleum,coal products.	11	126	212	...	...	3	5	6	...	...	354
355	Rubber products	1086	1001	1213	...	...	38	36	37	...	...	355
356	Plastic products n.e.c..	2307	2052	2604	...	...	55	49	52	...	...	356
361	Pottery,china etc	980	939	889	...	...	20	21	19	...	...	361
362	Glass and products	698	649	647	...	...	25	23	22	...	...	362
369	Non-metal products n.e.c	8453	7610	7021	...	...	124	106	92	...	...	369
371	Iron and steel	1246	1244	1283	...	...	121	115	116	...	...	371
372	Non-ferrous metals	837	709	567	...	...	33	31	26	...	...	372
381	Metal products	24490	23887	15783	...	...	224	210	168	...	...	381
382	Machinery n.e.c.	6081	5575	14689	...	...	129	119	153	...	...	382
3825	Office,computing etc..	28	28	26	...	...	4	3	2	...	...	3825
383	Electrical machinery ...	2614	2522	2615	...	...	144	140	135	...	...	383
3832	Radio,television etc..	519	390	508	...	...	43	43	41	...	...	3832
384	Transport equipment	1583	1404	1413	...	...	227	226	225	...	...	384
3841	Shipbuilding, repair..	120	102	173	...	...	53	51	50	...	...	3841
3843	Motor vehicles	1084	999	956	...	...	145	144	145	...	...	3843
385	Professional goods	497	495	531	...	...	10	9	9	...	...	385
390	Other industries	1710	1483	2286	...	...	25	22	27	...	...	390
3	Manufacturing	158261	148375	152078	...	...	2357	2202	2197	...	...	3
410	Electricity,gas,steam ..	1110	1053	1000	...	...	64	69	64	...	...	410
4101	Electricity	1073	1019	968	...	...	60	61	60	...	...	4101
420	Water works and supply .	14006	13674	13822	...	...	29	29	29	...	...	420
4	Electricity,gas etc	15116	14727	14822	...	...	93	98	93	...	...	4
2-4	All industry	177571	167164	170805	...	...	a/ 2540	a/ 2389	a/ 2378	...	...	2-4

Note. For limitation of coverage and differences in classification, see country note.

a/ Total of industries shown.

SPAIN

ISIC	INDUSTRY	3. AVERAGE NUMBER OF EMPLOYEES (THOUSANDS)					4. WAGES AND SALARIES OF EMPLOYEES a/ (BILLION PESETAS)					ISIC
		1981	1982	1983	1984	1985	1981	1982	1983	1984	1985	
210	Coal mining	52	54	47	...	...	76.7	b/ 89.7	77.5	...	...	210
220	Petroleum and gas	...	...	...	...	...	0.7	b/ 0.8	0.7	...	...	220
230	Metal ore mining	10	8	9	...	...	12.9	b/ 13.5	12.1	...	...	230
290	Other mining	26	26	24	...	...	24.0	b/ 26.6	21.5	...	...	290
2	Mining, quarrying .	c/ 88	c/ 88	c/ 80	...	...	114.3	b/ 130.6	111.8	...	...	2
311/2	Food products	251	238	235	...	...	166.3	179.4	196.7	...	...	311/2
313	Beverages	66	59	60	...	...	55.3	63.1	73.4	...	...	313
314	Tobacco	12	12	12	...	...	11.0	12.5	14.1	...	...	314
321	Textiles	156	143	137	...	...	99.6	104.0	113.7	...	...	321
3211	Spinning,weaving etc..	74	69	83	...	...	47.2	50.2	71.9	...	...	3211
322	Wearing apparel	95	84	83	...	...	51.5	53.4	58.7	...	...	322
323	Leather and products ...	20	18	17	...	...	14.2	14.3	15.8	...	...	323
324	Footwear	52	43	38	...	...	29.8	28.6	27.9	...	...	324
331	Wood products	79	68	66	...	...	44.7	43.1	46.4	...	...	331
332	Furniture, fixtures	79	67	64	...	...	47.5	46.1	49.0	...	...	332
341	Paper and products	48	44	43	...	...	42.3	44.3	49.0	...	...	341
3411	Pulp,paper etc.	19	19	18	...	...	19.6	22.2	23.4	...	...	3411
342	Printing,publishing	76	74	67	...	...	64.3	71.7	72.6	...	...	342
351	Industrial chemicals ...	53	51	45	...	...	57.8	62.7	60.5	...	...	351
3511	Basic excl fertilizers	23	21	18	...	...	25.9	27.7	24.8	...	...	3511
3513	Synthetic resins etc .	17	18	15	...	...	18.4	21.3	21.5	...	...	3513
352	Other chemical products.	74	72	76	...	...	75.3	84.4	100.1	...	...	352
3522	Drugs and medicines ..	34	34	32	...	...	36.1	41.1	44.0	...	...	3522
353	Petroleum refineries ...	9	9	10	...	...	21.0	b/ 24.0	20.3	...	...	353
354	Petroleum,coal products.	3	5	6	...	...	3.5	b/ 8.4	7.2	...	...	354
355	Rubber products	37	35	36	...	...	32.1	35.6	40.6	...	...	355
356	Plastic products n.e.c..	50	48	51	...	...	39.9	43.2	50.5	...	...	356
361	Pottery,china etc	19	20	18	...	...	14.1	16.4	16.4	...	...	361
362	Glass and products	24	23	21	...	...	23.1	24.3	25.9	...	...	362
369	Non-metal products n.e.c	118	98	86	...	...	89.6	87.0	85.0	...	...	369
371	Iron and steel	120	115	115	...	...	123.9	132.7	147.5	...	...	371
372	Non-ferrous metals	32	30	26	...	...	31.5	34.8	34.4	...	...	372
381	Metal products	201	187	155	...	...	161.0	171.3	158.9	...	...	381
382	Machinery n.e.c.	125	115	139	...	...	109.5	116.1	153.9	...	...	382
3825	Office,computing etc..	4	3	2	...	...	3.6	4.0	3.6	...	...	3825
383	Electrical machinery ...	142	138	133	...	...	131.7	146.1	155.3	...	...	383
3832	Radio,television etc..	43	44	40	...	...	40.4	46.2	46.9	...	...	3832
384	Transport equipment	226	226	224	...	...	221.5	245.8	276.4	...	...	384
3841	Shipbuilding, repair..	53	51	50	...	...	50.2	57.7	55.1	...	...	3841
3843	Motor vehicles	144	144	145	...	...	143.6	154.3	181.7	...	...	3843
385	Professional goods	10	8	8	...	...	7.9	8.1	9.1	...	...	385
390	Other industries	24	20	25	...	...	16.1	15.7	22.3	...	...	390
3	Manufacturing	2201	2050	1996	...	...	1786.0	1917.1	2081.6	...	...	3
410	Electricity,gas,steam ..	64	64	64	...	...	120.2	b/ 146.1	128.5	...	...	410
4101	Electricity	60	60	60	...	...	113.0	b/ 137.7	121.3	...	...	4101
420	Water works and supply .	21	22	21	...	...	19.4	22.2	23.5	...	...	420
4	Electricity,gas etc	85	86	85	...	...	139.6	168.3	152.0	...	...	4
2-4	All industry	c/ 2374	c/ 2224	c/ 2161	...	...	2039.9	2216.0	2345.4	...	...	2-4

Note. For limitation of coverage and differences in classification, see country note.

a/ Mining and electricity and major groups 353 and 354 include contributions to social security scheme.
b/ Up to 1982, including supplements to wages and salaries. c/ Total of industries shown.

ISIC	INDUSTRY	5. SUPPLEMENTS TO WAGES AND SALARIES (BILLION PESETAS) 1981	1982	1983	1984	1985	6. AVERAGE NUMBER OF OPERATIVES (THOUSANDS) 1981	1982	1983	1984	1985	ISIC
210	Coal mining	...	...	23.9	...	...	44	45	46	...	...	210
220	Petroleum and gas	...	...	0.2	...	...	...	...	...	...	...	220
230	Metal ore mining	...	...	3.7	...	...	8	7	7	...	...	230
290	Other mining	...	...	6.7	...	...	22	21	20	...	...	290
2	Mining, quarrying .	...	...	34.5	...	...	a/ 74	a/ 73	a/ 73	...	...	2
311/2	Food products	51.6	57.6	63.8	...	...	191	187	180	...	...	311/2
313	Beverages	18.1	18.6	21.4	...	...	42	40	38	...	...	313
314	Tobacco	2.8	3.4	3.8	...	...	11	11	11	...	...	314
321	Textiles	30.9	34.1	37.6	...	...	133	122	117	...	...	321
3211	Spinning,weaving etc..	14.5	16.9	24.0	...	...	64	59	71	...	...	3211
322	Wearing apparel	17.2	17.1	19.0	...	...	81	72	70	...	...	322
323	Leather and products ...	4.4	4.5	4.8	...	...	18	15	15	...	...	323
324	Footwear	10.2	9.3	9.2	...	...	47	39	34	...	...	324
331	Wood products	14.1	14.1	15.5	...	...	72	62	60	...	...	331
332	Furniture, fixtures	14.7	14.5	15.8	...	...	70	59	56	...	...	332
341	Paper and products	13.2	13.9	15.5	...	...	39	35	35	...	...	341
3411	Pulp,paper etc.	6.2	7.0	7.4	...	...	16	15	15	...	...	3411
342	Printing,publishing	17.0	19.3	21.6	...	...	62	59	52	...	...	342
351	Industrial chemicals ...	20.8	22.3	19.8	...	...	38	34	31	...	...	351
3511	Basic excl fertilizers	8.9	10.0	8.2	...	...	16	14	12	...	...	3511
3513	Synthetic resins etc .	6.9	7.1	6.7	...	...	13	12	11	...	...	3513
352	Other chemical products.	24.1	27.3	30.8	...	...	39	38	37	...	...	352
3522	Drugs and medicines ..	11.4	13.2	13.6	...	...	14	14	13	...	...	3522
353	Petroleum refineries ...	...	...	7.4	...	...	5	5	5	...	...	353
354	Petroleum,coal products.	...	...	2.3	...	...	2	4	5	...	...	354
355	Rubber products	11.0	12.7	13.4	...	...	29	28	28	...	...	355
356	Plastic products n.e.c..	13.7	13.7	16.1	...	...	42	38	40	...	...	356
361	Pottery,china etc	4.6	5.4	5.2	...	...	17	17	15	...	...	361
362	Glass and products	8.7	8.8	8.7	...	...	19	18	17	...	...	362
369	Non-metal products n.e.c	26.6	27.7	28.2	...	...	98	84	73	...	...	369
371	Iron and steel	40.7	44.3	46.5	...	...	90	86	85	...	...	371
372	Non-ferrous metals	9.9	11.6	12.0	...	...	24	23	19	...	...	372
381	Metal products	49.7	55.0	51.8	...	...	164	153	126	...	...	381
382	Machinery n.e.c.	34.1	35.4	46.5	...	...	93	85	106	...	...	382
3825	Office,computing etc..	1.1	1.1	1.1	...	...	2	1	1	...	...	3825
383	Electrical machinery ...	41.2	46.7	50.0	...	...	100	96	91	...	...	383
3832	Radio,television etc..	12.4	14.2	15.2	...	...	27	28	25	...	...	3832
384	Transport equipment	70.2	77.2	78.9	...	...	170	171	170	...	...	384
3841	Shipbuilding, repair..	16.0	18.0	12.3	...	...	38	37	36	...	...	3841
3843	Motor vehicles	48.9	48.6	57.0	...	...	109	111	111	...	...	3843
385	Professional goods	2.5	2.6	3.0	...	...	7	6	6	...	...	385
390	Other industries	5.0	4.9	7.0	...	...	20	17	21	...	...	390
3	Manufacturing	a/ 557.0	a/ 602.0	655.6	...	...	1723	1604	1543	...	...	3
410	Electricity,gas,steam ..	...	...	41.9	...	...	35	35	35	...	...	410
4101	Electricity	...	...	39.6	...	...	34	34	33	...	...	4101
420	Water works and supply .	5.3	5.8	6.2	...	...	11	13	13	...	...	420
4	Electricity,gas etc	...	...	48.1	...	...	46	48	48	...	...	4
2-4	All industry	...	...	738.2	...	...	a/ 1843	a/ 1725	a/ 1664	...	...	2-4

Note. For limitation of coverage and differences in classification, see country note.

a/ Total of industries shown.

ISIC	INDUSTRY	7. WAGES AND SALARIES OF OPERATIVES a/ (BILLION PESETAS)					8. HOURS WORKED BY OPERATIVES (MILLIONS)					ISIC
		1981	1982	1983	1984	1985	1981	1982	1983	1984	1985	
210	Coal mining	...	71.1	61.5	...	...	68	71	69	...	...	210
220	Petroleum and gas	0.5	0.6	0.5	...	...	...	...	...	...	...	220
230	Metal ore mining	...	9.6	7.8	...	...	13	12	11	...	...	230
290	Other mining	...	21.4	17.1	...	...	38	36	33	...	...	290
2	Mining, quarrying .	...	102.7	86.9	...	...	b/ 119	b/ 119	b/ 113	...	...	2
311/2	Food products	117.6	127.3	138.8	...	...	360	345	324	...	...	311/2
313	Beverages	36.5	37.7	41.8	...	...	80	74	70	...	...	313
314	Tobacco	9.8	11.1	12.5	...	...	18	17	18	...	...	314
321	Textiles	79.4	82.8	90.1	...	...	244	220	210	...	...	321
3211	Spinning,weaving etc..	37.8	40.3	57.4	...	...	114	106	124	...	...	3211
322	Wearing apparel	40.3	40.9	44.9	...	...	148	133	126	...	...	322
323	Leather and products ...	11.6	11.6	12.9	...	...	33	28	27	...	...	323
324	Footwear	26.1	24.7	24.2	...	...	87	72	62	...	...	324
331	Wood products	39.4	32.3	40.7	...	...	135	117	110	...	...	331
332	Furniture, fixtures	40.0	38.7	41.2	...	...	132	112	104	...	...	332
341	Paper and products	31.5	33.0	36.3	...	...	74	66	63	...	...	341
3411	Pulp,paper etc.	14.8	16.7	17.4	...	...	31	29	26	...	...	3411
342	Printing,publishing	47.8	52.3	51.0	...	...	117	110	95	...	...	342
351	Industrial chemicals ...	35.0	38.3	36.9	...	...	70	63	55	...	...	351
3511	Basic excl fertilizers	14.7	16.0	14.8	...	...	29	25	21	...	...	3511
3513	Synthetic resins etc .	12.1	14.0	13.9	...	...	24	23	20	...	...	3513
352	Other chemical products.	31.1	33.9	39.6	...	...	69	63	65	...	...	352
3522	Drugs and medicines ..	11.9	13.3	13.8	...	...	26	25	22	...	...	3522
353	Petroleum refineries ...	...	9.8	9.1	...	...	9	8	8	...	...	353
354	Petroleum,coal products.	...	5.0	5.5	...	...	4	7	8	...	...	354
355	Rubber products	23.1	25.2	28.5	...	...	53	49	49	...	...	355
356	Plastic products n.e.c..	29.3	31.3	36.2	...	...	77	70	71	...	...	356
361	Pottery,china etc	11.7	13.6	13.3	...	...	31	32	27	...	...	361
362	Glass and products	16.9	17.5	18.4	...	...	37	34	30	...	...	362
369	Non-metal products n.e.c	78.0	69.1	66.4	...	...	192	159	134	...	...	369
371	Iron and steel	85.8	92.1	102.3	...	...	161	151	147	...	...	371
372	Non-ferrous metals	22.0	24.1	23.4	...	...	46	41	34	...	...	372
381	Metal products	123.1	130.7	120.1	...	...	306	281	224	...	...	381
382	Machinery n.e.c.	76.0	79.5	106.1	...	...	170	154	187	...	...	382
3825	Office,computing etc..	2.2	1.4	1.5	...	...	3	2	2	...	...	3825
383	Electrical machinery ...	82.4	89.4	93.8	...	...	178	185	158	...	...	383
3832	Radio,television etc..	22.8	25.8	26.3	...	...	48	46	45	...	...	3832
384	Transport equipment	160.0	183.8	192.7	...	...	283	279	276	...	...	384
3841	Shipbuilding, repair..	36.5	41.8	36.8	...	...	66	64	51	...	...	3841
3843	Motor vehicles	102.5	115.6	126.9	...	...	176	173	185	...	...	3843
385	Professional goods	5.1	5.0	5.6	...	...	13	11	11	...	...	385
390	Other industries	13.5	12.3	16.8	...	...	36	31	37	...	...	390
3	Manufacturing	b/ 1273.0	1353.0	1449.1	...	...	3163	2892	2730	...	...	3
410	Electricity,gas,steam ..	59.2	70.2	62.8	...	...	67	65	63	...	...	410
4101	Electricity	57.2	67.8	60.4	...	...	64	63	60	...	...	4101
420	Water works and supply .	10.6	12.1	14.0	...	...	22	23	23	...	...	420
4	Electricity,gas etc	69.8	82.3	76.8	...	...	89	88	86	...	...	4
2-4	All industry	...	1538.0	1612.8	...	...	b/ 3371	b/ 3099	b/ 2929	...	...	2-4

Note. For limitation of coverage and differences in classification, see country note.

a/ Mining and electricity and major groups 353 and 354 include contributions to social security scheme.
b/ Total of industries shown.

ISIC	INDUSTRY	9. QUANTITY OF ELECTRICITY CONSUMED (MILLION KWH) 1981	1982	1983	1984	1985	10. OUTPUT IN FACTOR VALUES (BILLION PESETAS) 1981	1982	1983	1984	1985	ISIC
210	Coal mining	886	924	1003	...	...	134	174	189	...	...	210
220	Petroleum and gas	9	24	18	...	...	24	41	90	...	...	220
230	Metal ore mining	785	668	748	...	...	42	42	56	...	...	230
290	Other mining	640	651	628	...	...	65	70	78	...	...	290
2	Mining, quarrying .	2321	2267	2397	...	...	265	327	413	...	...	2
311/2	Food products	3091	3001	3390	...	...	1948	2174	2568	...	...	311/2
313	Beverages	586	542	559	...	...	416	471	549	...	...	313
314	Tobacco	68	55	59	...	...	115	122	160	...	...	314
321	Textiles	1810	1592	1747	...	...	553	547	640	...	...	321
3211	Spinning,weaving etc..	1212	1032	1441	...	...	306	291	409	...	...	3211
322	Wearing apparel	191	179	187	...	...	233	244	274	...	...	322
323	Leather and products ...	117	112	102	...	...	92	88	106	...	...	323
324	Footwear	118	127	91	...	...	140	139	153	...	...	324
331	Wood products	821	751	642	...	...	233	217	254	...	...	331
332	Furniture, fixtures	340	290	318	...	...	198	193	214	...	...	332
341	Paper and products	2737	2862	2778	...	...	322	346	386	...	...	341
3411	Pulp,paper etc.	2475	2593	2502	...	...	168	190	201	...	...	3411
342	Printing,publishing	237	228	221	...	...	220	254	281	...	...	342
351	Industrial chemicals ...	6275	6300	6103	...	...	579	662	708	...	...	351
3511	Basic excl fertilizers	3791	3971	3826	...	...	262	305	301	...	...	3511
3513	Synthetic resins etc .	1424	1443	1410	...	...	193	232	272	...	...	3513
352	Other chemical products.	768	552	608	...	...	487	542	682	...	...	352
3522	Drugs and medicines ..	273	272	225	...	...	202	229	251	...	...	3522
353	Petroleum refineries ...	1024	1060	1219	...	...	1132	1330	1654	...	...	353
354	Petroleum,coal products.	84	118	164	...	...	64	109	126	...	...	354
355	Rubber products	624	607	591	...	...	156	154	193	...	...	355
356	Plastic products n.e.c..	819	854	871	...	...	226	244	318	...	...	356
361	Pottery,china etc	216	258	193	...	...	44	51	55	...	...	361
362	Glass and products	584	562	567	...	...	99	107	120	...	...	362
369	Non-metal products n.e.c	4810	4883	4651	...	...	575	554	537	...	...	369
371	Iron and steel	9704	9890	10303	...	...	693	775	886	...	...	371
372	Non-ferrous metals	7257	5108	3207	...	...	321	354	432	...	...	372
381	Metal products	1203	1315	1309	...	...	695	753	707	...	...	381
382	Machinery n.e.c.	515	530	650	...	...	480	503	653	...	...	382
3825	Office,computing etc..	13	13	21	...	...	27	36	34	...	...	3825
383	Electrical machinery ...	968	933	977	...	...	561	658	752	...	...	383
3832	Radio,television etc..	130	138	152	...	...	164	199	232	...	...	3832
384	Transport equipment	1583	1626	1868	...	...	1020	1175	1446	...	...	384
3841	Shipbuilding, repair..	264	266	232	...	...	186	248	224	...	...	3841
3843	Motor vehicles	1161	1190	1479	...	...	738	808	1091	...	...	3843
385	Professional goods	26	25	20	...	...	27	28	34	...	...	385
390	Other industries	91	91	121	...	...	83	81	113	...	...	390
3	Manufacturing	46672	44451	43516	...	...	11712	12875	15001	...	...	3
410	Electricity,gas,steam ..	5961	5975	6069	...	...	948	1147	1331	...	...	410
4101	Electricity	5907	5914	6003	...	...	868	1050	1218	...	...	4101
420	Water works and supply .	1205	1215	1448	...	...	63	74	79	...	...	420
4	Electricity,gas etc	7166	7190	7517	...	...	1011	1221	1410	...	...	4
2-4	All industry	56159	53908	53430	...	...	12988	14423	16824	...	...	2-4

Note. For limitation of coverage and differences in classification, see country note.

ISIC	INDUSTRY	11. VALUE ADDED IN FACTOR VALUES (BILLION PESETAS) 1981	1982	1983	1984	1985	12. GROSS FIXED CAPITAL FORMATION TOTAL (BILLION PESETAS) 1981	1982	1983	1984	1985	ISIC
210	Coal mining	70.1	88.8	96.2	...	...	...	...	28.3	...	...	210
220	Petroleum and gas	20.3	36.2	85.6	...	...	...	...	0.4	...	...	220
230	Metal ore mining	19.0	20.3	29.9	...	...	...	...	4.9	...	...	230
290	Other mining	36.1	35.9	40.5	...	...	...	...	6.0	...	...	290
2	Mining, quarrying	145.5	181.2	252.2	...	...	...	...	39.6	...	...	2
311/2	Food products	449.3	509.1	586.3	...	...	44.5	46.2	56.9	...	...	311/2
313	Beverages	158.2	183.9	216.4	...	...	13.6	15.5	18.2	...	...	313
314	Tobacco	58.9	56.4	63.6	...	...	2.2	0.9	1.3	...	...	314
321	Textiles	210.0	220.5	251.7	...	...	17.3	20.6	18.9	...	...	321
3211	Spinning, weaving etc.	102.4	107.1	157.3	...	...	8.3	11.4	12.7	...	...	3211
322	Wearing apparel	111.1	117.4	124.0	...	...	6.0	3.8	3.7	...	...	322
323	Leather and products	28.7	28.9	34.0	...	...	1.2	1.3	1.7	...	...	323
324	Footwear	56.9	54.8	61.0	...	...	1.7	1.3	1.6	...	...	324
331	Wood products	94.0	95.0	106.0	...	...	9.7	8.6	8.1	...	...	331
332	Furniture, fixtures	95.1	92.4	99.9	...	...	5.4	4.1	4.9	...	...	332
341	Paper and products	103.6	112.4	128.1	...	...	12.4	16.5	16.7	...	...	341
3411	Pulp, paper etc.	53.3	62.9	67.0	...	...	7.8	10.8	9.1	...	...	3411
342	Printing, publishing	117.0	137.9	158.3	...	...	8.6	9.5	10.6	...	...	342
351	Industrial chemicals	151.3	181.3	198.7	...	...	20.1	16.9	19.5	...	...	351
3511	Basic excl fertilizers	72.8	90.6	99.2	...	...	10.0	9.7	11.1	...	...	3511
3513	Synthetic resins etc	42.9	57.7	62.1	...	...	4.7	3.8	4.0	...	...	3513
352	Other chemical products	191.3	213.4	257.7	...	...	14.1	17.7	19.6	...	...	352
3522	Drugs and medicines	89.8	97.5	104.3	...	...	4.8	6.4	8.2	...	...	3522
353	Petroleum refineries	96.4	202.5	300.9	...	...	...	...	18.3	...	...	353
354	Petroleum, coal products	18.7	31.8	30.8	...	...	...	...	0.9	...	...	354
355	Rubber products	76.7	73.3	72.6	...	...	5.5	5.0	5.8	...	...	355
356	Plastic products n.e.c.	86.0	88.2	116.4	...	...	7.6	8.0	9.8	...	...	356
361	Pottery, china etc	27.6	32.0	32.2	...	...	2.3	3.7	6.2	...	...	361
362	Glass and products	52.8	56.8	64.3	...	...	5.3	5.6	5.6	...	...	362
369	Non-metal products n.e.c	234.2	221.5	231.6	...	...	31.5	24.9	21.8	...	...	369
371	Iron and steel	237.5	269.1	297.3	...	...	49.7	25.6	29.0	...	...	371
372	Non-ferrous metals	76.5	82.0	115.1	...	...	38.3	6.0	7.5	...	...	372
381	Metal products	333.2	350.0	316.9	...	...	28.3	21.9	22.1	...	...	381
382	Machinery n.e.c.	225.7	239.9	321.9	...	...	14.1	12.8	19.8	...	...	382
3825	Office, computing etc.	11.4	14.1	15.7	...	...	2.5	3.0	2.2	...	...	3825
383	Electrical machinery	274.6	303.0	349.1	...	...	14.7	17.7	23.9	...	...	383
3832	Radio, television etc.	89.4	101.7	119.3	...	...	3.7	4.1	6.2	...	...	3832
384	Transport equipment	335.4	410.2	447.3	...	...	a/ 26.9	a/ 27.5	a/ 32.0	...	...	384
3841	Shipbuilding, repair	51.2	99.5	106.6	...	...	...	-	3.8	...	...	3841
3843	Motor vehicles	240.7	258.1	283.2	...	...	25.0	25.7	26.9	...	...	3843
385	Professional goods	15.1	16.0	18.1	...	...	0.5	1.0	0.7	...	...	385
390	Other industries	35.8	35.1	50.5	...	...	2.4	2.5	4.5	...	...	390
3	Manufacturing	3951.6	4414.8	5050.7	...	...	b/ 383.9	b/ 325.1	389.6	...	...	3
410	Electricity, gas, steam	339.4	348.3	401.2	...	...	...	...	412.0	...	...	410
4101	Electricity	323.1	327.4	370.5	...	...	347.3	412.0	412.0	...	...	4101
420	Water works and supply	34.5	39.2	43.2	...	...	7.5	12.7	13.2	...	...	420
4	Electricity, gas etc	373.9	387.5	444.4	...	...	...	...	425.2	...	...	4
2-4	All industry	4471.0	4983.5	5747.3	...	...	...	...	854.4	...	...	2-4

Note. For limitation of coverage and differences in classification, see country note.

a/ Up to 1982, excluding shipbuilding and manufacture of railroad equipment (ISICs 3841 and 3842). Beginning 1983, excluding ISIC 3842.

b/ Total of industries shown.

13. INDEX NUMBERS OF INDUSTRIAL PRODUCTION (1980 = 100)

ISIC	INDUSTRY		1976	1977	1978	1979	1981	1982	1983	1984	1985	RATE a/	ISIC
210	Coal mining		61	69	75	80	118	131	132	131	133	9.0	210
220	Petroleum and gas		110	59	50	71	77	95	185	139	130	1.9	220
230	Metal ore mining		71	72	77	78	112	102	106	129	124	6.4	230
290	Other mining		94	103	101	100	112	97	97	106	99	0.6	290
2	Mining, quarrying .		69	73	77	82	114	120	126	128	127	7.0	2
311/2	Food products												311/2
313	Beverages		84	88	94	99	104	104	111	112	117	3.7	313
314	Tobacco												314
321	Textiles		100	97	97	103	90	92	94	92	96	-0.5	321
3211	Spinning,weaving etc..		...	...	...	...	...	...	...	...	...	...	3211
322	Wearing apparel	b/	124	116	114	110	90	94	90	88	86	-4.0	322
323	Leather and products ...		123	125	144	139	126	133	138	153	152	2.4	323
324	Footwear	b/	...	...	...	...	...	...	...	...	...	...	324
331	Wood products		99	97	102	105	95	97	96	91	84	-1.8	331
332	Furniture, fixtures		...	...	...	...	...	...	...	...	...	...	332
341	Paper and products	c/	77	77	80	87	97	93	100	107	104	3.4	341
3411	Pulp,paper etc.		...	...	...	...	...	...	...	...	...	...	3411
342	Printing,publishing	c/	...	...	...	...	...	...	...	...	...	...	342
351	Industrial chemicals ...	d/	86	90	97	101	102	98	98	103	106	2.4	351
3511	Basic excl fertilizers		...	...	...	...	...	...	...	...	...	...	3511
3513	Synthetic resins etc .		...	...	...	...	...	...	...	...	...	...	3513
352	Other chemical products.	d/	...	...	...	...	...	...	...	...	...	...	352
3522	Drugs and medicines ..		...	...	...	...	...	...	...	...	...	...	3522
353	Petroleum refineries ...		100	97	97	97	96	88	89	96	98	-0.2	353
354	Petroleum,coal products.		...	...	...	...	...	...	...	...	...	...	354
355	Rubber products		78	98	96	102	101	96	97	100	105	3.4	355
356	Plastic products n.e.c..												356
361	Pottery,china etc												361
362	Glass and products		96	103	109	103	98	94	95	90	85	-1.3	362
369	Non-metal products n.e.c												369
371	Iron and steel		89	91	92	94	99	99	101	105	107	2.1	371
372	Non-ferrous metals												372
381	Metal products		92	102	101	98	98	93	94	87	89	-0.4	381
382	Machinery n.e.c.		105	103	105	90	108	98	88	90	98	-0.8	382
3825	Office,computing etc..		116	107	121	120	76	52	44	37	31	-13.6	3825
383	Electrical machinery ...		96	110	114	101	102	92	90	93	95	-0.1	383
3832	Radio,television etc..		68	110	125	98	97	79	86	87	95	3.8	3832
384	Transport equipment		109	123	107	99	93	96	98	87	90	-2.1	384
3841	Shipbuilding, repair..		178	185	130	115	104	110	69	35	37	-16.0	3841
3843	Motor vehicles		74	97	98	96	83	89	108	110	119	5.4	3843
385	Professional goods		68	85	89	62	81	95	95	93	98	4.1	385
390	Other industries		...	...	...	...	...	...	...	...	...	...	390
3	Manufacturing		93	98	100	100	98	96	99	100	101	0.9	3
410	Electricity,gas,steam ..		84	86	91	97	100	103	106	109	116	3.7	410
4101	Electricity		...	...	...	...	...	...	...	...	...	...	4101
420	Water works and supply .		.	.	.	.	.	.	.	.	.	.	420
4	Electricity,gas etc		...	...	...	...	...	...	...	...	...	...	4
2-4	All industry		91	96	98	99	99	98	101	101	104	1.5	2-4

a/ Annual growth rate 1976-1985.
b/ Major group 324 is included in 322.
c/ Major group 342 is included in 341.
d/ Major group 352 is included in 351.

SRI LANKA

The information in the tables, except for the indexes, is based on the reply to the United Nations Questionnaire on General Industrial Statistics from the Department of Census and Statistics, Colombo.

Data for the years shown are from two different sources: those for 1981 are derived from the annual survey of manufacturing industries, conducted since 1978 by the Department of Census and Statistics; those for 1982 are from the results of the 1983 Census of Industry. The coverage of each annual survey is based on the list of manufacturing establishments that completed a satisfactory survey questionnaire in the preceding year. Although in principle the 1981 survey coverage was limited to public and registered private establishments with ten or more employees, the survey results shown here also include data for 250 esablishments with less than ten employees. The 1982 census data refer to all industrial establishments with five or more persons engaged, and are based on a complete enumeration.

The annual surveys are carried out by mail, with follow-ups by field enumerators in certain cases. The 1983 Census of Industry was carried out through direct interviews by field enumerators. Neither of the data sets has been adjusted for non-response.

The national indusrial classification is the same as the present version of the ISIC. The reference period is the calendar year. Where an establishment has supplied data for a financial year other than the calendar year, such data are assigned to the calendar year in which the major part of the financial year falls.

The number of establishments is the number of units engaged in one industrial activity at one location. Where an enterprise is engaged in more than one industrial activity at the same or different locations, a separate count is made for each type of activity at each location. Employment data for 1981 refer to 30 June; figures for 1982 refer to the average number of persons engaged.

Output for 1981 is the value of all goods produced by the establishment, at ex-factory prices, excluding indirect taxes but including the value of discounts, and value added is the difference between the value of output and the cost of direct inputs (raw materials, electricity and fuels). For 1982, the output data also include receipts for goods sold in the same condition as purchased, as well as for contract work, repairs, installation work and other industrial services, and value added is calculated as the difference between output and all industrial inputs. Valuation of the 1982 data is at purchasers' prices, i.e. including all charges invoiced to the customer by the establishment (indirect taxes, transport costs) and excluding the value of any subsidies received by the establishment, as well as customer rebates, discounts and allowances.

The indexes of industrial production are compiled by the Department of Census and Statistics and provided in response to the United Nations Questionnaire on Indexes of Industrial Production. The indexes cover, in principle, all major industrial establishments.

Related national publication:
<u>Report on the Survey on Manufacturing Industries</u>, (annual), published by the Department of Census and Statistics. Colombo.

ISIC	INDUSTRY	1. NUMBER OF ESTABLISHMENTS a/ (NUMBER) 1981	*1982	1983	1984	1985	2. AVERAGE NUMBER OF EMPLOYEES a/ (NUMBER) b/ 1981	c/ *1982	1983	1984	1985	ISIC
210	Coal mining	...	-	...	...	...	...	-	...	...	...	210
220	Petroleum and gas	...	-	...	...	...	...	-	...	...	...	220
230	Metal ore mining	...	-	...	...	...	...	-	...	...	...	230
290	Other mining	...	1812	...	...	...	...	22931	...	...	...	290
2	Mining, quarrying .	...	1812	...	...	...	...	22931	...	...	...	2
311/2	Food products	138	2877	...	...	...	13480	94837	...	...	...	311/2
313	Beverages	15	51	...	...	...	3723	3666	...	...	...	313
314	Tobacco	6	2769	...	...	...	3150	60585	...	...	...	314
321	Textiles	214	2728	...	...	...	33193	69533	...	...	...	321
3211	Spinning,weaving etc..	137	...	...	...	...	26178	...	...	...	...	3211
322	Wearing apparel	90	388	...	...	...	24753	38462	...	...	...	322
323	Leather and products ...	19	75	...	...	...	818	1712	...	...	...	323
324	Footwear	9	40	...	...	...	1654	2099	...	...	...	324
331	Wood products	13	645	...	...	...	5135	15067	...	...	...	331
332	Furniture, fixtures	26	517	...	...	...	1497	6612	...	...	...	332
341	Paper and products	53	87	...	...	...	6380	4831	...	...	...	341
3411	Pulp,paper etc.	6	-	...	...	...	5021	-	...	...	...	3411
342	Printing,publishing	16	265	...	...	...	4319	8218	...	...	...	342
351	Industrial chemicals ...	18	46	...	...	...	2366	4530	...	...	...	351
3511	Basic excl fertilizers	13	...	...	...	...	1216	...	...	...	...	3511
3513	Synthetic resins etc .	-	-	...	...	...	-	...	...	...	...	3513
352	Other chemical products.	117	190	...	...	...	5681	6540	...	...	...	352
3522	Drugs and medicines ..	13	-	...	...	...	914	...	...	...	...	3522
353	Petroleum refineries ...	2	3	...	...	...	5660	5538	...	...	...	353
354	Petroleum,coal products.	3	-	...	...	...	85	-	...	...	...	354
355	Rubber products	75	633	...	...	...	7357	35084	...	...	...	355
356	Plastic products n.e.c..	50	39	...	...	...	2327	2406	...	...	...	356
361	Pottery,china etc	13	129	...	...	...	2619	6715	...	...	...	361
362	Glass and products	9	26	...	...	...	648	1621	...	...	...	362
369	Non-metal products n.e.c	64	1767	...	...	...	9674	29847	...	...	...	369
371	Iron and steel	6	30	...	...	...	1973	3084	...	...	...	371
372	Non-ferrous metals	5	8	...	...	...	598	66	...	...	...	372
381	Metal products	104	449	...	...	...	4506	10136	...	...	...	381
382	Machinery n.e.c.	38	64	...	...	...	3504	2297	...	...	...	382
3825	Office,computing etc..	1	...	...	...	...	93	...	...	...	...	3825
383	Electrical machinery ...	30	42	...	...	...	2429	2882	...	...	...	383
3832	Radio,television etc..	4	...	...	...	...	192	...	...	...	...	3832
384	Transport equipment	24	78	...	...	...	1309	2634	...	...	...	384
3841	Shipbuilding, repair..	4	...	...	...	...	485	...	...	...	...	3841
3843	Motor vehicles	13	...	...	...	...	609	...	...	...	...	3843
385	Professional goods	19	9	...	...	...	977	321	...	...	...	385
390	Other industries	36	285	...	...	...	1734	3661	...	...	...	390
3	Manufacturing	1212	14240	...	...	...	151549	422984	...	...	...	3
410	Electricity,gas,steam ..	...	13	...	...	...	...	10679	...	...	...	410
4101	Electricity	...	...	...	...	...	...	...	...	...	...	4101
420	Water works and supply .	...	67	...	...	...	...	1314	...	...	...	420
4	Electricity,gas etc	...	80	...	...	...	...	11993	...	...	...	4
2-4	All industry	...	16132	...	...	...	...	457908	...	...	...	2-4

a/ Establishment coverage differs from year to year; see introductory country mote.
b/ At 30 June of the year indicated.
c/ Average number of persons engaged.

ISIC	INDUSTRY	3. WAGES AND SALARIES OF EMPLOYEES a/ (MILLION RUPEES)					4. OUTPUT IN FACTOR VALUES a/ (MILLION RUPEES)					ISIC
		1981	*1982	1983	1984	1985	1981	*1982	1983	1984	1985	
210	Coal mining	...	-	...	...	...	...	-	...	...	...	210
220	Petroleum and gas	...	-	...	...	...	...	-	...	...	...	220
230	Metal ore mining	...	-	...	...	...	...	-	...	...	...	230
290	Other mining	...	73	...	...	...	...	494	...	...	...	290
2	Mining, quarrying .	...	73	...	...	...	...	494	...	...	...	2
311/2	Food products	121	583	...	...	...	1694	11699	...	...	...	311/2
313	Beverages	29	52	...	...	...	365	670	...	...	...	313
314	Tobacco	69	159	...	...	...	1440	3138	...	...	...	314
321	Textiles	232	432	...	...	...	1508	2833	...	...	...	321
3211	Spinning,weaving etc..	194	...	...	...	...	1201	...	...	...	...	3211
322	Wearing apparel	166	280	...	...	...	1567	2188	...	...	...	322
323	Leather and products ...	8	14	...	...	...	52	59	...	...	...	323
324	Footwear	19	20	...	...	...	106	103	...	...	...	324
331	Wood products	64	140	...	...	...	249	1144	...	...	...	331
332	Furniture, fixtures	13	36	...	...	...	34	142	...	...	...	332
341	Paper and products	57	53	...	...	...	501	667	...	...	...	341
3411	Pulp,paper etc.	47	...	...	...	...	353	...	...	...	...	3411
342	Printing,publishing	54	109	...	...	...	230	723	...	...	...	342
351	Industrial chemicals ...	32	64	...	...	...	874	1806	...	...	...	351
3511	Basic excl fertilizers	14	...	...	...	...	88	...	...	...	...	3511
3513	Synthetic resins etc .	-	-	...	...	...	-	-	...	...	...	3513
352	Other chemical products.	71	90	...	...	...	869	1337	...	...	...	352
3522	Drugs and medicines ..	13	-	...	...	...	104	...	...	...	...	3522
353	Petroleum refineries ...	75	122	...	...	...	10008	11419	...	...	...	353
354	Petroleum,coal products.	-	-	...	...	...	10	-	...	...	...	354
355	Rubber products	92	175	...	...	...	739	1404	...	...	...	355
356	Plastic products n.e.c..	18	16	...	...	...	220	258	...	...	...	356
361	Pottery,china etc	33	107	...	...	...	165	347	...	...	...	361
362	Glass and products	6	17	...	...	...	66	117	...	...	...	362
369	Non-metal products n.e.c	123	247	...	...	...	1050	1919	...	...	...	369
371	Iron and steel	32	50	...	...	...	435	373	...	...	...	371
372	Non-ferrous metals	8	...	...	...	...	90	1	...	...	...	372
381	Metal products	38	68	...	...	...	273	404	...	...	...	381
382	Machinery n.e.c.	36	33	...	...	...	232	259	...	...	...	382
3825	Office,computing etc..	1	...	...	...	...	5	...	...	...	...	3825
383	Electrical machinery ...	22	23	...	...	...	293	309	...	...	...	383
3832	Radio,television etc..	2	...	...	...	...	9	...	...	...	...	3832
384	Transport equipment	10	27	...	...	...	53	196	...	...	...	384
3841	Shipbuilding, repair..	5	...	...	...	...	17	...	...	...	...	3841
3843	Motor vehicles	4	...	...	...	...	13	...	...	...	...	3843
385	Professional goods	4	2	...	...	...	18	11	...	...	...	385
390	Other industries	15	32	...	...	...	107	308	...	...	...	390
3	Manufacturing	1447	2951	...	...	...	23248	43834	...	...	...	3
410	Electricity,gas,steam ..	...	311	...	...	...	...	2611	...	...	...	410
4101	Electricity	...	...	...	...	...	...	...	...	...	...	4101
420	Water works and supply .	...	21	...	...	...	...	90	...	...	...	420
4	Electricity,gas etc	...	332	...	...	...	...	2701	...	...	...	4
2-4	All industry	...	3356	...	...	...	...	47029	...	...	...	2-4

a/ Establishment coverage differs from year to year; see introductory country mote.

ISIC	INDUSTRY	5. VALUE ADDED IN FACTOR VALUES a/ (MILLION RUPEES)					6. GROSS FIXED CAPITAL FORMATION TOTAL a/b/ (MILLION RUPEES)					ISIC
		1981	*1982	1983	1984	1985	1981	*1982	1983	1984	1985	
210	Coal mining	...	-	...	...	...	...	-	...	...	...	210
220	Petroleum and gas	...	-	...	...	...	...	-	...	...	...	220
230	Metal ore mining	...	-	...	...	...	...	-	...	...	...	230
290	Other mining	...	436	...	...	...	...	66	...	...	...	290
2	Mining, quarrying .	...	436	...	...	...	...	66	...	...	...	2
311/2	Food products	352	4625	...	...	...	85	314	...	...	...	311/2
313	Beverages	105	266	...	...	...	46	25	...	...	...	313
314	Tobacco	1142	2975	...	...	...	14	17	...	...	...	314
321	Textiles	426	1717	...	...	...	94	97	...	...	...	321
3211	Spinning,weaving etc..	335	...	...	...	...	31	...	...	...	...	3211
322	Wearing apparel	402	844	...	...	...	79	74	...	...	...	322
323	Leather and products ...	17	35	...	...	...	2	11	...	...	...	323
324	Footwear	42	43	...	...	...	9	28	...	...	...	324
331	Wood products	99	763	...	...	...	47	35	...	...	...	331
332	Furniture, fixtures	14	85	...	...	...	2	9	...	...	...	332
341	Paper and products	141	140	...	...	...	16	25	...	...	...	341
3411	Pulp,paper etc.	107	...	...	...	...	6	...	...	...	...	3411
342	Printing,publishing	73	404	...	...	...	72	103	...	...	...	342
351	Industrial chemicals ...	175	447	...	...	...	46	98	...	...	...	351
3511	Basic excl fertilizers	35	...	...	...	...	35	...	...	...	...	3511
3513	Synthetic resins etc .	-	...	...	...	...	-	...	...	...	...	3513
352	Other chemical products.	289	527	...	...	...	74	123	...	...	...	352
3522	Drugs and medicines ..	42	...	...	...	...	10	...	...	...	...	3522
353	Petroleum refineries ...	350	1109	...	...	...	103	100	...	...	...	353
354	Petroleum,coal products.	2	...	...	...	...	1	-	...	...	...	354
355	Rubber products	309	733	...	...	...	82	148	...	...	...	355
356	Plastic products n.e.c..	60	71	...	...	...	22	37	...	...	...	356
361	Pottery,china etc	81	182	...	...	...	4	46	...	...	...	361
362	Glass and products	32	53	...	...	...	4	20	...	...	...	362
369	Non-metal products n.e.c	418	874	...	...	...	115	165	...	...	...	369
371	Iron and steel	36	144	...	...	...	39	24	...	...	...	371
372	Non-ferrous metals	24	1	...	...	...	18	-	...	...	...	372
381	Metal products	98	173	...	...	...	33	46	...	...	...	381
382	Machinery n.e.c.	92	112	...	...	...	90	246	...	...	...	382
3825	Office,computing etc..	3	...	...	...	...	-	...	...	...	...	3825
383	Electrical machinery ...	139	139	...	...	...	22	41	...	...	...	383
3832	Radio,television etc..	6	...	...	...	...	3	...	...	...	...	3832
384	Transport equipment	24	82	...	...	...	2	14	...	...	...	384
3841	Shipbuilding, repair..	13	...	...	...	...	1	...	...	...	...	3841
3843	Motor vehicles	6	...	...	...	...	1	...	...	...	...	3843
385	Professional goods	9	7	...	...	...	-	-	...	...	...	385
390	Other industries	29	168	...	...	...	34	32	...	...	...	390
3	Manufacturing	4980	16719	...	...	...	1155	1878	...	...	...	3
410	Electricity,gas,steam ..	...	1499	...	...	...	...	764	...	...	...	410
4101	Electricity	...	...	...	...	...	...	...	...	...	...	4101
420	Water works and supply .	...	21	...	...	...	...	151	...	...	...	420
4	Electricity,gas etc	...	1520	...	...	...	...	915	...	...	...	4
2-4	All industry	...	18675	...	...	...	...	2859	...	...	...	2-4

a/ Establishment coverage differs from year to year; see introductory country mote.
b/ Capital expenditure.

7. INDEX NUMBERS OF INDUSTRIAL PRODUCTION (1980 = 100)

ISIC	INDUSTRY	1976	1977	1978	1979	1981	1982	1983	1984	1985	a/ RATE	ISIC
210	Coal mining	...	...	...	...	...	...	...	...	...	...	210
220	Petroleum and gas	...	...	...	...	...	...	...	...	...	...	220
230	Metal ore mining	...	...	...	...	...	...	...	...	...	...	230
290	Other mining	...	...	...	...	...	...	...	...	...	...	290
2	Mining, quarrying .	...	...	...	...	...	...	...	...	...	...	2
311/2	Food products	55	60	68	111	111	113	...	...	...	e/ 12.7	311/2
313	Beverages											313
314	Tobacco	89	93	98	129	106	107	...	...	...	e/ 3.1	314
321	Textiles .... b/	92	105	110	73	125	128	...	...	...	e/ 5.7	321
3211	Spinning,weaving etc..	...	...	...	...	...	...	...	...	...	...	3211
322	Wearing apparel .... b/c/	79	72	86	94	120	124	...	...	...	e/ 7.8	322
323	Leather and products ...	65	73	94	110	124	125	...	...	...	e/ 11.5	323
324	Footwear .... c/	...	...	...	...	...	...	...	...	...	...	324
331	Wood products	124	99	87	45	97	98	...	...	...	e/ -3.8	331
332	Furniture, fixtures	...	...	...	...	...	...	...	...	...	...	332
341	Paper and products	109	242	232	144	103	107	...	...	...	e/ -0.3	341
3411	Pulp,paper etc.	...	...	...	...	...	...	...	...	...	...	3411
342	Printing,publishing	...	...	...	...	...	...	...	...	...	...	342
351	Industrial chemicals ... d/	113	161	207	149	114	119	...	...	...	e/ 0.9	351
3511	Basic excl fertilizers	...	...	...	...	...	...	...	...	...	...	3511
3513	Synthetic resins etc .	...	...	...	...	...	...	...	...	...	...	3513
352	Other chemical products. d/	...	...	...	...	...	...	...	...	...	...	352
3522	Drugs and medicines ..	...	...	...	...	...	...	...	...	...	...	3522
353	Petroleum refineries ...	...	...	...	...	...	...	...	...	...	...	353
354	Petroleum,coal products.	...	...	...	...	...	...	...	...	...	...	354
355	Rubber products	54	48	56	73	85	86	...	...	...	e/ 8.1	355
356	Plastic products n.e.c..	...	...	...	...	...	...	...	...	...	...	356
361	Pottery,china etc											361
362	Glass and products	35	36	47	80	93	94	...	...	...	e/ 17.9	362
369	Non-metal products n.e.c											369
371	Iron and steel	64	53	60	78	80	82	...	...	...	e/ 4.2	371
372	Non-ferrous metals											372
381	Metal products	101	139	86	125	106	110	...	...	...	e/ 1.4	381
382	Machinery n.e.c.	...	...	...	...	...	...	...	...	...	...	382
3825	Office,computing etc..	...	...	...	...	...	...	...	...	...	...	3825
383	Electrical machinery ...	...	...	...	...	...	...	...	...	...	...	383
3832	Radio,television etc..	...	...	...	...	...	...	...	...	...	...	3832
384	Transport equipment	...	...	...	...	...	...	...	...	...	...	384
3841	Shipbuilding, repair..	...	...	...	...	...	...	...	...	...	...	3841
3843	Motor vehicles	...	...	...	...	...	...	...	...	...	...	3843
385	Professional goods	...	...	...	...	...	...	...	...	...	...	385
390	Other industries	386	434	476	389	1176	1181	...	...	...	e/ 20.5	390
3	Manufacturing	76	77	83	92	107	110	...	...	...	e/ 6.4	3
410	Electricity,gas,steam ..	...	...	...	...	...	...	...	...	...	...	410
4101	Electricity	...	...	...	...	...	...	...	...	...	...	4101
420	Water works and supply .	...	...	...	...	...	...	...	...	...	...	420
4	Electricity,gas etc	...	...	...	...	...	...	...	...	...	...	4
2-4	All industry	...	...	...	...	...	...	...	...	...	...	2-4

a/ Annual growth rate 1976-1985.
b/ Some textile manufacturing is included in major group 322.
c/ Major group 324 is included in 322.
d/ Major group 352 is included in 351.
e/ Annual growth rate 1976-1982.

SURINAME

The information in the tables is based on the reply to the United Nations Questionnaire on General Industrial Statistics from the Algemeen Bureau voor de Statistiek, Paramaribo. The concepts, definitions and classification by branches of industry are generally in accordance with United Nations standards.

The data in the tables are derived from the quarterly industrial survey covering all industrial establishments conducted by the above-mentioned statistical office. The statistics are compiled according to the present version of ISIC. Manufacturing data are available only for selected industries.

ISIC	INDUSTRY	1. AVERAGE NUMBER OF PERSONS ENGAGED a/ (NUMBER)					2. WAGES AND SALARIES OF EMPLOYEES a/ (MILLION GUILDERS)					ISIC
		1981	1982	1983	1984	1985	1981	1982	1983	1984	1985	
210	Coal mining	-	-	-	-	-	-	-	-	-	-	210
220	Petroleum and gas	-	-	-	97	126	-	-	-	1.6	2.3	220
230	Metal ore mining	6045	5583	5089	4630	4448	161.8	184.5	189.4	205.5	189.6	230
290	Other mining	54	78	80	80	28	0.5	1.0	0.9	0.9	0.2	290
2	Mining, quarrying .	6099	5661	5169	4807	4602	162.3	185.5	190.3	208.0	192.1	2
311/2	Food products	2930	3163	3190	3120	3330	28.6	33.5	33.6	32.5	41.3	311/2
313	Beverages	308	497	431	338	527	3.8	4.5	5.6	4.9	9.5	313
314	Tobacco	81	80	80	79	82	2.1	2.1	2.5	2.8	2.8	314
321	Textiles	...	...	...	...	...	...	...	...	...	...	321
3211	Spinning,weaving etc..	...	...	...	...	...	...	...	...	...	...	3211
322	Wearing apparel	393	378	430	449	422	2.5	2.6	3.0	2.8	4.3	322
323	Leather and products ...	-	-	-	-	-	-	-	-	-	-	323
324	Footwear	163	150	155	172	207	1.1	1.2	1.4	1.5	2.0	324
331	Wood products	1445	1469	1500	1383	1585	16.5	18.9	17.9	19.5	20.2	331
332	Furniture, fixtures	128	134	224	199	194	0.7	0.9	2.3	1.2	1.2	332
341	Paper and products	28	27	27	31	36	0.2	0.1	0.1	0.2	0.2	341
3411	Pulp,paper etc.	...	...	...	...	...	...	...	...	...	...	3411
342	Printing,publishing	208	142	100	109	113	2.5	2.1	1.8	2.1	2.0	342
351	Industrial chemicals ...	...	...	...	...	...	...	...	...	...	...	351
3511	Basic excl fertilizers	...	...	...	...	...	...	...	...	...	...	3511
3513	Synthetic resins etc .	...	...	...	...	...	...	...	...	...	...	3513
352	Other chemical products.	242	255	258	272	332	3.5	4.2	4.7	5.5	7.9	352
3522	Drugs and medicines ..	...	...	...	...	...	...	...	...	...	...	3522
353	Petroleum refineries ...	-	-	-	-	-	-	-	-	-	-	353
354	Petroleum,coal products.	-	-	-	-	-	-	-	-	-	-	354
355	Rubber products	-	-	-	-	-	-	-	-	-	-	355
356	Plastic products n.e.c..	79	86	92	107	77	0.8	0.8	1.5	1.5	1.0	356
361	Pottery,china etc											361
362	Glass and products	495	556	434	480	466	5.7	6.7	5.6	5.6	5.5	362
369	Non-metal products n.e.c											369
371	Iron and steel	-	-	-	-	-	-	-	-	-	-	371
372	Non-ferrous metals	-	-	-	-	-	-	-	-	-	-	372
381	Metal products	34	32	31	31	31	0.4	0.4	0.4	0.5	0.5	381
382	Machinery n.e.c.	...	...	...	...	5	...	...	...	...	-	382
3825	Office,computing etc..	...	...	...	...	...	...	...	...	...	...	3825
383	Electrical machinery ...	...	...	...	...	...	...	...	...	...	...	383
3832	Radio,television etc..	...	...	...	...	...	...	...	...	...	...	3832
384	Transport equipment	...	...	...	...	...	...	...	...	...	...	384
3841	Shipbuilding, repair..	57	53	...	...	...	0.8	0.9	...	...	...	3841
3843	Motor vehicles	-	-	-	-	-	-	-	-	-	-	3843
385	Professional goods	16	17	17	17	17	0.1	0.1	0.2	0.2	0.2	385
390	Other industries	...	...	...	...	...	...	...	...	...	...	390
3	Manufacturing	...	...	...	...	...	...	...	...	...	...	3
410	Electricity,gas,steam .. b/	746	776	806	816	805	17.1	20.3	22.4	25.0	25.9	410
4101	Electricity	746	776	806	816	805	17.1	20.3	22.4	25.0	25.9	4101
420	Water works and supply .	536	544	539	543	530	5.1	6.1	6.9	6.9	7.8	420
4	Electricity,gas etc b/	1282	1320	1345	1359	1335	22.2	26.4	29.3	31.9	33.7	4
2-4	All industry	...	...	...	...	...	...	...	...	...	...	2-4

a/ Manufacturing: selected industries only.

b/ Excluding gas and steam.

3. OUTPUT IN FACTOR VALUES a/ (MILLION GUILDERS)

ISIC	INDUSTRY	1981	1982	1983	1984	1985	ISIC
210	Coal mining	-	-	-	-	-	210
220	Petroleum and gas	-	-	-	12	17	220
230	Metal ore mining	773	711	626	494	426	230
290	Other mining	2	5	6	1	1	290
2	Mining, quarrying .	775	716	632	507	444	2
311/2	Food products	147	177	203	213	235	311/2
313	Beverages	30	61	48	70	71	313
314	Tobacco	18	22	26	26	28	314
321	Textiles	...	...	...	...	...	321
3211	Spinning,weaving etc..	...	...	...	...	...	3211
322	Wearing apparel	8	9	9	9	9	322
323	Leather and products ...	-	-	-	-	-	323
324	Footwear	6	5	6	7	9	324
331	Wood products	31	30	26	25	28	331
332	Furniture, fixtures	2	3	6	9	6	332
341	Paper and products	2	2	1	1	2	341
3411	Pulp,paper etc.	...	...	...	...	...	3411
342	Printing,publishing	7	6	5	5	5	342
351	Industrial chemicals ...	...	...	...	...	...	351
3511	Basic excl fertilizers	...	...	...	...	...	3511
3513	Synthetic resins etc .	...	...	...	...	...	3513
352	Other chemical products.	18	19	22	23	30	352
3522	Drugs and medicines ..	...	...	...	...	...	3522
353	Petroleum refineries ...	-	-	-	-	-	353
354	Petroleum,coal products.	-	-	-	-	-	354
355	Rubber products	-	-	-	-	-	355
356	Plastic products n.e.c..	5	6	11	9	5	356
361	Pottery,china etc						361
362	Glass and products	37	38	30	35	36	362
369	Non-metal products n.e.c						369
371	Iron and steel	-	-	-	-	-	371
372	Non-ferrous metals	-	-	-	-	-	372
381	Metal products	1	1	1	1	1	381
382	Machinery n.e.c.	...	...	...	...	-	382
3825	Office,computing etc..	...	...	...	...	...	3825
383	Electrical machinery ...	...	...	...	...	...	383
3832	Radio,television etc..	...	...	...	...	...	3832
384	Transport equipment	...	...	...	...	...	384
3841	Shipbuilding, repair..	3	3	1	-	-	3841
3843	Motor vehicles	-	-	-	-	-	3843
385	Professional goods	1	1	1	1	1	385
390	Other industries	...	...	...	...	...	390
3	Manufacturing	...	...	...	...	...	3
410	Electricity,gas,steam .. b/	83	83	80	77	78	410
4101	Electricity	83	83	80	77	78	4101
420	Water works and supply .	7	9	17	17	17	420
4	Electricity,gas etc b/	90	92	97	94	95	4
2-4	All industry	...	...	...	...	...	2-4

a/ Manufacturing: selected industries only.

b/ Excluding gas and steam.

The information in the tables is based on the reply to the United Nations Questionnaire on General Industrial Statistics from the Central Statistical Office, Mbabane. The concepts, definitions and classification by branches of industry are generally in accordance with United Nations standards.

The data are derived from the census of industries and the census of small industries which together cover all establishments regardless of size. The inquiry is carried out by mail supplemented by interview, if needed. In the tables, adjustments have been made for non-response. The figures are based on the national classification but are arranged according to the present version of ISIC as far as details permit. The reference period is the calendar year. However, financial-year coverage of certain respondents is accepted and incorporated in the calendar year in which the major part of the financial year falls.

The number of persons engaged relates to the average number of employees only. Part-time employees and those absent temporarily are included. Wages and salaries include employers' contribution to pension and other social insurance schemes.

Output is calculated as the sum of (a) sales of goods produced, (b) work and services performed for others, (c) net change in stocks of finished goods and work in progress, (d) net value of goods sold in the same condition as purchased, (e) value of own account construction of fixed assets and (f) other receipts excluding rent and interest. Estimates of value added represent the value arrived at by deducting total input from output. The input consists of the cost of (a) materials, fuels, lubricants, electricity and water consumed, (b) contract, repair and maintenance work done by others and (c) all other expenses excluding compensation of employees, depreciation, rent and interest payments. Valuation of output and value added is in factor values.

Related national publications:
Census of Industrial Production (annual); Annual Statistical Bulletin, both published by the Central Statistical Office, Mbabane.

ISIC	INDUSTRY	1. NUMBER OF ESTABLISHMENTS a/b/ (NUMBER) 1981	1982	1983	1984	1985	2. AVERAGE NUMBER OF EMPLOYEES b/ (NUMBER) 1981	1982	1983	1984	1985	ISIC
210	Coal mining	...	...	...	...	...	...	...	...	...	...	210
220	Petroleum and gas	...	...	...	...	...	...	...	...	...	...	220
230	Metal ore mining	...	...	...	...	...	...	...	...	...	...	230
290	Other mining	...	...	...	...	...	...	...	...	...	...	290
2	Mining, quarrying .	3	3	3	...	...	2683	2569	2362	...	...	2
311/2	Food products	11	10	9	...	...	4704	4629	4173	...	...	311/2
313	Beverages	4	4	4	...	...	366	383	385	...	...	313
314	Tobacco	-	-	-	...	...	-	-	-	...	...	314
321	Textiles .... c/	35	33	34	...	...	942	720	633	...	...	321
3211	Spinning,weaving etc..	...	...	...	...	...	...	...	...	...	...	3211
322	Wearing apparel .... c/	...	...	...	...	...	...	...	...	...	...	322
323	Leather and products ... c/	...	...	...	...	...	...	...	...	...	...	323
324	Footwear	-	-	-	...	...	-	-	-	...	...	324
331	Wood products	[14	14	14]	...	...	[2201	2436	2370]	...	...	331
332	Furniture, fixtures				...	...				...	...	332
341	Paper and products ..... d/	13	11	11	...	...	1418	1484	1719	...	...	341
3411	Pulp,paper etc.	...	...	...	...	...	...	...	...	...	...	3411
342	Printing,publishing .... d/	...	...	...	...	...	...	...	...	...	...	342
351	Industrial chemicals ... e/	10	13	13	...	...	451	580	511	...	...	351
3511	Basic excl fertilizers	...	...	...	...	...	...	...	...	...	...	3511
3513	Synthetic resins etc .	...	...	...	...	...	...	...	...	...	...	3513
352	Other chemical products. e/	...	...	...	...	...	...	...	...	...	...	352
3522	Drugs and medicines ..	...	...	...	...	...	...	...	...	...	...	3522
353	Petroleum refineries ... e/	...	...	...	...	...	...	...	...	...	...	353
354	Petroleum,coal products. e/	...	...	...	...	...	...	...	...	...	...	354
355	Rubber products	-	-	-	...	...	-	-	-	...	...	355
356	Plastic products n.e.c.. e/	...	...	...	...	...	...	...	...	...	...	356
361	Pottery,china etc	-	-	-	...	...	-	-	-	...	...	361
362	Glass and products	[12	11	9]	...	...	[382	441	362]	...	...	362
369	Non-metal products n.e.c				...	...				...	...	369
371	Iron and steel	-	-	-	...	...	-	-	-	...	...	371
372	Non-ferrous metals	-	-	-	...	...	-	-	-	...	...	372
381	Metal products	23	23	22	...	...	554	572	465	...	...	381
382	Machinery n.e.c. .... f/	3	4	4	...	...	559	547	452	...	...	382
3825	Office,computing etc..	...	...	...	...	...	...	...	...	...	...	3825
383	Electrical machinery ... f/	...	...	...	...	...	...	...	...	...	...	383
3832	Radio,television etc..	...	...	...	...	...	...	...	...	...	...	3832
384	Transport equipment	-	-	-	...	...	-	-	-	...	...	384
3841	Shipbuilding, repair..	...	...	...	...	...	...	...	...	...	...	3841
3843	Motor vehicles	...	...	...	...	...	...	...	...	...	...	3843
385	Professional goods	-	-	-	...	...	-	-	-	...	...	385
390	Other industries	6	7	7	...	...	160	168	180	...	...	390
3	Manufacturing	131	130	127	...	...	11737	11960	11250	...	...	3
410	Electricity,gas,steam ..	...	...	...	...	...	...	...	...	...	...	410
4101	Electricity	...	...	...	...	...	...	...	...	...	...	4101
420	Water works and supply .	...	...	...	...	...	...	...	...	...	...	420
4	Electricity,gas etc g/	2	2	2	...	...	943	943	1282	...	...	4
2-4	All industry g/	136	135	132	...	...	15363	15472	14894	...	...	2-4

a/ Electricity and water: number of enterprises.
b/ All establishments. Calendar year.
c/ Major groups 322 and 323 are included in 321.
d/ Major group 342 is included in 341.
e/ Major groups 352 to 354 and 356 are included in 351.
f/ Major group 383 is included in 382.
g/ Excluding gas and steam.

ISIC	INDUSTRY	3. WAGES AND SALARIES OF EMPLOYEES a/b/ (THOUSAND EMALANGENI) 1981	1982	1983	1984	1985	4. OUTPUT IN FACTOR VALUES b/ (THOUSAND EMALANGENI) 1981	1982	1983	1984	1985	ISIC
210	Coal mining	...	...	...	...	...	...	...	...	...	...	210
220	Petroleum and gas	...	...	...	...	...	...	...	...	...	...	220
230	Metal ore mining	...	...	...	...	...	...	...	...	...	...	230
290	Other mining	...	...	...	...	...	...	...	...	...	...	290
2	Mining, quarrying .	9954	10008	9756	...	...	25812	24970	26710	...	...	2
311/2	Food products	14765	19239	17708	...	...	160110	164206	186972	...	...	311/2
313	Beverages	1389	1721	2135	...	...	13947	18254	21947	...	...	313
314	Tobacco	-	-	-	...	...	-	-	-	...	...	314
321	Textiles .... c/	2000	1592	1645	...	...	21679	18969	17597	...	...	321
3211	Spinning,weaving etc..	...	...	...	...	...	...	...	...	...	...	3211
322	Wearing apparel .... c/	...	...	...	...	...	...	...	...	...	...	322
323	Leather and products ... c/	...	...	...	...	...	...	...	...	...	...	323
324	Footwear	-	-	-	...	...	-	-	-	...	...	324
331	Wood products	[4273	5052	5158]	...	...	[21161	22203	20726]	...	...	331
332	Furniture, fixtures				...	...				...	...	332
341	Paper and products ..... d/	8809	10320	11053	...	...	63671	67594	68214	...	...	341
3411	Pulp,paper etc.	...	...	...	...	...	...	...	...	...	...	3411
342	Printing,publishing .... d/	...	...	...	...	...	...	...	...	...	...	342
351	Industrial chemicals ... e/	3345	4058	5470	...	...	55628	67363	52319	...	...	351
3511	Basic excl fertilizers	...	...	...	...	...	...	...	...	...	...	3511
3513	Synthetic resins etc .	...	...	...	...	...	...	...	...	...	...	3513
352	Other chemical products. e/	...	...	...	...	...	...	...	...	...	...	352
3522	Drugs and medicines ..	...	...	...	...	...	...	...	...	...	...	3522
353	Petroleum refineries ... e/	...	...	...	...	...	...	...	...	...	...	353
354	Petroleum,coal products. e/	...	...	...	...	...	...	...	...	...	...	354
355	Rubber products	-	-	-	...	...	-	-	-	...	...	355
356	Plastic products n.e.c.. e/	...	...	...	...	...	...	...	...	...	...	356
361	Pottery,china etc	-	-	-	...	...	-	-	-	...	...	361
362	Glass and products	[795	917	677]	...	...	[6695	9817	7932]	...	...	362
369	Non-metal products n.e.c				...	...				...	...	369
371	Iron and steel	-	-	-	...	...	-	-	-	...	...	371
372	Non-ferrous metals	-	-	-	...	...	-	-	-	...	...	372
381	Metal products	1929	1891	2365	...	...	14934	15260	15662	...	...	381
382	Machinery n.e.c. .... f/	1588	2281	1742	...	...	15839	20240	11241	...	...	382
3825	Office,computing etc..	...	...	...	...	...	...	...	...	...	...	3825
383	Electrical machinery ... f/	...	...	...	...	...	...	...	...	...	...	383
3832	Radio,television etc..	...	...	...	...	...	...	...	...	...	...	3832
384	Transport equipment	-	-	-	...	...	-	-	-	...	...	384
3841	Shipbuilding, repair..	...	...	...	...	...	...	...	...	...	...	3841
3843	Motor vehicles	...	...	...	...	...	...	...	...	...	...	3843
385	Professional goods	-	-	-	...	...	-	-	-	...	...	385
390	Other industries	243	286	309	...	...	525	490	589	...	...	390
3	Manufacturing	39136	47357	48262	...	...	374189	404396	403199	...	...	3
410	Electricity,gas,steam ..	...	...	...	...	...	...	...	...	...	...	410
4101	Electricity	...	...	...	...	...	...	...	...	...	...	4101
420	Water works and supply .	...	...	...	...	...	...	...	...	...	...	420
4	Electricity,gas etc g/	3579	4210	4339	...	...	14927	20446	22948	...	...	4
2-4	All industry g/	52669	61575	62357	...	...	414928	449812	452857	...	...	2-4

a/ Including employers' contributions to pension and other social insurance schemes.
b/ All establishments. Calendar year.
c/ Major groups 322 and 323 are included in 321.
d/ Major group 342 is included in 341.
e/ Major groups 352 to 354 and 356 are included in 351.
f/ Major group 383 is included in 382.
g/ Excluding gas and steam.

ISIC	INDUSTRY		5. VALUE ADDED IN FACTOR VALUES a/ (THOUSAND EMALANGENI) 1981	1982	1983	1984	1985	6. GROSS FIXED CAPITAL FORMATION TOTAL a/ (THOUSAND EMALANGENI) 1981	1982	1983	1984	1985	ISIC
210	Coal mining		...	...	...	...	...	...	...	...	...	...	210
220	Petroleum and gas		...	...	...	...	...	...	...	...	...	...	220
230	Metal ore mining		...	...	...	...	...	...	...	...	...	...	230
290	Other mining		...	...	...	...	...	...	...	...	...	...	290
2	Mining, quarrying .		15103	14407	15710	...	...	1129	211	284	...	...	2
311/2	Food products		38809	39515	43273	...	...	14418	15633	1699	...	...	311/2
313	Beverages		3758	5052	6155	...	...	1905	3487	2289	...	...	313
314	Tobacco		-	-	-	...	...	-	-	-	...	...	314
321	Textiles	b/	2416	2252	1638	...	...	3499	647	191	...	...	321
3211	Spinning,weaving etc..		...	...	...	...	...	...	...	...	...	...	3211
322	Wearing apparel	b/	...	...	...	...	...	...	...	...	...	...	322
323	Leather and products ...	b/	...	...	...	...	...	...	...	...	...	...	323
324	Footwear		-	-	-	...	...	-	-	-	...	...	324
331	Wood products		[6466	8134	5514]	...	...	[424	293	1376]	...	...	331
332	Furniture, fixtures					...	...				...	...	332
341	Paper and products	c/	17954	18337	13768	...	...	3317	2903	4377	...	...	341
3411	Pulp,paper etc.		...	...	...	...	...	...	...	...	...	...	3411
342	Printing,publishing	c/	...	...	...	...	...	...	...	...	...	...	342
351	Industrial chemicals ...	d/	11914	18486	10174	...	...	2234	17304	248	...	...	351
3511	Basic excl fertilizers		...	...	...	...	...	...	...	...	...	...	3511
3513	Synthetic resins etc .		...	...	...	...	...	...	...	...	...	...	3513
352	Other chemical products.	d/	...	...	...	...	...	...	...	...	...	...	352
3522	Drugs and medicines ..		...	...	...	...	...	...	...	...	...	...	3522
353	Petroleum refineries ...	d/	...	...	...	...	...	...	...	...	...	...	353
354	Petroleum,coal products.	d/	...	...	...	...	...	...	...	...	...	...	354
355	Rubber products		-	-	-	...	...	-	-	-	...	...	355
356	Plastic products n.e.c..	d/	...	...	...	...	...	...	...	...	...	...	356
361	Pottery,china etc		-	-	-	...	...	-	-	-	...	...	361
362	Glass and products		[1319	1482	2435]	...	...	[227	1809	230]	...	...	362
369	Non-metal products n.e.c					...	...				...	...	369
371	Iron and steel		-	-	-	...	...	-	-	-	...	...	371
372	Non-ferrous metals		-	-	-	...	...	-	-	-	...	...	372
381	Metal products		5113	4918	4356	...	...	1453	2624	617	...	...	381
382	Machinery n.e.c.	e/	f/ 1450	2547	2108	...	...	52	150	63	...	...	382
3825	Office,computing etc..		...	...	...	...	...	...	...	...	...	...	3825
383	Electrical machinery ...	e/	...	...	...	...	...	...	...	...	...	...	383
3832	Radio,television etc..		...	...	...	...	...	...	...	...	...	...	3832
384	Transport equipment		-	-	-	...	...	-	-	-	...	...	384
3841	Shipbuilding, repair..		...	...	...	...	...	...	...	...	...	...	3841
3843	Motor vehicles		...	...	...	...	...	...	...	...	...	...	3843
385	Professional goods		-	-	-	...	...	-	-	-	...	...	385
390	Other industries		f/ 235	f/ 110	f/ 246	...	...	27	-15	-6	...	...	390
3	Manufacturing		89434	100833	89667	...	...	27556	44835	11084	...	...	3
410	Electricity,gas,steam ..		...	...	...	...	...	...	...	...	...	...	410
4101	Electricity		...	...	...	...	...	...	...	...	...	...	4101
420	Water works and supply .		...	...	...	...	...	...	...	...	...	...	420
4	Electricity,gas etc	g/	7178	8659	9334	...	...	11424	24166	36006	...	...	4
2-4	All industry	g/	111715	123899	114711	...	...	40109	69212	47374	...	...	2-4

a/ All establishments. Calendar year.
b/ Major groups 322 and 323 are included in 321.
c/ Major group 342 is included in 341.
d/ Major groups 352 to 354 and 356 are included in 351.
e/ Major group 383 is included in 382.
f/ Value added is less than corresponding wages and salaries due to operating losses.
g/ Excluding gas and steam.

SWEDEN

The information on industrial activity is based on the reply to the United Nations Questionnaire on General Industrial Statistics from Statistics Sweden, Stockholm. The concepts, definitions and classification by branches of industry are generally in accordance with United Nations standards.

The estimates are derived from annual inquiries into mining, manufacturing and the electricity, gas and water industries. All industries in these major divisions are surveyed except sand and clay pits (ISIC 290), manufacture of ice (ISIC 311/2), publishing not related to printing (ISIC 342), manufacture of crushed stone for road laying (ISIC 369) and ship breaking yards (ISIC 3841). All establishments (except peat) are covered for mining and, in the case of manufacturing, establishments with an average of 5 or more persons engaged during the reference year are, in general, included. However, all dairies, distilleries, breweries and starch factories are included, irrespective of size. For electricity, practically all producers and redistributors of electricity are covered, including production and deliveries in establishments ancillary to other industrial establishments. All gas works are covered. The coverage for water supply is limited to water works supplying large communities and producing more than one million cubic metres annually.

The data are compiled according to the national scheme which is stated to be identical with the present version of ISIC through the 4-digit level.

The statistical unit is the establishment and classification is based on the composition of production measured by sales value of the output of different commodities. For establishments which combine production and reselling of goods in the same condition as purchased, only the production activity is included. Data are based upon direct returns from producers.

The estimates of persons engaged include working proprietors, salaried employees and wage earners. Homeworkers are not included and payments to homeworkers are not included in wages and salaries. These payments, however, are included in the estimates of value added. Salaried employees are enumerated as of one day in August or September and numbers of wage earners represent averages. All estimates shown for operatives relate to wage earners.

The concept of output represents the ex-factory sales value of goods produced and services rendered, excluding indirect taxes. Value added is calculated as the value of output less the cost of materials and supplies, purchased fuels and electricity consumed and contract and commission work done by others. The cost of maintenance work is not deducted.

The data on gross fixed capital formation relate to the value of purchases of new fixed assets and alterations and repairs of a capital nature, including own-account construction. Fixed capital formation in new establishments not yet in operation is included. Transactions are recorded at the time of delivery except for buildings and other construction where the value of work completed during the reference period is recorded.

The indexes of industrial production are compiled by Statistics Sweden and provided in response to the United Nations Questionnaire on Indexes of Industrial Production. In principle, the indexes cover establishments with 5 or more persons engaged in manufacturing and all establishments engaged in mining, electricity, gas and water.

Related national publications:
<u>Industri, Del 1</u> (annual); <u>Statistisk Arsbok For Sverige</u>; <u>Statistiska Meddelanden</u>, all published by Statistics Sweden, Stockholm.

ISIC	INDUSTRY	1. NUMBER OF ESTABLISHMENTS a/ (NUMBER)					2. AVERAGE NUMBER OF PERSONS ENGAGED a/ (THOUSANDS)					ISIC
		1981	1982	1983	1984	1985	1981	1982	1983	1984	1985	
210	Coal mining	-	-	-	-	-	-	-	-	-	-	210
220	Petroleum and gas	-	-	-	-	-	-	-	-	-	-	220
230	Metal ore mining	31	29	32	34	35	11.5	10.9	10.3	9.4	9.5	230
290	Other mining	84	85	80	76	78	1.6	1.5	1.5	1.4	1.5	290
2	Mining, quarrying .	115	114	112	110	113	13.1	12.4	11.8	10.8	11.0	2
311/2	Food products	872	842	815	809	797	64.6	63.0	62.5	62.2	62.2	311/2
313	Beverages	42	40	37	35	35	4.6	4.4	4.3	4.2	4.3	313
314	Tobacco	4	4	4	4	4	1.6	1.5	1.5	1.4	1.4	314
321	Textiles	323	311	298	289	283	18.7	17.3	16.5	16.5	16.2	321
3211	Spinning,weaving etc..	106	101	98	95	91	8.3	7.0	6.8	6.9	6.6	3211
322	Wearing apparel	349	311	292	278	266	13.2	12.2	11.4	11.3	10.8	322
323	Leather and products ...	40	36	35	33	30	2.0	2.0	1.9	1.8	1.6	323
324	Footwear	79	68	64	52	45	2.5	2.2	2.0	1.5	1.4	324
331	Wood products	1293	1211	1180	1158	1124	51.5	47.7	46.6	46.2	44.4	331
332	Furniture, fixtures	331	314	305	302	300	12.5	11.5	11.5	11.7	11.8	332
341	Paper and products	216	212	208	211	213	59.3	56.3	55.3	55.0	54.9	341
3411	Pulp,paper etc.	96	91	88	85	85	47.4	44.8	43.1	42.6	42.4	3411
342	Printing,publishing	864	858	853	865	874	43.7	42.7	42.6	42.4	42.6	342
351	Industrial chemicals ...	156	151	152	156	155	19.4	18.5	18.5	18.4	17.8	351
3511	Basic excl fertilizers	72	69	71	71	68	10.1	10.0	10.1	9.8	9.8	3511
3513	Synthetic resins etc .	84	82	81	85	87	9.3	8.5	8.4	8.5	8.0	3513
352	Other chemical products.	154	152	152	149	151	24.4	24.7	24.5	25.7	25.0	352
3522	Drugs and medicines ..	22	29	23	24	26	8.2	8.2	8.6	9.3	9.4	3522
353	Petroleum refineries ...	6	6	6	6	5	1.7	1.7	1.7	1.7	1.6	353
354	Petroleum,coal products.	27	29	29	31	35	1.5	1.6	1.5	1.5	1.7	354
355	Rubber products	91	82	81	78	84	9.5	8.8	8.8	8.9	9.1	355
356	Plastic products n.e.c..	266	268	260	273	271	11.7	11.0	10.8	11.8	12.5	356
361	Pottery,china etc	21	21	21	21	21	3.1	3.4	3.3	3.2	3.1	361
362	Glass and products	46	39	39	39	42	4.2	3.8	3.8	4.0	4.2	362
369	Non-metal products n.e.c	391	359	341	334	328	18.3	16.8	15.1	14.4	14.3	369
371	Iron and steel	87	86	81	80	79	48.9	44.3	40.1	37.5	36.7	371
372	Non-ferrous metals	88	80	80	82	82	12.3	11.5	11.6	12.3	11.9	372
381	Metal products	1642	1573	1546	1585	1556	74.9	70.6	69.6	71.3	71.6	381
382	Machinery n.e.c.	1225	1196	1167	1176	1190	113.9	107.5	102.3	103.9	104.6	382
3825	Office,computing etc..	57	53	47	47	55	7.7	6.3	6.3	7.2	8.5	3825
383	Electrical machinery ...	436	419	419	415	420	78.9	75.8	74.8	75.2	76.3	383
3832	Radio,television etc..	94	91	90	94	89	38.1	35.9	35.3	36.0	38.9	3832
384	Transport equipment	500	497	496	494	487	113.8	113.8	106.2	107.8	111.3	384
3841	Shipbuilding, repair..	97	90	85	87	82	21.2	19.8	16.5	15.4	13.6	3841
3843	Motor vehicles	265	266	268	263	263	66.8	67.6	64.6	68.0	72.7	3843
385	Professional goods	157	149	154	148	139	9.9	9.7	10.1	10.4	10.7	385
390	Other industries	115	109	105	107	101	4.9	4.4	4.2	4.1	4.0	390
3	Manufacturing	9821	9423	9220	9210	9117	825.5	788.7	763.0	766.3	768.0	3
410	Electricity,gas,steam ..	720	705	694	688	699	26.7	27.6	27.9	28.0	27.9	410
4101	Electricity	b/ 714	b/ 699	b/ 689	683	691	b/ 26.5	b/ 27.3	b/ 27.6	27.7	27.7	4101
420	Water works and supply .	130	126	126	126	126	1.3	1.3	1.3	1.3	1.2	420
4	Electricity,gas etc	850	831	820	814	825	28.0	28.9	29.2	29.3	29.1	4
2-4	All industry	10786	10368	10152	10134	10055	866.6	830.0	804.0	806.4	808.1	2-4

a/ Manufacturing: establishments with 5 or more persons engaged. b/ Including steam.

ISIC	INDUSTRY	3. AVERAGE NUMBER OF EMPLOYEES a/ (THOUSANDS)					4. WAGES AND SALARIES OF EMPLOYEES a/ (MILLION KRONOR)					ISIC
		1981	1982	1983	1984	1985	1981	1982	1983	1984	1985	
210	Coal mining	-	-	-	-	-	-	-	-	-	-	210
220	Petroleum and gas	-	-	-	-	-	-	-	-	-	-	220
230	Metal ore mining	11.5	10.9	10.3	9.4	9.5	924	917	927	971	1035	230
290	Other mining	1.6	1.5	1.5	1.4	1.5	118	119	124	133	148	290
2	Mining, quarrying .	13.1	12.4	11.8	10.8	11.0	1042	1036	1051	1104	1183	2
311/2	Food products	64.6	63.0	62.4	62.2	62.2	4329	4540	4826	5226	5639	311/2
313	Beverages	4.6	4.4	4.3	4.2	4.3	363	369	390	423	478	313
314	Tobacco	1.6	1.5	1.5	1.4	1.4	118	122	127	137	136	314
321	Textiles	18.7	17.3	16.5	16.5	16.2	1154	1141	1187	1288	1393	321
3211	Spinning,weaving etc..	8.3	7.0	6.8	6.9	6.6	530	468	502	550	576	3211
322	Wearing apparel	13.2	12.2	11.4	11.2	10.8	736	704	711	759	773	322
323	Leather and products ...	2.0	2.0	1.9	1.8	1.6	122	128	132	136	135	323
324	Footwear	2.5	2.2	2.0	1.5	1.4	146	139	131	108	107	324
331	Wood products	51.5	47.7	46.5	46.1	44.4	3442	3409	3596	3855	4010	331
332	Furniture, fixtures	12.5	11.5	11.5	11.6	11.8	777	777	828	920	1014	332
341	Paper and products	59.3	56.3	55.3	55.0	54.9	4484	4549	4873	5525	6029	341
3411	Pulp,paper etc.	47.4	44.8	43.1	42.6	42.4	3622	3662	3871	4401	4771	3411
342	Printing,publishing	43.7	42.7	42.5	42.4	42.6	3775	3940	4194	4600	4994	342
351	Industrial chemicals ...	19.4	18.5	18.5	18.4	17.8	1537	1585	1717	1888	1983	351
3511	Basic excl fertilizers	10.1	10.0	10.1	9.8	9.8	830	894	983	1068	1132	3511
3513	Synthetic resins etc .	9.3	8.5	8.4	8.5	8.0	708	691	735	820	851	3513
352	Other chemical products.	24.4	24.7	24.5	25.7	25.0	1992	2156	2300	2602	2811	352
3522	Drugs and medicines ..	8.2	8.2	8.6	9.3	9.4	706	752	849	995	1099	3522
353	Petroleum refineries ...	1.7	1.7	1.7	1.7	1.6	156	168	194	206	205	353
354	Petroleum,coal products.	1.5	1.6	1.5	1.5	1.7	117	128	137	153	197	354
355	Rubber products	9.5	8.8	8.8	8.9	9.1	646	643	687	756	833	355
356	Plastic products n.e.c..	11.7	11.0	10.8	11.8	12.5	761	763	810	981	1136	356
361	Pottery,china etc	3.1	3.4	3.3	3.2	3.1	189	217	234	256	266	361
362	Glass and products	4.2	3.8	3.8	4.0	4.2	284	287	302	348	395	362
369	Non-metal products n.e.c	18.3	16.8	15.1	14.4	14.3	1369	1336	1266	1321	1452	369
371	Iron and steel	48.9	44.3	40.1	37.5	36.7	3782	3797	3751	3704	3910	371
372	Non-ferrous metals	12.3	11.5	11.6	12.3	11.9	906	917	979	1111	1171	372
381	Metal products	74.9	70.6	69.5	71.3	71.5	5159	5251	5634	6325	6777	381
382	Machinery n.e.c.	113.9	107.5	102.3	103.8	104.5	8494	8702	9036	9974	11020	382
3825	Office,computing etc..	7.7	6.3	6.3	7.2	8.5	599	556	601	717	1004	3825
383	Electrical machinery ...	78.9	75.8	74.8	75.2	76.3	5910	6259	6732	7389	7070	383
3832	Radio,television etc..	38.1	35.9	35.3	36.0	38.9	2903	2941	3169	3509	3798	3832
384	Transport equipment	113.8	113.8	106.1	107.8	111.3	8430	9029	8938	10165	11489	384
3841	Shipbuilding, repair..	21.2	19.8	16.5	15.4	13.6	1720	1585	1457	1482	1396	3841
3843	Motor vehicles	66.8	67.6	64.6	68.0	72.7	4674	5213	5207	6158	7376	3843
385	Professional goods	9.9	9.7	10.1	10.4	10.7	753	793	900	1029	1449	385
390	Other industries	4.9	4.4	4.2	4.1	4.0	317	302	311	343	359	390
3	Manufacturing	825.5	788.7	762.5	765.9	767.8	60248	62151	64923	71528	77231	3
410	Electricity,gas,steam ..	26.7	27.6	27.9	28.0	27.8	2232	2442	2690	2914	3143	410
4101	Electricity	b/ 26.5	b/ 27.3	b/ 27.6	27.7	27.6	b/ 2208	b/ 2416	b/ 2664	2891	3114	4101
420	Water works and supply .	1.3	1.3	1.3	1.3	1.2	103	106	111	118	125	420
4	Electricity,gas etc	28.0	28.9	29.2	29.3	29.0	2335	2548	2801	3032	3268	4
2-4	All industry	866.6	830.0	803.5	806.0	807.8	63625	65735	68775	75664	81682	2-4

a/ Manufacturing: establishments with 5 or more persons engaged. b/ Including steam.

ISIC	INDUSTRY	5. AVERAGE NUMBER OF OPERATIVES a/ (THOUSANDS)					6. WAGES AND SALARIES OF OPERATIVES a/ (MILLION KRONOR)					ISIC
		1981	1982	1983	1984	1985	1981	1982	1983	1984	1985	
210	Coal mining	-	-	-	-	-	-	-	-	-	-	210
220	Petroleum and gas	-	-	-	-	-	-	-	-	-	-	220
230	Metal ore mining	8.9	8.5	8.1	7.4	7.4	643	650	651	691	744	230
290	Other mining	1.3	1.2	1.1	1.1	1.1	85	85	89	95	100	290
2	Mining, quarrying .	10.2	9.7	9.2	8.5	8.5	728	735	740	786	844	2
311/2	Food products	48.6	47.1	46.2	46.4	46.6	2906	3043	3199	3480	3769	311/2
313	Beverages	3.2	3.0	2.9	2.8	3.0	227	228	239	259	295	313
314	Tobacco	1.2	1.1	1.0	1.0	1.0	71	74	74	78	75	314
321	Textiles	14.7	13.7	13.0	13.1	12.9	803	787	822	897	973	321
3211	Spinning,weaving etc..	6.4	5.5	5.3	5.4	5.2	360	321	348	382	404	3211
322	Wearing apparel	10.8	10.0	9.4	9.3	9.1	542	515	525	562	576	322
323	Leather and products ...	1.6	1.6	1.5	1.4	1.3	89	94	97	101	100	323
324	Footwear	2.2	1.9	1.7	1.3	1.2	115	109	102	85	83	324
331	Wood products	41.5	38.2	37.5	37.4	35.8	2565	2515	2696	2908	3023	331
332	Furniture, fixtures	10.2	9.3	9.4	9.6	9.8	584	579	619	702	769	332
341	Paper and products	45.5	42.8	42.0	42.1	41.6	3111	3115	3351	3847	4214	341
3411	Pulp,paper etc.	36.6	34.3	33.0	32.6	32.3	2540	2535	2694	3090	3362	3411
342	Printing,publishing	25.1	24.3	24.1	24.1	24.3	1972	2047	2163	2344	2574	342
351	Industrial chemicals ...	12.4	12.1	12.1	11.6	11.1	838	883	965	1028	1103	351
3511	Basic excl fertilizers	6.3	6.2	6.3	5.8	5.7	449	480	532	544	611	3511
3513	Synthetic resins etc .	6.1	5.8	5.8	5.8	5.4	388	403	433	485	492	3513
352	Other chemical products.	12.4	12.3	11.8	12.1	11.9	765	827	857	936	1030	352
3522	Drugs and medicines ..	3.0	2.9	2.9	3.1	3.2	177	186	200	235	255	3522
353	Petroleum refineries ...	0.9	0.9	1.0	0.9	0.9	74	80	91	99	101	353
354	Petroleum,coal products.	1.0	1.0	1.0	1.0	1.1	67	73	79	89	109	354
355	Rubber products	6.8	6.3	6.4	6.5	6.6	401	393	429	475	529	355
356	Plastic products n.e.c..	8.9	8.2	8.1	9.0	9.7	500	493	529	642	763	356
361	Pottery,china etc	2.4	2.6	2.6	2.5	9.4	132	149	164	179	179	361
362	Glass and products	3.4	3.1	3.1	3.3	3.4	205	210	223	259	295	362
369	Non-metal products n.e.c	13.0	11.7	10.8	10.4	10.3	857	823	809	853	929	369
371	Iron and steel	35.8	32.5	29.0	28.0	27.3	2452	2461	2402	2498	2671	371
372	Non-ferrous metals	9.2	8.6	8.9	9.4	9.1	609	617	668	760	809	372
381	Metal products	57.0	53.3	52.5	53.7	53.3	3499	3519	3770	4232	4520	381
382	Machinery n.e.c.	74.6	69.5	65.7	66.7	67.9	4669	4756	4887	5435	5925	382
3825	Office,computing etc..	4.7	3.7	3.5	4.1	5.1	291	245	246	306	402	3825
383	Electrical machinery ...	47.0	44.1	42.4	42.9	42.9	2798	2882	2977	3269	3431	383
3832	Radio,television etc..	21.5	20.0	18.8	19.3	19.6	1256	1243	1281	1406	1579	3832
384	Transport equipment	79.9	80.0	76.1	77.5	81.5	5042	5468	5551	6384	7180	384
3841	Shipbuilding, repair..	15.6	14.7	12.0	11.0	9.7	1062	1024	927	926	866	3841
3843	Motor vehicles	48.5	49.0	48.6	51.3	56.3	2891	3243	3390	4071	4878	3843
385	Professional goods	5.8	5.5	5.6	5.5	6.5	349	359	379	405	517	385
390	Other industries	3.7	3.2	3.0	2.9	2.8	204	188	192	211	220	390
3	Manufacturing	578.8	547.9	528.8	532.4	535.3	36446	37287	38859	43017	46762	3
410	Electricity,gas,steam ..	10.8	11.1	10.9	10.8	10.4	839	899	966	1012	1068	410
4101	Electricity	b/ 10.8	b/ 11.1	b/ 10.9	10.7	10.3	b/ 835	b/ 895	b/ 963	1009	1062	4101
420	Water works and supply .	0.6	0.6	0.6	0.6	0.6	48	49	51	56	59	420
4	Electricity,gas etc	11.4	11.7	11.5	11.4	11.0	887	948	1017	1068	1127	4
2-4	All industry	600.4	569.3	549.5	552.3	554.8	38061	38970	40616	44871	48733	2-4

a/ Manufacturing: establishments with 5 or more persons engaged. b/ Including steam.

ISIC	INDUSTRY	7. HOURS WORKED BY OPERATIVES a/ (MILLIONS) 1981	1982	1983	1984	1985	8. QUANTITY OF ELECTRICITY CONSUMED a/ (MILLION KWH) 1981	1982	1983	1984	1985	ISIC
210	Coal mining	-	-	-	-	-	-	-	-	-	-	210
220	Petroleum and gas	-	-	-	-	-	-	-	-	-	-	220
230	Metal ore mining	12	11	12	11	10	1890	1793	1905	2044	2330	230
290	Other mining	2	2	2	2	2	84	88	89	93	90	290
2	Mining, quarrying .	14	13	14	13	12	1974	1881	1994	2137	2420	2
311/2	Food products	72	70	69	69	69	1499	1523	1649	1757	1855	311/2
313	Beverages	6	5	5	5	5	110	113	115	128	151	313
314	Tobacco	2	2	1	1	1	22	23	23	23	23	314
321	Textiles	22	20	19	19	19	260	266	286	291	335	321
3211	Spinning,weaving etc..	10	8	8	8	8	135	130	138	142	159	3211
322	Wearing apparel	16	14	14	13	13	38	38	39	40	44	322
323	Leather and products ...	2	2	2	2	2	20	23	25	26	25	323
324	Footwear	3	3	3	2	2	16	14	13	11	12	324
331	Wood products	65	60	60	59	57	1378	1364	1469	1559	1627	331
332	Furniture, fixtures	16	15	14	15	15	131	134	145	152	168	332
341	Paper and products	66	63	62	63	63	14081	13279	14832	16481	16820	341
3411	Pulp,paper etc.	53	50	48	49	48	13836	13045	14516	16157	16497	3411
342	Printing,publishing	40	39	38	39	39	318	336	348	358	394	342
351	Industrial chemicals ...	19	18	18	17	17	4088	4044	4617	4800	4905	351
3511	Basic excl fertilizers	10	10	10	9	9	3022	3174	3605	3798	3822	3511
3513	Synthetic resins etc .	9	9	9	9	8	1066	870	1011	1002	1082	3513
352	Other chemical products.	18	18	17	17	17	352	366	436	497	497	352
3522	Drugs and medicines ..	4	4	4	4	4	127	130	146	188	185	3522
353	Petroleum refineries ...	1	1	1	2	2	297	307	340	434	495	353
354	Petroleum,coal products.	2	2	2	2	2	77	80	79	88	101	354
355	Rubber products	10	9	9	9	10	193	197	205	232	280	355
356	Plastic products n.e.c..	13	12	12	13	14	296	299	319	373	408	356
361	Pottery,china etc	3	4	4	4	4	74	77	94	95	114	361
362	Glass and products	5	5	5	5	5	159	165	171	185	193	362
369	Non-metal products n.e.c	20	18	17	16	16	934	933	923	918	931	369
371	Iron and steel	53	49	45	42	41	5060	4856	4958	5471	5480	371
372	Non-ferrous metals	14	13	13	14	13	2241	2279	2385	2474	2514	372
381	Metal products	87	81	80	82	82	1177	1208	1308	1433	1493	381
382	Machinery n.e.c.	112	105	101	103	104	1284	1280	1331	1453	1565	382
3825	Office,computing etc..	7	6	5	6	8	63	64	62	63	89	3825
383	Electrical machinery ...	67	64	62	64	62	921	954	952	994	1219	383
3832	Radio,television etc..	29	27	27	28	28	236	246	266	264	325	3832
384	Transport equipment	115	116	112	114	120	1494	1574	1652	1753	1982	384
3841	Shipbuilding, repair..	23	21	18	16	14	252	263	253	242	242	3841
3843	Motor vehicles	68	70	71	75	83	1003	1034	1081	1177	1385	3843
385	Professional goods	9	8	8	8	10	55	51	56	63	88	385
390	Other industries	5	5	4	4	4	39	42	42	44	42	390
3	Manufacturing	863	821	797	806	808	36619	35825	38812	42133	43761	3
410	Electricity,gas,steam ..	17	17	17	17	17	4879	5854	9000	11064	10671	410
4101	Electricity	b/ 17	b/ 17	b/ 17	17	17	b/ 4865	b/ 5841	b/ 8985	11048	10655	4101
420	Water works and supply .	1	1	1	1	2	349	345	339	345	363	420
4	Electricity,gas etc	18	18	18	18	19	5228	6199	9339	11409	11034	4
2-4	All industry	895	852	829	837	839	43821	43905	50145	55679	57215	2-4

a/ Manufacturing: establishments with 5 or more persons engaged. b/ Including steam.

ISIC	INDUSTRY	9. OUTPUT IN FACTOR VALUES a/ (BILLION KRONOR)					10. VALUE ADDED IN FACTOR VALUES a/ (BILLION KRONOR)					ISIC
		1981	1982	1983	1984	1985	1981	1982	1983	1984	1985	
210	Coal mining	-	-	-	-	-	-	-	-	-	-	210
220	Petroleum and gas	-	-	-	-	-	-	-	-	-	-	220
230	Metal ore mining	3.00	3.25	4.11	4.97	5.69	1.89	2.20	2.89	3.54	4.06	230
290	Other mining	0.56	0.59	0.65	0.71	0.73	0.40	0.42	0.47	0.49	0.52	290
2	Mining, quarrying .	3.56	3.84	4.76	5.68	6.42	2.29	2.62	3.36	4.03	4.58	2
311/2	Food products	42.20	48.60	53.29	59.79	64.58	12.76	13.72	15.42	16.23	18.13	311/2
313	Beverages	3.04	3.52	3.95	4.19	4.74	1.44	1.70	1.95	1.95	2.15	313
314	Tobacco	0.81	1.05	1.14	1.32	1.48	0.52	0.72	0.72	0.80	0.93	314
321	Textiles	4.64	4.95	5.68	6.27	6.92	2.31	2.41	2.75	2.94	3.26	321
3211	Spinning,weaving etc..	1.97	1.91	2.32	2.58	2.79	1.05	0.96	1.16	1.25	1.40	3211
322	Wearing apparel	2.14	2.08	2.20	2.38	2.51	1.18	1.13	1.21	1.29	1.35	322
323	Leather and products ...	0.54	0.64	0.77	0.92	0.91	0.24	0.26	0.30	0.34	0.34	323
324	Footwear	0.50	0.50	0.48	0.43	0.44	0.24	0.24	0.23	0.20	0.21	324
331	Wood products	20.19	21.07	25.06	27.69	27.50	8.09	8.34	10.08	10.92	9.93	331
332	Furniture, fixtures	3.37	3.56	4.03	4.57	5.38	1.69	1.72	1.89	2.09	2.45	332
341	Paper and products	33.38	34.96	41.98	50.75	51.19	11.75	13.10	16.51	20.81	19.19	341
3411	Pulp,paper etc.	28.25	29.31	35.04	43.06	42.64	9.50	10.61	13.42	17.53	15.53	3411
342	Printing,publishing	12.44	13.92	15.76	17.90	19.97	8.37	9.37	10.53	11.83	13.05	342
351	Industrial chemicals ...	11.88	13.70	17.50	19.62	19.64	4.10	4.92	6.11	7.04	7.24	351
3511	Basic excl fertilizers	6.88	7.92	10.00	10.99	11.01	b/ 2.53	b/ 2.97	b/ 3.75	b/ 4.19	4.40	3511
3513	Synthetic resins etc .	4.99	5.78	7.49	8.63	8.62	1.57	1.95	2.36	2.85	2.83	3513
352	Other chemical products.	10.07	11.06	12.75	14.21	15.92	5.43	6.25	7.21	8.26	9.38	352
3522	Drugs and medicines ..	2.90	3.39	4.24	4.97	5.56	2.10	2.54	3.21	3.70	4.08	3522
353	Petroleum refineries ...	20.24	23.26	28.83	29.39	29.91	1.02	2.00	3.50	2.86	3.41	353
354	Petroleum,coal products.	2.12	2.53	2.92	3.65	3.81	0.60	0.71	0.81	1.06	1.05	354
355	Rubber products	2.45	2.70	3.16	3.54	3.93	1.27	1.36	1.54	1.76	1.94	355
356	Plastic products n.e.c..	3.30	3.52	4.17	5.20	5.91	1.70	1.80	2.07	2.60	2.87	356
361	Pottery,china etc	0.54	0.69	0.79	0.79	0.89	0.39	0.48	0.54	0.53	0.61	361
362	Glass and products	1.28	1.46	1.72	1.82	1.97	0.74	0.81	0.96	0.99	1.07	362
369	Non-metal products n.e.c	6.19	6.60	6.76	7.39	7.93	3.40	3.74	3.77	4.12	4.39	369
371	Iron and steel	17.65	20.24	22.90	26.44	28.93	6.92	7.80	8.76	9.16	10.20	371
372	Non-ferrous metals	7.63	8.43	10.82	11.35	11.26	1.95	2.12	2.73	2.89	2.85	372
381	Metal products	21.63	23.11	26.38	30.80	33.71	11.79	12.23	13.66	16.22	17.62	381
382	Machinery n.e.c.	34.08	36.29	41.99	47.88	54.76	18.47	19.30	21.36	24.41	27.40	382
3825	Office,computing etc..	2.72	2.81	3.77	4.49	6.42	1.37	1.40	1.66	1.87	2.54	3825
383	Electrical machinery ...	22.17	24.98	28.92	32.73	34.01	13.02	14.72	17.20	19.17	18.34	383
3832	Radio,television etc..	11.11	12.41	14.92	17.40	18.29	6.90	7.63	9.20	10.68	9.97	3832
384	Transport equipment	40.57	47.28	52.26	56.03	65.52	16.80	20.44	21.86	22.00	27.13	384
3841	Shipbuilding, repair..	6.87	7.90	7.62	5.23	6.67	3.41	4.01	4.32	2.52	3.60	3841
3843	Motor vehicles	27.79	32.40	37.58	42.66	48.21	9.74	12.21	13.50	14.96	17.81	3843
385	Professional goods	2.78	3.09	3.71	4.27	5.82	1.74	1.88	2.25	2.46	3.44	385
390	Other industries	1.20	1.20	1.31	1.44	1.46	0.66	0.63	0.67	0.72	0.75	390
3	Manufacturing	329.10	364.99	421.23	472.76	511.00	138.59	153.90	176.59	195.65	210.68	3
410	Electricity,gas,steam ..	40.87	45.41	51.72	57.45	69.67	16.37	17.60	21.15	24.39	27.38	410
4101	Electricity	c/ 40.66	c/ 45.19	c/ 51.51	57.23	69.33	c/ 16.31	c/ 17.54	c/ 21.10	24.32	27.31	4101
420	Water works and supply .	1.17	1.31	1.42	1.51	1.61	1.05	1.18	1.29	1.37	1.45	420
4	Electricity,gas etc	42.04	46.72	53.14	58.96	71.28	17.42	18.78	22.44	25.76	28.83	4
2-4	All industry	374.70	415.55	479.13	537.40	588.70	158.30	175.30	202.39	225.44	244.09	2-4

a/ Manufacturing: establishments with 5 or more persons engaged. b/ Including group 3512.
c/ Including steam.

ISIC	INDUSTRY	11. GROSS FIXED CAPITAL FORMATION TOTAL a/b/ (MILLION KRONOR)					12. GROSS FIXED CAPITAL FORMATION MACHINERY AND EQUIPMENT a/b/ (MILLION KRONOR)					ISIC
		1981	1982	1983	1984	1985	1981	1982	1983	1984	1985	
210	Coal mining .... c/	...	...	...	...	...	...	...	...	...	...	210
220	Petroleum and gas ...... c/	...	...	...	...	...	...	...	...	...	...	220
230	Metal ore mining	648	595	346	366	386	372	316	242	273	295	230
290	Other mining .... c/	81	108	151	199	231	72	86	144	169	199	290
2	Mining, quarrying .	729	703	497	565	617	444	402	386	442	494	2
311/2	Food products	1529	1452	1721	1897	2120	1133	1194	1355	1358	1552	311/2
313	Beverages	[220	145	230	211	322	188	128	216	157	267]	313
314	Tobacco											314
321	Textiles	278	244	231	288	270	218	202	204	246	220	321
3211	Spinning,weaving etc..	...	...	...	...	...	...	...	...	...	...	3211
322	Wearing apparel	51	63	42	50	59	43	57	39	40	50	322
323	Leather and products ...	13	14	20	35	25	7	11	16	30	16	323
324	Footwear	34	20	9	11	20	18	12	8	10	12	324
331	Wood products	1045	855	1186	1547	1225	779	696	945	1167	905	331
332	Furniture, fixtures	148	142	171	170	291	97	102	124	136	225	332
341	Paper and products	3530	3188	3391	4091	6057	2912	2706	3062	3451	5165	341
3411	Pulp,paper etc.	3238	2923	3044	3720	5704	2685	2505	2748	3111	4846	3411
342	Printing,publishing	713	591	642	752	840	602	515	577	631	721	342
351	Industrial chemicals ...	800	912	1086	1169	1404	674	855	977	1055	1219	351
3511	Basic excl fertilizers	...	...	...	...	...	...	...	...	...	...	3511
3513	Synthetic resins etc .	...	...	...	...	...	...	...	...	...	...	3513
352	Other chemical products.	525	582	847	992	1249	396	416	629	718	899	352
3522	Drugs and medicines ..	...	...	...	...	...	...	...	...	...	...	3522
353	Petroleum refineries ...	[275	574	965	220	259	262	556	936	210	241]	353
354	Petroleum,coal products.											354
355	Rubber products	126	99	201	258	260	110	90	169	195	191	355
356	Plastic products n.e.c..	229	204	272	456	644	181	186	246	388	559	356
361	Pottery,china etc	24	25	31	47	56	21	20	29	44	45	361
362	Glass and products	75	67	67	77	111	64	62	53	65	96	362
369	Non-metal products n.e.c	398	359	317	386	435	297	290	270	324	394	369
371	Iron and steel	1427	948	735	960	1225	1213	824	682	888	1140	371
372	Non-ferrous metals	321	222	271	413	499	268	194	244	311	418	372
381	Metal products	1235	1040	1189	1825	1746	985	839	989	1337	1329	381
382	Machinery n.e.c.	1850	1660	1742	2190	2977	1427	1289	1434	1627	2210	382
3825	Office,computing etc..	...	...	...	...	...	...	...	...	...	...	3825
383	Electrical machinery ...	1094	1177	1391	1637	1952	865	987	1200	1430	1643	383
3832	Radio,television etc..	...	...	...	...	...	...	...	...	...	...	3832
384	Transport equipment	1879	2004	2261	3360	4006	1387	1488	1634	2637	3016	384
3841	Shipbuilding, repair..	119	134	101	168	113	73	91	82	96	75	3841
3843	Motor vehicles	...	...	...	...	...	...	...	...	...	...	3843
385	Professional goods	121	142	151	166	231	100	108	141	140	189	385
390	Other industries	40	41	57	74	188	37	40	48	61	108	390
3	Manufacturing	17980	16770	19226	23282	28471	14284	13867	16227	18656	22830	3
410	Electricity,gas,steam ..	8584	9842	11421	11213	12158	3629	3820	6718	7171	7074	410
4101	Electricity	7369	8015	8884	8691	9135	3455	3580	5971	6574	5969	4101
420	Water works and supply .	...	...	...	...	...	...	...	...	...	...	420
4	Electricity,gas etc	...	...	...	...	...	...	...	...	...	...	4
2-4	All industry	...	...	...	...	...	...	...	...	...	...	2-4

a/ Manufacturing: establishments with 5 or more persons engaged. b/ Excluding used fixed assets.
c/ Major groups 210 and 220 are included in 290.

13. VALUE OF STOCKS AT END OF PERIOD
TOTAL a/
(MILLION KRONOR)

ISIC	INDUSTRY	1981	1982	1983	1984	1985	ISIC
210	Coal mining	-	-	-	-	-	210
220	Petroleum and gas	-	-	-	-	-	220
230	Metal ore mining	632	499	815	504	521	230
290	Other mining	130	197	158	187	172	290
2	Mining, quarrying .	762	696	973	692	693	2
311/2	Food products	4936	5874	6161	6307	6804	311/2
313	Beverages	697	758	804	836	843	313
314	Tobacco	503	739	664	797	699	314
321	Textiles	1438	1620	1731	1927	2077	321
3211	Spinning,weaving etc..	...	...	...	...	...	3211
322	Wearing apparel	595	620	677	651	794	322
323	Leather and products ...	163	168	210	244	229	323
324	Footwear	174	159	155	152	120	324
331	Wood products	5519	5287	5708	6487	6216	331
332	Furniture, fixtures	888	897	996	1127	1289	332
341	Paper and products	5809	6409	6633	6779	6777	341
3411	Pulp,paper etc.	4934	5572	5770	5721	5729	3411
342	Printing,publishing	729	767	974	1070	1245	342
351	Industrial chemicals ...	2142	2244	2515	2954	3030	351
3511	Basic excl fertilizers	...	...	...	...	...	3511
3513	Synthetic resins etc .	...	...	...	...	...	3513
352	Other chemical products.	2158	2448	b/ 4125	4134	4691	352
3522	Drugs and medicines ..	...	...	...	...	...	3522
353	Petroleum refineries ...	2558	2801	3042	2587	2648	353
354	Petroleum,coal products.	609	713	669	676	732	354
355	Rubber products	581	611	693	709	746	355
356	Plastic products n.e.c..	584	666	891	908	948	356
361	Pottery,china etc	224	234	252	293	293	361
362	Glass and products	298	306	307	348	430	362
369	Non-metal products n.e.c	1016	1012	1100	1105	1140	369
371	Iron and steel	6445	6304	5872	6462	6139	371
372	Non-ferrous metals	1547	1766	2447	2179	2335	372
381	Metal products	7854	8506	b/ 7274	8118	7938	381
382	Machinery n.e.c.	17104	17436	16331	17610	18608	382
3825	Office,computing etc..	...	...	...	...	...	3825
383	Electrical machinery ...	10593	10670	10708	12367	14581	383
3832	Radio,television etc..	...	...	...	...	...	3832
384	Transport equipment	16093	17175	17162	17253	18679	384
3841	Shipbuilding, repair..	4760	4831	3650	3977	4144	3841
3843	Motor vehicles	...	...	...	...	...	3843
385	Professional goods	933	964	1070	1239	1333	385
390	Other industries	556	527	495	502	515	390
3	Manufacturing	92746	97681	99666	105821	111879	3
410	Electricity,gas,steam ..	...	...	...	...	...	410
4101	Electricity	...	...	...	...	...	4101
420	Water works and supply .	...	...	...	...	...	420
4	Electricity,gas etc	...	...	...	...	...	4
2-4	All industry	...	...	...	...	...	2-4

a/ Manufacturing: establishments with 5 or more persons engaged.
b/ Owing to reclassification of establishments, the figure is not strictly comparable with those for previous years.

14. INDEX NUMBERS OF INDUSTRIAL PRODUCTION (1980 = 100)

ISIC	INDUSTRY	1976	1977	1978	1979	1981	1982	1983	1984	1985	a/ RATE	ISIC
210	Coal mining	-	-	-	-	-	-	-	-	-	...	210
220	Petroleum and gas	-	-	-	-	-	-	-	-	-	...	220
230	Metal ore mining	108	92	80	101	83	70	85	98	115	0.7	230
290	Other mining .... b/	98	99	99	102	101	98	99	100	100	0.2	290
2	Mining, quarrying . b/	106	93	83	101	86	74	87	99	114	0.8	2
311/2	Food products	99	97	97	98	100	102	102	104	103	0.4	311/2
313	Beverages	101	102	102	102	95	96	97	95	106	0.5	313
314	Tobacco	108	99	95	98	95	100	96	98	93	-1.6	314
321	Textiles	131	119	106	106	93	90	91	94	99	-3.1	321
3211	Spinning,weaving etc..	...	...	...	...	...	...	...	...	...	...	3211
322	Wearing apparel	165	133	102	102	91	81	79	78	74	-8.5	322
323	Leather and products ...	142	127	118	111	101	104	107	110	100	-3.8	323
324	Footwear	136	127	106	104	85	78	68	58	68	-7.4	324
331	Wood products	102	99	101	104	91	91	96	98	94	-0.9	331
332	Furniture, fixtures	113	108	105	109	78	75	77	85	85	-3.1	332
341	Paper and products	92	87	94	101	98	93	102	108	107	1.7	341
3411	Pulp,paper etc.	...	...	...	...	...	...	...	...	...	...	3411
342	Printing,publishing	92	93	95	100	99	99	102	109	112	2.2	342
351	Industrial chemicals ...	99	94	99	105	94	99	110	112	111	1.3	351
3511	Basic excl fertilizers	...	...	...	...	...	...	...	...	...	...	3511
3513	Synthetic resins etc .	...	...	...	...	...	...	...	...	...	...	3513
352	Other chemical products.	77	76	77	79	105	105	111	113	116	4.7	352
3522	Drugs and medicines ..	...	...	...	...	...	...	...	...	...	...	3522
353	Petroleum refineries ...	90	89	90	98	99	90	109	108	103	1.5	353
354	Petroleum,coal products.	109	97	91	95	107	109	114	135	122	1.3	354
355	Rubber products	116	112	104	106	91	89	94	103	117	0.1	355
356	Plastic products n.e.c..	100	96	99	97	93	92	98	109	113	1.4	356
361	Pottery,china etc	128	117	108	112	90	101	110	103	98	-2.9	361
362	Glass and products	98	100	100	100	89	95	103	105	109	1.2	362
369	Non-metal products n.e.c	108	99	95	101	87	84	80	82	81	-3.1	369
371	Iron and steel	95	85	88	103	93	96	99	109	105	1.1	371
372	Non-ferrous metals	91	89	94	99	94	97	101	104	105	1.6	372
381	Metal products	97	93	88	93	98	94	96	105	104	0.8	381
382	Machinery n.e.c.	105	99	96	103	98	94	98	108	118	1.3	382
3825	Office,computing etc..	...	...	...	...	...	...	...	...	...	...	3825
383	Electrical machinery ...	95	92	86	93	108	108	115	124	133	3.8	383
3832	Radio,television etc..	...	...	...	...	...	...	...	...	...	...	3832
384	Transport equipment	128	115	106	109	102	108	109	111	110	-1.7	384
3841	Shipbuilding, repair..	204	171	139	117	104	108	100	87	68	-11.5	3841
3843	Motor vehicles	...	...	...	...	...	...	...	...	...	...	3843
385	Professional goods	85	78	75	81	98	98	103	109	112	3.1	385
390	Other industries	112	102	98	101	95	87	85	82	82	-3.4	390
3	Manufacturing	102	96	95	100	98	97	102	107	109	0.7	3
410	Electricity,gas,steam ..	86	88	95	99	110	110	126	130	...	d/ 5.3	410
4101	Electricity	...	...	...	...	...	...	...	...	...	...	4101
420	Water works and supply .	109	105	119	120	99	99	98	98	...	d/ -1.3	420
4	Electricity,gas etc	...	...	...	...	...	...	...	...	...	...	4
2-4	All industry b/c/	102	96	94	100	98	97	102	107	109	0.7	2-4

a/ Annual growth rate 1976-1985.
b/ Excluding clay and sand pits.
c/ Excluding electricity, gas, steam and water.
d/ Annual growth rate 1976-1984.

SWITZERLAND

The information on industrial activity is based on the reply to the United Nations Questionnaire on General Industrial Statistics from the Office federal de l'industrie, des arts et metiers et du travail (OFIAMT), Berne. The concepts, definitions and classification by branches of industry are generally in accordance with United Nations standards.

The data are compiled according to the Labour Law of 1964, effective 1 February 1966, covering labour in industry, handicrafts and trade. Industry, as defined by this Law, covers all industrial establishments using automatic processes or presenting particular dangers to the life or health of the worker and all other establishments employing at least 6 production workers. Purely family concerns are exempt and military establishments, which are subject to special provisions, are not included in the tabulations. All personnel engaged by the establishment are included, rather than persons subject to special legal provisions only. The estimates are compiled according to an activity classification whereby certain industrial activities performed by non-industrial enterprises solely for their own use are not included. It should be noted that the employment numbers for 1982 are not fully comparable with those for previous years owing to modifications in enumeration methods.

The estimates, which are derived from information compiled according to the national scheme, have been adjusted as far as possible to the present version of ISIC.

The estimates of persons engaged relate to a specific day in September.

The indexes of industrial production are compiled by the Office federal de l'industrie, des arts et metiers et du travail (OFIAMT), Berne and provided in response to the United Nations Questionnaire on Indexes of Industrial Production.

Related national publications:
La Vie economique, published by the Departement federal de l'economie publique, Berne.

SWITZERLAND

ISIC	INDUSTRY	1. NUMBER OF ESTABLISHMENTS a/ (NUMBER)					2. AVERAGE NUMBER OF PERSONS ENGAGED a/b/ (THOUSANDS)					ISIC
		1981	1982	1983	1984	1985	1981	c/ 1982	1983	1984	1985	
210	Coal mining	...	...	...	...	...	...	...	...	...	...	210
220	Petroleum and gas	...	...	...	...	...	...	...	...	...	...	220
230	Metal ore mining	...	...	...	...	...	...	...	...	...	...	230
290	Other mining	...	...	...	...	...	...	...	...	...	...	290
2	Mining, quarrying .	...	...	...	...	...	...	...	...	...	...	2
311/2	Food products	501	482	474	467	472	45.1	57.0	54.3	47.9	48.9	311/2
313	Beverages	118	114	105	99	98	7.3	8.7	8.3	7.7	7.6	313
314	Tobacco	44	41	32	27	24	4.2	4.3	4.3	3.8	3.6	314
321	Textiles	664	584	566	538	527	41.5	37.6	35.8	34.7	34.5	321
3211	Spinning,weaving etc..	398	374	334	349	346	28.5	26.3	26.6	25.3	25.2	3211
322	Wearing apparel	449	419	390	361	353	17.5	17.3	15.8	14.7	14.4	322
323	Leather and products ...	87	82	77	74	74	2.4	2.2	2.0	1.8	1.9	323
324	Footwear	63	61	57	54	53	6.1	5.2	4.9	4.9	5.0	324
331	Wood products	551	568	554	547	546	17.1	18.0	17.9	17.8	18.2	331
332	Furniture, fixtures	276	260	249	239	233	10.6	11.9	11.3	9.5	9.3	332
341	Paper and products	175	167	166	165	168	16.4	16.3	16.1	15.1	15.4	341
3411	Pulp,paper etc.	36	36	36	34	34	7.9	7.3	8.5	7.7	7.7	3411
342	Printing,publishing	755	746	732	715	704	41.5	41.4	41.1	40.2	40.1	342
351	Industrial chemicals ... d/	369	348	347	339	345	66.6	70.1	68.6	65.9	67.4	351
3511	Basic excl fertilizers	...	...	...	...	...	...	...	...	...	...	3511
3513	Synthetic resins etc .	32	28	27	26	29	6.0	5.8	5.5	5.5	5.7	3513
352	Other chemical products. d/	...	...	...	...	...	...	...	...	...	...	352
3522	Drugs and medicines ..	...	...	...	...	...	...	...	...	...	...	3522
353	Petroleum refineries ...	6	9	9	7	8	0.4	0.7	0.7	0.6	0.7	353
354	Petroleum,coal products.	14	14	14	14	18	0.3	0.6	0.6	0.6	0.6	354
355	Rubber products	34	31	30	30	29	2.9	2.8	2.8	2.8	2.7	355
356	Plastic products n.e.c..	266	273	268	264	273	13.1	13.8	13.7	13.7	14.3	356
361	Pottery,china etc	28	20	18	17	16	2.8	2.1	2.0	1.9	1.8	361
362	Glass and products	56	57	56	56	56	3.8	4.0	3.8	3.8	3.8	362
369	Non-metal products n.e.c	274	279	263	274	282	12.9	14.6	14.3	14.2	13.7	369
371	Iron and steel	44	67	65	60	61	11.2	12.8	11.4	10.1	10.8	371
372	Non-ferrous metals	116	100	100	99	97	14.9	13.7	13.3	13.0	13.0	372
381	Metal products	1144	1110	1097	1084	1061	60.2	60.3	58.3	57.7	57.2	381
382	Machinery n.e.c. .... e/	1415	1395	1347	1329	1321	206.0	210.0	203.0	195.9	200.3	382
3825	Office,computing etc..	13	24	26	25	24	2.7	4.5	3.9	3.6	3.6	3825
383	Electrical machinery ... e/	...	...	...	...	...	...	...	...	...	...	383
3832	Radio,television etc..	44	32	30	31	28	2.4	2.2	2.2	2.3	2.2	3832
384	Transport equipment	128	108	103	99	100	16.1	16.3	13.9	13.6	15.1	384
3841	Shipbuilding, repair..	...	...	...	...	3	...	...	...	...	0.1	3841
3843	Motor vehicles	39	35	33	30	31	5.8	4.7	3.5	3.0	3.1	3843
385	Professional goods	961	888	839	791	772	60.2	52.7	48.6	43.8	46.3	385
390	Other industries	115	128	128	126	128	6.3	9.1	9.8	9.3	9.8	390
3	Manufacturing	8653	8351	8086	7875	7819	687.4	703.5	676.6	645.0	656.4	3
410	Electricity,gas,steam ..	...	...	...	...	...	...	...	...	...	...	410
4101	Electricity	...	...	...	...	...	...	...	...	...	...	4101
420	Water works and supply .	...	...	...	...	...	...	...	...	...	...	420
4	Electricity,gas etc	...	...	...	...	...	...	...	...	...	...	4
2-4	All industry	...	...	...	...	...	...	...	...	...	...	2-4

a/ Establishments subject to the Labour Law; see country note. b/ In September of the year indicated.
c/ Data are not comparable with those for previous years due to change in enumeration method.
d/ Major group 352 is included in 351. e/ Major group 383 is included in 382.

3. INDEX NUMBERS OF INDUSTRIAL PRODUCTION (1980 = 100)

ISIC	INDUSTRY		1976	1977	1978	1979	1981	1982	1983	1984	1985	a/ RATE	ISIC
210	Coal mining		...	...	...	...	...	...	...	...	...	...	210
220	Petroleum and gas		...	...	...	...	...	...	...	...	...	...	220
230	Metal ore mining		...	...	...	...	...	...	...	...	...	...	230
290	Other mining		...	...	...	...	...	...	...	...	...	...	290
2	Mining, quarrying		...	...	...	...	...	...	...	...	...	...	2
311/2	Food products												311/2
313	Beverages		90	93	93	95	100	101	100	101	101	1.3	313
314	Tobacco												314
321	Textiles		95	96	96	99	98	96	96	102	105	1.1	321
3211	Spinning,weaving etc.		...	...	...	...	...	...	...	...	...	...	3211
322	Wearing apparel		104	105	99	94	97	93	90	88	86	-2.1	322
323	Leather and products	b/	73	82	86	96	93	90	92	99	106	4.2	323
324	Footwear		...	...	...	...	...	...	...	...	...	...	324
331	Wood products		84	94	91	96	97	89	89	94	95	1.4	331
332	Furniture, fixtures		...	...	...	...	...	...	...	...	...	...	332
341	Paper and products		80	87	93	99	99	97	98	102	105	3.1	341
3411	Pulp,paper etc.		...	...	...	...	...	...	...	...	...	...	3411
342	Printing,publishing		96	94	95	92	108	112	116	123	136	3.9	342
351	Industrial chemicals	c/	92	91	94	98	104	103	109	115	123	3.3	351
3511	Basic excl fertilizers		...	...	...	...	...	...	...	...	...	...	3511
3513	Synthetic resins etc		...	...	...	...	...	...	...	...	...	...	3513
352	Other chemical products.	c/	...	...	...	...	...	...	...	...	...	...	352
3522	Drugs and medicines		...	...	...	...	...	...	...	...	...	...	3522
353	Petroleum refineries		...	...	...	...	...	...	...	...	...	...	353
354	Petroleum,coal products.		...	...	...	...	...	...	...	...	...	...	354
355	Rubber products	b/	...	...	...	...	...	...	...	...	...	...	355
356	Plastic products n.e.c.		...	...	...	...	...	...	...	...	...	...	356
361	Pottery,china etc												361
362	Glass and products		84	92	91	96	100	93	92	94	94	1.3	362
369	Non-metal products n.e.c												369
371	Iron and steel		81	90	88	96	98	91	90	98	101	2.5	371
372	Non-ferrous metals												372
381	Metal products	d/	84	87	92	91	97	92	88	88	94	1.3	381
382	Machinery n.e.c.												382
3825	Office,computing etc.		...	...	...	...	...	...	...	...	...	...	3825
383	Electrical machinery	d/	...	...	...	...	...	...	...	...	...	...	383
3832	Radio,television etc.		...	...	...	...	...	...	...	...	...	...	3832
384	Transport equipment	d/	...	...	...	...	...	...	...	...	...	...	384
3841	Shipbuilding, repair.		...	...	...	...	...	...	...	...	...	...	3841
3843	Motor vehicles		...	...	...	...	...	...	...	...	...	...	3843
385	Professional goods		120	127	115	96	89	60	58	62	72	-5.5	385
390	Other industries												390
3	Manufacturing		89	93	94	95	99	94	94	97	103	1.6	3
410	Electricity,gas,steam		76	96	89	95	107	108	108	102	114	4.6	410
4101	Electricity		...	...	...	...	...	...	...	...	...	...	4101
420	Water works and supply		...	...	...	...	...	...	...	...	...	...	420
4	Electricity,gas etc		...	...	...	...	...	...	...	...	...	...	4
2-4	All industry	e/	88	93	93	95	99	96	95	97	103	1.8	2-4

a/ Annual growth rate 1976-1985.
b/ Major group 355 is included in 323.
c/ Major group 352 is included in 351.
d/ Major groups 383 and 384 are included in 381 and 382 combined.
e/ Excluding mining and water works and supply.

SYRIAN ARAB REPUBLIC

The information in the tables, except for the indexes, is based on the reply to the United Nations Questionnaire on General Industrial Statistics from the Central Bureau of Statistics, Office of the Prime Minister, Damascus. The concepts, definitions and classification by branches of industry are generally in accordance with United Nations standards.

The data in the tables are derived from the survey of industrial establishments undertaken annually by the Central Bureau of Statistics. The inquiry is carried out by means of field interview by trained enumerators. Establishments with 10 or more persons engaged are completely enumerated, while those with fewer than 10 persons engaged are covered on a sample basis. The figures in the tables refer to all establishments, irrespective of size, except home industries. However, the directory of establishments used in the annual industrial surveys has not been brought up to date and consequently does not strictly reflect the situation of existing establishments. It should be noted that the table for number of establishments refers to the private sector only. Data for other tables refer to both the public and private sector unless otherwise footnoted.

The data in the tables are based on the national classification system, which follows the preceding version of ISIC. They have been adjusted by the Central Bureau of Statistics to represent the present version as far as details permitted. It should be noted that the manufacturing estimates include repair services for the general public (ISIC major division 9).

Value added refers to the net domestic product and valuation of output and value added is in factor values.

The indexes of industrial production are compiled by the Central Bureau of Statistics and provided in response to the United Nations Questionnaire on Indexes of Industrial Production. The indexes cover, in principle, all major industries.

Related national publication:

<u>Statistical Abstract</u> (annual), published by the Central Bureau of Statistics, Office of the Prime Minister, Damascus.

ISIC	INDUSTRY	1. NUMBER OF ESTABLISHMENTS a/ (NUMBER) 1981	1982	1983	1984	1985	2. AVERAGE NUMBER OF PERSONS ENGAGED (THOUSANDS) 1981	1982	1983	b/ 1984	1985	ISIC
210	Coal mining	-	-	-	-	...	-	-	-	-	...	210
220	Petroleum and gas	...	...	...	...	...	...	...	...	...	...	220
230	Metal ore mining	-	-	-	-	...	-	-	-	-	...	230
290	Other mining	...	...	...	...	...	...	...	...	...	...	290
2	Mining, quarrying	192	201	201	204	...	14.5	14.9	14.3	13.0	...	2
311/2	Food products					...	35.7	35.8	...		...	311/2
313	Beverages	[7602	7974	8001	8029]	...	4.5	4.5	...	[67.9]	...	313
314	Tobacco					...	9.9	9.9	...		...	314
321	Textiles	c/ 14906	c/ 15116	c/ 15115	c/ 15126	...	48.5	48.6	c/ 65.0	c/ 62.4	...	321
3211	Spinning,weaving etc.	...	...	...	...	...	22.7	22.8	...	...	...	3211
322	Wearing apparel	c/	c/	c/	c/	...	4.9	5.0	c/	c/	...	322
323	Leather and products	c/	c/	c/	c/	...	2.9	3.1	c/	c/	...	323
324	Footwear	c/	c/	c/	c/	...	10.0	10.1	c/	c/	...	324
331	Wood products	[9901	9942	10094	10294]	...	6.1	6.1	[22.0	24.2]	...	331
332	Furniture, fixtures					...	13.6	13.7			...	332
341	Paper and products	d/ 562	d/ 579	d/ 581	d/ 590	...	1.3	1.4	d/ 3.6	d/ 3.9	...	341
3411	Pulp,paper etc.	...	...	...	...	...	...	...	...	...	...	3411
342	Printing,publishing	d/	d/	d/	d/	...	2.9	3.0	d/	d/	...	342
351	Industrial chemicals	e/ 1788	e/ 1855	e/ 1866	e/ 1899	...	f/ 14.5	f/ 14.6	e/ 19.0	e/ 19.1	...	351
3511	Basic excl fertilizers	...	...	...	...	...	...	...	...	...	...	3511
3513	Synthetic resins etc	...	...	...	...	...	...	...	...	...	...	3513
352	Other chemical products	e/	e/	e/	e/	...	f/	f/	e/	e/	...	352
3522	Drugs and medicines	...	...	...	...	...	...	...	...	...	...	3522
353	Petroleum refineries	e/	e/	e/	e/	...	[5.6	5.6]	e/	e/	...	353
354	Petroleum,coal products	e/	e/	e/	e/	...			e/	e/	...	354
355	Rubber products	e/	e/	e/	e/	...	2.3	2.4	e/	e/	...	355
356	Plastic products n.e.c.	e/	e/	e/	e/	...	2.0	2.1	e/	e/	...	356
361	Pottery,china etc					...	1.7	1.7			...	361
362	Glass and products	[5841	5930	5957	5973]	...	2.5	2.6	[28.4	30.0]	...	362
369	Non-metal products n.e.c					...	17.7	17.7			...	369
371	Iron and steel	[4	5	2	2]	...	[1.5	1.4	19.6	2.0]	...	371
372	Non-ferrous metals					...					...	372
381	Metal products	[g/ 11696	g/ 11281	g/ 11781	g/ 12281]	...	11.6	11.7	[g/ 31.0	g/ 32.8]	...	381
382	Machinery n.e.c.					...	3.1	3.2			...	382
3825	Office,computing etc.	...	...	...	...	...	...	...	...	...	...	3825
383	Electrical machinery	g/	g/	g/	g/	...	2.5	2.6	g/	g/	...	383
3832	Radio,television etc.	...	...	...	...	...	1.1	1.0	...	...	...	3832
384	Transport equipment	g/	g/	g/	g/	...	1.0	1.1	g/	g/	...	384
3841	Shipbuilding, repair	...	...	...	...	...	...	...	...	...	...	3841
3843	Motor vehicles	...	...	...	...	...	...	...	...	...	...	3843
385	Professional goods	-	-	-	-	...	-	-	-	-	...	385
390	Other industries	1504	1524	1524	1524	...	3.4	3.4	2.0	2.6	...	390
3	Manufacturing h/	53804	54206	54921	55718	...	209.7	211.3	i/ 190.6	244.9	...	3
410	Electricity,gas,steam j/	205	225	1	1	...	14.9	16.1	18.7	17.4	...	410
4101	Electricity	205	225	1	1	...	14.9	16.1	18.7	17.4	...	4101
420	Water works and supply	1	1	225	225	...	3.6	3.9	4.1	4.3	...	420
4	Electricity,gas etc j/	206	226	226	226	...	18.5	20.0	22.8	21.7	24.0	4
2-4	All industry h/i/	54202	54633	55348	56148	...	242.7	246.2	i/ 227.7	279.6	...	2-4

a/ Private sector only.
b/ Public sector only
c/ Major groups 322 to 324 are included in 321.
d/ Major group 342 is included in 341.
e/ Major groups 352 to 356 are included in 351.
f/ Major group 352 is included in 351.
g/ Major groups 383 and 384 are included in 381 and 382 combined.
h/ Including repair services.
i/ Excluding major groups 311/2, 313 and 314.
j/ Excluding gas and steam.

ISIC	INDUSTRY	3. WAGES AND SALARIES OF EMPLOYEES (MILLION POUNDS) 1981	1982	1983	a/ 1984	1985	4. OUTPUT IN FACTOR VALUES (MILLION POUNDS) 1981	1982	1983	1984	1985	ISIC
210	Coal mining	-	-	-	-	...	-	-	-	-	...	210
220	Petroleum and gas	...	...	...	...	...	...	...	...	...	...	220
230	Metal ore mining	-	-	-	-	...	-	-	-	-	...	230
290	Other mining	...	...	...	...	...	...	...	...	...	...	290
2	Mining, quarrying	...	...	457.0	448.0	...	8306	7040	6591	6652	...	2
311/2	Food products	[			]	...	[			]	...	311/2
313	Beverages	689.4	689.4	767.0	567.0	...	4422	4305	5237	6013	...	313
314	Tobacco	]			]	...	]			]	...	314
321	Textiles	b/ 1346.9	b/ 1453.6	c/ 709.0	c/ 630.0	...	c/ 4761	c/ 4322	c/ 5192	c/ 5557	...	321
3211	Spinning,weaving etc.	...	...	...	...	...	...	...	...	...	...	3211
322	Wearing apparel	b/	b/	c/	c/	...	c/	c/	c/	c/	...	322
323	Leather and products	53.8	61.2	c/	c/	...	c/	c/	c/	c/	...	323
324	Footwear	86.1	92.3	c/	c/	...	c/	c/	c/	c/	...	324
331	Wood products	...	...	[82.0	23.0]	...	[1038	946	1032	1158]	...	331
332	Furniture, fixtures	...	...			...					...	332
341	Paper and products	18.5	19.9	d/ 46.0	d/ 21.0	...	d/ 154	d/ 270	d/ 299	d/ 313	...	341
3411	Pulp,paper etc.	...	...	...	...	...	...	...	...	...	...	3411
342	Printing,publishing	47.8	48.1	d/	d/	...	d/	d/	d/	d/	...	342
351	Industrial chemicals	e/ 217.5	e/ 219.0	f/ 349.0	f/ 357.0	...	f/ 11229	f/ 12121	f/ 11779	f/ 12908	...	351
3511	Basic excl fertilizers	...	...	...	...	...	...	...	...	...	...	3511
3513	Synthetic resins etc	...	...	...	...	...	...	...	...	...	...	3513
352	Other chemical products.	e/	e/	f/	f/	...	f/	f/	f/	f/	...	352
3522	Drugs and medicines	...	...	...	...	...	...	...	...	...	...	3522
353	Petroleum refineries	[83.9	138.7]	f/	f/	...	f/	f/	f/	f/	...	353
354	Petroleum,coal products.			f/	f/	...	f/	f/	f/	f/	...	354
355	Rubber products	34.5	34.6	f/	f/	...	f/	f/	f/	f/	...	355
356	Plastic products n.e.c.	32.7	34.1	f/	f/	...	f/	f/	f/	f/	...	356
361	Pottery,china etc	...	...	[	]	...	[			]	...	361
362	Glass and products	...	...	332.0	307.0	...	890	1899	2325	2625	...	362
369	Non-metal products n.e.c	...	...	]	]	...	]			]	...	369
371	Iron and steel	[36.3	31.3	37.0	39.0]	...	[343	286	334	329]	...	371
372	Non-ferrous metals					...					...	372
381	Metal products g/	...	...	[235.0	128.0]	...	[1316	3228	3479	2247]	...	381
382	Machinery n.e.c.	...	...			...					...	382
3825	Office,computing etc.	...	...	...	...	...	...	...	...	...	...	3825
383	Electrical machinery	44.8	59.4	g/	g/	...	g/	g/	g/	g/	...	383
3832	Radio,television etc.	17.8	19.6	...	...	...	...	...	...	...	...	3832
384	Transport equipment	18.2	20.1	g/	g/	...	g/	g/	g/	g/	...	384
3841	Shipbuilding, repair	...	...	...	...	...	...	...	...	...	...	3841
3843	Motor vehicles	...	...	...	...	...	...	...	...	...	...	3843
385	Professional goods	-	-	-	-	...	-	-	-	-	...	385
390	Other industries	...	40.8	10.0	-	...	92	898	917	398	...	390
3	Manufacturing h/	...	...	2567.0	2072.0	...	24245	28275	30594	31548	...	3
410	Electricity,gas,steam i/	298.0	313.0	413.0	374.0	...	...	...	...	...	...	410
4101	Electricity	298.0	313.0	413.0	374.0	...	...	...	...	...	...	4101
420	Water works and supply	15.0	47.1	134.0	59.3	...	...	...	...	...	...	420
4	Electricity,gas etc	i/ 313.0	i/ 360.1	i/ 547.0	i/ 433.3	...	833	901	1457	1604	...	4
2-4	All industry h/	...	...	i/ 3571.0	i/ 2953.3	...	33384	36216	38642	39804	...	2-4

a/ Public sector only
b/ Major group 322 is included in 321.
c/ Major groups 322 to 324 are included in 321.
d/ Major group 342 is included in 341.
e/ Major group 352 is included in 351.
f/ Major groups 352 to 356 are included in 351.
g/ Major groups 383 and 384 are included in 381 and 382 combined.
h/ Including repair services.
i/ Excluding gas and steam.

5. VALUE ADDED IN FACTOR VALUES a/ (MILLION POUNDS)

ISIC	INDUSTRY		1981	1982	1983	1984	1985	ISIC
210	Coal mining		...	...	...	...	...	210
220	Petroleum and gas		...	...	...	...	...	220
230	Metal ore mining		...	...	...	...	...	230
290	Other mining		...	...	...	...	...	290
2	Mining, quarrying .		...	6298	5852	5910	...	2
311/2	Food products		...	[		]	...	311/2
313	Beverages		...	466	395	313	...	313
314	Tobacco		...	[		]	...	314
321	Textiles	b/	...	1113	1132	867	...	321
3211	Spinning,weaving etc..		...	...	...	...	...	3211
322	Wearing apparel	b/	...	...	...	...	...	322
323	Leather and products ...	b/	...	...	...	...	...	323
324	Footwear	b/	...	...	...	...	...	324
331	Wood products		...	[397	427	574]	...	331
332	Furniture, fixtures		...				...	332
341	Paper and products	c/	...	118	85	78	...	341
3411	Pulp,paper etc.		...	...	...	...	...	3411
342	Printing,publishing	c/	...	...	...	...	...	342
351	Industrial chemicals ...	d/	...	1041	817	1471	...	351
3511	Basic excl fertilizers		...	...	...	...	...	3511
3513	Synthetic resins etc .		...	...	...	...	...	3513
352	Other chemical products.	d/	...	...	...	...	...	352
3522	Drugs and medicines ..		...	...	...	...	...	3522
353	Petroleum refineries ...	d/	...	...	...	...	...	353
354	Petroleum,coal products.	d/	...	...	...	...	...	354
355	Rubber products	d/	...	...	...	...	...	355
356	Plastic products n.e.c..	d/	...	...	...	...	...	356
361	Pottery,china etc		...	[		]	...	361
362	Glass and products		...	595	829	1002	...	362
369	Non-metal products n.e.c		...	[		]	...	369
371	Iron and steel		...	[39	56	75]	...	371
372	Non-ferrous metals		...				...	372
381	Metal products	e/	...	[1397	1581	683]	...	381
382	Machinery n.e.c.		...				...	382
3825	Office,computing etc..		...	...	...	...	...	3825
383	Electrical machinery ...	e/	...	...	...	...	...	383
3832	Radio,television etc..		...	...	...	...	...	3832
384	Transport equipment	e/	...	...	...	...	...	384
3841	Shipbuilding, repair..		...	...	...	...	...	3841
3843	Motor vehicles		...	...	...	...	...	3843
385	Professional goods		...	-	-	-	...	385
390	Other industries		...	135	334	99	...	390
3	Manufacturing	f/	...	5301	5656	5162	...	3
410	Electricity,gas,steam ..		...	...	...	...	...	410
4101	Electricity		...	...	...	...	...	4101
420	Water works and supply .		...	...	...	...	...	420
4	Electricity,gas etc		...	-137	85	-173	...	4
2-4	All industry	f/	...	11462	11593	10899	...	2-4

a/ Net domestic product.
b/ Major groups 322 to 324 are included in 321.
c/ Major group 342 is included in 341.
d/ Major groups 352 to 356 are included in 351.
e/ Major groups 383 and 384 are included in 381 and 382 combined.
f/ Including repair services.

6. INDEX NUMBERS OF INDUSTRIAL PRODUCTION (1980 = 100)

ISIC	INDUSTRY	1976	1977	1978	1979	1981	1982	1983	1984	1985	a/ RATE	ISIC
210	Coal mining	...	...	...	...	...	...	...	...	...	...	210
220	Petroleum and gas	...	...	...	...	...	...	...	...	...	...	220
230	Metal ore mining	...	...	...	...	...	...	...	...	...	...	230
290	Other mining	...	...	...	...	...	...	...	...	...	...	290
2	Mining, quarrying .	112	102	103	103	104	108	102	113	101	-1.1	2
311/2	Food products											311/2
313	Beverages	[87	85	93	91	105	154	180	184	...	f/ 9.8]	313
314	Tobacco											314
321	Textiles .... b/	103	97	104	102	101	110	134	151	...	f/ 4.9	321
3211	Spinning,weaving etc..	...	...	...	...	...	...	...	...	...	...	3211
322	Wearing apparel	...	...	...	...	...	...	...	...	...	...	322
323	Leather and products ... b/	...	...	...	...	...	...	...	...	...	...	323
324	Footwear	...	...	...	...	...	...	...	...	...	...	324
331	Wood products	[86	114	105	87	118	120	117	96	...	f/ 1.4]	331
332	Furniture, fixtures											332
341	Paper and products	58	78	86	81	118	193	320	329	...	f/ 24.2	341
3411	Pulp,paper etc.	...	...	...	...	...	...	...	...	...	...	3411
342	Printing,publishing	...	...	...	...	...	...	...	...	...	...	342
351	Industrial chemicals ... c/	40	48	57	66	137	153	153	170	...	f/ 19.8	351
3511	Basic excl fertilizers	...	...	...	...	...	...	...	...	...	...	3511
3513	Synthetic resins etc .	...	...	...	...	...	...	...	...	...	...	3513
352	Other chemical products. c/	...	...	...	...	...	...	...	...	...	...	352
3522	Drugs and medicines ..	...	...	...	...	...	...	...	...	...	...	3522
353	Petroleum refineries ... c/	...	...	...	...	...	...	...	...	...	...	353
354	Petroleum,coal products. c/	...	...	...	...	...	...	...	...	...	...	354
355	Rubber products .... c/	...	...	...	...	...	...	...	...	...	...	355
356	Plastic products n.e.c.. c/	...	...	...	...	...	...	...	...	...	...	356
361	Pottery,china etc	...	...	...	...	...	...	...	...	...	...	361
362	Glass and products	[52	65	68	84	114	137	165	194	...	f/ 17.9]	362
369	Non-metal products n.e.c											369
371	Iron and steel	...	...	...	...	...	...	...	...	...	...	371
372	Non-ferrous metals	...	...	...	...	133	105	127	123	...	g/ 5.3	372
381	Metal products	...	...	...	...	[d/ 105	d/ 117	d/ 108	d/ 87	...	g/ -3.4]	381
382	Machinery n.e.c.	...	...	...	...							382
3825	Office,computing etc..	...	...	...	...	...	...	...	...	...	...	3825
383	Electrical machinery ... d/	...	...	...	...	...	...	...	...	...	...	383
3832	Radio,television etc..	...	...	...	...	...	...	...	...	...	...	3832
384	Transport equipment .... d/	...	...	...	...	...	...	...	...	...	...	384
3841	Shipbuilding, repair..	...	...	...	...	...	...	...	...	...	...	3841
3843	Motor vehicles	...	...	...	...	...	...	...	...	...	...	3843
385	Professional goods	...	...	...	...	...	...	...	...	...	...	385
390	Other industries	...	...	...	...	...	...	...	...	...	...	390
3	Manufacturing	77	83	89	87	117	138	151	163	...	f/ 9.8	3
410	Electricity,gas,steam ..	...	...	...	...	...	...	...	...	...	...	410
4101	Electricity	46	56	71	87	117	141	227	248	...	f/ 23.4	4101
420	Water works and supply .	71	78	85	86	115	114	119	133	...	f/ 8.2	420
4	Electricity,gas etc	51	60	73	87	119	136	156	226	183	15.3	4
2-4	All industry e/	84	82	88	92	116	119	139	144	136	5.5	2-4

a/ Annual growth rate 1976-1985.
c/ Major groups 352 to 356 are included in 351.
e/ Excluding gas and steam.
g/ Annual growth rate 1980-1984.
b/ Major group 323 is included in 321.
d/ Major groups 383 and 384 are included in 381 and 382 combined.
f/ Annual growth rate 1976-1984.

TRINIDAD AND TOBAGO

The information in the tables, except for the indexes, is based on the reply to the United Nations Questionnaire on General Industrial Statistics from the Central Statistical Office, Port-of-Spain. The concepts and definitions are generally in accordance with United Nations standards.

The data in the tables are derived from the survey of business establishments conducted by the Central Statistical Office on a sample basis and relate to establishments with 10 or more persons engaged. The selection of establishments is made from a viewpoint of the national economy in consideration of the size of employment and the contribution to the total output. The inquiry is carried out through field interview by enumerators.

The data in the tables are based on the national classification system which is a modified version of ISIC and are available only in a broad grouping of industries. Establishments primarily engaged in repair work (ISIC major division 9) are included in manufacturing and classified according to the type of product repaired. The data for ISIC 353 and 354 combined include extraction of crude petroleum (ISIC 220), asphalt mining and refining (ISIC 290), servicing and marketing of petroleum products (ISIC major division 6) and petroleum exploration (ISIC major division 8) in addition to petroleum refining and manufacture of petroleum products.

The reference period is basically the calendar year, but financial-year coverage is accepted and incorporated in the calendar year in which the major part of the financial year falls. The number of employees relates to the last week in November of the reference year.

The indexes of industrial production are compiled by the Central Statistical Office and provided in response to the United Nations Questionnaire on Indexes of Industrial Production.

Related national publications:

Quarterly Economic Report; Annual Statistical Digest; Business Surveys (annual), all published by the Central Statistical Office, Port-of-Spain.

ISIC	INDUSTRY		1. NUMBER OF ESTABLISHMENTS a/ (NUMBER) 1981	1982	1983	1984	1985	2. AVERAGE NUMBER OF EMPLOYEES a/b/ (THOUSANDS) 1981	1982	1983	1984	1985	ISIC
210	Coal mining		...	...	...	...	...	...	...	...	...	...	210
220	Petroleum and gas		...	...	...	...	...	...	...	...	...	...	220
230	Metal ore mining		...	...	...	...	...	...	...	...	...	...	230
290	Other mining		...	...	...	...	...	...	...	...	...	...	290
2	Mining, quarrying .		...	...	...	...	...	...	...	...	...	...	2
311/2	Food products		[	]	...	...	...	[	]	...	...	...	311/2
313	Beverages		85	79	...	...	...	8.9	9.7	...	...	...	313
314	Tobacco		[	]	...	...	...	[	]	...	...	...	314
321	Textiles	c/	98	78	...	...	...	5.3	3.8	...	...	...	321
3211	Spinning,weaving etc..		...	...	...	...	...	...	...	...	...	...	3211
322	Wearing apparel	c/	...	...	...	...	...	...	...	...	...	...	322
323	Leather and products ...	c/	...	...	...	...	...	...	...	...	...	...	323
324	Footwear	c/	...	...	...	...	...	...	...	...	...	...	324
331	Wood products		[82	54]	...	...	...	[2.3	2.0]	...	...	...	331
332	Furniture, fixtures				...	...	...			...	...	...	332
341	Paper and products	d/	57	48	...	...	...	2.8	2.8	...	...	...	341
3411	Pulp,paper etc.		...	...	...	...	...	...	...	...	...	...	3411
342	Printing,publishing	d/	...	...	...	...	...	...	...	...	...	...	342
351	Industrial chemicals ...	e/	55	46	...	...	...	4.2	4.4	...	...	...	351
3511	Basic excl fertilizers		...	...	...	...	...	...	...	...	...	...	3511
3513	Synthetic resins etc .		...	...	...	...	...	...	...	...	...	...	3513
352	Other chemical products.	e/	...	...	...	...	...	...	...	...	...	...	352
3522	Drugs and medicines ..		...	...	...	...	...	...	...	...	...	...	3522
353	Petroleum refineries ...	f/	[74	56]	...	...	...	[17.0	17.8]	...	...	...	353
354	Petroleum,coal products.				...	...	...			...	...	...	354
355	Rubber products		-	-	...	...	...	-	-	...	...	...	355
356	Plastic products n.e.c..	g/	...	...	...	...	...	...	...	...	...	...	356
361	Pottery,china etc	e/	...	...	...	...	...	...	...	...	...	...	361
362	Glass and products	e/	...	...	...	...	...	...	...	...	...	...	362
369	Non-metal products n.e.c	e/	...	...	...	...	...	...	...	...	...	...	369
371	Iron and steel		-	-	...	...	...	-	-	...	...	...	371
372	Non-ferrous metals		-	-	...	...	...	-	-	...	...	...	372
381	Metal products	h/	[94]	...	...	...	...	[9.1]	...	...	...	...	381
382	Machinery n.e.c.			...	...	...	...		...	...	...	...	382
3825	Office,computing etc..		...	...	...	...	...	...	...	...	...	...	3825
383	Electrical machinery ...	h/	...	...	...	...	...	...	...	...	...	...	383
3832	Radio,television etc..		...	...	...	...	...	...	...	...	...	...	3832
384	Transport equipment	h/	...	...	...	...	...	...	...	...	...	...	384
3841	Shipbuilding, repair..		...	...	...	...	...	...	...	...	...	...	3841
3843	Motor vehicles		...	...	...	...	...	...	...	...	...	...	3843
385	Professional goods	g/	[33]	...	...	...	...	[1.7]	...	...	...	...	385
390	Other industries			...	...	...	...		...	...	...	...	390
3	Manufacturing	f/i/	578	...	...	...	...	51.3	...	...	...	...	3
410	Electricity,gas,steam ..		...	...	...	...	...	...	...	...	...	...	410
4101	Electricity		...	...	...	...	...	...	...	...	...	...	4101
420	Water works and supply .		...	...	...	...	...	...	...	...	...	...	420
4	Electricity,gas etc		...	...	...	...	...	...	...	...	...	...	4
2-4	All industry		...	...	...	...	...	...	...	...	...	...	2-4

a/ Establishments with 10 or more persons engaged.
b/ In the last week of November.
c/ Major groups 322 to 324 are included in 321.
d/ Major group 342 is included in 341.
e/ Major groups 352 and 361 to 369 are included in 351.
f/ Including petroleum exploration and extraction, production of petro-chemicals, marketing and distribution of petroleum products and asphalt mining.
g/ Major group 356 is included in 385 and 390 combined.
h/ Major groups 383 and 384 are included in 381 and 382 combined.
i/ Including repair services for the general public.

3. INDEX NUMBERS OF INDUSTRIAL PRODUCTION (1980 = 100)

ISIC	INDUSTRY	1976	1977	1978	1979	1981	1982	1983	1984	1985	a/ RATE	ISIC
210	Coal mining	...	...	...	...	...	...	...	...	...	...	210
220	Petroleum and gas	...	...	...	...	...	...	...	...	...	...	220
230	Metal ore mining	...	...	...	...	...	...	...	...	...	...	230
290	Other mining	...	...	...	...	...	...	...	...	...	...	290
2	Mining, quarrying .	...	...	...	...	...	...	...	...	...	...	2
311/2	Food products	117	109	104	108	97	91	104	113	98	-1.9	311/2
313	Beverages	94	91	86	88	99	110	108	103	87	-0.9	313
314	Tobacco	93	90	90	78	86	106	105	110	104	1.2	314
321	Textiles	101	95	90	89	76	66	57	55	43	-9.1	321
3211	Spinning,weaving etc..	...	...	...	...	...	...	...	...	...	...	3211
322	Wearing apparel	...	...	...	...	...	...	...	...	...	...	322
323	Leather and products ... b/	...	...	...	...	...	...	...	...	...	...	323
324	Footwear	139	98	120	110	96	79	88	77	57	-9.4	324
331	Wood products	149	145	147	138	98	94	104	106	51	-11.2	331
332	Furniture, fixtures	50	48	34	76	61	69	34	38	27	-6.6	332
341	Paper and products	50	70	66	81	91	81	63	60	70	3.8	341
3411	Pulp,paper etc.	...	...	...	...	...	...	...	...	...	...	3411
342	Printing,publishing	113	131	143	137	198	191	181	167	166	4.4	342
351	Industrial chemicals ...	130	106	94	106	71	88	103	72	62	-7.9	351
3511	Basic excl fertilizers	...	...	...	...	...	...	...	...	...	...	3511
3513	Synthetic resins etc .	...	...	...	...	...	...	...	...	...	...	3513
352	Other chemical products.	80	76	80	95	96	83	98	58	68	-1.8	352
3522	Drugs and medicines ..	...	...	...	...	...	...	...	...	...	...	3522
353	Petroleum refineries ...	...	...	...	...	...	...	...	...	...	...	353
354	Petroleum,coal products.	...	...	...	...	...	...	...	...	...	...	354
355	Rubber products	...	...	...	...	...	...	...	...	...	...	355
356	Plastic products n.e.c.. b/	...	...	...	...	...	...	...	...	...	...	356
361	Pottery,china etc	...	...	...	...	...	...	...	...	...	...	361
362	Glass and products	...	...	...	...	...	...	...	...	...	...	362
369	Non-metal products n.e.c	95	103	104	98	102	120	150	131	107	1.3	369
371	Iron and steel	...	...	...	...	...	...	...	...	...	...	371
372	Non-ferrous metals	...	...	...	...	...	...	...	...	...	...	372
381	Metal products	39	61	74	94	101	92	508	411	402	29.6	381
382	Machinery n.e.c.	...	...	...	...	...	...	...	...	...	...	382
3825	Office,computing etc..	...	...	...	...	...	..	...	...	...	...	3825
383	Electrical machinery ...	49	68	79	78	91	110	117	97	64	3.0	383
3832	Radio,television etc..	...	...	...	...	...	...	...	...	...	...	3832
384	Transport equipment	108	111	116	102	106	86	95	100	58	-6.7	384
3841	Shipbuilding, repair..	...	...	...	...	...	...	...	...	...	...	3841
3843	Motor vehicles	...	...	...	...	...	...	...	...	...	...	3843
385	Professional goods	...	...	...	...	...	...	...	...	...	...	385
390	Other industries .... b/	125	93	97	113	116	96	91	78	79	-5.0	390
3	Manufacturing ..... c/	83	93	92	94	89	91	105	104	...	d/ 2.9	3
410	Electricity,gas,steam ..	...	...	...	...	...	...	...	...	...	...	410
4101	Electricity	...	...	...	...	...	...	...	...	...	...	4101
420	Water works and supply .	...	...	...	...	...	...	...	...	...	...	420
4	Electricity,gas etc	...	...	...	...	...	...	...	...	...	...	4
2-4	All industry	...	...	...	...	...	...	...	...	...	...	2-4

a/ Annual growth rate 1976-1985.
b/ Major groups 323 and 356 are included in 390.
c/ Excluding oil, sugar and ship and boat building and repairs.
d/ Annual growth rate 1976-1984.

TURKEY

The information on industrial activity is based on the reply to the United Nations Questionnaire on General Industrial Statistics from the State Institute of Statistics, Ankara. The concepts, definitions and classification by branches of industry are generally in accordance with United Nations standards.

In general, the estimates are derived from the annual manufacturing survey compiled by the State Institute of Statistics. The manufacturing survey covers all establishments in the public sector and establishments in the private sector with 10 or more persons engaged up to 1982 but with 25 or more beginning 1983.

The national classification scheme used in compiling the estimates follows the present version of ISIC.

The employment estimates relate generally to annual averages. They are based on the number of production workers and other employees in four months of the year, and the number of active owners, partners and unpaid family workers for one period. The data include apprentices who work for no pay, or very little, in order to learn a craft. Homeworkers are not counted; payments to homeworkers are included in the cost of contract work done by others. Wages and salaries relate to the gross payments made for work done, including bonuses and premiums and payments in kind. However, wages and salaries of operatives for mining exclude payments in kind.

The concept of output represents the sum of (a) the value of sales of goods and electricity produced by the establishment, (b) receipts for services rendered to others, (c) the value of fixed assets produced by the establishment for its own use, (d) the value of sales of goods purchased and resold without further processing, and (e) miscellaneous receipts (repair, maintenance, construction, installation income, sales of by-products, scrap etc.); adjustments are made for changes in the value of stocks of finished and semi-finished goods. The valuation includes excise and production taxes and any charges for delivery performed by the establishment.

Value added is the difference between output and the cost of the following inputs: raw materials, components and containers; products bought and sold without further processing; fuels and electricity, and payments for manufacturing work done by others. Valuation is at delivered cost, defined as purchase price plus taxes and duties, transportation and loading expenses, all kinds of expenditures made before the goods are received, net of discounts. As input is measured on a received basis, adjustments are made for changes in stocks.

Gross fixed capital formation represents the value of the acquisition of new and used fixed assets, including assets produced by the establishment staff. Sales are not generally deducted.

The indexes of industrial production are compiled by the State Institute of Statistics and provided in response to the United Nations Questionnaire on Indexes of Industrial Production. In principle, the indexes cover both privately owned and publicly owned establishments.

Related national publications:
<u>Maden Istatistikleri</u> (Mining Statistics) (annual); <u>Yillik Imalat Sanayii Anket Sonuclari</u> (Annual Survey of the Manufacturing Industry); <u>Turkiye Istatistik Yilligi</u> (Statistical Yearbook of Turkey), all published by the State Institute of Statistics, Ankara.

ISIC	INDUSTRY	1. NUMBER OF ESTABLISHMENTS a/ (NUMBER) 1981	b/ 1982	1983	1984	1985	2. AVERAGE NUMBER OF PERSONS ENGAGED a/ (THOUSANDS) 1981	b/ 1982	1983	1984	1985	ISIC
210	Coal mining	...	...	...	...	...	...	...	...	...	...	210
220	Petroleum and gas	...	...	...	...	...	...	...	...	...	...	220
230	Metal ore mining	...	...	...	...	...	...	...	...	...	...	230
290	Other mining	...	...	...	...	...	...	...	...	...	...	290
2	Mining, quarrying .	...	...	...	...	...	...	...	...	...	...	2
311/2	Food products	1861	1951	800	794	...	118.7	124.2	110.4	119.8	...	311/2
313	Beverages	91	98	67	70	...	11.6	11.5	11.8	12.4	...	313
314	Tobacco	42	50	55	51	...	47.0	44.5	47.5	47.7	...	314
321	Textiles	1248	1255	685	660	...	168.9	173.8	172.8	180.7	...	321
3211	Spinning,weaving etc..	823	809	462	453	...	143.3	146.5	148.5	154.8	...	3211
322	Wearing apparel	339	389	212	231	...	14.0	18.6	19.9	22.0	...	322
323	Leather and products ...	172	178	71	75	...	5.1	5.7	4.2	4.3	...	323
324	Footwear	108	107	40	34	...	5.6	5.6	5.6	5.2	...	324
331	Wood products	210	226	106	105	...	12.8	13.8	12.5	12.4	...	331
332	Furniture, fixtures	119	131	48	44	...	3.8	4.0	3.3	3.5	...	332
341	Paper and products	151	150	89	88	...	18.7	18.9	18.7	19.8	...	341
3411	Pulp,paper etc.	29	27	22	23	...	12.4	12.5	12.7	13.6	...	3411
342	Printing,publishing	244	234	95	97	...	10.8	11.4	10.0	11.0	...	342
351	Industrial chemicals ...	115	118	74	77	...	23.7	24.5	25.6	27.8	...	351
3511	Basic excl fertilizers	74	75	40	42	...	7.0	7.2	7.1	7.6	...	3511
3513	Synthetic resins etc .	17	21	16	17	...	7.3	9.2	8.3	9.7	...	3513
352	Other chemical products.	329	333	161	166	...	20.9	22.1	20.2	20.7	...	352
3522	Drugs and medicines ..	78	85	59	58	...	8.5	9.5	9.6	9.9	...	3522
353	Petroleum refineries ...	5	5	4	4	...	7.2	7.1	6.9	3.9	...	353
354	Petroleum,coal products.	39	39	26	25	...	3.2	3.5	3.8	3.5	...	354
355	Rubber products	181	203	93	88	...	10.8	12.9	10.3	9.9	...	355
356	Plastic products n.e.c..	402	399	140	130	...	12.7	13.6	9.3	9.7	...	356
361	Pottery,china etc	42	50	30	33	...	8.6	8.6	9.3	10.2	...	361
362	Glass and products	62	64	36	34	...	11.0	12.4	12.1	12.9	...	362
369	Non-metal products n.e.c	506	500	323	328	...	40.4	39.5	37.3	39.0	...	369
371	Iron and steel	327	316	186	184	...	54.4	55.3	54.0	46.1	...	371
372	Non-ferrous metals	169	167	79	75	...	20.9	21.8	20.0	21.6	...	372
381	Metal products	837	856	355	356	...	39.4	41.7	37.0	37.7	...	381
382	Machinery n.e.c.	621	673	308	311	...	49.7	53.0	47.6	47.7	...	382
3825	Office,computing etc..	14	15	9	9	...	0.7	0.9	0.7	0.8	...	3825
383	Electrical machinery ...	405	407	224	218	...	31.4	33.4	32.7	35.1	...	383
3832	Radio,television etc..	55	63	35	37	...	7.7	8.7	9.2	10.4	...	3832
384	Transport equipment	418	405	214	210	...	49.8	49.7	49.7	52.0	...	384
3841	Shipbuilding, repair..	40	43	24	22	...	9.5	8.9	6.4	6.0	...	3841
3843	Motor vehicles	348	336	175	175	...	29.3	30.4	31.5	34.0	...	3843
385	Professional goods	50	61	30	31	...	2.0	2.1	1.9	2.0	...	385
390	Other industries	101	92	54	56	...	3.9	4.1	4.1	4.4	...	390
3	Manufacturing	9194	9457	4605	4575	...	807.0	837.3	798.5	823.0	...	3
410	Electricity,gas,steam ..	...	...	...	...	...	...	...	...	...	...	410
4101	Electricity	...	...	...	...	...	...	...	...	...	...	4101
420	Water works and supply .	...	...	...	...	...	...	...	...	...	...	420
4	Electricity,gas etc	...	...	...	...	...	...	...	...	...	...	4
2-4	All industry	...	...	...	...	...	...	...	...	...	...	2-4

a/ Manufacturing: all establishments in the public sector and those with 25 or more persons engaged in private sector.
b/ Manufacturing: up to 1982, all establishments in the public sector and those with 10 or more persons engaged in private sector.

ISIC	INDUSTRY	3. AVERAGE NUMBER OF EMPLOYEES a/ (THOUSANDS)					4. WAGES AND SALARIES OF EMPLOYEES a/ (BILLION LIRAS)					ISIC
		1981	b/ 1982	1983	1984	1985	1981	b/ 1982	1983	1984	1985	
210	Coal mining	...	...	...	...	...	...	...	...	...	...	210
220	Petroleum and gas	...	...	...	...	...	...	...	...	...	...	220
230	Metal ore mining	...	...	...	...	...	...	...	...	...	...	230
290	Other mining	...	...	...	...	...	...	...	...	...	...	290
2	Mining, quarrying .	...	...	...	...	...	...	...	...	...	...	2
311/2	Food products	116.3	121.6	109.6	119.3	...	44.04	58.61	67.69	93.15	...	311/2
313	Beverages	11.6	11.4	11.8	12.4	...	6.35	7.78	10.53	12.91	...	313
314	Tobacco	47.0	44.4	47.5	47.7	...	26.03	26.13	37.36	47.36	...	314
321	Textiles	167.8	172.8	172.4	180.4	...	57.82	75.94	101.46	141.10	...	321
3211	Spinning,weaving etc..	142.6	145.8	148.3	154.6	...	50.69	66.47	90.49	124.19	...	3211
322	Wearing apparel	13.7	18.4	19.8	21.9	...	2.59	5.15	7.83	11.53	...	322
323	Leather and products ...	5.0	5.4	4.2	4.3	...	1.50	1.94	2.06	2.54	...	323
324	Footwear	5.5	5.5	5.6	5.2	...	2.40	2.70	3.41	3.55	...	324
331	Wood products	12.6	13.5	12.5	12.5	...	4.38	5.73	6.92	8.80	...	331
332	Furniture, fixtures	3.6	3.8	3.3	3.4	...	0.72	0.99	1.23	2.08	...	332
341	Paper and products	18.6	18.8	18.6	19.8	...	9.74	13.69	16.15	22.02	...	341
3411	Pulp,paper etc.	12.4	12.5	12.7	13.6	...	7.26	10.22	11.72	16.37	...	3411
342	Printing,publishing	10.6	11.3	9.9	10.9	...	4.80	7.42	9.09	12.03	...	342
351	Industrial chemicals ...	23.7	24.5	25.6	27.8	...	16.20	19.60	25.02	36.65	...	351
3511	Basic excl fertilizers	7.1	7.2	7.0	7.6	...	3.82	5.12	5.62	8.77	...	3511
3513	Synthetic resins etc .	7.3	8.0	8.3	9.7	...	5.27	6.25	8.80	14.24	...	3513
352	Other chemical products.	20.7	21.9	20.2	20.7	...	11.87	15.81	19.58	27.23	...	352
3522	Drugs and medicines ..	8.5	9.5	9.6	9.9	...	5.90	7.69	9.72	13.29	...	3522
353	Petroleum refineries ...	7.2	7.1	6.9	3.9	...	5.70	7.44	7.51	6.44	...	353
354	Petroleum,coal products.	3.2	3.5	3.8	3.5	...	2.49	3.17	4.46	5.59	...	354
355	Rubber products	10.6	12.7	10.2	9.8	...	5.71	9.03	9.34	11.92	...	355
356	Plastic products n.e.c..	12.3	13.3	9.3	9.6	...	4.13	5.72	6.52	8.60	...	356
361	Pottery,china etc	8.6	8.6	9.3	10.2	...	3.48	4.70	5.88	8.58	...	361
362	Glass and products	10.9	12.3	12.1	12.9	...	6.01	8.88	11.24	15.91	...	362
369	Non-metal products n.e.c	39.9	39.0	37.0	38.7	...	14.69	20.83	24.34	36.21	...	369
371	Iron and steel	54.2	55.1	54.0	46.0	...	40.37	47.60	60.06	64.62	...	371
372	Non-ferrous metals	20.8	21.6	20.0	21.6	...	10.70	14.09	16.58	23.76	...	372
381	Metal products	38.5	40.9	36.5	37.5	...	15.65	20.33	25.46	33.86	...	381
382	Machinery n.e.c.	49.1	52.4	46.8	47.6	...	26.05	33.92	40.01	55.69	...	382
3825	Office,computing etc..	0.7	0.9	0.7	0.8	...	0.30	0.50	0.58	0.83	...	3825
383	Electrical machinery ...	31.1	33.1	32.6	35.0	...	15.34	21.39	28.01	41.59	...	383
3832	Radio,television etc..	7.7	8.6	9.2	10.4	...	4.71	6.52	9.35	13.02	...	3832
384	Transport equipment	49.5	49.4	49.6	52.0	...	28.25	35.21	44.81	60.14	...	384
3841	Shipbuilding, repair..	9.5	8.9	6.4	6.0	...	7.02	7.13	6.80	7.68	...	3841
3843	Motor vehicles	29.0	30.1	31.4	33.8	...	14.37	20.04	28.60	40.79	...	3843
385	Professional goods	1.9	2.1	1.9	1.9	...	0.65	0.89	1.13	1.25	...	385
390	Other industries	3.9	4.0	4.0	4.4	...	1.17	1.31	1.95	3.03	...	390
3	Manufacturing	798.4	828.4	795.0	820.9	...	368.83	476.00	595.63	798.14	...	3
410	Electricity,gas,steam ..	...	...	...	...	...	...	...	...	...	...	410
4101	Electricity	...	...	...	...	...	...	...	...	...	...	4101
420	Water works and supply .	...	...	...	...	...	...	...	...	...	...	420
4	Electricity,gas etc	...	...	...	...	...	...	...	...	...	...	4
2-4	All industry	...	...	...	...	...	...	...	...	...	...	2-4

a/ Manufacturing: all establishments in the public sector and those with 25 or more persons engaged in private sector.
b/ Manufacturing: up to 1982, all establishments in the public sector and those with 10 or more persons engaged in private sector.

ISIC	INDUSTRY	5. SUPPLEMENTS TO WAGES AND SALARIES a/ (MILLION LIRAS) 1981	c/ 1982	1983	1984	1985	6. AVERAGE NUMBER OF OPERATIVES a/b/ (THOUSANDS) 1981	c/ 1982	1983	1984	1985	ISIC
210	Coal mining	...	...	...	...	...	...	...	...	...	...	210
220	Petroleum and gas	...	...	...	...	...	...	...	...	...	...	220
230	Metal ore mining	...	...	...	...	...	...	...	...	...	...	230
290	Other mining	...	...	...	...	...	...	...	...	...	...	290
2	Mining, quarrying .	...	...	...	...	...	...	...	...	...	...	2
311/2	Food products	16336	21732	26733	34182	...	92.1	98.1	80.5	86.8	...	311/2
313	Beverages	2791	3415	4538	5284	...	6.5	7.0	6.5	6.6	...	313
314	Tobacco	10138	10353	13802	19565	...	41.7	41.3	41.5	42.4	...	314
321	Textiles	21572	30303	39576	51006	...	175.8	148.4	146.9	154.8	...	321
3211	Spinning,weaving etc..	19695	27806	36264	45967	...	152.9	124.6	126.2	132.3	...	3211
322	Wearing apparel	567	966	1762	2439	...	12.7	11.2	17.5	19.2	...	322
323	Leather and products ...	351	400	519	589	...	5.0	5.2	3.6	3.8	...	323
324	Footwear	1155	1182	1169	904	...	5.2	4.3	4.8	4.3	...	324
331	Wood products	1274	1684	2123	3103	...	10.1	11.9	10.0	10.1	...	331
332	Furniture, fixtures	133	154	231	558	...	3.1	3.3	2.8	2.9	...	332
341	Paper and products	4909	6983	8048	10777	...	14.9	15.0	12.6	13.3	...	341
3411	Pulp,paper etc.	3752	5102	6147	8729	...	11.4	9.7	8.3	9.1	...	3411
342	Printing,publishing	2147	2741	3145	4337	...	8.1	8.4	6.8	7.2	...	342
351	Industrial chemicals ...	8302	8547	12068	17203	...	15.8	17.3	17.4	18.7	...	351
3511	Basic excl fertilizers	2175	2241	2712	3873	...	4.9	5.4	5.2	5.5	...	3511
3513	Synthetic resins etc .	3108	5810	6151	6634	...	5.4	6.1	6.4	7.5	...	3513
352	Other chemical products.	4711	5982	7649	9857	...	14.2	13.7	12.3	12.8	...	352
3522	Drugs and medicines ..	2378	2953	3409	4449	...	5.3	5.6	5.5	5.5	...	3522
353	Petroleum refineries ...	3081	4091	5191	2604	...	4.7	3.4	4.7	2.7	...	353
354	Petroleum,coal products.	1214	1523	1930	2238	...	2.0	2.4	2.6	2.3	...	354
355	Rubber products	2214	2839	3463	5194	...	8.7	10.5	8.3	7.8	...	355
356	Plastic products n.e.c..	1166	1897	1941	2457	...	10.7	11.0	7.1	7.5	...	356
361	Pottery,china etc	1063	2087	2633	3363	...	7.3	7.6	8.2	8.8	...	361
362	Glass and products	2617	3785	4888	6894	...	8.0	9.8	9.2	10.2	...	362
369	Non-metal products n.e.c	6454	7741	9881	14533	...	34.0	30.3	27.8	29.2	...	369
371	Iron and steel	21543	25723	32460	37276	...	46.4	61.3	42.1	36.1	...	371
372	Non-ferrous metals	4113	5330	6931	8504	...	22.5	27.8	12.7	14.5	...	372
381	Metal products	6345	7290	9564	11684	...	43.2	49.4	29.6	30.9	...	381
382	Machinery n.e.c.	11699	16320	15649	24263	...	39.2	39.0	36.7	37.8	...	382
3825	Office,computing etc..	127	168	240	495	...	0.5	0.6	0.5	0.6	...	3825
383	Electrical machinery ...	5749	7506	10312	16615	...	24.2	25.8	25.2	26.7	...	383
3832	Radio,television etc..	2067	2315	3345	5188	...	5.6	6.6	7.0	7.9	...	3832
384	Transport equipment	13219	15721	18372	24453	...	39.4	38.7	38.2	40.8	...	384
3841	Shipbuilding, repair..	3825	3840	4765	4060	...	7.3	4.9	4.1	4.1	...	3841
3843	Motor vehicles	6424	7928	10666	22750	...	22.5	24.6	24.3	26.7	...	3843
385	Professional goods	151	158	388	298	...	1.7	1.8	1.6	1.6	...	385
390	Other industries	238	339	519	902	...	3.1	3.6	3.5	3.8	...	390
3	Manufacturing	155252	196792	245485	321082	...	700.3	707.5	620.7	643.6	...	3
410	Electricity,gas,steam ..	...	...	...	...	...	...	...	...	...	...	410
4101	Electricity	...	...	...	...	...	...	...	...	...	...	4101
420	Water works and supply .	...	...	...	...	...	...	...	...	...	...	420
4	Electricity,gas etc	...	...	...	...	...	...	...	...	...	...	4
2-4	All industry	...	...	...	...	...	...	...	...	...	...	2-4

a/ Manufacturing: all establishments in the public sector and those with 25 or more persons engaged in private sector.
b/ Manufacturing: numbers in December.
c/ Manufacturing: up to 1982, all establishments in the public sector and those with 10 or more persons engaged in private sector.

ISIC	INDUSTRY	7. WAGES AND SALARIES OF OPERATIVES a/ (BILLION LIRAS) 1981	1982 b/	1983	1984	1985	8. HOURS WORKED BY OPERATIVES a/ (MILLIONS) 1981	1982 b/	1983	1984	1985	ISIC
210	Coal mining	...	...	...	...	...	...	...	...	...	...	210
220	Petroleum and gas	...	...	...	...	...	...	...	...	...	...	220
230	Metal ore mining	...	...	...	...	...	...	...	...	...	...	230
290	Other mining	...	...	...	...	...	...	...	...	...	...	290
2	Mining, quarrying .	...	...	...	...	...	...	...	...	...	...	2
311/2	Food products	34.49	45.91	47.21	64.26	...	221.5	227.0	187.7	192.6	...	311/2
313	Beverages	3.68	4.75	5.38	6.46	...	15.8	16.8	16.0	16.1	...	313
314	Tobacco	26.03	23.67	32.28	38.48	...	100.9	94.6	95.7	106.4	...	314
321	Textiles	47.38	62.71	82.55	115.02	...	410.6	345.7	342.1	359.7	...	321
3211	Spinning,weaving etc..	41.72	54.89	73.97	101.47	...	357.3	290.4	294.2	307.6	...	3211
322	Wearing apparel	2.18	4.55	6.35	9.30	...	28.0	39.7	39.2	43.8	...	322
323	Leather and products ...	1.42	1.81	1.78	2.20	...	10.8	11.9	8.3	8.6	...	323
324	Footwear	2.22	2.49	2.87	2.88	...	12.0	9.9	10.9	10.1	...	324
331	Wood products	3.70	4.88	5.44	6.72	...	23.7	27.2	23.4	24.3	...	331
332	Furniture, fixtures	0.54	0.89	1.01	1.62	...	6.9	7.5	6.4	6.6	...	332
341	Paper and products	7.16	11.34	11.17	16.03	...	39.8	36.1	30.4	32.6	...	341
3411	Pulp,paper etc.	5.03	8.34	8.11	12.31	...	28.2	24.5	20.5	22.5	...	3411
342	Printing,publishing	3.67	6.35	5.83	7.98	...	19.8	20.6	15.8	18.3	...	342
351	Industrial chemicals ...	10.95	13.70	17.18	22.81	...	41.5	45.1	44.5	49.3	...	351
3511	Basic excl fertilizers	2.76	3.74	3.88	5.08	...	12.2	13.3	12.3	13.5	...	3511
3513	Synthetic resins etc .	3.94	4.76	6.80	10.34	...	15.6	17.1	18.2	20.9	...	3513
352	Other chemical products.	8.06	10.43	10.58	15.36	...	32.1	32.0	28.7	29.7	...	352
3522	Drugs and medicines ..	4.22	4.96	4.86	6.67	...	11.8	12.0	13.0	13.1	...	3522
353	Petroleum refineries ...	3.38	4.41	3.96	4.25	...	10.2	8.6	9.3	7.4	...	353
354	Petroleum,coal products.	1.55	2.56	2.96	3.50	...	4.2	4.9	5.2	5.1	...	354
355	Rubber products	4.70	6.79	6.61	8.38	...	20.1	24.0	21.4	18.1	...	355
356	Plastic products n.e.c..	2.92	4.00	4.31	5.69	...	30.1	25.1	17.1	16.7	...	356
361	Pottery,china etc	2.48	4.01	4.68	6.70	...	15.9	17.9	20.5	23.0	...	361
362	Glass and products	4.54	6.18	7.87	11.10	...	19.1	21.5	22.3	24.2	...	362
369	Non-metal products n.e.c	11.70	16.20	17.61	24.52	...	76.7	69.7	65.6	69.0	...	369
371	Iron and steel	35.77	37.73	48.92	49.92	...	115.1	124.2	110.3	87.8	...	371
372	Non-ferrous metals	8.50	11.33	8.27	15.40	...	42.4	40.3	25.6	34.1	...	372
381	Metal products	13.19	17.39	18.25	25.31	...	74.1	82.8	69.5	72.9	...	381
382	Machinery n.e.c.	21.17	27.38	28.28	39.18	...	88.1	93.8	86.4	88.5	...	382
3825	Office,computing etc..	0.24	0.41	0.44	0.59	...	1.2	1.5	1.4	1.5	...	3825
383	Electrical machinery ...	12.47	17.14	20.07	28.63	...	55.1	56.8	54.6	60.9	...	383
3832	Radio,television etc..	3.82	5.24	6.67	8.52	...	12.4	14.7	14.1	16.2	...	3832
384	Transport equipment	24.01	26.91	30.18	43.43	...	87.5	84.7	88.2	91.9	...	384
3841	Shipbuilding, repair..	4.18	4.25	4.11	4.81	...	16.5	11.0	9.7	9.3	...	3841
3843	Motor vehicles	10.75	15.84	19.23	28.81	...	50.2	52.6	57.8	61.6	....	3843
385	Professional goods	0.61	0.66	0.95	1.01	...	3.9	3.9	3.9	3.8	...	385
390	Other industries	1.03	1.27	1.49	2.29	...	7.1	8.3	7.6	10.4	...	390
3	Manufacturing	299.50	377.43	434.04	578.43	...	1613.0	1580.6	1506.6	1511.9	...	3
410	Electricity,gas,steam ..	...	...	...	...	...	...	...	...	...	...	410
4101	Electricity	...	...	...	...	...	...	...	...	...	...	4101
420	Water works and supply .	...	...	...	...	...	...	...	...	...	...	420
4	Electricity,gas etc	...	...	...	...	...	...	...	...	...	...	4
2-4	All industry	...	...	...	...	...	...	...	...	...	...	2-4

a/ Manufacturing: all establishments in the public sector and those with 25 or more persons engaged in private sector.
b/ Manufacturing: up to 1982, all establishments in the public sector and those with 10 or more persons engaged in private sector.

ISIC	INDUSTRY	9. QUANTITY OF ELECTRICITY CONSUMED (MILLION KWH)					10. OUTPUT IN PRODUCERS' PRICES a/ (BILLION LIRAS)					ISIC
		1981	1982	1983	1984	1985	1981	b/ 1982	1983	1984	1985	
210	Coal mining	...	...	...	...	...	...	...	...	...	...	210
220	Petroleum and gas	...	...	...	...	...	...	...	...	...	...	220
230	Metal ore mining	...	...	...	...	...	...	...	...	...	...	230
290	Other mining	...	...	...	...	...	...	...	...	...	...	290
2	Mining, quarrying .	...	...	...	...	...	...	...	...	...	...	2
311/2	Food products	893	1058	1030	1018	...	583	776	919	1536	...	311/2
313	Beverages	59	57	57	57	...	61	77	101	142	...	313
314	Tobacco	35	40	49	43	...	124	248	313	455	...	314
321	Textiles	1693	1845	1965	2199	...	418	594	797	1220	...	321
3211	Spinning,weaving etc..	1544	1670	1798	1989	...	350	486	675	1034	...	3211
322	Wearing apparel	33	24	34	27	...	36	56	128	214	...	322
323	Leather and products ...	22	25	19	19	...	15	22	26	43	...	323
324	Footwear	14	14	12	11	...	14	17	19	26	...	324
331	Wood products	118	136	142	156	...	30	43	59	81	...	331
332	Furniture, fixtures	6	7	7	9	...	9	10	12	18	...	332
341	Paper and products	701	972	918	1132	...	72	103	123	213	...	341
3411	Pulp,paper etc.	658	936	878	1082	...	47	67	82	142	...	3411
342	Printing,publishing	24	28	25	28	...	39	59	69	111	...	342
351	Industrial chemicals ...	1187	1524	1667	1428	...	213	284	364	613	...	351
3511	Basic excl fertilizers	230	506	450	348	...	37	61	58	107	...	3511
3513	Synthetic resins etc .	410	499	528	483	...	61	99	140	217	...	3513
352	Other chemical products.	72	82	100	116	...	141	180	228	354	...	352
3522	Drugs and medicines ..	28	31	42	48	...	60	74	103	158	...	3522
353	Petroleum refineries ...	284	331	299	342	...	741	1127	1284	1954	...	353
354	Petroleum,coal products.	7	11	12	13	...	73	89	159	219	...	354
355	Rubber products	126	155	137	156	...	54	82	101	160	...	355
356	Plastic products n.e.c..	98	125	119	99	...	50	69	71	113	...	356
361	Pottery,china etc	72	89	102	113	...	13	20	30	49	...	361
362	Glass and products	122	196	151	193	...	33	59	73	112	...	362
369	Non-metal products n.e.c	1716	1981	1621	1993	...	147	196	204	301	...	369
371	Iron and steel	1484	1834	2463	2146	...	229	356	518	705	...	371
372	Non-ferrous metals	1108	1126	949	823	...	84	111	148	247	...	372
381	Metal products	168	173	188	180	...	102	139	184	276	...	381
382	Machinery n.e.c.	214	332	365	225	...	167	236	309	550	...	382
3825	Office,computing etc..	1	2	2	1	...	2	3	2	4	...	3825
383	Electrical machinery ...	118	122	188	140	...	119	166	258	454	...	383
3832	Radio,television etc..	10	14	19	18	...	25	41	94	190	...	3832
384	Transport equipment	185	226	237	277	...	170	257	370	544	...	384
3841	Shipbuilding, repair..	10	16	14	15	...	17	23	19	29	...	3841
3843	Motor vehicles	148	178	191	230	...	135	215	324	467	...	3843
385	Professional goods	4	5	3	3	...	3	5	6	8	...	385
390	Other industries	9	11	13	20	...	9	11	16	30	...	390
3	Manufacturing	10572	12529	12872	12966	...	3750	5393	6894	10750	...	3
410	Electricity,gas,steam ..	...	...	...	...	...	...	...	...	...	...	410
4101	Electricity	...	...	...	...	...	...	...	...	...	...	4101
420	Water works and supply .	...	...	...	...	...	...	...	...	...	...	420
4	Electricity,gas etc	...	...	...	...	...	...	...	...	...	...	4
2-4	All industry	...	...	...	...	...	...	...	...	...	...	2-4

a/ Manufacturing: all establishments in the public sector and those with 25 or more persons engaged in private sector.
b/ Manufacturing: up to 1982, all establishments in the public sector and those with 10 or more persons engaged in private sector.

ISIC	INDUSTRY	11. VALUE ADDED IN PRODUCERS' PRICES a/ (BILLION LIRAS) 1981	1982 b/	1983	1984	1985	12. GROSS FIXED CAPITAL FORMATION TOTAL a/c/ (MILLION LIRAS) 1981	1982 b/	1983	1984	1985	ISIC
210	Coal mining	...	...	...	...	...	...	...	...	...	...	210
220	Petroleum and gas	...	...	...	...	...	...	...	...	...	...	220
230	Metal ore mining	...	...	...	...	...	...	...	...	...	...	230
290	Other mining	...	...	...	...	...	...	...	...	...	...	290
2	Mining, quarrying .	...	...	...	...	...	...	...	...	...	...	2
311/2	Food products	150.8	189.1	204.7	329.6	...	9034	24493	28117	55920	...	311/2
313	Beverages	41.7	51.3	67.9	96.0	...	2376	3730	12137	4452	...	313
314	Tobacco	61.1	178.0	186.7	284.8	...	208	1852	658	1511	...	314
321	Textiles	162.2	226.5	296.0	454.3	...	19390	30083	48733	88599	...	321
3211	Spinning,weaving etc..	135.3	184.5	251.4	383.6	...	15654	24863	41583	73051	...	3211
322	Wearing apparel	10.4	17.5	36.6	63.2	...	707	1592	2725	3717	...	322
323	Leather and products ...	4.3	6.0	6.3	10.4	...	148	222	616	1596	...	323
324	Footwear	4.3	5.2	6.2	9.1	...	173	801	77	3260	...	324
331	Wood products	9.5	13.3	20.7	25.2	...	2163	3500	1449	1399	...	331
332	Furniture, fixtures	3.5	3.8	4.4	7.5	...	163	260	397	395	...	332
341	Paper and products	20.1	33.3	44.5	66.8	...	3412	4618	3719	22220	...	341
3411	Pulp,paper etc.	11.4	21.1	30.4	46.9	...	3056	3272	1264	19444	...	3411
342	Printing,publishing	17.1	24.2	33.1	54.6	...	1093	8948	10512	1272	...	342
351	Industrial chemicals ...	61.9	95.1	102.4	164.9	...	6233	19853	33494	87944	...	351
3511	Basic excl fertilizers	12.8	21.7	24.3	48.7	...	1109	7374	7501	24902	...	3511
3513	Synthetic resins etc .	16.5	27.6	45.0	69.3	...	3507	10774	10878	40630	...	3513
352	Other chemical products.	51.2	63.0	69.9	115.8	...	3106	5036	7110	10979	...	352
3522	Drugs and medicines ..	22.1	24.8	34.5	54.0	...	1339	2724	3121	5799	...	3522
353	Petroleum refineries ...	371.9	459.2	449.4	452.8	...	12178	29428	10250	15964	...	353
354	Petroleum,coal products.	19.2	24.6	42.2	49.3	...	1355	2058	2662	4016	...	354
355	Rubber products	21.3	29.5	36.0	55.2	...	2408	1485	4818	7979	...	355
356	Plastic products n.e.c..	12.4	21.6	20.1	30.1	...	1053	1962	3884	5791	...	356
361	Pottery,china etc	8.1	11.3	18.2	28.8	...	413	902	1482	3711	...	361
362	Glass and products	16.6	31.4	37.9	54.3	...	11877	1816	3356	12078	...	362
369	Non-metal products n.e.c	70.8	83.2	89.6	116.6	...	4959	7154	12098	36449	...	369
371	Iron and steel	87.1	96.3	155.1	153.9	...	32942	20309	36348	20950	...	371
372	Non-ferrous metals	22.0	31.0	43.4	73.5	...	7707	6152	10690	25253	...	372
381	Metal products	42.7	59.5	73.0	106.6	...	4034	6417	6580	10707	...	381
382	Machinery n.e.c.	62.3	89.9	101.8	162.1	...	14378	9982	16442	22624	...	382
3825	Office,computing etc..	0.8	1.0	0.8	1.4	...	105	18	49	13	...	3825
383	Electrical machinery ...	50.4	70.4	100.0	178.0	...	3411	6809	24108	30083	...	383
3832	Radio,television etc..	11.5	20.3	35.9	67.2	...	393	1344	2804	7006	...	3832
384	Transport equipment	68.4	105.6	142.7	198.6	...	7206	18058	13659	49219	...	384
3841	Shipbuilding, repair..	12.9	18.6	11.9	17.8	...	717	2769	2936	3653	...	3841
3843	Motor vehicles	46.2	77.3	119.3	161.4	...	5986	14475	9858	43957	...	3843
385	Professional goods	1.4	2.7	2.7	3.5	...	70	214	250	290	...	385
390	Other industries	3.2	4.4	7.6	11.5	...	289	641	1359	4508	...	390
3	Manufacturing	1455.9	2026.9	2399.1	3357.0	...	152486	218375	297730	532886	...	3
410	Electricity,gas,steam ..	...	...	...	...	...	...	...	...	...	...	410
4101	Electricity	...	...	...	...	...	...	...	...	...	...	4101
420	Water works and supply .	...	...	...	...	...	...	...	...	...	...	420
4	Electricity,gas etc	...	...	...	...	...	...	...	...	...	...	4
2-4	All industry	...	...	...	...	...	...	...	...	...	...	2-4

a/ Manufacturing: all establishments in the public sector and those with 25 or more persons engaged in private sector.
b/ Manufacturing: up to 1982, all establishments in the public sector and those with 10 or more persons engaged in private sector.
c/ The value of sales is not deducted.

ISIC	INDUSTRY	13. GROSS FIXED CAPITAL FORMATION MACHINERY AND EQUIPMENT a/b/ (MILLION LIRAS)					14. VALUE OF STOCKS AT END OF PERIOD TOTAL a/ (BILLION LIRAS)					ISIC
		1981	c/ 1982	1983	1984	1985	1981	c/ 1982	1983	1984	1985	
210	Coal mining	...	...	...	...	...	...	...	...	...	...	210
220	Petroleum and gas	...	...	...	...	...	...	...	...	...	...	220
230	Metal ore mining	...	...	...	...	...	...	...	...	...	...	230
290	Other mining	...	...	...	...	...	...	...	...	...	...	290
2	Mining, quarrying	...	...	...	...	...	...	...	...	...	...	2
311/2	Food products	6039	14010	17110	41776	...	150.9	189.4	252.5	352.1	...	311/2
313	Beverages	1837	2384	7901	3688	...	11.3	13.4	15.4	21.0	...	313
314	Tobacco	134	177	2267	1027	...	56.1	77.9	113.7	123.5	...	314
321	Textiles	16757	22629	39105	75947	...	114.9	126.5	184.6	264.8	...	321
3211	Spinning,weaving etc.	13533	18223	34751	62139	...	99.4	106.1	153.8	226.2	...	3211
322	Wearing apparel	517	1246	2142	2503	...	6.3	11.2	19.4	24.3	...	322
323	Leather and products	116	184	504	1049	...	4.1	5.2	5.9	8.3	...	323
324	Footwear	120	131	101	3205	...	2.8	4.7	5.8	8.0	...	324
331	Wood products	1849	2663	1266	1031	...	10.5	14.5	17.9	28.9	...	331
332	Furniture, fixtures	90	184	238	310	...	3.7	2.0	3.3	4.0	...	332
341	Paper and products	2842	3930	2544	15865	...	15.6	17.6	19.3	40.5	...	341
3411	Pulp,paper etc.	2634	2871	2753	13804	...	12.3	12.7	14.7	33.5	...	3411
342	Printing,publishing	833	1872	3404	1659	...	4.9	6.8	8.0	10.2	...	342
351	Industrial chemicals	13053	15973	19873	79874	...	41.2	39.5	55.2	94.8	...	351
3511	Basic excl fertilizers	5364	6114	6159	23075	...	8.2	9.5	8.7	17.0	...	3511
3513	Synthetic resins etc	3145	8519	8323	36961	...	11.3	14.5	23.9	41.9	...	3513
352	Other chemical products	1633	3347	5137	7314	...	29.2	32.5	39.5	62.6	...	352
3522	Drugs and medicines	762	1660	1999	3449	...	15.9	16.6	20.7	31.5	...	3522
353	Petroleum refineries	7534	7456	5315	3683	...	62.6	87.9	109.8	162.2	...	353
354	Petroleum,coal products	458	1864	1963	3219	...	11.7	13.2	22.2	27.9	...	354
355	Rubber products	2134	2137	3842	6666	...	8.8	13.3	14.9	21.1	...	355
356	Plastic products n.e.c.	834	1619	3460	4612	...	8.1	11.7	11.8	15.8	...	356
361	Pottery,china etc	717	749	1353	3128	...	4.1	4.9	7.3	10.4	...	361
362	Glass and products	1273	1188	1855	7045	...	5.8	10.2	11.9	22.0	...	362
369	Non-metal products n.e.c	3441	5137	9288	24205	...	19.1	29.5	31.7	47.4	...	369
371	Iron and steel	8007	13871	31970	17500	...	60.3	71.7	111.1	129.1	...	371
372	Non-ferrous metals	7126	8506	9887	7677	...	31.2	24.6	38.9	64.0	...	372
381	Metal products	2823	5127	5427	9611	...	25.3	32.4	40.6	51.8	...	381
382	Machinery n.e.c.	3143	8254	13374	18313	...	48.1	72.3	76.9	111.2	...	382
3825	Office,computing etc.	73	61	49	14	...	0.2	0.4	0.5	0.8	...	3825
383	Electrical machinery	2175	3010	16602	23655	...	28.5	37.5	51.9	83.9	...	383
3832	Radio,television etc.	232	1203	2335	4320	...	6.1	10.8	16.1	28.1	...	3832
384	Transport equipment	5304	7697	10091	35141	...	41.2	63.2	92.3	117.6	...	384
3841	Shipbuilding, repair.	296	1153	1232	977	...	4.6	7.3	10.8	13.1	...	3841
3843	Motor vehicles	4741	5517	8285	32954	...	26.4	41.7	63.9	85.8	...	3843
385	Professional goods	21	131	160	182	...	1.0	1.5	1.0	1.5	...	385
390	Other industries	230	511	1201	3129	...	2.0	2.7	4.5	6.3	...	390
3	Manufacturing	91040	135987	217380	403014	...	809.3	1017.8	1367.3	1915.2	...	3
410	Electricity,gas,steam	...	...	...	...	...	...	...	...	...	...	410
4101	Electricity	...	...	...	...	...	...	...	...	...	...	4101
420	Water works and supply	...	...	...	...	...	...	...	...	...	...	420
4	Electricity,gas etc	...	...	...	...	...	...	...	...	...	...	4
2-4	All industry	...	...	...	...	...	...	...	...	...	...	2-4

a/ Manufacturing: all establishments in the public sector and those with 25 or more persons engaged in private sector.
b/ The value of sales is not deducted.
c/ Manufacturing: up to 1982, all establishments in the public sector and those with 10 or more persons engaged in private sector.

15. INDEX NUMBERS OF INDUSTRIAL PRODUCTION (1980 = 100)

ISIC	INDUSTRY	1976	1977	1978	1979	1981	1982	1983	1984	1985	a/ RATE	ISIC
210	Coal mining	113	109	110	103	110	110	107	114	120	0.7	210
220	Petroleum and gas	110	116	117	122	102	100	95	90	90	-2.2	220
230	Metal ore mining	168	169	136	109	119	122	101	144	144	-1.7	230
290	Other mining .... b/	91	87	79	91	124	136	135	179	231	10.9	290
2	Mining, quarrying .	117	118	110	105	111	113	107	121	132	1.3	2
311/2	Food products .... c/	94	103	104	93	106	154	163	152	136	4.2	311/2
313	Beverages	111	115	115	97	93	96	93	83	78	-3.8	313
314	Tobacco	94	103	99	118	145	133	104	105	104	1.1	314
321	Textiles	...	...	...	...	...	...	...	...	...	...	321
3211	Spinning,weaving etc..	...	...	...	...	...	...	...	...	...	...	3211
322	Wearing apparel	...	...	...	...	...	...	...	...	...	...	322
323	Leather and products ...	...	...	...	...	...	...	...	...	...	...	323
324	Footwear	...	...	...	...	...	...	...	...	...	...	324
331	Wood products	...	...	...	...	...	...	...	...	...	...	331
332	Furniture, fixtures	...	...	...	...	...	...	...	...	...	...	332
341	Paper and products	103	113	101	100	122	132	131	162	156	4.7	341
3411	Pulp,paper etc.	...	...	...	...	...	...	...	...	...	...	3411
342	Printing,publishing	...	...	...	...	...	...	...	...	...	...	342
351	Industrial chemicals ...	...	...	...	...	...	...	...	...	...	...	351
3511	Basic excl fertilizers	...	...	...	...	...	...	...	...	...	...	3511
3513	Synthetic resins etc .	...	...	...	...	...	...	...	...	...	...	3513
352	Other chemical products.	...	...	...	...	...	...	...	...	...	...	352
3522	Drugs and medicines ..	...	...	...	...	...	...	...	...	...	...	3522
353	Petroleum refineries ...	...	...	...	...	...	...	...	...	...	...	353
354	Petroleum,coal products.	...	...	...	...	...	...	...	...	...	...	354
355	Rubber products	...	...	...	...	...	...	...	...	...	...	355
356	Plastic products n.e.c..	...	...	...	...	...	...	...	...	...	...	356
361	Pottery,china etc	...	...	...	...	...	...	...	...	...	...	361
362	Glass and products	95	112	111	120	138	148	157	156	170	6.7	362
369	Non-metal products n.e.c d/	99	108	119	107	117	123	106	122	137	3.7	369
371	Iron and steel	86	80	92	105	92	104	98	133	148	6.2	371
372	Non-ferrous metals	...	...	...	...	...	...	...	...	...	...	372
381	Metal products	...	...	...	...	...	...	...	...	...	...	381
382	Machinery n.e.c.	...	...	...	...	...	...	...	...	...	...	382
3825	Office,computing etc..	...	...	...	...	...	...	...	...	...	...	3825
383	Electrical machinery ...	...	...	...	...	...	...	...	...	...	...	383
3832	Radio,television etc..	...	...	...	...	...	...	...	...	...	...	3832
384	Transport equipment	...	...	...	...	...	...	...	...	...	...	384
3841	Shipbuilding, repair..	...	...	...	...	...	...	...	...	...	...	3841
3843	Motor vehicles	...	...	...	...	...	...	...	...	...	...	3843
385	Professional goods	...	...	...	...	...	...	...	...	...	...	385
390	Other industries	...	...	...	...	...	...	...	...	...	...	390
3	Manufacturing	86	98	99	101	110	131	127	142	139	5.5	3
410	Electricity,gas,steam ..	...	...	...	...	...	...	...	...	...	...	410
4101	Electricity	78	88	93	97	100	114	117	132	147	7.3	4101
420	Water works and supply .	...	...	...	...	...	...	...	...	...	...	420
4	Electricity,gas etc	...	...	...	...	...	...	...	...	...	...	4
2-4	All industry	87	98	100	100	109	125	122	137	139	5.3	2-4

a/ Annual growth rate 1976-1985.
b/ Sulphur mining only.
c/ Sugar factories and refineries and slaughtering only.
d/ Cement only.

UNION OF SOVIET SOCIALIST REPUBLICS

The information on industrial activity is based on the reply to the United Nations Questionnaire on General Industrial Statistics from the Central Statistical Board of the USSR, Moscow. The concepts, definitions and classification by branches of industry are generally in accordance with United Nations standards.

The estimates are based on regular monthly and annual reports of enterprises. The statistical unit is the industrial enterprise or the industrial unit of the non-industrial enterprise; industrial units of collective farms and small subsidiary industrial enterprises, however, are not covered.

The estimates, which are based on the national classification, are shown in the most appropriate category of ISIC. The following industries are excluded: (a) prospecting and drilling for minerals, crude petroleum and natural gas, and preparing sites for extraction, (b) publishing, (c) gas distribution, (d) secondary processing of ferrous metals and (e) water supply. It should be noted that the manufacture of fur products (ISIC 322) is included in ISIC 323.

Employment numbers are annual averages of monthly figures and relate to persons engaged in the industrial activities of enterprises classified under mining, manufacturing, electricity and gas. They comprise production workers, apprentices, engineers and technicians, office staff, minor service personnel and guards.

Output relates to the value of the output of industry at enterprise prices of each year, excluding tax; the value of resale of commodities without further processing is not included.

The estimates of wages and salaries relate to the annual wage fund of all industrial-production personnel, including all kinds of bonuses. Payments in kind and social benefits are excluded.

The estimates of gross fixed capital formation represent acquisitions of new fixed assets and relate to the "productive" investments of industrial enterprises, valued at constant prices of 1 January 1969; the investments of industrial enterprises in dwellings, public utilities, social facilities and other "non-productive" assets are not included. The data are based on the national classification, which includes logging; commercial fishing; repair of motor vehicles, household appliances, furniture and footwear; repair and restoration of knitted goods and apparel; film copying and cleaning and dyeing.

The indexes of industrial production are compiled by the Central Statistical Board of the USSR and provided in response to the United Nations Questionnaire on Indexes of Industrial Production.

Related national publication:
<u>Narodnoe Khozyaistvo SSSR</u> (National Economy of the USSR) (annual), published by the Central Statistical Board of the USSR, Moscow.

ISIC	INDUSTRY	1. NUMBER OF ENTERPRISES a/ (NUMBER) 1981	1982	1983	1984	1985	2. AVERAGE NUMBER OF EMPLOYEES a/ (THOUSANDS) 1981	1982	1983	1984	1985	ISIC
210	Coal mining	[b/ 852	b/ 853	b/ 854	b/ 863	b/ 878]	1077	1105	[1293	1298]	...	210
220	Petroleum and gas						162	166			...	220
230	Metal ore mining	[1070	1070	1081	1087	1083]	c/d/ 191	c/d/ 194	...	...	...	230
290	Other mining						c/ 736	c/ 743	...	...	...	290
2	Mining, quarrying .	1922	1923	1935	1950	1961	2166	2208	...	...	...	2
311/2	Food products	7390	7538	7644	7765	[	2691	2717	[	]	...	311/2
313	Beverages	1696	1726	1760	e/	9700]	370	374	3129	3156	...	313
314	Tobacco	85	88	87	86		40	40			...	314
321	Textiles	1979	1996	2003	2009	2020	2232	2210	2189	2189	...	321
3211	Spinning,weaving etc..	...	...	...	...	...	...	...	...	...	...	3211
322	Wearing apparel	5149	5118	5156	4961	4952	2272	2250	2229	2209	...	322
323	Leather and products ...	263	266	266	267	269	199	199	[693	687]	...	323
324	Footwear	398	406	417	414	420	494	494			...	324
331	Wood products	[				]	791	791	791	797	...	331
332	Furniture, fixtures	2260	2275	2258	2271	2283	535	535	540	544	...	332
341	Paper and products						290	293	295	297	...	341
3411	Pulp,paper etc.	...	...	...	...	...	...	...	...	...	...	3411
342	Printing,publishing .... f/	...	...	...	...	...	...	...	...	...	...	342
351	Industrial chemicals ...	g/ 1480	g/ 1493	g/ 1499	g/ 1504	g/ 1511	1138	1148	h/ 2186	h/ 2203	...	351
3511	Basic excl fertilizers	...	...	...	...	...	...	...	...	...	...	3511
3513	Synthetic resins etc .	...	...	...	...	...	...	...	...	...	...	3513
352	Other chemical products.	g/	g/	g/	g/	g/	i/ 592	i/ 597	h/	h/	...	352
3522	Drugs and medicines ..	...	...	...	...	...	...	...	...	...	...	3522
353	Petroleum refineries ...	b/	b/	b/	b/	b/	i/	i/	h/	h/	...	353
354	Petroleum,coal products.	b/	b/	b/	b/	b/	i/	i/	h/	h/	...	354
355	Rubber products	g/	g/	g/	g/	g/	310	313	h/	h/	...	355
356	Plastic products n.e.c..	g/	g/	g/	g/	g/	128	130	h/	h/	...	356
361	Pottery,china etc	[329	333	337	339	337]	237	241	[378	374]	...	361
362	Glass and products						133	135			...	362
369	Non-metal products n.e.c	3200	3234	3217	3263	3243	2068	2088	2126	2124	...	369
371	Iron and steel	410	408	409	412	413	d/ 1029	d/ 1044	d/ 1073	d/ 1052	...	371
372	Non-ferrous metals	...	...	...	...	...	...	...	...	...	...	372
381	Metal products .... j/	[8094	8180	8273	8367	8417	14880	15011	15125	15353]	...	381
382	Machinery n.e.c.										...	382
3825	Office,computing etc..	...	...	...	...	...	...	...	...	...	...	3825
383	Electrical machinery ... j/	...	...	...	...	...	...	...	...	...	...	383
3832	Radio,television etc..	...	...	...	...	...	...	...	...	...	...	3832
384	Transport equipment .... j/	...	...	...	...	...	...	...	...	...	...	384
3841	Shipbuilding, repair..	...	...	...	...	...	...	...	...	...	...	3841
3843	Motor vehicles	...	...	...	...	...	...	...	...	...	...	3843
385	Professional goods ..... j/	...	...	...	...	...	...	...	...	...	...	385
390	Other industries .... f/	3845	3856	3857	e/ 5639	3878	d/ 1259	d/ 1271	...	...	...	390
3	Manufacturing	36578	36917	37183	37297	37443	31688	31881	...	...	...	3
410	Electricity,gas,steam ..	1432	1433	1422	1428	1434	790	816	831	851	...	410
4101	Electricity	...	...	...	...	...	...	...	...	...	...	4101
420	Water works and supply .	.	.	.	.	.	.	.	.	.	...	420
4	Electricity,gas etc	1432	1433	1422	1428	1434	790	816	831	851	...	4
2-4	All industry	39932	40273	40540	40675	40838	34644	34905	...	...	...	2-4

Note: Estimates are based on the national classification of industry.

a/ Excluding industrial units of collective farms and small subsidiary industrial enterprises.
b/ Major groups 353 and 354 are included in 210 and 220 combined.
c/ Non-ferrous ore mining is included in major group 290.
d/ Part of major group 230 is included in 371 and part in 390.
e/ Major group 313 is included in 390
f/ Printing is included in major group 390.
g/ Major groups 352, 355 and 356 are included in 351.
h/ Major groups 352 to 356 are included in 351.
i/ Major groups 353 and 354 are included in 352.
j/ Major groups 383 to 385 are included in 381 and 382 combined.

ISIC	INDUSTRY		3. WAGES AND SALARIES OF EMPLOYEES a/b/ (ROUBLES) 1981	1982	1983	1984	1985	4. HOURS WORKED BY OPERATIVES a/c/ (MILLIONS) 1981	1982	1983	1984	1985	ISIC
210	Coal mining		304	332	330	331	342	1847	1895	[2228	2236]	...	210
220	Petroleum and gas		250	256	263	271	296	288	295			...	220
230	Metal ore mining	d/	235	241	245	249	256	e/ 333	e/ 333	...	...	...	230
290	Other mining	d/	234	242	243	255	261	1304	1316	...	...	...	290
2	Mining, quarrying .		273	291	293	307	306	3772	3844	...	...	...	2
311/2	Food products		164	170	174	180	[	5073	5122	[		...	311/2
313	Beverages		148	151	153	f/	181	702	710	5901	5952	...	313
314	Tobacco		169	171	174	177	]	73	73		]	...	314
321	Textiles		162	167	175	178	183	3984	3945	3908	3907	...	321
3211	Spinning,weaving etc..		...	...	...	...	...	...	...	...	...	...	3211
322	Wearing apparel		139	141	142	145	150	4071	4032	3994	3958	...	322
323	Leather and products ...		170	174	176	180	185	360	360	[1245	1234]	...	323
324	Footwear		165	170	173	179	186	885	885			...	324
331	Wood products		184	190	195	199	207	1467	1467	1467	1478	...	331
332	Furniture, fixtures		184	191	195	200	205	974	974	983	991	...	332
341	Paper and products		195	200	206	212	217	536	542	546	549	...	341
3411	Pulp,paper etc.		...	...	...	...	...	...	...	...	...	...	3411
342	Printing,publishing	g/	...	...	...	...	...	...	...	...	...	...	342
351	Industrial chemicals ...		185	189	192	198	202	2007	2025	h/ 3860	h/ 3890	...	351
3511	Basic excl fertilizers		...	...	...	...	...	...	...	...	...	...	3511
3513	Synthetic resins etc .		...	...	...	...	...	...	...	...	...	...	3513
352	Other chemical products.		i/ 187	i/ 192	i/ 193	i/ 198	i/ 202	i/ 1063	i/ 1072	h/	h/	...	352
3522	Drugs and medicines ..		...	...	...	...	...	...	...	...	...	...	3522
353	Petroleum refineries ...		i/	i/	i/	i/	i/	i/	i/	h/	h/	...	353
354	Petroleum,coal products.		i/	i/	i/	i/	i/	i/	i/	h/	h/	...	354
355	Rubber products		191	195	197	202	208	545	550	h/	h/	...	355
356	Plastic products n.e.c..		174	179	180	187	192	214	217	h/	h/	...	356
361	Pottery,china etc		170	174	178	181	184	422	429	[680	672]	...	361
362	Glass and products		182	185	190	193	197	243	247			...	362
369	Non-metal products n.e.c		184	189	194	199	204	3787	3824	3894	3889	...	369
371	Iron and steel		218	222	227	232	237	e/ 1858	e/ 1885	e/ 1937	e/ 1900	...	371
372	Non-ferrous metals		...	...	...	...	...	...	...	...	...	...	372
381	Metal products	j/	[192	199	202	208	215	27096	27335	27543	27958]	...	381
382	Machinery n.e.c.											...	382
3825	Office,computing etc..		...	...	...	...	...	...	...	...	...	...	3825
383	Electrical machinery ...	j/	...	...	...	...	...	...	...	...	...	...	383
3832	Radio,television etc..		...	...	...	...	...	...	...	...	...	...	3832
384	Transport equipment	j/	...	...	...	...	...	...	...	...	...	...	384
3841	Shipbuilding, repair..		...	...	...	...	...	...	...	...	...	...	3841
3843	Motor vehicles		...	...	...	...	...	...	...	...	...	...	3843
385	Professional goods	j/	...	...	...	...	...	...	...	...	...	...	385
390	Other industries	g/	205	209	213	f/ 217	223	e/ 2189	e/ 2210	...	...	...	390
3	Manufacturing		183	189	192	198	203	57549	57904	...	...	...	3
410	Electricity,gas,steam ..		194	200	201	204	210	1470	1518	1546	1583	...	410
4101	Electricity		...	...	...	...	...	...	...	...	...	...	4101
420	Water works and supply .		.	.	.	.	.	.	.	.	.	...	420
4	Electricity,gas etc		194	200	201	204	210	1470	1518	1546	1583	...	4
2-4	All industry		190	196	199	205	211	62791	63266	...	...	...	2-4

a/ Excluding industrial units of collective farms and small subsidiary industrial enterprises.
b/ Monthly average per employee.
c/ Hours worked by employees.
d/ Non-ferrous ore mining is included in major group 290.
e/ Part of major group 230 is included in 371 and part in 390.
f/ Major group 313 is included in 390
g/ Printing is included in major group 390.
h/ Major groups 352 to 356 are included in 351.
i/ Major groups 353 and 354 are included in 352.
j/ Major groups 383 to 385 are included in 381 and 382 combined.

ISIC	INDUSTRY	5. OUTPUT (BILLION ROUBLES) 1981	1982	1983	1984	1985	6. GROSS FIXED CAPITAL FORMATION TOTAL a/ (MILLION ROUBLES) 1981	1982	1983	1984	1985	ISIC
210	Coal mining	[19.8	34.4	34.7	35.0]	...	2370	2557	2788	2838	2905	210
220	Petroleum and gas					...	10656	11855	13074	13740	15502	220
230	Metal ore mining	[12.0	15.9	16.0	16.3]	...	b/	b/	b/	...	...	230
290	Other mining					...	c/	c/	c/	c/	c/	290
2	Mining, quarrying	31.8	50.3	50.7	51.3	...	...	...	...	...	...	2
311/2	Food products	97.9	104.1	110.3	115.2	...	[				]	311/2
313	Beverages	16.8	17.7	18.4	d/	...	3604	3667	3848	4076	4085	313
314	Tobacco	3.6	3.8	4.3	4.9	...						314
321	Textiles	63.8	72.7	73.8	73.5	...	1480	1512	1619	1503	1413	321
3211	Spinning,weaving etc.	...	...	...	...	...	...	...	...	...	...	3211
322	Wearing apparel	30.1	30.9	30.9	31.8	...	165	167	171	178	177	322
323	Leather and products	3.6	4.2	3.9	3.9	...	[224	216	258	277	291]	323
324	Footwear	5.2	5.5	5.7	5.9	...						324
331	Wood products	[			]	...	[1474	1419	1454	1468	1554]	331
332	Furniture, fixtures	18.8	22.3	23.4	24.3	...						332
341	Paper and products					...	615	646	634	528	552	341
3411	Pulp,paper etc.	...	...	...	...	...	...	...	...	...	...	3411
342	Printing,publishing	...	...	e/	...	...	214	238	272	255	256	342
351	Industrial chemicals f/	64.4	75.5	79.2	82.0	...	5205	5181	5338	5595	5152	351
3511	Basic excl fertilizers	...	...	...	...	...	...	...	...	...	...	3511
3513	Synthetic resins etc	...	...	...	...	...	...	...	...	...	...	3513
352	Other chemical products. f/	...	...	...	...	...	...	...	...	...	...	352
3522	Drugs and medicines	...	...	...	...	...	...	...	...	...	...	3522
353	Petroleum refineries f/	...	...	...	...	...	...	...	...	...	...	353
354	Petroleum,coal products. f/	...	...	...	...	...	...	...	...	...	...	354
355	Rubber products f/	...	...	...	...	...	...	...	...	...	...	355
356	Plastic products n.e.c.. f/	...	...	...	...	...	...	...	...	...	...	356
361	Pottery,china etc	[3.2	3.3	3.5	3.6]	...	[137	168	183	147	142]	361
362	Glass and products					...						362
369	Non-metal products n.e.c	20.5	24.8	25.7	26.3	...	c/ 2306	c/ 2161	c/ 2412	c/ 2247	c/ 2404	369
371	Iron and steel	...	...	g/	...	...	b/ 3257	b/ 3396	b/ 3456	b/ 3597	b/ 3041	371
372	Non-ferrous metals	...	...	g/	...	...	h/	h/	h/	h/	h/	372
381	Metal products i/	[175.9	182.4	193.5	205.0]	...	[13657	13759	14567	15292	15969]	381
382	Machinery n.e.c.					...						382
3825	Office,computing etc..	...	...	...	...	...	...	...	...	...	...	3825
383	Electrical machinery i/	...	...	...	...	...	...	...	...	...	...	383
3832	Radio,television etc..	...	...	...	...	...	...	...	...	...	...	3832
384	Transport equipment i/	...	...	...	...	...	...	...	...	...	...	384
3841	Shipbuilding, repair..	...	...	...	...	...	...	...	...	...	...	3841
3843	Motor vehicles	...	...	...	...	...	...	...	...	...	...	3843
385	Professional goods i/	...	...	...	...	...	...	...	...	...	...	385
390	Other industries	e/g/ 64.6	e/g/ 79.5	e/g/ 82.6	d/e/g/ 104.0	...	b/h/ 4653	b/h/ 4588	b/h/ 4813	b/h/ 5043	b/h/ 5346	390
3	Manufacturing	568.4	626.7	655.2	680.4	...	...	...	...	...	...	3
410	Electricity,gas,steam	19.5	25.5	26.0	27.3	...	5251	5235	5578	5929	6664	410
4101	Electricity	...	...	...	...	...	...	...	...	...	...	4101
420	Water works and supply	.	.	.	.	...	.	.	.	.	.	420
4	Electricity,gas etc	19.5	25.5	26.0	27.3	...	5251	5235	5578	5929	6664	4
2-4	All industry	619.7	702.5	731.9	759.0	...	55268	56765	60465	62713	65453	2-4

a/ AT constant prices of 1 January 1984.
b/ Part of major group 230 is included in 371 and part in 390.
c/ Major group 290 is included in 369.
d/ Major group 313 is included in 390
e/ Printing is included in major group 390.
f/ Major groups 352 to 356 are included in 351.
g/ Major groups 371 and 372 are included in 390.
h/ Major group 372 is included in 390.
i/ Major groups 383 to 385 are included in 381 and 382 combined.

7. INDEX NUMBERS OF INDUSTRIAL PRODUCTION (1980 = 100)

ISIC	INDUSTRY		1976	1977	1978	1979	1981	1982	1983	1984	1985	a/ RATE	ISIC
210	Coal mining		100	101	101	100	98	100	101	102	104	0.4	210
220	Petroleum and gas	b/	83	88	92	96	102	105	106	108	108	3.0	220
230	Metal ore mining		98	100	101	99	98	98	100	101	103	0.6	230
290	Other mining		89	93	95	98	104	104	110	113	115	2.9	290
2	Mining, quarrying .	b/	94	96	98	99	101	102	104	106	108	1.6	2
311/2	Food products		91	95	99	100	101	106	111	115	122	3.3	311/2
313	Beverages		86	88	89	97	105	107	110	115	119	3.7	313
314	Tobacco		84	87	90	91	107	110	123	135	140	5.8	314
321	Textiles		90	94	97	98	103	103	104	104	106	1.8	321
3211	Spinning,weaving etc..		...	...	...	...	...	...	...	...	...	...	3211
322	Wearing apparel		83	86	90	94	104	104	105	109	111	3.3	322
323	Leather and products ...		94	96	97	98	100	100	94	96	96	0.2	323
324	Footwear		84	88	93	97	103	105	108	113	118	3.8	324
331	Wood products		97	99	101	98	102	106	111	114	116	2.0	331
332	Furniture, fixtures		83	88	93	95	106	110	116	122	130	5.1	332
341	Paper and products		95	98	102	97	104	107	113	118	123	2.9	341
3411	Pulp,paper etc.		...	...	...	...	...	...	...	...	...	...	3411
342	Printing,publishing		...	...	...	...	...	...	...	...	...	...	342
351	Industrial chemicals ...		81	87	92	94	106	110	117	124	130	5.4	351
3511	Basic excl fertilizers		...	...	...	...	...	...	...	...	...	...	3511
3513	Synthetic resins etc .		...	...	...	...	...	...	...	...	...	...	3513
352	Other chemical products.	c/	85	89	94	96	103	105	107	110	111	3.0	352
3522	Drugs and medicines ..		...	...	...	...	...	...	...	...	...	...	3522
353	Petroleum refineries ...	c/	...	...	...	...	...	...	...	...	...	...	353
354	Petroleum,coal products.	c/	...	...	...	...	...	...	...	...	...	...	354
355	Rubber products		86	92	95	98	102	106	109	112	117	3.5	355
356	Plastic products n.e.c..		76	82	88	94	114	119	126	136	147	7.6	356
361	Pottery,china etc		80	86	91	95	105	112	118	120	122	4.8	361
362	Glass and products		76	84	88	96	105	110	115	120	126	5.8	362
369	Non-metal products n.e.c		95	97	100	99	102	104	108	111	115	2.1	369
371 372	Iron and steel .... Non-ferrous metals		[94	96	98	99	101	102	107	110	112	2.0]	371 372
381 382	Metal products .... Machinery n.e.c.	d/	[74	80	88	94	105	111	118	126	134	6.8]	381 382
3825	Office,computing etc..		...	...	...	...	...	...	...	...	...	...	3825
383	Electrical machinery ...	d/	...	...	...	...	...	...	...	...	...	...	383
3832	Radio,television etc..		...	...	...	...	...	...	...	...	...	...	3832
384	Transport equipment	d/	...	...	...	...	...	...	...	...	...	...	384
3841	Shipbuilding, repair..		...	...	...	...	...	...	...	...	...	...	3841
3843	Motor vehicles		...	...	...	...	...	...	...	...	...	...	3843
385	Professional goods	d/	...	...	...	...	...	...	...	...	...	...	385
390	Other industries		...	...	...	...	...	...	...	...	...	...	390
3	Manufacturing	e/f/	83	88	92	96	103	106	111	116	121	4.3	3
410	Electricity,gas,steam ..		84	87	91	95	102	105	109	115	120	4.0	410
4101	Electricity		...	...	...	...	...	...	...	...	...	...	4101
420	Water works and supply .		.	.	.	.	.	.	.	.	.	.	420
4	Electricity,gas etc		...	...	...	...	...	...	...	...	...	...	4
2-4	All industry	e/g/	85	90	94	97	104	106	111	115	120	3.9	2-4

a/ Annual growth rate 1976-1985.
b/ Excluding prospecting and drilling of oil and natural gas wells.
c/ Major groups 353 and 354 are included in 352.
d/ Major groups 383 to 385 are included in 381 and 382 combined.
e/ Including commercial fishing and the processing and cold storage of fish and fish products by factory-type vessels.
f/ Excluding publishing.
g/ Including logging, motion picture production, cleaning and dyeing; excluding publishing and gas distribution.

The information on industrial activity is based on the reply to the United Nations Questionnaire on General Industrial Statistics from the Central Statistical Office, London. The concepts, definitions and classification by branches of industry are generally in accordance with United Nations standards. The estimates cover the United Kingdom of Great Britain and Northern Ireland; the Channel Islands and the Isle of Man are excluded.

The estimates are generally derived from the results of the annual census of production conducted by the Business Statistics Office of the Department of Trade and Industry for Great Britain and by the Department of Commerce, Belfast, for Northern Ireland. The censuses cover establishments engaged in mining, manufacturing and electricity, gas and water supply. The annual censuses are conducted within the framework of a sampling scheme introduced in 1978. Beginning with the 1980 census, forms were despatched to all establishments employing 100 persons or more and, in general, to samples of 1 in 2 of those employing 50-99 and 1 in 4 of those employing 20-49. The results presented cover all establishments as they include estimates for non-respondents, unsatisfactory returns and establishments not selected for the census.

The statistical unit is the establishment, defined as the smallest unit which can provide the information normally required for an economic census. Typically the establishment embraces all the activities carried on at a single address, including those which are ancillary to the principal activity. Establishments are asked to exclude from their returns all particulars relating to any department not engaged in production, for example, merchanting, transport, warehousing, for which separate accounts are kept; otherwise, non-production activities are included. Particulars relating to head offices mainly engaged in the administration of production units are included; where head office activity covers more than one return, details are included in the principle return.

The estimates are based on the national classification scheme (1980 version) but, except in the case of electricity consumed, data have been converted to the present version of ISIC. Normally establishments are classified to industries on the basis of major activity, measured by sales of the principal products.

The estimates of persons engaged include persons regarded as self-employed for national insurance purposes and members of their families who work in the business for at least half the normal number of working hours without receiving a fixed wage or salary. The number of employees is the average number of persons on the pay-roll during the year, whether employed full-time or part-time, comprising (a) administrative, technical and clerical employees and (b) all other employees (operatives), broadly defined as manual wage earners. The figures include persons engaged in non-production activities such as merchanting or factoring and canteen workers where particulars in respect of these activities could not be excluded from the return. Homeworkers are excluded.

The amounts shown for wages and salaries represent payments made to employees during the year, including overtime payments, bonuses, and commissions, whether paid regularly or not. No deduction is made for income tax, insurance, contributory pensions etc. The values of any payments in kind, travelling expenses, lodging allowances etc. are excluded. The estimates of supplements to wages and salaries include employers' contributions to national insurance as well as commercial insurance premiums to provide pensions, superannuation or other retirement benefits, sickness benefits, personal accident benefits, disability or death benefits for employees or former employees or their dependents. Contributions to the running costs of canteens, social centres, children's and holiday homes etc. for employees, former employees and their dependents are also included.

Data on electricity consumed are compiled by the Department of Energy. The estimates are presented by broad groupings of the national classification.

The estimates of output represent the value of production, including work done. It is calculated as the value of sales and work done adjusted for changes in the value of work in progress and stocks of finished goods during the year. Included are goods made by the establishment covered by the returns, goods made for it by other establishments or homeworkers from materials given out, capital items produced for use in the establishment (or for hiring out or leasing), goods sold without being subjected to any manufacturing process, waste products and the value of other industrial and non-industrial services rendered (receipts for repairs and maintenance, installation work, technical research and studies, provision of transport and revenue from renting out buildings, plant, machinery etc., staff facilities such as canteens, the right to use patents, trade marks etc.). The valuation used is at net selling value (excluding value-added tax), whether on an ex-works or delivered basis. However, the estimates presented have been adjusted to exclude customs and excise duties etc. and to include any subsidies received by the industry.

Value added is the difference between output as defined above and corresponding purchases, adjusted for changes in value of stocks of fuel and raw materials, and payments for work given out to other establishments and for repair and maintenance work. The input values exclude value-added tax. The value-added estimates are gross of payments for non-industrial services, licensing of motor vehicles and rates.

Gross fixed capital formation represents the cost incurred during the year, in the values charged to capital accounts, for new and used fixed assets less disposals. The proceeds of items disposed of exclude amounts written off for items scrapped. The value of work produced by establishments for their own use is included. Capital expenditure in respect of establishments where production had not started before the end of the year is also included, as is the value of progress payments for fixed assets on order but not completed at the end of the year. Deductible value-added tax is excluded but non-deductible value-added tax on motor cars acquired is included.

The indexes of industrial production are compiled by the Central Statistical Office and provided in response to the United Nations Questionnaire on Indexes of Industrial Production. The coverage, in principle, includes all establishments.

Related national publications:

<u>Report on the Census of Production</u> (Business Monitor series), published by the Business Statistics Office, Department of Trade and Industry, London. <u>Annual Abstract of Statistics</u>, published by the Central Statistical Office, London.

ISIC	INDUSTRY	1. NUMBER OF ESTABLISHMENTS (NUMBER) 1981	1982	1983	1984	1985	2. AVERAGE NUMBER OF PERSONS ENGAGED (THOUSANDS) 1981	1982	1983	1984	1985	ISIC
210	Coal mining	a/ 206	a/ 195	a/ 180	a/ 177	...	267	255	235	216	...	210
220	Petroleum and gas	129	161	176	203	...	25	28	29	33	...	220
230	Metal ore mining	36	34	34	15	...	1	1	1	1	...	230
290	Other mining	1089	1079	1055	717	...	21	21	13	11	...	290
2	Mining, quarrying .	1460	1469	1445	1112	...	315	305	278	261	...	2
311/2	Food products	6051	5893	5968	9450	...	525	505	489	507	...	311/2
313	Beverages	666	646	642	717	...	99	90	84	79	...	313
314	Tobacco	30	30	27	33	...	33	31	30	27	...	314
321	Textiles	5106	4822	4788	5943	...	301	276	265	266	...	321
3211	Spinning,weaving etc..	2317	2186	2137	2186	...	141	129	118	117	...	3211
322	Wearing apparel	7214	6273	6124	9178	...	239	222	214	228	...	322
323	Leather and products ...	1590	1388	1383	1524	...	29	26	25	24	...	323
324	Footwear	591	542	537	730	...	58	52	50	51	...	324
331	Wood products	6628	6441	6552	6532	...	99	97	96	86	...	331
332	Furniture, fixtures	5051	4781	4800	6054	...	110	103	100	101	...	332
341	Paper and products	1961	1937	1961	2996	...	177	164	159	158	...	341
3411	Pulp,paper etc.	212	256	255	361	...	39	35	34	33	...	3411
342	Printing,publishing	11984	11252	11362	17299	...	307	295	288	299	...	342
351	Industrial chemicals ...	1448	1463	1477	1708	...	178	165	151	151	...	351
3511	Basic excl fertilizers	796	791	800	895	...	113	112	102	103	...	3511
3513	Synthetic resins etc .	492	490	504	608	...	45	33	31	31	...	3513
352	Other chemical products.	1667	1594	1605	1900	...	174	169	164	164	...	352
3522	Drugs and medicines ..	342	327	329	385	...	70	69	68	68	...	3522
353	Petroleum refineries ...	49	47	47	42	...	17	15	14	12	...	353
354	Petroleum,coal products.	168	156	156	156	...	13	12	11	11	...	354
355	Rubber products	680	654	670	595	...	82	76	71	69	...	355
356	Plastic products n.e.c..	3202	3164	3228	4185	...	139	129	129	134	...	356
361	Pottery,china etc	558	599	607	607	...	46	41	40	43	...	361
362	Glass and products	634	607	630	706	...	46	42	41	40	...	362
369	Non-metal products n.e.c	3867	3792	3741	3162	...	134	128	128	123	...	369
371	Iron and steel	3471	3261	3150	3017	...	258	227	191	180	...	371
372	Non-ferrous metals	1125	1077	1089	1120	...	85	76	67	65	...	372
381	Metal products	11288	10976	10948	13219	...	402	378	360	349	...	381
382	Machinery n.e.c.	16629	14962	14934	21011	...	739	666	620	597	...	382
3825	Office,computing etc..	300	308	349	964	...	39	36	40	44	...	3825
383	Electrical machinery ...	5768	5594	5628	8919	...	596	557	546	560	...	383
3832	Radio,television etc..	2356	2317	2358	3397	...	278	260	258	272	...	3832
384	Transport equipment	4186	4094	4082	4144	...	746	681	627	592	...	384
3841	Shipbuilding, repair..	1240	1201	1189	1485	...	118	114	100	91	...	3841
3843	Motor vehicles	2344	2291	2285	1967	...	369	325	302	288	...	3843
385	Professional goods	2406	2352	2367	2336	...	92	90	81	80	...	385
390	Other industries	3354	3084	3060	7331	...	75	70	64	74	...	390
3	Manufacturing	107372	101481	101563	134614	...	5799	5383	5105	5070	...	3
410	Electricity,gas,steam ..	...	...	...	...	...	272	262	252	246	...	410
4101	Electricity	b/ 210	b/ 194	b/ 185	b/ 11	...	168	161	156	153	...	4101
420	Water works and supply .	101	56	63	87	...	43	50	47	45	...	420
4	Electricity,gas etc	...	...	...	...	...	315	312	299	291	...	4
2-4	All industry	...	...	...	...	...	6423	5995	5677	5622	...	2-4

a/ Colliery units or mines in active production.

b/ Number of generating stations.

ISIC	INDUSTRY	3. AVERAGE NUMBER OF EMPLOYEES (THOUSANDS)					4. WAGES AND SALARIES OF EMPLOYEES a/ (MILLION POUNDS)					ISIC
		1981	1982	1983	1984	1985	1981	1982	1983	1984	1985	
210	Coal mining	267	255	235	216	...	1915	1966	1852	896	...	210
220	Petroleum and gas	25	28	29	33	...	240	283	345	407	...	220
230	Metal ore mining	1	1	1	1	...	9	10	10	15	...	230
290	Other mining	21	20	13	11	...	139	149	102	93	...	290
2	Mining, quarrying .	314	304	278	261	...	2303	2408	2309	1411	...	2
311/2	Food products	523	503	487	506	...	2710	2864	3010	3311	...	311/2
313	Beverages	99	90	84	79	...	663	660	670	675	...	313
314	Tobacco	33	31	30	27	...	252	262	288	301	...	314
321	Textiles	299	275	264	266	...	1287	1292	1348	1469	...	321
3211	Spinning,weaving etc..	140	128	118	117	...	629	633	638	691	...	3211
322	Wearing apparel	236	220	211	228	...	810	830	855	989	...	322
323	Leather and products ...	28	26	25	24	...	127	126	130	134	...	323
324	Footwear	58	52	50	51	...	260	256	263	288	...	324
331	Wood products	96	94	92	86	...	522	560	608	593	...	331
332	Furniture, fixtures	108	101	98	100	...	610	618	661	718	...	332
341	Paper and products	176	163	159	158	...	1086	1121	1186	1276	...	341
3411	Pulp,paper etc.	39	35	34	33	...	256	259	275	286	...	3411
342	Printing,publishing	299	288	284	299	...	2171	2317	2514	2898	...	342
351	Industrial chemicals ...	178	164	151	151	...	1481	1488	1471	1549	...	351
3511	Basic excl fertilizers	112	112	102	103	...	937	1026	1007	1063	...	3511
3513	Synthetic resins etc .	45	33	31	31	...	377	288	295	302	...	3513
352	Other chemical products.	173	168	164	164	...	1126	1214	1301	1398	...	352
3522	Drugs and medicines ..	70	69	68	68	...	456	506	552	600	...	3522
353	Petroleum refineries ...	17	15	14	12	...	161	161	165	163	...	353
354	Petroleum,coal products.	13	12	11	11	...	92	97	97	79	...	354
355	Rubber products	81	76	71	69	...	477	493	522	534	...	355
356	Plastic products n.e.c..	138	128	129	134	...	774	793	871	987	...	356
361	Pottery,china etc	46	41	40	43	...	219	216	228	266	...	361
362	Glass and products	46	42	40	40	...	308	314	322	332	...	362
369	Non-metal products n.e.c	133	127	127	123	...	837	890	974	1008	...	369
371	Iron and steel	257	226	190	180	...	1680	1604	1486	1511	...	371
372	Non-ferrous metals	85	75	67	65	...	546	524	500	535	...	372
381	Metal products	396	372	357	349	...	2371	2469	2547	2705	...	381
382	Machinery n.e.c.	731	660	616	597	...	4612	4651	4662	4929	...	382
3825	Office,computing etc..	38	36	40	44	...	308	295	350	418	...	3825
383	Electrical machinery ...	594	556	545	560	...	3494	3648	3841	4328	...	383
3832	Radio,television etc..	277	260	258	271	...	1695	1779	1901	2217	...	3832
384	Transport equipment	745	680	626	592	...	4906	4915	4891	5049	...	384
3841	Shipbuilding, repair..	118	114	100	91	...	759	827	764	762	...	3841
3843	Motor vehicles	369	325	302	288	...	2397	2318	2353	2470	...	3843
385	Professional goods	91	89	80	80	...	511	568	561	590	...	385
390	Other industries	74	68	62	73	...	342	348	340	424	...	390
3	Manufacturing	5753	5342	5074	5067	...	34435	35299	36312	39039	...	3
410	Electricity,gas,steam ..	272	262	252	246	...	2219	2347	2447	2475	...	410
4101	Electricity	168	161	156	153	...	1448	1494	1570	1576	...	4101
420	Water works and supply .	43	50	47	45	...	309	386	414	429	...	420
4	Electricity,gas etc	315	312	299	291	...	2528	2733	2861	2904	...	4
2-4	All industry	6377	5953	5646	5619	...	39264	40441	41482	43353	...	2-4

a/ Excluding payments in kind.

ISIC	INDUSTRY	5. SUPPLEMENTS TO WAGES AND SALARIES (MILLION POUNDS)					6. AVERAGE NUMBER OF OPERATIVES a/ (THOUSANDS)					ISIC
		1981	1982	1983	1984	1985	1981	1982	1983	1984	1985	
210	Coal mining	648	615	688	500	...	241	230	212	194	...	210
220	Petroleum and gas	48	54	71	79	...	...	...	...	...	...	220
230	Metal ore mining	2	1	1	2	...	1	1	1	1	...	230
290	Other mining	25	28	19	16	...	17	16	10	9	...	290
2	Mining, quarrying .	723	698	779	597	...	...	...	...	...	...	2
311/2	Food products	473	490	477	500	...	414	398	387	406	...	311/2
313	Beverages	133	135	130	121	...	68	63	57	54	...	313
314	Tobacco	54	59	58	54	...	24	22	21	18	...	314
321	Textiles	208	198	190	194	...	237	218	209	212	...	321
3211	Spinning,weaving etc..	103	98	94	95	...	113	103	95	95	...	3211
322	Wearing apparel	123	119	114	125	...	198	183	177	193	...	322
323	Leather and products ...	22	20	19	18	...	23	21	20	20	...	323
324	Footwear	43	39	38	40	...	48	43	41	43	...	324
331	Wood products	88	95	93	86	...	69	68	68	63	...	331
332	Furniture, fixtures	94	95	91	95	...	82	76	74	77	...	332
341	Paper and products	196	196	195	199	...	129	119	116	115	...	341
3411	Pulp,paper etc.	47	46	46	46	...	29	26	26	24	...	3411
342	Printing,publishing	389	404	404	438	...	164	157	153	160	...	342
351	Industrial chemicals ...	339	349	342	327	...	108	99	91	90	...	351
3511	Basic excl fertilizers	223	250	247	225	...	66	66	60	59	...	3511
3513	Synthetic resins etc .	77	59	57	60	...	30	22	20	20	...	3513
352	Other chemical products.	235	242	246	262	...	92	90	87	87	...	352
3522	Drugs and medicines ..	104	111	116	123	...	36	34	34	33	...	3522
353	Petroleum refineries ...	49	48	47	40	...	12	10	9	8	...	353
354	Petroleum,coal products.	16	15	15	14	...	9	9	8	8	...	354
355	Rubber products	88	88	81	80	...	58	54	48	48	...	355
356	Plastic products n.e.c..	134	133	132	146	...	100	91	92	98	...	356
361	Pottery,china etc	39	39	38	42	...	38	34	33	36	...	361
362	Glass and products	59	57	54	53	...	34	31	30	29	...	362
369	Non-metal products n.e.c	153	159	164	158	...	96	90	90	89	...	369
371	Iron and steel	327	303	275	272	...	191	167	141	133	...	371
372	Non-ferrous metals	108	98	85	83	...	61	54	49	48	...	372
381	Metal products	401	399	388	398	...	281	262	251	247	...	381
382	Machinery n.e.c.	807	788	748	744	...	450	399	368	358	...	382
3825	Office,computing etc..	52	49	59	65	...	16	14	16	17	...	3825
383	Electrical machinery ...	583	587	584	638	...	358	330	325	333	...	383
3832	Radio,television etc..	272	276	282	318	...	154	141	142	148	...	3832
384	Transport equipment	901	867	840	809	...	514	463	420	398	...	384
3841	Shipbuilding, repair..	140	147	142	138	...	90	86	75	67	...	3841
3843	Motor vehicles	438	398	392	357	...	274	239	220	215	...	3843
385	Professional goods	97	102	92	94	...	57	55	48	48	...	385
390	Other industries	58	56	51	61	...	54	50	45	54	...	390
3	Manufacturing	6217	6180	5991	6091	...	3969	3656	3458	3474	...	3
410	Electricity,gas,steam ..	644	650	677	662	...	139	133	128	123	...	410
4101	Electricity	378	372	398	381	...	95	90	87	84	...	4101
420	Water works and supply .	67	74	80	81	...	24	26	23	23	...	420
4	Electricity,gas etc	711	724	757	743	...	163	159	151	146	...	4
2-4	All industry	7651	7602	7527	7431	...	...	...	...	...	...	2-4

a/ Employees working in ancillary departments not engaged in production (eg. transport organizations, warehouses etc.) are in genera excluded.

ISIC	INDUSTRY	7. WAGES AND SALARIES OF OPERATIVES a/ (MILLION POUNDS) 1981	1982	1983	1984	1985	8. QUANTITY OF ELECTRICITY CONSUMED b/ (BILLION KWH) 1981	1982	1983	c/ 1984	1985	ISIC
210	Coal mining	1679	1719	1605	658	...	5.8	5.8	5.7	3.9	4.9	210
220	Petroleum and gas	...	...	...	...	...						220
230	Metal ore mining	7	8	8	12	...	[1.8	1.8	1.8	2.0	2.0]	230
290	Other mining	106	113	81	73	...						290
2	Mining, quarrying .	...	...	...	...	...	7.6	7.6	7.5	5.9	7.1	2
311/2	Food products	1986	2092	2190	2439	...						311/2
313	Beverages	428	423	421	421	...	[7.1	7.0	6.1	8.4	8.6]	313
314	Tobacco	160	160	177	181	...						314
321	Textiles	930	931	979	1067	...	d/ 4.4	e/ 4.2	e/ 4.1	e/ 3.3	e/ 3.3	321
3211	Spinning,weaving etc..	467	469	474	514	...	...	...	...	...	...	3211
322	Wearing apparel	602	611	635	745	...	d/	e/	e/	e/	e/	322
323	Leather and products ...	92	91	94	98	...	[0.2]	e/	e/	e/	e/	323
324	Footwear	196	193	198	219	...		e/	e/	e/	e/	324
331	Wood products	350	377	415	402	...						331
332	Furniture, fixtures	442	442	473	520	...	[0.9	0.9]	[f/ 6.0	f/ 5.4	f/ 5.7]	332
341	Paper and products	748	766	807	859	...	4.0	g/ 5.0				341
3411	Pulp,paper etc.	186	185	194	203	...	...	...	...	...	...	3411
342	Printing,publishing	1201	1273	1357	1569	...	1.2	g/	f/	f/	f/	342
351	Industrial chemicals ...	797	798	802	822	...	h/ 17.7	h/ 17.2	h/ 16.7	h/ 17.8	h/ 18.4	351
3511	Basic excl fertilizers	491	537	534	546	...	...	...	...	...	...	3511
3513	Synthetic resins etc .	220	174	179	179	...	...	...	...	...	...	3513
352	Other chemical products.	505	539	571	612	...	h/	h/	h/	h/	h/	352
3522	Drugs and medicines ..	191	203	216	234	...	...	...	...	...	...	3522
353	Petroleum refineries ...	99	101	96	98	...	2.8	2.6	2.4	3.4	3.2	353
354	Petroleum,coal products.	63	67	65	46	...	0.1	0.1	0.1	-	-	354
355	Rubber products	312	324	320	344	...	1.3	1.3	1.4	i/	i/	355
356	Plastic products n.e.c..	511	514	566	651	...	h/	h/	h/	h/	h/	356
361	Pottery,china etc	168	165	177	208	...	[2.9	2.9	3.0]			361
362	Glass and products	217	221	225	229	...				[6.5	6.9]	362
369	Non-metal products n.e.c	577	608	670	712	...	1.9	1.8	1.9			369
371	Iron and steel	1197	1138	1051	1075	...	11.2	10.4	10.1	9.1	9.1	371
372	Non-ferrous metals	369	357	346	368	...	8.0	6.1	6.1	6.4	6.5	372
381	Metal products	1560	1622	1665	1777	...	3.4	[j/ 15.9	j/ 16.0	j/ 17.7	j/ 18.4]	381
382	Machinery n.e.c.	2566	2529	2493	2651	...	k/ 7.0					382
3825	Office,computing etc..	106	88	112	121	...	...	...	...	...	...	3825
383	Electrical machinery ...	1823	1872	1977	2193	...	k/	j/	j/	j/	j/	383
3832	Radio,television etc..	789	810	879	1000	...	...	...	...	...	...	3832
384	Transport equipment	3101	3065	2992	3116	...	6.0	j/	j/	j/	j/	384
3841	Shipbuilding, repair..	552	594	544	523	...	...	...	...	...	...	3841
3843	Motor vehicles	1628	1560	1568	1708	...	...	...	...	...	...	3843
385	Professional goods	279	296	283	303	...	[5.0	5.2	5.9	i/ 6.7	i/ 6.3]	385
390	Other industries	211	216	208	263	...						390
3	Manufacturing	21490	21791	22253	23988	...	85.1	80.6	79.8	84.7	86.4	3
410	Electricity,gas,steam ..	1028	1065	1101	1138	...	18.4	18.5	19.9	20.5	...	410
4101	Electricity	714	744	783	777	...	18.2	18.3	19.8	20.3	...	4101
420	Water works and supply .	159	179	182	198	...	3.8	4.0	4.1	4.3	...	420
4	Electricity,gas etc	1187	1244	1283	1336	...	22.2	22.5	24.0	24.8	...	4
2-4	All industry	...	...	...	...	...	114.9	110.7	111.3	113.8	...	2-4

a/ Excluding payments in kind.
b/ The estimates are compiled by the Department of Energy and are based on the national classification.
c/ Beginning 1984, data are compiled according to the 1980 edition of the UK Standard Industrial Classification, unadjusted.
d/ Major group 322 is included in 321.
e/ Major groups 322 to 324 are included in 321.
f/ Major group 342 is included in 331 to 341 combined.
g/ Major group 342 is included in 341.
h/ Major groups 352 and 356 are included in 351.
i/ Major group 355 is included in 385 and 390 combined.
j/ Major groups 383 and 384 are included in 381 and 382 combined.
k/ Major group 383 is included in 382.

ISIC	INDUSTRY	9. OUTPUT IN FACTOR VALUES (BILLION POUNDS) 1981	1982	1983	1984	1985	10. VALUE ADDED IN FACTOR VALUES (BILLION POUNDS) 1981	1982	1983	1984	1985	ISIC
210	Coal mining	4.38	4.56	4.08	1.46	...	3.40	3.47	3.09	0.97	...	210
220	Petroleum and gas	12.26	14.36	16.78	22.54	...	11.89	...	...	...	...	220
230	Metal ore mining	0.02	0.02	0.03	0.04	...	0.01	0.02	0.02	0.03	...	230
290	Other mining	0.80	0.92	0.73	0.63	...	0.56	0.66	0.54	0.44	...	290
2	Mining, quarrying .	17.46	19.86	21.62	24.67	...	15.86	...	...	...	...	2
311/2	Food products	22.88	24.74	26.42	30.32	...	7.08	7.71	8.32	8.84	...	311/2
313	Beverages	5.32	5.42	5.84	5.96	...	2.46	2.56	2.76	2.73	...	313
314	Tobacco	1.43	1.64	1.67	1.69	...	0.94	1.11	1.12	1.07	...	314
321	Textiles	5.59	5.74	6.17	6.91	...	2.35	2.35	2.59	2.82	...	321
3211	Spinning,weaving etc..	2.75	2.85	3.04	3.48	...	1.13	1.14	1.24	1.36	...	3211
322	Wearing apparel	2.90	3.03	3.17	3.67	...	1.44	1.49	1.56	1.81	...	322
323	Leather and products ...	0.64	0.65	0.71	0.80	...	0.25	0.22	0.25	0.28	...	323
324	Footwear	0.87	0.86	0.89	0.98	...	0.47	0.45	0.47	0.52	...	324
331	Wood products	2.78	3.06	3.59	3.29	...	1.01	1.12	1.36	1.17	...	331
332	Furniture, fixtures	2.31	2.43	2.63	2.89	...	1.16	1.18	1.25	1.36	...	332
341	Paper and products	5.10	5.36	5.78	6.56	...	2.17	2.20	2.44	2.68	...	341
3411	Pulp,paper etc.	1.45	1.50	1.64	1.94	...	0.48	0.48	0.55	0.62	...	3411
342	Printing,publishing	7.32	7.95	8.32	9.79	...	4.63	5.05	5.27	6.19	...	342
351	Industrial chemicals ...	11.82	12.16	14.16	16.08	...	3.74	3.79	4.68	5.41	...	351
3511	Basic excl fertilizers	7.93	8.45	9.63	10.91	...	2.49	2.58	3.09	3.69	...	3511
3513	Synthetic resins etc .	2.29	1.99	2.57	2.92	...	0.58	0.52	0.80	0.87	...	3513
352	Other chemical products.	6.84	7.52	8.21	9.16	...	3.42	3.82	4.07	4.61	...	352
3522	Drugs and medicines ..	2.64	3.05	3.27	3.67	...	1.54	1.83	1.93	2.18	...	3522
353	Petroleum refineries ...	12.34	13.19	13.76	16.09	...	1.73	1.43	1.62	1.31	...	353
354	Petroleum,coal products.	0.91	1.07	0.95	0.82	...	0.26	0.26	0.22	0.18	...	354
355	Rubber products	1.95	1.91	2.00	2.13	...	0.92	0.95	0.97	1.02	...	355
356	Plastic products n.e.c..	3.43	3.65	4.18	4.92	...	1.66	1.75	2.01	2.22	...	356
361	Pottery,china etc	0.61	0.61	0.67	0.79	...	0.40	0.40	0.45	0.53	...	361
362	Glass and products	1.11	1.13	1.17	1.33	...	0.61	0.60	0.60	0.71	...	362
369	Non-metal products n.e.c	4.52	5.15	5.88	6.04	...	2.34	2.63	3.05	3.21	...	369
371	Iron and steel	7.74	7.52	7.78	8.62	...	2.76	2.56	2.82	3.09	...	371
372	Non-ferrous metals	3.56	3.56	4.01	4.38	...	0.91	0.89	1.15	1.17	...	372
381	Metal products	9.18	10.10	10.63	11.14	...	4.49	4.92	5.24	5.35	...	381
382	Machinery n.e.c.	17.17	18.24	18.84	21.17	...	8.91	9.33	9.56	10.39	...	382
3825	Office,computing etc..	1.46	1.74	2.30	3.28	...	0.82	0.95	1.15	1.40	...	3825
383	Electrical machinery ...	13.28	14.57	16.06	18.77	...	6.75	7.47	8.03	9.28	...	383
3832	Radio,television etc..	6.46	7.17	8.20	10.06	...	3.39	3.75	4.12	4.92	...	3832
384	Transport equipment	18.43	19.21	20.62	21.49	...	7.86	8.14	8.75	9.03	...	384
3841	Shipbuilding, repair..	2.04	2.27	2.01	2.14	...	1.16	1.18	1.03	1.14	...	3841
3843	Motor vehicles	10.16	10.66	12.05	12.64	...	3.92	3.98	4.38	4.68	...	3843
385	Professional goods	1.75	2.11	2.00	2.18	...	0.94	1.14	1.12	1.23	...	385
390	Other industries	1.49	1.45	1.57	2.02	...	0.73	0.72	0.73	0.94	...	390
3	Manufacturing	173.22	184.01	197.67	219.99	...	72.39	76.24	82.46	89.15	...	3
410	Electricity,gas,steam ..	14.64	16.09	16.97	18.06	...	6.98	8.21	7.95	6.22	...	410
4101	Electricity	9.77	10.48	10.80	11.26	...	4.96	5.70	5.31	3.52	...	4101
420	Water works and supply .	1.23	1.53	1.57	1.61	...	0.98	1.24	1.28	1.27	...	420
4	Electricity,gas etc	15.87	17.62	18.54	19.67	...	7.96	9.45	9.23	7.49	...	4
2-4	All industry	206.55	221.49	237.83	264.33	...	96.21	...	...	...	...	2-4

ISIC	INDUSTRY	11. GROSS FIXED CAPITAL FORMATION TOTAL (MILLION POUNDS)					12. GROSS FIXED CAPITAL FORMATION MACHINERY AND EQUIPMENT (MILLION POUNDS)					ISIC
		1981	1982	1983	1984	1985	1981	1982	1983	1984	1985	
210	Coal mining	688	718	604	331	...	364	373	351	272	...	210
220	Petroleum and gas	2882	3081	2875	3160	...	1067	1242	1310	1163	...	220
230	Metal ore mining	1	1	2	3	...	2	-	2	3	...	230
290	Other mining	41	52	48	36	...	37	44	36	33	...	290
2	Mining, quarrying .	3612	3852	3529	3530	...	1470	1659	1699	1471	...	2
311/2	Food products	582	704	776	906	...	493	575	642	734	...	311/2
313	Beverages	263	251	236	285	...	182	179	185	219	...	313
314	Tobacco	36	61	63	64	...	37	50	57	58	...	314
321	Textiles	124	138	151	208	...	109	122	141	197	...	321
3211	Spinning,weaving etc..	63	62	79	113	...	57	58	74	107	...	3211
322	Wearing apparel	53	58	81	99	...	43	47	67	82	...	322
323	Leather and products ...	9	7	10	13	...	8	6	8	11	...	323
324	Footwear	11	17	16	20	...	8	12	13	17	...	324
331	Wood products	56	53	89	102	...	40	49	77	86	...	331
332	Furniture, fixtures	48	57	69	90	...	39	42	58	67	...	332
341	Paper and products	210	197	223	295	...	184	184	206	267	...	341
3411	Pulp,paper etc.	79	66	77	90	...	63	63	71	78	...	3411
342	Printing,publishing	252	227	273	405	...	210	200	250	358	...	342
351	Industrial chemicals ...	705	703	772	858	...	595	616	673	753	...	351
3511	Basic excl fertilizers	576	597	638	710	...	476	515	551	614	...	3511
3513	Synthetic resins etc .	97	61	67	75	...	90	58	63	73	...	3513
352	Other chemical products.	384	382	382	420	...	255	284	289	320	...	352
3522	Drugs and medicines ..	239	211	226	244	...	147	148	163	168	...	3522
353	Petroleum refineries ...	403	230	189	177	...	384	223	183	174	...	353
354	Petroleum,coal products.	19	20	17	20	...	17	19	15	16	...	354
355	Rubber products	52	50	60	74	...	46	49	57	68	...	355
356	Plastic products n.e.c..	149	154	207	291	...	130	140	181	249	...	356
361	Pottery,china etc	24	19	26	32	...	21	16	22	25	...	361
362	Glass and products	47	45	58	74	...	45	39	54	68	...	362
369	Non-metal products n.e.c	196	222	280	378	...	170	196	248	329	...	369
371	Iron and steel	244	198	239	272	...	228	195	231	255	...	371
372	Non-ferrous metals	105	81	65	76	...	82	72	55	71	...	372
381	Metal products	274	255	247	358	...	231	222	257	301	...	381
382	Machinery n.e.c.	507	520	539	661	...	401	441	452	590	...	382
3825	Office,computing etc..	62	60	101	115	...	36	42	69	97	...	3825
383	Electrical machinery ..	479	502	577	854	...	383	430	510	725	...	383
3832	Radio,television etc..	283	290	349	562	...	213	235	302	465	...	3832
384	Transport equipment	785	703	744	901	...	590	614	663	768	...	384
3841	Shipbuilding, repair..	131	66	88	131	...	53	50	56	71	...	3841
3843	Motor vehicles	474	468	498	596	...	405	419	467	552	...	3843
385	Professional goods	48	59	70	92	...	39	52	58	74	...	385
390	Other industries	40	54	40	56	...	34	40	36	49	...	390
3	Manufacturing	6105	5967	6499	8081	...	5004	5114	5688	6931	...	3
410	Electricity,gas,steam ..	2042	2687	2314	2902	...	1672	2221	2081	1981	...	410
4101	Electricity	1432	1953	1517	1766	...	1097	1538	1315	1390	...	4101
420	Water works and supply .	323	452	489	491	...	38	44	60	85	...	420
4	Electricity,gas etc	2365	3139	2803	3393	...	1710	2265	2141	2066	...	4
2-4	All industry	12082	12958	12831	15004	...	8184	9038	9529	10468	...	2-4

13. VALUE OF STOCKS AT END OF PERIOD
TOTAL
(MILLION POUNDS)

ISIC	INDUSTRY	1981	1982	1983	1984	1985	ISIC
210	Coal mining	845	879	796	751	...	210
220	Petroleum and gas	...	...	...	...	...	220
230	Metal ore mining	3	9	2	3	...	230
290	Other mining	65	71	49	38	...	290
2	Mining, quarrying .	...	...	...	...	...	2
311/2	Food products	2159	2246	2426	2552	...	311/2
313	Beverages	1922	1953	2031	2164	...	313
314	Tobacco	420	477	428	518	...	314
321	Textiles	1200	1185	1214	1349	...	321
3211	Spinning,weaving etc..	571	565	575	665	...	3211
322	Wearing apparel	597	602	628	734	...	322
323	Leather and products ...	165	141	146	149	...	323
324	Footwear	147	145	147	161	...	324
331	Wood products	567	573	684	630	...	331
332	Furniture, fixtures	380	367	359	398	...	332
341	Paper and products	784	764	821	973	...	341
3411	Pulp,paper etc.	244	236	250	295	...	3411
342	Printing,publishing	889	880	871	983	...	342
351	Industrial chemicals ...	1930	1880	2043	2203	...	351
3511	Basic excl fertilizers	1285	1306	1371	1471	...	3511
3513	Synthetic resins etc .	408	321	371	383	...	3513
352	Other chemical products.	1412	1527	1629	1805	...	352
3522	Drugs and medicines ..	655	736	810	882	...	3522
353	Petroleum refineries ...	1883	1657	1583	1726	...	353
354	Petroleum,coal products.	241	246	213	214	...	354
355	Rubber products	360	373	339	358	...	355
356	Plastic products n.e.c..	503	500	564	650	...	356
361	Pottery,china etc	147	142	138	165	...	361
362	Glass and products	216	210	200	223	...	362
369	Non-metal products n.e.c	669	686	682	724	...	369
371	Iron and steel	1679	1467	1491	1621	...	371
372	Non-ferrous metals	813	713	765	723	...	372
381	Metal products	2265	2302	2374	2620	...	381
382	Machinery n.e.c.	5301	5375	5487	5743	...	382
3825	Office,computing etc..	415	456	538	774	...	3825
383	Electrical machinery ...	3698	3757	4159	4678	...	383
3832	Radio,television etc..	1831	1836	2142	2584	...	3832
384	Transport equipment	8360	8243	8653	8920	...	384
3841	Shipbuilding, repair..	2382	2325	2396	2356	...	3841
3843	Motor vehicles	2268	2245	2549	2584	...	3843
385	Professional goods	551	610	606	638	...	385
390	Other industries	448	477	456	526	...	390
3	Manufacturing	39706	39498	41137	44148	...	3
410	Electricity,gas,steam ..	2184	2735	2753	2544	...	410
4101	Electricity	2061	2593	2610	2407	...	4101
420	Water works and supply .	-	-	-	-	...	420
4	Electricity,gas etc	2184	2735	2753	2544	...	4
2-4	All industry	...	...	...	...	...	2-4

14. INDEX NUMBERS OF INDUSTRIAL PRODUCTION (1980 = 100) a/b/

ISIC	INDUSTRY	1976	1977	1978	1979	1981	1982	1983	1984	1985	RATE c/	ISIC
210	Coal mining	...	...	97	97	97	93	90	33	66	-5.4 d/	210
220	Petroleum and gas	16	47	69	99	110	126	138	147	150	28.2	220
230	Metal ore mining	206	227	180	169	118	119	115	139	140	-4.2	230
290	Other mining	124	123	116	113	90	104	97	96	98	-2.6	290
2	Mining, quarrying	41	62	78	99	107	117	125	118	129	13.6	2
311/2	Food products	96	98	99	100	99	103	104	105	104	0.9	311/2
313	Beverages	...	...	100	103	96	96	97	99	98	-0.3 d/	313
314	Tobacco	92	91	98	97	97	91	90	90	83	-1.1	314
321	Textiles	...	...	121	118	92	90	92	94	97	-3.1 d/	321
3211	Spinning, weaving etc.	...	...	...	...	...	...	...	...	...	...	3211
322	Wearing apparel	...	...	108	111	92	94	97	104	110	0.3 d/	322
323	Leather and products	...	...	137	124	94	87	95	98	89	-6.0 d/	323
324	Footwear	110	116	115	114	88	86	87	88	91	-2.1	324
331	Wood products	...	...	[115	117	90	89	96	96	94	-2.8 d/]	331
332	Furniture, fixtures	...	...									332
341	Paper and products	...	...	110	112	93	88	90	92	91	-2.7 d/	341
3411	Pulp, paper etc.	...	...	...	...	...	...	...	...	...	...	3411
342	Printing, publishing	93	97	100	105	95	93	92	98	101	0.9	342
351	Industrial chemicals	...	...	108	112	99	96	106	113	118	1.3 d/	351
3511	Basic excl fertilizers	...	...	...	...	...	...	...	...	...	...	3511
3513	Synthetic resins etc	...	...	...	...	...	...	...	...	...	...	3513
352	Other chemical products	...	...	106	106	99	102	107	112	118	1.5 d/	352
3522	Drugs and medicines	...	...	...	...	...	...	...	...	...	...	3522
353	Petroleum refineries	110	106	110	113	93	94	96	100	100	-1.1	353
354	Petroleum, coal products	...	...	116	116	95	92	89	71	88	-3.9 d/	354
355	Rubber products	...	...	114	113	86	79	82	79	84	-4.3 d/	355
356	Plastic products n.e.c.	95	102	106	111	95	99	110	121	125	3.1	356
361	Pottery, china etc	109	121	121	113	90	82	87	92	95	-1.5	361
362	Glass and products	103	105	108	111	92	90	95	95	96	-0.8	362
369	Non-metal products n.e.c	...	...	110	110	89	90	95	95	93	-2.4 d/	369
371	Iron and steel	...	...	141	142	107	106	102	103	110	-3.5 d/	371
372	Non-ferrous metals	...	...	109	110	95	89	92	101	103	-0.8 d/	372
381	Metal products	...	...	112	114	97	101	103	105	105	-0.9 d/	381
382	Machinery n.e.c.	...	...	109	107	86	87	88	96	107	-0.3 d/	382
3825	Office, computing etc.	...	...	...	...	...	...	...	...	...	...	3825
383	Electrical machinery	...	...	104	103	94	98	105	113	116	1.6 d/	383
3832	Radio, television etc.	...	...	...	...	...	...	...	...	...	...	3832
384	Transport equipment	...	...	108	105	94	90	90	87	91	-2.4 d/	384
3841	Shipbuilding, repair	...	...	...	...	...	...	...	...	...	...	3841
3843	Motor vehicles	...	...	...	...	...	...	...	...	...	...	3843
385	Professional goods	95	98	104	103	101	94	95	101	110	1.6	385
390	Other industries	...	...	131	125	91	84	76	81	80	-6.8 d/	390
3	Manufacturing	107	109	110	110	94	94	97	101	104	-0.3	3
410	Electricity, gas, steam	89	93	96	102	99	98	100	94	104	1.7	410
4101	Electricity	...	...	...	...	...	...	...	...	...	...	4101
420	Water works and supply	95	97	100	103	98	102	102	103	104	1.0	420
4	Electricity, gas etc	90	93	97	102	99	98	100	95	104	1.6	4
2-4	All industry	95	100	103	107	96	99	102	103	108	1.4	2-4

a/ These figures do not include an adjustment to correct mixed sales and production data to true production index numbers.
b/ Consequently, they are not comparable whith the United Kingdom's 'output of the production industries' series.
c/ Annual growth rate 1976-1985. d/ Annual growth rate 1978-1985.

UNITED REPUBLIC OF TANZANIA

The information in the tables is based on the reply to the United Nations Questionnaire on General Industrial Statistics from the Bureau of Statistics, Ministry of Finance and Planning, Dar es Salaam. The concepts, definitions and classification by branches of industry are generally in accordance with United Nations standards.

The data in the tables are derived from the survey of industrial production undertaken by the Bureau of Statistics annually since 1966. The survey covers establishments with 10 or more persons engaged in mining, manufacturing and the generation, transmission and distribution of electric energy. The inquiry is conducted by mail with a follow-up by field visits. The mining sector includes the extraction of salt from sea-water, diamond mining and other mining; quarrying is not covered. Nearly 60 per cent of mining activity is attributed to either salt extraction or mica mining. For manufacturing, establishments owned by government departments or corporations of the East African Community are excluded. For electricity, all establishments included in the survey are branches of the Tanzania Electric Supply Co., Ltd. The survey of industrial production covers mainland Tanzania (former Tanganyika) only. The statistics are compiled according to the present version of ISIC.

The reference period is basically the calendar year, except in the case of gross fixed capital formation. Where only data for a financial year are available for establishments of certain industries, such data are incorporated in data for the calendar year in which the major part of the financial year falls. Estimates for gross fixed capital formation relate to the financial year ending in the reference year.

The employment data have been calculated by adding the number on all working days and dividing by the total number of working days. Wages and salaries relate to payments made in cash to employees for work done for the establishment, including overtime payments, commissions and other allowances.

Output is the sum of (a) value of products and by-products, (b) value of services or work done for others, (c) sales value of goods sold in the same condition as purchased and (d) net value of work in progress. Value added is the difference between output and industrial production costs comprising the cost of materials and supplies consumed, electricity, fuels and lubricants purchased, goods resold without further processing, work done by others and other costs for repair, maintenance and transport. Valuation of output and value added is in factor values.

Gross fixed capital formation is the total expenditure on land, buildings, machinery, equipment, vehicles and other fixed assets, including own-account construction of fixed assets, less the value of corresponding sales.

Related national publication:
<u>Survey of Industrial Production</u> (annual), published by the Bureau of Statistics, Ministry of Finance and Planning, Dar es Salaam.

ISIC	INDUSTRY	1. NUMBER OF ESTABLISHMENTS a/ (NUMBER)					2. AVERAGE NUMBER OF PERSONS ENGAGED a/ (NUMBER)					ISIC
		1981	1982	1983	1984	1985	1981	1982	1983	1984	1985	
210	Coal mining	1	1	1	...	...	...	...	...	...	...	210
220	Petroleum and gas	-	-	-	...	...	-	-	-	...	...	220
230	Metal ore mining	-	-	-	...	...	-	-	-	...	...	230
290	Other mining	27	28	29	...	...	...	...	...	...	...	290
2	Mining, quarrying .	29	29	30	...	...	4274	4333	4559	...	...	2
311/2	Food products	145	156	147	...	...	21901	25306	22194	...	...	311/2
313	Beverages	13	15	15	...	...	3032	2999	3651	...	...	313
314	Tobacco	3	3	3	...	...	3434	3190	3375	...	...	314
321	Textiles	79	80	82	...	...	33212	28266	32351	...	...	321
3211	Spinning,weaving etc..	48	46	48	...	...	24174	20902	23444	...	...	3211
322	Wearing apparel	63	63	68	...	...	4187	4207	3988	...	...	322
323	Leather and products ...	12	12	12	...	...	1829	1634	1702	...	...	323
324	Footwear	13	13	13	...	...	3335	3404	3540	...	...	324
331	Wood products	72	68	73	...	...	3378	3550	4121	...	...	331
332	Furniture, fixtures	60	60	61	...	...	2044	1939	1953	...	...	332
341	Paper and products	8	8	8	...	...	1668	1682	1649	...	...	341
3411	Pulp,paper etc.	2	2	2	...	...	632	651	624	...	...	3411
342	Printing,publishing	49	49	49	...	...	2589	2530	2529	...	...	342
351	Industrial chemicals ...	10	11	11	...	...	3451	3240	3253	...	...	351
3511	Basic excl fertilizers	5	5	5	...	...	2114	1860	1844	...	...	3511
3513	Synthetic resins etc .	-	-	-	...	...	-	-	-	...	...	3513
352	Other chemical products. b/	32	33	37	...	...	2721	2816	3022	...	...	352
3522	Drugs and medicines ..	-	-	-	...	...	-	-	-	...	...	3522
353	Petroleum refineries ... b/	...	...	...	...	...	...	...	...	...	...	353
354	Petroleum,coal products.	-	-	-	...	...	-	-	-	...	...	354
355	Rubber products	9	9	9	...	...	1368	1341	962	...	...	355
356	Plastic products n.e.c..	5	4	5	...	...	770	693	669	...	...	356
361	Pottery,china etc				...	...				...	...	361
362	Glass and products	[23	16	19]	...	...	[3714	2732	3088]	...	...	362
369	Non-metal products n.e.c				...	...				...	...	369
371	Iron and steel	[5	5	5]	...	...	[1336	1286	1293]	...	...	371
372	Non-ferrous metals				...	...				...	...	372
381	Metal products	43	38	45	...	...	3022	2747	2743	...	...	381
382	Machinery n.e.c.	15	16	15	...	...	1128	1151	1167	...	...	382
3825	Office,computing etc..	-	-	-	...	...	-	-	-	...	...	3825
383	Electrical machinery ...	7	6	10	...	...	1085	1037	1328	...	...	383
3832	Radio,television etc..	...	...	...	...	...	...	...	...	...	...	3832
384	Transport equipment	26	20	25	...	...	4911	4730	4766	...	...	384
3841	Shipbuilding, repair..	...	...	...	...	...	...	...	...	...	...	3841
3843	Motor vehicles	20	17	19	...	...	3306	3253	3161	...	...	3843
385	Professional goods	-	-	-	...	...	-	-	-	...	...	385
390	Other industries	13	15	13	...	...	840	840	887	...	...	390
3	Manufacturing	705	700	725	...	...	104955	101320	104231	...	...	3
410	Electricity,gas,steam ..	...	...	...	...	...	...	...	...	...	...	410
4101	Electricity	22	23	23	...	...	6269	7725	6587	...	...	4101
420	Water works and supply .	...	...	...	...	...	...	...	...	...	...	420
4	Electricity,gas etc	...	...	...	...	...	...	...	...	...	...	4
2-4	All industry	...	...	...	...	...	...	...	...	...	...	2-4

a/ Establishments with 10 or more persons engaged.

b/ Major group 353 is included in 352.

ISIC	INDUSTRY	3. AVERAGE NUMBER OF EMPLOYEES a/ (NUMBER)					4. WAGES AND SALARIES OF EMPLOYEES a/b/ (MILLION SCHILLINGS)					ISIC
		1981	1982	1983	1984	1985	1981	1982	1983	1984	1985	
210	Coal mining	...	...	...	...	...	...	...	...	...	...	210
220	Petroleum and gas	-	-	-	...	...	-	-	-	...	...	220
230	Metal ore mining	-	-	-	...	...	-	-	-	...	...	230
290	Other mining	...	...	...	...	...	...	...	...	...	...	290
2	Mining, quarrying .	4256	4303	4538	...	...	44.6	46.4	60.1	...	...	2
311/2	Food products	21686	25186	22080	...	...	177.6	224.5	227.8	...	...	311/2
313	Beverages	3029	2991	3641	...	...	45.4	53.0	66.3	...	...	313
314	Tobacco	3434	3190	3375	...	...	26.1	26.3	45.3	...	...	314
321	Textiles	33197	28160	32335	...	...	281.1	258.2	282.8	...	...	321
3211	Spinning,weaving etc..	24169	20899	23439	...	...	207.4	180.7	205.7	...	...	3211
322	Wearing apparel	4116	4134	3890	...	...	36.6	36.4	43.7	...	...	322
323	Leather and products ...	1823	1626	1695	...	...	22.7	24.1	28.1	...	...	323
324	Footwear	3328	3397	3533	...	...	39.3	45.3	69.5	...	...	324
331	Wood products	3325	3477	4065	...	...	31.3	33.6	38.9	...	...	331
332	Furniture, fixtures	1978	1878	1882	...	...	17.0	18.7	17.9	...	...	332
341	Paper and products	1667	1682	1648	...	...	21.1	22.9	20.0	...	...	341
3411	Pulp,paper etc.	632	521	624	...	...	8.0	9.6	6.3	...	...	3411
342	Printing,publishing	2532	2455	2455	...	...	33.7	35.1	43.5	...	...	342
351	Industrial chemicals ...	3449	3238	3251	...	...	36.7	39.8	45.3	...	...	351
3511	Basic excl fertilizers	2114	1860	1844	...	...	14.7	17.4	23.5	...	...	3511
3513	Synthetic resins etc .	-	-	-	...	...	-	-	-	...	...	3513
352	Other chemical products. c/	2698	2797	2989	...	...	53.4	55.9	60.7	...	...	352
3522	Drugs and medicines ..	-	-	-	...	...	-	-	-	...	...	3522
353	Petroleum refineries ... c/	...	...	...	...	...	...	...	...	...	...	353
354	Petroleum,coal products.	-	-	-	...	...	-	-	-	...	...	354
355	Rubber products	1358	1330	951	...	...	15.9	15.8	24.7	...	...	355
356	Plastic products n.e.c..	765	692	663	...	...	10.5	10.1	9.4	...	...	356
361	Pottery,china etc				...	...				...	...	361
362	Glass and products	[3699	2722	3081]	...	...	[33.6	25.5	52.3]	...	...	362
369	Non-metal products n.e.c				...	...				...	...	369
371	Iron and steel	[1336	1286	1293]	...	...	[18.2	18.4	15.7]	...	...	371
372	Non-ferrous metals				...	...				...	...	372
381	Metal products	2989	2713	2697	...	...	47.2	39.2	54.1	...	...	381
382	Machinery n.e.c.	1114	1140	1154	...	...	15.4	16.2	16.3	...	...	382
3825	Office,computing etc..	-	-	-	...	...	-	-	-	...	...	3825
383	Electrical machinery ...	1079	1034	1317	...	...	17.2	15.2	27.0	...	...	383
3832	Radio,television etc..	...	...	...	...	...	...	...	...	...	...	3832
384	Transport equipment	4896	4725	4756	...	...	56.0	54.7	57.8	...	...	384
3841	Shipbuilding, repair..	...	...	...	...	...	...	...	...	...	...	3841
3843	Motor vehicles	3291	3248	3151	...	...	38.6	37.9	40.3	...	...	3843
385	Professional goods	-	-	-	...	...	-	-	-	...	...	385
390	Other industries	828	818	869	...	...	10.1	10.5	12.2	...	...	390
3	Manufacturing	104326	100671	103620	...	...	1046.1	1079.4	1259.3	...	...	3
410	Electricity,gas,steam ..	...	...	...	...	...	...	...	...	...	...	410
4101	Electricity	6269	7725	6587	...	...	81.2	101.6	120.4	...	...	4101
420	Water works and supply .	...	...	...	...	...	...	...	...	...	...	420
4	Electricity,gas etc	...	...	...	...	...	...	...	...	...	...	4
2-4	All industry	...	...	...	...	...	...	...	...	...	...	2-4

a/ Establishments with 10 or more persons engaged.
b/ Excluding payments in kind.
c/ Major group 353 is included in 352.

ISIC	INDUSTRY	5. AVERAGE NUMBER OF OPERATIVES a/ (NUMBER) 1981	1982	1983	1984	1985	6. WAGES AND SALARIES OF OPERATIVES a/b/ (MILLION SCHILLINGS) 1981	1982	1983	1984	1985	ISIC
210	Coal mining	...	...	...	...	...	...	...	...	...	...	210
220	Petroleum and gas	-	-	-	...	...	-	-	-	...	...	220
230	Metal ore mining	-	-	-	...	...	-	-	-	...	...	230
290	Other mining	...	...	...	...	...	...	...	...	...	...	290
2	Mining, quarrying .	3261	3308	3452	...	...	23.4	24.3	33.2	...	...	2
311/2	Food products	15858	18475	16943	...	...	113.8	161.8	143.3	...	...	311/2
313	Beverages	1114	1110	1330	...	...	29.8	19.1	34.5	...	...	313
314	Tobacco	2352	2157	2167	...	...	16.8	15.2	27.3	...	...	314
321	Textiles	28331	23685	27733	...	...	198.9	181.0	189.3	...	...	321
3211	Spinning,weaving etc..	20218	17365	19796	...	...	147.6	126.0	136.0	...	...	3211
322	Wearing apparel	3655	3685	3478	...	...	27.5	27.5	32.3	...	...	322
323	Leather and products ...	1345	1177	1165	...	...	12.7	15.4	17.7	...	...	323
324	Footwear	2371	2346	2460	...	...	15.5	18.3	31.9	...	...	324
331	Wood products	2817	2915	3296	...	...	21.3	24.5	27.2	...	...	331
332	Furniture, fixtures	1658	1568	1572	...	...	12.6	14.2	12.6	...	...	332
341	Paper and products	1358	1359	1309	...	...	16.5	16.1	14.3	...	...	341
3411	Pulp,paper etc.	520	521	481	...	...	6.8	6.1	4.5	...	...	3411
342	Printing,publishing	1986	1908	1917	...	...	23.2	24.8	31.9	...	...	342
351	Industrial chemicals ...	2835	2736	2767	...	...	25.6	27.2	29.9	...	...	351
3511	Basic excl fertilizers	1807	1678	1681	...	...	10.8	13.3	16.6	...	...	3511
3513	Synthetic resins etc .	-	-	-	...	...	-	-	-	...	...	3513
352	Other chemical products. c/	2039	2172	2291	...	...	28.4	28.6	29.2	...	...	352
3522	Drugs and medicines ..	-	-	-	...	...	...	...	...	...	...	3522
353	Petroleum refineries ... c/	...	...	...	...	...	...	...	...	...	...	353
354	Petroleum,coal products.	-	-	-	...	...	-	-	-	...	...	354
355	Rubber products	616	594	416	...	...	6.4	6.5	5.6	...	...	355
356	Plastic products n.e.c..	489	429	384	...	...	5.7	5.4	4.9	...	...	356
361	Pottery,china etc	[		]	...	...	[		]	...	...	361
362	Glass and products	2214	1607	2381	...	...	17.8	12.3	36.5	...	...	362
369	Non-metal products n.e.c	[		]	...	...	[		]	...	...	369
371	Iron and steel	[1045	1004	1022]	...	...	[12.1	10.8	11.4]	...	...	371
372	Non-ferrous metals				...	...				...	....	372
381	Metal products	2378	2013	2112	...	...	30.9	26.1	32.5	...	...	381
382	Machinery n.e.c.	831	860	862	...	...	8.1	8.7	8.5	...	...	382
3825	Office,computing etc..	-	-	-	...	...	-	-	-	...	...	3825
383	Electrical machinery ...	841	770	945	...	...	8.4	8.8	13.1	...	...	383
3832	Radio,television etc..	...	...	...	...	...	...	...	...	...	...	3832
384	Transport equipment	3570	3486	3486	...	...	36.2	36.3	38.6	...	...	384
3841	Shipbuilding, repair..	...	...	...	...	...	...	...	...	...	...	3841
3843	Motor vehicles	2257	2246	2173	...	...	22.5	23.0	24.9	...	...	3843
385	Professional goods	-	-	-	...	...	-	-	-	...	...	385
390	Other industries	675	655	710	...	...	7.9	8.1	8.7	...	...	390
3	Manufacturing	80378	76711	80746	...	...	676.1	696.7	781.2	...	...	3
410	Electricity,gas,steam ..	...	...	...	...	...	...	...	...	...	...	410
4101	Electricity	4374	6045	4835	...	...	23.9	51.0	61.9	...	...	4101
420	Water works and supply .	...	...	...	...	...	...	...	...	...	...	420
4	Electricity,gas etc	...	...	...	...	...	...	...	...	...	...	4
2-4	All industry	...	...	...	...	...	...	...	...	...	...	2-4

a/ Establishments with 10 or more persons engaged.
c/ Major group 353 is included in 352.
b/ Excluding payments in kind.

ISIC	INDUSTRY	7. OUTPUT IN FACTOR VALUES a/ (MILLION SCHILLINGS)					8. VALUE ADDED IN FACTOR VALUES a/ (MILLION SCHILLINGS)					ISIC
		1981	1982	1983	1984	1985	1981	1982	1983	1984	1985	
210	Coal mining	...	...	...	...	...	...	...	...	...	...	210
220	Petroleum and gas	-	-	-	...	...	-	-	-	...	...	220
230	Metal ore mining	-	-	-	...	...	-	-	-	...	...	230
290	Other mining	...	...	...	...	...	...	...	...	...	...	290
2	Mining, quarrying .	388	277	322	...	...	175.1	108.1	118.5	...	...	2
311/2	Food products	2266	2306	2589	...	...	560.7	684.7	638.2	...	...	311/2
313	Beverages	465	928	878	...	...	109.4	...	186.7	...	...	313
314	Tobacco	255	250	552	...	...	104.2	102.4	278.2	...	...	314
321	Textiles	2054	1735	1991	...	...	730.0	...	648.4	...	...	321
3211	Spinning,weaving etc..	1214	901	1126	...	...	475.3	...	410.5	...	...	3211
322	Wearing apparel	424	467	480	...	...	81.4	84.2	100.9	...	...	322
323	Leather and products ...	174	176	204	...	...	37.4	52.9	44.8	...	...	323
324	Footwear	281	313	414	...	...	63.3	91.2	116.3	...	...	324
331	Wood products	207	187	211	...	...	100.1	67.4	...	...	...	331
332	Furniture, fixtures	138	137	150	...	...	45.8	32.9	38.2	...	...	332
341	Paper and products	157	174	174	...	...	66.5	65.4	70.6	...	...	341
3411	Pulp,paper etc.	36	35	45	...	...	11.4	...	14.6	...	...	3411
342	Printing,publishing	345	387	450	...	...	127.5	111.5	148.8	...	...	342
351	Industrial chemicals ...	422	363	438	...	...	88.8	144.2	156.6	...	...	351
3511	Basic excl fertilizers	87	85	170	...	...	38.2	32.0	49.4	...	...	3511
3513	Synthetic resins etc .	-	-	-	...	...	-	-	-	...	...	3513
352	Other chemical products. b/	621	666	725	...	...	229.0	261.1	232.2	...	...	352
3522	Drugs and medicines ..	-	-	-	...	...	-	-	-	...	...	3522
353	Petroleum refineries ... b/	...	...	...	...	...	...	...	...	...	...	353
354	Petroleum,coal products.	-	-	-	...	...	-	-	-	...	...	354
355	Rubber products	263	268	280	...	...	94.8	94.9	56.5	...	...	355
356	Plastic products n.e.c..	130	117	118	...	...	51.4	45.9	41.5	...	...	356
361	Pottery,china etc	[		]	...	...	[		]	...	...	361
362	Glass and products	440	311	363	...	...	129.6	137.8	178.4	...	...	362
369	Non-metal products n.e.c	]		]	...	...	]		]	...	...	369
371	Iron and steel	[370	364	376]	...	...	[100.8]	...	[111.3]	...	...	371
372	Non-ferrous metals				...	...		...		...	...	372
381	Metal products	493	549	681	...	...	137.2	166.3	214.9	...	...	381
382	Machinery n.e.c.	68	73	65	...	...	26.3	28.5	26.3	...	...	382
3825	Office,computing etc..	-	-	-	...	...	-	-	-	...	...	3825
383	Electrical machinery ...	261	217	381	...	...	34.9	52.9	57.6	...	...	383
3832	Radio,television etc..	...	...	...	...	...	...	...	...	...	...	3832
384	Transport equipment	872	936	870	...	...	162.9	216.2	199.4	...	...	384
3841	Shipbuilding, repair..	...	...	...	...	...	...	...	...	...	...	3841
3843	Motor vehicles	809	875	807	...	...	143.6	198.3	180.1	...	...	3843
385	Professional goods	-	-	-	...	...	-	-	-	...	...	385
390	Other industries	119	114	108	...	...	26.1	23.5	27.6	...	...	390
3	Manufacturing	10825	11038	12498	...	...	3108.1	c/ 2463.9	d/ 3573.4	...	...	3
410	Electricity,gas,steam ..	...	...	...	...	...	...	...	...	...	...	410
4101	Electricity	528	539	759	...	...	317.3	271.0	416.1	...	...	4101
420	Water works and supply .	...	...	...	...	...	...	...	...	...	...	420
4	Electricity,gas etc	...	...	...	...	...	...	...	...	...	...	4
2-4	All industry	...	...	...	...	...	...	...	...	...	...	2-4

a/ Establishments with 10 or more persons engaged.
b/ Major group 353 is included in 352.
c/ Excluding major groups 313, 321, 371 and 372.
d/ Excluding major group 331.

9. GROSS FIXED CAPITAL FORMATION
TOTAL a/b/
(MILLION SCHILLINGS)

ISIC	INDUSTRY	1981	1982	1983	1984	1985	ISIC
210	Coal mining	...	...	...	...	...	210
220	Petroleum and gas	-	-	-	...	...	220
230	Metal ore mining	-	-	-	...	...	230
290	Other mining	...	...	...	...	...	290
2	Mining, quarrying	4.4	4.4	12.2	...	...	2
311/2	Food products	77.4	60.0	83.9	...	...	311/2
313	Beverages	70.7	54.7	83.6	...	...	313
314	Tobacco	15.0	11.6	20.7	...	...	314
321	Textiles	124.9	96.2	138.7	...	...	321
3211	Spinning,weaving etc.	17.7	13.6	79.7	...	...	3211
322	Wearing apparel	17.1	13.2	12.3	...	...	322
323	Leather and products	8.3	6.5	4.5	...	...	323
324	Footwear	133.6	103.1	18.5	...	...	324
331	Wood products	5.1	3.8	4.3	...	...	331
332	Furniture, fixtures	5.4	3.9	12.3	...	...	332
341	Paper and products	4.7	3.6	4.6	...	...	341
3411	Pulp,paper etc.	2.6	0.1	0.4	...	...	3411
342	Printing,publishing	18.5	14.4	42.1	...	...	342
351	Industrial chemicals	1.7	1.4	18.7	...	...	351
3511	Basic excl fertilizers	6.7	5.0	6.5	...	...	3511
3513	Synthetic resins etc	-	-	-	...	...	3513
352	Other chemical products. c/	10.8	8.2	47.6	...	...	352
3522	Drugs and medicines	-	-	-	...	...	3522
353	Petroleum refineries ... c/	...	...	...	...	...	353
354	Petroleum,coal products.	-	-	-	...	...	354
355	Rubber products	5.8	4.4	19.2	...	...	355
356	Plastic products n.e.c.	8.9	6.6	2.8	...	...	356
361	Pottery,china etc	[		]	...	...	361
362	Glass and products	131.4	101.5	37.5	...	...	362
369	Non-metal products n.e.c				...	...	369
371	Iron and steel	[53.1	40.9	2.7]	...	...	371
372	Non-ferrous metals				...	...	372
381	Metal products	39.9	30.7	13.7	...	...	381
382	Machinery n.e.c.	16.9	13.1	12.5	...	...	382
3825	Office,computing etc.	-	-	-	...	...	3825
383	Electrical machinery	28.4	21.9	15.8	...	...	383
3832	Radio,television etc.	...	...	...	...	...	3832
384	Transport equipment	79.2	61.4	85.8	...	...	384
3841	Shipbuilding, repair.	...	...	...	...	...	3841
3843	Motor vehicles	17.6	13.8	24.3	...	...	3843
385	Professional goods	-	-	-	...	...	385
390	Other industries	1.9	1.3	1.7	...	...	390
3	Manufacturing	858.7	662.4	683.5	...	...	3
410	Electricity,gas,steam	...	...	...	...	...	410
4101	Electricity	995.3	65.8	346.8	...	...	4101
420	Water works and supply	...	...	...	...	...	420
4	Electricity,gas etc	...	...	...	...	...	4
2-4	All industry	...	...	...	...	...	2-4

a/ Data relate to the financial year ending in the year indicated.
b/ Establishments with 10 or more persons engaged.
c/ Major group 353 is included in 352.

UNITED STATES OF AMERICA

The information on industrial activity is based on the reply to the United Nations Questionnaire on General Indusrial Statistics from the Statistical Policy Office, Office of Information and Regulatory Affairs, in the Office of Management and Budget, Washington, D.C. The concepts, definitions and classification by branches of industry are generally in accordance with United Nations standards.

The estimates for mining are derived from the 1982 quinquennial census of mineral industries. The census covers all mining establishments with one or more paid employees. The estimates for manufacturing are derived from the quinquennial census of manufactures and annual survey of manufactures carried out by the Bureau of the Census. The quinquennial census covers years ending in 2 and 7 and covers all establishments with at least one employee. The annual survey uses a sample of approximately 55,000 establishments, representing a coverage of about two-thirds of total manufacturing employment in the United States. The annual survey and census exclude establishments which are owned and operated by the Government. Privately operated government establishments are included. In most industries, the administrative records were used for establishments with fewer than 5 employees. However, the size criteria varied by industry, and in a few industries, these records were used for all establishments with fewer than 20 employees. Data for electricity, gas and water supply (including sanitary services) are primarily based on statistics for privately owned utilities, compiled by regulatory agencies. These are the basic source materials used to prepare gross product originating estimates for this industry by the Bureau of Economic Analysis. That agency also conducts a plant and equipment expenditure survey which includes data for the above industry.

The national classification system defines an industry as a number of establishments producing a single product or a closely related group of products. An establishment is classified in a particular industry if its production of this product or product group exceeds in value its production of any other product group. In a few instances, the industry classification of an establishment is determined not only by its product group but also by the processes employed in making the product.

The estimates shown in the tables are based on the 1972 and 1977 supplement of the national industrial classification (SIC). They have been adjusted to the present version of ISIC at the 4-digit level of the national scheme. It should be noted that the following activities are excluded from the national concept of manufacturing: small-scale processing activities carried on as a secondary activity in agriculture; custom work to the individual order of household consumers (custom tailoring, woodworking, making of orthopaedic appliances etc.); some repair activities (reupholstery and furniture repair, tyre retreading etc.) and repair shops of railroads; production of coke for own use by public utility companies; manufacturing by retail establishments selling most of their products on premise to household consumers (bakeries, ice cream stores etc.); and manufacturing by construction contractors at the site (for example, production of paving materials).

The employment estimates for manufacturing refer to the average number of all full-time and part-time employees on the pay-rolls of operating establishments. The annual figure is an average of four quarterly observations for production workers, based on the 12th of March, May, August and November, plus the March 12th figure for all other employees. Estimates covering electricity, gas and water are averages of 12 monthly figures.

Wages and salaries are the gross earnings paid during the year, including dismissal pay, paid bonuses, vacation and sick-leave pay, and the cash equivalent of compensation paid in kind. Supplements to wages and salaries comprise (a) legally required expenditures, primarily employers' contributions to Federal old age and survivors' insurance, unemployment compensation and workmen's compensation, and (b) payments for voluntary programmes. The latter include all programmes not specifically required by legislation and cover the employer portion of such plans as insurance premiums, supplemental accident and sickness insurance and unemployment compensation, pension welfare, stock purchase and deferred profit-sharing plans. Excluded are such items as company-operated cafeterias, in-plant medical services, free parking lots, discounts on employee purchases, uniforms and work clothing for employees.

The estimates of output relate to the value of shipments, comprising the value of all products of the establishments, the value of goods shipped in the same condition as received and receipts for industrial work done on materials owned by others or industrial services rendered to others. The estimates for manufacturing are adjusted for changes in inventories but the relatively minor value of fixed assets produced in the plant is not included although activities relating to this item are covered in the data on employees, wages and salaries and gross fixed capital formation. The value of goods shipped is at net selling value f.o.b. plant after discounts and allowances. Freight charges, and excise and sales taxes are excluded.

Value added for manufacturing is calculated as the difference between output and the value of input on a consumed basis, comprising the costs of materials and supplies, goods shipped in the same condition as received, contract and commission work done by others, repair and maintenance work done by others and chargeable to current account, fuels and electricity purchased.

Gross fixed capital formation relates to expenditure on new plant and equipment only, including major alterations and capitalized repairs and improvements. For manufacturing, expenditures at plants not yet in operation are included. Land on which the structure site is not to be included, although the capitalized site improvements, such as roads, tracks, parking lots, fences and utilities are included.

The estimates of value of stocks are aggregates of establishment data. Prior to 1982, respondents are permitted to value inventories using any generally accepted accounting method (FIFO, LIFO, market, etc.). Beginning with the 1982 Census of Manufactures, respondents are required to report their inventories at cost or market value. As a result, the 1982 data for inventories, value added and output by manufacture are not fully comparable with those for previous years.

The indexes of industrial production are compiled by the Board of Governors of the Federal Reserve System. The indexes are compiled according to the national industrial classification which is generally comparable to the present version of ISIC.

Related national publications:

1982 Census of Manufactures; Annual Survey of Manufactures; Statistical Abstract of the United States (annual), all published by the Bureau of the Census, U.S. Department of Commerce, Washington, D.C. Federal Reserve Bulletin, published by the Board of Governors, Federal Reserve System, Washington, D.C.

UNITED STATES OF AMERICA

ISIC	INDUSTRY	1. NUMBER OF ESTABLISHMENTS (NUMBER)					2. AVERAGE NUMBER OF EMPLOYEES a/ (THOUSANDS)					ISIC
		1981	1982	1983	1984	1985	1981	1982	1983	1984	1985	
210	Coal mining	...	4665	...	...	...	...	244	...	...	...	210
220	Petroleum and gas	...	28351	...	...	...	...	278	...	...	...	220
230	Metal ore mining	...	1121	...	...	...	...	66	...	...	...	230
290	Other mining	...	5579	...	...	...	...	108	...	...	...	290
2	Mining, quarrying .	...	39716	...	...	...	...	696	...	...	...	2
311/2	Food products	...	19889	...	...	...	1323	1305	1268	1263	1249	311/2
313	Beverages	...	2241	...	...	...	188	183	178	174	171	313
314	Tobacco	...	163	...	...	...	61	58	55	52	49	314
321	Textiles	...	13259	...	...	...	951	897	905	895	840	321
3211	Spinning,weaving etc..	...	2803	...	...	...	475	427	422	411	376	3211
322	Wearing apparel	...	17876	...	...	...	1097	1019	1036	978	887	322
323	Leather and products ...	...	1727	...	...	...	79	68	66	59	52	323
324	Footwear	...	912	...	...	...	143	128	120	107	92	324
331	Wood products	...	18147	...	...	...	478	419	454	462	446	331
332	Furniture, fixtures	...	11691	...	...	...	419	387	397	431	423	332
341	Paper and products	...	6381	...	...	...	636	606	605	613	604	341
3411	Pulp,paper etc.	...	1168	...	...	...	257	248	242	248	248	3411
342	Printing,publishing	...	53406	...	...	...	1270	1292	1301	1325	1360	342
351	Industrial chemicals ...	...	4067	...	...	...	464	443	422	413	401	351
3511	Basic excl fertilizers	...	2334	...	...	...	261	251	242	235	228	3511
3513	Synthetic resins etc .	...	606	...	...	...	147	141	134	132	128	3513
352	Other chemical products.	...	7974	...	...	...	459	464	465	467	466	352
3522	Drugs and medicines ..	...	1281	...	...	...	170	166	168	167	164	3522
353	Petroleum refineries ...	...	433	...	...	...	109	108	104	95	86	353
354	Petroleum,coal products.	...	1889	...	...	...	43	43	43	43	42	354
355	Rubber products	...	1796	...	...	...	222	203	198	203	201	355
356	Plastic products n.e.c..	...	11653	...	...	...	469	479	486	528	541	356
361	Pottery,china etc	...	910	...	...	...	40	37	37	37	34	361
362	Glass and products	...	1865	...	...	...	166	153	151	145	138	362
369	Non-metal products n.e.c	...	13770	...	...	...	384	341	337	351	348	369
371	Iron and steel	...	3582	...	...	...	724	558	480	505	449	371
372	Non-ferrous metals	...	3172	...	...	...	286	245	239	249	244	372
381	Metal products	...	35686	...	...	...	1469	1366	1329	1374	1360	381
382	Machinery n.e.c.	...	53331	...	...	...	2484	2287	2095	2157	2093	382
3825	Office,computing etc..	...	2169	...	...	...	387	404	421	428	407	3825
383	Electrical machinery ...	...	16727	...	...	...	1983	1946	1920	2058	2030	383
3832	Radio,television etc..	...	9470	...	...	...	1198	1230	1231	1330	1334	3832
384	Transport equipment	...	10583	...	...	...	1877	1711	1742	1849	1899	384
3841	Shipbuilding, repair..	...	2566	...	...	...	220	205	180	179	175	3841
3843	Motor vehicles	...	4535	...	...	...	791	706	755	865	871	3843
385	Professional goods	...	8045	...	...	...	611	624	608	612	604	385
390	Other industries	...	15553	...	...	...	397	367	358	340	313	390
3	Manufacturing	...	336728	...	...	...	18832	17737	17399	17785	17422	3
410	Electricity,gas,steam ..	...	...	...	...	...	...	...	...	...	...	410
4101	Electricity	...	...	...	...	...	...	...	...	...	...	4101
420	Water works and supply .	...	...	...	...	...	...	...	...	...	...	420
4	Electricity,gas etc b/	...	...	...	...	...	849	...	...	...	...	4
2-4	All industry	...	...	...	...	...	...	...	...	...	...	2-4

a/ Manufacturing: excluding central administrative offices and auxiliary units.
b/ Including sanitary services.

ISIC	INDUSTRY	3. WAGES AND SALARIES OF EMPLOYEES a/ (BILLION DOLLARS)					4. SUPPLEMENTS TO WAGES AND SALARIES a/ (BILLION DOLLARS)					ISIC
		1981	1982	1983	1984	1985	1981	1982	1983	1984	1985	
210	Coal mining	...	6.64	...	...	...	...	2.73	...	...	...	210
220	Petroleum and gas	...	8.49	...	...	...	...	1.24	...	...	...	220
230	Metal ore mining	...	1.80	...	...	...	...	0.50	...	...	...	230
290	Other mining	...	2.24	...	...	...	...	0.48	...	...	...	290
2	Mining, quarrying .	...	19.17	...	...	...	...	4.95	...	...	...	2
311/2	Food products	20.96	22.08	22.49	23.17	23.77	4.60	5.07	5.26	5.59	5.73	311/2
313	Beverages	3.73	4.01	4.11	4.18	4.31	0.78	0.89	0.91	0.97	0.99	313
314	Tobacco	1.22	1.32	1.35	1.35	1.37	0.38	0.42	0.45	0.45	0.45	314
321	Textiles	11.63	11.28	12.46	12.90	12.77	2.05	2.10	2.32	2.45	2.44	321
3211	Spinning,weaving etc..	5.95	5.48	6.08	6.07	5.79	1.01	1.00	1.11	1.14	1.09	3211
322	Wearing apparel	9.90	10.05	10.65	10.37	9.86	1.45	1.55	1.71	1.70	1.64	322
323	Leather and products ...	0.90	0.85	0.88	0.81	0.76	0.16	0.15	0.16	0.16	0.15	323
324	Footwear	1.42	1.33	1.31	1.20	1.07	0.25	0.25	0.25	0.25	0.22	324
331	Wood products	6.62	6.15	7.06	7.54	7.67	1.36	1.32	1.51	1.63	1.66	331
332	Furniture, fixtures	5.18	5.09	5.58	6.35	6.54	0.88	0.90	1.02	1.16	1.25	332
341	Paper and products	12.64	12.95	13.79	14.88	15.35	2.75	2.88	3.16	3.36	3.44	341
3411	Pulp,paper etc.	6.13	6.35	6.72	7.31	7.64	1.39	1.42	1.56	1.67	1.72	3411
342	Printing,publishing	20.61	22.71	24.21	26.23	28.17	3.49	3.98	4.32	4.68	5.06	342
351	Industrial chemicals ...	11.05	11.41	11.55	12.15	12.36	2.79	2.90	3.00	3.12	2.87	351
3511	Basic excl fertilizers	6.54	6.80	6.94	7.22	7.30	1.69	1.76	1.80	1.90	1.74	3511
3513	Synthetic resins etc .	3.35	3.45	3.54	3.77	3.86	0.86	0.88	0.96	0.95	0.87	3513
352	Other chemical products.	9.25	10.15	10.66	11.41	11.99	2.04	2.31	2.46	2.64	2.70	352
3522	Drugs and medicines ..	3.71	3.97	4.23	4.47	4.71	0.79	0.88	0.96	1.01	1.04	3522
353	Petroleum refineries ...	3.19	3.40	3.44	3.33	3.07	0.86	0.92	0.93	0.91	0.78	353
354	Petroleum,coal products.	0.89	0.94	0.97	1.05	1.06	0.19	0.20	0.21	0.24	0.24	354
355	Rubber products	4.17	4.01	4.21	4.66	4.71	1.10	1.11	1.19	1.27	1.33	355
356	Plastic products n.e.c..	6.88	7.59	8.10	9.34	10.01	1.41	1.63	1.77	2.04	2.14	356
361	Pottery,china etc	0.61	0.60	0.62	0.65	0.65	0.14	0.14	0.16	0.17	0.16	361
362	Glass and products	3.17	3.14	3.27	3.32	3.30	0.87	0.87	0.91	0.90	0.92	362
369	Non-metal products n.e.c	6.80	6.36	6.63	7.25	7.52	1.41	1.43	1.48	1.58	1.61	369
371	Iron and steel	18.27	14.12	12.53	13.66	12.72	5.55	5.13	4.82	4.55	4.43	371
372	Non-ferrous metals	6.30	5.66	5.80	6.31	6.22	1.67	1.63	1.70	1.80	1.75	372
381	Metal products	25.53	25.36	25.63	27.87	28.79	5.50	5.79	5.91	6.31	6.50	381
382	Machinery n.e.c.	50.42	48.86	47.33	52.42	53.18	10.73	11.31	10.94	11.84	11.88	382
3825	Office,computing etc..	8.24	9.44	10.62	11.89	12.09	1.56	1.90	2.14	2.36	2.38	3825
383	Electrical machinery ...	36.72	39.27	41.92	47.64	49.32	8.09	9.07	9.76	11.12	11.35	383
3832	Radio,television etc..	23.05	25.97	28.37	32.38	34.05	4.90	5.73	6.34	7.24	7.48	3832
384	Transport equipment	45.08	43.25	47.61	53.90	58.57	12.99	13.10	13.87	15.13	16.11	384
3841	Shipbuilding, repair..	4.33	4.33	3.93	4.10	4.10	1.00	1.05	0.95	1.00	1.00	3841
3843	Motor vehicles	19.42	17.69	21.00	25.60	27.51	6.57	6.39	6.89	7.86	8.13	3843
385	Professional goods	11.56	12.88	13.47	14.32	14.67	2.33	2.65	2.82	3.03	3.01	385
390	Other industries	5.37	5.39	5.38	5.55	5.41	0.94	1.04	1.05	1.07	1.04	390
3	Manufacturing	340.07	340.21	353.01	383.81	395.19	76.76	80.74	84.05	90.12	91.85	3
410	Electricity,gas,steam ..	...	...	...	...	...	...	...	...	...	...	410
4101	Electricity	...	...	...	...	...	...	...	...	...	...	4101
420	Water works and supply .	...	...	...	...	...	...	...	...	...	...	420
4	Electricity,gas etc b/	19.69	...	...	...	...	4.75	...	...	...	...	4
2-4	All industry	...	...	...	...	...	...	...	...	...	...	2-4

a/ Manufacturing: excluding central administrative offices and auxiliary units.
b/ Including sanitary services.

ISIC	INDUSTRY	5. AVERAGE NUMBER OF OPERATIVES (THOUSANDS)					6. WAGES AND SALARIES OF OPERATIVES (BILLION DOLLARS)					ISIC
		1981	1982	1983	1984	1985	1981	1982	1983	1984	1985	
210	Coal mining	...	195	...	...	...	...	5.11	...	...	...	210
220	Petroleum and gas	...	114	...	...	...	...	3.05	...	...	...	220
230	Metal ore mining	...	45	...	...	...	...	1.18	...	...	...	230
290	Other mining	...	79	...	...	...	...	1.50	...	...	....	290
2	Mining, quarrying .	...	433	...	...	...	...	10.84	...	...	...	2
311/2	Food products	978	958	927	926	912	13.93	14.55	14.70	15.08	15.41	311/2
313	Beverages	91	89	86	83	80	1.78	1.89	1.94	1.98	2.01	313
314	Tobacco	49	45	42	39	37	0.89	0.96	0.96	0.93	0.94	314
321	Textiles	815	762	773	764	713	8.89	8.55	9.54	9.81	9.62	321
3211	Spinning,weaving etc..	417	373	370	361	328	4.78	4.36	4.89	4.84	4.59	3211
322	Wearing apparel	951	871	871	832	764	7.39	7.33	7.66	7.47	7.14	322
323	Leather and products ...	66	55	53	48	41	0.63	0.57	0.57	0.54	0.50	323
324	Footwear	126	113	106	94	80	1.11	1.03	1.01	0.92	0.82	324
331	Wood products	401	349	383	390	375	4.99	4.67	5.41	5.71	5.77	331
332	Furniture, fixtures	343	316	327	355	346	3.67	3.61	3.98	4.50	4.62	332
341	Paper and products	487	461	460	468	462	8.82	9.04	9.71	10.52	10.78	341
3411	Pulp,paper etc.	196	188	184	188	187	4.47	4.61	4.93	5.37	5.54	3411
342	Printing,publishing	720	711	723	733	742	10.45	11.31	12.05	12.92	13.55	342
351	Industrial chemicals ...	293	272	261	255	246	6.28	6.33	6.48	6.79	6.82	351
3511	Basic excl fertilizers	156	146	141	137	131	3.56	3.63	3.72	3.86	3.83	3511
3513	Synthetic resins etc .	101	94	91	90	87	2.05	2.05	2.15	2.28	2.32	3513
352	Other chemical products.	260	259	259	260	259	4.28	4.62	4.85	5.17	5.43	352
3522	Drugs and medicines ..	86	84	84	82	79	1.47	1.56	1.62	1.65	1.74	3522
353	Petroleum refineries ...	73	71	67	61	56	2.01	2.06	2.15	2.03	1.92	353
354	Petroleum,coal products.	28	29	28	29	28	0.51	0.56	0.58	0.62	0.61	354
355	Rubber products	172	154	152	157	154	2.94	2.76	2.93	3.30	3.26	355
356	Plastic products n.e.c..	370	368	376	416	424	4.45	4.93	5.30	6.14	6.53	356
361	Pottery,china etc	33	31	31	30	27	0.45	0.44	0.46	0.47	0.47	361
362	Glass and products	136	125	124	120	113	2.45	2.42	2.54	2.58	2.58	362
369	Non-metal products n.e.c	294	253	254	266	264	4.66	4.31	4.51	4.98	5.15	369
371	Iron and steel	567	416	364	391	347	13.60	10.00	8.96	9.98	9.30	371
372	Non-ferrous metals	221	184	182	192	186	4.47	3.92	4.06	4.49	4.36	372
381	Metal products	1111	1006	985	1033	1018	17.01	16.45	16.68	18.25	18.78	381
382	Machinery n.e.c.	1644	1431	1312	1379	1315	29.09	26.40	25.09	28.39	28.07	382
3825	Office,computing etc..	171	173	185	183	156	2.62	2.88	3.31	3.51	3.17	3825
383	Electrical machinery ...	1286	1215	1198	1296	1241	19.44	19.63	20.62	23.74	23.93	383
3832	Radio,television etc..	718	709	703	768	742	10.84	11.56	12.30	14.21	14.47	3832
384	Transport equipment	1291	1156	1181	1281	1302	28.21	26.31	29.34	33.70	36.41	384
3841	Shipbuilding, repair..	175	161	139	141	135	3.21	3.19	2.77	2.88	2.83	3841
3843	Motor vehicles	637	560	611	708	713	14.92	13.31	16.24	20.05	21.69	3843
385	Professional goods	368	363	348	358	348	5.54	5.92	6.10	6.53	6.69	385
390	Other industries	295	269	267	251	228	3.27	3.24	3.21	3.32	3.19	390
3	Manufacturing	13469	12332	12140	12507	12108	211.21	203.81	211.39	230.86	234.66	3
410	Electricity,gas,steam ..	...	...	...	...	...	...	...	...	...	...	410
4101	Electricity	...	...	...	...	...	...	...	...	...	...	4101
420	Water works and supply .	...	...	...	...	...	...	...	...	...	...	420
4	Electricity,gas etc	...	...	...	...	...	...	...	...	...	...	4
2-4	All industry	...	...	...	...	...	...	...	...	...	...	2-4

ISIC	INDUSTRY	7. HOURS WORKED BY OPERATIVES (MILLIONS) 1981	1982	1983	1984	1985	8. OUTPUT a/b/ (BILLION DOLLARS) 1981	c/ 1982	1983	1984	1985	ISIC
210	Coal mining	...	375	...	...	...	...	28.0	...	...	...	210
220	Petroleum and gas	...	238	...	...	...	...	176.0	...	...	...	220
230	Metal ore mining	...	84	...	...	...	...	5.2	...	...	...	230
290	Other mining	...	161	...	...	...	...	9.0	...	...	...	290
2	Mining, quarrying .	...	858	...	...	...	...	218.2	...	...	...	2
311/2	Food products	1934	1857	1818	1812	1777	240.1	246.0	251.3	263.4	263.0	311/2
313	Beverages	181	176	172	165	161	32.3	34.6	36.2	36.7	38.4	313
314	Tobacco	91	84	78	73	68	13.1	16.1	16.3	17.5	18.5	314
321	Textiles	1589	1427	1514	1486	1387	60.8	58.2	66.2	69.7	67.3	321
3211	Spinning,weaving etc..	829	705	745	712	644	29.8	26.9	30.8	31.2	29.1	3211
322	Wearing apparel	1690	1549	1562	1462	1310	40.9	43.1	44.4	45.2	43.7	322
323	Leather and products ...	111	101	97	89	77	4.3	3.9	4.1	4.0	3.6	323
324	Footwear	228	197	189	165	143	6.1	5.6	5.6	5.2	4.7	324
331	Wood products	773	657	745	759	736	33.2	29.4	36.3	39.1	39.2	331
332	Furniture, fixtures	656	584	621	688	664	20.3	19.5	22.1	25.0	25.5	332
341	Paper and products	994	923	934	961	944	80.7	80.0	84.3	95.4	93.4	341
3411	Pulp,paper etc.	408	386	384	397	392	40.5	39.6	41.4	48.0	46.1	3411
342	Printing,publishing	1343	1313	1339	1379	1384	77.5	85.8	93.1	104.0	112.2	342
351	Industrial chemicals ...	597	542	521	519	500	113.6	97.8	105.7	116.2	109.9	351
3511	Basic excl fertilizers	320	295	284	279	269	66.0	55.1	59.0	64.6	61.7	3511
3513	Synthetic resins etc .	199	183	179	181	174	31.0	28.2	33.1	35.7	33.4	3513
352	Other chemical products.	509	505	507	507	506	70.8	74.6	80.5	86.8	91.0	352
3522	Drugs and medicines ..	167	163	160	153	151	22.4	24.7	27.6	29.2	31.5	3522
353	Petroleum refineries ...	152	148	141	132	120	215.4	197.8	181.3	177.6	167.0	353
354	Petroleum,coal products.	57	57	59	60	58	9.1	9.5	10.1	11.4	11.7	354
355	Rubber products	332	291	296	313	301	19.3	18.2	19.8	21.9	21.6	355
356	Plastic products n.e.c..	717	705	740	826	837	34.4	36.9	40.3	48.1	49.8	356
361	Pottery,china etc	63	56	57	58	52	1.8	1.8	1.9	2.1	2.0	361
362	Glass and products	263	243	244	234	225	12.8	12.6	13.2	13.6	13.9	362
369	Non-metal products n.e.c	585	497	510	538	535	33.8	30.7	33.8	37.9	39.2	369
371	Iron and steel	1085	740	687	767	687	87.5	57.0	56.6	65.8	60.9	371
372	Non-ferrous metals	435	351	354	385	370	49.2	38.5	43.4	45.8	40.1	372
381	Metal products	2201	1944	1933	2047	2014	114.6	109.6	111.7	123.2	125.4	381
382	Machinery n.e.c.	3240	2729	2527	2715	2580	211.4	194.8	187.8	225.6	224.6	382
3825	Office,computing etc..	329	337	367	362	307	38.3	43.3	48.5	61.6	61.2	3825
383	Electrical machinery ...	2481	2307	2306	2525	2396	147.0	152.4	162.8	195.0	196.1	383
3832	Radio,television etc..	1379	1358	1362	1502	1432	84.0	93.6	101.5	123.1	124.4	3832
384	Transport equipment	2518	2237	2380	2676	2666	218.0	214.6	256.6	300.6	318.3	384
3841	Shipbuilding, repair..	351	319	269	277	263	13.3	13.3	12.2	13.1	12.8	3841
3843	Motor vehicles	1223	1068	1259	1529	1490	125.7	120.7	159.4	193.9	203.3	3843
385	Professional goods	717	696	671	698	676	48.8	51.6	53.7	60.0	61.3	385
390	Other industries	556	500	492	474	430	25.8	25.6	24.8	26.2	24.7	390
3	Manufacturing	26098	23416	23494	24513	23604	2022.6	1946.2	2043.9	2263.0	2266.9	3
410	Electricity,gas,steam .. d/e/	...	...	...	...	...	203.2	...	...	...	...	410
4101	Electricity .... e/	...	...	...	...	...	101.0	...	...	...	...	4101
420	Water works and supply .	...	...	...	...	...	...	...	...	...	...	420
4	Electricity,gas etc	...	...	...	...	...	...	...	...	...	...	4
2-4	All industry	...	...	...	...	...	...	...	...	...	...	2-4

a/ Manufacturing: in factor values. Electricity and gas: in producers' prices.
b/ Electricity and gas: value of sales.
c/ Beginning 1982, data are not fully comparable with those for previous years owing to the change in valuation of inventories.
d/ Excluding steam.
e/ Privately owned utility companies.

ISIC	INDUSTRY	9. VALUE ADDED IN FACTOR VALUES a/ (BILLION DOLLARS)					10. GROSS FIXED CAPITAL FORMATION TOTAL b/ (BILLION DOLLARS)					ISIC
		1981	c/ 1982	1983	1984	1985	1981	1982	1983	1984	1985	
210	Coal mining	...	1.82	...	...	...	...	3.16	...	...	...	210
220	Petroleum and gas	...	13.49	...	...	...	...	35.41	...	...	...	220
230	Metal ore mining	...	0.31	...	...	...	...	1.13	...	...	...	230
290	Other mining	...	0.62	...	...	...	...	1.15	...	...	...	290
2	Mining, quarrying .	...	16.24	...	...	...	...	40.85	...	...	...	2
311/2	Food products	68.05	74.41	78.24	82.57	87.96	4.58	5.16	4.29	4.98	5.78	311/2
313	Beverages	12.76	14.01	15.25	15.46	16.16	1.43	1.57	1.52	1.45	1.27	313
314	Tobacco	6.43	8.96	9.78	10.79	11.89	0.73	0.70	0.65	0.67	0.67	314
321	Textiles	24.02	23.39	26.88	28.30	26.91	1.89	1.76	1.79	2.30	2.14	321
3211	Spinning,weaving etc..	11.68	10.39	12.03	12.30	11.47	1.22	1.16	1.19	1.41	1.28	3211
322	Wearing apparel	21.48	21.63	22.45	23.25	22.15	0.50	0.50	0.43	0.52	0.45	322
323	Leather and products ...	1.95	1.74	1.79	1.71	1.57	0.09	0.06	0.06	0.05	0.05	323
324	Footwear	3.21	2.96	2.99	2.73	2.47	0.11	0.07	0.06	0.07	0.06	324
331	Wood products	12.47	10.92	14.15	15.38	15.39	1.33	1.04	0.86	1.25	1.20	331
332	Furniture, fixtures	10.64	10.29	11.70	12.88	13.25	0.45	0.42	0.41	0.55	0.56	332
341	Paper and products	32.35	33.38	35.43	40.88	40.39	5.36	5.10	4.35	5.30	6.28	341
3411	Pulp,paper etc.	16.37	16.30	17.37	20.94	19.74	3.61	4.02	3.24	3.91	4.58	3411
342	Printing,publishing	49.35	54.42	60.06	67.02	73.05	3.08	3.21	3.24	3.99	4.72	342
351	Industrial chemicals ...	41.94	35.67	41.22	46.00	43.36	7.13	6.45	4.69	4.77	5.20	351
3511	Basic excl fertilizers	25.50	21.17	23.72	26.41	26.03	4.39	4.07	3.20	2.89	3.06	3511
3513	Synthetic resins etc .	10.23	9.40	12.40	13.68	12.20	1.61	1.68	1.16	1.43	1.63	3513
352	Other chemical products.	39.33	43.29	47.17	50.79	54.28	2.40	2.72	2.57	2.98	3.06	352
3522	Drugs and medicines ..	14.88	16.98	19.37	20.57	22.72	1.05	1.25	1.19	1.43	1.47	3522
353	Petroleum refineries ...	24.02	19.25	17.88	12.74	13.89	4.94	6.32	4.32	3.49	3.04	353
354	Petroleum,coal products.	2.58	2.82	3.16	3.41	3.45	0.22	0.26	0.26	0.28	0.40	354
355	Rubber products	9.60	9.28	10.41	10.93	10.97	0.66	0.57	0.49	0.67	0.87	355
356	Plastic products n.e.c..	16.37	17.94	19.40	23.25	24.74	1.56	1.63	1.29	2.13	2.56	356
361	Pottery,china etc	1.20	1.17	1.30	1.37	1.30	0.07	0.08	0.07	0.06	0.09	361
362	Glass and products	7.12	6.81	7.28	7.34	7.66	0.66	0.75	0.54	0.58	0.84	362
369	Non-metal products n.e.c	16.54	15.00	16.74	18.99	19.88	1.86	1.48	1.14	1.73	1.84	369
371	Iron and steel	33.53	21.49	21.84	26.88	24.07	4.35	3.10	2.61	2.45	2.86	371
372	Non-ferrous metals	14.02	9.85	12.06	12.72	11.44	1.83	1.47	1.60	1.53	1.65	372
381	Metal products	56.21	54.19	55.29	60.61	61.81	3.63	3.07	2.61	3.33	3.59	381
382	Machinery n.e.c.	114.86	106.20	100.15	117.83	115.55	9.01	8.76	6.61	8.28	8.55	382
3825	Office,computing etc..	21.17	23.39	24.47	29.27	27.33	2.35	2.65	2.61	3.39	3.43	3825
383	Electrical machinery ...	81.52	86.46	93.50	111.83	111.22	6.85	7.79	7.45	10.14	10.64	383
3832	Radio,television etc..	49.19	55.45	61.38	73.87	73.56	4.74	5.72	5.73	8.05	8.29	3832
384	Transport equipment	87.88	89.08	105.24	121.28	128.23	11.65	7.61	5.28	8.47	11.24	384
3841	Shipbuilding, repair..	7.36	7.51	6.82	7.36	7.21	0.45	0.50	0.34	0.43	0.38	3841
3843	Motor vehicles	39.28	38.41	52.38	61.34	63.98	8.96	4.73	2.50	4.74	6.87	3843
385	Professional goods	31.49	33.67	35.26	39.87	40.28	2.02	2.10	1.80	2.30	2.58	385
390	Other industries	13.28	13.36	12.82	13.79	13.06	0.57	0.57	0.50	0.59	0.60	390
3	Manufacturing	834.20	821.64	879.44	980.60	996.38	78.96	74.32	61.49	74.91	82.79	3
410	Electricity,gas,steam ..	...	...	...	...	...	...	...	...	...	...	410
4101	Electricity	...	...	...	...	...	...	...	...	...	...	4101
420	Water works and supply .	...	...	...	...	...	...	...	...	...	...	420
4	Electricity,gas etc d/	64.14	...	...	...	...	38.40	...	...	...	...	4
2-4	All industry	...	...	...	...	...	...	...	...	...	...	2-4

a/ Electricity, gas and water: contributions to the gross domestic product.
b/ Excluding used fixed assets.
c/ Beginning 1982, data are not fully comparable with those for previous years owing to the change in valuation of inventories.
d/ Including sanitary services.

ISIC	INDUSTRY	11. GROSS FIXED CAPITAL FORMATION MACHINERY AND EQUIPMENT a/b/ (BILLION DOLLARS) 1981	1982	1983	1984	1985	12. VALUE OF STOCKS AT END OF PERIOD TOTAL (BILLION DOLLARS) 1981	c/ 1982	1983	1984	1985	ISIC
210	Coal mining	...	...	...	...	...	...	1.85	...	...	...	210
220	Petroleum and gas	...	...	...	...	...	...	5.78	...	...	...	220
230	Metal ore mining	...	...	...	...	...	...	1.58	...	...	...	230
290	Other mining	...	...	...	...	...	...	1.84	...	...	...	290
2	Mining, quarrying .	...	...	...	...	...	...	11.05	...	...	...	2
311/2	Food products	3.68	4.12	3.44	4.03	4.65	18.60	19.47	20.15	20.43	19.81	311/2
313	Beverages	1.03	1.25	1.13	1.15	1.01	3.46	4.09	3.91	3.97	4.20	313
314	Tobacco	0.40	0.48	0.51	0.49	0.51	4.62	6.11	7.18	6.87	6.23	314
321	Textiles	1.58	1.48	1.53	1.93	1.84	8.24	8.23	9.18	9.36	8.83	321
3211	Spinning,weaving etc..	1.05	1.00	1.05	1.24	1.13	3.83	3.64	3.97	4.07	3.71	3211
322	Wearing apparel	0.35	0.38	0.33	0.38	0.35	5.85	5.66	6.07	6.57	6.35	322
323	Leather and products ...	0.07	0.05	0.05	0.03	0.03	0.66	0.65	0.68	0.71	0.66	323
324	Footwear	0.08	0.05	0.04	0.05	0.04	0.86	0.84	0.84	0.79	0.75	324
331	Wood products	1.04	0.86	0.71	0.98	1.03	4.76	4.59	5.20	5.16	5.14	331
332	Furniture, fixtures	0.31	0.29	0.28	0.40	0.40	3.09	3.24	3.60	3.91	3.80	332
341	Paper and products	4.82	4.59	3.94	4.82	5.71	8.45	8.92	9.17	10.08	9.86	341
3411	Pulp,paper etc.	3.28	3.69	3.00	3.63	4.24	3.88	4.22	4.15	4.67	4.72	3411
342	Printing,publishing	2.49	2.68	2.70	3.28	3.75	6.12	7.04	7.59	8.47	8.49	342
351	Industrial chemicals ...	6.37	5.68	4.16	4.29	4.60	13.12	14.26	14.35	14.78	14.17	351
3511	Basic excl fertilizers	3.92	3.63	2.84	2.64	2.74	7.80	8.39	8.25	8.46	7.91	3511
3513	Synthetic resins etc .	1.40	1.45	1.03	1.23	1.40	3.08	3.64	3.99	4.16	4.12	3513
352	Other chemical products.	1.75	2.02	1.85	2.17	2.24	9.11	9.89	10.31	11.11	11.63	352
3522	Drugs and medicines ..	0.73	0.89	0.84	0.99	0.99	3.61	3.81	4.03	4.23	4.36	3522
353	Petroleum refineries ...	2.99	3.89	2.85	2.11	1.86	9.58	16.20	13.87	13.31	12.85	353
354	Petroleum,coal products.	0.18	0.21	0.24	0.25	0.36	0.86	0.98	1.19	1.03	1.06	354
355	Rubber products	0.55	0.47	0.42	0.58	0.73	2.30	2.56	2.46	2.66	2.71	355
356	Plastic products n.e.c..	1.31	1.38	1.04	1.78	2.12	4.12	4.64	4.91	5.51	5.68	356
361	Pottery,china etc	0.05	0.06	0.06	0.04	0.07	0.29	0.32	0.37	0.36	0.35	361
362	Glass and products	0.56	0.63	0.44	0.50	0.74	1.93	2.14	2.21	2.21	2.18	362
369	Non-metal products n.e.c	1.54	1.27	0.96	1.51	1.56	4.08	4.25	4.36	4.51	4.45	369
371	Iron and steel	3.84	2.83	2.36	2.22	2.56	15.20	14.34	12.66	12.74	11.29	371
372	Non-ferrous metals	1.49	1.18	1.35	1.31	1.39	9.25	8.64	8.35	8.25	7.21	372
381	Metal products	2.88	2.46	2.11	2.76	2.97	18.93	20.07	20.52	21.14	20.42	381
382	Machinery n.e.c.	7.19	6.98	5.56	6.79	7.18	43.65	48.52	45.61	49.10	46.03	382
3825	Office,computing etc..	1.80	2.00	2.18	2.74	2.89	9.20	9.98	10.51	13.22	11.85	3825
383	Electrical machinery ...	5.27	5.91	6.00	8.29	8.54	29.12	31.45	32.59	38.53	38.54	383
3832	Radio,television etc..	3.51	4.16	4.53	6.50	6.55	17.88	19.37	20.63	25.47	25.81	3832
384	Transport equipment	10.41	6.09	4.13	6.84	8.90	37.54	42.36	43.74	50.20	51.76	384
3841	Shipbuilding, repair..	0.30	0.29	0.22	0.25	0.22	1.94	1.82	1.36	1.53	1.49	3841
3843	Motor vehicles	8.34	4.02	2.20	4.23	5.88	9.74	9.26	11.03	12.72	12.84	3843
385	Professional goods	1.51	1.65	1.41	1.87	2.08	9.42	10.93	11.19	12.16	12.35	385
390	Other industries	0.43	0.43	0.37	0.47	0.46	4.59	5.00	4.93	4.91	4.76	390
3	Manufacturing	64.17	59.37	49.97	61.32	67.68	277.80	305.39	307.19	328.83	321.56	3
410	Electricity,gas,steam ..	...	...	...	...	...	...	...	...	...	...	410
4101	Electricity	...	...	...	...	...	...	...	...	...	...	4101
420	Water works and supply .	...	...	...	...	...	...	...	...	...	...	420
4	Electricity,gas etc	13.17	...	...	...	...	...	...	...	...	...	4
2-4	All industry	...	...	...	...	...	...	...	...	...	...	2-4

a/ Including sanitary services.
b/ Excluding used fixed assets.
c/ Beginning 1982, data are not fully comparable with those for previous years owing to the change in valuation of inventories.

13. INDEX NUMBERS OF INDUSTRIAL PRODUCTION (1980 = 100)

ISIC	INDUSTRY		1976	1977	1978	1979	1981	1982	1983	1984	1985	a/ RATE	ISIC
210	Coal mining		80	83	78	92	96	97	93	106	106	3.2	210
220	Petroleum and gas		84	88	94	91	110	98	88	91	89	0.6	220
230	Metal ore mining		112	97	111	116	113	76	74	84	82	-3.4	230
290	Other mining		89	94	99	104	97	84	92	109	111	2.5	290
2	Mining, quarrying .		87	89	92	95	104	97	92	99	97	1.2	2
311/2	Food products		89	93	95	99	102	101	104	109	112	2.6	311/2
313	Beverages		81	87	93	98	102	100	104	107	107	3.1	313
314	Tobacco		98	94	99	98	102	98	94	96	96	-0.2	314
321	Textiles		97	97	99	105	98	90	102	100	100	0.3	321
3211	Spinning,weaving etc..		98	93	94	99	98	86	97	96	95	-0.3	3211
322	Wearing apparel	b/	99	106	106	106	95	85	92	99	97	-0.2	322
323	Leather and products ...	b/c/	112	112	112	112	106	92	94	99	85	-3.0	323
324	Footwear		107	98	99	97	94	83	84	75	68	-4.9	324
331	Wood products	c/	107	114	117	116	99	94	114	125	130	2.2	331
332	Furniture, fixtures		91	97	104	108	105	101	114	127	130	4.0	332
341	Paper and products		88	91	96	100	103	100	109	115	116	3.1	341
3411	Pulp,paper etc.		90	92	94	98	103	99	106	112	110	2.3	3411
342	Printing,publishing		88	91	94	98	103	103	109	122	126	4.1	342
351	Industrial chemicals ...		83	90	98	105	103	88	102	108	111	3.3	351
3511	Basic excl fertilizers		84	87	92	102	100	84	93	99	98	1.7	3511
3513	Synthetic resins etc .		79	88	97	109	107	95	113	121	129	5.6	3513
352	Other chemical products.	c/	82	89	93	99	106	102	106	112	120	4.3	352
3522	Drugs and medicines ..		78	86	89	97	109	109	114	120	130	5.8	3522
353	Petroleum refineries ...		100	108	109	108	98	92	90	93	93	-0.8	353
354	Petroleum,coal products.		100	106	111	112	97	88	94	94	91	-1.0	354
355	Rubber products		102	121	121	119	109	101	110	125	123	2.1	355
356	Plastic products n.e.c..		69	79	91	101	106	99	116	132	138	8.0	356
361	Pottery,china etc	d/	...	...	...	...	...	...	...	...	...	...	361
362	Glass and products		89	92	100	102	101	95	94	98	97	1.0	362
369	Non-metal products n.e.c	d/	92	99	108	113	100	85	98	110	114	2.4	369
371	Iron and steel		113	112	122	122	108	67	77	86	83	-3.4	371
372	Non-ferrous metals		103	104	110	113	102	83	92	102	102	-0.1	372
381	Metal products		92	98	106	111	102	86	90	102	107	1.7	381
382	Machinery n.e.c.	e/	83	88	94	101	105	92	92	112	114	3.6	382
3825	Office,computing etc..		69	75	87	95	113	108	118	142	149	8.9	3825
383	Electrical machinery ...		78	84	92	101	103	98	107	126	123	5.2	383
3832	Radio,television etc..		105	112	117	102	103	87	101	120	108	0.3	3832
384	Transport equipment		95	104	113	116	99	90	101	118	126	3.2	384
3841	Shipbuilding, repair..		104	109	110	103	101	90	91	105	103	-0.1	3841
3843	Motor vehicles		109	124	134	134	103	92	115	139	147	3.4	3843
385	Professional goods	e/	86	91	98	102	100	95	93	102	103	2.0	385
390	Other industries	c/	98	100	102	104	104	92	99	100	98	0.0	390
3	Manufacturing		85	92	99	103	102	94	102	114	117	3.6	3
410	Electricity,gas,steam ..		91	93	96	99	100	98	98	103	105	1.6	410
4101	Electricity		89	93	97	98	101	100	103	108	103	1.6	4101
420	Water works and supply .		.	.	.	.	.	.	.	.	.	.	420
4	Electricity,gas etc		...	...	...	...	...	...	...	...	...	...	4
2-4	All industry		85	92	98	102	102	95	101	112	114	3.3	2-4

a/ Annual growth rate 1976-1985.
b/ Manufacture of leather gloves is included in major group 323.
c/ Dressing and dyeing of furs, mortician's goods, matches and candles are included in major group 390.
d/ Major group 361 is included in 369.
e/ Manufacture of electrical measuring instruments is included in major group 382.

URUGUAY

The information in the tables, except for the indexes, is based on the reply to the United Nations Questionnaire on General Industrial Statistics from the Direccion General de Estadistica y Censos, Secretaria de Planeamiento, Coordinacion y Difusion, Montevideo. The concepts, definitions and classification by branches of industry are generally in accordance with United Nations standards.

The data in the tables are derived from the annual sampling survey of manufacturing industries conducted by the Direccion General de Estadistica y Censos. The inquiry is carried out on all establishments with 50 or more persons engaged of the enterprises located in Montevideo and the domestic enterprises whose offices are located in Montevideo, and establishments with 5 to 49 persons engaged which are located in Montevideo area. The estimation of national data has been made on the basis of the results of the II Censo Economico Nacional taken for 1978. The data in the tables cover establishments with 5 or more persons engaged. The statistics are compiled according to the national classification system which follows the present version of ISIC.

Output is the sum of the value of products manufactured, net change between the beginning and the end of the year in the value of work in progress, value of industrial services rendered to others, value of goods sold without transformation, value of fixed assets produced by the establishment for its own use and receipts from non-industrial services rendered to others. Value added is the difference between the value of output and the value of input, comprising the costs of materials, supplies, fuels, goods sold without transformation, work done by others, electricity purchased and other expenses (including items of a non-industrial nature). The estimates are valued in producers' prices, i.e. including value-added tax and other indirect taxes and excluding subsidies (reimbursement on exports etc.).

The indexes of industrial production are compiled by the Departamento de Investigaciones Economicas del Banco Central del Uruguay and provided in response to the United Nations Questionnaire on Indexes of Industrial Production. The indexes cover, in principle, all industrial establishments with a gross value of output of more than 20 000 pesos in 1956.

Related national publication:
<u>Encuesta Anual de Produccion, Sector Industrial</u> (annual), published by the Direccion General de Estadistica y Censos, Secretaria de Planeamiento, Coordinacion y Difusion, Montevideo.

ISIC	INDUSTRY	1. AVERAGE NUMBER OF PERSONS ENGAGED a/ (THOUSANDS)					2. AVERAGE NUMBER OF EMPLOYEES a/ (THOUSANDS)					ISIC
		1981	1982	1983	1984	1985	1981	1982	1983	1984	1985	
210	Coal mining	...	...	...	...	...	...	...	...	...	...	210
220	Petroleum and gas	...	...	...	...	...	...	...	...	...	...	220
230	Metal ore mining	...	...	...	...	...	...	...	...	...	...	230
290	Other mining	...	...	...	...	...	...	...	...	...	...	290
2	Mining, quarrying .	...	...	...	...	...	...	...	...	...	...	2
311/2	Food products	36.6	36.4	37.1	35.3	36.0	36.5	36.3	37.1	35.3	36.0	311/2
313	Beverages	6.5	6.1	5.4	5.3	5.4	6.5	6.1	5.4	5.3	5.4	313
314	Tobacco	0.9	0.7	0.7	0.7	0.7	0.9	0.7	0.7	0.7	0.7	314
321	Textiles	19.4	14.2	13.3	15.6	16.5	19.4	14.2	13.3	15.6	16.5	321
3211	Spinning,weaving etc..	12.6	10.1	10.3	11.9	12.5	12.6	10.9	10.3	11.9	12.5	3211
322	Wearing apparel	11.9	7.2	8.3	9.6	10.4	12.0	7.2	8.3	9.6	10.4	322
323	Leather and products ...	7.7	5.2	5.6	5.7	5.3	7.7	5.2	5.6	5.7	5.3	323
324	Footwear	4.6	2.5	2.3	2.6	2.1	4.5	2.5	2.3	2.6	2.1	324
331	Wood products	3.3	3.1	2.4	1.9	2.3	3.3	3.1	2.4	1.9	2.3	331
332	Furniture, fixtures	1.2	1.0	0.5	0.6	0.6	1.2	1.0	0.5	0.6	0.6	332
341	Paper and products	3.5	2.9	2.9	3.0	3.4	3.5	2.9	2.9	3.0	3.4	341
3411	Pulp,paper etc.	2.0	1.6	1.6	1.8	1.9	2.0	1.6	1.6	1.8	1.9	3411
342	Printing,publishing	5.7	5.0	4.7	4.7	4.7	5.6	4.9	4.7	4.7	4.7	342
351	Industrial chemicals ...	2.1	1.4	1.2	1.3	1.5	2.1	1.4	1.2	1.3	1.5	351
3511	Basic excl fertilizers	1.4	0.8	0.8	0.8	0.9	1.3	0.8	0.8	0.8	0.9	3511
3513	Synthetic resins etc .	0.3	...	...	0.1	0.1	0.3	...	...	0.1	0.1	3513
352	Other chemical products.	7.2	7.0	6.6	6.7	6.7	7.2	7.0	6.6	6.7	6.7	352
3522	Drugs and medicines ..	3.4	3.3	3.2	3.1	3.1	3.3	3.2	3.2	3.1	3.1	3522
353	Petroleum refineries ...	2.2	1.9	1.5	1.5	1.6	2.2	1.9	1.5	1.5	1.6	353
354	Petroleum,coal products.	0.2	...	...	...	...	0.2	...	...	...	...	354
355	Rubber products	3.1	2.6	2.4	2.5	2.6	3.1	2.5	2.3	2.5	2.6	355
356	Plastic products n.e.c..	3.7	3.0	2.9	3.1	3.1	3.6	3.0	2.9	3.1	3.1	356
361	Pottery,china etc	2.0	1.3	0.9	1.3	1.2	2.0	1.3	0.9	1.3	1.2	361
362	Glass and products	1.9	1.4	1.3	1.1	1.1	1.9	1.4	1.3	1.1	1.1	362
369	Non-metal products n.e.c	4.5	3.9	3.7	3.5	3.0	4.4	3.9	3.7	3.5	3.0	369
371	Iron and steel	2.2	1.4	1.2	1.1	1.0	2.2	1.4	1.2	1.1	1.0	371
372	Non-ferrous metals	0.5	0.3	0.3	0.3	0.3	0.5	0.3	0.3	0.3	0.3	372
381	Metal products	7.9	6.2	4.9	4.9	4.9	7.9	6.2	4.9	4.9	4.9	381
382	Machinery n.e.c.	2.1	1.7	1.3	1.6	1.4	2.1	1.7	1.3	1.6	1.4	382
3825	Office,computing etc..	...	...	...	0.1	0.1	...	...	...	0.1	0.1	3825
383	Electrical machinery ...	5.6	3.7	3.3	3.3	2.9	5.5	3.7	3.3	3.3	2.9	383
3832	Radio,television etc..	0.1	0.7	0.5	0.5	0.2	1.0	0.7	0.5	0.5	0.2	3832
384	Transport equipment	6.3	4.0	1.8	2.2	2.4	6.3	4.0	1.8	2.2	2.4	384
3841	Shipbuilding, repair..	1.1	0.9	...	...	...	1.0	0.9	...	...	...	3841
3843	Motor vehicles	4.6	2.9	1.6	1.7	1.8	4.6	2.8	1.6	1.7	1.8	3843
385	Professional goods	-	0.1	0.1	0.2	0.2	-	0.1	0.1	0.2	0.2	385
390	Other industries	1.3	1.0	0.8	1.0	1.1	1.3	0.9	0.8	1.0	1.1	390
3	Manufacturing	154.1	125.2	117.4	120.6	122.4	153.6	124.8	117.3	120.6	122.4	3
410	Electricity,gas,steam .. b/	10.9	...	...	...	...	10.9	10.6	10.7	...	...	410
4101	Electricity .... b/	10.6	...	...	10.6	...	10.6	10.3	10.4	10.6	...	4101
420	Water works and supply . b/	5.1	...	...	...	...	5.1	...	...	...	...	420
4	Electricity,gas etc b/	16.0	...	...	...	...	16.0	...	...	...	...	4
2-4	All industry	...	...	...	...	...	...	...	...	...	...	2-4

a/ Establishments with 5 or more persons engaged.

b/ At 31 December of the year indicated.

ISIC	INDUSTRY	3. WAGES AND SALARIES OF EMPLOYEES a/ (MILLION NEW PESOS)					4. AVERAGE NUMBER OF OPERATIVES a/ (THOUSANDS)					ISIC
		1981	1982	1983	1984	1985	1981	1982	1983	1984	1985	
210	Coal mining	...	...	...	...	...	...	...	...	...	...	210
220	Petroleum and gas	...	...	...	...	...	...	...	...	...	...	220
230	Metal ore mining	...	...	...	...	...	...	...	...	...	...	230
290	Other mining	...	...	...	...	...	...	...	...	...	...	290
2	Mining, quarrying .	...	...	...	...	...	...	...	...	...	...	2
311/2	Food products	1959	2476	3270	3836	7819	28.7	28.7	29.7	27.9	28.6	311/2
313	Beverages	492	599	700	885	1899	4.4	4.0	3.4	3.4	3.4	313
314	Tobacco	111	117	149	246	361	0.7	0.5	0.5	0.5	0.5	314
321	Textiles	894	832	1090	1884	3792	16.3	10.3	10.9	13.0	13.8	321
3211	Spinning,weaving etc..	679	664	883	1577	3086	10.0	7.7	8.5	9.9	10.6	3211
322	Wearing apparel	495	387	527	785	1702	10.4	6.1	7.3	8.6	9.1	322
323	Leather and products ...	365	368	513	665	1339	6.4	4.5	4.9	5.0	4.5	323
324	Footwear	158	111	129	192	291	4.1	2.2	2.1	2.4	1.9	324
331	Wood products	171	160	149	169	322	2.7	2.5	2.0	1.5	1.7	331
332	Furniture, fixtures	56	52	39	40	79	1.0	0.8	0.4	0.4	0.4	332
341	Paper and products	228	216	288	472	990	2.7	2.3	2.4	2.5	2.8	341
3411	Pulp,paper etc.	143	129	173	308	642	1.6	1.3	1.3	1.4	1.5	3411
342	Printing,publishing	359	453	513	609	1171	2.8	2.6	2.6	2.6	2.7	342
351	Industrial chemicals ...	191	157	184	275	602	1.3	0.9	0.8	0.8	1.0	351
3511	Basic excl fertilizers	118	84	109	152	344	0.8	0.6	0.5	0.6	0.6	3511
3513	Synthetic resins etc .	27	...	...	26	57	0.2	...	...	0.1	0.1	3513
352	Other chemical products.	683	921	1153	1486	2886	3.5	3.6	3.2	3.3	3.3	352
3522	Drugs and medicines ..	383	494	682	847	1621	1.5	1.4	1.3	1.4	1.4	3522
353	Petroleum refineries ...	177	201	199	241	582	1.4	1.2	1.1	1.1	1.1	353
354	Petroleum,coal products.	24	...	...	...	...	0.1	...	...	...	...	354
355	Rubber products	272	259	298	413	814	2.3	1.6	1.5	1.6	1.7	355
356	Plastic products n.e.c..	213	224	258	336	640	2.8	2.2	2.2	2.4	2.4	356
361	Pottery,china etc	103	99	113	182	350	1.4	0.9	0.6	1.0	0.9	361
362	Glass and products	120	113	132	139	313	1.6	1.2	1.0	0.8	0.8	362
369	Non-metal products n.e.c	312	370	404	443	800	3.4	2.9	2.7	2.6	2.2	369
371	Iron and steel	119	116	113	157	273	2.0	1.2	0.9	0.8	0.8	371
372	Non-ferrous metals	27	18	27	24	57	0.4	0.2	0.2	0.2	0.2	372
381	Metal products	471	479	460	542	1061	6.3	4.8	3.7	3.7	3.8	381
382	Machinery n.e.c.	145	133	124	195	344	1.5	1.4	1.0	1.1	1.0	382
3825	Office,computing etc..	...	...	...	25	47	...	...	...	0.1	0.1	3825
383	Electrical machinery ...	361	329	353	459	793	4.1	2.6	2.4	2.5	2.3	383
3832	Radio,television etc..	54	55	43	70	45	0.7	0.4	0.3	0.3	0.1	3832
384	Transport equipment	502	414	282	431	889	4.9	2.8	1.0	1.4	1.6	384
3841	Shipbuilding, repair..	80	90	...	...	...	0.9	0.8	...	...	...	3841
3843	Motor vehicles	374	299	261	340	697	3.6	1.9	0.9	1.0	1.2	3843
385	Professional goods	-	8	11	21	30	-	0.1	0.1	0.2	0.2	385
390	Other industries	56	58	60	83	191	1.0	0.7	0.6	0.7	0.8	390
3	Manufacturing	9064	9670	11538	15210	30390	118.2	92.8	89.2	92.0	93.5	3
410	Electricity,gas,steam ..	...	...	...	...	...	b/ 6.0	b/ 5.7	b/ 5.7	...	...	410
4101	Electricity	604	794	971	1352	...	b/ 5.9	b/ 5.6	b/ 5.6	b/ 5.8	...	4101
420	Water works and supply .	...	...	...	...	...	...	...	...	...	...	420
4	Electricity,gas etc	...	...	...	...	...	...	...	...	...	...	4
2-4	All industry	...	...	...	...	...	...	...	...	...	...	2-4

a/ Establishments with 5 or more persons engaged.

b/ At 31 December of the year indicated.

ISIC	INDUSTRY	5. WAGES AND SALARIES OF OPERATIVES a/ (MILLION NEW PESOS)					6. HOURS WORKED BY OPERATIVES a/ (MILLIONS)					ISIC
		1981	1982	1983	1984	1985	1981	1982	1983	1984	1985	
210	Coal mining	...	...	...	...	...	...	...	...	...	...	210
220	Petroleum and gas	...	...	...	...	...	...	...	...	...	...	220
230	Metal ore mining	...	...	...	...	...	...	...	...	...	...	230
290	Other mining	...	...	...	...	...	...	...	...	...	...	290
2	Mining, quarrying .	...	...	...	...	...	...	...	...	...	...	2
311/2	Food products	1211	1537	2046	2337	4982	61.1	59.4	61.1	55.4	57.2	311/2
313	Beverages	270	303	333	428	963	11.0	9.2	7.4	7.3	7.4	313
314	Tobacco	59	60	75	93	174	1.3	0.9	0.9	0.9	0.9	314
321	Textiles	562	451	653	1090	2497	31.9	19.1	22.7	27.1	27.5	321
3211	Spinning,weaving etc..	407	351	532	887	2048	20.8	14.6	18.3	21.4	21.2	3211
322	Wearing apparel	355	271	388	590	1294	19.1	11.8	15.4	18.4	18.0	322
323	Leather and products ...	264	285	393	513	1029	12.1	10.3	11.4	11.5	10.3	323
324	Footwear	118	83	100	146	228	7.2	4.2	4.4	4.9	3.7	324
331	Wood products	111	104	100	114	226	5.4	4.2	3.4	3.3	2.9	331
332	Furniture, fixtures	41	39	26	25	62	4.9	1.4	0.7	0.8	0.8	332
341	Paper and products	143	134	191	324	669	6.4	4.9	5.3	5.9	5.8	341
3411	Pulp,paper etc.	91	84	118	216	433	3.9	2.8	3.1	3.5	3.3	3411
342	Printing,publishing	158	197	229	278	527	6.0	5.6	5.3	5.4	5.5	342
351	Industrial chemicals ...	79	71	73	111	280	3.1	2.0	1.7	1.9	2.3	351
3511	Basic excl fertilizers	49	42	48	68	169	2.0	1.3	1.3	1.3	1.5	3511
3513	Synthetic resins etc .	13	...	...	11	27	0.5	...	...	0.2	0.2	3513
352	Other chemical products.	199	281	324	435	876	7.6	7.6	6.8	7.1	7.2	352
3522	Drugs and medicines ..	93	116	149	194	401	3.0	3.0	2.7	2.8	2.9	3522
353	Petroleum refineries ...	106	113	128	157	393	2.8	2.8	2.3	2.4	2.6	353
354	Petroleum,coal products.	6	...	...	...	...	0.2	...	...	...	...	354
355	Rubber products	164	111	133	202	405	5.1	2.9	2.9	3.3	3.4	355
356	Plastic products n.e.c..	121	121	141	192	382	5.7	4.6	4.7	5.3	5.2	356
361	Pottery,china etc	52	48	51	103	185	3.2	1.7	1.4	2.3	2.0	361
362	Glass and products	78	71	81	87	200	3.2	2.4	2.1	1.7	1.8	362
369	Non-metal products n.e.c	192	222	236	267	502	7.3	6.3	5.5	5.5	4.6	369
371	Iron and steel	79	80	78	93	164	3.0	2.4	2.0	1.8	1.6	371
372	Non-ferrous metals	20	11	14	13	35	0.8	0.4	0.4	0.4	0.4	372
381	Metal products	301	288	257	310	648	12.8	9.3	7.1	7.4	7.6	381
382	Machinery n.e.c.	91	92	82	122	212	4.3	2.9	2.0	2.4	1.9	382
3825	Office,computing etc..	...	...	...	15	29	...	...	...	0.1	0.2	3825
383	Electrical machinery ...	202	165	194	267	448	8.7	5.1	4.9	5.2	4.6	383
3832	Radio,television etc..	30	24	21	43	25	1.5	0.8	0.6	0.7	0.2	3832
384	Transport equipment	343	210	97	181	427	10.7	5.1	2.0	2.9	3.4	384
3841	Shipbuilding, repair..	68	66	...	...	...	1.7	1.3	...	...	...	3841
3843	Motor vehicles	241	135	92	144	335	8.2	3.5	1.8	2.3	2.6	3843
385	Professional goods	-	5	8	16	22	-	0.2	0.3	0.4	0.3	385
390	Other industries	38	33	33	48	123	2.1	1.4	1.1	1.4	1.6	390
3	Manufacturing	5363	5386	6464	8542	17953	247.0	188.1	185.2	192.3	190.5	3
410	Electricity,gas,steam ..	...	...	...	...	...	...	...	...	...	...	410
4101	Electricity	...	...	...	...	...	...	...	...	...	...	4101
420	Water works and supply .	...	...	...	...	...	...	...	...	...	...	420
4	Electricity,gas etc	...	...	...	...	...	...	...	...	...	...	4
2-4	All industry	...	...	...	...	...	...	...	...	...	...	2-4

a/ Establishments with 5 or more persons engaged.

ISIC	INDUSTRY	7. OUTPUT b/c/ (MILLION NEW PESOS)					8. VALUE ADDED a/b/c/ (MILLION NEW PESOS)					ISIC
		1981	1982	1983	1984	1985	1981	1982	1983	1984	1985	
210	Coal mining	...	...	...	...	...	...	...	...	...	...	210
220	Petroleum and gas	...	...	...	...	...	...	...	...	...	...	220
230	Metal ore mining	...	...	...	...	...	...	...	...	...	...	230
290	Other mining	...	...	...	...	...	...	...	...	...	...	290
2	Mining, quarrying .	...	...	...	...	...	...	...	...	...	...	2
311/2	Food products	18081	20579	37098	53011	95057	5218	7549	12230	13832	27008	311/2
313	Beverages	4630	4828	5344	8104	15702	2682	3044	3208	4811	9282	313
314	Tobacco	2177	2604	3326	5106	8368	1698	2019	2744	4200	6896	314
321	Textiles	4994	3694	8997	18974	30391	2369	1703	3248	8061	13854	321
3211	Spinning,weaving etc..	3701	2922	7519	16205	25209	1720	1341	2724	6962	11513	3211
322	Wearing apparel	2523	1471	3279	6416	11649	765	491	1214	1856	4326	322
323	Leather and products ...	1764	2653	6486	12013	16345	668	1312	2150	4918	7744	323
324	Footwear	704	463	1099	1766	2438	262	194	517	607	823	324
331	Wood products	700	639	743	1358	1790	356	335	353	622	817	331
332	Furniture, fixtures	252	210	202	323	389	97	126	80	153	185	332
341	Paper and products	1269	1212	2499	5431	9470	565	527	1159	2780	4718	341
3411	Pulp,paper etc.	734	669	1512	3808	6139	336	303	359	2336	3726	3411
342	Printing,publishing	1036	1413	1798	2932	5768	517	670	661	1205	2705	342
351	Industrial chemicals ...	1548	1172	1927	3773	7402	751	458	739	1526	2686	351
3511	Basic excl fertilizers	840	479	854	1431	2853	497	273	466	799	1533	3511
3513	Synthetic resins etc .	180	...	...	358	703	85	...	...	145	255	3513
352	Other chemical products.	3421	4903	6800	12251	22855	1712	2539	3148	5907	11335	352
3522	Drugs and medicines ..	1558	2294	3240	5674	10950	828	1351	1603	2844	5997	3522
353	Petroleum refineries ...	9882	10322	13806	27838	49774	4375	3425	1906	9360	19719	353
354	Petroleum,coal products.	95	...	...	...	...	44	...	...	...	...	354
355	Rubber products	922	793	1630	3155	5579	449	493	937	1904	3487	355
356	Plastic products n.e.c..	1043	936	1549	2616	5134	464	419	747	1095	2537	356
361	Pottery,china etc	407	416	552	1221	1443	271	287	369	774	727	361
362	Glass and products	528	398	573	763	1642	262	200	246	426	748	362
369	Non-metal products n.e.c	1628	1692	2226	3142	4921	913	953	1166	1606	2385	369
371	Iron and steel	417	483	933	1662	2850	165	199	444	762	1431	371
372	Non-ferrous metals	106	67	163	285	576	46	24	75	189	318	372
381	Metal products	1919	1589	1939	3284	6095	1088	907	1053	1624	3289	381
382	Machinery n.e.c.	532	353	396	883	1659	362	192	261	597	1229	382
3825	Office,computing etc..	...	...	...	130	243	...	...	...	113	216	3825
383	Electrical machinery ...	1850	1283	1770	3529	5648	912	644	1020	1628	3170	383
3832	Radio,television etc..	457	401	182	893	782	253	186	83	267	401	3832
384	Transport equipment	2952	1619	1215	4028	8515	1199	755	489	1570	3884	384
3841	Shipbuilding, repair..	137	206	...	...	...	85	166	...	...	...	3841
3843	Motor vehicles	2396	1340	1141	3215	6698	948	556	460	1231	3003	3843
385	Professional goods	-	26	48	144	194	-	15	28	80	103	385
390	Other industries	175	160	198	500	918	102	107	103	302	562	390
3	Manufacturing	65555	65978	106596	184508	322572	28312	29587	40295	72395	135968	3
410	Electricity,gas,steam ..	...	...	...	...	...	...	...	...	...	...	410
4101	Electricity	...	...	...	...	...	...	...	...	...	...	4101
420	Water works and supply .	...	...	...	...	...	...	...	...	...	...	420
4	Electricity,gas etc	...	...	...	...	...	...	...	...	...	...	4
2-4	All industry	...	...	...	...	...	...	...	...	...	...	2-4

a/ Net of non-industrial costs.
b/ Establishments with 5 or more persons engaged.
c/ In producers' prices.

9. INDEX NUMBERS OF INDUSTRIAL PRODUCTION (1980 = 100)

ISIC	INDUSTRY		1976	1977	1978	1979	1981	1982	1983	1984	1985	a/ RATE	ISIC
210	Coal mining		...	...	...	...	...	...	...	...	...	...	210
220	Petroleum and gas		...	...	...	...	...	...	...	...	...	...	220
230	Metal ore mining		...	...	...	...	...	...	...	...	...	...	230
290	Other mining		...	...	...	...	...	...	...	...	...	...	290
2	Mining, quarrying		...	...	...	...	...	...	...	...	...	...	2
311/2	Food products		92	92	92	93	108	106	103	94	104	1.4	311/2
313	Beverages		81	83	87	100	109	94	79	72	74	-1.0	313
314	Tobacco		86	84	85	100	109	101	79	86	82	-0.5	314
321	Textiles		71	79	84	99	90	53	71	86	85	2.0	321
3211	Spinning,weaving etc.		...	...	...	...	...	...	...	...	...	...	3211
322	Wearing apparel	b/	89	100	110	101	89	58	70	82	72	-2.3	322
323	Leather and products		97	115	115	83	96	94	108	104	87	-1.2	323
324	Footwear	b/	...	...	...	...	...	...	...	...	...	...	324
331	Wood products		...	...	...	...	...	...	...	...	...	...	331
332	Furniture, fixtures		...	...	...	...	...	...	...	...	...	...	332
341	Paper and products		60	69	84	97	87	71	71	87	80	3.2	341
3411	Pulp,paper etc.		...	...	...	...	...	...	...	...	...	...	3411
342	Printing,publishing		66	79	82	92	103	88	74	71	72	1.0	342
351	Industrial chemicals	c/	77	81	92	117	97	80	70	76	76	-0.1	351
3511	Basic excl fertilizers		...	...	...	...	...	...	...	...	...	...	3511
3513	Synthetic resins etc		...	...	...	...	...	...	...	...	...	...	3513
352	Other chemical products.	c/	...	...	...	...	...	...	...	...	...	...	352
3522	Drugs and medicines		...	...	...	...	...	...	...	...	...	...	3522
353	Petroleum refineries		[105	99	106	101	94	95	78	79	74	-3.8]	353
354	Petroleum,coal products.												354
355	Rubber products		66	80	89	97	79	35	43	49	47	-3.7	355
356	Plastic products n.e.c..	d/	...	...	...	...	...	...	...	...	...	...	356
361	Pottery,china etc												361
362	Glass and products		[74	83	85	99	89	64	50	50	46	-5.1]	362
369	Non-metal products n.e.c												369
371	Iron and steel		...	...	...	...	...	...	...	...	...	...	371
372	Non-ferrous metals		...	...	...	...	...	...	...	...	...	...	372
381	Metal products		74	85	86	108	85	65	52	52	54	-3.4	381
382	Machinery n.e.c.		...	...	...	...	...	...	...	...	...	...	382
3825	Office,computing etc..		...	...	...	...	...	...	...	...	...	...	3825
383	Electrical machinery		45	54	54	74	96	66	35	44	44	-0.2	383
3832	Radio,television etc..		...	...	...	...	...	...	...	...	...	...	3832
384	Transport equipment		56	58	72	91	78	49	36	43	46	-2.2	384
3841	Shipbuilding, repair..		...	...	...	...	...	...	...	...	...	...	3841
3843	Motor vehicles		...	...	...	...	...	...	...	...	...	...	3843
385	Professional goods	d/	[74	78	82	112	79	65	61	67	69	-0.8]	385
390	Other industries												390
3	Manufacturing	e/	82	86	91	98	95	79	74	76	...	g/ -0.9	3
410	Electricity,gas,steam		...	...	...	...	...	...	...	...	...	...	410
4101	Electricity		...	...	...	...	...	...	...	...	...	...	4101
420	Water works and supply		...	...	...	...	...	...	...	...	...	...	420
4	Electricity,gas etc		79	83	90	93	105	107	109	110	...	g/ 4.2	4
2-4	All industry	f/	82	86	91	97	96	81	76	78	...	g/ -0.6	2-4

a/ Annual growth rate 1976-1985.
c/ Major group 352 is included in 351.
e/ Including mining.
g/ Annual growth rate 1976-1984.
b/ Major group 324 is included in 322.
d/ Major group 356 is included in 385 and 390 combined.
f/ Excluding electricity, gas and water.

VENEZUELA

The information in the tables, except for the indexes, is based on the reply to the United Nations Questionnaire on General Industrial Statistics from the Oficina Central de Estadistica e Informatica, Presidencia de la Republica, Caracas. The concepts, definitions and classification by branches of industry are generally in accordance with United Nations standards.

The data in the tables are derived from industrial surveys conducted monthly by the statistical office mentioned above. The inquiry covers establishments with 5 or more persons engaged. The data shown in the tables are based on the national classification system which follows the present version of ISIC.

The concepts and definitions of wages and salaries of employees are in conformity with international standards. Wages and salaries of operatives do not include overtime payments, bonuses, subsidies to support family etc., since these payments are not available separately for operatives.

Output is the sum of the value of all products sold, the net change in the value of stocks of finished goods and work in progress between the beginning and the end of the year, receipts for industrial services rendered to others and receipts from the sale of scrap and waste. Value added is calculated as the value of output less the value of inputs into the manufacturing process of goods. Valuation of output and value added is in producers' prices.

Gross fixed capital formation is the total value of acquisitions of fixed assets, new and used, and own-account construction of fixed assets during the year less the value of corresponding sales.

The indexes of industrial production are compiled by the Banco Central de Venezuela and provided in response to the United Nations Questionaire on Indexes of Industrial Production.

Related national publications:
Anuario Estadistico; Encuesta Industrial (annual), both published by the Oficina Central de Estadistica e Informatica, Presidencia de la Republica, Caracas.

VENEZUELA

ISIC	INDUSTRY	1. NUMBER OF ESTABLISHMENTS a/ (NUMBER)					2. AVERAGE NUMBER OF PERSONS ENGAGED a/ (THOUSANDS)					ISIC
		1981	1982	1983	1984	1985	1981	1982	1983	1984	1985	
210	Coal mining	...	...	...	...	...	...	...	...	...	...	210
220	Petroleum and gas	...	...	...	...	...	...	...	...	...	...	220
230	Metal ore mining	...	...	...	...	...	...	...	...	...	...	230
290	Other mining	...	...	...	...	...	...	...	...	...	...	290
2	Mining, quarrying .	...	...	...	...	...	...	...	...	...	...	2
311/2	Food products	2092	2313	2311	2377	2392	69.3	77.5	74.0	76.3	77.3	311/2
313	Beverages	129	129	133	127	127	16.0	15.9	16.2	14.6	15.0	313
314	Tobacco	32	26	26	37	36	4.1	3.8	3.5	4.4	3.8	314
321	Textiles	201	180	192	215	219	21.0	22.0	21.2	22.9	24.6	321
3211	Spinning,weaving etc..	114	...	...	133	133	17.0	...	...	19.1	20.7	3211
322	Wearing apparel	1069	1021	1039	939	936	30.5	27.7	28.4	28.3	29.7	322
323	Leather and products ...	116	108	112	124	115	3.4	3.6	3.8	4.2	3.8	323
324	Footwear	696	683	702	567	575	18.0	16.6	16.8	15.4	15.2	324
331	Wood products	330	302	296	306	288	7.2	6.6	6.7	7.5	7.0	331
332	Furniture, fixtures	749	928	965	839	848	13.0	14.6	15.0	13.0	12.9	332
341	Paper and products	112	89	95	106	99	13.1	10.9	10.9	12.0	12.3	341
3411	Pulp,paper etc.	33	...	...	38	37	7.1	...	...	7.2	7.9	3411
342	Printing,publishing	700	717	718	637	635	17.0	16.8	17.5	17.1	16.8	342
351	Industrial chemicals ...	102	100	108	115	114	8.4	10.6	10.2	10.0	10.3	351
3511	Basic excl fertilizers	60	...	...	73	70	5.0	...	...	5.1	4.7	3511
3513	Synthetic resins etc .	27	...	...	27	32	2.0	...	...	2.1	2.5	3513
352	Other chemical products.	253	251	251	286	287	26.1	24.9	23.5	24.1	24.6	352
3522	Drugs and medicines ..	75	...	...	67	69	9.0	...	...	7.0	7.5	3522
353	Petroleum refineries ...	18	16	17	16	12	7.1	7.0	6.9	7.2	6.5	353
354	Petroleum,coal products.	18	16	15	22	21	0.7	0.9	0.9	1.0	1.0	354
355	Rubber products	56	54	51	57	56	5.4	5.6	4.9	5.9	5.3	355
356	Plastic products n.e.c..	390	415	419	391	411	18.0	18.5	17.4	17.2	18.8	356
361	Pottery,china,etc	35	30	28	32	25	3.0	2.6	2.1	2.2	1.9	361
362	Glass and products	82	87	88	81	84	5.0	6.1	5.5	5.7	5.7	362
369	Non-metal products n.e.c	564	564	545	523	510	19.3	20.2	18.9	19.3	18.6	369
371	Iron and steel	128	116	116	133	136	26.0	24.1	28.5	24.3	25.2	371
372	Non-ferrous metals	69	67	72	84	86	7.0	7.2	8.9	9.3	9.7	372
381	Metal products	1233	1236	1239	1163	1147	31.4	30.8	30.8	26.5	27.7	381
382	Machinery n.e.c.	234	212	213	241	242	15.0	13.6	13.4	13.7	11.4	382
3825	Office,computing etc..	...	...	...	-	-	...	...	...	-	-	3825
383	Electrical machinery ...	209	204	209	206	220	15.0	15.7	14.2	12.4	13.6	383
3832	Radio,television etc..	49	...	...	48	49	4.2	...	...	2.7	3.1	3832
384	Transport equipment	248	244	244	259	251	23.1	24.7	21.9	20.5	20.5	384
3841	Shipbuilding, repair..	19	...	...	19	20	1.1	...	...	1.1	1.0	3841
3843	Motor vehicles	212	...	...	222	211	22.0	...	...	19.1	19.1	3843
385	Professional goods	41	35	35	43	43	1.6	2.6	1.8	1.9	1.9	385
390	Other industries	176	161	157	167	169	4.2	4.1	4.0	4.8	4.8	390
3	Manufacturing	10082	10304	10396	10093	10084	428.9	435.2	427.8	421.7	425.9	3
410	Electricity,gas,steam ..	...	...	...	...	...	...	...	...	...	...	410
4101	Electricity	...	...	...	...	...	...	...	...	...	...	4101
420	Water works and supply .	...	...	...	...	...	...	...	...	...	...	420
4	Electricity,gas etc	...	...	...	...	...	...	...	...	...	...	4
2-4	All industry	...	...	...	...	...	...	...	...	...	...	2-4

a/ Establishments with 5 or more persons engaged.

ISIC	INDUSTRY	3. AVERAGE NUMBER OF EMPLOYEES a/ (THOUSANDS)					4. WAGES AND SALARIES OF EMPLOYEES a/ (MILLION BOLIVARES)					ISIC
		1981	1982	1983	1984	1985	1981	1982	1983	1984	1985	
210	Coal mining	...	...	...	...	...	...	...	...	...	...	210
220	Petroleum and gas	...	...	...	...	...	...	...	...	...	...	220
230	Metal ore mining	...	...	...	...	...	...	...	...	...	...	230
290	Other mining	...	...	...	...	...	...	...	...	...	...	290
2	Mining, quarrying	...	...	...	...	...	...	...	...	...	...	2
311/2	Food products	65.1	72.9	69.5	71.5	72.7	2931	3526	3482	3708	4318	311/2
313	Beverages	16.0	15.4	15.5	14.1	14.5	943	931	1004	1050	1145	313
314	Tobacco	4.0	3.6	3.4	4.4	3.7	246	233	236	303	353	314
321	Textiles	20.3	21.5	20.7	22.5	24.1	1046	1051	1046	1202	1506	321
3211	Spinning,weaving etc.	17.0	...	...	18.8	20.4	914	...	...	1057	1327	3211
322	Wearing apparel	29.1	26.1	26.8	26.8	28.2	1059	933	998	1101	1327	322
323	Leather and products	3.3	3.4	3.6	4.0	3.6	119	115	129	142	153	323
324	Footwear	16.2	15.6	15.8	14.5	14.3	568	535	540	525	606	324
331	Wood products	7.2	6.1	6.1	7.0	6.5	214	208	223	258	263	331
332	Furniture, fixtures	12.7	13.1	13.6	11.6	11.5	434	503	527	464	522	332
341	Paper and products	13.0	10.6	10.6	11.7	12.0	684	633	649	786	807	341
3411	Pulp,paper etc.	7.0	...	...	7.1	7.7	397	...	...	525	535	3411
342	Printing,publishing	16.7	15.5	16.2	16.0	15.7	886	892	978	988	1108	342
351	Industrial chemicals	8.1	10.3	9.9	9.7	9.9	647	857	881	748	850	351
3511	Basic excl fertilizers	4.5	...	...	4.9	4.5	373	...	...	361	396	3511
3513	Synthetic resins etc	2.0	...	...	2.0	2.4	121	...	...	152	210	3513
352	Other chemical products	25.6	23.9	22.4	23.1	23.5	1607	1656	1733	1892	2124	352
3522	Drugs and medicines	8.4	...	...	6.7	7.1	533	...	...	537	676	3522
353	Petroleum refineries	7.1	7.0	6.8	7.2	6.4	697	775	996	892	902	353
354	Petroleum,coal products	0.7	0.9	0.9	0.9	0.9	40	44	49	63	66	354
355	Rubber products	5.2	5.5	4.7	5.7	5.1	274	351	311	509	521	355
356	Plastic products n.e.c.	17.0	17.5	16.6	16.3	18.0	740	789	812	830	985	356
361	Pottery,china etc	3.0	2.5	2.0	2.1	1.9	149	143	115	106	129	361
362	Glass and products	4.5	5.9	5.3	5.5	5.5	228	310	306	350	381	362
369	Non-metal products n.e.c	18.3	19.1	17.8	18.3	17.7	864	939	998	1047	1108	369
371	Iron and steel	25.4	23.6	28.0	23.9	24.8	1427	1810	2100	1756	2258	371
372	Non-ferrous metals	7.0	7.1	8.7	9.0	9.5	410	442	555	737	671	372
381	Metal products	29.2	28.7	28.6	24.4	25.6	1268	1341	1359	1208	1407	381
382	Machinery n.e.c.	14.0	13.1	12.9	13.1	10.9	697	689	711	719	669	382
3825	Office,computing etc.	...	...	...	-	-	...	...	...	-	-	3825
383	Electrical machinery	14.2	15.0	13.6	11.9	13.0	822	914	963	749	878	383
3832	Radio,television etc.	4.2	...	...	2.5	3.0	261	...	...	154	177	3832
384	Transport equipment	22.5	24.1	21.3	19.8	19.8	1301	1504	1524	1393	1505	384
3841	Shipbuilding, repair	1.1	...	...	1.1	1.0	43	...	...	54	59	3841
3843	Motor vehicles	21.1	...	...	18.4	18.4	1247	...	...	1328	1432	3843
385	Professional goods	1.6	2.5	1.7	1.8	1.9	94	134	82	117	148	385
390	Other industries	4.0	3.8	3.7	4.5	4.5	171	165	194	212	237	390
3	Manufacturing	411.0	414.3	406.7	401.3	405.7	20566	22423	23501	23855	26947	3
410	Electricity,gas,steam	...	...	...	...	...	...	...	...	...	...	410
4101	Electricity	...	...	...	...	...	...	...	...	...	...	4101
420	Water works and supply	...	...	...	...	...	...	...	...	...	...	420
4	Electricity,gas etc	...	...	...	...	...	...	...	...	...	...	4
2-4	All industry	...	...	...	...	...	...	...	...	...	...	2-4

a/ Establishments with 5 or more persons engaged.

ISIC	INDUSTRY	5. AVERAGE NUMBER OF OPERATIVES a/ (THOUSANDS) 1981	1982	1983	1984	1985	6. WAGES AND SALARIES OF OPERATIVES a/b/ (MILLION BOLIVARES) 1981	1982	1983	1984	1985	ISIC
210	Coal mining	...	...	...	...	...	...	...	...	...	...	210
220	Petroleum and gas	...	...	...	...	...	...	...	...	...	...	220
230	Metal ore mining	...	...	...	...	...	...	...	...	...	...	230
290	Other mining	...	...	...	...	...	...	...	...	...	...	290
2	Mining, quarrying .	...	...	...	...	...	...	...	...	...	...	2
311/2	Food products	49.0	55.5	53.5	54.9	55.4	960	1274	1251	1303	1489	311/2
313	Beverages	10.0	9.3	9.2	8.5	8.7	223	251	283	248	264	313
314	Tobacco	2.0	1.7	1.6	2.4	1.7	53	47	50	75	81	314
321	Textiles	17.0	17.7	17.0	19.0	20.4	475	457	447	480	631	321
3211	Spinning,weaving etc..	14.0	...	...	15.8	17.2	415	...	...	415	550	3211
322	Wearing apparel	25.2	22.9	23.4	23.6	24.9	518	470	489	554	637	322
323	Leather and products ...	3.0	3.1	3.3	3.7	3.2	57	61	67	77	80	323
324	Footwear	15.3	14.6	14.7	13.3	13.0	333	322	315	290	320	324
331	Wood products	6.0	5.4	5.5	6.2	5.8	110	115	125	140	139	331
332	Furniture, fixtures	11.0	11.9	12.2	10.3	10.3	215	268	288	239	272	332
341	Paper and products	10.0	8.1	7.8	8.6	8.8	231	216	224	266	278	341
3411	Pulp,paper etc.	5.3	...	...	5.3	5.6	133	...	...	175	189	3411
342	Printing,publishing	11.0	10.6	10.6	10.9	10.6	291	315	325	327	373	342
351	Industrial chemicals ...	4.2	5.2	5.1	5.1	5.3	122	185	181	171	183	351
3511	Basic excl fertilizers	2.4	...	...	2.6	2.4	67	...	...	88	90	3511
3513	Synthetic resins etc .	0.9	...	...	1.2	1.4	30	...	...	36	46	3513
352	Other chemical products.	13.1	13.0	11.6	13.1	12.5	319	351	342	389	417	352
3522	Drugs and medicines ..	4.5	...	...	3.7	3.7	106	...	...	107	135	3522
353	Petroleum refineries ...	3.4	3.3	3.3	3.5	3.0	111	115	124	153	132	353
354	Petroleum,coal products.	0.5	0.7	0.7	0.7	0.8	14	18	18	26	23	354
355	Rubber products	4.2	4.4	3.9	4.6	4.2	105	131	121	187	167	355
356	Plastic products n.e.c..	14.0	14.5	13.7	13.4	14.7	273	327	317	328	379	356
361	Pottery,china etc	2.3	2.1	1.6	1.7	1.5	69	66	51	44	49	361
362	Glass and products	4.0	4.7	4.2	4.4	4.5	93	117	110	118	146	362
369	Non-metal products n.e.c	15.0	15.5	14.1	14.1	13.8	356	402	412	407	415	369
371	Iron and steel	17.0	15.4	17.2	14.8	15.3	448	464	517	548	477	371
372	Non-ferrous metals	5.0	4.3	5.0	5.6	5.7	112	117	133	225	207	372
381	Metal products	24.0	23.6	23.4	19.9	20.5	539	608	611	513	583	381
382	Machinery n.e.c.	10.2	9.9	9.6	9.6	8.2	222	274	272	258	235	382
3825	Office,computing etc..	...	...	...	-	-	...	...	...	-	-	3825
383	Electrical machinery ...	10.0	10.0	8.8	8.4	9.6	221	267	244	239	280	383
3832	Radio,television etc..	2.4	...	...	1.7	2.1	48	...	...	42	54	3832
384	Transport equipment	17.0	17.8	15.2	14.8	14.7	453	563	501	438	487	384
3841	Shipbuilding, repair..	0.9	...	...	0.9	0.8	25	...	...	35	35	3841
3843	Motor vehicles	16.0	...	...	13.6	13.5	424	...	...	397	444	3843
385	Professional goods	1.0	1.5	1.1	1.2	1.2	23	36	22	28	31	385
390	Other industries	3.0	2.9	2.7	3.5	3.4	60	66	64	75	87	390
3	Manufacturing	307.4	309.6	300.0	299.8	301.7	7006	7903	7904	8146	8862	3
410	Electricity,gas,steam ..	...	...	...	...	...	...	...	...	...	...	410
4101	Electricity	...	...	...	...	...	...	...	...	...	...	4101
420	Water works and supply .	...	...	...	...	...	...	...	...	...	...	420
4	Electricity,gas etc	...	...	...	...	...	...	...	...	...	...	4
2-4	All industry	...	...	...	...	...	...	...	...	...	...	2-4

a/ Establishments with 5 or more persons engaged.

b/ Excluding overtime payments, bonuses and family allowances.

ISIC	INDUSTRY	7. QUANTITY OF ELECTRICITY CONSUMED a/ (MILLION KWH)					8. OUTPUT IN PRODUCERS' PRICES a/ (MILLION BOLIVARES)					ISIC
		1981	1982	1983	1984	1985	1981	1982	1983	1984	1985	
210	Coal mining	...	...	...	...	...	...	...	...	...	...	210
220	Petroleum and gas	...	...	...	...	...	...	...	...	...	...	220
230	Metal ore mining	...	...	...	...	...	...	...	...	...	...	230
290	Other mining	...	...	...	...	...	...	...	...	...	...	290
2	Mining, quarrying	...	...	...	...	...	...	...	...	...	...	2
311/2	Food products	...	935	1045	821	1001	23628	29740	30930	35603	42567	311/2
313	Beverages	...	147	179	192	168	7820	7334	9486	9676	10478	313
314	Tobacco	...	15	15	7	29	2934	3398	3412	3597	5332	314
321	Textiles	...	317	320	360	365	3542	4268	4461	6813	8463	321
3211	Spinning,weaving etc.	...	...	...	337	338	2925	...	...	5874	7323	3211
322	Wearing apparel	...	60	63	59	64	5422	4528	4810	6271	6672	322
323	Leather and products	...	22	24	25	32	659	696	732	1063	1369	323
324	Footwear	...	25	28	26	33	2341	2418	2458	2671	3072	324
331	Wood products	...	44	43	48	55	1139	1271	1310	1444	1410	331
332	Furniture, fixtures	...	44	45	39	121	1912	2385	2401	2126	2423	332
341	Paper and products	...	417	453	479	311	4180	3802	4017	6148	6659	341
3411	Pulp,paper etc.	...	...	...	440	276	2376	...	...	4123	4567	3411
342	Printing,publishing	...	82	95	76	90	3520	3614	3931	4259	4833	342
351	Industrial chemicals	...	1084	1846	340	458	3576	5095	5098	7190	8468	351
3511	Basic excl fertilizers	...	...	...	160	24	1735	...	...	3052	3091	3511
3513	Synthetic resins etc	...	...	...	92	226	1082	...	...	2313	2966	3513
352	Other chemical products	...	154	162	262	252	7457	8502	8945	11208	12924	352
3522	Drugs and medicines	...	...	...	33	43	1940	...	...	2204	3116	3522
353	Petroleum refineries	...	518	619	824	576	24005	21275	23598	34202	39659	353
354	Petroleum,coal products	...	4	4	5	6	237	285	298	518	602	354
355	Rubber products	...	84	75	102	109	1425	1535	1527	2864	2775	355
356	Plastic products n.e.c.	...	240	256	270	441	3802	4076	4175	5138	5849	356
361	Pottery,china etc	...	19	17	26	25	450	484	435	400	412	361
362	Glass and products	...	135	116	93	71	1059	1289	1198	1733	1854	362
369	Non-metal products n.e.c	...	1345	773	708	541	4024	4963	4517	4715	5239	369
371	Iron and steel	...	489	376	1112	4989	6540	8624	8543	10542	13461	371
372	Non-ferrous metals	...	494	1048	5071	488	3281	2769	4845	7722	8651	372
381	Metal products	...	229	228	203	234	5987	7293	6935	7452	9060	381
382	Machinery n.e.c.	...	63	72	61	76	3205	3377	3663	3865	4049	382
3825	Office,computing etc.	...	...	...	-	-	...	...	...	-	-	3825
383	Electrical machinery	...	132	110	95	112	3986	4048	3767	4424	5550	383
3832	Radio,television etc.	...	...	...	15	15	1199	...	...	970	1293	3832
384	Transport equipment	...	175	192	178	193	11176	11700	9937	11031	13677	384
3841	Shipbuilding, repair.	...	...	...	4	3	190	...	...	237	257	3841
3843	Motor vehicles	...	...	...	173	187	10938	...	...	10716	13314	3843
385	Professional goods	...	8	8	13	13	344	637	459	605	536	385
390	Other industries	...	16	20	18	24	881	821	960	1124	1241	390
3	Manufacturing	...	7297	8232	11513	10877	138532	150227	156848	194404	227285	3
410	Electricity,gas,steam	...	...	...	...	...	...	...	...	...	...	410
4101	Electricity	...	...	...	...	...	...	...	...	...	...	4101
420	Water works and supply	...	...	...	...	...	...	...	...	...	...	420
4	Electricity,gas etc	...	...	...	...	...	...	...	...	...	...	4
2-4	All industry	...	...	...	...	...	...	...	...	...	...	2-4

a/ Establishments with 5 or more persons engaged.

ISIC	INDUSTRY	9. VALUE ADDED IN PRODUCERS' PRICES a/ (MILLION BOLIVARES) 1981	1982	1983	1984	1985	10. GROSS FIXED CAPITAL FORMATION TOTAL a/ (MILLION BOLIVARES) 1981	1982	1983	1984	1985	ISIC
210	Coal mining	...	...	...	...	...	...	...	...	...	...	210
220	Petroleum and gas	...	...	...	...	...	...	...	...	...	...	220
230	Metal ore mining	...	...	...	...	...	...	...	...	...	...	230
290	Other mining	...	...	...	...	...	...	...	...	...	...	290
2	Mining, quarrying .	...	...	...	...	...	...	...	...	...	...	2
311/2	Food products	6987	9028	9633	9912	11974	1010	856	1057	1264	1454	311/2
313	Beverages	4720	4405	5995	5853	6271	982	994	604	625	467	313
314	Tobacco	1426	2837	2713	2767	4475	51	30	26	44	49	314
321	Textiles	1832	2148	2354	3295	3789	184	245	104	227	532	321
3211	Spinning,weaving etc..	1556	...	...	2933	3332	155	...	...	179	450	3211
322	Wearing apparel	1668	1904	2099	2321	2694	39	33	39	89	193	322
323	Leather and products ...	271	303	297	429	433	25	22	31	62	50	323
324	Footwear	1038	1105	1096	1011	1182	71	87	80	81	116	324
331	Wood products	516	496	581	624	600	52	43	58	60	67	331
332	Furniture, fixtures	874	1043	1063	904	1068	57	41	24	29	57	332
341	Paper and products	1998	1639	1827	2695	2674	210	114	159	125	470	341
3411	Pulp,paper etc.	1065	...	...	1994	2019	172	...	...	79	425	3411
342	Printing,publishing	1842	1816	1978	2012	2246	175	130	150	167	341	342
351	Industrial chemicals ...	1756	2873	2839	3479	3733	217	258	735	400	550	351
3511	Basic excl fertilizers	939	...	...	1632	1538	130	...	...	233	162	3511
3513	Synthetic resins etc .	375	...	...	841	1140	39	...	...	57	223	3513
352	Other chemical products.	3867	4824	4265	6019	6678	315	2549	432	395	476	352
3522	Drugs and medicines ..	1051	...	...	1336	1853	82	...	...	138	144	3522
353	Petroleum refineries ...	14909	11376	13510	22858	27254	1470	5818	619	806	654	353
354	Petroleum,coal products.	112	119	147	203	224	21	21	44	37	44	354
355	Rubber products	795	863	845	1602	1410	131	37	23	76	150	355
356	Plastic products n.e.c..	1980	2039	1999	2269	2613	245	241	232	328	417	356
361	Pottery,china etc	307	378	342	286	295	28	21	13	16	22	361
362	Glass and products	628	782	717	961	988	102	112	64	62	115	362
369	Non-metal products n.e.c	2325	2926	2623	2806	2834	268	348	240	159	203	369
371	Iron and steel	2445	4268	4408	5488	6411	1430	578	2804	464	380	371
372	Non-ferrous metals	1531	1085	2474	4392	3354	87	66	2090	187	496	372
381	Metal products	2939	3525	3362	3224	3769	334	180	406	322	527	381
382	Machinery n.e.c.	1459	1478	1693	1786	1808	152	108	105	603	154	382
3825	Office,computing etc..	...	...	...	-	-	...	...	...	-	-	3825
383	Electrical machinery ...	1847	1859	1880	2035	2301	210	187	114	160	240	383
3832	Radio,television etc..	533	...	...	466	548	80	...	...	34	63	3832
384	Transport equipment	3188	3822	2845	2581	3646	231	438	263	300	287	384
3841	Shipbuilding, repair..	95	...	...	128	152	6	...	...	18	4	3841
3843	Motor vehicles	3070	...	...	2414	3457	223	...	...	281	282	3843
385	Professional goods	204	395	273	301	196	13	39	33	48	48	385
390	Other industries	420	370	434	509	611	17	15	20	50	56	390
3	Manufacturing	63884	69706	74292	92622	105531	8127	13611	10569	7186	8615	3
410	Electricity,gas,steam ..	...	...	...	...	...	...	...	...	...	...	410
4101	Electricity	...	...	...	...	...	...	...	...	...	...	4101
420	Water works and supply .	...	...	...	...	...	...	...	...	...	...	420
4	Electricity,gas etc	...	...	...	...	...	...	...	...	...	...	4
2-4	All industry	...	...	...	...	...	...	...	...	...	...	2-4

a/ Establishments with 5 or more persons engaged.

11. INDEX NUMBERS OF INDUSTRIAL PRODUCTION (1980 = 100)

ISIC	INDUSTRY	1976	1977	1978	1979	1981	1982	1983	1984	1985	a/ RATE	ISIC
210	Coal mining	...	...	...	...	...	...	...	...	...	...	210
220	Petroleum and gas	...	...	...	...	...	...	...	...	...	...	220
230	Metal ore mining	...	...	...	...	...	...	...	...	...	...	230
290	Other mining	...	...	...	...	...	...	...	...	...	...	290
2	Mining, quarrying	...	...	...	...	...	...	...	...	...	...	2
311/2	Food products	57	65	71	82	114	127	136	171	212	15.7	311/2
313	Beverages	50	60	67	81	127	144	151	161	175	14.9	313
314	Tobacco	41	43	49	70	105	111	106	96	119	12.6	314
321	Textiles	85	81	93	95	112	103	109	166	185	9.0	321
3211	Spinning, weaving etc.	...	...	...	...	...	...	...	...	...	...	3211
322	Wearing apparel	74	76	87	97	92	96	104	142	140	7.3	322
323	Leather and products	64	74	74	88	112	115	114	155	204	13.7	323
324	Footwear	...	...	...	...	...	...	...	...	...	...	324
331	Wood products	67	67	75	88	105	100	100	110	122	6.9	331
332	Furniture, fixtures	63	83	95	110	79	85	84	96	110	6.4	332
341	Paper and products	51	57	66	75	118	133	141	193	205	16.7	341
3411	Pulp, paper etc.	...	...	...	...	...	...	...	...	...	...	3411
342	Printing, publishing	76	80	97	107	107	122	119	155	205	11.7	342
351	Industrial chemicals	54	64	70	81	110	110	102	163	191	15.1	351
3511	Basic excl fertilizers	...	...	...	...	...	...	...	...	...	...	3511
3513	Synthetic resins etc	...	...	...	...	...	...	...	...	...	...	3513
352	Other chemical products	54	56	61	69	98	110	106	142	176	14.0	352
3522	Drugs and medicines	...	...	...	...	...	...	...	...	...	...	3522
353	Petroleum refineries [	66	71	85	88	120	121	116	110	143	9.0]	353
354	Petroleum, coal products											354
355	Rubber products	64	63	70	81	112	116	107	110	171	11.5	355
356	Plastic products n.e.c.	...	...	...	...	...	...	...	...	...	...	356
361	Pottery, china etc	...	...	...	...	...	...	...	...	...	...	361
362	Glass and products	...	...	...	...	...	...	...	...	...	...	362
369	Non-metal products n.e.c	52	65	79	97	107	118	98	101	120	9.7	369
371	Iron and steel	41	67	83	96	112	132	107	124	119	12.6	371
372	Non-ferrous metals	...	...	...	...	...	...	...	...	...	...	372
381	Metal products	62	78	89	106	100	108	106	130	156	10.8	381
382	Machinery n.e.c.	66	70	87	91	125	112	122	166	184	12.1	382
3825	Office, computing etc.	...	...	...	...	...	...	...	...	...	...	3825
383	Electrical machinery	64	67	75	86	101	104	93	105	101	5.2	383
3832	Radio, television etc.	...	...	...	...	...	...	...	...	...	...	3832
384	Transport equipment	79	84	100	91	119	127	100	115	129	5.6	384
3841	Shipbuilding, repair	...	...	...	...	...	...	...	...	...	...	3841
3843	Motor vehicles	...	...	...	...	...	...	...	...	...	...	3843
385	Professional goods	...	...	...	...	...	...	...	...	...	...	385
390	Other industries	50	63	71	75	88	94	102	118	110	9.2	390
3	Manufacturing b/	57	65	73	84	109	120	121	155	...	c/ 13.3	3
410	Electricity, gas, steam	...	...	...	...	...	...	...	...	...	...	410
4101	Electricity	...	...	...	...	...	...	...	...	...	...	4101
420	Water works and supply	.	.	.	.	.	.	.	.	.	.	420
4	Electricity, gas etc	...	...	...	...	...	...	...	...	...	...	4
2-4	All industry	...	...	...	...	...	...	...	...	...	...	2-4

a/ Annual growth rate 1976-1985.
b/ Excluding footwear; including cold storage and motion picture production.
c/ Annual growth rate 1976-1984.

The information on industrial activity is based on the reply to the United Nations Questionnaire on General Industrial Statistics from the Federal Statistical Office, Belgrade. The concepts, definitions and classification by branches of industry have been adjusted as far as possible to comply with United Nations standards.

The estimates are derived from regular monthly and annual statistical reports and periodic surveys of industrial activity carried out by the Federal Statistical Office. All estimates relate to industrial activities in the socialist sector, classified according to the national organizational concept. Industrial activities of non-industrial organizations and of arts and crafts organizations are not included. The statistical unit is the enterprise, an economic organization of which the prevailing activity is industrial production.

The estimates are compiled by the Federal Statistical Office for orientation purposes only; they are based on the national classification, which is not comparable with ISIC. The data are arranged, for the most part by estimation, to represent the categories of ISIC. The estimates reflect organizational changes due to the integration and disintegration of existing organizations as well as the formation of new organizations and liquidation of old ones.

The estimates of employment represent annual averages of all workers and administrative personnel. Apprentices are excluded; working proprietors and unpaid family workers are not found in the socialist sector.

Wages and salaries represent personal income after deduction for social insurance contributions and taxes. The figures include personal receipts recorded by the organization as operating expenditure, covering such items as daily allowances, travel lump sums and field work allowances.

The estimates of value added relate to social product at current prices. Social product is calculated as the difference between value of production, including turnover tax, and material expenditure. It is defined as the sum of net personal receipts, contribution to accumulation and similar funds and depreciation.

The estimates of gross fixed capital formation relate to investments put in place during the reference year regardless of the time of payment.

The indexes of industrial production are compiled by the Federal Statistical Office and provided in response to the United Nations Questionnaire on Indexes of Industrial Production. In principle, the indexes cover the production of non-military goods of publicly owned establishments.

Related national publications:

Statisticki Bilten (issued intermittently during the year with the results of the annual surveys); Statisticki Godisnjak Yugoslavije (Statistical Yearbook of the Socialist Federal Republic of Yugoslavia); Statistical Pocket Book of Yugoslavia, all published by the Federal Statistical Office, Belgrade.

ISIC	INDUSTRY	1. NUMBER OF ENTERPRISES (NUMBER)					2. AVERAGE NUMBER OF PERSONS ENGAGED a/ (THOUSANDS)					ISIC
		1981	1982	1983	1984	1985	1981	1982	1983	1984	1985	
210	Coal mining	141	146	147	150	136	57	58	61	64	67	210
220	Petroleum and gas	9	11	11	10	16	4	5	5	5	5	220
230	Metal ore mining	78	81	84	82	83	33	33	36	37	38	230
290	Other mining	267	261	247	235	219	36	36	35	34	35	290
2	Mining, quarrying .	495	499	489	477	454	130	132	137	140	145	2
311/2	Food products	1077	1104	1099	1084	1055	185	191	196	206	214	311/2
313	Beverages	231	226	224	212	203	38	38	39	38	39	313
314	Tobacco	90	98	99	99	97	17	18	19	19	19	314
321	Textiles	709	722	722	716	690	231	239	244	255	264	321
3211	Spinning,weaving etc..	319	326	323	326	313	133	136	137	142	146	3211
322	Wearing apparel	520	531	529	525	531	138	145	150	161	177	322
323	Leather and products ...	128	127	128	126	127	25	25	26	27	29	323
324	Footwear	219	222	219	215	215	71	75	79	85	93	324
331	Wood products	567	571	558	538	514	103	106	107	108	107	331
332	Furniture, fixtures	503	506	506	492	485	94	96	98	100	103	332
341	Paper and products	189	194	200	195	192	41	44	44	45	46	341
3411	Pulp,paper etc.	78	80	81	80	80	21	22	23	23	24	3411
342	Printing,publishing	740	758	766	725	703	72	74	76	75	76	342
351	Industrial chemicals ...	245	267	265	265	260	45	51	51	55	58	351
3511	Basic excl fertilizers	175	188	185	182	177	25	28	27	29	32	3511
3513	Synthetic resins etc .	70	79	80	83	83	20	23	24	26	27	3513
352	Other chemical products.	228	234	246	241	239	45	45	49	50	52	352
3522	Drugs and medicines ..	64	61	67	64	62	14	14	15	16	16	3522
353	Petroleum refineries ...	27	30	28	28	31	11	12	13	13	14	353
354	Petroleum,coal products.	29	29	28	26	26	5	6	6	6	6	354
355	Rubber products	104	103	101	102	100	31	32	32	34	35	355
356	Plastic products n.e.c..	246	256	254	254	246	36	37	37	37	36	356
361	Pottery,china etc	55	59	58	57	54	16	17	17	17	16	361
362	Glass and products	73	76	77	76	68	20	21	22	22	23	362
369	Non-metal products n.e.c	513	519	518	496	472	89	90	91	91	90	369
371	Iron and steel	310	305	323	326	321	109	103	109	114	117	371
372	Non-ferrous metals	91	93	95	91	93	28	31	32	33	36	372
381	Metal products	979	1011	1014	1015	997	221	229	231	232	237	381
382	Machinery n.e.c.	747	782	791	788	781	185	192	198	202	208	382
3825	Office,computing etc..	...	...	...	...	...	...	...	...	...	...	3825
383	Electrical machinery ...	512	533	543	535	543	159	164	168	171	180	383
3832	Radio,television etc..	57	64	65	62	65	23	24	23	22	23	3832
384	Transport equipment	403	412	415	398	386	153	158	162	164	166	384
3841	Shipbuilding, repair..	86	86	87	81	82	26	26	28	27	28	3841
3843	Motor vehicles	...	...	...	...	...	...	...	...	...	...	3843
385	Professional goods	50	52	55	55	55	11	12	13	14	14	385
390	Other industries	73	73	69	69	65	11	12	11	11	12	390
3	Manufacturing	9658	9893	9930	9749	9549	2190	2263	2320	2385	2467	3
410	Electricity,gas,steam .. b/	582	609	628	628	630	81	86	90	92	96	410
4101	Electricity	446	458	475	477	482	66	69	73	75	79	4101
420	Water works and supply .	351	363	369	378	386	32	33	35	37	38	420
4	Electricity,gas etc b/	933	972	997	1006	1016	113	119	125	129	134	4
2-4	All industry b/	11086	11364	11416	11232	11019	2433	2514	2582	2654	2746	2-4

a/ Number of employees; working proprietors and unpaid family workers are not found in the socialist sector.
b/ Excluding steam.

ISIC	INDUSTRY	3. WAGES AND SALARIES OF EMPLOYEES a/ (BILLION DINARS)					4. SUPPLEMENTS TO WAGES AND SALARIES (MILLION DINARS)					ISIC
		1981	1982	1983	1984	1985	1981	1982	1983	1984	1985	
210	Coal mining	9.4	12.5	16.8	25.6	47.8	2933	3833	5266	8385	15856	210
220	Petroleum and gas	0.9	1.1	1.5	2.0	3.9	313	431	574	764	1586	220
230	Metal ore mining	4.6	5.8	8.3	12.3	24.4	1364	1738	2516	4415	7382	230
290	Other mining	4.4	5.5	6.5	9.4	21.3	1318	1665	1954	2951	5638	290
2	Mining, quarrying .	19.2	24.9	33.1	49.2	97.3	5928	7667	10310	16515	30462	2
311/2	Food products	23.4	30.0	39.7	59.6	109.5	7730	10242	13720	20219	39691	311/2
313	Beverages	4.9	6.1	7.7	11.2	21.7	1515	1952	2443	3727	7447	313
314	Tobacco	2.1	2.6	3.7	5.3	10.2	677	861	1188	1806	3637	314
321	Textiles	25.2	32.3	43.4	66.6	116.1	7955	10360	14244	22211	39907	321
3211	Spinning,weaving etc..	14.9	18.8	24.9	37.7	65.8	4679	6021	8193	12632	22667	3211
322	Wearing apparel	13.7	18.1	25.6	40.3	74.7	4268	5670	8103	12951	25131	322
323	Leather and products ...	3.1	4.1	5.5	8.4	16.2	987	1321	1797	2707	5485	323
324	Footwear	7.8	10.0	14.4	23.3	46.3	2502	3227	4548	7450	15482	324
331	Wood products	12.1	15.0	19.0	28.4	52.1	3758	4643	5837	9054	17121	331
332	Furniture, fixtures	10.7	13.3	17.1	25.7	46.5	3245	4130	5209	7949	14790	332
341	Paper and products	5.6	7.0	8.9	13.7	25.7	1837	2310	2932	4579	8887	341
3411	Pulp,paper etc.	3.0	3.8	4.8	7.5	14.0	993	1284	1628	2555	4938	3411
342	Printing,publishing	12.3	15.4	20.1	28.2	50.4	3409	4425	5795	8224	14975	342
351	Industrial chemicals ...	6.7	8.8	11.3	18.4	35.6	2104	2871	3672	6066	12344	351
3511	Basic excl fertilizers	3.7	5.0	6.4	9.7	20.0	1235	1687	2154	3483	7068	3511
3513	Synthetic resins etc .	2.9	3.8	5.0	8.7	15.6	869	1184	1518	2583	5276	3513
352	Other chemical products.	6.7	8.0	11.5	17.0	31.6	2121	2566	3806	5710	10855	352
3522	Drugs and medicines ..	2.1	2.4	3.4	4.9	9.1	660	784	1122	1660	3171	3522
353	Petroleum refineries ...	1.9	2.4	3.2	4.8	9.8	624	798	1087	1628	3531	353
354	Petroleum,coal products.	0.8	1.0	1.5	2.1	4.1	269	327	467	708	1217	354
355	Rubber products	3.8	4.9	6.5	9.8	18.7	1159	1447	1974	3012	6303	355
356	Plastic products n.e.c..	4.8	5.8	7.7	11.8	19.5	1499	1877	2497	3875	6588	356
361	Pottery,china etc	1.8	2.6	2.8	4.0	7.1	580	755	900	1238	2314	361
362	Glass and products	2.4	3.2	3.9	5.7	10.6	791	1030	1245	1794	3693	362
369	Non-metal products n.e.c	11.2	13.8	17.3	24.5	76.8	3624	4412	5499	8007	14923	369
371	Iron and steel	14.8	18.4	24.2	37.7	69.0	4868	5819	7630	11815	22716	371
372	Non-ferrous metals	4.1	5.6	7.8	12.6	25.2	1324	1751	2422	4254	7959	372
381	Metal products	30.3	39.2	50.3	74.2	139.4	9309	11999	15561	23406	45968	381
382	Machinery n.e.c.	27.9	36.4	48.1	71.1	135.4	8696	11531	15447	23153	45505	382
3825	Office,computing etc..	...	...	...	...	...	...	...	...	...	...	3825
383	Electrical machinery ...	21.2	27.1	36.0	54.3	111.7	6594	8497	11407	17136	36602	383
3832	Radio,television etc..	3.2	4.3	5.2	7.0	18.3	993	1313	1590	2084	4575	3832
384	Transport equipment	20.5	26.6	35.8	54.5	101.6	6459	8449	11181	17544	34388	384
3841	Shipbuilding, repair..	4.2	5.5	7.7	11.7	23.7	1267	1753	2353	3625	7750	3841
3843	Motor vehicles	...	...	...	...	...	...	...	...	...	...	3843
385	Professional goods	1.5	1.9	2.8	4.5	8.3	507	627	931	1485	2738	385
390	Other industries	1.5	1.8	2.3	3.5	6.5	480	628	791	1203	2289	390
3	Manufacturing	282.9	361.6	478.3	721.1	1380.2	88891	114525	152333	232911	452486	3
410	Electricity,gas,steam .. b/	12.8	17.0	22.7	33.3	66.1	4183	5651	7552	11544	23330	410
4101	Electricity	10.7	14.1	18.9	27.9	55.8	3505	4722	6354	9792	19909	4101
420	Water works and supply .	3.9	5.0	6.6	9.9	18.7	1235	1591	2105	3099	6483	420
4	Electricity,gas etc b/	16.7	22.0	29.3	43.2	84.8	5418	7242	9657	14643	29813	4
2-4	All industry b/	318.8	408.5	540.7	813.6	1562.3	100237	129434	172300	264069	512761	2-4

a/ After deduction for social insurance contributions and taxes. Including personal receipts chargeable to operating costs.
b/ Excluding steam.

ISIC	INDUSTRY	5. AVERAGE NUMBER OF OPERATIVES (THOUSANDS)					6. HOURS WORKED BY OPERATIVES (MILLIONS)					ISIC
		1981	1982	1983	1984	1985	1981	1982	1983	1984	1985	
210	Coal mining	46	46	48	52	53	87	86	91	97	99	210
220	Petroleum and gas	3	3	3	3	3	5	6	6	5	6	220
230	Metal ore mining	25	25	27	27	28	45	46	49	50	50	230
290	Other mining	29	29	28	27	28	56	54	52	50	53	290
2	Mining, quarrying .	103	103	106	109	112	193	192	198	202	208	2
311/2	Food products	139	142	145	156	161	266	267	277	297	310	311/2
313	Beverages	25	26	27	27	27	50	50	52	52	53	313
314	Tobacco	13	13	14	14	14	24	26	27	28	28	314
321	Textiles	182	188	192	201	208	325	335	340	363	376	321
3211	Spinning,weaving etc..	105	109	109	113	115	187	192	192	203	208	3211
322	Wearing apparel	109	114	119	129	141	193	199	211	228	250	322
323	Leather and products ...	19	19	19	20	22	35	35	35	37	30	323
324	Footwear	57	61	64	69	75	107	112	110	125	138	324
331	Wood products	84	87	88	89	88	155	164	163	165	164	331
332	Furniture, fixtures	70	72	73	74	76	131	133	133	135	139	332
341	Paper and products	30	31	33	34	33	56	58	60	61	61	341
3411	Pulp,paper etc.	15	15	16	17	17	28	29	31	32	31	3411
342	Printing,publishing	54	54	56	55	56	100	100	104	106	105	342
351	Industrial chemicals ...	30	34	34	37	39	56	62	64	69	74	351
3511	Basic excl fertilizers	16	18	18	19	20	30	34	33	36	40	3511
3513	Synthetic resins etc .	14	15	17	18	19	26	28	31	33	35	3513
352	Other chemical products.	27	27	29	31	32	49	49	53	55	58	352
3522	Drugs and medicines ..	7	8	8	9	10	13	14	14	15	18	3522
353	Petroleum refineries ...	6	6	7	8	8	12	12	12	15	16	353
354	Petroleum,coal products.	4	4	4	4	4	7	7	8	8	8	354
355	Rubber products	22	23	23	25	25	42	42	39	45	46	355
356	Plastic products n.e.c..	26	27	27	27	26	49	50	48	48	47	356
361	Pottery,china etc	13	13	13	13	13	24	25	24	24	24	361
362	Glass and products	16	17	18	18	18	29	30	32	32	33	362
369	Non-metal products n.e.c	69	70	70	71	70	134	134	134	136	135	369
371	Iron and steel	77	74	79	84	85	141	134	146	157	159	371
372	Non-ferrous metals	19	21	23	23	25	36	40	41	42	45	372
381	Metal products	155	160	162	161	164	283	287	287	289	304	381
382	Machinery n.e.c.	114	118	124	124	128	206	206	225	227	236	382
3825	Office,computing etc..	...	...	...	...	...	...	...	...	...	...	3825
383	Electrical machinery ...	103	104	107	109	115	185	188	192	196	212	383
3832	Radio,television etc..	14	14	13	13	13	25	26	23	23	24	3832
384	Transport equipment	97	100	103	105	106	175	177	174	180	183	384
3841	Shipbuilding, repair..	16	17	17	17	18	29	31	30	31	33	3841
3843	Motor vehicles	...	...	...	...	...	...	...	...	...	...	3843
385	Professional goods	8	8	8	8	9	14	14	15	16	18	385
390	Other industries	8	8	8	8	9	14	15	14	15	15	390
3	Manufacturing	1576	1621	1669	1724	1777	2898	2951	3020	3151	3267	3
410	Electricity,gas,steam .. a/	50	53	57	59	61	99	106	115	120	125	410
4101	Electricity	40	43	46	48	51	81	86	94	98	103	4101
420	Water works and supply .	20	20	22	24	25	39	41	44	48	50	420
4	Electricity,gas etc a/	70	73	79	83	86	138	147	159	168	175	4
2-4	All industry a/	1749	1797	1854	1916	1975	3229	3290	3377	3521	3650	2-4

a/ Excluding steam.

ISIC	INDUSTRY	7. QUANTITY OF ELECTRICITY CONSUMED (MILLION KWH)					8. OUTPUT (BILLION DINARS)					ISIC
		1981	1982	1983	1984	1985	1981	1982	1983	1984	1985	
210	Coal mining	722	729	860	889	931	37.8	50.0	69.0	121.8	218.8	210
220	Petroleum and gas	50	54	60	82	112	21.8	30.5	43.5	69.6	140.9	220
230	Metal ore mining	889	983	1098	1074	1190	30.1	40.5	67.4	112.3	224.7	230
290	Other mining	317	389	375	351	404	22.6	28.0	33.7	52.4	97.9	290
2	Mining, quarrying .	1978	2155	2393	2396	2637	112.3	149.0	213.6	356.1	682.3	2
311/2	Food products	1336	1345	1399	1530	1842	354.9	474.1	695.4	1082.2	1761.4	311/2
313	Beverages	216	221	224	217	232	50.2	68.6	90.1	131.0	252.1	313
314	Tobacco	55	56	59	59	69	22.7	34.0	49.4	70.1	168.1	314
321	Textiles	1394	1385	1391	1471	1541	166.8	213.9	318.8	543.2	957.8	321
3211	Spinning,weaving etc..	1131	1132	1152	1205	1254	103.2	131.1	196.4	332.8	584.1	3211
322	Wearing apparel	140	151	161	176	217	73.1	99.3	141.7	236.3	415.6	322
323	Leather and products ...	88	93	95	105	137	26.8	41.4	72.2	117.7	215.1	323
324	Footwear	74	77	84	95	128	47.4	64.7	108.0	201.7	372.2	324
331	Wood products	651	696	717	729	768	85.5	102.3	130.3	215.1	396.1	331
332	Furniture, fixtures	369	388	401	449	525	66.8	82.1	109.0	184.0	326.1	332
341	Paper and products	1531	1521	1617	1731	1781	74.9	90.6	123.0	215.7	403.7	341
3411	Pulp,paper etc.	1432	1404	1498	1607	1644	45.0	55.9	78.1	138.0	256.6	3411
342	Printing,publishing	195	194	191	186	213	64.7	86.7	114.4	158.7	283.1	342
351	Industrial chemicals ...	2332	2496	2510	2899	3069	107.0	141.2	217.0	442.9	793.1	351
3511	Basic excl fertilizers	1761	1854	1847	2161	2257	69.0	91.2	139.4	276.7	520.2	3511
3513	Synthetic resins etc .	570	642	663	738	812	38.0	50.0	77.6	166.2	272.9	3513
352	Other chemical products.	158	158	190	201	245	85.1	103.0	168.0	270.7	493.0	352
3522	Drugs and medicines ..	57	59	68	71	98	26.4	30.6	49.8	80.9	153.7	3522
353	Petroleum refineries ...	373	397	423	473	430	160.0	197.3	311.9	581.1	976.9	353
354	Petroleum,coal products.	161	169	148	147	149	24.5	32.9	52.8	81.6	160.5	354
355	Rubber products	251	257	256	277	302	38.7	46.9	73.2	138.8	263.4	355
356	Plastic products n.e.c..	300	309	305	327	331	45.9	58.4	85.9	145.9	212.1	356
361	Pottery,china etc	140	137	136	142	148	10.8	13.5	17.2	28.1	49.2	361
362	Glass and products	258	286	300	336	383	16.6	22.4	27.0	45.9	87.8	362
369	Non-metal products n.e.c	1917	1931	2007	1994	2021	80.1	98.6	133.3	217.3	407.7	369
371	Iron and steel	5517	5352	5894	6301	6456	212.1	254.5	442.8	759.5	1464.6	371
372	Non-ferrous metals	4846	5673	6055	6298	6658	91.4	119.0	182.4	312.0	612.4	372
381	Metal products	965	1099	1011	1010	1140	193.9	258.6	348.3	555.9	1082.2	381
382	Machinery n.e.c.	525	570	582	649	681	153.2	206.7	290.5	475.6	934.1	382
3825	Office,computing etc..	...	...	...	...	...	...	...	...	...	...	3825
383	Electrical machinery ...	611	650	641	682	798	168.9	220.9	316.2	544.3	1144.2	383
3832	Radio,television etc..	39	39	30	30	34	22.5	30.5	43.9	65.6	152.4	3832
384	Transport equipment	551	564	573	577	679	180.0	244.3	348.2	556.2	1068.9	384
3841	Shipbuilding, repair..	91	95	92	95	128	26.3	37.6	60.4	103.7	223.6	3841
3843	Motor vehicles	...	...	...	...	...	...	...	...	...	...	3843
385	Professional goods	25	28	26	31	31	7.6	10.4	15.7	26.7	49.8	385
390	Other industries	26	27	27	30	36	11.6	14.5	19.4	29.5	53.6	390
3	Manufacturing	25005	26230	27423	29122	31010	2621.2	3400.8	5002.1	8367.7	5404.8	3
410	Electricity,gas,steam .. a/	4254	4503	4911	5123	5502	157.8	210.5	318.1	576.3	1069.8	410
4101	Electricity	4167	4407	4808	5013	5384	128.9	169.3	250.4	461.9	851.9	4101
420	Water works and supply .	184	190	195	200	215	16.4	21.5	33.4	51.9	93.8	420
4	Electricity,gas etc a/	4438	4693	5106	5323	5717	174.2	232.0	351.5	628.2	1163.6	4
2-4	All industry a/	31421	33078	34922	36841	39364	2907.7	3781.8	5567.2	9352.0	7250.7	2-4

a/ Excluding steam.

ISIC	INDUSTRY	9. VALUE ADDED a/ (BILLION DINARS)					10. GROSS FIXED CAPITAL FORMATION TOTAL (MILLION DINARS)					ISIC
		1981	1982	1983	1984	1985	1981	1982	1983	1984	1985	
210	Coal mining	24.2	31.7	43.7	79.3	131.2	7863	10826	22179	47645	102668	210
220	Petroleum and gas	15.7	22.0	29.8	47.9	88.8	2592	3047	4995	8730	25934	220
230	Metal ore mining	12.1	17.0	27.3	47.1	85.9	12401	15158	12769	16926	26866	230
290	Other mining	11.5	14.3	17.0	25.9	49.9	2915	3416	4316	4574	10720	290
2	Mining, quarrying .	63.5	85.0	117.8	200.2	355.8	25771	32447	44259	77875	166188	2
311/2	Food products	67.2	86.9	134.2	198.5	393.9	19511	26706	38699	47754	79351	311/2
313	Beverages	16.5	21.0	29.6	44.9	95.3	3145	3035	4176	4507	7147	313
314	Tobacco	6.0	8.9	14.4	21.0	59.6	404	756	1014	1707	3427	314
321	Textiles	68.3	88.7	129.0	259.9	385.7	6575	8921	15271	23770	51396	321
3211	Spinning,weaving etc..	41.6	53.0	76.4	124.6	223.6	3829	5242	8628	15721	33062	3211
322	Wearing apparel	31.1	43.1	65.7	108.2	193.9	1997	3928	4404	9716	21990	322
323	Leather and products ...	8.6	13.5	20.2	30.6	62.4	732	1272	2214	2577	5900	323
324	Footwear	18.0	22.9	36.3	66.1	135.8	1396	2077	2529	5962	10720	324
331	Wood products	31.4	36.5	48.3	79.2	143.2	5016	5379	6091	8044	16125	331
332	Furniture, fixtures	24.1	29.2	39.2	66.2	118.4	3186	3790	4419	7182	16972	332
341	Paper and products	21.0	26.1	32.3	58.2	106.4	4168	8246	5663	9359	8674	341
3411	Pulp,paper etc.	11.6	15.9	19.5	36.5	64.4	3327	7181	4607	8123	6062	3411
342	Printing,publishing	30.5	40.0	52.1	68.3	124.9	2391	2056	2864	3252	4637	342
351	Industrial chemicals ...	23.8	33.2	47.1	104.3	170.6	32341	36085	51892	73796	90689	351
3511	Basic excl fertilizers	14.0	19.7	26.1	59.7	103.9	25209	28073	43442	66227	82506	3511
3513	Synthetic resins etc .	9.8	13.6	20.9	44.5	66.8	7132	8012	8450	7569	8183	3513
352	Other chemical products.	25.6	31.5	49.8	74.2	141.8	3761	3761	5901	8876	19321	352
3522	Drugs and medicines ..	8.5	10.3	15.8	23.0	50.8	1248	585	1859	2042	5762	3522
353	Petroleum refineries ...	14.2	15.6	21.7	46.2	112.1	9937	10654	10483	9451	15003	353
354	Petroleum,coal products.	3.3	5.6	8.3	13.1	27.4	1151	1434	1170	803	1123	354
355	Rubber products	11.2	13.9	17.5	35.0	72.8	2428	1843	2586	3684	7239	355
356	Plastic products n.e.c..	15.2	19.0	27.6	43.7	69.8	3848	3375	3141	5086	6532	356
361	Pottery,china etc	4.8	5.6	5.9	10.4	19.5	1562	1414	732	1158	2297	361
362	Glass and products	6.5	8.7	9.2	15.6	30.6	1646	2411	1190	3300	6013	362
369	Non-metal products n.e.c	31.7	37.7	47.5	71.4	138.7	8857	8557	7787	8661	17989	369
371	Iron and steel	43.0	55.9	88.4	149.3	270.2	18565	21192	21449	28219	107052	371
372	Non-ferrous metals	15.2	23.6	43.6	75.1	137.5	9761	7789	9364	17196	23400	372
381	Metal products	76.5	103.6	137.5	213.9	426.0	12149	17248	19344	29848	43362	381
382	Machinery n.e.c.	64.3	90.1	127.8	204.4	395.3	10611	12549	16325	21157	38152	382
3825	Office,computing etc..	...	...	...	...	...	...	...	...	...	...	3825
383	Electrical machinery ...	57.7	79.1	110.3	182.0	417.2	10355	11151	12733	19164	44879	383
3832	Radio,television etc..	8.7	13.8	17.1	24.4	61.5	759	1649	1858	2100	6166	3832
384	Transport equipment	55.1	77.4	110.3	173.8	341.1	9289	10798	15860	21438	39686	384
3841	Shipbuilding, repair..	10.5	15.7	27.2	42.6	97.7	665	1350	2084	3175	6329	3841
3843	Motor vehicles	...	...	...	...	...	...	...	...	...	...	3843
385	Professional goods	3.8	5.1	7.7	13.3	25.0	563	850	924	734	1625	385
390	Other industries	4.4	5.7	8.0	12.1	23.9	353	1498	1518	1302	1887	390
3	Manufacturing	779.0	1028.1	1469.5	2438.9	4639.0	185698	218775	269743	377703	692588	3
410	Electricity,gas,steam .. b/	62.8	86.5	106.1	192.4	340.2	53272	64544	75646	103782	36144	410
4101	Electricity	56.2	76.5	92.6	172.4	304.0	47880	57101	68351	93984	18742	4101
420	Water works and supply .	9.8	12.9	18.5	27.6	47.5	9971	13445	16003	26966	39259	420
4	Electricity,gas etc b/	72.6	99.4	124.6	220.0	387.7	63243	77989	91649	130748	75403	4
2-4	All industry b/	915.1	1212.5	1711.9	2859.1	5382.5	274712	329211	405651	586326	934179	2-4

a/ Social product including turnover taxes.

b/ Excluding steam.

11. GROSS FIXED CAPITAL FORMATION
MACHINERY AND EQUIPMENT
(MILLION DINARS)

ISIC	INDUSTRY	1981	1982	1983	1984	1985	ISIC
210	Coal mining	3053	4254	13674	29509	67879	210
220	Petroleum and gas	946	997	1520	4250	10514	220
230	Metal ore mining	4023	5063	5678	9284	15289	230
290	Other mining	1688	2036	2658	2706	7074	290
2	Mining, quarrying .	9710	12350	23530	45749	100756	2
311/2	Food products	9603	12084	18587	23362	44234	311/2
313	Beverages	1682	1743	2437	2806	5043	313
314	Tobacco	267	494	547	681	2150	314
321	Textiles	4325	5473	10914	17710	37004	321
3211	Spinning,weaving etc..	2784	3698	6469	12381	25761	3211
322	Wearing apparel	939	1660	2117	4715	9906	322
323	Leather and products ...	369	565	1156	1452	3115	323
324	Footwear	610	958	1332	3551	6450	324
331	Wood products	2404	2902	3810	4558	10173	331
332	Furniture, fixtures	1436	2071	2454	4091	10723	332
341	Paper and products	2417	5359	3066	6069	6817	341
3411	Pulp,paper etc.	2004	4886	2401	5268	4990	3411
342	Printing,publishing	1214	1090	1917	2299	3666	342
351	Industrial chemicals ...	14288	14547	18962	30074	45363	351
3511	Basic excl fertilizers	10707	10403	15498	26091	39468	3511
3513	Synthetic resins etc .	3581	4144	3464	3983	5894	3513
352	Other chemical products.	1706	2135	3595	5235	11820	352
3522	Drugs and medicines ..	555	336	1372	1406	4399	3522
353	Petroleum refineries ...	5133	7343	7872	7244	11777	353
354	Petroleum,coal products.	602	481	524	494	662	354
355	Rubber products	933	943	1525	2296	4657	355
356	Plastic products n.e.c..	2244	1928	1974	3436	3875	356
361	Pottery,china etc	1171	855	628	695	1198	361
362	Glass and products	769	1152	705	2151	4507	362
369	Non-metal products n.e.c	4941	5262	4698	5594	11178	369
371	Iron and steel	8869	12317	15033	17003	52366	371
372	Non-ferrous metals	4887	4850	4421	9824	17540	372
381	Metal products	6287	9431	11024	20430	26974	381
382	Machinery n.e.c.	5476	7183	9382	12682	23343	382
3825	Office,computing etc..	...	...	...	...	...	3825
383	Electrical machinery ...	5240	5736	6072	12979	29652	383
3832	Radio,television etc..	474	837	604	1181	3845	3832
384	Transport equipment	5631	5612	10225	14774	24098	384
3841	Shipbuilding, repair..	261	519	849	1625	3756	3841
3843	Motor vehicles	...	...	...	...	...	3843
385	Professional goods	258	415	596	498	1212	385
390	Other industries	129	814	1071	855	1299	390
3	Manufacturing	93830	115403	146644	217558	410802	3
410	Electricity,gas,steam .. a/	20127	26500	34523	45531	96685	410
4101	Electricity	18033	22982	31519	41522	89555	4101
420	Water works and supply .	1003	1441	1832	3101	5344	420
4	Electricity,gas etc a/	21130	27941	36355	48632	102029	4
2-4	All industry a/	124670	155694	206529	311939	613587	2-4

a/ Excluding steam.

12. INDEX NUMBERS OF INDUSTRIAL PRODUCTION (1980 = 100)

ISIC	INDUSTRY	1976	1977	1978	1979	1981	1982	1983	1984	1985	a/ RATE	ISIC
210	Coal mining	84	88	88	93	109	113	121	130	141	5.9	210
220	Petroleum and gas	91	95	98	99	109	110	104	101	107	1.8	220
230	Metal ore mining	87	96	97	98	99	102	105	111	109	2.5	230
290	Other mining	81	86	94	100	103	102	104	100	112	3.7	290
2	Mining, quarrying .	88	91	93	97	103	105	107	109	115	3.0	2
311/2	Food products	78	84	92	100	104	103	104	113	110	3.9	311/2
313	Beverages	71	82	86	92	103	118	112	106	100	3.9	313
314	Tobacco	93	98	95	103	105	106	111	98	107	1.6	314
321	Textiles	78	83	86	94	104	100	100	107	109	3.8	321
3211	Spinning,weaving etc..	78	83	86	94	104	103	103	110	...	b/ 4.4	3211
322	Wearing apparel	83	86	89	96	105	107	108	114	122	4.4	322
323	Leather and products ...	82	88	89	96	106	104	104	107	114	3.7	323
324	Footwear	81	84	86	92	111	112	116	129	138	6.1	324
331	Wood products	77	88	91	102	105	104	103	104	116	4.7	331
332	Furniture, fixtures	78	85	88	92	95	94	95	105	96	2.3	332
341	Paper and products	69	80	87	95	107	104	107	111	111	5.4	341
3411	Pulp,paper etc.	69	80	88	95	106	134	137	143	...	b/ 9.5	3411
342	Printing,publishing	80	83	89	96	101	99	98	100	105	3.1	342
351	Industrial chemicals ...	70	82	83	92	104	96	108	112	115	5.7	351
3511	Basic excl fertilizers	69	81	82	91	112	112	118	124	...	b/ 7.6	3511
3513	Synthetic resins etc .	...	...	...	...	...	...	...	...	...	...	3513
352	Other chemical products.	66	73	87	92	113	111	120	135	140	8.7	352
3522	Drugs and medicines ..	67	75	92	94	120	117	135	134	...	b/ 9.1	3522
353	Petroleum refineries ...	72	85	92	104	90	92	94	97	91	2.6	353
354	Petroleum,coal products.	62	64	73	92	98	95	100	107	105	6.0	354
355	Rubber products	63	77	86	97	108	103	106	110	118	7.2	355
356	Plastic products n.e.c..	57	72	83	93	105	110	104	96	95	5.8	356
361	Pottery,china etc	76	86	87	92	124	123	105	124	120	5.2	361
362	Glass and products	61	64	77	85	117	125	130	178	207	14.5	362
369	Non-metal products n.e.c	62	68	74	93	103	102	102	101	97	5.1	369
371	Iron and steel	73	82	93	99	112	109	117	126	131	6.7	371
372	Non-ferrous metals	87	91	98	98	103	103	106	112	117	3.3	372
381	Metal products	71	76	88	97	104	113	109	106	109	4.9	381
382	Machinery n.e.c.	69	75	88	97	107	108	114	116	120	6.3	382
3825	Office,computing etc..	...	...	...	...	...	...	...	...	...	...	3825
383	Electrical machinery ...	68	80	93	101	103	105	110	117	124	6.9	383
3832	Radio,television etc..	...	...	...	...	...	...	...	...	...	...	3832
384	Transport equipment	79	86	92	100	102	103	115	134	138	6.4	384
3841	Shipbuilding, repair..	136	125	103	101	104	105	112	140	...	b/ 0.4	3841
3843	Motor vehicles	110	127	140	155	158	160	159	166	...	b/ 5.3	3843
385	Professional goods	75	70	102	110	100	106	107	130	144	7.5	385
390	Other industries	80	89	98	109	115	108	105	114	125	5.1	390
3	Manufacturing	74	81	88	96	105	104	105	112	114	4.9	3
410	Electricity,gas,steam ..	74	83	87	93	101	103	109	116	119	5.4	410
4101	Electricity	...	...	...	...	...	...	...	...	...	...	4101
420	Water works and supply .	.	.	.	.	.	.	.	.	.	.	420
4	Electricity,gas etc	...	...	...	...	...	...	...	...	...	...	4
2-4	All industry	75	82	89	96	104	103	105	111	114	4.8	2-4

a/ Annual growth rate 1976-1985.

b/ Annual growth rate 1976-1984.

The information in the tables, except for the indexes, is based on the reply to the United Nations Questionnaire on General Industrial Statistics from the Central Statistical Office, Harare. The concepts, definitions and classification by branches of industry are generally in accordance with United Nations standards.

The data in the tables are derived from the census of production taken annually by the Central Statistical Office. The census covers all public and private establishments engaged in mining, quarrying, manufacturing, electricity and water supply. The inquiry is conducted by mail with assistance by field staff when required. The basic unit from which returns are collected is the establishment; head offices and depots are included if their main functions are ancillary to the establishment's individual activities, but are not counted as additional units of production. When only a part of an establishment's activities falls within the scope of the census, the establishment is included if the proportion of its total sales revenue from industrial activities is more than 50 per cent of its total sales revenue. Enterprises which are both agricultural and industrial are excluded from the census since it is usually not possible to isolate entirely the manufacturing activity of the enterprise. Such exclusions are mainly the manufacturing activities of sugar and citrus estates. Prospecting and preparation of sites for mineral extraction undertaken by the Ministry of Mines is also excluded. Sawmills operated in forest reserves are generally covered. African home industries in the tribal areas are not included and African industries in the urban areas are not well covered because of difficulties in the collection of data. Establishments with annual output of less than 2 000 dollars and establishments mainly in the nature of "self-employed", such as dressmakers, tailors, cabinet makers etc. are not covered. These deficiencies are not considered to be significant. Many of the figures published in official reports are revised in subsequent reports in the light of more accurate or more complete information from later surveys.

The estimates are based on the national classification scheme, which is comparable with the present version of ISIC. It should be noted that smelting of copper and nickel is included in metal ore mining (ISIC 230), petroleum refineries (ISIC 353) and manufacture of miscellaneous products of petroleum and coal (ISIC 354) are included in the manufacture of industrial chemicals (ISIC 351) and that the manufacture of leather and products of leather (ISIC 323) is included in ISIC 385 and 390 combined.

The reference period for the census is the financial year of the individual establishment; the estimates in the tables relate to aggregates of returns covering a 12-month period ending anywhere between 30 June of the year indicated and 29 June of the following year. The majority of the returns relate to the twelve months beginning 1 April of the year indicated.

The number of employees relates to the annual average number of persons on the pay-roll whether they are employed full-time or part-time, including working proprietors and family members if they are paid a definite wage or salary. Wages and salaries include employers' contributions to pension, medical aid or similar schemes. Output represents the total value of sales, adjusted for changes in the value of stocks of goods produced, plus charges made for repairs, work on customers' materials etc. (excluding non-operating revenue such as commission and dividends), the value of goods sold in the same condition as purchased and the value of capital works undertaken by the establishment's own employees. Value added is the balance remaining from output after deduction of the cost of (a) materials, supplies and fuels consumed, (b) water and electricity purchased, (c) work given out and (d) goods sold in the same condition as purchased. Both output and value added are valued in factor values. Gross fixed capital formation refers to the sum of all expenditures on fixed assets, less receipts from the disposal of fixed assets during the reference year. Fixed capital formation in new establishments not yet in operation and progress payments for fixed assets on order are included.

The indexes of industrial production are compiled by the Central Statistical Office and provided in response to the United Nations Questionnaire on Indexes of Industrial Production.

Related national publications:
The Census of Production (annual); Monthly Digest of Statistics, both published by the Central Statistical Office, Harare.

ISIC	INDUSTRY		1. AVERAGE NUMBER OF EMPLOYEES a/ (THOUSANDS) 1981	1982	1983	1984	1985	2. WAGES AND SALARIES OF EMPLOYEES a/b/ (MILLION DOLLARS) 1981	1982	1983	1984	1985	ISIC
210	Coal mining	c/	...	...	...	...	...	...	...	...	...	...	210
220	Petroleum and gas		-	-	-	...	...	-	-	-	...	...	220
230	Metal ore mining	d/	38.2	35.7	32.3	...	...	83.8	96.6	106.9	...	...	230
290	Other mining	c/	22.7	21.6	16.9	...	...	64.0	72.7	58.9	...	...	290
2	Mining, quarrying .	d/	60.9	57.3	49.2	...	...	147.8	169.3	165.8	...	...	2
311/2	Food products		25.2	26.3	27.0	...	...	72.4	90.8	103.9	...	...	311/2
313	Beverages		6.8	7.5	7.3	...	...	25.3	31.8	34.0	...	...	313
314	Tobacco		5.3	5.7	6.2	...	...	16.9	19.6	21.8	...	...	314
321	Textiles		20.4	20.8	20.6	...	...	44.6	51.8	56.9	...	...	321
3211	Spinning,weaving etc..	e/	15.1	15.5	15.2	...	...	32.9	37.7	40.5	...	...	3211
322	Wearing apparel		16.1	16.5	14.8	...	...	35.5	41.4	38.7	...	...	322
323	Leather and products ...	f/	...	...	...	...	...	...	...	...	...	...	323
324	Footwear		5.1	5.3	5.1	...	...	14.0	17.5	18.6	...	...	324
331	Wood products		8.8	6.4	5.5	...	...	16.4	16.1	18.9	...	...	331
332	Furniture, fixtures		5.8	6.5	5.2	...	...	13.2	12.0	12.5	...	...	332
341	Paper and products		3.4	4.1	4.7	...	...	13.0	17.4	24.3	...	...	341
3411	Pulp,paper etc.		...	...	...	...	...	...	...	...	...	...	3411
342	Printing,publishing		5.0	5.4	4.5	...	...	24.8	29.5	26.7	...	...	342
351	Industrial chemicals ...	g/	3.3	3.4	3.5	...	...	17.3	20.9	24.4	...	...	351
3511	Basic excl fertilizers	h/	0.8	0.9	0.9	...	...	4.7	5.8	6.6	...	...	3511
3513	Synthetic resins etc .		...	...	...	...	...	...	...	...	...	...	3513
352	Other chemical products.		4.4	4.5	4.6	...	...	21.3	26.1	30.6	...	...	352
3522	Drugs and medicines ..		...	...	...	...	...	...	...	...	...	...	3522
353	Petroleum refineries ...	g/	...	...	...	...	...	...	...	...	...	...	353
354	Petroleum,coal products.	g/	...	...	...	...	...	...	...	...	...	...	354
355	Rubber products		2.4	2.3	1.7	...	...	9.4	11.1	9.8	...	...	355
356	Plastic products n.e.c..		2.5	2.7	4.0	...	...	8.5	10.0	18.1	...	...	356
361	Pottery,china etc		[		]	...	...	[		]	...	...	361
362	Glass and products		7.8	7.8	7.1	...	...	20.0	24.6	27.1	...	...	362
369	Non-metal products n.e.c					...	...				...	...	369
371	Iron and steel	d/	[15.5	15.5	15.6]	...	...	[60.8	68.6	79.0]	...	...	371
372	Non-ferrous metals					...	...				...	...	372
381	Metal products		[21.6	21.4	16.0]	...	...	[71.5	81.0	65.5]	...	...	381
382	Machinery n.e.c.					...	...				...	...	382
3825	Office,computing etc..		...	...	...	...	...	...	...	...	...	...	3825
383	Electrical machinery ...		5.3	5.3	5.8	...	...	16.2	19.7	24.9	...	...	383
3832	Radio,television etc..		...	...	...	...	...	...	...	...	...	...	3832
384	Transport equipment		5.1	5.2	6.5	...	...	15.7	20.4	34.5	...	...	384
3841	Shipbuilding, repair..		...	...	...	...	...	...	...	...	...	...	3841
3843	Motor vehicles		3.8	4.1	4.6	...	...	12.7	16.4	21.9	...	...	3843
385	Professional goods	f/	[3.2	3.4	2.9]	...	...	[9.0	10.0	10.5]	...	...	385
390	Other industries					...	...				...	...	390
3	Manufacturing	d/	173.0	176.0	168.6	...	...	525.8	620.3	680.7	...	...	3
410	Electricity,gas,steam ..	i/	5.2	4.8	5.4	...	...	26.4	31.3	33.5	...	...	410
4101	Electricity		5.2	4.8	5.4	...	...	26.4	31.3	33.5	...	...	4101
420	Water works and supply .		0.5	0.5	0.5	...	...	1.4	1.5	1.6	...	...	420
4	Electricity,gas etc	i/	5.7	5.3	5.9	...	...	27.8	32.8	35.1	...	...	4
2-4	All industry	i/	239.6	238.6	223.7	...	...	701.4	822.4	881.6	...	...	2-4

a/ Figures relate to financial years of individual establishments ending at different times between 30 June of the year indicated and 29 June of the following year.
b/ Including employers' contributions to pension, medical aid and similar schemes.
c/ Major group 210 is included in 290.
d/ Smelting of copper and nickel is included in major group 230.
e/ Including manufacture of carpets.
f/ Major group 323 is included in 385 and 390 combined.
g/ Major groups 353 and 354 are included in 351.
h/ Including manufacture of petroleum products and gasses.
i/ Excluding gas and steam.

ISIC	INDUSTRY		3. OUTPUT IN FACTOR VALUES a/ (MILLION DOLLARS) 1981	1982	1983	1984	1985	4. VALUE ADDED IN FACTOR VALUES a/ (MILLION DOLLARS) 1981	1982	1983	1984	1985	ISIC
210	Coal mining	b/	...	...	...	...	...	...	...	...	...	...	210
220	Petroleum and gas		-	-	-	...	..	-	-	-	...	...	220
230	Metal ore mining	c/	257.5	249.6	426.3	...	...	149.0	125.2	279.6	...	...	230
290	Other mining	b/	192.1	193.2	205.1	...	...	124.7	121.5	141.0	...	...	290
2	Mining, quarrying .	c/	449.6	442.8	631.4	...	...	273.7	246.7	420.6	...	...	2
311/2	Food products		614.7	809.2	967.0	...	...	153.3	200.7	274.1	...	...	311/2
313	Beverages		128.2	165.0	288.4	...	...	70.2	86.4	220.2	...	...	313
314	Tobacco		67.3	75.6	133.9	...	...	43.4	47.8	111.9	...	...	314
321	Textiles		313.8	304.5	329.9	...	...	122.4	107.9	115.4	...	...	321
3211	Spinning,weaving etc..	d/	259.9	252.4	271.8	...	...	96.6	81.0	88.8	...	...	3211
322	Wearing apparel		144.5	147.9	132.6	...	...	68.9	72.6	64.1	...	...	322
323	Leather and products ...	e/	...	...	...	...	...	...	...	...	...	...	323
324	Footwear		58.9	67.4	68.3	...	...	32.8	39.4	39.5	...	...	324
331	Wood products		56.4	50.1	58.0	...	...	30.6	26.2	26.8	...	...	331
332	Furniture, fixtures		53.3	52.3	52.2	...	...	24.3	25.1	26.0	...	...	332
341	Paper and products		68.1	81.3	101.7	...	...	27.4	32.2	43.5	...	...	341
3411	Pulp,paper etc.		...	...	...	...	...	...	...	...	...	...	3411
342	Printing,publishing		80.5	88.4	90.4	...	...	48.9	53.5	56.8	...	...	342
351	Industrial chemicals ...	f/	203.6	222.0	223.2	...	...	58.4	55.7	35.5	...	...	351
3511	Basic excl fertilizers	g/	31.5	35.3	38.7	...	...	14.0	11.3	12.4	...	...	3511
3513	Synthetic resins etc .		...	...	...	...	...	...	...	...	...	...	3513
352	Other chemical products.		136.5	149.6	198.5	...	...	64.3	76.5	97.0	...	...	352
3522	Drugs and medicines ..		...	...	...	...	...	...	...	...	...	...	3522
353	Petroleum refineries ...	f/	...	...	...	...	...	...	...	...	...	...	353
354	Petroleum,coal products.	f/	...	...	...	...	...	...	...	...	...	...	354
355	Rubber products		54.8	57.1	51.8	...	...	25.0	26.8	27.1	...	...	355
356	Plastic products n.e.c..		44.5	48.9	83.5	...	...	22.6	25.5	43.9	...	...	356
361	Pottery,china etc		[		]	...	...	[		]	...	...	361
362	Glass and products		88.0	95.9	107.5	...	...	51.2	56.6	64.6	...	...	362
369	Non-metal products n.e.c					...	...				...	...	369
371	Iron and steel	c/	[279.7	259.2	324.1]	...	...	[114.0	90.0	140.3]	...	...	371
372	Non-ferrous metals					...	...				...	...	372
381	Metal products		[294.7	326.0	273.7]	...	...	[147.1	163.1	138.3]	...	...	381
382	Machinery n.e.c.					...	...				...	...	382
3825	Office,computing etc..		...	...	...	...	...	...	...	...	...	...	3825
383	Electrical machinery ...		82.5	96.8	111.9	...	...	37.5	45.5	61.8	...	...	383
3832	Radio,television etc..		...	...	...	...	...	...	...	...	...	...	3832
384	Transport equipment		79.2	99.7	145.4	...	...	34.9	38.2	80.2	...	...	384
3841	Shipbuilding, repair..		...	...	...	...	...	...	...	...	...	...	3841
3843	Motor vehicles		65.2	79.1	112.6	...	...	28.9	30.8	61.2	...	...	3843
385	Professional goods	e/	[41.6	38.5	43.5]	...	...	[19.4	19.3	21.8]	...	...	385
390	Other industries					...	...				...	...	390
3	Manufacturing	c/	2890.8	3235.4	3785.5	...	...	1196.6	1289.0	1688.8	...	...	3
410	Electricity,gas,steam ..	h/	174.8	196.1	274.1	...	...	76.6	83.2	116.4	...	...	410
4101	Electricity		174.8	196.1	274.1	...	...	76.6	83.2	116.4	...	...	4101
420	Water works and supply .		17.0	21.8	38.5	...	...	13.3	17.4	30.2	...	...	420
4	Electricity,gas etc	h/	191.8	217.9	312.6	...	...	89.9	100.6	146.6	...	...	4
2-4	All industry	h/	3532.2	3896.1	4729.5	...	...	1560.2	1636.3	2256.0	...	...	2-4

a/ Figures relate to financial years of individual establishments ending at different times between 30 June of the year indicated and 29 June of the following year.
b/ Major group 210 is included in 290.
c/ Smelting of copper and nickel is included in major group 230.
d/ Including manufacture of carpets.
e/ Major group 323 is included in 385 and 390 combined.
f/ Major groups 353 and 354 are included in 351.
g/ Including manufacture of petroleum products and gasses.
h/ Excluding gas and steam.

5. GROSS FIXED CAPITAL FORMATION
TOTAL a/
(MILLION DOLLARS)

ISIC	INDUSTRY		1981	1982	1983	1984	1985	ISIC
210	Coal mining	b/	...	...	...	...	...	210
220	Petroleum and gas		-	-	-	...	...	220
230	Metal ore mining	c/	88.6	30.3	31.8	...	...	230
290	Other mining	b/	44.3	64.0	55.9	...	...	290
2	Mining, quarrying .	c/	132.9	94.3	87.7	...	...	2
311/2	Food products		34.3	27.8	46.0	...	...	311/2
313	Beverages		15.9	10.7	13.7	...	...	313
314	Tobacco		1.7	5.2	15.7	...	...	314
321	Textiles		45.7	24.0	14.0	...	...	321
3211	Spinning,weaving etc..	d/	40.0	22.5	12.4	...	...	3211
322	Wearing apparel		6.3	3.3	2.5	...	...	322
323	Leather and products ...	e/	...	...	...	...	...	323
324	Footwear		3.2	2.8	2.7	...	...	324
331	Wood products		3.0	2.2	2.1	...	...	331
332	Furniture, fixtures		2.8	1.5	3.1	...	...	332
341	Paper and products		4.5	6.1	2.9	...	...	341
3411	Pulp,paper etc.		...	...	...	...	...	3411
342	Printing,publishing		7.8	15.2	13.3	...	...	342
351	Industrial chemicals ...	f/	7.4	8.3	5.3	...	...	351
3511	Basic excl fertilizers	g/	1.9	1.9	2.3	...	...	3511
3513	Synthetic resins etc .		...	...	...	...	...	3513
352	Other chemical products.		5.9	12.2	10.9	...	...	352
3522	Drugs and medicines ..		...	...	...	...	...	3522
353	Petroleum refineries ...	f/	...	...	...	...	...	353
354	Petroleum,coal products.	f/	...	...	...	...	...	354
355	Rubber products		3.4	3.8	4.8	...	...	355
356	Plastic products n.e.c..		6.6	2.4	7.8	...	...	356
361	Pottery,china etc		[			...	...	361
362	Glass and products		7.5	4.7	6.6]	...	...	362
369	Non-metal products n.e.c					...	...	369
371	Iron and steel	c/	[20.9	8.8	10.1]	...	...	371
372	Non-ferrous metals					...	...	372
381	Metal products		[17.2	19.3	12.2]	...	...	381
382	Machinery n.e.c.					...	...	382
3825	Office,computing etc..		...	...	...	...	...	3825
383	Electrical machinery ...		4.1	3.2	4.8	...	...	383
3832	Radio,television etc..		...	...	...	...	...	3832
384	Transport equipment		5.1	5.2	9.1	...	...	384
3841	Shipbuilding, repair..		...	...	...	...	...	3841
3843	Motor vehicles		3.2	4.2	8.5	...	...	3843
385	Professional goods	e/	[1.8	1.7	3.9]	...	...	385
390	Other industries					...	...	390
3	Manufacturing	c/	205.1	168.4	191.5	...	...	3
410	Electricity,gas,steam ..	h/	21.0	26.0	115.3	...	...	410
4101	Electricity		21.0	26.0	115.3	...	...	4101
420	Water works and supply .		3.3	4.2	-	...	...	420
4	Electricity,gas etc	h/	24.3	30.2	115.3	...	...	4
2-4	All industry	h/	362.3	292.9	394.5	...	...	2-4

a/ Figures relate to financial years of individual establishments ending at different times between 30 June of the year indicated and 29 June of the following year.
b/ Major group 210 is included in 290.
c/ Smelting of copper and nickel is included in major group 230.
d/ Including manufacture of carpets.
e/ Major group 323 is included in 385 and 390 combined.
f/ Major groups 353 and 354 are included in 351.
g/ Including manufacture of petroleum products and gasses.
h/ Excluding gas and steam.

6. INDEX NUMBERS OF INDUSTRIAL PRODUCTION (1980 = 100)

ISIC	INDUSTRY		1976	1977	1978	1979	1981	1982	1983	1984	1985	a/ RATE	ISIC
210	Coal mining		...	...	...	...	...	...	...	...	...	...	210
220	Petroleum and gas		...	...	...	...	...	...	...	...	...	...	220
230	Metal ore mining		...	...	...	...	...	...	...	...	...	...	230
290	Other mining		...	...	...	...	...	...	...	...	...	...	290
2	Mining, quarrying .		113	108	102	102	96	96	93	97	97	-1.7	2
311/2	Food products		85	93	89	96	108	124	127	120	114	3.3	311/2
313	Beverages		[90	84	85	88	89	92	90	87	95	0.6]	313
314	Tobacco												314
321	Textiles		74	74	73	79	112	119	109	124	175	10.0	321
3211	Spinning,weaving etc..		...	...	...	...	...	...	...	...	...	...	3211
322	Wearing apparel	b/	86	83	75	84	128	119	109	98	112	3.0	322
323	Leather and products ...		...	...	...	...	...	...	...	...	...	...	323
324	Footwear	b/	...	...	...	...	...	...	...	...	...	...	324
331	Wood products		[79	67	66	82	103	86	82	82	82	0.4]	331
332	Furniture, fixtures												332
341	Paper and products	c/	77	72	77	86	112	112	106	102	112	4.3	341
3411	Pulp,paper etc.		...	...	...	...	...	...	...	...	...	...	3411
342	Printing,publishing	c/	...	...	...	...	...	...	...	...	...	...	342
351	Industrial chemicals ...	d/	81	80	80	83	117	118	121	113	122	4.7	351
3511	Basic excl fertilizers		...	...	...	...	...	...	...	...	...	...	3511
3513	Synthetic resins etc .		...	...	...	...	...	...	...	...	...	...	3513
352	Other chemical products.	d/	...	...	...	...	...	...	...	...	...	...	352
3522	Drugs and medicines ..		...	...	...	...	...	...	...	...	...	...	3522
353	Petroleum refineries ...	d/	...	...	...	...	...	...	...	...	...	...	353
354	Petroleum,coal products.		...	...	...	...	...	...	...	...	...	...	354
355	Rubber products		...	...	...	...	...	...	...	...	...	...	355
356	Plastic products n.e.c..		...	...	...	...	...	...	...	...	...	...	356
361	Pottery,china etc												361
362	Glass and products		[107	87	70	87	118	110	105	98	105	-0.2]	362
369	Non-metal products n.e.c												369
371	Iron and steel												371
372	Non-ferrous metals	e/	[91	79	78	90	105	96	95	88	100	1.1]	372
381	Metal products												381
382	Machinery n.e.c.												382
3825	Office,computing etc..		...	...	...	...	...	...	...	...	...	...	3825
383	Electrical machinery ...	e/	...	...	...	...	...	...	...	...	...	...	383
3832	Radio,television etc..		...	...	...	...	...	...	...	...	...	...	3832
384	Transport equipment		91	86	75	86	155	178	146	117	97	0.7	384
3841	Shipbuilding, repair..		...	...	...	...	...	...	...	...	...	...	3841
3843	Motor vehicles		...	...	...	...	...	...	...	...	...	...	3843
385	Professional goods		...	...	...	...	...	...	...	...	...	...	385
390	Other industries		67	72	71	77	96	80	77	50	64	-0.5	390
3	Manufacturing		86	81	79	87	109	109	106	101	112	3.0	3
410	Electricity,gas,steam ..		...	...	...	...	...	...	...	...	...	...	410
4101	Electricity		124	86	99	93	100	91	95	97	111	-1.2	4101
420	Water works and supply .		.	.	.	.	.	.	.	.	.	.	420
4	Electricity,gas etc		...	...	...	...	...	...	...	...	...	...	4
2-4	All industry		92	85	83	88	106	105	102	100	108	1.8	2-4

a/ Annual growth rate 1976-1985.
b/ Major group 324 is included in 322.
c/ Major group 342 is included in 341.
d/ Major groups 352 and 353 are included in 351.
e/ Major group 383 is included in 371 to 382 combined.

PART TWO: INTERNATIONAL TABLES

INDEX NUMBERS OF INDUSTRIAL PRODUCTION AND EMPLOYMENT

The tables which follow present series of index numbers of industrial production and employment for the world, its major regions and selected country groupings for the years 1973-1985. Separate series are shown for each division of industry, or for certain major groups combined, as well as for the major divisions of industry according to the International Standard Industrial Classification of All Economic Activities (ST/STAT/SER.M/4 Rev.2). 1/ Except for a few, at the major group level, these series are similar to those published on a quarterly basis in the United Nations Monthly Bulletin of Statistics (Industrial Production) and on an annual basis in the United Nations Statistical Yearbook (Industrial Production and Employment).

The indexes are calculated from 1973. Each series is compiled by use of the Laspeyres formula, that is, the indexes are base-weighted arithmetic averages. The weight base years used are 1980 for 1978 and subsequent years and 1975 for 1973-1978. Value-added estimates, generally in factor values, for each of these years are used in weighting. The indexes based on 1975 are linked to those based on 1980 at 1978.

The indexes are calculated in three major stages. For the market economies, the indexes for each two-digit and for certain three-digit ISIC groups of mining, manufacturing and electricity, gas and water are first calculated for the developed and developing market economies of each region as well as for all countries of the region. Secondly, the resulting division or major group indexes are combined into indexes for these groups of countries for all mining, light and heavy manufacturing, all manufacturing, electricity, gas and water and industrial activity as a whole. Thirdly, the indexes for the developed and developing market economies of each region are combined into indexes for the various categories of mining, manufacturing and electricity, gas and water for all countries with developed and developing market economies. The two sets of indexes are then combined to yield the indexes for all market economies and these, in turn, are combined with similarly derived indexes for the USSR and European centrally planned economies to yield indexes for the world as a whole.

The national indexes used in compiling the indexes for the various categories of industrial activity shown are generally the corresponding indexes officially compiled by the country. In weighting the national indexes at the major group and division levels, the total value added in the industry, including handicrafts, is used in each case. The national indexes are adjusted to ISIC where necessary, in order to make the coverage of the combined indexes as homogeneous as possible. In a number of instances, countries make special calculations or make the necessary detailed information available to the Statistical Office. Where no official indexes are available, indicators for important industry groups are compiled by the Statistical Office on the basis of published data on commodity production. These country group indexes are then rebased to 1980 or 1975 where necessary and combined by the use of 1980 or 1975 weighting coefficients compiled by the Statistical Office.

For countries with market economies, the estimates of value added used for weighting purposes are derived, in most cases, from the results of industrial censuses or other inquiries relating to 1975 and 1980 or proximate years. These census results are adjusted to ISIC and projected to the bench-mark years where necessary. The estimates of value added in units of national currency are then converted to U.S. dollars. For 1975, the estimate for industry as a whole for the USSR is made in terms of U.S. dollars by applying the 1975 ratio of industrial output in the USSR to that of the United States (estimated by the Central Bureau of Statistics of the USSR) to the 1975 estimate of total value added for the United States. For the rest of the European centrally planned countries, overall dollar estimates for 1975 are derived by multiplying the corresponding USSR estimates in U.S. dollars by the estimated ratios of gross industrial production in each country to gross industrial production in the USSR. The derived totals are then distributed among ISIC divisions, major groups or combinations of major groups, on the basis of national indicators.

For 1980, the estimates of value added for the centrally planned economy countries are made using official data supplied by the statistical authorities or from data (number of persons engaged in industrial activity, average wages and salaries, cost structure, industrial origin of net material product and so forth) extracted from national publications. The value added estimates are computed separately for their components, "compensation of employees including contribution to social insurance, operating surplus and consumption of fixed capital" and adjusted to ISIC major groups. Efforts are made to ensure consistency with international standards. Estimates in national currencies have been converted to U.S. dollars by using official exchange rates.

The elementary series used in compiling the indexes for major groups are, in general, indexes for the corresponding category, or its subdivisions, compiled by national statistical authorities. Adjustments are made, when necessary, to align the national industrial classification with ISIC. In the case of the USSR and European countries of centrally planned economies, the indexes that serve as elementary series measure the movement in gross industrial output valued at constant enterprise prices, excluding turnover taxes. In the case of the market economies, most of the national indexes used as elementary series indicate trends in value added at constant prices, in most instances, in factor values.

Index numbers of industrial employment

The indexes are calculated from 1973. The weight base years used are 1980 for 1978 and subsequent years and 1975 for 1973-1978. The indexes based on 1975 are linked to those based on 1980 at 1978. Each series is compiled by use of the Laspeyres formula, that is, the indexes are base-weighted arithmetic averages.

The procedure used in the compilation of world indexes of employment is the same as that used for the world production indexes. For each division, major group or combination of major groups, of mining, manufacturing, and electricity, gas and water, indexes for individual countries are multiplied by the appropriate weight. The products are summed to derive aggregates and indexes for each division, major group or combination of major groups for the countries with developed and developing market economies and for each geographical area shown and then combined to yield aggregates and indexes for the market economies as a whole. The aggregates are combined with aggregates for the USSR and European countries of centrally planned economies to yield aggregates and indexes for each division, major group or combination of major groups, for the world as a whole. The aggregates for the constituent divisions or major groups are summed to derive the corresponding indexes for all mining, light, heavy and total manufacturing, electricity, gas and water and total industrial activity. The elementary series used in compiling the indexes for each division, major group or combination of major groups, consist of national indexes or absolute figures of employment. Available series of national indexes are given preference where these series relate to the average number of persons engaged during the year and cover the same field of industrial units as the national indexes of industrial production used as indicators for the indexes of world production. Substitute series are based on the number of persons engaged during one period of the year, or the average number of employees or operatives during the year. As in the case of national production indexes, adjustments are sometimes required to bring the industrial classification or the national data on employment into line with ISIC.

The indexes are designed to measure trends in the average number of persons engaged. Estimates of number of persons engaged, including working proprietors and active business partners, unpaid family workers as well as employees, are used as weighting coefficients. These data are obtained, in most cases, from the results of industrial censuses or other inquiries. In order to make the coverage of the weights and the indexes coincide as closely as possible, the figures are adjusted to ISIC and projected to the base years where necessary.

1/ United Nations publication, Sales No. E.68.XVII.8

1. INDEX NUMBERS OF INDUSTRIAL PRODUCTION

World a/

1980=100

ISIC	BRANCH OF ACTIVITY	% WEIGHT (1980)	1973	1974	1975	1976	1977	1978	1979	1981	1982	1983	1984	1985	Annual growth rate (73-85)
210	Coal mining................................	1.9	90	89	93	94	94	94	97	100	102	101	100	105	1.3
220	Crude petroleum and natural gas............	11.3	96	97	89	99	104	104	109	89	81	79	81	78	-1.7
230	Metal ore mining...........................	1.3	102	103	97	99	101	98	100	100	95	95	100	102	0.0
290	Other mining...............................	1.2	81	85	84	90	95	95	100	100	94	97	104	105	2.2
2	Mining and quarrying..............	15.7	92	94	91	99	102	102	106	92	86	85	86	85	-0.7
31	Food, beverages and tobacco............	10.7	80	82	84	88	92	95	99	102	104	106	110	114	3.0
321	Textiles...................................	4.4	91	91	88	95	95	97	100	99	97	99	101	103	1.0
322-324	Wearing apparel, leather and footwear....	3.4	86	87	89	94	96	98	101	100	98	99	102	102	1.4
33	Wood products and furniture............	3.2	92	91	86	94	98	100	103	97	94	100	103	104	1.0
34	Paper, printing and publishing.........	4.9	86	87	80	87	90	94	98	100	100	105	112	116	2.5
341	Paper and paper products...................	2.2	88	89	78	86	89	94	99	100	98	104	111	112	2.0
35	Chemical, petroleum, plastic products..	11.2	76	80	76	85	91	96	101	101	100	105	111	115	3.6
353-354	Petroleum and coal products.............	2.1	86	86	84	92	96	99	102	99	98	99	100	102	1.4
355-356	Rubber and plastic products.............	2.4	79	80	74	85	91	96	101	99	98	104	113	116	3.2
36	Non-metallic mineral products..........	3.5	82	85	82	88	91	96	100	98	95	97	100	101	1.8
37	Basic metal industries.................	6.0	94	97	87	94	95	100	104	99	89	91	98	99	0.4
38	Metal products, machinery and equipment	29.1	76	78	76	82	88	93	98	102	99	103	112	119	3.8
383	Electrical machinery......................	6.1	70	74	70	78	83	90	96	103	105	113	130	137	5.8
384	Transport equipment........................	6.8	82	82	81	89	94	99	102	101	98	102	108	114	2.8
31-33, 342 355-56, 39	Light manufacturing..................	28.2	83	85	83	90	93	96	100	100	100	103	107	110	2.4
341, 351-54 36-38	Heavy manufacturing..................	49.6	79	82	78	85	89	95	100	101	90	101	110	114	3.1
3	Manufacturing.....................	77.8	80	83	79	86	90	95	100	101	98	102	109	113	2.9
4	Electricity, gas and water.........	6.5	74	77	79	85	88	93	97	102	103	107	113	118	4.0
2-4	ALL INDUSTRY.................	100.0	82	84	81	88	92	96	100	99	97	100	105	109	2.4

a/ Excluding Albania, China, Democratic People's Republic of Korea and Viet Nam.

1. INDEX NUMBERS OF INDUSTRIAL PRODUCTION

Centrally planned economies a/

1980=100

ISIC	BRANCH OF ACTIVITY	% WEIGHT (1980)	1973	1974	1975	1976	1977	1978	1979	1981	1982	1983	1984	1985	Annual growth rate (73-85)
210	Coal mining	4.3	88	90	93	94	97	98	99	98	102	105	107	109	1.8
220	Crude petroleum and natural gas	1.8	70	76	81	87	91	96	97	102	104	106	107	108	3.7
230	Metal ore mining	0.5	83	88	87	87	90	90	92	89	90	93	93	96	1.2
290	Other mining	1.2	72	77	86	88	93	95	98	104	104	108	112	113	3.8
2	Mining and quarrying	7.8	77	81	86	90	94	97	98	100	102	105	107	108	2.9
31	Food, beverages and tobacco	16.5	79	85	89	90	94	97	100	101	103	108	111	117	3.3
321	Textiles	7.7	76	80	85	89	93	97	98	101	100	102	103	106	2.8
322-324	Wearing apparel, leather and footwear	5.4	70	75	80	85	88	92	95	103	103	105	108	112	4.0
33	Wood products and furniture	2.4	73	78	84	89	93	97	97	101	104	110	114	118	4.1
34	Paper, printing and publishing	1.5	...	...	...	...	...	...	...	...	...	...	...	...	...
341	Paper and paper products	0.9	75	79	85	90	95	98	97	102	105	110	115	119	3.9
35	Chemical, petroleum, plastic products	12.4	63	69	77	83	88	94	96	102	105	110	114	118	5.4
353-354	Petroleum and coal products	3.6	66	72	79	85	90	96	97	101	103	106	108	109	4.3
355-356	Rubber and plastic products	2.0	66	72	79	85	89	94	97	103	106	111	117	122	5.2
36	Non-metallic mineral products	4.0	72	78	84	89	93	97	98	102	104	108	111	114	3.9
37	Basic metal industries	5.7	76	81	86	90	94	97	99	100	101	105	109	111	3.2
38	Metal products, machinery and equipment	30.4	54	61	68	74	81	88	94	104	109	115	123	132	7.7
383	Electrical machinery	4.2	52	59	66	72	79	86	94	105	109	117	127	139	8.5
384	Transport equipment	4.1	55	62	68	75	81	89	95	106	110	114	121	130	7.4
31-33, 342 355-56, 39	Light manufacturing	36.8	73	78	83	87	91	95	97	100	102	106	109	114	3.8
341, 351-54 36-38	Heavy manufacturing	51.4	60	66	73	79	85	91	96	103	107	112	119	125	6.3
3	Manufacturing	88.2	64	71	76	82	87	93	96	102	105	110	115	120	5.4
4	Electricity, gas and water	4.0	69	73	78	85	87	92	95	102	105	108	114	119	4.6
2-4	ALL INDUSTRY	100.0	66	71	77	82	88	93	96	102	104	109	114	119	5.0

a/ Bulgaria, Czechoslovakia, German Democratic Republic, Hungary, Poland, Romania and the USSR.

1. INDEX NUMBERS OF INDUSTRIAL PRODUCTION

Market economies a/

1980=100

ISIC	BRANCH OF ACTIVITY	% WEIGHT (1980)	1973	1974	1975	1976	1977	1978	1979	1981	1982	1983	1984	1985	Annual growth rate (73-85)
210	Coal mining	1.4	91	88	93	92	93	90	95	102	102	99	95	102	1.0
220	Crude petroleum and natural gas	13.5	88	88	80	89	93	105	109	89	80	78	80	77	-1.1
230	Metal ore mining	1.5	102	102	95	98	99	98	100	101	96	95	100	102	0.0
290	Other mining	1.2	87	89	83	91	97	96	101	98	92	95	102	102	1.3
2	Mining and quarrying	17.6	97	98	90	99	102	102	107	91	84	83	84	83	-1.3
31	Food, beverages and tobacco	9.4	81	82	83	87	91	94	98	102	104	106	109	112	2.7
321	Textiles	3.6	98	95	90	98	96	97	101	98	95	98	100	101	0.2
322-324	Wearing apparel, leather and footwear	2.9	96	95	93	101	100	101	103	99	96	97	99	98	0.2
33	Wood products and furniture	3.4	97	95	86	96	99	101	104	97	92	98	102	102	0.4
34	Paper, printing and publishing	5.7	87	88	80	87	90	94	99	100	100	104	112	115	2.4
341	Paper and paper products	2.5	89	90	77	86	89	94	99	100	98	104	110	112	1.9
35	Chemical, petroleum, plastic products	10.9	80	82	76	85	92	96	102	100	98	104	110	114	3.0
353-354	Petroleum and coal products	1.7	94	92	86	94	98	100	104	98	96	96	97	98	0.4
355-356	Rubber and plastic products	2.5	81	82	74	84	91	96	102	99	97	103	112	115	3.0
36	Non-metallic mineral products	3.4	87	88	80	88	91	96	100	97	92	94	97	98	1.0
37	Basic metal industries	6.1	100	101	87	94	95	100	106	99	86	88	96	96	-0.3
38	Metal products, machinery and equipment	28.8	84	86	79	86	90	95	99	101	97	100	110	116	2.7
383	Electrical machinery	6.5	77	79	70	80	84	90	96	103	104	112	130	137	4.9
384	Transport equipment	7.4	91	88	85	92	97	101	103	100	97	100	107	112	1.8
31-33, 342 355-56, 39	Light manufacturing	26.2	88	88	85	92	94	97	101	100	99	102	106	109	1.8
341, 351-54 36-38	Heavy manufacturing	49.2	85	87	79	86	91	96	100	100	96	99	107	111	2.2
3	Manufacturing	75.4	86	88	81	89	92	96	101	100	97	100	107	111	2.2
4	Electricity, gas and water	7.0	75	77	79	85	88	93	98	102	103	107	113	118	3.8
2-4	ALL INDUSTRY	100.0	88	88	83	90	94	97	102	99	95	97	103	106	1.6

a/ Developed market economies and developing market economies.

1. INDEX NUMBERS OF INDUSTRIAL PRODUCTION

Developed market economies a/

1980=100

ISIC	BRANCH OF ACTIVITY	% WEIGHT (1980)	1973	1974	1975	1976	1977	1978	1979	1981	1982	1983	1984	1985	Annual growth rate (73-85)
210	Coal mining................................	1.6	92	89	93	93	93	90	95	101	101	97	92	100	0.7
220	Crude petroleum and natural gas............	4.9	68	69	69	72	80	88	95	106	101	100	105	106	3.8
230	Metal ore mining...........................	1.2	113	109	103	105	106	100	102	100	92	94	100	101	-0.9
290	Other mining...............................	1.1	90	92	83	87	91	95	101	98	90	93	98	97	0.6
2	Mining and quarrying..............	8.8	82	82	80	83	87	91	96	103	99	98	101	103	1.9
31	Food, beverages and tobacco............	9.2	84	86	86	90	92	96	99	101	101	103	105	107	2.0
321	Textiles...................................	3.3	104	99	92	101	99	98	102	97	93	95	96	97	-0.6
322-324	Wearing apparel, leather and footwear....	3.0	102	100	98	105	105	104	105	97	94	94	96	94	-0.7
33	Wood products and furniture............	3.7	101	98	88	98	101	102	105	96	91	97	101	100	-0.1
34	Paper, printing and publishing.........	6.7	88	88	80	88	90	94	99	100	99	104	111	114	2.2
341	Paper and paper products...................	2.9	91	92	78	87	89	94	100	100	97	103	110	110	1.6
35	Chemical, petroleum, plastic products..	11.2	83	86	78	89	93	98	104	100	96	102	108	111	2.4
353-354	Petroleum and coal products..............	1.5	106	103	96	103	106	106	109	95	89	87	89	88	-1.5
355-356	Rubber and plastic products..............	2.7	85	84	75	86	93	98	103	99	97	103	111	115	2.6
36	Non-metallic mineral products..........	3.6	92	92	82	90	92	97	101	96	90	92	95	95	0.3
37	Basic metal industries.................	7.0	106	107	90	98	97	102	107	99	84	87	94	94	-1.0
38	Metal products, machinery and equipment	34.3	86	87	79	86	90	95	100	101	97	100	110	116	2.5
383	Electrical machinery.......................	7.7	79	80	71	80	85	90	96	103	104	113	130	137	4.7
384	Transport equipment........................	8.8	93	89	84	93	98	101	104	101	97	101	107	112	1.6
31-33, 342 355-56, 39	Light manufacturing..................	26.9	92	91	86	93	96	98	102	99	97	100	104	105	1.1
341, 351-54 36-38	Heavy manufacturing..................	56.3	88	89	80	88	92	96	101	100	95	98	107	110	1.9
3	Manufacturing......................	83.2	89	90	82	90	93	97	101	100	96	99	106	109	1.7
4	Electricity, gas and water.........	8.0	78	80	81	87	90	94	98	101	102	105	110	115	3.3
2-4	ALL INDUSTRY.................	100.0	88	89	82	89	92	96	101	100	96	99	106	109	1.8

a/ North America (Canada and the United States of America), Europe (excluding centrally planned economies and Yugoslavia), Australia, Israel, Japan, New Zealand and South Africa.

1. INDEX NUMBERS OF INDUSTRIAL PRODUCTION

Developing market economies a/

1980=100

ISIC	BRANCH OF ACTIVITY	% WEIGHT (1980)	1973	1974	1975	1976	1977	1978	1979	1981	1982	1983	1984	1985	Annual growth rate (73-85)
210	Coal mining	0.5	73	78	86	91	92	95	96	109	112	116	126	134	5.2
220	Crude petroleum and natural gas	42.1	111	111	98	111	115	111	115	82	72	70	70	66	-4.2
230	Metal ore mining	2.5	94	99	91	93	97	96	97	102	100	98	100	105	0.9
290	Other mining	1.7	74	77	82	98	111	97	101	99	97	99	109	113	3.6
2	Mining and quarrying	46.8	108	108	97	109	113	110	113	84	74	73	74	70	-3.6
31	Food, beverages and tobacco	10.3	70	71	75	80	86	91	97	106	112	113	121	128	5.2
321	Textiles	4.7	84	86	87	93	93	96	98	101	101	104	108	111	2.4
322-324	Wearing apparel, leather and footwear	2.6	74	80	82	89	88	92	96	105	104	106	114	114	3.7
33	Wood products and furniture	2.0	70	76	76	80	88	91	98	99	98	105	108	113	4.1
34	Paper, printing and publishing	2.4	77	79	76	81	85	90	95	101	103	105	114	132	4.6
341	Paper and paper products	1.1	72	75	69	76	81	88	95	101	104	107	119	124	4.6
35	Chemical, petroleum, plastic products	9.7	66	69	69	74	84	89	94	102	107	112	119	124	5.4
353-354	Petroleum and coal products	2.3	72	72	67	79	84	90	96	104	109	113	113	119	4.3
355-356	Rubber and plastic products	1.6	68	72	72	80	83	88	93	96	99	103	114	115	4.5
36	Non-metallic mineral products	2.9	62	68	71	78	84	90	95	103	103	101	105	111	5.0
37	Basic metal industries	3.1	60	67	67	73	80	88	97	98	100	100	112	115	5.6
38	Metal products, machinery and equipment	10.4	62	68	71	77	82	88	95	98	96	97	109	115	5.3
383	Electrical machinery	2.5	52	59	63	73	78	88	95	100	102	110	126	130	7.9
384	Transport equipment	2.7	69	78	80	81	82	90	95	92	90	94	107	109	3.9
31-33, 342 355-56, 39	Light manufacturing	23.6	74	76	78	84	87	93	97	103	105	108	116	125	4.5
341, 351-54 36-38	Heavy manufacturing	25.6	64	69	70	76	83	89	95	101	102	103	113	118	5.2
3	Manufacturing	49.2	69	72	74	79	86	91	96	102	103	106	114	122	4.9
4	Electricity, gas and water	4.0	52	58	63	71	77	85	93	105	112	120	131	138	8.5
2-4	ALL INDUSTRY	100.0	84	86	84	91	97	99	104	94	90	91	96	98	1.3

a/ Caribbean, Central and South America, Africa (other than South Africa), Asian Middle East and East and South-East Asia (other than Israel and Japan) and Yugoslavia.

1. INDEX NUMBERS OF INDUSTRIAL PRODUCTION

North America a/

1980=100

ISIC	BRANCH OF ACTIVITY	% WEIGHT (1980)	1973	1974	1975	1976	1977	1978	1979	1981	1982	1983	1984	1985	Annual growth rate (73-85)
210	Coal mining	1.6	71	71	77	79	82	78	92	97	97	93	108	108	3.6
220	Crude petroleum and natural gas	8.8	88	88	86	84	89	93	93	108	98	88	92	91	0.3
230	Metal ore mining	1.2	122	117	106	113	109	98	103	104	81	82	94	95	-2.1
290	Other mining	0.8	91	94	81	90	95	98	104	97	82	89	104	105	1.2
2	Mining and quarrying	12.4	89	89	86	87	91	92	94	105	95	88	95	94	0.5
31	Food, beverages and tobacco	7.5	81	83	83	88	92	95	98	102	100	103	107	109	2.5
321	Textiles	2.4	102	95	88	96	95	99	105	98	90	102	100	100	-0.2
322-324	Wearing apparel, leather and footwear	2.6	96	93	89	101	104	105	105	96	86	91	96	93	-0.3
33	Wood products and furniture	3.9	100	95	86	100	105	110	111	101	95	112	123	127	2.0
34	Paper, printing and publishing	8.0	87	87	79	88	91	95	98	103	100	108	117	120	2.7
341	Paper and paper products	3.6	91	91	77	88	91	96	100	102	98	107	113	114	1.9
35	Chemical, petroleum, plastic products	10.8	78	81	74	85	93	99	105	104	95	103	111	115	3.3
353-354	Petroleum and coal products	1.6	98	96	95	101	108	110	108	98	92	90	93	92	-0.5
355-356	Rubber and plastic products	2.1	77	81	70	83	96	104	110	108	100	113	129	131	4.5
36	Non-metallic mineral products	2.6	91	92	82	92	97	106	110	100	87	96	105	108	1.4
37	Basic metal industries	6.3	124	121	97	108	109	117	118	106	72	82	91	88	-2.8
38	Metal products, machinery and equipment	34.1	89	89	78	88	94	101	107	102	92	97	113	116	2.2
383	Electrical machinery	6.7	83	84	69	79	84	92	101	104	98	107	124	121	3.2
384	Transport equipment	9.2	101	94	84	96	105	114	116	99	90	101	118	126	1.9
31-33, 342 355-56, 39	Light manufacturing	24.1	88	88	83	92	97	100	103	102	97	105	112	114	2.2
341, 351-54 36-38	Heavy manufacturing	55.3	91	91	80	89	95	102	107	103	90	96	109	112	1.8
3	Manufacturing	79.4	90	90	81	91	96	102	106	102	92	99	110	112	1.8
4	Electricity, gas and water	8.2	84	84	85	88	92	95	98	101	100	103	109	110	2.3
2-4	ALL INDUSTRY	100.0	89	89	81	89	95	100	104	102	93	98	108	110	1.8

a/ Canada and the United States of America.

1. INDEX NUMBERS OF INDUSTRIAL PRODUCTION

Caribbean, Central and South America

1980=100

ISIC	BRANCH OF ACTIVITY	% WEIGHT (1980)	1973	1974	1975	1976	1977	1978	1979	1981	1982	1983	1984	1985	Annual growth rate (73-85)
210	Coal mining................................	0.2	62	66	72	75	87	96	104	113	115	125	133	135	6.7
220	Crude petroleum and natural gas...........	12.1	90	86	80	82	86	92	100	101	98	96	98	96	0.5
230	Metal ore mining..........................	3.4	81	90	81	86	91	92	95	102	105	106	112	115	3.0
290	Other mining..............................	1.1	60	61	70	75	77	81	96	97	91	91	99	98	4.2
2	Mining and quarrying..............	16.8	87	85	80	82	87	92	99	101	99	98	101	101	1.2
31	Food, beverages and tobacco...........	18.2	71	74	77	81	86	89	98	104	106	105	109	114	4.0
321	Textiles..................................	5.2	87	90	87	90	91	93	100	94	92	89	92	95	0.7
322-324	Wearing apparel, leather and footwear....	3.7	82	87	86	90	90	92	98	99	94	88	91	93	1.0
33	Wood products and furniture...........	3.0	74	77	76	77	84	88	98	98	95	92	94	95	2.1
34	Paper, printing and publishing.........	4.4	82	85	81	85	88	92	95	97	98	98	105	130	3.9
341	Paper and paper products..................	2.1	70	75	68	74	78	85	95	96	100	102	112	117	4.4
35	Chemical, petroleum, plastic products..	14.0	70	72	73	80	83	87	94	101	102	102	108	115	4.2
353-354	Petroleum and coal products.............	3.6	69	70	68	78	82	90	93	108	107	105	103	119	4.6
355-356	Rubber and plastic products.............	2.6	71	76	74	82	81	84	93	90	88	92	98	100	2.9
36	Non-metallic mineral products..........	4.7	63	69	72	78	83	89	95	98	93	84	85	87	2.7
37	Basic metal industries.................	5.7	62	70	66	69	79	87	97	91	91	89	99	98	3.9
38	Metal products, machinery and equipment	17.2	66	72	73	78	82	84	93	88	79	71	77	82	1.8
383	Electrical machinery......................	3.5	60	66	70	76	80	85	91	86	84	77	81	90	3.4
384	Transport equipment.......................	4.6	69	79	79	77	77	84	94	75	70	69	74	75	0.7
31-33, 342 355-56, 39	Light manufacturing..................	36.8	76	80	80	84	87	90	98	100	99	98	102	107	2.9
341, 351-54 36-38	Heavy manufacturing..................	41.1	66	71	72	77	82	86	94	94	91	86	92	97	3.3
3	Manufacturing.....................	77.9	70	74	75	80	84	88	96	97	95	91	96	102	3.2
4	Electricity, gas and water.........	5.3	55	61	64	70	77	84	92	104	108	114	122	127	7.2
2-4	ALL INDUSTRY.................	100.0	72	75	76	80	84	88	96	98	96	94	99	103	3.0

1. INDEX NUMBERS OF INDUSTRIAL PRODUCTION

Asia a/

1980=100

ISIC	BRANCH OF ACTIVITY	% WEIGHT (1980)	1973	1974	1975	1976	1977	1978	1979	1981	1982	1983	1984	1985	Annual growth rate (73-85)
210	Coal mining	0.5	89	90	96	97	97	99	97	106	108	107	114	120	2.5
220	Crude petroleum and natural gas	29.9	120	123	108	125	126	121	120	81	67	66	66	61	-5.5
230	Metal ore mining	0.7	86	84	82	85	91	92	95	103	97	83	81	81	-0.5
290	Other mining	1.3	74	77	77	95	109	92	100	101	103	107	115	118	4.0
2	Mining and quarrying	32.4	115	118	106	120	123	118	118	83	70	68	69	64	-4.8
31	Food, beverages and tobacco	6.7	78	76	80	84	90	96	99	106	113	116	122	128	4.2
321	Textiles	4.3	93	89	89	96	95	99	98	102	101	106	108	109	1.3
322-324	Wearing apparel, leather and footwear	1.7	88	88	88	97	96	99	99	107	107	112	119	117	2.4
33	Wood products and furniture	2.1	102	97	91	99	101	104	104	94	92	98	95	98	-0.3
34	Paper, printing and publishing	4.0	...	...	...	...	...	...	...	...	...	...	...	...	...
341	Paper and paper products	1.6	86	83	74	86	86	92	99	98	101	106	115	120	2.8
35	Chemical, petroleum, plastic products	9.4	74	75	70	76	87	94	99	100	104	111	120	122	4.3
353-354	Petroleum and coal products	2.9	88	86	78	90	95	96	102	99	101	106	108	106	1.6
355-356	Rubber and plastic products	2.2	85	77	72	81	85	93	98	99	103	109	119	121	3.0
36	Non-metallic mineral products	3.0	83	81	74	82	87	93	97	100	100	104	109	113	2.6
37	Basic metal industries	6.8	86	85	76	85	86	90	99	96	95	95	104	106	1.8
38	Metal products, machinery and equipment	22.7	71	71	63	71	77	84	91	107	109	117	138	148	6.3
383	Electrical machinery	6.5	58	57	50	64	69	79	88	113	122	145	187	205	11.1
384	Transport equipment	5.3	77	79	77	80	83	83	85	108	102	99	110	114	3.3
31-33, 342 355-56, 39	Light manufacturing	20.5	85	81	81	88	91	97	100	102	104	108	115	121	3.0
341, 351-54 36-38	Heavy manufacturing	41.3	75	75	67	75	81	88	94	103	105	111	126	133	4.9
3	Manufacturing	61.8	77	77	71	79	84	91	96	103	105	110	122	129	4.4
4	Electricity, gas and water	5.8	67	69	73	81	85	92	97	103	107	114	123	129	5.6
2-4	ALL INDUSTRY	100.0	88	88	82	91	96	100	103	96	94	97	105	108	1.7

a/ Asian Middle East and East and South-East Asia.

1. INDEX NUMBERS OF INDUSTRIAL PRODUCTION

Asia excluding Israel and Japan a/

1980=100

ISIC	BRANCH OF ACTIVITY	% WEIGHT (1980)	1973	1974	1975	1976	1977	1978	1979	1981	1982	1983	1984	1985	Annual growth rate (73-85)
210	Coal mining................................	0.8	76	81	91	94	95	96	96	109	112	113	124	133	4.8
220	Crude petroleum and natural gas............	59.7	120	123	109	125	126	121	120	81	67	66	66	60	-5.6
230	Metal ore mining...........................	1.3	80	80	78	81	88	89	94	103	96	81	78	78	-0.2
290	Other mining...............................	1.1	58	63	78	124	155	94	102	107	118	125	142	153	8.4
2	Mining and quarrying..............	62.9	117	120	107	123	124	119	119	82	69	68	68	63	-5.0
31	Food, beverages and tobacco............	5.6	67	65	70	78	85	92	97	111	128	132	148	162	7.6
321	Textiles..................................	4.7	79	80	85	93	91	98	96	105	103	112	116	117	3.3
322-324	Wearing apparel, leather and footwear....	1.8	69	75	83	93	91	96	95	111	112	126	138	134	5.7
33	Wood products and furniture............	1.2	58	71	72	82	93	94	94	98	103	133	132	146	8.0
34	Paper, printing and publishing.........	1.2	...	...	...	...	...	...	...	...	...	...	...	...	...
341	Paper and paper products..................	0.6	74	76	72	77	85	92	95	112	116	123	146	151	7.6
35	Chemical, petroleum, plastic products..	8.3	65	69	67	70	88	94	96	104	112	122	130	133	6.2
353-354	Petroleum and coal products..............	4.2	80	78	68	83	90	93	100	102	108	97	117	117	3.2
355-356	Rubber and plastic products..............	1.2	64	67	70	76	85	96	94	103	115	121	141	140	6.7
36	Non-metallic mineral products..........	2.0	59	66	70	78	86	94	96	109	117	125	135	145	7.8
37	Basic metal industries.................	1.8	55	63	68	81	84	92	99	110	116	122	138	147	8.5
38	Metal products, machinery and equipment	6.5	50	75	65	81	81	95	97	112	117	135	161	169	10.7
383	Electrical machinery......................	2.1	37	46	52	65	74	90	97	110	113	136	162	162	13.1
384	Transport equipment.......................	1.6	62	71	77	88	88	99	94	120	122	134	163	166	8.6
31-33, 342 355-56, 39	Light manufacturing..................	16.1	71	70	75	82	87	96	98	108	114	124	139	155	6.7
341, 351-54 36-38	Heavy manufacturing..................	18.0	59	66	67	73	85	94	97	108	115	127	142	149	8.0
3	Manufacturing.....................	34.1	65	68	71	77	86	95	97	108	114	126	141	152	7.3
4	Electricity, gas and water.........	3.0	52	58	64	73	79	87	95	107	118	130	146	157	9.6
2-4	ALL INDUSTRY.................	100.0	93	96	92	103	109	110	111	92	86	89	95	96	0.3

a/ Asian Middle East and East and South-East Asia.

1. INDEX NUMBERS OF INDUSTRIAL PRODUCTION

Europe a/

1980=100

ISIC	BRANCH OF ACTIVITY	% WEIGHT (1980)	1973	1974	1975	1976	1977	1978	1979	1981	1982	1983	1984	1985	Annual growth rate (73-85)
210	Coal mining	1.9	112	103	107	101	99	96	97	102	100	96	76	88	-1.2
220	Crude petroleum and natural gas	3.8	30	32	36	48	63	77	97	102	108	119	127	132	13.1
230	Metal ore mining	0.2	118	119	108	108	102	96	99	93	85	88	96	95	-1.8
290	Other mining	0.8	94	95	87	90	93	95	100	99	95	94	96	95	0.1
2	Mining and quarrying	6.7	68	67	68	73	79	85	97	101	103	108	108	114	4.4
31	Food, beverages and tobacco	10.8	85	86	86	90	92	95	98	101	102	103	104	106	1.9
321	Textiles	3.8	103	101	93	102	99	96	102	96	94	92	94	97	-0.5
322-324	Wearing apparel, leather and footwear	3.8	106	105	104	108	106	104	106	98	98	96	96	96	-0.8
33	Wood products and furniture	4.0	96	97	85	95	97	96	101	94	89	89	90	87	-0.8
34	Paper, printing and publishing	5.9	91	92	81	88	90	94	100	98	97	99	105	105	1.2
341	Paper and paper products	2.6	92	96	81	88	90	94	100	99	97	101	107	108	1.4
35	Chemical, petroleum, plastic products	12.0	87	91	82	92	95	98	104	98	96	101	106	109	1.9
353-354	Petroleum and coal products	1.5	113	108	95	104	103	103	110	92	87	85	85	85	-2.4
355-356	Rubber and plastic products	3.0	86	86	79	89	94	96	102	95	95	98	103	108	1.9
36	Non-metallic mineral products	4.2	92	93	84	90	92	94	99	94	90	91	91	89	-0.3
37	Basic metal industries	6.0	104	107	91	96	95	98	104	97	90	89	95	97	-0.6
38	Metal products, machinery and equipment	34.0	89	92	87	92	94	96	98	99	98	98	100	106	1.5
383	Electrical machinery	7.8	83	88	83	88	93	95	97	99	100	102	109	117	2.9
384	Transport equipment	8.7	92	88	87	95	98	98	101	100	102	103	100	104	1.0
31-33, 342 355-56, 39	Light manufacturing	29.9	93	94	89	95	96	98	101	98	97	97	100	101	0.7
341, 351-54 36-38	Heavy manufacturing	55.8	90	93	86	92	94	96	100	98	96	97	100	105	1.3
3	Manufacturing	85.7	91	94	87	94	94	97	100	98	96	97	100	103	1.0
4	Electricity, gas and water	7.6	75	78	79	86	88	93	98	101	102	105	109	116	3.7
2-4	ALL INDUSTRY	100.0	88	91	85	92	93	96	100	99	97	99	101	105	1.5

a/ Excluding centrally planned economies.

1. INDEX NUMBERS OF INDUSTRIAL PRODUCTION

European Economic Community

1980=100

ISIC	BRANCH OF ACTIVITY	% WEIGHT (1980)	1973	1974	1975	1976	1977	1978	1979	1981	1982	1983	1984	1985	Annual growth rate (73-85)
210	Coal mining	2.1	118	107	111	105	100	96	97	101	99	95	74	86	-2.6
220	Crude petroleum and natural gas	3.5	35	38	39	50	68	80	101	104	110	121	127	131	11.6
230	Metal ore mining	0.2	140	134	129	120	115	99	97	91	81	80	89	83	-4.3
290	Other mining	0.8	96	98	86	90	93	95	101	99	94	93	95	92	-0.4
2	Mining and quarrying	6.6	72	71	70	74	82	87	99	102	104	108	105	110	3.6
31	Food, beverages and tobacco	10.9	85	87	86	91	91	95	99	101	102	103	105	107	1.9
321	Textiles	4.0	105	102	94	104	99	97	102	96	94	92	94	96	-0.8
322-324	Wearing apparel, leather and footwear	3.9	110	109	106	110	107	105	107	97	98	96	95	94	-1.3
33	Wood products and furniture	3.5	97	97	85	98	98	97	101	94	88	88	88	84	-0.9
34	Paper, printing and publishing	5.2	91	92	79	88	90	95	101	98	96	97	103	102	1.0
341	Paper and paper products	2.1	93	96	80	88	91	95	100	98	97	100	106	106	1.1
35	Chemical, petroleum, plastic products	12.3	88	94	83	95	97	99	105	98	96	100	105	108	1.7
353-354	Petroleum and coal products	1.6	118	112	97	106	104	104	111	91	86	82	82	82	-3.0
355-356	Rubber and plastic products	3.1	88	88	80	91	95	97	102	95	95	98	103	108	1.7
36	Non-metallic mineral products	4.3	95	95	86	93	93	96	99	93	89	90	89	87	-0.7
37	Basic metal industries	6.1	107	110	90	98	95	99	104	97	89	87	92	94	-1.1
38	Metal products, machinery and equipment	34.6	89	91	86	93	94	96	99	99	98	98	100	106	1.5
383	Electrical machinery	8.2	85	88	83	89	93	96	97	98	100	102	108	115	2.6
384	Transport equipment	9.2	92	86	85	94	97	98	101	100	101	102	99	103	1.0
31-33, 342 355-56, 39	Light manufacturing	29.7	93	94	90	96	97	98	102	98	97	97	99	100	0.6
341, 351-54 36-38	Heavy manufacturing	56.3	96	95	87	94	95	97	100	98	96	97	99	103	0.6
3	Manufacturing	86.0	95	94	87	94	96	97	101	98	96	97	99	102	0.6
4	Electricity, gas and water	7.4	75	78	78	86	88	93	98	100	101	104	107	114	3.6
2-4	ALL INDUSTRY	100.0	90	92	85	93	94	96	101	98	97	98	100	104	1.2

1. INDEX NUMBERS OF INDUSTRIAL PRODUCTION

European Free Trade Association

1980=100

ISIC	BRANCH OF ACTIVITY	% WEIGHT (1980)	1973	1974	1975	1976	1977	1978	1979	1981	1982	1983	1984	1985	Annual growth rate (73-85)
210	Coal mining................................	0.1	199	215	181	200	181	173	126	111	124	165	159	200	0.0
220	Crude petroleum and natural gas............	6.5	12	11	27	39	42	67	81	96	96	113	130	136	21.5
230	Metal ore mining...........................	0.5	124	130	106	114	96	88	104	95	83	94	102	113	-0.8
290	Other mining...............................	0.6	90	92	91	92	91	91	98	96	104	108	111	115	2.1
2	Mining and quarrying..............	7.7	39	39	46	55	55	71	84	96	96	112	126	134	10.8
31	Food, beverages and tobacco............	10.4	89	90	87	90	93	94	98	100	101	100	101	101	1.1
321	Textiles...................................	2.7	107	108	95	99	97	95	99	97	91	88	92	94	-1.1
322-324	Wearing apparel, leather and footwear....	2.9	103	100	96	101	98	94	96	99	96	93	93	93	-0.9
33	Wood products and furniture............	6.8	99	98	87	89	93	94	99	93	90	92	95	94	-0.4
34	Paper, printing and publishing.........	11.4	97	98	87	90	89	93	98	101	99	106	113	116	1.5
341	Paper and paper products...................	6.6	93	99	80	84	84	90	99	100	95	103	110	111	1.5
35	Chemical, petroleum, plastic products..	9.8	84	88	80	87	88	91	97	101	100	107	115	119	3.0
353-354	Petroleum and coal products..............	0.7	103	100	101	106	106	106	112	102	110	118	120	121	1.4
355-356	Rubber and plastic products..............	2.2	88	90	84	85	91	91	98	95	93	96	104	111	2.0
36	Non-metallic mineral products..........	3.5	92	93	79	81	84	86	94	97	96	97	99	104	1.0
37	Basic metal industries.................	5.0	95	100	90	90	89	94	104	97	95	103	111	110	1.2
38	Metal products, machinery and equipment	30.3	90	95	95	92	93	92	95	100	99	99	103	110	1.7
383	Electrical machinery.......................	4.4	76	87	88	88	91	90	95	107	108	113	121	132	4.7
384	Transport equipment........................	4.8	101	103	107	110	105	99	100	100	104	104	104	107	0.5
31-33, 342 355-56, 39	Light manufacturing..................	30.7	98	97	91	93	95	95	98	98	97	97	100	102	0.3
341, 351-54 36-38	Heavy manufacturing..................	53.2	89	95	88	89	89	91	96	100	98	101	106	111	1.9
3	Manufacturing......................	83.9	92	95	89	90	91	92	97	99	98	100	104	108	1.4
4	Electricity, gas and water.........	8.4	77	79	84	83	90	93	99	106	107	114	118	126	4.2
2-4	ALL INDUSTRY.................	100.0	88	90	87	88	89	91	96	99	98	102	107	111	2.0

1. INDEX NUMBERS OF INDUSTRIAL PRODUCTION

Oceania a/

1980=100

ISIC	BRANCH OF ACTIVITY	% WEIGHT (1980)	1973	1974	1975	1976	1977	1978	1979	1981	1982	1983	1984	1985	Annual growth rate (73-85)
210	Coal mining................................	4.7	73	83	83	88	92	96	96	117	124	136	148	161	6.8
220	Crude petroleum and natural gas............	2.5	96	106	107	112	116	116	119	102	96	90	84	78	-1.7
230	Metal ore mining...........................	7.4	108	107	112	106	116	110	108	102	117	121	127	147	2.7
290	Other mining...............................	1.4	104	103	94	92	89	100	98	106	102	104	106	105	0.1
2	Mining and quarrying..............	16.0	96	99	101	99	106	106	105	106	114	119	125	137	3.0
31	Food, beverages and tobacco...........	13.7	96	100	97	98	99	101	98	102	100	100	101	101	0.4
321	Textiles...................................	2.7	115	84	105	98	97	99	100	100	92	90	88	86	-2.4
322-324	Wearing apparel, leather and footwear....	3.0	92	78	83	79	81	87	93	99	88	87	86	85	-0.7
33	Wood products and furniture............	4.3	103	83	93	90	93	86	95	95	92	90	89	88	-1.3
34	Paper, printing and publishing.........	6.8	90	93	84	89	91	93	97	105	141	164	193	227	8.0
341	Paper and paper products..................	2.2	89	79	76	83	85	90	98	93	90	88	86	83	-0.6
35	Chemical, petroleum, plastic products..	8.8	93	94	86	95	90	95	100	100	97	96	95	94	0.1
353-354	Petroleum and coal products.............	0.8	94	94	95	99	103	102	103	102	100	100	100	101	0.6
355-356	Rubber and plastic products.............	2.8	117	123	99	106	96	98	95	99	92	90	90	88	-2.4
36	Non-metallic mineral products..........	3.5	100	94	95	92	94	91	97	102	91	89	88	87	-1.2
37	Basic metal industries.................	8.3	91	111	92	99	93	96	98	95	79	73	68	64	-2.9
38	Metal products, machinery and equipment	21.3	111	90	100	92	92	99	102	103	86	81	78	74	3.3
383	Electrical machinery......................	3.3	114	103	100	94	81	84	92	97	78	78	78	78	-3.1
384	Transport equipment.......................	6.2	119	118	118	116	103	115	108	111	108	108	108	109	-0.7
31-33, 342 355-56, 39	Light manufacturing..................	31.8	99	94	94	95	95	96	97	102	105	110	116	123	1.8
341, 351-54 36-38	Heavy manufacturing..................	41.3	101	94	94	94	92	96	101	100	87	83	80	77	2.2
3	Manufacturing.....................	73.1	100	94	94	94	93	96	99	101	95	95	96	97	-0.2
4	Electricity, gas and water.........	10.9	66	79	73	87	85	90	94	105	108	114	120	126	5.5
2-4	ALL INDUSTRY.................	100.0	96	92	93	93	95	97	100	102	100	101	103	106	0.8

a/ Australia and New Zealand.

2. INDEX NUMBERS OF INDUSTRIAL EMPLOYMENT

World a/

1980=100

ISIC	BRANCH OF ACTIVITY	% WEIGHT (1980)	1973	1974	1975	1976	1977	1978	1979	1981	1982	1983	1984	1985	Annual growth rate (73-84)
210	Coal mining	1.8	95	95	97	97	97	97	99	101	102	103	103	...	0.7
220	Crude petroleum and natural gas	0.5	74	77	80	83	86	90	94	108	112	112	116	...	4.2
230	Metal ore mining	31.0	107	105	101	103	103	100	100	97	93	92	91	...	-1.5
290	Other mining	1.2	...	...	...	...	...	...	...	...	...	...	...	...	...
2	Mining and quarrying	4.5	96	97	97	97	98	97	99	101	100	100	100	...	0.4
31	Food, beverages and tobacco	13.9	81	85	86	92	95	96	97	101	101	101	102	...	2.1
321	Textiles	9.9	96	99	98	98	98	100	100	95	94	93	91	...	-0.5
322-324	Wearing apparel, leather and footwear	8.8	82	83	87	96	98	100	102	100	99	100	100	...	1.8
33	Wood products and furniture	6.2	92	94	93	95	95	98	99	98	98	102	106	...	1.3
34	Paper, printing and publishing	4.4	94	95	93	95	95	97	99	100	98	99	100	...	0.6
341	Paper and paper products	1.7	98	100	97	99	99	99	100	100	97	97	98	...	0.0
35	Chemical, petroleum, plastic products	7.4	88	91	91	92	95	97	100	100	98	98	99	...	1.1
353-354	Petroleum and coal products	1.0	...	...	...	...	...	...	...	...	...	...	...	...	...
355-356	Rubber and plastic products	2.5	89	90	88	92	95	96	100	100	98	99	102	...	1.2
36	Non-metallic mineral products	5.5	91	92	92	93	95	98	99	100	101	98	99	...	0.8
37	Basic metal industries	4.1	100	101	100	99	99	100	101	98	95	91	91	...	-0.8
38	Metal products, machinery and equipment	30.0	92	93	92	94	96	98	100	100	97	97	98	...	0.6
383	Electrical machinery	6.9	...	...	...	...	...	...	...	...	...	...	...	...	...
384	Transport equipment	7.2	...	...	...	...	...	...	...	...	...	...	...	...	...
31-33, 342 355-56, 39	Light manufacturing	46.2	88	90	91	94	97	98	100	99	98	99	100	...	1.2
341, 351-54 36-38	Heavy manufacturing	46.3	92	94	93	95	96	98	100	100	98	97	97	...	0.5
3	Manufacturing b/	92.5	91	92	92	95	96	98	100	99	98	98	98	...	0.7
4	Electricity, gas and water	3.0	81	82	85	87	91	94	97	103	106	108	113	...	3.1
2-4	ALL INDUSTRY	100.0	91	92	92	95	97	98	100	99	98	98	99	...	0.8

a/ Excluding Albania, China, Democratic People's Republic of Korea and Viet Nam.

b/ Excluding printing and publishing for the USSR.

2. INDEX NUMBERS OF INDUSTRIAL EMPLOYMENT

Centrally planned economies a/

1980=100

ISIC	BRANCH OF ACTIVITY	% WEIGHT (1980)	1973	1974	1975	1976	1977	1978	1979	1981	1982	1983	1984	1985	Annual growth rate (73-85)
210	Coal mining	3.7	94	92	93	93	94	96	98	102	105	107	109	111	2.4
220	Crude petroleum and natural gas	0.4	96	96	95	95	96	96	98	107	108	114	118	121	1.9
230	Metal ore mining	0.6	96	97	97	98	97	98	99	100	101	104	104	105	0.8
290	Other mining	1.8	...	...	...	...	...	...	...	...	...	...	...	...	...
2	Mining and quarrying	6.5	96	95	97	95	96	97	99	102	104	106	108	109	1.1
31	Food, beverages and tobacco	9.1	93	95	96	97	99	100	100	101	101	101	102	102	0.8
321	Textiles	7.4	98	99	99	100	100	100	100	100	98	97	96	96	-0.2
322-324	Wearing apparel, leather and footwear	8.3	94	95	96	97	98	99	99	101	100	100	100	100	0.5
33	Wood products and furniture	4.3	100	101	101	100	101	101	101	100	100	100	100	100	0.0
34	Paper, printing and publishing	2.1	95	96	97	97	98	99	99	100	98	98	98	98	0.3
341	Paper and paper products	1.0	94	95	96	96	97	98	99	100	100	101	101	102	0.7
35	Chemical, petroleum, plastic products	6.6	90	92	97	96	97	98	99	101	102	102	102	102	1.0
353-354	Petroleum and coal products	1.2	...	...	...	...	...	...	...	...	...	...	...	...	...
355-356	Rubber and plastic products	1.4	87	90	91	95	95	97	98	101	102	102	104	104	1.5
36	Non-metallic mineral products	6.5	93	95	99	98	99	100	100	100	100	93	94	92	-0.1
37	Basic metal industries	3.7	94	95	97	96	97	99	99	100	100	102	102	104	0.8
38	Metal products, machinery and equipment	40.7	87	89	90	93	96	97	99	101	101	102	102	103	1.4
383	Electrical machinery	4.6	...	...	...	...	...	...	...	...	...	...	...	...	...
384	Transport equipment	5.0	...	...	...	...	...	...	...	...	...	...	...	...	...
31-33, 342 355-56, 39	Light manufacturing	34.1	94	96	97	98	100	100	100	101	100	100	100	100	0.5
341, 351-54 36-38	Heavy manufacturing	57.1	89	91	93	95	97	98	99	101	101	101	101	102	1.1
3	Manufacturing b/	91.2	90	92	94	95	97	98	99	101	101	100	101	101	1.0
4	Electricity, gas and water	2.3	87	89	90	92	94	95	97	102	105	107	108	111	2.0
2-4	ALL INDUSTRY	100.0	90	92	94	95	97	98	99	101	101	101	101	102	1.0

a/ Bulgaria, Czechoslovakia, German Democratic Republic, Hungary, Poland, Romania and the USSR.

b/ Excluding printing and publishing for the USSR.

2. INDEX NUMBERS OF INDUSTRIAL EMPLOYMENT

Market economies a/

1980=100

ISIC	BRANCH OF ACTIVITY	% WEIGHT (1980)	1973	1974	1975	1976	1977	1978	1979	1981	1982	1983	1984	1985	Annual growth rate (73-84)
210	Coal mining................................	1.2	96	97	101	101	99	98	100	100	100	98	97	...	0.1
220	Crude petroleum and natural gas...........	0.6	67	71	76	79	83	88	94	109	113	112	115	...	5.0
230	Metal ore mining...........................	1.2	108	106	101	103	103	100	100	97	92	90	89	...	-1.7
290	Other mining...............................	0.9	...	...	...	...	...	...	...	...	...	...	...	...	...
2	Mining and quarrying..............	3.9	97	98	98	99	99	97	99	100	98	97	96	...	-0.1
31	Food, beverages and tobacco...........	15.5	80	82	85	91	95	96	97	101	101	101	102		2.2
321	Textiles...................................	10.7	96	99	98	98	98	100	100	94	93	92	90	...	-0.6
322-324	Wearing apparel, leather and footwear....	9.0	78	80	84	95	97	100	102	100	99	99	100	...	2.3
33	Wood products and furniture...........	6.7	91	92	91	93	93	97	99	98	98	102	106	...	1.4
34	Paper, printing and publishing.........	5.2	95	95	93	95	95	97	99	100	99	99	100	...	0.5
341	Paper and paper products..................	2.0	98	101	97	99	100	99	100	100	96	97	97	...	-0.1
35	Chemical, petroleum, plastic products..	7.7	90	92	92	93	96	97	100	99	97	98	99	...	0.9
353-354	Petroleum and coal products.............	0.9	...	...	...	...	...	...	...	...	...	...	...	...	...
355-356	Rubber and plastic products.............	2.9	88	88	86	90	93	95	100	99	97	99	101	...	1.3
36	Non-metallic mineral products..........	5.2	90	89	89	91	93	97	99	100	101	100	101	...	1.0
37	Basic metal industries.................	4.3	100	102	100	99	99	100	101	97	94	88	88	...	-1.2
38	Metal products, machinery and equipment	26.5	94	95	92	94	96	98	100	99	95	95	96	...	0.2
383	Electrical machinery.......................	7.6	...	...	...	...	...	...	...	...	...	...	...	...	...
384	Transport equipment........................	7.9	...	...	...	...	...	...	...	...	...	...	...	...	...
31-33, 342 355-56, 39	Light manufacturing..................	50.1	86	88	89	94	96	98	100	99	98	99	100	...	1.4
341, 351-54 36-38	Heavy manufacturing..................	42.8	94	95	95	95	96	98	100	99	96	95	96	...	0.2
3	Manufacturing.....................	92.9	91	92	92	94	96	98	100	99	97	97	98	...	0.7
4	Electricity, gas and water.........	3.2	80	81	83	86	91	94	97	103	106	108	114	...	3.3
2-4	ALL INDUSTRY.................	100.0	91	92	92	94	96	98	100	99	98	98	98	...	0.7

a/ Developed market economies and developing market economies.

2. INDEX NUMBERS OF INDUSTRIAL EMPLOYMENT

Developed market economies a/

1980=100

ISIC	BRANCH OF ACTIVITY	% WEIGHT (1980)	1973	1974	1975	1976	1977	1978	1979	1981	1982	1983	1984	1985	Annual growth rate (73-85)
210	Coal mining................................	1.3	107	102	99	99	102	99	102	98	98	92	87	85	-1.9
220	Crude petroleum and natural gas............	0.4	53	58	61	64	69	77	77	114	122	115	116	117	6.8
230	Metal ore mining...........................	1.0	102	96	91	96	108	96	98	102	96	94	94	93	-0.8
290	Other mining...............................	0.8	104	119	112	108	108	101	104	96	90	84	82	80	-2.2
2	Mining and quarrying...............	3.5	95	97	96	97	98	96	99	101	98	93	92	90	-0.4
31	Food, beverages and tobacco............	9.9	101	101	99	99	101	101	100	98	96	97	95	95	-0.5
321	Textiles...................................	6.4	129	122	116	114	110	107	105	92	86	88	82	79	-4.0
322-324	Wearing apparel, leather and footwear....	6.4	114	110	106	107	105	104	103	96	90	90	88	86	-2.3
33	Wood products and furniture............	5.7	108	107	101	103	103	103	103	94	88	90	87	85	-2.0
34	Paper, printing and publishing.........	7.2	101	101	98	98	98	99	100	99	96	97	97	98	-0.2
341	Paper and paper products..................	2.7	106	109	103	104	103	102	101	98	93	93	92	92	-1.2
35	Chemical, petroleum, plastic products..	8.9	100	102	98	99	99	100	101	98	96	95	96	95	-0.4
353-354	Petroleum and coal products.............	1.2	...	...	...	...	...	...	...	...	...	...	...	...	...
355-356	Rubber and plastic products.............	3.5	98	97	91	94	96	99	101	99	95	98	100	99	0.1
36	Non-metallic mineral products..........	4.1	110	109	104	103	103	103	103	97	91	90	88	84	-2.2
37	Basic metal industries.................	5.5	115	116	111	108	106	104	103	96	88	79	78	75	-3.5
38	Metal products, machinery and equipment	37.4	101	101	96	97	98	100	101	98	94	94	95	95	-0.5
383	Electrical machinery......................	11.7	...	...	...	...	...	...	...	...	...	...	...	...	...
384	Transport equipment.......................	11.9	...	...	...	...	...	...	...	...	...	...	...	...	...
31-33, 342 355-56, 39	Light manufacturing..................	38.1	108	106	102	102	102	102	102	96	92	93	91	90	-1.5
341, 351-54 36-38	Heavy manufacturing..................	55.1	102	103	98	98	98	100	101	98	93	92	92	92	-0.9
3	Manufacturing.....................	93.2	105	104	100	100	101	101	102	97	93	92	92	91	-1.2
4	Electricity, gas and water.........	3.3	89	90	92	93	94	96	98	102	103	104	103	104	1.3
2-4	ALL INDUSTRY.................	100.0	104	104	100	100	101	101	101	97	93	93	92	91	-1.1

a/ North America (Canada and the United States of America), Europe (excluding centrally planned economies and Yugoslavia), Australia, Israel, Japan, New Zealand and South Africa.

2. INDEX NUMBERS OF INDUSTRIAL EMPLOYMENT

Developing market economies a/

1980=100

ISIC	BRANCH OF ACTIVITY	% WEIGHT (1980)	1973	1974	1975	1976	1977	1978	1979	1981	1982	1983	1984	1985	Annual growth rate (73-84)
210	Coal mining	1.1	90	96	100	100	95	96	97	102	102	107	110	...	1.8
220	Crude petroleum and natural gas	0.7	78	82	86	91	93	96	98	105	107	109	114	...	3.5
230	Metal ore mining	1.5	114	115	109	109	107	104	101	93	88	88	84	...	-2.7
290	Other mining	1.1	...	...	...	...	...	...	...	...	...	...	...	...	...
2	Mining and quarrying	4.4	97	99	99	99	99	98	99	100	98	100	101	...	0.4
31	Food, beverages and tobacco	21.9	69	70	77	86	91	93	95	102	103	104	105	...	3.9
321	Textiles	15.7	82	90	91	91	93	97	98	95	96	94	94	...	1.2
322-324	Wearing apparel, leather and footwear	12.0	55	69	70	71	72	98	102	103	104	105	108	...	6.3
33	Wood products and furniture	7.8	74	79	82	84	84	91	96	101	106	112	123	...	4.7
34	Paper, printing and publishing	3.0	81	81	83	88	91	93	98	103	105	106	107	...	2.6
341	Paper and paper products	1.2	75	69	82	88	91	93	97	106	104	107	110	...	3.6
35	Chemical, petroleum, plastic products	6.3	71	75	80	85	90	92	98	101	100	101	104	...	3.5
353-354	Petroleum and coal products	0.6	...	...	...	...	...	...	...	...	...	...	...	...	...
355-356	Rubber and plastic products	2.1	67	69	77	82	86	88	99	101	99	101	105	...	4.2
36	Non-metallic mineral products	6.5	74	74	78	82	88	93	96	103	108	108	111	...	3.8
37	Basic metal industries	2.9	68	71	79	83	92	92	97	100	107	108	109	...	4.4
38	Metal products, machinery and equipment	13.9	70	74	77	82	85	92	98	101	99	98	99	...	3.2
383	Electrical machinery	2.9	...	...	...	...	...	...	...	...	...	...	...	...	...
384	Transport equipment	3.4	...	...	...	...	...	...	...	...	...	...	...	...	...
31-33, 342 355-56, 39	Light manufacturing	63.8	72	76	80	88	92	95	98	100	102	103	105	...	3.5
341, 351-54 36-38	Heavy manufacturing	28.7	74	77	81	85	89	93	97	102	102	102	104	...	3.1
3	Manufacturing	92.5	72	76	80	87	91	94	98	101	102	102	105	...	3.5
4	Electricity, gas and water	3.1	...	...	...	...	...	...	...	...	...	...	...	...	...
2-4	ALL INDUSTRY	100.0	73	77	81	88	91	94	98	101	102	103	105	...	3.4

a/ Caribbean, Central and South America, Africa (other than South Africa), Asian Middle East and East and South-East Asia (other than Israel and Japan) and Yugoslavia.

2. INDEX NUMBERS OF INDUSTRIAL EMPLOYMENT

North America a/

1980=100

ISIC	BRANCH OF ACTIVITY	% WEIGHT (1980)	1973	1974	1975	1976	1977	1978	1979	1981	1982	1983	1984	1985	Annual growth rate (73-85)
210	Coal mining...............................	1.1	67	86	83	105	111	86	104	92	96	86	83	80	1.5
220	Crude petroleum and natural gas...........	1.1	49	73	59	85	91	76	86	116	124	115	114	114	7.3
230	Metal ore mining..........................	0.7	89	102	98	103	101	91	97	104	82	69	67	60	-3.2
290	Other mining..............................	0.6	95	98	92	94	96	97	101	97	90	89	90	89	-0.5
2	Mining and quarrying..............	3.5	70	76	80	83	86	86	96	103	102	93	92	89	2.0
31	Food, beverages and tobacco...........	8.1	101	78	99	77	78	101	101	99	96	95	96	95	-0.5
321	Textiles..................................	4.7	118	113	104	106	106	106	105	100	88	89	90	86	-2.6
322-324	Wearing apparel, leather and footwear....	6.6	115	111	102	107	106	106	103	99	92	92	93	89	-2.1
33	Wood products and furniture...........	4.9	101	98	87	98	102	107	109	100	90	96	101	101	0.0
34	Paper, printing and publishing.........	9.4	92	93	88	91	93	97	100	102	99	99	104	107	1.3
341	Paper and paper products..................	3.4	99	101	92	97	99	100	102	100	94	94	97	97	-0.2
35	Chemical, petroleum, plastic products..	8.7	96	97	91	95	97	101	103	102	98	98	102	102	0.5
353-354	Petroleum and coal products..............	0.8	95	98	98	99	100	104	105	107	104	98	94	89	-0.5
355-356	Rubber and plastic products..............	3.4	92	92	80	88	97	103	107	102	96	100	110	111	1.6
36	Non-metallic mineral products..........	3.0	107	107	96	100	103	107	108	100	88	88	92	92	-1.2
37	Basic metal industries.................	5.1	114	116	104	102	103	106	109	98	80	73	76	70	-4.0
38	Metal products, machinery and equipment	40.2	92	93	84	89	92	98	103	100	92	90	97	97	0.4
383	Electrical machinery......................	9.3	92	93	81	81	89	95	101	102	96	97	106	105	1.1
384	Transport equipment.......................	8.5	100	96	87	94	98	105	109	97	91	94	101	104	0.3
31-33, 342 355-56, 39	Light manufacturing..................	35.7	103	86	94	84	86	103	103	100	94	96	99	98	-0.4
341, 351-54 36-38	Heavy manufacturing..................	57.0	97	88	89	83	86	100	104	100	92	90	95	94	-0.3
3	Manufacturing.....................	92.7	99	88	91	84	86	101	104	100	93	92	96	96	-0.2
4	Electricity, gas and water.........	3.8	87	93	89	93	95	94	97	105	104	107	107	110	2.0
2-4	ALL INDUSTRY.................	100.0	97	97	90	94	96	100	103	100	94	92	97	96	-0.1

a/ Canada and the United States of America.

2. INDEX NUMBERS OF INDUSTRIAL EMPLOYMENT

Caribbean, Central and South America

1980=100

ISIC	BRANCH OF ACTIVITY	% WEIGHT (1980)	1973	1974	1975	1976	1977	1978	1979	1981	1982	1983	1984	1985	Annual growth rate (73-84)
210	Coal mining................................	0.4	...	...	...	...	...	...	...	...	...	...	...	...	...
220	Crude petroleum and natural gas............	1.2	72	75	78	81	84	89	96	101	107	112	121	...	4.8
230	Metal ore mining...........................	2.5	...	...	...	...	...	...	...	...	...	...	...	...	...
290	Other mining...............................	1.6	...	...	...	...	...	...	...	...	...	...	...	...	...
2	Mining and quarrying..............	5.7	...	...	...	...	...	...	...	...	...	...	...	...	...
31	Food, beverages and tobacco...........	21.5	79	82	89	90	94	94	97	99	100	101	102	...	2.4
321	Textiles..................................	7.2	102	102	103	104	103	102	102	95	90	84	81	...	-2.1
322-324	Wearing apparel, leather and footwear....	9.3	76	81	86	92	93	97	99	98	94	92	92	...	1.8
33	Wood products and furniture...........	6.4	...	...	...	...	...	...	...	...	...	...	...	...	...
34	Paper, printing and publishing.........	4.8	77	81	83	87	90	93	98	96	92	90	88	...	1.2
341	Paper and paper products..................	1.9	81	87	87	90	93	96	99	96	92	90	89	...	0.9
35	Chemical, petroleum, plastic products..	8.9	86	89	94	98	101	96	100	98	97	95	95	...	0.9
353-354	Petroleum and coal products.............	1.0	...	...	...	...	...	...	...	...	...	...	...	...	...
355-356	Rubber and plastic products.............	3.0	100	104	109	110	112	92	98	96	97	98	99	...	-0.1
36	Non-metallic mineral products..........	6.3	76	81	85	90	94	97	99	95	90	84	81	...	0.6
37	Basic metal industries................	3.9	70	78	83	89	94	96	100	95	93	90	84	...	1.7
38	Metal products, machinery and equipment	20.7	77	87	92	93	92	92	96	95	85	77	73	...	-0.5
383	Electrical machinery......................	3.7	...	...	...	...	...	...	...	...	...	...	...	...	...
384	Transport equipment.......................	5.0	...	...	...	...	...	...	...	...	...	...	...	...	...
31-33, 342 355-56, 39	Light manufacturing..................	51.8	81	84	90	93	95	96	98	98	96	95	95	...	1.5
341, 351-54 36-38	Heavy manufacturing..................	38.7	78	84	90	93	94	95	98	96	89	82	79	...	0.9
3	Manufacturing.....................	90.5	79	83	89	92	94	95	98	97	93	89	88	...	1.0
4	Electricity, gas and water.........	3.8	...	...	...	...	...	...	...	...	...	...	...	...	...
2-4	ALL INDUSTRY.................	100.0	79	84	89	92	94	95	98	97	93	91	90	...	1.2

2. INDEX NUMBERS OF INDUSTRIAL EMPLOYMENT

Asia a/

1980=100

ISIC	BRANCH OF ACTIVITY	% WEIGHT (1980)	1973	1974	1975	1976	1977	1978	1979	1981	1982	1983	1984	1985	Annual growth rate (73-84)
210	Coal mining................................	1.1	93	98	102	102	96	97	97	103	103	107	109	...	1.4
220	Crude petroleum and natural gas............	0.4	91	93	97	101	100	98	95	104	103	104	106	...	1.4
230	Metal ore mining...........................	0.5	104	105	104	104	104	99	96	99	95	97	96	...	0.7
290	Other mining...............................	0.6	102	103	99	94	99	93	96	110	108	110	114	...	1.0
2	Mining and quarrying..............	2.6	78	100	83	100	99	97	96	104	102	105	107	...	2.9
31	Food, beverages and tobacco...........	19.7	70	74	77	77	92	94	95	102	103	106	106	...	3.8
321	Textiles..................................	16.2	88	93	93	93	93	98	99	93	95	96	93	...	0.5
322-324	Wearing apparel, leather and footwear....	11.6	55	59	70	88	95	100	103	103	105	107	108	...	6.3
33	Wood products and furniture............	8.0	82	83	87	86	86	93	97	98	105	113	122	...	3.7
34	Paper, printing and publishing.........	3.4	93	91	93	94	95	98	100	102	104	110	108	...	1.4
341	Paper and paper products..................	1.3	87	92	92	96	97	97	99	104	104	109	110	...	2.2
35	Chemical, petroleum, plastic products..	6.0	78	79	83	87	89	94	98	101	103	106	108	...	3.0
353-354	Petroleum and coal products..............	0.5	...	...	...	...	...	...	...	...	...	...	...	...	...
355-356	Rubber and plastic products..............	2.4	73	72	77	81	84	91	100	102	102	109	111	...	3.9
36	Non-metallic mineral products..........	6.2	82	80	82	84	88	94	96	102	109	112	114	...	3.0
37	Basic metal industries.................	3.0	91	90	95	93	95	98	98	100	107	110	110	...	1.7
38	Metal products, machinery and equipment	17.9	89	88	87	91	91	94	98	102	103	108	109	...	1.9
383	Electrical machinery......................	4.6	...	...	...	...	...	...	...	...	...	...	...	...	...
384	Transport equipment.......................	3.9	...	...	...	...	...	...	...	...	...	...	...	...	...
31-33, 342 355-56, 39	Light manufacturing..................	62.9	76	79	83	89	93	96	98	99	101	105	105	...	3.0
341, 351-54 36-38	Heavy manufacturing..................	32.0	87	86	87	90	92	95	98	102	104	108	110	...	2.2
3	Manufacturing.....................	94.9	79	82	85	90	93	96	98	100	102	106	107	...	2.8
4	Electricity, gas and water.........	2.5	77	80	77	89	97	91	96	102	110	112	125	...	4.5
2-4	ALL INDUSTRY.................	100.0	80	83	85	90	93	96	98	100	103	106	107	...	2.7

a/ Asian Middle East and East and South-East Asia.

2. INDEX NUMBERS OF INDUSTRIAL EMPLOYMENT

Asia excluding Israel and Japan a/

1980=100

ISIC	BRANCH OF ACTIVITY	% WEIGHT (1980)	1973	1974	1975	1976	1977	1978	1979	1981	1982	1983	1984	1985	Annual growth rate (73-84)
210	Coal mining	1.3	91	97	101	101	96	96	96	103	104	109	112	...	1.9
220	Crude petroleum and natural gas	0.5	91	92	97	101	100	98	94	94	103	104	106	...	1.4
230	Metal ore mining	0.6	97	96	99	99	99	97	96	99	95	98	97	...	0.0
290	Other mining	0.6	...	...	...	...	...	...	...	...	...	...	...	...	...
2	Mining and quarrying	3.0	95	97	99	99	97	96	96	104	103	107	109	...	1.2
31	Food, beverages and tobacco	22.4	65	70	74	86	92	93	94	103	104	106	108	...	4.7
321	Textiles	18.2	81	91	90	93	94	97	98	94	97	96	96	...	1.6
322-324	Wearing apparel, leather and footwear	13.6	50	55	66	86	99	99	103	106	107	110	113	...	7.7
33	Wood products and furniture	8.4	74	77	81	81	82	90	95	101	111	119	135	...	5.6
34	Paper, printing and publishing	2.3	86	84	85	91	94	96	100	108	111	115	118	...	2.9
341	Paper and paper products	1.0	72	74	77	86	91	92	97	110	111	117	121	...	4.8
35	Chemical, petroleum, plastic products	5.5	65	68	75	81	86	92	98	102	104	106	109	...	4.8
353-354	Petroleum and coal products	0.5	...	...	...	...	...	...	...	...	...	...	...	...	...
355-356	Rubber and plastic products	1.9	57	59	67	73	78	87	100	102	104	106	111	...	6.2
36	Non-metallic mineral products	6.7	75	74	77	80	86	92	95	104	113	115	119	...	4.3
37	Basic metal industries	2.4	73	73	83	84	88	96	96	102	114	118	122	...	4.8
38	Metal products, machinery and equipment	11.8	71	74	76	81	87	91	99	103	105	107	111	...	4.1
383	Electrical machinery	2.7	...	...	...	...	...	...	...	...	...	...	...	...	...
384	Transport equipment	2.8	...	...	...	...	...	...	...	...	...	...	...	...	...
31-33, 342 355-56, 39	Light manufacturing	68.9	69	75	79	86	91	95	98	101	104	105	108	...	4.2
341, 351-54 36-38	Heavy manufacturing	25.5	72	73	77	81	87	92	97	103	108	110	114	...	4.3
3	Manufacturing	94.4	70	74	78	85	89	94	98	101	105	107	110	...	4.2
4	Electricity, gas and water	2.3	71	66	70	77	85	88	94	103	112	116	132	...	5.8
2-4	ALL INDUSTRY	100.0	71	75	79	85	90	94	98	101	105	107	110	...	4.1

a/ Asian Middle East and East and South-East Asia.

2. INDEX NUMBERS OF INDUSTRIAL EMPLOYMENT

Europe a/

1980=100

ISIC	BRANCH OF ACTIVITY	% WEIGHT (1980)	1973	1974	1975	1976	1977	1978	1979	1981	1982	1983	1984	1985	Annual growth rate (73-85)
210	Coal mining	1.5	114	111	111	107	106	103	101	99	97	93	89	86	-2.3
220	Crude petroleum and natural gas	0.2	70	85	71	75	83	82	82	106	116	119	127	132	5.4
230	Metal ore mining	0.3	97	108	109	115	111	105	101	98	92	94	92	91	-0.5
290	Other mining	0.9	121	119	117	111	109	109	108	98	93	84	81	78	-3.6
2	Mining and quarrying	2.9	113	121	111	107	106	104	103	99	96	92	89	86	-2.2
31	Food, beverages and tobacco	10.4	102	102	99	99	101	101	101	98	97	95	94	94	-0.7
321	Textiles	6.5	127	122	118	114	112	107	105	94	87	85	84	81	-3.7
322-324	Wearing apparel, leather and footwear	6.9	117	111	110	109	105	103	103	94	88	86	86	84	-2.7
33	Wood products and furniture	5.9	108	108	103	103	102	101	100	95	90	88	86	84	-2.1
34	Paper, printing and publishing	6.0	107	108	104	102	101	100	100	97	94	92	91	90	-1.4
341	Paper and paper products	2.3	112	112	107	105	104	102	101	95	92	89	88	87	-2.1
35	Chemical, petroleum, plastic products	9.5	102	104	101	101	101	101	100	96	93	91	91	90	-1.0
353-354	Petroleum and coal products	0.5	...	...	...	...	...	...	...	...	...	...	...	...	...
355-356	Rubber and plastic products	3.5	102	102	96	97	98	98	99	96	93	91	90	89	-1.1
36	Non-metallic mineral products	4.6	109	109	105	103	103	102	102	95	91	88	86	82	-2.4
37	Basic metal industries	6.0	112	113	110	108	105	101	101	94	89	78	76	74	-3.4
38	Metal products, machinery and equipment	36.5	105	106	103	102	103	102	101	96	93	91	90	89	-1.4
383	Electrical machinery	8.2	...	...	...	...	...	...	...	...	...	...	...	...	...
384	Transport equipment	9.2	...	...	...	...	...	...	...	...	...	...	...	...	...
31-33, 342 355-56, 39	Light manufacturing	38.3	110	108	105	104	104	102	101	96	92	90	89	88	-1.8
341, 351-54 36-38	Heavy manufacturing	55.4	106	107	104	103	103	102	101	96	92	89	88	87	-1.6
3	Manufacturing	93.7	107	107	104	103	103	102	101	96	92	89	88	87	-1.7
4	Electricity, gas and water	3.4	89	90	94	94	95	96	98	101	102	102	101	101	1.1
2-4	ALL INDUSTRY	100.0	107	107	104	103	103	102	101	96	92	90	89	88	-1.6

a/ Excluding centrally planned economies.

2. INDEX NUMBERS OF INDUSTRIAL EMPLOYMENT

European Economic Community

1980=100

ISIC	BRANCH OF ACTIVITY	% WEIGHT (1980)	1973	1974	1975	1976	1977	1978	1979	1981	1982	1983	1984	1985	Annual growth rate (73-85)
210	Coal mining	1.7	115	111	111	109	106	103	101	98	96	92	86	82	-2.8
220	Crude petroleum and natural gas	0.1	58	63	64	68	74	78	90	102	112	116	122	128	6.8
230	Metal ore mining	0.2	137	127	127	126	117	111	102	94	84	86	82	80	-4.4
290	Other mining	0.8	129	128	122	115	112	111	110	97	91	81	78	75	-4.4
2	Mining and quarrying	2.8	117	114	113	109	107	105	103	98	95	89	86	82	-2.9
31	Food, beverages and tobacco	10.4	104	103	100	98	102	101	101	98	95	93	93	92	-1.0
321	Textiles	6.5	136	130	123	118	114	109	106	93	86	83	81	78	-4.5
322-324	Wearing apparel, leather and footwear	6.9	129	123	117	113	109	105	103	92	86	83	83	80	-3.9
33	Wood products and furniture	5.5	112	111	105	104	103	102	100	94	88	85	84	81	-2.7
34	Paper, printing and publishing	5.7	112	111	106	103	101	100	100	97	93	91	90	89	-1.9
341	Paper and paper products	2.2	116	116	111	107	105	103	102	95	91	88	87	85	-2.6
35	Chemical, petroleum, plastic products	9.7	103	105	102	102	102	101	101	96	92	89	89	87	-1.4
353-354	Petroleum and coal products	0.5	...	...	...	...	...	...	...	...	...	...	...	...	...
355-356	Rubber and plastic products	3.6	102	103	97	97	98	98	99	95	92	90	89	88	-1.2
36	Non-metallic mineral products	4.7	116	114	108	106	105	103	102	95	90	86	83	80	-3.0
37	Basic metal industries	6.1	117	118	114	112	109	104	102	93	88	76	73	70	-4.2
38	Metal products, machinery and equipment	37.0	107	108	104	102	103	102	102	95	91	89	88	87	-1.7
383	Electrical machinery	8.6	...	...	...	...	...	...	...	...	...	...	...	...	...
384	Transport equipment	9.6	...	...	...	...	...	...	...	...	...	...	...	...	...
31-33, 342 355-56, 39	Light manufacturing	37.8	115	113	107	105	105	103	102	95	90	88	87	85	-2.5
341, 351-54 36-38	Heavy manufacturing	56.1	109	110	106	104	104	103	102	95	91	88	86	84	-2.1
3	Manufacturing	93.9	112	112	107	105	105	103	102	95	91	88	86	85	-2.3
4	Electricity, gas and water	3.3	93	94	99	98	97	97	98	100	102	100	99	98	0.4
2-4	ALL INDUSTRY	100.0	112	112	107	105	105	103	102	95	91	88	87	85	-2.3

2. INDEX NUMBERS OF INDUSTRIAL EMPLOYMENT

European Free Trade Association

1980=100

ISIC	BRANCH OF ACTIVITY	% WEIGHT (1980)	1973	1974	1975	1976	1977	1978	1979	1981	1982	1983	1984	1985	Annual growth rate (73-85)
210	Coal mining................................	0.2	131	128	123	116	117	110	100	108	98	93	87	85	-3.5
220	Crude petroleum and natural gas............	0.2	55	59	62	69	75	84	93	131	135	132	150	155	9.0
230	Metal ore mining...........................	0.7	108	109	111	113	110	102	103	97	92	87	83	80	-2.5
290	Other mining...............................	0.8	107	107	101	101	99	104	106	97	96	90	85	84	-2.0
2	Mining and quarrying..............	1.8	102	103	101	102	101	101	102	103	100	95	93	92	-0.9
31	Food, beverages and tobacco............	10.8	97	106	96	107	107	99	99	101	106	104	100	100	0.2
321	Textiles..................................	4.1	119	114	106	105	103	101	100	95	88	80	80	77	-3.6
322-324	Wearing apparel, leather and footwear....	5.0	114	111	107	107	105	104	102	96	92	89	85	83	-2.6
33	Wood products and furniture............	8.4	108	106	99	99	100	99	99	96	94	92	89	90	-1.5
34	Paper, printing and publishing.........	10.3	100	100	97	99	98	97	98	98	95	93	93	93	-0.6
341	Paper and paper products..................	5.8	103	105	103	104	103	99	99	98	92	89	88	86	-1.5
35	Chemical, petroleum, plastic products..	8.0	98	99	95	96	96	97	98	98	98	97	97	98	0.0
353-354	Petroleum and coal products.............	0.4	...	...	...	...	...	...	...	...	...	...	...	...	...
355-356	Rubber and plastic products.............	2.5	105	105	97	101	101	101	102	97	95	92	93	94	-0.9
36	Non-metallic mineral products..........	3.5	110	109	104	101	101	100	100	97	95	93	92	90	-1.7
37	Basic metal industries.................	6.2	104	106	104	104	101	98	99	98	96	88	84	84	-1.8
38	Metal products, machinery and equipment	36.7	99	103	100	100	100	99	99	99	97	94	93	94	-0.4
383	Electrical machinery......................	5.6	...	...	...	...	...	...	...	...	...	...	...	...	...
384	Transport equipment.......................	7.7	...	...	...	...	...	...	...	...	...	...	...	...	...
31-33, 342 355-56, 39	Light manufacturing..................	38.3	107	105	100	101	101	100	100	98	97	94	92	92	-1.2
341, 351-54 36-38	Heavy manufacturing..................	56.4	100	101	100	96	94	98	99	99	97	93	92	93	-0.6
3	Manufacturing......................	94.7	103	104	100	101	100	99	99	98	97	94	92	92	-0.9
4	Electricity, gas and water.........	3.5	84	89	85	91	98	97	98	101	104	104	104	104	1.8
2-4	ALL INDUSTRY..................	100.0	102	102	99	100	99	99	99	98	97	94	92	93	-0.8

2. INDEX NUMBERS OF INDUSTRIAL EMPLOYMENT

Oceania a/

1980=100

ISIC	BRANCH OF ACTIVITY	% WEIGHT (1980)	1973	1974	1975	1976	1977	1978	1979	1981	1982	1983	1984	1985	Annual growth rate (73-85)
210	Coal mining	1.6	83	83	92	97	100	100	96	110	124	128	124	...	3.7
220	Crude petroleum and natural gas	0.2	...	...	...	...	...	...	...	...	...	...	...	...	...
230	Metal ore mining	2.3	97	103	107	100	100	93	93	106	106	98	95	...	-0.2
290	Other mining	0.7	102	101	101	101	90	100	100	109	100	100	100	...	-0.2
2	Mining and quarrying	4.8	93	95	101	99	100	97	96	108	111	108	107	...	1.3
31	Food, beverages and tobacco	16.1	97	98	98	99	99	99	96	98	97	96	94		-0.3
321	Textiles	3.8	113	114	112	114	106	102	100	95	94	87	87	...	-2.4
322-324	Wearing apparel, leather and footwear	6.0	104	104	102	101	96	95	99	95	96	88	89	...	-1.4
33	Wood products and furniture	6.6	97	101	100	101	101	96	97	101	105	93	93	...	-0.4
34	Paper, printing and publishing	8.3	101	103	100	96	96	96	97	101	101	99	98	...	-0.3
341	Paper and paper products	2.4	103	106	103	98	100	98	99	98	97	92	89	...	-1.3
35	Chemical, petroleum, plastic products	7.8	106	110	103	100	100	98	101	99	100	94	92	...	-1.3
353-354	Petroleum and coal products	0.4	...	...	...	...	...	...	...	...	...	...	...	...	...
355-356	Rubber and plastic products	3.5	103	110	100	98	98	93	96	97	98	90	86	...	-1.6
36	Non-metallic mineral products	3.4	106	121	111	114	113	102	101	107	103	91	87	...	-1.8
37	Basic metal industries	6.0	99	102	102	98	99	94	96	103	102	89	83	...	-1.6
38	Metal products, machinery and equipment	29.1	104	110	109	105	101	98	99	99	101	90	86	...	-1.7
383	Electrical machinery	4.6	...	...	...	...	...	...	...	...	...	...	...	...	...
384	Transport equipment	9.0	...	...	...	...	...	...	...	...	...	...	...	...	...
31-33, 342 355-56, 39	Light manufacturing	43.1	100	102	100	100	98	97	97	98	99	94	93	...	-0.7
341, 351-54 36-38	Heavy manufacturing	45.4	103	108	106	102	100	98	100	100	101	91	87	...	-1.5
3	Manufacturing	88.5	101	105	103	101	99	97	98	99	100	92	90	...	-1.0
4	Electricity, gas and water	6.7	92	94	92	90	89	99	97	102	112	114	114	...	2.0
2-4	ALL INDUSTRY	100.0	100	104	102	100	99	97	98	100	101	95	92	...	-0.8

a/ Australia and New Zealand

كيفية الحصول على منشورات الأمم المتحدة

يمكن الحصول على منشورات الأمم المتحدة من المكتبات ودور التوزيع في جميع أنحاء العالم . استعلم عنها من المكتبة التي تتعامل معها أو اكتب إلى : الأمم المتحدة ، قسم البيع في نيويورك أو في جنيف .

如何购取联合国出版物

联合国出版物在全世界各地的书店和经售处均有发售。请向书店询问或写信到纽约或日内瓦的联合国销售组。

HOW TO OBTAIN UNITED NATIONS PUBLICATIONS

United Nations publications may be obtained from bookstores and distributors throughout the world. Consult your bookstore or write to: United Nations, Sales Section, New York or Geneva.

COMMENT SE PROCURER LES PUBLICATIONS DES NATIONS UNIES

Les publications des Nations Unies sont en vente dans les librairies et les agences dépositaires du monde entier. Informez-vous auprès de votre libraire ou adressez-vous à : Nations Unies, Section des ventes, New York ou Genève.

КАК ПОЛУЧИТЬ ИЗДАНИЯ ОРГАНИЗАЦИИ ОБЪЕДИНЕННЫХ НАЦИЙ

Издания Организации Объединенных Наций можно купить в книжных магазинах и агентствах во всех районах мира. Наводите справки об изданиях в вашем книжном магазине или пишите по адресу: Организация Объединенных Наций, Секция по продаже изданий, Нью-Йорк или Женева.

COMO CONSEGUIR PUBLICACIONES DE LAS NACIONES UNIDAS

Las publicaciones de las Naciones Unidas están en venta en librerías y casas distribuidoras en todas partes del mundo. Consulte a su librero o diríjase a: Naciones Unidas, Sección de Ventas, Nueva York o Ginebra.

Litho in United Nations, New York
05000H
United Nations publication
40836—September 1987—3,275
(only hardbound edition for sale)
Sales No. E.87.XVII.8
ISBN 92-1-161288-8
ISBN 92-1-161289-6 (Vols. I and II the set)
ST/ESA/STAT/SER.P/24 (Vol.I)